DICTIONARY OF
ARCHITECTURE &
CONSTRUCTION

DICTIONARY OF ARCHITECTURE & CONSTRUCTION

2200 illustrations

Third Edition

Edited by

Cyril M. Harris

Professor Emeritus of Architecture
Columbia University

McGraw-Hill

New York   San Francisco   Washington, D.C.   Auckland   Bogotá
Caracas   Lisbon   London   Madrid   Mexico City   Milan
Montreal   New Delhi   San Juan   Singapore
Sydney   Tokyo   Toronto

Library of Congress Cataloging-in-Publication Data

Dictionary of architecture & construction / edited by Cyril M. Harris.
   —3rd ed.

       p.   cm.
   Includes index.
   ISBN 0-07-135178-7
   1. Architecture—Dictionaries.   2. Building—Dictionaries.
   I. Title: Dictionary of architecture and construction.
   II. Harris, Cyril M., (date).
   NA31.H32 2000
   720'.3—dc21

                                    99-056285

McGraw-Hill

*A Division of The **McGraw·Hill** Companies*

ISBN 0-07-135178-7

*The sponsoring editor for this book was Wendy Lochner and the
production supervisor was Pamela A. Pelton. It was set in Goudy
by North Market Street Graphics.*

Printed and bound by R. R. Donnelley & Sons Company.

 This book was printed on recycled, acid-free paper containing
a minimum of 50% recycled, de-inked fiber.

PREFACE

The first edition of the *Dictionary of Architecture and Construction*, published in 1975, included more definitions of terms in architecture and construction than any other dictionary of its kind. Because of the accuracy and clarity of these definitions, it has been accepted as the authority on architectural terminology, not only by general and professional users, but in many courts of law throughout the world. A greatly expanded second edition was published in 1993. Now extensively revised, updated, and further expanded to include a total of approximately 24,500 definitions and over 200 additional illustrations, this comprehensive third edition brings users the broadest possible coverage of the language of architecture and construction.

The publication of the third edition represents the culmination of 33 years of work by the Editor. No individual, or even a small group, can bring expert knowledge to all of the widely diverse specialties that are now associated with architecture and building construction. In the preparation of this edition, detailed coverage of terms has been made possible by building on the work of standards groups and technical committees of professional societies and trade associations, whose valuable assistance is recognized in the Acknowledgments. As was noted in the first editon of this *Dictionary*, the following individuals, each of them specialists in their own field, provided the necessary expertise required for a comprehensive and authoritative work: Walter F. Aikman; William H. Bauer; Bronson Binger, A.I.A.; Donald Edward Brotherson, A.I.A.; Robert Burns, A.I.A.; A. E. Bye, F.A.S.L.A.; Richard K. Cook, Ph.D.; William C. Crager, C.S.P.; Frank L. Ehasz, Ph.D., P.E.; Francis Ferguson, A.I.A., A.I.P.; Frederick G. Frost, F.A.I.A.; Alfred Greenberg, P.E.; John Hagman; Michael M. Harris, F.A.I.A.; R. Bruce Hoadley, D.For.; Jerome S. B. Iffland, P.E.; George C. Izenour, A.I.E.E.E.; Curtis A. Johnson, M.Sc., P.E.; Edgar Kaufmann, Jr., H.A.I.A.; Thomas C. Kavanaugh, Sc.D.; Robert L. Keeler; George Lacancellera, C.S.I.; Paul Lampl, M.A., A.I.A.; Valentine A. Lehr, M.S.C.E., P.E.; Robert E. Levin, Ph.D., P.E.; George W. McLellan; Emily Malino, A.I.D.; Roy J. Mascolino, R.A.; Donald E. Orner, P.E.; John Barratt Patton, Ph.D.; Albert J. Rosenthal, L.L.B.; Henry H. Rothman, F.F.C.S.; James V. Ryan, M.S.; John E. Ryan, P.E., S.F.P.E.; Reuben Samuels, P.E., F.A.S.C.E.; Joseph Schein, A.I.A.; Joseph M. Shelley, B.S.Arch.; Kenneth Alexander Smith, A.I.A., P.E.; Perry M. Smith, P.E., Fred G. Snook, M.S.; Carl A. Swanson, B.C.E., C.S.I.; Kenneth Thomas, M.Sc., C.Eng.; Charles W. Thurston, Ph.D., P.E.; Marvin Trachtenberg, Ph.D.; Everard M. Upjohn, M.Arch.; Oliver B. Volk; Byron G. Wels. This group of experts, who came from widely diverse backgrounds, included practicing architects, professional engineers, architectural historians, art historians, professors of architecture, specification writers, craftsmen, contractors, safety experts, and a legal scholar. To all of them, I owe a continuing debt of gratitude. In addition, special thanks go to a colleague for many years in the Graduate School of Architecture of Columbia University, Professor Adolf K. Placzek, Avery Librarian Emeritus, for his helpfulness, scholarship and insights.

Cyril M. Harris

ACKNOWLEDGMENTS

The Editor wishes to express his appreciation to the following organizations for their permission to reproduce selected definitions or illustrations from their publication. In addition to the specific permissions credited herein, a number of other organizations and publications have authorized the reproduction of definitions or illustrations without formal acknowledgment.

Special thanks are due to the American Institute of Architects for permitting selected definitions to be reproduced from the AIA *Glossary of Construction Industry Terms*. In all instances, no further reproduction is authorized.

A number of the definitions in this dictionary have been selected and reproduced with permission from copyrighted publications of the American National Standards Institute (ANSI) and the American Society for Testing and Materials (ASTM); for more detailed information in a specific field, readers should consult applicable ANSI standards and the *ASTM Book of Standards*. Extracts have been reproduced from the following publications of the British Standards Institution, London W1A 2BS: BS565, BS 3921, and CP 121.

Permission has been granted to reproduce material from the following publications: *The Asphalt Handbook* of the Asphalt Institute; *Facts and Figures* of the Pioneer Division, Portec Inc.; *CPM in Construction, A Manual for General Contractors* of the Association of General Contractors of America; *Brick and Tile Engineering* by H. C. Plummer, Structural Clay Products Institute; *Ceramic Glossary* of the American Ceramic Society; Plastics Glossary of the *Modern Plastics* magazine, McGraw-Hill; *Timber Construction Manual* of the American Institute of Timber Construction, published by John Wiley & Sons; *Woodworking Technology* by J. J. Hammond et al., published by McKnight & McKnight; *Fundamentals of Business Law*, published by Callaghan & Co.; *Product Line Dictionary*, Canadian Construction Information Corp.; *Glossary of Architectural Metal Terms* of the National Association of Architectural Metals Manufacturers; *ASCE Manual of Engineering Practice, No. 34*; *ASHRAE Guide and Data Books*.

The following organizations have granted their permission to reproduce definitions or illustrations from their publications: Aluminum Association; American Institute of Steel Construction; American Iron and Steel Institute; Architectural Aluminum Manufacturers Association; Copper Development Association; Revere Copper and Brass Co.; The Steel Company of Canada; Steel Joist Institute; Zinc Institute, Inc.; National Fire Protection Association; Illuminating Engineering Society; National Builder's Hardware Association; American Concrete Institute (ACI), SP-4, 318-71, SP-19, ACI Committee 504 Report on Sealants, and the ACI Committee 531 Report on Concrete Masonry Structures.

I thank William A. Pierson for his photograph of Round Arch style.

At McGraw-Hill, Inc., I acknowledge the help of and thank Margaret Lamb, editing manager in McGraw-Hill's Technical Group, and Wendy Lochner, senior editor for architecture books. At North Market Street Graphics, I thank Tom Laughman, editing supervisor for this edition.

ABOUT THE EDITOR

Cyril M. Harris is Professor Emeritus of Architecture at Columbia University, where he was chairman of the Division of Architectural Technology for 10 years and is currently Special Lecturer in the Graduate School of Architecture, Planning, and Preservation. He is also the Charles Batchelor Professor Emeritus of Electrical Engineering at Columbia. He has received the A.I.A. Medal of the American Institute of Architects, the Gold Medal and the Sabine Medal of the Acoustical Society of America, the Gold Medal of the Audio Engineering Society, the Franklin Medal of the Franklin Institute, and the Pupin Medal for Service to the Nation from Columbia University; he is a member of both the National Academy of Sciences and the National Academy of Engineering. Professor Harris has received international recognition for his work in acoustical design of auditoriums, including the Metropolitan Opera House, Benaroya Hall in Seattle, Orchestra Hall in Minneapolis, the John F. Kennedy Center for the Performing Arts in Washington, D.C., and the National Centre for the Performing Arts in Bombay. He received his Ph.D. in physics from M.I.T. and has been awarded honorary doctorates from Northwestern University and the New Jersey Institute of Technology. Other books written or edited by Dr. Harris include *American Architecture: An Illustrated Encyclopedia*, published by W. W. Norton; *Illustrated Dictionary of Historic Architecture*, Dover Publications, Inc.; and *Shock and Vibration Handbook*, McGraw-Hill, Inc., now in its fourth edition.

DICTIONARY OF ARCHITECTURE & CONSTRUCTION

Å   Abbr. for **angstrom**.

A   **1.** Abbr. for **ampere**, a unit of electric current. **2.** Abbr. for **area**.

AA   Abbr. for the "Architectural Association," the largest school of architecture in England; address 34–36 Bedford Square, London, WC1B 3ES.

AAA   Abbr. for "Architectural Aluminum Association."

AAI   Abbr. for "Architectural Association of Ireland."

AAMA   Abbr. for "Architectural Aluminum Manufacturers Association."

A&E   See **architect-engineer**.

Aaron's rod   An ornament or molding consisting of a straight rod from which pointed leaves or scroll work emerge on either side, at regular intervals.

abaciscus   **1.** A **tessera**, as used in mosaic work. Also called **abaculus**. **2.** A small **abacus**.

abaculus   See **abaciscus, 1.**

abacus   The uppermost member of the capital of a column; often a plain square slab, but sometimes molded or otherwise enriched.

abacus   *A*

abamurus   A buttress, or a second wall added to strengthen another.

abate   **1.** To remove material, as in stone carving. **2.** In metalwork, to cut away or beat down so as to show a pattern or figure in low relief.

abated   Said of a surface that has been cut away or beaten down so as to show a pattern or figure in low relief; also see **relief**.

abatement   The wastage of wood when lumber is sawed or planed to size.

abat-jour   Any beveled aperture, or a skylight, in a wall or in a roof to admit light from above.

abaton   A sanctuary not to be entered by the public; a holy of holies.

abat-sons   Descriptive of a surface said to reflect sound downward.

abat-vent   **1.** Louvers that are placed in an exterior wall opening to permit light and air to enter, but break the wind. **2.** A sloping roof. **3.** In the **French Vernacular architecture** of New Orleans, an extension of a roof over a sidewalk.

abat-voix   In a church, a sound reflector behind and over a pulpit.

abbey   A monastery or convent; particularly the church thereof.

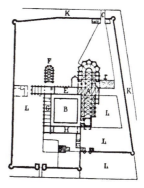

abbey: Plan of abbey of St. Germain-des-Prés, Paris, 13th cent. *A*, church; *B*, cloister; *C*, city gate; *E*, chapter house; *F*, chapel; *G*, refectory; *H*, cellars and presses; *I*, abbot's lodging; *K*, ditches; *L*, gardens

abbreuvoir   Same as **abreuvoir**.

ABC   **1.** Abbr. for "aggregate base course." **2.** Abbr. for "Associated Builders and Contractors."

A-block   A hollow, concrete masonry unit with one end closed and the opposite end open, having a web between, so that two cells are formed when the block is laid in a wall.

Abney level   A **hand level** used for measuring vertical angles; comprised of a small telescope, bubble tube, and graduated vertical arc.

above-grade building volume   The volume of a building (in cubic feet or in cubic meters) measured from the average adjoining grade level to the average roof level, and from outside to outside of exterior walls, but not including breezeways, porches, or terraces.

abrade   To wear away or scrape off a surface, especially by friction.

Abrams' law   A statement applying to given concrete materials and conditions of test: For a mixture of workable consistency, the strength of concrete provided by the mixture is determined by the ratio of the amount of water to the amount of cement.

abrasion   A surface discontinuity caused by roughening or scratching.

abrasion resistance   The ability of a surface to resist being worn away or to maintain its original appearance when rubbed with another object.

abrasion resistance index   A measure of the abrasion resistance of a vulcanized material or synthetic rubber compound relative to that of a standard rubber compound under specified conditions.

abrasive   A hard substance for removing material by grinding, lapping, honing, and polishing. Common abrasives include silicon carbide, boron carbide, diamond, emery, garnet, quartz, tripoli, pumice, diatomite, metal shot, grit, and various sands; usually adhered to paper or cloth.

abraum   A red ocher used to stain mahogany.

abreuvoir   In masonry, a joint or interstice between stones, to be filled with mortar or cement.

ABS   Abbr. for **acrylonitrile-butadiene-styrene**.

abscissa   In the plane Cartesian coordinate system, the horizontal coordinate of a point on a plane; the x-coordinate, obtained by measuring the distance from the point to the y-axis along a line parallel to the x-axis.

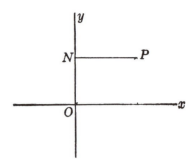

abscissa: *P*, any point; *NP*, abscissa

absidiole   Same as **apsidiole**.

absolute humidity   The mass of water vapor per unit volume of air.

absolute pressure   The sum of the **gauge pressure** plus **atmospheric pressure**.

absolute volume   **1.** Of a granular material, the total volume of the particles, including the permeable and impermeable voids, but excluding the spaces between the particles. **2.** Of fluid, the volume which the fluid occupies. **3.** The displacement volume of an ingredient of concrete or mortar.

absorbed moisture   Moisture that has entered a solid material by absorption and has physical properties not substantially different from ordinary water at the same temperature and pressure. Also see **absorption**.

absorbent   A material which, owing to an affinity for certain substances, extracts one or more such substances from a liquid or gas with which it is in contact, and which changes physically or chemically, or both, during the process.

absorber   **1.** A device containing liquid for absorbing refrigerant vapor or other vapors. **2.** In an **absorption system**, that part of the low-pressure side of the system which is used for absorbing refrigerant vapor. **3.** That part of a solar collector whose primary function is to absorb radiant solar energy.

absorbing well, dry well, waste well   A well used for draining off surface water and conducting it underground, where it is absorbed.

absorptance   In illumination engineering, the ratio of the absorbed flux to the incident flux.

absorption   **1.** The process by which a liquid, or a mixture of gases and liquid, is drawn into and tends to fill permeable pores in a porous solid material; usually accompanied by a physical change, chemical change, or both, of the material. **2.** The increase in weight of a porous solid body resulting from the penetration of liquid into its permeable pores. **3.** The increase in weight of a brick or tile unit when immersed in either cold or boiling water for a stated length of time; expressed as a percentage of the weight of the dry unit. **4.** The process by which radiant energy, which is incident on a surface, is converted to other forms of energy. **5.** See **sound absorption**.

absorption bed A pit of relatively large dimensions which is filled with coarse aggregate and contains a distribution pipe system; used to absorb the effluent of a septic tank.

absorption coefficient See **sound absorption coefficient**.

absorption field, disposal field A system of trenches containing coarse aggregate and distribution pipes through which septic-tank effluent may seep into the surrounding soil.

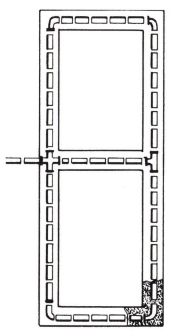

absorption field composed of absorption trenches
Extent of coarse aggregate indicated by shaded area

absorption rate, initial rate of absorption The weight of water absorbed when a brick is partially immersed for one minute; usually expressed in grams per minute or ounces per minute.

absorption system A **refrigeration system** in which the refrigerant gas evolved in the evaporator is taken up in an absorber and (upon the application of heat) released in a generator.

absorption trench A trench containing coarse aggregate and a **distribution tile** pipe through which septic-tank effluent may flow, covered with earth.

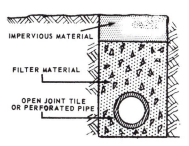

absorption trench

absorption-type liquid chiller Equipment utilizing a generator, condenser, absorber, evaporator, pumps, controls, and accessories to cool water, or other secondary liquid, using absorption techniques.

ABS plastic A plastic of acrylonitrile-butadiene-styrene; has good resistance to impact, heat, and chemicals; esp. used for piping.

abstract of title An outline history of the ownership of a parcel of land, from the original grant, with changes in title, and with a statement of all mortgages, liens, encumbrances, etc., affecting the property.

abut To adjoin at an end; to be contiguous.

abutment A masonry mass (or the like) which receives the thrust of an arch, vault, or strut.

abutment A

3

abutment piece   See **solepiece**.

abuttals   Those boundaries of one piece of land that abut on adjacent pieces.

abutting joint   A joint between two pieces of wood, in which the direction of the grain in one piece is at an angle (usually 90°) to the grain in the other.

abutting tenon   One of two tenons which are inserted in a common mortise from opposite sides, so as to touch each other.

ac, a-c, a.c.   Abbr. for "alternating current."

AC   **1.** On drawings, abbr. for "alternating current." **2.** On drawings, abbr. for **armored cable**. **3.** Abbr. for **air conditioning**. **4.** Abbr. for "asbestos cement."

acacia   Same as **gum arabic**.

Acadian cottage   Same as **Cajun cottage**.

acanthus   A common plant of the Mediterranean, whose leaves, stylized, form the characteristic decoration of capitals of Corinthian and Composite orders. In scroll form it appears on friezes, panels, etc.

acanthus

ACB   **1.** Abbr. for **asbestos-cement board**. **2.** Abbr. for "air circuit breaker."

accelerated life test   A test in which one or more parameters (e.g., temperature) is increased or decreased beyond its normal or rated value to determine the resulting deterioration within a reasonable time period.

accelerated weathering   A laboratory testing technique to determine, in a relatively short time, the **weather resistance** of a paint film or other exposed surface.

accelerating admixture   An **admixture** that speeds the setting and/or the early strength development of hydraulic concrete.

acceleration   **1.** The rate of change of the velocity of a moving body. **2.** The rate of change, esp. the quickening of the natural progress of a process, such as hardening, setting, or strength development of concrete.

acceleration of gravity (g)   The acceleration produced by the force of gravity at the surface of the earth. (By international agreement the value of g is 386.089 inches per second square = 32.1740 feet per second square = 9.80665 meters per second square.)

acceleration stress   In a wire rope (or the like), the additional stress imposed as a result of the acceleration of the load.

accelerator   **1.** A substance which, when added to concrete, mortar, or grout, increases the rate of hydration of a hydraulic cement, shortens the time of set, or increases the rate of hardening or strength development. **2.** A substance, added with a curing agent, to speed a vulcanization process and enhance the physical properties of a vulcanized material. **3.** Same as **accelerating admixture**.

accent lighting   Any directional lighting which emphasizes a particular object or draws attention to a particular area.

acceptable water pressure   See **maximum acceptable pressure** and **minimum acceptable pressure**.

acceptance   See **final acceptance**.

acceptance test   A test conducted by a purchaser (or an agent thereof) (a) to determine if the material, devices, or equipment delivered conforms to the purchase contract specifications and/or (b) to determine the degree of uniformity of the product supplied by the vendor.

access   A means of approach, e.g., a road, street, or walk.

access door   A door, usually small, which is provided through a finished construction, as

access door

into a duct, through a ceiling, behind a wall, in a large piece of mechanical equipment, etc.; used to provide a means of inspection of equipment or services housed within.

access eye   See **cleanout, 1.**

access floor   Same as **raised floor.**

access flooring system   See **raised flooring system.**

accessibility standards   See **Americans with Disabilities Act** and **Uniform Federal Accessibility Standards.**

accessible   **1.** Allowing physical contact, as by means of an easily removable cover or door or a part of the building structure or finish materials. **2.** Providing access to a fixture, appliance, or piece of equipment; removal of a cover, panel, plate, or similar obstruction may be required. **3.** Said of a building, facility, or site that can be approached, entered, and used by a physically disabled person.

accessible means of egress   A path of travel, usable by a mobility-impaired person, that leads to a **public way.**

accessible route   A continuous unobstructed path, connecting all accessible spaces and rooms in a building, which can be negotiated by all physically disabled persons.

accessory building   A secondary building, whose use is incidental to that of the main building located on the same plot.

accessory use   The use or occupancy incidental to the principal use or occupancy of a building.

access panel   A removable panel (usually secured with screws) in a frame which is usually mounted in a ceiling or wall; provides access to a concealed item that does not require frequent attention.

access plate   A removable plate (usually bolted in place) that provides access to an area that seldom requires attention; permits inspection of an otherwise inaccessible area.

access stair   A stair, from one floor level to another, which does not serve as a required exit stair. Also see **exterior stair.**

accident   A sudden, unexpected event identifiable as to time and place. Also see **occurrence.**

accidental air   See **entrapped air.**

acclivity   The upward slope of a hillside.

accolade   An ornamental treatment, used over an arch, a door, or a window, composed of two ogee curves meeting in the middle; often a richly decorated molding.

accolade

accordion door   **1.** Any fabric-faced door which is hung from an overhead track and folds back like the bellows of an accordion. **2.** A hinged door consisting of a system of panels which are hung from an overhead track. When the door is open, the faces of the panels close flat against each other; when the door is closed, the edges of adjacent panels butt against (or interlock with) each other to form a solid barrier.

accordion partition   A fabric-faced partition which is hung from an overhead track and folds back like the bellows of an accordion.

accouplement   The placement of columns or pilasters close together, in pairs.

accrued depreciation   **1.** The reduction in actual value of property over a period of time, as a result of wear and tear, obsolescence, etc. **2.** The accumulated reductions in the stated value of property over a period of time, entered on balance sheets for accounting or tax purposes.

accumulator   **1.** In a refrigeration system, a storage chamber for low-side liquid refrigerant; also called a **surge drum** or **surge header. 2.** In a refrigerant circuit, a vessel whose volume is used to reduce pulsation.

ACD   Abbr. for **automatic closing device.**

ACE   Abbr. for "Architects Council of Europe."

acetone   A highly flammable solvent which evaporates rapidly; used in lacquers, paint removers, thinners, etc.

acetylene A colorless gas, when mixed with oxygen, burns at a temperature of about 3500°C; used in welding.

acetylene torch A torch, used in welding and in metal cutting, which is operated by compressed acetylene gas and oxygen.

AC generator A generator which produces alternating current when driven by a **prime mover**.

Achaemenid architecture An architecture developed under the Achaemenid rulers of Persia (6th to 4th cent. B.C.) by a synthesis and eclectic adaptation of architectural elements which included those of surrounding countries. In the hypostyle hall it achieved a highly original new building type.

achromatic Said of architecture that is without color, for example, the white buildings of **Greek Revival**.

achromatic color White light; a color that does not elicit hue.

ACI Abbr. for "American Concrete Institute."

acid-etched Said of a metallic surface (e.g., a nail) that has been treated in an acid bath to provide a rough surface.

acidic Said of igneous rocks containing more than 65% silica.

aciding The light etching of a cast-stone surface.

acid lead Fully refined lead to which a small amount of copper has been added; 99.9% pure.

acid neutralizer A device installed in a drainage system into which the discharge of acid is probable; neutralizes the discharge sufficiently to permit it to enter the drainage system safely.

acid polishing The polishing of a glass surface by acid treatment.

acid resistance The degree to which a surface, such as porcelain enamel, will resist attack by acids.

acid-resistant brick Brick suitable for use in contact with chemicals; usually laid with acid-resistant mortars.

acid-resistant cast-iron pipe A **cast-iron** pipe containing between 14.25 and 15% silicon and small amounts of manganese, sulfur, and carbon; manufactured in the same dimensions as cast-iron pipe.

acid soil Soil having an acid reaction; usually a soil having a **pH value** of less than 6.6.

acisculis A mason's small pick, with a flat face and pointed peen.

acorn A small ornament in the shape of a nut of the oak tree; sometimes used as a finial, pendant, or decorative element within a broken pediment, or as a decoration on a carved panel.

acorn

acous 1. Abbr. for **acoustical**. 2. Abbr. for **acoustics**.

acoustic, acoustical The qualifying adjectives *acoustic* and *acoustical* have the following meanings: arising from, actuated by, containing, producing, or related to sound. In general, *acoustic* is used when the term being qualified designates something that has the properties, dimensions, or physical characteristics associ-

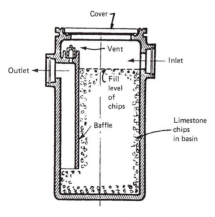

acid neutralizer

ated with sound waves; *acoustical* is used when the term being qualified does not explicitly designate something that has the properties, dimensions, or physical characteristics of sound (e.g., acoustical engineering). However, sometimes these two terms are used interchangeably.

acoustical barrier   See **sound barrier**.

acoustical board   See **acoustical ceiling board**.

acoustical ceiling   A ceiling covered by, or formed of, an **acoustical material**.

acoustical ceiling board   An acoustical material in board form, designed primarily for suspended ceiling application.

acoustical ceiling system   A structural system for supporting an acoustical ceiling; may incorporate lighting fixtures and air diffusers.

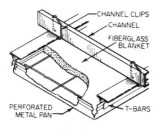

acoustical ceiling system

acoustical door   A solid, heavy door which is gasketed along the top and sides; usually has an **automatic door bottom**; especially constructed to reduce noise transmission through it; usually carries a **sound transmission class** (STC) rating, which is a measure of its sound insulation value.

acoustical duct lining   See **duct lining**.

acoustical insulation board   A porous material in board form, designed or used as an acoustical material or as an element in a sound-insulation construction.

acoustical lay-in panel   An acoustical ceiling board designed to be laid into an exposed grid suspension system.

acoustical material   Any material especially designed to absorb sound.

acoustical model   A model of an auditorium or room used to study certain acoustical properties of the full-sized enclosure, such as the distribution of sound pressure, the paths of sound rays, and focusing effects.

acoustical panel   Same as **acoustical lay-in panel**.

acoustical plaster   A special low-density sound-absorptive plaster, applied in the form of a finish-coat, to provide a continuous finished surface.

acoustical power   See **sound power**.

acoustical sprayed-on material   An acoustical material applied by a spray process to form a continuous finished surface.

acoustical tile   An acoustical material in board form, often having unit dimensions of 24 in. by 24 in. (approx. 61 cm by 61 cm) or less. Usually used on ceilings but also may be applied to sidewalls.

acoustics   **1.** The science of sound, including the generation, transmission, and effects of sound waves. **2.** The totality of those physical characteristics of an auditorium or room (such as the size and shape of elements on the walls or ceiling which scatter sound, the amount of sound absorption, and noise level within the room) which affect an individual's perception, and his judgment, of the quality of speech and music produced in the room.

acph   Abbr. for "air changes per hour."

acquiescence   **1.** An act of concurrence by adjoining property owners which resolves a boundary dispute or establishes a common boundary, where the definite or more accurate position of same has not or cannot be defined by survey. **2.** The tacit consent of one owner, by not interposing a formal objection, to what might be an encroachment by an adjoining property owner over a questionable boundary.

acre   A unit of land measurement equal to 43,560 sq ft or 4046.85 sq m; 1 sq mile (2.59 sq km) equals 640 acres.

acre-foot   The amount of water required to cover an area of 1 acre to a depth of 1 foot; equivalent to 43,560 cubic feet (4046.9 m^3); sometimes used as a measure of materials in place (e.g., gravel).

acrolith   A statue or sculptured figure in which only the head, hands, and feet are of stone, the rest being usually of wood.

acropodium   **1.** An elevated pedestal bearing a statue, particularly if raised from the substructure on supports. **2.** The plinth of a statue if resting on supports.

acropolis **1.** The elevated stronghold of a Greek city, usually with the temple of the patron divinity. **2.** (*cap.*) The Acropolis of Athens. **3.** Any elevated group of buildings serving as a civic symbol.

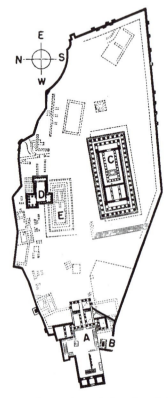

acropolis: Acropolis at Athens. A, Propylaea; B, Temple of Niké Apteros; C, Parthenon; D, Erechtheum; E, foundations of old Temple of Athena 6th cent. B.C.

acroterion, acroter, acroterium **1.** Strictly, a pedestal at the corners or peak of a roof to support an ornament. **2.** More usually, the ornament itself.

acroterion, 1

acroterion, 2

acrylic fiber A synthetic fiber manufactured by polymerizing acrylonitrile.

acrylic paint A type of **latex paint** made from **acrylic resins;** also called acrylic latex paint.

acrylic resin, acrylate resin One of a group of thermoplastic resins made from esters of acrylic acid; exceptionally tough, stable, resistant to chemicals, and transparent; used as a binder, in sheet form, as an air-curing adhesive, and as the main ingredient in some caulks and sealants.

acrylonitrile-butadiene-styrene (ABS) A plastic used for piping in drainage systems, storm sewers, and underground electrical conduit.

ACS Abbr. for "American Ceramic Society."

ACT. On drawings, abbreviation for "actual."

act curtain, act drop, front curtain, house curtain A curtain, behind the asbestos curtain in a theatre, which closes the proscenium and serves as an indication of the beginning or end of an act or scene.

act drop See **act curtain.**

acting area That part of a theatre stage floor on which the actors perform.

acting area light A spotlight used to illuminate a selected acting area.

acting level A platform above the theatre stage floor which is used for acting.

actinic glass A glass having a yellow tint which reduces the transmission of infrared and ultraviolet rays; sometimes used in factory windows or skylights.

action hinge Same as **double-acting hinge.**

activated alumina A form of aluminum oxide

which adsorbs moisture readily and is used as a drying agent.

activated carbon   See **activated charcoal**.

activated charcoal, activated carbon   Charcoal obtained by carbonizing organic material, usually in the absence of air; usually in granular or powdered form; highly effective in adsorbing odors in air or in removing colors in solution.

activated rosin flux   A flux having a resin or rosin base and containing an additive to increase wetting by the solder.

activated sludge   Sewage sediment that has been subjected to vigorous aeration and the action of microorganisms.

activator   Same as **catalyst**.

active earth pressure   The component of pressure in a horizontal direction which a mass of earth exerts on a wall.

active leaf, active door   In a door having a pair of leaves, that leaf to which the latching or locking mechanism is attached; usually the leaf that is permitted to open first; sometimes both leaves are active.

active sludge   A **sludge, 3** which is rich in destructive bacteria; useful in breaking down fresh sewage.

active solar energy system   A building subsystem in which solar energy is collected and is transferred predominantly by mechanical equipment (fans, pumps) powered by energy not derived from solar radiation. Compare with **passive solar energy system**.

active sound attenuator   A special type of **sound attenuator** that incorporates a sound source which generates sound waves intended to cancel some of the noise generated by the fans in an **HVAC** system.

activity   In **CPM** terminology, a task or item of work that must be performed in order to complete a project.

activity duration   In **CPM** terminology, the amount of time estimated as required to accomplish an **activity**.

actual start of construction   The first placement of permanent construction of a building on a site, such as pile driving, or the pouring of slabs or footings.

acuminated   Finished in a point, as a lofty Gothic roof.

acute angle   An angle of less than 90°.

acute arch, lancet arch   A sharply pointed arch whose centers are farther apart than the width of the arch.

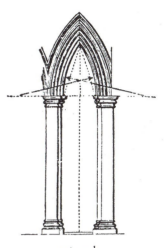

acute arch

a.d.   Abbr. for "air-dried."

AD   **1.** Abbr. for "air-dried." **2.** Abbr. for **access door**. **3.** Abbr. for **area drain**. **4.** Abbr. for "as drawn."

ADA   Abbr. for **Americans with Disabilities Act**.

Adamesque style   An inexact term implying a derivation from the **Adam style**, but having possible differences depending on the time and location of application.

Adam Revival   See **Colonial Revival**.

Adam style   An architectural style based on the work of Robert Adam (1728–1792) and his brothers, predominant in England in the late 18th century and strongly influential in the U.S.A., Russia, and elsewhere. It is characterized by clarity of form, use of color, subtle detailing, and unified schemes of interior design. Basically Neoclassical, it also adapted Neo-Gothic, Egyptian, and Etruscan motifs. (*See illustration p. 10.*)

adapt   To make suitable for a particular purpose or new requirements or conditions, by means of modifications or changes.

adaptability   The capacity of building spaces and elements for being altered or being added to for specific needs, as, for example, to accommo-

Adam style fireplace

date the needs of persons with and without disabilities.

adaptable dwelling unit One of a number of dwelling units that is on an **accessible route** and equipped so it may be converted to be used, with a minimum of structural change, by all categories of physically disabled persons.

adaptation The process by which the eye changes sensitivity and becomes accustomed to more or less light than it was exposed to during an immediately preceding period.

adapter **1.** A device for matching and properly connecting items, tubing, or devices (especially electric) which are of different size, operating characteristics, or design. **2.** A device that enables different sizes or types of plugs, pipes, etc., to be joined.

adapter

adaptive use The extensive alteration, restoration, and/or renovation of an existing structure or building so that it will serve a new purpose.

ADC Abbr. for "Air Diffusion Council."

ADD. **1.** On drawings, abbr. for **addendum. 2.** On drawings, abbr. for **addition.**

added lean-to Same as **integral lean-to.**

addendum A written or graphic instrument issued prior to the execution of the **contract** which modifies or interprets the bidding documents, including **drawings,** and **specifications,** by additions, deletions, clarifications or corrections; becomes part of the **contract documents** when the construction contract is executed.

addition **1.** A floor or floors, a room, wing, or other expansion to an existing building. **2.** In building code usage: Any new construction which increases the height or floor area of an existing building or adds to it (as a porch or attached garage). **3.** An amount added to the **contract sum** by a **charge order;** also see **extra.**

additional services The professional services which may, upon the owner's request or approval, be rendered by the architect in addition to the basic services identified in the **owner-architect agreement.**

additive A material, used in very small quantity, to modify a specific property of another material or otherwise improve its characteristics; used in paints, plasters, mortars, etc.

additive alternate An alternate bid resulting in an addition to the same bidder's **base bid.** Also see **alternate bid.**

additus maximus In an ancient Roman amphitheatre, a main entrance.

addorsed, adorsed Said of animals or figures placed back to back in decorative sculpture.

addorsed dolphins

addressable system A fire alarm system whose integrity can be monitored and which provides easy identification of the location of an alarm condition; also provides for remote testing and monitoring of the sensitivity of the detectors from a control panel.

ADF In the lumber industry, abbr. for "after deducting freight."

ADH On drawings, abbr. for **adhesive**.

adherend A body which is held to another by an adhesive.

adhesion **1.** The joining of two surfaces as pieces of wood, metal, plastic, or other construction materials, by means of a viscous, sticky composition such as cement or glue. **2.** The sticking together of two surfaces by means of physical and chemical forces such as those which bind a paint film to a surface.

adhesion-type ceramic veneer Thin sections of ceramic veneer held in place by the adhesion of mortar to unit and backing, requiring no metal anchors; not more than 1¼ in. (3.2 cm) in overall thickness. Also see **anchored-type ceramic veneer**.

adhesive A substance capable of holding materials together by bonding the surfaces that are in contact.

adhesive failure The separation of two surfaces joined by an adhesive, either by a force less than that specified by the manufacturer or by service conditions.

adiabatic Occurring without the gain or loss of heat.

adiabatic curing The curing of concrete or mortar in which adiabatic conditions are maintained during the curing period.

Adirondack Rustic style See **Rustic style**.

adit An entrance or passage.

adjoining grade elevation The average elevation of the final grade adjoining all exterior walls of a building, calculated from grade elevations taken at intervals (usually 10 ft or 3 m) around the perimeter of the building.

adjustable base anchor A device used to hold a doorframe above the finished floor.

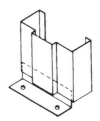

adjustable base anchor

adjustable doorframe A doorframe which has an adjustable jamb so that it can be installed in walls of different thicknesses.

adjustable hanger A **hanger** having a provision for adjusting its length.

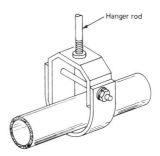

adjustable hanger

adjustable multiple-point suspension scaffold **1.** See **mason's adjustable multiple-point suspension scaffold**. **2.** See **stone-setter's adjustable multiple-point suspension scaffold**.

adjustable proscenium On a theatre stage, an inner proscenium which is variable in height, width, or position; may be hung from rigging overhead or floor-mounted.

adjustable shelving Shelving supported by metal clips or other movable supports, making it possible to adjust the height of individual shelves.

adjustable shore, adjustable steel prop   A vertical **shore** used to support reinforced concrete beams and slab forms; usually all metal or a combination of wood and metal; can be raised or lowered within certain limits.

adjustable-speed motor   An electric motor in which the speed can be varied gradually over a considerable range, but which, once adjusted, remains virtually unaffected by the **load, 3**.

adjustable square, double square   A **try square** whose arm is at right angles to the handle; the position of the arm may be moved so as to form an L or a T.

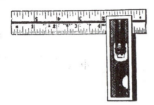

adjustable square

adjustable wrench   Any one of several types of wrenches having one jaw fixed and the other adjustable; set to the desired size by means of a knurled screw.

MONKEY   CRESCENT

adjustable wrenches

administration of the construction contract   See **construction phase—administration of the construction contract**.

administrative authority   The individual, official, board, department, or agency established and authorized by a city, county, state, or political subdivision created by law to administer and enforce the provisions of a code.

admixture   A material other than water, aggregates, lime, or cement, used as an ingredient of concrete or mortar, and added to the batch immediately before or during its mixing; used as a water repellent, as a coloring agent, as a **retarder** or **accelerator** (to modify its setting rate), etc.

adobe   A heavy soil, composed largely of clay and silt in sufficient quantities to form a matrix in which sand particles are firmly imbedded; water is added, and straw, manure, and fragments of tile are sometimes combined with this mixture to provide increased mechanical strength and cohesion when it dries. It can be used as a plaster or be formed into bricks, often shaped by hand in a wooden form, then sun-dried; widely used in **Spanish Colonial architecture** and its derivatives. Adobe brick walls are often limeplastered to improve resistance to weather; a coating such as slaked lime acts as a stabilizing agent.

adobe blasting   Same as **mud-capping**.

adobe brick   Large, roughly molded, sundried clay brick, usually of varying sizes.

adobe quemado   An adobe brick that has been kiln-dried at a temperature lower than that required to produce a **hard-burnt brick**; usually deep red in color, relatively soft, and rough in texture.

ADS   Abbr. for "automatic door seal."

adsorbed water   **1.** Water which is held on the surfaces of a material by electrochemical forces; its physical properties are substantially different from those of absorbed water or chemically combined water at the same temperature and pressure. **2.** Water which is bound to soil particles as a result of the attraction between electrical charges on their surfaces and water molecules.

adsorbent   A material (such as **activated charcoal**) which has the ability to extract certain substances from gases, liquids, or solids by causing the substances to adhere to its internal surface without changing the adsorbent physically or chemically.

adsorption   The action of a material in extracting a substance from the atmosphere (or a mixture of gases and liquids) and gathering it on the surface in a condensed layer; the process is not accompanied by physical or chemical change.

advance slope grouting   **Grouting** by a technique in which the front of the mass of grout is forced to move horizontally through preplaced aggregate.

advance slope method   A method of concrete placement in which the face of the fresh concrete moves forward as the concrete is placed; the face of the fresh concrete is not vertical.

adverse possession   Occupation of property by one not the true owner, openly, notoriously, and continuously. See **statute of limitations; squatter's right; proscription**.

advertisement curtain   On the stage of a theatre, a curtain which bears advertisements; usually behind the **asbestos curtain**, but sometimes (rarely) the asbestos itself.

advertisement for bids   The published public notice soliciting bids for a construction project. Most frequently used to conform to legal requirements pertaining to projects to be constructed under public authority, and usually published in newspapers of general circulation in those districts from which the public funds are derived.

adytum, adyton   **1.** The inner shrine of a temple reserved for the priests. **2.** The most sacred part of a place of worship.

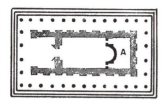

adytum: plan of a Roman temple, showing the adytum at A

adz   A cutting tool whose thin arching blade is perpendicular to the handle; used for the rough-shaping of wood.

adze   British term for **adz**.

A/E   Abbr. for **architect-engineer**.

AEA   Abbr. for "Aluminum Extruders Association."

aedes   **1.** In Roman antiquity, any edifice or a minor shrine, not formally consecrated. **2.** Now, any chapel or temple.

adz

aedicula   **1.** A canopied niche flanked by colonnettes intended as a shelter for a statue or as a shrine. **2.** A door or window framed by columns or pilasters and crowned with a pediment. **3.** Diminutive of **aedes**. **4.** A small chapel.

aegicranes   Sculptured representations of the heads or skulls of goats or of rams; used as decorations on ancient altars, friezes, etc.

aegicranes

aerarium   In ancient Rome, the public treasury.

aerate   To introduce air into soil or water by natural or artificial means.

aerated concrete   See **cellular concrete**.

aerated plastic   Same as **foamed plastic**.

aeration   Exposing a substance to circulating air.

aerator fitting   A device which introduces air into an exiting stream of water.

aerial cable   An overhead electric cable (field-assembled at a construction site) which is attached to poles or other supporting structures.

aerial photograph, aerophoto   A photograph taken from a vehicle in flight.

aerial photomap   An aerial photograph or photomosaic to which is added basic mapping information such as place names, boundaries, etc.

aerial photomosaic   A composite of aerial photographs depicting a portion of the earth's surface.

aerodynamic noise   Noise resulting from the flow of air; often generated in an air-conditioning system when an airstream encounters protuberances, rough surfaces, and/or blunt edges.

aerofilter   A bed of coarse material used for the rapid filtering of sewage; recirculation of the **effluent** may be employed.

aerograph   A spray gun for paint.

aerophoto   An **aerial photograph**.

aerosol paints   Paints which are packaged in a pressurized container for spray application. Pressure is supplied by compressed liquefied gas.

aes   In ancient Rome or Greece: copper, tin, or any alloy of these metals.

aetoma, aetos   A **pediment**, or the **tympanum** of a pediment.

A/F   In a portland cement mixture, the abbr. for "molar or weight ratio of aluminum oxide to iron oxide."

affronted, affronté   Said of animals or figures facing each other, as in pediments, overdoors, etc.

affronted

AFNOR   Abbr. for "Association Française de Normalisation."

A-frame   A three-piece rigid structural frame in the shape of the upright capital letter A.

A-frame house   A house, usually constructed of wood, with a roof that extends steeply downward from both sides of a central ridge, almost to the building foundation; the roof is supported by a rigid structural framework in the shape of the capital letter **A**. One or both end walls of the house are often almost completely glazed. Much of the living area on the ground floor is open to the underside of the roof; the bedrooms are frequently located on a balcony directly under the roof; often, there is an exterior deck at one end or both ends of the house. Also see **rafter house**.

A-frame house

African cherry   See **makore**.

African ebony   See **ebony**.

African mahogany   Same as **khaya**.

African rosewood   See **bubinga**.

after cooler   A device that cools compressed air after it is fully compressed.

afterfilter, final filter   In an air-conditioning system, a high-efficiency filter located near a **terminal unit**.

afterflaming   The continued flaming combustion of a material after the exposing flame has been removed.

after-flush   The residue of water in a toilet flush tank after it has been flushed; after flushing, the residue gradually drains from the flush tank to seal the trap.

afterglow   The glow in a material after the removal of an external source of fire to which it is exposed, or after the cessation (natural or induced) of flames.

aftertack, residual tack The lingering tack or stickiness of a paint film which remains over a long period of time.

AG **1.** Abbr. for "above grade." **2.** Abbr. for "against the grain."

AGA Abbr. for "American Gas Association."

agalma In ancient Greece, any work of art dedicated to a god.

agba A large central African tree with rather lightweight wood of a creamy to pinkish brown color. Used for plywood, interior millwork, and carpentry.

AGC Abbr. for "Associated General Contractors."

age hardening An aging process in certain metals, at room temperature, which results in increased strength and hardness.

ageing British variant of **aging**.

agency **1.** A relationship by which one party, usually the **agent**, is empowered to enter into binding transactions affecting the legal rights of another party, usually called the **principal**, as, for example, entering into a contract or buying or selling property in his name or on his behalf. **2.** An administrative branch of government (federal, state, or local).

agent One who is empowered to enter into binding transactions on behalf of another (usually called the **principal**).

age softening The loss of strength and hardness at room temperature which takes place in certain alloys owing to spontaneous reduction of residual stresses in the strainhardened structure.

agger **1.** In ancient Rome, an earthwork; an artificial mound or rampart. **2.** The fill for a road over low ground.

agglomeration The collecting together of tiny suspended particles into a mass of larger size, one which will settle more rapidly.

AGGR On drawings, abbr. for **aggregate**.

aggradation The addition of a material to the earth's surface to promote the uniformity of a grade or slope.

aggregate **1.** An inert granular material such as natural sand, manufactured sand, gravel, crushed gravel, crushed stone, vermiculite, per-

lite, and air-cooled blast-furnace slag, which when bound together into a conglomerate mass by a matrix forms concrete or mortar. **2.** An inert granular material that may be added to gypsum plaster.

aggregate bin A structure designed for storing and dispensing dry granular construction materials such as sand, crushed stone, and gravel; usually has a hopper-like bottom that funnels the material to a gate under the structure.

aggregate blending The mixing of two or more **aggregates** so as to obtain different aggregate properties.

aggregate interlock The projection of aggregate particles or portions thereof from one side of a joint or crack in concrete into recesses in the other side so as to effect load transfer in compression and shear, and maintain mutual alignment.

aggregate strength The strength of a wire rope determined by summing the individual breaking strength of the strands of which it is fabricated.

agiasterium In the early church, that part of a basilica in which the altar was set up.

aging, *Brit.* **ageing** **1.** The progressive change in a chemical and physical material with increased age; in natural rubber and synthetic elastomers, usually marked by a deterioration caused by oxidation. Also see **age hardening, age softening**. **2.** The storing of varnish to improve clarity and gloss.

agitating lorry British term for **agitating truck**.

agitating speed The rate of rotation of the drum or blades of a truck mixer or other device used for agitation of mixed concrete.

agitating truck, *Brit.* **agitating lorry** A vehicle carrying a drum in which freshly mixed concrete can be conveyed from the point of mixing to that of placing, the drum being rotated continuously so as to agitate the contents.

agitation **1.** The process of providing gentle motion in mixed concrete, just sufficient to prevent segregation or loss of plasticity. **2.** The mixing and homogenization of slurries or finely ground powders by air or mechanical means.

agitator **1.** A mechanical device used to mix a liquid contained in a vessel. **2.** A device for maintaining plasticity and preventing segregation of mixed concrete by agitation.

agitator body A truck-mounted drum for transporting freshly mixed concrete; rotating internal paddles or rotation of the drum prevents the setting of the mixture prior to its delivery at the site.

agitator body

AGL Abbr. for "above ground level."

agnus dei Any image or representation of a lamb as emblematic of Christ, esp. such a representation with a halo and supporting the banner of the cross.

agnus dei

agora The chief meeting place or marketplace in an ancient Greek city.

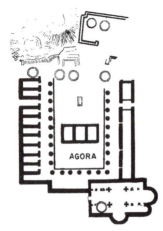

agora: plan of the agora of Antiphellus

agrafe, agraffe The voussoir or keystone of an arch, especially when carved as a cartouche.

agrafe

agreement 1. A meeting of minds. 2. A legally enforceable promise or promises between two or among several persons. 3. On a construction project, the document stating the essential terms of the construction contract which incorporates by reference the other **contract documents**. 4. The document setting forth the terms of the contract between the architect and owner or between the architect and a consultant. 5. An arrangement indicating the intent of a **contract** but not necessarily fulfilling all the enforceable provisions of it. Also see **agreement form, contract**.

agreement form A document setting forth in printed form the general provisions of an **agreement** with spaces provided for insertion of specific data relating to a particular project.

Agrément Board See **British Board of Agrément**.

agricultural drain Same as **agricultural pipe drain**.

agricultural lime A hydrated lime which is used to condition soil.

agricultural pipe drain A system of porous or perforated pipes laid in a trench filled with gravel (or the like); used for draining subsoil.

aguilla An obelisk, or the spire of a church tower.

Ah Abbr. for "ampere-hour."

aha Same as **ha-ha**.

AHU Abbr. for **air-handling unit**.

AIA Abbr. for "American Institute of Architects."

AIEE   Abbr. for "American Institute of Electrical Engineers."

aiguille   A slender form of drill used for boring or drilling a blasthole in rock.

aileron   A half gable, such as that which closes the end of a penthouse roof or of the aisle of a church.

AIMA   Abbr. for "Acoustical and Insulating Materials Association."

air balancing   A procedure used to adjust the flow of air in an **HVAC** system so as to meet the design goals for airflow throughout the system.

air barrier   A membrane that acts as a resistance to air leakage.

air-blown mortar   Same as **shotcrete**.

air blowpipe   A pipe which emits a jet of air; used to clean an area of debris.

airborne sound   Sound that reaches a point in a building by propagation from the source through air.

air-bound   Said of a pipe or apparatus in which the presence of a pocket of air prevents or reduces the desired liquid flow in the pipe or apparatus. Also see **air lock, 2**.

air break   In a drainage system, a piping arrangement in which a drain from an appliance, device, or fixture discharges into the open air and then into another fixture, receptacle, or interceptor; used to prevent back **siphonage** or **backflow**.

air brick   A perforated brick or perforated metal unit of brick size which is built into a wall; used for ventilation.

airbrush   A small tool used for the fine-spray application of paint, dye, watercolor pigment, or ink by compressed air.

airbrush

air chamber   In a water piping system near a valve or faucet, a vertical pipe stub which is sealed at the top and contains air; the entrapped air provides a cushion when the valve is closed

suddenly, thereby eliminating the noise of **water hammer**.

air changes   A measure of the volume of air supplied to or exhausted from a building (or room); usually expressed in terms of the number of complete changes of air per hour in the room or space under consideration.

air circuit breaker   A type of **circuit breaker** utilized in commercial buildings at medium voltage; the word "air" refers to the insulating medium between contacts in the circuit breaker.

air circulation   Natural or imparted motion of air.

air cleaner   A device (such as an air washer, air filter, electrostatic precipitator, or charcoal filter) which removes airborne impurities such as dust, smoke, or fumes.

air cock   Same as **pet cock**.

air compressor   A machine which draws in air at atmospheric pressure, then compresses it to pressures higher than atmospheric and delivers it at a rate sufficient to operate pneumatic tools or equipment.

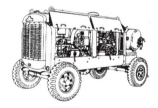

air compressor

AIR COND   On drawings, abbr. for "air condition."

air conditioner   A device for providing **air conditioning**.

air conditioning   **1.** The process of treating air so as to control simultaneously its temperature, humidity, cleanliness, and distribution within an interior space such as a room or building. **2.** Same as definition **1**, but also controlling odor and noise.

air-conditioning duct   See **air duct**.

air-conditioning grille   Same as **inserted grille**.

air-conditioning lock   A type of window lock requiring a special key or wrench to open it; used where the window is to be opened only for special purposes, such as cleaning.

air-conditioning lock

air-conditioning system An assembly of components for the treatment of air, controlling its temperature, humidity, cleanliness, and distribution within an air-conditioned space. Types of systems differ, but the basic components may include: outside-air intake, preheater, return-air intake, filters, dehumidifier, heating coil, humidifier, fans, ductwork, air outlets, air terminals, refrigeration machine, piping, pumps, and water or brine. See **heating, ventilating, and air-conditioning system**.

air-conditioning unit Same as **room air conditioner**.

air content The volume of air voids in cement paste, mortar, or concrete, exclusive of pore space in aggregate particles, usually expressed as a percentage of total volume of the mixture.

air control valve Same as **air maintenance device**.

air-cooled blast-furnace slag The material resulting from solidification of molten blast-furnace slag under atmospheric conditions. Also see **blast-furnace slag**.

air-cure To vulcanize at ordinary room temperatures, or without the aid of heat.

air curtain A stream of high-velocity temperature-controlled air which is directed downward, across an opening; excludes insects, exterior drafts, etc.; prevents the transfer of heat across it, and makes it possible to air-condition a space having an open entrance; used in exterior doors, on loading platforms, etc.

air diffuser An air distribution outlet, usually located in the ceiling and consisting of deflecting vanes discharging supply air in various directions and planes, and arranged to promote mixing of the air which is supplied to the room with the air already in the room.

air diffuser

air-distributing acoustical ceiling A suspended acoustical ceiling in which the board, perforated metal, or tile is provided with small, evenly distributed mechanical perforations through the material; designed to provide a desired flow of air from a pressurized plenum above.

air door Same as **air curtain**.

air drain An empty space left around the external foundation wall of a building to prevent the earth from lying against it and causing dampness.

air-dried lumber, natural-seasoned lumber Wood dried by exposure to air under natural conditions; usually has a moisture content not greater than 24%.

air drill Same as **pneumatic drill**.

air drying The process of drying slowly under ambient conditions of temperature and humidity, as in the natural seasoning of lumber or the hardening of paint.

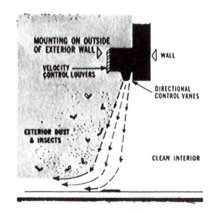

air curtain or air door

air duct A duct, usually fabricated of metal, fiber glass, or concrete; used to transfer air from one location to another.

air eliminator In a piping system, a device used to remove air from water, steam, or a refrigerant.

air-entrained concrete Concrete made with air-entraining cement or an air-entraining agent. Same as **cellular concrete**.

air entraining Descriptive of the capability of a material or process to develop a system of minute bubbles of air in cement paste, concrete, or mortar.

air-entraining admixture An **admixture** that causes the development of air bubbles in concrete or mortar during its mixture.

air-entraining agent An addition for hydraulic cement or an admixture for concrete or mortar which causes air to be incorporated in the form of minute bubbles in the concrete or mortar during mixing, usually to increase its workability and frost resistance.

air-entraining hydraulic cement Hydraulic cement which contains an air-entraining agent in an amount such as to cause air to be entrained in the mortar, within specified limits.

air entrainment The occlusion of air in the form of tiny bubbles (generally smaller than 1 mm) during the mixing of concrete or mortar; used to improve its workability.

air-exhaust ventilator **1.** An air-exhaust unit used to carry away odors and fumes from a stove, griddle, etc.; may contain a grease-extracting device or an air filter; sometimes includes a fire-extinguishing device. **2.** Any air-exhaust unit used to carry away dirt particles, odors, or fumes (as in an industrial plant); the ventilator may be mechanically actuated or of the gravity type.

air filter Any device used to remove solid and/or gaseous pollutants from air.

airflow vane Same as **turning vane**.

air flue See **flue**.

air-fuel ratio The ratio of the volume (or weight) of air being furnished for combustion to the volume (or weight) of the fuel.

air gap **1.** The unobstructed vertical distance between the lowest opening of a faucet (or the like) which supplies a plumbing fixture (such as tank or wash bowl) and the level at which the fixture will overflow. **2.** In a drainage system, the unobstructed vertical distance between the outlet of a waste pipe and the **flood-level** rim of the

receptacle into which it discharges. **3.** A gap in an electric or magnetic circuit; usually acts as a high-resistance path in the circuit.

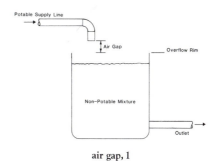

air gap, 1

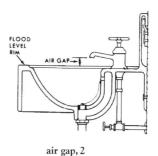

air gap, 2

air grating **1.** A fixed metal grille on the exterior of a building through which air is brought into, or discharged from, the building for purposes of ventilation. **2.** An **air diffuser**.

air gun **1.** Same as **spray gun**. **2.** See **shotcrete gun**.

air hammer, pneumatic hammer A portable tool, driven percussively by air pressure, into which is set a chisel, hammer, or the like.

air-handling luminaire Same as **air-light troffer**.

air-handling system An air-conditioning system in which an **air-handling unit** provides part of the treatment of the air.

air-handling unit; packaged fan equipment An assembly of air-conditioning components (such as fans, cooling coils, filters, humidifiers, and dampers) integrated into a self-contained package and often installed as a single unit, which is connected to system of metal ductwork that distributes the conditioned air.

air hole In the foundation of a house, an opening that provides ventilation for a **crawl space**.

air house Same as **pneumatic structure**.

air-inflated structure Same as **pneumatic structure**.

air inlet In an air-conditioning system, a device through which air is exhausted from a room or building.

air intake Same as **outside-air intake**.

air lance A rod-shaped device for directing a high-velocity stream of compressed air; used to clean away debris from a surface.

air leakage **1.** The volume of air which flows through a closed window or door in a given length of time as a result of the difference in air pressure on its opposite faces. **2.** In ductwork, air which escapes from a joint, coupling, etc. **3.** The undesired leakage or uncontrolled passage of air from a ventilation system. **4.** The flow of uncontrolled air through cracks or openings in an enclosure within a building (such as a HVAC plenum) or through the surfaces which enclose the building.

airless spraying, hydraulic spraying The spraying of paint by means of high fluid pressure and special equipment.

air lift **1.** Equipment for lifting slurry or dry powder through pipes by means of compressed air. **2.** The use of compressed air, introduced in water at the bottom of an open-ended cased pile or cell of a cofferdam, to rid it of loose material.

air-lift pump A type of pump for raising water from a well, consisting of a pipe which surrounds another of smaller diameter; compressed air is injected into the smaller pipe, causing water to rise up the larger pipe.

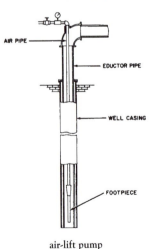

air-lift pump

air-light troffer In an air-conditioning system, a unit which combines the functions of a light fixture and an air **terminal unit**.

air line A duct, hose, or pipe that supplies compressed air to a pneumatic tool or piece of equipment.

air lock **1.** A space which is designed to isolate an air conditioned space from another space to which it is connected. **2.** In a pump or piping system, the stoppage of flow resulting from the presence of trapped air. **3.** An enclosure with control doors between two rooms that permits the ingress and egress from one room to another while permitting minimal air movement between rooms.

air-lock strip The weather stripping which is fastened to the edges of each wing of a revolving door.

air maintenance device A valve required to introduce air into a tank which stores water under pressure.

air meter A device for measuring the air content of concrete and mortar.

air-mixing plenum In an air-conditioning system, a chamber in which the recirculating air is mixed with air from outdoors.

air monitoring During the removal of asbestos in buildings, the measurement of asbestos fiber content in the air.

air motor An air-operated device used to open or close a **damper, 1** or valve.

air moving device See **fan**.

air outlet In an air-conditioning system, a device at the end of a duct through which air is supplied to a space.

air permeability test A test for the measurement of the fineness of powdered materials, such as portland cement.

air pipe A seldom-used synonym for **vent pipe**.

airplane bungalow A **Craftsman style** bungalow having a gable whose face is parallel to the main ridge of the roof; its second floor is a single room.

air pocket An air-filled volume within a section of piping (or an apparatus) which is normally filled with liquid.

air pressure-reducing valve See **pressure-reducing valve**.

air pressure relief vent A **relief vent**.

air pump A pump used to exhaust or to compress air, or force it through another apparatus. Also see **air compressor**.

air purge valve A device which eliminates trapped air from a piping system.

air receiver On an air compressor, the air storage tank.

air register Same as **register**.

air regulator A device for regulating airflow, as in the burner of a furnace.

air reheater In a heating system, any device used to add heat to the air circulating in the system.

air release valve A **valve**, usually manually operated, which is used to release air from a water pipe or fitting.

air right The legal property right for use of the space above a specified elevated plane; usually includes the right to ground support but excludes other rights to ground use, e.g., the right to construct a building over a railroad track.

air-ring In the placement of **shotcrete**, a perforated manifold through which air is introduced into the flow of material.

air-seasoned lumber See **air-dried lumber**.

air separator An apparatus for separating ground-up materials pneumatically into various sizes.

air-set To allow material to harden under normal atmospheric pressure and temperature.

air shaft, air well A ventilating shaft; a roofless enclosed area within a building or between buildings; may have openings such as windows.

air shutter A device for regulating the quantity of air being mixed with gas for combustion.

air-slaked Said of a surface that is wetted by the exposure to moisture in air.

air slaking Absorption by quicklime or cement of moisture and carbon dioxide from the atmosphere, causing the material to change its chemical composition.

air-supported structure See **pneumatic structure**.

air tap Same as **air vent**.

air terminal In a lightning protection system, the combination of a metal rod and its brace or footing, on the upper part of a structure.

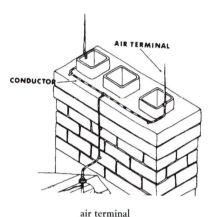

air terminal

air terminal unit In air-conditioning, same as **terminal unit**.

air test A test that applies uniform air pressure throughout a drainage system being tested for leakage. This test is recommended in lieu of a **water test** when there is a danger of water freezing during the test.

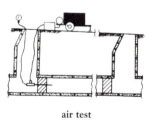

air test

air test, pneumatic test A test for leaks in drainage systems, in soil, waste, and ventilating pipe systems, or in ductwork; all openings are sealed, and compressed air is introduced into the system; air leakage is indicated by means of a U-gauge or other suitable pressure gauge.

air tight Said of an enclosure or barrier that does not permit the passage of air.

air-to-air resistance The resistance provided by the wall of a building to the flow of heat. See **thermal conductance** and **thermal resistance**.

air-to-air transmission coefficient See **thermal transmittance**.

air trap Same as **trap, 1**.

air vent In a water distribution system, a **vent** for releasing trapped air; usually located at the highest point in the system.

air ventilation The quantity of air which must be supplied to maintain the desired quality of air within a space.

air vessel **1.** An enclosed volume of air which uses the compressibility of air to minimize **water hammer**. **2.** An enclosed chamber using the compressibility of air to promote a more uniform flow of water in a piping system.

air void A space which is filled with air in cement paste, mortar, or concrete. Also see **entrapped air, entrained air**.

air washer A water spray system or device for cleaning, humidifying, or dehumidifying the air.

air-water jet **1.** A jet of air and water mixed, which leaves a nozzle at high velocity; used in cleaning the surfaces of concrete or rock. **2.** In cleaning concrete or rock surfaces, a high-velocity jet consisting of a mixture of air and water.

air-water storage tank A water storage tank in which the air, above the water, is compressed.

airway A passage for ventilation between thermal insulation and roof boards.

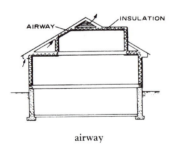

airway

air well See **air shaft**.

AISC Abbr. for "American Institute of Steel Construction."

AISI Abbr. for "American Iron and Steel Institute."

aisle **1.** A longitudinal passage between sections of seats in an auditorium or church. **2.** In a church, the space flanking and parallel to the nave; usually separated from it by columns, intended primarily for circulation but sometimes containing seats.

aisleway A passage or walkway within a factory, storage building, or shop permitting the flow of inside traffic. Also see **aisle**.

AITC Abbr. for "American Institute of Timber Construction."

aiwan A reception hall in an ancient Parthian building.

ajarca In southern Spain, an ornament in brick walls, formed of patterns, a half brick deep, more or less complicated.

a jour, ajouré Pierced, perforated, or cut out to form a decorative opening in wood, stone, metal, or other material.

AL On drawings, abbr. for **aluminum**.

ala **1.** An alcove or small room opening off the atrium of an ancient Roman house. **2.** A small room on each side of a **cella**.

alabaster Fine-grained, translucent variety of very pure gypsum, generally white or delicately shaded.

A-labeled door A door carrying a certification from the Underwriters' Laboratories, Inc. that it meets the requirements for a **class-A door**.

alameda A shaded public walk or promenade.

alarm valve See **wet alarm valve**.

alatorium **1.** A piazza, corridor, or covered walk. **2.** The flank of a building.

albani stone A pepper-colored stone used in buildings in ancient Rome before the introduction of marble.

albarium A white lime used for stucco; made by burning marble.

albronze Same as **aluminum bronze**.

album In ancient Roman architecture, a space on the surface of a wall covered with white plaster, located in a public place, on which public announcements and records, etc. were written.

alburnum Same as **sapwood**.

alcazar A Moorish or Spanish fortress or castle.

alclad A metal product clad with an aluminum or aluminum-alloy coating, usually as a protection against corrosion.

alcove A small recessed space, opening directly into a larger room.

alder A moderately light-colored, light-weight hardwood that changes to flesh color or light brown when dried; often stained to simulate cherry, mahogany or walnut; often used as plywood core and crossbanding.

aleatorium In ancient Roman architecture, a room in which dice games were played.

ale house In an early British or American community: a village tavern licensed to sell alcoholic beverages.

alette **1.** A minor wing of a building. **2.** A door jamb. **3.** A rear pilaster, partially visible within a cluster of columnar elements. **4.** The wing of the pier on both sides of an engaged column.

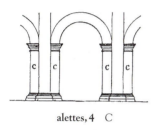

alettes, 4   C

Alexandrian work Same as **opus Alexandrinum**.

Alexandrinum opus Same as **opus Alexandrinum**.

Alhambra A fortress and palace built by the Moorish kings of Granada in southern Spain, completed in the 14th century.

alicatado Tile work which is executed with **azulejos**; used to decorate pavements and walls, especially in patios.

alidade The part of a surveying instrument which consists of a sighting device, with index, and reading or recording accessories.

alienation The transfer of title to real property by one person to another.

aliform Having a wing-like shape or extensions.

aligning punch A punch used for lining up mating holes prior to riveting or bolting; a **drift punch**.

aligning punch

alignment **1.** An adjustment in a straight line. **2.** The theoretical, definitive lines that establish the position of construction (such as a building) or the shape of an individual element (such as a curved or straight beam). **3.** In highway and other surveys, the ground plan depicting direction of the route as distinguished from a profile, which shows the vertical element. **4.** In prehistoric building, formal alleys of standing stones, as at Carnac in France.

alipterion In ancient Roman architecture, a room used by bathers for anointing themselves.

alite A principal constituent of portland-cement clinker; primarily tricalcium silicate, but includes small amounts of magnesium oxide, aluminum oxide, ferric oxide, and other oxides.

alive Same as **live, 1**.

alkali Any of the various chemically active bases such as the soluble salts of metals, e.g., the water-soluble salts of sodium and potassium which occur in constituents of concrete and mortar that may result in deleterious expansion.

alkali-aggregate reaction A chemical reaction in mortar or concrete between alkalies from portland cement or other sources and certain constituents of some aggregates; under certain conditions, deleterious expansion of the concrete or mortar may result.

alkaline soil Soil containing soluble salts of magnesium, sodium, or the like, and having a **pH value** of between 7.3 and 8.5.

alkali reactivity Of a concrete aggregate, its susceptibility to **alkali-aggregate reaction**.

alkali resistance **1.** The degree to which a paint resists reaction with alkaline materials such as lime, cement, plaster, soap, etc.; a necessary property for paints in bathrooms, kitchens, laundries. **2.** The degree to which a porcelain enamel will resist attack by aqueous alkaline solutions.

alkali-silica reaction In portland cement, the reaction between the alkalies and particular siliceous rocks and/or minerals which are present in some aggregates; may result in abnormal expansion and cracking of concrete under service conditions.

alkali soil A soil, with salts injurious to plant life, having a **pH value** of 8.5 or higher.

alkyd paint A paint using an alkyd resin as the vehicle for the pigment.

alkyd resin One of a group of thermoplastic synthetic resins; used in bonding materials, in adhesives, and in paints and varnishes.

allée A broad walk, planted with trees on either side, usually at least twice as high as the width of the walk.

allège A part of a wall which is thinner than the rest, esp. the spandrel under a window.

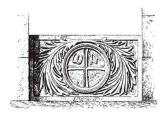

allège

allegory A figurative representation in which the meaning is conveyed symbolically.

allegory: Cathedral of Worms, 13th cent. The beast with four heads symbolizes the Four Gospels

Allen head A screw having a hexagonally shaped recess in its head.

Allen wrench A wrench for Allen head screws; a steel bar, hexagonal in shape, which is bent to form a right angle.

Allen wrench

alley **1.** A service way providing a secondary public means of access to abutting properties; a narrow passageway between or behind buildings, sometimes permitting traffic for only one lane of cars. **2.** A garden walk between rows of trees; an **allée**.

all-heart lumber Lumber that is all **heartwood**, entirely free of **sapwood**.

alligator hide A surface condition on porcelain enamel, characterized by an extreme roughness; a severe case of **orange peel**.

alligatoring **1.** The splitting of a film of paint in a pattern resembling an alligator skin, caused by shrinkage of a coat of paint applied over a semiplastic or thermoplastic undercoat; also called **crocodiling**. **2.** Surface cracking, due to oxidation and shrinkage stresses, which shows as repetitive mounding of an asphalt surface in a pattern resembling the hide of an alligator; occurs only in unsurfaced bitumen exposed to the weather.

alligator shears, lever shears Wide-jawed shears, resembling the jaws of an alligator, used to cut sheets of metal; operated by a foot lever.

alligator wrench A wrench having V-shaped, fixed serrated jaws; used to turn cylindrical parts, esp. in fitting pipe.

all-in aggregate See **bank-run gravel**.

all-in contract Same as **turn-key job**.

allotment garden Any privately or publicly owned garden area which has been divided into plots for assignment to individuals for their use.

allover A pattern covering an entire surface; usually one which is repeated.

ALLOW. On drawings, abbr. for "allowance."

allowable bearing value, allowable soil pressure, allowable bearing capacity The maximum permissible pressure on foundation soil that provides adequate safety against rupture of the soil mass or movement of the foundation of such magnitude as to impair the structure that imposes the pressure.

allowable load The load which induces the maximum permissible unit stress at a critical section of a structural member.

allowable pile bearing load The maximum permissible load on a pile that provides adequate safety against movement of such magnitude that would endanger the structure supported by the pile.

allowable pile load The allowable concentrically applied load which is permitted along the central axis of a pile.

allowable soil pressure See **allowable bearing value**.

allowable stress In the design of structures, the maximum unit stress permitted under working loads by codes and specifications.

allowance **1.** See **cash allowance**. **2.** See **contingency allowance**.

alloy A composition of two or more metals fused together, usually to obtain a desired property.

alloy steel Steel containing one or more alloying elements other than carbon, such as chromium, molybdenum, or nickel, which have been added (in an amount exceeding a specified minimum) to impart particular physical, mechanical, or chemical properties.

all-rowlock wall See **rowlock cavity wall**.

all-stretcher bond A masonry **bond, 6** showing only **stretchers** on the face of the brick wall; same as **stretcher bond**.

allure See **alure**.

alluvial deposit Earth, sand, gravel, or other rock or mineral materials transported and laid down by flowing water.

alluvium Gravel, sand, silt, soil, or other material that is deposited by running water.

ALM On drawings, abbr. for "alarm."

almariol A storage place for ecclesiastical vestments; an **ambry**.

almary See **ambry**.

almehrabh In Arabian architecture, a niche in a mosque which marks the direction of Mecca.

almemar, almemor **1.** A **bema, 2. 2.** In a synagogue, a desk on which the Torah is placed while being read to the congregation.

almena An indented **trapezium** serving as an embattled parapet.

almena

almery See **ambry**.

almond An **aureole** of elliptical form.

almonry A building or part thereof where alms are distributed.

almshouse **1.** A building in which charity was distributed to the poor; found in England and in some early American settlements and cities; also see **poorhouse**. **2.** An **almonry**.

alpha brass An alloy containing 51 to 61% copper and 39 to 45% zinc; used in hot-water systems because of its corrosion resistant properties.

alpha gypsum A specially processed gypsum having low consistency and high compressive strength, often exceeding 5,000 lb per sq in. (352 kg per sq cm).

ALS Abbr. for "American Lumber Standards."

ALT On drawings, abbr. for "alternate."

altar **1.** An elevated table, slab, or structure, often of stone, rectangular or round, for religious rites, sacrifices, or offerings. **2.** The Communion table in certain churches.

altar

altar frontal   An ornamental hanging or panel for the front of an altar.

altar of repose   In a Roman Catholic church, a side altar, repository, or storage niche where the Host is kept from Maundy Thursday to Good Friday.

altarpiece   A decorative screen, painting, or sculpture above the back of an altar.

altar rail   A low rail or barrier in front of the altar, running transversely to the main axis of the church and separating the officiating clergy from the other worshipers.

altar screen   A richly decorated partition of stone, wood, or metal, separating the altar from the space behind it.

altar slab, altar stone   A flat stone or slab forming the top of an altar.

altar tomb   A raised tomb, or monument covering a tomb, whose shape resembles an altar.

alteration   Construction in a building which may change the structural parts, mechanical equipment, or location of openings, but does not increase the overall area of dimensions of the building.

alterations   **1.** A construction project (or portion of a project) comprising revisions within or to prescribed elements of an existing structure, as distinct from additions to an existing structure. **2.** Remodeling.

alternate bid   The amount stated in the bid to be added to or deducted from the amount of the **base bid** if the corresponding change in project scope or alternate materials and/or methods of construction is accepted.

alternating current   An electric current that varies periodically in value and direction, first flowing in one direction in the circuit and then flowing in the opposite direction; each complete repetition is called a **cycle**, and the number of repetitions per second is called the **frequency**.

alternating sprinkler system   A fire **sprinkler system** that can be changed from a **wet-pipe sprinkler system** in the summer to a **dry-pipe sprinkler system** in the winter.

alternator   A generator of alternating current which is produced by the turning of its rotor.

ALTN   On drawings, abbr. for "alteration."

alto-rilievo, alto-relievo   See **high relief**.

alum   A chemical compound added to gypsum plaster to make the plaster harden faster.

ALUM.   On drawings, abbr. for **aluminum**.

alumina   The oxide of aluminum; an important constituent of the clays used in brick, tile, and refractories.

aluminium   British term for **aluminum**.

aluminize, *Brit.* **aluminise**   To apply a surface coating of aluminum to another metal or other base material, usually by spraying or dipping in molten aluminum. On steel, such coatings greatly increase corrosion resistance.

aluminous cement   See **calcium aluminate cement**.

aluminum, *Brit.* **aluminium**   A lustrous, silver-white, nonmagnetic, lightweight metal which is very malleable; has good thermal and electrical conductivity; a good reflector of both heat and light. In construction, most aluminum is used in alloy form because of added strength; further strengthened by heat treatment; used in extrusions, castings, and sheets. Excellent resistance to oxidation; often anodized for better corrosion resistance, surface hardness, and/or architectural color requirements.

aluminum brass   Brass to which aluminum has been added to increase its corrosion resistance.

aluminum bronze   A copper-aluminum alloy, usually with 3 to 11% aluminum; may contain additional additives; has good corrosion resistance and may be cast or coldworked.

aluminum door A door having aluminum stiles and rails; usually glazed.

aluminum foil Very thin aluminum sheet (less than 0.006 in. or 0.15 mm); usually used for thermal insulation and vapor barriers.

aluminum oxide Same as **alumina**.

aluminum paint A paint made with aluminum paste and a film-forming vehicle (such as a varnish); a good heat and light reflector; has good water impermeability.

aluminum powder Small flakes of aluminum metal obtained by stamping or ball-milling foil in the presence of a fatty lubricant, such as stearic acid, which causes the flakes to orient in a pattern to give high brilliance. Usually supplied in paste form wetted with mineral spirits.

aluminum-silicon bronze An alloy consisting chiefly of copper with aluminum and silicon added to give it greater strength and hardness.

aluminum window Any window constructed principally of aluminum, the components of which usually are extruded.

alure, allure, alur A gallery or passage, as along the parapets of a castle, around the roof of a church, or along a cloister.

alure A

ALV Symbol for **alarm valve**.

alveated Having the vaulted shape of a beehive.

alveus In ancient Rome, a bath constructed in the floor of a room, the upper part of it projecting above the floor, the lower part being sunk into the floor itself.

ALY On drawings, abbr. for **alloy**.

amado In traditional Japanese architecture, a type of shutter made of sliding wooden panels which (when not in use) slide into a box-like storage cabinet attached to the exterior of the building at one side of the opening; usually set in place in the evening.

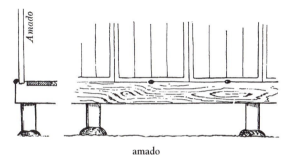

amado

AMB Abbr. for "asbestos mill-cut board."

ambient lighting In any given area, the general background illumination.

ambient noise The all-encompassing, average background **noise** associated with a given environment, often a composite of sounds from many sources near and far, of many different types, e.g., the general background noise in a neighborhood or in an auditorium.

ambient pressure In a water distribution system, the normal operating pressure at any particular location in the system.

ambient temperature The temperature of the surrounding air.

ambitus 1. A small niche in underground Roman or Greek tombs, forming a receptacle for a cinerary urn. 2. In the Middle Ages, such a niche, but enlarged to admit a coffin. 3. In the Middle Ages, the consecrated ground surrounding a church.

ambo, ambon 1. In early Christian churches, a pulpit for reading or chanting the Gospels or the Epistles. 2. In contemporary Balkan or Greek churches, a large pulpit or reading desk. (*See illustration on p. 28.*)

ambo, 1

ambrices In ancient Roman construction, the cross laths inserted between the rafter and tiles of a roof.

ambry, almary, almery, aumbry **1.** A cupboard or niche in a chancel wall for the utensils of the Eucharist; an **armarium**. **2.** A storage place, storeroom, closet, or pantry.

ambry, 1

ambulatory **1.** A passageway around the apse of a church, or for circumambulating a shrine. **2.** A covered walk of a cloister.

ambulatory church A church having a domed center bay which is surrounded on three sides by aisles.

ambulatory, 2

AMCA Abbr. for "Air Movement and Control Association."

AMD On drawings, abbr. for "air-moving device."

amended water Water to which a **surfactant** has been added.

American basement A floor of a building partly above and partly below grade level, often serving as the entrance level to the building. Also see **basement**. Also called a walk-out basement.

American bond Same as **common bond**; same as **English garden-wall bond**.

American Bracketed style A term occasionally used for the **Italianate style**.

American Chateauesque style See **Chateauesque style**.

American Colonial architecture A term usually applied to colonial buildings constructed in America by English immigrants to the New World; often classified according to region *in America*.

In early *colonial New England*, the typical house was **timber-framed** with hewn-and-pegged joints; exterior walls were sometimes covered with hard plaster, then clad with clapboard or weatherboards. Unpretentious houses commonly had a single room with a loft space above; more prosperous houses, often one and a half or two stories high and one or two rooms deep, usually were built on the **hall-and-parlor plan**, with one room on each side of an interior wall containing a massive, centrally located fireplace and a large high chimney; on the façade, **drops** were often suspended from the underside of an overhanging second floor. Many of these early houses had a steeply pitched **gable roof** and a **side gable**, or a **hipped roof** with eaves having no significant overhang; unglazed window openings were covered with solid-wood shutters, later replaced by narrow casement windows having small **quarrels**; heavy battened doors. Also see **saltbox house, stone ender, whale house**. Occasionally called Early Colonial architecture.

In the *colonial South* and along the *mid-Atlantic coast*, single-room houses of the early settlers were often similar to the **one-room plan** houses in New England, with a clay-and-sticks chimney. Later, as the houses became larger, they usually followed a hall-and-parlor plan or a **center-hall plan**. Exterior walls were usually brick, with hand-split shingles on the roof; a massive decorative brick or stone exterior chimney at one or both gabled end walls, with **corbeled chimney caps**. **Pent roofs** were common in the mid-Atlantic area. For colonial architecture constructed by immigrants other than the English, see **Dutch Colonial architecture, French Colonial architecture, German Colonial architecture, Spanish Colonial architecture**.

American Colonial Revival An **architectural mode** usually based on architectural prototypes in the English colonies in America, but often including features not found or rarely present in those prototypes. Buildings in this classification are usually characterized by a façade often featuring a Classical cornice; cupola; widow's walk; colonial detailing; bevel siding or a smooth brick wall finish with fine joints; brickwork often set in a **Flemish bond** pattern; splayed lintels; a hipped, gabled, or gambrel roof covered with slate tiles or wood shingles; louvered shutters; double-hung rectangular sash windows with multiple panes in both the upper and lower sashes; symmetrically arrayed windows in the façade; a fanlight over the main entry door and sidelights on each side of door; the front door commonly crowned by a pediment, extending forward and supported on columns so as to form an entry porch.

American four-square house **1.** A one- or two-story house having a square floor plan consisting of four rooms (one in each corner), a **hipped roof**, and an off-center entry door; most popular from about 1905 to 1915. **2.** A **Prairie box**, primarily in the years between about 1900 to 1920, having a low-pitched hipped roof and a symmetrical façade.

American Institute of Architects (AIA) A professional organization, founded in 1857, whose purpose is to establish and promote professionalism and accountability on the part of its members, and to promote architectural design excellence. Address: 1735 New York Avenue NW, Washington, DC 20006.

American International style See **International style** and **Contemporary style**.

American linden See **basswood**.

American Mansard style A seldom-used synonym for **Second Empire style**. Also see **Mansard style**.

American method of application A method of applying rectangular roofing shingles which provides double coverage with a head lap, but no side lap.

American National Standards Institute An independent organization of trade associations, technical societies, professional groups, and consumer organizations; establishes and publishes standards; formerly known as the United States of America Standards Institute (USASI or ASI), and previously as the American Standards Association (ASA).

American Renaissance Revival A term occasionally used for **Italian Renaissance Revival**.

American Rundbogenstil Same as **Round Arch style**.

American Society of Landscape Architects (ASLA) The professional organization of landscape architects in America, founded in 1899. Address: 4401 Connecticut Avenue NW, Washington, DC 20008.

American Society for Testing and Materials A nonprofit organization that establishes standard tests and specifications for construction materials; such tests and specifications usually are referred to by the abbreviation ASTM followed by a numerical designation. Address: 100 Bar Harbor Drive, West Conshohocken, PA 19428.

American standard beam A type of I-beam of hot-rolled structural steel; designated by the prefix S placed before the size of the member.

American standard channel A C-shaped structural member of hot-rolled structural steel; designated by the prefix C placed before the size of the member.

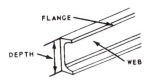

American standard channel

American standard pipe threads In the U.S.A., standard pipe threads for commonly used sizes of pipe for water, gas, or steam; formerly called **Briggs standard pipe threads**.

American Standards Association See **American National Standards Institute**.

Americans with Disabilities Act (ADA) A federal law, enacted in 1990, requiring that public accommodations be accessible to those having physical disabilities; this law mandates that existing physical barriers be replaced or modified so there are no impediments to access by the physically disabled. For detailed information, write the U.S. Equal Employment Opportunities Commission, 1801 L Street, NW, Washington, DC 20507. See American National Standards Institute (ANSI) Standard A117.1-1992. Also see **Uniform Federal Accessibility Standards** and **physical disability**.

American table of distances A table giving safe distances for the storage of explosives, as approved by the Institute of the Makers of Explosives.

American Tudor style See **Tudor Revival**.

American wire gauge, American standard wire gauge, Brown and Sharpe gauge A system used in the U.S.A. for designating wire diameter in electrical wiring or the thickness of aluminum, brass, and copper sheets; ranges from 6/0 (0.58 in. or 16.3 mm) to 40 (0.0031 in. or 0.079 mm).

Amer Std Abbr. for "American Standard."

amino plastic Any plastic made of compounds derived from ammonia.

ammeter An instrument for measuring the rate of flow of electricity, usually expressed in amperes.

ammonia A chemical used as a refrigerant, esp. in large low-temperature refrigeration systems (as in ice skating rinks) because of its high efficiency.

ammonium chloride See **sal ammoniac**.

amorini Same as **putti**.

amorino, amoretto A winged cherub.

amorphous Said of rock having no crystal structure.

amortizement The sloping top of a buttress or projecting pier.

amortizement

amount of mixing The designation of the extent of mixer action employed in combining the ingredients for concrete or mortar; for *stationary mixers*: the mixing time; for *truck mixers*: the number of revolutions of the drum or blades at mixing speed, after the intermingling of the cement with water and aggregates.

amp Abbr. for **ampere**.

ampacity The current-carrying capacity of a wire or cable, expressed in **amperes**.

amperage The flow of electric current in a circuit, expressed in amperes.

ampere The International Standard unit for electrical current. A unit of the rate of flow of electric current; an electromotive force of 1 volt acting across a resistance of 1 ohm results in a current flow of 1 ampere.

amphiprostyle Marked by columns in porticoes only at the front and back (of a classical temple), not on the sides.

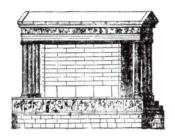

amphiprostyle

amphistylar Said of a classical temple having columns across the length of both sides or across both ends.

amphitheatre, amphitheater **1.** A circular, semicircular, or elliptical auditorium in which a central arena is surrounded by rising tiers of seats. **2.** (*Brit.*) The first section of seats in the gallery of a theatre. **3.** Any outdoor theatre, esp. of the classical Greek type.

amphithura A curtain divided in the center, closing the entrance through the iconostasis of a Greek church.

amplitude Of oscillation or vibration, the maximum displacement from the mean position.

amusement park A commercially operated park with entertainment features such as roller coasters, shooting galleries, merry-go-rounds, refreshment stands, etc.

amyl acetate, banana oil A solvent for lacquers and paints; has a strong banana-like odor.

amylin See **dextrin**.

anaglyph An embellishment carved or chased in low relief. Also see **bas-relief**.

analemma **1.** A retaining wall at the side of an ancient Greek or Roman theatre. **2.** Any raised construction which serves as a support or rest.

analogion, analogium **1.** A reading desk, lectern, or ambo. **2.** In the Eastern church, a stand on which choir books rest.

anamorphosis A drawing which appears to be distorted unless viewed from a particular angle or with a special device.

anamorphosis

anatase See **titanium dioxide**.

anathyrosis A Greek method of fitting masonry without mortar by carefully dressing the contact edges of the blocks, leaving the center rough and slightly recessed.

anchor, anchorage **1.** A device such as a metal rod, wire, or strap, for fixing one object to another, as specially formed metal connectors used to fasten together timbers, masonry, trusses, etc. **2.** In prestressed concrete, a device to lock the stressed tendon in position so that it will retain its stressed condition. **3.** In precast concrete construction, a device used to attach the precast units to the building frame. **4.** In slabs on grade, or walls, a device used to fasten to rock or adjacent structures to prevent movement of the slab or wall with respect to the foundation, adjacent structure, or rock. **5.** A support which holds one end of a timber fast. **6.** A device used to secure a window or doorframe to the building structure; usually adjustable in three dimensions; also see **doorframe anchor**. **7.** See **jamb anchor, masonry anchor**, etc. **8.** The anchor-shaped dart in the egg-and-dart molding; also called **anchor dart**. **9.** A device used in a piping system to secure the piping to a structure; typically provided by a metal insert in an overhead concrete slab or beam. **10.** A wrought-iron clamp, of Flemish origin, on the exterior side of a brick building wall that is connected to the opposite wall by a steel tie-rod to prevent the two walls from spreading apart; these clamps were often in the shape of numerals indicating the year of construction, or letters representing the owner's initials, or were simply fanciful designs.

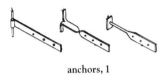

anchors, 1

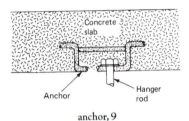

anchor, 9

Concrete slab
Anchor
Hanger rod

medieval **anchors**, 10

anchorage **1.** In **posttensioning**, a device which anchors the tendons to the posttensioned concrete member. **2.** In **pretensioning**, a device used to anchor the tendons temporarily during the hardening of the concrete. **3.** Same as **anchor**, 3.

anchorage bond stress The forces in a steel bar divided by the product of the perimeter and the **embedment length**.

anchorage deformation, anchorage slip The shortening of **tendons** in prestressed concrete due to the deformation of the anchorage or slippage of the tendons in the anchorage device when the prestressing force is transferred to the anchorage device.

anchorage device Any device used in **anchorage**.

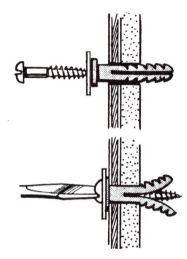

anchorage device

anchorage loss Same as **anchorage deformation.**

anchorage system A group of interacting **anchors** and elements.

anchorage zone **1.** In **posttensioning**, the region adjacent to the anchorage for the tendon which is subjected to secondary stresses as a result of the distribution of the prestressing force. **2.** In **pretensioning**, the region in which transfer bond stresses are developed.

anchor block A block of wood, replacing a brick in a wall to provide a nailing or fastening surface.

anchor bolt, foundation bolt, hold-down bolt **1.** A steel bolt usually fixed in a building structure with its threaded portion projecting; used to secure frameworks, timbers, machinery bases, etc. **2.** See **brick anchor**.

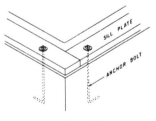

anchor bolt

anchor cable A cable or line, one end of which is held in a fixed position.

anchor dart See **anchor**, 8.

anchored-type ceramic veneer Ceramic veneer which is attached to a backing by grout and nonferrous metal anchors; minimum overall thickness is 1 in. (2.54 cm).

anchor line Same as **anchor cable**.

anchor log A timber which serves as a **dead man**.

anchor pile A pile behind a retaining wall to which tie-back rods or cables are connected.

anchor plate A square metal plate used as floor tile in industrial plants.

anchor rod A threaded metal rod used with various types of hangers to support ductwork, piping, etc.

anchor tie Same as **anchor, 1**.

ancient light (*Brit.*) A window which is legally entitled to the continuous access to light by virtue of having had continuous access to light for many years in the past.

ancillary One of a group of buildings having a secondary or dependent use, such as an annex.

ancon, (*pl.*) **ancones** **1.** A scrolled bracket or **console, 1** which supports a cornice or entablature over a door or window. **2.** A projecting boss on a column **drum** or wall block.

anda The hemispherical dome of a **stupa**.

andron, andronitis **1.** In ancient Greece, the part of a building used by men, esp. the banquet room. **2.** A passage beside the tablinum in a Roman house.

anechoic room A room whose boundaries absorb almost completely sound waves which are incident upon them; practically no sound is reflected from the boundaries.

anemometer An instrument for measuring the velocity of airflow.

angel beam A **hammer beam** of a medieval roof truss; so called because it often had an angel carved on its surface.

angel light A small triangular **light, 1** between subordinate arches of the tracery of a window, esp. in the English Perpendicular style.

angiosperm A class of seed plants (having seeds enclosed in an ovary) which includes most of the world's flowering plants.

angiportus In ancient Rome, a narrow road passing between two houses or a row of houses, or an alley leading to a single house.

angle **1.** The figure made by two lines that meet. **2.** The difference in direction of such intersecting lines, or the space within them. **3.** A projecting or sharp corner. **4.** A secluded area resembling a corner; a nook. **5.** An L-shaped metal member; an **angle iron**. **6.** See **bevel angle**. **7.** A fitting on a gutter for rainwater which changes the gutter's direction.

angle bar **1.** An upright bar at the meeting of two faces of a polygonal window, bay window, or bow window. **2.** An **angle iron**.

angled bay window A **bay window** that is triangular in plan and protrudes outward from a wall.

angle bead **1.** A **corner bead**. **2.** A strip, usually of metal or wood, set at the corner of a plaster

ancon, 1

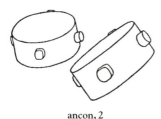

ancon, 2

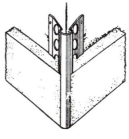

angle bead, 2

wall to protect the corner or serve as a guide to float the plaster flush with it; a type of **angle staff**.

angle blasting Sandblasting, or the like, at an angle of less than 90°.

angle block, glue block A small block of wood used to fasten adjacent pieces, usually at right angles, or glued into the corner of a wooden frame to stiffen it.

angle board A board whose surface is cut at a desired angle; serves as a guide for cutting and/or planing other boards at the same angle.

angle bond A tie used to bond masonry work at wall corners.

angle brace **1.** A strip of material which is fixed across a frame to make it rigid, as a wood strip which is nailed temporarily across the corners of a window frame or doorframe to maintain squareness during shipment or in handling before permanent installation; also called an **angle tie**. **2.** An **angle iron**. **3.** A special **brace** which is used for drilling where there is insufficient room for an ordinary brace handle to turn.

angle bracket A projecting bracket which is not at right angles to the wall.

angle brick Any brick having an oblique shape to fit an oblique, salient corner.

angle buttress One of two buttresses at right angles to each other, forming the corner of a structure.

angle capital A capital at a corner column, esp. an Ionic capital where the four volutes project equally on the diagonals, instead of being in two parallel planes; used by both Greeks and Romans.

angle capital

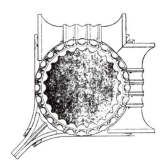

Plan of an Ionic **angle capital**

angle chimney A chimney placed so that the sides of the chimney form an angle with the side walls of a room.

angled chimney stacks See **diagonal chimney stacks**.

angle cleat Same as **angle clip**.

angle clip A short strip of angle iron used to secure structural elements at right angles.

angle closer A special-shaped brick used to close the bond at the corner of a wall.

angle collar A cast-iron pipe fitting which has a socket at each end for joining with the spigot ends of two pipes that are not in alignment.

angle column A column placed at the corner of a building, as at the corner of a portico; may be freestanding or engaged.

angle corbel An L-shaped **corbel plate** forming a right-angle bend, the vertical surface of which is fastened to the wall; the horizontal surface is used to support a building component.

angled bay window A **bay window** that is triangular in plan and protrudes outward from a wall.

angled chimney stacks See **diagonal chimney stacks**.

angle divider A square for setting or bisecting angles; one side is an adjustable hinged blade; when set at 90°, it can be used as a **try square**.

angle dozer A **bulldozer** with its blade set at an angle to push the earth to one side.

angledozer Same as **bulldozer**.

angled stair A stair in which successive flights are at an angle of other than 180° to each other (often at 90°), with an intermediate platform between them.

angle fillet A wooden strip, triangular in cross section, which is used to cover the internal joint between two surfaces meeting at an angle of less than 180°.

angle fireplace A fireplace across one corner of a room; for example, see **fogón**.

angle float A trowel having two edge surfaces bent at 90°; used to finish corners in freshly poured concrete and in plastering.

angle float

angle gauge A template used to set or check angles in building construction.

angle globe valve A type of **globe valve** intended for use at a point in a water distribution system where the piping changes direction by 90°; saves the cost of an extra elbow and provides an additional point of control of water flow.

angle hip tile An **arris hip tile**.

angle iron, angle bar An L-shaped iron or steel bar or structural steel member.

angle joint A joint between two pieces of lumber which results in a change in direction, such as a **dovetail joint** or a **mortise-and-tenon joint**.

angle lacing A system of lacing in which angle irons are used in place of bars.

angle leaf In medieval architecture, a carved claw or **spur, 1** which projects from the lower **torus** of a column, so as to cover one of the projecting corners of the square plinth beneath.

angle-lighting luminaire A luminaire whose light distribution is asymmetric with respect to a direction of specific interest.

angle modillion A **modillion** at the corner of a cornice.

angle newel A **landing newel**.

angle niche A niche formed at the corner of a building; common in medieval architecture.

angle of illumination The angle between the axis of an illuminator and a perpendicular to the surface being illuminated.

angle of repose The maximum angle with the horizontal at which a mass of material, as in a cut or embankment, will lie without sliding; the angle

between the horizontal and the maximum slope that a soil assumes through natural processes.

angle of rest Same as **angle of repose**.

angle paddle A hand tool used to finish a plastered surface.

angle pier A **pier, 2** at the intersection of two walls, constructed on the external angle.

angle post In half-timber construction, the corner post.

angle rafter A **hip rafter**.

angle rib **1.** In decorative work, a molding that ornaments an **angle**. **2.** In **Gothic architecture**, one of the diagonal **ribs, 1** that divides each of the rectangles of a vault.

angle ridge A **hip rafter**.

angle-roll Same as **bowtell**.

angle section A structural steel member having an L-shaped cross section.

angle shaft **1.** A column within the right-angled recesses of Norman door and window jambs. **2.** A decorative member, such as a colonnette or enriched corner bead, attached to an external angle of a building.

angle staff, staff angle A vertical strip of wood or metal at the exterior angle of two plastered surfaces and flush with them; protects the plastering and serves as a guide for floating the plaster; a **corner bead, 2**.

angle stile A narrow strip of wood used to conceal the joint between a wall and a vertical wood surface which makes an angle with the wall, as at the edge of a corner cabinet.

angle stone Same as **quoin**.

angle strut An angle-shaped structural member which is designed to carry a compression load.

anglet A groove, usually containing an angle of 90°.

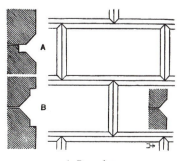

A, B, **anglet**

angle tie See **angle brace, 1**.

angle tile A **tile, 1** that forms an angle; used to cover a **hip, 1** (ridge) of a roof; sometimes used in **weather tiling** (tile hanging) to cover the corner of a building.

angle trowel A **margin trowel**.

angle valve A valve for controlling the flow of a liquid or air; the fluid leaves at right angles to the direction in which it enters the valve.

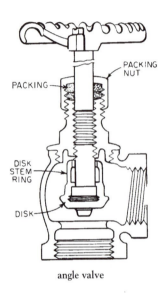

angle valve

angle volute See **angle capital**.

Anglo-Italian Villa style A term occasionally used for the **Italianate style**.

Anglo-Saxon architecture The pre-Romanesque architecture of England before the Norman Conquest (1066 A.D.), which survived for a short time thereafter; characterized by massive walls and round arches; a belt course or pilaster strips; triangular arches; **long-and-short work**.

angstrom A funit of length; used to express electromagnetic wavelengths; $1 \text{ Å} = 10^{-10}$ meter $= \frac{1}{10}$ nanometer. *Abbr.* Å.

angular aggregate Aggregate, the particles of which possess well-defined edges formed at the intersection of roughly planar faces.

angular frequency (ω) The **frequency** of a periodic quantity multiplied by 2π; expressed in radians.

angular hip tile Same as **angle tile**.

Anglo-Saxon architecture

angular pediment   A **pediment** having a horizontal cornice and slanting sides that meet in a point at the top so as to form a triangle; also called a triangular pediment.

angular pediment

anhydrite   A natural mineral calcium sulfate, used in the manufacture of portland cement to control the set.

anhydrous calcium sulfate, dead-burnt gypsum   Gypsum from which all the water of crystallization has been removed.

anhydrous gypsum plaster   Plaster which has a greater percentage of the water of crystallization removed than normal gypsum plasters; used as a finish plaster. Requires the addition of an accelerator to produce a set.

anhydrous lime   See **lime**.

animal black   A black pigment made by charring of animal bones; sometimes used in paints, although **carbon black** generally is preferred for tinting strength and blackness. Available in three grades: boneblack, drop black, and ivory black.

animal glue, hide glue   A glue made from the bones, hide, horns, and connective tissues of animals; when used hot, it develops strong bonds; has poor water resistance.

ANL   On drawings, abbr. for "anneal."

annealed glass   Glass that has cooled slowly as it exits the float line during its production, thereby minimizing residual internal stresses.

annealing   A process of holding a material at an elevated temperature, but below its melting point, to permit the relieving of internal stresses in the material.

annex, annexe   A subsidiary structure near or adjoining a larger principal building.

annexation   The acquisition of new territory by a governmental authority, such as a city or state.

annual plant   A plant whose life cycle is completed in a single growing season.

annual ring, growth ring   A layer of wood produced during one year of a tree's growth.

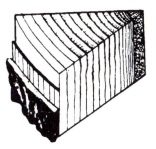

annual rings

annular   Said of a ring-shaped structure or object.

annular molding   Any molding which is circular in plan, such as the **torus**.

annular vault   A **barrel vault** in the shape of a ring, instead of a straight line; covers a space of which the plan is formed by the area between two concentric circles, or any portion of such a space.

annulated column   A shaft or cluster of shafts fitted, at intervals, with rings.

annulet   A small molding, usually circular in plan and square or angular in section; esp. one of the fillets encircling the lower part of the Doric capital above the necking.

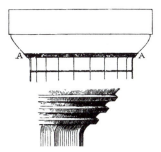

annulets: A, of a Doric capital. Shown enlarged in lower figure

annunciator   **1.** A signaling device, usually electrically operated, giving an audible signal and a visual indication when energized by pressing a button. **2.** See **car annunciator**.

ANOD   On drawings, abbr. for **anodize**.

anode   In an electric system to protect underground iron pipes or structures from electrochemical action, a metallic rod which is driven in the ground; direct current is passed through the rod to the earth, and then through the iron pipe or structure, in a direction opposite to that resulting from the electrochemical properties of the soil.

anodic coating   The surface finish resulting from anodizing; may be transparent or colored by the use of a dye or pigment in the anodizing process.

anodize   To provide a hard, noncorrosive, electrolytic, oxide film on the surface of a metal, particularly aluminum, by electrolytic action.

anse de panier   Same as **basket-handled arch**.

ANSI   Abbr. for **American National Standards Institute**.

anta (*pl.* **antae**)   A **pilaster** or a rectangular **pier** formed by a thickening at the end of a wall, usually projecting into a façade or portico; its capital and base usually differ from those on columns within the portico. Antae usually occur in pairs, with one on each side of the portico. If there are columns within the portico that are between the antae, they are said to be *in antis*. Also see **distyle in antis**.

antae   A

anta cap   The capital of an **anta**.

antebellum   Dating before or existing before the U.S. Civil War (1861–1865).

antecabinet   A room, often spacious and elegant, leading to a private audience room or cabinet.

antechamber   **1.** A room preceding a chamber. **2.** A **foyer**, **lobby**, or **vestibule**.

antechapel   A separate entrance space, as a porch or vestibule, in front of a chapel.

antechoir   The space, more or less enclosed, between the inner and outer gates of the choir screen.

antechurch   A deep narthex at the front of a church, usually with a nave and side aisles.

antecourt   An entrance court or outer court which precedes the principal court, as at Versailles; a forecourt.

antefix   **1.** A decorated upright slab used in classical architecture and derivatives to close or conceal the open end of a row of tiles which cover the joints of roof tiles. **2.** A similar ornament on the ridge of a roof.

antefix, 1

antemural   The outerworks or wall surrounding and protecting a castle.

antenave   A narthex or porch of any description leading into the nave of a church.

antepagment   The stone or stucco decorative dressing enriching the jambs and head of a doorway or window; same as **architrave, 1**.

antependium   A hanging which was suspended over and in front of the altar in medieval churches.

antepodium   A seat behind the dais in a choir, reserved for the clergy.

anteport   A preliminary portal; an outer gate or door.

anteportico   An outer porch or a portico in front of the main portico in a classical temple.

anterides   In ancient Greek and Roman architecture, a structure to strengthen another; a type of buttress placed against an outer wall, esp. in subterranean construction.

anteroom   A room adjacent to a larger, more important one; frequently used as a waiting area.

anthemion, honeysuckle ornament   A common Greek ornament based upon the

anthemion

honeysuckle or palmette. Used singly on stelae or antefixes, or as a running ornament on friezes, etc.

antic, antic work   A grotesque sculpture consisting of animal, human, and foliage forms incongruously run together and used to decorate molding terminations and many other parts of medieval architecture. Sometimes synonymous with **grotesque** or **arabesque**.

antic

anticorrosive paint   A paint formulated with a corrosive-resistant pigment (such as lead chromate, zinc chromate, or red lead) and a chemical and moisture-resistant binder; used to protect iron and steel surfaces.

anticum   The front of a classical building, as distinguished from the posticum; same as **pronaos**.

antidesiccant   Material applied to plants prior to transplanting to reduce the amount of moisture lost from transpiration.

antiflooding interceptor   Same as **backwater valve**.

antifreeze sprinkler system   A **wet-pipe sprinkler system** whose piping is filled with an antifreeze solution. When the system is activated, the antifreeze solution is discharged, followed by a discharge of water from the water supply to which it is connected.

antifriction bearing   Any bearing having the capability of reducing friction effectively.

antifriction latch bolt   In builders' hardware, a latch bolt designed to reduce friction as the bolt engages the **strike plate**.

antimonial lead, hard lead, regulus metal   An alloy containing 10 to 25% antimony and the balance lead; antimony increases the tensile strength and hardens the lead; used in roofing, tank lining, and **cladding, 2**.

antimony oxide   A white opaque pigment used in paints and plastics to provide flame-retardant properties. It has better opacity than extenders but is not as good as titanium dioxide.

antimony yellow   See **Naples yellow**.

antiparabema   One of two chapels at the entrance end of a Byzantine church.

antipumping   A feature that prevents the reclosing of a **circuit breaker** until the cause of the closing has been corrected.

antique crown, eastern crown   A heraldic device consisting of a headband with an indefinite number of pointed rays projecting from it.

antique crown

antiquing, broken-color work A technique of handling wet paint to expose parts of the undercoat, by combing, graining, or marbling.

antiquum opus Same as **opus incertum**.

antis, in See **in antis**.

anti-sing lamp Same as **low-noise lamp**.

anti-siphon An adjective applied to a mechanical device, such as a valve, that eliminates **siphonage**.

anti-siphon trap See **deep-seal trap**.

antislip paint A paint with a high coefficient of friction, caused by addition of sand, wood flour, or cork dust; used on steps, porches, and walkways to prevent slipping.

antismudge ring A frame attached around the perimeter of a ceiling-mounted **air diffuser**, which minimizes the formation of rings of dirt on the ceiling.

antistatic agent An agent which minimizes static electricity in plastics; may consist of chemical additives or metallic devices connected to an electrical ground.

anti-sun glass See **coated glass** and **tinted glass**.

AP Abbr. for "access panel."

APA Abbr. for "American Plywood Association."

apadana The columnar audience hall in a Persian palace.

apartment 1. A room or suite of rooms designed to be lived in, containing at least one bathroom; is separated from, and is usually one of, many similar units within a multiple dwelling. 2. A building containing at least three such dwelling units; an **apartment house**. Also see **efficiency apartment, garden apartment, apartment hotel**.

apartment hotel 1. A hotel which rents living quarters suitable for light housekeeping and supplies hotel services. 2. An apartment house which supplies living quarters suitable for light housekeeping and has public dining facilities.

apartment house See **apartment, 2**.

apartments (*Brit.*) A group of rooms used as a dwelling by one person or one family.

APC On drawings, abbr. for "acoustical plaster ceiling."

apex In architecture or construction, the highest point, peak, or tip of any structure.

apex stone, saddle stone The uppermost stone in a gable, pediment, vault, or dome; usually triangular, often highly decorated.

apodyterium A room in Greek or Roman baths, or in the palaestra, where the bathers or those taking part in gymnastic exercises undressed and dressed.

aponsa A **shed roof** having rafters that are let into (or rest upon) a wall.

apophyge 1. That part of a column where the shaft of the column springs from its base or where the shaft terminates at its **capital**; usually molded in a concave sweep; also called a scape or congé. 2. The hollow (i.e., **scotia**) beneath the **echinus** of some Classical capitals.

apophyge, 1

apophyge, 2

aposthesis Same as **apophyge**.

apostilb A unit of **luminance** equal to $(1/\pi)$ candela per square meter.

apotheca In ancient Greece and Rome, a storeroom of any kind, but esp. one for storing wine.

appareille The slope or ascent to the platform of a bastion.

apparent brightness See **brightness**.

apparent candlepower Of an extended light source at a specified distance: the candlepower of a point source which produces the same illumination at that distance.

apparent density 1. The mass per unit volume of in-place thermal insulation. 2. The mass per unit volume (or the weight per unit volume) of a material, including the voids which are inherent in the material.

APPD   On drawings, abbr. for **approved**.

appentice, pent, pentice   A minor structure built against the side of a building, with a roof of single slope; a **penthouse, 3**.

appentice

appliance, appliance equipment   Any device (other than industrial) which utilizes gas or electricity as a fuel to produce air-conditioning, heat, light, refrigeration, or to perform one or more functions such as dishwashing; usually built in a standard size or type and installed or connected as a unit.

appliance lamp   An electric lamp designed for high-temperature service.

appliance outlet   See **outlet**.

appliance panel   In electric systems, a metal housing containing two or more devices (such as **fuses**) for protection against excessive current in circuits which supply portable electric appliances with current.

appliance regulator   A regulator for controlling and maintaining a uniform pressure of gas supplied to an appliance.

application for payment   The contractor's written request for payment of amount due for completed portions of the **work, 1** and, if the contract so provides, for materials delivered and suitably stored pending their incorporation into the work.

applied molding   A molding that is nailed on, laid on, or otherwise fastened to a surface, rather than cut into the surface itself.

applied trim   Supplementary and separate decorative strips of wood or moldings applied to the face or sides of a frame, as on a doorframe.

appliqué   **1.** An accessory decorative feature applied to an object or structure. **2.** In ornamental work, one material affixed to another.

appraisal   An evaluation or estimate (preferably by a qualified professional appraiser) of the market or other value, cost, utility, or other attribute of land or other facility.

approach-zone district   In zoning, a classification which identifies all that area outward from the end of, or approach to, a runway in which the height of structures or other hazards to aircraft is restricted.

approved   **1.** Referring to materials, devices, or construction accepted by the authority having jurisdiction, by reason of tests or investigations conducted by it or by an agency satisfactory to the authority, or by reason of accepted principles or tests by national authorities or technical or scientific organizations. **2.** Referring to occupancy or use, accepted by the authority having jurisdiction by reason of the submission of adequate proof of conformity with the basic requirements of the code under which the authority functions.

approved equal   Material, equipment, or method approved by the architect for use in the **work, 1** as being acceptable as an equivalent in essential attributes to the material, equipment, or method specified in the **contract documents**.

approved ground   A **ground** (such as the steel framework of a building, a concrete-encased electrode, or a ground ring) that meets the requirements of the National Electrical Code or other applicable code.

approving authority   The individual agency, board, department, or official established and authorized by a political subdivision (e.g., state, province, county, city, or parish) which is created by law to administer and enforce specified requirements.

APPROX   On drawings, abbr. for "approximate."

appurtenance   **1.** Any built-in, nonstructural portion of a building, such as doors, windows, ventilators, electrical equipment, partitions, etc. **2.** An incidental property right, as a **right-of-way**.

appurtenant structure A structure attached to the exterior of a building or erected on the roof, usually designed to support service equipment or to support a billboard or the like.

APPX On drawings, abbr. for "appendix."

apron **1.** A flat broad piece of finished lumber or trim placed directly under a windowsill. **2.** A flat piece of wood mounted under the base of a cabinet. **3.** Same as **counterflashing**. **4.** Same as **apron flashing**. **5.** Paneling on the exterior of a building which serves as a protection against weather or as a decorative feature. **6.** That portion of a concrete slab which extends beyond the face of a building on adjacent ground, as the extension of a garage floor. **7.** A vertical panel at the back of a sink or lavatory. **8.** In a theatre, that part of a stage which projects into the audience area beyond the proscenium and curtain line; a **forestage**.

apron flashing **1.** The **flashing** that covers the joint between a vertical surface and a sloping roof, as at the lower edge of a chimney. **2.** The flashing that diverts water from a vertical surface into a gutter.

apron lift A hydraulic or mechanical lift which extends the fixed **apron** of a stage in front of a proscenium opening.

apron lining The piece of boarding which covers the rough **apron piece** of a staircase.

apron molding See **apron, 2.**

apron piece, pitching piece A horizontal wood beam, fixed into a wall and projecting horizontally, which supports the ends of carriage pieces, roughstrings, and joists at the landings of a wooden staircase.

apron rail A **lock rail** having a raised ornamental molding.

apron stage In a proscenium theatre, an extension of the fixed apron (in front of a proscenium opening) by means of a platform or by an **apron lift**.

apron wall In an exterior wall, a panel which extends downward from a windowsill to the top of a window below.

apse A semicircular (or nearly semicircular) or semipolygonal space, usually in a church, terminating an axis and intended to house an altar.

apse aisle An aisle or ambulatory extending around an apse or chevet.

apse

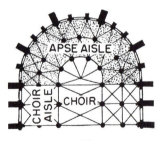

apse aisle

apse chapel A chapel opening from an apse; such a radial chapel is a conspicuous feature of French Gothic architecture.

apsidal Pertaining to an apse or similar to one.

apsidiole A small apsidal chapel, esp. one projecting from an apse.

apsis The semicircular termination of any rectangular chamber; an **apse**.

APT **1.** On drawings; abbr. for **apartment**. **2.** Abbr. for Association for Preservation Technology.

apteral Descriptive of a classical temple or similar building that has no columns along the sides but may have a portico at one or both ends.

APW On drawings, abbr. for "architectural projected window."

aqueduct A channel for supplying water; often underground, but treated architecturally on high arches when crossing valleys or low ground.

aqueduct

aquifer A water-bearing formation of gravel, permeable rock, or sand that is capable of providing water, in usable quantities, to springs or wells.

aquila A **tympanum** decorated with carvings.

AR **1.** On drawings, abbr. for "as required." **2.** On drawings, abbr. for "as rolled."

arabesque **1.** Intricate overall pattern of geometric forms or stylized plants used in Muhammadan countries. **2.** Overall decorative pattern of acanthus scrolls, swags, candelabrum shafts, animal or human forms, on panels or pilasters, in Roman and Renaissance architecture. **3.** A species of ornament of infinite variety used for enriching flat surfaces or moldings, either painted, inlaid, or carved in low relief.

arabesque

Arabic arch A **horseshoe arch**.

araeostyle Same as **areostyle**; see **intercolumniation**.

araeosystyle, areosystyle Alternately **systyle** and **araeostyle**; having an intercolumniation alternately of two and four diameters.

arbitration The binding resolution of disputes by one or more neutral persons (usually called "arbitrators"), as a substitute for judicial proceedings; may be invoked only by agreement of the parties to the dispute, but such agreement may be arrived at before there is an actual dispute, as, for example, through a clause in a contract between them, or after a dispute has arisen. Arbitration proceedings characteristically are less formal than those in court, and the rules of evidence and most rules of substantive law that would be invoked by a court are not applied.

arbor **1.** A light, open structure having a lattice framework, usually supporting intertwined vines or flowers; a shaded, leafy recess, often formed by tree branches. **2.** See **counterweight arbor**. **3.** The rotating shaft of a circular saw, spindle molder, shaper, etc.

arboretum An informally arranged garden, usually on a large scale, where trees are grown for display, educational, or scientific purposes.

arc **1.** The luminous column of gas in an arc discharge; caused by the flow of electric current between separated electrodes in a gas. **2.** See **carbon-arc spotlight**. **3.** Any part of the circumference of a circle. **4.** An angular measure.

arca custodiae In ancient Roman architecture, a type of cell for the confinement of prisoners.

arcade **1.** A line of counterthrusting arches raised on columns or piers. Also see **blind arcade, coupled arcade, interlacing arcade, intersecting arcade, surface arcade, wall arcade**. **2.** A covered walk with a line of such arches along one or both long sides. **3.** A covered walk with shops and offices along one side, and a line of such arches on the other. Also see **stoa**. **4.** A covered walk, lit from the top, lined with shops or offices on one or more levels.

arcading A line of arches, raised on columns, that are represented in relief as decoration of a solid wall; sometimes seats are incorporated in the composition. (*See illustration on p. 44.*)

arcading

arcae In ancient Roman architecture, the gutters of the **cavaedium**.

arcature 1. Arcading. 2. An ornamental, miniature arcade.

arc-boutant Same as **flying buttress**.

arc cutting A process of cutting or removing metal by melting it with the heat produced between an electrode and the metal being cut.

arc de triomphe Same as **triumphal arch**.

arc discharge An electric discharge characterized by the production of light, high cathode-current densities, and a low voltage drop at the cathode.

arc doubleau An arch, usually very massive, carried across a wide space, to support a groined vault or to stiffen a barrel vault.

arcella A cheese room, in medieval architecture.

arc formeret The wall arch or wall rib, or the corresponding rib coming next to the arcade between nave and aisle, or the like, as in Gothic vaulting.

arc gouging A groove or bevel formed in metal as a result of arc cutting.

arch A construction that spans an opening; usually curved; often consists of wedge-shaped blocks (**voussoirs**) having their narrower ends toward the opening. Arches vary in shape, from those that have little or no curvature to those that are acutely pointed. For special types of arches, see **acute arch, anse de panier, arrière-voussure, back arch, basket-handle arch, bell arch, blind arch, camber arch, catenary arch, cinquefoil arch, compound arch, cusped arch, diminished arch, discharging arch, Dutch arch, elliptical arch, equilateral arch, flat arch, Florentine arch, foil arch, French arch, garden arch,** gauged arch, Gothic arch, horseshoe arch, inverted arch, jack arch, keel arch, keystone arch, lancet arch, Mayan arch, memorial arch, miter arch, Moorish arch, ogee arch, pointed arch, Queen Anne arch, raking arch, rampant arch, rear arch, relieving arch, round arch, rowlock arch, safety arch, sconcheon arch, secondary arch, segmental arch, semicircular arch, semielliptical arch, shouldered arch, skew arch, straight arch, three-centered arch, transverse arch, trefoil arch, triangular arch, triumphal arch, Tudor arch, two-centered arch.

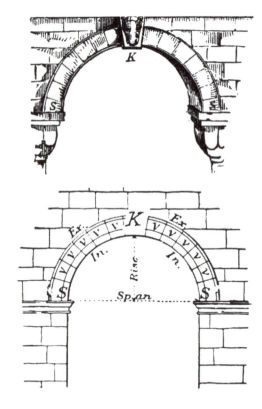

arch: *Ex* Estrados; *In* intrados; *K* keystone; *S* springers; *v* voussoirs

ARCH. On drawings, abbr. for **architect, architecture,** or **architectural**.

arch band Any narrow elongated surface forming part of, or connected with, an arch.

arch bar A curved wrought-iron or steel bar used to support the weight of the masonry above a fireplace or window opening.

arch beam   Same as **arched beam**.

arch brace   A curved brace, usually used in pairs to support a roof frame and give the effect of an arch.

arch brick, compass brick, featheredge brick, radial brick, radiating brick, radius brick, voussoir brick   **1.** A wedge-shaped brick used in arch or circular construction; its two larger faces are inclined toward each other. **2.** Extremely hard-burnt brick from an arch of a scove kiln.

arch buttress   Same as **flying buttress**.

arch center   Formwork to support the voussoirs of an arch during construction.

arch corner bead   A corner bead which is cut on the job; used to form and reinforce the curved portion of arch openings.

arched barrel roof   Same as **barrel roof**.

arched beam   A beam whose upper surface is slightly curved.

arched buttress   Same as **flying buttress**.

arched construction   A method of construction relying on arches and vaults to support walls and floors.

arched corbel table   In Early Christian and Romanesque architecture and derivatives, a raised band (often at the top of a wall) composed of small arches resting on corbels, the arcading regularly punctuated by junctures with pilaster strips.

arched dormer   A dormer having an approximately semicylindrical roof; the head of the upper sash in the dormer may be either round-topped or flat-topped.

archeion   See **archivium**.

archeria   In medieval fortifications, an aperture through which an archer or longbowman might discharge arrows.

archiepiscopal cross   A cross with two transverse arms, the longer one nearer the center.

arching   **1.** The transfer of **stress** from a yielding part of a soil mass to adjoining less-yielding or restrained parts of the mass. **2.** A system of arches. **3.** The arched part of a structure.

architect   **1.** A person trained and experienced in the design of buildings and the coordination and supervision of all aspects of the construction of buildings. **2.** A designation reserved, usually by law, for a person or organization professionally qualified and duly licensed to perform architectural services, including analysis of project requirements, creation and development of the project design, preparation of drawings, specifications, and bidding requirements, and general administration of the construction contract. An architect usually renders services that require the application of art, science, and the aesthetics of design to the construction of buildings, including their components and appurtenances and the spaces around them, taking into account the safeguarding of life, health, property, and public welfare; often includes consultation, evaluation, planning, the provision of preliminary studies, designs, and construction documents; and may also include construction management, and the administration of construction documents.

architect-engineer   An individual or firm offering professional services as both architect and engineer; term generally used in government contracts, particularly those with the federal government.

architect-in-training   Same as **intern architect**.

architectonic   Related or conforming to technical architectural principles.

architect's approval   The architect's written or imprinted acknowledgment that materials, equipment, or methods of construction are acceptable for use in the **work, 1**, or that a contractor's request or claim is valid.

architect's scale   A **scale** having graduations along its edges so that scale drawings can be measured directly in feet (or meters); usually triangular in shape.

architectural   **1.** Pertaining to architecture, its features, characteristics, or details. **2.** Pertaining to materials used to build or ornament a structure, such as mosaic, bronze, etc.

architectural area   Total floor area of a building calculated from its exterior surfaces or from the center line of a common wall between two buildings; usually excludes open terraces. Roofed areas such as porches or arcades are calculated at one-half actual area.

architectural bronze   An alloy containing 57% copper, 40% zinc, 2.75% lead, 0.25% tin;

used for extruded moldings and forgings. Not technically a bronze.

architectural coating A coating which is usually intended for on-site application of interior and/or exterior surfaces of buildings.

architectural concrete **1.** Reinforced concrete used for structural and ornamental work. **2.** In nonconcrete frame structures, the exposed concrete used for aesthetic effects.

architectural details The relatively small elements of design and finish of a building.

architectural drawing One of a number of drawings prepared by an architect for a construction project, e.g., plans, elevations, and details.

architectural fountain A system of pumps, tubes, pipes, controls, valves, and nozzles through which water is forced under pressure to produce ornamental jets, spouts, or showers; often lighted for special nighttime effects.

architectural glass Any of several types of **configurated glass**.

architectural hardware See **finish hardware**.

architectural millwork, custom millwork Ready-made millwork as obtained from the mill, especially fabricated to meet the specifications for a particular job, as distinguished from standard or stock items or sizes.

architectural mode An inexact classification for buildings that share selected architectural features but, unlike an **architectural style**, may not share consistency of design, form, or ornamentation with other buildings similarly classified. When such buildings seemingly emulate an earlier prototype (for example, **American Colonial Revival**), important architectural details that characterize the prototype are often either omitted or exaggerated in size or importance; furthermore, other design elements may be added (such as a type of dormer, chimney, or window) that never existed in the prototype; or characteristic building materials of the prototype may be replaced with newer types of materials. Compare with **architectural style**.

architectural projected window A window in which the basic frame and hinged **sash (ventilator, 2)** members are made of heavier steel than that used in a **commercial projected window**.

architectural section See **section, 2**.

architectural style A classification characterizing buildings that share many common attributes, including similarity in general appearance, in the arrangement of major design elements in ornamentation, in the use of materials, and in form, scale, and structure. Such styles are often related to a particular period of time, geographical region, country of origin, or religious tradition, or to the architecture of an earlier period. Often, a term that includes the word *style* (such as **Santa Fe style**) is an **architectural mode** rather than an architectural style.

architectural terra-cotta A hard-burnt, glazed or unglazed clay unit used in building construction; plain or ornamental; machine-extruded or hand-molded; usually larger in size than brick or facing tile. Also see **ceramic veneer**.

architectural volume The cubic content of a building calculated by multiplying the floor area by the height. For foundations, the average depth of footing to the **finish floor** is used. For roofs (other than flat roofs), the average height is used.

architecture **1.** The art and science of designing and building structures, or large groups of structures, in keeping with aesthetic and functional criteria. **2.** Structures built in accordance with such principles.

architrave **1.** In the classical orders, the lowest member of the entablature; the beam that spans from column to column, resting directly upon their capitals. Also see **order**. **2.** The ornamental

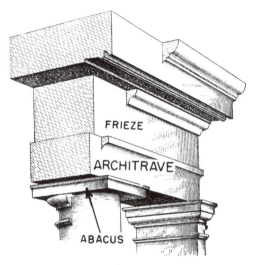

architrave

moldings around the faces of the jambs and lintel of a doorway or other opening; an **antepagment**.

architrave block   Same as **skirting block**.

architrave cornice   An entablature in which the cornice rests directly on the architrave, the frieze being omitted.

archivium   In ancient Greece and Rome, a building in which archives of a city or state were deposited; also called **archeion** or **tabularium**.

archivolt   An **architrave** modified by being carried around a curved opening instead of a rectangular one; an ornamental molding or band of moldings on the face of an arch following the contour of the extrados.

archivolt

archivoltum   A medieval conduit or receptacle for waste materials, as a sewer or cesspool.

arch order   **1.** In Roman architecture, arches enframed by engaged columns and entablatures. **2.** In medieval architecture, successive vertical planes of arches and colonettes set one within another.

arch rib   **1.** In Romanesque architecture, a transverse rib crossing the nave or aisle at right angles to its length. **2.** A principal load-bearing member of a ribbed arch.

arch ring   In an arched structure, the curved member that sustains the principal load.

arch stone   Same as **voussoir**.

arch surround   A seldom-used term for a decorative border around an arch; same as **archivolt**.

arch truss   A **truss** having an arched upper chord (concave downward) and a straight bottom chord; there are vertical hangers between the two chords.

archway   A passage through or under an arch, esp. when long, as under a **barrel vault**.

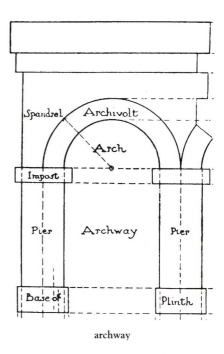

archway

arc light   A high-intensity light source produced by an arc, usually, between two metal electrodes or between two carbon rods; also see **carbon-arc spotlight**.

arcosolium   An arched recess or sepulchral cell in a Roman subterranean burial place or catacomb.

arcs doubleaux   Same as **arch band**.

arc spotlight   See **carbon-arc spotlight**.

arcuated   Based on, or characterized by, arches or archlike curves or vaults. It is common to distinguish between trabeated (beamed) and arcuated buildings.

arcuatio   In ancient Rome, a structure formed by means of arches or arcades and employed to support a construction of any kind, such as an aqueduct.

arcus ecclesiae   In medieval architecture, the arch by which the nave of the church was divided from the choir or chancel.

arcus presbyterii   In medieval architecture, the arch over the **tribune, 2**.

arcus toralis   The lattice separating the choir from the nave in a basilica.

ARC W, ARC/W   On drawings, abbr. for **arc weld**.

arc weld

arc weld A **weld** in which the heat of fusion is supplied by an electric arc.

arc welding The joining of metal parts by fusion, in which the necessary heat is produced by means of an electric arc, sometimes accompanied by the use of a **filler metal** and/or the application of pressure.

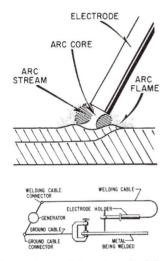

arc welding: *above*, with bare electrodes; *below*, circuit

are An area equal to 100 sq m.

area **1.** Measurement of surface within specified boundaries. **2.** Space either within or outside a structure or location, designated for a specific purpose, as recreation and/or parking area. **3.** An uninterrupted interior space. **4.** An areaway. **5.** The cross-sectional area of steel reinforcement.

area drain A receptable designed to collect surface or rainwater from an open area.

area grouting The grouting of an area in which (closely spaced) shallow holes have been drilled in a pattern in bedrock. This grouting has the effect of strengthening the upper portions of the bedrock and making it less pervious.

area light **1.** A source of light with significant dimensions in two directions, such as a window or luminous ceiling. **2.** A light used to illuminate large areas.

area method A method of estimating probable total construction cost by multiplying the adjusted gross floor area by a predetermined cost per unit of area.

area of refuge A floor area with direct access to a **horizontal exit** or supplemental vertical exit where persons unable to use stairs can remain temporarily in safety to await instructions or assistance during emergency evacuation of the building.

area of steel See **area, 5**.

area separation wall A fire-rated partition designed to prevent the spread of fire from an adjoining occupancy.

area wall A retaining wall around an **areaway**.

areaway An open subsurface space adjacent to a building used to admit light and air or as a means of access to a basement or crawl space.

arena **1.** An acting space of any shape surrounded by seats. **2.** A type of theatre not having a proscenium, the spectators' seats, rising in tiers, wholly surrounding the stage. **3.** The sanded central area in a Roman amphitheatre or circus, surrounded by the seats. **4.** Any building, indoor or outdoor, for sports events, etc.

arenaceous Composed primarily of sand; sandy.

arena theatre See **arena, 2**.

arena vomitory A **vomitory** through a section of seats which provides a special access, for actors, to an arena stage.

areostyle, araeostyle See **intercolumniation, 2**.

argillaceous Composed primarily of clay or shale; clayey.

argillite A rock containing chiefly clay materials; derived from claystone, siltstone, or shale; used locally as building stone, although rarely produced commercially.

ARI Abbr. for "Air-Conditioning and Refrigeration Institute."

aris See **arris**.

ark An ornamental, enclosed repository in a synagogue for the scrolls of the Torah.

arkose Sandstone containing 25% or more feldspar grains in abundance; used as building stone.

armarium Same as **ambry**.

armature **1.** The heavy-current winding of a motor or generator. **2.** The winding in a solenoid or relay. **3.** Structural ironwork in the form of framing or bars (commonly employed in medieval buildings) used to reinforce slender columns, or to consolidate canopies or hanging members such as bosses, and in tracery.

arm conveyor A conveyor for building materials in the form of an endless belt or chain, to which are attached projecting arms or shelves which carry the materials.

armored cable, metal-clad cable Two or more individually insulated electric conductors having a common outer protective covering of metal. Also see **BX**.

armored clamp A fitting which grips the armor of a cable where the armor terminates or where the cable enters a junction box.

armored faceplate A tamperproof **faceplate** or **lock front**, mortised in the edge of a door to cover the lock mechanism.

armored front In builders' hardware, a **lock front** which consists of two plates: the **under plate** (an unfinished plate fastened to the case) and the **finish plate** (a plate which covers the cylinder setscrews, thus protecting them from tampering, and which is fastened to the under plate); used on mortise locks.

armored plywood Plywood which is faced on one or both sides with metal sheeting.

armored wood Metal-clad wood.

armor plate A metal plate which protects the lower part of a door from kicks and scratches; similar to a **kickplate** but covering the door to a greater height, usually 39 in. (1 m) or more from the bottom of the door.

armor-plate glass See **bullet-resisting glass, tempered glass**.

armory **1.** A building used for military training or storage of military equipment. **2.** A weapons-manufacturing plant.

aromatic cedar See **eastern red cedar**.

arrester **1.** At the top of an incinerator or chimney, a wire screen which prevents sparks or burning material from leaving the stack. **2.** See **lightning arrester**. **3.** See **surge arrester**. **4.** See **water-hammer arrester**. **5.** A **lightning arrester**.

arrière-voussure, rear arch **1.** A **rear vault**; an arch or vault in a thick wall carrying the thickness of the wall, esp. one over a door or window frame. **2.** A relieving arch behind the face of a wall.

arris, aris **1.** An external angular intersection between two planar faces (an edge), or two curved faces, as in moldings or between two

arrière-voussure

flutes on a Doric column or between a flute and the fillet on an Ionic or a Corinthian column. **2.** The sharp edge of a brick.

arris fillet A triangular **batten** used to tilt up the lowest course of slates on a roof, at the edge of gutters.

arris gutter A V-shaped wooden gutter fixed to the eaves of a building.

arris hip tile, angle hip tile A special roof tile having an L-shaped cross section, made to fit over the hip of a roof.

arris rail A rail of triangular section, usually formed by slitting diagonally a strip of square section; the broadest surface forms the base.

arrissing tool A tool similar to a **float**, but having a form suitable for rounding an edge of freshly placed concrete.

arris tile Any angularly shaped tile.

arrisways, arriswise Diagonally, in respect to the manner of laying tiles, slates, bricks, or timber.

arrow diagram In **CPM**, an arrangement of arrows, representing **activities**, that describe a project.

arrow loop, loophole A vertical slit for archers in medieval fortification walls, with jambs deeply splayed toward the interior.

arrow loop

ARS On drawings, abbr. for **asbestos roof shingles**.

ART. On drawings, abbr. for "artificial."

Art Deco A decorative style stimulated by the Paris Exposition International des Arts Decoratifs et Industrielles Modernes of 1925, widely used in the architecture of the 1930s, including skyscraper designs such as the Chrysler Building in New York; characterized by sharp angular or zigzag surface forms and ornaments. Also referred to as **Style Moderne**.

artemiseion A building or shrine dedicated to the worship of Artemis.

arterial vent A **vent** serving a building drain and a public sewer.

art glass A type of colored glass used in windows during the late 19th and early 20th centuries; characterized by unusual combinations of hues and special effects in transparency and opaqueness.

article **1.** A subdivision of a document. **2.** In project specifications, the primary subdivision of the section, often further subdivided into paragraphs, subparagraphs, and clauses.

articulated drop chute A drop chute, for a falling stream of concrete, which consists of a vertical succession of tapered metal cylinders, so designed that the lower end of each cylinder fits into the upper end of the one below.

articulated structure A structure which permits relative motion to occur between its parts (e.g., by means of one or more sliding or hinged joints).

artifact See **building artifact**.

artificial daylight Light provided by an artificial source which has a spectral distribution approximating that of natural daylight at a correlated color temperature.

artificial horizon A device for indicating the horizon, as a bubble, pendulum or the flat surface of a liquid.

artificially dried See **kiln-dried**.

artificial marble See **artificial stone**.

artificial monument A relatively permanent object used to identify the location of a survey station or corner.

artificial sky A dome (usually hemispherical) illuminated by concealed light sources; used to illustrate and study daylighting techniques on architectural models placed near the center of the hemisphere.

artificial stone A mixture of stone chips or fragments, usually embedded in a matrix of mortar, cement, or plaster; the surface may be ground, polished, molded, or otherwise treated to simulate stone; variously called **art marble, artificial marble, cast stone, marezzo, patent stone**, and **reconstructed stone**.

art marble See **artificial stone**.

Art Moderne An architectural style found principally in houses constructed in the 1930s, following the earlier Art Deco style. Common characteristics may include smooth stuccoed wall surfaces; flat roofs; architectural details that emphasize the horizontal appearance of the building; rounded exterior corners; **ribbon windows** that may continue around a corner; glass blocks; an asymmetrical façade. The jagged version of this style is sometimes called Zigzag Moderne. Also see **International style**. Compare with **Art Deco** and **Streamline Moderne**.

Art Nouveau A style of decoration in architecture and applied art developed principally in France and Belgium toward the end of the 19th cent.; characterized by organic and dynamic forms, curving design, and whiplash lines. The German version is called *Jugendstil*, the Austrian variant *Sezession*; in Italy one speaks of *Stile Liberty*, in Spain of *Modernismo*.

Arts and Crafts Movement A group of architects and artisans who emphasized the importance of craftsmanship and high standards in all architectural details; greatly influenced by the outstanding work of William Morris and his company of craftsmen near London. Beginning in the late 19th century and extending into the early 20th century, this movement had a significant impact in America on the **Prairie style** with its low-pitched roofs and widely overhanging eaves, and on the **Craftsman style**. In particular, excellent craftsmanship and superior detailing was embraced in the designs of the architects Charles Sumner Greene (1868–1957) and his brother Henry Mather Greene (1870–1954) of Pasadena, California, whose work exemplified architectural details carried to a high art.

art window A term sometimes applied to a window having its upper and lower sashes of different sizes, with the upper sash containing a number of small panes of colored glass.

arx The fortress or citadel of an ancient town.

AS Abbr. for **automatic sprinkler**.

ASA Abbr. for "American Standards Association;" see **American National Standards Institute**.

asarotum A type of painted pavement used by the ancient Romans before their use of mosaic work.

asb 1. Abbr. for **apostilb**. 2. Abbr. for **asbestos**.

ASBC Abbr. for "American Standard Building Code."

asbestos abatement, asbestos removal The procedures used in eliminating the release of asbestos fibers or in removing materials containing asbestos (e.g., the process of encapsulation). Also see **air monitoring, HEPA filter**, and **wet cleaning**.

asbestos, asbestos fiber Fine, flexible, non-combustible, inorganic fiber obtained from natural hydrous magnesium silicate; can withstand high temperatures without change; a poor heat conductor; is fabricated into many forms either alone or with other ingredients.

asbestos blanket Asbestos fibers (alone or in combination with other fibers) stitched, bonded, or woven into flexible blanket form; used for high-temperature insulation or for fire and flame barriers.

asbestos board See **asbestos-cement board**.

asbestos-cement board, asbestos-cement wallboard, asbestos sheeting A dense, rigid, board containing a high proportion of asbestos fibers bonded with portland cement; resistant to fire, flame, and weathering; has low resistance to heat flow. Used as a building material in sheet form and corrugated sheeting.

asbestos-cement cladding Asbestos-cement board and component wall systems, directly supported by wall framing, forming a wall or wall facing.

asbestos curtain, fire curtain, safety curtain A curtain which closes the stage of a theatre from the auditorium automatically in case of fire, preventing the spread of flame and smoke; usually fabricated of woven asbestos and steel wire, it may be nonrigid, semirigid, or rigid.

asbestos felt A product made by saturating felted asbestos with asphalt or other suitable binder, such as a synthetic elastomer.

asbestos fiber See **asbestos**.

asbestos joint runner, pouring rope An asbestos rope, wrapped around a pipe and then clamped in position; used to hold molten lead which is poured in a caulked joint.

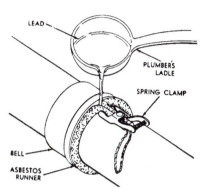

asbestos joint runner

asbestos plaster A fireproof insulating material generally composed of asbestos with bentonite as the binder.

asbestos roofing Roofing or wall cladding sheets made of asbestos cement; may be plain, corrugated, or variously patterned. Also see **asbestos cement board**.

asbestos roof shingle A fire-resisting roofing shingle, composed largely of asbestos.

asbestos runner Same as **asbestos joint runner**.

asbestos structural roofing Heavy **asbestos-cement board** directly supported by roof framing, forming a roof deck and providing a roof surface for cladding.

ASC Abbr. for "asphalt surface course."

ASCE Abbr. for "American Society of Civil Engineers."

ascendant See **chambranle**.

ash A hard, strong, straight-grained hardwood of the eastern U.S.A. having good shock resistance and bending qualities; used as flooring, trim, and decorative veneer.

ash dump An opening in the floor of a fireplace or firebox through which ashes are swept to an ashpit below.

ashlar **1.** Squared building stone. **2. Ashlar masonry**. **3.** A vertical stud between the floor beams and rafters of a garret.

ashlar anchor Same as, or functioning as, a **cramp**.

ashlar brick, rock-faced brick A brick whose face has been hacked to resemble roughly hacked stone.

ashlaring **1.** Ashlars, collectively. **2.** In garrets, the short wood upright pieces between the floor beams and rafters, to which wall lath is attached.

ashlar line A horizontal line at the exterior face of a masonry wall.

ashlar masonry Masonry composed of rectangular units of burnt clay or shale, or stone, generally larger in size than brick and properly bonded, having sawn, dressed, or squared beds and joints laid in mortar.

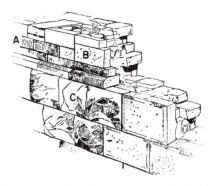

ashlar masonry: A, random-range quarry-faced ashlar; B, random-range dressed-faced ashlar; C, coursed quarry-faced ashlar; D, coursed dressed ashlar with margin draft; E, bonder in ashlar; f, rubble filling back of ashlar

ashlar piece A vertical stud between the floor beams and rafters of a garret.

ashlar veneer A **veneer wall** constructed of ashlar masonry.

ashlering See **ashlaring**.

ashpan A metal receptacle beneath a grating for collection and removal of ashes.

ashpit A chamber located below the fireplace or firebox for the collection and removal of ashes.

ashpit door A cast-iron door providing access to an ashpit for ash removal.

ASHRAE Abbr. for "American Society of Heating, Refrigerating and Air-Conditioning Engineers."

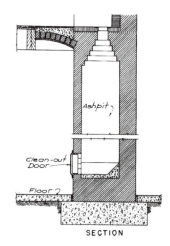

ashpit

ASI Abbr. for "Architects and Surveyors Institute."

Asiatic base A type of **Ionic base**; consists of a lower disk with horizontal fluting or scotias (there may be a plinth below the disk) and an upper torus decorated with horizontal fluting on relief; developed in Asia minor.

Asiatic water closet A water closet which has its bowl nearly flush with the floor so that the user adopts a squatting position; widely used in some parts of Asia.

ASID Abbr. for "American Society of Interior Designers."

asistencia In **Spanish Colonial architecture**, a chapel usually having no permanent priest but relying on the part-time assistance of visiting *padres*.

askarel A synthetic electrically insulating liquid which is nonflammable; when decomposed by an electric arc, the gaseous products also are nonflammable.

ASLA Abbr. for **American Society of Landscape Architects**.

ASME Abbr. for "American Society of Mechanical Engineers."

aspasticum An apartment or place adjoining the ancient churches or basilicas in which the bishop or presbyters received visits of devotion or in which ceremonies or business was conducted.

aspect The direction which a building faces with respect to the points of a compass.

aspect ratio 1. In any rectangular configuration (such as the cross section of a rectangular duct), the ratio of the longer dimension to the shorter. 2. In a rectangular configuration, the ratio of the long-side to the short-side.

aspersorium A holy-water stoup or font.

ASPH On drawings, abbr. for **asphalt**.

asphalt 1. A dark brown to black cementitious material, solid or semisolid, in which the predominating constituents are bitumens which occur in nature. 2. A similar material obtained artificially in refining petroleum; used in built-up roofing systems as a waterproofing agent. 3. A mixture of such substances with an aggregate for use in paving.

asphalt- Also see **asphaltic**.

asphalt binder course See **binder course, 1**.

asphalt block A paving block composed of a mixture of 88 to 92% crushed stone and the balance **asphaltic cement**.

asphalt cement Asphalt that is refined to meet specifications for paving, industrial, and special purposes; see **asphaltic cement**.

asphalt color coat An asphalt surface treatment with a cover of mineral aggregate which has been selected to produce a desired color.

asphalt concrete See **asphaltic concrete**.

asphalt cutter A powered machine having a rotating abrasive blade; used to saw through bituminous surfacing material.

asphalt-emulsion slurry seal A mixture of slow-setting emulsified asphalt, fine aggregate, and mineral filler, with water added to produce a slurry consistency.

asphalt felt See **breather-type asphalt felt**.

asphalt filler See **asphalt joint filler**.

asphalt fog seal An **asphalt surface treatment** consisting of a light application of liquid asphalt without a mineral aggregate cover.

asphalt heater A piece of equipment for raising the temperature of bitumen used in paving; usually the bitumen circulates through tubes inside a chamber heated by a burner.

asphaltic Also see **asphalt**.

asphaltic base course In asphalt pavement, a foundation layer consisting of mineral aggregate bound together with asphaltic material.

asphaltic cement, asphalt cement A specially prepared asphalt, free of water and mate-rial foreign to asphalt; contains less than 1% ash; must be heated to a fluid condition for use; an asphalt specially prepared as to quality and consistency for direct use in the manufacture of bituminous pavements.

asphaltic concrete, asphalt paving, black top A mixture of asphalt and graded aggregate widely used as paving material over a prepared base; normally placed, shaped, and compacted while hot, but can be prepared for placement without heat. Also see **cold mix**.

asphaltic felt See **asphalt prepared roofing**. Also see the specific type of felt, as **mineral-surfaced felt**, **sanded flux-pitch felt**, etc.

asphaltic macadam A pavement similar to **macadam** but having asphalt as the binder in place of tar.

asphaltic mastic, mastic asphalt A viscous mixture of asphalt and a filler material such as fine sand or asbestos; hardens when exposed to air; used as an adhesive, as a sealant at joints, and in waterproofing.

asphalting The process of applying asphalt for various construction purposes, as in waterproofing basements and roof decks.

asphalt intermediate course Same as **binder course, 1**.

asphalt joint filler An asphaltic product used for filling cracks and joints in pavement and other structures.

asphalt lamination A laminate of sheet material, such as paper or felt, which uses asphalt as the adhesive.

asphalt leveling course A course (of an asphalt-aggregate mixture) of variable thickness used to eliminate irregularities in contour of an existing surface, prior to the placement of a superimposed layer.

asphalt macadam See **asphaltic macadam**.

asphalt mastic See **asphaltic mastic**.

asphalt overlay One or more courses of asphalt construction on an existing pavement; generally includes an asphalt leveling course to correct the contour of the old pavement.

asphalt paint A liquid asphaltic product sometimes containing small amounts of other materials such as lampblack, aluminum flakes, and mineral pigments.

asphalt panel See **premolded asphalt panel**.

asphalt paper A paper sheet material that has been coated, saturated, or laminated with asphalt to increase its toughness and its resistance to water.

asphalt pavement A pavement consisting of a surface course of mineral aggregate, coated and cemented together with asphalt cement on supporting courses.

asphalt pavement sealer A compound applied to asphalt pavements to protect the surface from deterioration, from weathering, and from petroleum products.

asphalt pavement structure All of the courses of asphalt-aggregate mixtures placed above the subgrade or improved subgrade.

asphalt paving See **asphaltic concrete**.

asphalt plank A plank which is fabricated of a mixture of asphalt fiber and mineral filler, often reinforced with steel or fiberglass mesh; sometimes contains mineral grits to provide a sandpaper texture.

asphalt prepared roofing, asphaltic felt, cold-process roofing, prepared roofing, rolled roofing, rolled strip roofing, roofing felt, sanded bituminous felt, saturated felt, self-finished roofing felt A roofing material manufactured by saturating a dry felt with asphalt and then coating the saturated felt with a harder asphalt mixed with a fine mineral, glass-fiber, asbestos, or organic stabilizer; available in the form of rolls. All or part of the weather side may be covered with mineral granules or with powdered talc or mica. The reverse side is covered with a material suitable to prevent sticking in the roll. The granule-surfaced material may be used as **cap sheet** in **built-up roofing**.

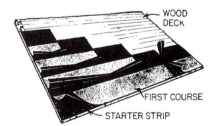

Installing **asphalt prepared roofing**

asphalt prime coat An initial application of an **asphalt primer**, usually as preparation for a superimposed treatment or construction.

asphalt primer A liquid material of low viscosity which upon application to a nonbituminous surface is completely absorbed; used to waterproof existing surfaces and to prepare them as a base for an asphalt course.

asphalt roofing See **asphalt-prepared roofing**.

asphalt seal coat A bituminous coating, with or without aggregate, applied to the surface of a pavement to waterproof and preserve the surface and to improve the texture of a previously applied bituminous surface.

asphalt-shingle nail Same as **roofing nail**.

asphalt shingles, composition shingles, strip slates Shingles manufactured from saturated roofing felts (rag, asbestos, or fiber glass) coated with asphalt and having mineral granules on the side exposed to the weather.

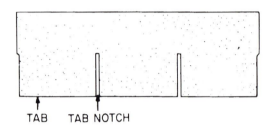

TAB   TAB NOTCH

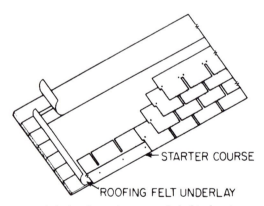

STARTER COURSE

ROOFING FELT UNDERLAY

asphalt shingles: *above*, an asphalt shingle strip; *below*, installing asphalt shingles

asphalt soil stabilization The treatment of naturally occurring nonplastic or moderately plastic soil with liquid asphalt at normal temperatures to improve the load-bearing qualities of the soil.

asphalt surface course A top course of asphalt pavement.

asphalt surface treatment The application of asphaltic materials to any type of pavement surface or road surface, with or without a cover of mineral aggregate.

asphalt tack coat A light coating of liquid asphalt on an existing asphalt surface or on a portland cement concrete surface; used to ensure a bond between the old surface and the overlaying course.

asphalt tile A resilient, low-cost floor tile composed of asbestos fibers, finely ground limestone fillers, mineral pigments, and asphaltic or resinous binders. Requires waxing and buffing; set in mastic over wood or concrete subfloor; is not greaseproof unless specially treated.

asphaltum 1. Natural **asphalt**. 2. In painting, asphalt from residues of crude mineral oil.

aspiration In an air-conditioned room, the pulling of room air into the moving air-stream which is discharging from a diffuser.

aspirator A device which draws a stream of liquid or air through it by means of suction which is produced by the flow of a fluid through an orifice.

ASR Abbr. for "automatic sprinkler riser."

Assam psychrometer A **psychrometer**, shielded from radiation, in which the air is blown over the bulbs of the two thermometers with a small fan.

ASSE Abbr. for "American Society of Sanitary Engineering."

assemblage of orders Same as **supercolumniation**; also see **orders**.

assembling bolt A threaded bolt for holding together temporarily the several parts of a structure during riveting.

assembly building A building used for the gathering of persons for the purposes of amusement, deliberation, dining, drinking, education, entertainment, instruction, or awaiting transportation.

assembly occupancy Occupancy of a room, hall, or building by people gathered for a purpose, such as church, restaurant, or bus station.

assembly space A gathering place (such as an auditorium, exclusive of a stage) that is occupied by numbers of persons during major periods of occupancy; some building codes consider every tier of seating in an auditorium to be a separate assembly space.

asser In ancient carpentry: 1. The ribs or brackets of an arched ceiling. 2. The purlins or rafters of a roof. 3. A beam or joist.

assessed valuation The value of a property as determined by a municipality for real estate tax purposes; often this valuation is less than the true market value of the property.

assessment A tax, charge, or levy on property: 1. as a means of computing real estate tax; 2. to pay for specific services or improvements.

assessment ratio Of a property, the ratio between its market value and its assessed value.

assignment 1. The transfer of a legal right. 2. In the case of a lease, the transfer of the right of the tenant to the entire property leased and for the entire term remaining; also see **sublease**.

assize 1. A cylindrical block of stone forming one unit in a column. 2. A course of stonework.

associate In an architectural firm, a member of an architect's staff who has a special employment agreement.

associate architect, associated architect An architect who has a temporary partnership, joint venture, or employment agreement with another architect to collaborate in the performance of services for a specific project or series of projects. Also see **joint venture**.

assommoir A gallery built over a door or passage of a fortified place, from which stones and heavy objects could be hurled down on the enemy.

ASST On drawings, abbr. for "assistant."

assumption of mortgage The purchaser of property may promise the vendor that he will assume the obligation to keep up the mortgage payments. In such event, the mortgagee may generally enforce this promise against the purchaser, and in addition to his right to foreclose in the event of nonpayment the mortgagee may also recover from the purchaser (or from the vendor) any deficiency between the proceeds of the foreclosure sale and the amount still owing on the mortgage. Also see **subject to mortgage**.

Assyrian architecture Architecture of the Assyrian empire (centered between the Tigris and Upper and Lower Zab rivers in southwest Asia); was expressive of its might, as conquerors of Mesopotamia and much of the adjacent countries between the 9th and 7th centuries B.C. Mud

astler

brick was used as the building material, although stone was available; stone was used only for carved revetments and monumental decorative sculptures. Excavations have uncovered large palaces and temple complexes with their ziggurats as well as extensive fortifications.

Assyrian architecture: decorative relief

Assyrian architecture: colored tiling from Khorsabad

Assyrian architecture: head

Assyrian architecture: pavement slab at Nimrud
(end of 9th cent. B.C.)

astler   Old English term for **ashlar.**

ASTM   Abbr. for **American Society for Testing Materials.**

astragal   **1.** A **bead,** usually half-round, with a fillet on one or both sides. It may be plain, but the term is more correctly used to describe the classical molding consisting of a small convex molding decorated with a string of beads or bead-and-reel shapes. **2.** A plain **bead molding.** Also called **roundel, baguette,** or **chaplet. 3.** A member, or combination of members, fixed to one of a pair of doors or casement windows to cover the joint between the meeting stiles and to close the clearance gap; provides a weather seal, minimizes the passage of light and noise, and retards the passage of smoke or flame during a fire. Also see **overlapping astragal, split astragal.** (*See illustration p. 57.*)

astragal, 1:   in Greek architecture

An overlapping **astragal, 3**

atlas

astragal front   A **lock front** which is shaped to fit the edge of a door having an astragal molding.

astragal joint   A spigot-and-socket joint used on a lead **downspout** (or the like), where the socket incorporates ornamental moldings called astragals.

astreated   Decorated with star-like ornaments.

astylar   Columnless; usually describing a façade without columns, pilasters, or the like.

asylum   A building or group of buildings that serves as a refuge for the mentally ill.

AT.   **1.** Abbr. for **asphalt tile**. **2.** On drawings, abbr. for "airtight."

atadura   In Mayan architecture, a façade molding, above and below a continuous horizontal decorative frieze on the exterior of a building.

ataracea   Inlaid woodwork of various colors.

ATC   **1.** On drawings, abbr. for **architectural terra-cotta**. **2.** On drawings, abbr. for "acoustical tile ceiling."

atelier   **1.** An artist's workshop. **2.** A place where artwork or handicrafts are produced by skilled workers. **3.** A studio where the fine arts, including architecture, are taught.

ATF   On drawings, abbr. for "asphalt-tile floor."

Athenaeum   A temple or place dedicated to Athene, or Minerva; specifically an institution founded at Rome by Hadrian for the promotion of literary and scientific studies, and imitated in the provinces.

atlantes   See **atlas**.

atlas, *pl.* **atlantes**   A figure (or figures) of a man used in place of a column to support an entablature; also called a **telamon**.

atm   Abbr. for "atmosphere."

atmospheric pressure, barometric pressure   The pressure exerted by the earth's atmosphere; under standard conditions equal to 14.7 lb per sq in. (1.01×10^6 pascals) equivalent to the pressure exerted by a column of mercury 29.9 in. (76.0 cm) high.

atmospheric-pressure steam curing   Same as **atmospheric steam curing**.

atmospheric steam curing   The **steam curing** of concrete or cement products at atmospheric pressure, usually at a maximum ambient temperature between 100 to 200°F (40 to 95°C).

atmospheric-type vacuum breaker   A **backflow preventer** containing a float check, check seat, and an air inlet port. As water flows through this device, it causes the float check to rise off a seat, thereby permitting the flow of water. If pressure is lost upstream or if the flow of water is turned off, the float check falls, thereby allowing air to enter the line and preventing backflow.

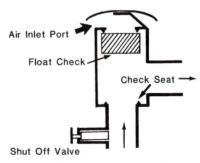

atmospheric-type vacuum breaker

atomization The formation of tiny droplets or a very fine spray, as produced by impinging jets of air on a small stream of paint in spray painting.

atomizing-type humidifier A humidifier in which tiny particles of water are introduced into a stream of air.

atrio A walled forecourt in California mission architecture.

atriolum **1.** In ancient Rome, a small atrium. **2.** A small antechamber forming the entrance of a tomb.

atrium In a contemporary building, a vertical opening (or series of openings), usually centrally located, that connects three or more floors; may be covered at the top. Most codes do not permit its use as an enclosed stairway, elevator hoistway, or utility shaft.

attached column An **engaged column**.

attached garage **1.** A garage which has at least one wall (or part of one wall) in common with a building. **2.** A garage which is connected to a building, as by a covered porch.

attached house A house that is joined to one (or more) adjacent house(s) by a **party wall**.

attachment plug A device which is inserted into a receptacle to establish the electric connection between the conductors which are wired to the receptacle and the conductors of the flexible cord attached to the plug.

atrium, 1

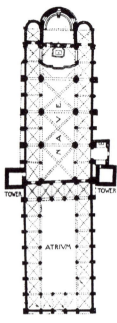

atrium, 2

attemperator See **coil**.

attenuation See **sound attenuation**.

attenuator See **sound attenuator**.

Atterberg limits In plastic soils, the water contents (determined by standard tests) which define the boundaries between the different states of consistency of plastic soils. Also see **liquid limit, plastic limit, shrinkage limit**.

Atterberg test A test for determining the plasticity of soils.

attic **1.** A **garret**. **2.** In classic building, a story built above the wall cornice. **3.** (*cap.*) Pertaining to the district of Attica in Greece. **4.** The ornamental construction above an **entablature;** often decorated. **5.** The space between the ceiling framing of the topmost story and the underside of the roof framing.

Attic base The base of a column of the Ionic order consisting of an upper **torus** and a lower torus, with a **scotia** and two narrow fillets between them.

attic order Small pillars or pilasters decorating the exterior of an **attic, 2**.

attic story See **attic, 2**.

attic tank An open tank which is installed above the highest plumbing fixture in a building

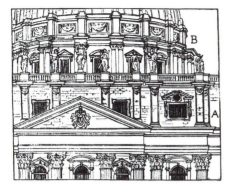

attic, 2: of St. Peter's, Rome; A, attic of main edifice; B, attic of the dome

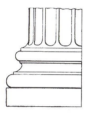

Attic base

(e.g., in the attic) and which supplies water to the fixtures by gravity; the filling of the tank is controlled by a float valve.

Atticurge Said of a doorway having jambs which are inclined slightly inwards, so that the opening is wider at the threshold than at the top.

attic ventilator A mechanical fan, located in the attic space of a residence; usually moves large quantities of air at a relatively low velocity.

attorney-in-fact A person authorized to act for or in behalf of another person or organization, to the extent prescribed in a written instrument known as a **power of attorney**.

aud Abbr. for **auditorium**.

audio accumulator An audio listening device used to detect sounds of breaking and entering a building or a secure area within a building. False alarms are minimized by a circuit design that delays activation of an alarm until a predetermined number of sound detections have been "accumulated" within a selected time period.

audio frequency Any **frequency** of oscillation of a sound wave which is audible; usually in the range between 15 and 20,000 Hz (cycles per second).

audio-visual aids Equipment and/or materials used in training, demonstrations, or teaching, which employs sight and sound simultaneously.

auditorium That part of a theatre, school, or public building which is set aside for the audience for listening and viewing.

auditorium seating Manufactured row chairs for stepped, level, or inclined floors in rooms or areas occupied by an audience.

auditory In ancient churches, that part of the church where the people usually stood to be instructed in the gospel; now called the **nave**.

auger **1.** A hand-held carpenter's tool for boring holes in wood, similar to, but larger than, a **gimlet**; has a long steel bit usually not larger than 1 in. (25 mm) in diameter. **2.** A rotary drill, usually powered, for cutting circular holes in earth or rock.

auger bit A bit having a square tang, fitted into and rotated by a brace; used for drilling holes in wood.

augered pile A concrete pile which is cast-in-place in a hole drilled by an auger; may be belled at the bottom; suitable in dry soil.

Augustaeum A building or temple dedicated to the deified Augustus.

aula In ancient architecture, a court or hall, esp. an open court attached to a house.

auleolum A small church or chapel.

aumbry See **ambry**.

aureole A pointed oval frame or glory around the head or body of a sacred figure; the radiance surrounding it.

auricular Said of the shape of an ornament of organic and dynamic forms that resemble the ear.

authority See **administrative authority**.

authority having jurisdiction A federal, state, local, or other regional department, or an individual such as a fire chief, fire marshal, chief of a fire prevention bureau (or labor department or health department), building official, electrical inspector, or other individual having statutory authority. For insurance purposes, the "authority having jurisdiction" may be an insurance inspection department or rating bureau, or other representative of an insurance company. In many circumstances the property owner or a delegated agent assumes the role of the authority having jurisdiction; at government installations, the commanding officer or departmental official may be the "authority having jurisdiction."

AUTO On drawings, abbr. for "automatic."

autoclave A pressure vessel in which an environment of steam at high pressure may be produced, usually at a high temperature; used in the curing of concrete products and in the testing of hydraulic cement for soundness.

autoclave curing Steam curing of concrete products, sand-lime brick, asbestos cement products, hydrous calcium silicate insulation products, or cement in an autoclave at maximum ambient temperatures generally between 340 and 420°F (170 and 215°C).

autoclaving cycle **1.** In autoclave curing, the time interval between the start of the temperature-rise period and the end of the blowdown period. **2.** A schedule of the time and temperature-pressure conditions of periods which make up the cycle.

auto court A **motel**.

autogenous healing A natural process of closing and filling cracks in concrete or mortar while it is kept damp.

autogenous volume change The change in volume produced by continued hydration of cement, exclusive of effects of external forces or change of water content or temperature.

automatic Said of a door, window, or other opening protective device that is so constructed and arranged that, when actuated by a predetermined temperature or rise in temperature, it will operate as intended.

automatic batcher A **batcher** for concrete which is actuated by a single starter switch, opens automatically at the start of the weighing operations of each material, and closes automatically when the designated weight of each material has been reached.

automatic circuit breaker See **circuit breaker**.

automatic circuit recloser A self-controlled device for automatically interrupting and reclosing an alternating current circuit with a predetermined sequence of opening and reclosing, followed by resetting, hold closed, or lockout operation.

automatic closing device See **closing device**.

automatic control valve A valve designed to control the flow of steam, water, gas, or other fluids, by means of a variable orifice which is positioned by an operator in response to signals from a sensor or controller.

automatic door **1.** A power-operated door that closes when subject to an abnormally high ambient temperature, an unusual rate of temperature rise, or an abnormal smoke condition. **2.** A power-operated door that opens when a person or automobile approaches.

automatic door bottom A movable plunger, in the form of a horizontal bar at the bottom of a door, which drops automatically when the door is closed; when closed, a horizontal protruding

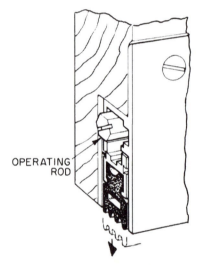

OPERATING ROD

automatic door bottom

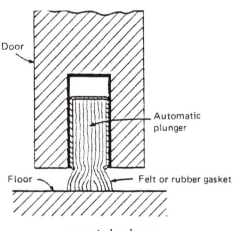

Door

Automatic plunger

Floor

Felt or rubber gasket

automatic door bottom

operating rod strikes the door jamb, thereby actuating the plunger, sealing the threshold and reducing noise transmission.

automatic dry-pipe sprinkler system A **sprinkler system** in which the piping up to the sprinkler heads is either filled with compressed air or air at atmospheric pressure; the water supply is controlled by an acceptable dry-pipe valve; also see **dry-pipe sprinkler system**.

automatic dry standpipe system A **standpipe system** in which all piping is either filled with compressed air or air at atmospheric pressure; the water enters the system through a control valve that is actuated either automatically by a reduction of air pressure within the system or by the manual activation of a remote control located at each fire-hose station.

automatic elevator, self-service elevator An elevator which starts and stops automatically in response to the pushing of a button at one of the landings or in the car.

automatic fire-alarm system A **fire-alarm system** which detects the presence of a fire and automatically initiates a signal indicating its detection.

automatic fire detector An alarm-initiating device that automatically detects heat, smoke, or other products of combustion.

automatic fire-extinguishing system An approved system of devices and equipment that automatically detects a fire and then discharges an approved fire-extinguishing agent onto or in the area of the fire.

automatic fire pump A pump which provides the required water pressure in a fire standpipe or sprinkler system; when the water pressure in the system drops below a preselected value, a sensor causes the pump to start, and to stop the pump when the pressure is restored.

automatic fire-suppression system An engineered system using carbon dioxide (CO_2), a foam wet or dry chemical, a halogenated extinguishing agent, or a clean extinguishing agent, in an **automatic sprinkler system** to detect and automatically suppress a fire through fixed piping and nozzles.

automatic fire vent 1. A device installed in the roof of a large single-story building which operates automatically in the event of fire, providing an opening to the outdoors; removes smoke and confines the fire so that it can be fought more effectively. 2. See **smoke and fire vent**.

automatic flushing system A water tank system which provides automatically for the periodic flushing of urinals or other plumbing fixtures, or of pipes having too small a slope to drain effectively.

automatic gas shutoff device In a **gas-fired water heater**, a device that shuts off the gas supply if the water temperature in the heater exceeds a predetermined limit.

automatic load shedding The automatic disconnection of a part of the electrical load in a building when there is an **outage** of the main power supplied to the building; this action reduces the total load placed on an emergency power generator.

automatic operation In an elevator: an operation whereby the starting of the elevator car is effected in response to the momentary actuation of operating devices at the landing, and/or in response to any automatic starting mechanism; and whereby the car is stopped automatically at the landings.

automatic operator A power-operated door-activating device and control, actuated by approaching traffic or a remote switch.

automatic smoke alarm system An alarm system whose **smoke detectors** initiate and transmit an alarm automatically.

automatic smoke vent See **smoke and fire vent**.

automatic sprinkler A **sprinkler head** having a nozzle which is normally closed, but opens when exposed to a predetermined quantity of heat—either by the melting of a fusible element or by the rupturing of a liquid-filled glass bulb.

automatic sprinkler system 1. A **fire-protection sprinkler system** connected to a suitable water supply; designed to provide an immediate and continuous flow of water automatically in case of fire. 2. A fire sprinkler system that reacts to fire without the need for human intervention; a type of automatic **fire-protection sprinkler system**.

automatic threshold closer Same as **automatic door bottom**.

automatic transfer switch 1. A combination of an electrically operated, double-throw transfer switch and a control panel. Under normal circumstances, the connected load is energized from the utility source. Upon failure of this source, the transfer switch automatically connects the load to an emergency power generator until power supplied by the utility is restored, at which time it reconnects the load to the utility source. **2.** In an electric circuit, a **switch** which automatically transfers a specific load from the normal source to an emergency source if the former fails or if the voltage of the normal source drops below a preset minimum.

automatic water supply A water supply system whose operation is not dependent on any manual setting of any items of equipment, such as operating valves, starting pumps, or connectors.

automatic wet-pipe sprinkler system A **sprinkler system** in which all piping and sprinkler heads, at all times, are filled with water under pressure; the system discharges immediately when a sprinkler head operates, and the water continues to flow until the system is shut off.

auto-suppression system A British term for a protection system that activates automatically when a fire is detected; an **automatic sprinkler system**.

aux Abbr. for "auxiliary."

auxiliary dead latch, auxiliary latch bolt, deadlocking latch bolt, trigger bolt A supplementary latch in a lock which automatically deadlocks the main latch bolt when the door is closed.

auxiliary energy subsystem An energy source (other than the sun), used to supplement or provide backup for the output provided by a solar energy system.

auxiliary rafter Above a **principal rafter,** a second principal rafter, occasionally used in a large **queenpost truss**.

auxiliary reinforcement In a prestressed structural member, any reinforcement in addition to that whose function is **prestressing**.

auxiliary rim lock A secondary or extra lock that is surface-mounted on a door to provide additional security.

auxiliary rope-fastening device A device attached to an elevator car, to a counterweight, or to the overhead dead-end rope-hitch support; automatically supports the car or counterweight in case the fastening for the wire rope (cable) fails.

available short-circuit current The maximum electric current delivered by the electric power system to a **fault** at a given point in a circuit.

avalanche protector A barrier that prevents loose material from sliding into the tracks or wheels of any type of excavation or digging machine.

avant-corps That part of a building which projects prominently from the main mass, e.g., a pavilion.

AVE On drawings, abbr. for "avenue."

aventurine Glass (or glazes) containing colored spangles of nonglassy material.

avenue **1.** A wide street, usually planted with trees; generally straight. **2.** A way of approach or access.

average bond stress The force in a steel **reinforcing bar** divided by the product of its perimeter and its embedded length.

average concrete Concrete that is made without artificial aggregates or admixtures; its strength is not established by tests but is assumed to be the value derived from its **water-cement ratio**.

average-end-area method A procedure for calculating the volume of earthwork between two cross sections; the cross-sectional areas are averaged and multiplied by the distance between cross sections to determine the volume.

average frequency of occurrence The average number of years between storms that will produce rainfall rates equaling or exceeding a given amount; sometimes called the "return period."

average grade Within a building construction site, the arithmetic average of the elevations of various ground surfaces within the site.

average haul The average distance that a grading material is moved from **cut** to **fill**.

AVG On drawings, abbr. for "average."

avodire, white mahogany A west African wood, pale yellow to white in color; soft to hard; light in weight to moderately heavy; frequently ribbon-striped. Used for interior finish, plywood, and paneling.

AW   Abbr. for "actual weight."

A/W   Abbr. for "all-weather."

award   A communication from an **owner** accepting a bid or negotiated proposal. An award creates legal obligations between the parties.

A-weighted sound level   The sound level measured with a **sound-level meter** using *A-weighting*, which alters the sensitivity of the sound-level meter with respect to frequency so that the sound-level meter is less sensitive at frequencies where the ear is less sensitive; usually used in specifying permissible sound levels in buildings.

AWG   On drawings, abbr. for **American wire gauge**.

AWI   Abbr. for "Architectural Woodwork Institute."

awl   A pointed tool used for piercing holes in thin wood, hardboard, etc.

awning   A roof-like covering of canvas, or the like, often adjustable, over a window, door, etc., to provide protection against the sun, rain, and wind.

awning blind   A **blind** which is hinged at the top; can swing outward and be fixed in position by a stay.

awning blind

awning window   A window consisting of a number of top-hinged horizontal sashes one above the other, the bottom edges of which swing outward; operated by one control device.

AWPA   Abbr. for "American Wood-Preservers' Association."

AWS   **1.** Abbr. for "all wood screws." **2.** Abbr. for "American Welding Society."

A.W.W.I.   Abbr. for "American Wood Window Institute."

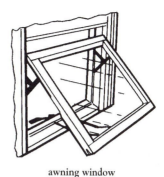

awning window

ax   **1.** A sharp-edged steel tool for splitting wood, hewing timber, etc. **2.** An **axhammer**.

ax, 1

axed arch   An arch which is constructed of bricks that have been roughly cut into a wedge shape.

axed brick, rough-axed brick   A brick, shaped with an ax, that has not been trimmed; when laid, the joints for such bricks are thicker than those for gauged brick.

axed work   (*Brit.*)   A hand-dressed stone surface showing toolmarks made by an ax, pick, or bushhammer.

axhammer   An ax for spalling or dressing rough stone; has either one cutting edge and one hammer face or two cutting edges.

axial-flow fan   **1.** One of the following types of fans: vaneaxial, tubeaxial, or propeller. Such fans impart energy to the air by giving it a twisting motion. They are specified by blade shape, ratio of hub-to-tip diameter, pitch of the blades, and number of blades. Guide vanes may be added to straighten the flow and increase the efficiency. **2.** See **centrifugal fan**. (*See illustration p. 64.*)

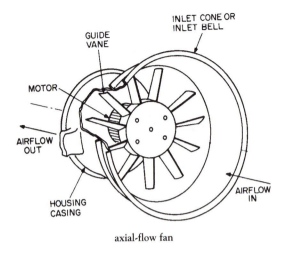

axial-flow fan

axial force   See **axial load**.

axial force diagram   In statics, a graphical representation of the **axial load** acting at each section of a structural member, plotted to scale and with proper sign as an ordinate at each point of the member and along a reference line representing the length of the member.

axial load, axial force   The resultant longitudinal internal component of force which acts perpendicular to the cross section of a structural member and at its centroid, producing uniform stress.

axis   A straight line indicating center of symmetry of a solid or plane figure.

axle pulley   See **sash pulley**.

axle-steel reinforcing bar   A **reinforcing bar** fabricated from carbon-steel axles of railroad cars.

Axminster carpet   A carpet having pile which is attached to the carpet backing by inserting the tufts by rows between the warp threads and then binding them by means of the filling; this method of carpet construction permits intricate design and almost any number of colors to be used.

axonometric projection   A form of orthographic projection in which a rectangular object, projected on a plane, shows three faces. One of two general divisions of pictorial projection (the other being **oblique projection**); often divided into three types: isometric, dimetric and trimetric.

ayaka   A type of pillar, placed on a platform attached to a Buddhist **stupa**.

azimuth   In plane surveying, a horizontal angle measured clockwise from north meridian to the direction of an object or fixed point.

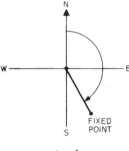

azimuth

azimuth traverse   A survey traverse in which the direction of the measured course is determined by azimuth and verified by back azimuth; to initiate this type of traverse, it is necessary to have a reference meridian.

azotea   In Spanish architecture, the terrace or platform on the roof of a house.

Aztec architecture   The architecture of the Aztecs in Mexico, succeeding the Mayans, from the 14th cent. until the Spanish conquest in the 16th cent.

azulejo   An earthenware tile of Spanish manufacture, painted and enameled in rich colors, esp. one having a metallic luster.

B

B Abbr. for **beam**.

B&B In the lumber industry, abbr. for "grade B and better."

B&S **1.** On drawings, abbr. for "beams and stringers." **2.** On drawings, abbr. for "bell and spigot." **3.** On drawings, abbr. for **Brown and Sharpe gauge**.

B1S **1.** Abbr. for "banded one side." **2.** Abbr. for "bead one side."

B2E Abbr. for "banded two ends."

B2S **1.** Abbr. for "banded two sides." **2.** Abbr. for "bead two sides." **3.** Abbr. for "bright two sides."

B2S1E Abbr. for "banded two sides and one end."

B3E Abbr. for "beveled on three edges."

B4E Abbr. for "beveled on four edges."

BA Abbr. for "bright annealed."

Babylonian architecture In ancient Babylon, architecture characterized by: mud-brick construction; walls articulated by pilasters and recesses, sometimes faced with burnt and glazed brick; narrow rooms, mostly covered with flat timber and mud roofs; and the extensive use of bitumen in drain and pavement construction and as mortar.

back **1.** The rear, reverse, unseen, more remote, or less important part of a structure, tool, or object. **2.** The support for a more prominent or visible element; e.g., the back of wallboard is the surface to be plastered. **3.** The top or exposed side of a slate, tile, or the like, in contrast to the bed. **4.** The ridge or top of a horizontal member or structure like a joist, rafter, or roof. **5.** A principal rafter. **6.** The extrados or top surface of an arch, often buried in the surrounding masonry. **7.** A low-grade veneer used for the back ply in plywood construction. **8.** The wainscoting below the sash frame of a window, extending to the floor.

back arch Same as **arrière-voussure**.

backband A piece of millwork used around a rectangular window or door casing to cover the gap between the casing and the wall or as a decorative feature. Also called a **backbend**.

backband

backbar A work surface behind (and at the same height as) a liquor or service bar; usually has cabinets under the work surface which are used for storage, for the display of bottles and glassware, or for refrigerated coolers.

backbend **1.** Same as **backband**. **2.** At the outer edge of a metal door or window frame, the face which returns to the wall surface.

backboard A temporary board on the outside of a scaffold.

back boxing See **back lining, 1**.

back-brush To repaint a surface, which has just been painted, with a return stroke.

back check In a hydraulic **door closer, 1** a mechanism which slows the speed with which a door may be opened.

back choir Same as **retrochoir**.

backcloth Same as **backdrop**.

back counter A work surface behind the front serving counter of a restaurant, usually containing short-order cooking equipment, storage cabinets, storage shelves, etc.

back-draft damper A **damper, 1** having blades which are actuated by gravity, permitting air to pass through them in one direction only.

backdrop On the theatre stage, a large, taut, flat canvas, usually hung from the grid at the rear of the stage to mask the backstage area.

back edging Cutting a glazed ceramic pipe by first chipping through the glaze around the perimeter and then chipping the pipe below until it is cut through.

backer strip An asphalt-coated water-repellent strip which is applied behind the joint where the vertical edges of two shingles meet.

backfill Soil which is replaced in an area that has been excavated previously.

back fillet The **return** of the margin of a groin, doorjamb, or window jamb when it projects beyond a wall.

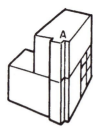

back fillet   A

backfill concrete A non-structural concrete used to prepare a surface to receive structural concrete, to fill excavated pockets in rocks, or to correct over-excavation.

backfilling, backfill 1. Rough masonry built behind a facing or between two faces. 2. Filling over the extrados of an arch. 3. Brickwork in spaces between structural timbers. Also see **nogging**. 4. Soil or crushed stone used to fill the space between the excavation or sheeting and the exterior of a structure, or around the foundation walls to provide means for water to drain away from a foundation.

back flap, back fold, back shutter The leaf in a window shutter that folds behind the exposed leaf of the shutter; that part of a window shutter that folds into a recess in the window casing.

backflap hinge, flap hinge A hinge having a flat plate or strap which is screwed to the face of a shutter or door.

backflow 1. The flow of water or other liquids, mixtures, or substances into the distributing pipes of a potable supply of water from any other than its intended source. Also see **back siphonage**. 2. Any flow in a direction opposite to the natural or intended direction of flow.

backflow connection Any arrangement of pipes, plumbing fixtures, drains, etc., in which **backflow** can occur.

backflow preventer A device used to prevent water (or other liquids) from being siphoned into a potable water system.

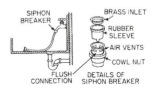

backflow preventer   for a hose connection

backflow valve See **backwater valve**.

back fold See **backflap**.

back form See **top form**.

background noise The total **noise** from all sources other than a particular one of interest.

back gutter A gutter installed on the uphill side of a chimney on a sloping roof; used to divert water around the chimney.

back hearth, inner hearth That part of the hearth, or floor, which is contained within the jambs of the fireplace.

backhoe An excavating machine for cutting trenches; a boom-mounted bucket moves toward the machine, cutting the ground like a hoe; then the machine turns away from the cut to permit the operator to dump the spoil.

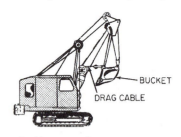

backhoe   attachment on a crane

backhouse, back building 1. A privy or outhouse. 2. A structure that stands behind a building to which it is a subsidiary.

backing 1. The bevel given the upper edge of a **hip rafter**. 2. Fitting pieces of furring onto joists to provide a level surface for laying floorboards. 3. Shaping the back of **lining** so that it lies flat against a wall. 4. The unexposed or unfinished inner face of a wall. **5.** Coursed masonry which is built over the extrados of an arch. **6.** Stone used for random rubble walls. **7. A backing brick**. **8.** The earth backfill of a retaining wall. **9.** In welding, a material (such as asbestos) used in backing up a joint during welding. **10.** A **backup strip**. **11.** See **carpet backing**.

backing board   In a **suspended acoustical ceiling**, a flat sheet of gypsum board to which acoustical tile is attached by adhesive or mechanical means.

backing brick   A relatively low-quality brick used behind face brick or other masonry.

backing coat   A coat of plaster other than the **finish coat**.

backing ring   A **backing** in the form of a ring, used during the welding of piping at butt joints.

backing up   In masonry, the laying of **backing brick**.

back jamb   See **back lining, 1**.

backjoint   In masonry, a rabbet such as that made on the inner side of a chimneypiece to receive a slip.

backlighting   The illumination of an object from the rear.

back lining   **1.** A thin wood strip which lines a window casing, next to the wall and opposite the pulley stile, and provides a smooth surface for the working of the weighted sash; also called **back boxing** or a **back jamb**. **2.** That piece of framing forming the back recess for boxing shutters.

back lintel   A lintel which supports the backing of a masonry wall, as opposed to the lintel supporting the facing material.

back-mop   To mop the back or underside of roofing felts with asphalt or tar when laying a built-up roof.

back mortaring   Same as **backplastering** and **pargetting, 3**.

back-nailing   Nailing the plies of a built-up roof to the substrate (in addition to hot mopping) to prevent slippage.

back nut   **1.** A threaded nut, one side of which is dished to retain a grommet; used in forming a watertight pipe joint. **2.** A locking nut on the shank of a pipe fitting, tap, or valve.

back observation   Same as **backsight**.

back-paint   To paint the reverse or hidden side of an object, usually for protection against the weather.

backplastering   A coat of plaster applied to the back side of lath, opposite the finished surface.

backplate   A plate, usually metal or wood, which serves as a backing for a structural member.

backplate lamp holder   A lamp holder, integrally mounted on a plate, which is designed for screwing to a flat surface.

back pressure   Pressure developed in opposition to the flow of liquid or gas in a pipe, duct, conduit, etc.; due to friction, gravity, or some other restriction to flow of the conveyed fluid.

back-pressure valve   See **check valve**.

back putty, bed glazing   The bedding of glazing compound which is placed between the face of glass and the frame or sash containing it.

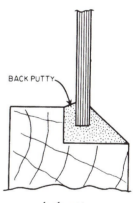

back putty

backsaw   A saw having a metal strip along its back to stiffen it; has many small teeth for fine, accurate sawing, as for miters.

backsaw

backset   **1.** The horizontal distance from the face of a lock or latch to the center of the keyhole, knob, or lock cylinder. **2.** Same as **setback**.

back shore   In **raking shores**, an outer member under a **rider shore** that temporarily supports the side of a building.

back shutter   See **backflap**.

backsight   In surveying, a sight on a previously established survey point or line.

back siphonage   The flowing back of used, contaminated, or polluted water from a plumbing fixture or vessel into the pipe which feeds it; due to reduced pressure in the pipe.

back siphonage preventer   See **vacuum breaker**.

backsplash   A protective panel on the wall behind a sink or counter; an **apron, 7**.

backstage   The entire area behind the fire wall of the stage of a theatre, including *the* rear of the *stage*, storage areas, and dressing rooms.

back stay   Same as **brace, 1**.

back-to-back house   A house with a **party wall** at the rear as well as along the sides.

backup   **1.** That part of a masonry wall behind the exterior facing. **2.** A compressible material used behind a sealant to reduce its depth and to support the sealant against sag or indentation. **3.** Overflow in a drain or piping system, due to stoppage. **4.** A condition where waste water flows back into another fixture or compartment or water line (but does not flow back into the potable water system).

backup protection   In an electrical system, a type of protection initiated by a sensing device that detects a failure of a protective element (such as a circuit breaker); in that event, the next upstream protective device takes over the protective function.

backup strip, lathing board   A wood strip which is fixed at the corner of a partition or wall to provide a nailing surface for ends of lath.

back veneer   In veneer plywood, the layer of veneer on the side of a plywood sheet which is opposite the **face veneer**—usually of lower quality.

back veneer

back vent   An individual vent for a plumbing fixture located on the downstream (sewer) side of a **trap, 1** to protect the trap against siphonage.

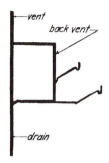

back vent

backwater valve, backflow valve   A type of **check valve** in a drainage pipe; reversal of flow causes the valve to close, thereby cutting off flow.

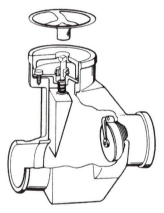

backwater valve

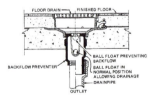

backwater valve: installation

bacterial corrosion   A corrosion which results from substances (e.g., ammonia or sulfuric acid) produced by the activity of certain bacteria.

badger   **1.** A tool used inside a pipe or culvert to remove excess mortar or deposits. **2.** A **badger plane**.

badger plane   A hand plane, the mouth of which is cut obliquely from side to side, so that it can work close up to a corner.

badigeon A filler or patching material used in masonry or wood work.

baffle 1. A plate used to control the flow of a liquid. 2. An opaque or translucent plate used to shield a light source from direct view at certain angles; a **light baffle**. 3. A flat deflector or obstruction designed to reduce sound transmission. 4. A plate that retards and/or changes the direction of the flow of air, air-gas mixtures, or flue gases.

bag, sack A quantity of portland cement: 94 lb in the United States, 87.5 lb in Canada, 112 lb (50.8 kg) in the United Kingdom, and 50 kg in most countries using the metric system.

bagasse A by-product of sugar cane after the juice has been extracted; used as a fuel and also as the principal component in cellulose-cane acoustical tile.

bag molding The application of pressure on a material during molding so that it takes the shape of a curved, rigid die. The material, contained within the die and a flexible cover, is deformed by changes of pressure within the enclosure.

bagnette A **bead molding**.

bagnio 1. A bathing establishment. 2. A brothel. 3. A Turkish prison.

bag plug An inflatable drain stopper; when inflated, it acts to seal a pipe; usually located at the lowest point of the piping system.

bag trap An S-shaped **trap, 1** in which the vertical inlet and outlet pipes are in alignment.

bag trap

bague An annular molding encircling the shaft of a column or pillar, either half-way between the base and capital or at lesser intervals.

baguette A small, convex molding.

bahut 1. In a masonry wall or parapet, the rounded upper course. 2. A low wall surmounting a cornice to carry the roof structure.

baignoire A box in a theatre in the lowest tier.

bail 1. The wall of an outer court of a feudal castle. 2. A hinged loop that is used for lifting.

bailey 1. The open area within a medieval fortification; in complex sites the alley between the several layers of walls is called an "outer bailey"; the central area, the "inner bailey." 2. The outer wall of a feudal castle.

baked finish A paint or varnish finish obtained by baking, usually at temperatures above 150°F (65°C), thereby developing a tough, durable film.

bake house A small subsidiary structure having one or more ovens used exclusively for baking of bread and pastries; once especially found in religious communities and on plantations; usually located away from the principal dwelling to reduce the risk of setting it on fire.

bake oven An oven constructed of bricks, usually having a circular or oval dome; often located within the hearth of the principal fireplace of a colonial home, usually in a corner of the hearth and a few feet above it. Bake ovens were once an integral part of the fireplace construction; some were heated by glowing charcoal or embers that were swept out before the unbaked loaves were inserted and the iron oven door closed. Also called a beehive oven, bread oven, brick oven, or Dutch oven.

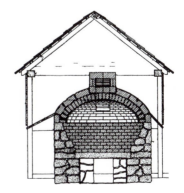

bake oven (longitudinal section)

baking, stoving The use of heat on fresh paint films to speed the evaporation of thinners and to promote the reaction of binder components so as to form a hard polymeric film.

balance arm On a **projected window**, a side supporting arm which is constructed so that the center of gravity of the sash is not changed appreciably when opened.

balance beam, balance bar A long beam, attached to a gate (or drawbridge, etc.) so as to counterbalance the weight of the gate during opening or closing.

balanced circuit A three-wire electric circuit in which the load is the same on each side of the neutral wire.

balanced construction A plywood or sandwich-panel construction which has an odd number of plies laminated together so that the construction is identical on both sides of a plane through the center of the panel.

balanced door A door so arranged that it is held either open or closed by weights.

balanced earthwork **Cut and fill** work in which the amount of fill equals the amount of material excavated.

balanced ladder A ladder held in a vertical position by guides with a weight attached equal to the weight of the ladder.

balanced load **1.** A load connected to an electric circuit (as a three-wire system) so that the currents taken from each side of the system are equal and the power factors are equal. **2.** The load at which there is simultaneous crushing of concrete and yielding of tension steel.

balanced reinforcement An amount and distribution of steel reinforcement in a flexural reinforced concrete member such that the allowable tensile stress in the steel and the allowable compressive stress in the concrete are attained simultaneously.

balanced sash In a double-hung window, a sash which opens by being raised or lowered and whose weight is balanced with counterweights or with pretensioned springs so that little force is required to lift the sash.

balanced step, dancing step, dancing winder One of a series of **winders** arranged so that the width of each winder tread (at the narrow end) is almost equal to the tread width in the straight portion of the adjacent stair flight.

balance pipe A pipe connection used to equalize the pressure at two points in a piping system.

balancing A procedure for adjusting the mass distribution of a rotor so that vibration of the journals, or the forces on the bearings, are reduced or controlled.

balancing plug cock See **balancing valve**.

balancing valve, balancing plug cock A **valve** used in a pipe for controlling fluid flow; not usually used to shut off the flow.

balaneion A Greek term for a bath.

balaustre, canary wood A South American glossy wood; quite hard, heavy; yellowish brown, orange, or purplish brown in color.

BALC On drawings, abbr. for **balcony**.

balconet A pseudo-balcony; a low ornamental railing to a window, projecting but slightly beyond the threshold or sill.

balcony **1.** A projecting platform on a building, sometimes supported from below, sometimes cantilevered; enclosed with a railing or balustrade. **2.** A projecting gallery in an auditorium; a seating area over the main floor. **3.** An elevated platform used in a permanent stage setting in a theatre.

balcony outlet In a vertical rainwater pipe that passes through an exterior balcony, a fitting which provides an inlet for the drainage of rainwater from the balcony.

balcony rail See **rail, 2**.

balcony stage A balcony used as a playing area, as in the Elizabethan theatre.

baldachin, baldacchino, baldachino, baldaquin, ciborium An ornamental canopy over an altar, usually supported on columns, or a similar form over a tomb or throne.

bald roof See **smooth-surfaced roof**.

balection molding See **bolection molding**.

bale house **1.** See **straw bale house**. **2.** An obsolete term for **warehouse**.

bale tack Same as **lead tack**.

balistraria In medieval battlements, a cross-shaped aperture through which crossbowmen shot arrows.

balk, baulk **1.** A squared timber used in building construction. **2.** A low ridge of earth that marks a boundary line.

balk tie A **balk, 1** which joins the wall posts of a timber roof, preventing the walls from spreading.

balistraria

ball and flower   See **ballflower**.

ballast   **1.** Coarse stone, gravel, slag, etc., used as an underlayer for poured concrete. **2.** A device used to provide the required starting voltage and operating current for fluorescent, mercury, or other electric-discharge lamps. **3.** Class P: A ballast for a fluorescent lamp which meets the requirements of the **Underwriters' Laboratories, Inc.**; includes an automatic resetting thermal protector to remove the ballast from the circuit if its temperature exceeds a specified value. **4.** Same as **constant-wattage ballast**.

ballast factor   The ratio of the luminous output of a lamp when operated on a **ballast** to its luminous output when operated under standardized rating conditions.

ballast noise rating   A measure of the noise generated by a fluorescent lamp ballast; designated by letters from A (the quietest) through F (the noisiest).

ball-bearing hinge   A hinge which is equipped with ball bearings between the hinge knuckles in order to reduce friction.

ball breaker   Same as **wrecking ball**.

ball catch   A door fastener having a contained metal ball which is under pressure from a spring; the ball engages a striking plate and keeps the door from opening until force is applied.

ball-check valve   A spring-operated **check valve** in a piping system; when the fluid flows in one direction, pressure against a movable ball allows fluid to pass; when the direction of flow is reversed, the ball is forced against a seat, thereby stopping the flow.

ball cock   A **float valve** with a spherical float.

ball float   A floating device, usually approx. spherical in shape, which is used to operate a **ball valve**.

ballflower   A spherical ornament composed of three conventionalized petals enclosing a ball, usually in a hollow molding, popular in the English Decorated style.

ballflower

balling up   In welding, the formation of globules of molten brazing filler metal or flux as a result of failure to wet adequately the metal being welded.

ballium   The court of open space within a medieval fortification; a **bailey**.

ball joint   A joint in which one part has a ball-shaped end that is held in a spherical shell attached to the other, thereby permitting the axis of one part to be set at any angle with respect to the other.

balloon   A globe or round ball, placed on the top of a pillar, pediment, pier, or the like, which serves as a **crown, 1**.

balloon framing, balloon frame   A system of framing a wooden building; all vertical structural elements of the exterior bearing walls and partitions consist of single studs which extend

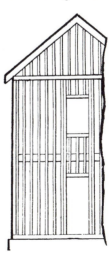

balloon framing

the full height of the frame, from the top of the soleplate to the roof plate; all floor joists are fastened by nails to studs. Compare with **braced framing**.

balloon-payment loan A type of loan agreement, whether or not secured by a mortgage, in which the final payment due at maturity is much larger in amount than each of the periodic payments required during the life of the loan.

ball peen hammer A hammer having a hemispherical **peen**.

ball peen hammer

ball-penetration test An ASTM test method used as a measure of the consistency of concrete; a metal weight having a hemispherically shaped bottom is placed on the smooth level surface of the concrete, and the depth to which it sinks is measured.

ballroom A large social hall expressly designed for dancing, but frequently used for dining or large meetings.

ball test **1.** See **Kelly ball test**. **2.** In a **drain**, a test for freedom from obstruction and for circularity; a ball (less than the diameter of the drain by a specified amount) is rolled through the drain.

ball valve A valve for regulating the flow of fluids by a movable ball which fits in a spherical seat.

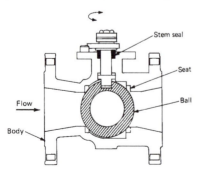

ball valve

balnea, *pl.* of **balneum** Roman baths, usually the great public ones.

balnearium In ancient Rome, a private bathroom.

balsa, corkwood The lightest of all woods, with density of about 7 to 10 lb per cu ft (110 to 160 kg per cu m); used for the core of lightweight sandwich panels, models, etc.

balteus **1.** The band in the middle of the bolster of an Ionic capital. **2.** The band joining the volutes of an Ionic capital. **3.** One of the passages dividing the auditorium of ancient Roman theatres and amphitheatres horizontally into upper and lower zones.

baluster, banister **1.** One of a number of short vertical members, often circular in section, used to support a stair handrail or a coping. **2.** *(pl.)* A **balustrade**. **3.** The roll forming the side of an Ionic capital; a **bolster, pulvinus**.

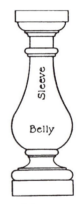

baluster, 1

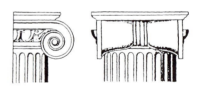

baluster, 3

baluster column **1.** A column shaped somewhat like a baluster, with a short, massive shaft. **2.** A short, thick-set column in a subordinate position, as in the windows of early Italian campanili.

baluster shaft Same as **baluster column**.

baluster side On an Ionic capital, the return face (having the form of a concave roll), reaching from volute to volute.

baluster side

balustrade An entire railing system (as along the edge of a balcony) including a top rail and its balusters, and sometimes a bottom rail.

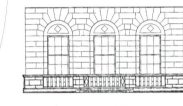

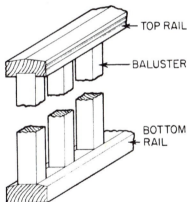

balustrade

balustrum Same as **altar rail**.

bamli In the architecture of India, a court or courtyard.

banana oil See **amyl acetate**.

banco In Spanish architecture and its derivatives, a built-in seat.

band 1. Any horizontal flat member or molding or group of moldings projecting slightly from a wall plane and usually marking a division in the wall. Also called **band molding** or **band course**. 2. A small, flat molding, broad, but of small projection, rectangular or slightly convex in profile, used to decorate a surface either as a continuous strip or formed into various shapes. Also called **fillet**, **list**. 3. A **fascia** on the architrave of an entablature.

bandage A strap, band, ring, or chain placed around a structure to secure and hold its parts together, as around the springing of a dome.

band clamp A two-piece metal clamp, secured by bolts at both ends; used to hold riser pipes.

band course Same as **belt course**.

banded architrave In late neoclassic architecture in England, Italy, and France, an **architrave, 2** interrupted at intervals by smooth projecting blocks, between which are set the molded portions of the architrave.

banded column A column with **drums** that alternate in size, color, or degree of ornamentation.

banded column

banded impost In medieval architecture, an impost with horizontal moldings, the section of the molding of the arch above being similar to that of the shaft below.

banded impost

banded pilaster   A **pilaster** decorated in the manner of a banded column.

banded rustication   Courses of masonry, alternating smooth ashlar with rustication, in Renaissance architecture and derivatives.

banded surround   A **surround** (i.e., a decorative architectural element around a doorway, fireplace, or window) that is banded, usually by adjacent masonry blocks that are of two different sizes; for example, see **Gibbs surround**.

bandelet   **1.** An **annulet**. **2.** A small flat molding.

banderol, banderole, bannerol   A decorative representation of a ribbon or long scroll, often bearing an emblem or inscription.

banding   **1.** Wood edging for veneered doors or panels; normally used at the edge of plywood or coreboard constructions. **2.** One or more decorative wood strips; decorative inlay. **3.** Metal, plastic, or fiber straps to tie bundles together. **4.** The strapping of the top of a timber pile to prevent its splitting while being driven.

banding plane   A carpenter's plane used to cut grooves and to inlay strings and bands in straight and circular work.

band iron   A thin metal strap used as a form tie, a hanger, etc.

bandlet   Same as **bandelet**.

band molding   A **band, 1**.

band saw   A saw consisting of an endless, toothed steel belt which runs between two wheels, one of which is machine-powered.

band shell   A sound-reflective construction, usually in the open air, to direct sound from performers on a stage to an audience.

band window   One of a horizontal series of three windows or more, separated only by **mullions**, that form a horizontal band across the façade of a building; for example, see **frieze-band window**. Most commonly found in buildings erected after 1900. Also called a ribbon window.

banister   **1.** A handrail for a staircase. **2.** A **baluster**.

bank   **1.** A mass of soil rising above a digging level. **2.** An establishment which receives, lends, and exchanges money and carries out other financial transactions.

bank barn   A two-story barn usually built into the slope of a hill and oriented so that the ground floor is protected from the prevailing wind. An inclined driveway leads to a large sliding door on the upper floor, which contains an area set aside for threshing grain, storing grain, and storing animal feed. The level below provides housing for animals and is entered at ground level from an enclosed yard. In the United States, sometimes called a German barn, Pennsylvania barn, or Pennsylvania Dutch barn. Also see **barn, forebay barn, Swiss barn, Yankee barn**.

bank barn

bank cubic yard   (or **meter**) A unit to express the volume of **bank material**.

bank depository   A safe on the exterior of a building which receives deposits after business hours.

banker   The bench or table upon which bricklayers and stonemasons prepare and shape their material.

banker-mark   In medieval construction, a mark cut in a dressed stone to identify the stonecutter.

bank gravel   See **bank-run gravel**.

bank house   See **German Colonial architecture**.

bank material   Soil or rock in place before excavation or blasting.

bank measure   **1.** A measure of the volume of a mass of soil or rock, before excavation, in its natural position. **2.** The measurement of earth material *in situ* (i.e., in its original place in the ground).

bank metres   The number of cubic metres of material in its original place in the ground.

bank-run gravel, bank gravel, run-of-bank gravel   Aggregate taken directly from natural deposits; contains both large and small stones.

bank sand Compared to lake sand, a sand having sharp edges so that when used in plastering it results in a better bond and greater plaster strength.

bank yards The number of cubic yards of material in its original place in the ground.

bannerol See **banderol**.

banner vane A weather vane having the shape of a banner; balanced by a weight on the other side of the banner.

banner vane

banquet hall A room used for dining, social gatherings, or meetings accommodating large numbers of people.

banquette **1.** A long, upholstered seat built in against a wall. **2.** A raised, narrow walk along a roadway. **3.** A term once used in some parts of the American South for a sidewalk.

banquette cottage In New Orleans in the early 19th century, a small town house located flush against a sidewalk.

baptistery A building or part of one wherein the sacrament of baptism is administered.

bar **1.** One of the thin strips of wood or metal forming the several divisions of a sash or a wood panel door, employed to receive the glass. **2.** A solid metal product having a square, rectangular, or other simple symmetrical cross-sectional shape and a length much greater than its width. **3.** A counter over which liquor and other beverages are served; may be equipped with a footrail if stools are not provided. **4.** A steel **reinforcing bar**. **5.** A unit of pressure equal to 10^5 pascals, 10^5 newtons per square meter, or 10^6 dynes per square centimeter. **6.** One of a number of thin strips of wood or metal forming the several divisions of a window sash or a wood-paneled door. **7.** Same as **iron mantel, 3**.

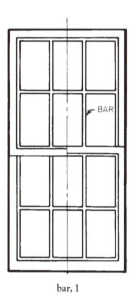

bar, 1

baraban In early Russian architecture, same as **drum, 2**.

barbacan See **barbican**.

barb bolt, rag bolt A bolt having jagged edges to prevent its being withdrawn from the object into which it is driven.

barbed Said of a shank (e.g., that of a nail) which has been provided with repetitive ridges or indentations which may be shallow or deep, oblique or crosswise, diagonal or perpendicular.

barbed wire, barbwire Two or more wires twisted together with sharp hooks or points (or a single wire furnished with barbs); used for fences.

bar bending In reinforced concrete construction, the process of bending **reinforcing bars** to various shapes.

barbican, barbacan The outer defense work of a castle or town, frequently a watchtower at the gate.

barbican

barbwire See **barbed wire**.

bar chair See **bar support**.

bar clamp A clamping device used in carpentry; consists of a long bar with adjustable clamping jaws.

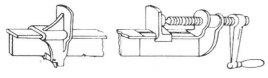

bar clamp

bare Descriptive of a piece of material which is smaller than the specified dimensions; scant.

bare conductor An electrical conductor having no covering or electrical insulation.

barefaced tenon, bareface tenon A **tenon** having a shoulder cut on one side only.

bargain and sale deed A **deed** in which the grantor represents that he has some interest in the property being conveyed, without warranting that he has a clear unencumbered title. Such a deed often includes a warranty that the grantor did not encumber the property or convey away any part of the title during his period of ownership. Also see **quitclaim deed**; **warranty deed**.

bargeboard, gableboard, vergeboard A board which hangs from the projecting end of a roof, covering the gables; often elaborately carved and ornamented in the Middle Ages.

bargeboard

barge couple 1. One of the two rafters that support that part of a gable roof which projects beyond the gable wall. 2. One of the rafters (under the barge course) which serve as grounds for the barge boards and carry the plastering or boarding of the soffits; also called a **barge rafter**.

barge course 1. The coping of a wall, formed by a course of bricks set on edge. 2. In a tiled roof, the part of the tiling which projects beyond the principal rafters (**bargeboards**) where there is a gable.

barge rafter Same as **barge couple, 2**.

barge spike, boat spike A long spike, square in cross section, used in timber construction.

barge stone One of the stones, generally projecting, which form the sloping top of a gable built of masonry.

bar iron A strong, malleable iron, available in the form of bars, which can be beaten into various shapes by blacksmiths to form tools, horseshoes, hardware, and highly decorative ironwork. See **wrought iron**.

barite A mineral used in concrete as an aggregate, esp. for the construction of high-density radiation shielding; also called **barium sulfate**.

barium plaster A special mill-mixed gypsum plaster containing barium salts; used to plaster walls of x-ray rooms.

barium sulfate See **barite**.

bar joist An open-web steel **joist** consisting of a single bar, bent in a zigzag pattern, and welded at its points of contact to upper and lower **chords**.

bark The protective outer layer of a tree, composed of inner, conductive cells and outer corklike tissue.

bark mill A small building that was once used for processing bark used in dyeing and tanning.

bark pocket, inbark, ingrown bark A small quantity of bark, nearly or entirely enclosed in wood.

barley-sugar column (*Brit.*) A **spiral column**.

bar mat A network of steel **reinforcing bars** assembled in two or more layers and welded or tied together.

bar molding A rabbeted molding applied to the edge of a counter or bar to serve as a **nosing**.

bar molding

barn A farm building, most often rectangular (but occasionally circular or polygonal), for housing farm animals, storing farm equipment, threshing grain, and storing grain, hay, and other agricultural produce. Barn construction usually depends on such factors as the local climate and traditions, building materials available, the skills and time required for construction, and the cost. For some examples, see **bank barn, basement barn, circular barn, connected barn, Connecticut barn, crib barn, double barn, Dutch barn, English barn, forebay barn, four-crib barn, German barn, hex barn, New England connected barn, octagon barn, Pennsylvania barn, Pennsylvania Dutch barn, potato barn, raised barn, round barn, side-hill barn, Sweitzer barn, Swiss barn, three-bay barn, tobacco barn, Yankee barn**.

barn-door hanger A hanger for an exterior sliding door; consists of a frame which moves along a horizontal track, supported by rollers.

barn-door stay A small wheel which rolls along a horizontal track and guides the movement of a barn door.

barn raising In the United States before the 20th century, a cooperative effort in which the elements of the framework for a large barn were assembled and lifted into place. The walls were supported by sections of a massive timber framework, called **bent frames**. First, the cellar was dug and the barn floor constructed. Next, the bent frames were assembled on the ground adjacent to the barn by fitting the various components of the frame together and fastening them with wood pegs driven into previously drilled holes. Finally, at the appropriate locations, each bent frame was raised into an upright position by the use of long poles with steel points (*barn pikes*) and then interconnected with other bent frames. See the illustration under **bent frame** showing how the bent frames were raised, an action that required considerable manpower and therefore the assistance of neighbors; this collaborative effort is also known as a *barn raising* or *raising bee*.

barometric damper An automatic adjustable device for regulating the draft through a fuel-burning appliance, thereby making operation of the appliance nearly independent of the chimney draft over its normal range of operation.

barometric draft regulator A **damper** usually installed in the breeching between a boiler and chimney; permits air to enter the breeching automatically as required, to maintain a constant overfire draft in the combustion chamber.

barometric pressure See **atmospheric pressure**.

Baroque A European style of architecture and decoration which developed in the 17th cent. in Italy from late Renaissance and Mannerist forms, and culminated in the churches, monasteries, and palaces of southern Germany and Austria in the early 18th cent. It is characterized by interpenetration of oval spaces, curved surfaces, and conspicuous use of decoration, sculpture, and color. Its late phase is called *Rococo*. The style prevailing in the restrained architectural climate of England and France can be called *Baroque* classicism.

bar post One of the posts driven into the ground to form the sides of a field gate.

barracks Permanent or temporary housing for soldiers or, less often, groups of workmen.

bar-rail molding Same as **bar molding**.

barreaux Wood bars forming a latticework between wall posts in **French Vernacular architecture** of Louisiana and environs; provided a structural support for **infilling** set between structural timbers.

barred-and-braced gate A gate with a diagonal brace to reinforce the horizontal timbers.

barred gate A gate with one or more horizontal timber rails.

barrel 1. A weight measure for portland cement in the U.S.A., corresponding to 376 pounds net; this measure is now obsolete. 2. (*U.S.A.*) A vessel which holds 31½ gal of liquid. 3. That portion of a pipe having a constant bore and wall thickness.

barrel arch An arch formed of a curved solid plate or slab, as contrasted with one formed with individual curved members or ribs.

barrel bolt, tower bolt A door bolt which moves in a cylindrical casing; not driven by a key.

barrel ceiling A ceiling of semicylindrical shape.

barrel drain Any drain which is cylindrical in shape.

barrel fitting A short length of threaded connecting pipe, as a **nipple**.

barreling, tumbling The application of paint to small articles by tumbling them in a barrel containing paint.

barrel nipple A **barrel fitting** threaded at each end.

barrel roof, barrel shell roof 1. A roof of semicylindrical section; capable of spanning long distances parallel to the axis of the cylinder. 2. A **barrel vault**.

barrel vault, barrel roof, cradle vault, tunnel vault, wagonhead vault, wagon vault A masonry vault of plain, semicircular cross section, supported by parallel walls or arcades and adapted to longitudinal areas.

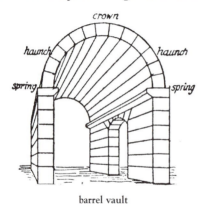

barrel vault

barricade An obstruction to deter the passage of persons or vehicles.

barrow 1. A **wheelbarrow**. 2. An elongated artificial mound protecting a prehistoric chamber tomb or **passage grave**.

barrow run A temporary pathway of wood planks or sheets to provide a smooth access for wheeled materials-handling carriers on a building site.

bar sash lift A type of handle, attached to the bottom rail of a sash, for raising or lowering it.

bar schedule A tabulation of the reinforcement used in reinforced concrete, showing the number, shape, size, and dimensions of each element that is required.

bar screen A coarse screening device used to separate large pieces of stone from smaller pieces, which fall through the spaces between equally spaced **bars, 2**.

bar size section A hot-rolled angle, channel, tee, or zee having its greatest cross-sectional dimension less than 3 in. (7.6 cm).

bar spacing The center-to-center distance (perpendicular to the longitudinal axis) between parallel **reinforcing bars**.

barstone One of two upright stones, placed on each side of a fireplace (before the invention of grates) to receive the ends of a metal bar.

bar strainer A screening device consisting of a bar or a number of parallel bars; used to prevent objects from entering a drain; also see **bar screen**.

bar support, bar chair A device used to support and/or hold steel **reinforcing bars** in proper position before or during the placement of concrete.

bartizan On a fortified wall, a small overhanging structure with lookout holes and loops, often at a corner or near an entrance gateway.

bar tracery A pattern formed by interlocking bars of stone within the arch of a Gothic window.

bar-type grating An open grid assembly of metal bars in which the **bearing bars** (running in one direction) are spaced by rigid attachment to **cross bars**.

barway A gate opened by moving a bar or bars.

barytes Same as **barite**.

basalt A dark, fine-grained, igneous rock used extensively for paving stones, but rarely for building stone.

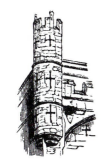

bartizan

bar tracery

bascule   A structure that rotates about an axis, as a seesaw, with a counter balance (for the weight of the structure) at one end.

base   **1.** The lowest (and often widest) visible part of a building, often distinctively treated. A base is distinguished from a foundation or footing in being visible rather than buried. **2.** A low, thickened section of a wall; a **wall base**. Also see **socle**. **3.** Lower part of a column or pier, wider than the shaft, and resting on a plinth, pedestal, podium, or stylobate. Also see **Asiatic base, Attic base**. **4.** A **baseboard**; skirting. **5.** A preparation for a finished surface, as for flooring, stucco, paint, etc.; a surface to which the base coat of plaster is applied. Also see **backing, ground**. **6.** In paint, either the medium or the main chemical ingredient. **7.** In asphaltic or portland cement concrete paving, the prepared bottom course of crushed stone or gravel upon which subsequent courses are laid; serves to distribute localized wheel loads over a larger subbase and hence to improve load-bearing capacity.

base anchor   The metal piece attached to the base of a doorframe for the purpose of securing the frame to the floor; either fixed or adjustable.

basebead   Same as **base screed**.

base bid   The amount of money stated in the bid as the sum for which the bidder offers to perform the **work, 1** not including that work for which **alternate bids** are also submitted.

base bid specifications   The specifications listing or describing only those materials, equipment, and methods of construction upon which the **base bid** must be predicated, exclusive of any **alternate bids**. Also see **specifications** and **closed specifications**.

base block   **1.** A block of any material, generally with little or no ornament, forming the lowest member of a base, or itself fulfilling the functions of a base, as a member applied to the foot of a door or to window trim. **2.** A rectangular block at the base of a casing or column which the baseboard abuts; usually slightly thicker than either the **casing** or **baseboard**. **3.** A **skirting block**.

baseboard, mopboard, scrubboard, skirting board, washboard   A flat projection from an interior wall or partition at the floor, covering the joint between the floor and wall and protecting the wall from kicking, mopping, etc. It may be plain or molded; a **base, 4**.

CORINTHIAN	IONIC
COMPOSITE	ATTIC
TUSCAN	ROMAN DORIC

bases, 3

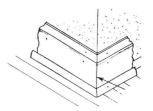

baseboard

baseboard heater   A heating system in which the heating elements are installed in panels along the baseboard of a wall.

baseboard raceway   A channel having a removable cover, sometimes installed along a baseboard in an existing building to house wiring. Removal of the cover provides easy access to the wiring.

baseboard radiator unit   A heating unit which is designed to replace a baseboard along a wall; water or steam flows directly behind the face of the unit (or heat is supplied to the face by electric heating elements directly behind it); heat from the face is transmitted to the room. In the finned-tube type, the fins are heated by water or steam flowing through the tube; this heat is delivered to the room through slots in the face of the unit.

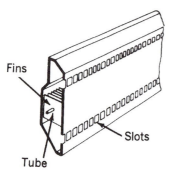

baseboard radiator unit

base cap   See **base molding**.

base clip   Same as **base anchor**.

base coat   **1.** All plaster applied before the finish coat; may be a single coat or a scratch coat and a brown coat. **2.** The first coat applied to a surface, as paint; a prime coat. **3.** An initial coat applied to a wood surface before staining or otherwise finishing it.

base coat floating   The spreading, compacting, and smoothing of the base coat of plaster so that it is finished to a reasonably true plane.

base course   **1.** A foundation or footing course, as the lowest course in a masonry wall. **2.** A layer of selected material of planned thickness, constructed on the subgrade or subbase for the purpose of serving one or more functions such as distributing load, providing drainage, minimizing frost action, etc. **3.** The lowest layer in a pavement construction.

base-court, basse-cour   **1.** A yard or ward behind the outer bailey of a castle. **2.** On a farm, a service yard often reserved for fowl. **3.** A lesser or service courtyard in any building. **4.** (*Brit.*) A lower court of law.

base elbow   A cast-iron pipe elbow having a baseplate or flange cast on it, by which it is supported.

base exchange   Same as **cation-exchange softening** of water.

base flashing   **1.** The **flashing** provided by upturned edges of a watertight membrane on a roof. **2.** Any metal or composition flashing at the joint between a roofing surface and a vertical surface, such as a wall or parapet.

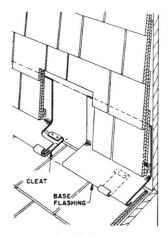

base flashing

base line   A surveyed line which has been established with more than usual care, and to which surveys are referred for coordination and correlation.

base map   In urban planning, a map indicating the significant existing physical features of an area, i.e., streets, rivers, parks, railroads, etc., and serving as a foundation for all subsequent mapping.

basement   **1.** Usually the lowest story of a building, either partly or entirely below grade. Also see **cellar, American basement**. **2.** The lower part of the wall or walls of any building. **3.** The substructure of a column or arch. Frequently, the applicable building code specifies that only one floor level shall be classified as a basement. Also see **American basement, English basement, French basement, raised basement, walk-out basement**.

basement barn A term sometimes used for **bank barn**.

basement house A house whose rooms are mainly located above ground level but whose entrance, from the exterior, is at ground level or one floor above.

basement soil See **subgrade, 1**.

basement stair A stairway connecting the basement or cellar with the level of the living area.

basement wall A foundation wall which encloses a usable area under a building.

basement window A window in the basement of a residence.

base metal The metal to be welded or soldered (as distinguished from **filler metal** which is deposited during the joining process).

base molding Molding used to trim the upper edge of interior baseboard; a **base cap**.

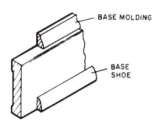

base molding and base shoe

baseplate **1.** A metal plate used to distribute a nonuniform load. **2.** A metal plate on which a column rests. **3.** A metal plate used as a foundation for heavy machinery; a **bed plate**.

base ply In roofing: the layer of felt secured to the deck over which a built-up roof is applied.

base screed A metal screed having expanded or short perforated flanges; acts as a dividing strip between plaster and cement; provides a **ground** (guide) to indicate proper thickness of plaster and cement.

base sheet Saturated and/or coated felt sheeting which is laid as the first ply in a built-up roofing membrane.

base shoe, base shoe molding, floor molding, shoe molding, carpet strip A molding used next to the floor on interior baseboard.

base shoe corner A molding piece or block applied in the corner of a room to eliminate the need for mitering the **base shoe**.

base table A **base molding, 2**.

base tee A **pipe tee** with a connected baseplate for supporting it.

base tile The lowest course of tiles in a tiled wall.

basic creep In concrete construction, **creep** occurring without the migration of moisture to (or from) the concrete.

basic insulation level (BIL) The insulation capability of an item of electrical equipment (e.g., a transformer) to withstand specified voltage surges.

basic services The services performed by an architect during the following five phases of a project: schematic design; design development; construction documents; bidding or negotiation; and contract administration.

basil Same as **bezel**.

basilica **1.** A Roman hall of justice, typically with a high central space lit by a clerestory and lower aisles all around it, and with apses or exedrae for the seats of the judges. **2.** The form of the early Christian church, a central high nave with clerestory, lower aisles along the sides only, with a semicircular apse at the end. Often preceded by a vestibule (narthex) and atrium. In larger basilicas, there are often transepts, and sometimes five aisles.

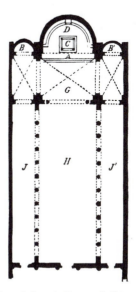

basilica: Typical plan. A, D, apse; B, B´, secondary apse; C, high altar; D, bishop's throne; G, transept; H, nave; J, J´, aisles

basin   **1.** A somewhat shallow vessel for holding water (or the like). **2.** A shallow tank or natural or artificial depression containing water.

basket   See **bell, 1**.

basket capital   A **capital** having a shape similar to an inverted bell that is ornamented with surface work similar to **basket weave**.

basket-handle arch, basket arch   A flattened arch whose ellipse-like shape is determined by three arcs that are interconnected, each arc being drawn from a different center of curvature; also called a semielliptical arch or an elliptical arch.

basket-handle arch

basket newel   A **newel** at one end of a handrail at the bottom of a flight of stairs; has the overall shape of a tall cylindrical basket.

basket weave   A checkerboard pattern of bricks, flat or on edge.

basket weave

basket-weave bond   A brick **bond** arrangement having a checkerboard pattern.

bas-relief, basso-relievo, basso-rilievo   A carving, embossing, or casting moderately protruded from the background plane; low relief.

basse-cour   See **base-court**.

basso-rilievo, basso-relievo   See **bas-relief**.

basswood, American linden   A cream-colored, fine-textured, moderately low-density wood of North America; used extensively for plywood, lumber core, and trim.

bas-taille   Same as **bas-relief**.

bastard   A nonstandard item; one of irregular or abnormal size or shape or of inferior quality.

bastard ashlar, bastard masonry   **1.** Stone, in thin blocks, used to face a brick or rubble wall; square-hewn and laid to resemble **ashlar**. **2.** Ashlar stones which are only roughly dressed at the quarry.

bastard bond   Same as **header bond**.

bastard file   One of four principal classifications of files which are graded according to coarseness (coarse, bastard, second, smooth).

bastard granite   A quarry term for gneissic granites; not considered a true granite; used in wall construction.

bastard joint   Same as **blind joint**.

bastard masonry   See **bastard ashlar**.

bastard pointing   See **bastard tuck pointing**.

bastard-sawn   See **plain-sawn**.

bastard spruce   Same as **Douglas fir**.

bastard stucco   Plaster applied in three coats: a scratch, a brown, and a finish coat.

bastard tuck pointing, bastard pointing   An imitation **tuck pointing** in which the external face is parallel to the wall, but projects slightly and casts a shadow.

bastel house, bastille house, bastle house   A partly fortified house whose lowest story usually is vaulted.

bastide   **1.** A medieval settlement built for defense purposes and generally laid out with a geometric plan, esp. in France. **2.** A small rural dwelling in southern France.

bastide, 1

bastille, bastile   **1.** A fortification or castle, frequently used as a prison. **2.** A tower or bulwark in the fortifications of a town.

bastille house   A **bastel house**.

bastion   A defense work, round, rectangular, or polygonal in plan, projecting from the outer wall of a fortification, principally to defend the adjacent perimeter.

bastle house See **bastel house**.

baston, baton, batoon **1.** A **torus**. **2.** See **batten**.

bat **1.** A piece of brick with one undamaged end; also called a "brickbat." **2.** A unit of **batt insulation**. **3.** A piece of wood used as a brace. **4.** A **batten**.

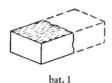

bat, 1

Bataan mahogany Same as **tanguile**.

bat bolt A bolt barbed or jagged at the butt, or tang, to give it a firmer hold.

batch **1.** A quantity of concrete or mortar mixed at one time. **2.** A quantity of adhesive mixed at one time.

batch box A container of known volume used to measure and mix the constituents of a batch of concrete, plaster, or mortar, to ensure proper proportions.

batched water The mixing water added to a concrete or mortar mixture before or during the initial stages of mixing.

batcher A device for measuring ingredients for a batch of concrete.

batching Weighing or measuring the volume of the ingredients of a batch of concrete or mortar, and then introducing these ingredients into a mixer.

batch mixer A machine that mixes grout, mortar, or concrete in batches in contrast to one that mixes continuously.

batch plant An operating installation of equipment including **batchers** and **mixers** as required for batching or for batching and mixing concrete materials; also called a **mixing plant** when mixing equipment is included.

batement light A window with its lower edge cut diagonally rather than horizontally so as to fit an arch or rake below; esp. used in **perpendicular tracery**.

bath **1.** An open tub used as a fixture for bathing. **2.** The room containing the bathtub. **3.** *(pl.)* The Roman public bathing establishments, consisting of hot, warm, and cool plunges, sweat rooms, athletic and other facilities; **balnea, thermae**.

bathhouse **1.** A building equipped with bathing facilities. **2.** A small structure containing dressing rooms or lockers for bathers, as at the seaside.

bathroom A room containing a water closet, a lavatory, and a bathtub and/or shower.

bathroom cabinet Same as **medicine cabinet**.

bathtub A tub for bathing, usually a fixed plumbing installation designed for one person.

bat insulation Same as **batt insulation**.

baton A **batten**.

bâtons rompus Short, straight pieces of convex molding, as those forming Norman or Romanesque chevrons and zigzags.

batoon A **batten**.

batt A unit of **batt insulation**.

batted work, broad tooled A hand-dressed stone surface scored from top to bottom in narrow parallel strokes, (usually 8 to 10 per inch) (20 to 25 per centimeter), by use of a batting tool. The strokes may be vertical or oblique.

batten **1.** A narrow strip of wood applied to cover a joint along the edges of two parallel boards in the same plane. **2.** A strip of wood fastened across two or more parallel boards to hold them together; also called a **cross batten**. **3.** A flat strip of wood attached to a wall as a base for lathing, plastering, etc.; also called a **furring strip**. **4.** In roofing, a wood strip applied over boards or roof structural members; used as a base for the attachment of slate, wood, or clay-tile shingles. **5.** See **board and batten**. **6.** A board usually 2 in. (5 cm) to 4 in. (10 cm) thick and usually used as a lathing support or in flooring. **7.** A steel strip used to secure metal flooring on a fire escape. **8.** On a theatre stage, a strip of wood to frame, stiffen, or reinforce a flat, or to fasten several flats together. **9.** On a theatre stage, length of hollow metal of round, square, or rectangular cross section used in connection with stage rigging to hang scenery or lighting equipment, such as a **pipe batten** or **lighting batten**.

battenboard See **coreboard**.

battened column A column consisting of two longitudinal shafts, rigidly connected to each other by batten plates.

battened door A wood door without **stiles** which is constructed of vertical boards held together by horizontal **battens, 2**, on the back side. Also called a **batten door, ledged door**, and **unframed door**.

battened door

battened shutters Solid, unframed, window shutters held together by horizontal **battens, 2**; similar in construction to small **battened doors.**

battened wall, strapped wall A wall to which battens have been affixed.

battening Narrow battens or wood strips attached to a wall for the purpose of receiving lath and plaster.

batten plate, stay plate A steel plate used to join two parallel components (such as flanges or angles) of a built-up structural column, girder, or strut; designed to transmit shear between the two components.

batten roll, conical roll In metal roofing, a roll joint formed over a triangular-shaped wood piece.

batten seam A seam in metal roofing which is formed around a wood strip.

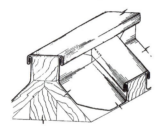

batten seam

batter To incline from the vertical. A wall is said to batter when it recedes as it rises.

batter board **1.** One of a pair of horizontal boards which are nailed (at right angles to each other) to three posts set beyond the corners of a building excavation; used to indicate a desired location; strings, fastened to these boards, are used to indicate the exact corner of a building. **2.** One of the boards set across a pipe trench to carry a cord or wire **grade line**.

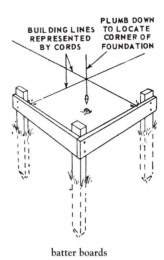

batter boards

batter brace, batter post A diagonal brace which reinforces one end of a truss.

battered A term descriptive of a surface that is inclined or tilted with respect to the vertical; for example, a **battered wall**.

battered wall A wall having a **batter**.

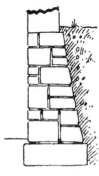

battered wall

batter level A device for measuring the inclination of a slope.

batter pile, brace pile, spur pile A pile driven at an inclination to the vertical to provide resistance to horizontal forces.

batter post **1.** See **batter brace**. **2.** A post at one side of a gateway or at a corner of a building for protection against vehicles.

batter rule In constructing a battered wall, a device for regulating the inclination.

batter stick A tapered board which is hung vertically; used to test the batter of a wall surface.

battery **1.** A combination of two or more electric cells capable of storing and supplying direct current by electrochemical means. **2.** Any group of two or more similar adjacent plumbing fixtures which discharge into a common horizontal waste or soil branch.

batting tool A mason's chisel usually 3 to 4½ in. (7.6 to 11.4 cm) wide, used to dress stone to a striated surface. See **batted work**.

batt insulation A flexible blanket-type thermal insulation, commonly used as insulation between studs or joists in frame construction; also used as an acoustical material or a component in sound-insulating construction. Usually made from rock, slag, or glass fibers. Sometimes has a vapor barrier on one side or is entirely enclosed in paper with a vapor barrier on one side. Nominally 16 (40.6 cm) or 24 in. (61 cm) wide, and approx. 1 to 6 in. (2.5 to 15 cm) thick.

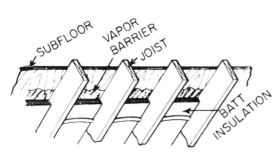

batt insulation installed on underside of subfloor

battlement, embattlement **1.** A fortified parapet with alternate solid parts and openings, termed respectively "merlons" and "embrasures" or "crenels" (hence crenelation). Generally for defense, but employed also as a decorative motif. **2.** A roof or platform serving as battle post. **3.** A decorative motif having the general shape of a battlement.

battlement

Bauhaus A school of design established in Weimar, Germany, by Walter Gropius in 1919. The term became virtually synonymous with modern teaching methods in architecture and the applied arts, and with a functional aesthetic for the industrial age; often characterized by emphasis on functional design, the use of a repetitive interval between members of the framework of a building, and the maintenance of purely geometric forms. Often, major building components such as bays, doors, and windows are placed to coincide with this repetitive interval, although the building itself may be asymmetrical.

baulk Same as **balk**.

baulk-tie See **balk-tie**.

bawn **1.** A fortified enclosure, often of mud or stone, surrounding a farmyard or castle; esp. in Ireland. **2.** A fortified house (especially during the 17th century) with massive walls, designed to serve as a haven of refuge in the event of an enemy attack; also see **garrison house**.

bay **1.** Within a structure, a regularly repeated spatial element defined by beams or ribs and their supports. **2.** A protruded structure with a bay window. **3.** The free or light space between sash bars. **4.** In landscape architecture, a recess or alcove formed by plants in a design. **5.** In plastering, the distance between **screeds** employed for working the floating of plaster.

bayle The open space contained between the first and second walls of a fortified castle; a **bailey, 1**.

bay leaf A stylized laurel leaf used in the form of a garland to decorate torus moldings.

bayonet holder, bayonet socket A type of lamp holder which provides mechanical support and electric connections for an electric light bulb; esp. used in Great Britain.

bayonet saw Same as **saber saw**.

bay stall (*Brit.*)   A built-in window seat.

bayt   **1.** A Muslim dwelling, generally for one family, e.g., a tent or house. **2.** In the early Muslim palace complex, a separate dwelling unit.

bay window   A window that protrudes from a wall, usually bowed, canted, polygonal, segmental, semicircular, or square-sided in plan; typically one story in height, although sometimes higher; occasionally corbeled out from the face of the wall, as an oriel; also see **angled bay window, bow window, cant window.**

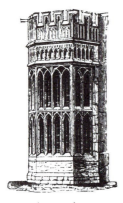

bay window

bazaar   A marketplace where goods are exposed for sale; esp. in the East, consisting either of small shops or stalls in a narrow street or series of streets, or of a certain section of town under one roof and divided into narrow passageways.

b/b₀   Symbol for **course-aggregate factor**.

bbl   Abbr. for "barrel."

BC   Abbr. for "building code."

BCM   Abbr. for "broken cubic meter."

BCY   Abbr. for "broken cubic yard."

bd.   In the lumber industry, abbr. for "board."

bd. ft.   In the lumber industry, abbr. for "board foot."

bdl   In the lumber industry, abbr. for "bundle."

beacon house   Same as **lighthouse**.

bead   **1.** A **bead molding**. **2.** A narrow wood strip, molded on one edge, against which a door or window sash closes; a **stop bead**. **3.** A strip of metal or wood used around the periphery of a pane of glass to secure it in a frame, ventilator, or sash; a **stop**. **4.** A pearl-shaped carved decoration on moldings or other ornaments, usually in

series, or in conjunction with other shapes; a **beading**. Also see **bead and reel molding**. **5.** A molding decorated with **beading**; an **astragal, 1** or **chaplet**. **6.** Used in combination with other terms to describe the function or position of a beaded molding, such as **quirk bead, angle bead, corner bead**, etc. **7.** The act of carving or running a bead; **beading**. **8.** In metal roofing or flashing, the shape formed by folding a narrow strip of the edge flat or rolling it into a tube in order to stiffen or fasten the metal. **9.** A factory-formed light-gauge metal strip having one or two expanded or short perforated flanges and variously shaped noses; used at the perimeter of plastered surface as a casing bead or plaster stop, and at corners to reinforce the edge. **10.** A hardened drop of excess paint or varnish. **11.** A narrow, convex strip of sealant, such as caulking or glazing compound. **12.** A **weld bead**.

bead, butt and square   Similar to **bead and butt** but having the panels flush on the beaded face only, and showing square reveals on the other.

bead and butt, bead butt, bead butt work   Framed work in which the panel is flush with the framing and has a bead run on two edges in the direction of the grain; the ends are left plain.

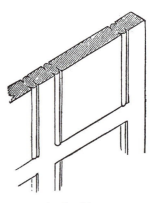

bead and butt

bead and flush panel   See **beadflush panel**.

bead and quirk   See **quirk bead**.

bead and reel, reel and bead   A semiround convex molding decorated with a pattern of disks alternating with round or elongated beads.

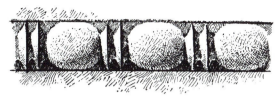

bead and reel

bead butt, bead butt work See **bead and butt**.

beaded clapboard See **clapboard**.

beadflush panel, bead-and-flush panel A panel which is flush with the surrounding framing and finished with a flush bead on all edges of the panel.

bead house A dwelling for poor religious people, located near the church in which the founder was interred, and for whose soul the beadsmen or beadswomen were required to pray.

beading Collectively the bead moldings used in ornamenting a given surface; also see **bead**.

beading plane, bead plane A plane having a curved cutting edge for shaping beads in wood.

bead-jointed Said of a carpentry joint having a bead along the edge of one piece to make the joint less conspicuous.

bead molding 1. A small, convex molding of semicircular or greater profile; also called a **half round**; a **roundel**; a **baguette**. 2. Same as **paternoster**.

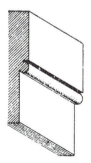

bead molding

bead plane See **beading plane**.

bead weld Same as **surfacing weld**.

beadwork Same as **beading**.

beakhead An ornament; any of several fantastic, animal-like heads with tapered, down-pointed beaks; frequently used in richly decorated Norman doorways. Also see **catshead**.

beakhead molding, bird's-beak molding Same as **beak molding, 2**.

beaking joint A joint formed by several **heading joints** occurring in one continuous line; esp. used in connection with the laying of floor planks.

beak molding 1. A pendant fillet with a channel behind it on the edge of a corona, larmier, or stringcourse, etc., so called because in profile it resembles a bird's beak. 2. A molding enriched with carved birds' heads or beaks.

beak molding

beam 1. A structural member whose prime function is to carry transverse loads, as a joist, girder, rafter, or purlin. The term *beam* may be modified by an adjective indicating its location; as, for example, an *end beam* or *side beam*. See **anchor beam, binding beam, breastsummer beam, camber beam, ceiling beam, collar beam, cross beam, dragon beam, floor beam, ground beam, hammer beam, I-beam, laced beam, perimeter beam, summerbeam, tie beam, top beam, wind beam**. 2. A group of nearly parallel rays of light.

beam anchor, joist anchor, wall anchor A metal **tie** used to anchor a beam or joist to a wall, or to tie a floor securely to a wall.

beam-and-column construction Same as **post-and-lintel construction**.

beam-and-girder construction A system of floor construction in which the load is distributed by slabs to spaced beams and girders.

beam-and-slab floor A floor system in which a concrete floor slab is supported by **reinforced concrete** beams.

beam bearing plate   A foundation plate (usually of metal) placed beneath the end of a beam, at its point of support, to distribute the end load at the point.

beam blocking   **1.** Boxing-in or covering a joist, beam, or girder to give the appearance of a larger beam. **2.** Strips of wood used to create a false beam.

beam bolster   A rod which provides support for steel reinforcement in formwork for a reinforced concrete beam.

beam bottom   The **soffit** of a beam.

beam box   Same as **wall box**.

beam brick   A face brick which is used to bond to a poured-in-place concrete lintel.

beam ceiling   **1.** A ceiling, usually of wood, made in imitation of exposed floor beams with the flooring showing between. **2.** The underside of a floor, showing the actual beams, and finished to form a ceiling.

beam-column   A beam which transmits an axial load as well as a transverse load.

beam compass   An instrument used to draw large circles or arcs of circles for full-sized working drawings; has a long horizontal bar on which two movable heads slide to and fro, one of which carries a pencil, and the other a sharp-pointed pin or tracer, the distance between them determining the radius of the circle.

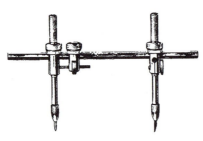

beam compass

beam divergence (*Brit.*)   Same as **beam spread**.

beam fill, beam filling   Masonry, brickwork, or cement fill, usually between joists or horizontal beams at their supports; provides increased fire resistance.

beam form   A **form** which gives the necessary shape, support, and finish to a concrete beam.

beam hanger   **1.** A strap, wire, or other hardware device which supports framework from structural members. **2.** A **stirrup, 4**.

beam infilling   See **infilling**.

beam iron   Same as **beam anchor**.

beam pocket   **1.** In a vertical structural member, an opening to receive a beam. **2.** An opening in the form for a column or girder where the form for an intersecting beam is framed.

beam saddle   Same as **beam hanger**.

beam side   In a concrete form for a beam, the side panels of the form.

beam spread   The angle between two directions (on opposite sides of the axis of a light beam, and in the same plane as the beam axis) in which the light intensity equals a stated percent of a maximum reference intensity.

beam test   A test of the flexural strength (modulus of rupture) of concrete from measurements on a standard unreinforced concrete beam.

bearer   **1.** Any horizontal beam, joist, or member which supports a load. **2.** A support for a landing or winder in a stair. **3.** The ribbon board in balloon framing, which supports second-floor joists. **4.** A horizontal member of a scaffold upon which the platform rests and which may be supported by ledgers.

bearer bracket   Same as **roofing bracket**.

bearing   **1.** A **bearer**. **2.** That portion of a beam, truss, or other structural member which rests on the supports. **3.** The support for a shaft, axle, or trunnion. **4.** In surveying, the horizontal angle between a line and a reference meridian adjacent to the quadrant in which the line lies.

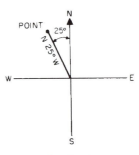

bearing, 4

bearing bar   **1.** A wrought-iron bar placed on masonry to provide a level support for floor joists. **2.** A load-carrying bar which supports a grating and which extends in the direction of the grating span.

bearing bar centers The distance between centers of bearing bars in a metal grating.

bearing block A block which distributes a load on the surface beneath the block.

bearing capacity **1.** The load per unit area that can be supported safely by the ground. **2.** See **pile bearing capacity**. **3.** The pressure that can be exerted on soil or soil rock without excessive yield. **4.** Of a pile, the load required to produce a condition of failure.

bearing distance, span The length of a beam between its bearing supports.

bearing partition See **load-bearing partition**.

bearing pile A **pile** which carries a vertical load.

bearing plate A steel slab which is placed under a beam, column, girder, or truss to distribute the end reaction from the beam to its support.

bearing pressure The pressure on a **bearing, 2**; the load on a bearing surface divided by its area.

bearing stratum The rock or soil stratum (a) which carries the load transferred to it by a caisson, pile, or the like or (b) on which a concrete footing or mat bears.

bearing strength **1.** The maximum load that a column, footing, joint, or wall can sustain at failure, divided by the effective bearing area. **2.** The non-destructive limit of a pipe load; used to determine its supporting strength in the field.

bearing stress See **bearing pressure**.

bearing test A field or laboratory test to determine the bearing capacity of a soil sample, individual pile, pile foundation, or the like.

bearing wall A wall capable of supporting an imposed load. Also called a structural wall or loadbearing wall.

beaumontage A resin, beeswax, and shellac mixture used for filling small holes or cracks in wood or metal.

Beaux-Arts style A grandiose architectural style as taught at the Ecole des Beaux Arts in Paris primarily in the 19th century, widely applied until 1930 to large public buildings such as courthouses, libraries, museums, railroads, and to some pretentious residences. Characteristics often include formalism in design, symmetrical plans, heavily rusticated arched masonry, ashlar stone bases with rusticated stonework, especially on the ground floor and raised basement levels; sculptured figures; a massive and symmetric façade, often with a projecting central pavilion; a monumental attic story; commonly decorated with dentils; enriched entablatures; monumental flights of stairs; classical columns often set in close pairs; banded columns, engaged columns, coupled pilasters; highly decorated pilastered parapets; balconies; sculptured spandrels; decorative brackets; sculptured figures; ornamental details such as cartouches, floral patterns, Greek key designs, ornamental keystones, medallions; elaborately decorated panels, and the like; the roof, commonly a flat or low-pitched, hipped, or a mansard roof; often, domes and rotundas; rectangular windows symmetrically placed, with lintels overhead; arched dormers, balustraded windows, pedimented windows, or windows with balconets; doors, commonly paneled with a glass-paneled canopy over the primary entryway, flanked by columns or pilasters; a wrought-iron grille on the exterior side of the entry door. Also called Beaux-Arts Classicism.

beaver board Same as **composition board**.

bed **1.** In masonry and bricklaying, the side of a masonry unit on which it lies in the course of the wall—the underside when placed horizontally. **2.** The layer of mortar on which a masonry unit is set. **3.** The lower surface or side of a slate. **4.** To set a glass pane in place with putty. **5.** In layered stone used for building, a surface parallel to the stratification. **6.** A layer (stratum) of rock between two bedding planes.

bed chamber An apartment or chamber intended for a bed, or for sleeping and resting.

bedding **1.** Mortar, putty, or other substance used to secure a firm and even bearing, as putty laid in the rabbet of a window frame, or mortar used to lay bricks. **2.** A base which is prepared in soil or concrete for laying masonry or concrete.

bedding coat The plaster coat which receives aggregate or other decorative material, impinged or embedded in its surface before it sets.

bedding course **1.** The first layer of mortar at the bottom of masonry. **2.** A **cushion course**.

bedding dot   A small spot of plaster built out to the face of a finished wall or ceiling; serves as a screed for leveling and plumbing in the application of plaster.

bedding plane   The surface at which two beds, layers, or strata join in stratified rocks.

bedding plants   Annual and subtropical plants used for seasonal effects in landscaping.

bedding stone   A flat marble slab used by masons to check the flatness of rubbed bricks.

bed glazing   See **back putty**.

bed joint   **1.** A horizontal layer of mortar on which masonry units are laid. **2.** One of the radial joints in an arch. **3.** A horizontal crack in a massive rock.

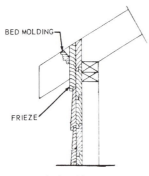

bed joint, 1

bed molding   **1.** A molding of the cornice of an entablature situated beneath the corona and immediately above the frieze. **2.** The lowest member of a band of moldings. **3.** Any molding under a projection, as between eaves and sidewalls.

bed molding, 3

bed place   An alcove into which a bed is located; found, for example, in many houses in Europe and their derivatives.

bedplate   A plate, frame, or platform which supports a heavy object such as a machine or furnace; a **baseplate**.

bed putty   Same as **back putty**.

bedrock   The hard, solid rock at the earth's surface or underlying surface soil; can be utilized as a firm foundation for a building.

bedroom   A room suitably furnished for sleeping.

bed sill   A horizontal timber at the base of a building of timber-framed construction; the timber rests on, or is set into, the ground; same as **groundsill, 2**.

bed surface   Of a brick, the *in situ* non-vertical surface intended to be joined by mortar.

bed-type filter   In a water supply line, a filter containing a porous medium through which the water is forced as a result of the water pressure; used for the removal or reduction of suspended solid contaminants.

beech, beechwood   A moderately high-density, fine-grained, durable, strong hardwood of North America and Europe. Whitish to light red-brown in color; used for small wood-turned parts and flooring.

beehive oven   Same as **bake oven**.

beehive tomb, tholos tomb   A monumental underground tomb in the form of a beehive, used in the Mycenaean period.

beetle   A heavy mallet or rammer; used for driving stones into pavement, for driving wedges, etc.; a **maul**.

beggin, begging   **1.** A dwelling of larger size than a cottage. **2.** In the north of England and in Scotland, a house. **3.** A term especially applied to a hut covered with mud or turf.

beit hilani   **1.** In northern Syria, a type of palace in the first millenium B.C. having a forward section with two large transverse rooms, a portico with one to three columns, and a throne room. **2.** In ancient Assyrian architecture, the pillared portico of a **beit hilani, 1**.

bel   A unit of level which denotes the ratio between two quantities proportional to power; the number of bels equals the logarithm of this ratio, to the base 10; 1 bel = 10 decibels.

belection   See **bolection molding**.

Belfast roof   A **bowstring roof**.

Belfast truss   A **bowstring truss**, for large spans, which is constructed entirely of timber components; the upper member is bent, and the lower member is horizontal.

belfry **1.** A **bell tower**, either attached to a church or standing alone. **2.** A timber framework in a steeple that supports a bell.

Belgian block A type of paving stone generally cut in a truncated, pyramidal shape; laid with the base of the pyramid down.

Belgian truss See **Fink truss**.

belite A constituent of portland cement clinker; when pure, known as dicalcium silicate.

bell **1.** The body of a Corinthian capital or a Composite capital, with the foliage removed; also called a **vase** or **basket**. **2.** The portion of a pipe which is enlarged to receive the end of another pipe of the same diameter for the purpose of making a joint; also called a **hub**.

bell, 1

bell, 1

bell-and-spigot joint, bell-and-socket joint, spigot-and-socket joint A connection between two sections of pipe, the straight spigot end of one section is inserted in the flared-out end of the adjoining section; the joint is sealed by a caulking compound or with a compressible ring.

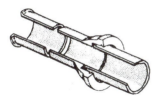

bell-and-spigot joint

bell arch A round arch supported on large **corbels**, giving rise to a bell-shaped appearance.

bell arch

bell cage The timber framework which supports the bells in a belfry or steeple.

bell canopy A gable roof to shelter a bell.

bell capital **1.** A bell-shaped **capital**. **2.** The bell-shaped core of a Corinthian capital to which the leaves and volutes appear to be attached.

bellcast eaves Same as **flared eaves**.

bellcast roof Same as a **bell roof**.

bell cote A small belfry astride the ridge of a church roof, often crowned with a small spire.

bell deck The belfry floor above the lower rooms in a tower.

belled caisson A **caisson** having an enlarged base.

belled excavation A part of a shaft or footing excavation, usually near the bottom and bell-shaped.

belled pier A **pier** having an enlarged end at the bottom of its shaft, often in the shape of a bell-like truncated cone.

bellexion molding See **bolection molding**.

bellflower A bell-shaped floral ornament; commonly, one of a string of such decorative elements.

bell gable A **wall gable** having one or more openings for bells.

bell house A tower-like building for housing bells, esp. in Ireland.

bellied Having a convex or bulging form.

belling In pier, caisson, or pile construction enlarging the base of a foundation element to increase its bearing area at the bearing stratum.

bell joint See **bell-and-spigot joint.**

bellows expansion joint In a run of piping, a joint formed with flexible metal bellows which compress or stretch to compensate for linear expansion or contraction of the run of piping.

bell pull A device once used to summon servants in an elegant home; in each room, the bell pull consisted of a small handle connected to a wire that was mechanically connected to a bell in the servants' quarters. Thus, a pull on the handle rang a bell in the servants' quarters; each bell pull produced a sound of different pitch, identifying the room calling for service.

bell roof A roof having a cross section similar to that of a bell, flaring out at its lower edge.

bell roof

bell tower A tall structure supporting one or more bells; may be part of a building or an independent structure; also see **belfry.**

bell transformer A small transformer which supplies power, at low voltage, for operating a doorbell or the like.

bell trap A type of bell-shaped trap used in floor drains; its use is prohibited by the National Plumbing Code.

bell turret A small tower, usually topped with a spire or pinnacle, and containing one or more bells.

bell wire Small-diameter wire of low current-carrying capacity; covered with insulating material rated at 30 volts or less.

belowstairs In the basement.

belt conveyor A power-driven endless belt that runs on idler wheels; used to carry building materials, etc.

belt course 1. A horizontal band of masonry extending horizontally across the façade of a

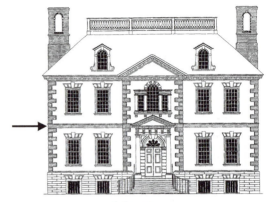
belt course

building and occasionally encircling the entire perimeter; usually projects beyond the face of the building and may be molded or richly carved. Also called a stringcourse or band course; called a **sill course** if set at windowsill level. 2. A horizontal board across front face or around a building, often having a molding.

belt-driven machine Any machine powered by an external source connected to the machine by one or more belts.

belt loader A machine used in excavation; a layer of earth is removed with a cutting edge or rotating auger; then the excavated material is elevated by means of a conveyor belt so that it can be loaded into a hauling unit; a separate prime mover usually is required to move the machine forward.

belt sander A portable tool having a power-driven abrasive-coated continuous belt; used to smooth surfaces.

belvedere 1. A rooftop pavilion from which a vista can be enjoyed. 2. A **gazebo.** 3. A **mirador.**

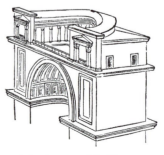
belvedere, 1 of the Vatican

bema **1.** A transverse space in a church a few steps above the floor of the nave and aisles, and separating them from the apse. **2.** In a synagogue, a raised pulpit from which the Torah (Holy Bible) is read.

bematis Same as **diaconicon, 1.**

bench **1.** A long seat, usually of wood, with or without a back, usually for several persons. **2.** A **berm, 6. 3.** Same as **pretensioning bed.**

bench brake A bench-mounted machine used for bending sheet metal.

benched foundation Same as **stepped foundation.**

bench end A terminal wood facing on a church pew, often decorative.

bench hook, side hook Any device used on a carpenter's bench to keep work from moving toward the rear of the bench.

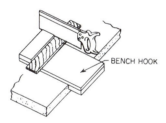

bench hook

benching **1.** Concrete laid on the side slopes of drainage channels where the slopes are interrupted by manholes, etc. **2.** Concrete laid on sloping sites as a safeguard against sliding. **3.** Concrete laid along the sides of a pipeline to provide additional support.

bench mark In surveying, a marked reference point on a permanent, fixed object, such as a metal disk set in concrete, whose elevation (above or below an adopted datum) is known and from which the elevation of other points or objects may be determined.

bench plane A **plane, 1** used primarily in benchwork on flat surfaces, as a block plane or jack plane.

bench sander A stationary power tool (usually mounted on a table or stand) which is equipped with a rotating abrasive disk or belt; used to smooth surfaces of material held against it.

bench stake Same as **stake, 1.**

bench stop A bench hook which is used to fasten work in place, often by means of a screw.

bench table A projecting course of masonry at the foot of an interior wall, or around a column; generally wide enough to form a seat.

bench table

bench terrace A level step cut into a hillside grade.

bench trimmer, trimming machine, guillotine A machine for cutting the ends of two pieces of wood to any desired angle.

bench vise An ordinary **vise, 1** fixed to a bench, which is used to hold a material or component while it is being worked on.

benchwork Any work performed at a bench rather than on machines or in the field.

bend See **pipe bend.**

bender For pipes, see **hickey, 2.**

bending beam See **tie beam.**

bending iron A tool used to straighten or to expand flexible pipe, esp. lead pipe.

bending moment The **moment** which produces bending at a section of a beam or other structural member; equal to the sum of moments taken about the center of gravity of that section.

bending pin One of a number of pins in a curved line which are used in bending lead pipe.

bending schedule A chart showing the shapes and dimensions of every reinforcing bar and the number of bars required on a particular job; prepared by the designer or detailer of the reinforced concrete structure.

bending strength The ability of a structural member to resist breakage when subject to one or more external forces that cause it to bend.

bend radius   The smallest radius of curvature into which a material can be bent without damage.

beneficial occupancy   The use of a project or portion thereof for the purpose intended.

beneficiation   The improvement in the physical or chemical properties of a material by the removal or modification of undesirable components or impurities which it contains.

benefits (mandatory and customary)   The personnel benefits required by law (such as social security, workmen's compensation, and disability insurance), and by custom (such as sick leave, holidays, and vacation), and those which are optional with the individual firm (such as life insurance, hospitalization programs, pension plans, and similar benefits).

benitier   A basin for holy water, usually set at the entrance to a church.

bent   1. Same as **bent frame**. 2. A rhizomatous grass, used where a resilient velvety texture is required.

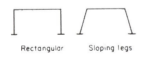

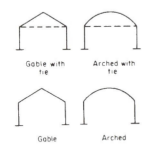

bents, 1

bent approach   An arrangement of two gateways not in line, so that it is necessary to make a sharp turn to pass through the second; for privacy in houses or temples, for security in fortifications.

bent bar   A longitudinal **reinforcing bar** which is bent to pass from one face of a structural member to the other face.

bent chisel   Same as **corner chisel**.

bent ferrule   A **ferrule** having a 90° bend.

bent frame   One of a number of sections in a timber framework that is transverse to the length of a large barn or house of timber-frame construction; each section, usually designed to carry both lateral and vertical loads, was commonly constructed on the ground and then raised to its upright position with the assistance of neighbors, as described under **barn raising**.

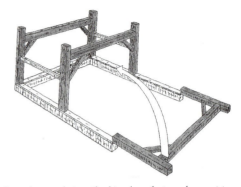

bent frame   being tilted in place during a barn raising

bent grass   See **bent, 2**.

bentonite   A clay, formed from decomposed volcanic ash, with a high content of the mineral montmorillonite; has the capability of absorbing a considerable amount of water, and swells accordingly.

bent shoe   A **base shoe** molding which is bent on a radius.

bentwood   Wood formed to shape by bending, rather than by carving or machining.

Berlin blue   See **Prussian blue, 2**.

berliner, palladiana   A type of terrazzo topping using small and large pieces of marble paving, usually with a standard terrazzo matrix between pieces.

berm   1. A continuous bank of earth alongside a road; a shoulder. 2. A continuous bank of earth piled against a masonry wall. 3. A strip of ground, formed into a ledge to support beams or pipes. 4. The horizontal surface between a moat and the exterior slope of a fortified rampart. 5.

In earth excavation work, that portion of the excavation, usually sloped, left at the perimeter and removed as the sheeting and bracing are installed. **6.** A narrow terrace or shelf built into an embankment, or the like, which breaks the continuity of an otherwise long slope.

besant See **bezant**.

bestiary In a medieval church, a group of carved or painted creatures, often highly imaginative and symbolic.

BET. On drawings, abbr. for "between."

bethel A place of worship.

Bethell process A process for preserving wood by impregnating the cells with creosote under pressure.

béton A kind of concrete; a mixture of lime, sand, and gravel.

béton armé Same as **reinforced concrete**.

béton brut Concrete as it appears when the framework is removed, so that the concrete surface reflects the framework joints, wood grain, and fasteners around which it was poured; often deliberately retained for architectural effect. See **Brutalism**.

bettering house An archaic term for **poorhouse**.

bev In the lumber industry, abbr. for "beveled."

bevel **1.** The angle which one surface of a body makes with another surface when they are not at right angles. **2.** See **door bevel**. **3.** See **lock bevel**. **4.** A **bevel square**.

bevel angle In welding, the angle which is formed between the prepared edge of a member and a plane perpendicular to the surface of the member.

bevel board A board cut to any required bevel; used in framing a roof, stairway, or other angular wood construction.

bevel chisel A chisel for cutting wood, having its cutting edge at an angle with the sides.

bevel collar Same as **angle collar**.

bevel cut Any cut not at right angles.

beveled See **bevel**.

beveled closer See **king closer**.

beveled edge Of a door; a vertical door edge which has a slope of ⅛ in. (0.3 cm) in 2 in. (5 cm) from a plane perpendicular to the door face.

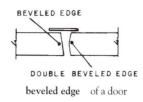

beveled edge of a door

beveled halving, bevel halving A **half-lap joint** in which the abutting surfaces are cut at an angle to the plane of the timbers.

beveled joist A floor joist having its upper edges beveled.

beveled pipe A pipe which has one end angled so that it mates with a complementary pipe end.

beveled-rabbeted window stool A **window stool** which is rabbeted with a beveled profile to match the slope of the sill of the window frame.

beveled siding See **clapboard**.

beveled washer A metal washer having a bevel on one side, permitting a bolt or rod to pass through it but providing full bearing against a nut.

bevel jack A device for holding wood moldings in cutting a miter.

bevel joint In carpentry, a joint in which two pieces meet at other than a right angle.

bevel protractor A graduated semicircular **protractor** having a pivoted arm; used for measuring or marking off angles.

bevel protractor

bevel siding See **clapboard**.

bevel square A carpenter's tool, similar to a **square** but having a blade that can be adjusted to any angle.

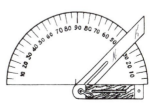

setting a **bevel square**

bezant, besant, byzant   An ornament shaped like a coin or disk; sometimes used in a series in decorative molding designs.

bezant

bezel, basil   The bevel or sloping edge of a cutting tool, as an ax or chisel.

BFP   Abbr. for **backflow preventer**.

Bh   Abbr. for **Brinell hardness**.

Bhn   Abbr. for **Brinell hardness number**.

bhp   Abbr. for **brake horse power**.

biaxial bending   The bending of a member about two perpendicular axes simultaneously.

bib, bibb   See **bibcock**.

bibcock, bib, bibb, bib tap   A **faucet** or **stopcock** which has its nozzle bent downward.

bibcock

bibliotheca   A library; a place to keep books.

bib nozzle   Same as **bibcock**.

bib tap   Same as **bibcock**.

bib valve   An ordinary **bibcock** which is closed by screwing down a handle, thereby closing a washer disk onto a seating in the valve.

bicoca   A turret or watchtower.

bicycle-wheel roof   A roof structural system whose main structural members radiate from the center to the perimeter of the building, resembling a bicycle wheel.

bid   **1.** An offer to perform the work described in a contract at a specified cost. **2.** A complete and properly signed proposal to do the **work, 1** or designated portion thereof for the sums stipulated therein, supported by data called for by the bidding requirements.

bid bond   A form of bid security executed by the bidder as principal and by a surety. Also see **bid security** and **surety**.

bid date   The date established by the owner or the architect for the receipt of bids. Also see **bid time**.

bidder   One who submits a bid for a prime contract with the **owner**, as distinct from a subbidder who submits a bid to a prime bidder. A bidder is not a **contractor** on a specific project until a contract exists between him and the owner.

bidding documents   The advertisement or invitation to bid, **instructions to bidders**, the bid form, and the proposed **contract documents** including any **addenda** issued prior to receipt of bids.

bidding or negotiation phase   The fourth phase of the architect's **basic services**, during which competitive bids or negotiated proposals are sought as the basis for awarding a contract.

bidding period   The calendar period beginning at the time of issuance of bidding requirements and **contract documents** and ending at the prescribed bid time. Also see **bid time**.

bidding requirements   Those documents providing information and establishing procedures and conditions for the submission of bids. They consist of the notice to bidders or advertisement for bids, instructions to bidders, invitation to bid, and sample forms. Also see **bidding documents**.

bidet   A low, basin-like plumbing fixture on which the user sits; used to wash the posterior parts of the body.

bid form   A form furnished to a bidder to be filled out, signed, and submitted as his bid.

bid guarantee   Same as **bid security**.

bid letting   See **bid opening**.

bid opening   The opening and tabulation of bids submitted by the prescribed bid time and in conformity with the prescribed procedures. Also see **bid time**.

bid price The sum stated in the bid for which the bidder offers to perform the **work, 1.**

bid security The deposit of cash, certified check, cashier's check, bank draft, money order, or **bid bond** submitted with a bid and serving to guarantee to the owner that the bidder, if awarded the contract, will execute such contract in accordance with the bidding requirements and the **contract documents.**

bid time The date and hour established by the owner or the architect for the receipt of bids. Also see **bid date.**

biennial plant A plant whose life cycle is completed in two growing seasons.

bifolding door A door having two pairs of leaves, each pair consisting of an outer and an inner leaf which are hinged together; each inner leaf (the one nearest the center line) is hung from an overhead track; each outer leaf is pivoted at the jamb.

biforate Having two doors or windows.

bifrons Having two fronts or faces looking in two directions, as a double **herm.**

bifrons

bifronted Same as **bifrons.**

biga A chariot similar to a **quadriga** but drawn by two horses.

BIL See **basic insulation level.**

bilection molding See **bolection molding.**

billet **1.** A common Norman or Romanesque molding formed by a series of circular (but occasionally square) cylinders, disposed alternately with the notches in single or multiple rows. **2.** A steel slab which is placed under a column to distribute the load, as from the column to the sup-

billet, 1

porting masonry. **3.** A timber which is sawn on three sides and left rounded on the fourth. **4.** A wood block from which smaller pieces of structural lumber can be cut.

bill of materials Same as **quantity survey.**

bill of quantities Same as **quantity survey.**

bimah A **bema, 2.**

bimetallic element A device formed of two metals which are bonded together, each having a different coefficient of thermal expansion; used in temperature-indicating and temperature-controlling devices.

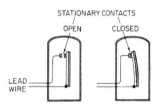

bimetallic element in a thermostat

bin A container for storing loose materials, such as sand or crushed rock.

binder **1.** A cementing material, either hydrated cement or a product of cement or lime and reactive siliceous material, for holding loose material together. **2.** A component of an adhesive composition that is primarily responsible for the adhesive forces which hold two bodies together. **3.** A **binding agent. 4.** A **soil binder. 5.** A **binding joist. 6.** A **binding stone. 7.** Any member which binds together components of a framing structure.

binder course, binding course **1.** In asphaltic concrete paving, an intermediate course between the course base and the surfacing material; consists of intermediate-size aggregate bound by bituminous material. **2.** A row of masonry units laid between, and used to bind, an inner and an outer wall.

binder soil Material consisting primarily of fine soil particles (fine sand, silt, clay, and colloids); has good binding properties. Also called **clay binder.**

binding agent That liquid portion of a paint which solidifies and binds together the pigment particles and develops adhesion to the painted surface.

binding beam Any timber which serves to tie together various parts of a frame. See **summerbeam**.

binding course See **binder course**.

binding joist, binder A beam which supports the common joists of a wood floor above and the ceiling joists below; commonly, joins two vertical posts.

binding piece A piece of lumber which is nailed between two opposite beams or joists to prevent lateral deflection; a **straining beam**.

binding post A post attached to an electric cable, wire, or apparatus, for making a connection to it conveniently.

binding post

binding rafter A longitudinal timber which supports the roof rafters between the ridge and the eaves, as a **purlin**.

binding screw A type of **setscrew**.

binding stone A stone which bonds masonry together, as a perpend; a **binder, 6**.

binnacle An obsolete term for a dwelling place.

biparting door A double door having two leaves (one on each side of the center line of the door) which slide in the same plane and meet at the center line.

birch A moderately strong, high-density wood of North America and northern Europe, yellowish white to brown in color; its uniform texture and figure are well suited for veneer, flooring, and turned wood products.

birdbath A small puddle of water occurring at a low spot in paving.

bird peck A small spot or hole in wood usually caused by a woodpecker. Subsequent tree growth develops distorted grain around the injury.

bird's-beak molding See **beak molding, 2**.

bird screen A screen fixed to the top of a chimney to prevent the entry of birds. See **rain cap**.

bird screen

bird's eye An eye-shaped figure in wood formed by small sharp depressions in the growth rings. Found particularly in sugar maple but also in other wood species.

bird's-eye lamp See **incandescent direct-light lamp**.

bird's-eye maple Wood of the sugar maple tree, cut so as to produce a wavy grain with numerous small, decorative, circular markings.

bird's-mouth 1. A notch cut across the grain at one end of a timber for its reception on the edge of another piece, such as a **wall plate**. 2. The angle between two components, usually between 90 and 180 degrees.

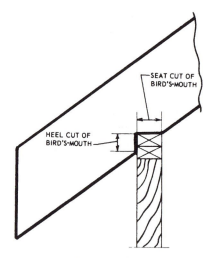

bird's-mouth, 1

bird's-mouth joint A wood joint formed by a cut into the end of a timber to fit over a cross timber; for example, cut into a rafter.

bisellium   In ancient Rome, a seat of honor, or a state chair, reserved for persons of note or persons who had done special service for the state.

bisomus   A sarcophagus with two compartments.

bit   **1.** A small tool which fits in the chuck of a brace or drill, and by which it is rotated—thereby cutting or boring a hole. **2.** The projecting blade of a key which is cut in a manner to actuate the tumblers and permit the lock bolts to be operated. **3.** That part of a soldering iron which transfers heat and solder to the joint. **4.** The cutting edge of a **plane**.

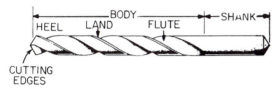

bit, 1

bitbrace   A **brace, 3**.

bite   In glazing, the distance by which the inner edge of a frame (or a stop) overlaps the edge of the glass or panel.

bit gauge, bit stop   A metal piece temporarily fixed to a **bit** to prevent drilling too deeply in a blind hole.

bit key   A key having a projecting blade or wing which engages with and actuates the bolt and tumblers of a lock.

bit stock   A **brace, 3**.

bit stop   See **bit gauge**.

bitumen   A semisolid mixture of complex hydrocarbons derived from coal or petroleum, as coal-tar pitch or asphalt; before application, usually dissolved in a solvent, emulsified, or heated to a liquid state.

bituminized fiber pipe   A lightweight drainage pipe fabricated of cellulose fiber combined with coal tar.

bituminous cement   A black substance available in solid, semisolid, or liquid states at normal temperatures; composed of mixed indeterminate hydrocarbons; appreciably soluble only in carbon disulfide or other volatile liquid hydrocarbon; esp. used in sealing **built-up roofing** and between joints and in cracks of concrete pavements.

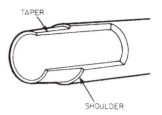

bituminized fiber pipe

bituminous coating   An asphalt or tar compound used to provide a protective finish for a surface.

bituminous distributor   A truck equipped with a tank body and with a system for pumping hot tar, road oil, or other bituminous material through a perforated spray bar at the rear; used to lay down a surface coating of the bituminous material.

bituminous emulsion   A suspension of minute globules of bituminous material in water (or of minute globules of water in a liquid bituminous material); used as a protective coating against weather, esp. where appearance is not important.

bituminous felt   See **asphalt prepared roofing**.

bituminous grout   A mixture of bituminous material and aggregate such as sand; liquefies when heated; suitable for pouring in joints or cracks as a sealant; cures in air.

bituminous paint   A low-cost paint containing asphalt or coal tar, a thinner, and drying oils; used to waterproof concrete and to protect piping where bleeding of the asphalt is not a problem.

bituminous varnish   A dark-colored varnish (either of the oil or spirit type) that contains bituminous ingredients.

BK SH   On drawings, abbr. for "book shelves."

BL   On drawings, abbr. for **building line**.

B/L   Abbr. for "bill of lading."

B-labeled door   A door carrying a certification from the Underwriters' Laboratories, Inc. that it meets the requirements for a **class-B door**.

black ash mortar, black mortar   A mixture of high-calcium lime, water, and ashes or clinker which relies on its pozzolanic properties for its hard set.

blackbody   **1.** A body whose radiation at each wavelength is the maximum possible for any electromagnetic radiator at that temperature. **2.** A body that absorbs all light which is incident on it and consequently looks black.

black bolt A hot-formed bolt covered with black scale, not of uniform diameter; used in steel construction.

black diapering Same as **diaperwork**.

black ebony See **ebony**.

black japan A high-quality bituminous paint used as a metal varnish.

black light Invisible ultraviolet electromagnetic energy near the visible spectrum; useful for exciting fluorescent paints, dyes, etc., so that they become visible.

black light fluorescent lamp A fluorescent lamp whose phosphor is designed to emit **black light**.

black locust See **locust**.

black mortar See **black ash mortar**.

blackout switch On a theatre stage, a master switch that extinguishes all stage lights simultaneously.

black plate Uncoated cold-rolled steel in sheets, usually 12 in. (30.5 cm) to 32 in. (81.3 cm) in width.

blacksmith shop A shop where iron bars are forged into objects such as tools, and where horses are fitted with horseshoes.

blacktop See **asphaltic concrete**.

blade **1.** The flat metal surface of a trowel with which plaster is applied. **2.** The cutting part of a knife, plane, etc. **3.** The broad, slightly concave surface of a bulldozer, or the like, which pushes the material being moved. **4.** One of the principal rafters of a roof.

blade frequency The number of times fan blades pass a given point per second; equals the number of blades in the fan multiplied by the fan speed in revolutions per second.

Blaine apparatus An apparatus for measuring the surface area of a finely ground cement, or the like, on the basis of its air permeability.

Blaine fineness The fineness of a powdered material, such as cement, as determined by the Blaine apparatus; usually expressed as a surface area in square centimeters per gram.

Blaine test A test for determining the fineness of cement, or other fine material, on the basis of

the permeability to air of a sample of the material prepared under specified conditions.

blanc fixe A fine-grained barium sulfate, used as white pigment in paints.

blandel Same as **apostilb**.

blank arcade Same as **blind arcade**.

blank door **1.** A recess in a wall, having the appearance of a door; usually used for symmetry of design. **2.** A door which has been sealed off but is still visible.

blanket encumbrance A lien or mortgage which is applied proportionately to every lot within a subdivision.

blanket grouting See **area grouting**.

blanket insulation Thermal insulation, commonly fabricated of fibrous glass material, with or without confining envelope, facings, or coatings; in properly selected density and thickness, can conform to curved or irregular surfaces of equipment, large-diameter piping, or tanks; also used as an acoustical material behind a facing material or as a component in sound-insulating construction.

blank flange A flange without bolt holes; otherwise complete.

blank jamb A vertical member of a door-frame which has not been prepared to receive hardware.

blank wall, blind wall, dead wall A wall whose whole surface is unbroken by a window, door, or other opening.

blank window, blind window, false window **1.** A recess in an external wall, having the external appearance of a window. **2.** A window, which has been sealed off but is still visible.

blast area The area in which the loading of explosives and the blasting operations take place.

blast cleaning Any cleaning process, such as sandblasting, in which an abrasive is directed at the surface with high velocity.

blast freezer An upright freezer in which air, at a very low temperature, is circulated by blowers; used to freeze foods in minimum time.

blast-furnace slag The nonmetallic product, consisting essentially of silicates and aluminosilicates of calcium and other bases, which is developed in a molten condition simultaneously with iron in a blast furnace. The solidified product is further classified by the process by which it was brought from the molten state; also see **air-cooled blast-furnace slag, expanded blast-furnace slag, granulated blast-furnace slag**.

blast-furnace slag cement See **portland blast-furnace slag cement**.

blast heater A heater consisting of a set of heat-transfer coils (or sections) through which air is drawn or forced by a fan at relatively high velocities.

blast hole A hole drilled into rock in which an explosive charge is to be placed.

blasthole drill A drill which cuts holes in rock for the placement of explosives.

blasting Using explosives to loosen rock or other closely packed materials.

blasting agent According to OSHA: a material or mixture consisting of a fuel and oxidizer used for blasting, but not classified as an explosive and in which none of the ingredients is classified as an explosive, provided the furnished product cannot be detonated with a No. 8 test blasting cap when confined.

blasting cap A metallic tube closed at one end, containing a charge of one or more detonating compounds, and designed for and capable of detonation from the sparks or flame from a safety fuse inserted and crimped into the open end.

blasting mat A heavy, flexible covering (usually made of woven-wire rope or cordage); covers an area during blasting, to prevent rock or earth fragments from flying about.

blast-resistant door A steel door which has been fabricated to resist dynamic stresses caused by blast pressures up to 3,000 lb per sq in. (211 kg per sq cm).

bldg Abbr. for **building**.

bleachers A **grandstand** (or section within a grandstand) where the seats are usually not provided with backrests.

bleacher seating A stand of tiered planks providing undivided space for seating.

bleaching A chemical or photochemical reaction which whitens or removes color from a surface.

bleb A blister or small bubble in a fluid or in a material (such as glass) that has solidified.

bled timber Wood from trees tapped for resin. Although appearance may be affected, strength is usually not.

bleeder A small valve used to drain fluid from a pipe, radiator, vessel, etc.

bleeder pipe, bleeder tile A pipe, usually of structural clay, for carrying water from a drainage tile to a drain or sewer.

bleeding 1. The upward penetration of a coloring pigment from a substrate through a topcoat of paint. 2. The oozing of grout from below a road-surfacing material to the surface in hot weather. 3. Exudation of one or more components of a sealant, with possible absorption by adjacent porous surfaces. 4. The autogenous flow of mixing water within, or its emergence from, newly placed concrete or mortar; caused by the settlement of the solid materials within the mass or by drainage of mixing water; also called **water gain**. 5. The diffusion of coloring matter through a coating from the substrate, or the discoloration that arises from such a process.

bleeding capacity The ratio of the volume of water which is released by **bleeding, 4** to the volume of mortar or paste.

bleeding rate The rate at which water is released by **bleeding, 4** from mortar or paste.

bleeding test A test (ASTM C232) for measuring the tendency for water to rise to the surface of freshly placed concrete.

bleed-through, strike-through Discoloration in the face plies of wood veneer constructions caused by oozing of glue through the face veneers.

blemish In wood, marble, etc., usually a minor appearance defect that does not necessarily affect durability or strength.

blended cement A mixture of portland cement and other material such as granulated blast-furnace slag, pozzolan, hydrated lime, etc., combined either during or after the finish grinding of the cement at the mill.

blended lamp Same as **self-ballasted lamp**.

blender A soft round-tipped paintbrush used for blending colors and smoothing out brush marks left by coarser brushes.

blending In hot-water systems, the mixing of hot water with cold water in order to raise the cold-water temperature. Blending usually takes place at the point of use.

blending valve   A three-way valve which permits liquid entering the valve to be mixed with liquid that recirculates through the valve; used to obtain a desired liquid temperature.

blight   In plants, a fungus disease causing them to wither.

blighted area   Any area which has become an economic and aesthetic liability to a community.

blind   **1.** A device to obstruct vision or keep out light; usually a shade, a screen, or an assemblage of light panels or slats. **2.** A solid disk inserted in a pipe joint or union to prevent the flow of water during the repair of a water distribution system.

blind alley   A road, alley, or passageway open at one end only. Also see **cul-de-sac**.

blind arcade   A decorative row of arches applied to a wall as a decorative element, esp. in Romanesque buildings.

blind arcade

blind arch   An arch in which the opening is permanently closed by wall construction.

blind area   An area built around the outside of a basement wall to prohibit penetration of moisture.

blind attic   An attic space, floored but unfinished inside. Also see **loft, 1.**

blind casing, subcasing   A rough window frame or subcasing to which trim is added.

blind door   **1.** Same as **blank door. 2.** A louvered door.

blind dovetail   Same as **secret dovetail.**

blind drain   A drain which is not connected to a sewage system.

blind fast   A catch for securing a blind or a shutter, in either an open or a closed position.

blind flange   A flange which closes the end of a pipe.

blind floor   Same as **subfloor.**

blind header   **1.** A masonry unit having the appearance, but not the full length, of a **header. 2.** A clipped header.

blind hoistway   A **hoistway** that does not have a hoistway door at every floor.

blind hole   A hole which is drilled only partway through the thickness of the material.

blinding   **1.** A thin layer of lean concrete or of fine gravel or sand applied to a surface to fill voids and to provide a smoother, cleaner, drier, or more durable finish; esp. fine gravel or sand over freshly placed asphaltic concrete. **2.** Sprinkling small stone chips over a freshly tarred road. **3.** Placing a material over piping to completely cover it. **4.** Compacting of soil directly over a **drain tile**, thereby reducing its tendency to move into the tile.

blind joint   **1.** A type of masonry joint in **double Flemish bond**; a thin line joint between two stretchers (this line bisects a header in the course directly below). **2.** A **joint**, no part of which is visible.

blind lancet   A **blind arch** in the shape of a **lancet.**

blind mortise, stopped mortise   A mortise whose depth is less than the thickness of the piece into which it is cut, so that it does not pass through it.

blind-mortise-and-tenon joint, stub mortise and tenon   A joint combining a **blind mortise** and a **stub tenon**; neither is visible in the assembled joint.

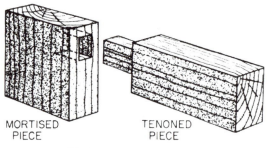

MORTISED PIECE   TENONED PIECE

blind-mortise-and-tenon joint

blind nailing, concealed nailing, secret nailing   **1.** Nailing in such a way that the nail-

blind nailing

heads are not visible on the face of the work. **2.** In finished roofing, the use of nails that are not exposed to the weather.

blind nipple A **nipple**, one end of which is capped.

blind pocket A pocket in the ceiling at a **window head** to accommodate a Venetian blind when it is raised.

blind row In an auditorium, a row of seats having its first seat at a side aisle and its last seat at a side wall.

blind seat A seat in an auditorium having an obstructed or partially obstructed view of the stage.

blind slat An obliquely-set slat (as in a shutter), which serves to shed rain but to admit light.

blind stop A rectangular molding used in the assemblage of a window frame; nailed between the outside trim and the outside sashes, it serves as a stop for storm sashes and screens and assists in preventing air infiltration.

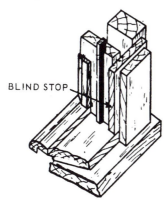

BLIND STOP

blind stop

blindstory **1.** A floor level without exterior windows. **2.** The triforium of a Gothic church, or derivatives.

blind tenon A **tenon** which does not pass all the way through a **mortise**.

blind tracery Tracery adorning a wall or panel but not pierced through.

blind wall A **blank wall**.

blind window See **blank window**.

blister **1.** A roughly circular or elongated unbonded area between plies of laminated constructions, as in wood veneer. Usually caused by entrapped moisture. Also called **steam blow**. **2.** A spongy raised portion of a roofing membrane, where separation of the felts has occurred or the membrane is not bonded to the substrate as a result of the expansion of water and air trapped in the membrane. **3.** A raised spot on the surface of the metal caused by expansion of gas in a subsurface zone during thermal treatment. **4.** A raised area on the surface of a molded plastic caused by the pressure of internal gases on its incompletely hardened surface. **5.** See **blistering**. **6.** A convex, raised area on the surface of a pipe which indicates an internal separation.

blister figure, quilted figure A quilt-like pattern in wood veneer, usually caused by a nonuniform grain structure.

blistering **1.** Small blisters, bubbles, or bulges in a plaster finish coat; results from applying a finish coat over too damp a base coat, or from troweling on plaster too soon; also called **turtleback**. **2.** See **blister**. **3.** The irregular raising of a thin layer at the surface of placed mortar or concrete during or soon after completion of the finishing operation, or, in the case of pipe, after spinning. **4.** In the firing of a ceramic, the development of enclosed or broken macroscopic vesicles or bubbles in a body or glaze or other coating.

blk **1.** Abbr. for "block." **2.** Abbr. for "black."

BLKG On drawings, abbr. for **blocking**.

BLO On drawings, abbr. for **blower**.

bloated Swollen, as in certain lightweight aggregates for concrete, as a result of processing.

bloated clay Clay which has expanded during firing, owing to entrapped air or the breakdown of sulfides or other ingredients in the clay; light and porous; suitable for insulating aggregate in lightweight concrete. Also see **expanded clay**.

blocage Masonry that is composed of irregularly shaped stones laid in a mass of mortar.

block **1.** A masonry unit; a **concrete block**. **2.** (*Brit.*) A walling unit which exceeds in length, width, or height the dimensions specified for a brick. **3.** A solid piece of wood or other material. **4.** A plank or timber which serves as bridging

block and tackle

block, 6

between joists or the like. **5.** In quarrying, the large piece of stone, generally squared, that is taken from the quarry to the mill for sawing, slabbing, and further working. **6.** A mechanical device which encloses one or more pulleys, through which chains or ropes pass, usually for hoisting. **7.** A small area of city or town which is bounded by neighboring and intersecting streets; the length of a side of such an area. **8.** (*Brit.*) A large building which is divided into a number of units, as a block of flats.

block and tackle A pulley **block, 6** together with rope or cable, used to raise or shift a load.

block beam A flexural structural member, composed of individual concrete blocks which are joined together by **prestressing**.

blockboard See **coreboard; strip core.**

block bond Same as **common bond.**

block bonding In joining one part of a brick wall to another, the use of several courses of brickwork.

block bridging, solid bridging, solid strutting Short members (boards) which are fixed vertically between floor joists to stiffen the joists.

block bridging

block capital Same as **cushion capital.**

block cornice A cornice used in Italian architecture; usually consists of a bed molding, a range of block modillions or corbels, and a corona or cornice (the bed molding may be omitted).

block flooring Blocks of wood which are used as paving or flooring.

blockholing The breaking of boulders by firing a charge of explosive that has been loaded in a drill hole.

blockhouse **1.** A fortified structure used to furnish protection against enemy attack in frontier areas, usually at a location of strategic importance; often square or polygonal in plan; typically constructed of hewn timbers having dovetailed notches at the corners to provide strong rigid joints; commonly, an overhanging upper story; often masonry walls on the ground story with log construction above, or entirely of log construction; frequently, a **pyramidal roof**; usually a few small windows with heavy shutters; **loophole** openings through the walls permit the firing of guns over a wide range of angles. **2.** A reinforced concrete structure that provides shelter against the hazards of heat, blast, or nuclear radiation.

blockhouse

block-in-course Hammer-dressed stones (which may vary in length) having square faces, laid with close joints, in courses not exceeding 12 in. (30 cm) in height; used in heavy engineering masonry construction.

block-in-course bond In a brick arch of concentric rings which is divided in sections, a bond within a section formed through the full depth of the **archivolt** by a block of bonded brick or by a voussoir inserted at intervals; ties together the concentric rings.

blocking **1.** Pieces of wood used to secure, join, or reinforce members, or to fill spaces between them. **2.** A method of bonding two adjoining or intersecting walls, not built at the same time, by means of offsets whose vertical dimensions are not less than 8 in. (20 cm). **3.** The sticking together of two painted surfaces when pressed together. **4.** An undesired adhesion between touching layers of a material, as occurs under moderate pressure during storage or use. **5.** Small blocks of wood used for shimming. **6.** Wood which is built into a roofing system above the deck but below the membrane and flashing; used to stiffen the deck around the opening, to serve as a stop for thermal insulation, and to serve as a nailer for attachment of the membrane or flashing.

blocking chisel A broad-edged chisel made in a number of sizes, shapes, and weights; a **bolster, 4.**

blocking course **1.** A plain finishing course of masonry directly above a cornice. **2.** A **string course.**

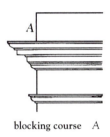

blocking course A

block insulation A rigid or semirigid slab of thermal insulation.

block modillion See **modillion.**

blockout In a concrete structure under construction, a space where concrete is not to be placed.

block plan A small-scale simplified plan of a building, indicating its location and surroundings.

block plane A small **plane,** held in one hand; the angle of the cutting blade is low (usually about 20°); esp. used to clean up end grain and miters.

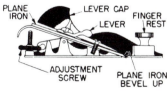

block plane

block quoin A **quoin** formed by bricks, distinguished decoratively from adjacent masonry by a contrasting appearance or by a projecting pattern.

block tin In plumbing: pure tin.

blockwork Masonry of concrete block and mortar.

bloom **1.** The formation of a thin film of material on the surface of paint causing it to appear lower in gloss and milky in color. It varies in composition depending on the nature of the paint, drying conditions, etc., and may sometimes be removed with a damp cloth. **2.** A type of **efflorescence** that appears on brickwork. **3.** A discoloration or change in appearance of the surface of a rubber product (as sulfur bloom and wax bloom) caused by the migration of a liquid or solid to the surface. **4.** A defect on a freshly varnished surface, appearing as a cloudy film.

blooming See **bloom, 4.**

blow **1.** See **throw, 1. 2.** The eruption of water and sand inside a **cofferdam,** causing flooding.

blowback A characteristic of a safety valve; the difference between the pressure at which it opens and the pressure at which it closes automatically, after the excess pressure has been released.

blow count **1.** The number of blows required to drive an object into soil. **2.** In soil borings, the number of blows required to advance a sample spoon 6 in. (15.2 cm) or 12 in. (30.5 cm). **3.** In pile driving, the number of blows required to advance the pile 12 in. (30.5 cm) or the number of blows per unit distance of advance.

blowdown period In an **autoclave,** the time taken to reduce the pressure from its maximum value to atmospheric pressure.

blower A **fan,** usually one for heavy-duty application, e.g., a fan that forces fresh air through a duct system to an underground excavation.

blow hole **1.** Same as **gas pocket. 2.** Same as **bug hole.**

blowing **1.** See **popping. 2.** The upward movement of soil material at the base of an excavation or cofferdam as a result of groundwater pressure.

blowlamp British term for **blowtorch.**

blown asphalt Asphalt that is treated by blowing air through it at elevated temperature to give it characteristics desired for certain special uses such as roofing, pipe coating, undersealing portland cement concrete pavements, membrane envelopes, and hydraulic applications.

blown joint, blow joint A plumbing joint in a lead pipe, formed with the use of a blowtorch.

blown oil A fatty oil that has been oxidized by blowing air through it while it is hot; sometimes mixed with mineral oil for use as a lubricant; used in paints and varnishes because oxidation increases its drying power and viscosity.

blow-off On a boiler, an outlet to permit the discharge of accumulated deposits from water.

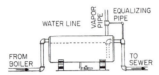

a tank which receives discharge from a boiler **blow-off**

blowout Same as **blowing, 2**.

blowtorch, *Brit.* **blowlamp** A small torch which generates a high-intensity flame; used for heating soldering irons, burning off paint, etc.

blow-up Localized buckling or shattering of rigid pavement caused by excessive longitudinal pressure.

BLR On drawings, abbr. for **boiler**.

blub A small hole in a mold or plaster cast, formed by trapped air.

blue asbestos Same as **riebeckite asbestos**.

blue brick, sewer brick, Staffordshire blue A brick of high strength whose blue color results from firing in a kiln in a flame of low oxygen content.

blued Said of a steel nail surface that has been heated so that its surface takes on an oxidized bluish hue.

blue lias lime *(Brit.)* A hydraulic lime obtained by burning blue lias limestone. When mixed with water, it has a set which is not characteristic of regular limes.

blue metal A hard rock, bluish in color, which is crushed and used in **macadam**.

blue print A reproduction of a drawing by means of a contact printing process on light-sensitive paper, producing a negative image

consisting of white lines on a blue background; esp. refers to such reproductions of architectural drawings or working drawings used on construction sites.

blue stain A dark stain in the sapwood of some species of trees, usually caused by a fungus; it does not weaken the wood; also called **sap stain**.

bluestone A hard, fine-grained, commonly feldspathic and micaceous sandstone or siltstone of dark greenish to bluish gray color that splits readily along bedding planes to form thin slabs; commonly used to pave surfaces for pedestrian traffic. A variety of **flagstone**.

blue top A stake which is driven into the ground, the top of which indicates the grade level.

bluing The addition of a small amount of clean blue colorant to a white paint to promote the visual perception of whiteness.

blunt arch An arch rising to a slight point, struck from two centers within the arch.

blunt arch

blushing A white or grayish cast on high-gloss paint; results from the precipitation of binder solids owing to incompatibility with water, oil, or solvent.

B/M On drawings, abbr. for **bill of materials**.

b.m. In the lumber industry, abbr. for **board measure**.

BM **1.** On drawings, abbr. for **bench mark**. **2.** On drawings, abbr. for **beam**.

board **1.** Lumber less than 2 in. (5 cm) thick and between 4 in. (10 cm) and 12 in. (30 cm) in width; a board less than 4 in. (10 cm) wide may be classified as a **strip**. **2.** Short for **switchboard**. **3.** A box-office ticket board or seating chart.

board-and-batten construction Wall construction for a timber-framed house in which the exterior covering consists of closely spaced boards set vertically, with narrow wood strips covering the joints between the boards.

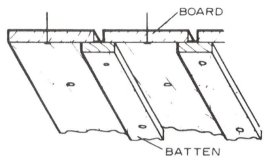

board and batten

board-and-batten door Same as **battened door**.

board and brace A type of carpentry work consisting of boards which are grooved along both edges and have thinner boards fitted between them.

board butt joint In **shotcrete** construction, a joint which is formed by sloping the gunned surface to meet a board laid flat.

boarded door A **batten door**.

boarded wall An exterior wall of a building of **wood-frame construction** having boards commonly applied horizontally, although vertically positioned boards are found occasionally.

board fence A fence constructed of boards that are spaced horizontally and fastened to square lumber posts; widely used in the past, but now usually found only in upscale rural communities because of its relatively high cost.

board foot A unit of cubic content used in measuring lumber; equal in volume to an area of 1 square foot having a thickness of 1 inch.

board house 1. A house of **board-and-batten construction**, **board-on-board construction**, or the like. 2. A timber-framed one-room cottage, sheathed with vertical cypress boards, in Florida during the late 16th century when it was a Spanish colony; had battened doors, a dirt floor, and a gable roof of thatched palm leaves with a hole along the ridge as an outlet for smoke from a fireplace directly below it.

boarding Boards used as **sheathing**.

boardinghouse A house that rents furnished rooms and provides meals for boarders in exchange for the payment of a weekly or monthly charge; especially used by workers and transients in mill towns primarily from the 18th to the early 20th centuries.

boarding in The process of nailing boards on the outer frame of a house, as a facing.

boarding joist A **joist** to which floor boarding is nailed.

boarding school A high school or elementary school which has living accommodations for its students.

board insulation, insulating board, insulation board Rigid or semirigid thermal insulation having a thickness small in comparison to other dimensions; density usually about 4 to 16 lb per cu ft (64 to 256 kg per cu m); low structural strength.

board lath See **gypsum lath, wood lath, insulation lath**.

board measure A system of measuring lumber: In the U.S.A. the term **board foot** is used; in many countries using the SI system of units, the term **board metre** is used.

board metre A unit of cubic content used in measuring lumber, equal in volume to an area of 1 square metre having a thickness of 25 millimeters.

board of trade unit In Britain, a unit of electrical energy consumption equal to 1 kilowatt-hour.

board-on-board construction Wall construction for a **timber-framed house** having an exterior covering consisting of a double layer of vertical boards of approximately the same width; usually, the boards in the second layer are placed so as to cover the joints between the boards in the first layer.

board rule A measuring device for finding the number of board feet in a board without calculation.

board sheathing A **sheathing** of board, usually tightly spaced, but some roof constructions use open spacing between boards. (See illustration p. 108.)

boardwalk A walkway made of boards or planks, often a promenade along a shore or beach.

boast To rough-hew stone, preparing it for carving.

boasted ashlar A type of **ashlar masonry** having a boasted surface.

boasted work A dressed (usually by hand) stone surface showing roughly parallel narrow

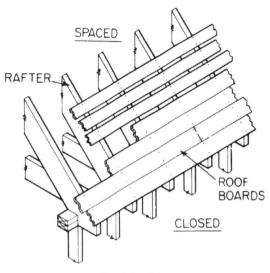

board sheathing

bochka

chisel grooves, not uniform in width and not carried across the face of the stone.

boaster   A flat, steel mason's chisel used in the dressing of stone.

boat dock   See **scenery wagon**.

boathouse   A structure for storing boats when not in use; generally built at the water's edge, often partly over the water; sometimes has provisions for social activities.

boat spike   Same as **barge spike**.

boatswain's chair   A seat supported by slings attached to a suspended rope, designed to accommodate one workman in a sitting position.

bob   Same as **plumb bob**.

bobache   See **bobeche**.

bobeche, bobache   The collar fitted to a lamp holder as on a chandelier and from which glass prisms may be suspended.

BOCA   Abbr. for "Building Officials and Code Administrators."

BOCA National Building Code   A national **building code** in the United States prepared by the Building Officials and Code Administrators International. Address: 4051 W. Flossmoor Road, Country Club Hills, IL 60478. Also see **Uniform Building Code**.

bochka   In early Russian architecture, a wooden roof whose peak has the shape of a horizontal

cylinder with the upper side surface extending into a pointed ridge.

bodhika   In Indian architecture, the capital of a column.

bodied linseed oil   **Linseed oil** which has been thickened in viscosity by processing with chemicals or heat; the viscosity may vary from raw linseed oil to almost a gel.

bodily injury   Physical injury, sickness, or disease sustained by a person. Also see **personal injury**.

body   The principal volume of a building, such as the nave of a church.

body coat   In painting, the final coat on a surface.

bodying in, bodying up   A process in French polishing for building up the thickness of the finish by numerous applications of varnish, rubbing each one smooth and level.

b of b   Abbr. for "back of board."

bog   Wet, soft, and spongy ground, where the soil is composed mainly of decayed and decaying vegetable matter.

bog house   A synonym for **outhouse**.

bogie   On a theatre stage, a hanger for an overhead track, from which scenery, flats, or panels are suspended.

bog plant   A plant which lives continuously in wet soil, but not in stagnant water.

boil   A wet run of material at the bottom of an excavation or under the sheeting of an excavation.

boiled oil, pale-bodied oil   Any oil, but esp. linseed oil, which has been partially polymerized by heating at about 500°F (260°C) together with driers to promote rapid drying.

boiler   A closed vessel in which a liquid is heated or vaporized by the direct application of heat to the outside of the vessel.

boiler blow-off   Same as **blow-off**.

boiler blow-off tank   A vessel designed to receive the discharge from a boiler blow-off outlet where the discharge is cooled to a temperature low enough to permit its safe entry into the drainage system.

boiler compound   A chemical added to water in a boiler to prevent corrosion, foaming, or the formation of **boiler scale**.

boiler horsepower   A unit of measurement of the power of a steam boiler; equivalent to the evaporation of 34.5 lb of water per hour into dry saturated steam from and at 212°F.

boiler jacket   The covering of thermal insulation around a boiler.

boiler plate   **1.** Plates of steel used for making boilers and tanks. **2.** The accessories and appurtenances associated with a boiler plant. **3.** Those portions of the **specifications** that commonly apply to most buildings, so are commonly reproduced from one set of specifications to another.

boiler return trap   A device used to return **condensate** to a low-pressure boiler when it cannot flow into the boiler by gravity.

boiler room   A room in which one or more steam or hot-water boilers and associated equipment are located.

boiler scale   Metal from the inner surfaces of a boiler which decomposes and flakes off (in much the same manner as rust forms).

boiler steel   A medium-hardness steel which is rolled into plates 0.25 in. (0.6 cm) to 1.5 in. (3.8 cm) thick; used in fabricating boilers.

boiling   Same as **blowing, 2**.

boiling tub, maturing bin   A large tub used to slake high-calcium or magnesium quicklime to form a lime putty.

boiserie   Wood paneling on interior walls, usually floor to ceiling; as a rule enriched by carving, gilding, painting, or, rarely, inlaying. Also see **paneling, wainscot**.

bolection molding, balection, belection, bellexion, bilection, bolexion   A molding projecting beyond the surface of the work which it decorates, as that covering the joint between a panel and the surrounding stiles and rails; often used to conceal a joint where the joining surfaces are at different levels.

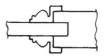

bolection molding

bollard   A low single post, or one of a series, usually stone, set to prevent motor vehicles from entering an area.

bolster   **1.** A short horizontal timber or steel member placed on top of a column to support and decrease the span of beams or girders. **2.** One of the rolls forming the sides of an Ionic capital, joining the volutes of the front and rear faces; a **baluster** or **pulvinus**. **3.** In centering an arch, a crosspiece which connects the ribs and supports the voussoirs. **4.** A **blocking chisel** for masonry work. **5.** A horizontal piece of wood or a timber that caps a column, pillar, or post to provide greater bearing area for supporting a load imposed from above; often highly decorative.

bolster, 4

bolster work   A form of rusticated masonry; courses of masonry which are curved or bow outward like the sides of a **cushion, 1**.

bolt   **1.** A metallic pin or rod having a head at one end and an external thread on the other for

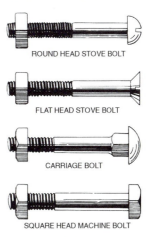

ROUND HEAD STOVE BOLT

FLAT HEAD STOVE BOLT

CARRIAGE BOLT

SQUARE HEAD MACHINE BOLT

bolts, 1

screwing up a nut; used for holding members or parts of members together. **2.** A short section cut from a tree trunk. **3.** A short log from which veneer is peeled.

bolt blank, screw blank A bolt having a fixed head, but no threads or nuts; intended for a subsequent threading operation.

bolted pressure switch In an electrical circuit, a type of knife-blade switch having jaws into which the knife blades fit under heavy pressure when the switch is closed; this pressure assures a low-resistance electrical connection.

boltel See **bowtell**.

bolt head The enlarged shape which is preformed on one end of a bolt to provide a bearing surface.

bolting mill In days before commercial flour was readily available, a small building in which flour was sifted.

bolt shooting See **stud shooting**.

bolt sleeve In concrete construction, a tube which surrounds a bolt in a concrete wall to prevent the concrete from sticking to the bolt.

BOM Abbr. for **bill of materials**.

bombé Swelling out; having a convex shape.

bona fide bid A bid submitted in good faith, complete and in prescribed form which meets the conditions of the bidding requirements and is properly signed by someone legally authorized to sign such bid.

bond **1.** A financial guarantee by a surety company that work will be completed as described in a contract. Also see **bid bond, completion bond, contract bond, labor and material payment bond, performance bond, surety bond**. **2.** See **roofing bond**. **3.** The adhesive strength that prevents delamination of the plies of a built-up roofing membrane. **4.** The union of materials by their adhesive or cohesive properties. **5.** See **bond timber**. **6.** An arrangement of masonry units (**headers** and **stretchers**) laid in a pattern that provides a brick wall with strength, stability, and in some cases, beauty, depending on the pattern. For descriptions of various masonry bonds, see **American bond, basketweave bond, Chinese bond, common bond, Dutch bond, English bond, English Cross bond, English garden wall bond, Flemish bond, Flem-**ish garden wall bond, flying bond, header bond, in-and-out bond, monk bond, raking stretcher bond, rat-trap bond, rowlock bond, running bond, silver-lock bond, stack bond, stretcher bond, Sussex bond, Yorkshire bond**. **7.** A low-resistance electric conductor which joins two adjacent metal parts or structures.

bond area The area of interface between two elements across which adhesion develops (or may develop), as between concrete and reinforcing steel.

bond-beam block A hollow concrete masonry unit with portions depressed to form a continuous channel in which reinforcing steel can be placed for embedment in grout. A **lintel block** sometimes is used as a bond-beam block.

bond blister A blister at the interface between the coating and core of metal clad products.

bond breaker **1.** A material used to prevent a sealant from bonding to the bottom of a joint. **2.** A material used to prevent adhesion of newly placed concrete and the substrate. **3.** A material to facilitate independent movement between two units that would otherwise behave monolithically.

bond coat **1.** A coat of bonding agent or plaster to provide a bond for succeeding coats of plaster. **2.** A coat of primer used as a sealer or to ensure adhesion of the paint to the surface.

bond course A course of headers or bondstones to bond the facing masonry to the backing masonry.

bonded member A structural member of **prestressed concrete** in which the tendons are bonded to the concrete either directly or by means of grouting.

bonded post tensioning In prestressed concrete, grouting the annular spaces around a **tendon** after it is stressed, thereby bonding the tendon to the concrete.

bonded tendon In prestressed concrete, a prestressing **tendon** which is bonded to the concrete either directly or by means of grouting.

bonder A masonry unit that bonds; also called a **bondstone**.

bonderized Said of a metal surface that has been phosphate-coated.

bond face That part of the joint face to which a **field-molded sealant** is bonded.

bond header   In masonry, a **bondstone** that extends the full thickness of the wall; also called a **throughstone**.

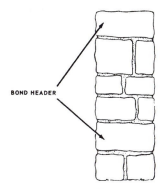

BOND HEADER

bond header

bonding   **1.** The connecting together of all the electrical grounds in a system to eliminate differences in ground potential between them. **2.** The interconnecting of **cable sheaths** and sheaths of adjacent conductors so there is no potential difference between the metal parts which are grounded. **3.** The connecting of a gas pipe system to an acceptable **grounding electrode** as specified by the National Electrical Code or other applicable code.

bonding agent   A chemical substance applied to a suitable substrate to create a bond between it and a succeeding layer, as between a subsurface and a terrazzo topping or between a surface and the plaster that is applied to it.

bonding brick   A brick that acts as a **bondstone.**

bonding capacity   **1.** An indication of a contractor's credit rating. **2.** The maximum amount of money a bonding company will extend in contract bonds to a building contractor.

bonding compound   See **dressing compound.**

bonding conductor   Same as **bonding jumper.**

bonding jumper   **1.** A conductor used to provide **bonding** between metal parts of a system. **2.** A reliable conductor which ensures that there is good electrical conductivity between the metal parts to which it is connected.

bonding layer   A layer of mortar, usually ⅛ to ½ in. (3 to 13 mm) thick, which is spread on a moist and prepared, hardened concrete surface prior to laying fresh concrete.

bonding stone   Same as **bondstone.**

bond length   Obsolete term for **development length.**

bond plaster, concrete bond plaster   A mill-mixed gypsum plaster containing a small percentage of lime; just before application it is mixed with water only and then applied to a maximum thickness of ¼ in. (0.6 cm) over prepared concrete surfaces. It serves as the bond between the concrete and succeeding coats of gypsum plaster.

bond prevention   **1.** In pretensioned construction, measures taken to prevent selected tendons from becoming bonded to the concrete for a predetermined distance from the ends of flexural members. **2.** Measures taken to prevent adhesion of concrete or mortar to surfaces against which it is placed.

bondstone, bonder   In stone masonry, a stone usually set with its longest dimension perpendicular to the wall face so as to tie the masonry wall to the wall backing. A very large bondstone may be set with its long dimension parallel to the wall face and still serve as a bonder if its width is sufficiently large to tie to the wall backing.

bond strength   **1.** The resistance to separation of mortar and concrete from reinforcing steel (or other materials) with which it is in contact. **2.** All forces that resist separation, such as adhesion, friction due to shrinkage, and longitudinal shear in the concrete engaged by the bar deformations. **3.** The applied unit load in tension, compression, flexure, peeling, impact, cleavage, or shear required to break an adhesive assembly, with failure occurring in or near the plane of the bond.

bond stress   **1.** The force of adhesion per unit area of contact between two bonded surfaces, such as between concrete and a steel **reinforcing bar.** **2.** The shear stress at the surface of a reinforcing bar which prevents relative movement between the bar and the surrounding concrete.

bond timber   A timber built into a brick or stone wall in a horizontal position, for the purpose of strengthening it or for tying it together during construction; serves as a bonding course and as a means for securing the battening and bracketing.

bone black   See **animal black.**

bone-dry wood   See **ovendry wood.**

bone house   See **ossuary**.

boning in (*Brit.*)   In surveying, locating and driving pegs in the ground so that their tops are in a line marking a desired gradient.

bonnet   **1.** A **chimney cap**. **2.** A frame of wire netting over a chimney to prevent the escape of sparks. **3.** Same as **bird screen**. **4.** A cap placed over a **pile** to prevent damage to the pile while it is being driven. **5.** The small roof over a bay window. **6.** A covering over an exterior door or window to provide shelter and/or a decorative element; also see **pent**.

bonnet hip tile, cone tile   A tile that resembles a woman's bonnet; used to cover the hip on a hip roof.

bonnet roof   A roof having a double slope on all four sides, the lower slope being less steep than the upper slope; often extends over an open-sided raised porch to provide excellent shade for the house and protection against rain. Especially found in **French Vernacular architecture**.

bonnet roof

bonus-and-penalty clause   A provision in the construction contract for payment of a bonus to the contractor for completing the **work, 1** prior to a stipulated date, and a charge against the contractor for failure to complete the work by such stipulated date.

bonus clause   A provision in the construction contract for additional payment to the contractor as a reward for completing the **work, 1** prior to a stipulated date.

book matching, herringbone matching   The assembling of wood veneers from the same **flitch** so that successive sheets are alternated face up and face down. In figured wood, side-by-side sheets show a symmetrical mirror image about the joints between adjoining sheets.

boom   **1.** A cantilevered or projecting structural member (such as a beam or spar) which is used

book matching

to support, hoist, or move a load. **2.** The projecting member at the front of a crane or derrick which is used for this purpose.

boom hoist   A hoist which has a spar attached to a mast; used to lift and move a load.

booster compressor   A **compressor** which discharges into the suction line of another compressor.

booster fan   An auxiliary fan which increases the air pressure in a system; used to provide additional capability to handle peak exhaust (or supply) loads in an air-conditioned space such as a theatre lobby; also used to supply air to furnaces.

booster heater   An auxiliary water heater which is installed in the hot-water piping system to provide additional heat in one part of the system.

booster pump   An auxiliary pump which is used in a piping system to increase or maintain the pressure in the system.

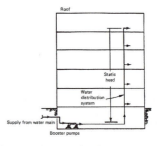

simplified diagram of a water distributor system employing a **booster pump**

booster transformer   An electric **transformer** used to raise the voltage of an electric circuit.

boot   The flange and metal casing around a pipe that passes through a roof.

booth   **1.** A fixed seating unit in a restaurant or bar; usually consists of a table between (or partially surrounded by) seats which have high backs. **2.** See **lighting booth**.

boot lintel   A **lintel** designed to carry a layer of facing brickwork.

boot scraper   A horizontal metal plate set in a small frame, once located near the front steps of most buildings; used to scrape dirt or mud from the bottoms of shoes or boots before entering the building; common before the advent of paved streets.

border   In a theatre, a strip of material which is stretched horizontally over the top of a stage, usually on rigging; used to mask the flies, lights, and other objects of scenery or overhead machinery.

borderlight   A horizontal strip of lights, hung parallel to the proscenium of a theatre; used to provide general stage illumination.

border stone   Same as **curbstone**.

bore   **1.** The inside diameter of a pipe, valve, or other fitting. **2.** The circular hole made by boring.

bored latch   A latch intended for installation in a circular hole in a door.

bored lock   A lock intended for installation in a circular hole in a door.

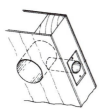

a door prepared for installation of a **bored lock**

bored pile   Same as **cast-in-place pile**.

bored well   A well constructed by boring a hole in the ground with an auger and installing a casing.

borehole   See **boring**.

boring, borehole   A hole drilled in the ground to obtain soil samples for evaluation and to obtain information about the strata.

borning room   In colonial New England houses, a small room (adjacent to the warm kitchen or **keeping room**) in which babies were born and sometimes kept during infancy.

boron-loaded concrete   High-density concrete having a boron-containing admixture or aggregate to act as a neutron attenuator. Also see **radiation-shielding concrete**.

borrow   Material taken from one location for use as **fill** elsewhere.

borrowed light   **1.** A frame in an interior partition which is glazed, thereby permitting light from one interior space to fall in another. **2.** The light which is transmitted through such glazing.

borrow pit   A bank or pit from which earth is taken for use as **fill** elsewhere.

bosket   A grove; a thicket or small grouping of trees in a garden, park, or the like.

bosquet   Same as **bosket**.

boss   **1.** A projecting, usually richly carved ornament placed at the intersection of ribs, groins, beams, etc., or at the termination of a molding. **2.** In masonry, a roughly shaped stone set to project for carving in place. **3.** To hammer sheet metal to conform to an irregular surface. **4.** A protuberance on a pipe, fitting, or part designed to add strength, to facilitate alignment during assembly, to provide for fastenings, etc.

boss, 1

bossage   In masonry, projecting, rough-finished stone left during construction for carving later in final decorative form.

bossing   The shaping of soft sheet metal, such as lead, so that it will conform to the surface to which it is applied; also called **dressing**.

bossing mallet A mallet used for striking a metal surface in **bossing**.

bossing stick A tool used in shaping sheet lead for a tank lining.

Boston hip, Boston ridge, shingle ridge finish A style of finishing a shingle, slate, or tile **hip roof**; the shingles are laid in two parallel rows which overlap at the hip; alternate courses overlap in opposite directions, providing a weatherproof joint.

Boston hip

bosun's chair A suspended seat for one person, supported by a rope, sometimes used instead of a scaffold for minor jobs; its height may be adjusted by a powered winch or block and tackle.

botanical garden A garden in which a variety of plants are collected and grown for scientific study and display; often includes greenhouses for tropical material.

bothie, bothy **1.** A small cottage or hut, especially in northern England, Scotland, or Ireland. **2.** A house for accommodating a number of workers for the same company, farmer, or employer.

bottle Old English term for **bowtell**.

bottle brick A hollow brick which is shaped so that it may be mechanically interconnected with similar units; may be laid with steel reinforcement.

bottle-nose curb, bottle-nose drip On a sheet-lead roof, an edge which is rounded to form a drip.

bottlery A room for the storage of bottled goods such as beer and ale.

bottom arm The arm mechanism which is attached to the bottom rail of a door, connecting it to the spindle of a **floor closer** or pivot.

bottom bolt A bolt at the bottom of a door; locks by slipping into a socket in the floor; may be held in the raised position by a catch.

bottom car clearance The clear vertical distance from the floor of an **elevator pit** to the lowest structural or mechanical part, equipment, or device installed beneath the **elevator car platform** (except for guide shoes or rollers, safety jaw assemblies, and platform aprons or guards) when the car rests on its fully compressed **buffers**.

bottom chord The lower longitudinal member of a truss.

bottom heave The upward movement of soil in the base of an especially large excavation.

bottom lateral bracing The lateral bracing in the plane of the bottom chords of a truss.

bottomless hole A hole which passes completely through a material.

bottom plate Same as **sole plate**.

bottom rail **1.** The lowest horizontal structural member of the frame of a door or window that interconnects its vertical members. **2.** The lower rail in a **balustrade**.

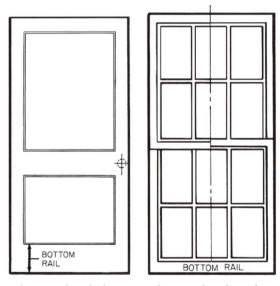

bottom rail: of a door   bottom rail: of a window

bottom register A register located close to the floor, along a wall.

bottom shore In a series of **raking shores** which support a wall, the member that is nearest the wall face.

bottom stone Same as **footing stone**.

boudoir See **chamber, 1**.

boulder A naturally rounded rock fragment larger than 10 in. (25 cm) in diameter; used for crude walls and foundations, generally in mortar.

boulder clay　See **till**.

boulder ditch　A **French drain**.

boulder wall　A wall constructed of boulders set in mortar.

boule　A **plain-sawn** log which has been reassembled in the original log form, but with spacers between adjacent slabs.

bouleuterion　**1.** In ancient Greece, a place of assembly, esp. for a public body. **2.** In modern Greece, a chamber for the sitting of a legislative body or the building in which such a chamber is situated.

boulevard　An important thoroughfare, often with a center divider planted with trees and grass, or similarly planted dividers between curbings and sidewalks.

boultine, boultel　See **bowtell**.

boundary　See **land boundary**.

boundary marker　A marker or inscribed stone that designates some type of boundary; for example, see **meridian stone**.

boundary survey　A mathematically closed diagram of the complete peripheral boundary of a site, reflecting dimensions, compass bearings and angles. It should bear a licensed land surveyor's signed certification, and may include a **metes and bounds** or other written description.

bouquet　The floral or foliated ornament forming the extreme top of a finial, knob, hip, or the like.

Bourdon gauge　A pressure gauge containing a curved metal tube which tends to straighten when subject to internal pressure; this movement is translated into readings on a graduated dial.

bousillage, bouzillage　A mixture of clay and Spanish moss or clay and grass; used as a plaster to fill the spaces between structural framing; particularly found in **French Vernacular architecture** of Louisiana of the early 1700s. A series of wood bars (*barreaux*), set between the posts, helped to hold the plaster in place. Bousillage, molded into bricks, was also used as **infilling** between posts; then called *briquette-entre-poteaux*. Also see **pierrotage.**

bouteillerie　See **buttery**.

boutel, boutell　See **bowtell**.

bow　**1.** The longitudinal curvature of a rod, bar, or piece of tubing or lumber. **2.** A flexible rod for laying large curves to any desired curvature. **3.** Old English term for **flying buttress**.

bow, 1

bow compass　A compass, one leg of which carries a pencil or pen; the legs are connected by a bow-shaped spring instead of a joint; used to draw arcs or circles.

bow divider　A **bow compass**, each leg of which terminates in a point; used to transfer measurements from one part of a drawing to another.

bowed roof　Same as **segmental roof**.

bower　**1.** A rustic dwelling, generally of small scale and picturesque nature. **2.** In a large medieval residence, the private chamber of the lady. **3.** A sheltered recess in a garden.

bower, 3

bow girder　A **girder** at a "corner" of a building having a curved façade.

bowl An open-top diffusing glass or plastic enclosure used to shield a light source from direct view and to redirect or scatter the light.

bowl capital A plain **capital** shaped like a bowl.

bowled floor A floor which slopes downward toward a central area, as toward a stage in a theater.

bowling green A carefully maintained, level piece of lawn, originally reserved for the game of bowls (bowling).

bow saw A saw having a narrow blade which is held taut in a bowed frame.

bow-shaped See **double-bellied**.

bowstring beam, bowstring girder, bowstring truss A **beam, girder**, or **truss** having one curved member in the shape of a bow (often circular or parabolic in shape) and a straight or cambered member which ties together the two ends of the bow.

bowstring roof, Belfast roof A roof supported by bowstring trusses.

bowtell, boltel, boultine, boutell, bowtel, edge roll 1. A plain, convex molding, usually three-quarters of a circle in section. 2. A **torus** or **round molding**. 3. The shaft of a clustered pillar. 4. A **roll molding**. 5. A **quarter round** or **ovolo**.

bow window, compass window A rounded **bay window**; projects from the face of a wall in a plan which is the segment of a circle.

box 1. A private seating area for spectators in an auditorium, usually located at the front or side of a mezzanine or balcony; may contain movable, rather than fixed, chairs. 2. An enclosure for mounting an electric device and its associated circuit conductors or for splicing, pulling in, or terminating conductors.

box-and-strip construction, box construction A relatively simple, economical wall construction once used in the United States for small houses and dependencies; has an exterior appearance similar to that of **board-and-batten construction**. The walls are constructed of closely-spaced, wide, upright boards, approximately 1 inch (2.5 cm) thick; the cracks between the boards are covered with vertical battens only on the exterior surface of the boards. The **sillplates** are secured on a foundation consisting of flat stones.

box beam, box girder A hollow beam, usually rectangular in section; if fabricated of steel, the sides are steel plates welded together, or they may be riveted together by steel angles at the corners.

box bolt A sliding bolt which is rectangular in cross section; attached to a door at the edge, it slides into a receptacle to secure the door.

box casing The inner lining of the **cased frame** of a window.

box chisel A chisel, one end of which is notched; used to pry open boxes that are nailed.

box column A hollow, built-up column, constructed of wood, usually rectangular or square in section.

box column

box culvert A culvert, usually of reinforced concrete, which is rectangular in cross section.

box dam Same as **cofferdam**.

box dovetail See **common dovetail**.

box drain An underground drain which is rectangular in cross section; usually constructed of concrete or brick.

boxed cornice, box cornice, closed cornice A hollow cornice, built up of boards, moldings, shingles, etc., so that the lower ends of

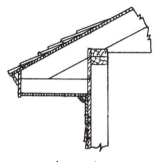

box cornice

the rafters are not visible. Also called a closed cornice.

boxed eaves That part of a roof that projects beyond the exterior wall (i.e., the **eaves**), which is enclosed by boards and/or moldings so that the rafters are not visible.

boxed frame See **cased frame**.

boxed gutter Same as **box gutter**.

boxed heart, boxed pith A timber sawn so that the heart of the log falls within its faces.

boxed mullion A hollow mullion which houses sash counterweights in a window frame; built up from boards so as to provide a solid appearance.

boxed pith A piece of lumber cut so as to enclose the soft central core (i.e., the **pith**) within the four faces of the piece.

boxed shutter Same as **boxing shutter**.

boxed stair Same as **box stair**.

boxed stringer Same as **close string**.

box frame 1. A structural frame composed of cells which are side by side and/or in vertical tiers; the cross-walls act as bearing walls, carrying the loads to the foundation; also called **cellular framing** or **cross-wall construction**. 2. A structural frame having floors and walls consisting of monolithic reinforced-concrete slabs. 3. A **cased frame**.

box garden A garden divided into sections by hedges of boxwood.

box girder See **box beam**.

box gutter A rectangularly shaped wood **gutter** that is set into and partially below the lower edge of a roof; usually lined with sheet lead or asphalt.

box-head window A window constructed so that the sashes can slide vertically up into the head (or above it) to provide maximum opening for ventilation.

box house A house having gables on its end walls; usually two or three rooms wide and two rooms deep.

boxing 1. A box-like enclosure or recess at the side of a window frame which receives a **boxing shutter** when it is folded. 2. A **cased frame**. 3. The mixing of paint by pouring it from one can to another. 4. Continuing a **fillet weld** around a

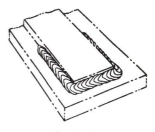

boxing, 4

corner of a member as an extension of the principal weld.

boxing shutter, folding shutter A window shutter which can be folded into the **boxing** or recess at the side.

box lewis Assembly of metal components, some or all tapered upward, inserted into a downward-flaring hole (**lewis hole**) cut into the tops of columns or other heavy masonry units for hoisting.

box lock A metal door lock commonly encased in a flat rectangular box, often fabricated of brass; mounted on the interior surface of a door.

box nail A nail similar to a **common nail** but thinner; has a long shank which may be smooth or barbed.

box office A room or booth with one or more windows facing a theatre lobby or public area; used for sale of tickets.

box out To form an opening or pocket in concrete by means of a box-like form.

box pew A church pew screened or enclosed by a high back and sides.

box pile A pile which is fabricated from two deep-arch **sheet piles**, steel channels or the like, and welded along their lines of contact; the enclosed space may be filled with concrete or left open.

box scarf A **scarf joint** used between lengths of wooden gutter; the reduced end of one length is fitted into the recessed end of the next, producing a flush joint which is secured by paint and screws.

box section Said of a concrete pipe having a rectangular cross section.

box sill A type of **sill, 1** used in frame construction; a header joist, nailed to the ends of the floor joists, rests on the sill. (*See illustration p. 118.*)

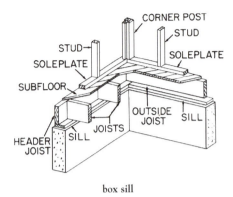

box sill

box stair, closed stair An interior staircase constructed with a **close string** on both sides, often enclosed by walls or partitions with door openings at various floor levels.

box stall, loose-box In barns or stables, an individual compartment in which an animal may move about freely.

box staple On a doorpost, a socket which receives the end of a lock bolt which secures the door.

box stool A stool with a compartment beneath a hinged lid or seat.

box stoop A high **stoop** making a quarter turn, reached by a flight of stairs along a building front.

box strike plate, box strike A metal plate on a doorframe into which the bolt of a door lock projects, and which provides a complete housing that protects the bolt opening from tampering.

box stringer Same as a **close string**.

box up To encase with boards, as in the nailing of sheathing boards over studs.

boxwinder A staircase whose entrance is concealed behind a door next to a fireplace; sometimes architecturally balanced by a pantry door on the opposite side of the fireplace; often found in elegant homes in the 18th and 19th centuries.

boxwood A fine-grained, very hard, dense wood, white to light yellow in color; esp. used for turned work and inlay.

box wrench A wrench, usually double-ended, that has a closed socket which fits over the head of a bolt or a nut.

BP **1.** On drawings, abbr. for **blueprint**. **2.** On drawings, abbr. for **baseplate**. **3.** On drawings, abbr. for **bearing pile**.

BPG Abbr. for "beveled plate glass."

BR On drawings, abbr. for **bedroom**.

bracciale A projecting metal bracket, having a socket and ring for holding a flagstaff, torch, or the like; esp. used on Renaissance palaces in Florence and Siena.

brace **1.** A metal or wood member which is used to stiffen or support a structure; a strut which supports or fixes another member in position or a tie used for the same purpose. **2.** An **angle brace**. **3.** A tool having a handle, crank, and chuck; used for holding a bit or auger and rotating it to drill a hole by hand; also called a **bit stock**. **4.** A **raker, 2**.

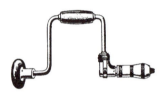

brace, 3

brace block A block of wood used to lock in place adjacent layers of a built-up wood beam.

braced Strengthened or well interlaced and linked together by **bracing**.

braced arch An openwork truss in the form of an arch.

braced door See **framed door**.

braced excavation An **excavation** whose perimeter is retained by **sheeting**.

braced frame, braced framing, full frame **1.** The frame of a building in which the resistance to lateral forces or to frame instability is provided by diagonal bracing, K-bracing, or other type of bracing. **2.** Heavy, braced wood framing for a structure which uses **girts** that are mortised into solid posts; the posts are full frame height, with one-story-high studs between, usually diagonally braced.

brace molding The molding formed by joining two ogees with the convex ends together and in section resembling the brace used as a symbol in printing. Also see **keel molding**.

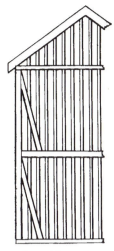

braced frame, 1

brace piece　A **mantelpiece**.

brace pile　See **batter pile**.

brace table, brace scale, brace measure
A table indicating the length of hypotenuses for right isosceles triangles with legs of various lengths; used by carpenters in cutting wood braces to length.

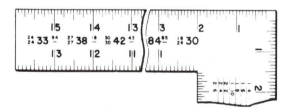

brace table:　on a steel square

bracing　**1.** Structural elements installed to provide restraint or support (or both) to other members, so that the complete assembly forms a stable structure; may consist of knee braces, cables, rods, struts, ties, shores, diaphragms, rigid frames, etc., singly or in combination. **2.** Collectively, the braces so used.

brack　See **cull**.

bracket　**1.** Any overhanging member projecting from a wall or other body to support a weight (such as a cornice) acting outside the wall. **2.** A **knee brace** which connects a post or **batter brace** to an overhead strut.

bracket, 1

3. A projecting electrical wall fitting. **4.** A short board attached to the carrying member on the underside of a stair supporting the tread. **5.** A decorative detail attached to the spring of a stair under the overhanging edge of the treads. Also see **eaves bracket, stair bracket, step bracket, wall bracket**.

bracket baluster　A metal baluster whose base is bent at right angles and built into the string of a masonry stair.

bracket capital　**1.** A capital extended by brackets, lessening the clear span between posts, often seen in Near Eastern, Muslim, Indian, and some Spanish architecture. **2.** Same as **bolster, 1**.

bracketed cornice　A deep cornice supported by a series of decorative brackets, often in pairs.

bracketed eaves　See **eaves bracket**.

cottage with **bracketed eaves**

bracketed hood　A projecting surface over a window or door that is supported by brackets; provides some shelter or serves as ornamentation. (*See illustration p. 120.*)

bracketed stair　A flight of open string stairs; one with decorative brackets on the exposed outer string and under the return nosing of treads. (*See illustration p. 120.*)

bracketed hood   above a door

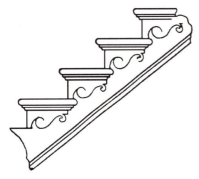

bracketed stair

bracketed string An open string having, secured to its face, bracket-shaped pieces which appear to support the overlapping treads.

Bracketed style A term occasionally used for the **Italianate style**.

bracketing **1.** Any system of brackets. **2.** An arrangement of wooden brackets employed as a skeleton support to plasterwork, moldings, or other plaster ornamental details.

bracket pile One of a series of **piles** which are driven into the ground adjacent to a foundation to support it; brackets, which are welded to the piles, and which extend under the foundation, transfer the structural load from the foundation to the piles.

bracket saw A handsaw used for cutting curved shapes.

bracket scaffold, bracket staging A scaffold which is supported by metal brackets which are attached to the building.

bracket valve A **stop valve** whose body incorporates a supporting bracket for piping which it controls.

brad **1.** A small finishing nail, usually of the same thickness throughout, with a head that is almost flush with the sides or a head that projects slightly to one side. **2.** A tapering, square-bodied finishing nail with a countersunk head.

brad, 1

brad awl A small awl used to make starter holes for brads or screws.

brad punch, brad set A **nail set** for small finishing nails or brads.

brad pusher A tool used to hold and insert a brad into the surface of wood in an inaccessible location.

brad set, brad setter See **brad punch**.

bragger A **corbel**.

braided wire An electrical conductor which is composed of many fine wires braided or twisted together.

braid pattern Same as **guilloche**.

brake horse power (bhp) The useful mechanical power supplied by an engine as determined by a friction brake or an absorption dynamometer that is applied to the shaft or flywheel of the engine.

branch In plumbing, a pipe which originates in or discharges into a main, submain, riser, or stack.

branch cell A plumbing fitting in a line which is at an angle to the main pipeline, usually at a right angle.

branch circuit The portion of an electric wiring system that extends beyond the final overcurrent device (such as a fuse) protecting the circuit.

branch conductor In a lightning protection system, a conductor that branches off at an angle from a continuous run of the conductor.

branch drain A drain pipe connecting the soil line or plumbing fixtures in a building to the main line.

branch duct   An air duct which branches from a main duct; at this point the main duct is reduced in cross-sectional area.

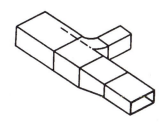

branch duct

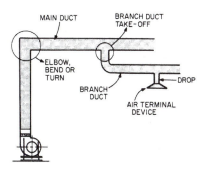

branch duct: installation

branch fitting   A fitting used to connect one or more branch pipes to a main pipe.

branch interval   A length of soil stack or waste stack which is usually one story high, but not less than 8 ft (2.4 m), within which the horizontal branches from one story of a building are connected to a stack.

branch joint   **1.** A joint taken off a main pipeline. **2.** The **wiped joint** used where one pipe branches from another.

branch knot   A knot in wood formed as a result of two or more branches originating from the same point.

branch line   **1.** A water supply line which connects one or more fixtures with the main supply, with a riser, or with another branch. **2.** A pipe in which fire sprinklers (i.e., sprinkler heads) are placed.

branch pipe   A length of pipe which has one or more branches.

branch rib   Same as **lierne rib**.

branch sewer   A sewer that receives sewage from a relatively small area.

branch tracery   A form of Gothic tracery in Germany in late 15th and early 16th cent.; made to imitate rustic work with boughs and knots.

branch vent   **1.** A vent connecting one or more individual vents with a **vent stack** or **stack vent**. **2.** A vent pipe to which are connected two or more pipes that vent plumbing fixtures.

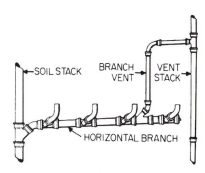

branch vent, 1

brander   To apply furring.

brandering   See **cross-furring**.

brandishing   Same as **brattishing**.

brandrith   A fence or rail around the opening of a well.

brashy, short-grained   Descriptive of weak, brittle wood that has little resistance to shock or bending and usually breaks quite abruptly.

brass   **1.** Any copper alloy having zinc as the principal alloying element, but often with small quantities of other elements. **2.** A plate of brass with memorial inscription and sometimes an effigy engraved on it, set into a church floor to mark a tomb. (*See illustration p. 122.*)

brass pipe   Pipe manufactured from an alloy containing 85 percent copper and 15 percent zinc. The advantages and disadvantages of brass pipe are similar to those for copper tubing, except that brass pipe can be used in a drain pipe under pressure and that the joints between brass pipes can be screwed or soldered.

brattice, bretesse, bretêche   In medieval fortifications, a tower or bay of timber construction. (*See illustration p. 122.*)

brass, 2

brattice

brattishing, brandishing, bretisement A decorative cresting at the top of a Gothic screen, panel, parapet, or cornice, generally in the form of openwork of a stylized floral design.

braze To join two pieces of metal by a hard, nonferrous filler metal, usually in rod or wire form, having a melting temperature above 800°F (427°C).

brazed joint A gastight and watertight metal-pipe joint formed by **brazing**; often used in copper piping systems.

brazier A receptacle containing burning coal or coke; sometimes used to dry out a building.

Brazilian rosewood, palisander A variegated, hard, heavy wood having shades of brown and violet or red with black streaks; used for turned articles and decorative paneling.

brazing solder Same as **hard solder**.

brc Abbr. for **brace**.

brcg Abbr. for **bracing**.

bread room In medieval times, a room fitted with shelves for loaves of bread and biscuits, and bins for flour and confectionery; was part of the **buttery**.

break A change in direction of a plane; usually in reference to a wall.

breakaway wall A wall that is not part of the structural support of a building to which it is attached; deliberately intended (through its design and construction) to collapse under specific lateral loading forces without causing damage to the elevated portion of the building or to the supporting foundation system.

breakdown voltage The voltage at which an **electrical insulation** ruptures, thereby destroying its insulating value and permitting current flow.

breaker A rock-crushing machine in which small particles are produced by impact or by fracture between movable jaws.

breaker ball, headache ball A heavy, rounded metal weight which is swung from a crane line; used to demolish masonry or concrete structures.

breakfast nook A nook where light meals are taken; usually has a built-in table and seating.

break-glass call-point A British term for a **fire alarm box**.

break-in In bricklaying, a cutout in a brick wall, to form an aperture for the insertion of a timber.

breaking down, conversion The process of sawing logs into boards.

breaking ground Initial excavation work, indicating the start of construction.

breaking joints Any arrangement of structural units, esp. masonry units, such that the vertical joints between adjacent units do not follow a vertical line, but are staggered.

breaking load, failure load, fracture load, ultimate load The load which, if placed upon a structure or test piece, is just great enough to break it.

breaking radius The minimum radius of curvature that a piece of wood (or plywood) can be bent without breaking.

break-out The transfer of acoustic energy from the interior of an **HVAC** duct, through the duct walls, to the space surrounding the duct.

breast **1.** A projecting part of a wall, as at a chimney. **2.** That portion of a wall between the floor and a window above. **3.** The underside of a handrail, beam, rafter, or the like.

breast beam See **breastsummer**.

breast board One of a number of boards used to retain the face of an excavation.

breast drill A hand-operated drill having a piece against which the chest is braced to provide additional force.

breast drill

breast lining The interior wooden paneling between a windowsill and the baseboard below.

breast molding **1.** The molding on a window sill or on the breast of a wall. **2.** Paneling beneath a window.

breastsummer, breast beam, bressummer, brestsummer A horizontal beam which spans a wide opening (a **lintel**) in an external wall; a **summer, 3.**

breast timber Same as **wale**.

breast wall, face wall **1.** A **retaining wall**. **2.** A parapet which is breast high.

breastwork **1.** Masonry work for a chimney breast. **2.** The parapet of a building. **3.** A defensive wall, hastily constructed, about breast high.

breather-type asphalt felt An underlayment sheet material, saturated with asphalt, which permits the transmission of water vapor; often used as underlayment for asbestos-cement shingles.

breccia Any stone composed of angular fragments embedded and consolidated in a finer ground. Numerous marbles owe their distinctive appearance to brecciation.

breech fitting See **breeching fitting**.

breeching **1.** The duct or pipe connecting the exhaust-gas discharge from a boiler furnace, or other fuel-burning equipment, to a stack. **2.** A **breeching fitting**.

breeching fitting, breech fitting, breeching A Y-shaped symmetrical pipe fitting in which the flow in two parallel pipes is united in one pipe.

breeze See **pan breeze**.

breeze block A concrete masonry unit using **pan breeze** as aggregate.

breeze brick Brick made from **pan breeze** and portland cement; often built into ordinary brickwork because of its good nail-holding capability.

breezeway A covered passageway, open to the outdoors, connecting two cabins, two parts of a house, or between a house and a garage; sometimes serves as an outdoor sitting area; also called a dogtrot.

bressummer See **breastsummer**.

brestsummer See **breastsummer**.

bretessé See **brattice**.

bretisement Same as **brattishing**.

BRG On drawings, abbr. for **bearing**.

brick A solid masonry unit, usually of clay, molded into a rectangular shape while plastic, and then treated in a kiln at an elevated temperature

brick anchor

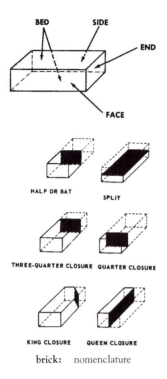

brick: nomenclature

to harden it, so as to give it mechanical strength and to provide it with resistance to moisture; after being removed from the kiln, the brick is said to be *burnt, hard-burnt, kiln-burnt, fired,* or *hard-fired.* Bricks laid lengthwise in a wall are called **stretchers**; bricks laid crosswise to a wall are called **headers**. Bricks differ in color, ranging from dark red to rose and salmon, and from pink to blue-black and purple, depending on the type of clay and on the temperature of the kiln in which they were burnt. Various types of patterns common in laying bricks are described under **bond**. The current American brick is typically about 8 inches (20.3 cm) long, 3¾ inches (8.26 cm) wide, and 2¼ inches (5.7 cm) thick; other countries tend to produce bricks with their own standard dimensions. For specific types of brick, see **adobe quemado, air brick, angle brick, arch brick, axed brick, brindled brick, building brick, bull stretcher, burnt brick, cant brick, capping brick, closer, common brick, compass brick, concrete brick, coping brick, cownose brick, dogleg brick, dog-tooth course, Dutch brick, engineered brick, engineering brick, firebrick, fired brick, flooring brick, gauged brick, glass brick, glazed brick, hard-burnt brick, hollow brick, kiln-fired brick, molded brick, mortar, mud**

brick, pug-mill brick, pressed brick, radius brick, rough-axed brick, rubbed brick, rustic brick, sailor, salmon brick, sand-faced brick, sand-lime brick, semiengineering brick, soft brick, soldier, solid brick, standard brick, stock brick, twin brick, unburnt brick, vitrified brick, wire-cut brick. See **bond** for a description of brickwork patterns. Also see **adobe** for a description of sun-dried brick.

brick anchor   A device made of deformed metal stripping, designed to be embedded in the structural concrete of a building to support brick or other veneer facing material.

brick and brick   A method of laying brick so that units touch each other; mortar is used only to fill surface irregularities.

brick-and-half wall   A brick wall whose thickness equals one **header** plus one **stretcher**.

brick-and-stud work   See **brick nogging**.

brick ax   Same as **brick hammer**.

brickbat   A **bat, 1**.

brick beam   A lintel formed by several courses of bricks and held together by iron straps.

brick bond   Same as **bond, 6**.

brick cement   A waterproof cement used in masonry work.

brick core   The rough brickwork that fills the space between a timber lintel and soffit of a **discharging arch**.

brick earth   A loamy impure clay used for brickmaking.

brick face   That surface of a brick which is intended for use as the exposed surface of a masonry structure.

brick facing   See **brick veneer**.

brick filling   In **half-timbered construction**, brick laid between the heavy structural timbers to provide thermal insulation, fire resistance, and increased structural rigidity.

brick gauge   A standard height of brick courses, e.g., four courses in a height of 12 in. (30 cm).

brick hammer, bricklayer's hammer   A steel tool, one end of which has a flat square surface used as a hammer, for breaking bricks, driving nails, etc.; the other end forms a chisel peen used for dressing bricks.

bricking up   Filling up door or window openings with brick.

brick hammer

bricklayer's hammer See **brick hammer**.

bricklayer's square scaffold A scaffold composed of framed wood squares which support a platform; limited to light and medium duty.

bricklaying Laying brick and filling all joints, as well as cleaning, grouting and pointing, and waterproofing.

brick masonry See **brickwork**.

brick molding A wood molding used to cover the gap between a door or window frame and the masonry reveal into which the frame is set.

brick nogging, brick-and-stud work Brickwork laid in the spaces between timbers in a wood-frame wall; also see **nogging**.

brick on bed A brick in an ordinary brick wall, all courses of which are laid on the largest side.

brick on edge A brick laid on its narrow edge.

brick oven See **bake oven**.

brick seat A ledge on a footing or wall which supports a course of masonry.

brick set A **bolster** for cutting brick.

brick slip A solid tile, either cut from one face of a brick or specifically manufactured to similar dimensions; usually about 1 in. (2.5 cm) thick. Used to simulate brickwork construction either for prefabrication or in facing in situ concrete members.

brick tile A tile with one of its faces molded so that it appears to be the face or end of a brick.

brick trimmer A brick arch abutting against the wood trimming joist in front of a fireplace, used to support the hearth; a trimmer arch of brick.

brick trowel A **trowel** having a flat, triangle-shaped steel blade in an offset handle used to

brick trowel

pick up and spread mortar. The narrow end of the blade is called the "point"; the wide end, the "heel."

brick tumbling See **tumbling course**.

brick veneer, brick facing A facing of brick laid against the front side of an exterior wall but not bonded to it; provides a decorative, durable wall surface. Such bricks typically are laid lengthwise, so this type of construction is relatively thin, economical, and easy to lay.

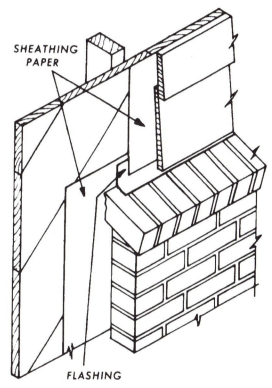

SHEATHING PAPER

FLASHING

brick veneer

brickwork, brick masonry Masonry of brick and mortar. Also see **skintled brickwork, reinforced-grouted brick masonry, rendered brickwork**.

brickwork column An isolated vertical load-bearing member whose width is not more than four times its thickness.

brickwork cube A cube of brickwork, 9 in., (22.86 cm) on each side, used widely for quality control tests in Great Britain for load-bearing brickwork constructions.

brickwork movement joint   A joint designed to permit relative movement between a brick wall and its adjacent structure without impairing the functional integrity of the structure.

bridal cable   An **anchor cable** which is perpendicular to the line of pull.

bridal hitch   The connection between a bridle cable and a **pulley block** or **sheave block**.

bridge   **1.** A structure that spans a depression or provides a passage between two points which are at a height above the ground affording a passage for pedestrians, vehicles, etc. **2.** At a demolition or construction site, a scaffold built over the adjacent sidewalk to protect pedestrians and motor vehicles from falling material or debris. **3.** In the backstage of a theatre, a platform or gallery (of fixed or adjustable height), over or alongside the stage; used by scene painters (see **paint bridge**), lighting operators (see **light bridge**), and stagehands.

bridgeboard   A notched board which supports the treads and risers of wooden stairs; an open or cut stringer.

bridge crane   A traveling overhead hoisting machine which spans fixed side rails that are part of a building structure or are erected to support the crane; the hoisting unit also may travel laterally between the rails; used to handle materials in such a location as a machine shop or fabricating plant.

bridged floor   A floor using **common joists** for support.

bridged gutter   A gutter formed by boards which are supported on a beam and are covered with lead sheeting or other suitable material.

bridge joint   In carpentry, see **bridle joint, 1.**

bridge-over   Said of a member (such as a joist) which is laid across parallel lines of support.

bridge stone   A flat stone providing passage over a gutter or areaway.

bridgewall   A low firebrick separating wall in a furnace.

bridging   A brace, or a system of braces, placed between joists (or the like) to stiffen them, to hold them in place, and to help distribute the load.

bridging floor   A floor supported by **common joists**, without girders.

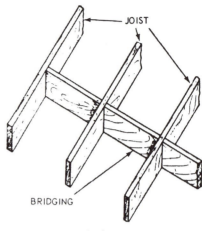

bridging

bridging joist   Same as **common joist**.

bridging piece   A wooden member fastened between or across floor joists to stiffen them or to carry a partition.

bridle iron   Same as **hanger, 2.**

bridle joint   In carpentry: **1.** A joint formed by two timbers, of which one is hollowed out to receive the end of the other (with recessed sides). **2.** A joint in which two tongues project from the sides of the tenoned member; these tongues fit into corresponding slots in the mortised member.

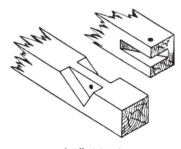

bridle joint, 1

bridle path, riding trail   A path, cleared and compacted, reserved for riding horses and barred to vehicles.

Briggs standard   See **American standard pipe threads**.

bright   Descriptive of freshly cut lumber or veneer which is not discolored.

bright dip   A dip used to give a bright surface to brasses; often a mixture of sulfuric acid, nitric acid, hydrochloric acid, and water.

bright glaze   A colorless or colored ceramic glaze having high gloss.

brightness   That attribute of visual perception in accordance with which a surface appears to emit more light or less light. Now called **luminance**.

brightness meter   A common expression for a **luminance meter**.

brilliance   The clarity, strength, and brightness of a color or varnish.

brindled brick   Brick having a brown mottled surface; sometimes used as facing brick.

brine   In a refrigeration system, any liquid used as a heat transfer medium which remains as a liquid and which has either a flashpoint above 150°F (66°C) or no flashpoint; usually a water solution of inorganic salts.

Brinell hardness   A measure of resistance of a material to indentation; obtained by use of a machine which presses a standard hard steel or carbide ball into the material, under standard loading conditions; expressed by the **Brinell hardness number**—the higher the number, the harder the material.

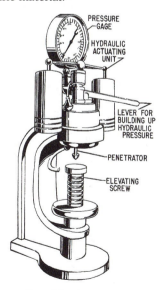

Brinell hardness tester

Brinell hardness number   A measure of Brinell hardness; obtained by dividing the load

expressed in kilograms (applied to a ball, usually 10 mm in diameter), by the area of indentation, expressed in square millimeters.

briquette, briquet   A molded specimen of mortar with enlarged extremities and reduced center having a cross section of definite area, used for the measurement of tensile strength of mortar.

briquette-entre-poteaux   In **French Vernacular architecture** of Louisiana, a relatively inexpensive, porous brick that was once used to fill the spaces between upright posts and diagonal braces in a home of **timber-framed construction**; often found in **poteaux-en-terre houses**; usually the entire brick-filled exterior surface was finished with a coat of lime plaster to protect the surface; then often covered with clapboard. Many two-story town houses and houses of well-to-do planters had basement walls of brick and upper walls of briquette-entre-poteaux. Also see **bousillage**.

brisance   The crushing or shattering effect of a high explosive.

brise-soleil   A fixed or movable device, such as fins or louvers, designed to block the direct entrance of sun rays into a building.

bristle brush   A brush made with animal hair (usually from hogs) or with synthetic fibers.

Bristol glaze   A raw ceramic glaze containing zinc oxide, often used in terra-cotta.

British Board of Agrément   An independent British organization, which operates under government sanction, for testing, assessing, and issuing certificates concerning the performance of new building materials (or old materials used in new ways), components, products, and/or building systems.

British Standard, British Standard specification   A specification of grades, qualities, sizes, etc., of materials, components, etc., published by the **British Standards Institution**.

British Standards Institution   A national organization (corresponding to the **American National Standards Institute** and the **American Society for Testing Materials**) which establishes and publishes standard specifications.

British thermal unit   The amount of heat required to raise the temperature of 1 pound of water by 1 degree Fahrenheit. *Abbr.* Btu.

brittle **1.** Descriptive of a material which fractures under low stress without appreciable deformation. **2.** Descriptive of a paint film unable to withstand stretching or scratching without breaking or becoming otherwise deformed.

brittle fracture Said of a fracture that takes place with no prior ductile deformation.

brittleheart Decayed or brittle wood at the center of a log.

BRK On drawings, abbr. for **brick**.

BRKT On drawings, abbr. for **bracket**.

brl Abbr. for **barrel**.

broach **1.** In quarrying, to free stone blocks from the ledge by cutting out the webbing between holes drilled close together in a row. **2.** To finish a stone surface with broad diagonal parallel grooves cut by a pointed chisel. **3.** A half pyramid above the corners of a square tower to provide a transition to an octagonal spire. **4.** A spire sometimes springing from a tower without an intermediate parapet. **5.** Any pointed ornamental structure.

broached spire Same as **broach, 1**.

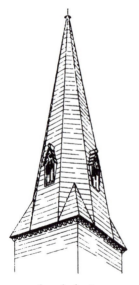

broached spire

broached work See **broach, 2**.

broach post Same as **king post**.

broach stop See **chamfer**.

broadax An ax having a large, broad blade; used for the roughdressing of timber.

broad glass Same as **cylinder glass**.

broad knife, stripping knife A knife with a square-edged, wedge-shaped blade for removing paint or wallpaper; similar to a putty knife but with a wider blade.

broadloom Seamless carpet of any weave, woven on a wide loom, usually 6 to 18 ft (1.8 to 5.5 m) wide.

broad stone Same as **ashlar**.

broad tool A wide steel chisel used to finish-dress stone.

broad tooled See **batted work**.

brob A wedge-shaped spike used to secure the end of a timber which butts against the side of another.

broken arch A form of segmental arch in which the center of the arch is omitted and is replaced by a decorative feature; usually applied to a wall above the entablature over a door or window.

broken ashlar See **random work, 2**.

broken-color work See **antiquing**.

broken edge An edge of a metal sheet containing cracks, splits, or tears.

broken-flight stair Same as **dogleg stair**.

broken gable A vertical surface at the end of a building having a **broken-pitch roof**; extends from the level of the cornice to the ridge of the roof. It is not triangularly shaped, as in the case of a roof having a single pitch on each side of the ridge.

broken joints Vertical masonry joints which are staggered to provide better bond and added structural strength, no unit being directly above another.

broken-joint tile A curved roof tile which overlaps only the tile in the course immediately below.

broken pediment **1.** A **pediment** whose sloping or curving sides terminate before reaching the pediment's highest point, resulting in an opening that is often filled with an urn, cartouche, or other ornament; sometimes called an open pediment or broken-apex pediment. **2.** A **pediment** with sloping or curving sides whose base is broken in the middle; also called a broken-base pediment.

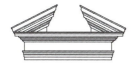
broken pediment

broken-pitch roof   A roof having more than one pitch on each side of a central ridge.

broken rangework   Stone masonry laid in horizontal courses of different heights, any one course of which may be broken (at intervals) into two or more courses.

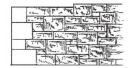
broken rangework

broken-scroll pediment   Same as **swan's-neck pediment**.

broken-stripe veneer   A variation of **ribbon-stripe veneer** in which the stripes are intermittent; produced by interwoven grain which is quarter-cut.

broken white   A toned-down white paint, usually cream-colored.

bronteum   In ancient Greek and Roman theatres, a device for producing the noise of thunder, generated by the impact of stones against the inside of a heavy vase designed for this purpose.

bronze   **1.** An alloy of copper and tin. **2.** Any alloy, bronze in color, having a substantial admixture of copper to modify the properties of the principal element, as aluminum bronze, magnesium bronze, etc.

bronzing   **1.** A form of **chalking** on a paint film, caused by weathering; appears varicolored when viewed at different angles. **2.** The application of a coating of metal bronze powder.

broom   **1.** To press a layer of roofing material against bitumen which has just been applied, in order to achieve proper and complete bond between the roofing plies. **2.** To brush the scratch coat of plaster with a broom to improve the mechanical adhesion of the brown coat, thus producing a **broom finish**. **3.** To spread the head of a timber pile by impact.

broom finish   **1.** The surface texture obtained by stroking a broom over freshly spread concrete or plaster. **2.** See **broom, 2**.

brooming   See **broom**.

brotch   A thin piece of a tree branch which is bent in a U-shape; used for fastening thatch on roofs; also called a **buckle** or **spar**.

Brown and Sharpe gauge   See **American wire gauge**.

brown coat, floating coat   The coat of roughly finished plaster beneath the finish coat; in three-coat work, the second coat of plaster, applied over a scratch coat and covered by the finish coat; in two-coat work, the base-coat plaster applied over lath or masonry; may contain a greater proportion of aggregate than the **scratch coat**.

brown-glazed brick   See **salt-glazed brick**.

browning   Same as **brown coat**.

brownmillerite   A mineral compound occurring in portland cement and high-alumina cement; consists of an oxide of calcium, aluminum, and iron.

brownout   **1.** To complete the application of a base-coat plaster. **2.** The setting of base-coat plaster, which darkens, or browns, as it sets. **3.** The dimming of lights as a consequence of a reduction of voltage furnished to a section of a city (or an entire city) by the electrical utility.

brown rot   A fungus that destroys wood cellulose, leaving a brown powdery residue behind.

brown stain   A chocolate brown stain produced by fungus in the **sapwood** of some pine trees.

brownstone   **1.** A dark brown or reddish brown arkosic sandstone, quarried and used extensively for building in the eastern U.S.A. during the middle and late nineteenth cent. **2.** A dwelling faced with brownstone, often a **row house**.

browpiece   A beam over a door; a **breastsummer**.

brow post   Same as **crossbeam**.

browsing room   A section of a library reserved for users to examine and casually read a collection of books, magazines, or documents.

BRS   On drawings, abbr. for **brass**.

Br Std   Abbr. for **British Standard**.

Brunswick black   A type of **bituminous paint**.

Brunswick blue   See **Prussian blue**.

Brunswick green, lead chrome green A light green powder; a pigment consisting of lead chromate and iron blue pigments.

brush **1.** An implement made of natural or artificial bristles which are attached to a handle or back; used for cleaning or painting a surface. **2.** An electric conductor (such as a strip of copper or a carbon rod) which provides electrical contact between a rotating and stationary element in a current motor or generator.

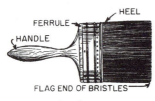

brush, 1

brushability The property of a paint or varnish which enables it to be applied smoothly by brushing.

brushed surface Said of a concrete surface that has been stroked with a stiff brush when the concrete is freshly placed or slightly hardened.

brush finish, brushed finish A finish produced by a rotating wire brush.

brush graining An imitation effect of wood grain; produced by drawing a clean dry brush through a dark liquid stain, applied over a dry, light base coat.

brush mark A small ridge or valley produced in a paint film by the combing action of the bristles of a brush.

brushout The application of paint on a small surface for testing.

brush rake An attachment with heavy-duty tines, which is fixed to the front of a tractor or other prime mover; used in land clearing to gather and pile debris.

Brussels carpet **1.** A carpet made of several colors of worsted yarn, fixed in backing of strong linen thread; the pile forms a pattern of uncut loops. **2.** An inexpensive, single-colored substitute for the above.

Brutalism, New Brutalism A style of modern architecture, primarily in the 1960s, emphasizing heavy, monumental, stark concrete forms and raw surfaces; may show patterns of the rough wood formwork used in casting the concrete (*béton brut*). Buildings in this style are often suggestive of massive sculptures.

BRZ On drawings, abbr. for **bronze**.

BRZG On drawings, abbr. for "brazing."

BS **1.** Abbr. for "**British Standard**" published by the **British Standards Institution**; each standard is designated by the letters BS followed by a number. **2.** On drawings, abbr. for "both sides." **3.** Abbr. for "beam spacer."

BSCP Abbr. for "British Standard Code of Practice."

BSI **1.** Abbr. for **British Standards Institution**. **2.** Abbr. for "Building Stone Institute."

BSMT On drawings, abbr. for **basement**.

BSR Abbr. for "building space requirements."

BSS Abbr. for "British Standard Specification."

bstd Abbr. for "bastard."

BTB Abbr. for "bituminous treated base."

Btr., btr In the lumber industry, abbr. for "better."

Btu Abbr. for **British thermal unit**.

bubble glass Glass in which decorative bubbles have been introduced during manufacture.

bubbling Bubbles of entrapped air or solvent vapors which protrude from a paint surface; formed either on application or during drying of the paint film.

bubile A structure to house cows.

bubinga, African rosewood A west African wood, light red to violet in color, often with purple stripes, frequently figured; hard, high density; used as interior finish and for decorative paneling.

buck **1.** A **door buck**. **2.** A **sawhorse**.

bucket An attachment for a materials-handling or excavating machine that digs or carries loose materials such as earth, gravel, stone, or concrete; may be shaped like a scoop, with provision for opening and closing for convenience in unloading.

bucket loader See **chain-bucket loader** and **tractor loader**.

bucket trap A mechanical, buoyancy-operated steam trap which is designed to prevent steam from passing through the trap; makes use of an inverted or upright cup.

bucket-wheel excavator An excavating machine having a rotating wheel fitted with toothed-edged buckets; used to dig a layer of earth and load it onto a conveyor belt as the machine moves forward under its own power.

buck frame, core frame A wood frame which is built into a partition, constructed on wood studs, to receive a door lining; a **subframe**.

bucking Sawing felled trees into logs.

buckle **1.** Distortion of the surfaces of a beam or girder under load; caused by unequal distribution of weight, temperature, or moisture, or the lack of uniform texture. **2.** Distortion of the surface of a sheet of material, such as a bulge or wrinkle in **asphalt prepared roofing**. **3.** A **brotch**.

buckler An ornament used in the decoration of friezes; sometimes circular or lozenge-shaped.

buckler

buckling load, *Brit.* **crippling load** The **axial load** at which a perfectly straight column or structural member starts to bend.

buck opening A **rough opening**.

bucksaw A saw consisting of a blade set in an H-shaped frame; used for cutting wood on a **sawhorse**.

buck scraper A type of earth scraper; when filled, the scoop is raised from the ground by runners on each side.

buckstay **1.** A vertical member, usually in cross-connected pairs, reinforcing the side walls of an arched masonry furnace or flue to take the thrust of an arch. **2.** Any similar brace member.

bucranium, bucrane A sculptured ornament representing the head or skull of an ox, often garlanded; frequently used on Roman Ionic and Corinthian friezes.

bucranium

bud **1.** To graft a plant by inserting a bud of one plant into the stock of another. **2.** An element in a Corinthian capital.

bud, 2

bud capital Same as **lotus capital**.

buff **1.** To clean and polish a surface so that a high luster results. **2.** To grind down and/or polish a floor finish of terrazzo or other exposed-aggregate concrete.

Buffalo box See **curb box**.

buffer **1.** A device, apparatus, or material which reduces mechanical shock due to impact. **2.** A device located at the bottom of an elevator hoistway, designed to stop a car or counterweight from descending beyond its normal limit of travel; motion beyond this limit is taken up by storing or by absorbing and dissipating the kinetic energy of the car or counterweight. Also see **oil buffer, spring buffer**. **3.** Any type of barrier that limits the scattering of rock as a result of blasting.

buggy, concrete cart A two-wheeled or four-wheeled cart, often motor-driven, usually rubber-tired, for transporting small quantities of concrete from hoppers or mixers to forms.

bug holes Small regular or irregular cavities, usually not exceeding ⅝ in. (15 mm) in diameter, resulting from entrapment of air bubbles in the surface of formed concrete during placing and compaction.

builder The individual or firm who is the employer of craftsman required for erecting a building in accordance with the plans and specifications prepared by the architect and who carries the responsibility for doing so.

builders' guide, builders' handbook, builders' manual See **pattern book**.

builders' hardware See **finish hardware**.

builder's jack A bracket attached to a windowsill, which projects outside the window; used to support a scaffold.

builder's level **1.** A **level, 1** which is set in a long wood or alloy frame. **2.** A simple type of **tilting level** or **dumpy level**.

builder's risk insurance A specialized form of property insurance to cover **work, 1** in the course of construction. Also see **property insurance**.

Builders' Shed style Same as **Shed style**.

builder's staging A heavy scaffold which is constructed of square timbers, braced together; usually used for the handling of heavy materials.

builder's tape A **tape measure**; in the U.S.A., usually 50 ft or 100 ft long, contained in a circular case.

building A more or less enclosed and permanent structure for housing, commerce, industry, etc., distinguished from mobile structures and those not intended for occupancy. Also see **accessory building**.

building alteration See **alteration**.

building area The total area of a site which is covered by buildings as measured on a horizontal plane at ground level. Terraces and uncovered porches usually are excluded from this total, although the stipulations of a mortgage lender or governmental program may require their inclusion.

building artifact An element in a building which demonstrates human workmanship, such as a stained-glass window.

building block A rectangular masonry unit, other than a brick, made of burnt clay, cement, concrete, glass, gypsum, or any other material suitable for use in building construction.

building board Any sheet of building material, often faced with paper or vinyl; suitable for use as a finished surface on walls, ceilings, etc.

building brick, common brick Brick for building purposes, not esp. treated for texture or color.

building code A collection of rules and regulations adopted by authorities having appropriate jurisdiction to control the design and construction of buildings, alteration, repair, quality of materials, use and occupancy, and related factors of buildings within their jurisdiction; contains minimum architectural, structural, and mechanical standards for sanitation, public health, welfare, safety, and the provision of light and air. Also see **Uniform Building Code** and **BOCA National Building Code**.

building combined drain A **building drain** which conveys both sewage and storm water.

building combined sewer A **building sewer** which conveys both sewage and storm water.

building component **1.** A building element which uses industrial products that are manufactured as independent units capable of being joined with other elements. **2.** According to the **NEC**, any subsystem, subassembly, or other system designed for use in (or integral with) a structure or part of a structure, which can include electrical, fire protection, mechanical, plumbing, and structural systems and other systems affecting health and safety.

building conservation The management of a building to prevent its decay, destruction, misuse, or neglect; may include the recording of the history of the building and conservation measures applied.

building construction The fabrication and erection of a building by assembling or combining **building components**, subsystems, or systems.

building construction joint See **construction joint, 2**.

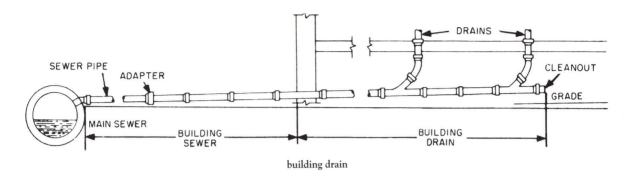

building drain

building coverage The fraction or percentage of a site's total area which is taken up by buildings.

building drain That part of the lowest piping of a drainage system which receives the discharge from soil pipes, waste pipes, and other drainage pipes inside the walls of the building and conveys the discharge by gravity to the building sewer outside the building wall.

building-drainage system All piping provided for carrying waste water, sewage, or other drainage from the building to the street sewer or place of disposal.

building envelope See **envelope, 1**.

building environment The combination of conditions that may influence, modify, or otherwise affect a person, piece of equipment, or system in a building (for example, lighting, noise, temperature, relative humidity, and/or odors).

building foundation See **foundation, 1**.

building grade The ground elevation, which is established by the appropriate authority, regulating the height of a building.

building gravity drainage system A **building-drainage system** which drains by gravity into the building sewer.

building heat-loss factor A measure of the rate of heat loss of a building; expressed in Btu per degree day (joules per degree day). The number of degree days is multiplied by this factor to obtain the heat energy requirements during that period.

building height The vertical distance measured from curb or grade level to the highest level of a flat or mansard roof, or to the average height of a pitched, gabled, hip, or gambrel roof; in general, bulkheads, penthouses, etc., are excluded provided they are relatively low and do not occupy a large percentage of the area of the roof upon which they are located.

building house drain Same as **building drain**.

building improvement See **improvement**.

building inspector A member of a building department, usually of a municipality, who inspects construction to determine if it conforms to both the requirement of the building code and the approved plans; one who inspects occupied buildings for violations of the building code.

building insulation See **thermal insulation**.

building lime, finish lime, mason's lime Lime used in plastering or masonry work.

building line A line established by law or agreement usually parallel to a property line, beyond which a structure may not extend. This restriction generally does not apply to uncovered entrance platforms, terraces, and steps.

building main The water-supply pipe, including fittings and accessories, from the water main or other source of supply to the first branch of the water-distributing system.

building maintenance The actions of ensuring that a building remains in working condition by preserving it from deterioration, decline, or failure.

building material Any material used in construction, such as steel, concrete, brick, masonry, glass, wood, etc.

building official An official designated by the appointing authority, whatever his official title, to enforce the provisions of the applicable building code and other applicable laws.

Building Officials and Code Administrators International See **BOCA National Building Code**.

building paper A heavy, relatively cheap, durable paper, such as **asphalt paper**, used in building construction, esp. in frame construction, to improve thermal insulation and weather protection and to act as a vapor barrier. Special types are: **sheathing paper**, used between sheathing and siding; **floor lining paper**, used between rough and finish floors.

building permit A written authorization to an applicant (usually a builder) for a specific project allowing him to proceed with construction; granted by the municipal agency having jurisdiction after plans have been filed, reviewed.

building preservation The process of applying measures to maintain and sustain the existing materials, integrity, and form of a building, including its structure and **building artifacts**.

building protection The application of measures designed to preserve a building and its contents from deterioration, damage (from fire, water, etc.) and unauthorized intrusion.

building reconstruction The reproduction by new construction following the exact form and details of a no longer existing building or artifact as it once appeared.

building regulations British term for **building code**.

building rehabilitation The returning of a building to a useful state by repair, alteration, and modification.

Building Research Establishment A government-financed building research organization in the U.K.

building restoration The accurate reestablishment of the form and details of a building, its artifacts, and the site on which it is located, usually as it appeared at a particular time; may require the removal of later work or the reconstruction of earlier work which had been removed.

building restriction Any one of a number of restrictions, imposed on the construction of a building or the use of land; may be included in a code or in other documents, e.g., a **restrictive covenant**; may be statutory or contractual.

building restriction line A line, defined by local ordinances, beyond which structures may not be erected; usually parallel to the street line.

building retrofit The addition of new building materials, building elements, and components not provided in the original construction.

building sanitary drain See **sanitary drain**.

building sanitary sewer A **building sewer** which conveys sewage but does not convey storm water.

building section Any portion of a building, such as a room, floor, or floors, that is within the limits of fire divisions.

building service chute A vertical or inclined tube or channel that conveys and controls the fall of objects such as mail, laundry, and garbage to a lower level.

building services The utilities and services supplied and distributed within a building generally related to the building environment, including: heating, air-conditioning, lighting, water supply services, drainage services, electrical supply, gas supply, fire protection, and security protection.

building sewer That part of the horizontal piping of a drainage system which extends beyond the ends of the building drain and receives the discharge of the building drain and conveys it to a public sewer, private sewer, individual sewage disposal system, or other point of disposal.

building site See **site**.

building stone Any stone which may be used in building construction: granite, limestone, marble, etc.

building storm drain A **building drain** that conveys only storm water.

building storm sewer **1.** A **building sewer** which conveys only storm water. **2.** The horizontal piping of a storm drainage system which extends from the **building storm drain**, receives its discharge, and conveys it to the public storm sewer or other point of disposal.

building subdrain That portion of a building drainage system which does not drain by gravity into a **building sewer**; wastes from the subdrain are collected in a sump and discharged by a pump.

building subhouse drain Same as **building subdrain**.

building subsystem **1.** A complete group of elements or set of parts that form and function as a unit within a finished building. **2.** An assemblage of components that perform a specific function in a building, e.g., an air-conditioning system consisting of its components such as a fan, ductwork, air diffusers, and controls.

building survey A detailed report of the present condition of a building, including its appearance and structural integrity; for example, may include illustrations of the façade and other walls, and analyses such as the condition of the masonry.

building surveyor British term for an individual who has received special training in various aspects of building construction such as: planning of construction projects, building construction techniques, construction costs, and the legal aspects of building construction. There is no direct counterpart for this position in the U.S.A. Also see **Chartered Building Surveyor**.

building system According to the **NEC**: plans, specifications, and documentation for a system of manufactured building or for a type of system of **building components, 2.** including variations thereof as are specifically permitted by regulation, and which variations are submitted as part of the building system or amendment thereto. **3.** An assembly of integrated **building subsystems** satisfying the functional requirements of a building. Also see **closed building system, industrialized building system, open building system**.

building tile See **structural clay tile**.

building trades Specialized skills connected with building construction, such as carpentry, masonry, plumbing, plastering.

building trap, main trap A **running trap** on the outlet side of a building drain (on the sewer side of all drain connections); prevents the passage of odors between the common sewer and the plumbing of the building.

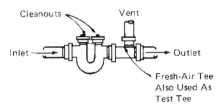

building trap

building unit A unit (such as a building brick or a structural clay tile), the specifications for which include measures of its durability, strength, and other structural characteristics, but not the specifications related to its appearance.

building volume See **above-grade building volume**.

build up To apply successive layers to form a thicker mass.

built beam Same as **built-up beam**.

built environment The aggregate of the physical surroundings and conditions constructed by human beings, in contrast to those surroundings and conditions resulting from the **natural environment**.

built-in Built as an integral part of a larger construction, as furniture which is especially fitted in a building.

built-on-the-job Fabricated completely on the jobsite, as joinery fabricated from lumber of standard sizes.

built rib Same as **built-up rib**.

built-up **1.** Assembled by fastening a number of parts together. **2.** Fabricated of several layers, thicknesses, or pieces which are laminated or fastened together.

built-up air casing A field-fabricated enclosure around an air-handling system, usually built on a waterproof concrete base which has a curb around it with floor drains, or built on a floor which is sloped toward drainpipe openings.

built-up beam **1.** A beam made of structural metal units (such as plates and angles) which are riveted, bolted, or welded together. **2.** A beam of precast concrete units which are joined by shear connectors. **3.** A **flitch beam**. **4.** A timber made up of several pieces fastened together, forming one of larger dimensions.

built-up beam on a post

built-up fan equipment A term applied to an **HVAC system** in which the fan is selected as an individual component and integrated in the installation with other separate elements of the system such as coils, air filters, and control dampers for regulating the proportioning of outside, exhaust, and return air.

built-up girder Same as **built-up beam**.

built-up rib A rib made of laminations of timber of various sizes.

built-up roofing, composition roofing, felt-and-gravel roofing, gravel roofing A continuous roof covering made up of laminations or plies of saturated or coated roofing felts, alternated with layers of asphalt or coal-tar pitch and surfaced with a layer of gravel or slag in a heavy coat of asphalt or coal-tar pitch or finished with a **cap sheet**; generally used on flat or low-pitched roofs. Also see **tar-and-gravel roofing**.

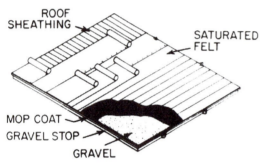

built-up roofing

built-up string A curved stair string formed of wood members fastened together by counter cramps.

built-up timber Same as **built-up beam, 4**.

bulb In lighting, see **lamp bulb, light bulb**.

bulb angle An **angle iron**, one side of which thickens toward the edge, forming a bulbous rib.

bulb angle

bulb bar A steel or iron bar, one side of which thickens toward an edge, forming a bulbous rib at that edge.

bulb of pressure Same as **pressure bulb**.

bulb pile A **pedestal pile**.

bulb shape See **lampbulb**.

bulb tee A **tee, 3** the web of which thickens toward the edge, forming a bulbous rib.

bulk cement Cement which is transported and delivered in bulk (usually in specially constructed vehicles) instead of in bags.

bulk density The weight of a material (including solid particles and any contained water) per unit volume including voids.

bulkhead 1. A structure on the roof of a building covering a water tank, shaft, or service equipment. 2. A structure, as on a roof, covering a stairwell or other opening, to provide adequate headroom. 3. A retaining structure to prevent earth movement into a dredged area. 4. A horizontal or inclined door giving access from the outside of a house to a cellar or to a shaft. 5. The member of an entrance frame which forms a base for a sidelight adjacent to a door. 6. In a concrete form, a partition which blocks fresh concrete from one section of the form or closes the end of the form (as at a construction joint).

bulkhead

bulkhead packer A **refuse compactor** in which the refuse is compacted within the unit itself, into a specific volume, in one or more bags.

bulking The increase in the bulk volume of a quantity of a material in a moist condition over the volume of the same quantity dry; also called **moisture expansion**.

bulking factor The ratio of the volume of moist sand to the volume of the sand when dry.

bulking value A measure of the specific gravity of a pigment, usually expressed as gallons per 100 lb or liters per kilogram.

bulk modulus of elasticity, modulus of volume elasticity A number expressing a material's resistance to elastic changes in volume; the ratio between a pressure that acts on a material (to change its volume) and the fractional change in volume so produced, within the elastic limit of the material.

bulk oxygen system   An assembly of equipment (such as oxygen storage containers, pressure regulators, safety devices, vaporizers, manifolds, and interconnecting piping) for supplying a regulated flow of oxygen to a pipeline, as at a hospital; the oxygen may be stored as a liquid or gas in either stationary or portable containers.

bulk specific gravity   The ratio of (a) the mass of a volume of material (including the mass of the water within the voids, but excluding the voids between particles) at a stated temperature to (b) the mass of an equal volume of distilled water at a stated temperature.

bulk strain, volume strain   The ratio of the change in volume of a body to its original volume, as a result of stress applied to the body.

bulk strength   The mechanical strength per unit volume of a solid.

bulla   A circular metal boss used by the ancient Romans as a decoration for fastening parts of doors; often highly ornamented.

bulla

bull clam   A **bulldozer** having a curved bowl or bucket attached to the front of the blade.

bulldog clip   Same as a **sleeper clip**.

bulldog plate   See **toothed plate**.

bulldozer   A tractor or other prime mover equipped with a blade attached by arms or brackets to its front end; used in pushing or piling earth or rock.

bullet catch   A fastener which holds a door in place by means of a projecting spring-actuated steel ball which is depressed when the door is closed.

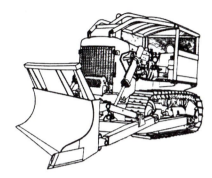

bulldozer

bulletin board   A surface used for the display of announcements, information, and the like, usually attached with thumbtacks.

bulletproof glass   See **bullet-resisting glass**.

bullet-resisting glass   A laminated assembly consisting of four or more sheets of glass stacked alternately with layers of a transparent plastic resin, then bonded under heat and pressure.

bull float   A tool or machine used to smooth unformed surfaces of freshly placed concrete.

bull float

bull header, bull head   **1.** In masonry, a **header** with one corner rounded; used as a **quoin** in brick window sills and at doorways. **2.** A **header** which is laid on edge so that the end of the masonry unit is exposed.

bullhead tee, bullheaded tee   **1.** In plumbing, a **pipe tee** which is connected to a branch that is longer than the main run. **2.** A plumbing tee which has an outlet larger than the opening on the run. (*See illustration p. 138.*)

bullion   Same as **bull's eye**.

bullnose, bull's-nose   **1.** A blunt or curved outside corner, as the corner made by two walls. **2.** A structural member or trim having a rounded edge, as on stair treads, window sills, doors, etc. **3.** In plastering, a metal bead used on exterior corners

bullnose block

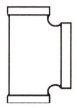

bullhead tee, 2

where rounded edges are required. **4.** A small, hand-held carpenter's plane with the cutting edge set near the front of the grip.

bullnose block   A brick or concrete masonry unit having one or more rounded exterior corners.

bullnose block

bullnosed plane   See **bullnose, 4.**

bull-nosed step   A step, usually lowest in a flight, having one or both ends rounded to a semicircle and projecting beyond the face of the stair string or strings. The semicircular projection extends beyond and around the newel post.

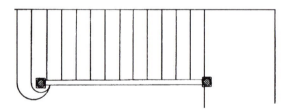

bull-nosed step

bullnose stretcher   See **bull stretcher.**

bullnose trim   Same as **bullnose, 2.**

bull-point   A pointed steel hand drill, which is struck with a hammer; used to chip off small pieces of masonry or rock.

bull's-eye   **1.** A figure or ornament of concentric bands. **2.** A round or oval aperture, open, louvered, or glazed; an **oculus** or **oeil-de-boeuf.** **3.** The enclosure of such an aperture, a double-

bull's-eye, 2

arched frame with two or four key voussoirs. **4.** A glass disk formed with a raised center.

bull's-eye window   **1.** A glazed round aperture, glazed with thickened concentric circles of glass; same as glazed **bull's-eye, 2;** also called an oculus, oxeye window, or *oeil-de-boeuf*. **2.** An aperture similar to **1.**, but unglazed; may be open or louvered.

bull's head   Same as **bucranium.**

bull stretcher, bullnose stretcher   **1.** In masonry, a **stretcher** having a **bullnose** along the longest dimension for laying along an edge, as along a sill. **2.** Any stretcher which is laid on edge to show its broad face.

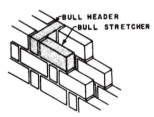

bull stretcher, 2 and bull header, 2

bulwark   A strong defensive wall structure, generally low enough to permit defensive fire.

bumper   **1.** A device (other than an **oil buffer** or **spring buffer**) designed to stop an elevator car or counterweight from descending beyond its normal limit of travel; the car strikes the bumper, which absorbs the impact. **2.** On a doorframe, a **rubber silencer** to reduce noise caused by the slamming of a door.

bumper bar   See **guard bar**.

bumper guard   See **guard bar**.

bund   A continuous, low wall or embankment along a body of water.

bundled bars   A group of parallel **reinforcing bars** (not exceeding four in number) in contact with each other, enclosed in stirrups or ties; used as reinforcement in reinforced concrete.

bundle of lath   A quantity of lath for plastering, etc. Usually, wood strips: 50 pieces, 5/16 in. by 1½ in. by 48 in. (0.16 cm by 3.81 cm by 121.9 cm); gypsum lath: 6 sheets, 16 in. by 48 in. (40.6 cm by 121.9 cm).

bundle pier   A Gothic pier in which the plan takes a continuous undulating and breaking outline, giving the appearance of a dense bundle of rising forms rather than the distinct shafts of the **compound pier**.

bungalow   A small one-story or one-and-a-half-story house, usually having a low profile and of **wood-frame construction**, often having a porch. Although found elsewhere, such houses were relatively low in cost in the early 20th century in America because they could be built according to plans taken from available pattern books, or could be purchased as early as 1908 as precut boards and timbers ready for assembly. Sometimes called a bungaloid-style house. Also see **prefabricated house**.

bungalow court   A group of three or more detached, one-story, single-family dwellings, arranged with common utilities and accessories under a common ownership.

bungalow sash   The upper sash of a **double-hung window** that has been divided by **muntins** into a number of long vertical panes; the lower sash is undivided.

bungalow siding   Clapboarding having a minimal width of 8 in. (20 cm).

bunk   A built-in, usually narrow, bed.

bunker   **1.** A compartment bin, often elevated, for storage of aggregates, sand, coal, etc. **2.** A space in a refrigerator for ice or a cooling element.

bunker fill roof   In adobe construction of the American Southwest, a flat roof supported by roof beams of heavy logs stripped of their bark; wood sheathing is laid on the roof beams, which

is then covered with building paper, earth fill, then a second layer of building paper, asphalt, and gravel.

buon fresco   See **fresco**.

buoyant foundation   A **foundation** of reinforced concrete whose weight, together with that of the imposed loads, is approximately equal to the weight of the displaced soil and/or water.

burden   **1.** Earthy material, rock, etc., which overlays bedrock. **2.** In blasting, the distance between the blasting charge and the free face of the material to be blasted.

burglar alarm system   An electronic system designed to detect unauthorized entry into or within a premise. The system may be activated by the closure of a switch (for example, by stepping on a mat, opening a window, etc.), by the interruption of a photoelectric beam, or by a **motion detector**.

buried cable   An underground cable which is installed so that it cannot be removed without disturbing the soil.

buried plate electrode   A plate of iron, steel, or nonferrous material, at least 0.06 inch (1.5 mm) thick which has a surface area of at least 2 square feet (0.2 m²) which is buried in exterior soil; usually used where conditions do not permit the driving of a **ground rod** into the soil.

burl   **1.** An abnormal growth or protuberance on a tree. Also called **knur, knurl**. **2.** Wood veneer cut from burls.

burlap, *Brit.* **hessian canvas**   A coarse woven fabric of jute, hemp, or, less commonly, flax, for use as a water-retaining covering in curing concrete surfaces or as a reinforcement in plaster.

burned joint   A joint formed by fitting the end of one lead pipe into the flared end of another lead pipe. Heat is then applied evenly around the perimeter, melting the overlapping edges and fusing them together.

burner   That part of a furnace, boiler, etc., where the flame is produced.

burning   The flame cutting of metal plates to a desired shape.

burning-brand test   A fire test of roof coverings in which specified burning wooden brands are fastened to a sloping roof deck test specimen while exposed to a specified wind; one of three fire tests usually applied to roof coverings. Also see **intermittent-flame-exposure test**.

burning off Heat-softening an age-dried paint film by use of an acetylene torch or blowtorch to permit its removal by scraping.

burning rate A measure of the tendency of plastics to burn at given temperatures. Certain plastics, such as those based on shellac, burn readily at comparatively low temperatures. Others melt or disintegrate without actually burning, or burn only if exposed to direct flame.

burnish To polish by friction; to make smooth and lustrous.

burnishing Raising the gloss of a surface by rubbing.

burn rate The rate at which a material will burn after the ignition heat source has been removed.

burnt brick Brick that has been treated in a kiln at an elevated temperature to harden it, give it mechanical strength, and improve its resistance to moisture. Compare with **unburnt brick**.

burnt lime See **lime**.

burnt sienna **Sienna** which has been calcined.

burnt umber See **umber**.

burr **1.** A waste brick from the kiln which has been partially fused. **2.** A batch of bricks fused together. **3.** A rough or sharp edge left on metal by a cutting tool. **4.** Same as **burl, 1.**

bursting strength **1.** A measure of the ability of a sheet to resist rupture when pressure is applied to one side by a specified instrument under specified conditions. **2.** Of a pipe or fitting, the internal pressure required to result in its failure.

burst pressure Of a **valve**, the maximum pressure which can be slowly applied to the valve (e.g., at room temperature, for 30 seconds) without causing it to rupture.

bus **1.** A **busbar**. **2.** A heavy, rigid electrical conductor that serves as a common connection between the source of electric power and the load circuits.

busbar A heavy, rigid electrical conductor (usually uninsulated copper or aluminum) which serves as an interconnection between power-handling devices (such as switches and circuit breakers) or as a common connection between several circuits.

bus duct, busway A prefabricated conduit which is used to enclose and protect **bus** running through it.

bush hammer A hammer having a serrated face containing many pyramid-shaped points; used to dress a concrete or stone surface; originally a hand tool but now usually power driven.

bush hammer

bush-hammered concrete Concrete having an exposed aggregate finish; usually obtained with a power-operated bushhammer which removes (by percussive cutting) the sand-cement matrix about the aggregate particles to a depth ranging from $\frac{1}{16}$ to $\frac{1}{4}$ in. (1.59 to 6.35 mm).

bushhammer finish A stone or concrete surface dressed with a bushhammer; used decoratively or to provide a roughened traction surface for treads, floors, and pavements.

bushing **1.** In plumbing, a pipe fitting which is threaded on both the inside and the outside so that it can be used to connect two pipes (or other fittings) of different sizes. **2.** A sleeve which screws into, or is otherwise fastened to, an opening in order to prevent mechanical abrasion or damage to a cable, rod, or the like, which passes through it.

business district That area of a town or city used for commercial purposes, which is usually defined and limited by zoning ordinances.

busway   See **bus duct**.

butcher block, chopping block   An assembly of rectangular blocks of hardwood which are edge-glued, joined by dowels, and then pressed together hydraulically; esp. used as a work surface in a kitchen.

butler's pantry   A small service room, situated between a kitchen and dining room, usually equipped with a sink and cupboards, a small stove, and often with a supplementary refrigerator and appliances.

butlery (*Brit.*)   Buttery; butler's pantry.

butment   Same as **abutment**.

butment cheek   The face of a material surrounding a mortise, and abutted by the shoulders surrounding the tenon.

butt   **1.** A short length of roofing material. **2.** The thick end of a shingle. **3.** A **butt hinge**.

butt and break   The staggering of butt-lath joints on framing members to add greater strength to a wall and to reduce plaster cracking.

butt-and-miter joint   A carpentry joint having a butt on the top half of the face and a miter on the lower half.

butt casement hinge   A type of **butt hinge** commonly used on casement sashes.

butt chisel   A wood chisel with a short blade, esp. used for setting hardware on doors and doorframes.

butt chisel

butted frame   A doorframe which has a thickness less than or equal to the thickness of the wall in which it is set; the frame butts against the wall opening.

butt end   The thicker end of a timber, handle, etc.

butt-end treatment   A technique of preserving timber posts by soaking the ends (which may be exposed to soil and/or water) in wood-preservative chemicals such as creosote or pentachlorophenol dissolved in a fluid such as diesel fuel oil.

butter   **1.** To smooth on plastic roofing cement or roofing adhesive with a trowel, as on a flashing. **2.** To apply mortar as to a masonry unit, with a trowel.

buttercup yellow   See **zinc chromate**.

butterflies   Color imperfections in lime-putty finish. If unscreened lime has lumps which are not broken up in mixing, white spots occur in the finish as the lumps break down in troweling the plaster on the wall.

butterfly   See **butterfly wedge**.

butterfly hinge   A decorative hinge having the appearance of a butterfly.

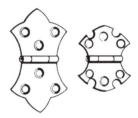

butterfly hinges

butterfly nut   A **wing nut**.

butterfly roof   A roof shape which has two surfaces that rise from the center to the eaves with a valley in the center; resembles the wings of a butterfly.

butterfly spring   A light metal spring, set over the pin of a door hinge, which acts as closer.

butterfly tie   Same as **butterfly wall tie**.

butterfly valve   A valve used to control the flow of fluids; two disks are hinged on a common shaft to control flow through the port, permitting flow only in one direction. (*See illustration p. 142.*)

butterfly wall tie   A **wall tie** manufactured from heavy steel wire and shaped like a figure 8.

butterfly wedge, butterfly   A double **dovetail** for joining two boards at their edges.

buttering   Spreading mortar on a masonry unit with a trowel.

buttering trowel   A small trowel used to spread mortar on a brick before it is laid. (*See illustration p. 142.*)

butternut, white walnut   A moderately soft, medium-textured, low-density wood of light to pale brown color. The walnut-like grain is used particularly for decorative veneer.

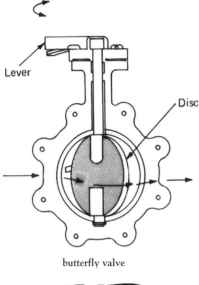

Lever

Disc

butterfly valve

buttering trowel

buttery **1.** Pantry or wine cellar; formerly a medieval storeroom for provisions (originally *bouteillerie*). **2.** (*Brit.*) Dispensary of provisions, esp. food and drink, to college students.

buttery hatch Semiclosed screen between a buttery and the hall.

butt fusion A method of joining plastic pipe, sheet, or other similar forms of a thermoplastic resin wherein the two ends to be joined are heated to the molten state and then rapidly pressed together to form a homogeneous bond.

butt gauge See **marking gauge**.

butt hinge A door or window hinge consisting of two rectangular metal plates which are joined with a pin; in large hinges of this type the pin is removable, whereas in small hinges it usually is fixed; fastened to butting surfaces, such as the face of the jamb and the edge of a door.

butt hinge

butt-hung door A door hung on **butt hinges**, as opposed to pivots.

butt joint **1.** A plain, square joint between two members, where the contact surfaces are cut at right angles to the faces of the pieces; the two pieces are fitted squarely against each other rather than lapped; also see **oblique butt joint**. **2.** A joint in which the structural units being joined abut each other so that under movement any sealant is in tension or compression between the joint faces.

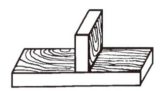

butt joint formed by two boards

welded **butt joint**

button **1.** A small projecting member such as a piece of wood or metal; used to fasten the frame of a door or window. **2.** A **turn button**.

button catch Same as **button, 1**.

buttonhead The head of a bar, bolt, rivet, or screw which is hemispherical in shape; usually the head is less than a full hemisphere and has a flat bearing surface.

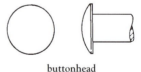

buttonhead

button punching Punch-like crimping at regular intervals along the lap of adjacent metal decking panels; used to lock the panels together.

button set A **rivet set** used to give a rivet head a button shape.

buttonwood Same as North American **sycamore**.

buttress An exterior mass of masonry set at an angle to or bonded into a wall which it strengthens or supports; buttresses often absorb lateral thrusts from roof vaults. Also see **flying buttress, hanging buttress.**

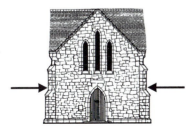

buttresses

buttress pier **1.** A pier acting as a buttress by receiving lateral thrusts. **2.** The part of a buttress which rises above the point of thrust of a vault.

buttress tower A tower which flanks an arched entrance and acts, or appears to act, as a buttress.

butt splice A **butt joint, 1** which is secured by nailing a piece of wood to each side of a joint.

butt splice

butt stile See **hanging stile, 1.**

butt strap A metal strap or plate which covers and secures both pieces of a **butt joint, 1.**

butt veneer, stump veneer Curly figured veneer cut from the root or stump of a tree.

butt weld A welded **butt joint, 1.**

buttwood, stump wood Wood cut from the base or stump of a tree.

butyl stearate A colorless oleaginous material, practically odorless, used as damp-proofing for concrete.

buzz saw Same as **circular saw.**

BV Abbr. for **butterfly valve.**

BW Abbr. for **butt weld.**

BX, BX cable A flexible, multi-conductor **armored cable** having an outer protective covering consisting of a helically wound steel strip; used for connections to electric equipment and in wiring houses.

BX

by-altar A subordinate altar.

bypass Any device (such as a pipe or duct) for directing flow around an element instead of through it.

bypass valve A valve (usually in a closed position) which is used as the control device in a **bypass.**

bypass vent A **vent stack** which runs parallel to a soil stack (or a waste stack) and is connected to it at frequent intervals.

byre A stable for livestock; a cow shed.

byzant See **bezant.**

Byzantine arch Same as **horseshoe arch.**

Byzantine architecture The architecture of the Byzantine or Eastern Roman Empire which developed from Early Christian and late Roman antecedents in the 4th cent., flourished principally in Greece, but spread widely and lasted throughout the Middle Ages until the fall of Constantinople to the Turks (1453). It is characterized by large pendentive-supported domes, round arches and elaborate columns, richness in decorative elements, and color. The most famous example is the Hagia Sophia in Istanbul (532–537).

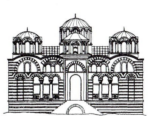

Byzantine architecture

Byzantine Revival

Byzantine Revival The reuse of Byzantine forms in the second half of the 19th century; an architectural mode found to a limited extent that borrows special features of **Byzantine architecture**, including pendentive-supported domes, round arches, elaborately decorated columns, and capitals.

a capital in Byzantine architecture

C

1/C Abbr. for "single conductor."

2/C Abbr. for "two conductor."

C **1.** On drawings, abbr. for **course**. **2.** Abbr. for **centigrade** or "Celsius."

C&Btr. In the lumber industry, abbr. for "grade C and better."

Caaba Same as **Kaaba**.

CAB Abbr. for **cement-asbestos board**.

CAB. On drawings, abbr. for **cabinet**.

cabaña **1.** An open or tent-like structure at a swimming pool or at the shore. **2.** Originally, a simple Spanish dwelling resembling a hut or cabin.

cabanne A primitive one-room dwelling used by the early French pioneers in the Mississippi Valley as a temporary shelter; had a framework consisting of poles with branches woven between them; a steeply pitched gable roof, thatched with palmetto fronds or bark attached to a wood framework; somewhat similar to the **palma hut** in Florida.

cabin A simple one-story cottage or hut, often of relatively crude construction; see **center-hall cabin, continental cabin, dog-run cabin, dogtrot cabin, double-pen cabin, log cabin, possum-trot cabin, saddlebag cabin, single-pen cabin, stone cabin, tourist cabin, vertical log cabin, Virginia cabin.**

cabin court A **motel**, usually consisting of individual cabins.

cabinet **1.** A private room for study or conference. **2.** A suite of rooms for exhibiting scientific and artistic curiosities. **3.** A case or box-like assembly consisting of shelves, doors, and drawers and primarily used for storage. **4.** An enclosure having a front hinged door or doors, for housing of electrical devices or conductor connections.

cabinet drawer kicker See **drawer kicker**.

cabinet drawer runner See **drawer runner**.

cabinet drawer stop See **drawer stop**.

cabinet file A single-cut **file**, half-round on one side, flat on the other.

cabinet filler A wood member which closes the space between cabinets and adjacent walls or ceilings.

cabinet finish A varnished or polished hardwood interior finish as distinguished from a painted softwood finish.

cabinet heater A heater containing a heating element enclosed in a metal cabinet, usually with an intake grille below, and an outlet for the heated air above; often contains a fan.

cabinet jamb A steel doorframe in three or more pieces applied as the finished frame over a **rough buck**.

cabinet lock A **spring bolt**.

cabinet scraper A flat steel blade used for smoothing a wood surface after it has been planed, or for scraping paint, etc., from the surface.

cabinet window A type of projecting window or bay window for the display of goods in shops; much used early in the 19th cent.

cabinet work Joinery often of fine quality, as in the construction of built-in cabinets and shelves.

cable **1.** An electric conductor consisting of a group of smaller-diameter conductor strands twisted together. **2.** A group of electric conductors which are insulated from each other. **3.** Any heavy rope or wire line used for support, for exerting a force, or for controlling a mechanism. **4.** One of the reedings which are set into the flutes of a pilaster or column.

cable bond An electrical connection (a) between the armor or sheath of one cable and that of an adjacent cable, (b) across a joint in the armor or sheath of a cable, or (c) between the armor or sheath and the earth.

cable conduit See **conduit, 1**. Also see **cable duct**.

cabled fluting, ribbed fluting, stopped flute A molding of convex section formed in the flutes of a column, usually in the lower third of the shaft.

cable duct A rigid metal duct through which insulated electric conductors are run, generally conductors carrying large currents; for underground installations, concrete pipes usually are used.

cable grip A device temporarily connected to the end of a cable to assist in pulling the cable during its installation.

cable jacket The protective covering over the core, insulation, or sheath of a cable.

cable molding See **cabling**.

cable pulling compound A substance which facilitates the pulling of wires through a cable duct or conduit.

cable rack Same as **ladder cable tray**.

cable roof A structural system consisting of a roof-deck and covering which are supported by cables.

cable sheath A single layer or multiple layers of a protective covering over a cable.

cable support box In an installation of electric conduit that runs vertically, a box which provides support for the cables within the conduit so as to limit the strain on them from their own weight.

cable-supported construction A structure that is held in equilibrium by cables.

cable tray An assembly of metalwork which is used to support insulated electric conductors; similar in function to a metal **cable duct**, but consisting of a ladder-like metal framework on the bottom and sides, with the top open.

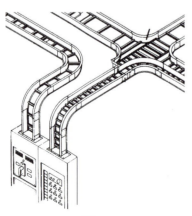

cable tray

cable vault An underground structure used in pulling or splicing electric cables which are laid underground.

cableway An apparatus for moving material, sometimes used at construction sites; usually a wire rope which is suspended between two points, from which buckets, or the like, are hung and pulled along.

cabling, cable molding **1.** An ornament formed like a cable, showing twisted strands. **2.** The convex filling of the lower part of the flutes of classical columns. Also see **rope molding, reeding**.

cabling, 1

Cabot's quilt An insulating material consisting of dried eelgrass held between layers of cloth or paper; once used as thermal insulation, now little used.

CAB plastic See **cellulose acetate butyrate plastic**.

cab-tire cable A flexible cable having a heavy rubber or neoprene outer sheathing.

CAD Abbr. for **computer-aided design**.

cadastral survey A survey relating to land boundaries and subdivisions, made to create units suitable for transfer or to define the limitations of title.

cadmium plating An electroplating which provides a corrosion-resistant coating on metal.

cadmium yellow A strong yellow pigment, cadmium sulfide, characterized by good permanence; used in paints.

caementicius In ancient Rome, irregular masonry built of rough quarry stones not squared or shaped in any way.

Caen stone A stone from Caen (in Normandy) used in some medieval buildings in England.

caer- A prefix signifying a fortified wall, castle, or city, occurring in place names in Wales and parts of western and northern England.

cage **1.** Any rigid, reinforced assembly, ready for placing in position. **2.** A metal enclosure for balcony spotlights. **3.** A chantry or chapel screened by open **tracery**.

caged beam A **beam** enclosed in a **casing, 2,** usually by a fire-rated construction.

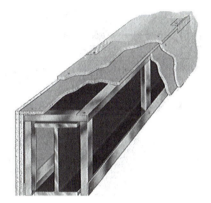

caged beam

caged column A **column** enclosed in a **casing, 2,** usually by a fire-rated material; also see **column casing**.

caher In Ireland, ancient stonework thought to have been intended for defensive work for a church or for several sacred buildings.

cairn A pile of stones heaped up for a landmark, memorial, or monument; a **tumulus**.

caisson **1.** A watertight structure or chamber, within which work is carried on in building foundations or structures below water level. **2.** A sunken panel, esp. in a vaulted ceiling or the inside of a cupola; a **coffer**.

caisson drill An auger-like machine (or an attachment for a crane) used in foundation work to cut a vertical or inclined circular shaft in the earth for a building footing which is carried to solid material beneath.

caisson pile A cast-in-place pile; made by driving a tube into the ground, emptying the tube, then filling with concrete.

Cajun cottage, Cajun cabin A simple dwelling built by immigrants (*Acadians*) from the Maritime Provinces of Canada who, from about 1760 to 1790, settled largely in the bayou dis-

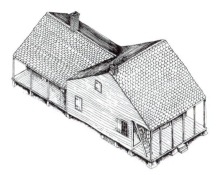

Cajun cottage

tricts of southern Louisiana where their descendants are now usually referred to as *Cajuns*. In the early 1800s, the typical Cajun cottage was built on **groundsills**, supported on cypress blocks or brick piers; usually characterized by a shingle-covered, moderately steep end-gabled roof; hand-riven clapboard **siding**; rooms positioned in a relatively straight line from the front to the back of the house; French doors at the front and rear to promote the flow of air through the house; a porch across the front, commonly without a railing; usually a steep stairway from one end of the porch to a loft above; battened doors; battened shutters on the windows.

caking In paints, the formation of a hard dense mass of pigment which is difficult to disperse by hand agitation.

CAL On drawings, abbr. for "calorie."

calathus The basket-shaped or bell-shaped core of a capital, esp. Corinthian.

calcareous Containing calcium carbonate or, less generally, containing the element calcium.

calcimine, kalsomine A low-cost wash coating consisting of glue and whiting (usually powdered calcium carbonate) mixed with water, sometimes tinted; used on plaster or masonry-type surfaces.

calcine To heat a substance below the temperature of fusion to drive off chemically combined water or to alter its chemical and physical characteristics.

calcined gypsum A gypsum that has been partially dehydrated by heating.

calcite A mineral form of calcium carbonate; the principal constituent of limestone, chalk, and marble; usually a major raw material used in portland cement manufacture.

calcite streak A former fracture or parting (in limestone) that has been recemented and annealed by deposition of calcite.

calcium aluminate cement, aluminous cement, *(Brit.)* **high-alumina cement** The product obtained by pulverizing clinker, consisting essentially of hydraulic calcium aluminates resulting from fusing or sintering a suitably proportioned mixture of aluminous and calcareous materials.

calcium carbonate A low-density white pigment for use in paint; provides little opacity; used mainly to provide bulk and flatness.

calcium chloride A chemical salt used in plastic concrete as an accelerator.

calcium hydroxide Same as **hydrated lime, 2**.

calcium oxide See **lime**.

calcium silicate brick A **sand-lime brick**.

calcium silicate insulation Hydrated calcium silicate with inorganic fiber reinforcement, molded into rigid shapes.

calcium stearate A product of the reaction of lime and stearic acid; used as an integral water repellant in concrete.

calcium sulfate Anhydrite or gypsum dihydrate which has been calcined to the point at which all the water of crystallization has been removed.

calcium sulfate cement A cement that depends primarily on the hydration of calcium sulfate for its setting and hardening properties; includes **Keene's cement, Parian cement, plaster of paris**.

calcium sulfate hemihydrate Gypsum which has been calcined to the point at which 75% of the water of crystallization has been removed.

calculated live load **1.** The live load which is specified by the applicable building code. **2.** The actual load applied in service.

calculon A brick 21.9 cm long, 17.8 cm wide, and 6.6 cm high.

caldarium The hot plunge in a Roman bath.

calefactory A heated common room in a monastery.

calendar A sculptured or painted emblematic series of the months.

calendar   from portal of Amiens Cathedral, 13th cent.

calf's-tongue molding, calves'-tongue molding A molding consisting of a series of pointed tongue-shaped elements all pointing in the same direction or toward a common center when around an arch.

calf's-tongue molding

caliber The nominal internal diameter of a pipe. In contrast, the outside diameter is specified for brass and copper tubing and for brass and copper pipe of other than iron-pipe sizes.

calibre Same as **caliber**.

caliche Gravel, sand, or desert debris cemented by porous calcium carbonate or other salts.

caliduct **1.** A duct or pipe for conveying hot air, hot water, or steam for heating. **2.** In the ancient Roman systems of furnace heating, a hot-air flue, usually of terra-cotta or built up with brick partitions and tile facings.

California bearing ratio A ratio used in determining the bearing capacity of a foundation; defined as the ratio of the force per unit area required to penetrate a soil mass with a 3 sq in. (19.4 sq cm) circular piston at the rate of 0.05 in. (1.27 mm) per min to the force required for corresponding penetration of a standard crushed-rock base material; usually determined at a penetration of 0.1 in. (2.54 mm).

California bungalow, California Craftsman A loosely used term applied to a small one-story or one-and-a-half-story wood bungalow, often in the **Craftsman style**; widely found in California from about 1890 to 1920 as well as in other areas of the United States.

California ranch house   See **ranch house**.

caliper   An instrument, resembling a pair of dividers, with adjustable legs for measuring the diameter or the thickness of bodies. Also see **inside caliper** and **outside caliper**.

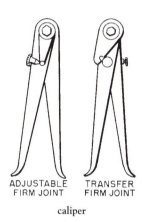

ADJUSTABLE FIRM JOINT   TRANSFER FIRM JOINT

caliper

caliper stage   In a theatre, a stage having side arms, which may be used for acting, on both sides of the main stage or apron.

calking   Same as **caulking**.

calliper   Same as **caliper**.

call loan   A loan that is payable at any time on the demand of the lender; in some instances, the borrower may also have the right to repay the loan at any time he chooses.

call point   See **fire-alarm box**.

calorie   The heat required to raise the temperature of 1 gram of water 1°C.

calorific value   The amount of heat liberated by the combustion of a unit weight (or if a gas, a unit volume) of fuel.

calorifier (*Brit.*)   A storage vessel, not open to the atmosphere, in which a supply of water is heated.

calotte   A dome, cupola, or structure of similar form, as a cup-shaped ceiling, the head of an alcove, etc.

calves'-tongue molding   See **calf's-tongue molding**.

calyon   Flint or pebble-stone; used in building walls, etc.

calyx   An ornament resembling the outer protective covering of a flower; found, for example, in the Corinthian capital.

cam   In a lock, a rotating piece attached to the end of the cylinder plug to engage the locking mechanism.

CAM   On drawings, abbr. for **camber**.

camara   Same as **camera**.

camber   **1.** A slight convex curvature built into a truss or beam to compensate for any anticipated deflection so that it will have no sag when under load. Also see **bow**. **2.** A slight convex curvature of any surface, e.g., to facilitate the runoff of water.

camber arch   An **arch** having little rise; essentially a flat arch having a slightly upward curve toward its midpoint.

camber beam   A beam curved slightly upward toward the center.

camber board   A template which performs the same function as a **camber diagram**.

camber diagram   A diagram, used in construction, which indicates the specified **camber** at all points along the length of a truss or beam.

camber piece, camber slip   A slightly curved wood board used as a support in laying a brick arch having a small rise.

camber window   A window arched at the top.

cambium   The cellular layer of wood tissue between the bark and sapwood of a tree.

cambium

camboge   A concrete masonry unit with transverse openings; used in tropical architecture, often decoratively, to permit ventilation while excluding sunlight, as in a **brise-soleil**.

came   A slender rod of cast lead, with or without grooves, used in casements and stained-glass windows, to hold together the panes or pieces of glass.

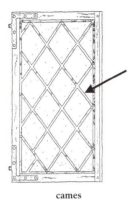

cames

campanile

camelback truss   A truss having a broken outline for the upper chord, composed of a series of straight segments, taking the humped shape of a camel's back.

camelhair mop   A soft-haired brush which is used for varnishing, gilding, and filling in narrow spaces.

camera   **1.** In ancient architecture, an arched roof, ceiling, or covering; a vault. **2.** A room having an arched ceiling; a vaulted room. **3.** A small room, small hall, or chamber.

camerated   Having an arched or vaulted appearance.

camera vitrea   A vaulted ceiling, having its surface lined with plates of glass.

cam handle, locking handle   In a window having a **sash (ventilator, 2)** which swings about pivots, a handle which locks the sash in a closed position by wedging it against a keeper.

campanario   In **Mission architecture**, a belfry or a pierced wall that serves as a belfry, with a bell usually hung in an arched opening.

campaniform   Bell-shaped.

campanile   A bell tower, usually freestanding.

campanulated   Bell-shaped.

camp ceiling   **1.** A ceiling shaped like the interior of a truncated pyramid. **2.** The ceiling within the roof of a building, the sides of which are sloped, following the line of the rafters, but the center of which is flat.

camp sheeting   **Sheetpiling** used for foundation work in sandy soil.

can   Abbr. for **canvas**.

Canadian Standards Association   A nonprofit organization which establishes and publishes standards; its tests and approvals are accepted by the electrical inspection authorities in Canada.

canal, canalis   A channel or groove, as a hollow between the fillets of the volutes of an Ionic capital.

canale   In **Spanish Colonial architecture**, a **waterspout** used to drain rainwater from an essentially flat roof; it projects through, and beyond, the face of the parapet around the roof.

canaliculus   A small channel or groove, as a fluting carved on the face of a **triglyph**.

canary whitewood   Same as **tulipwood, 1**.

canary wood   See **balaustre**.

cancela   In Spanish architecture and its derivatives, a large gate often of ironwork or a massive wood gate, usually decorated with **spindlework** or a lattice grille.

cancelli   Barred screens in a basilica, separating the clergy from the laity, in Early Christian architecture.

candela   The International Standard unit of luminous intensity; closely approximates the formerly accepted unit known as the "international candle."

candelabrum **1.** A movable candle lampstand with central shaft and, often, branches or a decorative representation thereof. **2.** A lighting device designed as an architectural fixture, composed as in definition 1, above. Also see **lamppost**.

candela per unit area See **luminance**.

candle beam In old churches, a horizontal beam, bar, or rail furnished with prickets for holding candles, each of which has a saucer or tray to catch the drippings; placed over or near the altar, and also at the entrance to the choir or chancel, where the rood beam or rood screen was placed in richer churches.

candlepower (cp) The luminous intensity of a light source, expressed in candelas. *Abbr.* cp. Also see **apparent candlepower**.

candle-snuffer roof Same as **conical roof**.

cane bolt A heavy cane-shaped bolt with the top bent at right angles; installed at the bottom of a door.

cane bolt

canephora, canephorus **1.** Ornament representing a maiden (youth) bearing a basket of ceremonial offerings on the head. **2.** A **caryatid** with basket on her head; used either as a support or as a freestanding garden ornament.

cannelated Said of a surface that is fluted or grooved.

canonnière A hole left in a retaining wall to permit water in the earth behind the wall to drain through it.

canopy **1.** A decorative **hood** above a niche, pulpit, choir stall, or the like. **2.** A covered area which extends from the wall of a building, protecting an entrance or loading dock.

canopy of honor Same as **celure**.

canopy roof A roof, often over a balcony or porch, that is suggestive of the curvature of a suspended cloth canopy.

cant **1.** A salient corner. **2.** A line or surface angled in relation to another, as a sloped wall. **3.** Masonry "on cant" is laid with joints sloping between front and back surfaces; the vertical joints are laid normally. **4.** A log partly or wholly squared off.

cant bay A bay erected on a plan of canted outline.

cant-bay window A **cant window**.

cant board A board which is laid so as to cant a surface, as under the first row of shingles on a roof, or to support lead sheeting on each side of a valley gutter; a **cant strip**.

cant brick See **splay brick**.

canted Having a **cant, 2**; said of a wall, etc.

canted molding A wood **raking molding**.

canted wall A **cant wall**.

cantharus A fountain or basin in the atrium or courtyard before ancient and some Oriental churches, where persons could wash before entering the church.

cantherius A principal rafter in an ancient wooden roof.

cantilever **1.** A beam, girder, structural member, truss, or structural member or surface that projects horizontally beyond its vertical support, such as a wall or column. **2.** A projecting bracket used for carrying the cornice or extended eaves of a building.

cantilever arch An arch that is supported by flat projections on opposing walls.

cantilever beam A **beam** which is supported only at one end.

cantilever footing A **footing** having a tie beam to another footing to balance a structural load not symmetrically located with respect to the footing.

cantilever form Same as **slip form**.

cantilever retaining wall See **cantilever wall**.

cantilever steps Steps built into the wall at one end, but supported at the other end only by the steps below.

cantilever truss A **truss** overhanging its support at one end and anchored at the other.

cantilever wall A reinforced concrete wall which resists overturning by the use of **cantilever footings**.

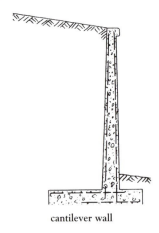

cantilever wall

canting strip A **water table, 1**.

cant molding A square or rectangular molding with the outside face beveled.

canton A corner of a building decorated with a projecting masonry course, a pilaster, or similar feature.

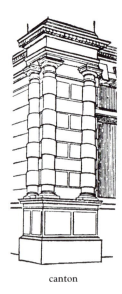

canton

cantoned Ornamented at the corners with projecting pilasters.

cantoned pier Same as **pilier cantoné**.

cantoria A church choir gallery.

cantoris Of (or belonging to) the cantor or precantor, for example—the cantoris side of the choir in a church; the left or north side as one faces the altar.

cant strip **1.** A beveled strip of wood or other material used esp. under built-up roofing where the roofing turns up, providing a gradual transition; used to prevent the cracking of roofing applied over it; as **arris fillet. 2.** A **tilting fillet**; a **doubling piece. 3.** A **cant board**.

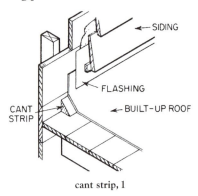

cant strip, 1

cant wall A wall canted on plan.

cant window, cant-bay window A bay window erected on a plan of canted outline; the sides of the window are at an angle with respect to the wall; also see **angled bay window**.

cant window

CANV On drawings, abbr. for **canvas**.

canvas A closely woven cloth of cotton, hemp, or flax; sometimes adhered to a wall or deck to serve as a substrate for paint; used to cover roof decks that are walking surfaces or sun decks.

canvas wall A plastered wall to which a layer of canvas has been applied to serve as a base for wallpaper.

cap **1.** Usually, the topmost member of any vertical architectural element, often projecting, with a drip as protection from the weather, e.g., the coping of a wall, top of a pedestal or buttress, the lintel of a door, etc. **2.** A layer of concrete placed over rock in the bottom of foundation excavations to level the exposed surface, prevent its deterioration by weathering, and protect it from other damage. **3.** The upper member of a column, pilaster, door cornice, molding, and the like; also called **cap trim, wainscot cap, dado cap, chair rail cap, capital. 4.** A fitting used to close the top end of a tubular newel. **5.** A **blasting cap**. **6.** A fitting used to close the end of a pipe. **7.** A plane surface which is bonded to the bearing surface of a test specimen during its strength testing to ensure a uniform load distribution.

capacitance The quantitative measure of the electric-energy storage capability of a **capacitor**; usually measured in farads or microfarads (10^{-6} farads).

capacitance alarm A device which is electrically connected to a protected metal enclosure (such as a safe, vault, file, or security cabinet) so that the enclosure itself becomes part of a balanced-capacitance circuit. A person approaching the protected cabinet unbalances the electrical circuit and activates a security alarm.

capacitor An electric component which consists of conducting plates insulated from each other by a layer of dielectric material; introduces **capacitance** into a circuit.

capacitor motor A single-phase induction motor with its main winding connected to a source of power and having an auxiliary winding connected in series with a **capacitor** to facilitate starting.

capacity **1.** See **carrying capacity**. **2.** The volume contained in a vessel. **3.** The maximum or minimum water flow obtainable under given conditions (e.g., specified conditions of pressure, temperature, and velocity).

capacity insulation The ability of masonry to store heat; depends on its mass, density, and specific heat.

cap block Same as **drive cap**.

cap cable In prestressed concrete, a short cable introduced to prestress the zone of negative bending.

Cape Ann house A rectangular house, commonly one or one and a half stories high, that is similar to a **Cape Cod house**, but has a shingled **mansard roof** rather than a shingled **gable roof**.

Cape Ann house

cape chisel A long **cold chisel** which has a long taper and a narrow cutting edge; used for cutting keyways and the like.

Cape Cod house A colonial one-and-a-half-story rectangular house of wood-frame construction that originated on Cape Cod, Massachusetts. Usually characterized by: a massive central chimney serving all fireplaces; a gable roof; a roof covering and exterior wall covering of hand-split wood shingles, left unpainted to weather to a gray color; double-hung windows on the first story and often on the gable-end walls; paneled doors; a partial basement. Cape Cod houses are of three types: **full Cape house**, which has two windows on each side of the front door; **three-quarter Cape house**, which has two windows on one side of the

Cape Cod house

front door and a single window on the other side; and a **half Cape house**, which has two windows on one side of the front door and none on the other.

Cape house   A term used in some parts of New England for a **Cape Cod house.**

cap flashing   Same as **counterflashing**.

capilla mayor   The principal chapel in Spanish churches.

capillary action, capillarity   **1.** The movement of a liquid in the interstices of soil or other porous material, as a result of surface tension. **2.** The phenomenon responsible for dry soil sucking up moisture above the ground water level. Also see **capillary flow.**

capillary break   A space between two surfaces which is purposely made wide enough to prevent the movement of moisture through the space by capillary action.

capillary flow   The flow of moisture through a capillary pore system, as in concrete.

capillary groove   A groove formed between two building components to prevent **capillary action** between them.

capillary joint   Same as **sweat joint**.

capillary migration   See **capillary flow**.

capillary space   In cement paste, any space not occupied by anhydrous cement or cement gel. Air bubbles, whether entrained or entrapped, are not considered to be part of the cement paste.

capillary tube   A tube of small internal diameter; used in refrigeration as a control for the flow of liquid refrigerant, or as an expansion device between the condenser and evaporator; or used to transmit pressure from the sensitive bulb of a temperature control to the operating element.

capillary water   Water, above the water table, held there by capillary action.

capital   The topmost structural member of a column, pilaster, anta, or the like, often decorated;

capital: nomenclature

may support an **architrave, 1** or may be surmounted by an impost. See illustrations under the various **orders**; also see **angle capital, basket capital, bracket capital, bud capital, Byzantine capital** (illustrated under Byzantine architecture), **Composite capital, Corinthian capital, corner capital, cushion capital, Doric capital, Hathoric capital, protomaic capital, Ionic capital, lotus capital, palm capital, scalloped capital, water-leaf capital**.

capitals

capitol   Official meeting place for a legislative body.

cap molding, cap trim   **1.** Molding or trim which embellishes the top of a dado. **2.** Molding, at the head of a window or door, above the simple trim of the casing.

cappella del coro   The **choir**, or chapel of the choir.

capping   Any architectural member serving as a **cap, 1**, such as a **coping**.

capping brick   Same as **coping brick**.

capping piece, cap piece, cap plate   A piece of timber covering the heads of a series of uprights or other vertical structure.

capping plane   A plane used for rounding the upper surface of wooden railings.

cap plate   **1.** A **capping piece**. **2.** The top plate on a steel column or post; usually supports a load.

cap rail   A **rail, 1** fastened to the uppermost member of a railing system.

capreolus   In an ancient timber roof, a brace or strut; a king post or tie beam.

cap screw   **1.** A screw which is threaded along its entire length and has a chamfered point; it is driven into a hole and secured without a nut. **2.** Same as **tap bolt**.

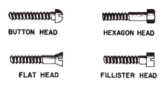

BUTTON HEAD   HEXAGON HEAD

FLAT HEAD   FILLISTER HEAD

cap screws

cap sheet   A coated felt, usually mineral-surfaced; used as the top ply of a built-up roofing membrane. See **asphalt prepared roofing**.

capstone   **1.** Any single stone in a **coping**. **2.** A stone placed at the top of a stone arch.

captain's house   In colonial New England, a house having a truncated hipped roof and chimneys at both gable ends; has a **widow's walk** and/or a cupola on the roof.

captain's walk   See **widow's walk**.

cap trim   See **cap molding**.

car   See **elevator car**.

caracole   A **spiral stair**.

car annunciator   An electric device in an elevator car which provides a visual indication of floor landings.

carapa, crabwood, Surinam mahogany, West Indian mahogany   A pale to reddish brown wood of South America and Africa; moderately hard and heavy, with straight grain and medium texture; used for general construction and in plywood.

caravansary, caravanserai   **1.** In the middle east, a building or inn for the overnight lodging of travelers by caravan; usually enclosed by a solid wall and entered through a large gate. **2.** By extension, any large inn or hotel.

interior of a **caravansary**

carbonaceous   Said of rock containing organic matter.

carbon-arc cutting   An arc-cutting process in which the severing of metal is effected by melting with the heat of an arc produced between the carbon electrode and the metal being cut.

carbon-arc lamp   A high-intensity electric-discharge lamp employing an arc discharge between carbon electrodes.

carbon-arc spotlight   A spotlight employing a high-intensity **arc light** source.

carbon-arc welding   An arc-welding process wherein coalescence is produced by heating with an arc between a carbon electrode and the work.

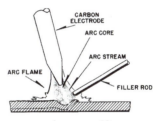

CARBON ELECTRODE
ARC CORE
ARC STREAM
ARC FLAME
FILLER ROD

carbon-arc welding

carbonation   The reaction between carbon dioxide and calcium compounds, esp. in cement paste, mortar, or concrete, to produce calcium carbonate.

carbon black   A synthetically produced black pigment, almost pure carbon; used to color paint and concrete because of its high shading strength. Also see **animal black**.

carbon dioxide–extinguishing system   A **fire-extinguishing system** in which the extinguishing agent is carbon dioxide supplied from a pressurized vessel through fixed pipes and nozzles; includes an automatic **fire detection system** and an actuating mechanism.

carbon steel   **1.** Steel having no specified minimum content of alloying elements. **2.** Steel having a specified minimum copper content not exceeding 0.40%. **3.** Steel having a maximum specified content as follows: manganese 1.65%, silicon 0.60%, copper 0.60%.

carcase   Same as **carcass**.

carcass, carcase   **1.** The framework of a building before the addition of sheathing or other covering. **2.** The frame or main parts of a structure unfinished and unornamented, lacking masonry, brickwork, floors, carpentry, plastering, inside trim, etc.

carcass flooring The frame of timbers which supports the floorboards above and the ceiling below.

carcass roofing A framework of timber which spans a building and carries the boarding and other covering.

carcer **1.** A prison. **2.** A starting stall in a Roman circus for horse or chariot races. **3.** The dens for beasts in an amphitheatre.

card frame, card plate A metal frame, attached to a door or drawer, which holds a name card or label.

cardo A hinge or pivot, used in ancient construction to hang a door.

car door See **elevator car door**.

car door contact, gate contact An electric device which prevents movement of an elevator car unless its door (or gate) is in the closed position.

care, custody, and control Describes a standard exclusion in liability insurance policies. Under this exclusion, the liability insurance does not apply to damage to property in the care or custody of the insured, or to damage to property over which the insured is for any purpose exercising physical control.

car-frame sling Same as **elevator car-frame sling**.

carillon **1.** A bell tower; a **campanile**. **2.** A set of fixed bells, usually hung in a tower and struck by hammers.

carnarvon arch A lintel supported on corbels.

carnauba wax A hard, high-melting-point wax; used in wood polishes and coatings to produce a matte finish.

carnel, crenelle Same as the embrasure of a **battlement**.

carnificina In ancient Rome, a subterranean dungeon in which criminals were tortured and in many cases executed.

carol An area in a cloister set off by screens, partitions, or railings; similar in use to a **carrel**.

Carolean Said of the periods of the reigns of King Charles I (1625–1649) and Charles II (1660–1685) of England; also called Caroline.

Carolingian architecture The pre-Romanesque architecture of the late 8th and 9th cent. in France and Germany, based on Roman forms. So called after the emperor Charlemagne (768–814). The cathedral of Aachen is the best-known example.

carolytic, carolitic Descriptive of a column having a **foliated** shaft.

carousel packer An automatic **refuse compactor** in which compacted waste materials are compacted and packaged in bags arrayed along a circular carriage; designed for high-volume and/or for long, unattended operation.

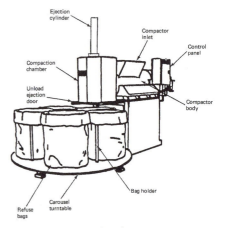

carousel packer

car park (*Brit.*) A **parking lot**.

Carpenter Gothic, Carpenter Gothic Revival A mid-19th century architectural style in which highly decorative woodwork and Gothic motifs were applied to otherwise simple homes or churches in America, usually designed and constructed by carpenters and builders; often asymmetric in plan. Buildings in this style are often characterized by: a façade that promotes vertical emphasis, such as by pointed arches that extend into the gables; Gothic motifs such as foliated ornaments, pinnacles with battlements, crockets, decorative brackets, foils, towers, turrets, and wall dormers suggestive of Gothic architecture; often, an entry porch having a flattened Gothic or Tudor arch; a steeply pitched roof or gabled roof, often with a gable at the center of the façade or with intersecting gables; lacy, highly ornate bargeboards and finials decorating the gables and dormers; decorative shingle patterns on the roof; high, ornamental chimney stacks; often, clusters of chimney pots; bay windows, casement windows with diamond-shaped or rectangular-shaped panes, lancet windows, ogee-arch windows, oriel windows, stained-glass windows, triangular arch windows often with mullions and relatively thin **tracery**; label moldings; often elaborately paneled entry doors in a Gothic motif; a wood-paneled door or a battened door suggestive of the medieval period, sometimes bordered with sidelights. Occasionally called Carpenter's Gothic.

Carpenter Gothic

carpenter's brace　Same as **brace, 3**.

carpenter's bracket scaffold　A scaffold consisting of wood or metal brackets supporting a platform.

carpenter's finish, *Brit.* **joiner's finish**　Finish work by a carpenter, including the laying of the finish flooring, the construction of stairs, the fitting and installation of doors and windows, exposed cabinet work and moldings, etc., but excluding rough finish work such as framing.

carpenters' guides, carpenters' handbooks　See **pattern book**.

carpenter's level　An instrument used by a carpenter to determine a horizontal or a vertical

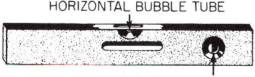

carpenter's level

line; consists of a **spirit level** set in a straight bar of wood or metal.

carpenter's punch　A **nail set**.

carpenter's square, framing square　A flat, steel **square** commonly used in carpentry.

carpenter's square

carpentry　A building trade which includes cutting, framing, and joining the timbers or woodwork of a building or structure.

carpet　A heavy, durable floor covering, usually of woven, knitted, or needle-tufted fabric; commonly installed with tacks or staples, or by adhesives.

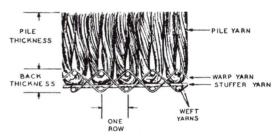

carpet　construction

carpet backing　The material on the underside of carpet; usually made of cotton, carpet rayon, kraft cord, or jute; may have a coating of latex.

carpet bedding　Beds in which small annual plants with ornamental foliage or flowers, and perhaps gravel-filled sections as well, are arranged in patterns to be seen from above.

carpet cushion　Same as **carpet underlayment**.

carpet density　The number of rows of pile tufts per inch, lengthwise.

carpet fiber　The material of which the yarn of the carpet pile is made, as wool, acetate, acrylic, cotton, nylon, polyester, polypropylene, rayon, etc.

carpet float   A wood float, covered with a piece of dense-pile carpet; used in plastering to produce a fine-grained texture in a sand finish.

carpet pile   The tufts of yarn that stand erect from the base of the carpet and whose ends form the surface; the ends may be cut or looped.

carpet pile height   The height of the pile yarn above the backing material; usually expressed in inches or millimeters.

carpet pitch   The number of warp yarn ends per inch crosswise of the loom; usually expressed in terms of the number of pile yarn ends in a 27-in. (68.6-cm) width of carpet.

carpet strip   **1.** A molding used to fasten the edge of carpeting. **2.** A strip of wood (approximately equal to the carpet thickness) installed on the floor at the threshold of a door.

carpet stuffers   Extra yarn, usually jute, which is run lengthwise through the center of the fabric of carpet backing to add thickness and weight.

carpet underlayment   A padding material, laid directly on the floor, over which carpet is installed; usually manufactured of hair felt, foam rubber, hair felt and jute, sponge rubber, or some other combination of these materials.

carpet warp   Yarn which runs lengthwise of the fabric, passing alternately over and under the weft yarns.

carpet weft   Yarn which runs across the width of the carpet, from selvage to selvage.

car platform   Same as **elevator car platform**.

carport   A covered automobile shelter associated with a separate dwelling. It has one or more sides open to the weather.

carreau   A single glass or encaustic tile, usually square or diamond-shaped, used in ornamental glazing.

carrefour   **1.** An open place from which a number of streets or avenues radiate. **2.** By extension, any crossroad or junction. **3.** A public square or plaza.

carrel, cubicle   A small individual compartment or alcove in a library, used for semiprivate study.

carrelage   Tiling; esp. the decorative tiling in terra-cotta used in the Middle Ages for floors, etc.; imitated in modern times.

carriage   **1.** An inclined beam which supports the steps or adds support between the **strings** of a wooden staircase, usually between the wall and outer string. Also called a **carriage piece, horse, roughstring**. **2.** In theatre stage equipment, a counterweight arbor. **3.** A movable frame on which some other movable part or object is supported.

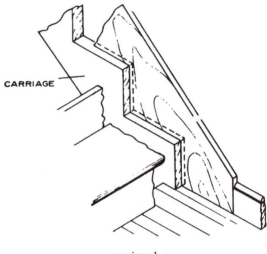

carriage, 1

carriage bolt   A threaded bolt having a circular head, an oval or flat bearing surface, and a means (such as a square shoulder under the head) of preventing rotation of the bolt.

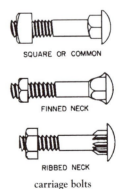

carriage bolts

carriage clamp   A type of C-clamp used in carpentry.

carriage house   See **coach house**.

carriage piece   See **carriage, 1**.

carriage porch A roofed structure over a driveway at the door to a building, protecting from the weather those entering or leaving a vehicle. Also see **porte cochere**.

carriage shed A rough, roofed structure having one or more open sides; once used as a temporary shelter for horse-drawn carriages, as in the yard of a church.

carriageway (*Brit.*) A road designed to carry vehicular as opposed to pedestrian traffic; specifically, the actual traffic lanes of such a road as distinct from median strips or shoulders.

carrier **1.** A mobile prime mover for transporting construction machines; also may serve as the working base or undercarriage of the machine. **2.** A container attached to or hung from a trolley for moving a load from one point to another on a construction site. **3.** A **carrier angle** or **carrier bar** which supports treads formed from metal grating.

carrier angle An angle iron connected to the inside face of a stair stringer to form a supporting ledge for the end of a tread or riser.

carrier bar A flat metal bar which is used in the same way as a carrier angle.

carrying capacity Of an electric cable or wire, same as **ampacity**.

carrying channel In suspended ceiling construction, a three-sided metal member used to support the entire ceiling assembly.

carrying freezer A cold-storage room, where the temperature usually is maintained between −20°F (−28.9°C) and 20°F (−6.7°C).

carry up In masonry and brickwork, to build up a wall to a specified height.

car safety See **elevator car safety**.

car-switch operation Operation of an **elevator car** in which the movement and direction of travel of the car are directly and solely under the control of the operator by means of a manually operated car switch or continuous-pressure buttons in the car.

cart house An enclosure, such as a shed, for sheltering two-wheeled horse-drawn vehicles that are intended for two passengers.

cartload The quantity a cart will carry, usually ¼ to 1 cu yd (approx. 0.2 to 0.8 cu m).

carton pierre A mixture of glue, whiting, paperpulp, and chalk; molded, dried, and finished to form durable, usually interior, architectural embellishments imitating stone, metal, etc.; a kind of **papier-mâché** used for making lightweight cast ornaments where plaster would be too heavy.

cartoon A drawing or painting made as a detailed model, often full-scale, of an architectural embellishment.

cartouche **1.** An ornamental tablet often inscribed or decorated, and framed with elaborate scroll-like carving. **2.** A modillion of curved form. **3.** In Egyptian hieroglyphics and derivatives, a frame around the Pharaoh's name.

cartouche, 1

cartridge Same as **cartouche**.

cartridge fuse A **fuse** enclosed in a cylindrical tube, which protects an electric circuit against the excessive flow of current.

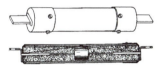

cartridge fuse: a section of the enclosed fuse is shown in the lower figure

cartridge heater An electric heating coil, enclosed in a metal case shaped like a cartridge.

cartridge-type filter A **water filter** in the form of a cartridge. (*See illustration p. 160.*)

carved work **1.** In stonework, hand-cut ornamental features which cannot be applied from pattern. **2.** In brickwork, carving, usually on bricks of larger than ordinary size. (*See illustration p. 160.*)

carvel joint A flush joint between adjacent planks.

caryatid A supporting member serving the function of a pier, column, or pilaster and carved

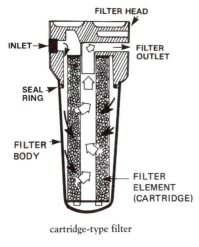

cartridge-type filter

carved work, 1: an Early English carved capital

or molded in the form of a draped, human, female figure. See **canephora**.

casa del campo In Spanish architecture and its derivatives, a one-story country house usually built around a patio, constructed primarily of adobe and wood; had a **mission tile** roof having a central ridge, or a shed roof having a single shallow pitch, usually with considerable overhang to provide shade.

casa del pueblo, casa del poblador In Spanish Colonial architecture of the 18th and 19th centuries, a house in a village or town usually constructed of adobe brick that has been plastered and whitewashed; had a mission tile roof supported by beams that penetrated the walls, and wood-framed casement windows, with the windows facing the street protected by grilles or gratings.

casa del rancho In Spanish Colonial architecture and its derivatives, especially in the 18th and 19th centuries, the main dwelling of a ranch that usually included: a large courtyard entered by way of a massive wooden gate; a **corral**; a partially enclosed or fully enclosed patio; living quarters for all members and servants of the household, housing for domestic animals, and associated storage spaces.

casa de tablas Same as **tabla house**.

cascade refrigerating system A **refrigeration system** consisting of two or more refrigerant circuits, each with a pressure-imposing element, condenser, and evaporator; the evaporator of one circuit cools the condenser of the other circuit, which is at a lower temperature.

case **1.** To cover one building material with another. **2.** Same as **casing, 1. 3.** The housing containing a lock mechanism. **4.** A unit in which food is displayed and protected; often partially constructed of clear glass or plastic and thermally insulated; usually counter-top or wall-mounted.

case bay That section of a floor or roof between two principals or girders.

cased beam **1.** A beam having a **casing, 2. 2.** Same as **caged beam**.

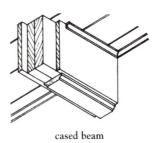

cased beam

cased column Same as **caged column**.

cased frame, boxed frame, box frame The wood frame of a **double-hung window**; has hollow jambs or mullions which contain the sash counterweights.

cased glass, case glass, overlay glass Glass formed of two or more fused layers of different colors; the top layer may be cut, permitting a lower layer to show through.

cased opening, trimmed opening An opening between rooms which is finished with doorjambs and trim but does not have a door hung in it.

cased post A post having a **casing, 2**.

cased sash-frame A **cased frame**.

case-hardened **1.** Said of a piece of material fabricated of steel or iron alloy whose surface has been hardened by a special process: first by carburization and then by heat treatment. **2.** Said of timber whose outer layers have dried too rapidly during seasoning.

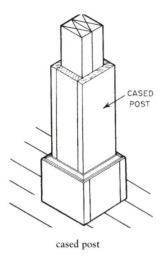

cased post

case-hardened glass Same as **tempered glass**.

case-hardening **1.** In timber, a condition in which the outer layers have dried without shrinkage, causing stress between the inner and outer layers. **2.** Producing a hard surface layer on steel, as by carburizing, cyaniding, carbonitriding, nitriding, induction hardening, and flame hardening.

casein A protein; the chief nitrogenous ingredient of milk.

casein glue Glue made from milk protein; esp. used in carpentry and joinery.

casein paint A paint which uses an emulsion of casein as adhesive and binder.

case lock A surface-mounted lock, such as a **box lock**.

casemate A vault or chamber in a bastion, having openings for the firing of weapons.

casemate wall A city or fortress enclosure consisting of an outer and an inner masonry wall braced by transverse masonry partitions, which divide the interstitial space into a series of chambers for fill or storage.

casement **1.** A window **sash (ventilator, 2)** which swings open along its entire length; usually on hinges fixed to the sides of the opening into which it is fitted; see **casement window**. **2.** A deep hollow molding, used chiefly in cornices.

casement adjuster A device for holding a **casement** in any open position. Also see **casement stay**.

casement combination window A **combination window, 2**, one element of which is a casement window.

casement door A **French door**.

casement hinge A hinge on which a **casement, 1** is hung; also see **butt casement hinge, close-up casement hinge, extension casement hinge**.

casement stay In a casement window, a bar used to hold a **casement**, in any of several fixed, open positions. Also see **peg stay**.

casement ventilator A **casement, 1**, which opens like a door, supported on hinges, pivots, or friction hinge mechanisms.

casement window A window having at least one **casement, 1**; may be used in any combination with **fixed lights**.

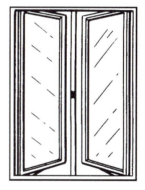

casement window

case mold A shell made of plaster to hold various parts of a plaster mold in proper position; also used to prevent distortion when pouring gelatin or wax molds.

case steel The outside skin on steel produced by **case-hardening**.

casework The aggregate assembled parts (including framework, finish, doors, drawers, etc.) which make up a case or cabinet.

cash allowance An amount established in the **contract documents** for inclusion in the **contract sum** to cover the cost of prescribed items not specified in detail, with provision that variations between such amount and the finally determined cost of the prescribed items will be reflected in **change orders** appropriately adjusting the **contract sum**.

cashel In Ireland, an enclosing wall of rough stone, once intended as defensive work for a church or for several sacred buildings; a **caher**.

casing **1.** The exposed trim molding, framing, or lining around a door or window; may be either flat or molded. **2.** Finished millwork, of uniform profile, which covers pipes or encases a structural member such as a post or beam. **3.** A pipe section used to line a hole; may be driven, drilled, or dropped into place; also called a **shell**. **4.** Of a pump, the housing that encloses the impeller.

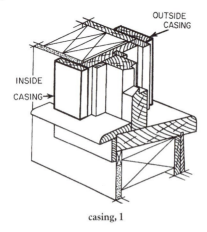

casing, 1

casing bead A **bead** applied to edges of a plaster surface to provide a stop or a separation between two dissimilar materials.

casing-bead doorframe A doorframe having a metal casing bead which serves as a **ground** for plastering.

casing knife In paperhanging, a knife used to trim wallpaper around casings, at moldings, baseboards, etc.

casing nail A slender nail with a small, slightly flared head used for finishing work.

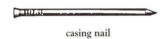

casing nail

casing-off The elimination of the frictional forces between a portion of a **pile, 1** and the surrounding soil by the use of a sleeve between the pile and the soil.

casino **1.** A clubhouse or public room, esp. used for gambling. **2.** A clubhouse or public room used for dancing. **3.** A summerhouse or lodge; a retreat.

Cassel brown See **Vandyke brown**.

cassoon A deep panel or coffer in a ceiling or soffit.

cast, staff In plastering, a shape, usually decorative, made in a mold and then fastened in place.

castable refractory A packaged, dry mixture of hydraulic cement (generally calcium aluminate cement) and specially selected and proportioned refractory aggregates which, when mixed with water, produces refractory concrete or mortar.

castellated **1.** Bearing the external fortification elements of a castle, in particular, battlements, turrets, etc. **2.** Ornamented with a battlement-like or crenelated pattern.

castellum A reservoir, often of architectural nature, at the end of an aqueduct, for distributing the water into various channels.

casting See **founding**.

casting plaster A finely ground plaster with special additives; used in casting work. The additives produce hardness and control shrinkage or expansion.

cast-in-place concrete, cast-in-situ concrete, in situ concrete Concrete which is deposited in the place where it is required to harden as part of the structure, as opposed to precast concrete.

cast-in-place pile A concrete pile which is concreted either with a casing or without a casing at its permanent location, as opposed to a precast concrete pile.

cast-in-situ concrete Same as **cast-in-place** concrete.

cast iron An iron alloy, usually including carbon and silicon; a large range of building products are made of this material by pouring the molten metal into sand molds and then machining. Has high compressive strength, but low tensile strength.

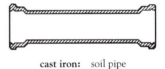

cast iron: soil pipe

cast-iron architecture In building construction, cast iron used in combination with wrought iron for the **framing** of commercial buildings and for the components of **cast-iron fronts**; used primarily before the advent of **steel-frame construction**. Usually characterized by: prefabricated cast-iron components, repetitive modules, and large windows, in contrast to earlier masonry façades in which large windows were impractical because they weakened the wall into which they were set.

cast-iron boiler   A boiler furnished in sections of cast iron, usually assembled at the place of installation; the capacity of the boiler may be increased by adding more sections.

cast-iron front   A load-bearing façade composed of prefabricated parts, commonly used on commercial buildings ca. 1850–1870.

cast-iron lacework   Mass-produced decorative ironwork of intricate design, formed by the casting process and therefore relatively inexpensive compared with wrought-iron work.

cast-iron pipe, cast-iron soil pipe   A pipe fabricated of an iron alloy containing carbon and silicon; usually lined with cement or coal-tar enamel and coated externally with one of a variety of materials to reduce corrosion by soils; known technically as **gray cast-iron pipe**.

cast-iron register   See **mantel register**.

cast-iron stove   See **Franklin stove**.

castle   A stronghold; a building or group of buildings intended primarily to serve as a fortified post; a fortified residence of a prince or nobleman.

cast molding   A molding of plaster, cement, or other such material which is cast in a mold in sections and set in place after it has hardened.

castrum   An ancient fortified town, castle, or fort.

cast staff   In plastering, a shape, usually decorative, made in a mold and then fastened in place.

cast stone   See **artificial stone**.

CAT.   On drawings, abbr. for "catalog."

catabasis, catabasion   See **katabasis**.

catacomb   Underground passageways used as cemeteries, with niches for sarcophagi or smaller ones for cinerary urns.

catacumba   The atrium or courtyard of a basilican church.

catafalque   A draped and canopied stage or scaffold, usually erected in a church, on which is placed the coffin or effigy of a deceased person.

catalyst   **1.** A substance which accelerates a chemical reaction but appears to remain unchanged itself. **2.** A hardener that accelerates cure of adhesives either with or without heat. Used primarily with synthetic resins.

catalytically-blown asphalt   A **blown asphalt** produced by using a catalyst during the blowing process.

cat-and-clay chimney   Same as **stick-and-clay chimney**.

catch   A device for fastening a door or gate; usually opened manually from one side only.

catch basin   A reservoir, esp. for catching and retaining surface drainage over a large area, in which sediment may settle.

catch drain   A drain running along sloping ground to catch and convey the water flowing over the surface.

catch pit   Same as **catch basin**.

catch platform   A platform or other construction projection from the face of a building, from which it is supported; used to protect individuals and property from falling debris during construction.

catenary   The curve formed by a flexible cord hung between two points of support.

catenary arch   An arch which takes the form of an inverted catenary.

catenated   Decorated by a chain-like motif.

catface   A rough depression, flaw, or blemish in a plaster finish coat.

cathead   A notched wedge placed between two formwork members meeting at an oblique angle.

cathedra   The bishop's throne, set at the end of the apse in Early Christian churches.

cathedra

cathedral

cathedral The home church of a bishop, usually the principal church in a diocese.

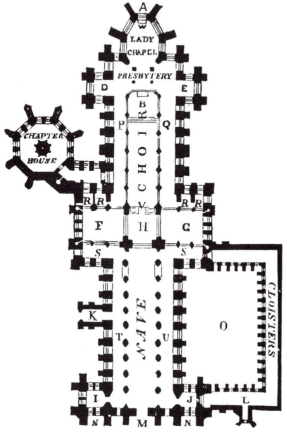

cathedral: plan of Wells Cathedral. *A,* apse; *B,* altar; *D, E,* eastern transept; *F, G,* western transept; *H,* central tower; *I, J,* western towers; *K,* north porch; *L,* library; *M,* western doorway; *N, N,* western side doors; *O* cloister yard; *P, Q,* north and south aisles of choir; *S, S,* east and west aisles of transept; *T, U,* north and south aisles of nave; *R, R,* chapels; *V,* rood screen; *W,* altar of lady chapel

cathedral glass Translucent sheet glass which is unpolished.

Catherine-wheel window A round window with radial mullions. A **rose window, wheel window**.

cathetus The axis of a cylinder, esp. the axial line passing through the eye of an Ionic volute.

cathodic corrosion Same as **galvanic corrosion**.

cathodic protection, electrolytic protection A method of protecting a ferrous metal

structure, which is embedded in water or moist soil, from corrosion due to galvanic action; usually by attaching it to a metal rod which is more electronegative than the structure, or by counteracting the current which is the source of corrosion by another one (in the opposite direction) which just balances it.

cation-exchange softening The softening of water by the removal of dissolved ionic contaminants in hard water (such as scale-forming magnesium and calcium ions) and their replacement with sodium ions, which are more soluble.

cat ladder, duckboard, gang boarding, roof ladder A plank with a series of small strips nailed across it; hung on a sloping roof under repair to provide a footing for workmen and to protect the surface.

cat's eye A **pin knot** smaller than ¼ in. (0.6 cm) in diameter.

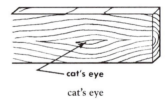

cat's eye

catshead An ornament consisting of an animal-like head, similar to a **beakhead**.

catshead

catslide **1.** The long sloping roof at the rear of a **saltbox** or **catslide house**. **2.** The term used in southern U.S.A. for a **saltbox house**.

catstep See **corbiestep**.

CATW On drawings, abbr. for **catwalk**.

catwalk A narrow fixed walkway providing access to an otherwise inaccessible area or to lighting units, light bridges, etc.; used above an excavation, around a high building, above the ceiling of an auditorium or theatre, or around a stagehouse.

caul A flat sheet of metal or wood used as a protective layer of plywood, particleboard, fiberboard, etc., during the forming, pressing, and shaping operations.

cauliculus, caulicole Any one of the ornamental stalks rising between the leaves of a Corinthian or Composite capital, from which the volutes spring.

caulis One of the main stalks of leaves which spring from between the acanthus leaves of the second row on each side of the typical Corinthian capital, and which are carried up to support the volutes at the angles.

caulk To fill a joint, crack, etc., with **caulking**.

caulked joint A type of joint used for cast-iron pipe having hub-and-spigot ends. After the spigot-end of one pipe is placed inside the hub-end of the other, a rope of oakum or hemp is packed into the annular space around the spigot end until the packing is about 1 inch (2.5 cm) below the top. Then molten lead is poured into the annular space on top of the rope. Finally, the lead is pounded farther into the joint with a caulking iron.

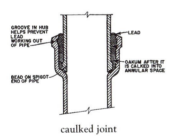

caulked joint

caulked rivet A **rivet** which has not been properly driven so as to fit tightly in the hole, but to which a seeming tightness has been given by turning the edge of the head under with a **cold cut** or similar tool.

caulking, calking **1.** A resilient mastic compound, often having a silicone, bituminous, or rubber base; used to seal cracks, fill joints, prevent leakage, and/or provide waterproofing; also see **caulking compound. 2.** Another term for **cogging.**

caulking cartridge An expendable container made of plastic, fiberboard, or metal; filled with caulking compound, for use in a caulking gun. A common type is 2 in. (5 cm) in diameter, approx. 8 in. (20 cm) long, and fitted with a plastic nozzle.

caulking compound A soft putty-like material intended for sealing joints in buildings and other structures, preventing leakage, or providing a seal at an expansion joint; usually available in two consistencies: "gun grade," for use with a caulking gun, and "knife grade," for application with a putty knife.

caulking ferrule A **ferrule**, usually of brass, which is caulked.

caulking gun A device for applying caulking compound by extrusion. In a hand gun, the required pressure is supplied mechanically by hand; in a pressure gun, the pressure required usually is greater and is supplied pneumatically.

caulking recess In plumbing, a recess (or counterbore) in the back of a flange into which lead can be caulked, for water pipe connections and the like.

causeway **1.** A paved road or passage raised above surrounding low ground. **2.** Such a passage ceremonially connecting the valley temple with the pyramid in Egyptian architecture.

caustic dip The immersion of metal in a chemical solution for cleaning purposes.

caustic embrittlement A type of embrittlement in the metal at joints and the ends of tubes in steam boilers; due to the chemical composition of the boiler water; may lead to failure of the metal.

caustic etch, frosted finish A decorative matte texture produced on aluminum alloys by an etching treatment in an alkaline solution, generally caustic soda.

caustic lime See **lime**.

cavaedium **1.** An inner courtyard in a Roman house. **2.** An **atrium**.

cavalier A raised portion of a fortress for commanding adjacent defenses or for the placement of weapons.

cavasion A term, used many years ago, for an excavation for the foundation of a building.

cavea The semicircular, tiered seating area of an ancient (esp. Roman) theatre.

cavel Same as **kevel**.

cavetto, gorge, hollow, throat, trochilus A hollow member or round concave molding containing at least the quadrant of a circle, used in cornices and between the tori of bases, etc.

Erroneously called "scotia," which has a noncircular curvature.

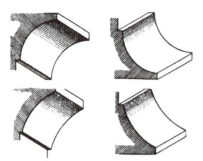

examples of a **cavetto**

cavetto cornice   See **Egyptian gorge**.

cavil   Same as **kevel**.

cavitation   A phenomenon in the flow of water consisting in the formation and the collapse of cavities in water.

cavitation damage   The pitting of concrete caused by implosion (collapse) of bubbles in flowing water.

cavity barrier   Same as **fire stop**.

cavity batten   A piece of wood placed within a cavity wall during construction to catch mortar droppings.

cavity fill   A material placed in the air space in a hollow or double wall or in a floor-ceiling assembly to improve its sound- or heat-insulation qualities.

cavity flashing   A continuous sheet of waterproofing material which is installed across the gap of a cavity wall.

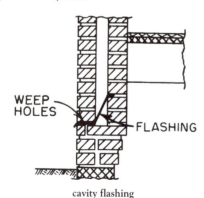

cavity flashing

cavity tray   A British term for **cavity flashing**.

cavity wall, hollow masonry wall, hollow wall   An exterior wall, usually of masonry, consisting of an outer and inner withe separated by a continuous air space, but connected together by wire or sheet-metal ties. The dead air space provides improved thermal insulation.

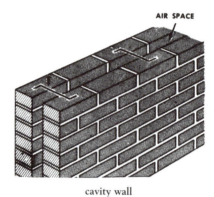

cavity wall

cavity wall tie   A rigid, corrosive-resistant metal tie which bonds two withes of masonry.

cavo-rilievo, cavo-relievo   See **sunk relief**.

CB   Abbr. for **catch basin**.

CB1S   Abbr. for "center beam one side."

CB2S   Abbr. for "center beam two sides."

CBM   Abbr. for "Certified Ballast Manufacturers Association."

CBR   Abbr. for **California bearing ratio**.

C/B ratio, saturation coefficient   The ratio of the weight of water absorbed by a masonry unit during immersion in cold water to weight absorbed during immersion in boiling water; an indication of the probable resistance of brick to freezing and thawing.

c-c   Abbr. for "center-to-center."

cc, CC   Abbr. for "cubic centimeter."

C-clamp   A steel clamp, shaped like the letter C; used to hold, under pressure, two materials placed between the top of the open end of the C and a flattened end of a screw shaft which is threaded through the other end of the C.

C-clamp

CCTV Abbr. for "closed-circuit television."

CCTV surveillance system See **closed-circuit TV surveillance system**.

CCW On drawings, abbr. for "counter-clockwise."

cd Abbr. for **candela**.

cedar A durable softwood generally noted for decay resistance; includes **western red cedar, incense cedar, eastern red cedar.**

cedro In Spanish Colonial architecture, one of many unsplit peeled, relatively straight, red cedar saplings supported by **vigas;** used in ceiling construction.

ceil **1.** To provide with a ceiling. **2.** To provide with a wainscot finish; to sheathe internally.

ceiling The overhead surface of a room, usually a covering or decorative treatment used to conceal the floor above or the roof.

ceiling area lighting Lighting in which the entire ceiling acts as one large **luminaire**, as, for example, a luminous ceiling.

ceiling beam Same as **ceiling joist**.

ceiling binder An intermediate support for ceiling joists.

ceiling cable distribution system A cable distribution system in which cable is run through the space between a suspended or false ceiling and the structural floor above it.

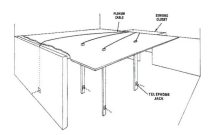

ceiling cable distribution system

ceiling cornice Same as **cove molding**.

ceiling diffuser, ceiling outlet **1.** Any **air diffuser** (usually round, square, rectangular, or linear) which is located in the ceiling; used to provide a horizontal distribution pattern of air over a zone occupied by people.

ceiling fitting Same as **surface-mounted luminaire**.

ceiling flange Same as **escutcheon, 2**.

ceiling floor The framework for a ceiling beneath, but not for the floor above.

ceiling hook A hook having a wood screw formed in its base.

ceiling hook

ceiling joist **1.** Any **joist** which carries a ceiling. **2.** One of several small beams to which the ceiling of a room is attached. They are mortised into the sides of the binding joists, nailed to the underside of these joists, or suspended from them by straps.

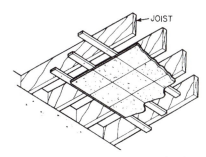

ceiling joists   carrying an acoustical ceiling

ceiling light A **borrowed light, 1**, horizontally located in a ceiling to provide light below.

ceiling medallion, ceiling ornament, ceiling rose A ceiling ornament, usually cast in plaster; often a luminaire or chandelier is hung from its center; see **medallion, 2**.

ceiling outlet **1.** A **ceiling diffuser**. **2.** A small metal box, mounted at ceiling level, in which electric conductors terminate; used to support a lighting fixture or other ceiling-mounted electric appliance.

ceiling plenum In an air-conditioning system, the space between a hung ceiling and the underside of a floor slab above, where this space is used as a plenum for return air.

ceiling ratio In illumination engineering, the ratio of the luminous flux which reaches the ceiling directly to the upward component of the flux provided by a **luminaire**.

ceiling sound transmission In a suspended ceiling construction, the transmission of sound between adjoining rooms by way of the path consisting of the ceiling of each room and the continuous plenum over, and common to, both rooms.

ceiling sound transmission class, ceiling STC A single-number rating of the sound-insulating value of a suspended ceiling between adjacent rooms.

ceiling sprinkler A **fire sprinkler** (head) of special design, intended for installation in ceilings; includes sprinklers of the recessed, flush, and concealed types.

ceiling STC Same as **ceiling sound transmission class**.

ceiling strap A strip of wood, nailed to the underside of floor joists or rafters, from which a ceiling is suspended or fastened.

ceiling strut An adjustable vertical member which extends from the head of a doorframe to construction above; used to hold the frame in a fixed position prior to wall construction; also see **strut guide**.

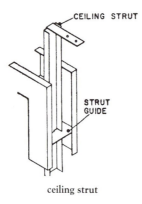

ceiling strut

ceiling suspension system A system of metal members designed to support a suspended ceiling, typically an acoustical ceiling. Also may be designed to accommodate lighting fixtures or air diffusers.

ceiling switch Same as **chain-pull switch**.

ceilure See **celure**.

celature Engraved, chased, or embossed decoration on metal.

cell **1.** See **core**. **2.** A single small cavity surrounded partially or completely by walls. **3.** A segment of a ribbed vault. **4.** The small sleeping apartment of a monk or a prisoner. **5.** In electri-

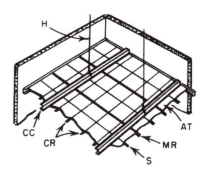

ceiling suspension system: *AT*, acoustical tile; *CC*, carrying channel; *CR*, cross runners; *H*, hanger wire; *MR*, main runner; *S*, spline

cal systems, a single raceway of a cellular or underfloor duct system. **6.** In electrical batteries, a single voltage-producing component used in series with other similar components to provide the desired output voltage.

cella, naos The sanctuary of a classical temple, containing the cult statue of the god.

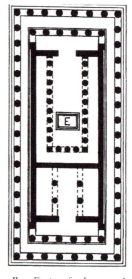

cella *E*, site of cult statue A

cellar **1.** A room (or several rooms, or the entire basement floor) that is partially or entirely below grade; relatively cool in the summer and above freezing in the winter; often used as storage space; provides some thermal insulation airspace between the ground or concrete slab and the flooring of the wood floor above. **2.** That part of a building having at least half of its clear height below grade. Also see **earth cellar, root cellar, storm cellar, basement**.

cellar bulkhead, cellar cap Same as **bulkhead, 4**.

cellar door A **bulkhead, 4**, often sloping or nearly horizontal.

cellar hole The excavation for a cellar or the open remains of a cellar.

cellarino In the Roman or Renaissance Tuscan or Doric orders of architecture, the neck or necking beneath the ovolo of the capital.

cellar sash A window **sash** set into the foundation wall of a building, usually just below the horizontal member or surface that provides bearing and anchorage for the wall above.

cellarway Passage to or through one or more cellars.

cellula **1.** In ancient Rome, a small sanctuary in the interior of a small temple. **2.** Any small chamber or storeroom.

cellular brick (*Brit.*) A brick or block in which holes, closed at one end, exceed 20% of the volume.

cellular cofferdam A self-sustaining **cofferdam** fabricated of interlocking steel sheet piling; has separate inside and outside walls.

cellular concrete, aerated concrete A light-weight product consisting of portland cement, cement-silica, cement-pozzolan, lime-pozzolan, or lime-silica pastes, or pastes containing blends of these ingredients and having a homogeneous cell structure, produced by gas-forming chemicals or foaming agents.

cellular construction Construction with concrete elements in which part of the interior concrete is replaced by voids.

cellular-core door See **mesh-core door**.

cellular floor A floor having hollow openings in it that provide ready-made raceways for dis-

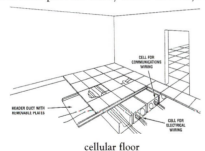

cellular floor

tributing wiring for telecommunications and electric power.

cellular framing See **box frame, 1**.

cellular glass See **foam glass**.

cellular material Any material that contains many cells (either open or closed, or both) dispersed throughout the mass.

cellular plastic A plastic containing numerous cells disposed uniformly throughout its mass.

cellular polystyrene An insulation composed principally of a polymerized styrene resin which has been processed to form a rigid foam having a closed-cell structure.

cellular raceway A hollow space, in a modular floor system, suitable for use as a raceway for electric conductors.

cellular rubber A rubber product containing cells that are either open and interconnecting or closed and not interconnecting.

cellular striation In a cellular material, such as plastic, a layer of cells that differ greatly from the characteristic cell structure of the material.

celluloid A relatively tough thermoplastic material made from plasticized cellulose nitrate with camphor; inflammable, easily molded, readily dyed, not light-stable.

cellulose A naturally occurring polysaccharide made up solely of glucose units and found in most plants; the main constituent of dried woods, jute, flax, hemp, ramie, etc.; cotton is almost pure cellulose; used in the manufacture of a wide variety of synthetic building materials.

cellulose acetate A material of the ester family derived by conversion of cellulose; used in the production of synthetic lacquers, coatings, plastics, and thermal insulation.

cellulose acetate butyrate (CAB) plastic A plastic compound of cellulose acetate butyrate ester and plasticizer and other ingredients.

cellulose enamel Lacquer made with nitrocellulose. Also see **lacquer**.

cellulose fiber tile An acoustical tile formed of cellulose fiber.

cellulose lacquer A **lacquer** having a cellulose derivative base.

cellulose nitrate A material formed by the reaction of cellulose fibers with nitric and sulfuric acids. Those with lower nitrogen content are used as binders in lacquers and are very inflammable. A high nitrogen content results in **nitrocellulose**, an explosive.

cellure See **celure**.

Celsius scale Same as **centigrade** scale.

Celtic cross A cross with a long vertical shaft and short horizontal arms, and with a circle struck from their intersection, joining all four.

Celtic cross

celure, ceilure, cellure A decorative ceiling, esp. over the chancel, in medieval church architecture or derivatives. **2.** A paneled canopy above an altar or crucifix.

CEM On drawings, abbreviation for **cement**.

cem ab Abbr. for **cement-asbestos board**.

cement **1.** A material or a mixture of materials (without aggregate) which, when in a plastic state, possesses adhesive and cohesive properties and hardens in place. Frequently, the term is used incorrectly for concrete, e.g., a "cement" block for concrete block. See also **portland cement**. **2.** A calcined combination of limestone and clay, combined with an **aggregate** that reacts chemically when water is added; after this reaction occurs, the mixture hardens in place as it dries, resulting in a stonelike material. Although the ancient Romans developed a cement that could harden under water (called *hydraulic cement*), there was little information in

modern times on how to produce such a cement until the mid-1700s when experiments in England led to the development of a cement that could set quickly, in or out of water. Also see **hydraulic cement, portland cement, Roman cement, water cement**.

cement-aggregate ratio The ratio, by weight or volume, of cement to aggregate.

cement-asbestos board A dense, rigid, noncombustible board containing a high proportion of asbestos fibers which are bonded with portland cement; highly resistant to weathering; also called **asbestos-cement board**.

cementation The setting of a cement.

cement bacillus See **ettringite**.

cement block See **concrete block**.

cement brick Brick fabricated from a mixture of cement and sand; molded under pressure and steam-cured at a temperature of 200°F (93°C); used behind **face brick** where it will not be exposed to acid or alkaline conditions.

cement clinker See **clinker, 1**.

cement-coated nail A nail which is coated with cement to increase its holding power.

cement content, cement factor The quantity of cement contained in a unit volume of concrete or mortar, preferably expressed as weight, but frequently given as bags of cement per cubic yard of concrete, e.g., a 6½-bag mix.

cement factor See **cement content**.

cement fillet, weather fillet Mortar which provides a weathertight seal in a corner between roofing slates and a wall; used in place of **flashing**.

cement gel A colloid comprising the largest part of the porous mass of mature hydrated cement paste.

cement gravel Gravel bound into a mass by clay, calcium carbonate, silica, or some other binding agent.

cement grout See **grout**.

cement gun A device for applying cement mortar as a fine spray; uses compressed air as the propellant.

cementitious Having cementing properties.

cementitious material A material (with or without an aggregate) that provides plasticity, cohesive, and adhesive properties when it is mixed with water—properties that are necessary for its placement and formation into a rigid mass.

cementitious mixture   A mixture of mortar, concrete, or grout that contains hydraulic cement.

cement mixer   See **concrete mixer**.

cement mortar   A mixture of cement, lime, sand, or other aggregates with water; used for plastering over masonry or to lay blocks. The lime adds plasticity and resistance to moisture. Also see **mortar**.

cement paint, concrete paint   **1.** A paint consisting generally of white portland cement and water, pigments, hydrated lime, water repellents, or hygroscopic salts; usually applied over masonry surfaces as a waterproofing. **2.** A paint formulated to be resistant to the alkali in the cement surface over which it is applied.

cement paste   A mixture of cement and water.

cement plaster   **1.** Plaster with portland cement as the binder; sand and lime are added on job. Used for exterior work or in wet or high-humidity areas. **2.** In some regions, **gypsum plaster**.

cement rendering   The application of a portland cement and sand mix over a surface; has rather poor weather resistance.

cement rock, cement stone   A clayey limestone whose percentage composition of alumina, lime, and silica is about that of cement; may be used without the addition of other earth materials.

cement screed   A **screed** of cement mortar.

cement slurry   A mixture of cement and water, still in the liquid state; injected into prepacked aggregate or used as a wash over a surface.

cement stucco   Same as **stucco**.

cement temper   Portland cement used as an additive in lime plaster to improve its strength and durability.

cement-water paint   Same as **cement paint**.

cement-wood floor   A poured floor of a mixture of portland cement, sand, and sawdust.

cemetery beacon   In Europe in the 12th and 13th centuries, a model of a lighthouse having an altar.

cem. fin.   Abbr. for "cement finish."

CEM FL   On drawings, abbr. for "cement floor."

CEM MORT   On drawings, abbr. for **cement mortar**.

CEM PLAS   On drawings, abbr. for **cement plaster**.

cen   Abbr. for "center" or "central."

cenaculum   In ancient Rome, a small informal dining room, often on an upper story.

cenatio   In ancient Rome, the formal dining room in a house, sometimes even in a separate annex.

cenotaph   A monument erected in memory of one not interred in or under it.

center   **1.** The center ply in plywood. **2.** The core in a laminated construction. **3. Centering**. **4.** The center about which an arc of a circle is drawn, equidistant from all points on the arc.

center bit   A tool for boring holes in wood, held by a **brace**; the cutting end consists of a sharp point (or threaded center spur) for fixing the center of the hole, a projecting scoring edge for marking the circumference of the hole, and a sharp lip for cutting away the wood inside the circumference.

center bit   showing cutting end

center flower   A molded plaster **centerpiece**.

center-gabled pediment   A **pediment** on a gable located at the center of a façade; may be flush with the front wall or project forward from it.

center gutter   Same as **valley gutter**.

center-hall cabin, central-hall cabin   A cabin having two rooms that are separated by a hallway; often, there is an exterior chimney on each end wall. Compare with **dogtrot cabin** and **saddlebag cabin**.

center-hall plan   In American Colonial architecture, the floor plan of a house usually having two rooms symmetrically situated on each side of a centrally located hallway; a stair in the hallway led to the loft space above. Essentially a **hall-and-parlor plan** with a hallway separating the two rooms.

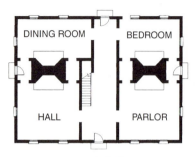

center-hall plan

center-hung door, center-pivoted door A door which is supported by and swings about a pivot recessed in the floor at a point located on the center line of the door's thickness; the door may be of the single-swing or double-acting type.

center-hung sash A window sash hung on its centers so that it swings about a horizontal axis.

centering A temporary structure upon which the materials of a vault or arch are supported in position until the work becomes self-supporting.

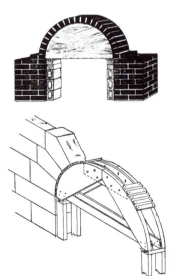

centering: two types

center line A line representing an axis of symmetry; usually shown on drawings as a broken line.

center-matched Said of tongue-and-grooved lumber with its tongue-and-groove at the center of the piece rather than offset as in **standard matched**.

center nailing The nailing of slates (at a point just above their middle) along a line which is slightly above the head of the slates in the course below.

center of gravity, center of mass A point within a body such that, if the whole mass of the body were concentrated there, the attraction of gravity would remain the same.

center of mass See **center of gravity**.

center of twist See **shear center**.

centerpiece An ornament placed in the middle of something, as a decoration in the center of the ceiling.

center pivot Of a door: a pivot having its axis on the thickness center line of the door, normally about 2¾ in. (7 cm) from the hinge jamb.

center-pivoted door See **center-hung door**.

centerplank, heart plank Usually a quarter-sawn hardwood board cut near the center of a log.

center punch A hand-held punch consisting of a steel rod, one end of which has a sharp point; used to mark a point on metal, indicating where a hole is to be drilled.

center punch

center rail The horizontal **door rail** which separates the upper and lower panels of a recessed panel-type door; usually located at lock height.

centers See **centering**.

center shaft Of a revolving door, the vertical shaft to which the **wings** are attached.

center stringer A **string, 1**, which is located under a flight of stairs at its midpoint and which supports its treads by cantilever action.

center-to-center, on center The distance between the center line of one element, member, part, or component (as a stud or joist) and the center line of the next.

centi A prefix indicating division by 100.

centigrade The thermometer scale, divided into 100 degrees, in which 0°C is the freezing point of water and 100°C is the boiling point.

centigrade heat unit Same as **pound-calorie**.

centimeter In the metric system, a measure of length equal to a hundredth part of a meter, or 0.3937+ in.; abbreviated cm; an inch equals 2.54 cm.

central air-conditioning system An **air-conditioning system** in which the air is treated by equipment at one or more central locations outside the spaces served, and conveyed to and from these spaces by means of fans and pumps through ducts and pipes.

central air-handling unit An **air-handling unit** in which treated air is distributed to a number of spaces by means of ductwork.

central fan system A mechanical system of air conditioning in which air is treated by equipment outside the area served and distributed by means of ductwork.

central-hall plan, central-passage plan Same as **center-hall plan**.

central heating system A system in which heat is supplied to all areas of a building from a central plant through a network of ducts or pipes.

centrally located chimney, central chimney An **interior chimney**, often massive in size, located near the middle of a house, to provide heat for the entire house during the winter.

central-mixed concrete Concrete that is completely mixed in a stationary mixer, from which it is transported to the delivery point.

central mixer A stationary concrete mixer from which the freshly mixed concrete is transported to the work.

central pavilion A centrally located, prominent projection from the façade of a monumental public building or stately home; often two stories high and domed, and architecturally accented by more elaborate decorative elements.

central-plant refrigeration system A **refrigeration system** in which the cooling medium is distributed to remote locations from a central location, generally containing multiple refrigeration compressors and circulating pumps.

central station An office to which one or more types of alarm systems in a building are connected; operators monitor and provide supervisory control of these systems; may be provided with direct lines to fire or police departments, or to other outside agencies.

centric load, concentric load A load which passes through the centroid of the cross section of a structural member and acts normal to the cross section.

centrifugal compressor A compressor in which compression is obtained by the use of a **centrifugal pump**.

centrifugal fan A fan, within a scroll-type housing, which receives air along the axis and discharges it radially; may be either belt-driven or connected directly to a motor.

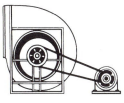
centrifugal fan

centrifugally-cast concrete See **spun concrete**.

centrifugal pump A pump in which the pressure is imparted to the fluid by centrifugal force produced by a rotating impeller.

centrifugal pump

centroid The point which may be considered the center of a two-dimensional figure; the **center of gravity** of an area.

centry-garth A burying ground or cemetery.

CEQ Abbr. for "Council on Environmental Quality."

CER On drawings, abbr. for **ceramic**.

ceramic Any of a class of products, made of clay or a similar material, which are subjected to a high temperature during manufacture or use, as porcelain, stoneware, or terra-cotta; typically a ceramic is a metallic oxide, boride, carbide, or nitride, or a mixture or compound of such materials.

ceramic aggregate Ceramic products in lump or fragment form, usually colored, used in making ornamental concrete.

ceramic bond A bond between materials which are exposed to temperatures approaching the fusion point of the mixture, as a result of thermochemical reaction between the materials.

ceramic coating An inorganic, essentially nonmetallic protective coating on metal, suitable for use at or above red heat.

ceramic color glaze, ceramic glaze An opaque, colored glaze of satin or gloss finish; obtained by coating the clay body with a compound of metallic oxides, chemicals, and clays, either by spraying or by dipping, and then burning at high temperatures; the glaze is fused to the body, making them inseparable.

ceramic-faced glass Glass which during the heat-strengthening process has colored ceramic frit permanently fused to one surface.

ceramic mosaic tile An unglazed tile, formed by either the dust-pressed or the plastic method, usually ¼ to ⅜ in. (0.64 to 0.95 cm) thick, and having a facial area of less than 6 sq in. (38.7 sq cm); usually mounted on sheets to facilitate setting; may be either of porcelain or of natural clay.

ceramic veneer An architectural terra-cotta having a ceramic glazed surface; the dimensions of its face are usually large compared with its thickness; the backside glazing is either scored or ribbed, making it easier to attach the ceramic veneer to a wall or other surface.

cercis The wedge-like or trapezoidal section of seats between two of the stepped passageways in a Greek theatre.

ceroma In a Greek or Roman bath, a room where bathers and wrestlers were anointed with oil thickened with wax.

certificate for payment A statement from the architect to the owner confirming the amount of money due the contractor for work accomplished or materials and equipment suitably stored, or both.

certificate of insurance A memorandum issued by an authorized representative of an insurance company stating the types, amounts, and effective dates of insurance in force for a designated insured.

certificate of occupancy A document issued by governmental authority certifying that all or a designated portion of a building complies with the provisions of applicable statutes and regulations, and permitting occupancy for its designated use. Also called an occupancy permit or a certificate of use and occupancy permit.

certification A declaration in writing that a particular product or service complies with a specification or stated criterion.

certified ballast A fluorescent lamp **ballast** which adheres to performance standards set by the Certified Ballast Manufacturers Association.

Certified Ballast Manufacturers Association An independent organization of fluorescent lamp ballast manufacturers.

certified output rating Same as **gross output**.

certosa A monastery of the Carthusian monks, esp. in Italy.

cesspit Same as **cesspool**.

cesspool **1.** A lined and covered excavation in the ground which receives the discharge of domestic sewage or other organic wastes from a drainage system, so designed as to retain the organic matter and solids, but permitting the liquids to seep through the bottom and sides; also called a **leaching cesspool** or **pervious cesspool**. **2.** (*Brit.*) A wooden box, usually lead-lined, constructed in a roof or gutter, to collect rainwater, which then passes to a downpipe.

cesspool

CF **1.** Abbr. for "cost and freight." **2.** Abbr. for "cooling fan."

cfm Abbr. for "cubic feet per minute."

CFR Abbr. for Code of Federal Regulations.

CG **1.** Abbr. for "coarse grain." **2.** On drawings, abbr. for "ceiling grille." **3.** Abbr. for "corner guard." **4.** Abbr. for **center of gravity**.

CG2E Abbr. for "center groove two edges."

chafer house Old English term for ale house.

chaff house A subsidiary building used on a farm to store fodder, such as corn husks, cut hay, or the like.

chain A land surveyor's standard distance-measuring device. Also see **Gunter's chain**.

chain block, chain fall, chain hoist A **tackle**, fitted with an endless chain for hoisting a heavy load by hand; often suspended from an overhead track.

chain bolt At the top of a door, a spring bolt which is actuated by a chain attached to it.

chain bond Masonry construction which is bonded together by an embedded iron bar or chain.

chain bucket loader A **bucket-wheel excavator** in which the buckets are on a roller chain.

chain course A bond course formed by stone headers which are held together by cramps.

chain door fastener A device attached to a door and its jamb which limits the door opening to the length of the chain.

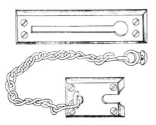

chain door fastener

chain-driven machine A machine connected by chain to a reversible motor or engine; for example, a chain-driven elevator.

chaînes A type of wall decoration used in 17th century French domestic architecture; consists of vertical bands of rusticated masonry which divides the façades into panels or bays.

chain fall See **chain block**.

chain hoist See **chain block**.

chaining In surveying, the measuring of a distance by use of a **chain** or tape.

chaining pin, surveyor's arrow, taping arrow, taping pin A metal pin used in surveying for marking taped measurements on the ground.

chain intermittent fillet weld Two lines of intermittent **fillet welds** on a joint, one line being approximately opposite the other.

chain intermittent fillet weld

chain link fence A fence made of heavy steel wire fabric (usually coated with zinc, or the like) which is interwoven in such a way as to provide a continuous mesh without ties or knots, except at the selvage; the wire fabric is held in place by metal posts.

chain molding A molding carved with a representation of a chain.

chain-pipe vise A portable vise used to hold pipe in the jaw by means of a chain.

chain pipe wrench, chain tongs A plumber's wrench for turning pipe, consisting of a lever arm which has sharp teeth that engage the pipe and a short, adjustable chain which is wrapped around the pipe and holds the pipe securely.

chain pipe wrench

chain-pull switch An electric switch, used in interior wiring, which is operated by pulling a chain or cord; usually mounted on the ceiling.

chain pump A pump consisting of an endless chain, fitted at intervals with disks, which moves through a pipe; used to raise sludge.

chain riveting Riveting in which the rivets are set in parallel adjacent rows along the seam and are not staggered.

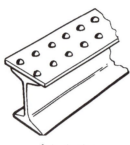

chain riveting

chain saw A power-driven saw, usually hand-held, for cutting wood; a protruding arm carries an endless chain, into which the cutting teeth are set.

chain saw

chain scale A draftman's scale or an engineer's scale which is graduated in inches, which are further subdivided by 10 and multiples of 10.

chain timber A large **bond timber.**

chair 1. A **bar support.** 2. A metal frame, built into a thin partition wall and the floor to support a sanitary fixture (such as a washbasin or water closet) clear of the floor.

chair board Same as **chair rail.**

chair house Same as **cart house.**

chair rail A horizontal strip usually of wood, affixed to a plaster wall at a height which prevents the backs of chairs from damaging the wall surface.

chair rail cap See **cap, 3.**

chaitya A Buddhist or Hindu sanctuary, shrine, or temple.

chaitya hall A hall of worship adjacent to a Buddhist monastery.

chalcedony A submicroscopic variety of fibrous quartz, generally translucent and containing variable amounts of opal; reacts with alkalies in portland cement.

chalcidicum, chalcidic 1. A portico, or hall supported by columns, or any addition of like character connected with any ancient basilica; hence a similar addition to a Christian church. 2. In a Christian basilica, the narthex. 3. In ancient Roman architecture, a building for judicial functions.

chalcidium A committee room off the main part of an ancient Roman lawcourt (basilica).

chalet 1. A timber house especially found in the Alps, distinguished by the exposed and decorative use of structural members, balconies, and stairs. Upper floors usually project beyond the stories below. 2. Any building of similar design. See **Swiss cottage architecture.**

chalk A soft limestone, usually white, gray, or buff in color, composed chiefly of the calcareous remains of marine organisms.

chalkboard A marking surface, primarily for use with chalk, which is cleanable and reusable.

chalkboard trim A chalkboard frame, operating hardware, and accessories.

chalked See **chalky.**

chalking The formation of a powdery surface condition from the disintegration of a binder or elastomer, as in a coating such as cement paint. The binder is decomposed and the pigment is loosely bound on the surface and resembles chalk when the finger is rubbed over it; caused by weathering or an otherwise destructive environment.

chalk line 1. A light cord rubbed with chalk and stretched over a surface to mark a straight line. 2. A line so marked.

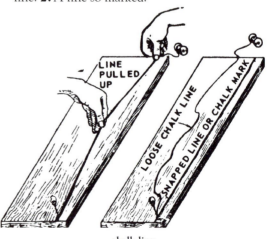

chalk line

chalky, chalked   Descriptive of the condition of a porcelain enameled surface that has lost its natural gloss and become powdery.

CHAM   On drawings, abbr. for **chamfer**.

chamber   **1.** A room used for private living, conversation, consultation, or deliberation, in contrast to more public and formal activities. Also see **bedroom, boudoir, cabinet, closet, den, parlor, solar, study**. **2.** A room for such use which has acquired public importance, e.g., the senate chamber, an audience chamber. **3.** *(Brit., pl.)* A suite of rooms for private dwelling. **4.** *(pl.)* A suite of rooms for deliberation and consultation (juristic). **5.** A space equipped or designed for a special function, mechanical or technological, e.g., a torture chamber, a combustion chamber.

chamber story   In a house, a floor completely occupied by bedrooms; also called chamber floor.

chamber test   A fire test for floor coverings, developed by Underwriters' Laboratories, Inc., in which speed and distance of flame spread are measured.

chamber tomb   See **passage grave**.

chambranle   A structural feature, often ornamental, enclosing the sides and top of a doorway, window, fireplace, or similar opening. The top piece or lintel is called the *transverse* and the side pieces or jambs the *ascendants*.

chambrel   An obsolete term for **gambrel**.

chamfer   **1.** A bevel or cant, such as a small splay at the external angle of a masonry wall. **2.** A **wave molding**. **3.** A groove or furrow. **4.** An oblique surface produced by beveling an edge or corner, usually at a 45° angle, as the edge of a board or masonry surface.

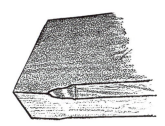

chamfer, 4

chamfer bit   A **bit** for beveling the upper edge of a hole.

chamfered rustication   Rustication in which the smooth face of the stone parallel to the wall is deeply beveled at the joints so that, where two stones meet, the chamfering forms an internal right angle.

chamferet, chamfret   **1.** A hollow chamfer. **2.** A hollow channel or gutter.

chamfer plane   A carpenter's plane esp. used for beveling edges; has a V-groove along the bottom or adjustable guides to facilitate the cutting of chamfers.

chamfer stop   **1.** Any ornamentation which terminates a **chamfer**. **2.** A **stop chamfer**.

chamfer strip   A **cant strip**.

champ   A defined surface ready for carving.

chancel   The sanctuary of a church, including the choir; reserved for the clergy.

chancel aisle   The side aisle of a chancel in a large church; it usually passes around the apse, forming a deambulatory.

chancel arch   An arch which, in many churches, marks the separation of the chancel or sanctuary from the nave or body of the church.

chancel arch

chancellery, chancellory   **1.** A chancellor's office or a building containing one. **2.** The official premises of a diplomatic envoy abroad.

chancel rail   The railing or barrier in place of a chancel screen by which the chancel is separated from the nave.

chancel screen   Screen dividing the chancel from the nave.

chancery   A building or suite of rooms designed to house any of the following: a lawcourt with

chandelier

special functions, archives, a secretariat, a chancellery.

chandelier A **luminaire** suspended from the ceiling; usually ornate or branched with the lamps visible.

chandlery, chandry A storage room for lighting supplies and devices, required before gas or electricity was available.

chandry See **chandlery**.

change In building construction, an authorized alteration or deviation from the design or scope of work as originally defined by the contract documents.

change of use An alteration in the permitted use of an existing building; such a change may result in the imposition of other provisions of the applicable code, for example, those governing means of egress from the building.

change order A written order to the **contractor** signed by the **owner** and the **architect**, issued after the execution of the contract, authorizing a **change** in the work or an adjustment in the **contract sum** or the **contract time** as originally defined by the contract documents; may add to, subtract from, or vary the scope of work. A change order may be signed by the architect alone (provided he has written authority from the owner for such procedure and that a copy of such written authority is furnished to the contractor upon request), or by the contractor if he agrees to the adjustment in the contract sum or the contract time.

changeover point The temperature at which the thermal transmission loss to the outside of a building equals the heat gain in the interior, so that cooling or heating is not required.

changes in the work Changes ordered by the **owner** consisting of additions, deletions, or other revisions within the general scope of the **contract**, the **contract sum** and the **contract time** being adjusted accordingly. All **changes in the work**, except those of a minor nature not involving an adjustment to the contract sum or the contract time, should be authorized by **change order**. Also see **field order**.

channel **1.** A structural or rolled steel shape used in steel construction. **2.** A decorative groove, in carpentry or masonry. **3.** An enclosure containing the ballast, starter, lamp holders,

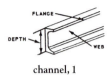
channel, 1

and wiring for a fluorescent lamp, or a similar enclosure on which filament lamps (usually tubular) are mounted.

channel bar See **channel iron**.

channel beam A structural member having a U-shaped cross section.

channel block A hollow concrete masonry unit with portions depressed to form a continuous channel for reinforcing steel and grout.

channel block

channel clip **1.** In a **ceiling suspension system**, a metal clip which is hung from a channel and to which a perforated metal pan is attached. **2.** A special fastener made of light-gauge sheet metal or wire for the attachment of gypsum lath, or the like, to steel channels.

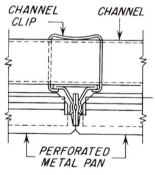
channel clip, 1

channel glazing A method of window glazing which uses removable, surface-mounted, U-shaped metal stops or beads to fix the glass in place.

channeling A series of grooves in an architectural member, such as a column.

channel iron, channel bar A rolled iron or steel bar whose U-shaped cross section is formed

channeling

by a broad central section, called a "web," with a flange on either side.

channel pipe A drain pipe having a half or three-quarter circular cross section; open along the top.

channel runner A heavy horizontal member in suspended ceiling construction.

channel section Same as **channel, 1**.

chantlate A piece of wood fastened to the rafters at the eaves and projecting beyond the wall, so as to prevent rainwater from trickling down the face of the wall.

chantry A chapel within a church, endowed for religious services for the soul of the donor or others he may designate.

chantry chamber The room or rooms used by the priest(s) attached to a **chantry**.

chapel **1.** A small area within a larger church, containing an altar and intended primarily for private prayer. **2.** A room or a building desig-

chapel, 1

nated for religious purposes within the complex of a school, college, hospital, or other institution. **3.** A small secondary church in a parish.

chapel of ease A church built within the bounds of a parish for the attendance of those who cannot reach the parish church conveniently.

chapel royal The chapel of a royal castle or palace.

chapiter Same as **capital**.

chaplet An **astragal** or **bead molding**, sometimes enriched with carved foliage.

chapter house A place for business meetings of a religious or fraternal organization; occasionally also contains living quarters for members of such a group.

chaptrel A small capital of a vaulting shaft.

chaptrel

charcoal filter A filter for removing odors, vapors, and dust particles from air, employing **activated charcoal** as the filter element.

charette **1.** The intense effort to complete an academic architectural problem within a specified time. **2.** The time in which this work is done.

charge The quantity of **refrigerant** in a refrigeration system.

charging Feeding materials into a concrete or mortar mixer, furnace, or other receptacle where they will be further treated or processed.

charging chute An enclosed vertical chute with doors through which waste material is dropped down and fed into an incinerator.

charging door A door to an incinerator through which waste is passed into the combustion chamber.

Charleston house An 18th- or early-19th-century town house in Charleston, South Carolina; usually Georgian or Greek Revival style, two stories high, with the first story often well above ground level. Such houses were of two types. The first and more common type, called a *single house*, was long and narrow, a single room deep, built with its long side perpendicular to the street; on the long side facing a garden was a two-tiered colonnaded porch onto which all rooms opened; the entrance was by a flight of stairs leading from the street up to the porch. The second type, called a *double house*, had a façade facing the street and was two rooms deep, boxlike in shape, and had a portico with a classical two-tiered porch at the middle of the façade.

charnel house   A building or chamber for the deposit of the bones of the dead.

Charonian steps, Charon's staircase   In the early Greek theatre, a flight of steps from the middle of the stage to the orchestra; used by characters from the underworld.

Charpy test   A single-blow impact test utilizing a falling pendulum which breaks a specimen, usually notched, supported at both ends.

Chartered Building Surveyor   A **building surveyor** who is a member of the Royal Institution of Chartered Surveyors.

Chartered Institution of Building Services   A British organization whose members are concerned with services within a building related to the building environment, including: heating, air-conditioning, lighting, acoustical, water supply services, drainage services, electrical supply, gas supply, fire protection, and security protection.

charterhouse   A Carthusian monastery.

chartophylacium   A place for the safe keeping of records and other valuable documents.

chartreuse   A monastery of the Carthusian monks, esp. in France.

chase   **1.** A continuous recess built into a wall to receive pipes, ducts, etc.; a **wall chase**. **2.** A groove cut in a masonry wall to receive a pipe, conduit, etc. **3.** To decorate metalwork by tooling on the exterior surface.

chase bonding   Joining old masonry work to new by means of a bond having a continuous vertical recess the full height of the wall.

chase mortise, pulley mortise   A **stub mortise** which is larger than the tenon inserted into it; one side of the mortise is sloped, permitting the tenon to be inserted sideways; used where exterior clearance is limited.

chase wedge   A wedge-shaped tool with a handle; used for bossing sheet lead.

chasovnya   In early Russian architecture, a chapel which is a detached structure.

chasse   A container for a saint's relics.

chat   A stony mineral material, occurring with mineral ore; very similar to **chert**.

château   **1.** A castle or imposing country residence of nobility in old France. **2.** Now, any French country estate.

château, 1

château d'eau   At the termination of an aqueduct, a reservoir architecturally embellished as a public fountain.

Châteauesque style, Château style, Châteauesque Revival   An opulent architectural style patterned after the design of monumental French chateaus of the 16th century; popular in the late 19th century and beyond. Buildings were usually characterized by a façade having masonry walls; an attic story; a single balcony or continuous balconies; prominent use of vertical elements such as pilasters; wall dormers with gables that might break the roof line; cross gables; a **belt course**; an ornately **hipped roof**

Châteauesque style

either steeply pitched to a ridge and/or truncated by a horizontal surface; cast-iron **cresting** on the roof; through-the-cornice wall dormers; roof dormers with pedimented parapets, pinnacles, and spires; a cylindrical corner turret having a conical roof; tall, decorative chimneys and ornamental chimney caps; windows, frequently in pairs, divided by heavy stone mullions; oriels; semicircular bay windows; exterior door set arches; often a canopy was provided over the entry door.

châtelet   A castle of small scale.

chat-sawn finish   In stone masonry cutting, the moderately rough surface resulting from the use of coarse chat (crushed chert) as the abrasive agent carried by the gang saw blades.

chattel   **1.** Any article of property not consisting of or affixed to land; movable property. **2.** Same as **1**, above, plus any interest in land that is less than a **freehold**. When this nomenclature is used, the term *chattel personal* is employed to designate movables such as goods and money, and *chattel real* to designate less-than-freehold interests in real property, such as leasehold interests for a term of years.

chattel mortgage   A security interest in a chattel as collateral for the payment of a loan.

chatter marks   Intermittent transverse marks on a material due to vibration during rolling, extrusion, cutting, or drawing.

chattra   Atop a **stupa**, a stone umbrella symbolizing dignity; composed of a stone horizontally oriented disk on a vertical pole.

chattravali   Similar to a **chattra**, but having three horizontally oriented stone disks; a triple umbrella; see illustration for **stupa**.

chauntry   Same as **chantry**.

cheapener   An **extender** in paint; not necessarily cheap; more expensive extenders may be used to provide such properties as hardness, wearability, gloss control, and improved brushability.

check   **1.** A small crack running parallel to the grain in wood and across the rings; usually

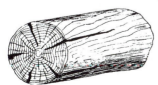

check, 1

caused by shrinkage during drying; in veneers, may improve the appearance. **2.** A minute crack in steel which has been cooled too abruptly. **3.** An attachment that limits movement, such as a **door check**. **4.** See **checking**.

check cracks   See **checking**.

check dam   A barrier in an erodible channel to control the flow of water.

checked back   Having a rabbet; receding.

checker, chequer   One of the squares in a check pattern, contrasted to its neighbors by color or texture; often only two effects are alternated, as in a chessboard. Also see **diaper**.

checkered plate   **1.** A cast steel or iron plate having square, flat projections suggestive of a checkerboard. **2.** A **floor plate**.

checkerwork   In a wall or pavement, a pattern formed by laying masonry units so as to produce a checkerboard effect.

checkerwork

check fillet   On a roof, a curb used to divert or control the flow of rainwater.

checking, check cracks, map cracks, shelling   **1.** Shallow cracks at closely spaced but irregular intervals on the surface of mortar or concrete. **2.** Small cracks in a film of paint or varnish which do not completely penetrate to the substrate or the previous coat. The cracks are in a pattern roughly similar to a checkerboard. **3.** In plastering, in a lime finish coat, fine spiderweb cracks or fissures; usually caused by insufficient troweling or undergauging. **4.** See **check**.

checking floor hinge   A door pivot, fixed in the floor, which includes a mechanism for controlling the speed of the door as it closes. (*See illustration p. 182.*)

checking resistance   The ability of a paint coating, or the like, to resist slight breaks that do

check lock

checking floor hinge

not penetrate to the previously applied coating or substrate.

check lock A small lock whose function is to check the bolt of a larger lock that secures a door.

check nut Same as **locknut, 2**.

check rail In a double-hung window, a horizontal **meeting rail** esp. one which overlaps the other meeting rail.

checkroom A **cloakroom, 3**.

check stop A strip or molding used to hold a sliding element in place, as at the bottom sash of a double-hung window.

check strip A **parting bead**.

check throat A groove cut on the underside of a windowsill or doorsill to prevent the passage of drops of rainwater to the wall.

check valve, back-pressure valve, reflux valve An automatic valve which permits liquid to flow in only one direction. Also see **nonreturn valve**.

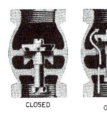

CLOSED   OPEN

check valve

cheek A narrow upright face forming the end or side of an architectural or structural member, or one side of an opening.

cheek boards In concrete formwork, the boards on the sides of the form.

cheek cut, side cut An oblique angular cut at the lower end of a jack rafter or the upper end of any rafter so that it can fit tightly against a hip rafter or valley rafter.

cheesiness The characteristic of a partially dried paint film which results in tearing and crumbling when pulled with the fingernail.

chemical bond A bond obtained as a result of cohesion between layers of similar crystalline materials, owing to the formation and the interlocking of crystals.

chemical brown stain See **kiln brown stain**.

chemical closet See **chemical toilet**.

chemical flux cutting An **oxygen-cutting** process wherein the severing of metals is effected by the use of a chemical flux to facilitate cutting.

chemical grout A fluid used in the **chemical stabilization** of soils.

chemically foamed plastic A cellular plastic whose structure is produced by gases generated from the chemical interaction of its constituents, as a **foamed plastic**.

chemically prestressed cement An **expansive cement** which contains a higher percentage of expansive component than shrinkage-compensating cement.

chemically prestressed concrete A concrete made with **expansive cement** and reinforcement under conditions such that tensile stress is induced in the reinforcement as a result of the expansion of the cement, so as to produce prestressed concrete.

chemical plaster Same as **patent plaster, 2**.

chemical-resistant paint A specially formulated paint finish which utilizes binders and pigments that are unaffected by chemicals.

chemical stabilization The injection of chemicals into a soil to improve its strength and decrease its permeability.

chemical staining Treatment of wood with chemicals to obtain color change and enhance grain contrast.

chemical toilet, *Brit.* **chemical closet** A toilet without conventional water and drain connections; contains a fluid, usually with a disinfectant and deodorant, which neutralizes waste matter chemically.

chemin-de-ronde A continuous gangway behind a rampart, providing a means of communication along a fortified wall.

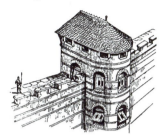

chemin-de-ronde

cheneau 1. A gutter at the eaves of a building, esp. one that is ornamented. 2. An ornamented **crest, 2** or cornice.

chequer See **checker**.

cherry An even-textured, moderately high-density wood of the eastern U.S.A., rich red-brown in color; takes a high luster; used for cabinetwork and paneling.

cherry mahogany See **makore**.

cherry picker A machine for lifting men or materials on a platform at the end of an extendable boom; usually mounted on a carrier with wheels to provide mobility.

chert A very fine-grained dense rock consisting of chalcedony or opal, often with some quartz, and sometimes with calcite, iron oxide, organic matter, or other impurities; has a homogeneous texture and white, gray, or black color; some of its constituents may react with cement alkalies and therefore may be undesirable as concrete aggregate for exposed concrete in northern climates.

chestnut A light, coarse-grained, medium-hard timber; used for ornamental work and trim.

cheval-de-frise, *pl.* **chevaux-de-frise** Sharply pointed nails or spikes set into the top of a barrier.

chevet The apse, ambulatory, and radiating chapels of a church.

chevron 1. A V-shaped stripe pointing up or down, used singly or in groups in heraldry and on

chevron, 2

uniforms; hence, any ornament so shaped. 2. A molding showing a zigzag sequence of these ornaments in Romanesque architecture or derivatives; a **dancette** or **zigzag molding**.

chevron pattern A V-shaped zigzag pattern used as an ornament in brickwork bond.

chevron slat A V-shaped slat used in an opening to provide privacy and ventilation.

Chicago Commercial style See **Commercial style**.

Chicago cottage A small, narrow, inexpensive, quickly built **cottage** set on a brick foundation with its lower story partially below ground level; characterized by **balloon framing**, clapboard exterior walls, an exterior stair between the street and a second-story entrance, an attic above the second story; developed for speculation in Chicago in the mid- to late 1800s.

Chicago School A group of highly influential architects, including Adler and Sullivan, Burnham and Root, William LeBaron Jenney, and their followers in Chicago in the latter part of the 19th century. The School's central philosophy was that architectural design should be of its time rather than based on the past. This group initially applied its philosophy to both skyscrapers and homes, but its greatest and most lasting influence was in the design of skyscrapers, and its greatest achievements were in structural design. Also see **Prairie School**.

Chicago window A large plate-glass window in a commercial building with an operable window on each side to provide ventilation; because of its large size, it provided greater natural illumination than earlier windows. Widely used in high buildings in Chicago in the late 19th century.

chicken house See **poultry house**.

chicken ladder Same as **crawling board**.

chicken wire A light-weight, galvanized wire netting having a hexagonal mesh.

chien A standard unit of floor space or bay of a Chinese dwelling.

chien-assis A small unglazed **dormer** window used to provide light and ventilation in an attic below a sloping roof; especially used in the middle ages.

chigi On the roof of a Shinto temple, a decorative pair of curved timbers that extend above and beyond the roof ridge, crossing at the ridge.

chilled-water refrigeration system A **refrigeration system** employing water as the circulating liquid.

chilling On a painted or varnished surface, a clouding of the surface or a reduction of luster as a result of the movement of cold air over the drying surface.

CHIM On drawings, abbr. for **chimney**.

chimney An incombustible vertical structure containing one or more flues to provide draft for fireplaces, and to carry off gaseous products of combustion to the outside air from fireplaces, furnaces, or boilers. Also see **clay-and-sticks chimney, double chimney, double-shouldered chimney, end chimney, flush chimney, mud-and-sticks chimney, outside chimney, pilastered chimney, sloped-offset chimney, stepped-back chimney, sticks-and-clay chimney, diagonal chimney stacks**.

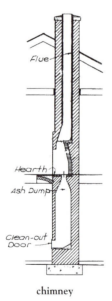

chimney

chimney apron A nonferrous metal flashing built into the chimney masonry and roofing at the penetration of the roof by the chimney.

chimney arch The arch over the opening of a fireplace, supporting the breast.

chimney back See **fireback**.

chimney bar, turning bar A wrought-iron or steel lintel which is supported by the sidewalls and carries the masonry above the fireplace opening. If curved, it is known as an **arch bar**.

chimney block A solid concrete masonry unit with curved faces, intended for use with other similar units in laying up a round flue.

chimney board Same as **fireboard**.

chimney bond A **stretcher bond** used in internal construction in chimneys.

chimney breast, chimney piece A projection into a room of fireplace walls forming the front portion of the chimney stack.

chimney can A **chimney pot**.

chimney cap, bonnet 1. An abacus or cornice forming a crowning termination of a chimney. 2. A rotary device, moved by the wind, which facilitates the escape of smoke by turning the exit aperture away from the wind, preventing the entry of rain or snow and improving the draft. 3. A **chimney hood**.

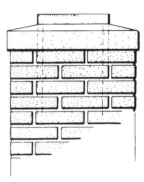

chimney cap, 1

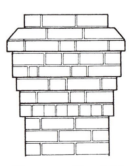

chimney cap with **corbel**, 1

chimney cheek The sides of a fireplace opening which generally support the mantelpiece.

chimney connector A pipe or metal breeching which connects and makes the transition from furnaces and boilers to the flue of a chimney.

chimney corner, inglenook, roofed ingle An area adjacent to the hearth, usually provided with seating.

chimney cowl A revolving metal ventilator over a flue which induces updrafts and prevents downdrafts; a **chimney cap, 2**.

chimney crane A pivoted arm of cast iron attached to the rear wall of the fireplace upon which to hang pots for cooking.

chimney crane   (1796)

chimney cricket A small false roof built over the main roof behind a chimney; used to provide protection against water leakage where the chimney penetrates the roof.

chimney crook, chimney hook In a fireplace, a cast-iron bar, hooked at the lower end and adjustable in length, upon which to suspend pots from a crane or other support.

chimney effect, flue effect, stack effect The tendency of air or gas in a shaft or other vertical passage to rise when heated, owing to its lower density compared with that of the surrounding air or gas.

chimney flue See **flue**.

chimney foundation A very large substructure, in a cellar, that supported the load of a huge fireplace and massive **centrally located chimney** and transmitted this load to the earth or rock below; such a foundation was necessarily immense because of the heavy load of the fireplace above it. Usually rectangular in shape and constructed of brick, stone, fieldstone, stone rubble, or some combination thereof.

chimney girt In a timber-framed house, a structural framing timber that served as a main horizontal support between **chimney posts**.

chimney gutter A preformed nonferrous metal flashing, used for waterproofing where a chimney pierces a pitched roof.

chimneyhead The top of a chimney.

chimney hood A covering which protects a chimney opening.

chimney hood

chimney hook A device for hanging pots for cooking; see **chimney crane**.

chimney jamb One of the two vertical sides of a fireplace opening.

chimney lining See **flue lining**.

chimney lug Same as **randle bar**.

chimney mantel See **mantelpiece, chimney piece**.

chimney pent A small structure, set flush between two exterior brick chimneys located on an end wall of a house; covered by a small narrow sloping roof at the level of the ground floor ceiling, buttressing the chimneys.

chimney pent

chimney piece An ornament over and around a fireplace framing the mantel or the casing of the chimney breast.

chimney post In a **timber-framed house**, one of the wood posts providing the main vertical structural supports at the front and rear sides of a chimney.

chimney pot, chimney can A cylindrical pipe of brick, terra-cotta, or metal placed atop a

chimney pot

chimney to extend and thereby increase the draft.

chimney shaft   That part of a chimney which is carried above the roof of a building of which it forms a part.

chimney stack   **1.** A group of chimneys carried up together. **2.** A very tall chimney, usually round in cross section, attached to factories, mills, etc.

chimney stalk   Same as **chimney stack**.

chimney throat, chimney waist   The narrowest portion of a chimney flue, between the "gathering" (or upward contraction above the fireplace) and the flue proper; often where the damper is located.

chimney tile   Same as **fireplace tile**; see also **Dutch tile**.

chimney top   That part of a chimney that extends above the roof or crowns the chimney stack.

chimney tun   A **chimney stack**.

chimney waist   Same as **chimney throat**.

chimney wing   Same as **chimney cheek**.

China grass cloth   Same as **grass cloth**.

china sanitary ware   Glazed, vitrified, **sanitary ware**.

China white   See **silver white, 2**.

China wood oil   See **tung oil**.

chinbeak molding   One consisting of a convex followed by a concave profile, with or without a fillet below or between, as an inverted ogee, or an ovolo, fillet, and cove.

Chinese architecture   A highly homogeneous traditional architecture which repeated throughout the centuries established types of simple, rectangular, low-silhouetted buildings constructed according to fixed canons of proportions and construction methods. Stone and brick were used for structures demanding strength and permanence, such as fortifications, enclosure walls, tombs, pagodas, and bridges. Otherwise buildings were mostly constructed in a wooden framework of columns and beams supported by a platform, with nonbearing curtain or screen walls. The most prominent feature of the Chinese house was the tile-covered gabled roof, high-pitched and upward-curving with widely overhanging eaves resting on multiple brackets. Separate roofs over porches surrounding the main buildings or, in the case of pagodas, articulating each floor created a distinctive rhythmical, horizontal effect.

Chinese blue   **1.** A pigment in the iron blue family. **2.** One type of **Prussian blue**.

Chinese bond   Same as **rat-trap bond**.

Chinese Chippendale   Descriptive of lattice patterns suggestive of Chinese motifs designed by Thomas Chippendale (1718–1779), England's most widely known furniture maker of his time. Such designs were a combination of horizontal, vertical, and diagonal lines, forming geometric patterns, usually within a rectangular frame; especially used in railing systems.

Chinese fret   A lattice pattern of Chinese motif described under **Chinese Chippendale**.

Chinese lacquer, Japanese lacquer, lacquer   A hard-wearing varnish drawn from natural sources, as from the Japanese varnish tree.

Chinese white   A paint using zinc oxide as the principal pigment.

chink   In a wall, a crack or fissure of greater length than breadth.

chinking   The material used to fill chinks (i.e., long cracks, openings, or fissures), especially between logs that form the exterior walls of log cabin construction. Where the cracks are small, the filling material is often mud or plaster; where the cracks are large, the filling may include wood chips, pebbles, straw, or small sticks.

chinking board   A board used to cover **chinking** in an exterior wall.

chinoiserie   A Western European and English architectural and decorative fashion employing Chinese ornamentation and structural elements, particularly in 18th cent. Rococo design.

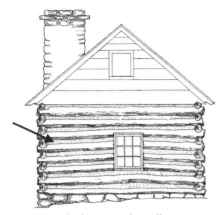

chinking in a log wall

chip A broken fragment of marble or other mineral aggregate, screened to a specified size.

chip ax A small ax for chipping timber or stone into shape.

chipboard See **particleboard**.

chip carving Hand-decorating a wood surface by slicing away chips, forming incised geometric patterns.

chip cracks, eggshelling Same as **checking** except that the edges of the cracks are raised or pulled away from the plaster base, resulting in the loss of bond.

chipped grain A wood surface from which small bits have been ripped as a result of defective planing or machine work.

chipper See **paving breaker**.

chipping Treatment of a hardened concrete surface by chiseling.

chipping resistance Of a paint coating (or the like), the ability of one or more coats to resist the removal of any portion of its surface as a result of impacts.

chisel A hand tool with a cutting edge on one end of a metal blade (usually steel); used in dressing, shaping, or working wood, stone, metal, etc.; usually driven with a hammer or mallet. Also see **cold chisel** and **wood chisel**.

chisel

chisel bar A heavy, steel hand bar with a chisel edge on one end.

chisel knife A knife with a square edge, usually 1½ in. (3.8 cm) or less in width, used to scrape off paint or wallpaper in areas where a wider-edged stripping knife would not be suitable.

chisel pattern A pattern of shingles or tiles on a roof in which the bottom corners of the shingles or tiles are clipped at an angle.

chlorinated paraffin wax A viscous liquid or solid used as a plasticizer or in flame-retardant paints.

chlorinated polyvinyl chloride (PVC) A plastic, widely used for piping in both hot- and cold-water systems and in drainage systems—especially where corrosion may be a problem.

chlorinated rubber A white powder containing 67% rubber by weight, produced by the reaction of chlorine and rubber; used in plastics, adhesives, and corrosion- and acid-resistant paints.

chock A wedge or block used to prevent an object from moving.

choir That part of a church, between the sanctuary and the nave, usually occupied by a group of singers.

choir

choir aisle An aisle parallel to and adjoining the choir.

choir loft A balcony choir area.

choir rail A railing separating the choir from the nave or the crossing.

choir screen, choir enclosure A screen wall, railing, or partition of any type dividing the choir from the nave, aisles, and crossing. (*See illustration p. 188.*)

choir stall A seat with arms and a high back, often covered with a canopy, for clergy and singers.

choir wall A wall between piers and under an arcade screening the choir from the aisles.

choir screen

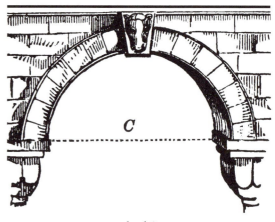

chord, 3

choltry   Same as **choultry**.

chomper   Same as **split-face machine**.

chopping block   See **butcher block**.

choragic monument   In ancient Greece, a commemorative structure, erected by the successful leader in the competitive choral dances in a Dionysiac festival, upon which was displayed the bronze tripod received as a prize; such monuments sometimes were further ornamented by renowned artists.

choragium   In ancient Greece and Rome, a large space behind a theatre stage where the chorus rehearsed and where stage properties were kept.

choraula   Rehearsal room in a church for a choir.

chord   **1.** A principal member of a truss which extends from one end to the other, primarily to resist bending; usually one of a pair of such members. **2.** The straight line between two points on a curve. **3.** The span of an arch.

chord modulus   See **modulus of elasticity**.

choultry   **1.** A caravansary. **2.** In India, a large village hall or place of assembly.

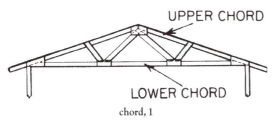

UPPER CHORD

LOWER CHORD

chord, 1

chrismatory   A niche close to a church font which holds the consecrated oil for baptism.

chrismon   Christ symbol composed of the first two letters of the Greek word for Christ, chi and rho; a "Christogram."

Christian door   In Colonial New England, the paneled front door of a house in which the stiles and rails of the door form a pattern suggestive of a cross, the two lower stiles and rails form a pattern vaguely suggestive of an open book, representing the Bible. Also called a cross-and-bible door.

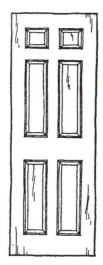

Christian door

Christogram   See **chrismon**.

chromate   To coat a metal surface with a rust-inhibiting primer of lead or zinc chromate.

chromaticity The color quality of light definable by its dominant (or complementary) wavelength and its purity, taken together.

chrome green 1. A green pigment made by blending lead chromate yellow and iron blue pigments. 2. Chromium oxide.

chrome steel A very hard wear-resistant steel having a high elastic limit; usually contains 2% chromium and from 0.8 to 2% carbon.

chrome yellow, Leipzig yellow A family of inorganic yellow pigments, principally lead chromate, but blended with lead sulfate or other lead salts to produce a range of yellow-to-orange pigments.

chromium A hard, brittle metal resistant to corrosion, workable when annealed, gray-white in color; used in alloys, esp. steel, and in plating.

chromium oxide A durable green pigment having good alkali resistance; rather expensive and sparingly used.

chromium plating A plating with chromium used to provide a protective finish which is extremely resistant to corrosion and a surface of extreme hardness; used for decorative purposes because of the smooth surface and ability to take a high polish.

chromium steel Same as **chrome steel**.

chronic-disease hospital An institution which provides facilities and services primarily for chronically ill patients who require long-term care.

chryselephantine Made of gold and ivory; descriptive of statues of divinities, like Zeus at Olympia, with ivory for the flesh and gold for the drapery, on a wooden armature.

CHU Abbr. for **centigrade heat unit**.

chuck A device with adjustable jaws used for centering and holding a cutting bit, drill bit, etc.

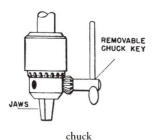

chuck

chuff A brick which has been rendered useless while in the kiln.

chuff brick See **salmon brick**.

church An edifice or place of assemblage specifically set apart for Christian worship.

church house A building used for the social and secular activities of a parish.

church stile Old English for **pulpit**.

churn drill A drill whose cutting action is achieved by raising and dropping a chisel bit.

churn molding Same as **zigzag molding**.

Churrigueresque style A Spanish decorative style, often used in the late 17th century and the first half of the 18th century, characterized by elaborate and lavish **Baroque** ornamentation and detailing; named after the Spanish architect José Churriguera (1655–1725); also see **Mission architecture, Plateresque architecture, Spanish Colonial architecture**.

upper façade of a chapel in the **Churrigueresque style**

chute An open-top trough through which bulk materials are conveyed and lowered by gravity.

chymol See **gemel**.

CI On drawings, abbr. for **cast iron**.

ciborium A **baldachin**.

CIBS Abbr. for "Chartered Institution of Building Services."

CIE Abbr. for "Commission Internationale de l'Eclairage" (International Commission on Illumination).

cif Abbr. for "cost, insurance, and freight."

cilery The ornamental carving, such as foliage, around the capital of a column.

cill British term for **sill**.

cillery Same as **cilery**.

cima See **cyma**.

cimbia A band or fillet around the shaft of a column.

cimborio A lantern or cupola above or nearly above the high altar in Spanish architecture.

cimeliarch The treasury of a church for storing valuables such as ceremonial garb and holy objects.

cinch See **lead pipe cinch**.

cincture, girdle A ring of moldings around the top or bottom of the shaft of a column, separating the shaft from the capital or base; a fillet around a post. Also see **necking**.

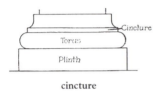

cincture

cinder block, *Brit.* **clinker block** A lightweight masonry unit made of cinder concrete; widely used for interior partitions.

cinder concrete A lightweight concrete made with cinders as the coarse aggregate.

cinders 1. Blast-furnace slag or similar material from volcanoes. 2. Ashes, esp. from soft coal.

cinerarium A depository for urns containing the ashes of the dead.

Cinquecento architecture Renaissance architecture of the 16th cent. in Italy.

cinquefoil A five-lobed pattern divided by **cusps**; also see **foil**.

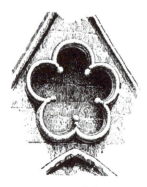

cinquefoil

cinquefoil arch A cusped arch having five foliations worked on the **intrados**.

cinquefoil arch

CIOB Abbr. for "Chartered Institute of Building."

CIP Abbr. for "cast-iron pipe."

cippus A small pillar for commemorative inscriptions, boundary markers, gravestones, etc.

CIR 1. On drawings, abbr. for "circle" or "circular." 2. On drawings, abbr. for "circuit."

CIR BKR On drawings, abbr. for **circuit breaker**.

CIRC On drawings, abbr. for "circumference."

circle end A **starting step** having the shape of a half circle.

circle-on-circle face See **circular-circular face**.

circle trowel A trowel having a concave or convex blade; used in plastering curved surfaces.

circline lamp A **fluorescent lamp** tube bent in the form of a circle; the entire lamp forms a toroid.

circuit 1. A continuous electrical path, or a system of conductors, through which an electric current is intended to flow. 2. An assembly of pipes and fittings, forming part of a hot-water system, through which water circulates.

circuit breaker An electric device for opening and closing a circuit, designed to open the circuit automatically upon flow of a predetermined value of abnormally high current; may be repeatedly reclosed and reused as an automatic overcurrent protection device without replacement of any components.

circuit controller Any type of device used to close and/or open an electrical circuit.

circuit vent In plumbing, a **branch vent** which serves two or more traps and extends from in

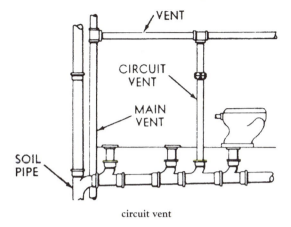

circuit vent

front of the last fixture connection of a horizontal branch to the **vent stack**.

circular arch   An arch whose intrados takes the form of a segment of a circle.

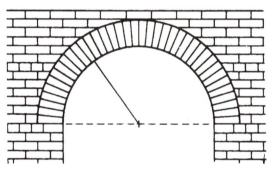

circular arch

circular barn   A barn having a circular plan; requires less building material than a rectangular barn enclosing the same volume, but usually costs somewhat more to construct. Also called a cylindrical barn or a round barn.

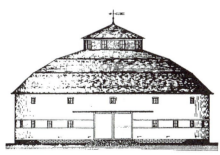

circular barn

circular-circular face, circle-on-circle face   In stonework, carpentry, and joinery: a face worked to convex spherical shape, presenting a curved outline in both plan and elevation.

circular-circular sunk face, circle-on-circle sunk face   Same as **circular-circular face** but presenting a concave outline, in both plan and section.

circular cutting and waste   A measure of the excess tiling, flooring, roofing material, etc., that must be discarded when a curved floor or roof is laid.

circular face   In stonework, a face worked to convex circular shape.

circular mil-foot   A unit electric conductor having a cross-sectional area of 1 circular mil and a length of 1 ft.

circular mill   The area of a circle having a diameter of 1 mil ($\frac{1}{1,000}$ in.); used in specifying wire size; equals an area of 0.00051 sq mm.

circular miter   The **miter** formed by the intersection of a curved and a straight piece.

circular plane   Same as **compass plane**.

circular saw   A power-operated saw in the form of a circular steel blade with teeth along the perimeter. Also see **table saw**.

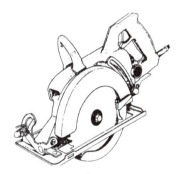

circular saw

circular spike   A type of metal timber connector having a series of sharp teeth in a circle; the teeth dig into the wood as a bolt is tightened, thereby preventing lateral motion. (*See illustration p. 192.*)

circular stair   Same as **spiral stair**; a stair having a cylindrical staircase.

circular sunk face   In stonework, a face worked to concave circular shape; the opposite of **circular face**.

circular spike

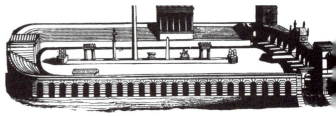

circus

circular window A large window having the shape of a full circle; often has decorative elements within the circle disposed in a radial manner.

circular work See **compass work**.

circulating head, circulating pressure A measure of the pressure available in a hot-water supply system for circulating water around the convection circuit.

circulating water system A system in which the same water circulates around a closed loop; sometimes a small amount must be added to make up for losses.

circulation **1.** The traffic pattern through an area or building. **2.** In a building, a scheme providing for a smooth, economical, and functional flow of traffic. **3.** A means of travel through a building, such as doors, corridors, stairs, and elevators. **4.** The continuous flow of a liquid or gas within a closed circuit.

circulation pipe A pipe forming part of the primary or secondary circuit of a hot-water system.

circulation-type hot-water supply system A supply system which circulates water through a storage tank and one or more gas-fired heaters by means of a pump; circulation improves the transfer of heat and the temperature distribution within the system.

circumvallate To surround an area with a wall or ramparts.

circus, hippodrome In ancient Rome, a roofless enclosure for chariot or horse racing and for gladiatorial shows; usually a long oblong with one rounded end and a barrier down the center; seats for the spectators usually on both sides and around one end.

CIRIA Abbr. for "Construction Industry Research and Information Association of the U.K."

cissing, sissing **1.** A slight shrinkage of a glossy paint coat resulting in small cracks through which the undercoat may be seen; a mild form of **crawling, 2**. **2.** A process for preparing a wood surface for graining by wetting with a sponge.

cist Same as **cistvaen**.

cistern An artificial reservoir or tank for storing water at atmospheric pressure (such as rainwater collected from a roof) for use when required.

cistern head Same as **leader head**.

cistvaen, kistvaen A Celtic sepulchral chamber of flat stones set together like a box, and covered by a tumulus.

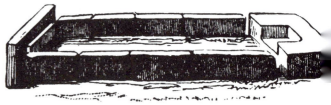

cistvaen

citadel A fortress or castle in or near a city, intended to keep the inhabitants in subjugation, or, in case of a siege, to supply a final refuge.

city plan A large-scale, comprehensive map of a city delineating streets, important buildings, and other urban features compatible with the scale of the map.

city planning, town planning, urban planning Planning a future community, or the guidance and shaping of the expansion of a present community, in an organized manner and with an organized layout, taking into account such considerations as convenience for its inhabitants, environmental conditions, social requirements, recreational facilities, esthetic design, and economic feasibility; includes a study of present requirements and conditions, as well as projections for the future; such planning usually includes proposals for its implementation. See **community planning**.

civery See **severy**.

civic center An area of a city where municipal buildings are grouped; esp. includes the city hall, court house(s), public library, and other public buildings such as a municipal auditorium, art gallery, etc.

civic crown, civic wreath In ancient Rome, an honorary ornament, consisting of a garland of oak leaves, on a monument to one who had saved the life of a Roman citizen in battle.

civil engineer An engineer trained in the design of static structures such as buildings, roads, tunnels, and bridges and the control of water and its contaminants.

CKT On drawings, abbr. for "circuit."

CKT BKR On drawings, abbr. for **circuit breaker**.

CL Abbr. for **center line**.

C-labeled door A door carrying a certification from the Underwriters' Laboratories, Inc. that it meets the requirements for a **class-C door**.

clachan A small village or hamlet in Scotland or Ireland.

clack valve A type of **check valve** in which the controlling element is hinged on one edge, opening for flow in one direction and closing when the flow is reversed.

clack valve

clad Said of a surface that is surface sheathed.

clad alloy An alloy having metallurgically bonded surface coating; applied as corrosion protection, for surface appearance, for use in brazing, etc.

clad brazing sheet A metal sheet which is clad, on one or both sides, with a brazing **filler metal**.

cladding **1.** See **siding**. **2.** A metal coating which is bonded to another metal; see **clad alloy**. **3.** In welding, the deposition of **filler metal** on a

metal surface to obtain desired properties or dimensions; also called **surfacing**. **4.** A nonstructural material (or the surface formed by such a material) used as the exterior covering for the carcass or framework of a building. **5.** The surface on which shingles, tiles, or clapboards are fastened. Also see **siding** and **veneer**.

clairecolle See **clearcole**.

clairvoyée, claire-voie An ironwork screen, openwork fence, gate, or grille through which a vista can be enjoyed.

clam The bucket of a **clamshell**.

clamp A wood and/or metal device designed to hold components firmly, esp. during gluing, machining, soldering, welding, etc.

clamp

clamp brick A stock brick which has been held in a clamp while being burned in a kiln.

clamping plate A metal connector which is bolted to a joint of a wooden frame to strengthen it; a type of **timber connector**.

clamping plate

clamping screw See **screw clamp**.

clamping time The period of time a glued joint must be tightly held during curing.

clamp nail A specialized fastener used to pull and to hold mitered joints together.

clamshell **1.** A wood molding, the profile of which resembles that of a clamshell. **2.** A bucket used on a crane or derrick for handling granular materials. Its jaw-like halves close and open by cable or hydraulic action. (*See illustration p. 194.*)

clapboard, bevel siding, lap siding A wood siding commonly used as an exterior cov-

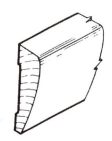

clamshell, 1

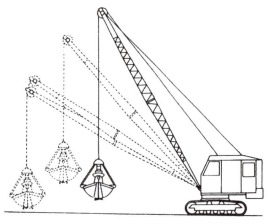

clamshell, 2

ering on a building of frame construction; applied horizontally and overlapped, with the grain running lengthwise; thicker along the lower edge than along the upper.

clapboard gauge, siding gauge A device used to space clapboards so that they are applied parallel to each other.

clapboard house A term occasionally used as a synonym for **Virginia house**.

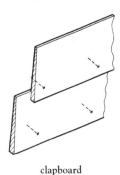

clapboard

clapper In fire **sprinkler systems**, a type of sealing assembly.

clapper valve Same as **clack valve**.

clapping stile Same as **lock stile**.

clarification drawing A graphic interpretation of the **drawings** or other **contract documents** issued by the architect as part of an **addendum, modification, change order,** or **field order**.

Clarke beam A type of **built-up** wood beam consisting of joists or planks which are bolted together and then reinforced with wood pieces nailed along both edges of the joint.

clasp nail Same as **cut nail**.

class As applied to concrete: a characterization according to some quality (such as compressive strength) or usage.

class A, B, C, D, E, F A classification applied to fire doors, fire windows, roof coverings, interior finishes, places of assembly, etc., to indicate gradations of fire safety. See **fire-endurance, fire-door rating**.

class-A door A door having a 3-hr fire-endurance rating, suitable for use as a closure in a class-A opening.

class-B door A door having a 1- or 1½-hr fire-endurance rating, suitable for use as a closure in a class-B opening, such as fire exits and passageways.

class-C door A door having a ¾-hr fire-endurance rating, suitable for use as a closure in a class-C opening.

class-D door A door having a 1½-hr fire-endurance rating, suitable for use as a closure in a class-D opening in an exterior wall.

class-E door A door having a ¾-hr fire-endurance rating, suitable for use as a closure in a class-E opening in an exterior wall.

Classical architecture The architecture of Hellenic Greece and Imperial Rome on which the Italian Renaissance and subsequent styles such as the Baroque and the Classic Revival based their development. The Five Orders are a characteristic feature. See illustrations under **order**.

Classical order See **order**.

Classical Revival style An architectural style, used in many major public buildings from about 1770 to 1830 and beyond; typified by simplicity, dignity, monumentality, and purity of design; based primarily on the use of Roman forms of classical antiquity, although later examples exhibit some characteristics of the **Greek Revival style** which followed. Sometimes called Early Classical Revival, Jeffersonian Classicism, Neoclassical Revival, or Roman Classicism. Buildings in this style were usually rectangular in plan, two rooms deep, gable-fronted, with the long side of the house commonly facing the street; they commonly exhibit many of the following attributes: a symmetrical form sometimes similar to a classical temple; two stories high, often with one- or two-story wings; walls of brick, stucco, stone, or wood construction; typically, a two-story monumental portico, painted white, with a triangular pediment, frequently with a semicircular window set within its tympanum; a pedimented roof, usually supported by four columns on square bases; an entablature above the columns; a low hipped roof, occasionally partially hidden by balustrades; usually five-**ranked;** a paneled door beneath a semicircular or elliptical fanlight. Classical Revival architecture reemerged in popularity from about 1895 to 1940, with modifications, as described under **Neoclassical style**.

classic box A **Colonial revival** house having a hipped roof and a full-width front porch.

classicism In architecture, principles that emphasize the correct use not only of Roman and Greek, but also of Italian Renaissance models.

Classic Revival A term often used as a synonym for the **Classical Revival style**.

classified excavation An excavation in which there are separate prices for **common excavation** and for **rock excavation**; compare with **unclassified excavation**.

class P ballast See **ballast**.

classroom window A window which is twice as wide as an ordinary window, usually having two or more side-by-side **hopper lights** and a single **fixed light** above them.

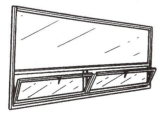

classroom window

clathri A lattice of bars, as of cages for animals or gratings for windows.

clause In the AIA documents, a subdivision of a subparagraph, identified by four numerals, e.g., 3.3.10.1.

claustral, cloistral Pertaining to a cloister.

clavel, clavis A keystone of an arch.

clavis See **clavel**.

claw bar See **pinch bar**.

claw chisel A chisel with a serrated cutting edge; used in cutting stone.

claw hammer A carpenter's hammer with a flat striking face; the other end of the head is curved, and divided into two claws for pulling nails.

claw hatchet See **shingling hatchet**.

claw plate A **timber connector** which is round in shape.

claw plate

clay A fine-grained, cohesive, natural earthy material; plastic when sufficiently wet; rigid when dried; vitrified when heated in a kiln to a sufficiently high temperature; used in making brick, as **wall infilling**, and as daub in **wattle-and-daub**.

clay-and-hair mortar A plastic mixture of clay and water to which animal hair is added to improve the mechanical strength of the resulting mortar after it has dried.

clay-and-sticks chimney A chimney constructed of clay or mud and sticks, and then coated on the interior with clay, mud, or plaster to provide some protection against setting the chimney on fire; used in homes in many frontier areas where bricks, stones, and lime mortar were not available.

clay binder See **binder soil**.

clay brick A solid masonry unit made of clay, usually formed into a rectangular unit while in the plastic state and treated in a kiln at an elevated temperature to harden it.

clay cable cover A fired-clay covering for underground electric cables.

clay content Of a heterogeneous material such as soil or a natural concrete aggregate, the percentage of clay by weight.

clay masonry unit A building unit, larger than a brick, composed of burnt clay, shale, **fire clay**, or some mixture thereof.

clay-mortar mix Masonry mortar which has been plasticized by the addition of finely ground clay.

clay pipe See **vitrified-clay pipe**.

clay puddle See **puddle**.

clay size That portion of fine-grained soil that is finer than 0.002 millimeter.

clay spade An attachment for a pneumatic **paving breaker**, with a wide, flat chisel-like working blade that cuts through cohesive material like clay.

clay tile **1.** A roofing tile of hard, burnt clay. **2.** In flooring, a **quarry tile**.

cleading The boards lining the sides of an excavation, pit, or shaft.

cleanability The property of a paint film which permits easy removal of dirt, stains, and other surface contamination.

clean agent In a **fire suppression system**, any electrically nonconducting, volatile, or gaseous extinguishant that does not leave a residue when it evaporates.

clean aggregate Fine or coarse aggregate, free of such material as clay, silt, or organic substances.

clean back In masonry, the visible end of a stone laid as a bondstone.

cleaning eye A **cleanout**.

cleaning sash, cleaning ventilator The movable part of a window which opens only for cleaning the window; usually unlocked with a special key or wrench.

cleanout **1.** A pipe fitting with a removable plug which provides access for inspection or cleaning of the pipe run. Also called an **access eye or cleaning eye**. **2.** An opening at the base of a chimney, stack, or breeching for the removal of dust, soot, etc. **3.** An opening in concrete forms for removing debris; closed before the concrete is placed.

cleanout door **1.** An **ashpit door**. **2.** A door providing access to a soil pipe, the base of a column form, or the like. **3.** A **soot door**.

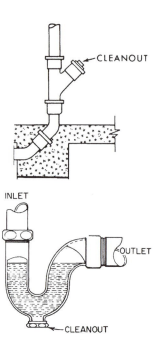

cleanout, 1: *above:* for cleaning pipe run; *below:* for a P-trap

clean power Electric power having a relative absence of electrical noise and harmonics so that its voltage waveform is essentially a sine wave.

clean room An assembly room for precision products whose quality would be affected by dust, lint, or airborne pathogens; usually has smooth room surfaces to prevent dust collection; air precipitators or filters keep dust, lint, etc., to a specified minimum level.

clean stuff Same as **clear lumber**.

clean timber British term for **clear lumber**.

clear The net distance, free from interruption, between any two surfaces or areas.

clearage Same as **clearance**.

clearance **1.** Open space between two elements of a building to aid in proper placement, to compensate for minor inaccuracies in cutting, or to allow unobstructed movement between parts. **2.** The space or distance allowed for anchorage or erection processes or to accommodate dimensional variations in the building structure. **3.** See **door clearance**.

clear ceramic glaze Said of an inseparable ceramic glaze that is firebonded and translucent or tinted with a lustrous finish.

clearcole, clairecolle **1.** A primer consisting of glue, water, and white lead or whiting. **2.** A clear coating used in application of gold leaf.

clear glaze A colorless or colored transparent ceramic glaze. Also see **ceramic color glaze**.

clear height A vertical height providing an unobstructed **clearance, 1**.

clearing The cutting down of bushes and trees and the digging and removal of their roots and stumps.

clearing arm A branch provided on a drain to facilitate the clearing of obstructions with a drain rod.

clear lumber, clean timber, clears, clear stuff, clear timber, free stuff Wood free of knots and other defects.

clear span The distance between the two inside faces of the supports of a span.

clearstory Same as **clerestory window**.

cleat A small block or strip of wood nailed on a member or on a surface; used to support a brace or to hold a member or object in place temporarily.

cleat wiring Electric wiring on cleats or insulated supports which are mounted on a wall or other surface, leaving the wiring exposed; conduits or raceways are not used.

cleat wiring

cleavage **1.** In rocks, a tendency to split along parallel, generally closely spaced surfaces as, for example, in slate. **2.** In some stone industries, the splitting along the depositional layering. **3.** The rupturing of adhesive bonds between rigid materials; a prying action. **4.** A tendency in some woods to split along closely spaced parallel planes, as in shingles.

cleavage plane In a crystalline material, such as certain types of rocks, a plane along which splitting takes place most easily.

cleave board Same as **rived board**.

cleft timber Timber which has been split along the grain to approximate dimensions.

cleithral Same as **clithral**.

clench See **clinch**.

clench bolt See **clinch bolt**.

clenching, clench nailing The hammering over of the point of a nail against a wood face to secure its adhesion under rough usage.

clench nail See **clinch nail**.

clerestory, clerestory window **1.** An upper zone of wall pierced with windows that admit light to the center of a lofty room. **2.** A window so placed. (*See illustration p. 198.*)

clerestory, 2   A

clerk of the works Same as **project representative**.

clevis An iron (or a link in a chain) bent into the form of a horseshoe, stirrup, or letter U, with holes in the ends to receive a bolt or pin. (*See illustration p. 198.*)

CLG On drawings, abbr. for **ceiling**.

climbing crane A hoisting device used in the erection of high-rise buildings; a vertical mast is fastened to structural members of the building framework and is moved up as the structure rises during construction; a horizontal boom, equipped with a winch and hoist line, is swung from the top of the vertical mast.

climbing form A concrete form which is raised vertically for succeeding **lifts, 6** of concrete in a given structure, usually supported on anchor bolts or rods embedded in the top of the previous lift; the form is moved only after an

clinch

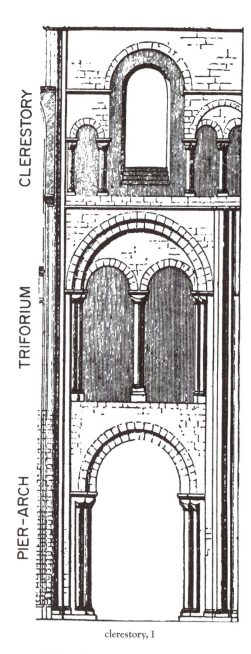

CLERESTORY

TRIFORIUM

PIER-ARCH

clerestory, 1

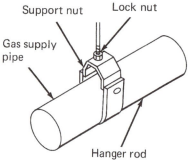

clevis hanger

entire lift is placed and partially hardened; not the same as a **slip form**, which moves during the placement of concrete.

clinch, clench To secure or fasten a nail, staple, screw, etc., by hammering the protruding point so that it is bent over.

clinch bolt, clench bolt A bolt with one end designed to be bent over, to prevent withdrawal.

clinch joint Same as **lap joint, 2** secured with **clinch nails**.

clinch nail, clench nail Any nail designed for clinching after driving.

clinic **1.** A facility, independent or part of a hospital, in which ambulatory patients receive diagnostic and therapeutic medical and surgical care. **2.** Single-focus or general-purpose units of the entire facility, such as the cardiac clinic or the pediatric clinic.

clink **1.** A short pointed steel bar; used, by striking with a sledgehammer, to break up pavement or road surfaces. **2.** One of many small cracks in steel due to differential expansion in heating. **3.** A sealed edge between adjacent sheets of flexible-metal roofing material.

clinker **1.** A partially fused product of a kiln, which is ground for use in cement; also called **cement clinker**. **2.** A vitrified or partially vitrified residue of coal which has been burnt in a furnace; used as an aggregate in **cinder block**. **3.** A **clinker brick**.

clinker block British term for **cinder block**.

clinker brick A very hard-burnt brick whose shape is distorted, owing to nearly complete vitrification; used for paving.

clinometer An instrument for measuring vertical angles.

clip **1.** A portion of a brick cut to length. **2.** A special fastener made of light-gauge sheet metal or wire for the attachment of gypsum lath to channel or steel studs. **3.** A small device, usually of metal, for holding larger parts in place, either by friction or by mechanical action, as a spring device of metal used to hold glass in a window.

clip angle, lug angle A short angle iron that takes a portion of the stress of any member.

clip bond A bond formed by clipping of the inside corners of **facing brick** laid as **stretchers** so as to form notches for the insertion of diagonal **headers**.

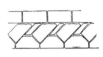

clip bond

clipeus An ornamental disk of marble or other material, in the shape of a shield; often sculptured in relief, hung in the intercolumniations of the atria of ancient Roman dwellings.

clip joint A mortar joint which is thicker than usual; used to bring a masonry course to a required height.

clipped eaves Eaves that do not overhang the face of a wall by more than the width of the gutter.

clipped gable See **jerkinhead**.

clipped header, false header A half-brick placed to look like a **header** for purposes of establishing a brickwork pattern, as in Flemish bond.

clipped lintel A **lintel** which is intermittently attached to a structural member; the structural member assists the lintel in carrying the load.

clithral In early Greek architecture, having a roof that forms a complete covering; said of certain temples, as distinguished from **hypaethral**.

CLKG On drawings, abbr. for **caulking**.

CLO On drawings, abbr. for **closet**.

cloaca An underground conduit for drainage; a sewer, esp. in ancient Rome.

cloak rail On a closet wall, a board on which hooks are attached for hanging clothes.

cloakroom 1. A room for the deposit or checking of outer clothing. 2. A small lounge outside a legislative chamber where coats may be hung. 3. A room for checking packages or baggage, as in a theatre, railway station, or airport. 4. (Brit.) A washroom and toilet.

clochan A type of primitive building peculiar to Ireland, usually having a beehive form, constructed of the masonry usually neither dressed nor cemented; a single stone covers the apex.

clochan   houses in County Kerry

cloisonne A surface decoration in which differently colored enamels or glazes are separated by fillets applied to the design outline. For porcelain enamel, the fillets are wire secured to the metal body; for tile and pottery, the fillets are made of ceramic paste, squeezed through a small-diameter orifice.

cloister A covered walk surrounding a court, usually linking a church to other buildings of a monastery.

cloistered arch Same as **coved vault**.

cloistered vault A **coved vault**.

cloister garth The courtyard within a cloister.

cloistral See **claustral**.

clone One of a series of plants that is reproduced by cuttings or other vegetative methods for several generations.

close 1. An enclosed space around or at the side of a building; esp. the neighborhood of a cathedral. 2. A narrow lane leading from a street.

close-boarded, close-sheeted 1. Covered with square-edge boards that are laid in close contact with each other, as in roofing or siding. 2. Said of fencing which is completely filled with vertical boards having no spaces between them.

close-contact glue A glue which requires very closely joined surfaces.

close couple See **couple-close**.

close-coupled tank and bowl A **flush tank** which is separate from, but attached to, a toilet bowl. (See illustration p. 200.)

close-cut Descriptive of a hip (or valley) on a slate, shingle, or tile roof in which the pieces are cut to meet exactly on the hip (or valley).

closed building system A building system in which only its own subsystems, its own sub-

close-coupled tank and bowl

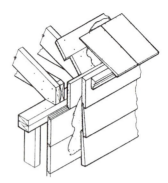

closed cornice, 2

assemblies, and its own components are interchangeable.

closed cell In a material such as foam rubber or foam plastic, one of many air spaces (cells) totally enclosed by its walls and hence not interconnecting with other cells.

closed-cell foam A cellular plastic in which the cells do not interconnect.

closed-circuit grouting Injecting grout into a hole (which intersects fissures or voids to be filled) with sufficient volume and pressure so that more grout is fed to the hole than is taken up, the excess grout being returned to the pumping plant for recirculation.

closed-circuit TV surveillance system A system comprised of a TV camera and a monitor connected by a **coaxial cable**; designed to provide visual surveillance; often an important adjunct to a building security system.

closed construction Said of a **building component**, **building system**, or **building** which is manufactured in such a way that various portions cannot be readily inspected at the installation site without their disassembly or destruction.

closed cornice **1.** A **box cornice**. **2.** A wood cornice which projects only slightly and has no soffit, having only a frieze board and crown molding.

closed eaves Eaves in which projecting roof members are not visible, being closed from view by boarding.

closed impeller In a pump, an **impeller** having two shrouds (i.e., two disks enclosing the impeller vanes). Such a pump usually requires little maintenance and usually retains its operat-

ing efficiency longer than a pump having an **open impeller**.

closed list of bidders See **invited bidders**.

closed mortise Same as **blind mortise**.

closed newel The central shaft of a turning stair when constructed as a continuous enclosing wall, either hollow or solid.

closed shaft A shaft roofed or enclosed at the top.

closed sheathing See **closed sheeting**.

closed sheeting, closed sheathing, tight sheeting A continuous frame with vertical or horizontal sheathing planks placed side by side to form a continuous retaining wall used to hold up the face of an excavation.

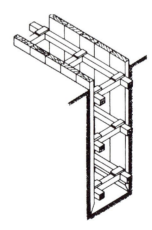

closed sheeting

closed shelving In cabinets, shelving which is concealed by a door.

closed specifications Specifications stipulating the use of specific products or processes without provision for substitution. Also see **base bid specifications**.

closed stair A **box stair**.

closed stair string Same as **close string**.

closed string Same as **close string**.

closed string stair A stair constructed with **close strings** so that the treads are not visible from a side view of the stair.

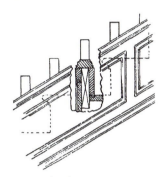

closed string stair

closed system A heating or refrigeration piping system in which the circulating water or brine is completely enclosed and under pressure above atmospheric.

closed valley Same as **concealed valley**.

closed water piping system A water piping system in which a check valve or other device prevents the return of water to the water supply system.

close-grained, close-grown See **narrow-ringed**.

close nipple A **nipple** having no shoulder (i.e., no unthreaded portion) and having the shortest possible length permitted by standard practice.

close nipple

closer 1. The last brick, block, stone, or tile laid in a horizontal course; may be either a complete unit or one trimmed on the site. 2. A stone course running from one windowsill to another (a variety of stringcourse). Also see **king closer, queen closer**.

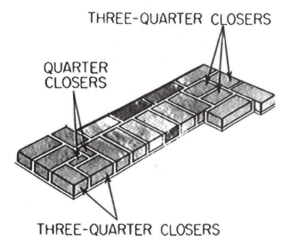

closer, 1

closer mold A temporary wood form used as a guide in cutting brick to a specific size.

closer reinforcement A metal plate which is applied to a door or frame to provide additional strength for the attachment of a **door closer**.

closer reinforcing sleeve A plate which reinforces the rabbeted soffit and both faces of a doorframe.

close-sheeted See **close-boarded**.

close sheeting Same as **closed sheeting**.

close string, close stringer, closed stringer, curb string, housed string A staircase **string** whose upper edge is straight and parallel to its lower edge; the tread and riser ends are housed in the face of the string and are concealed.

close studding Construction in which the studs are placed relatively close and the intervening spaces are plastered.

closet 1. A small enclosed storage area. 2. A small private room, often off a bedroom.

closet bolt A bolt having a low circular head of extra large diameter which is cupped on the underside so that it is sealed against the surface when the bolt is tightened; used to fasten a water closet bowl to the floor.

close timbering The lining of an excavation or trench with boards having no space between them.

closet lining Red cedar boards whose odor repels moths; used to line closets.

close tolerance A tolerance closer than **standard tolerance**.

closet pole, closet rod A straight, round rod installed in a clothes closet to hold clothes hangers.

closet screw A long screw having a detachable head; used to fasten a water closet bowl to the floor.

closet valve The valve which controls the flushing cycle of a tank-type water closet.

close-up casement hinge A hinge similar to an **extension casement hinge** but having its hinge pin closer to the face of the **casement, 1**.

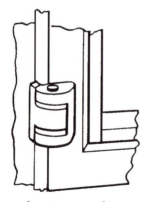

close-up casement hinge

closing costs Those costs incidental to a transfer of title from seller to buyer and execution of a mortgage on a property, e.g., legal and recording fees and title insurance.

closing device, automatic closing device, self-closing device 1. A mechanism designed to ensure that an open fire door will close and latch in the event of a fire. **2.** A device which ensures that a door will return to its closed position after being opened.

closing ring A metal ring fastened to a door; used to pull it shut.

closing stile Same as **lock stile**.

closure bar Of a stair, a flat metal bar connected to the top and/or bottom surface or edge

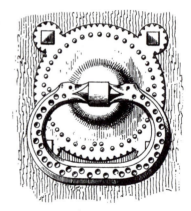

closing ring

of a stringer along a wall; used to close gaps between the stringer and the wall.

closure strip A preformed asphalt or elastomeric filler strip used to close the opening in corrugated sheets at eaves, the lower edge of siding, at window beads, and the like.

clothes chute A **laundry chute**.

cloudiness The lack of clarity or transparency in a paint or varnish film.

clout 1. A metal plate attached to a moving wood member to protect it from abrasion. **2.** A **clout nail**.

clout nail A nail having a large flat head, a round shank, and a long side point or duckbill point; used for fastening sheet metal, asphalt-prepared roofing, plasterboard, etc.

clr., Clr, Clr. In the lumber industry, abbr. for "clear."

CLS Abbr. for "Canadian lumber sizes."

clunch A stiff, rigid clay or a chalk, used in early British construction.

clustered column A number of columns which are grouped together and physically connected so they act as a single structural element.

clustered pier A **pier, 1** composed of a number of shafts grouped together, usually around a central, more massive, shaft or core.

cluster housing Dwellings grouped closely together to form relatively compact units. The space between clusters usually is allocated to pedestrian circulation and cooperative recreational use. This pattern normally results in a

clustered column

higher density of land use than that of a conventional subdivision layout.

clutch A device which permits the drive train of a machine to be connected to, or disconnected from, a prime source of power; usually operates on a mechanical principle with friction surfaces that can be joined or separated, but other types include a fluid coupler.

cm Abbr. for "centimeter."

CM Abbr. for "center matched."

CMP On drawings, abbr. for "corrugated metal pipe."

CMU Abbr. for **concrete masonry unit**.

CND On drawings, abbr. for **conduit**.

CNRC Abbr. for "Canadian National Research Council."

CO 1. Abbr. for **change order**. 2. Abbr. for **certificate of occupancy**. 3. Abbr. for **cleanout**. 4. Abbr. for **cutout**.

coach bolt Same as **carriage bolt**.

coach house, carriage house A building or part thereof for housing carriages when not in use.

coach-mounting steps A small elevated platform on which a person would step when mounting or dismounting from a coach or carriage; often set near the entrance to a house.

coach screw See **lag bolt**.

coak 1. A projection from the end of a piece of wood or timber which fits into a hole in another piece to join them. 2. A dowel or hardwood pin through overlapping timbers.

coalescence The formation of a film of resinous or polymeric material when water evaporates from an emulsion or latex system, permitting contact and fusion of adjacent latex particles.

coal house A subsidiary building for the storage of coal; often connected to a blacksmith's shop.

coal-tar felt A felt that has been saturated with refined coal-tar pitch.

coal-tar pitch, tar A dark brown to black hydrocarbon obtained by the distillation of coke-oven tar; softening point near 150°F (65°C); used in **built-up roofing** as a waterproofing agent.

coaming A frame or curb around an opening in a roof or floor, raised above the surrounding level to prevent the flow of water into the opening.

coarse aggregate Aggregate retained on a 4.76-mm (No. 4) sieve. Also see **crushed gravel, crushed stone, gravel, pea gravel**.

coarse filter In an air-conditioning system, same as **prefilter**.

coarse fraction That fraction of the solid particles in a soil sample having grain sizes larger than a No. 200 sieve, i.e., greater than 0.003 inch (0.075 mm) in diameter.

coarse-grained 1. See **wide-ringed**. 2. See **coarse-textured**.

coarse stuff A mixture of lime putty, hair, and sand; used as a base-coat plaster.

coarse-textured, coarse-grained, open-grained Descriptive of wood having an open, porous cell structure that usually requires filling to provide a smooth finish.

coat A single layer of plaster, paint, or any type of material applied to a surface.

coated bar A **reinforcing bar** that has been coated to increase its resistance to corrosion.

coated base sheet, coated base felt A roofing material consisting of asphalt-saturated felt which is coated with a harder viscous asphalt to increase its impermeability to moisture significantly.

coated electrode, light-coated electrode
A filler-metal **electrode** used in arc welding which consists of a metal wire having a light coating to stabilize the arc.

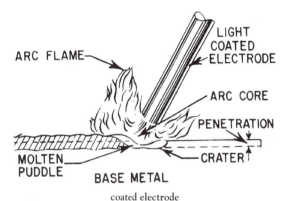

coated electrode

coated glass   Glass having a coating designed to admit light over most of the visible range but to block light in the ultraviolet and infrared ranges; the coating reflects some of heat generated within a building so that it remains in the building instead of largely being transmitted through the window, thereby effecting a saving of heat during the winter; often applied on glazing in a **double window** construction.

coated nail   An enameled nail, **cement-coated nail** or **mechanically galvanized nail**.

coating   A layer of material which is applied to a surface to decorate, preserve, protect, seal, or smooth the substrate; usually applied by brushing, spraying, mopping, troweling, or dipping.

coat rack   A storage rack for coats and hats; may include a boot rack, umbrella stand, and drip tray.

coatroom   1. A **cloakroom**. 2. A room for the deposit or checking of outer garments.

coaxial cable   1. A cable consisting of two concentric conductors (an inner conductor and an outer conductor) insulated from each other by a dielectric; commonly used for the transmission of high-speed electronic data and/or video sig-

coaxial cable

nals. 2. A single transmission cable having a concentric conductor and shielding; used for communications transmission, such as for television signals.

cob   A mixture of straw, gravel, and unburnt clay; used esp. for walls.

cobble, cobblestone   1. A rock fragment between 2½ and 10 in. (64 and 256 mm) in diameter, used for rough paving, walls, and foundations. 2. Coarse aggregate for concrete, having a nominal size in the range 3 to 6 in. (75 to 150 mm).

cob wall   A wall formed of unburnt clay mixed with chopped straw, gravel, and occasionally with layers of long straw, in which the straw acts as a bond.

cobwebbing   Formation of strands, resembling cobwebs, of dried or semidried paint when expelled from a spray gun; usually caused by highly polymerized binders.

cochlea   1. A tower for a spiral staircase. 2. A **spiral stair**.

cochleary, cochleated   Spirally or helically twisted, as a spiral stair.

cocina   In Spanish architecture, a kitchen.

cock   1. See **faucet**. 2. A **stopcock**.

cock bead   A bead which is not flush with the adjoining surface but is raised above it.

cocking   1. Same as **cogging**. 2. Tipping sideways.

cocking piece   See **sprocket**.

cockle-shell cupboard   Same as **shell-headed cupboard**.

cockle stair   A **spiral stair**.

cockloft   A garret under a roof, above the highest ceiling. Also see **loft, 2**.

cockscomb   A **drag**.

cockspur fastener   A fastener on a casement window.

coctile   Made by baking, as porcelain or a brick.

code   1. A legal instrument adopted within a political jurisdiction (such as a town, county, state, province, parish, etc.) that prescribes the minimum acceptable levels of the design, construction, installation, and performance of materials, components, devices, items of equipment, appliances used in a building, or building systems and/or subsystems. 2. A published body of rules and regulations for building practices, materials, and installations, designed to protect the health, welfare, and safety of the public, such as a **building code**, health code, etc. Codes established by municipal, state, or federal authorities usually have the power of law.

coded fire-alarm system　A **fire-alarm system** in which an alarm signal is sounded in a predetermined coded sequence, usually indicating the area in a building where the alarm has been initiated.

code of practice　A technical document setting forth standards of good construction for various materials and trades.

COEF　On drawings, abbr. for "coefficient."

coefficient of beam utilization　The ratio of the luminous flux reaching a specified area from a floodlight or similar luminaire to the total luminous flux of the beam.

coefficient of discharge　**1.** The ratio of the actual discharge of water through an opening to its corresponding theoretical value. **2.** The ratio of **effective area** to the **free area** of an air diffuser.

coefficient of elasticity　Same as **modulus of elasticity**.

coefficient of expansion　The change in dimension of a material per unit of dimension per degree change in temperature.

coefficient of friction　The ratio of the force causing a body to slide along a plane (in the direction of sliding) to the normal force pressing the two surfaces together.

coefficient of heat transmission　Same as **coefficient of thermal transmission**.

coefficient of light transmission　See **luminous transmittance**.

coefficient of performance　**1.** In a heat pump, the dimensionless ratio of heat produced to the energy supplied. **2.** In a refrigerating unit, the dimensionless ratio of the heat removed to the energy expended in removing it.

coefficient of runoff　In the design of storm-water drainage systems, a coefficient which accounts for storm-water losses attributed to evaporation, infiltration, and surface depressions.

coefficient of static friction　The **coefficient of friction** where the force in the direction of sliding is that necessary to initiate sliding.

coefficient of subgrade friction　The **coefficient of friction** between a slab and the subgrade on which it rests.

coefficient of subgrade reaction　The ratio of load per unit area on soil to the corresponding deformation.

coefficient of thermal expansion　Same as **coefficient of expansion**.

coefficient of thermal transmission　The amount of heat transferred through a unit area of a partition per hour, per degree temperature difference between the air on the two sides; e.g., the number of Btu per square foot per hour per degree Fahrenheit.

coefficient of utilization, _Brit._ **utilization factor.**　The ratio of luminous flux received on the work plane to the total luminous flux emitted by the source.

coefficient of variation　The **standard deviation** expressed as a percentage of the average.

coelanaglyphic relief　Carving in relief in which no part of the figure represented projects beyond the surrounding plane.

coenaculum　In ancient Roman houses, the dining room or supper room, or any of the upper rooms in which food was eaten.

coenatio　Same as **cenatio**.

coenobium　A community of monks living under one roof.

coffer, lacunar　**1.** One panel in **coffering**. **2.** A **caisson, 2**.

cofferdam　A temporary watertight enclosure around an area of water or water-bearing soil, in which construction is to take place, bearing on a stable stratum at or above the foundation level of new construction. The water is pumped from within to permit free access to the area.

coffering　**1.** Ceiling with deeply recessed panels, often highly ornamented. **2.** Similar effects executed in marble, brick, concrete, plaster, or stucco. Also see **caisson, 2**. (_See illustration p. 206._)

coffer panel　One of the many panels in **coffering, 1**.

cog　In a **cogged joint**, the solid portion which is left in a timber after it has been notched.

cogeneration　In a building, the on-site electric power generation utilizing both the electri-

cogged joint

coffering, 1

cal power and steam or hot water which is developed; in some municipalities in the U.S.A., if excess electrical power is generated, it may be sold to the utility.

cogged joint A carpentry joint formed by two crossed structural timbers, each of which is notched at the place where they cross.

cogged joint

cogging, cocking The joining of two timbers which are notched, cogged, or indented.

cohesion **1.** The molecular forces of attraction by which the body of an adhesive or sealant is held together; the internal strength of an adhesive or a sealant. **2.** Of soil particles, the sticking together of particles whose forces of attraction exceed the forces that tend to separate them.

cohesionless soil A soil which when unconfined has no significant cohesion when submerged, and no significant strength when air-dried.

cohesive failure The tearing apart of a sealant as the joint expands if its adhesive (bond) capabilities exceed its cohesive capabilities.

cohesive soil A soil which when unconfined has appreciable cohesion when submerged, and considerable strength when air-dried.

coign See **quoin.**

coil A **heat exchanger** in the form of pipe or tubing in any of various configurations; fins may be attached to dissipate heat; also called an **attemperator.**

coiled expansion loop Same as **expansion bend.**

coin, quoin **1.** The corner of a building. **2.** The stones or bricks which form the corner. **3.** A wedge.

coke grating A special grating fitted into an ordinary fireplace to burn No. 3 grade coke, ½ to 1¼ in. (1.3 to 3.1 cm) size, generally fitted with an integral gas burner to facilitate lighting of fuel.

COL On drawings, abbr. for **column.**

colarin Same as **collarino.**

cold-air return In an air-conditioning system in a house of wood frame construction, a return air duct which utilizes the space between joists.

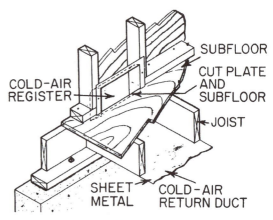

cold-air return

cold bending, cold gagging The bending of metal without the application of heat, as the bending of metal pipe.

cold bridge Any type of break in a continuous thermal insulation barrier, leaving an opening that "short-circuits" the thermal insulation.

cold-cathode lamp An **electric-discharge lamp** which produces light by means of a **glow discharge;** operates at relatively low current and high voltage; has cylindrical electrodes which operate at a low temperature.

cold cellar Part of a cellar where root crops are stored during the winter at cold, but above-freezing, temperatures.

cold check The formation of fine cracks in wood finishes when subjected to cycles of heat and cold.

cold chisel   A chisel with a cutting edge formed of tempered steel; for cutting metal which has not been softened by heating.

cold chisel

cold cut, cold cutter   A **cold chisel** mounted on a handle like a hammer; struck with a maul.

cold-drawn   Descriptive of metal which has been drawn through a set of dies designed to reduce its cross-sectional area without heating the metal. The process is used in the fabrication of rod, tubing, and wire.

cold-driven rivet   A **rivet** that is driven cold, without preheating.

cold-finished bar   A metal bar, brought to its final dimensions by **cold-working**, which results in improved surface finish and dimensional tolerance.

cold-finished steel   Carbon steel which has been cleaned and pickled and then rolled or drawn through dies to produce a dimensionally accurate section with an improved surface finish (and often with other improved properties).

cold flow   **1.** The permanent deformation of a material under constant stress. **2.** At room temperature, the continuing dimensional change under static load that follows initial instantaneous deformation.

cold-formed member   A structural steel member formed without the application of heat.

cold-formed steel construction   That type of construction made up entirely, or in part, of steel structural members cold-formed to shape from sheet or strip steel, such as roof deck, floor and wall panels, floor joists, studs, roof joists, or other structural elements.

cold gagging   See **cold bending**.

cold glue   A glue which is a **cold-setting adhesive**.

cold joint   A joint formed when a concrete surface hardens before the next batch of concrete is placed against it; characterized by a poor bond unless special procedures are observed.

cold-laid mixture   Any mixture which may be spread and compacted at normal atmospheric temperature.

cold mix   Asphaltic concrete for placement without heat; prepared with a relatively light and slow-curing asphalt; hardens to a state less firm and durable than hot-mixed asphaltic concrete.

cold molding   **1.** A procedure in which a composition is shaped at room temperature and cured by subsequent baking. **2.** The material used in this procedure.

cold patch   An application of asphaltic cold mix over a small area.

cold pie   Mortar in excess of that actually used in laying a masonry unit.

cold pressing   The bonding of components by pressure without the application of heat.

cold-process roofing   A bituminous roofing membrane which consists of layers of coated felts that have been bonded with cold-applied asphalt roof cement and surfaced with an emulsified or cutback asphalt roof coating. Also see **asphalt prepared roofing**.

cold riveting   Driving rivets cold, without preheating.

cold-rolled   Descriptive of metal that has been formed by rolling at room temperature, usually to obtain improved surface finish or higher tensile strength.

cold room   A room where low temperatures are maintained; a refrigeration room.

cold saw   A saw for cutting metal at ordinary room temperatures, as a metal-cutting circular saw.

cold set   A type of short steel chisel having a flat edge; used in cutting bars, flattening sheet-metal seams, etc.

cold-setting adhesive   An adhesive that sets at temperatures below 68°F (20°C).

cold-shortness   Brittleness in metal at room temperatures.

cold shut   In a casting, a defect having the appearance of a fold or wrinkle.

cold-solder   To solder without the application of heat, as with copper amalgam.

cold solder joint   A faulty joint in electric wiring which results from the application of insufficient heat at the joint; the solder merely covers the joint and is not physically united with it.

cold-start lamp   Same as **instant-start fluorescent lamp**.

cold-storage cooler An insulated room which is artificially cooled but whose temperature is never below 30°F (–1.1°C).

cold-storage door A heavy, thermally insulated door, fully gasketed at the frame; used on refrigerators and freezers.

cold strength Of refractory concrete, the compressive or flexural strength determined prior to firing.

cold-water paint A mixture of pigment and binder dissolved or dispersed in cold water.

cold welding The joining of metals (such as aluminum) at room temperature by subjecting thoroughly cleaned metal surfaces to pressure; coalescence is produced solely by the application of mechanical force.

cold-worked steel Descriptive of steel which has been rolled, drawn, or twisted at normal ambient temperatures; used for steel bars and wire in reinforcement for concrete.

cold working The plastic deformation of metal at or near room temperature; this shaping is usually carried out by drawing, pressing, rolling, or stamping.

coliseum See **colosseum**.

collapse Mechanical failure of cells in wood, usually caused by abnormal or forced drying.

collar **1.** A metal cap flashing for a vent pipe projecting above a roof deck. **2.** A raised band which encircles a metal shaft, a wood dowel, or a wooden leg. **3.** A raised section to reinforce a metal weld. **4.** A **collarino**. **5.** The reinforcing metal of a nonpressure **thermit weld**. **6.** Same as **escutcheon**.

collar beam, spanpiece, sparpiece, top beam, wind beam A horizontal member which ties together (and stiffens) two opposite common rafters, usually at a point about halfway up the rafters in a collar beam roof.

collar beam roof, collar roof A roof supported by rafters tied together by collar beams.

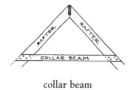

collar beam

collar brace A structural member which reinforces a collar beam in medieval roof framing.

collared hole A hole of shallow depth, drilled into a material to prevent slippage of the bit when a deeper hole is drilled.

collaring **1.** Pointing with cement mortar under the overhangs of tiles or slabs. **2.** The drilling of a **collared hole**.

collarino **1.** A **necking**, as on a classic Tuscan, Doric, or Ionic capital; also called a **collar, 4. 2.** An **astragal**.

collar joint **1.** The joint between a roof rafter and a **collar beam**. **2.** The vertical joint between masonry **withes**.

collar tie In wood roof construction, a timber which prevents the roof framing from changing its shape.

collected plants Plants that are gathered from sources other than a working nursery.

collecting safe area In an emergency, a **safe area** that receives occupants from the assembly space it serves, as well as from other safe areas.

collection hopper A cart with wheels used to funnel concrete into drop chutes and **elephant trunks**, which may or may not be attached; often used alone for placing concrete in shallow restricted areas.

collector See **solar thermal collector**.

collector street One which functions as a feeder from an area of limited traffic to a major street or highway.

Collegiate Gothic A secular version of Gothic architecture, characteristic of the older colleges of Oxford and Cambridge. Adopted in the late 19th and early 20th centuries by a number of other colleges in other countries.

colloid A gelatinous substance so finely divided that it remains in suspension when dispersed in a liquid.

colloidal concrete Concrete whose aggregate is bound by colloidal grout.

colloidal grout A grout which has artificially induced cohesiveness or ability to retain the dispersed solid particles in suspension.

colloidal mixer A **mixer** designed to produce colloidal grout.

collusion A secret agreement for illegal or fraudulent purposes.

Collegiate Gothic

colluviarium In ancient Rome, an opening made at regular intervals in an aqueduct, for ventilation.

Cologne earth, Cologne brown A type of **Vandyke brown** made from roasted American clays which contain ochre and bituminous matter.

colombage Half-timber construction.

colonette, colonnette **1.** A small column, usually decorative. **2.** In medieval architecture, a thin round shaft to give a vertical line in elevation, or as an element in a compound pier.

Colonial architecture Architecture transplanted from the motherland to overseas colonies. For examples see **American Colonial architecture, Dutch Colonial architecture, English Colonial architecture, French Colonial architecture, German Colonial architecture, Spanish Colonial architecture**. Compare with **Colonial Revival**.

colonial casing A type of decorative, exposed trim molding.

colonial casing

Colonial joint Same as **tooled joint**.

colonial panel door A door having stiles, rails, and a mutin which form frames around recessed panels.

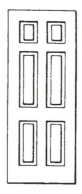

colonial panel door

Colonial Revival An **architectural mode** that reuses selected aspects of earlier colonial prototypes, especially from around 1870 onward. In the United States, when this term is used without reference to a country of origin (simply as *Colonial Revival*), it usually refers to **American Colonial Revival**, based on prototypes in the English colonies in America. Of these prototypes, the **Georgian** and the **Federal style** (*Adam style*) are the most widely imitated, giving rise to the terms Georgian Revival and Federal Revival (*Adam Revival*). Colonial Revival houses are usually the result of a rather free interpretation of their prototypes; they tend to be larger than, and may differ significantly from, the houses they seek to emulate, often exaggerating architectural details. For descriptions of other types of colonial revival architecture, see **Dutch Colonial Revival, Chateauesque style, French Eclectic architecture, Spanish Colonial Revival, Mission Revival, Pueblo Revival**. Also see **Neo-Colonial architecture**.

colonial siding Wide, square-edged siding boards used extensively in early American construction. Also see **weatherboarding**. (*See illustration p. 210.*)

colonnade A number of columns arranged in order, at intervals called **intercolumniation**, supporting an entablature and usually one side of a roof. (*See illustration p. 210.*)

colonnette See **colonette**.

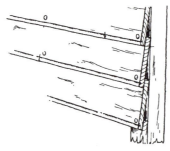

colonial siding

colonnade

colophony See **rosin**.

color (*perceived*) That attribute of visual perception that can be described by names such as yellow, red, blue, etc., or some combination of such names. (*of an object*) A characteristic of the appearance of an object, surface, etc., distinct from its form, gloss, shape, size, or position; depends on the spectral composition of the incident light, on the spectral reflectance or transmittance of the object, and on the spectral response of the observer.

color chart A chart showing a systematic array of colors or their representations.

color code A system of colors adopted for identification of pipes, cables, wiring, or the like.

colored aggregate Sand, gravel, or other aggregate chosen for the coloration it can impart to concrete in an exposed-aggregate finish.

colored cement A cement to which color pigment has been added.

colored concrete **1.** Concrete tinted during its mixing by colored cement or color pigments. **2.** Hardened concrete which has been subjected to a colored wash.

colored finishes In plastering, finish coats containing colored aggregates or color pigments; the color is intimately mixed throughout.

color frame A metal frame at the front of a luminaire, used to support transparent colored material, esp. in spotlights and floodlights.

coloring pigment **1.** See **pigment**. **2.** See **stainer**.

color pigment **1.** A natural or synthetic pigment or stainer, usually iron or chromium oxides, added to either mortar or block concrete. **2.** See **pigment, 1**.

color rendering index (CRI) A measure of the closeness with which a light approximates daylight having the same **color temperature**.

color retention The ability of a paint or varnish film to retain its original color appearance and not fade with age or exposure to sunlight.

color temperature Of a light source, the absolute temperature at which a **blackbody, 1** radiator must be operated to have a chromacity equal to that of the light source.

colossal column A **column** that is more than one story in height.

colossal order, giant order An order more than one story in height.

colossal pilaster A pilaster that extends the full height of a building containing two or more floors.

colosseum, coliseum **1.** (*cap.*) The Flavian amphitheatre in Rome. **2.** Any large Roman amphitheatre. **3.** Now, any large sports arena, open or roofed.

colour See **color**.

columbage In French Vernacular architecture of Louisiana, timber-framed construction with diagonal bracing of the framework; the space between the structural timbers was usually filled with **bousillage** or **pierrotage**.

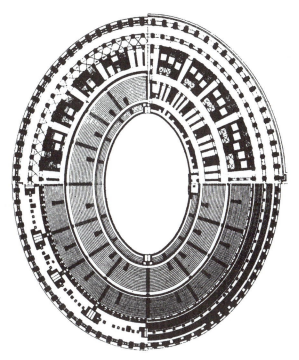

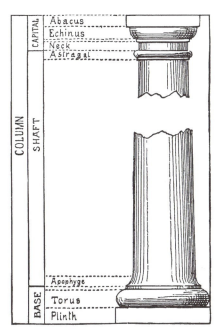

column, 2   Tuscan order

Colosseum, 1   showing seating and plan at various levels

columbarium   One or a series of niches, intended to receive human remains.

columbarium

columella   Same as **colonette**.

column   **1.** In structures, a relatively long, slender structural compression member such as a post, pillar, or strut; usually vertical, supporting a load which acts in (or near) the direction of its longitudinal axis. **2.** In classical architecture, a cylindrical support consisting of a base (except in Greek Doric), shaft, and capital; either monolithic or built up of drums the full diameter of the shaft. **3.** A pillar standing alone as a monument.

columna rostrata   Same as **rostral column**.

columna triumphalis   See **triumphal column**.

column baseplate   A horizontal plate beneath the bottom of a column; transmits and distributes the column load to the supporting material below the plate.

column capital   A mushroom-like enlargement of reinforced concrete, at the upper end of a column, designed and built to act as an integral unit with the column and the floor slab above so as to increase the shearing resistance.

column casing   Any form of enclosure of a steel column which provides a prescribed fire rating, e.g., a boxed enclosure fabricated of a fire-rated material, such as gypsum board; also see **caged beam**.

column clamp   A fastening device for a form for a concrete column, holding together the sides of the form.

column curve The graphical relationship between the axial strength of a column and its **slenderness ratio**.

column footing See **footing**.

column head Same as **column capital**.

columniation Systems of grouping columns in classical architecture. Also see **intercolumniation**.

column side In a form for a concrete column, one of the vertical panels.

column splice A splice which unites two columns.

column strip That portion of a flat slab, over the columns, which consists of the quarter panels on both sides of the column center line.

colymbethra In a Greek church, the room or font for administering baptism.

Com, Com. In the lumber industry, abbr. for "common."

comb **1.** Combing, 1. **2.** A **drag**, 1. **3.** Any tool used to produce **combing, 2, 3**.

COMB. On drawings, abbr. for "combination."

comb board A **saddle board** having notches along its upper edge.

comb cut Same as **plumb cut**.

combed Same as **dragged**.

combed-finish tile Tile whose face surfaces are altered by more or less parallel scratches in manufacture to give increased bond for mortar, plaster, or stucco.

combed joint A **finger joint**.

comb-grained See **edge-grained, quartersawn**.

combination column A column in which a structural steel member, designed to carry part of the load, is encased in concrete of such quality and in such manner that the combination of steel and concrete will carry the total load.

combination door An exterior door having interchangeable screen and glass storm-panel inserts; provides a glazed storm door in winter and a screened door in summer.

combination faucet A device in which the flow of water from hot and cold water pipes is controlled and is drawn from a common spout.

combination fixture A fixture which combines one or more kitchen sinks and laundry trays in a single unit.

combination faucet

combination frame In light wood-frame buildings, a combination of a full frame and a balloon frame.

combination ladder A portable ladder which may be used as a **stepladder, extension ladder, single ladder**, or **trestle ladder**.

combination plane **1.** A plane having interchangeable cutters for various applications in shaping. **2.** A plane having a guide which can be changed from one side to the other, or adjusted vertically.

combination pliers Slip-joint pliers having serrated faces for gripping rounded surfaces such as pipe, together with blades for cutting wire.

combination pliers

combination sheet In roofing, a fiberglass felt integrally attached to kraft paper.

combination square An adjustable carpenter's tool consisting of a steel rule which slides through an adjustable head; may be used as a **try square**, miter square, level, marking gauge, plumb, and straightedge.

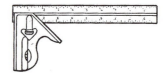

combination square

combination stair A stair in which access to the first landing is provided by a supplementary service stair as well as the main flight.

combination waste and vent system A special system of venting in which the waste piping is purposely oversized; intended as an economical means of providing adequate pro-

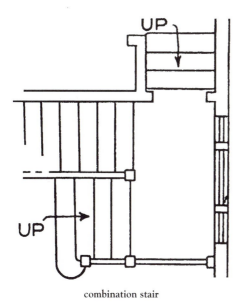

combination stair

tection of fixture traps against loss of seal in extensive installations where the individual venting of fixture drains would be impractical or uneconomical; serves both as a waste pipe and vent pipe.

combination window **1.** A window equipped with removable or interchangeable screen and glass sections that make it suitable for either summer or winter use. **2.** A window having several types of **sash**.

combined aggregate A mixture of fine and coarse aggregate for a concrete.

combined-aggregate grading The particle-size distribution of a mixture of fine and coarse aggregates.

combined building drain A building drain that conveys the drainage of both sewage and storm water.

combined building sewer A sewer that receives both storm water and sewage.

combined dry-pipe/preaction system A fire **sprinkler system** which combines automatic sprinklers (i.e., sprinkler heads) attached to a piping system containing air under pressure controlled by a fire detection system installed in the same areas as the sprinklers. See **dry-pipe sprinkler system** and **preaction sprinkler system**.

combined footing A **footing** which supports more than one column load.

combined frame A doorframe having fixed panes of glass flanking one or both sides of the door.

combined load Two or more different types of loads (such as dead load, live load, or wind load) on a structure, occurring simultaneously.

combined sewer A **sewer** which carries both sanitary sewage and storm water.

combined stresses A stress state which cannot be represented by a single component of stress.

combing **1.** In roofing, the topmost row of shingles which project above the ridge line; the uppermost ridge on a roof. **2.** Using a comb or stiff bristle brush to create a pattern by pulling through freshly applied paint. See **antiquing**. **3.** Scraping or smoothing a soft stone surface.

combplate The toothed portion of the stationary threshold plate at both ends of an escalator or moving walk, designed to mesh with the grooved surface of the moving steps or treadway.

combustibility The ease with which a material will burn when subject to heat.

combustible Capable of undergoing combustion in air, at pressures and temperatures that might occur during a fire in a building.

combustion Any chemical process that produces light and heat as either glow or flames.

combustion liquid A liquid having a flash point at or above 140°F (60°C) and below 200°F (93.4°C).

come-along A tool for spreading concrete, similar to a hoe; has a blade approx. 20 in. (50 cm) wide and 4 in. (10 cm) high.

comedor A dining room in a Spanish Colonial house.

comfort chart A chart which relates **effective temperature**, dry-bulb temperature, wet-bulb temperature, and air movement to human comfort; **comfort zones** are indicated on such a chart.

comfort station A building or part thereof where toilet and lavatory facilities are available for public use.

comfort zone The **effective temperature** range over which the majority of adults feel comfortable.

commercial bronze An alloy containing 90% copper, 10% zinc; so called because of its bronze color; esp. used in weatherstripping.

Commercial Italianate style See **Italianate style**.

commercial projected window A type of steel **projected window**; intended for commercial and industrial buildings which do not require interior trim or finishing around the window.

Commercial style A style of commercial architecture developed by the **Chicago School**, applied primarily to multistory office buildings and mercantile buildings constructed from about 1875 to 1930. Usually characterized by a **tripartite scheme** consisting of a *base* that is one to three stories high, a *shaft* many stories high; and a *cap*, usually one to three stories high that tops the structure; a flat roof; an overhanging cornice; unadorned fenestration, most often with large rectangular windows (for example, see **Chicago window**); bay windows with decorative **spandrels, 1**. Sometimes called Chicago Commercial style.

commercial tolerances The plus and/or minus allowances that are acceptable with a specified dimension.

Commission Internationale de l'Eclairage International Commission on Illumination. *Abbr.* CIE.

commode step One of two or more steps at the foot of a flight of stairs which have curved ends projecting beyond the string and surrounding the newel.

common A large plot of grassy, fenced-in, publicly owned land, generally at or near the center of a village or town; in earlier eras, once shared by the townspeople as a pasture.

common alloy An alloy that does not increase in strength when heat-treated but may be strengthened by strain hardening.

common area An area either within a building or outside a building which is intended for use of all occupants of the building or a group of buildings, but not for the free use of the general public.

common ashlar A pick- or hammer-dressed block of stone.

common bond A pattern of brickwork in which every third, fifth, sixth, or seventh **course**

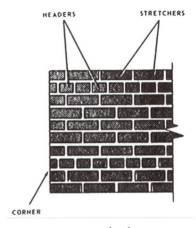

common bond

consists of headers (i.e., bricks laid horizontally with their lengths perpendicular to the face of the wall), and the other courses consist of stretchers (i.e., bricks laid horizontally so that their lengths are parallel to the face of the wall). This pattern is widely used because it can be laid relatively quickly.

common brass, high brass An alloy containing 65% copper, 35% zinc; the most common of commercial wrought brasses.

common brick Same as **building brick**.

common dovetail, box dovetail, through dovetail A dovetail joint in which the end grain shows on both members.

common dovetail

common excavation The excavation of material that does not require blasting, such as earth, in contrast to the excavation of solid rock.

common ground See **ground, 1**.

common house **1.** That part of a monastery in which a fire was kept for the monks during the winter. **2.** A one-room cottage in Spanish Colonial architecture of Florida, primarily in the first half of the 18th century. Characterized by: whitewashed **tabby** walls, a hipped roof that was thatched with palmetto fronds; and a smoke hole at the ridge of the roof; also see **Saint Augustine house**.

common joist, bridging joist A **joist** on which floorboards are laid; neither supports nor is supported by another joist.

common lap Shingle roofing in which alternate courses are offset one-half the width of a shingle.

common lime Either hydrated lime or quicklime; used in plastering.

common nail A cut or wire low-carbon steel nail, having a slender plain shank and a medium diamond point; used in work where finish is unimportant, as in framing.

common path of travel That portion of **exit access** that the occupants are required to traverse before two separate and distinct paths of travel to two **exits** are available.

common pitch In a spiral stair, the pitch of the **fliers** above and below the **winders**.

common purlin In **timber-framed construction**, one of a number of horizontal timbers that are parallel to the ridge of the roof, and joined to the **principal rafters** into which they are seated. The upper surfaces of the common purlins and the principal rafters are in the same plane. Also see **purlin**.

common rafter In wood-frame construction, one of a number of slanting structural members (extending from the **ridgeboard** down to the eaves) that support the roof; these members are usually of the same size and evenly spaced along the length of the roof ridge.

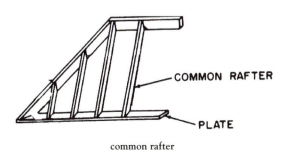

common rafter

common return An electrical conductor which serves as the electrical return for more than one circuit.

common room **1.** A room or lounge for the informal use of all members of a college. **2.** A room or lounge for the use of the patrons of an inn.

common vent See **dual vent**.

common wall See **party wall**.

communicating frame A double-rabbeted frame (with the rabbets on each side) prepared for two single-swing doors, one on each side of the frame, which open in opposite directions.

Communion table In Protestant churches, a table used instead of an altar in the Communion service.

community A group of people having common rights, privileges, or interests, or living in the same place under the same laws and regulations.

community center A building or group of public buildings for the social, cultural, and educational activities of a neighborhood or entire community.

community-facilities plan A graphic and written statement depicting a desirable pattern of public facilities (e.g., schools and parks) within an area, including their character, location, size, and service populations along with their suggested construction schedule.

community plan See **city plan** and **town plan**.

community planning The process of planning a future community, or the guidance and shaping of the expansion of a current community, in an organized manner and with an organized layout, taking into account such considerations as convenience for its inhabitants, environmental conditions, social requirements, recreational facilities, aesthetic design, and economic feasibility. Such planning includes a study of present requirements and conditions as well as projections for the future, and often includes proposals for implementing the plan.

COMP **1.** On drawings, abbr. for "compensate." **2.** On drawings, abbr. for "component." **3.** On drawings, abbr. for "composition."

compacted volume **1.** A measure of the volume of soil (or rocks) after its placement and compaction in a fill. **2.** The volume of a solid, such as soil, after it has been subjected to **compaction, 2**.

compacted yards The **compacted volume** measured in cubic yards.

compacting factor The ratio of the weight of concrete which fills a container of standard size and shape (when allowed to fall into it under standard conditions of test) to the weight of fully compacted concrete which fills the same container.

compaction **1.** The process of inducing a closer packing of the solid particles in freshly mixed concrete or mortar during placement by reducing the volume of voids, usually by vibration, centrifugation, tamping, or some combination of these actions. **2.** A similar manipulation of other cementitious mixtures, soils, aggregate, or the like.

compaction pile One of a group of piles, driven in a pattern, to compact a surface layer of loose granular soil to increase its bearing capacity.

compactor **1.** A machine that uses weight, vibration, or a combination of both, to achieve **compaction**. **2.** A motor-driven machine (usually having one or more rams) which reduces the volume of waste material by subjecting it to pressure and forces it into a removable container.

compactor, 1

companion flange **1.** A pipe flange which has been drilled so that it will fit the standard drilled holes in a flanged pipe or fitting. **2.** A pipe flange that is suitable for connection with a flanged valve or fitting.

company town A community whose inhabitants depend predominantly on a single company for their employment and for many of their personal and family needs. The company may own and provide housing, schools, shopping facilities, recreational facilities, as well as church and library facilities for its workers and their families.

compartment A small space within a larger enclosed area, often separated by partitions.

compartment ceiling A ceiling divided into panels, which are usually surrounded by moldings.

compartment wall British term for **fire wall**.

compass An instrument for drawing circles, measuring the distance between two points, etc.; consists of two pointed legs, movable on a joint or pivot, usually made so that one of the points can be detached for the insertion of a pen, extension, etc.

compass

compass brick An **arch brick**.

compass-headed arch A semicircular arch.

compass plane A plane having a curved baseplate (either concave or convex); for smoothing curved woodwork.

compass rafter A **rafter** which is curved on one or both sides.

compass roof **1.** A roof having curved rafters or ties. **2.** A form of timber roof in which the rafters, collar beams, and braces of each truss combine to form an arch.

compass saw A handsaw having a narrow blade; used to cut small intricate shapes or circles of small radius.

compass saw

compass survey A traverse survey which relies on the magnetic needle for orienting the sequence as a whole or for determining the bearings of the lines individually.

compass timber Timber that has been cut from a branch having a smooth curve of the required shape.

compass window **1.** A rounded bay window that projects from the face of a wall; in plan, it forms the segment of a circle; same as **bow window**. **2.** A semicircular **oriel window**. **3.** A window having a rounded, usually semicircular, upper member.

compass work, circular work Joinery which has circular forms within its overall design.

compatible materials In building construction, those materials that can exist in close proximity without affecting each other detrimentally.

compensation **1.** Payment for services rendered or products or materials furnished or delivered. **2.** Payment in satisfaction of claims for damages suffered.

compensator In fire **sprinkler systems**, a device intended to minimize false alarms caused by small increases in service pressure of the water supply.

COMPF On drawings, abbr. for "composition floor."

completed operations insurance Liability insurance coverage for injuries to persons or damage to property occurring after an operation is completed but attributed to that operation; does not apply to damage to the completed work itself. An operation is completed (a) when all operations under the contract have been completed or abandoned; or (b) when all operations at one project site are completed; or (c) when the portion of the work out of which the injury or damage arises has been put to its intended use by the person or organization for whom that portion of the work was done.

complete fusion In welding, fusion that has occurred over the entire base-metal surfaces exposed for welding and between all layers and **passes**.

completion bond, construction bond, contract bond The guarantee of a bonding company that a contractor will perform and deliver the work contracted for free of all encumbrances and liens.

completion date In the **contract documents**, the **date of substantial completion** of the work.

completion list See **inspection list**.

compluvium The aperture in the center of the roof of the atrium in a Roman house, sloping inward to discharge rainwater into a cistern or tank.

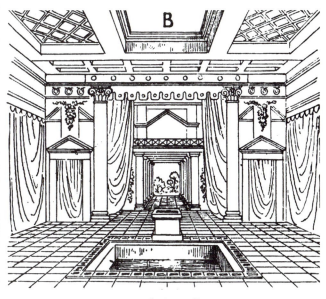

compluvium, *B*

compo **1.** Any composition material. **2.** Mortar made with an appropriate proportion of cement, lime, and sand. **3.** Various plastic cements and pastes which harden on exposure, as papier-mâché.

composite arch An arch whose curves are struck from four centers, as in English Perpendicular Gothic; a **mixed arch**.

composite beam A structural beam composed of different materials so interconnected that the beam responds to loads as a unit.

composite board A type of **hardboard**, esp. one fabricated for use in heat insulation.

Composite capital The topmost member of a column of the **Composite order**; a Roman adaptation of a Corinthian capital, being much more elaborate; consists of volutes and convex molding between them, somewhat similar to the **Ionic capital**; has a circle of acanthus leaves applied to the lower part of the bell used in the Corinthian capital. (*See illustration p. 218.*)

composite column A column in which a metal structural member is completely encased

composite construction

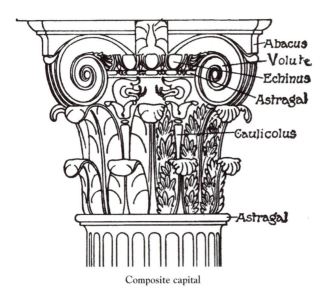

Composite capital

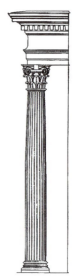

Composite order

in concrete containing special and longitudinal reinforcement.

composite construction A type of construction made up of different materials (such as concrete and structural steel) or of members produced by different methods (such as cast-in-place concrete and precast concrete).

composite door A door made of a core material which is faced and edged with steel, wood, or a plastic-laminated material.

composite fire door A flush-design fire door; consists of a manufactured core material with chemically impregnated wood edge banding and untreated wood face veneers, or laminated plastic faces, or surrounded by and encased in steel.

composite girder **1.** See **plate girder**. **2.** A girder of **composite construction**.

composite joint A joint employing more than one means to hold the elements together, e.g., welding and bolting.

Composite order In Classical architecture, one of the five Classical orders; combines characteristics of both the Corinthian and Ionic orders; similar to the Corinthian order, but much more embellished. The capital consists of **volutes** borrowed, with modifications, from the **Ionic capital**; the circle of acanthus leaves applied to the capital is borrowed from the **Corinthian capital**. See illustration under bases for an example of a base of the Composite order.

composite pile **1.** A **pile** comprised of different materials, e.g., concrete and wood. **2.** A pile comprised of steel members which are fastened together, end-to-end, to form a single pile.

composite sample A sample of material which is obtained by blending two or more individual samples.

composite structure A structural element in which different types of materials share a load.

composite truss A truss whose compressive members are timber and whose tension members are metal (usually steel).

composite wall A wall built of a combination of two or more masonry units of different types of materials that are bonded together, one forming the facing of the wall and the other the backup.

composition board A **building board** which is fabricated of wood fibers, under pressure and at an elevated temperature, usually with a binder.

composition joint A **bell-and-spigot joint** that is sealed with a combination of materials such as cement and hemp, rope and rosin, etc.

composition nail (*Brit.*) A brass nail used in roofing, esp. to fix tiles and slates.

composition roofing See **built-up roofing**.

composition shingles See **asphalt shingles**.

compost A mixture usually consisting largely of decomposed organic material; used for fertilizing soil.

compound arch An arch formed by concentric arches set within one another.

compound beam, built-up beam A rectangular beam composed of smaller timbers over which planks are nailed on each side; the composite unit is joined together by bolting or by gluing.

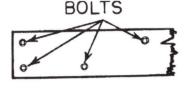

BOLTS

compound beam

compound pier, compound pillar A pier composed of a conjunction of colonettes, generally attached to a central shaft; a **clustered column**. Also see **bundle pier**.

compound rafter One of a pair of two rafters, one spaced above the other; the one below is usually called the secondary rafter.

compound shake Wood **shakes, 2** found in combination.

compound vault One whose construction appears to depend upon a pendant placed on each side, and within the walls that carry the main vault.

compound wall A wall which is constructed of more than one material; not of homogeneous construction.

COMPR **1.** On drawings, abbr. for "composition roof." **2.** On drawings, abbr. for "compress." **3.** On drawings, abbr. for "compressor."

compregnated wood, resin-treated wood Wood impregnated with a thermosetting resin, then subjected to heat and pressure to provide both resin curing and compression.

comprehensive general liability insurance A broad form of liability insurance covering claims for bodily injury and property damage which combines under one policy coverage for all liability exposures (except those specifically excluded) on a blanket basis and automatically covers new and unknown hazards that may develop; automatically includes contractual liability coverage for certain types of contracts.

comprehensive services Professional services performed by the architect in addition to the **basic services**, in such related areas as project analysis, programming, land use studies, feasibility investigations, financing, construction management, and special consulting services.

compressed cork Same as **corkboard**.

compressed fiberboard See **hardboard**.

compressed straw slab See **strawboard**.

compressed wood, densified wood Wood which has been impregnated with resin and subjected to a high pressure to increase its density and strength.

compressibility The relative resistance (e.g., of a soil mass) to a change in volume upon being subjected to a compressive stress.

compression **1.** The state of being compressed, or being shortened by a force. **2.** The change in length produced in a test specimen by a compressive load.

compression bearing joint A joint, between two structural members in compression, that transmits the compressive stress from one member to the other.

compression coupling A coupling used to connect sections of hubless pipe (i.e., pipe without a hub), acid-resistant cast-iron pipe, or glass-pipe; consists of an inner elastomeric gasket and an outer metallic sleeve, with an integral bolt used to tighten and compress the seal.

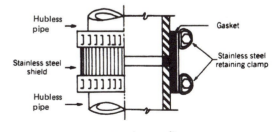

Hubless pipe

Gasket

Stainless steel shield

Stainless steel retaining clamp

Hubless pipe

compression coupling

compression faucet A faucet in which water flow is shut off by a flat disk that is screwed down onto its seat. (*See illustration p. 220.*)

compression flange The widened portion of a beam or girder, such as the horizontal portion of the cross section of a simple-span T-beam, which is shortened by bending under a normal load.

compression gasket

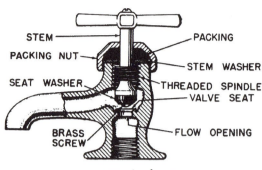

compression faucet

compression gasket A **gasket** designed for use under compression.

compression joint **1.** Any joint formed by a **fitting** designed to join piping or tubing by means of pressure. **2.** A **joint** having cup-shaped threaded nuts which, when tightened, compress tapered sleeves so they form a tight joint along the periphery of the tubing they connect.

compression loading A reduction in the thickness of an elastomeric element along the line of an externally applied force.

compression member Any member in which the primary stress is longitudinal compression.

compression molding A technique of thermoset molding; a molding compound is placed in a polished steel mold, and then heat and pressure are applied.

compression reinforcement Structural reinforcement which is designed to carry compressive stresses.

compression seal A material which provides a seal as a result of pressure between the faces of a joint.

compression set The permanent deformation of an elastomeric sealant, compressed so far that its internal structure is partially or completely destroyed and it no longer will assume its previous shape.

compression test On a specimen of mortar or concrete, a test to determine its **compressive strength**; in the U.S.A., unless otherwise specified, mortar test specimens are 2-in. cubes, and concrete test specimens are cylinders 6 in. in diameter and 12 in. high.

compression valve A valve in which water flow is shut off by a flat disk that is screwed down onto its seat.

compression wood Abnormal wood formed on the underside of branches and leaning trunks of softwoods; usually lower in strength; has unusual shrinkage characteristics.

compressive strain The **strain** caused by a compressive load.

compressive strength The maximum **compressive stress** which a material is capable of sustaining.

compressive stress **1.** The stress which resists the shortening effect of an external compressive force. **2.** For a test specimen: the compressive load per unit area of original cross section carried by the test specimen at any time during a compression test.

compressor A machine for compressing air or other gases which is a basic component in some refrigeration systems; draws vaporized **refrigerant** from the **evaporator** at a relatively low pressure, compresses it, and then discharges it to a **condenser**.

compressor-type liquid chiller Equipment utilizing a **compressor**, condensor, evaporator, controls, and accessories to cool water or other secondary liquid.

computer-aided design (CAD) The analysis and/or design, and/or modeling, and/or simulation, and/or layout of building design with the aid of a computer.

CONC **1.** On drawings, abbr. for **concrete**. **2.** On drawings, abbr. for "concentric."

concameration **1.** An arch or vault. **2.** An apartment; a chamber.

concave joint A recessed masonry joint, formed in mortar by the use of a curved steel

concave joint

jointing tool; because of its curved shape it is very effective in resisting rain penetration; used in areas subjected to heavy rains and high winds.

concealed Said of materials, components, controls, etc., that are rendered inaccessible by the finish or structure of a building.

concealed cleat A metal strap or cleat used to anchor sheet-metal roofing or flashing to the roof sheathing (or blocking); used to conceal the anchor under the sheet metal.

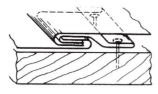

concealed cleat

concealed closer See **overhead concealed closer**.

concealed flashing On a roof, flashing which is entirely concealed by shingles.

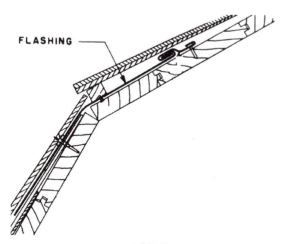

FLASHING

concealed flashing

concealed gutter A gutter built into the eaves of a roof, usually metal-lined.

concealed heating A system (such as a **panel heating** system) that employs heating elements which are concealed from view or are blended into the architectural features of a room.

concealed nailing 1. See **blind nailing**. 2. In roofing, see **nailing**.

concealed piping Piping which requires the removal of permanent construction to gain access to it.

concealed routing Routing at the bottom of a cabinet door or drawer to provide a means of opening and closing without pulls.

concealed suspension system A system for suspending an acoustical ceiling in which no suspension members are visible in the room.

concealed valley A type of **valley** on a roof; the shingles or slates are laid to the intersecting roof surfaces, covering the metal lining of the valley.

concentrated load A load acting on a very small area of a structure, as differentiated from a **distributed load**.

concentric Having a common center.

concentricity Conformance to a common center as, for example, the inner and outer walls of round tube.

concentric load See **centric load**.

concentric tendon One of a number of **tendons** which follow a line through the center of gravity of a prestressed concrete member.

concha 1. The semidome vaulting of an apse; also called a conch. 2. In Spanish architecture and its derivatives, a decorative element in the form of the interior of a sea scallop; see **shell-headed**.

concordant tendon In a statically indeterminate structure, a **tendon** that is coincident with the pressure line produced by the tendon.

concourse 1. An open space where several roads or paths meet. 2. An open space for accommodating large crowds in a building, as in a railway terminal.

concrete A composite stonelike material formed by mixing an **aggregate** (such as stones of irregular shape or crushed rock) with **cement** (which acts as the binding material) and water, then allowing the mixture to dry and harden; **portland cement**, now used in making concrete, was not developed until the 19th century. Also see **average concrete, cyclopean concrete, poured concrete, reinforced concrete**.

concrete admixture See **admixture**.

concrete aggregate See **aggregate**.

concrete agitation See **concrete vibration**.

concrete anchor   See **anchor**.

concrete block   A hollow or solid concrete masonry unit consisting of portland cement and suitable aggregates combined with water. Lime, fly ash, air-entraining agents, or other admixtures may be included. Sometimes incorrectly called **cement block**.

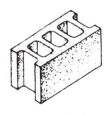

concrete block

concrete bond, concrete bond plaster   See **bond plaster**.

concrete border   **1.** On a theatre stage, the **lighting batten** nearest the proscenium. **2.** A curtain concealing the lighting batten nearest the proscenium.

concrete breaker   A compressed-air tool for breaking up concrete.

concrete brick   A solid concrete masonry unit, rectangular in shape, usually not larger than 4 in. by 4 in. by 12 in. (10 cm by 10 cm by 30 cm); made from portland cement and suitable aggregates; may include other materials.

concrete cart   See **buggy**.

concrete collar, doughnut   A collar of reinforced concrete which is placed around an existing column so that it can be jacked up; the shrinkage of the concrete causes it to grip the column firmly.

concrete column   A **column, 1** made of either reinforced or unreinforced concrete.

concrete curing blanket   See **curing blanket**.

concrete curing compound   A chemical compound which is applied to a concrete surface to prevent the loss of moisture during early stages of cement hydration.

concrete-encased beam   A steel beam that is totally encased in concrete which is cast integrally with the concrete slab.

concrete-encased electrode   See **encased electrode**.

concrete finishing machine   **1.** A machine mounted on flanged wheels which rides on forms or specially set tracks, used to finish concrete surfaces such as those of pavements. **2.** A portable power-driven machine for floating and finishing concrete floors and slabs.

concrete flatwork   Finishing operations on concrete floors and slabs.

concrete floor hardener   A liquid or dry mixture of chemicals, minerals, metals, and/or other synthetic materials which produces a dense wear-resistant and/or nonslip and/or colored surface on concrete floors.

concrete form   See **form**.

concrete form coating   See **form coating**.

concrete formwork   See **formwork**.

concrete frame construction   A structure consisting of concrete beams, girders, and columns which are rigidly joined.

concrete gun   A **spray gun** used in applying freshly mixed concrete; compressed air forces the concrete along a flexible hose and through a nozzle.

concrete hardener   An admixture that significantly alters the rate of hydration of concrete so as to increase its strength.

concrete insert   A plastic, wood fiber, or metal (often lead) plug, either built in a wall or ceiling or inserted by drilling; used as an anchor or support to hold attached loads.

concrete insert

concrete masonry   **1.** Construction consisting of concrete masonry units laid up in mortar or grout. **2.** Poured concrete construction.

concrete masonry unit   A block or brick cast of portland cement and suitable aggregate, with or without admixtures, and intended for laying up with other units as in normal stone masonry construction. Also see **A-block, breeze block, cinder block, concrete block, concrete brick**, etc.

concrete mixer, cement mixer A machine that mixes concrete ingredients by means of paddles or a rotating drum. Raw materials usually are introduced into the mixing drum through its open end and discharged by tilting the mixing drum to allow the concrete to pour out.

concrete nail A hardened-steel nail having a flat countersunk head and a diamond point; used for nailing to concrete or masonry.

concrete nail

concrete paint See **cement paint**.

concrete pile A concrete pile which is driven into the ground or otherwise placed; may be a precast pile, reinforced pile, or prestressed concrete pile.

concrete pipe A porous pipe, fabricated of concrete, used primarily for subsoil drainage.

concrete planer A self-propelled machine equipped with a series of rotating blades (or drums) for smoothing and leveling in refinishing old concrete pavement.

concrete plank A precast, prestressed, hollow-core concrete plank, usually relatively lightweight; used for floor and roof decking; may carry a structural topping.

concrete posttensioning See **posttensioning**.

concrete pump A machine that mixes concrete ingredients and then moves the concrete mixture through a hose to the point of placement. Also see **pneumatic placement**.

concrete reinforcement See **reinforcement**.

concrete retarder A material added to concrete to increase its setting time by decreasing the rate at which **hydration** takes place.

concrete saw A power-operated saw used in grooving uncured concrete (to prevent cracking) or in cutting hard concrete slabs.

concrete slab A flat, rectangular, reinforced concrete structural member; especially used for floors, roofs, pads, etc.

concrete vibrating machine A machine which compacts a layer of freshly mixed concrete by vibration.

concrete vibration Energetic agitation of freshly mixed concrete during placement by mechanical oscillation devices at moderately high frequency to assist in its consolidation.

concrete vibrator A device for agitating freshly mixed concrete during placement by mechanical oscillation at a moderately high frequency to assist in consolidation.

concreting paper A **building paper**.

concurrent loads Two or more elements of dead (or live) loads that, for purposes of design, are considered to act simultaneously.

condemnation 1. The process by which property of a private owner is taken for public use, without his consent, but upon the award and payment of just compensation, being in the nature of a forced sale. 2. A legal declaration that a piece of property or a building is unfit for use.

condensate The liquid formed by the condensation of a vapor; in steam heating, water is condensed from steam; in air conditioning, water is extracted from air.

condensate unit A packaged unit comprising a tank and pump which store and transfer condensed steam to a remote location.

condensation 1. In a refrigeration system, the process of changing the **refrigerant** into liquid by the extraction of heat. 2. See **surface condensation**.

condensation gutter, condensation channel, condensation groove, condensation trough A trough-like depression in the top of the interior sill of a glazed opening, to receive and carry off moisture forming on the indoor face of the glass.

condenser A heat-exchange device in a refrigeration system; consists of a vessel or arrangement of pipes or tubing in which refrigerant vapor is liquefied (condensed) by the removal of heat.

condenser tube Metal tubing manufactured to special requirements as to tolerances, finish, and temper; used in water cooling in a **heat exchanger**.

condensing unit In a refrigeration system, a single compact unit consisting of one or more power-driven **compressors, condensers, liquid receivers** (when required), and control accessories.

condition monitoring The measurement of various parameters (such as vibration, bearing temperature, oil pressure, and performance) related to the mechanical condition of machinery; this information is used to predict whether a breakdown is apt occur in the very near future.

conditions of acceptance Criteria establishing the limits within which the measured or observed characteristics of a test specimen must fall in order for it to comply with stated requirements.

conditions of the bid Conditions set forth in the **instructions to bidders**, the notice to bidders or advertisement for bids, the invitation to bidders, or other similar documents prescribing the conditions under which bids are to be prepared, executed, submitted, received, and accepted.

conditions of the contract Those portions of the **contract documents** which define, set forth, or relate to: contract terminology; the rights and responsibilities of the contracting parties and of others involved in the **work, 1**; requirements for safety and for compliance with laws and regulations; general procedures for the orderly prosecution and management of the work; payments to the contractor; and similar provisions of a general, nontechnical nature.

conditory A repository for storing things, esp. an underground vault for the dead.

condominium A form of real estate ownership of a multifamily residential dwelling. Each occupant has 100% ownership of his own apartment and partial ownership of common elements such as hallways, elevators, plumbing, etc. Also see **cooperative**.

conductance See **thermal conductance**.

conduction See **thermal conduction**.

conductive flooring Flooring which has been designed to eliminate or prevent electrostatic buildup and electrostatic or mechanical sparking.

conductive rubber A rubber which has been mixed with carbon black in fabrication; has sufficient electrical conductivity to prevent electrostatic buildup.

conductivity See **thermal conductivity, electrical conductivity**.

conductor **1.** A wire, cable, or device offering low resistance to the flow of electric current. **2.** A material that transmits heat readily. **3.** A **downspout**. **4.** Any vertical pipe which conveys rainwater, including one within a building.

conductor head See **leader head**.

conductor shielding A metallic sheath which surrounds an electric conductor.

conduit **1.** A tube or pipe used to protect electric wiring. **2.** A tube or pipe used for conveying fluid. **3.** Any channel intended for the conveyance of water, whether open or closed.

conduit body According to the **NEC**, a separate portion of an electrical conduit or tubing system that provides access through one or more removable covers to the interior of the system at a junction of two or more sections of the system or at a terminal point of the system.

conduit box See **junction box**.

conduit fitting **1.** An accessory for a **conduit, 1** system, such as a bushing or an access fitting. **2.** In an electrical conduit system, an accessory such as an access fitting or bushing.

conduit hanger See **hanger, 1**.

cone bolt See **cone-nut tie**.

cone-cut veneer Wood veneer that has been cut in a manner similar to the sharpening of a pencil, to obtain circular sheets of highly figured veneer.

cone-drum cyclorama See **rolling cyclorama**.

conehead rivet A rivet which has a head shaped like a truncated cylindrical cone.

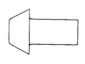

conehead rivet

cone-nut tie, cone bolt A type of **tie rod** used in a concrete form for a wall; has a cone at both ends; also acts as a spreader.

cone of depression A conically shaped depression in the soil around a point where an underground pump is located.

cone tile, cone hip tile See **bonnet hip tile**.

confession, confessio The tomb of a martyr or confessor; if an altar was erected over the grave, the name was also extended to the altar and to the subterranean chamber in which it stood; in later times a basilica was sometimes erected over the chamber and the entire building was known as a confession.

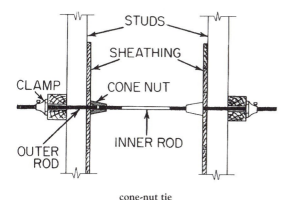

cone-nut tie

confessional A small booth furnished with a seat for a priest and with a window, screen, or aperture so that the penitent, who is outside, may whisper in the priest's ear without being seen.

confessional

configurated glass, figured glass Glass having an irregular surface in a pattern that has been rolled or formed during fabrication; used to obscure vision or to diffuse light.

configuration The spatial arrangement of wood particles, chips, flakes, or fibers used in **particleboard, fiberboard**, etc.

confined concrete A concrete which has closely-spaced special transverse reinforcement which restrains the concrete in directions perpendicular to the applied stress.

conflagration hazard The risk involved in the spread of fire by exterior exposure to and from adjoining structures or buildings.

confluent vent A **vent** serving more than one **fixture vent** or **stack vent**.

congé **1.** See **apophyge**. **2.** A quarter-round concave molding, tangent to a vertical surface and succeeded by a fillet parallel to that surface. **3.** In ceramic tile work, a **sanitary base** or **sanitary shoe**.

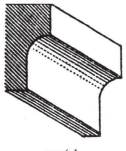

congé, 1

congelated Same as **frosted, 1**.

conglomerate Rock consisting of rounded pebbles which are cemented together with a finer material.

congregate residence A building (or portion thereof) containing facilities for living, sanitation, and sleeping as required by the applicable building code; may include facilities for cooking and/or eating for occupancy other than by a family. This classification includes, for example, convents, dormitories, fraternity or sorority houses, and shelters.

conical roll See **batten roll**.

conical roof A roof in the shape of an inverted cone, usually atop a cylindrical tower; also called a candle-snuffer roof, or witch's cap.

conical vault A **vault** having a cross section in the form of a circular arc, which is larger at one end than the other.

conical vault

conifer A cone-bearing tree or shrub of the gymnospermous order; a softwood which includes cypress, firs, pines, and spruce.

conisterium In ancient Greece and Rome, a room appended to a gymnasium or palaestra in which wrestlers were sprinkled with sand or dust after having been anointed with oil.

connected barn See **continuous house**.

connected load The electric load (in watts) on an electric system if all apparatus and equipment connected to the system are energized simultaneously.

Connecticut barn Same as **Yankee barn**.

connecting angle An **angle section** used to connect two structural members.

connecting block A plastic block containing metal wiring terminals; used to establish electrical connections.

connection In steel construction, a combination of joints capable of transmitting forces between two or more members.

connector **1.** In an electric circuit, a device for joining two or more conductors, by a low-resistance path, without the use of a permanent splice. **2.** A mechanical device for fastening together two or more pieces, members, or parts, including anchors, fasteners, or wall ties.

connector

connector plate In a **truss**, a prepunched toothed metal connector located at a joint or splice of a truss; designed to sustain the forces that occur at such a location.

consent of surety **1.** Written consent of the **surety** on a **performance bond** and/or **labor and material payment bond** to such contract changes as **change orders** or reductions in the contractor's retainage, or to final payment, or to waiving notification of contract changes. **2.** Written consent of the **surety**, to an extension of time in a **bid bond**.

conservation The overseeing and maintenance of a building to prevent or arrest its decay or destruction, usually by applying a variety of measures. See **building conservation** and **building preservation**.

conservatory **1.** A school for the teaching of music, drama, or other fine arts. **2.** A structure chiefly used for growing flowers, plants, and out-of-season fruits and vegetables under protected conditions; it is attached to a dwelling, in contrast to a greenhouse which serves the same purpose but is usually a separate structure in a garden or field. Also see **orangery, greenhouse,** and **hothouse**.

consistency **1.** The degree of firmness, or the relative ability of freshly mixed concrete, grout, or mortar to flow; usually measured by the **slump test** for concrete, and by the **flow test** for mortar, plaster, cement paste, or grout. Also see **viscosity**. **2.** The property of a cohesive soil that describes its physical state.

consistency index Same as **relative consistency**.

consistency limits Same as **Atterberg limits**.

consistometer An apparatus for measuring the **consistency** of grouts, cement pastes, mortars, or concrete.

consistory A chamber used for a church court.

console **1.** A decorative bracket in the form of a vertical scroll, projecting from a wall to support a cornice, a door or window head, a piece of sculpture, etc.; an **ancon**. **2.** The cabinet from which an organ is played, including the keyboards, pedals, stops, etc. **3.** A panel control desk or cabinet containing dials, meters, switches, and other apparatus for controlling mechanical, hydromechanical, or electrical equipment.

console lift A section of the floor area of a theater or auditorium that can be raised or lowered.

console table A table attached to a wall and supported on consoles.

consolidation **1.** The compaction of freshly placed concrete or mortar, usually by vibration, centrifugation, or tamping, to mold it within forms and around embedded parts and reinforcement and to eliminate voids other than entrained air. Also see **compaction**. **2.** The process whereby soil particles are packed more closely by the application of continued pressure.

consolidation grouting **1.** The injection of fluid grouting, usually portland cement and

console, 1

sand, into a compressible soil mass to displace it and form a structure for support. **2.** Same as **area grouting**.

consolidation settlement Of loaded clay, a settlement which takes place over a period of years.

con spec Abbr. for "construction specification."

CONST On drawings, abbr. for **construction**.

constant-voltage transformer A special transformer which is designed to provide constant voltage at its output, independent of voltage variations in the line to which its input is connected.

constant-wattage ballast A **ballast** used with a **high-intensity discharge lamp** to minimize the effects of voltage variations and to provide a high power-factor.

constratum In ancient Rome, a flooring constructed of planks.

construction **1.** All the on-site work done in building or altering structures, from land clearance through completion, including excavation, erection, and the assembly and installation of components and equipment. **2.** A structure. **3.** The manner in which something is built.

construction bolt Any one of a number of common steel bolts, used during construction as a temporary fastening device, such as a bolt to hold forms together.

construction bond A **completion bond**.

construction budget **1.** The sum established by the owner as available for construction of the project. **2.** The stipulated highest acceptable bid price or, in the case of a project involving multiple construction contracts, the stipulated aggregate total of the highest acceptable bid prices.

construction class A classification based on the fire-resistance ratings of the construction of a building or its parts.

construction cost The cost of all the construction portions of a project, generally based upon the sum of the construction contract(s) and other direct construction costs; does not include the compensation paid to the architect and consultants, the cost of the land, right-of-way, or other costs which are defined in the **contract documents** as being the responsibility of the **owner**.

construction documents The **working drawings** and **specifications**.

construction documents phase The third phase of the architect's **basic services**. In this phase the architect prepares from the approved design development documents, for approval by the **owner**, the **working drawings** and **specifications** and the necessary bidding information. In this phase the architect also assists the owner in the preparation of bidding forms, the **conditions of the contract**, and the form of agreement between the owner and the contractor.

construction equipment All machinery, derricks, hoists, ladders, materials-handling equipment, platforms, runways, safeguards and protective devices, and scaffolds, as well as other equipment, used in construction operations.

construction inspector See **project representative**.

construction joint **1.** A joint where two successive placements of concrete meet. **2.** A separation provided in a building which allows its component parts to move with respect to each other. The cause of such movement may be thermal, seismic, or wind loading.

construction loads The **loads, 1** during construction, to which a structure is subjected.

construction loan A loan to a builder for a short term, financing construction prior to permanent financing.

construction management The special management services performed by the architect or others during the **construction phase** of the project, under separate or special agreement with the owner. This is not part of the architect's **basic services**, but is an additional service sometimes included in **comprehensive services**.

construction phase—administration of the construction contract The fifth and final phase of the architect's **basic services**, which includes the architect's general administration of the construction contract(s). Also see **contract administration**.

construction survey See **engineering survey**.

construction wrench A wrench having an open end for turning nuts and bolts; the other end tapers to a blunt point which is used to align mating holes in steel construction.

constructive eviction The rendering of leased premises uninhabitable because of the landlord's improper acts of commission or omission; gives rise to the same legal consequences as an unlawful eviction. See **eviction**.

Constructivism A movement which originated in Moscow after 1917, primarily in sculpture, but with broad applications to architecture. The expression of construction was to be the basis for all building design, with emphasis on functional machine parts. Tatlin's project of a monument to the Third International in Moscow (1920) is the most famous example.

consulate A building or place where a consul conducts official business.

consultant An individual or organization engaged by the owner or the architect to render professional consulting services complementing or supplementing the architect's services.

CONT On drawings, abbr. for "continue."

contact A part which is an electric conductor and which provides a low-resistance path for current flow upon mating with another conducting part with which it is designed to operate.

contact adhesive, contact-bond adhesive, dry-bond adhesive An adhesive that is apparently dry to the touch and adheres instantaneously upon contact.

contact-bond adhesive See **contact adhesive**.

Constructivism: Tatlin's project

contact ceiling A ceiling that is secured directly to the construction above, without the use of furring channels.

contactor Any device for repeatedly opening and closing an electric power circuit.

contact pressure Pressure, produced by the weight of a footing and all the forces acting on it, which acts at and perpendicular to the contact area between the footing and the soil.

contact pressure adhesive An **adhesive** that is permanently tacky at room temperature and adheres to many types of surfaces upon contact, requiring little pressure in application.

contact splice A type of connection between **reinforcing bars** in reinforced concrete; the bars are lapped and are in direct contact.

container packer A **refuse compactor** that compresses refuse within a steel container. The container is latched to the compactor by special locking devices.

containment grouting Same as **perimeter grouting**.

contamination The introduction of sewage, wastes, and/or chemicals (or other material) into a potable water supply that render it unfit for its intended purpose.

Contemporary style An imprecise term applied to any of a number of **architectural**

modes popular from about the 1940s through the 1970s and beyond, sometimes included under the term *modern architecture*; often characterized by widely overhanging eaves, exposed roof beams, and front-facing gables with heavy piers that support the gables; often, a balcony with an overhanging sunscreen, roof decks, and a patio that may serve as an extension of the living area; another type has a façade and flat roof resembling that of the International style.

contents hazard classification The classification of the potential danger of building contents as ordinary, high, or low.

contextualism The "fitting-in" of a building with surrounding buildings so that it is in harmony with them, especially in terms of scale, form, mass, and color.

contignation A framework, as of beams.

continental cabin A one-and-one-half-story **log house** attributed to German-speaking immigrants to colonial America; usually consisted of a large room at the front of the house, a bedroom behind it, and a long narrow kitchen along one side. A sizable stove in the kitchen was used both for cooking and for heating the adjacent large room.

continental seating A seating arrangement in an auditorium in which the rows of seats are unbroken by aisles or crossovers; access to the rows is from an aisle at the end of the rows or from doors along the sidewalls.

contingency allowance A sum designated to cover unpredictable or unforeseen items of **work, 1** or changes subsequently required by the **owner**.

contingent agreement Any **agreement** under which the rights or obligations of a party are subject to the happening of a stated contingency, e.g., an agreement between an **owner** and an architect in which part or all of the architect's compensation is contingent upon the owner's obtaining funds for the project (such as by successful referendum, sale of bonds, or other financing), or upon some other specially prescribed condition.

continuous acoustical ceiling A suspended acoustical ceiling in which the top of a partition extends only to the lower surface of the ceiling.

continuous beam A beam which extends over three or more supports, joined together so

that, for a given load on one span, the effect on the other spans can be calculated.

continuous block core, edge-glued core, stave core A solid core consisting of blocks of wood which are bonded together and sanded to a smooth uniform thickness; used in wood doors, panels, etc.

continuous footing A **combined footing**, of prismatic or truncated shape, which supports two or more columns in a row.

continuous foundation A foundation which supports a number of independent loads.

continuous girder A girder with more than two supports.

continuous grading A particle-size distribution for material such as an aggregate in which all intermediate-size fractions are present, as opposed to gap grading.

continuous handrail Handrail for a **geometrical stair**.

continuous header A **top plate** consisting of timbers on end which are joined (along their lengths and at corners) to form a continuous, rigid framework around a structure, sufficiently strong to act as a lintel over wall openings.

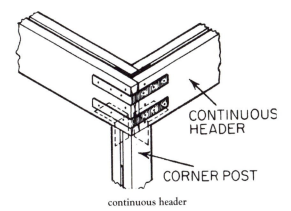

CONTINUOUS HEADER

CORNER POST

continuous header

continuous hinge, piano hinge A hinge having the same length as the moving part to which it is applied. (*See illustration p. 230.*)

continuous house A house that is connected to several other ancillary facilities such as a barn, privy, shed, and/or stable; advantageous in areas having a harsh winter climate because this arrangement permits the residents to use these

continuous hinge

dependencies without going outdoors. Compare with **telescope house**.

continuous impost In Gothic architecture, the moldings of an arch when carried down to the floor without interruption or anything to mark the impost point.

continuous impost

continuous kiln See **progressive kiln**.

continuous load Said of an electrical load in which the maximum current is expected to continue for at least 3 hours at a time.

continuously reinforced pavement A pavement having no transverse joints, except tied construction joints which are placed between successive days' concreting, with sufficient longitudinal reinforcement, adequately lapped to develop tensile continuity.

continuous mixer A mixer for concrete or mortar into which ingredients are fed without stopping and from which the mix is discharged in a continuous stream, in contrast to the periodic discharge of a **batch mixer**.

continuous-pressure electric elevator An electric elevator operated by means of push buttons in the elevator car and at landings, requiring that a button to be held manually to keep the car in motion.

continuous rating The maximum constant load that can be carried by a piece of electric equipment without exceeding a designated temperature rise.

continuous slab A slab which extends as a unit over three or more supports in a given direction.

continuous span A span which is formed of a series of consecutive spans (over three or more supports) that are continuously or rigidly connected so that bending moment may be transmitted from one span to the adjacent ones.

continuous string A string for a **geometrical stair**.

continuous truss A truss that extends over three or more supports.

continuous vent A vertical **vent** that is a continuation of a drain, a soil pipe, or a waste pipe to which the vent connects.

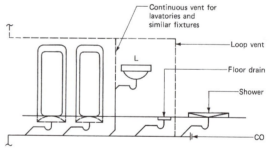

continuous vent

continuous waste A drain from two or more plumbing fixtures connected to a single trap.

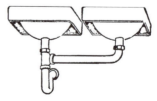

continuous waste

continuous waste-and-vent A waste pipe and a vent pipe which are in a straight line, the latter being a continuation of the former.

contour basin   A level basin on a sloping site to catch rainfall.

contour curtain   A theatre stage curtain which can be raised in separate folds by individual lines which are attached to its component sections, thereby controlling its shape or contour.

contour interval   The vertical distance between adjacent contour lines.

contour line   A line on a map or drawing representing points of equal elevation on the ground.

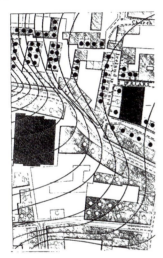

contour lines

contour map   A topographic map which portrays relief by the use of contour lines which connect points of equal elevation; the closer the spacing of the lines, the greater the relative slope.

CONTR   On drawings, abbr. for **contractor**.

contract   A legally enforceable promise or agreement between two or among several persons. Also see **agreement**.

contract administration   The duties and responsibilities of the architect during the **construction phase**.

contract bond   See **completion bond**.

contract date   Same as **date of agreement**.

contract documents   Those documents that comprise a **contract**, e.g., in a construction contract, the **owner-contractor agreement, conditions of the contract** (general, supplementary, and other conditions), plans and/or drawings, specifications, all addenda, modifications, and

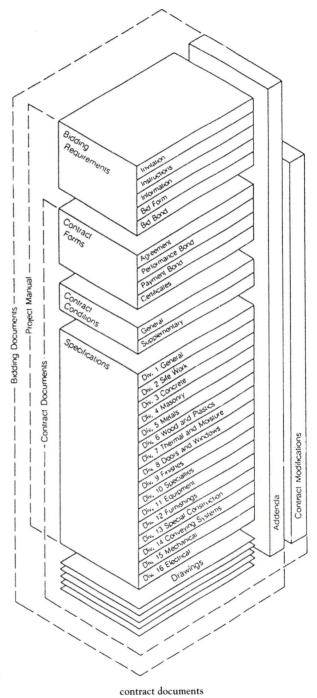

contract documents

changes thereto, together with any other items stipulated as being specifically included.

contracting officer The person designated as an official representative of the **owner** with specific authority to act in his behalf in connection with a project.

contraction Of concrete, the sum of volume changes occurring as the result of all processes affecting the bulk volume of a mass of concrete.

contraction joint 1. An **expansion joint, 1**. 2. A joint between adjacent parts of a structure which permits movement between them resulting from contraction.

contraction joint grouting The injection of grout into a contraction joint.

contract limit A limit line or perimeter line established on the **drawings** or elsewhere in the **contract documents** defining the boundaries of the site available to the contractor for construction purposes.

contract load The load specified in the contract for the purchase of an elevator, or the load specified in the application for the building permit.

contractor One who undertakes responsibility for the performance of construction work, including the provision of labor and materials, in accordance with plans and specifications and under a contract specifying cost and schedule for completion of the work; the person or organization responsible for performing the **work, 1** and identified as such in the **owner-contractor agreement**.

contractor's affidavit A certified statement of the **contractor**, properly notarized, relating to payment of debts and claims, release of liens, or similar matters requiring specific evidence for the protection of the **owner**. Also see **noncollusion affidavit**.

contractor's estimate 1. A forecast of **construction cost**, as opposed to a firm proposal, prepared by a **contractor** for a **project** or a portion thereof. 2. A term sometimes used to denote a contractor's application or request for a progress payment. Also see **application for payment**.

contractor's liability insurance Insurance purchased and maintained by the contractor to protect him from specified claims which may arise out of or result from his operations under the contract, whether such operations be by himself or by any subcontractor or by anyone directly or indirectly employed by any of them, or by anyone for whose acts any of them may be liable.

contractor's option A provision of the **contract documents** under which the contractor may select certain specified materials, methods, or systems at his own option, without change in the **contract sum**.

contractor's proposal See **bid**.

contract speed The speed specified in the contract for the purchase of an elevator, or the speed specified in the application for the building permit.

contract sum The price stated in the **owner-contractor agreement**, which is the total amount payable by the owner to the contractor for the performance of the **work, 1** under the **contract documents**; can be adjusted only by a **change order**.

contract time The period of time established in the **contract documents**, pursuant to other agreement between the parties, or by operation of law, within which the **work, 1** must be completed.

contractual liability Liability assumed by a party under a **contract** by express language, implication, or operation of law; includes not only the obligation of a party to perform in accordance with the contract but also such other obligations as may be assumed, e.g., those arising from indemnification or "hold harmless" clauses.

contractura The tapering of a column from bottom to top.

contraflexure point Same as **point of inflection**.

contrasted arch An arch, such as an **ogee arch**, containing a reverse curve.

contrast ratio The ratio of the reflectance of a dry paint film over a black substrate having 5 percent reflectance or less, to the reflectance of the same paint equivalently applied over a substrate having an 80 percent reflectance.

contrast sensitivity The ability to detect the presence of differences in luminance; the reciprocal of the **contrast threshold**.

contrast threshold 1. The minimum perceptible contrast for a given state of adaptation of the eye. 2. The luminance contrast which can barely be detected by an observer.

contre-imbrication An ornamental pattern on a surface formed by overlapping elements which are below the general line of the surface; in **imbrication** the overlapping elements stand out and are above the general line of the surface.

contrevents In **French Vernacular architecture**, same as wood **shutters**.

contributing chapel In Spanish Colonial architecture, a chapel usually having no permanent *padre* to officiate at religious ceremonies, relying instead on the part-time assistance of visiting priests.

control Any device for regulating a system or component during its normal (manual or automatic) operation; it is responsive, during automatic operation, to the property (such as pressure or temperature) whose magnitude is to be regulated.

control area A building (or portion thereof) in which exempted quantities of hazardous materials may be dispensed, handled, stored, or used.

control board, control desk, control panel control rack One or more panels comprised of an assembly of master switches, adjustable controls, indicating dials or numerical readouts, and the like, used to control and monitor the state of a remotely operated system (e.g., a lighting system, sound system, or air conditioning system) and equipment.

control desk A position in a library, public lobby, hospital, etc., where activities may be overseen or supervised.

control factor The ratio of the minimum compressive strength of a material, such as concrete, to the average compressive strength.

control joint A groove which is formed, sawed, or tooled in a concrete or masonry structure to regulate the location and amount of cracking and separation resulting from the dimensional change of different parts of the structure, thereby avoiding the development of high stresses.

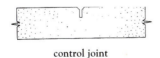

control joint

control-joint grouting The injection of grout into a control joint.

controlled fill Fill (intended as a bearing for a structural load) which is placed in layers, compacted, and tested to ensure that it meets specified compaction standards as determined by laboratory tests on a series of soil samples from the fill material.

controlled flow Said of a roof drainage system that regulates the drainage of rainwater so that it is essentially uniform.

controlled-flow roof drainage system A roof drainage system that permits rainwater to drain off a roof much more slowly than the rate at which it accumulates; after the storm has abated, the accumulation drains off at a controlled rate.

controlled low-strength material A material resulting in a compressive strength of no more than 1200 pounds per square inch (8300 kPa).

controller An electric device (or combination of devices) designed to initiate one or more functions of operation, such as starting, stopping, reversing, and speed changing, of the apparatus to which it is connected; operation may be manual or automatic.

control room, console room A small room, in or adjacent to an auditorium, having a view of the stage, in which the lighting or sound-control consoles are located.

control survey A **survey, 1** that provides horizontal and vertical positions of points to which supplementary surveys are adjusted.

control valve Any **valve** used to regulate fluid flow.

CONT W On drawings, abbr. for "continuous window."

conv. Abbr. for **convector**.

convalescent home A medical-care institution providing services for patients recovering from acute or postoperative conditions who do not require the level of skilled services provided by an extended-care facility or warrant custodial care such as that normally rendered in nursing homes.

convection Heat transmission, either natural or forced (by means of a fan), by currents of air resulting from differences in density due to temperature differences in the heated space.

convection heating Heating which results from the movement of air (or any other gas or liquid), carrying heat from the hotter to the cooler spaces.

convector A surface designed to transfer its heat to a surrounding fluid largely or wholly by convection; units for water or steam heating usually are installed against the wall or in a recess in the wall.

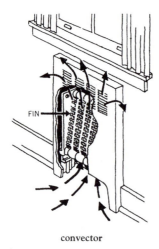

convector

convenience outlet A **receptacle outlet** which is mounted on the wall of a room to supply electricity for lamps, appliances, etc.

convenience receptacle Same as **receptacle**.

convent 1. A religious community: friars, monks, or nuns (now usually nuns). 2. A group of buildings occupied by such a community.

conventional design Design procedures using stresses or moments which have been determined by widely accepted methods.

conventional door Any door (including a kalamein door) except one of a special type, such as a fire door, a sound-attenuating door, or the like.

conventional sprinkler In a fire protection system, a **sprinkler** providing a spherical water distribution directed towards the floor and ceiling; directs 40 to 60 percent of the total water flow initially in a downward direction.

convento In Spanish architecture and its derivatives, a convent or monastery usually containing living quarters, workrooms, storerooms, a balcony, and patio.

conversion 1. See **breaking down**. 2. A change in the use of a building to another use which has different requirements according to code (e.g., different exit, fire-resistance, light and ventilation, loading, structural, or zoning requirements).

conversion burner A burner, together with its control unit, which is designed as a replacement for an existing boiler or furnace.

conversion factor A quantity by which the numerical value in one system of units must be multiplied to arrive at the numerical value in another system of units.

converted timber Timber sawn into lumber or boards.

converter A device or machine used to change alternating-current power to direct-current power or vice versa.

conveyance 1. The transfer of property from one person to another. 2. The document or instrument by which this transfer is effected.

conveying hose Same as **delivery hose**.

conveyor A motor-driven mechanism used for the continuous transport of material, e.g., an endless belt or series of rollers.

cooked glue Glue requiring heating before use.

cook house Same as **outkitchen**.

coolant See **cooling medium**.

cooler 1. A thermally insulated enclosure, kept at a reduced temperature by means of refrigeration. 2. An **air conditioner**.

coolhouse A greenhouse which is maintained at a cool temperature above freezing.

cooling medium, coolant A fluid which conducts heat from one or more heat sources and transports it to a **heat exchanger**, where the heat is removed and disposed of.

cooling range In a water-cooling device, the difference between the average temperature of the water entering the device and the average temperature of the water leaving it.

cooling tower A structure, usually on the roof of a building, over which water is circulated, so as to cool it evaporatively by contact with air.

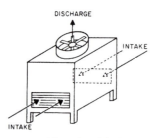

cooling tower   of the induced-draft, propeller type

cooperative   A form of real estate ownership of a multi-unit housing structure by a non-profit corporation which leases portions of the property to its stockholders. The stockholders are part owners of the corporation; they do not own their own apartments. Periodic payments, usually monthly, by stockholders are used to meet costs of ownership, such as mortgage payments, property maintenance, taxes, and repairs. Such shareholding by the tenant allows him to occupy a dwelling unit while not possessing direct title to it.

coopered joint   In a curved surface, a joint similar in appearance to a joint in a barrel.

COORD   On drawings, abbr. for "coordinate."

coordinator   A device used on a pair of exit doors to ensure that the **inactive leaf** is permitted to close before the active leaf; required on a door having an overlapping astragal.

cop   Same as **merlon**.

cop.   Abbr. for **coping**.

copal   Resin of natural origin used in varnishes to provide gloss and hardness.

copal varnish   A high-gloss varnish made with a drying oil, such as linseed oil, and copal.

cope   **1.** To cut or shape the end of a molded wood member so that it will cover and fit the contour of an adjoining member. **2.** To notch a steel beam, channel, etc., so that another member may be fitted against it. **3.** A **coping**. **4.** To form a **coping**.

cope chisel   Same as **cape chisel**.

coped joint, scribed joint   A joint between two moldings; one molding is cut to the profile of the second.

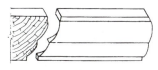

coped joint

copestone   Same as **coping stone**.

coping   A protective cap, top, or cover of wall, parapet, pilaster, or chimney; often of stone, terra-cotta, concrete, metal, or wood. May be flat, but commonly sloping, double-beveled, or curved to shed water so as to protect masonry below from penetration of water from above.

Most effective if extended beyond wall face and cut with a drip. Also see **featheredge coping**.

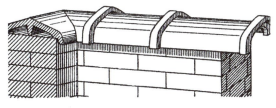

coping   of terra-cotta

coping block   A concrete masonry unit having a solid top, for use as a coping at the top and finishing course in wall construction.

coping brick   A brick which is specially manufactured for use as the top course in a **coping**; caps the top of an exposed wall.

coping course   A horizontal layer of masonry units that forms a **coping**.

coping saw   A light narrow-bladed saw with fine teeth, held in a U-shaped tension frame; used for cutting small curves in wood.

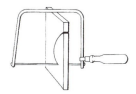

coping saw   used in cutting

coping stone, capstone, copestone   A stone which forms a coping.

copper   A lustrous reddish metal, highly ductile and malleable; has high tensile strength, is an excellent electrical and thermal conductor, is available in a wide variety of shapes; widely used for downspouts, electrical conductors, flashing, gutters, roofing, etc.

copper alloy   Metal having a specified copper content of less than 99.3% but more than 40% and having no other element in excess of the copper content (except in the case of certain copper-nickel-zinc alloys, in which zinc slightly exceeds the copper content).

copper bit, coppering bit   A gas-heated **soldering iron** used by plumbers.

copper fitting   A **fitting** (fabricated of wrought copper, cast brass, or bronze) which may be joined to copper or brass pipe by solder, screw threads, or a compression fit.

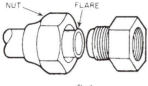

copper fitting

copper glazing Same as **copperlight glazing**.

copperlight glazing, copper glazing, electrocopper glazing, fire-retarding glazing A fire-retardant glazing consisting of a number of individual panes of glass which are separated by strips of electrically welded copper.

copperplating Depositing a protective layer of copper on the surface of another metal, either by the electrolytic method or by dipping.

copper roofing A flexible metal roof covering made of copper sheets, joined by seams. As the copper oxidizes, it develops a green coating on its surface called a **patina.**

copper sheet Copper roofing material used to cover flat, domed, or sloping roofs; usually weighs from ½ to 2 lb per sq ft (2.5 to 10 kg per sq m).

copper slate See **lead slate**.

coppersmith's hammer A hammer having a long, curved, ball-shaped peen; used to beat copper sheeting into the desired shape.

copper tube A seamless tube made from almost pure copper (99.9 percent); available only in drawn or soft form, with plain ends. Joints for this pipe can either be soldered or brazed. Also see **type-DWV tubing**.

coquillage A representation of the forms of seashells and the like, as a decorative carving.

coquina A soft limestone formed primarily of broken shells and coral; cut into blocks and used in construction.

cora A draped female figure used in architecture; a **caryatid**.

COR BD On drawings, abbr. for **corner bead**.

corbeil, corbeille An ornament resembling a basket, esp. a finial. Also see **calathus**.

corbel 1. In masonry, a projection or one of a series of projections, each stepped progressively outward with increasing height, and usually pro-

jecting from a wall or chimney; serves as a support for an overhanging member or **course, 1** above, or as a purely decorative element. **2.** A projecting stone that supports a superincumbent weight. **3.** A heavy bracket, often decorated, that is set into an adobe wall to act as a bearing surface to support a roof beam.

brick wall having a **corbel, 1**

corbel, 2

corbel arch Masonry built over a wall opening by uniformly advancing courses from each side until they meet at a midpoint. The stepped reveals may be smoothed, even arcuated, but no arch action is effected—not a true arch.

corbel course   A masonry course acting as a corbel, or an ornament of similar appearance. Also see **stringcourse**.

corbeled chimney cap   The crowning termination of a chimney in which successive courses of bricks step outward with increasing height.

corbel gable   Erroneous for **corbie gable**.

corbeling iron, corbel pin   A metal pin used (instead of corbeled brickwork) for carrying a **wall plate**.

corbel out   To build out one or more courses of brick or stone from the face of a wall, forming a support for timbers.

corbel piece   See **bolster**.

corbel pin   See **corbeling iron**.

corbel ring   Same as **annulet**.

corbel-step   Erroneous for **corbiestep**.

corbel table   A projecting stringcourse or masonry strip supported by corbels. Also see **arched corbel table**.

corbel table

corbel vault, corbeled vault   A masonry roof constructed from opposite walls, or from a circular base, by shifting courses slightly and regularly inward until they meet. The resulting stepped surface can be smoothed or curved, but no arch action is incurred.

corbie gable, crow gable, step gable   A gable having a stepped edge.

corbiestep, catstep, crowstep   The stepped edge of a gable masking a pitched roof, found in northern European masonry, 14th to 17th cent., and in derivatives.

cord   See **electric cord**.

corded door   An accordion door fabricated of narrow wood slats which are interconnected with cotton cord or fabric tapes; usually suspended from ceiling-mounted tracks.

cordon   A **stringcourse** or **belt course**.

core   1. The center of a plywood or crossbanded construction; it may consist of lumber (solid or glued) or particleboard; serves as a base for

corbiestep

veneer. 2. The internal structure in a **hollow-core door**. 3. The wood chips cut from a mortise. 4. The metal bar to which a handrail is attached. 5. The internal structure which serves as a base for complex plasterwork. 6. The molded open space in a concrete masonry unit. 7. The filling within a thick hollow stone wall. 8. The filling between a lintel and relieving arches. 9. A cylindrical sample of hardened concrete or rock obtained by means of a core barrel and drill. 10. A part of a multistory building, containing a variety of service and utility functions, as elevators, stairwells, etc. 11. That part of a magnetic circuit (usually steel or iron laminations) about which are wound coils in electromagnetic devices such as transformers, solenoids, relays, etc.; a **magnetic core**. 12. (*Brit.*) The conductor of a cable with its insulation, but not including any outer protective covering. 13. That portion of a **grille, 2** contained within the frame. 14. Of gypsum board, the hardened material filling the space between a face paper and a back paper; consists primarily of gypsum with additives. 15. (*British*) Same as **blockout**.

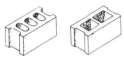
core, 6

core area   Of a grille for an air diffuser, the total area within the outer edges of the outer opening through which air can pass.

core barrel   The hollow cutting tool of a **core drill**; consists of a section of pipe which has a carbide insert or diamond cutting edge.

coreboard, *Brit.* **battenboard**   A wood-base panel used in plywood or laminated core constructions; the **core, 1**, to which **faces** are glued.

core boring   In the ground at a construction site, a core obtained with a rotating tool; used to determine the nature and/or thickness of the underlying rock.

cored beam   **1.** A beam having a partially hollow cross section. **2.** A beam from which core samples have been taken.

cored block, cored tile   A cast gypsum building unit.

cored cellular material   Cellular material containing a multiplicity of holes which are molded or cut into the material in some pattern, usually perpendicular to the largest surface, and extending part or all the way through the piece.

core drill   A drill used to remove a sample of rock in situ, for determining bedrock profiles or for obtaining a core for testing; the sample is retained in the **core barrel**.

core driver   A hardwood or steel cylinder which is the same size as a hole through which it is driven; used to clear the hole of chips.

core frame   See **buck frame**.

core hole   In a **structural clay tile**, same as **cell, 1**.

core module   A **module, 1** containing electrical, heating, plumbing, and related subsystems.

core sample   Same as **core, 9**.

core test   A compression test on a concrete sample cut from hardened concrete by means of a core drill.

coring   Removing a core from a concrete structure or rock foundation, for test purposes.

coring out   The process of removing droppings after a **parge coat** has been applied to the inside of a chimney shaft.

Corinthian capital   The uppermost member of a column of the Corinthian order.

Corinthian order   In Classical architecture, the slenderest and most ornate of the three original Greek **orders**; commonly has an elaborate cornice and a fluted shaft. For an illustration of a Corinthian base, see **bases**.

cork   The outer bark of the cork oak tree; lightweight, used as thermal insulation, for gaskets, and in vibration control.

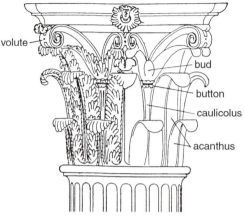

Corinthian capital

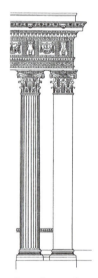

Corinthian order

corkboard   Cork granules molded to shape, compressed, and baked in a rectangular block or board shape or sheet form; usually 6 to 12 lb per cu ft (96 to 192 kg per cu m) in density; used for thermal insulation and vibration control.

corkscrew stair   A **spiral stair**.

cork tile   A resilient material composed mainly of granulated bark of the cork oak tree and synthetic resins. The surface is finished either with a protective coat of wax, lacquer, or resin or with a film of clear polyvinyl chloride laminated to the top surface for easier maintenance; the natural surface requires waxing and buffing, the vinylized surface buffing only; set in mastic over wood or concrete subfloor.

corkwood   See **balsa**.

corn.   Abbr. for **cornice**.

corncrib, corn house   A structure used for storing unhusked ears of corn; designed to provide adequate air circulation to ensure that freshly picked corn dries more or less uniformly during storage, so as to minimize spoilage. Found in a wide variety of sizes and shapes, but most often the sides slope inwardly so that the area is smaller at the bottom of the crib than at the top. Also called a corn loft.

corner   In land surveying, a point established for marking the boundaries of landed property either by an actual survey or by agreement between neighbors. Monuments or other objects may serve to designate intersection points of the boundary lines.

corner bead, angle bead, angle staff, corner guard, corner molding, plaster bead, staff bead   **1.** Any vertical molding, usually a plain, filleted, or quirked bead, used to protect the external angle of two intersecting surfaces. **2.** A strip of formed galvanized iron, sometimes combined with a strip of metal lath, placed on corners before plastering to reinforce them.

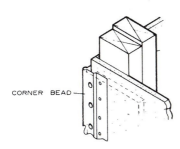

corner bead, 2

corner bit brace   Same as **angle brace, 3**.

corner block   **1.** See **corner return block**. **2.** A square, relatively flat wood block, often decoratively carved, placed at upper corners on each side of the wood framing around a door.

corner board   A board which is used as trim on the external corner of a wood-frame structure and against which the ends of the siding are fitted.

corner brace   A diagonal brace let into studs to reinforce corners of a wood-frame structure.

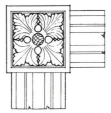

corner block, 2

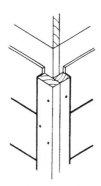

corner board

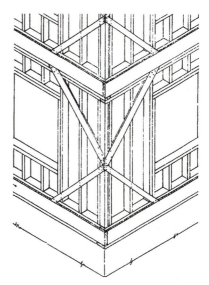

corner brace

corner bracket   A bracket which is connected to a doorframe jamb and head at the upper hinge corner, as a support for an exposed overhead door closer; used only on out-swinging doors.

corner capital   Same as **angle capital**.

corner chimney   A chimney whose face forms an angle across the intersection of two walls of a room, as in a **fogón**; occasionally called an angle chimney.

corner chisel A chisel having two cutting edges which meet at right angles; used for cutting corners of mortises.

corner clamp Same as **miter clamp**.

corner cupboard A cabinet built to fit into the corner of a room, its face forming a 45° angle with the adjacent walls.

corner drop A hand-carved or hand-turned wood ornament that is suspended from a corner of an overhanging second story of an early colonial American house. See **pendant, 2** and **turned drop**.

corner drop   suspended from a framed overhang

corner guard See **corner bead**.

corner lath See **corner reinforcement, 2**.

corner locking Any method of joining two timbers at a corner (for example, as in dovetailing) to form a rigid joint.

corner lot A lot of which at least two adjacent sides abut upon streets or public places, for their full length, which must not be less than a code-specified distance.

corner molding Same as **corner bead, 1**.

corner notch At a corner of a log cabin or log house, any one of several types of notches cut near an end of an exterior timber to form a rigid joint when mated with another appropriately notched timber set at right angles to it. See **diamond notch, double-saddle notch, dovetail notch, half-dovetail notch, half-cut notch, halved-and-lapped notch, lap notch, log notch, round notch, saddle notch, single notch, single-saddle notch, square notch, V-notch**.

corner pilaster An **engaged** pier or pillar, often with a capital and base, located at a corner of a building or colonnade.

corner post 1. In a timber structure, a post which is placed at a corner or return angle to provide for exterior or interior nailing. 2. A metal mullion member which connects two sheets of glass at an angle, forming a corner.

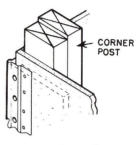

corner post, 1

corner reinforcement 1. In a knocked-down or welded doorframe assembly, the reinforcement at the junction of the head and jamb. 2. A strip of expanded-metal lath bent to form a 90° angle; used in an inside corner of a plaster wall, ceiling, etc., to prevent cracks in plastering. Also called **corner lath**. 3. See **exterior corner reinforcement**.

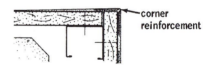

corner reinforcement, 2

corner return block, corner block A concrete masonry unit having a solid face at one end, as well as solid faces on the sides.

corner return block

cornerstone 1. A stone that forms a corner or angle in a structure. 2. A stone prominently situated near the base of a corner in a building, carrying information recording the dedicatory ceremonies, and in some instances containing or capping a vault in which contemporary memorabilia are preserved; a foundation stone.

cornerstone

corner stud Same as **corner post**.

corner tile A saddle-shaped tile used in covering the **hip** of a roof.

corner trap A trapdoor at the front of a theatre stage, through which an actor can appear or disappear.

corner trowel In plastering or masonry, a hand-held trowel used to shape either inside or outside corners.

corn house Same as **corncrib**.

cornice **1.** Any molded projection which crowns or finishes the part to which it is affixed. **2.** The third or uppermost division of an entablature, resting on the frieze. **3.** An ornamental molding, usually of wood or plaster, running round the walls of a room just below the ceiling; a **crown molding**; the molding forming the top member of a door or window frame. **4.** The exterior trim of a structure at the meeting of the roof and wall; usually consists of bed molding, soffit, fascia, and crown molding. For special types, see **architrave cornice, boxed cornice, bracketed cornice, cavetto cornice, closed cornice, eaves cornice, modillion cornice, open cornice**.

cornice

cornice lighting Lighting from sources which are shielded by a panel parallel to the wall and attached to the ceiling or to the upper edge of the wall and which distribute light over the wall.

cornice return The continuation of a cornice in a different direction, usually at right angles, as at the gable end of a house.

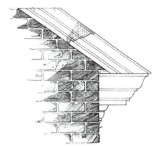

cornice return

coro An elaborate choir, at times almost an independent building, commonly placed to the west of the transept in a Spanish cathedral.

corona The overhanging vertical member of a cornice, supported by the bed moldings and crowned by the cymatium; usually with a **drip** to throw rainwater clear of the building. Also see **cornice**.

corona

corona lucis A circle or hoop of lights or candles for a church, either suspended or supported on a stand.

coronarium In ancient Rome, stucco work applied to the decoration of a cornice or projecting molding.

coronet A pedimental or other decoration wrought in relief on a wall above a window or door.

CORP On drawings, abbr. for "corporation."

Corporate style An austere style of industrial buildings used in New England during the early part of the 19th century; characterized by red brick walls in combination with white stone lintels; often gracefully proportioned.

corporation cock A valve which is placed in a water or gas service pipe of a building, near its junction with the public water or gas main. (*See illustration p. 242.*)

corporation stop Same as **corporation cock**.

241

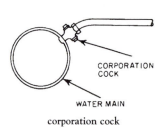

corporation cock

corps de logis   The central part of a château, large house, or mansion, not including the wings or subordinate parts.

corpse gate   Same as **lych-gate**.

corpsing   A shallow mortise in a plaster finish coat.

CORR   On drawings, abbr. for "corrugate" or "corrugated."

corral   An enclosure for livestock, commonly for horses.

corrected net fill   The **net fill** corrected for the reduction in volume resulting from compaction.

corredor   In Spanish architecture, a long, narrow porch or arcade that often covers the entire front and/or one or more sides of a house; or a corridor in the house.

corridor   **1.** A long interior passageway providing access to several rooms. **2.** A public means of access from several rooms or spaces to an exit. **3.** An enclosed passageway that limits the means of egress to a single path of travel. Also see **exit, passageway**.

corrosion   The deterioration of metal or of concrete by chemical or electrochemical reaction resulting from exposure to weathering, moisture, chemicals, or other agents in the environment in which it is placed.

corrosion inhibitor   Any of a number of materials used to prevent the oxidation of metals; may be a coating applied to the surface, a paint undercoat, or an element alloyed with the metal.

corrugated aluminum   **1.** See **corrugated metal**. **2.** When perforated, a facing for a sound-absorptive blanket in some acoustical ceiling constructions.

corrugated asbestos   A siding or roofing material fabricated in the form of corrugated **asbestos cement board**.

corrugated fastener, joint fastener   A steel fastening device used to join corner pieces in rough carpentry; one side of a small corrugated strip is sharpened so that it may be driven into the two wood pieces to be joined; used only where appearance is not important.

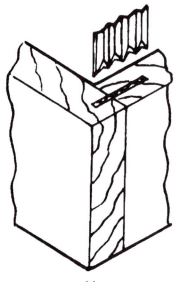

corrugated fastener

corrugated glass   Glass which has been corrugated to provide greater diffusion of light.

corrugated iron   Sheet steel (usually galvanized) which has been fabricated as a **corrugated metal**.

corrugated metal   Sheet metal which has been drawn or rolled into parallel ridges and furrows to provide additional mechanical strength; aluminum and galvanized sheet steel are widely used.

corrugated roofing   A roofing material in sheet form, usually of galvanized metal or cement asbestos, shaped into alternate ridges and valleys.

corrugated-roofing nail   Same as **roofing nail**.

corrugated tubing   Same as **flexible seamless tubing**.

cortile   An interior courtyard enclosed by the walls of a **palazzo** or other large building; often arcaded.

cortina In Spanish, literally, a curtain. In Spanish architecture or its derivatives, corbeled stonework directly below a balcony or windowsill.

Cosmati work Polychromatic patterns of stone, glass, or gilding set in marble; commonly applied in Italian Romanesque architecture.

cost breakdown See **schedule of values**.

cost of light See **lighting cost**.

cost-plus-fee agreement An agreement under which the contractor (in an **owner-contractor agreement**) or the architect (in an **owner-architect agreement**) is reimbursed for his direct and indirect costs and, in addition, is paid a fee for his services. The fee is usually stated as a stipulated sum or as a percentage of cost.

cot A small house or cottage.

cot bar A **glazing bar** which connects the radial bars of a fanlight.

cotloft (*Brit.*) See **loft, 2**.

cottage **1.** A relatively small house, often in a village, in the countryside, in a suburb, or at the seashore. **2.** A small vacation house. **3.** A dwelling, often temporary, that provides only basic shelter. **4.** An imposing mansion (as found in Newport, Rhode Island). Also see **banquette cottage, Cajun cottage, Chicago cottage, Dutch cottage, Normandy cottage, one-and-one-half bay cottage, one-bay cottage, one-room cottage, palma cottage, prairie cottage, raised cottage, tidewater cottage, two-bay cottage**.

cottage hospital **1.** An institution in which patients are housed in relatively small, home-like units, each providing eating and living space for a small group. **2.** (*Brit.*) A small hospital served by local nonspecialist physicians.

cottage orné A small, picturesque house in a rural or country setting, primarily in the late 18th and early 19th centuries. Some cottages were so classified because straight tree trunks were used as columns and selected parts of tree branches were used as brackets; others were placed in this category merely because their ornamentation was said to create a picturesque effect.

cottage roof A roof which has common rafters that rest on wall plates and are joined at their upper ends in a ridge; no principal beams are used.

Cottage style house **1.** A style of domestic architecture, usually of wood construction, popularized in the 19th century, primarily by the pattern books of architects Andrew Jackson Downing (1815–1852) and Alexander Jackson Davis (1803–1892); usually included many of the following characteristics: an asymmetric plan, walls of **board-and-batten construction**, balconies, decorative chimneys, steeply pitched roofs, and bay windows. **2.** A loose term infrequently applied to a **bungalow**.

Cottage style house

cottage window A **double-hung window** having its upper sash smaller than the lower sash; the upper pane is often decorated.

cotter A beveled piece of wood or steel, used as a wedge for fastening.

cotter pin A metal pin used for fastening; the split ends which project beyond the pin hole are bent back from the axis of the pin.

cotter pin: *above; below, installation*

cotton mats Cotton-filled quilts fabricated for use as a water-retaining covering in curing concrete surfaces.

coulisse, cullis **1.** A piece of channeled or grooved timber, as one in which a frame slides. **2.** An area backstage in the theatre, esp. between two wing flats.

council school (*Brit.*) An elementary or secondary school supported by public taxes; similar to public school in U.S.A.

count

count   In wire cloth, the number of openings per linear inch.

counter   **1.** A long horizontal surface used in stores, shops, banks, etc., for display of goods, for work-top areas, or for business transactions. **2.** The top or working surface of the base of a kitchen cabinet.

counter apse   An **apse** which is opposite another apse. Many such double apses have a crypt below the western apse.

counter arch   An arch used to counteract the thrust of another arch.

counterbalanced window   A double-hung window constructed so that the weights of the upper and lower sashes balance each other.

counterbalance system   Same as **counterweight system**.

counterbatten   **1.** A **batten** fixed to the backs of boards to stiffen them. **2.** A batten fixed to a boarded and felted roof; nailed over the rafters and parallel to them.

counterbore   To enlarge a hole to receive the head of a bolt or a nut.

counterbrace   A brace which counteracts the strain of another brace, as a web member of a truss.

counterbracing   A system of counterbraces.

counterceiling   Same as **false ceiling**.

counter cramp   A construction joint used to join segments of built-up stair stringers or counter tops. Slotted strips of wood are secured along the face of the stringers at the joint. Thin folding wedges are inserted in the slots to align the strips and thereby tighten the joint.

counterflashing, cover flashing, cap flashing   A strip of sheet metal, often built into masonry and turned down over other flashing; used to prevent water from entering the joints and the exposed upturned edges of **base flashing** on a roof.

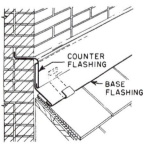

counterflashing

counterfloor   See **subfloor**.

counterfort   In masonry structures, a buttress, spur wall, pier, or projecting portion, extending upward from the foundation or from the inner face of a basement, abutment, or retaining wall to provide additional resistance to thrust.

counterfort wall   A **cantilever wall** that is reinforced with **counterforts** or buttresses.

counter gauge   Same as **mortise gauge**.

counterlathing   See **cross-furring**.

counterlight   A light or window directly opposite another.

countermure   A wall between the inner wall and outer wall of a fortification, either to provide additional defense or as an aid to the besieger.

counterscarp   The face of the ditch of a fortress sloping toward the defender.

countersink   A boring bit having a conical-shaped cutter; used to make a depression to receive the head of a screw or bolt so that it does not protrude above the surface.

countersink

countersunk bolt   A bolt having a circular head with a flat top and a conical bearing surface which tapers in from the top; when in place, the head is flush-mounted.

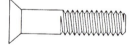

countersunk bolt

countersunk rivet   A rivet used in countersunk holes in which the point, while hot, is hammered down to fill the countersinking.

countervault   An **inverted arch**.

counterwall   **1.** A wall of a building that is adjacent to, but separated from, the end wall of a building; **party wall**. **2.** Same as **countermure**.

counterweight   **1.** A weight that just balances another weight. **2.** In a theatre stagehouse, a weight (usually of iron, sand, or shot) used to balance suspended scenery, or the like.

counterweight arbor A movable frame in which are stacked the modular counterweights of a **counterweight system**.

counterweighted window A window having sashes, each of which is counterbalanced with a weight.

counterweight safety See **elevator car safety**.

counterweight system A permanent, overhead, theatre stage rigging system; used to raise or lower scenery or lighting equipment which is counterbalanced by counterweights that ride in vertical tracks at the side of the stage.

counting house A building once used primarily for accounting and bookkeeping.

country seat A rural residence of some importance.

couple Two equal and opposite parallel forces, with different lines of action, tending to produce rotation of a body; their **moment** equals the product of the magnitude of one of the forces and the perpendicular distance between them.

couple-close, close couple A pair of opposite rafters which are connected by a collar beam or tie beam and are tied together at the apex.

coupled arcade An **arcade** supported on **coupled columns**.

coupled columns Two closely spaced **columns** that form a pair.

coupled columns

coupled pilasters Two closely spaced pilasters forming a pair.

coupled windows Two closely spaced windows which form a pair.

coupled windows

coupler A metal hardware device used to join frames and braces of tubular metal scaffolding.

couple roof, coupled roof A double-pitched roof, usually of narrow span, in which opposite rafters are not tied together; the walls resist the outward thrust.

coupling A short internally threaded section of pipe, used to join two pipes or conduits.

coupling

coupling pin A **pin, 1** which is used to connect lifts or tiers or formwork scaffolding vertically.

cour d'honneur The **forecourt** of a building, especially a monumental forecourt.

course **1.** A layer of masonry units running horizontally in a wall or, much less commonly, curved over an arch; it is bonded with mortar. **2.** A continuous row or layer of material, as shingles, tiles, etc. **3.** In concrete construction, one of several horizontal layers making up a **lift, 5**. For specific types, see **band course, base course, belt course, blocking course, bond course, coping course, corbel course, dog-tooth course, masonry course, random course, sill course,**

springing course, staggered course, stringcourse, tumbling course.

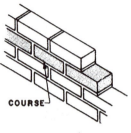

course, 1

coursed ashlar, range masonry, range-work, regular coursed rubble Ashlar masonry in which the stones are of equal height within each course; all courses need not be of the same height.

coursed masonry, course work Masonry construction in which the stones are laid in regular courses, not irregularly as in rough or random rubble.

coursed pattern A pattern formed by shingles that are laid in regular horizontal rows of equal height, each row overlapping the row below, with the vertical joints of one row usually falling approximately midway between those of the row below.

coursed rubble Masonry construction in which roughly dressed stones of random size are used, as they occur, to build up courses; the interstices between them are filled with smaller pieces, or with mortar.

coursed rubble

coursed square rubble Same as **random ashlar**.

coursed veneer In stone masonry, the use of veneer stones having equal height to form each continuous course, with horizontal joints extending the full length of the façade; the vertical joints are broken so that no two vertical joints form a continuous line.

course work See **coursed masonry**.

coursing joint A horizontal or arched mortar joint between two courses of masonry in a wall or arch.

court **1.** An open, uncovered, and unoccupied space partially or fully surrounded by walls or buildings. **2.** A courtroom. **3.** Residence of a dignitary or member of royalty and its enclosed grounds.

courthouse **1.** A building in which are contained rooms for courts of law, judges' chambers, offices of clerks of court, and, sometimes, other official offices. **2.** A building containing county administrative offices, often including the county jail.

courtroom The main room in a courthouse where the judge presides.

courtyard An open area that is partially or fully enclosed by one or more buildings and/or by walls. Courtyards that are enclosed or partially enclosed by walls are sometimes referred to as patios. Also see **placita**.

coussinet **1.** The stone which is placed on the impost of a pier to receive the first stone of an arch. **2.** The part of the front of an Ionic capital between the abacus and echinus.

cove A concave surface or molding, especially placed at the transition from a wall to the ceiling, or from a wall to the floor.

cove base A **congé, 2**.

cove bracketing A series of wood brackets or the framing set to receive the laths for a cove, as in constructing a **cove ceiling**.

coved base A trim piece at the base of a wall forming a concave rounded intersection with the floor.

coved ceiling A ceiling having a cove at its intersection with the wall.

coved eave That part of a roof that projects beyond the exterior wall, the underside of which is covered with a concave surface so that the rafters are not visible.

coved vault, cloistered arch, cloistered vault A vault composed of four quarter-cylindrical surfaces or coves, meeting in vertical diagonal planes, the axial sections of the vault being arched, and the horizontal courses diminishing in length from spring to crown.

cove ceiling

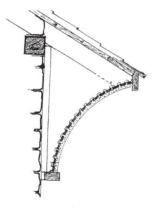

coved eave

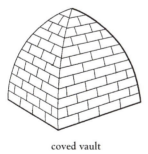

coved vault

cove header brick, cove header A brick having one end that is molded or shaped with a cove or concave curve.

cove lighting Lighting from sources which are out of sight, atop a wall molding; shielded by a ledge or horizontal recess, and which distribute light over the ceiling and upper walls.

covemold frame A steel doorframe having a cross section which is similar in shape to a wood doorframe with a cove molding at its outer edge.

cove molding, cavetto A molding having a concave face; often used as trim.

covenant See **restrictive covenant**.

cover **1.** In reinforced concrete, the least distance between the surface of the reinforcement and the outer surface of the concrete. **2.** That part of a tile or shingle which is covered by the next course.

coverage **1.** A measure of the area over which a gallon of paint may be spread at a given thickness, usually expressed as square feet per gallon at 1 mil dry film. **2.** The amount of surface that can be covered by a particular amount of roofing material.

cover block Same as **spacer**.

cover coat In ceramics, the layer of porcelain enamel normally applied over a ground coat.

covered bridge A roofed bridge, typically constructed of heavy timbers and trusses, enclosed or partially enclosed on its sides; especially found in regions having heavy snowfall.

covered joint A **lap joint**.

covered shaft An interior enclosed space that extends through one or more stories of a building, connecting openings in successive floors, or the floors and roof; must be covered at the top.

cover fillet See **cover molding**.

cover flange Same as **escutcheon**.

cover flap A hinged flap which covers boxing shutters.

cover flashing See **counterflashing**.

covering capacity Now replaced by **hiding power**.

covering power See **hiding power**.

cover molding, cover fillet Any plain or molded wood strip covering a joint, as between sections of paneling.

cover plants Plants, usually low-growing, used to cover soil so as to prevent its erosion.

cover plate **1.** A plate fastened on the flanges of a girder to give it additional cross section. **2.** A top or bottom plate of a **chord, 1**; also called **flange plate**.

coverstone A flat stone which is laid on a steel beam or girder and serves as a foundation for the masonry laid on it.

cover strip A thin strip used to cover a butt joint.

coving 1. **Coves**. 2. Vertical outward curve of an exterior wall, esp. to meet eaves or a jetty. 3. A concave molding along a rood beam to support a loft or gallery. 4. The curved or splayed jambs of a fireplace which narrows toward the back.

cow barn, cow house, cow shed A **dependency** used to house cattle.

cowl A protective hood on a vertical pipe (such as a soil stack or vent pipe); used to exclude rainwater and snow.

cownose brick A **brick** that is semicircular at one end.

cp Abbr. for **candlepower**.

CP On drawings, abbr. for **cesspool**.

CPFF Abbr. for "cost plus fixed fee."

CPM Abbr. for **critical path method**.

cpm Abbr. for "cycles per minute."

cps Abbr. for "cycles per second"; same as Hz, abbr. for **hertz**.

CPVC Abbr. for "chlorinated polyvinyl chloride."

CR 1. Abbr. for "cold-rolled." 2. Abbr. for "ceiling register."

Cr Abbr. for "cross."

crab A short shaft or axle, mounted on a frame, having squared ends to receive hand cranks; used to wind up a rope carrying a load.

crabwood See **carapa**.

crack A building defect consisting of complete or incomplete separation within a single element or between contiguous elements of constructions.

crack-control reinforcement Steel reinforcement in concrete construction to prevent cracks or to limit them to small, uniformly distributed ones.

cracked section A section which is either designed or analyzed on the assumption that concrete has no resistance to tensile stress.

cracking See **crazing, alligatoring, crawling, hairline cracking**.

cracking load That load which causes the tensile stress in a structural concrete member to exceed the tensile strength of the concrete.

crackle In painting, a paint or lacquer designed to develop a network of fine cracks when applied over a softer undercoat.

crack length The total length of all cracks measured along the outer edges of window frames and the inner faces of stops or beads around sash; used to determine the air infiltration of the entire window when the air-infiltration rate is known.

cradle See **chimney foundation**.

cradle roof A **barrel roof, 1**.

cradle vault Same as **barrel vault**.

cradling Timber framing for supporting the lath and plaster or masonry of a dome or vaulted ceiling.

Craftsman style A domestic architectural style in America in the first few decades of the 20th century, greatly influenced by the **Arts and Crafts movement**. Houses in this style were usually characterized by: a nonsymmetrical façade, typically sheathed with stucco, wood clapboard, or wood shingles, and less often with board and batten, brick, concrete block, or stone; often, masonry walls on the first story and clapboard or wood shingles on the second story; occasionally, a **battered** foundation; a gabled porch, recessed or trellised, facing the street; commonly a **porte cochère** at one side of the porch; usually a low to moderately pitched front-gabled roof; exposed roof rafters, beams, false beams, or triangular knee braces inserted as decorative elements under the gables; gabled dormers or **shed dormers** with exposed beams; double-hung windows or heavily framed casement windows. The interior commonly featured a high wainscot that was

Craftsman style: upper hall of a residence

integrated with the doors and windows as part of the structural decoration. The stairway from the living room to the floor above was often an important design element.

crail work Ornamental ironwork.

cramp **1.** A U-shaped metal fastening to hold adjacent units of masonry together, as in a parapet or wall coping; a **cramp iron**. **2.** A rectangular frame, with a tightening screw, used to compress joints between wood pieces during gluing. **3.** A device for holding a frame in place during construction.

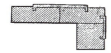

cramp, 1

cramp iron A **cramp, 1**.

crampon A lifting device (for rocks, timbers, etc.) having two steel spikes which grasp the load.

crandall A hammer-like tool having a number of sharp, pointed steel rods which are held in a slot at the end of a handle; used for dressing stone.

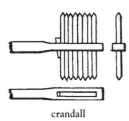

crandall

crane **1.** A machine for lifting or lowering a load and moving it horizontally, in which the hoisting mechanism is an integral part of the machine; classified by mounting, by boom configuration, and by lifting capacity. **2.** See **fireplace crane**.

crane boom See **boom, 2**.

crank arm operator Same as **roto operator**.

crank brace Same as **brace, 3**.

crapaudine door, center-pivoted door A door which rotates on pivots set into the lintel and the doorsill rather than about one vertical edge.

crash bar The cross bar of a **panic exit device**; serves as a push bar to actuate the panic hardware.

crane

cratchet An upright tree trunk having a natural fork at its upper end; the Y of the fork is used to support the **ridgepole** of the roof.

cratchet

cratering The formation of small craters in a paint film, caused by bursting bubbles of air which were trapped during application.

crawl The movement of paint in a wet paint film that does not remain evenly spread but redistributes itself after application, usually as a result of an imperfect bond with the surface.

crawler tractor An engine-driven vehicle that travels on segmented roller-chain tracks designed to reduce ground pressure and increase traction in loose footing; powered by a gasoline or diesel engine. (*See illustration p. 250.*)

crawling **1.** A defect in porcelain enamel, appearing as agglomerates or irregularly shaped "islands." **2.** A parting and contraction of the glaze on the surface of ceramic ware during dry-

crawler tractor

ing or firing, resulting in unglazed areas bordered by coalesced glaze.

crawling board A plank with cleats spaced and secured at equal intervals, for use by a worker on roofs; not designed for transporting material.

crawl space **1.** Any interior space of limited height, but sufficient to permit workmen access to otherwise concealed ductwork, piping, or wiring. **2.** In a building without a basement, an unfinished accessible space below the first floor which is usually less than a full story in height; normally enclosed by the foundation wall. **3.** A **creep trench**.

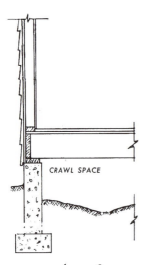

CRAWL SPACE

crawl space, 2

crawlway A **crawlspace** having one dimension that is many times larger than the other two.

crazing, cracking, craze cracks Fine, random cracks or fissures in a network on or under

a surface of plaster, cement, mortar, concrete, ceramic coating, or paint film; caused by shrinkage.

crease tile See **crest tile**.

creasing **1.** One or more courses of tiles or bricks laid upon the top of a wall or chimney with a projection of 1 to 2 in. (2.5 to 5 cm) for each course over the one below, to throw off water; if there is coping, it is placed above the creasing. Also called a **creasing course, tile creasing**. **2.** A layer of slates or of metal over a projecting string-course or window cap, serving as a flashing to prevent the infiltration of moisture.

creasing course Same as **creasing, 1**.

credence A small stand or shelf near an altar to hold the elements of the Eucharist: church vessels, service books, etc.

creep **1.** The continuing, time-dependent part of strain resulting from stress; the permanent and continuing dimensional deformation of a material under a sustained load, following the initial instantaneous elastic deformation. **2.** Slow movement of rock debris or soil, usually imperceptible except in observations of long duration. **3.** In structures, particularly of concrete, permanent deflection of structural framing or structural decking resulting from plastic flow under continued stress. **4.** In roofing, permanent elongation or shrinkage of a roofing membrane resulting from thermal or moisture changes. **5.** The flow of water along the interface between a structure and the surrounding soil or rock foundation.

creeper **1.** A brick in the wall adjacent to an arch, cut to conform to the curvature of the extrados. **2.** (*pl.*) Same as **crocket**.

creep strength The stress that produces a given rate of creep at a specified temperature.

creep trench A low underfloor horizontal passageway, usually less than 3¼ ft (1 m) high. Also see **crawl space**.

crematory, crematorium A building for the incineration of the human dead.

cremone bolt, cremorne bolt A type of hardware for locking French windows or the like; a rotating handle actuates sliding rods which move in opposite directions, extending from the edges of the window into sockets that are fixed in the frame.

cremorne bolt See **cremone bolt**.

crenation One of a series of rounded projections or teeth forming an edge.

crenel, crenelle An open space between the merlons of a **battlement**.

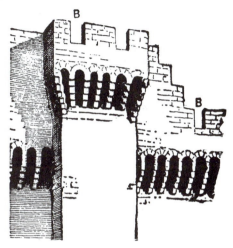

B, crenel

crenelated, crenellated 1. Having battlements. 2. Bearing an embattled pattern of repeated indentations.

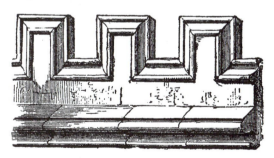

crenelated

crenelated molding, crenellated molding, embattled molding A molding notched or indented to represent merlons and embrasures in fortification.

crenelated molding

crenelet 1. A small crenel, whether in an actual battlement or in a decorative design imitating one. 2. A small **arrow loop**.

crenellation See **battlement**.

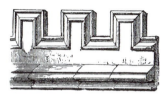

crenellation

Creole house A house developed by the Creoles (i.e., French-speaking persons of European ancestry born in the Gulf Coast or environs in the early 18th century) designed to provide reasonable comfort under the local conditions of high temperature and high humidity; usually rectangular in plan, with one or two rooms, a garret overhead; a **bonnet roof** or a roof having a single slope on each side of a central ridge; usually a **raised house** surrounded (or partially surrounded) by a full-length porch along one or both sides of the house; the rooms are entered through French doors from the porch. The floor on which the family lived was raised well above ground level to improve the air circulation. Compare with **Cajun cottage**.

Creole house

creosote An oily liquid obtained by distilling coal tar; used to impregnate wood (as a preservative) and to waterproof materials. Also called **dead oil** and **pitch oil**.

crepido A raised base on which other things are built or supported, as an ancient Roman temple or altar.

crepidoma The base courses (a stepped platform) of a classical (esp. Greek) temple. Also see **stylobate**.

crescent A building or series of buildings whose façades follow a concave arc of a circle or ellipse in plan.

crescent arch A **horseshoe arch**.

crescent truss A **truss** in which the top chord and the bottom chord are either both curved upward or both curved downward; having different radii of curvature, the chords intersect at the ends, forming a crescent profile; between the chords is a web.

crescent truss

cress tile See **crest tile**.

crest **1.** A finial. **2.** An ornament of a roof, a roof screen, wall, or aedicula, generally rhythmic and highly decorative, and frequently perforated; **cresting**.

crest, 2

cresting See **crest, 2**.

crest tile, crease tile, cress tile **1.** Tile which fits like a saddle on the ridge of a roof. **2.** Tile forming a **crest, 2**.

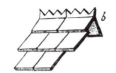

crest tiles, 1: *b*

crest tiles, 2

CRI Abbr. for "color rendering index."

crib **1.** A lining of a shaft, such as a framework of timbers. **2.** A framework constructed of squared timbers, steel, or concrete members; used as a retaining wall or to provide support for construction above. **3.** A partial enclosure for storing hay, corn, or the like; also see **corncrib**.

crib barn A crudely constructed barn once used to house animals or to store agricultural products; usually timber-framed, but sometimes built of logs. If constructed with one storage space, it was called a *single-crib barn*; if two storage spaces, a *double-crib barn*; if four storage spaces, a *four-crib barn*.

cribbing **1.** A system of **cribs, 2**. **2.** A framework of wood, concrete, or metal members which form open bins that are filled with crushed rock or pervious soil; used as a retaining structure for an earth embankment. **3.** A framework of timber mats, steel members or plates, etc., used as a support for mobile cranes, or the like.

cribbled Covered with dots, raised or sunk (describing a surface or background). Also see **scumbled**.

crib test A test for rating combustible properties of treated wood which is exposed to fire.

cribwork **1.** A construction of timber made by placing horizontal beams one above the other and fastening them together, each layer being at right angles to those above and below it. **2.** Same as **cribbing**.

crick A small **jackscrew**.

cricket, saddle A small saddle-shaped projection on a sloping roof; used to divert water around an obstacle such as a chimney.

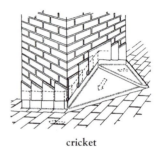

cricket

crimp **1.** To bend or warp. **2.** To offset a structural steel member so that it will fit over the flange of another member.

crimped copper Copper in sheets or strips having small transverse corrugations to provide for expansion, to increase rigidity, or to serve as ornamentation.

crimped wire A wire having a series of small curves in it; these deformations are provided to increase the capacity of the wire to bond to concrete.

crimping A process similar to corrugating, but providing a surface (essentially flat) with regularly spaced small ridges.

crinkle-crankle (*Brit.*) A serpentine wall, esp. in the 18th century. Same as **serpentine wall**.

crinkled On a porcelain enamel surface, a textural effect having the appearance of fine wrinkles or ridges.

crinkling See **wrinkling**.

cripple **1.** In a building frame, a structural element that is shorter than usual, as a stud above a door opening or below a windowsill. **2.** In roofing, a bracket that anchors at the ridge line and carries scaffold platforms for roofing workers.

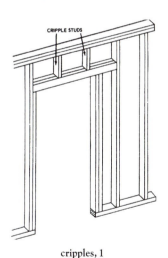

cripples, 1

cripple rafter A **jack rafter**.

cripple stud A **cripple, 1**.

cripple window (*Brit.*) A **dormer window**.

crippling load British term for **buckling load**.

criss A jig for forming crest tiles.

criterion **1.** A standard or rule on which a decision or judgment may be based, forming the basis for the establishment of acceptable limits of environmental conditions in buildings. **2.** An established **code**, measure, norm, or rule upon which a decision may be based.

critical angle An angle of pitch of stairs or a ramp which is considered uncomfortable and unsafe if exceeded; this angle is 50° for stairs and 20° for ramps.

critical density That unit weight of a saturated granular material above which it will gain strength and below which it will lose strength when subjected to rapid deformation.

critical height The maximum height at which a vertical cut in a cohesive soil will stand unsupported.

critical level The setting on a **backflow preventer** or **vacuum breaker** which determines its minimum permitted elevation above the **flood-level rim** of the fixture or receptacle served.

critical load The **load, 1** on a member or structure at which failure is likely to occur.

critical path method, CPM A system of project planning, scheduling, and control which combines all relevant information into a single master plan, permitting the establishment of the optimum sequence and duration of operations; the interrelation of all the efforts required to complete a construction project are shown; an indication is given of the efforts which are critical to timely completion of the project.

critical section In structures, that section or position where failure is most likely to occur.

critical slope The maximum angle with the horizontal at which a sloped bank of soil of given height will stand unsupported.

critical speed The angular speed of rotating machinery at which excessive vibration is produced; at this speed the periodic disturbing force coincides with a mechanical resonance of the shaft and/or of the machinery or its supports.

critical void ratio That **void ratio** which corresponds to the **critical density**.

crocidolite Same as **riebeckite asbestos**.

crocket In Gothic architecture and derivatives, an upward-oriented ornament, often vegetal in form, regularly spaced along sloping or vertical edges of emphasized features such as spires, pinnacles, and gables. (*See illustration p. 254.*)

crocket capital A capital having a series of **crockets**.

crocket

crocking A paint defect that permits color to be removed from a surface by rubbing.

crock tile A glazed clay drain tile, sometimes with bell-shaped ends.

crocodiling See **alligatoring, 1**.

croft An **undercroft**.

croisette Same as **crossette**.

cromlech **1.** A monument of prehistoric or uncertain date consisting of an enclosure formed by huge stones planted in the ground in a circle. **2.** A **dolmen**.

crook **1.** The warp of a board edge from a straight line drawn between the two ends; also called **edgebend** or **spring**. **2.** A piece of timber so warped; a **knee**.

crook rafter A **knee rafter**.

crop, crope A bunch of foliage worked or sculptured at the top of a spire, finial, or similar decorative member, and having a resemblance to the top of a plant.

crosette Same as **crossette**.

cross **1.** An object consisting primarily of two straight or nearly straight pieces forming right angles with one another; the usual symbol of the Christian religion. **2.** A monument or small building of any kind surmounted by a **cross, 1**, as a market cross. **3.** A **pipe cross**.

cross, 3

cross aisle **1.** In a church, a transverse aisle between pews. **2.** In an auditorium, an aisle usually parallel to rows of seats, connecting other aisles or an aisle and an exit.

cross-and-bible door Same as **Christian door**.

crossband, crossbanding, cross core **1.** In plywood, a veneer sheet whose grain is at right angles to the face veneer. **2.** Any decorative band whose grain is perpendicular to the principal surface.

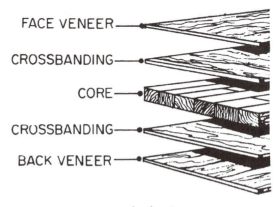

FACE VENEER

CROSSBANDING

CORE

CROSSBANDING

BACK VENEER

crossbanding, 1

cross bar In a grating, one of the connecting bars which extend across **bearing bars**, usually perpendicular to them; where they intersect the bearing bars, they are welded, forged, or mechanically locked to them.

cross bar centers In a metal grating, the distance between centers of the cross bars.

cross batten A **batten, 2**.

cross beam, crossbeam **1.** A large beam between two walls. **2.** A girder that holds the sides of a building together. **3.** Any beam that crosses another. **4.** A strut between the walings on opposite sides of an excavation. **5.** A beam which runs transversely to the center line of a structure. **6.** Any transverse beam in a structure, such as a joist.

cross-bedding In sedimentary rocks, inclined laminations or bedding which lends textural and color pattern to building stone of such material.

cross bond A masonry bond in which courses of **Flemish bond** alternate with courses of stretchers; the joints in the courses above and below the stretchers are opposite the centers of the stretchers.

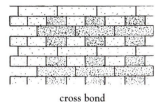

cross bond

cross brace Same as **X-brace**.

cross bracing **1.** Any system of bracing in which the diagonals intersect; also called X-bracing. **2.** Horizontal timbering which extends across an excavation so as to support a cofferdam or sheathing. **3.** Braces that cross from one column to the next to increase the load-bearing capacity of the combination.

cross break Separation in wood in a direction perpendicular to the normal grain direction.

cross bridging, diagonal bridging, herring-bone strutting Diagonal bracing (in pairs) between adjacent floor joists to prevent the joists from twisting.

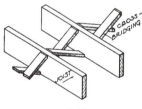

cross bridging

cross-church A cruciform church; one having a cross-shaped ground plan.

cross-connection **1.** A connection between two otherwise separate piping systems, one containing potable water and the other water which may be contaminated. **2.** In a fire-protection system, a piping connection from a **siamese connection** to a **standpipe** or to a sprinkler system.

cross core See **crossbanding**.

crosscut Cut at right angles to the grain.

crosscut saw A saw adapted by its filing and setting to cut across the grain of wood rather than with the grain.

crossette **1.** A decorative embellishment, such as a molding around one corner of a door, window,

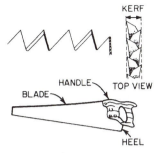

crosscut saw with details showing saw teeth

or fireplace opening, that somewhat resembles a squared-off ear; especially popular during the latter half of the 18th century; also called a **dog's ear**. **2.** A small projecting part of a **voussoir** (arch stone), which hangs upon an adjacent stone.

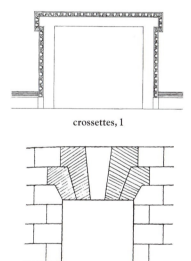

crossettes, 1

crossettes, 2

cross fall On the surface of the ground, the gradient across the width of a building.

cross fire, cross figure A **fiddleback** grain pattern.

crossflow filtration A water filtration process in which a semipermeable membrane is used to separate waterborne contaminants from the water. The bulk solution flows over and parallel to the filter surface, and under pressure, a portion of the water is forced through the membrane filter. (*See illustration p. 256.*)

cross-furring, brandering, counterlathing Strips, flat bands, or fillets which are applied on

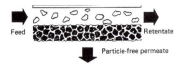

crossflow filtration

the undersides of joists to which lath (for plastering) is nailed; usually attached perpendicular to the main framing members.

cross gable   A gable which is set parallel to the ridge of the roof.

cross gables

cross-garnet hinge   A hinge shaped like the letter T; the longer part is fastened to the door leaf and the shorter to the frame.

cross girder   Any beam which unites longitudinal girders.

cross grain   Grain in wood not parallel with the long dimensions, or irregular gnarled grain.

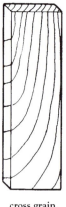

cross grain

cross-grained float   A wooden float having the grain of the wood parallel to the short side of the float. Used for leveling and scouring the surface of plaster or cement.

crosshairs   Crossed wires or etched lines on a reticule in the focal plane of the telescope of a surveying instrument.

cross house, cross-plan house   A masonry house having a cruciform plan (i.e., shaped like a cross); especially found in colonial Maryland and Virginia. At the front of the house, entry was through a front door in a two-story extension in the transverse direction of the cross; at the rear of this extension was an enclosed porch on the ground floor containing a small, steep stair leading to a room above. Meals were usually prepared in an **outkitchen** near the house.

cross house

crossing   **1.** In a church, the place where the nave and chancel cross the transept. **2.** A painting technique whereby freshly applied paint is rebrushed at right angles to the direction of application and then rebrushed at right angles again to provide even distribution of paint over the surface. **3.** Same as **crossbanding**.

cross joint   See **head joint**.

cross-laminated   Laminated so that some layers of material are oriented at right angles to the remaining layers with respect to the grain or to the direction in which tension is greatest.

crosslap joint   A joint connecting two wood members which cross each other; half the thick-

crosslap joint

ness of each is cut away so that the thickness at the joint is the same as that of each member.

crosslight Light received from windows at right angles to each other.

crosslighting Lighting an object from two opposite sides.

cross main Pipes which supply the **branch lines, 2**, either directly or through risers.

cross nogging Bracing between common joists which is arranged in a herringbone pattern.

crossover **1.** A connection between two pipes in the same water-supply system, or between two water-supply systems containing potable water. **2.** A pipe fitting shaped like the letter U with the ends turned outward; used where one pipe crosses another in the same plane; also called a **crossover fitting**. **3.** In an auditorium, a passage which usually parallels the rows of seats, forming a connection between aisles.

crossover fitting See **crossover, 2**.

cross panel A rectangular panel with its longest dimension in a horizontal direction.

cross peen hammer A hammer having a wedge-shaped **peen**.

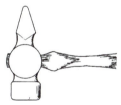

cross peen hammer

crosspiece Any piece of timber or beam crossing from wall to wall or running from one part to another.

cross quarters A cross-shaped ornamental flower in tracery.

crossrail In a panel door, any horizontal member other than those at the top and bottom of the door.

cross rib Same as **arch rib**.

cross riveting Same as **staggered riveting**.

cross runner In a **suspended acoustical ceiling**, a secondary member of the suspension system. Also see **cross-furring**.

cross section A representation of a building, or portion thereof, drawn as if it were cut verti-

cally to show its interior; often taken at right angles to the longitudinal axis of the building.

cross-sectional area See **net cross-sectional area**.

cross-sill A **sill, 1** oriented in a direction perpendicular to the length of the structure.

cross springer **1.** The diagonal arch of a ribbed groin vault. **2.** A transverse rib of a groined roof.

crosstalk Undesired signals in one electrical circuit as a result of electrical coupling with another circuit.

cross tee A light-gauge metal member, similar in shape to an inverted T; used to support the abutting ends of form boards in **insulating concrete** roof constructions.

cross tongue A tongue of wood (either cross-grained or plywood) used to join two timbers in a tenoned frame to provide additional strength.

cross valve A valve fitted on a transverse pipe between two parallel pipes in order to provide flow between them.

cross vault A vault formed by the intersection at right angles of two barrel vaults.

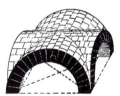

cross vault

cross ventilation The circulation of fresh air through open windows, doors, or other openings, which are in opposite sides of the room or rooms being ventilated.

crosswalk An area across a street or road esp. designated for pedestrians by special markings or paving materials.

cross-wall construction See **box frame, 1**.

cross welt, transverse seam In flexible-metal roofing, a seam between sheets; usually parallel to the gutter or to the ridge.

cross window A window in which the combination of a single mullion and a transom presents the appearance of a cross.

cross-wire weld A **weld** made between crossed wires or bars.

crotch The point where a tree branch joins the trunk.

crotchet Obsolete term for **crocket**.

crotch veneer Wood veneer cut from the **crotch** of a tree; often exhibits unusual and decorative grain patterns. Also see **curl**.

croud Same as **crowde**.

crowbar, crow A steel bar, one end of which is flattened; sometimes slightly bent; used for heavy prying, and as a lever for moving heavy objects.

crowde A crypt or cellar, especially of a church.

crowfoot 1. Colloquial term for **stylolite**. 2. A V-shaped marking on an architectural or engineering drawing, the apex of which indicates a reference point or the limit of a dimension.

crowfooted Having **corbiesteps**.

crowfooted gable, crow gable Same as **corbie gable**.

crown 1. Any upper terminal feature in architecture. 2. The top of an arch including the keystone, or of a vault. 3. The corona of a cornice, sometimes including elements above it. 4. The camber of a beam. 5. The central area of any convex surface. 6. A **crown molding**. 7. The high point at the center of a road's cross section. 8. The leafy top of a tree or shrub. 9. In plumbing, that part of a trap where the direction of flow changes from upward to downward.

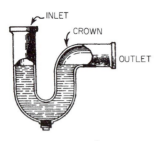

crown, 9

crown course A course of curved asbestos sheet or tile, used to cap the ridge of a roof.

crown glass A handmade glass of soda-lime composition, used for windows; manufactured in the early 19th century by a now-obsolete process in which a hollow sphere of glass was blown while still very soft, then spun to form a large, nearly flat circular disk. During the spinning process, ripple lines were formed in a pattern of concentric circles, with their center at the center of the spun disk; this central area was used in a **bull's eye window**. Also see **glass**.

crowning See **crown**.

crown molding Any molding serving as a corona or otherwise forming the crowning or finishing member of a structure.

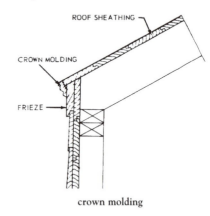

crown molding

crown plate 1. Same as **bolster**. 2. A longitudinal structural member at the apex of a roof that supports the upper ends of the rafters.

crown post Any vertical member in a roof truss, esp. a **king post**.

crown rafter In a hip roof, the central **common rafter**.

crown saw, cylinder saw, hole saw A rotary saw used to cut round holes; has teeth along the edge of a hollow cylinder.

crown steeple A decorative termination of a tower or turret, resembling a crown.

crown tile See **ridge tile**.

crown vent In plumbing a vent pipe which is connected at the **crown, 9** of a trap.

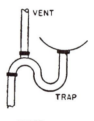

crown vent

crown weir   On the internal surface of a trap for a plumbing fixture, the highest point of the bottom surface at the **crown, 9.**

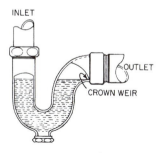

crown weir

crow's-foot   Same as **crowfoot.**

crowsfooting   A minor defect in paint whereby isolated unconnected wrinkles resembling a bird's foot are formed when a paint film dries.

crowstep   See **corbiestep.**

crowstep gable   Same as **corbie gable.**

crowstone   The top horizontal stone of a **corbie gable.**

CRT   Abbr. for "cathode ray tube."

cruciform   **1.** Cross-shaped. **2.** The characteristic plan for Gothic and other large churches formed by the intersection of nave, chancel, and apse with the transepts.

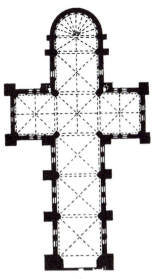

cruciform

cruck   One of a pair of naturally curved timbers, along the outer walls, that support the **ridge beam** of a timber-framed house or farm building.

crushed gravel   The product resulting from the artificial crushing of gravel with substantially all fragments having at least one fractured face. Also see **coarse aggregate.**

crushed stone, crushed rock   The product resulting from the artificial crushing of rocks, boulders, or large cobblestones, substantially all faces of which have been crushed. Also see **coarse aggregate.**

crusher-run aggregate   Aggregate that has been broken in a mechanical crusher and has not been subjected to any subsequent screening process.

crusher-run base   A base course for asphaltic or portland cement concrete paving consisting of **crusher-run aggregate.**

crushing strength   The ultimate strength of a brittle material (such as concrete) at which disintegration by crushing occurs; the greatest compressive stress it can withstand without fracture.

crush plate   **1.** An expendable strip of wood which is attached to the edge of a concrete form or to the intersection of fitted forms; used to protect the form from damage during pulling, prying, or other stripping operations. **2.** A **wrecking strip.**

crush-room (*Brit.*)   A **foyer.**

crutch, cruck   One of a pair of naturally curved timbers that rise from the outer walls to support the ridge beam, each crutch being called a **blade, 4**; joined at the top and connected by one or two tie beams, the resulting arched frame forming the unit in the framework of old English houses or farm buildings; pairs of crutches were placed at approximately equal intervals.

crutch house, cruck house   A medieval English house in which the roof is carried on pairs of **crutches.**

crypt   **1.** A story in a church below or partly below ground level and under the main floor, particularly of the chancel, often containing chapels and sometimes tombs. **2.** A hidden subterranean chamber or complex of chambers and passages. (*See illustration p. 260.*)

cryptocrystalline   A rock texture that is too fine to be discernible with an optical microscope.

cryptoporticus

crypt

cryptoporticus An enclosed gallery with walls and windows rather than columns, often partially underground for more constant temperature.

crystal glass A clear glass, made as nearly colorless as possible.

crystalline glaze A glaze containing macroscopic crystals.

crystallized finish A wrinkled paint finish caused by fast-drying vehicles containing oils which have not been gasproofed.

crystal palace **1.** An exhibition building constructed in large part of iron and glass in Hyde Park, London for the great exhibition of 1851. **2.** Any exhibition building similarly constructed.

CS **1.** Abbr. for "caulking seam." **2.** Abbr. for **cast stone**.

CSA Abbr. for **Canadian Standards Association**.

CSG On drawings, abbr. for **casing**.

CSI Abbr. for "Construction Specifications Institute."

CSK On drawings, abbr. for **countersink**.

CTB On drawings, abbr. for "cement treated base."

CTD On drawings, abbr. for "coated."

C to C On drawings, abbr. for **center-to-center**.

CTR On drawings, abbr. for **center**.

cu Abbr. for "cubic."

cubage The architectural volume of a building; the sum of the products of (*a*) the areas and (*b*) the height from the underside of the lowest floor construction system to the average height of the surface of the finished roof above, for the various parts of the building.

cubby **1.** A small closet or storage space. **2.** A diminutive room. **3.** A small snug hiding space.

cube strength In a test of the strength of portland cement, the load per unit area at which a concrete cube (of standard size) fails when tested in a specified manner.

cubical aggregate Angular aggregate most of whose particles have length, breadth, and thickness approximately equal.

cubicle **1.** A very small enclosed space. **2.** A **carrel**.

cubiculum **1.** In ancient Roman architecture, a bedchamber. **2.** A mortuary chapel attached to a church. **3.** A burial chamber having, on its walls, compartments for the reception of the dead.

cubic yard In the U.S.A., the customary unit for measuring the volume of embankments, refuse, etc.; equivalent to the volume of a cube, each edge of which measures 3 feet; equals a volume of 0.765 cubic meters.

cubic yard bank measurement (cybm) The number of **cubic yards** of material in its original place in the ground.

cubic yard compacted measurement (cycm) The number of **cubic yards** of excavated material after compaction.

cubiform capital Same as **cushion capital**.

cubit A linear unit of measurement used by the ancients; in ancient Egypt, equal to 20.62 in. (52.4 cm).

cu ft Abbr. for "cubic foot."

cu in. Abbr. for "cubic inch."

cul-de-four A half-dome or quarter-sphere vault, as over an apse or niche.

cul-de-lampe A pointed, pendant ornament used at the apex of a vault and to terminate protruding, elevated structures. Also see **drop, pendant**.

cul-de-sac A street, lane, or alley closed at one end, usually having an enlarged, somewhat circular area for turning around.

culina In ancient Rome, a kitchen.

cull, brack, wrack A piece of lumber or brick of a quality below the lowest accepted grade or below specifications.

cullis See **coulisse**.

cult temple A temple devoted to the worship of a divinity, as distinguished from a **mortuary temple**.

culver hole Same as **putlog hole**.

culvert A passage below ground level which permits the flow of water; often a large diameter metal or concrete pipe.

cu m Abbr. for "cubic meter."

cumar gum A synthetic resin, used in varnishes to provide alkali-resistant properties.

Cumberland house A one-story house, primarily found in Tennessee, of the general type described under **folk architecture**; usually had a gable on one or both ends of the house and a front porch that often served as the center of family activity.

cumulative batching Measuring more than one ingredient of a batch of concrete in the same container by bringing the batcher scale into balance at successive total weights as each ingredient is accumulated in the container.

cuneiform Having a wedge-shaped form; esp. applied to characters, or to the inscriptions in such characters, of the ancient Mesopotamians and Persians.

cuneiform pile A pile which is tapered or step-tapered.

cuneus 1. One of the wedge-shaped sections for spectators in an ancient theatre. 2. Same as **voussoir** or wedge.

cuniculus A low underground passage.

cup 1. The deviation of the face of a board from a plane. 2. A metal insert in a countersunk screw hole.

cup base A device to hold a cylindrically shaped steel column in place at its base.

cupboard An enclosed storage space with shelves, esp. for dishes, glassware, etc., usually placed in kitchens or pantries.

cup escutcheon On a sliding door, a plate which has a recess to provide a fingerhold; contains a **flush ring** flush with the surface of the plate.

cup joint A joint between two lead pipes in a straight line; the tapered end of one is fitted into the flared end of the other.

cupola 1. A domed roof or ceiling. 2. A domed structure, often set on a circular or polygonal

cupola

base on a roof or set on pillars; often glazed to provide light in the space below, or louvered to provide ventilation in that space.

cup shake A **shake** occurring between annual rings; a **ring shake**.

curb, *Brit.* **kerb** 1. A low wall of wood, metal, or masonry built around an opening in a roof or placed on the surface of a roof to support equipment. 2. A raised rim of concrete, stone, or metal which forms the edge of a street, sidewalk, or planted area. 3. A **purlin plate**.

curb box, curb-stop box, curb-valve box, Buffalo box A vertical sleeve which provides access to a buried **curb cock**; the cock is turned by a long key which is inserted through the sleeve to the cock.

curb cock, curb stop In a water-service pipe, a control valve for the water supply of a building, usually placed between the sidewalk and curb;

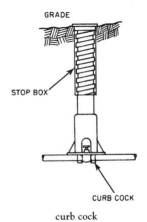

curb cock

used to shut off the water supply in case of emergency.

curb edger See **curb tool**.

curb form A specially shaped form for concrete, used in conjunction with a curb tool to give the desired shape and finish to a concrete curb.

curbing **1.** Material used for forming curbs. **2.** Slabs and blocks of stone or concrete set on edge, straight or curved, forming an upward projection; used as a **curb, 2**.

curbing machine A machine that extrudes a continuous strip of asphalt or concrete through a shaped template as it moves forward.

curb joint, *Brit.* **curb roll, knuckle joint** The horizontal joint that occurs at the intersection of the two slopes of a **curb roof**.

curb level **1.** The elevation of the street **grade, 2**, fixed by municipal authorities. **2.** The elevation at the point of the street grade that is opposite the center of the wall nearest to, and facing, the **street line**. **3.** The legally established level of the curb in front of a building, measured at midpoint of the line along the front.

curb line The line coincident with the face of the street curb adjacent to the roadway.

curb plate **1.** The wall plate of a circular or elliptical domical roof, or of a skylight. **2.** The plate which receives the upper rafters of a **curb roof**.

curb rafter One of the upper rafters of a **curb roof**.

curb roll **1.** Same as **curb joint**. **2.** A wood roll covered with lead at the intersection of the two sloped surfaces of a curb roof.

curb roof A roof, symmetric about the ridge, that slants downward and away from the ridge in two successive planes of differing slope, and usually has a raised horizontal curb where the roof changes slope.

curbstone A stone forming a curb or part of a curb.

curb stop See **curb cock**.

curb-stop box See **curb box**.

curb string, curb stair string Same as **close string**.

curb tool, curb edger A tool used to give the desired finish and shape to the exposed surfaces of a concrete curb.

curb-valve box See **curb box**.

curb roof

curdling The thickening of varnish in a can.

cure **1.** To change the physical properties of an adhesive or sealant by chemical reaction, which may be condensation, polymerization, or vulcanization; usually accomplished by the action of heat and catalyst, alone or in combination, with or without pressure. **2.** For concrete, see **curing**. **3.** To provide conditions conducive to the hydration process of stucco or portland cement. **4.** To provide a sufficient quantity of water and to maintain the proper temperature within a plaster to ensure cement hydration.

curf Same as **kerf**.

curia The council house in a Roman municipality.

curing Maintaining the humidity and temperature of freshly placed concrete during some definite period following placing, casting, or finishing to assure satisfactory hydration of the cementitious materials and proper hardening of the concrete.

curing agent A catalyst; a hardener.

curing blanket A built-up covering of sacks, matting, burlap, wet earth, sawdust, straw, or other suitable material placed over freshly finished concrete; such covering is moistened to supply water in the early hydration process, and tends to maintain a uniform temperature.

curing compound A liquid which is sprayed (or otherwise applied) to newly placed concrete which retards the loss of water during curing.

curing cycle **1.** See **autoclaving cycle**. **2.** See **steam-curing cycle**.

curing kiln See **steam box**.

curing membrane A sheet or layer of impervious material laid or sprayed over freshly poured concrete to restrict evaporation of mixing water so that the hydration process can be sustained. Also see **membrane curing**.

curing temperature The temperature to which an adhesive must be subject in order to ensure that it will cure satisfactorily; usually the time to effect a satisfactory cure (i.e., the *curing time*) is also specified.

curl A winding, swirling, or circling in the grain of wood, usually obtained from the **crotch** or fork of a tree; also see **fiddleback**.

curling The distortion of a member, originally linear or planar, so that it is curved in shape, e.g., the warping of a slab as a result of temperature differences.

current The flow of electricity in a circuit; the unit of measurement is the ampere.

current-carrying capacity The maximum current which an electric device is rated to carry without excessive overheating and consequent premature breakdown or combustion; also see **ampacity**.

curstable A course of stones with moldings cut on them. May be a **stringcourse** or part of a **cornice**.

curtail A spiral scroll-like termination of any architectural member, as at the end of a stair rail.

curtail plate A **plate, 2** that acts as a support for a **gambrel roof** where the roof changes pitch.

curtail step, scroll step A step, usually lowest in a flight, of which one end or both ends are rounded in a spiral or scroll shape which projects beyond the newel.

curtain board, draft curtain A substantial noncombustible curtain, hung tightly against a roof or ceiling along the perimeter of a special-hazard area; acts as a partition in directing heat and smoke within the curtained area toward vents and preventing the spread of fire.

curtain coating The application of paint by passing the object being coated under a continuous falling sheet of paint.

curtain drain Same as **intercepting drain**.

curtain grouting The injection of grouting below the surface, so as to create a mass of grout which is oriented transverse to the direction of anticipated water flow.

curtaining Gross sagging of a paint film, such that a pattern resembling the ruffles on a curtain is formed. Also see **sagging, 3**.

curtain line A line on a theatre stage, usually imaginary, where the **act curtain** touches the stage floor.

curtain set The set of rigging (lines, arbor, sheaves, operating line, etc.) associated with a curtain on a theatre stage.

curtain track A horizontal arrangement of continuous supports for draperies, permitting the draperies to be drawn along a track.

curtain wall **1.** In a tall building of **steel-frame construction**, an exterior wall that is non-load-bearing, having no structural function; also see **metal curtain wall**. **2.** In ancient fortifications, an enclosing wall or rampart connecting two bastions or towers.

curtain wall, 2

curtilage The ground adjacent to a dwelling and appertaining to it, as a yard, garden, or court.

curvature friction The friction resulting from bends or curves in the specified profile of post-tensioned tendons.

curved muntin A secondary framing member (i.e., a **muntin**) that is curved, usually at its upper end. (*See illustration p. 264.*)

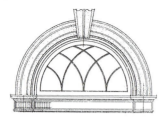

curved muntins

curved pediment Same as **segmental pediment**.

curvilinear gable Same as **multicurved gable**.

curvilinear parapet A **parapet** whose outline usually consists of a combination of several curved and straight lines, as, for example, in a **mission parapet**.

Curvilinear style The later, richer period of the Decorated style of English Gothic architecture, in the second half of the 14th cent.

curvilinear tracery See **flowing tracery**.

cusec A unit equal to one cubic foot per second.

cushion **1.** A convex element resembling a pad. **2.** A corbel for roofing, a padstone. **3.** Padding, as around glass, to reduce the effects of vibration and abrasion. **4.** A piece of timber acting as a cushion or buffer to resist or receive the force of another part of the framing; a **cushion piece**.

cushion capital **1.** A capital resembling a cushion that is pressed down because of weight on it. **2.** In medieval, esp. Norman, architecture, a cubic capital with its lower angles rounded off.

cushion capital, 2

cushion course **1.** A convex **fascia**. Also see **torus**. **2.** Same as **bedding course, 2**.

cushioned vinyl flooring Vinyl sheet flooring which has a resilient foam layer incorporated as part of its thickness.

cushion frieze A frieze that bulges outward at its sides, as found in the convex profile of the **frieze** in some Classical **orders**.

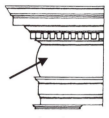

cushion frieze

cushion head, *Brit.* **pile helmet** A cap which covers and protects the head of a pile while it is being driven into the ground by a pile driver.

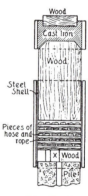

cushion head

cushion piece See **cushion, 4**.

cushion rafter See **auxiliary rafter**.

cusp **1.** The intersection of two arcs or foliations in a tracery. **2.** The figure formed by the intersection of tracery arcs. Also see **foil**.

types of **cusps**

cusped arch   See **foil arch**.

cuspidation   A system of ornamentation consisting of or containing cusps, as in a **multifoil** arch.

custom-built   Constructed on the jobsite from material which was not prefabricated, as distinguished from "factory-built."

custom-grade lumber   Normal- or middle-grade lumber, both with respect to material and quality of workmanship; intended for conventional high-quality work. Compare with **economy-grade lumber** and **premium-grade lumber**.

customhouse   A building where customs duties are received.

custom millwork   See **architectural millwork**.

cut   **1.** Excavated material. **2.** The void resulting from the excavation of material. **3.** The depth to which material is to be excavated to bring the surface to a predetermined grade. **4.** In the theatre, a long slot across the stage floor for the introduction or removal of scenery.

cut-and-cover   A method of laying a pipe (or constructing a tunnel) by excavating a trench, then laying the pipe (or constructing the tunnel lining), and finally covering it with excavated material.

cut and fill   The process of excavating, moving the excavated material to another location, and using it as **fill, 1**.

cut-and-mitered string   An **open string** of which the vertical edges of the notches are made to miter with the ends of the risers.

cut-and-mitered valley   A valley which is **close-cut**.

cut-and-rubbed brick   A **brick** that is cut to size and then rubbed to produce the required finish.

cutaway drawing   A pictorial representation of an object, showing its interior as if a slice of the object had been removed.

cutback asphalt   An organic, bituminous roof coating or flashing cement in a volatile solvent, applied without heat; also used for dampproofing and for priming concrete and masonry surfaces.

cut bracket   A **bracket**-shaped piece of board (for example, a **bracketed string**) used either for support or as a decoration.

cut brick   A roughly shaped brick, cut and trimmed with a bolster.

cut glass   A glass which has been decorated by grinding figures or patterns on its surface by abrasive means, followed by polishing.

cut line   In a theatre stage, a rope which can be cut in case of fire backstage, automatically dropping the **asbestos curtain** and/or opening the smoke hatches.

cut nail   A **nail** having a wedge shape, sheared from sheet steel; has a sheared-square, blunt point.

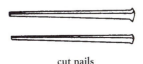

cut nails

cutoff   **1.** The prescribed elevation at which the top of a drive pile is cut. **2.** A structure, such as a wall, intended to eliminate or reduce percolation through porous strata.

cut-off elevation   Of a **pile**, the elevation of the top of the pile which is indicated on the contract drawing.

cutoff stop   On a doorframe, a **stop** which terminates above the floor line and has a closed end.

cut-off wall   A wall, constructed underground, designed to impede the flow of water.

cutout   **1.** Any opening in a masonry, metal, grating, or wood surface, as an opening in a doorframe to receive door hardware. **2.** A piece of material stamped out of sheet metal or other sheet material. **3.** A circuit breaker or valve for breaking an electrical or piping connection.

cutout box   In electric wiring, a metal enclosure that houses circuit breakers or fuses; is designed for surface mounting, with a swinging door or cover to provide easy access.

cut roof, terrace roof   A **pitched roof, 1**, which is truncated, forming a **flat roof, 1**; has no ridge.

cut splay   An oblique cutting of a brick to fit a slope, a splay, or the like.

cut stone   Building stone cut or machined to a specified size and shape, each piece fabricated to conform with drawings, for installation in a designated location in a finished structure.

cut string, cut stringer   Same as **open string**.

cutter, rubber A soft brick, sometimes used for facework because of the facility with which it can be cut or rubbed down.

cutting A short piece of lumber resulting from crosscutting or ripping operations.

cutting and waste See **circular cutting and waste**.

cutting gauge A tool with an adjustable stop similar to a **marking gauge** but with a cutting blade instead of a marking pin; used for cutting veneer and thin wood.

cutting in Careful use of a brush to paint the edge of a corner wall, ceiling area, door, or window frame.

cutting list A tabulation of the dimensions of wooden pieces or timbers required for a particular job.

cutting pliers Pliers with jaws having sharp edges esp. adapted for cutting wire.

cutting screed A tool with a sharp edge; used for trimming **shotcrete** to a finished outline.

cutting stock In stone milling, slabs of suitable size and thickness from which cut stone units are fabricated.

cutting torch A device used in oxygen, air, or powder cutting for controlling and directing the gases used for preheating and the oxygen or powder used for cutting the metal.

cut-work See **gingerbread**.

cu yd Abbr. for "cubic yard."

CV Symbol for **swing check valve**.

CV1S Abbr. for "center vee one side."

CV2S Abbr. for "center vee two sides."

CW **1.** On drawings, abbr. for "cold water." **2.** On drawings, abbr. for "clockwise." **3.** Abbr. for "cool white."

C/W Abbr. for **clerk of the works**.

cwt Abbr. for "hundred weight."

CWX Abbr. for "cool white deluxe."

cybm Abbr. for **cubic yard bank measurement**.

cycle See **alternating current**.

cycles per second A unit of **frequency**.

cycloid A curve generated by a point in the plane of a circle when the circle is rolled along a straight line, keeping always in the same plane.

cycloidal arch An arch whose intrados forms a cycloid.

cyclone cellar A covered area below grade; a place of refuge from dangerous windstorms. Also called a **storm cellar**.

cyclone collector A conical sheet-metal device for separating and collecting particles from the air by centrifugal force; used in exhaust systems, esp. in factories.

Cyclopean **1.** Describing prehistoric masonry, made of huge stone blocks laid without mortar. **2.** Megalithic.

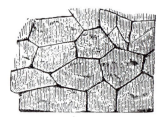

Cyclopean, 1 wall

cyclopean concrete Mass concrete in which large stones, each of 100 lb (45.4 kg) or more, are placed and embedded as the concrete is deposited; such a stone is called a **pudding stone** or **plum**; they are usually not less than 6 in. (15 cm) apart and not closer than 8 in. (20 cm) to any exposed surface. Also see **rubble concrete**.

cyclorama A curved **backdrop** at the rear of a theatre stage, sometimes extending around to the proscenium arch in a U-shape; usually painted to simulate the sky.

cyclostyle A circular colonnade which is open at the center.

cycm Abbr. for **cubic yard compacted measurement**.

cylinder In a lock, the cylindrically shaped assembly containing the tumbler mechanism and the keyway, which can be actuated only by the correct keys.

cylinder collar A plate or ring used under the head of the cylinder for a lock.

cylinder glass In the past, a type of relatively poor-quality **glass** made by blowing a cylinder of molten glass, dividing it lengthwise, and then rolling these sheets flat while the glass was still hot; much cheaper than the higher-quality crown glass then available; also called sheet glass.

cylinder lock A door lock in which the locking mechanism is contained in a cylinder that includes the keyhole but is separated from the lock case.

cylinder saw   See **crown saw**.

cylinder screw   In a lock mechanism the setscrew that prevents the cylinder from being turned after installation.

cylinder strength   Of concrete, same as compressive strength.

cylinder test   A test to determine the compressive strength of concrete by subjecting a concrete **test cylinder** to compression.

cylinder wrench   Same as **pipe wrench**.

cylindrical barn   Same as **circular barn**.

cylindrical lock   A **bored lock** which has a cylindrical case into which a separate latchbolt case fits.

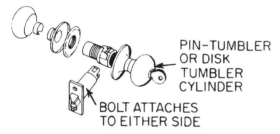
cylindrical lock

cylindrical stair   Same as **spiral stair**.

cylindrical vault   A **barrel vault**.

CYL L   On drawings, abbr. for **cylinder lock**.

cyma, cima   A molding having a profile of double curvature; one having an ogee profile.

cyma recta, Doric cyma   A molding of double curvature which is concave at the outer edge and convex at the inner edge.

cyma reversa, Lesbian cyma   A molding of double curvature which is convex at the outer edge and concave at the inner edge.

cyma recta   cyma reversa

cymatium   The crowning molding of a classical cornice, esp. when it has the form of a cyma, though it may also be an ovolo or cavetto; an **ogee**.

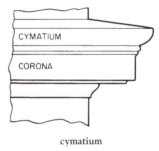
cymatium

cymbia   See **cimbia**.

cypress   A moderately strong, hard, and heavy softwood of the U.S.A.; its heartwood is naturally decay-resistant and is used for exterior and interior construction where durability is required.

cyrtostyle   A projecting curved portico, usually semicircular, having columns.

D

d Abbr. for **penny** (nail size).

D Abbr. for "down."

D&CM Abbr. for "dressed and center matched."

D&H In the lumber industry, abbr. for "dressed and headed."

D&M In the lumber industry, abbr. for "dressed and matched."

D&MB Abbr. for "dressed and matched beaded."

D&SM Abbr. for "dressed and standard matched."

D1S Abbr. for "dressed one side."

D2S Abbr. for "dressed two sides."

D2S&CM Abbr. for "dressed two sides and center matched."

D2S&M Abbr. for "dressed two sides and matched."

D2S&SM Abbr. for "dressed two sides and standard matched."

D4S Abbr. for "dressed on four sides."

dabber A soft brush used to apply varnishes.

dabbing, daubing Dressing a stone surface with a special pointed tool to produce a pitted appearance.

DAD On drawings, abbr. for **double-acting door**.

dado **1.** The middle portion of a pedestal between the base (or the plinth) and the surbase (or the cornice, cap, or entablement); also called **die**. **2.** The middle part (sometimes all parts) of a protective, ornamental paneling applied to the

lower walls of a room above the **baseboard**. **3.** A rectangular groove cut across the full width of a piece of wood to receive the end of another piece.

dado cap A **chair rail** or cornice at the top of a dado.

dado head A power-driven rotary cutter, usually consisting of two identical circular saws with a chipper between them; used in woodworking for cutting flat-bottomed grooves.

dado joint See **housed joint**.

dado rail A **chair rail**.

dagger A small Decorated tracery motif in the form of a distorted cusped lancet, with the foot pointed; a pointed oval-shaped opening in the tracery.

dagoba In Buddhist architecture, a monumental structure containing relics of Buddha or of some Buddhist saint.

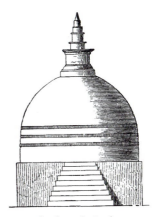

dagoba in Sri Lanka

daily noise dose See **noise dose**.

dairy See **milk house**.

dais A raised platform reserved for the seating of speakers or dignitaries. (*See illustration p. 270.*)

dalan In Persian and Indian architecture, a veranda, or sometimes a more stately reception hall, more or less open to the weather, with a roof carried on columns, or the like.

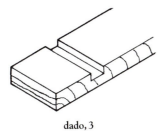

dado, 3

dais

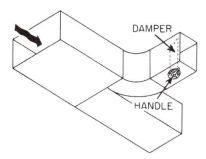

damper, 1

butterfly **damper, 1**

dallan Same as **dalan**.

dalle A slab or large tile of stone, baked clay, etc., esp. a tile of which the surface is incised or otherwise ornamented, such as the medieval sepulchral slabs set in the pavement and walls of churches.

damages See **liquidated damages**.

dammar, damar, dammer, gum dammar A naturally occurring resin; useful in paints and varnishes because of its light color.

damp check See **damp course**.

damp course, damp check, dampproof course In masonry, an impervious horizontal layer of material (as tile, dense limestone, metal, etc.) to prevent the capillary entrance of moisture from the ground or a lower course, but used also below copings, above roof level in chimneys, and elsewhere to stop downward seepage.

damper **1.** A device used to vary the volume of air passing through an air outlet, inlet, or duct; it does not significantly affect the shape of the delivery pattern. **2.** A pivoted cast-iron plate at fireplace throat, i.e., between fireplace and smoke chamber, to regulate draft. **3.** Same as **fireplace damper**.

damping The dissipation of energy with time, e.g., the dissipation of energy in a mechanical system whose free oscillations decrease with time, resulting in a decrease in its amplitude of vibration.

damping material A viscous material applied to a vibrating surface, such as a metal panel, to reduce the noise which it radiates.

dampproof course See **damp course**.

dampproofing **1.** A treatment of concrete or mortar to retard the passage or absorption of water, or water vapor, either by applying a suitable coating to exposed surfaces or by using a suitable admixture. **2.** A **damp course**. **3.** Applying a water-impervious material to a surface, such as a wall, to prevent the penetration of moisture.

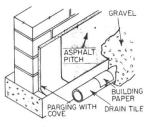

dampproofing, 3

dancers Colloquial term for **stairs.**

dancette See **chevron, 2; zigzag.**

dancing step See **balanced step.**

dancing winder See **balanced step.**

dao, paldao A variegated colored wood from the Philippines and New Guinea, having shades of gray, green, yellow, brown, and pink with dark streaks; moderately hard, heavy; used for cabinets, plywood, and interior finish.

dap A notch in a timber for receiving another timber or into which the head of a pile is fitted.

dar 1. In Indian and Persian architecture, a gateway. 2. In Oriental architecture, a dwelling.

darby, derby slicker 1. A float tool used in plastering, either wood or metal, about 4 in. (10 cm) wide and about 42 in. (approx. 1 m) long, with two handles; used to float or level the plaster base coat prior to application of the finish coat, or to level the plaster finish coat before floating or troweling. 2. A hand-manipulated straightedge usually 3 to 8 ft (1 to 2.5 m) long, used in the early-stage leveling operations of concrete finishing to supplement floating.

dart See **egg-and-dart molding; anchor, 8.**

dash-bond coat A thick slurry of portland cement, sand, and water dashed on surfaces with a paddle or brush to provide a base for a subsequent plaster coat.

date of agreement The date stated on the face of the **agreement.** If no date is stated, it may be the date on which the agreement is actually signed, if this is recorded, or it may be the date established by the award; also referred to as the **contract date.**

date of commencement of the work The date established in a **notice to proceed** or, in the absence of such notice, the date of the **agreement** or such other date as may be established therein or by the parties thereto.

date of substantial completion The date certified by the architect when the **work, 1** or a designated portion thereof is sufficiently complete, in accordance with the **contract documents,** so the owner may occupy the work or designated portion thereof for the use for which it is intended.

date stone A stone, imbedded in the walls of many old buildings, carved with the date of completion of the structure.

date stone

datum A level surface or point to which other levels are related; a reference in measuring elevations.

datum dimension A dimension that exactly locates a reference point, reference line, or reference plane.

datum line Same as **reference line.**

daub 1. A material such as clay, mortar, mud, or plaster (often mixed with straw), used as **infilling** between logs, as a coating over walls, or as plaster in **wattle-and-daub. 2.** To coat roughly with plaster or mud.

daubing 1. See **dabbing. 2.** A rough coating of plaster given to a wall by throwing plaster against it.

day One division in a window, as in a large church window.

day gate In a bank, an interior grille door to a safe-deposit vault; used when the main vault door is open.

daylight factor The ratio of the illumination at a point on a given plane to the illumination on a horizontal plane from the whole of an unobstructed sky of assumed or known luminance distribution; a measure of the daylight illumination at that point.

daylight glass A bluish glass, often colored with cobalt, used with incandescent lamps to produce the effect of daylight by absorbing excess radiation in the red part of the light spectrum.

daylight lamp 1. Any type of lamp which produces light whose spectral distribution approximates that of a specified daylight condition. 2. See **incandescent daylight lamp.**

daylight width, sight size, sight width The width of a glazed opening which admits light.

dB Abbr. for **decibel**.

dB(A) A unit of sound-level; a reading taken on the A-scale of a **sound-level meter**.

DB. Clg. Abbr. for "double-headed ceiling."

DBL On drawings, abbr. for "double."

DBT Abbr. for **dry-bulb temperature**.

dc, d-c, d.c., DC Abbr. for "direct current."

D-crack, D-line crack 1. In concrete surfaces, one of many fine, closely spaced cracks; often in random patterns. 2. In highway slabs, one of the fine cracks parallel to the edges, joints, and larger cracks or cutting diagonally across the corners.

DD On drawings, abbr. for **Dutch door**.

deactivation The reduction or removal of the corrosive qualities of water, usually by passing the water through a **deactivator** while hot.

deactivator A tank containing iron filings which removes active oxygen and other corrosive elements from water that passes through it.

dead Descriptive of electric wiring which is not connected to a source of voltage.

dead-air space Unventilated air space within a structure, as in a shaft, ceiling, or hollow wall.

dead bolt A type of door lock; the bolt, which is square in cross section, is operated by the door key or a turn piece.

dead bolt

dead-burnt gypsum See **anhydrous calcium sulfate**.

dead door Same as **blank door**.

dead end 1. A length of pipe leading from a soil, waste, or vent pipe, building drain, or build-ing sewer, which is terminated by a plug, cap, or other closed fitting; there is no circulation in this length of pipe, and no waste from a plumbing fixture is fed into it. 2. The point of fastening in a running rope system where the other end is fastened to a **rope drum**. 3. In concrete work, the end opposite that to which a load is applied. 4. A portion of a corridor in which the travel to an exit is in one direction only.

dead-end anchorage Anchorage at the end of a tendon which is opposite the jacking end.

deadening The use of **damping material**.

dead flue A **flue** that has been bricked-up or otherwise sealed off.

dead-front Descriptive of a piece of electric equipment so constructed that there are no parts which can be touched from the front of the assembly that are at a voltage different from that of the earth.

dead knot A knot that has lost its fibrous connection with the surrounding wood; it can easily loosen and fall out or be knocked out.

deadlatch Same as **night latch**.

dead leaf Same as **standing leaf**.

dead leg Same as **dead end**.

dead level Said of a roof surface having a declination of less than 2%.

deadlight See **fixed light**.

dead load 1. The weight of a structure itself, including the weight of fixtures or equipment permanently attached to it. 2. The load imposed on a pipe located in a trench and covered by infill; depends on the depth and width of the trench, and the density and character of the infill material.

deadlock 1. A lock equipped with a dead bolt only. 2. A lock in which a bolt is moved by means of a key or thumb turn, and is positively stopped in its projected position.

deadlocking latch bolt See **auxiliary dead latch**.

deadman A buried concrete block, log, plate, or the like, which serves as an anchorage, e.g., as an anchor for a tie to a retaining wall; depends on its own weight and passive pressure from the soil to hold it in place.

dead parking Long-term, unattended storage of a vehicle.

dead-piled Descriptive of lumber or panels stacked without spacers.

dead room A room characterized by an unusually large amount of sound absorption.

dead sand Sand that may be used as an underneath course for a finished layer of loose stones or gravel.

dead shore An upright piece of heavy timber used as a prop or support for a dead load during structural alterations to a building, esp. one of two supports for a **needle, 1**.

dead-soft temper The temper of sheet copper used for roofing.

dead wall A wall whose entire surface is unbroken by a door, window, or any other opening; a **blank wall**.

dead window Same as **blank window**.

deadwood **1.** Dead tree limbs or branches. **2.** Wood from dead trees.

deal **1.** (*U.S.A.*) Pine or fir lumber cut to a specified size, usually at least 3 in. (76 mm) thick and 9 in. (229 mm) wide. **2.** (*Brit.*) Square-sawn softwood lumber, 1⅞ in. (47.6 mm) to 4 in. (101.6 mm) thick and 9 in. (228.6 mm) to under 11 in. (279.4 mm) wide.

deambulatory **1.** An aisle extending around the apse of a church; an apse aisle. **2.** The ambulatory of a cloister, or the like.

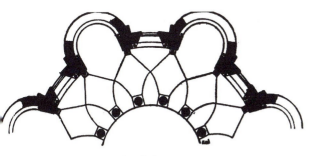

deambulatory, 1

de-bonding In pretensioned construction, a procedure used to prevent specific tendons from becoming bonded to the concrete for a specified distance from the ends of the flexural members.

debt service The periodic repayment of a loan, including both accrued interest and a portion of the principal.

DEC On drawings, abbr. for "decimal."

decal, decalcomania Colored designs on special paper for transfer to unglazed or glazed ceramic ware or glass.

decani side The south side of a church, i.e., the side on the right of one facing the altar.

decarburization The loss of carbon at the surface of **carbon steel** when it is heated for processing or in modifying its mechanical properties.

decastyle A building having a portico of ten columns, or rows of ten columns.

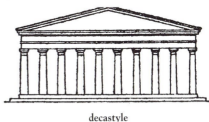

decastyle

decay See **brown rot, white rot**.

decayed knot See **unsound knot**.

decay rate **1.** At a given frequency, the rate at which the sound level in a room decreases after a source stops emitting sound; expressed in decibels per second (dB/s). **2.** Of sound waves in an enclosed space, the rate at which the sound-pressure level of **reverberation** decreases; usually expressed in decibels per second. **3.** Of a vibrating mechanical system, the rate at which some stated characteristic (such as the amplitude of vibration) decreases with time.

decenter To remove centering or shoring.

decibel The unit in which the **level, 4** of various acoustical quantities is expressed.

deciduous Descriptive of trees or shrubs, usually of temperate climates, that shed their leaves annually; characteristic of most hardwoods and a few softwoods.

deck **1.** The flooring of a building or other structure. **2.** A flat open platform, as on a roof. **3.** The structural surface to which a roof covering system is applied. **4.** The top section of a mansard or curb roof when it is nearly flat.

deck clip **1.** A metal fastening device used to attach roof-deck material to a structural frame. **2.** An H-shaped metal piece used between adjacent sheets of plywood decking to limit uneven deflections. **3.** Any device used to fasten thermal insulation to a roof-deck.

deck curb   A curb around the edge of a roof-deck.

deck dormer   A **hipped dormer** that has been truncated so that it has a flat, horizontal roof.

deck drain   A drain that is similar in all respects to a **roof drain** except that it generally has a flat strainer and is located in a flat area such as a patio, walkway, etc.

decking   **1.** The thick boards or planks used as structure flooring, usually for long spans between joists or for heavy service; also called **planking**. **2.** Light-gauge sheets of metal which are ribbed, fluted, or otherwise integrally stiffened for use in constructing a floor or roof. **3.** See **roof decking**.

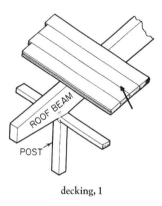

decking, 1

deck-on-hip   A flat roof capping a lower roof that is hipped.

deck paint   An enamel having a high degree of resistance to mechanical wear; esp. used on surfaces such as porch floors.

deck roof, deck-on-hip roof   A **hipped roof** that has been truncated to form a flat-topped roof.

deck screens   Two or more **screens, 3** placed one over the other.

Deconstructivist architecture   Architecture that seeks to arrive at new forms of expression by turning away from structural restraints and functional and thematic hierarchies, and toward often nonrectangular, fantastic, and seemingly disjointed designs. Such work often represents an application of the philosophical theories of Jacques Derrida in France, who

sought to arrive at new insights in literature by breaking apart literary texts into their contradic-

Decorated style

tory and hidden components of meaning; this philosophy has been applied in the late 20th century to architectural structures usually called deconstructivist architecture.

decor   The combination of materials, furnishings, and objects used in interior decorating to create an atmosphere or style.

Decorated style   The second of the three phases of English Gothic architecture, from ca. 1280 to after 1350, preceded by Early English and followed by the Perpendicular; characterized by rich decoration and tracery, multiple ribs and liernes, and often ogee arches. Its early development is called *Geometric*; its later, *Curvilinear*.

decorative block   A concrete masonry unit having special treatment of its exposed **face shell** for architectural effect; such treatment may consist of distinctive aggregates (with or without additional coloring) or of beveled recesses (for patterned appearance when illuminated obliquely).

decorative half-timbering   Timbers or boards that provide the appearance of **half-timbered construction** but whose function is ornamental rather than structural; also called false half-timbering.

decorative paint A **paint** which conceals the covered surface and provides a decorative and protective coating.

decorative stone Stone that functions as architectural decoration.

decoupling The separating of building elements to reduce the transfer of heat, sound, or physical loads from one element to another.

dedicated street A street, the title of which has been yielded by an owner, either permanently or temporarily, to the authorities for use of the street by the general public.

dedication cross A cross painted or carved on the wall of a church to indicate any one of the twelve spots touched with chrism by the bishop at the consecration ceremony of the church.

deduction The amount deducted from the **contract sum** by a **change order**.

deductive alternate An alternate bid resulting in a deduction from the same bidder's **base bid**. Also see **alternate bid**.

deed Any duly attested, written document executed under seal and delivered to effect a transfer, bond, or contract, such as a conveyance of real property or interest therein.

deed restriction A limitation on the use of land, which is set forth in a **deed** conveying the restriction.

deep bead See **draft bead**.

deep cutting, deeping The resawing of timber lengthwise, parallel to the faces.

deeping See **deep cutting**.

deep-seal trap, antisiphon trap In plumbing, a U-shaped trap having a **seal, 3** of 4 in. (10 cm) or more.

defect In wood, a fault that may reduce its durability, usefulness, or strength.

defective work Work not complying with the contract requirements.

deficiencies See **defective work**.

deflagration Burning; the rapid combustion of a substance, attended with an extremely sudden evolution of flame and vapor.

deflected tendons In a concrete member, tendons which have a curved trajectory with respect to the gravity axis of the member.

deflection **1.** Any displacement in a body from its static position, or from an established direction or plane, as a result of forces acting on the body. **2.** The deformation of a structural member as a result of loads acting on it.

deflection angle In surveying, a horizontal angle measured from prolongation of the preceding **transit line** to the next line; recorded as "right" if clockwise rotation and "left" if counterclockwise.

deflection limitation The maximum deflection permitted by code or by good practice.

deflectometer A device for measuring the amount of bending in a beam induced by a transverse load.

deformation Any change of form, shape, or dimensions produced in a body by a stress or force, without a breach of the continuity of its parts.

deformed bar, deformed reinforcing bar A steel **reinforcing bar** which is manufactured with surface deformations to provide a locking anchorage with surrounding concrete.

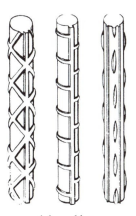

deformed bars

deformed metal plate A corrugated (or otherwise deformed) metal plate used in construction to form a vertical joint and to provide a mechanical interlock between the adjacent sections.

deformed reinforcement In reinforced concrete, **reinforcement, 1** consisting of reinforcing bars, reinforcing rods, deformed wire, welded wire fabric, and welded deformed wire fabric.

deformed tie bar   A deformed bar used as a **tie bar** to hold two slab elements in close contact.

defrosting   The removal of accumulated ice from a cooling element.

defurring   Same as **deliming**.

DEG   On drawings, abbr. for "degree."

degradation   Disintegration of a paint film by heat, moisture, sunlight, or natural causes.

degrades   Pieces of lumber which, during reinspection, prove to be of lower quality than originally classified.

degree   **1.** A **step**, as of a **stair**. **2.** A **stair**, or set of steps.

degree-day   A unit used in estimating the fuel consumption for a building; equal to the number of degrees that the mean temperature, for a 24-hour day, is below the "base temperature"; the base temperature is taken as 65°F (18.3°C) in the U.S.A. and as 60°F (15.6°C) in Great Britain.

degree of saturation   Same as **percent saturation**.

dehumidification   **1.** The condensation of water vapor from air by cooling below the **dew point**. **2.** The removal of water vapor from air by chemical or physical methods.

dehumidifier   Any device or apparatus for removing moisture from air.

dehydration   The removal of water vapor from air by the use of absorbing or adsorbing materials.

deionization   See **cation-exchange softening**.

DEL   On drawings, abbr. for "delineation."

delamination   A failure in a laminated structure characterized by the separation or loss of adhesion between plies, as in built-up roofing or glue-laminated timber.

delay cap   A **blasting cap** that explodes (as the result of an electrical current through it) at a set time after activation.

deliming   The removal of **scale, 8** on the inside of boilers or hot water heaters.

deliming tee   A **tee, 2** provided at the entry and outlet of a water heater to permit the temporary installation of deliming equipment periodically.

deliquescence   The absorption of water from the air by certain salts in plaster or brick; results in dark, damp areas on the surface.

delivery hose   A hose through which fresh concrete, mortar, or the like is pumped.

delivery point   See **point of service**.

delphinorum columnae   The two columns at one end of the spina of an ancient Roman circus, on which marble figures of dolphins were placed.

delta connection   A connection arrangement of a three-phase electrical transformer; the three windings are connected in series forming a closed circuit in the shape of a Greek capital delta. Compare with **wye connection**.

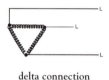

delta connection

delubrum   **1.** In ancient Roman architecture, a sanctuary or temple. **2.** The part of a classical temple containing the altar or a statue of the deity; the most sacred part of the temple.

deluge sprinkler system   **1.** A **dry-pipe sprinkler system** with open heads; is controlled by an automatic valve which is activated by smoke- or heat-sensitive devices; provides a dense, uniform coverage of water over the protected area. **2.** A fire sprinkler system using **open sprinklers** (i.e., open sprinkler heads). When the fire detection system is activated, the **deluge valve** opens, resulting in water being sprayed simultaneously from all of the open sprinklers; usually used for protection against rapidly spreading high-hazard fires.

deluge valve   A special valve that, under normal conditions, holds back the water from the piping of a **deluge sprinkler system**; a separate fire detection system is used to open this valve.

DEL V   symbol for **deluge valve**.

demand   **1.** The electric load on a system, integrated over a specific time interval; usually expressed in watts or kilowatts. **2.** The volume of gas per unit time (usually expressed in cubic feet per hour or liters per second) or the amount of heat (usually expressed in Btu per hour or megajoules per hour) required for the operation of one or more gas appliances. **3.** The rate of flow of water, usually expressed in gallons per minute (liters per second), furnished by a water supply system to various types of plumbing fixtures and water outlets under normal conditions.

demand factor The ratio of the **maximum demand** of a system to the total connected load of the system.

demand mortgage loan A **call loan** which is secured by a mortgage.

demicolumn Same as **half column**.

demilune Same as **ravelin**.

demimetope A half, or incomplete, **metope** in a Doric Frieze.

demi-relief, demi-relievo Same as **mezzo-relievo**.

demographic study A study of the size, distribution, and composition of, and changes within, a specified population group.

demolition The systematic destruction of a building, all or in part.

demountable partition, relocatable partition A nonload-bearing partition of dry construction, assembled from prefabricated components, which can be installed, removed, and then reinstalled at a different location; may be full height, from floor to ceiling, or partial height.

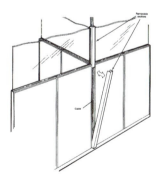

demountable partitions

den An indoor retreat, usually small, for work or leisure. Also see **chamber, 1**.

dendrology The branch of botany involving the study of trees and shrubs.

dense concrete Concrete containing a minimum of voids.

dense-graded aggregate An aggregate graded to produce low void content and maximum weight when compacted.

densified impregnated wood See **compressed wood**.

density The degree of aggregation; the quantity of any entity distributed over an area per unit of areal measure, e.g., persons per acre, families per acre, or dwelling units per square mile.

density control The control of the density of concrete in field construction to ensure that specified values, as determined by standard tests, are obtained.

denticulated, denticular Ornamented with dentils.

dentil One of a band of small, square, toothlike blocks forming part of the characteristic ornamentation of the Ionic, Corinthian, and Composite orders, and sometimes the Doric.

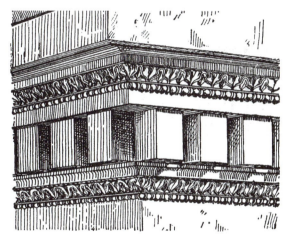

Ionic **dentils**

dentil band 1. A molding that occupies the position of a row of dentils in classical architecture. 2. A course of masonry that resembles a row of **dentils**; for example, in brickwork, the toothlike effect produced by the projection of alternate **headers** and smaller blocks.

dependency A subsidiary building near or adjoining a principal structure.

depeter Same as **depreter**.

depolished glass Any glass having a diffuse surface, usually produced by etching, sandblasting, etc.

deposited metal The **filler metal** that is added during a welding operation.

deposit for bidding documents Monetary deposit required to obtain a set of **construction documents** and bidding requirements, customarily refunded to bona fide bidders on return of the documents in good condition within a specified time.

depository See **bank depository**.

depot **1.** A place of deposit; a storehouse or warehouse. **2.** A railroad station; a building for the accommodation and shelter of passengers and the receipt and transfer of freight by the railroad.

depreciation factor The reciprocal of **maintenance factor**.

depressed arch A **drop arch**.

depression storage The quantity of storm water that is lost as a result of minor surface depressions in the ground.

depreter Stucco with a **rock dash** finish.

DEPT On drawings, abbr. for "department."

depth gauge A device for measuring the depth of a hole, cutout, groove, recess, etc.; usually consists of a graduated scale which slides through a crosspiece.

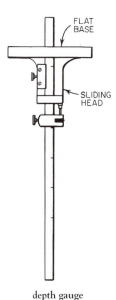

FLAT BASE

SLIDING HEAD

depth gauge

depth of fixity The depth below ground level at which the soil firmly holds a pile.

derating The reduction in the normal rating of equipment to account for abnormal environmental conditions to which the equipment may be subject.

derby, derby float See **darby**.

derrick A hoisting machine for heavy loads; usually has a vertical mast and a horizontal or sloping boom whose movement is controlled by wire rope; lifting power is supplied by a hoist line controlled by an independent hoist engine or motor; differs from a **crane** in that it has a boom rather than a jib.

descaling Removing **scale, 8** that forms on the inside of hot water heaters, boilers, etc.

desiccant Any absorbent or adsorbent, liquid or solid, that will remove water or water vapor from a material. In a refrigeration circuit, the desiccant should be insoluble in the refrigerant.

desiccation **1.** The use of a desiccant for drying. **2.** The use of heated air to remove moisture, as from timber in a kiln.

design **1.** To compose a plan for a building. **2.** The architectural concept of a building as represented by plans, elevations, renderings, and other drawings. **3.** Any visual concept of a man-made object, as of a work of art or a machine.

design development phase The second phase of the architect's **basic services**. In this phase the architect prepares (from the approved schematic design studies, for approval by the owner) the design development documents consisting of drawings and other documents to fix and describe the size and character of the entire project as to structural, mechanical and electrical systems, materials and such other essentials as may be appropriate; the architect also submits to the owner a further **statement of probable construction cost**.

design documents See **structural design documents**.

design load **1.** The total load on a structural system for the worst combination of loads and forces which it is designed to sustain. **2.** In an air-conditioning system, the maximum **heat load** which it is designed to handle. **3.** See **design ultimate load**.

design strength **1.** The load-bearing capacity of a member computed on the basis of the allowable stresses which are assumed in design. **2.** The assumed values for the strength of concrete, and the yield stress of steel on which the theoretical **ultimate strength** of a section is computed.

design ultimate load, factored load In structural design, the **working load** times the **load factor**.

desornamentado Said of architecture of 16th-century Spanish Renaissance architecture that is relatively simple.

destina **1.** A pillar or other support for a building. **2.** An aisle or small cell in a church.

destraria A late Latin term for **deambulatory**.

DET **1.** On drawings, abbr. for **detail**. **2.** On drawings, abbr. for "detached." **3.** Abbr. for "double end trimmed."

detached garage **1.** A garage which is completely surrounded by open space. **2.** A garage connected to a building by an uncovered terrace.

detached house A house that stands completely alone, not sharing a wall with another house.

detail **1.** A minor section of an architectural design or concept. **2.** A drawing, at a larger scale, of a part of another drawing, indicating in detail the design, location, composition, and correlation of the elements and materials shown.

detail drawing Same as **detail, 2**.

detailed estimate of construction cost A forecast of **construction cost** prepared on the basis of a detailed analysis of materials and labor for all items of **work, 1** as contrasted with an estimate based on current area, volume, or similar unit costs.

detector See **sensor**.

detention door A heavy steel door containing **fixed lights** of laminated glass protected by bars and muntins of tool-resistant steel; used in prisons and mental hospitals.

detention screen A window screen especially designed for institutions of detention; fabricated of screen mesh which is woven of large stainless steel wires; a massive steel frame holds the mesh under tension.

detention window A metal **awning window** esp. designed for institutions of detention. The **sashes (ventilators, 2)** are only 6 in. (15 cm) to 8 in. (20 cm) high and pivot on full-width hardened steel rods about 1 in. (2.5 cm) in diameter.

deterioration Of concrete, same as **disintegration**.

deterministic design Design which is based on the mechanical and physical properties of materials, building elements, and structures involved.

detonating cord A flexible cord having a high-explosive center core; when detonated, it then detonates other cap-sensitive explosives with which it is in contact.

detonator A **blasting cap, electric blasting cap, electric-delay blasting cap, or nonelectric-delay blasting cap**.

detritus Loose material which results from the disintegration of rock.

detritus tank In sanitary engineering, a settling tank through which sewage is passed for the removal of the heavier solids.

detrusion See **cleavage, 4**.

developed area An area of land upon which improvements have been made.

developed distance The shortest distance between two points that free air would travel as measured horizontally, vertically, or diagonally in a straight line or around corners.

developed length The length of a pipeline measured along the center line of the pipe and fittings.

development **1.** A tract of previously undeveloped land which is subdivided for housing and provided with all necessary utilities, such as roads, water, electricity, sewers, etc. **2.** A large-scale housing project. **3.** Any man-made change to improved or unimproved real estate, including but not limited to dredging, excavation or drilling operations, filling, or paving located within an area of special flood hazard.

development area (Brit.) An area in which the government encourages new and esp. diversified industry in order to promote industrial stability.

development bond stress Same as **anchorage bond stress**.

development length **1.** The minimum length of straight **reinforcing bar** or **reinforcing rod** which is required to anchor it in concrete. **2.** The length of embedded reinforcement required to develop the design strength at a critical section.

device In an electric system, a component that is intended to carry, but not consume, electric energy, e.g., a switch.

device function numbers Numbers (assigned by ANSI/IEEE Standard C37.02) that provide a convenient way of indicating the function of various types of electrical devices on drawings or in written material.

devil float, devil, nail float A wooden hand float with nails projecting from each corner; used to roughen the surface of plaster to provide a key for the next coat.

devil float

deviling Scratching or roughening plaster.

devitrification Crystallization in glass.

dewater To remove water from an excavated job site, usually by draining or pumping.

dewatering Pumping water from a site to maintain a dry and stable condition during construction.

dewpoint The temperature at which air becomes saturated with water vapor and below which moisture is likely to condense; varies with the amount of moisture contained in the air.

dextrin, amylin, starch gum A starch-like compound having strong adhesive properties; an amorphous, odorless, sweetish-tasting, white, water-soluble gum; used as a wallpaper adhesive.

DF 1. Abbr. for **daylight factor**. 2. On drawings, abbr. for **drinking fountain**.

DFI Abbr. for "Deep Foundations Institute."

dflct Abbr. for "deflection."

d.f.u. Abbr. for **drainage fixture unit**.

DHW Abbr. for **double-hung window**.

DIA On drawings, abbr. for "diameter."

diabase Rock having the same composition as basalt, but with larger crystals which are just visible to the unaided eye; also called **traprock**.

diaconicon 1. Originally a place where the deacons kept the vessels used for the church service. 2. In Greek churches, a sacristy to the right of the sanctuary.

DIAG 1. On drawings, abbr. for **diagonal**. 2. On drawings, abbr. for "diagram."

diaglyph 1. A relief engraved in reverse; an intaglio. 2. A **sunk relief**.

diagonal In a framed structure, an inclined member running across a **panel, 7**, e.g., as in a truss.

diagonal bond A type of **raking bond**, in thick masonry walls, consisting of a header course (usually every sixth course) with its bricks laid at a diagonal with the exterior and interior faces.

diagonal brace An inclined structural member in compression and/or tension; usually employed to stabilize a frame against horizontal forces, such as wind.

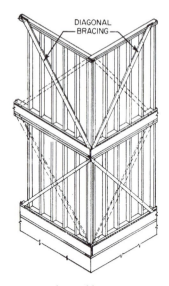

diagonal braces

diagonal bridging 1. See **crossbridging**. 2. See **bridging**. 3. A combination of horizontal **bridging** and **diagonals** in the same plane; spans between the top flange of one beam (or joist) and the bottom flange of the adjacent beam (or joist), in a plane perpendicular to both.

diagonal buttress One extending at 45° from the right-angle corner of two walls.

diagonal bridging, 2

diagonal chimney stacks Several brick chimney stacks that are square in cross section and oriented so that diagonals through them form a straight line; usually corbeled and joined at their tops.

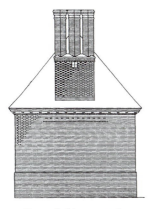

diagonal chimney stacks

diagonal crack An inclined crack, usually at about 45° to the center line, beginning at the tension surface of a concrete member.

diagonal grain A defect in lumber, usually the result of careless sawing, in which the wood grain is at an angle to the long dimension.

diagonal pitch In riveted joints having two or more rows of staggered rivets, the distance from one rivet in one row to the nearest rivet in the next row.

diagonal rib A rib crossing a bay or compartment of a vault on a diagonal.

diagonal sheathing A covering of wallboards nailed to exterior studs or rafters at an angle of approximately 45 degrees.

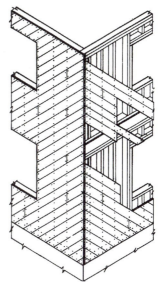

diagonal sheathing

diagonal slating, drop-point slating A method of laying shingles or slates so that the diagonal of each slate runs horizontally.

diagonal tension In **reinforced concrete** or **prestressed concrete**, the principal tensile stress resulting from the combination of vertical and horizontal stresses.

diametral compression test Same as **splitting tensile test**.

diamicton In ancient Roman architecture, a type of masonry wall construction having a hollow cavity filled with broken material of every description.

diamond-bond pattern Same as **diaperwork**.

diamond drill In exploratory drilling, a rotary drill having a coring bit which is studded with black diamonds.

diamond fret, lozenge fret, lozenge molding A molding consisting of fillets intersecting so as to form diamonds or rhombuses. (*See illustration p. 282.*)

diamond light, diamond pane A small pane of glass, either diamond-shaped or square-shaped, and set diagonally in lead **cames** in a window sash. Also called diamond glass. (*See illustration p. 282.*)

diamond matching, four-piece butt matching A method of cutting and piecing

two types of **diamond frets**

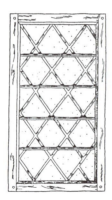

diamond lights

diaper

four adjacent, square-cut pieces of wood veneer so that a diamond pattern results at the center.

diamond-mesh lath A common type of expanded metal lath; used as a base for plaster.

diamond notch Same as **V-notch**.

diamond pattern On a roof, a pattern of tiles or shingles whose lower edges are V-shaped.

diamond slate An asbestos cement shingle or slate, approx. square in shape, with two corners nipped for use in **diagonal slating**.

diamond work See **diaperwork**.

diaper An allover pattern with motifs placed in a repeated design, esp. on a rectangular or diagonal grid.

diaperwork, diaper pattern A decorative masonry pattern formed by brick headers having a dark glazed finish exposed on one end; often laid in the flat unbroken surfaces of gable walls in repeated patterns of diamonds, crisscrossed lines, inverted V's, or chevrons; also called black diapering.

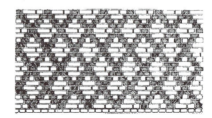

diaperwork

diaphragm **1.** A **diaphragm plate**. **2.** A floor slab, metal wall panel, roof panel, or the like, having a sufficiently large in-plane shear stiffness and sufficient strength to transmit horizontal forces to resisting systems.

diaphragm action Descriptive of a floor system in which all columns that frame into the floor from above and below are maintained in the same position relative to each other.

diaphragm plate A relatively thin, usually rectangular plate, used to stiffen a metal-framed structure; provides additional strength and rigidity.

diaphragm pump A pump in which the piston is replaced by a clamped diaphragm that is set in vibration by a reciprocating rod, attached at its center.

diaphragm valve A valve whose action is controlled by fluid pressure on a diaphragm.

diastyle See **intercolumniation**.

diathyrum A vestibule in an ancient Grecian house with the street door at one end and the door to the courtyard at the other.

diatomite, diatomaceous earth, kieselguhr A white or light gray, chalky, natural siliceous material; obtained by mining deposits of fossil remains of small marine life; used as an extender in paints, as an aggregate in lightweight concrete, as a waterproofing material in portland cement, as a filter for water, and as an abrasive.

diatoni **1.** In ancient Greek and Roman masonry construction, stones which extend the full thickness of the wall; same as **through stones**. **2. Quoins** which project from a wall and have two dressed faces.

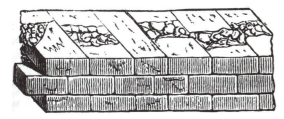

ancient construction with **diatoni**

diazoma The wide horizontal walkway between the lower and upper tiers of seats in a Greek theatre.

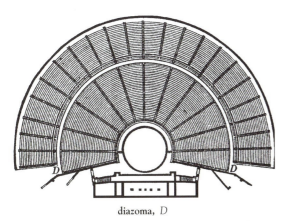

diazoma, *D*

dichroic reflector lamp An incandescent lamp (usually a **PAR lamp**) with a built-in light filter which colors the light or removes a significant part of the infrared power from the light beam.

dictyotheton A type of masonry used by the ancient Greeks; composed of square-cut stones, forming a network or chessboard pattern; similar to the **opus reticulatum** of the Romans.

die **1.** The middle portion of a pedestal between the base (or plinth) and the surbase; also called a **dado**. **2.** A tool for cutting threads on pipe, screws, etc.

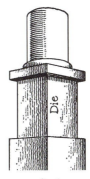

die, 1

dieback A condition often found in woody plant material where browning and death of the plant cells begin from the tip inward and may continue as far as the woody or perennial part of the plant.

die-cast Descriptive of a casting produced by forcing molten metal into a mold.

dielectric fitting In a water supply system, a special type of adapter (such as a **union**) used to connect a pipe containing copper with a pipe containing iron; used between dissimilar metals to prevent galvanic action from causing corrosion failure.

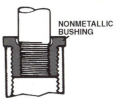

NONMETALLIC BUSHING

dielectric fitting

die line A longitudinal depression or protrusion formed on the surface of drawn or extruded material owing to imperfections on the die surface.

die-squared timber A timber having a square cross section, at least 4 in. (10 cm) on a side.

differential leveling The process of establishing the difference in elevation between any two points by using a **level, 1** and a leveling rod.

differential settlement Relative movement of different parts of a structure caused by uneven sinking of the structure.

diffuse light Light which is random in direction.

diffuse-porous wood A hardwood having pores of uniform size and distribution throughout each annual ring.

diffuser **1.** Any device, object, or surface that scatters light (or sound) from a source. **2.** For air-conditioning systems, see **air diffuser**.

diffuse reflection Reflection of light from a rough surface which scatters it in all directions.

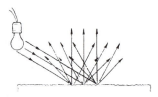

diffuse reflection

diffuse sound Sound is said to be perfectly diffuse in a room when the sound waves travel in all directions with equal probability and the sound level of the reflected sound is everywhere equal.

diffusing glass Glass having an irregular surface to diffuse light; may be fabricated in flat sheets by rolling or pressing, or in hollow shapes by blowing.

diffusing panel A translucent material, such as that covering the lamps in a luminaire, used to distribute light over an extended area and to conceal the lamps and interior of the luminaire.

diffusing surface A reflecting surface which scatters incident light or sound in all directions.

diffusion streak On a clad sheet, a surface streak which results from the diffusion of alloy-ing constituents into the coating from the core during thermal treatment.

dig-down pit Same as **sunken pit**.

digestion tank The first tank of a **septic tank** system in which organic material is processed.

diglyph A member having two vertical channels or grooves, without the two lateral half grooves which characterize the **triglyph**.

dike, dyke **1.** A dry stone wall. **2.** A long low dam. **3.** A bank of earth from an excavation. **4.** An earth embankment which acts as a cofferdam for keeping water out of an excavation.

dilatancy The expansion of cohesionless soils when subject to shearing deformation.

diluent A **thinner**.

diluent air Air which is induced or admitted into a flue in order to dilute the products of combustion.

DIM. On drawings, abbr. for "dimension."

dimension A geometric element in design, such as length, angle, or the magnitude of a quantity.

dimensionally stable Said of a building material whose dimensions remain relatively constant with changes in temperature and humidity.

dimensional stability The degree to which a material maintains its original dimensions when subjected to changes in temperature and humidity. See **equilibrium moisture content**.

dimension lumber, dimension stuff Lumber cut to a particular size and stocked for the building industry; usually 2 to 5 in. (5.1 to 12.7 cm) thick and 5 to 12 in. (12.7 to 30.5 cm) wide.

dimension ratio The average specified diameter of a pipe divided by the minimum specified wall thickness.

dimension shingles Shingles which are uniform, rather than random, in size.

dimension stock **1.** Square-edged lumber usually of timber size; softwoods are at least 4 by 12 in. (10.2 to 30.5 cm), and hardwoods at least 4 ½ in. (11.5 cm) thick. **2.** Timber from which dimension lumber is cut.

dimension stone Stone that is selected, trimmed, or cut to desired shapes and/or sizes for such uses as building stone, markers, paving blocks, flagging, or curbing.

dimension stuff See **dimension lumber**.

dimension work Masonry constructed with **dimension stone**.

diminished arch, skeen arch, skene arch An arch having less rise or height than a semicircle.

diminished bar A **glazing bar** or **muntin** shaped so as to appear thinner in cross section than it actually is.

diminished column A **column** having a greater diameter at its base than at its capital.

diminished stile, diminishing stile, gunstock stile A door stile having different widths above and below the **middle rail**, as in a glazed door in which the stile is narrower in the glazed portion.

diminishing courses On a roof: courses of tiles that diminish in height in going from the eaves to the ridge, thereby providing the appearance of greater height.

diminishing piece Same as **diminishing pipe**.

diminishing pipe, taper pipe A pipe of diminishing diameter which acts as a **reducer**.

diminishing rule A template used to establish the **entasis** of a column.

diminishing stile See **diminished stile**.

dimmer A device which varies the light intensity of a light source without appreciably affecting the spatial distribution of the light; usually an electric control device that varies the current flow and hence the light output of the lamp.

dimmer room A room in which are located the dimmers for controlling the lights for an auditorium or theatre.

DIN Abbr. for "Deutsche Industrie Normal" (Germany Industry Standard).

dinette A recess off a living room, foyer, or kitchen that is used for dining purposes.

dinging A single, rough coat of stucco on a wall; often scored with a tool to form imitation masonry joints.

dingle An obsolete term for a temporary enclosure constructed at the entrance to a building as protection against the weather.

dining bay, dining recess Same as **dinette**.

dining room The principal room used for meals, in which the family in a private house, or guests in a hotel, come together at mealtimes.

Diocletian window See **Venetian window**.

diorama **1.** A large painting, or a series of paintings, intended for exhibition to spectators in a darkened room in a manner to produce by optical illusions an appearance of reality. **2.** A building in which such paintings are exhibited.

diorite Medium- to coarse-grained rock composed essentially of plagioclase feldspar and ferromagnesium minerals.

dip Of a **trap, 1** the lowest portion of the inside top surface of the channel through the trap.

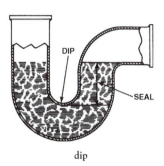

dip

dipcoat A paint or plastic coating which is applied by completely immersing an article in a tank of the coating; usually applied as a finishing or waterproof coating.

dip edge An edge on a metal **flashing** that is formed to promote the flow of water away from vertical surfaces.

diplinthius In ancient Roman construction, masonry which is two bricks thick.

dip solution Any chemical solution used to produce a specific color or finish on copper or copper alloys.

dipteral A classical temple having two rows of free columns, rather than a single row, surrounding the **cella**. Also see **peripteral, pseudodipteral**. (See illustration p. 286.)

dipylon **1.** In ancient Greece, a gate consisting of two separate gates placed side by side. **2.** (cap.) A gate of this type on the northwestern side of Athens.

direct-acting thermostat An instrument which activates a control circuit when a predetermined temperature is reached.

direct cross-connection **1.** A continuous **cross-connection** or interconnection such that the flow of water from one system to the other

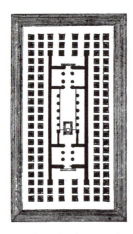

dipteral temple, shown in plan

may occur under the slightest pressure differential between the two piping systems. **2.** Any connection (such as a shutoff valve) between a potable water-supply line and a nonpotable source at which there is the possibility of contaminating the water supply should the valve (a) leak or (b) be opened when it should be closed.

direct current   In an electric circuit, a current that flows in one direction only. Also see **alternating current**.

direct cylinder   The tank of a **direct-fired water heater**.

direct dumping   The discharging of concrete directly into place from a crane bucket or mixer.

direct expense   All items of expense directly incurred by or attributable to a specific project, assignment, or task.

direct-fired air heater   An air heater in which all the heat of combustion is discharged into the airstream; used in factories, warehouses, etc., to raise the temperature of air, which is brought in from the outside, to room temperature.

direct-fired water heater   A water heater in which the source of heat (gas, oil, or electricity) is located at the water tank—in contrast to an **indirect water heater**.

direct glare   Glare resulting from high brightness or insufficiently shielded light sources in the field of view or from reflecting areas of high brightness.

direct glazing   Glazing that is set into a structure instead of into a frame mounted within a structural opening.

direct heating   Warming of a space by means of exposed heated surfaces (e.g., from a stove, fire, radiators, or pipes); both **radiant heating** and **convection heating** take place.

direct-indirect lighting   Lighting in which the luminaires are in the general diffuse category but emit little or no light at angles near a horizontal plane drawn through them.

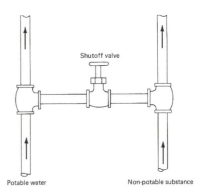

direct cross-connection

directional lighting   Lighting, predominantly from a preferred direction, which provides illumination on the **work plane** or on an object.

direct leveling   The determination of differences of elevation by a continuous series of short horizontal lines; the vertical distances from these lines to adjacent ground marks are determined by direct observations on graduated rods with a leveling instrument equipped with a **spirit level**.

direct lighting   Lighting in which luminaires distribute 90% to 100% of the emitted light in the direction of the surface to be illuminated, usually in a downward direction.

direct luminaire   A luminaire which emits 90% to 100% of its total output below a horizontal plane through it.

direct nailing   Same as **face nailing**.

direct-plunger elevator   A **hydraulic elevator** which has a piston (plunger) directly attached to the elevator car frame.

Directoire style   A transitional classicist style preceding the Empire style, named after the Directoire rule in France (1795–1799).

directory board   An information board with changeable letters or symbols.

direct personnel expense Salaries and wages of principals and employees engaged on a project, assignment, or task, including mandatory and customary benefits.

direct return system A piping arrangement for a heating system (or air-conditioning or refrigeration system) in which the heating (or cooling) fluid, after it has passed through each **heat exchanger**, is returned to the boiler (or evaporator) by the shortest direct path.

direct solar water-heating system A solar water-heating system in which water passes directly from the potable water supply, through the collectors and storage, to the hot-water supply.

direct sound The sound which travels directly from the source to the point of observation—no reflection of sound is involved.

direct sound level The **sound level** of the **direct sound** in a room.

direct stress Stress without bending or shear; only compressive or tensile stress.

direct system A heating, air-conditioning, or refrigeration system in which heat is exchanged directly with a surrounding material or space.

direct water heater Same as **direct-fired water heater**.

dirt-and-stick chimney, dirt chimney Same as **clay-and-sticks chimney**.

dirt-depreciation factor See **luminaire dirt-depreciation factor**.

dirt resistance The ability of a paint coating (or the like) to resist soiling by foreign material deposited on, or embedded in, the dried coating.

disability glare Glare that reduces visual performance and visibility and often is accompanied by discomfort.

disappearing stair, folding stair, loft ladder A swinging stair, usually a folding ladder, which enables passage to an attic space or loft. The stair is fixed to a trapdoor which, when closed, hides the stair from viewers below.

discharge coefficient See **coefficient of discharge**.

discharge head The energy per unit weight of fluid on the discharge side of a pump.

discharge lamp Any lamp that produces light by means of phosphors as a result of an electrical discharge through one or more gases or vapors within the lamp's envelope (e.g., see **fluorescent lamp**).

discharge opening The opening at the base of a **refuse chute** through which the refuse drops into a refuse container or refuse compactor.

discharge pipe Any pipe that conveys the discharge from plumbing fixtures, appliances, or the like.

discharging arch, relieving arch, safety arch An arch, usually segmental and often a blind arch, built above the lintel of a door or window to discharge the weight of the wall above the lintel to each side.

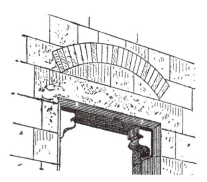

discharging arch

discoloration Any change in color from the original color or from the desired color.

discomfort glare Glare that produces discomfort but does not necessarily interfere with visual performance or visibility.

disconnecting means A device (usually a circuit breaker, a fused switch, or a fused circuit-breaker-assembly) that disconnects the conductors of an electric circuit from the source of supply.

disconnecting trap Same as **interceptor**.

discontinuous construction Construction in which there is no solid connection between the rooms of a building and the building structure; or between one section of a building and another; esp. used to prevent the transmission of noise along a solid path.

discontinuous easement An easement requiring for its exercise an action by one party, as a right-of-way.

discontinuous impost A **shafted impost**, where the arch moldings are different from the moldings of the pier from which the arch springs.

discontinuous impost

dished hole A hole whose upper edge has been enlarged.

dishing The grading of the surface of the ground or pavement, usually to promote drainage.

disintegration Of concrete or the like, the deterioration into small fragments or particles.

disk sander A **sanding machine** or a **power sander** which has a circular abrasive (usually sandpaper) disk which rotates; used for smoothing or polishing surfaces.

dispersant An admixture which is capable of maintaining finely ground materials in suspension; used as a slurry thinner or grinding aid.

dispersing agent An addition or admixture capable of increasing the fluidity of pastes, mortars, or concrete.

dispersion 1. Any gas, liquid, or solid containing finely dispersed particles in suspension. 2. A paint containing finely dispersed particles of pigment or latex.

displacement pile A solid pile or hollow pile whose lower end is closed so that in being driven, the pile displaces an equivalent soil volume (either by compaction or soil displacement).

displuviatum An atrium, the roof of which was sloped outward from the compluvium instead of toward it.

disposal field Same as **absorption field**.

disposal unit See **waste-disposal unit**.

dissolved solids See **solutes**.

distance block A wood block which separates two components from each other at a fixed distance.

distance separation For fire-protection requirements, the separation between an exterior wall of a building and an interior property line, or the center line of an adjacent street, or the exterior wall of another building; all measured at right angles to the exterior wall.

distegia Same as **episkenion**.

distemper A paint containing earth pigments, calcium carbonate, tinting colors, glue size, or casein, mixed with water; **tempera**.

distemper brush A wide flat paintbrush with long bristles; used in applying distempers, such as calcimine.

distillation A water purification process in which water is converted to a vapor by boiling it, and then reconverted to purified water by cooling the vapor.

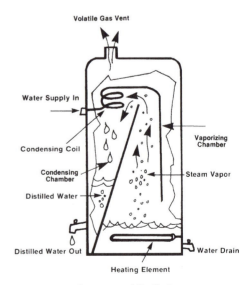

the process of **distillation**

distributed load A load which acts evenly over a structural member or over a surface that supports the load.

distribution The movement of freshly mixed concrete toward the point of placement, either by motorized tools or by hand.

distribution-bar reinforcement, distribution steel In a **reinforced concrete** slab, small-diameter steel **reinforcing bars**, usually at right angles to the main reinforcement; intended to spread a concentrated load on the slab and to prevent cracking.

distribution board Same as **distribution switchboard**.

distribution box **1.** In sanitary engineering, a box in which the flow of effluent from a septic tank is distributed equally into the **drain tile** lines that lead to the **absorption field**. **2.** A **junction box**.

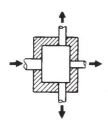

distribution box

distribution center A point in an electrical system in a building where secondary voltage (usually a low voltage) is distributed to different circuits within the building. Generally includes automatic overload protective devices that provide protection for the electric system in the event that the system is called upon to exceed its safe operating capacity; in that case, the system shuts down automatically.

distribution cutout In a primary circuit, an electrical **cutout, 3** which disconnects the circuit as a means of overcurrent protection.

distribution line In sanitary engineering, a line of **distribution tile**.

distribution panel Same as **panelboard**.

distribution reinforcement See **distribution-bar reinforcement**.

distribution steel See **distribution-bar reinforcement**.

distribution switchboard An electric switchboard used to distribute power within a building; enclosed in a metal box which includes circuit breakers, fuses, and switches.

distribution tile In a sewage-disposal system, clay or concrete tile pipe, laid with open joints, which carries **effluent** from a **distribution box**.

distribution transformer A transformer that reduces the primary voltage to a secondary (lower) voltage for distribution within a building.

district surveyor A British term for **building inspector**.

distyle Having two columns in front; used in describing a classical building.

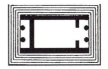

distyle, temple shown in plan

distyle in antis Having two columns in front between **antae**.

ditcher, ditching machine See **trencher**.

ditching machine

ditriglyph An interval between two columns such as to admit two triglyphs in the entablature instead of one, as usual.

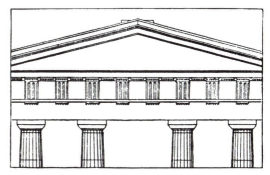

ditriglyph

DIV On drawings, abbr. for **division**.

divan **1.** In Muslim countries, a council room or hall for a court of justice. **2.** A smoking room.

diversion valve Same as **diverter**.

diversity The nonsimultaneous occurrence of maximum **demands** on any given part of a system.

diversity factor **1.** In an electric wiring system, the ratio of the sum of the individual maximum **demands** of the various subsystems to the maximum demand of the whole system. **2.** In a gas piping system, the ratio of the maximum *probable* demand to the maximum *possible* demand.

diverter A valve (sometimes motorized) at a junction of a **pipe tee**; used to change the flow from one branch to another.

divided door Same as **Dutch door**.

divided light Glass in a window or glazed door that is divided into smaller panes by secondary framing members; see **muntin**.

divided tenon Same as **double tenons, 1**.

dividers A pair of compasses having both legs terminating in points; used for measuring, transferring, or comparing distances between two points when a precise measurement is required; also used to scribe an arc, radius, or circle, and to compare or transfer measurements directly from a rule.

division One of the sixteen basic organizational subdivisions used in the AIA **uniform system** for construction specifications, data filing, and cost accounting.

division bar See **muntin**.

division wall See **fire wall, 1**.

diwan Same as **divan, 1**.

dkg Abbr. for "decking."

DL **1.** On drawings, abbr. for **dead load**. **2.** On drawings, abbr. for **deadlight**.

D-line crack See **D-crack**.

DN On drawings, abbr. for "down."

DO. On drawings, abbr. for "ditto."

doat See **dote**.

dobying Same as **mud-capping**.

dock **1.** A platform, usually the height of the floor or truck vans, which facilitates loading and unloading; a **loading dock**. **2.** Short for **scene dock**.

dock bumper A resilient bumper attached to a loading **dock, 1** to absorb truck impacts against it.

docked gable Same as **jerkinhead roof**.

document deposit See **deposit for bidding documents**.

dodecastyle Having twelve columns in the front row; said of buildings of classical type.

dog Same as **dog iron**.

dog anchor See **dog iron**.

dog bars Vertical rails in the lower portion of a gate.

dog-ear **1.** An external corner made by folding a sheet of material without cutting it. **2.** The corner of a sheet of material which is folded over. **3.** Same as **crossette**. **4.** The projections at the corners of a door or window casing.

dog-eared fold Same as **dog-ear**.

dogging device A mechanism which fastens the crossbar of a **panic exit device** in the fully depressed position.

dog iron, dog anchor A short bar of iron with its ends bent at right angles and pointed so as to hold together the two pieces into which they are driven.

dog iron

dogleg brick A special brick not having a rectangular shape; instead, the edge along the narrowest side is not a straight line but forms an obtuse angle. These bricks are especially used where the face of a wall forms an obtuse angle; this avoids the use of cut bricks and a mortar joint where the face of the wall changes direction; an **angle brick**.

dogleg chisel Same as **corner chisel**.

dog-leg pile A pile which has been bent or curved in driving.

dogleg stair, doglegged stair A half-turn stair which has no wellhole between successive flights; the rail and balusters of the upper and under flights fall in the same vertical plane.

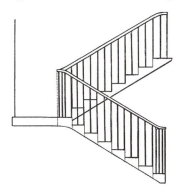

dogleg stair

dog nail **1.** A large nail having a head that projects considerably on one side. **2.** A wrought nail used for fastening door hinges.

dog-run cabin Same as **dogtrot cabin**.

dog's ear, dog ear Same as **crossette**.

dog shore A horizontal **shore** that is framed between vertical surfaces (without braces) such as between two buildings.

dog's tooth Same as **dogtooth**.

dog's-tooth course Same as **dog-tooth course**.

dogtooth, tooth ornament **1.** An ornament in medieval architecture and derivatives, of more or less elaborate motif, usually pyramidal with notched sides, the diagonal portions usually resembling petals or leaves which radiate from the raised point. **2.** A brick laid with its corners projecting from the wall face.

dog-tooth course A horizontal band of bricks, or **course,** that is laid diagonally on edge; each

dog-tooth course on a brick chimney

brick is set so that one corner projects from the face of the wall, often at an angle of 45 degrees; also called a dog's-tooth course.

dogtrot A **breezeway**.

dogtrot cabin A dwelling, often of log construction, consisting of two single-room cabins separated from each other by a covered open-air passageway (**dogtrot**); a common wood-shingled pitched roof typically covers both cabins, and each cabin has its own entrance and a chimney at its gable end. The dogtrot or breezeway not only serves to link the cabins, but also provides an outdoor sitting area. Also called a double-pen cabin.

dogtrot plan See **possum-trot plan**.

dolly **1.** A block of hardwood placed on the upper end of a pile; acts as an extension piece and as a cushion during pile driving. **2.** A tool for holding the head of a rivet and absorbing the impact while the other head is being driven. **3.** A low cart or truck used for transporting heavy or bulky equipment.

Dolly Varden siding Beveled wood **siding** which is rabbeted along the bottom edge.

dolmen, table stone A prehistoric tomb of standing stones, usually capped with a large horizontal slab.

dolomite **1.** A mineral form of calcium-magnesium carbonate; a constituent of some building limestones. **2.** Limestone consisting principally of the mineral dolomite; **dolostone**.

dolomitic lime A trade term and misnomer for **high-magnesium lime**; the product does not contain dolomite.

dolomitic limestone Limestone that contains more than 10% but less than 80% of the mineral dolomite.

dolostone See **dolomite, 2**.

dome **1.** A curved roof structure spanning an area; often spherical in shape. **2.** A square prefabricated pan form; used in two-way joist (**waffle**) concrete floor construction. **3.** A vault substantially hemispherical in shape, but sometimes slightly pointed or bulbous; a ceiling of similar form. Also see **geodesic dome** and **saucer dome**.

dome light A skylight having the shape of a shallow dome; often fabricated of glass or plastic;

may be set into a roof to provide supplementary daylighting below it.

domestic hot-water heater Packaged equipment which heats water for domestic purposes.

Domestic Revival style A style of architecture in England in the 19th century loosely patterned after elements of the Queen Anne style, Domestic Revival, and aspects of the Picturesque Movement as well as the Arts and Crafts Movement; often characterized by timber-framed houses, ornate bargeboards, brickwork in diaper patterns, tall decorative chimney stacks, and leaded windows; a forerunner of the **shingle style,** in which tiles were used rather than wood shingles. Also called Old English style.

domestic sewage See **sanitary sewage**.

domical Pertaining to, resembling, or characterized by a dome, as a domical church.

domical vault A **coved vault**.

dominant estate Where a restriction on use of one piece of real property is imposed in order to confer a benefit upon the owner of another, the former is called the **servient estate** and the latter the **dominant estate**. For example, if ownership of one field confers upon its owner the **easement** or right to walk across the field of a neighbor in order to reach the highway, the field whose owner has that right is the dominant estate and that which may be crossed is the servient estate.

donjon Same as **keep**.

dook A wood insert in a wall for attaching finishings.

door **1.** An entranceway. **2.** A barrier (usually solid) which swings, slides, tilts, or folds to close an opening in a wall or cabinet or the like. For additional definitions and illustrations of specific types, see **automatic door, balanced door, battened door, blank door, blind door, board-and-battened door, car door, casement door, cellar door, Christian door, class-A door, class-B door, class-C door, class-D door, class-E door, crapaudine door, cross-and-bible door, divided door, double-acting door, double door, double-margin door, Dutch door, dwarf door, Egyptian door, elevator car door, false door, fire door, flap door, flush door, folding door, framed door, French door, half door, Holy door, jib door, landing door, ledged-and-braced door, ledged door, overhung door, Palladian door, paneled door, pocket door, revolving door, roll-up door, sash**

door, scuttle door, sham door, single-acting door, sliding door, storm door, swinging door, trapdoor, unframed door, vertical plank door, weather door, wicket, witch door, z-braced battened door, zambullo door.

door band Same as **door bar**.

door bar A heavy bar across a door to prevent it from being opened, such as a plank dropped between metal holders on each side of the doorframe.

door bar

door bevel The bevel which is provided on the stile edge (lock edge) of a door so that the door may swing free of the doorframe; usually about 3° toward the **doorstop, 1**.

door bolt A manually operated sliding rod or bar attached to a door for locking it; a spring is not part of the locking mechanism.

door bolt

doorbrand **1.** A bar used to fasten a door. **2.** A strap hinge which holds in place the planks of a door.

door buck A wood or metal subframe, set in a wall, to which the finished frame is attached; also called a **rough buck** or **sub-buck**.

door bumper See **doorstop, 2**.

doorcap The wall area or decorative element directly above a doorway, often ornamented.

door casing, doorcase The finished frame surrounding a door; the visible frame.

door catch See **catch**.

door check Same as **door closer, 1**.

doorcheek A **doorjamb**.

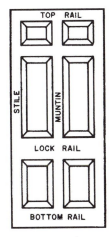

door nomenclature

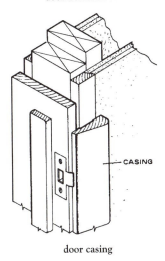

door casing

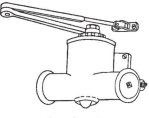

door closer, 1

door contact, door switch   An electric contacting device for opening and closing a circuit, which is attached to a doorframe and operated by opening or closing the door.

doorframe   An assembly built into a wall consisting of two upright members (**jambs**) and a head (**lintel**) over the doorway; encloses the

door class   See **class-A door**, **class-B door**, etc.

door clearance   **1.** The clearance between the bottom of a door and the finished floor. **2.** Same as **frame clearance**. **3.** The clearance between the meeting edges of a pair of doors.

door closer   **1.** A device combining a spring for closing and a compression chamber into which liquid or air escapes slowly, thus providing a means of controlling the speed of the closing action; also called a **door check**. **2.** In elevators, a device or assembly of devices which closes an opened car or hoistway door by the use of gravity or springs.

door closer bracket   A device which permits a **door closer, 1** to be installed on the doorframe, rather than directly on the door.

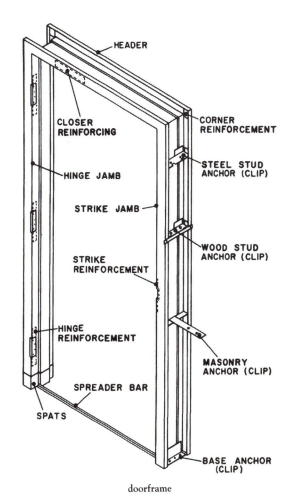

doorframe

doorway and provides support on which to hang the door.

doorframe anchor An adjustable device, fabricated of metal, used to attach a doorframe to the surrounding structure; also see **jamb anchor**.

door furniture (*Brit.*) Any functional or decorative fitting for a door, excluding the lock and hinges.

door grille A grille in a prepared door opening which allows air to pass through but restricts vision and acts as a partial barrier.

door hand See **hand**.

door head **1.** The uppermost member of a doorframe. **2.** A horizontal projection above a door.

doorhood

door head, England (15th cent.)

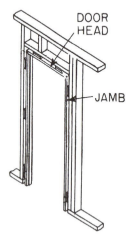

door head, doorjamb

door holder A device that holds a door open at selected positions.

doorhood A projecting covering over an external door to provide shelter from rain or snow.

door jack A frame for holding a wood door in place while it is off its hinges and being planed.

doorjamb, doorcheek, doorpost The vertical member on each side of a door.

door knob The knob or handle that releases the latch on a door, permitting it to be opened.

door knocker A hinged knob, bar, or ring of metal, attached to the outside of an exterior door, to enable a person to announce his presence.

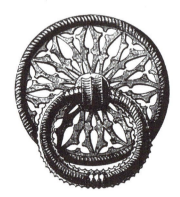

door knocker, England (15th cent.)

door latch See **latch**.

door light The glass area in a door.

door lining The finish of wood, metal, marble, etc., which surrounds the top and sides of a doorway.

door lock A device that prevents a door from being opened except with a key; for example, see **box locks** or **case locks**; also see **lock**.

door louver   In a door, an opening with a series of slats, blades, or piercings which permit the passage of air.

door mullion   The center vertical member of a double-door opening, set between two single active leaves; usually forms the strike side of each leaf; may be removable. Also see **mullion.**

doornail   **1.** A large-headed nail against which the knocker strikes. **2.** A large-headed nail used to decorate or strengthen a door.

door opening, opening size   The size of the doorframe opening measured from jamb to jamb and from floor line or threshold to head of frame; usually equal to the actual door size plus clearances.

door operator   On elevators, a device or assembly of devices which opens and closes a car door and/or hoistway door by power other than by hand, gravity, springs, or the movement of the car.

door pivot   See **pivot, 2.**

doorplate   A plate on the exterior side of a door which gives the name of the occupant, apartment number, or the like.

door pocket   The boxing or chamber in a wall which receives a sliding door when it is in the open position.

doorpost   **1.** See **doorjamb. 2.** A heavy post that frames one side of a doorway; in the past, doors were sometimes hinged directly to such a post instead of to a **doorframe.**

door rail   A horizontal cross member which forms part of the framework of a door; connects the hinge stile to the lock stile, both at the top and bottom of the door and at intermediate locations; may be exposed, as in paneled doors, or concealed, as in flush doors.

door roller   A hardware accessory, consisting of wheels on a track, which supports a sliding door.

door saddle   Same as **threshold, 1.**

door schedule   A tabulation, usually on a blueprint or in specifications, which lists all doors required on a job, indicating sizes, types, locations, and special requirements.

door screen   A wire screen panel fixed in a door to exclude insects but permit the passage of air; may be removable to permit replacement by a glazed panel in cold weather.

door set   An assembly of manufactured components of which a door is comprised, e.g., the door, door frame, door lining, etc.

doorsill   The horizontal board or metal plate on the floor directly beneath a door; covers the joint where two types of floor materials meet; also called a saddle.

doorstead   A **doorway,** including all components of the door and doorframe.

doorstep   A **step** at a door; often one of several at the exterior of an outer door.

door stile   A vertical structural member of the door itself; this is in contrast to a vertical structural member of the **doorframe,** which is called a **jamb.** The inner **stile** (i.e., the stile nearest the axis about which the door swings) is called the *hinge stile*; the outer stile is called the *lock stile*.

doorstone   The stepstone at the threshold of a door.

doorstop   **1.** A strip against which a door shuts in its frame. **2.** A device placed on a wall behind a door, or mounted on the floor, to prevent opening the door too wide; also called a **door bumper.**

door strip   A strip attached to the bottom edge of a door to cover the gap between the bottom edge and the doorsill.

door surround   A decorative element or structure around a doorway; for example, see **Gibbs surround.**

door sweep   See **sweep strip.**

door swing   See **hand.**

door switch   See **door contact.**

door track   A metal track or rail on which a sliding door moves.

door transom   A **transom, 2.**

door tree   The jamb or sidepiece of a door.

door trim   The casing or moldings used around a doorframe to conceal the crack or joint between the frame and wall or for decorative effects.

door unit   **1.** A door and frame assembly. **2.** As specified in building codes: the clear opening of each door in a required fire exit.

doorway   An opening in a wall, with a door, which provides a passageway into a room or building.

door window A **French door**.

dope **1.** A material added to a building material such as mortar or plaster to retard or accelerate the set. **2.** A material added to a batch of paint to adjust it to specifications. **3.** A solution of cellulose nitrate applied to a porous fabric as a protective coating. **4.** A compound used in making a pipe joint, as a lubricant and to ensure a leakproof joint.

Doric capital The topmost member of a column or pilaster of the **Doric order**.

Doric cyma A **cyma recta**.

Doric order In Classical architecture and derivatives, the column and entablature developed by the Dorian Greeks. Characterized by sturdy proportions, a simple capital, a frieze usually having regularly spaced **triglyphs** and **metopes,** and **mutules** in the cornice; plainer than the Corinthian order or the Ionic order (although the Tuscan order later introduced by the Romans was even plainer). The Roman Doric column has a base but is usually not fluted (see illustration of base, which follows); in contrast, the Greek Doric column is usually fluted but has no base. Compare with **Tuscan order**.

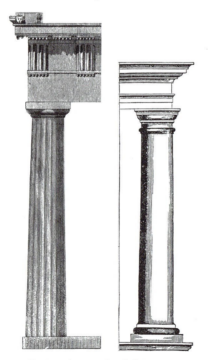

Doric order: *a*, Greek; *b*, Roman

dormant, dormant tree In a **timber-framed house**, a large horizontal beam that supports beams of a lesser size.

dormant window Same as **dormer**.

dormer, dormer window A structure projecting above a sloping roof, usually housing a vertical window. It is not part of the roof structure but is framed separately, and often provides daylight and ventilation for a room located in a garret or loft space. For definitions and illustrations of specific types, see **arched dormer, deck dormer, eyebrow dormer, flat-head dormer, gable dormer, hipped dormer, inset dormer, mission dormer, oval dormer, Palladian dormer, pedimented dormer, pitched-roof dormer, pointed dormer, polygonal dormer, recessed dormer, ridge dormer, round dormer, segmental dormer, shed dormer, through-the-cornice dormer, triangular dormer, wall dormer, watershed dormer**.

dormer cheek The vertical side of a dormer.

dormer window, dormer A vertical window which projects from a sloping roof, placed in a small gable.

dormer window

dormitory A place, building, or room to sleep in.

dorsal Same as **canopy**.

dorsel **1.** A canopy. **2.** Same as **reredos**.

dorter, dortour A dormitory, esp. in a monastery.

dosing tank In sanitary engineering, a collection tank for sewage which is subsequently discharged for further processing.

dossal Same as **reredos**.

dossel **1.** Same as **reredos**. **2.** A hanging of silk, satin, damask, or cloth of gold at the back of an altar of a church and sometimes also on the sides of the chancel.

dosseret A member or supplementary capital resting on the top of the capital of a column; see **impost block**; also called a double capital.

dot A small spot of plaster placed on a plastering surface, or a temporary nail; to assist the plasterer in leveling a wall and in obtaining proper plaster thickness.

dote, doat, doze A form of decay in which wood becomes soft and weak and has a dull lifeless appearance.

doty Said of timber which has decayed.

double-acting butt Same as **double-acting hinge**.

double-acting door A door that swings in both directions; see **swinging door**.

double-acting frame A doorframe which does not contain doorstops, thereby permitting installation of a double-acting door.

double-acting hinge A hinge which permits motion in either of two directions; used on swinging doors.

double-acting pump A reciprocal pump in which the reciprocating motion of a piston does work in both directions.

double angle Two L-shaped metal structural members which are fastened together, back to back.

double architrave An **architrave, 1** having two decorative bands around an opening (such as a door or window in a wall of a building); usually the bands are in different planes, separated by an ornamental molding.

double ax An ax having a two-edged blade.

double back See **double up**.

double bead Two beads, side by side; there is no other surface or molding between them.

double-bellied baluster A baluster whose upper half has the same profile as the lower half.

double-bend fitting In plumbing, an S-shaped pipe fitting.

double-beveled edge The edge of a door (along the lock stile) which is beveled from the center of the edge toward each door face.

double-break switch In electric wiring, a switch which opens a conductor at two points.

double bridging **Bridging** which is placed between adjacent joists at positions which divide the joists into three lengths.

double capital Same as **dosseret**.

double-center theodolite Same as **repeating theodolite**.

double chimney **1.** A pair of exterior chimneys, of approximately the same size, one on each side of a **gable end** of a house. **2.** The chimneys for two fireplaces that open back to back, serving two different rooms; commonly has two flues.

double church A church constructed in two stories, affording two places of worship, one above the other; a large hole in the floor of the upper church enables the two congregations to hear the same service.

double-cleat ladder Similar to a **single-cleat ladder**, but wider, with an additional center rail which allows for two-way traffic of workmen ascending and descending.

double cloister An **ambulatory** that is divided in two by a series of columns or piers.

double-cone molding A molding enriched with carved cones joined base to base and apex to apex.

double corner block, pier block, pilaster block A concrete masonry unit having solid rectangular end faces as well as solid rectangular side faces.

double corner block

double course, doubling course A double layer of shingles or the like, one over the other, providing a minimum coverage of two thicknesses. (*See illustration p. 298.*)

double-crib barn See **crib barn**.

double-cut file A file having two sets of cutting ridges, each set crossing the other; the ridges are diagonal with respect to the center line of the file.

double-cut saw A saw whose teeth have been cut so that the blade cuts on both the pull and the push strokes.

double decker A two-story house that provides living quarters for two families; it has one

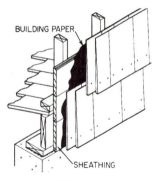

double course

apartment on each floor and a separate entrance for each family.

double-decker barn A barn having three levels (including a loft) that is built into a hillside having a steep slope.

double-decker porch See **two-tiered porch**.

double door Two single doors (leaves) hung in the same doorframe.

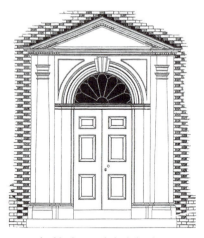

double door with fanlight above

double-dovetail key, hammerhead key A key made of hardwood which is used to join two timbers; has a dovetail on each end which is driven into a corresponding recess in each timber.

double eaves course Same as **double course**.

double egress frame A doorframe which is prepared to receive two single-acting doors swinging in opposite directions, both doors being of the same **hand**.

double-ended substation A electric **substation** consisting of two switchboards in one common assembly, separated physically and electrically by a "tie circuit breaker."

double-end-trimmed Descriptive of lumber which is sawn reasonably square on both ends.

double-entry stair Same as **double stair**.

double-extra-strong pipe A standard designation for steel pipe in which the thickness of the pipe wall has been increased beyond that of standard-weight pipe to provide double strength.

double-faced **1.** Descriptive of any joinery, as a molding, which is formed of two parts having faces in different planes. **2.** Any material which is finished on both sides.

double-faced hammer A hammer with a striking face at each end of the head.

double-faced ware, porcelain enamel ware Ware that has a finish coat on both surfaces.

double feathering The subdivision of large **cusps** into smaller ones.

double Flemish bond A brickwork pattern showing a **Flemish bond** on both faces of a wall.

double floor, double-joisted floor, framed floor A floor in which the **binding joists** support the **common joists** above and the ceiling below.

double format pavior A brick or tile made esp. for paving and having double the bed face, or double the longer face perpendicular to the bed face.

double-framed floor A **double floor** in which the **binding joists** are framed by girders.

double-framed roof A roof in which longitudinal members (such as a ridge beam and purlins) are used.

double framing Using twice the usual number of framing members to provide additional strength.

double-fronted lot A lot bounded by a street on the front and back.

double-gable roof An **M-roof**.

double glazing Two panes of glass, usually parallel, with an air space between; used to provide increased thermal and/or sound insulation.

doublehanded saw A saw operated by two men, one at each end.

double-headed nail, scaffold nail, form nail A nail having two heads, one above the other; the upper head is driven with a hammer, and it is used to withdraw the nail; the lower head bears on the surface into which the nail is driven; used on temporary structures such as scaffolds, formwork, etc.

double-headed nail

double header A **header joist** made of two pieces of lumber, fixed together by bolts or nails, to provide greater strength than a single piece.

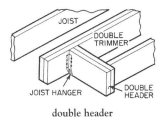

double header

double-hipped roof A **hipped roof** having a double slope; also see **bonnet roof**.

double house **1.** A pair of **semi-detached houses** having a plan that is symmetric on both sides of the common wall; each of the two units has its own entry. **2.** See **Cape Cod house**. **3.** See **Charleston house**.

double-hung window, double-hung sash window A window having two vertically sliding sashes, each closing a different part of the window; the weight of each sash is counterbalanced for ease of opening and closing.

double-intersection truss A **truss**, each panel of which has two intersecting diagonals.

double jack rafter A short rafter that joins a hip to a valley.

double-joisted floor See **double floor**.

double junction A fitting for a water pipe or a drainage pipe which has a branch on each side.

double lancet window A window having a mullion which is so shaped as to form two **lancets**.

double lath Wood lath, twice the normal thickness.

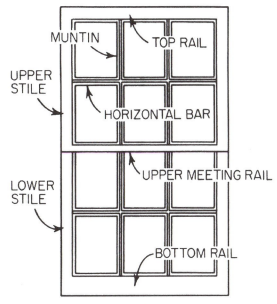

double-hung window: terminology

double lean-to roof A V-shaped roof formed by two lean-to roofs meeting at their low edge with a gutter at their intersection.

double-lock seam A type of seam between the edges of adjacent metal sheets; formed by making a double fold, then dressing down to form a seam.

double-lock seam

double-lock welt Same as **double-lock seam**.

double L stair A platform stair with two intermediate landings, one near the top and one near the bottom, with a 90° change of direction at each landing.

double-margin door A door having the appearance of a **double door**.

double measure In joinery, work which has molding on both sides.

double meeting rail A horizontal fixed **meeting rail** where two adjacent pivoted **sashes (ventilators, 2)** meet.

double meeting stile   The vertical equivalent of a **double meeting rail**.

double-molded   Said of doors that are molded on both sides of the framing.

double monastery   A monastery and a nunnery adjacent to each other, sharing the same church and under the rule of the same superior.

double offset   In plumbing, two changes of direction which are in succession in a continuous pipe.

double partition   A partition built with separated framing members for each face so as to form a cavity space in the center for purposes of sound insulation or to conceal sliding doors.

double-pen cabin   A log cabin having two adjacent rooms under a common roof; usually has a chimney at each end of the cabin; often a porch across the full width of the cabin. Also see **center-hall cabin, dogtrot cabin, saddlebag cabin**.

double-pile house   A house that is two rooms deep. Also see **pile, 2** and **single-pile house**.

double-pitched   Having a pitch in two directions, as a **gambrel roof**.

double-pitched roof   A roof having two flat slopes on each side of a central ridge; for example, see **gambrel roof**.

double-pitched skylight   A skylight which has two slopes and straddles the ridge of a roof.

double-pole scaffold   A scaffold supported from the base by a double row of uprights, independent of support from the walls and constructed of uprights, ledgers, horizontal platform bearers, and diagonal bracing.

double-pole switch   In electric wiring, a **switch** which has two blades (and associated contacts) for opening or closing both sides of a circuit simultaneously.

double porch   A two-tiered porch in which the porches on the first and second stories appear to be virtually identical in design.

double pour   In built-up roofing, two separate applications of a top coating of bitumen and surfacing; esp. used on level roofs designed to hold water.

double-quirked bead   See **quirk bead, 2**.

double-rabbeted frame   A doorframe having recesses along both sides so that a door can be hung on either side of the frame.

double raised panel   See **raised panel**.

double-rebated frame   Same as **double-rabbeted frame**.

double return stair, side flights   A stair having one flight from the main floor to an intermediate landing and two side flights from that landing to the floor above.

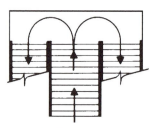

double return stair

double Roman tile   A **Roman tile** having an additional roll up the center of the tile that matches (and is parallel to) the roll at its edges.

double roof   A timber framing system in which the common rafters rest on **purlins** which provide intermediate support.

double-run stairs   Two separate **flights** that start and finish at the same levels, and cross each other about the center point of each stair.

double-saddle notch   At a corner of a log cabin, one of a pair of rounded notches cut on opposite sides of a horizontal log near one end; it forms a joint at the corner with a round unnotched log set at a right angle between such a pair of notched logs. Sometimes simply called a saddle notch; also see **notch**.

double shear   The shear to which a member is subject when the shearing stress is along two section planes.

double-shell tile   Ceramic tile with double faces separated by short webs.

double-shouldered chimney   Same as **stepped-back chimney**.

double skirting   A **baseboard** that is much higher than usual.

double square   See **adjustable square**.

double stair   An open stair having a pair of staircases leading down from a landing; usually designed to be impressive; compare with **double-return stair**.

double step A double notch cut into a tie beam which supports a rafter in a timber framing system.

double-strength glass Sheet glass having a thickness of between 0.118 in. (3.00 mm) and 0.113 in. (3.38 mm).

double-suction pump A pump having a spiral-shaped casing in which the water enters the impeller from *both* sides of the impeller so that hydraulic unbalance is practically eliminated.

double-sunk Recessed or lowered in two steps, as when a panel is sunk below the surface of a larger panel.

double surface treatment Two successive treatments applied to a surface, such as asphaltic material followed by a mineral aggregate.

double-swing door Same as **double-acting door**.

double-swing frame A doorframe which is prepared to receive a pair of single-acting doors, both of which swing in the same direction.

double T-beam A precast concrete member composed of two beams with a common slab across the top.

double tenons **1.** Two tenons, side by side, at one end of a member; also called a **divided tenon**. **2.** Two tenons, one at each end of a member, which are coaxial.

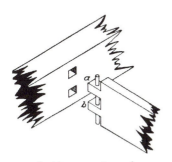

double tenons, 1: *a, b*

double-throw bolt A door bolt that can be projected beyond its first position, into a second (or fully extended) position to provide additional security.

double-throw switch In electric wiring, a **switch** which can charge the circuit connections by moving the switch blade from one of two sets of contact clips into the other.

double-tiered porch Same as **two-tiered porch**.

double-tier partition A partition which extends two stories in height.

double up, double back A method of applying plaster; first the plaster base coat is applied; then this is covered with plaster from the same mix before the base coat has set. A form of **two-coat work**.

double vault A vault, usually domical, consisting of an inner shell separated from a higher outer shell.

double vault

double wall A masonry wall composed of two walls with a space between them; the space may be filled with a material such as fiberglass to provide additional thermal insulation and sound insulation.

double-wall cofferdam A **cofferdam** formed by a double wall of **sheeting** (such as interlocking steel sections) and backfilled with soil or crushed stone.

double waste and vent Same as **dual vent**.

double-welded joint In **arc welding** and in **gas welding**, any joint welded on both sides.

double window **1.** Two windows, one outside the other, as a **storm window**, used to provide improved thermal and noise insulation. **2.** A window which is double glazed, with an air space between. **3.** Two windows, side by side, which form a single architectural unit.

double wrench A wrench having a set of jaws at each end.

doubling course See **double course**.

doubling piece　1. A **cant strip**. 2. A **tilting fillet**. 3. See **arris fillet**.

doubly prestressed concrete　Concrete which is prestressed in two directions that are mutually perpendicular.

doubly reinforced concrete　Concrete having both **compression reinforcement** and **tension reinforcement**.

doucine　A **cyma** molding.

doughnut　See **concrete collar**.

Douglas fir, Oregon pine, red fir, yellow fir　A strong, medium-density, medium- to coarse-textured softwood; widely used for plywood and as lumber and timber in construction work.

dovecote　A structure that houses doves or pigeons; often square, hexagonal, octagonal, or round in plan and one-and-a-half or two stories high; typically topped with a finial; once popular because the birds provided a tasty source of fresh meat. The interior is honeycombed with niches in which the birds may rest. Also called a pigeon house or *pigeonnier*.

dovetail　1. A splayed **tenon**, shaped like a dove's tail, broader at its end than at its base. 2. A joint formed by such a tenon which is fitted into the recess of a corresponding mortise.

dovetail, 1

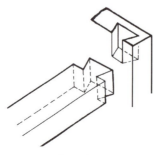

dovetail, 2

dovetail anchor slot　A slot which is nailed to a concrete form (the open end is against the wood); the ends of the slot are temporarily closed with a piece of wood or cellular foam. After the concrete is poured and the forms removed, the slot is used for anchoring masonry to the concrete.

dovetail baluster　A baluster having a dovetail base for attachment to the stair tread.

dovetail brick　A brick which has one end formed like a wedge; the other end has a recess to receive the wedge-like end of another brick.

dovetail cramp　A dovetail-shaped **cramp** for lifting masonry.

dovetail cutter　A rotary cutting tool, used to shape dovetails.

dovetail feather joint　A **double-dovetail key**.

dovetail half-lap joint, dovetail halved joint, dovetail halving joint　A joint formed by two members of equal thickness in which a **dovetail, 1** at the end of one member is fitted into a corresponding mortise in the second member; half the thickness of each is removed.

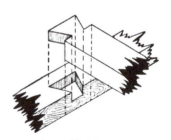

dovetail half-lap joint

dovetail hinge　Same as **butterfly hinge**.

dovetail joint　Same as **dovetail, 2**.

dovetail lath, dovetail sheeting　A type of metal lath, now called **rib lath**.

dovetail margin　Any band or strip which is dovetailed.

dovetail miter　Same as **secret dovetail**.

dovetail molding, triangular fret molding　A molding decorated with fretwork in the form of dovetails.

dovetail notch　At a corner of a log house, a notch in the shape of a **dovetail** at the end of a rectangular exterior timber; forms a strong, interlocking rigid joint when mated with an appropriately notched hewn timber at right angles to it. Compare with **half-dovetail notch**.

dovetail plane   A plane used for cutting tongues and grooves for dovetail joints.

dovetail saw   A small **tenon saw** having a very thin blade and fine teeth.

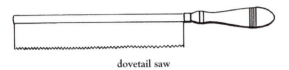

dovetail saw

dovetail sheeting   See **dovetail lath**.

dowel   A cylindrical wood or metal rod; used to secure two pieces of wood, stone, concrete, etc., by inserting it in a hole through the two members.

dowel-bar reinforcement   Short **reinforcing bars** of steel which extend approximately equally into two abutting pieces of concrete, to increase the strength of the joint.

dowel bit, spoon bit   A boring tool, the barrel of which is a half cylinder terminating in a conoidal cutting edge or radial point; used with a brace.

dowel joint   Any carpentry joint making use of dowels.

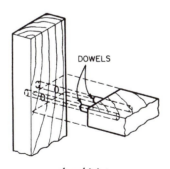

DOWELS

dowel joint

dowel lubricant   A lubricant applied to steel reinforcing bars in expansion joints to reduce bond with the concrete, so as to promote unrestrained longitudinal movement.

dowel pin   **1.** A dowel. **2.** A metal pin having a sharpened or deformed end used to fasten mortise-and-tenon joints.

dowel plate   A hardened steel plate containing holes of various diameters; used to cut dowels by driving pegs through the holes to remove excess wood.

dowel screw   A dowel having threads on both ends.

downcomer   **1.** A downspout. **2.** Any pipe in which the flow is substantially vertical.

down conductor   The vertical portion of an electric conductor used in a lightning protection system to provide a lightning current path from the air terminals to ground.

downdraft, *Brit.* **downdraught**   **1.** A downward current of air in a chimney or flue, often carrying smoke with it. **2.** A downward current of air resulting from the passage of air across a window surface, which cools it and increases its density so that it moves downward.

down-feed system   **1.** A piping arrangement for a heating (or air-conditioning or refrigeration) system, in which the heating (or cooling) fluid is circulated through supply mains that are above the levels of the heating (or cooling) units they serve. **2.** A water distribution system in which the water distribution main is located at the top of the pressure zone; the distribution-main supplies the risers that distributes water **downward** to the lowest point of the zone.

down lead   Same as **down conductor**.

downlight   A small direct **luminaire** (recessed, surface-mounted, or suspended) whose light is directed vertically downward.

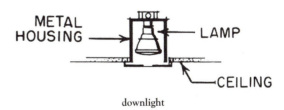

METAL HOUSING — LAMP

CEILING

downlight

downpipe   See **downspout**.

downspout, conductor, downcomer, downpipe, leader, rain leader, rainwater pipe   A vertical pipe, often of sheet metal, used to conduct water from a roof drain or gutter to the ground or cistern. (*See illustration p. 304.*)

downstage   The front part of a stage, nearest the audience.

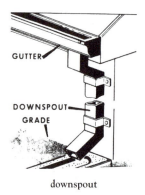

downspout

downstairs The lower floor or floors of a dwelling.

DOZ On drawings, abbr. for "dozen."

doze See **dote**.

dozer Same as **bulldozer**.

dozer shovel A **bulldozer** having a front-mounted bucket used for digging, loading, or pushing.

dozy See **doty**.

DP On drawings, abbr. for **dew point**.

dpc Abbr. for **dampproof course**.

d.p.c. brick A brick having an average water absorption not greater than 4.5% by weight.

dpm Abbr. for "dampproof membrane."

DR 1. On drawings, abbr. for **drain**. 2. Abbr. for **dressing room**. 3. Abbr. for **dining room**.

draft, *Brit.* **draught** 1. A current of air or gases, as an air current which flows through a flue, chimney, or heater; or a localized air current which results in more heat being withdrawn from a person's skin than is normally dissipated. 2. A narrow, dressed border around the face of a stone, usually about the width of a chisel edge; also called a **drafted margin** or **margin draft**.

draft bead, deep bead, sill bead, ventilating bead, window bead A small fillet or strip which is fixed to the sill of a double-hung window; permits ventilation at the meeting rail while avoiding a draft at the sill; also called a **draft stop**.

draft chisel Same as **drafting chisel**.

draft curtain See **curtain board**.

drafted margin See **draft**.

draft fillet In glazing where putty is not used, a fillet on which the glass rests.

draft hood 1. A device fitted into or on top of a flue to prevent downdrafts. 2. An open enclosure over a gas-fired furnace. Serves to create a stack effect which more readily mixes the exhaust gases with air and directs the mixture to the chimney; prevents back drafts from getting into the furnace.

drafting chisel A chisel esp. used for cutting a border or line at the edge of a stone.

drafting machine A device, used in drafting, that provides the combined functions of a T-square, scale, triangle, and protractor; it is attached to a drawing board or drawing table.

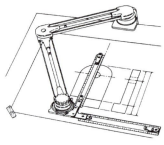

drafting machine

drafting pen A pen especially designed for use in mechanical drawing. See **drawing pen**.

drafting pen

draft regulator A device that maintains a desired draft in a gas appliance by automatically reducing the draft to the selected value.

draft stop A building material installed to prevent the movement of air, smoke, gases, and flame to other areas of the building through a large concealed passage, such as a suspended ceiling.

drag 1. A piece of sheet steel with a toothed edge along the long dimension; used to level and scratch plaster to produce a key for the next coat; a **comb**. 2. A tool consisting of a steel plate having a finely serrated edge; used to dress stone by dragging it back and forth across the surface.

dragged Said of an exposed surface over which a **drag** or **comb** has been pulled or worked to produce a textured surface.

dragging beam   Same as **dragon beam**.

dragging piece   Same as **dragon beam**.

dragline   A bucket attachment for a crane; used for removing earth by pulling the bucket toward the crane.

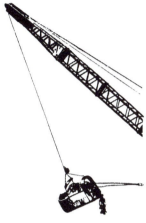

dragline

dragon beam, dragon piece   A short, horizontal piece of timber which bisects the angle formed by the **wall plate** at the corner of a wood-frame building; one end serves to receive and support the foot of a **hip rafter**; the other end is supported by a **dragon tie**.

dragon's blood   A naturally occurring deep red resin; used as a tinting material, principally in varnishes.

dragon summer   A **dragon beam** of unusually large size.

dragon tie   An **angle brace** which supports one end of a **dragon beam**.

drag shovel   Same as **backhoe**.

drain   1. Any pipe in a building-drainage system which carries waste water or water-borne waste. 2. Any pipe or channel for carrying waste water or storm water.

drainage   1. A **drainage system**, either artificial or natural. 2. The water that is drained off.

drainage envelope   The materials which completely surround a pipe, providing support and/or protection.

drainage fill   1. Lightweight concrete which is placed on roofs or floors to promote drainage. 2. A base course of granular material placed between a sub-grade and floor slab to retard the capillary rise of moisture.

drainage fitting, Durham fitting   A cast-iron, threaded fitting, used on drainage pipes; has a shoulder such as to present a smooth, continuous interior surface.

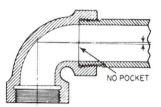

NO POCKET

drainage fitting

drainage fixture unit   Same as **fixture unit**.

drainage hole   An opening in a construction which permits unwanted water to drain away, e.g., from behind a retaining wall.

drainage piping   All or any part of the **drainpipe** of a plumbing system.

drainage system   The piping network within a structure which conveys sewage, rainwater, or other wastes from their point of origin to a point of disposal, such as a public sewer or a private treatment facility.

drainage tile   Same as **drain tile**.

drainboard, *Brit.* **draining board**   A work surface, adjacent to a sink, having a built-in pitch so that it drains into the sink.

drain cock   A small cock or faucet, at the lowest point in a tank, for draining off the liquid.

drain field   Same as **absorption field**.

drainpipe   1. Any pipe that serves as a **drain**. 2. Same as **downspout**.

drain spout   Same as **downspout**.

drain test   A **water test** or an **air test** of a drainage or vent system for leakage.

drain tile   A hollow tile, usually laid end to end as piping (with open joints) in soil in order to drain water-saturated soil, or used to permit fluid in the hollow-tile pipe to disperse into the ground (as in an absorption field).

drain trap   Same as **trap, 1**.

draped tenon   Same as **deflected tenon**.

drapery panel   1. See **linenfold**. 2. One unit of drapery.

drapery track   Same as **curtain track**.

draught   Same as **draft**.

draught excluder   A British term for **door strip**.

draught stop   Same as **fire stop**.

drawbar   A bar at the rear of a tractor to which may be fastened lines, ropes, towed machines, and other loads.

drawbolt   Same as **barrel bolt**.

drawbore   A hole in the tenon of a mortise-and-tenon joint which is not in line with the holes of the mortise; when a pin is driven through, the joint becomes tighter.

drawbridge   At the entrance of fortifications, a bridge over the moat or ditch, hinged and provided with a raising and lowering mechanism so as to hinder or permit passage.

drawbridge

draw cock   See **pet cock**.

draw curtain   A theatre curtain that moves horizontally, usually divided in the middle so that each half can be pulled to one side of the stage.

drawdown   The distance by which the **groundwater level** is lowered as a result of pumping.

drawer dovetail   See **lapped dovetail**.

drawer kicker   A wood piece which prevents a drawer from tilting downward when it is pulled out.

drawer roller   A device used to ease the sliding of a drawer open or shut, usually by means of a metal or fiber wheel rotating on a metal frame.

drawer runner, drawer slip   In drawer framing, one of a pair of strips on which the drawer slides.

drawer slide   A mechanism employing guides and rollers that support a drawer and permit its easy operation.

drawer stop   A block which stops the inward movement of a drawer when it has reached its proper position.

drawing room   A formal reception room, usually in a prominent location of a large home, mansion, or manor house.

drawings   The portion of the **contract documents** showing in graphic or pictorial form the design, location, and dimensions of the elements of a **project**.

draw-in system   In electric wiring, a system using conductors installed in conduits, ducts, raceways, and boxes, thereby permitting removal and replacement of any conductor without disturbing any part of the building structure or finish.

drawknife, drawshave   A woodworking tool consisting of a blade with a handle at each end; the tool is drawn over the surface toward the user.

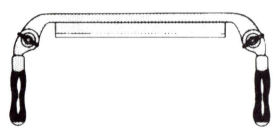

drawknife

drawn finish   A smooth, bright finish on metal tubing, wire, rod, bar, and strip; obtained by drawing the metal through a die.

drawn glass, flat-drawn glass, flat-drawn sheet glass   Sheet glass fabricated by the continuous drawing of the molten glass from a furnace; has fire-finished surfaces, not perfectly flat and parallel, resulting in some distortion.

drawn product   A product formed by pulling material through one or more dies.

drawn wire   Wire brought to final dimensions by being drawn through one or more dies.

drawshave   A **drawknife**.

dredge   **1.** A floating excavator for removing earth or rock from under water. Usually accomplished by clamshell, power shovel, or cutterhead combined with a suction line. **2.** To remove soil from an area under water.

drencher system   A **fire-protection sprinkler system** which provides a water spray to protect the exterior of a building against fire.

dress circle   In an opera house, theatre, or the like, a tier of seats above the main seating area—usually the first or lowest.

dressed   Descriptive of brick, lumber, or stone which has been prepared, shaped, or finished by cutting, planing, rubbing, or sanding one or more of its faces.

dressed and matched boards, D and M boards, dressed and matched lumber, planed matchboards, tongue-and-groove boards   Boards or lumber that has been planed smooth; cut so that a tongue along one edge fits into a groove cut along the edge of the adjacent piece.

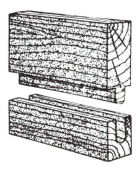

dressed and matched boards

dressed lumber, dressed stuff, surfaced lumber   Lumber having one or more of its faces planed smooth.

dressed size   The dimensions of a timber after sawing and planing; usually about ⅜ in. (0.95 cm) in thickness or ½ in. (1.27 cm) in width less than the nominal size.

dressed stone   Stone that has been worked to desired shape; the faces to be exposed are smooth; usually ready for installation.

dressed stuff   See **dressed lumber**.

dressed timber   See **dressed lumber**.

dresser   A plumber's tool used to flatten sheet lead and straighten lead pipe.

dresser coupling   A clamp-style **coupling** for unthreaded pipe.

dresser joint   A type of **Normandy joint**.

dressing, dressings   **1.** Projecting ornamental moldings and carved decorations of all kinds. **2.** Masonry or molding of better quality than the facing brick; used around openings or at corners of buildings; often made of gauged brick. **3.** Smoothing a stone surface. **4. Bossing**.

dressing compound, bonding compound   A hot- or cold-applied bituminous liquid used to coat exposed surfaces of roofing felt.

dressing room   A room used for changing costumes and applying makeup in a theatre, opera house, and the like.

dress plate   Same as **cover plate**.

DRG   On drawings, abbr. for "drawing."

drier   **1.** An additive which is mixed with paints and varnishes to speed their drying by absorbing oxygen from the air. **2.** See **soluble drier**. **3.** A device containing a desiccant, placed in a refrigerant circuit; used to collect and hold within the desiccant all water in the system in excess of the amount which can be tolerated in the circulating refrigerant.

drier scum   See **scum**.

drier white   Superficial discoloration of clayware during drying; usually caused by adherence of soluble salts to the surface of the ware.

drift   **1.** The lateral deflection of a building, due to wind or other loads. **2.** In a water spray device, the entrained unevaporated water carried from the device by air movement through it. **3.** See **driftpin, 2**. **4.** A deposit of loose materials such as gravel, rock fragments, clay and other soils which have been driven together by water, wind, or ice.

driftbolt   **1.** A short rod or square bar driven into holes bored in timber, for attaching adjacent sticks to each other or to piles; varies from 1 to 2 ft (0.3 to 0.6 m) in length; often provided with a head or with a sharpened end; also called a **drift**, or **driftpin**. **2.** A steel bolt used to drive out other bolts.

drifter A type of pneumatic, percussive rock drill.

drift index 1. The ratio of the lateral deflection of a building to its height. 2. The ratio of the lateral deflection of a story of a building to the height per story.

drift limitation See **drift index**.

driftpin 1. A square or round metal rod with no threads, driven into an undersized, prebored hole as a substitute for a bolt, screw, or other fastener. 2. A short, tapered rod for enlarging rivet holes or bringing them into line; also called a **drift**. 3. A **driftbolt**. 4. A tapered round rod used to align holes in two or more pieces of metal.

driftpin

drift plug 1. A hardwood cylindrical plug which is driven through a soft-metal pipe to straighten it. 2. A conical plug driven into one end of a soft-metal pipe to produce a flare.

drift punch A punch with long taper and blunt end for aligning holes.

drift punch

drill 1. A hand- or motor-driven rotary tool used with a **bit** for boring holes in a material. 2. A hand-held tool used to bore a hole in a material by striking one end with a series of blows. 3. A machine for boring holes in the ground or in rock, e.g., in obtaining rock-core samples.

drill bit Same as **bit, 1**.

drilled-in caisson A composite foundation column; consists of a heavy wall pipe which is concrete-filled; the upper end is locked into the structure, and the lower end is secured in a socket in rock.

drilled pier, drilled pile A concrete pier or pile that is cast in place in a hole that has been bored in soil or rock.

drilled pile Same as **augered pile**.

drill press A drilling machine mounted in a stand; a handle is used to lower the drill (which rotates about a vertical axis) into the work.

drinking fountain A fixture consisting of a shallow basin, together with a water jet, designed to provide potable water for human consumption.

drinking-water cooler A factory-made assembly containing a small refrigeration system and having the primary functions of cooling potable water and dispensing such water.

drip, headmold, hoodmold, label, throating, weather molding 1. The outermost projecting molding around the top of a door or window, to discharge rainwater. 2. A **throat, 2**. 3. A pipe, or a steam trap and a pipe considered as a unit, which conducts condensation from the steam side of a piping system to the water or return side of the system. 4. A container that is typically installed at a low point in a gas piping system to collect condensate (i.e., liquids that may form within the gas system).

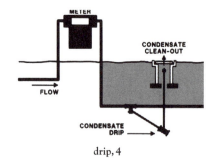
drip, 4

drip cap A horizontal molding, fixed to a door or window frame to divert the water from the top rail, causing it to drip beyond the outside of the frame.

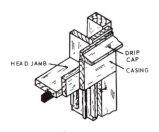
drip cap

drip channel A **throat, 2**.

drip course Same as **dripstone course**.

drip edge A strip which extends beyond other parts of a roof and which directs rainwater off the roof.

drip line An imaginary line described on the ground by the outer branch tips of a plant.

drip mold, drip molding Any molding so formed and located as to act as a **drip**.

drippage **1.** An accumulation of liquid by dripping. **2.** A dripping of water from the gutters or eaves of a house.

dripping eaves Sloping eaves which project beyond a wall and are not provided with a gutter so that water on the roof falls directly to the ground.

drip sink, lead safe A shallow **sink** set near floor level to receive the drip from a faucet or the like.

dripstone A **drip cap** made of stone.

dripstone course A continuous horizontal drip molding on a masonry wall.

dripstone

driptight Said of an enclosure constructed so that drops of liquid striking the enclosure (from a specified range of angles) cannot enter it.

drive band In pile driving, a steel band which encircles the head of a timber pile to prevent it from splitting when being driven.

drive cap A steel attachment placed over the top end of a **pile** to prevent damage while it is driven in the ground.

drive band

drive-in A retail business, bank, or motion-picture theatre, designed to permit its patrons to receive services while they remain in their automobiles.

driven pile Any **pile**, such as a precast pile, which is driven into position at its final position at the site.

driven well A well constructed by driving a pipe into the ground; usually fitted with a **well point** and screen.

drivepipe A pipe, one end of which is sharpened for driving it into the ground; used to obtain a sample in situ, to reach water, etc.

drive point Same as **well point**.

drivescrew, screw nail A type of metal fastener; a helically threaded nail, driven with a hammer; has a higher withdrawal resistance than a nail with a plain shank; some types may be removed with a screwdriver.

drive shoe A reinforcement placed at the bottom of a **pile** to prevent damage to the pile during driving.

driveway A private way or road, which is primarily for use by automobiles.

driving band See **drive band**.

driving machine The power unit which applies the necessary energy to raise and lower an elevator or dumbwaiter car or to drive an escalator, moving walk, or the like.

driving resistance The number of blows of a pile-driving hammer which are required to advance the point of a pile a specified distance into the subsoil.

drn Abbr. for **drain** or **drainage**.

dromos The long, deep entrance passageway to an ancient Egyptian tomb or a Mycenaean beehive tomb. (*See illustration p. 310.*)

309

droop

dromos

droop   The deviation from a preset value of a controlled liquid level, temperature, variable pressure, or differential pressure (at minimum controllable flow) when the flow through a regulator is gradually increased from its minimum controllable flow to its rated capacity.

drop   **1.** Any one of the guttae under the mutules or triglyphs of a Doric entablature. **2.** In a cabinet lock, the vertical dimension from the finished edge of the lock to the center of the cylinder or tube. **3.** In air conditioning, the vertical distance that a horizontally projected airstream falls from its original elevation when leaving an outlet, measured at the end of the **throw**. **4.** Same as **drop curtain**. **5.** Same as **drop panel**. **6.** Of a stair, a fitting used to close the bottom end of a tubular newel. **7.** Same as **pendant, 2**; also see **corner drop**. **8.** Same as **turned drop**.

drop apron   A strip of metal which is fixed vertically downward at eaves and gutters of a flexible-metal roof; acts as a **drip**.

drop arch   A pointed arch which is struck from two centers that are nearer together than the width of the arch, so that the radii are less than the span; a **depressed arch**.

drop black   See **animal black**.

drop bottom-seal   See **automatic door bottom**.

drop box   An electric outlet box hung from above, as in a theatre stagehouse where it is fed by a cable from the overhead **gridiron**.

drop ceiling   See **dropped ceiling**.

drop chute   A device used to confine or to direct the flow of a falling stream of concrete; may be articulated or may be fabricated of heavy rubberized canvas.

drop cloth   A large sheet of cloth, paper, or plastic which is spread over a floor, furniture, etc., as a protection against paint drippings and splatter.

drop cord   An electric-light cord suspended and energized from a ceiling outlet.

drop curtain   On the theatre stage, any curtain that moves up and down, rather than from side to side.

drop elbow   A pipe **elbow, 1** having lugs on the sides for attaching it to a support.

drop ell   Same as **drop elbow**.

drop escutcheon   An **escutcheon** having a pivoted plate which covers a keyhole.

drop hammer   A heavy weight for driving a **pile** into the ground; dropped by gravity along a set of guide rails onto the head of the pile.

drop handle   A door handle that hangs vertically when not in use; often fabricated of brass or wrought iron.

drop handle

drop-head window   A **double-hung window** whose lower sash can drop through the window sill into a pocket below the sill.

drop-in beam   A simple beam, usually supported by cantilever arms, with joints so placed that it can be installed by lowering it into position.

drop key plate   A **key plate** having a cover which swings over the key hole to protect it.

droplight   **1.** An electric lamp suspended from the ceiling on a flexible cord. **2.** An electric lamp, sometimes protected by a wire guard, etc., on the end of a flexible cord; used as a portable work light.

drop molding   A panel molding recessed below the surface of the surrounding styles and rails.

drop ornament   A tear-shaped pendant, or a representation thereof.

drop-out ceiling   A suspended ceiling system having **listed** translucent or opaque, heat-sensitive panels; when subject to heat, these panels drop from the suspension system, thereby exposing the sprinkler system installed above it.

drop panel   On the lower side of a flat concrete slab, the thickened portion which surrounds a column, column capital, or bracket.

drop panel form   A concrete **form** which is so erected as to provide the necessary support, shape, and finish for a drop panel.

dropped ceiling, drop ceiling   **1.** A suspended ceiling. **2.** See **soffit**.

dropped girder   A **girder** which is dropped below the floor joists and supports them.

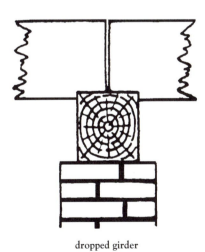

dropped girder

dropped girt, dropped girth   A **girt** which is dropped below the floor joists and supports them.

dropped roof   The roof of an addition to a house, usually a flat surface of single pitch with its upper edge somewhat below the eaves of the house.

drop-point slating   See **diagonal slating**.

drop ring   A ring which is used as a handle to operate a lock or latch; the ring remains in a dropped position when not in use, but it may be raised and pivoted about the spindle to operate the lock.

drop siding, novelty siding, rustic siding   An exterior wall cladding of wooden boards (or strips of other material such as aluminum or vinyl), which are tongued and grooved or rabbeted and overlapped so that the lower edge of each board interlocks with a groove in the board immediately below it.

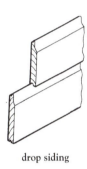

drop siding

drop tee   A **pipe tee** having lugs in the sides by which it can be attached to a support.

drop tracery   Tracery hanging from the soffit of an arch.

drop vent   In plumbing, a special individual **vent** which connects to a drain or vent pipe at a point below the fixture served.

drop window   A vertically sliding window in which the sash can descend into an opening below the sill so that the entire window is open for ventilation.

drop wire   The electric conductor extending from an outdoor pole to a building.

drove   A mason's chisel having a blade from 2 to 4 in. (5 to 10 cm) broad; a **boaster**.

drove chisel   Same as **boaster**.

drove work   Stone which has been dressed with a **drove**; same as **boasted work**.

drum   **1.** One of the cylinders of stone which form a column. **2.** A round or polygonal wall

drum hoist

drum, 1

below a dome, often pierced with windows. **3.** The bell of Composite or Corinthian capitals.

drum hoist   Same as **hoist, 2.**

drum paneling   A form of door construction in which the panels are flush on both sides and covered with cloth or leather.

drum trap   In plumbing, a cylindrical trap, with its axis in a vertical direction, having a cover plate which may be unscrewed for access; commonly used on the drainpipe from a bathtub or under a bathroom floor.

drum trap

drunken saw, wobble saw   A **circular saw** having a blade which is set so that it does not rotate in one plane; used to cut a groove or kerf.

drwl   Abbr. for **dry wall.**

dry area   A covered area, below grade, between a basement wall and a retaining wall beyond it; its function is to keep the basement wall dry.

dry-batch weight   The weight of the materials, excluding water, used to make a batch of concrete.

dry-bond adhesive   See **contact adhesive.**

dry-bulb temperature   The air temperature indicated by a **dry-bulb thermometer** after correction for the effects of **radiation.**

dry-bulb thermometer   **1.** An ordinary thermometer. **2.** The one of two thermometers in a **psychrometer** which has an unmoistened bulb.

dry concrete   Concrete having a low proportion of water so that the plastic mixture is relatively stiff; suitable for use in dry locations; esp. advantageous where large masses are poured and compacted and on sloping surfaces.

dry construction   The use of dry materials such as gypsum board, plywood, or wallboard in construction, without the application of plaster or mortar.

dry course   The first ply of built-up roofing laid directly over insulation or on a structural deck without the application of bitumen.

dry density   The density of soil, or the like, after it has been heated at a temperature of 221°F (105°C) to a dry condition.

dryer   See **drier.**

dry filter   A filter for cleaning air which removes dirt by straining or filtering the air through various types of screens, fiberglass, or the like.

dry gas   Gas having a moisture and hydrocarbon dew point below any normal temperature to which the gas piping will be exposed.

dry glazing   **1.** Any method of securing glass in a frame by use of a dry, preformed resilient gasket, without the use of a glazing compound. **2.** **Patent glazing.**

dry hydrate   A finely ground hydrated lime, made from calcium or from dolomitic limestone.

drying   The physical change of a liquid paint or varnish film which results in a hard surface, as a result of the loss of solvent, or a chemical reaction, or a combination of both. Also see **air drying, forced drying.**

drying agent   See **soluble drier.**

drying creep   **Creep** that results from drying.

drying inhibitor   A substance added to paints and varnishes to prevent too rapid drying or skin drying; used to promote a high gloss and to avoid a wrinkled film.

drying oil, paint oil   A vegetable oil which oxidizes easily on exposure to air and forms a hard, dry film; esp. useful in paints.

drying shrinkage   The contraction of plaster, cement paste, mortar, or concrete caused by loss of moisture.

dry joint A joint without mortar.

dry kiln An oven for drying and seasoning cut lumber.

dry laid Said of masonry that has been laid without the use of mortar.

dry lining The surfacing a wall with **gypsum lath**, without the application of wet plaster.

dry masonry Masonry laid without mortar.

dry mix A mixture of mortar or of concrete which contains little water in relation to its other components.

dry mixing Blending of solid materials for mortar or concrete prior to adding the mixing water.

dry-mix shotcrete **Shotcrete** which is conveyed pneumatically; most of the mixing water is added at the nozzle.

dry mortar A mortar whose constituents are so proportioned that it is markedly stiffer than usual, yet with sufficient water for hydration.

dryout A condition in gypsum plaster caused by water evaporating out of the plaster before it sets. Such plaster is soft, powdery, and usually light in color.

dry-pack To ram forcibly a slightly moist portland cement-aggregate mixture into a confined area, as into the space between the top of concrete pier underpinning and the bottom of the building being underpinned. Here the dry-pack serves as a low-shrinkage filler material that transmits the load of the building to the underpinning.

dry-packed concrete A concrete mixture sufficiently dry to be consolidated only by heavy ramming.

dry partition A partition erected and finished without the application of wet plaster.

dry-pipe sprinkler system **1.** A complete **fire-protection sprinkler system** with sprinkler heads in which there is no water unless the system is actuated (either automatically or manually) in case of fire; esp. used in areas subject to freezing temperatures, or to avoid the hazards of leaking or bursting pipes. **2.** A fire **sprinkler system** containing a network of pipes filled with air or nitrogen under pressure and equipped with an automatic sprinklers; when the sprinklers open, the air or nitrogen is released, thereby opening a valve (called a "dry-pipe valve") which permits water to enter the pipes and to flow out the opened sprinklers.

dry-pipe valve The control valve for a **dry-pipe sprinkler system** which activates the system; must be in a location where it is protected against mechanical injury and freezing.

dry-powder fire extinguisher One that discharges a fine, dry powder (usually sodium bicarbonate, potassium bicarbonate, or ammonium phosphate) by the pressure of a gas stored in the same container as the powder; generally suitable for class-B and class-C fires.

dry press A mechanical press for forming brick, cast stone, or other ceramic articles from slightly moistened granular mixtures; pressure is applied to both top and bottom of the die box.

dry-press brick Brick formed in molds under high pressures from relatively dry clay (5 to 7% moisture content).

dry-process enameling A porcelain enameling process in which the metal article is heated to a temperature above the maturing temperature of the coating; then the coating materials are applied to the hot metal, in the form of a dry powder, and fired.

dry return In a steam heating system, a return pipe which carries both water of condensation and air.

dry riser inlet Same as **fire department connection**.

dry riser system Same as **dry standpipe system**.

dry rising main British term for **dry standpipe**.

dry-rodded volume The volume which an aggregate occupies when compacted dry under the standardized conditions used in measuring unit weight of aggregate.

dry-rodded weight The weight per unit volume of an aggregate when compacted dry under standardized conditions.

dry rodding In measuring the weight per unit volume of coarse aggregates, the process of compacting dry material in a calibrated container by **rodding** under standardized conditions.

dry rot The decay of seasoned wood caused by fungi of a type capable of carrying water into the wood they infest.

dry rubble construction   Masonry of rubble which is laid without mortar.

dry saturated steam, dry steam   Steam containing no water in suspension.

dry shake   See **monolithic surface treatment**.

dry sheet   A nonbituminous felt or a light roofing paper applied between the roof-deck and the roofing material to prevent adherence of the roofing to the roof-deck and to isolate the roofing from movements of the roof-deck.

dry sprinkler   Same as **dry-pipe sprinkler system**.

dry sprinkler system   See **dry-pipe sprinkler system**.

dry-stacked surface-bonded wall   A wall built of a combination of two or more masonry units of different material bonded together, one forming the backup and the other the facing of the combination.

dry standpipe   A **standpipe** that is not normally filled with water but to which water can be supplied (through a **fire department connection**) in the event of fire.

dry standpipe system   A **standpipe system** that is normally dry.

dry steam   See **dry saturated steam**.

dry stock   See **dry wood**.

dry stone wall   A wall composed of stones not cemented with mortar.

dry strength   The strength of an adhesive joint determined immediately after drying under specified conditions, or after a period of conditioning in the standard laboratory atmosphere.

dry-tamp process   The placing of concrete or mortar by hammering or ramming a relatively dry mix into place.

dry topping   See **monolithic surface treatment**.

dry-type transformer   A transformer whose core and coils are not immersed in an insulating oil.

dry vent   A **vent** which carries neither water nor waterborne wastes.

dry-volume measurement   Measurement of the ingredients of grout, mortar, or concrete by their bulk volume.

dry wall   1. An interior wall, constructed with a **dry-wall finish** material such as gypsum board or plywood; also see **dry construction**. 2. In masonry construction, a self-supporting rubble or ashlar wall built without mortar.

dry-wall construction   Same as **dry construction**.

dry-wall finish   An interior covering material such as gypsum board or plywood, which is usually applied in large sheets or panels; does not require a water additive to apply.

dry-wall frame   A type of knocked-down door-frame; designed for installation in a wall which is constructed with studs and a dry sheet facing material (such as gypsum board) after the wall is erected.

dry wall partition   A partition constructed without the application of wet plaster.

dry weight   The dry density of a material multiplied by its volume.

dry well   1. A covered pit either with open-jointed lining or filled with coarse aggregate through which drainage from roofs, basement floors, foundation drain tiles, or areaways may seep or leach into the surrounding soil. 2. Same as **cesspool**. 3. An **absorbing well**.

dry wood   1. (U.S.A.) Wood dried to a moisture content of from 15 to 19%. 2. (Brit.) Wood dried to a moisture content of from 15 to 23%.

DS   On drawings, abbr. for **downspout**.

D.S., D/S, D/Sdg   Abbr. for **drop siding**.

DSGN   On drawings, abbr. for "design."

DT   On drawings, abbr. for **drum trap**.

DT&G   Abbr. for "double tongue and groove."

DU   On drawings, abbr. for **disposal unit**.

dual duct   A duct, having a continuous internal divider, to provide two individual raceways for installation of two separate electric wiring systems (such as one for electric power and one for a sound system).

dual-duct system   An air-conditioning system in which two supply ducts run to each space being conditioned, one for cold air, the other for warm air; at each individually controlled space, air from the two ducts is blended in a sheet-metal box (called a "mixing box") and then supplied to the conditioned space.

dual-duct terminal unit   Same as "mixing box"; see **dual-duct system**.

dual-element fuse   A **fuse** which has current-responsive elements of two different fusing characteristics in series.

dual-fiber cable **Optical fiber cable** composed of two single-fiber cables enclosed in an extruded plastic overjacket; may have a rip cord for peeling back the overjacket to access the fibers.

dual-fuel system A heating system in which the boiler can burn either of two fuels, usually oil and gas in the U.S.A.; usually one is the primary fuel and the other is used for standby purposes.

dual glazing Same as **double glazing**.

dual-head nail Same as **double-headed nail**.

dual-pitched roof A roof having a double slope on both sides of a central ridge; for example, a **gambrel roof**.

dual-temperature system A hot water system that supplies hot water at two different temperatures.

dual vent, common vent, unit vent In plumbing, a single **vent, 1** connected at the junction of two fixture drains, which serves as a vent for both.

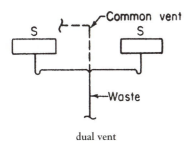

dual vent

dub To strike, cut, rub, or dress so as to make smooth, or of an equal surface.

dubbing out, dubbing **1.** Filling in hollow and irregular surfaces and leveling walls with plaster before regular plasterwork. **2.** Forming, very roughly, a plaster cornice, before the final plaster coat is applied.

duck See **mouse**.

duckboard **1.** A cat ladder. **2.** A wooden walkway across muddy ground, a wet floor, etc.

duckfoot bend Same as **rest bend**.

duck tape A tape of heavy cotton or synthetic fabric which is impregnated with a sealing compound, such as asphalt or an elastomer.

duct **1.** See **air duct**. **2.** In electric systems, a metallic or nonmetallic tube, (usually circular, oval, rectangular, or octagonal) for housing wires or cables; may be underground or embedded in concrete floor slabs.

duct furnace A **unit heater** having a burner and heat exchanger, but not a fan; located in a **duct system** which is provided with a fan for moving the air.

ductile Capable of being stretched or deformed without fracturing.

ductile-iron pipe A pipe that is fabricated of a cast-iron alloy in which graphite replaces the carbon that is present in **cast-iron**; provides the same advantages as cast-iron pipe along with the added advantage of a higher external load-bearing capacity; not as brittle as cast-iron pipe (thus permitting rougher handling) but higher in cost.

ductility index The ratio of the total deformation at maximum load to the elastic limit deformation.

duct lining A fiberglass blanket material used as a lining inside a sheet-metal duct of an air-conditioning system; reduces noise which is transmitted along the duct and provides thermal insulation.

duct sealing compound A resilient substance used to seal the ends of a cable duct or conduit.

duct sheet A coiled or flat sheet of a gauge width and thickness suitable for use in **ductwork**.

duct silencer Same as **sound attenuator**.

duct system A series of ducts and associated elbows, connectors, dampers, and air outlets used to convey air from a fan to the spaces served.

ductwork The ducts in a heating, ventilating, or air-conditioning system.

due care The standard of reasonable care, skill, ability, and judgment which, if not met, constitutes **negligence**; such a standard may be imposed by contract or by operation of law in the absence of a contract. This term implies the performance of duties and services by a professional which is consistent with the level of performance provided by reputable professionals in the same geographical area at the same period of time.

dugout A primitive shelter, often consisting of an excavation in a bank of sloping terrain that is roofed with bark laid over a pole framework, then covered with sod; also see **half-dugout**.

dug well A well for water, constructed by excavating a large-diameter shaft and installing a casing.

dumbbell tenement A multiple-dwelling substandard apartment building; commonly three to five stories high, containing relatively long narrow apartments within it; has windows only at the front and rear of each apartment. Shafts located on one or both sides of the apartment provide air and a little light in the rooms that do not face the front or rear of the building. The floor plan of each floor resembles the outline of a dumbbell. Also called a **railroad flat**.

dumbwaiter A hoisting and lowering mechanism within a building equipped with a relatively small car which moves in a vertical direction (in guides); used exclusively for carrying materials.

dummy cylinder For a door lock, a mock cylinder which has no operating mechanism.

dummy joint Same as **groove joint**.

dumped fill Excavated material, usually end-dumped from trucks, with no special effort made to spread or compact it.

dumpling A large unexcavated mass, usually at the center of an excavated area, which is left undisturbed; may be removed when the work nears completion.

dump truck Any type of truck whose body can be tilted to discharge its load.

dumpy level A surveying instrument used in the direct measurement of differences of elevation; consists of a telescope and a **spirit level** (which is parallel to the telescope and mounted below it); the telescope is permanently attached to leveling base.

dungeon 1. The principal and strongest tower of a castle; the **keep**. 2. A dim chamber in a medieval castle, usually at the base of the keep.

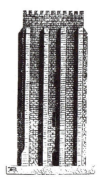

dungeon, 1

dunnage Members which form a structural support for a cooling tower, or the like, but which are not part of the building structure.

dunter machine See **surfacer, 3**.

duomo A cathedral; properly, an Italian cathedral.

duomo at Brescia, shown in section

DUP On drawings, abbr. for "duplicate."

duplex 1. A **duplex apartment**. 2. A **duplex house**.

duplex apartment A separate dwelling in an apartment building, having rooms on two levels, with self-contained vertical circulation.

duplex burner In a heating system, a gas burner having two sections which can either burn together at full load or be used singly for reduced heating.

duplex cable An electric cable consisting of two individually insulated conductors which are twisted together.

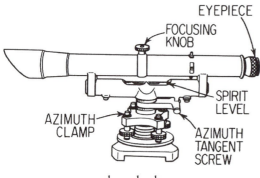

EYEPIECE
FOCUSING KNOB
SPIRIT LEVEL
AZIMUTH CLAMP
AZIMUTH TANGENT SCREW

dumpy level

duplex-head nail Same as **double-headed nail**.

duplex house, two-family house A house having quarters, with separate entrances, for two families; usually a two-story house with a separate apartment on each floor.

duplex outlet See **duplex receptacle**.

duplex receptacle In electric wiring, two **receptacles**, combined as a single unit, for installation in an **outlet box**.

duplex receptacle

durability The ability of a material, component, assembly, or building to resist weathering action, chemical attack, abrasion, and other conditions of service.

durability factor A measure of the change (with time) in the property of a material as a result of exposure to an influence which has the potential of causing deterioration; usually expressed as a percentage of the property before exposure.

duraluminum An alloy containing principally aluminum, approximately 4% copper, 0.2 to 0.75% magnesium, and 0.4 to 1% manganese; individual manufacturers may include small amounts of silicon and iron.

duramen See **heartwood**.

durbar In India, an audience hall in the palace of a prince.

Durham fitting See **drainage fitting**.

Durham system A soil or waste system where all piping is of threaded pipe, tube, or other such rigid construction, using recessed **drainage fittings**.

durn A vertical member on each side of a door, usually formed of a solid timber.

durometer An instrument for measuring the degree of hardness of a material; also see **shore hardness**.

dust board 1. A panel placed above a built-up cornice to prevent the entry of dust. 2. A paneled division between wooden drawers.

dust collector An accessory device used to prevent dust, which a tool or machine produces, from escaping into the surrounding air; suction forces the dust-laden air into a bag or chamber, where it is collected.

dust cover box Same as **plaster guard**.

dustfree Descriptive of the stage in the drying of a paint or varnish film at which dust will no longer stick to the surface.

dust-free time The time required for a freshly applied paint or compound to form a skin on its surface so that dust will not adhere to it.

dusting The development of a powdered material at the surface of hardened concrete.

dust-laying oil Oil of sufficiently low viscosity to be applied without preheating; may be a slow-curing asphaltic product or a nonvolatile petroleum distillate containing no asphalt; applied over unpaved surfaces.

dustproof So constructed or protected that the accumulation of dust will not interfere with successful operation.

dustproof strike A **strike plate** equipped with a spring plunger that completely fills the bolt hole when the bolt of the lock is not projected into it.

dust-tight Descriptive of an enclosure which is so constructed (with gaskets, etc.) as to prevent the entry of dust.

Dutch arch, French arch A flat arch in brick; most of the bricks slope outward from the middle of the arch (at the same angle on both sides of the centerline) and do not have radial joints. Properly not an arch. Same as **flat arch**.

Dutch barn 1. A distinctive type of front-gabled barn of **curtain wall, 1** construction, erected by early Dutch settlers in America; approximately square in plan; built on stone piers with a steeply pitched roof. Often sheathed with overlapping planks to shed water readily; the outer planks temporarily removable for maintenance; typically had a small **pent roof** directly over the entryway for wagons; **owl holes** near the peaks of the gables for ventilation and for access to the barn for mice-eating birds. 2. Same as **bank barn**. 3. Same as **hay barrack**.

Dutch bond 1. Same as **English cross bond**. 2. Same as **Flemish bond**.

Dutch brick

Dutch brick   A hard yellow brick often used in the interior of Dutch Colonial houses; commonly laid in the floor of the fireplace hearth that extended into the room. Occasionally, this term refers to a brick having a thickness of only about 1½ inches (3.8 cm). Also see **klinkart**.

Dutch Colonial architecture   A broad term describing the architecture prevalent in the Dutch-settled parts of America during the early part of the 17th century. The earliest houses were simple one-story, single-room permanent dwellings.

In *rural areas*, the design of houses depended primarily on available building materials. Where stone was abundant, houses were built with thick stone walls; where suitable clay was available, houses were built of brick, usually laid in a Flemish bond pattern; where timber was plentiful, the houses were of wood construction with **siding** of wide weatherboarding. Common characteristics included: a roof covering of wood shingles or tiles; steeply pitched gables with parapets; **Dutch gambrel roofs** with flared eaves having a considerable overhang; straight-line gables; a chimney located in a thick exterior wall at a gable end or gambrel end of the house; casement windows with small panes and battened shutters; a **Dutch door;** heavy plank floors, **bake ovens**.

In *urban areas* such as New Amsterdam, houses were typically two and a half or three and a half stories high, although those in which the owners also conducted a business on the ground floor and lived in the floors above were four or five stories high. Common characteristics included: thick exterior walls usually having a rough timber structure, faced with a brick veneer laid in a Flemish bond pattern with the facing secured to the timber framing by decorative wrought-iron **anchors**; where wood was plentiful, wide weatherboarding used as **siding** instead of brick facing; stone walls in regions where stone was commonly available; a parapeted gable-end wall often facing the street; typically, **corbie gables** or steeply pitched **straight-line gables**; often, a gambrel roof with flared eaves; usually, a brick chimney within the exterior walls, topped with a chimney cap; casement windows with small glass panes in **cames**; battened shutters (later replaced by double-hung windows); a **Dutch door** or paneled double door, often with a **transom light** above; usually an exterior **stoop** in front of the door.

Dutch Colonial Revival   Revival architecture from the late 19th century onward, loosely based on the Dutch Colonial prototypes described previously, including a gambrel roof, **flared eaves**, **Dutch doors**, and multipaned double-hung windows. Revival houses often retain many of the characteristics of their prototypes, but differ significantly as a result of modern additions such as a gambrel roof with dormers, wood shutters having decorative designs cut through the shutters, and **cross gambrels**.

Dutch diaper bond   Same as **English cross bond**.

Dutch door   A door consisting of two separate leaves, one above the other; the leaves may operate independently or together.

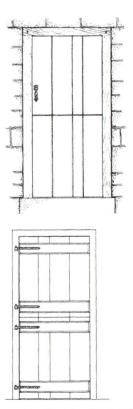

Dutch door: exterior elevation; interior elevation

Dutch door bolt A device which fastens together the upper and lower leaves of a Dutch door so that they open and close as a single unit.

Dutch gable **1.** Same as **Flemish gable**. **2.** A corbie **gable**.

Dutch gambrel roof A type of gambrel roof that has two flat surfaces on each side of the ridge of the roof. The initial downward slope from the roof ridge is an angle of about 22 degrees, then steepens to an angle of about 45 degrees. Near the lower end, the pitch is much less and the roof has **flared eaves**. Compare with **English gambrel roof, New England gambrel roof, Swedish gambrel roof**.

Dutch lap A method of applying shingles, slates, etc.; each shingle overlaps one below and one to the side.

Dutch lap

Dutch light A removable glazed sash, used in greenhouses.

dutchman **1.** A small piece or wedge inserted as filler to stop an opening. **2.** A small piece of material used to cover a defect, to hide a badly made joint, etc. **3.** A short lead nipple used to join two pipes which are otherwise not long enough to be joined.

Dutch method of application A method of applying rectangular roofing shingles which provides a lap at the top and one side, thereby forming a square or rectangular pattern.

Dutch oven Same as **bake oven**.

Dutch roof Occasionally, a synonym for a **Dutch gambrel roof**.

Dutch shutter A **shutter, 2** whose upper and lower sections can be opened and closed independently of each other.

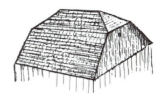

Dutch slice-hip roof

Dutch slice-hip roof A **Dutch gambrel roof** in which each end has been clipped off, as in a **jerkinhead** roof.

Dutch tile A flat, square, decorative tile from Holland often used on the faces of fireplaces; different colors were once available, but Delft blue tiles were probably the most popular.

DVTL On drawings, abbr. for **dovetail**.

dwang **1.** A crowbar or similar tool. **2.** A strut inserted between timbers to stiffen them.

dwarf door A door whose height is somewhat less than normal.

dwarf gallery A passage on the external surface of a wall screened by a small-scale arcade.

dwarf partition A partition which does not extend to full ceiling height.

dwarf rafter Same as **jack rafter**.

dwarf wainscoting Wainscot that is restricted to the lower part of a wall.

dwarf wall **1.** A wall of less height than a story of a building. **2.** A wall which supports the sleeper joists under the lowest floor of a building.

dwelling A building designed or used as the living quarters for one or more families.

dwelling unit One or more rooms in a building designed as living accommodations for one or more families.

dwg, DWG Abbr. for "drawing."

D-window **1.** Same as **semicircular fanlight**. **2.** A **semicircular window, 2**.

DWV Abbr. for "drainage, waste, and vent."

DWV tubing See **type-DWV tubing**.

dye A coloring material or compound that imparts color throughout a material by penetration.

dyke See **dike**.

Dymaxion House An unconventional lightweight house developed and patented in 1928 by

R. Buckminster Fuller (1895–1983); originally called the *4-D house,* and intended as a prefabricated unit. Octagonal or circular in plan, this experimental house was supported by a massive central shaft that housed all building services, such as electrical and plumbing systems.

dynamic analysis   The analysis of a structural system as a function of displacement under transient loading conditions.

dynamic balancing   See **balancing**.

dynamic load   Any load which is nonstatic, such as a wind load or a moving live load.

dynamic loading   Loading by a piece of machinery or equipment which imposes a load in addition to its static load, as a result of its vibration or movement.

dynamic modulus of elasticity   The modulus of elasticity of a test specimen which is computed from physical characteristics of the specimen (size, weight, and shape) and from its fundamental frequency of vibration.

dynamic penetration test   A **penetration test** in which penetration into the soil results from the application of a series of blows on a testing device.

dynamic pile formula   Any of several formulas by which the bearing capacity of a driven **pile** can be calculated from the energy of the pile hammer and the penetration of the pile under each blow.

dynamic resistance   The resistance of a pile (or the like) to blows from a pile hammer, expressed in blows per unit depth of penetration.

dynamics   That part of the science of mechanics which treats the motion of bodies and the action of forces in producing or changing their motion.

dyostyle   Same as **distyle**.

E

E   Symbol for "90° elbow."

E/A   Abbr. for "engineer/architect."

EA   Abbr. for "exhaust air."

eachea   One of a number of earthen or bronze vases described by Vitruvius as being installed under the seats of open-air theatres for "reinforcing" the voices of the actors; it is doubtful that such vases were employed.

eagle   A pediment of a Greek building.

E&CB1S   Abbr. for "edge and center bead one side."

E&CV1S   Abbr. for "edge and center vee one side."

E and OE   Abbr. for "errors and omissions excepted."

ear   **1.** Any small projecting member or part of a piece or structure, either decorative or structural. **2.** See **shoulder, 1**. **3.** Same as **crossette, 1**.

EAR lamp   An **incandescent lamp** part of whose envelope acts as an ellipsoidal reflector; used with small-aperture **downlights**.

earliest event occurrence time   In **CPM** terminology, the earliest point in time that all **activities** that precede the event will be completed.

Early Christian architecture   The final phase of Roman architecture from the 4th to the 6th cent., primarily in church building. Coeval with and related to the rise of Byzantine architecture.

Early Classical Revival   Occasionally, a synonym for the **Classical Revival style**, which was popular in America from about 1770 to 1830; the addition of the adjective *Early* is intended to differentiate this style from **Neoclassical style**, a later reuse of classical architecture between about 1895 and 1940.

Early English Colonial architecture   See **American Colonial architecture**.

Early English style   The first of the three phases of English Gothic architecture, from ca. 1180 to ca. 1280, based on Norman and French antecedents and succeeded by the Decorated

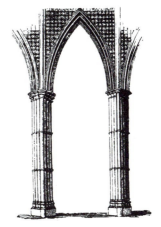

Early English style: Westminster Abbey

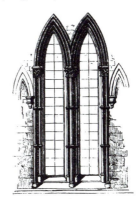

Early English style: window

Early English style: base

style. Often characterized by lancet windows without tracery.

early finish time In **CPM** terminology, the first day upon which no work is to be done for an **activity** assuming that it started on its **early start time**.

Early Gothic Revival See **Gothic Revival**.

Early Romanesque Revival A term occasionally used for **Romanesque Revival, 2**.

early start time In **CPM** terminology, the first day of the project, upon which work on an **activity** can begin if every preceding activity is finished as early as possible.

early stiffening See **false set**.

early strength The strength of concrete or mortar developed soon after placement, usually during the first 72 hr.

Early Victorian See **Victorian architecture**.

earlywood See **springwood**.

earth **1.** British term for **ground, 3**. **2.** See **soil, 1**.

earth auger An **auger, 2**.

earth berm See **berm**.

earth cellar A **cellar** that is dug into the face of steeply sloping ground, with its floor at approximately the same level as the ground at the entrance door; provides an effective place for storing food because the surrounding earth keeps the interior cool. Compare with **root cellar**.

earth dike Same as **dike, 4**.

earth drill Same as **auger, 2**.

earth electrode In electric wiring a metal plate, water pipe, or other type of conductor buried in the earth in a manner ensuring a good conductive path to the ground.

earthenware **1.** A glazed or unglazed nonvitreous ceramic whiteware, having an absorption of more than 3%. **2.** See **stoneware**.

earthfast Descriptive of a timber-framed structure that is supported on posts sunk in the ground, rather than supported by a foundation; also see **post-in-ground construction** and **poteaux-en-terre house**.

earth floor In many types of primitive dwellings, a floor providing a reasonably durable walking surface, and that was usually composed of a compacted mixture of earth, ashes, clay (if available), with additives such as lime, pebbles, or straw. Another addition—animal blood—was once

thought to improve the stability of the compacted soil. Also see **rammed earth**.

earthing conductor British term for **grounding electrode conductor**.

earthing lead British term for **grounding conductor**.

earth material Any rock, fill, natural soil, or combination thereof.

earth pigment, mineral pigment, natural pigment A pigment which is produced by physical processing of materials mined directly from the earth.

earth plate **1.** An **earth electrode** in the form of a buried metal plate. **2.** British term for **buried plate electrode**.

earth pressure **1.** The horizontal thrust which is exerted by retained earth. **2.** The pressure exerted on a structure, such as a wall, by the earth which it retains.

earthquake load The total force exerted on a structure by an earthquake.

earth roof See **sod roof**.

earth table Same as **ground table**.

earth-wall dwelling See **jacal, pueblo architecture, sod house**.

earthwork **1.** Operations connected with the movement of earth. **2.** A construction made of soil.

eased Said of a building component, any edge of which is slightly rounded, for example, as a stair **nosing**.

eased edge Any edge which is rounded slightly.

eased edge

easement **1.** A right of accommodation (for a specific purpose) in land owned by another, such as right-of-way or free access to light and air. **2.** A curve formed at the juncture of two members; forms a smooth transition between surfaces that would otherwise intersect at an angle. **3.** Those portions of stair handrails which are curved in the vertical plane only; an "easement curve."

easing **1.** Removal of material to enable a piece to be fitted into an allotted space. **2.** See **basement, 2**.

east end   The end of a church where the principal altar is placed; so called because medieval churches almost invariably had their sanctuaries at the east end and the main doors at the west end.

eastern crown   See **antique crown**.

eastern hemlock, hemlock spruce, spruce pine   Wood of a coniferous tree of eastern North America; moisture-resistant, soft, coarse, uneven-textured; splinters easily; inferior for use in construction.

Eastern method   See **pick and dip**.

eastern red cedar, aromatic cedar   A highly aromatic, moderately high-density, fine-textured wood of a distinctive red color with white streaks; widely used for fence posts, shingles, and mothproof closet linings.

Eastern Stick style   Same as **Stick style**; also see **Western Stick style**.

eastern water closet   Same as **Asiatic water closet**.

Easter sepulcher   In some churches, in which sacred elements are placed from Maundy Thursday to Easter. An embrasure on the left wall of the chancel.

Easter sepulcher

East Indian laurel   A dense, moderately hard wood; light to dark brown in color, with dark streaks; found in India and Burma. Used for cabinets, paneling, and interior finish; resembles black walnut.

East Indian rosewood   A hard, dense wood; purplish in color, with black streaks; used for decorative paneling and cabinets.

Eastlake ornamentation, Eastlake style   A style not of architecture but of ornamentation, associated with the English designer Charles Locke Eastlake (1836–1906). Decorative elements included: spindlework (especially balusters or posts turned on a lathe), perforated bargeboards and pediments, carved panels, large ornamental fanlike brackets, highly ornamental moldings, and decorative hardware fittings such as door knobs and locks.

east window   In church architecture, a window at the choir end of the church, which is commonly the **east end**.

eave lead   A lead **gutter, 1**.

eaves   That part of a roof that projects beyond the exterior wall; usually the lower edge of a sloped roof. Also see **bellcast eaves, boxed eaves, bracketed eaves, closed eaves, coved eaves, flared eaves, open eaves**.

eaves board   Same as **eaves fascia**.

eaves bracket   A bracket that supports the eaves of a roof; usually one of many, often in pairs.

eaves brackets

eaves channel   A channel or small gutter along the top of a wall; conveys the roof drippings to spouts or gargoyles.

eaves cornice   A **cornice** at the eaves of a roof.

eaves course   **1.** The first course of slates, shingles, or tiles at the eaves on a roof. **2.** Same as **double course**.

eaves fascia

eaves fascia A board that is nailed vertically at the ends of roof rafters; sometimes supports a gutter; also called a fascia board.

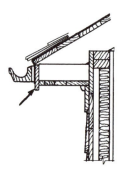

eaves fascia

eaves flashing A metal strip which is dressed into an eaves gutter, acting as **flashing**.

eaves gutter See **gutter, 1**.

eaves lath A strip of wood beneath the lowest course of shingles on a roof (i.e., at the eaves) that raises the lower edges of the shingles so they are nailed at the same slope as the shingles above them.

eaves plate A horizontal wood beam, at the eaves, which is supported at its ends by piers or posts; carries the lower ends of roof rafters.

eaves pole A **cant strip**.

eaves tile, starter tile Tile, usually shorter or plainer than the other roofing tile, used in the first course of tile along the eaves of a building.

eaves trough See **gutter, 1**.

EB1S Abbr. for "edge bead one side."

ebonize To blacken with paint or stain to look like ebony.

ebony Wood of a number of tropical species usually distinguished by its dark color, durability, and hardness; used for carving, ornamental cabinetwork, etc.

eccentric Not having the same center or center line.

eccentric head and shaft

eccentric fitting Any **fitting, 1** in which the center line is offset from that of the run of pipe.

eccentric load A load on a column or pile which is nonsymmetric with respect to the central axis, therefore producing a bending moment.

eccentric tendon In prestressed concrete, a **tendon** which follows a trajectory not coincident with the gravity axis of the member.

ecclesiasterion A hall for religious meetings.

ecclesiology The study of the furnishing and adornment of churches.

échauguette A **bartizan**.

echinus The convex projecting molding of eccentric curve supporting the abacus of the Doric capital. Hence the corresponding feature in capitals of other orders, which often had **egg-and-dart** ornamentation; any molding of similar profile or decoration. Also see **ovolo, bowtell**.

echinus: *E*

echinus and astragal An ornament similar to **egg and dart** with a **bead and reel** below it.

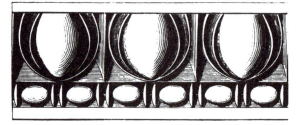

echinus and astragal at the Pantheon

echo Sound waves which have been reflected to a listener with sufficient magnitude and time delay so as to be perceived separately from those communicated directly to the listener.

eclectic architecture Architecture that combines elements and characteristics of a wide range of historic styles. See **Exotic Eclectic architecture,**

French Eclectic architecture, Neo-Eclectic architecture, Spanish Eclectic architecture.

Eclecticism   The selection of elements from diverse styles for architectural decorative designs, particularly during the second half of the 19th cent. in Europe and the U.S.A.

École des Beaux-Arts   The school in Paris that taught elaborate, historic, and eclectic architecture, designed on a monumental scale, based on classical architecture of Hellenic Greece and Imperial Rome, that adapted features of French architecture of the 16th, 17th, and 18th centuries; became a State institution in 1863 and still is the center of the teaching of architecture in France. Also see **Beaux-Arts style**.

economic rent   That rent on a property which is sufficient to pay all costs of operation, maintenance, and payment of mortgages (but not utilities and services).

economy brick   A cored, modular brick whose nominal dimensions are 4 in. by 4 in. by 8 in. (10.16 cm by 10.16 cm by 20.36 cm); actually about 3½ in. by 3½ in. by 7½ in. (8.89 cm by 8.89 cm by 19.05 cm).

economy-grade lumber   The lowest grade of lumber; intended for work where price is the primary consideration. Compare with **custom-grade lumber** and **premium-grade lumber**.

economy wall   A brick wall, 4 in. (10 cm) thick, back-mortared and strengthened at intervals by vertical pilasters to support floor or roof framing.

ecphora   The projection of any member or molding beyond the face of the member or molding directly below it.

ectype   A copy or image in relief or embossed.

edge-bar reinforcement   In concrete construction, tension steel used as reinforcement to strengthen insufficiently strong edges of a concrete slab.

edge beam   A stiffening beam at the edge of a slab.

edge-bedded   See **face-bedded**.

edgebend   British term for **crook, 1**.

edge clearance   The distance between the edge of a pane of glass or a panel and its surrounding frame, measured in the plane of the pane or panel.

edged tool   See **edge tool**.

edge form   A **form** to limit the horizontal spread of the freshly poured concrete on a flat surface or slab.

edge-glued core   See **continuous block core**.

edge-grained, comb-grained, quartersawn, rift-grained, vertical-grained   Descriptive of wood sawn so that the annual rings intersect the wide face at an angle of 45° or more.

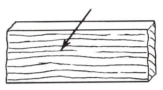

edge-grained

edge joint   **1.** A joint formed between two veneers or laminations, in the direction of the grain. **2.** A joint formed between two boards or plates which are side-by-side.

edge joint, 2 (welded)

edge molding, edging, edge strip   Any molding on the edge of a door, counter, or other relatively thin member.

edge nailing, edge toenailing   Nailing through the edges of boards, such as flooring, so that each board conceals the nailing in the adjacent one.

edge plate   On a door, an angle iron or a channel-shaped guard used to protect the edge of a door.

edge pull   A pull which is mortised into the edge of a sliding door.

edger   **1.** A finishing tool used on the edges of fresh concrete or plaster to provide a rounded

edger, 1

corner. **2.** A wood sanding machine for use along the edges of wood floors.

edge roll   See **bowtell**.

edge shafts   Shafts which sustain arches, united by their sides and back to the nearest wall or arch, so they appear to support their edge only; abundantly used in Norman architecture.

edge shafts

edge-shot   Planed on the edges, as a board.

edge spacer   In window construction, a spacer which (a) prevents edge contact and (b) positions laterally a pane of glass or panel within a supporting frame.

edgestone   A stone used for curbing.

edge toenailing   See **edge nailing**.

edge tool, edged tool   Any tool having a sharp cutting edge, such as a plane or chisel.

edge tracking   In painting with a roller, the trails that may result from either or both ends of the paint roller.

edge vent   One of the openings at the perimeter of a roof to relieve possible water-vapor pressure in the roof system.

edging   **1.** Edge molding. **2.** A plain or molded strip of metal, wood, or other material used to protect edges of a panel or hide the laminations as in plywood or roof sheathing; an edging strip. **3.** In concrete finishing, the process of rounding

the exposed edges of slabs to reduce the possibility of chipping or spalling.

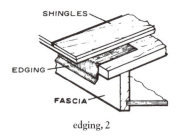

edging, 2

edging strip   Same as **edging, 2**.

edging trowel   Same as **edger, 1**.

edicule   An **aedicula**.

edifice   A large and important building.

Edison-base fuse   A fuse rated up to 30 amperes, contained in a small glass or ceramic container that screws into a socket; has a window for observing whether the fuse has "blown."

EDR   Abbr. for "equivalent direct radiation."

educational occupancy   The use of a building or buildings for the gathering of groups of six or more persons for purposes of instruction, including schools, universities, colleges, academies, nursery schools, and kindergartens.

EE   **1.** Abbr. for "eased edges." **2.** Symbol for "45° elbow."

eelgrass   An organic material composed of a dried grass-like sea plant; fabricated as a blanket, usually enclosed by kraft paper; the resulting enclosed air spaces provide resistance to heat flow; has been used as a thermal insulator.

effective area   The net area of an air outlet or air inlet through which air can pass; it is equal to the **free area** of the device times the **coefficient of discharge**.

effective area of reinforcement   In reinforced concrete, the product of the right cross-sectional area of the steel reinforcement by the cosine of the angle between its direction and the direction for which its effectiveness is considered.

effective bond   A bond in brickwork which is completed at the ends with a 2½-in. (5-cm) **closer**.

effective depth   Of a beam or slab section, the depth measured from the compression face to the centroid of the tensile reinforcement.

effective length Of a column, the distance between inflection points in the column when it bends.

effective opening The minimum cross-sectional area of the opening at the point of water-supply discharge, expressed in terms of diameter of a circle; if the opening is not circular, the diameter of a circle of equivalent cross-sectional area is given.

effective prestress The stress remaining in concrete due to **prestressing** after **loss of prestress**; includes the effect of the weight of the member, but excludes the effect of any superimposed load.

effective reinforcement That reinforcement which is assumed to be active in resisting applied stresses.

effective span The distance (measured from center to center) between supports for a beam, or the like.

effective stress In prestressed concrete, the stress remaining in the tendons after **loss of prestress** has occurred.

effective temperature An index which combines into a single figure the effects of temperature, humidity, and air movement on the sensation of warmth or cold felt by the human body; numerically equal to the temperature of still, **saturated air** which induces an identical sensation.

efficacy See **luminous efficacy**.

efficiency apartment A small apartment usually consisting of a single room used both as a living room and as a bedroom, together with a kitchen alcove and a bathroom.

effigy A representation or imitation of a person, in whole or in part, as a likeness in sculpture.

efflorescence An encrustation of soluble salts, commonly white, deposited on the surface of stone, brick, plaster, or mortar; usually caused by free alkalies leached from mortar or adjacent concrete as moisture moves through it.

effluent In sanitary engineering, a liquid which is discharged as waste, esp. the discharge from a **septic tank**.

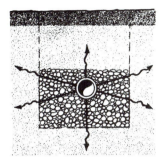

effluent discharging into soil

EG Abbr. for "edge (vertical) grain."

e.g. Abbr. for the Latin term "exempli gratia," which means *for example*.

egg and dart, echinus, egg and anchor, egg and arrow, egg and tongue An egg-shaped ornament alternating with a dart-like ornament, used to enrich ovolo and **echinus** moldings and also on bands. In the **egg-and-anchor, egg-and-arrow**, and **egg-and-tongue** moldings, the dart-like ornament is varied in form.

egg and dart

eggcrate diffuser A metal or plastic assembly, resembling an eggcrate, used below a lighting fixture to diffuse the light it provides.

eggcrate louver A **louver** having rectangular openings resembling the dividers used in egg containers.

eggshell, eggshelling A semimatte glaze or porcelain enamel surface resembling eggshell in texture; sometimes a defect.

eggshell gloss Low gloss of a paint film; slightly higher in gloss than a flat or matte finish but lower than a semigloss.

eggshelling See **chip cracks**.

egress An exit, or means of exiting. Also see **means of egress**.

Egyptian architecture The architecture of Egypt from the 3rd millennium B.C. to the Roman period. Its most outstanding achievements are its massive funerary monuments and temples built of stone for permanence, featuring only post-and-lintel construction and corbel vaults without arches and vaulting.

Egyptian door A door whose frame is narrower at the top than at the bottom, with doorjambs that are inclined inward at their tops with respect to the vertical.

Egyptian gorge, cavetto cornice The characteristic cornice of most Egyptian buildings, consisting of a large cavetto decorated with vertical leaves, and a roll molding below.

Egyptian Revival A mode of **Exotic Revival** architecture suggestive of the architecture of ancient Egypt; used primarily from about 1800 to 1850 and then again, though rarely, from about 1920 to 1930. Buildings in this style usually include some of the following characteristics and/or decorative elements: ashlar-finished exterior walls that are tilted inward at their tops

with respect to the vertical; window frames that are narrower at the top than at the bottom; **Egyptian doors**; lotus capitals; columns that bulge or that imitate papyrus stalks bundled by

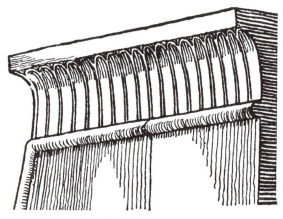

Egyptian gorge

Egyptian architecture: *above*, façade of Temple of Horus; *right*, column, Temple of Hathor

bands at the top and bottom of the columns; an **Egyptian gorge**; winged **sun disks**; an entrance portal flanked by a monumental gateway having slanting sidewalls.

EIC Abbr. for "Engineering Institute of Canada."

EIFS Abbr. for **exterior insulation and finishing system**.

EIS Abbr. for "environmental impact statement."

ejector, ejector pump **1.** A type of pump for ejecting liquid, as from a sump; induces fluid flow by entraining the liquid in the flow of a stream of air, steam, or water. **2.** A **cleanout, 1**.

ejector basin A receiving basin that collects sanitary waste discharge.

ejector grille (*Brit.*) **1.** A ventilating grille with slots shaped to force the air out in divergent streams. **2.** A British term for an **air diffuser**.

ejector vent A **vent pipe** used to convey air to a receiving basin that collects sanitary waste discharge.

EL On drawings, abbr. for **elevation**.

el See **ell**.

elaeothesium Same as **alipterion**.

elastic Descriptive of a material having the property of **elasticity**.

elastic arch An arch designed on the basis of the elastic theory of materials.

elastic constant **1.** See **modulus of elasticity**. **2.** See **Poisson's ratio**.

elastic deformation A change in shape without impairment of the elastic properties of a material.

elastic design A method of analysis in which the design of a structural member is based on a linear stress-strain relationship, assuming that the working stresses are only a fraction of the elastic limit of the material.

elasticity The property of a body that causes it to tend to return to its original shape after deformation (as stretching, compression, or torsion).

elastic limit The greatest stress which a material is capable of sustaining without permanent deformation upon complete release of the stress.

elastic loss In **pretensioned concrete**, the reduction in prestressing load resulting from the elastic shortening of the member.

elastic modulus Same as **modulus of elasticity**.

elastic shortening **1.** In a structural member, a decrease in the length (under an imposed load) which is linearly proportional to the load. **2.** In prestressed concrete, the shortening of a member which occurs immediately on application of forces induced by prestressing.

elastomer A macromolecular material (such as rubber or a synthetic material having similar properties) that returns rapidly to approximately the initial dimensions and shape after substantial deformation by a weak stress and release of the stress.

elastomeric Said of any material having the properties of an **elastomer**, as a roofing material which can expand and contract without rupture.

elastomeric bearing An expansion bearing fabricated of an **elastomer**, which permits movement of the structure it supports.

elbow **1.** A pipe, sheet metal, or conduit fitting having a bend, usually 90°; a 90° elbow is also called an **ell**. **2.** A **crossette, 1. 3.** A **shoulder, 1**.

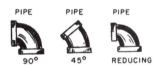

PIPE   PIPE   PIPE

90°   45°   REDUCING

PIPE TO TUBE (90°)

FEMALE   MALE

COPPER TO COPPER

45°   90°

elbows, 1

elbowboard **1.** An elbow rail. **2.** Same as **window stool**.

elbow catch A spring-loaded locking device commonly used to lock the **inactive leaf** of a pair of cabinet doors. When the inactive leaf closes, a hook on one end of the catch automatically engages a strike, thereby securing the door.

elbow rail   A strip of millwork fixed to a partition as an armrest; also called an **elbowboard**.

elec, ELEC   Abbr. for **electric** or **electrical**.

electric, electrical   The qualifying adjectives *electric* and *electrical* have the following meanings: containing, producing, arising from, actuated by, or related to electricity. In general, *electric* is used when the term being qualified designates something that has the properties, dimensions, or physical characteristics associated with electricity; *electrical* is used when the term being qualified does not explicitly designate something that has the properties, dimensions, or physical characteristics of electricity (e.g., electrical engineering). However, sometimes these two terms are used interchangeably.

electrical codes   See **National Electrical Code (NEC)** and **National Electrical Safety Code (NESC)**.

electrical conductivity   A measure of the ability of a material to conduct electric current.

electrical curing   The curing of concrete by the use of electrical heaters.

electrical distribution cutout   See **distribution cutout**.

electrical fault   See **fault**.

electrical insulation, insulating material   A material that is a very poor conductor of electricity.

electrical insulator   A component or device made from material having great enough resistance to the flow of electric current to be effectively considered as a nonconductor of current.

electrically supervised   Descriptive of an electric wiring system which utilizes the flow of a small current in the circuit (too small to actuate the apparatus being supplied) to energize an alarm signal upon failure of any device or equipment in the circuit.

electrical metallic conduit (EMC)   Conduit, usually fabricated of steel, which encloses electrical wiring, thereby protecting the wiring from outside damage. The difference between electrical metallic conduit and electrical metallic tubing (EMT) is that conduit is heavy-walled and usually has threaded ends; in contrast, tubing is thinner and is not threaded. Between these two is an intermediate metallic conduit (IMC), which is 25 percent lighter and less costly than EMT; it may be threaded or threadless.

electrical metallic tubing   A thin-walled metal raceway having a circular cross section; used to pull in or withdraw electric cables or wires after the tubing is installed in place; uses connectors and couplings other than the threaded type.

electrical nonmetallic tubing (ENT)   A round, corrugated plastic tube that is concealed in concrete, or it may be concealed in a ceiling construction having a fire rating of at least 15 minutes, provided the ceiling is not used as a plenum for return air.

electrical porcelain   Vitrified whiteware having an electrical insulating function.

electrical resistance   The physical property of a device, conductor, element, branch, or system, by virtue of which power is lost as heat when current flows through it; the physical property which an electric conductor exhibits to the flow of current; measured in ohms.

electrical resistivity, specific resistance   The resistance, in ohms, of an electric conductor of unit cross-sectional area and unit length.

electrical rod   Obsolete term for **lightning rod**.

electrical service connection   See **service connection**.

electrical tape   See **friction tape, thermoplastic insulating tape, thermoplastic protective tape**.

electric appliance   See **appliance**.

electric-arc welding   See **arc welding**.

electric blasting cap   A blasting cap designed for and capable of detonation by means of an electric current.

electric cable   See **cable, 1** and **cable, 2**.

electric cord   One or more flexible insulated electric conductors in a flexible insulating covering which is equipped with terminals.

electric-delay blasting cap   A cap designed to detonate at a predetermined time after electrical energy is applied to the ignition system.

electric device   See **device**.

electric-discharge lamp   A lamp which produces light when electric current flows through a vapor or a gas; may be designated by the gas filling which is responsible for the major part of the radiation (e.g., mercury lamp, neon lamp, etc.), by the physical dimensions or operating parameters (e.g., short-arc lamp, high-pressure lamp, etc.), or by its application (e.g., black-light lamp, bactericidal lamp, etc.).

electric drill   A hand-held electrically powered **drill, 1**; usually classified according to the capacity of the chuck; may be of either fixed or variable speed.

electric eye   See **photoelectric cell**.

electric heating element   A unit consisting of an electrical resistance material, insulated supports, and terminals for connection to a source of electric power; used as a heat source.

electricity meter   A device which measures and registers the integral of an electric quantity with respect to time, e.g., a **watt-hour meter**.

electric lock   A locking device in which the movement of a bolt or latch is actuated by the application of a voltage to the terminals of the device.

electric motor control   See **motor controller**.

electric operator   An electrically powered mechanism used to open or close a casement window, hatch, damper, or the like.

electric outlet   See **outlet**.

electric panel heating   See **panel heating**.

electric precipitator   Same as **electrostatic precipitator**.

electric receptacle   See **receptacle**.

electric resistance welding   See **resistance welding**.

electric sign   A fixed or portable self-contained, electrically illuminated appliance with words or symbols designed to convey information or attract attention.

electric space heater   A **space heater** in which electricity supplies the heat energy.

electric squib   An electrically actuated device used to ignite a charge in blasting operations.

electric stairway   Same as **escalator**.

electric strike   An electrical device that permits the release of a door at a remote location.

electric water heater   A water heater, usually fully automatic, having a storage tank with one or more electric heating elements, and with operating and safety controls.

electric welding   **1.** See **arc welding**. **2.** See **resistance welding**.

electroacoustics   The science of transforming acoustical energy into electric energy and vice versa, e.g., by means of microphones or loudspeakers.

electrochemical corrosion   Same as **galvanic corrosion**.

electrocopper glazing   See **copperlight glazing**.

electrode   **1.** In arc welding, the component in a welding circuit through which an electric current is conducted between the electrode holder and the arc. **2.** In resistance welding, the component through which the electric current in the welding machine passes (usually accompanied by pressure) directly to the work.

electrogalvanizing   Galvanizing by a process in which the zinc is deposited by an electroplating method.

electrogas welding   A method of **gas metal-arc welding** or **flux-cored arc welding** in which an external gas is supplied; for welding in a vertical position, the molding weld is confined by "welding shoes."

electrolier   A support for an electrically operated luminaire, esp. one that hangs, as a chandelier.

electroluminescence   The emission of light from a phosphor excited by electromagnetic energy.

electroluminescent lamp   A lamp in the form of a thin sheet, either rigid or flexible, which generates light by electroluminescence; characterized by low luminance and efficacy.

electrolysis   The decomposition of a chemical compound into its constituent parts by the passage of an electric current; this action leads to the decomposition of metals.

electrolytic copper   Copper that has been refined by electrolytic deposition; used for manufacture of tough pitch copper and copper alloys.

electrolytic corrosion   Same as **galvanic corrosion**.

electrolytic protection   See **cathodic protection**.

electromagnetic contactors   Electrically actuated devices to open and close electric power circuits.

electromagnetic interference   In the transmission or reception of communication signals,

electromotive force

the interference caused by the radiation of electromagnetic fields.

electromotive force The force which causes (or tends to cause) the movement of electricity in a conductor; the difference in potential between the terminals of an electric source.

electroplated Said of a metal surface having a thin electrochemical deposit of a metal such as brass, zinc, copper, cadmium, tin, or nickel; the metal deposit usually is the result of its immersion in an electrolytic bath.

electroslag welding A welding process in which the two surfaces to be welded are fused together by use of an electrically liquefied molten slag which melts both the **filler metal** and the two surfaces.

electrostatic air cleaner Same as **electrostatic precipitator**.

electrostatic precipitator A device installed in flues, and the like, to prevent smoke and dust particles from escaping to the atmosphere; the particles are given an electric charge as they pass through a charged screen; then they are attracted to one of two electrically charged plates through which they pass; from time to time they are removed from the plate.

electro-zinc plated See **galvanized**.

electrum A natural alloy of gold and silver, sometimes employed in the decorations of ancient temples and palaces.

elementary school, grade school An educational institution which offers instruction usually from the first year through the sixth or eighth year of schooling.

elemi A fragrant yellow-brown resin obtained from tropical trees; used in varnishes and lacquers.

elephant trunk A long cylindrical tube with a hopper-like top; used as a chute for concrete in placing the concrete in deep shafts or forms; the tube is kept filled with concrete, so that there is no free fall of material and resultant segregation of its constituents is avoided.

elevated water tank A **gravity water tank**.

elevated-water-tank system See **gravity water system**. A water supply system for a building in which water is pumped from the water main to an elevated water storage tank located above the highest and most hydraulically remote point in the water supply system; the height of the tank increases the pressure in the water distribution system.

elevation **1.** A drawing showing the vertical elements of a building, either exterior or interior, as a direct projection to a vertical plane. **2.** The vertical distance above or below some established reference level.

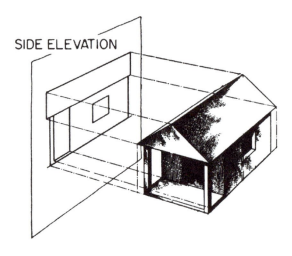

SIDE ELEVATION

elevation, 1

elevator A hoisting and lowering mechanism equipped with a car or platform which moves in guides in a vertical direction, and which serves two or more floors of a building or structure; also see **dumbwaiter**. Also see **freight elevator, hand elevator, hydraulic elevator, passenger elevator, power elevator, sidewalk elevator**.

elevator car The load-carrying unit of an elevator, including its platform, car frame, enclosure, and door or gate.

elevator car annunciator An electrical device that indicates the elevator landings where call buttons have been pressed.

elevator car door A door at the entrance to an elevator car.

elevator car-frame sling The supporting frame of an elevator to which are attached the car platform, guide shoes, elevator car safety, hoisting ropes (or sheaves), and/or associated equipment.

elevator car-leveling device Any mechanism or control that, when activated, will move the car to a landing and stop the car at such landing.

elevator car platform The structure which forms the floor of an elevator car and directly supports the load.

elevator car safety, counterweight safety A mechanical device attached to an elevator car frame or to the frame of the counterweight; slows down, stops, and holds the car or counterweight in the event of excessive speed or free fall of the car, or if the wire ropes slacken, break, or pull out of their fastenings.

elevator counterweight A **counterweight** carried by an elevator cable to balance the weight of an elevator cab; the counterweight travels upward when the cab travels downward, and vice versa; usually composed of steel plates stacked within a frame.

elevator hoistway See **hoistway**.

elevator interlock A device on each door at an elevator landing; prevents movement of an elevator unless the door is locked in the closed position.

elevator landing That portion of a floor, balcony, or platform adjacent to an elevator hoistway which is used to receive and discharge passengers or freight.

elevator machine beam, elevator sheave beam A steel beam, within an elevator machinery room, which is beneath and supports elevator equipment; usually directly over the elevator hoistway (shaft).

elevator pit That portion of an elevator shaft or hoistway extending below the level of the bottom landing saddle to provide for bottom overtravel and clearance, and for elevator parts that require space below the bottom limit of car travel.

elevator shaft An elevator **hoistway**.

elevator sheave beam See **elevator machine beam**.

elevator stage, drop stage, lift stage A theatre stage floor which moves vertically on an elevator, usually so that one set can quickly replace another; may consist of a single unit or articulated sections.

Elizabethan architecture The transitional style between Gothic and Renaissance in England, named after Elizabeth I (1558–1603); mainly country houses, characterized by large mullioned windows and strapwork ornamentation.

Elizabethan architecture

Elizabethan Manor style See **Tudor Revival**.

ell, el **1.** A secondary wing or extension of a building at right angles to its principal dimension. **2.** Same as **elbow**.

elliptical arch An arch having the shape of half an ellipse; in its construction, the ellipse is often approximated by three adjoining circular arcs.

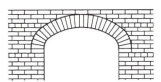

elliptical arch

elliptical fanlight A **fanlight** that has the shape of half an ellipse, often placed over a door; rods or bars radiating from a point are suggestive of the shape of an open fan. Also called a semi-elliptical fanlight.

elliptical stair A stair which winds about a solid elliptic **newel** or elliptically shaped **well, 1**.

elm A tough, strong, moderately high-density hardwood of brown color; often has twisted, interlocked grain. Common in cultivation for shade and ornament; used for decorative veneer, piles, and planks.

elongated piece A particle of aggregate having the ratio of its length to width greater than a specified value.

elongation See **strain**.

eluriation The conditioning of sludge from sanitary waste so that certain constituents are removed by successive decontaminations using fresh water or plant effuents, thereby reducing requirements for conditioning chemicals.

EM Abbr. for "end matched."

emarginated Having the margin broken by a notch or notches.

embankment A raised structure of earth, rocks, or gravel, usually intended to retain water or carry a roadway.

embattled, embattlemented Having battlements.

embattled molding A **crenelated molding**.

embattlement Same as **battlement**.

embedded column A column that is partly built within the face of a wall.

embedded reinforcement See **reinforcement, 1**.

embedding compound Same as **taping compound**.

embedment A steel component which is cast in concrete and used to transmit externally applied loads to the concrete structure.

embedment length The length of embedded steel **reinforcement, 1** provided beyond a critical section.

embellishment Ornamentation; adornment with decorative elements.

emblemata, emblema A type of inlaid work used by the early Romans to embellish floors, panels, and the like.

emblemata

emboss To raise or indent a pattern on the surface of a material; sometimes produced by the use of patterned rollers.

embow To form in a vault or arch.

embowed Having an outward-curving projection, as a bay window.

embrasure **1.** The crenels or intervals between the merlons of a battlement. **2.** An enlargement of a door or window opening, at the inside face of the wall, by means of splayed sides.

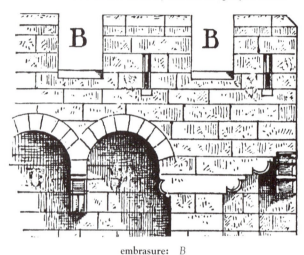

embrasure: B

EMC See **electric metallic conduit**.

emergency-exit lighting A system designed and maintained to assure necessary exit illumination in the event of failure of the normal lighting in the building.

emergency-exit window See **fire-escape window**.

emergency lighting Lighting designed to supply illumination which is essential to safety in the event of failure of the normal electric power supply.

emergency power generator See **standby power generator**.

emergency release On a door, a safety device other than a **panic exit device** which permits egress under emergency conditions.

emery A granular form of impure carborundum; used for grinding and polishing glass, stone, and metal surfaces.

emery cloth A cloth which is coated with powdered emery; used wet or dry (usually on metal) in a manner similar to that of sandpaper, esp. for fine smoothing or polishing.

emf Abbr. for **electromotive force**.

eminent domain The power or right of the nation or the state to take private property for public use, usually with reasonable compensation to the owner.

emission The radiation of energy (for example, electromagnetic, heat, light, or sound).

emissivity See **thermal emissivity**.

emittance The ratio of radiant flux emitted by a material to that emitted by a blackbody at the same temperature, under the same conditions.

Empire style The elaborate neoclassic style of the French First Empire (1804–1815).

emplecton A type of masonry commonly used by the Romans and Greeks, esp. in fortification walls, in which the exterior faces of the wall were built of ashlar in alternate headers and stretchers, and with the intervening space filled with rubble.

emplecton

employer's liability insurance Insurance protection for the employer against claims by employees for damages which arise out of injuries or diseases sustained in the course of their work and which are based on common law negligence rather than on liability under workmen's compensation acts.

emporium In ancient Roman towns, a large building in which foreign merchandise, imported by sea, was deposited until disposed of to retail dealers.

empty-cell process A method of impregnating wood with fluid preservatives under pressure.

EMT Abbr. for **electrical metallic tubing**.

emulsified asphalt An emulsion of **asphalt cement** and water containing small amounts of an emulsifying agent.

emulsifier A substance which modifies the surface tension of colloidal droplets, keeping them from coalescing and keeping them suspended.

emulsion 1. A mixture of liquids insoluble in one another, in which one is suspended in the other in the form of minute globules. 2. A mixture in which solid particles are suspended in a liquid in which they are insoluble, as a mixture of bitumen and water, with uniform dispersion of the bitumen globules. The cementing action needed in roofing and waterproofing takes place as the water evaporates.

emulsion glue A glue, usually cold-setting, made from emulsified synthetic polymers.

emulsion paint A paint composed of small beads of resin binder which are dispersed, along with pigments, in water. On evaporation of the water, the resin particles coalesce to form a film which adheres to the surface and binds the pigment particles.

emulsion sealant See **latex sealant**.

ENAM On drawings, abbr. for **enamel**.

enamel A paint made of finely ground pigments and a resin binder that dries to form a hard, smooth, glassy film having very little surface texture.

enameled brick See **glazed brick**.

encarpus A sculptured festoon of fruit and flowers.

encarpus

encased Said of a steel-framed structure in which all of the individual framing members are completely encased in cast-in-place concrete.

encased beam A metal **beam** enclosed in another material, usually concrete.

encased electrode An electrode encased in concrete (located within and near the bottom of a concrete footing or foundation); the electrode, which may consist of reinforcing bars or rods, must be in electrical contact with the earth.

encased knot A knot that is not intergrown with the surrounding wood; a **dead knot**.

encasement **1.** A rigid structure or pipe which surrounds a buried pipe, providing it with added support or protection. **2.** See **pile encasement**.

encastré Embedded.

encaustic **1.** Painted with a mixture of a paint solution and wax which, after application, is set by heat. **2.** Colors which have been applied to brick, glass, porcelain, and tile and set by the application of heat.

encaustic tile A tile for pavement and wall decoration, in which the pattern is inlaid or incrusted in clay of one color in a ground of clay of another color.

part of a Medieval pavement of **encaustic tiles**

enceinte **1.** The fortification wall of a castle or town. **2.** The area so enclosed.

enchased Descriptive of a variety of hammered metalwork in which a pattern in relief is produced by hammering down the background or depressed portions of the design.

enclosed fuse A **cartridge fuse**.

enclosed knot An unexposed knot completely covered by surrounding wood so that it does not appear on the surface.

enclosed platform The partially enclosed, raised portion of an assembly room, the ceiling of which is not more than a specified distance above the top of the proscenium opening; designed or used for the presentation of plays or other entertainment wherein scenery, drops, decorations, etc., may be used.

enclosed shaft Same as **covered shaft**.

enclosed stair Same as **box stair**.

enclosure wall **1.** Any non-load-bearing wall in skeleton construction; usually anchored to piers, columns, or floors; a **curtain wall**. **2.** The curved metal or glass partition surrounding a revolving door.

encorbelment The projection of each **course, 1** of masonry over the course below it.

encroachment The unauthorized extension of a building, or part thereof, on the land of another.

encumbrance A restriction on the use of **real property**, or an obligation to make a payment which is secured by real property and which does not prevent its conveyance.

end anchorage A mechanical device used to transmit prestressing force to the **reinforced concrete** in a posttensioned member.

endbeam See **beam**.

end-bearing pile A **pile** principally supported at its toe (point), which rests on or is embedded in a bearing stratum.

end-bearing sleeve A device which fits over the abutting ends of two steel **reinforcing bars**; used to assure transfer of axial compression only from one bar to the other.

end-bedded Same as **face-bedded**.

end block An enlarged end section of a member, designed to reduce anchorage stresses to allowable values.

endboard A wood board that closes off the end of a cornice where there is no **cornice return**.

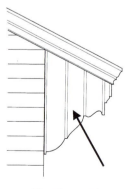

end board at cornice

end butt joint   Same as **end joint**.

end channel   A horizontal stiffener which is welded into the top and bottom of hollow-metal doors to provide strength and rigidity.

end checks   Checks that develop in the end grain of lumber during drying.

end chimney   A chimney located at an **end gable** of a house; may be either an **interior chimney** in which the outer surface is flush with an exterior wall, or an **exterior chimney** in which the chimney projects from the exterior of the end wall.

end-construction tile   Tile designed to receive its principal stress parallel to the axes of the cells; laid with axes of the cells in the vertical direction.

end distance   The distance between the end of a timber which is bolted and the center of the nearest bolt hole.

end gable   A **gable** at the end wall of a house.

end girt   A heavy timber that acts as a main horizontal support for the second floor in an early **timber-framed house**; it is located along one end of the house, for example, between a center post and each of the corner posts; serves to tie together various components of the timber framing. Also see illustration under **timber-framed house**.

end grain   The wood grain that is exposed when a cut is made at right angles to the grain.

end-grain core   Plywood or panel core composed of wood blocks sawn and glued so that the grain is at right angles to the faces of the panels.

end-grain nailing   Nailing into an end-grain surface of wood so that the shank of each nail is parallel to the grain.

end house   A house having one of its two ends facing the street.

end joint   1. A joint formed when boards are joined end to end, as a **butt joint**. 2. A joint, perpendicular to the grain, formed between two veneers. 3. A joint formed by the butt ends of two bricks which are connected with mortar.

end joint, 1   with fishplates

end lap   The amount of overlap in a lap joint, as at the end of a ply of roofing felt.

end lap joint   An **angle joint** formed by two members, each of which has been cut to half its thickness and lapped over the other.

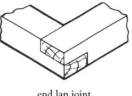

end lap joint

endless saw   Same as **band saw**.

end-matched   Said of boards or strips having a tongue along one end and a groove along the other.

endothermic   Said of a reaction which occurs with the absorption of heat.

end post   A post or a structural member which is in compression at the end of a truss.

end scarf   A **scarf joint** between two timbers formed by the insertion of one end into the other, similar to a **mortise and tenon joint**.

end scroll   Same as **volute**.

end stiffener   One of the vertical angles connected to the **web** of a beam or girder at its ends; used to stiffen the web and transfer the end shear to the shoe, baseplate, or supporting member.

end thrust   The force exerted by the end of a structural member.

endurance limit   In fatigue testing, the maximum stress which can be applied to a material for an infinite number of stress cycles without resulting in failure of the material.

energized   Connected to a source of voltage.

energy   The capacity to do work; the amount of work that a system is capable of doing.

energy cutoff device   A safety device used in a water heater to interrupt the flow of energy to the heater if the temperature or pressure exceeds a preset value anywhere within the water heating system; required by most codes to protect the water heater and to prevent possible associated equipment damage and/or loss of life.

enfilade   The alignment of a series of doors axially through a sequence of rooms.

enframement   Same as **surround, 1**.

engaged   Attached (or apparently attached) to a wall by being partly embedded or bonded to it; for example, an **engaged column**.

engaged bollard   A low post, partially incorporated in a wall or column surface; set to prevent motor vehicles from damaging the surface.

engaged column, attached column   A column partially built into a wall, not free-standing.

engaged columns

engaged porch   Same as **integral porch**.

engineer   A person trained and experienced in the profession of engineering; a person licensed to practice the profession by the authority in the area.

engineer-architect   See **architect-engineer**.

engineered brick   Brick having the nominal dimensions 3⅕ in. by 4 in. by 8 in. (8.13 cm by 10.16 cm by 20.36 cm).

engineering brick (*Brit.*)   Brick having a dense, strong, semivitreous body conforming to these limits: *Class A:* compressive strength 69.0×10^6 N per sq m; maximum water absorption 4.5%. *Class B:* compressive strength 48.5×10^6 N per sq m; maximum water absorption 7%.

engineering geology   The application of geology and its principles in the investigation and evaluation of naturally occurring rock and soil for use in the design of civil works.

engineering officer   A person designated, usually by a military component or a corporation, as having authoritative charge over certain specific engineering operations and duties.

engineering survey   A survey conducted to obtain essential information for planning an engineering project or developing and estimating its cost.

engineer-in-training   A designation prescribed by statute for a person qualified for professional engineering registration in all respects except the required professional experience.

engineer's chain   A distance measuring device used in land surveying consisting of a series of links; in the U.S.A., each link is 1 ft long; the length of the chain is 100 ft.

engineer's level   Any of a group of precision leveling instruments for establishing a horizontal line of sight; used to determine differences of elevation.

engineer's scale   A straightedge, divided uniformly into multiples of 10 divisions per inch so that drawings may be made with decimal values of distances, loads, forces, etc.

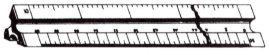

engineer's scale

English barn   **1.** A timber-framed barn built of wood or stone, usually connected to the house through a series of outbuildings. **2.** Same as **Yankee barn**.

English basement   In the United States, the lowest floor of a residential building that is partly below, but mostly above, grade; the principal entrance to the building is at the level of the floor above.

English bond   A brickwork pattern in which courses of **headers** and courses of **stretchers** alternate; forms a strong bond and is easy to lay.

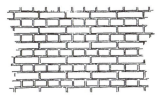

English bond

English cottage   A term occasionally used as a synonym for **cottage orné**.

English cross bond, Saint Andrew's cross bond   Similar to English bond, but the stretchers, in alternating courses, have their joints displaced by half the length of a stretcher.

English cross bond

English frame house   In colonial America, particularly along the mid-Atlantic coast in the middle and latter part of the 17th century, a **timber-framed house** whose construction followed the then-current traditional framing techniques used in England of massive timbers with very strong joints.

English gambrel roof   A **gambrel roof** in which the upper and lower slopes are of approximately equal length, but the lower slope is of much steeper pitch, usually about 60 degrees.

English garden   An informal garden whose plantings, walks, and pools do not form any recognizable plan and are deliberately lacking in symmetry. As a supposed imitation of natural scenery, paths tend to be sinuous rather than straight, and trees and bushes are casually arranged; the antithesis of a **formal garden**.

English garden wall bond   Like **common bond** except that **headers** occur every fourth course.

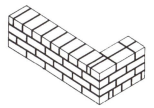

English garden wall bond

English Regency   See **Regency Revival** and **Regency style**.

English Revival, English Tudor style   See **Tudor Revival** and **Neo-Tudor**.

English tile   A single-lap, flat, smooth roofing tile having interlocking sides.

ENGR   On drawings, abbr. for "engineer."

engrailed   Scalloped with concave lines; cut along the edge with a series of small concave curves, usually of the same size.

ENGRG   On drawings, abbr. for "engineering."

enlucido   In Spanish architecture and its derivatives, a term descriptive of a surface that is plastered.

enneastyle   A term descriptive of a **portico** having nine columns in the front.

enplecton   Greek or Roman masonry consisting of cut stone facings with an infilling of rubble.

enriched   Having **embellishment**. Also see **entail**.

enriched: Corinthian base

ENT   See **electrical nonmetallic tubing**.

entablature   **1.** In Classical architecture and its derivatives, an elaborate horizontal band and molding supported by columns; horizontally divided into three basic elements: *architrave* (the lowest member), *frieze* (the middle member), and *cornice* (the uppermost member). The proportions and detailing of an entablature are different for each **order**, and are strictly prescribed. **2.** Any similar construction that crowns a wall, window, or doorway.

entablature   (Ionic)

entablement   **1.** The platform which is above the **dado** in a pedestal. **2.** An **entablature**.

entail   **1.** Engraved or carved work. **2.** Intaglio; inlay.

entasis   The intentional slight convex curving of the vertical profile of a tapered column; used to overcome the optical illusion of concavity that characterizes straightsided columns.

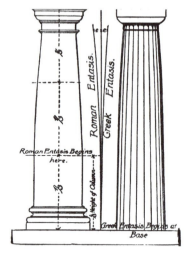

entasis: proportions are much exaggerated

enterclose   A passageway between two rooms or spaces in a building.

entrained air   Microscopic air bubbles intentionally incorporated in mortar or concrete during mixing, typically 10 to 1,000 μ in diameter and nearly spherical.

entrainment   See **secondary air motion**.

entrance   The point of entry into a building: an exterior door, a vestibule, or a lobby.

entrance hall   A large vestibule or hall at the main entryway to a Georgian style home; usually high-ceilinged and well-lighted; commonly subdivided by an elliptical arch into two rooms: a *reception hall*, and a *stair hall* that contains an elaborate **open-string** staircase.

entrapped air, accidental air   Voids in concrete, usually 1 mm or more in diameter, resulting from air not purposely entrained.

entrelacs   See **interlace**.

entresol   See **mezzanine, 1**.

entry   An entrance, small hall, or vestibule inside an exterior door.

entryway   An entrance passage. Also see **entry**.

envelope   **1.** The imaginary shape of a building indicating its maximum volume; used to check the plan and setback (and similar restrictions) with respect to zoning regulations. **2.** The folded-over, continuous edge formed by turning the lowest ply of a built-up roofing membrane over the top surface layer; prevents bitumen from dripping through the exposed edge joints and seepage of water into the insulation.

envenomation   The process by which deterioration occurs in the surface of a plastic close to or in contact with another surface; softening, discoloration, mottling, crazing, or similar effects may result

environment   See **built environment** and **natural environment**.

environmental design professions   The professions collectively responsible for the design of man's physical environment, including architecture, engineering, landscape architecture, urban planning, and similar environment-related professions.

environmental impact statement   A detailed analysis of the probable environmental consequences of proposed federal legislation, major federal actions, or large-scale construction making use of federal funds, likely to have significant effects on environmental quality; such a statement is required by the National Environmental Policy Act of 1969 (42 U.S.C. §4321 *et seq.*).

environmentally friendly   Said of a process or product that is not destructive to the environment.

ephebeion   A type of Greek gymnasium.

épi   The spire-shaped termination of a projecting point or angle of a roof.

épi

epicranitis, epikranitis   **1.** A molding marking the top of a wall or forming the top member of a cornice. **2.** An interior cornice.

epicranitis

epinaos   See opisthodomos.

episcenium   Same as episkenion.

episkenion, episcenium distegia   The upper story of the scene building in an ancient Greek or Roman theatre.

epistle side   The south side of a church when the altar is at the east end; the Epistle is read from that side of the altar.

epistomium   In ancient Rome, a cock or faucet of a water pipe.

epistyle, epistylium   An architrave.

epithedes   The upper member of the cornice of an entablature.

epiurus   In ancient Roman construction, a wood peg used as a nail.

epoxy   A class of synthetic, thermosetting resins which produce tough, hard, chemical-resistant coatings and excellent adhesives.

epoxy joint   In masonry, a visible joint filled with epoxy resin in place of mortar or caulking.

epoxy mortar   A mixture of a fine aggregate, epoxy resin, and a catalyst.

epoxy paint   A paint in which thermosetting resins are contained in a vehicle that results in a tough, very hard, chemically resistant coating; its components must be mixed immediately prior to use.

epoxy weld   In cut-stone fabrication, a joint at an inside angle, cemented by an epoxy resin, to form an apparent single unit between two pieces of stone.

épure

épure   A full-scale, detailed drawing.

EQ   On drawings, abbr. for "equal."

equalized settlement   The design of a foundation on the basis of equal settlement under a dead load, rather than uniform bearing pressure under a total load.

equalizing bed   Material (such as crushed rock) laid beneath a pipeline in a trench to provide a uniform support for the pipeline.

equilateral arch, equilateral pointed arch, three-pointed arch   A **two-centered arch** in which the chords of the curves just equal the span of the arch.

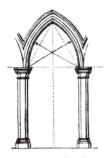

equilateral arch

equilateral roof   A roof with sides sloping at 60°, forming an equilateral triangle in cross section.

equilibrium   The state of being equally balanced; a state of a body in which the forces acting on it are equally balanced.

equilibrium moisture content   The moisture content of wood when it has reached equilibrium with the surrounding atmosphere; this state is highly dependent on relative humidity of the atmosphere.

EQUIP.   On drawings, abbr. for "equipment."

equipment ground   **1.** In electric wiring, a connection from the exposed metal parts of equipment housings to provide a path to ground in the event such parts become energized as a result of failure of the insulation of a conductor housed within the equipment; a ground connection to any noncurrent-carrying metal parts of a wiring installation or equipment, or both. **2.** A ground connector to (a) noncurrent-carrying metal parts of electrical equipment or (b) the metallic shields of a wiring installation, or both.

equipment regulator   In gas supply services, same as **appliance regulator**.

equity   The value of an owner's interest in property, computed by subtracting the amount of outstanding mortgages or liens from the total value of the property.

equivalent continuous sound level, average sound level (L_{eq})   The sound level, expressed in decibels, of a steady sound which has the same A-weighted sound energy as the time-varying sound over the averaging period.

equivalent duct diameter   The diameter of a round duct having approximately the same area as a rectangular duct; approximately equal to the square root of the product of the duct width times the duct height.

equivalent embedment length   The length of embedded reinforcement which can develop the same stress as that which can be developed by a hook or mechanical anchorage.

equivalent round   The diameter of a circle having a circumference equal to the outside perimeter of other than round tube.

equivalent temperature   An index similar to **effective temperature**, but not considering the effects of humidity.

equiviscous temperature   The temperature at which a bitumen attains the proper viscosity for **built-up roofing** application.

Erechtheum   A temple on the Acropolis in Athens; the most important monument of the Ionic style, including a fine example of a porch of caryatides.

Erechtheum: eastern elevation

erection   The hoisting and/or installing in place of the structural components of a building, usually using a crane, hoist, or other powered equipment.

erection bolt   A bolt in the form of a threaded rod with a head at one end, used to join structural components temporarily.

erection bracing Bracing which is installed during erection, to hold framework in a safe condition until sufficient permanent construction is in place to provide full stability.

erection drawing A shop drawing depicting the pieces or components of all or of a portion of a construction in their relative positions, properly lettered and numbered in order to facilitate the process of erection.

erection stress Stress which is induced by loads applied during erection of a structure.

erection tower At a construction site, a temporary framework used in hoisting building components or equipment.

ergastulum A Roman workhouse for slaves or debtors.

erosion **1.** The deterioration brought about by the abrasive action of fluids or solids in motion. **2.** The gradual deterioration of a paint film due to degradation of the binder, which results in chalking, or to mechanical abrasion, such as foot traffic.

erratum A correction of a printing, typographical, or editorial error.

errors and omissions insurance See **professional liability insurance**.

ERW Abbr. for **electric resistance welding**.

escalator, moving staircase, moving stairway A power-driven, inclined, continuous stairway used for raising or lowering passengers.

escape The curved part of the shaft of a column where it springs out of the base; the **apophyge, 1**.

escape lighting Lighting provided by an independent, self-contained source of light that activates when there is failure in the normal source of electric power.

escape stair, fire-escape stair An interior or exterior stair, required by law, which provides an escape route in the event of fire.

escarpment A steep slope in front of a fortification to impede the approach of an enemy.

escheat The assumption of ownership of property by the state if no other owner can be found.

esconson Same as **sconcheon**.

Escorial A palace of the kings of Spain, built by Philip II in the 16th cent. near Madrid.

escutcheon **1.** A protective plate surrounding the keyhole of a door, a light switch, etc.; also

called a **scutcheon**. **2.** A flange on a pipe, used to cover a hole in a floor through which the pipe passes. **3.** A protective or ornamental cover at the termination of a post, picket, or rail against a tread, floor, or wall.

key plate, **escutcheon, 1**

escutcheon pin A small nail, usually brass, used for fixing an **escutcheon**; often ornamental.

escutcheon pin

esonarthex The second narthex from the entrance, when two are present.

esp. Abbr. for "especially."

espadaña In **Mission architecture**, a decorative **gable end** of a church having a multicurved mission parapet; the gable end often has a false front, designed to be impressive; it usually does not house a bell.

espagnolette bolt Same as **cremone bolt**.

espalier **1.** A trelliswork of various forms on which the branches of fruit trees or fruit bushes are extended horizontally, in fan shape, etc., in a single plane, to secure a freer circulation of air for the plant and better exposure to the sun. **2.** A tree or plant so grown.

esplanade A level open space for walking or driving, often providing a view.

esquisse A first sketch or very rough design drawing showing the general features of a project.

Essex board measure On a special type of steel square used by carpenters, a chart which lists the number of board feet in a board 1 in. thick and of various standard sizes.

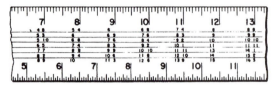

Essex board measure

EST On drawings, abbr. for **estimate**.

estate **1.** The property of a deceased at the time of death. **2.** A property interest, usually applied to land.

estimate **1.** See **detailed estimate of construction cost**. **2.** See **statement of probable construction cost**. **3.** See **contractor's estimate**.

estimated design load In a heating or air-conditioning system, the sum of the useful heat transfer, plus heat transfer from or to the connected piping, plus heat transfer occurring in any auxiliary apparatus connected to the system.

estimated maximum load In a heating or air-conditioning system, the calculated maximum heat transfer that the system may be called upon to provide.

estípite In Spanish and Latin-American Mannerist architecture and derivatives, a shaft of square cross section, tapering downward, frequently combined with other unusual elements, the whole used like an order.

estlar Old English term for **ashlar**.

estrade A platform or dais.

etch **1.** To cut away the surface of glass or metal with a strong acid or by abrasive action, usually in a decorative pattern. **2.** To remove the surface of cast stone with acid to expose the aggregate. **3.** To alter the surface texture of porcelain enamel by chemical attack.

ethylene glycol A type of alcohol, completely miscible in water, used in latex and water-based paints to provide stability when frozen; used in heating and cooling systems as a fluid for transferring heat.

ETL Abbr. for "Electrical Testing Laboratories, Inc."

Etruscan architecture The architecture of the Etruscan people in western central Italy from the 8th century B.C. until their conquest by the Romans in 281 B.C. Apart from some underground tombs and city walls, it is largely lost, but remains important for the influence of its construction methods on Roman architecture, e.g., the stone arch.

Etruscan architecture: Arch of Augustus, Perugia

ettringite A mineral, high in sulfate calcium sulfoaluminate; occurs naturally or is formed by sulfate attack on mortar and concrete; designated as a cement bacillus in older literature.

eucalyptus Wood of the eucalyptus tree, native to Australia and Tasmania, but many species now are grown elsewhere in the world; the physical characteristics and properties vary considerably with the species. Also see **gumwood**.

eucharistic window   Same as **squint, 1**.

euripus   **1.** In ancient Rome, any artificial pond or canal used to ornament a villa. **2.** A ditch around the arena of an amphitheater of a circus to prevent wild animals from escaping.

eurythmy   Harmony, orderliness, and elegance of proportions.

eustyle   See **intercolumniation**.

EV1S   Abbr. for "edge vee one side."

evaporable water   Water in set cement paste which is present in capillaries or held by surface forces; measured as that water which is removable by drying under specified conditions.

evaporation   Loss of vaporized water, solvent, etc., as from a paint film.

evaporation retarder   An organic liquid which, when spread on the water film on a concrete surface, retards the evaporation of water resulting from **bleeding, 5**.

evaporative cooling   Cooling accomplished by evaporating water (usually as a fine spray) in air; as a result, the dry-bulb temperature decreases and the humidity increases; this principle is used in cooling towers and in the cooling of buildings in hot, arid climates.

evaporative equilibrium, true wet-bulb temperature   The condition attained when the wetted wick of a wet-bulb thermometer has reached a stable and constant temperature when exposed to moving air in excess of 900 ft (274.3 m) per minute.

evaporator   That part of a refrigeration system in which refrigerant is vaporized, thereby taking up external heat and producing cooling.

evasé   Opened out, flared.

event   In a CPM **arrow diagram**, the starting point for an **activity**; occurs only when all work preceding it has been performed.

even-textured   Descriptive of wood of uniform texture with little difference in cell size between **springwood** and **summerwood**.

evergreen   Said of a plant or tree that retains its verdure through all the seasons, as the pine and other coniferous trees, the holly, rhododendron, etc.

eviction   Removal of a tenant from property. Eviction may be lawful, pursuant to authorization contained in the lease; it may be warranted by breaches on the part of the tenant, such as nonpayment of rent, or by other factors such as expiration of the lease by its own terms. Unlawful eviction normally will give the tenant a right to damages and in appropriate cases a right to be restored to possession of the property. Also see **constructive eviction**.

exastyle   Same as **hexastyle**.

EXC   On drawings, abbr. for "excavate."

excavation   **1.** The removal of earth from its natural position. **2.** The cavity resulting from the removal of earth.

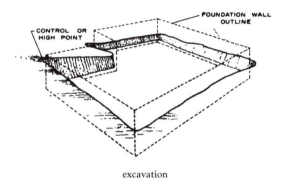

excavation

excavator   Any of a number of power-driven machines used to dig, move, and transport earth, gravel, etc.

exceedance probability   The probability of a storm occurring during any one year which equals or exceeds the rainfall rate used in the design of the storm-water drainage system.

excelsior, wood wool   Curly, fine shavings cut from wood.

excess condemnation   Condemnation of more property than is required for a specific public improvement.

excess joint   A joint in brickwork in which more mortar is applied in laying the joint than is required for a satisfactory masonry bond. Some of the mortar projects beyond the face of the wall, resulting in an irregular surface and, therefore, relatively poor weather protection at the mortar joint.

excess joint

exchequer To use or have a pattern of checkers.

excubitorium **1.** A gallery in a church where public watch was formerly kept at night on the eve of a festival. **2.** In a medieval monastery, an apartment for night watchers whose duty it was to call monks to their nocturnal devotions.

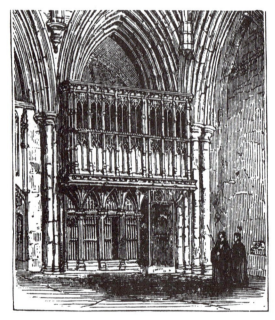

excubitorium, 1

exedra, exhedra **1.** A large niche or recess, usually with a bench or seats, semicircular or rectangular in plan and either roofed or unroofed. **2.**

exedra, 1

In a church, a large apsidal extension of an interior volume, normally on a main axis.

exfiltration **1.** The outward flow of air through a wall, joints, etc. **2.** In a sewer pipeline, the volume of flow leaving a pipeline into the surrounding soil.

exfoliated vermiculite Vermiculite which has been expanded, by a heat process, to many times its original volume; suitable for lightweight aggregate, particularly for insulating purposes; used as a thermal insulation.

exfoliation Peeling, swelling, or scaling of stone or mineral surfaces in thin layers; caused by chemical or physical weathering or by heat. Minerals such as vermiculite expand to many times their original size when heat-treated.

EXH On drawings, abbr. for "exhaust."

exhaust-air grease extractor See **grease extractor**.

exhaust fan A fan which withdraws air from a localized area or from a space in a building from which it is desired not to return the air to the central air-treatment system, as from a toilet.

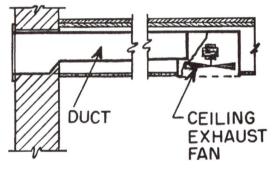

exhaust fan

exhaust fume hood A prefabricated cabinet which confines odoriferous, poisonous, or corrosive fumes for exhausting or filtered recirculation; esp. used in laboratories.

exhaust grille A **grille** through which air is exhausted from a conditioned space to the atmosphere.

exhaust-heat recovery system See **waste-heat recovery system**.

exhaust opening An **exhaust grille** or any type of opening through which air is exhausted from a space.

exhaust shaft   An outlet duct from an exhaust fan through which foul air or gases are expelled to the atmosphere.

exhaust ventilation   The removal of foul air from a space by a mechanical means, such as a fan; fresh air is allowed to enter through available or controlled openings.

EXIST.   On drawings, abbr. for "existing."

existing building   In regulations and in codes, a building which is already completed or which may be built under prior laws or regulations.

existing grade   The **grade, 2** prior to excavation or filling.

existing work   In regulations and in codes, such as a utility service or a system (or any part thereof) installed prior to the effective date of the applicable regulations or code.

exit   That portion of a means of egress which is separated from the rest of a building by walls, floors, doors, or other means and which provides a reasonably protected path of escape for the occupants of a building in the event of fire.

exit access   That portion of a **means of egress** which leads to an exit.

exit corridor   A corridor or enclosed passageway connecting a stairway, fire tower, or other required exit with a street or alley or with an open space communicating with a street or alley.

exit court   A yard or court providing egress to a **public way** for one or more required exits.

exit device   See **panic exit device**.

exit discharge   That portion of a **means of egress** between the termination of the exit at the exterior of a building and the ground level.

exit light   An illuminated sign used to identify an exit.

exit passageway   An enclosed **means of egress** connecting a required exit or exit court with a public way.

exonarthex   The **narthex** nearest the entrance, when two are present.

exostes   A **loggia** having a balcony.

exothermic   Said of a reaction that occurs with the evolution of heat.

exotic plant   A plant that is not native to the locality or region in which it is being grown.

Exotic Revival, Exotic Eclectic   A term descriptive of architecture based loosely on exotic prototypes, moderately popular primarily from about 1835 to 1890. See **Egyptian Revival, Moorish Revival, Oriental Revival, Swiss Cottage architecture**.

expanded blast-furnace slag, foamed blast-furnace slag   The lightweight cellular material obtained by controlled processing of molten blast-furnace slag with water, or with water and other agents such as steam or compressed air or both. Also see **blast-furnace slag**.

expanded cement   See **expansive cement**.

expanded clay   Clay which has been heated to a semiplastic condition and expanded to many times its original volume by the formation of internal gas; used as a lightweight aggregate.

expanded corner bead   A **corner bead** having wide expanded flanges that are easily flexed; provides increased reinforcement.

expanded corner bead

expanded glass   See **foam glass**.

expanded metal   A type of **metal lath** having an open mesh formed by slitting metal sheet; made in various patterns and metal thicknesses, with either a flat or an irregular surface.

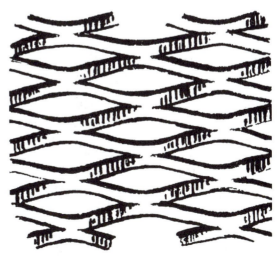

expanded metal

expanded-metal lath A **metal lath** used as a base on which to apply plaster; usually fabricated by slitting sheet metal and then stretching it to form openings through which plaster is troweled; the lath holds the plaster coat firmly in place.

expanded-metal partition A partition formed of heavy expanded-metal lath on thin framing or support members, both sides of which are plastered to form a solid assembly, usually about 1½ to 2½ in. (3.8 to 6.4 cm) thick.

expanded perlite A natural, volcanic, glassy, light, cellular material suitable for lightweight aggregate in concrete.

expanded plastic 1. See **cellular plastic**. 2. See **foamed plastic, 1**.

expanded polystyrene A foamed styrene plastic; has high resistance to heat flow; mechanical strength relatively high for such a light material.

expanded rubber Cellular rubber having closed cells, made from a solid rubber compound.

expanded shale Shale which has been heat-treated so that it expands to many times its original volume; used as a lightweight aggregate.

expanded slate Slate which has expanded to many times its original volume as a result of **exfoliation**; this heating process causes the formation of internal gas, producing a porous structure which is retained upon cooling so the material is suitable as a lightweight aggregate.

expanding bit Same as **expansion bit**.

expanding cement Same as **expansive cement**.

expanding pile A **pile** provided with a mechanical device at its lower end to expand the bottom so as to provide greater bearing and a higher resistance to uplift.

expanding vault A **conical vault**.

expansion The increase in length or volume of a material, or a body, caused by temperature, moisture, or other environmental condition.

expansion anchor Same as **expansion bolt**.

expansion attic An unfinished attic in a completed house, capable of being converted into livable area.

expansion bearing A support at the end of a span where provision is made for the expansion and contraction of the structure.

expansion bend, expansion loop A bend (usually in the form of a horseshoe or Ω) which is inserted in a pipe run to provide for the expansion of the pipe resulting from a temperature change.

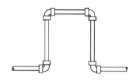

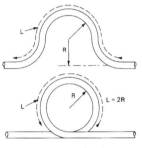

expansion bends

expansion bit, expansive bit A **bit**, of adjustable size, for cutting holes in wood.

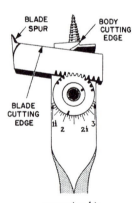

expansion bit

expansion bolt An anchoring device having an expandable socket that swells as a bolt is tightened into it; used in masonry walls for attaching timber, etc.

expansion coefficient See **coefficient of expansion**.

expansion coil An **evaporator** constructed of pipe or tubing.

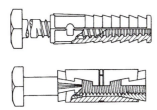

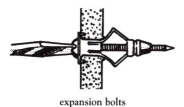

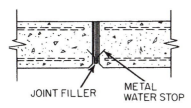

expansion bolts

expansion fastener Same as **expansion bolt**.

expansion joint **1.** A joint or gap between adjacent parts of a building, structure, or concrete work which permits their relative movement due to temperature changes (or other conditions) without rupture or damage. **2.** An **expansion bend**.

JOINT FILLER METAL WATER STOP

expansion joint, 1

expansion joint cover A prefabricated cover which serves to protect an **expansion joint, 1**; designed to accommodate relative movement between the surfaces on the two sides of the joint.

expansion joint filler See **joint filler, 2**.

expansion loop See **expansion bend**.

expansion shield Same as **expansion bolt**.

expansion sleeve A **pipe sleeve** which permits movement of the element that it houses.

expansion strip Material in an **expansion joint**.

expansion tank A tank in a hot-water heating system, above the heating tank, which allows for the increased volume of water when heated.

expansion valve In a refrigeration system, a valve for controlling the flow of refrigerant to the cooling element.

expansive bit See **expansion bit**.

expansive cement, sulfoaluminate cement A cement which when mixed with water forms a paste that tends to increase in volume, after setting, to a significantly greater degree than portland cement paste does; used to compensate for volume decrease due to shrinkage or to induce tensile stress in reinforcement. Classified as *Type K*: Contains anhydrous aluminosulfate burned simultaneously with a portland cement composition, or burned separately when it is to be interground with portland cement clinker or blended with portland cement, calcium sulfate, and free lime. *Type* M: A mixture of portland cement, calcium aluminate cement, and calcium sulfate. *Type* S: A portland cement containing a large computed tricalcium aluminate content, modified by an excess of calcium sulfate above usual optimum content.

expansive-cement concrete Concrete made with expansive cement in order to reduce or control volume changes during the curing period. Also see **self-stressing, shrinkage-compensating**.

expansive hydraulic cement A **hydraulic cement** that forms a paste when mixed with water, thereby increasing in volume by a controlled amount during the early hardening period which occurs after setting.

expansive soil Soil that tends to increase in volume as a result of an increase in its water content.

EXP BT On drawings, abbr. for **expansion bolt**.

expert witness A witness in a court case or other legal proceeding, or in an arbitration proceeding, who, by virtue of his experience, training, skill, and knowledge of a particular field or subject, is recognized as being especially qualified to render an informed opinion on matters relating to that field or subject.

expiatory chapel A chapel erected to expiate a murder or other great crime.

expletive Something used to fill up, as a piece of masonry used to fill a cavity.

exploded view A drawing, rendering, or the like showing the individual disassembled components of an apparatus, device, or machine; the parts are shown in their proper relationship with respect to their assembled position.

exploration The general activity undertaken to identify and classify the elements of which a soil mass is constituted.

explosion-proof Said of an enclosure that is capable of withstanding an explosion of a specified gas or vapor that may occur within it, and of preventing the ignition of the gas or vapor surrounding it.

explosive Any explosive chemical compound, mixture, or device, the primary or common purpose of which is to produce an explosion; i.e., with substantially instantaneous release of gas and heat, unless such compound, mixture, or device is otherwise specifically classified by the U.S. Department of Transportation. *Class A:* possessing detonating hazard, such as dynamite or nitroglycerin. *Class B:* possessing flammable hazard, such as propellant explosives. *Class C:* containing class A or class B explosives, but in restricted quantities.

explosive actuated gun See **stud gun**.

explosive rivet A rivet having an explosive-filled, hollow shank; the rivet is inserted, then the shank is exploded by striking it with a hammer.

exposed **1.** Said of an electrically **live part** which can be touched or approached nearer than a safe distance by a person; not suitably guarded, isolated, or insulated. **2.** Said of a system (such as gas piping or electrical wiring) which is visible in the finished structure.

exposed-aggregate finish A decorative finish for concrete work; achieved by removing the outer skin of mortar, generally before the concrete has fully hardened, and exposing the coarse aggregate.

exposed finish tile Tile whose surfaces are intended to be left exposed or painted; tile may be smooth, combed, or roughened.

exposed masonry Any masonry construction having no surface finish other than paint applied to the wall face.

exposed nailing See **nailing**.

exposed suspension system, grid system A system for suspending an acoustical ceiling in which the members supporting the acoustical material are visible in the room.

exposed suspension system

exposure Of a wood **shake**: same as **weather, 1**.

exposure hazard The probability that a building will be exposed to fire in surrounding or adjoining property.

exposure line An imaginary line drawn across a wood **shake**, dividing it so that the area above this line is the same area as that below it; the area below the line is that portion of the shake exposed to the weather.

expulsion fuse A fuse that uses the gases produced by an arc and the lining of the fuse holder to extinguish the arc produced when the fuse melts.

EXT On drawings, abbr. for "exterior."

extended-care facility An institution in which resident patients receive medical, nursing, and rehabilitative services for medical conditions less acute than those normally cared for in a general hospital. May be an independent building or a designated portion of a hospital.

extended coverage insurance **1.** See **property insurance**. **2.** See **steam boiler and machinery insurance**.

extended coverage sprinkler In a fire sprinkler system, a type of spray **sprinkler** (i.e., sprinkler head) which extends the usual maximum area of protection; **listed** as a special sprinkler.

extended pigments An organic pigment that has been diluted with an extender (e.g., calcium carbonate or blanc fixe).

extended-service lamp See **long-life lamp**.

extended surface Additional surface on a pipe or tube used in heat transfer, usually consisting of metal fins, disks, pins, or ribs.

extender **1.** A white, inert mineral pigment of low opacity; used in paints to provide bulk, texture, or a lower gloss or to reduce paint cost. Common extenders are calcium carbonate, silica, diatomaceous earth, talc, and clay. **2.** A substance added to synthetic resin adhesives to increase volume and reduce cost without affecting quality.

extensibility The capacity of a sealant to be stretched in tension.

extension A wing or structure added to an existing building.

extension bolt Same as **extension flush bolt**.

extension casement hinge On a casement window which has a **sash** (**ventilator, 2**) that swings outward, an exterior hinge so located that when the window is open clearance is provided on the hinge side to permit cleaning from the inside.

extension casement hinge

extension device Any device (excluding an adjustment screw) used to obtain vertical adjustment.

extension flush bolt A type of **flush bolt**; bolt head is connected to the operating mechanism by a rod inserted through a hole bored in the door.

extension flush bolt

extension ladder A ladder which has more than one section, each sliding within the other, so that it can be extended in length.

extension link A hardware device used to provide a long backset in the bored lock of a door.

extension rule A **rule** containing a calibrated sliding insert which may be extended.

extension trestle ladder A ladder which is self-supporting and adjustable in length; consists of a **trestle ladder** base and a vertically-adjustable **single ladder** which may be interlocked.

exterior balcony A landing or porch projecting from the wall of a building.

exterior chimney, external chimney A chimney located outside, and usually attached to, an exterior wall of a house at the gable end, gambrel end, or mansard end.

exterior corner reinforcement A preformed section of expanded sheet metal used to reinforce exterior stucco or plaster corners.

exterior finish The outer finish of a building which provides protection against weather or serves as a decorative element.

exterior glazed Said of glazing that has been set from the outside of the building.

exterior insulation and finishing system An exterior finish for a building composed of polystyrene foam covered with a synthetic stucco; this type of stucco (in contrast to traditional, porous cement-based stucco) is waterproof and is sprayed on.

exterior paint A paint with durable binder and pigments especially formulated to withstand exposure to weather.

exterior panel One of the panels of a flat concrete slab having at least one edge which does not join another panel.

exterior ramp A **ramp, 1** that is an appendage to a building, leading to a level above or below existing ground level.

exterior separation The distance from the outermost exterior wall of a building to the center line of an adjacent street or public space, or to an interior lot line, or to a line halfway between the exterior wall and the wall of another building on the same lot.

exterior stair A stair exposed to the outdoors; often it is a legally required exit.

exterior trim Any material applied to an exterior wall that, if removed or destroyed, will not reduce the structural stability of the building enclosure, and that is installed so as not to reduce the required fire-resistance rating of the enclosure. May include belt courses, cornices, fascias, gutters, half-timber work, overhanging eaves, shutters, surrounds, trellises, and moldings around doors and windows; does not include door and window frames and sashes.

exterior-type plywood   Plywood bonded with a fully waterproof glueline.

exterior wall, external wall, periphery wall   A wall which is part of the envelope of a building, thereby having one face exposed to the weather or to earth.

external dormer   See **dormer window**.

external thread   Same as **outside thread**.

external vibration   Energetic agitation of freshly mixed concrete by means of a vibrating device which is attached at selected positions on the concrete forms.

external wall   See **exterior wall**.

EXTR   On drawings, abbr. for "extrude."

extra   Performed work or a desired item of construction which is beyond the intent of the drawings and specifications contained in a construction contract; an item of **work, 1** involving additional cost. Also see **addition, 3**.

extractives   Substances in wood such as colorants, oils, tannins, resin, etc., that are not an integral part of the cell structure and can be removed with solvents.

extrados   The exterior curve or boundary of the visible face of the arch.

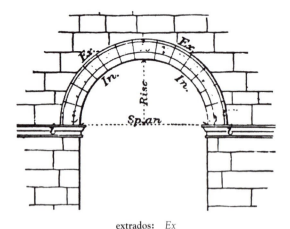

extrados: *Ex*

extradosed arch   One which has the extrados clearly marked, as a curve exactly or nearly parallel to the intrados; has a well-marked archivolt.

extra heavy   Said of a piping (usually cast iron) that is thicker than standard.

extra-high-pressure mercury lamp   A **mercury-vapor lamp** that operates at a partial pressure of about 10 atmospheres or higher.

extra-rapid-hardening cement   See **high-early-strength cement**.

extra services   See **additional services**.

extra-strong pipe   A standard designation for steel or wrought-iron pipe in which the wall thickness is greater than that of standard-weight pipe.

extra work   Any work not included in the contract documents; an **extra**.

extruded compactor   A type of **refuse compactor** that produces a continuously extruded cylinder of compacted refuse in a plastic casing, in a manner similar to that of sausage packed into a sausage casing. The casing is cut and sealed in convenient lengths for ease of handling.

extruded corner   A bay projecting where two masses of an edifice form a reentrant angle, and hence a convenient location for stairs.

extruded joint   In masonry work, a seldom-used term for **excess joint**.

extrusion   **1.** The process of producing metal shapes of a constant cross section by forcing the hot metal through an orifice in a die by means of a pressure ram. **2.** Any item made by this process.

extrusion coating   A thin film of molten resin which has been extruded and pressed onto a substrate to form a coating without an adhesive.

exudation   Any liquid or liquid-like material which oozes through a pore, crack, or opening in a concrete surface.

eye   **1.** The central roundel of a pattern or ornament. **2.** The circular (or nearly circular) central part of a volute, as in an Ionic capital. **3.** One of the smaller, more or less triangular, openings between the bars of Gothic tracery. **4.** An **oculus**, esp. one at the summit of a dome. **5.** A hole through material for access, to permit the passage of a pin, or to serve as a means of attachment.

eyebar   A bar with an eye at either one end or each end; used as a tension member in a steel truss; a pin passes through the eye, forming a joint.

eyebolt   A bolt having its head in the form of a loop or eye.

eyebrow, eyebrow dormer   A low **dormer**

eyebolt

that has no sides, the roofing courses being carried over the dormer in a continuous wavy line.

eyebrow eave   On a shingled roof, an eave that is carried over a door entry in a continuous wavy line.

eyebrow eave

eyebrow lintel   A **lintel** above a window, carried over the window in a continuous wavy line.

eyebrow monitor   See **trapdoor monitor**.

eyebrow window   **1.** A bottom-hinged, inward-opening window in the uppermost level of a house, usually under the front eaves; often one of a series of windows in the frieze of a Greek Revival style building. **2.** A window in an **eyebrow**.

eye-catcher   See **folly**.

eye-house   See **I-house**.

eyelet   **1.** In a medieval castle, a small opening for light, air, or the discharge of missiles, in a wall or parapet; a small **loophole**. **2.** A small hole in a wall.

eyelet

F

F   Abbr. for "Fahrenheit."

FA   **1.** On drawings, abbr. for "fresh air" duct section. **2.** Abbr. for "fire alarm."

FAB   On drawings, abbr. for "fabricate."

fabric   The basic elements making up a building; the carcass without finishings or decoration.

façade   The exterior face of a building which is the architectural front, sometimes distinguished from the other faces by elaboration of architectural or ornamental details.

façade gable   A **wall gable** on the architectural front of a building.

face   **1.** The exposed surface of a wall, masonry unit, or sheet of material. **2.** The surface of a unit designed to be exposed, as in finished masonry, or plywood having one side which is finished. **3.** The broad surface of a board, timber, or panel. **4.** The exposed vertical surface of an arch. **5.** The striking surface of a hammer. **6.** During a construction operation in a tunnel, the surface being excavated. **7.** To install a surface layer of one material on another, as to face a concrete block wall with brick.

face-bedded, edge-bedded   Stone set so that its laminae are vertical and parallel to the exposed face.

face brick   See **facing brick**.

face clearance   The distance between the face of a panel or light of glass and the nearest face of its retaining frame or stop, measured normal to the plane of the panel or glass.

faced block   A concrete masonry unit having a special ceramic, glazed, plastic, or polished, face surface.

faced plywood   Plywood faced with any sheet material other than wood.

faced wall   A wall in which the facing and backing are so bonded as to result in a common action under load.

face edge   See **work edge**.

face feed   In welding, the application of **filler metal** to the joint, usually by hand, during brazing or soldering.

face glazing   Glazing set in an L-shaped or rabbeted frame and fixed in place with a triangular bead of glazing compound.

face guard   A prefabricated strip, or the like, which protects the face of a wall or column against damage by carts, wagons, etc.

face hammer   A hammer having a cutting peen at one end and a flat striking face at the other; used in preparing stone for finer tool work.

face joint   A joint which is visible on the face of a masonry wall, usually more carefully pointed or struck than the others.

face mark   A pencil mark (X) which identifies the **work face** of a planed timber.

face measure   **1.** The measurement of the area of a board; **surface measure; superficial measure**. **2.** The **face width**.

face mix   A concrete mixture used for the exterior face of cast stone, superior in appearance and durability to the concrete cast immediately behind, to which it is fully bonded.

face mold   **1.** A template for marking the board out of which are cut ornamental handrailings, etc. **2.** A template for checking the shape of wood or stone surfaces.

face nailing   Nailing in which the nails are driven perpendicular to the face of the material.

face panel   In a **flush door** constructed of wood, a plywood panel, having a veneer finish, which is bonded to the core and/or crossbanding.

faceplate   Any protective plate, such as an **escutcheon** or the plate over a mortised lock.

face putty, front putty The putty on the exposed side of glass in a window frame; formed with a putty knife in the angle of the sash after the glass has been set in place.

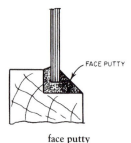

face putty

face shell The sidewall of a hollow concrete masonry unit.

face side See **work face**.

face stone Stone that is used as the **facing** of a building.

face string, finish string An **outer string**, usually of better material or finish than the rough-string which it covers; may be part of the actual construction or applied to the face of the supporting member.

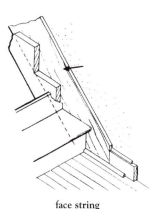

face string

facet **1.** One surface of a polyhedron. **2.** A flat surface between two column flutes, a fillet.

face-to-face dimension In a valve or fitting, the dimension from the face of the inlet port to the face of the outlet port.

facette Same as **facet**.

face velocity The velocity of air at the face of an **air diffuser** or **air terminal unit**.

face veneer Wood veneer selected for its decorative qualities rather than its strength.

face veneer

face wall **1.** A **retaining wall**. **2.** The front wall of a building.

face width The width of the face of a piece of dressed lumber.

facework See **facing**.

fachwerk The term used by German-speaking immigrants to America in the 18th and 19th centuries for **half-timbered construction**, i.e., the medieval system of braced timber framing of a house in which the space between the structural timbers is usually filled with brick or filled with a **nogging** consisting of clay mixed with chopped straw to act as a binder; then the exterior sides of the walls were coated with plaster (although the timbers were often left exposed).

facia See **fascia**.

facility All or any portion of a building, area, or structure, including the site on which it is located, wherein specific services are provided or activities are performed.

facing, facework **1.** A veneer of nonstructural material such as stone, terra-cotta, metal, stucco, plaster, and wood used to finish the surface of a rougher or less attractive material. **2.** Any material, forming a part of a wall, used as a finished

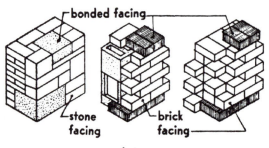

facing

surface; a **revetment**. **3.** On thermal insulation, the protective, functional, or decorative surface applied at the outermost layer of insulation.

facing bond Any **bond, 6** in which the face of the wall shows mostly stretchers.

facing brick, face brick Brick esp. made or selected to give an attractive appearance when used without rendering or plaster or other surface treatment of the wall; made of selected clays, or treated, to produce the desired color.

facing hammer A hammer having a notched, rectangular head; used for dressing concrete or stone.

facing pavoir A **hard burnt** brick, sometimes used as a **facing brick**.

factabling Same as **coping**.

factored load **1.** See **design ultimate load**. **2.** The product of the **nominal load** and a **load factor**.

factor of safety, safety factor **1.** The ratio of the ultimate stress of a structure or pressure vessel to the design working stress. **2.** The ratio of the ultimate breaking strength of a member or piece of material or equipment to the actual working stress or safe load when in use.

factory, *Brit.* **works** A building or group of buildings for the production or manufacture of goods.

factory-built house Same as **prefabricated house**.

factory lumber See **shop lumber**.

factory square An area of 10 square meters (108 square feet).

fadding Using a pad, called a "fad," to apply shellac.

fadeometer An apparatus for determining the resistance of resins and other materials to fading. It accelerates the fading by subjecting the article to high-intensity ultraviolet rays of approximately the same wavelength as those found in sunlight.

fading The loss of color of a paint film through exposure to sunlight and weather.

Fahrenheit scale A thermometric scale in which 32° denotes freezing and 212° the boiling point of water under normal pressure at sea level.

FAI Abbr. for **fresh-air intake**.

F.A.I.A. Abbr. for "Fellow of the American Institute of Architects."

faïence, faïence ware Any earthenware having a transparent glaze; formerly, any decorated earthenware with an opaque glaze.

faïence mosaics Ceramic faïence tile, less than 6 sq in. (38.7 sq cm) in facial area, usually about ⅜ in. (0.95 cm) thick.

faïence tile Glazed or unglazed ceramic tile which shows characteristic variations in the face, edges, and glaze that give a handicrafted, nonmechanical, decorative effect. Also see **majolica**.

failure In structural engineering, that condition of a structural element (or its material components) which renders it incapable of continuing the load-carrying function for which it was designed; may be caused by fracture or by excessive and permanent plastic deformation.

failure by rupture See **shear failure**.

failure load See **breaking load**.

fair-faced Said of a concrete surface which requires no further concrete treatment other than curing, on completion of the forming process.

fair-faced brickwork A neatly built, smooth surface of brickwork.

fair raking cutting Cutting exposed brickwork or facing at an angle to the horizontal, as the brickwork along a gable.

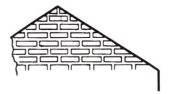

fair raking cutting

fall The slope of a pipe, conduit, or channel usually expressed in inches per foot (or centimeters per meter) or in percent.

fallback A reduction in the softening point of bitumen used in built-up roofing; may result from overheating.

falling door Same as **flap door**.

falling mold In joinery, a template used to control shaping of the surfaces of a handrailing.

falling stile Same as **lock stile**.

falling wainscot A movable partition that can be positioned to separate two adjacent rooms; hinged along its upper edge, at ceiling level, so that the partition can be swung up to the ceiling, thereby joining the two rooms as one.

fallout shelter A structure (or room therein) used for protection against harmful radiation due to radioactive fallout following a nuclear blast.

fall-pipe Same as **downspout**.

false arch One having the appearance of an arch, though not of arch construction, as a **corbel arch**.

false attic An architectural construction above the main cornice, concealing a roof, but not having windows or enclosing rooms.

false bearing Any bearing which is not directly upon a vertical support.

false body An apparently high viscosity in a paint which is considerably lowered when the paint is brushed or stirred.

false ceiling A secondary ceiling formed to provide space for services (such as ductwork) above it, to change room proportions, etc; also see **suspended ceiling**.

false door, blind door The representation of a door, inserted to complete a series of doors or to give symmetry; a **blank door**.

false ellipse A curve that approximates an ellipse, but is actually made up of several adjoining circular segments.

false front **1.** A front wall which extends beyond the sidewalls of a building to create a more imposing façade. **2.** A front wall that extends above the roof of a building; a **flying façade**.

false half-timbering A term descriptive of a wall construction that appears to be of **half-timbered construction**, but whose woodwork is merely decorative and serves no structural function.

false header See **clipped header**.

false heartwood Wood having the appearance of heartwood but not its properties.

false joint A groove routed (and generally pointed) in a solid block of stone to simulate a joint.

false overhang Same as **hewn overhang**.

false pile The additional length added to the top of a **driven pile**.

false plate Same as **wall plate**.

false proscenium A frame, on stage, directly behind the **proscenium arch**; used to expose a smaller stage area.

false roof A ceiling, esp. in an upper room or garret, which is shaped like a roof but is separated from the roof by a dead-air space.

false set, early stiffening, hesitation set, plaster set, premature stiffening, rubber set The rapid development of rigidity in a freshly mixed portland cement paste, mortar, or concrete without the generation of much heat; this rigidity can be dispelled and plasticity regained by further mixing without addition of water.

false tenon, inserted tenon A tenon of hardwood, inserted where the tenon of a jointed timber has insufficient strength.

false tongue See **spline**.

false window, blind window The representation of a window inserted to complete a series of windows or to give symmetry; a **blank window**.

false woodgraining Simulating a wood grain by painting the surface with a translucent stain, then working the stain into suitable patterns with graining brushes, combs, and rags to provide the appearance of wood; also called **faux bois**.

falsework Temporary bracing for supporting work under construction which cannot yet support itself.

family In urban planning, one or more persons occupying a single living unit.

fan **1.** An air-moving device composed of a wheel or blade and housing or orifice plate. **2.** During construction or demolition of a building, an upwardly projecting arrangement of scaffolding and netting that is intended to catch any debris that might otherwise fall to the ground. Also see **axial-flow fan, centrifugal fan, plenum fan, propeller fan, return fan, supply fan, tubeaxial fan, vaneaxial fan**.

fan-coil unit In air conditioning, a unit (which is located in the space being air conditioned) containing an air filter, air heating and/or cooling coils, and a centrifugal fan; the unit receives a supply of fresh air either from a central plant or from the outside by means of an exterior wall opening at the rear of the unit.

fane A temple, esp. one devoted to pagan worship.

fan Fink truss A form of **Fink truss** having subdiagonals that radiate outward from a central point.

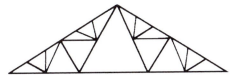

fan Fink truss

fan groin Same as **fan vault**.

fanlight A semicircular or semielliptical window over the opening of a door; commonly with radiating rods or bars suggestive of an open fan.

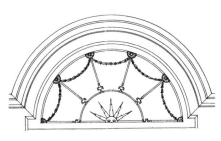

fanlight

fanlight catch A spring catch for locking a hinged window, provided with a means for attaching a controlling cord; esp. used on fanlights.

fan-powered terminal (FPT), fan-powered box In an air-conditioning system, a **variable air valve** with an auxiliary fan to mix induced air from a ceiling plenum with the primary air.

fan sash Same as **fanlight**.

fantail Any member or construction having a form resembling the construction of a fan, esp. applied to **centering** having radiating struts.

fan tracery, fanwork Tracery on the soffit of a vault whose ribs radiate like the ribs of a fan.

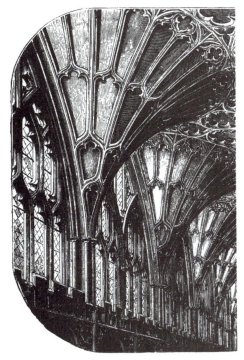

fan tracery

fan truss A truss which has struts supported at their feet by a common suspension member from which they radiate, diverging like the ribs of a fan.

fan vault A concave conical vault whose ribs, of equal length and curvature, radiate from the springing like the ribs of a fan.

fan vault

fan window   A **fanlight**.

fanwork   See **fan tracery**.

FAO   Abbr. for "finish all over."

FAR   Abbr. for **floor area ratio**.

farmstead   A farmhouse and its adjacent buildings and service areas.

fasces   A symbol of Roman authority consisting of a bundle of rods with an ax blade projecting from them.

fascia, facia   **1.** Any flat horizontal member or molding with little projection, as the bands into which the architraves of Ionic and Corinthian entablatures are divided. **2.** Any relatively narrow vertical surface (but broader than a fillet) which is projected or cantilevered or supported on columns or element other than a wall below. Also see **platband**.

fascia board   Same as **eaves fascia**.

fascia bracket   A bracket attached to an **eaves fascia** that supports a **gutter, 1**.

fasciate   Composed either of bands of molded fasciae, as in the Ionic architrave, or of bands of color.

fascine   A cylindrical bundle of brushwood or the like. Such bundles are used as a foundation mat or to protect a pier foundation from erosion.

fastener   A mechanical device, weld, or rivet for holding together two or more pieces, parts, members, or the like.

fastigium   **1.** The pediment of a portico, so-called in ancient architecture because it followed the form of the roof. **2.** The crest or ridge of a roof.

fast-joint butt   Same as **fast-pin hinge**.

fast-pin hinge   A hinge in which the pin is fastened permanently in place.

fast-pin hinge

fast-response sprinkler   A type of fire **sprinkler** (i.e., sprinkler head) having high thermal sensitivity, so that it responds at an early stage of fire development.

fast sheet   See **fixed light**.

fast-to-light   Descriptive of a material, such as a durable paint film, which does not fade when exposed to sunlight.

fast track   A method of construction management in which building construction begins before all construction details have been finalized in order to speed completion of the project.

fat   **1.** Material accumulating on a trowel during smooth troweling; used to fill in small imperfections. **2.** See **fat concrete, fat lime**, etc.

fat area   See **fat spot**.

fat board   A **mortarboard**.

fat clay   A clay having a high value of **liquid limit** and **plasticity index**.

fat concrete   A concrete containing a large proportion of mortar.

fat edge   A thick paint film on the edges of woodwork, moldings, or other painted surfaces having sharp external angles.

fatigue   The progressive structural change occurring in a localized area of a metal subjected to conditions of repeated cyclic stresses and strains considerably below the ultimate tensile strength; may result in cracks or complete fracture.

fatigue failure   The rupture of a material as a result of being subjected to repeated loadings at a stress substantially less than its strength under static conditions.

fatigue life   The number of cycles of loading of a specified character that a given specimen of material can sustain before failure occurs; a measure of the useful life of the material.

fatigue strength   A measure of the ability of a material or structural element to carry a load without failure when the loading is repeated a definite number of times.

fat lime, rich lime   **1.** A pure lime; either quicklime or hydrated lime. **2.** Lime putty having a good spread; used to fill voids in the finish coat as it is applied and troweled.

fat mix, rich mix   A concrete or mortar mixture containing a high ratio of binder to aggregate, thus providing better spread and workability.

fat mortar, rich mortar   Mortar containing a high percentage of cementitious compounds; sticky, adheres to a trowel.

fat spot, fat area A thick place in bituminous paving.

fattening The thickening of paint in a partially filled can after standing for a period of time.

fatty paint Paint which has thickened because of oxidation and polymerization of the drying-oil vehicle during storage.

fauces In the Roman house, passageways from the street to the atrium, or from the atrium to the peristyle.

faucet, bibcock, water tap A water outlet valve; also called a **cock**.

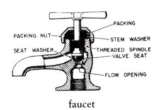

faucet

faucet ear In plumbing, a projection on a **bell, 2** which serves as a means of mechanical attachment.

fault A defect in the insulation or conductive capability of any component or device in an electric circuit, resulting in an interruption of current flow or in an unintended path of current flow of abnormal magnitude.

fault current An electrical current that flows from one conductor to ground (or to another conductor) because of an abnormal connection between the two.

faulting The differential vertical displacement of slabs or members which are adjacent to a joint or crack.

faux bois Same as **false woodgraining**; found, for example, in French Vernacular architecture.

faux marbre Hand-painted wood columns that appear to be marble.

favissa In ancient Rome, a crypt, cellar, or underground treasury.

favus A tile or slab of marble cut into a hexagonal shape, so as to produce a honeycomb pattern in pavements.

faying surface In welding, that surface of a member which is in contact with, or in close proximity to, another member to which it is to be joined.

fayre house Early nomenclature for a **timber-framed house**.

fbm In the lumber industry, abbr. for "foot board measure."

fc Abbr. for **footcandle**.

FD Abbr. for "floor drain."

FDB Abbr. for "forced-draft blower."

FDC Abbr. for "fire-department connection."

FDN On drawings, abbr. for **foundation**.

FE Abbr. for **fire escape**.

FEA Abbr. for "Federal Energy Administration."

feasibility study A detailed investigation and analysis conducted to determine the financial, economic, technical, or other advisability of a proposed project.

feather 1. In joinery, a projection (tongue) on the edge of a board which fits into the groove of another board, as in a tongue and groove. Also called a **spline**. 2. To produce a **featheredge**.

feather boarding A type of **siding** in which the edge of one board overlaps a small part of the board below it.

feather crotch Crotch veneer having a feathery grain pattern.

featheredge An edge of a surface, surface coating, or surface film, which tapers away in fineness.

featheredge board A board made thin on one edge, to overlap a part of the one next to it; also called a **clapboard**.

featheredge brick Same as **arch brick**.

featheredged coping, splayed coping, wedge coping Coping that slopes in only one direction (not ridged or gabled).

featheredge rule A metal or wood straightedge for working plaster; used for straightening angles. Usually about 2 to 6 ft (0.6 to 1.8 m) long, with a tapered edge.

feathering 1. Same as **foliation**. 2. The cusps in **tracery**.

feather joint A joint between two closely fitting boards which have been squared and butted against each other; a groove is cut along the length of each board in which a common tongue is fitted. (See illustration p. 362.)

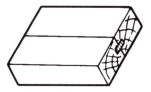

feather joint

feather tip   The thin, flimsy tip of a manufactured wood **shake**, usually uneven or with broken corners, usually caused by improper sawing of the shake.

feather tongue   Same as **cross tongue**.

featured edge   Of a gypsum board, the paperbound edge which provides special design or performance.

Federal Housing Administration   An agency of the government of the U.S.A. which insures loans made by private lending institutions for the purchase, rehabilitation, or construction of housing on private property.

Federal Revival   A loose term denoting American architecture, primarily from about 1870 to 1970, that reuses aspects of, and attempts to emulate, the earlier **Federal style**.

Federal style   An architectural style in the postcolonial era in America, from about 1780 to 1820 and beyond; noted for its clarity of form, simplicity, restraint, and subtle use of color, as well as its delicacy and lightness in detailing; greatly influenced by the work of Robert Adam (see **Adam style**). Buildings in this style are usually characterized by: a symmetric façade, often with a giant entrance portico (sometimes domed); commonly, brick construction with a Flemish bond pattern and thin mortar joints, or clapboard over timber framing with corner boards; a **belt course** separating the first story from the second; a cornice with moldings, friezes, quoins; classical decorative elements such as festoons, garlands, dentils, and egg-and-dart moldings; a side-gabled, center-gabled, or hipped roof of moderate pitch; a balustrade at the cornice line; centrally located chimneys in the northern states in America; exterior chimneys at the ends of the house in the southern states; double-hung windows; initially, stone lintels above the windows, frequently, louvered window shutters; elaborate doorways, including relatively thin columns, full-height **pilasters**, or framing to form

Federal style,   façade (1796)

an entryway; a **fanlight** or a row of rectangular panes over a paneled front door, often with **sidelights** on each side of the door. Often, little or no distinction is made between the terms Federal style and Adam style, as applied in the American colonies, because of their strong similarities.

Federal style,   door

Fed Spec   Abbr. for "Federal Specification."

fee   Remuneration for professional work.

feebly hydraulic lime   Lime obtained from limestone containing a low percentage of clay.

feeder   **1.** In power distribution, a group of electric conductors which originate at a main distribution center and supply one or more secondary distribution centers, one or more branch-circuit distribution centers, or a combination of these. **2.** In a water distribution system, a water pipe connecting an appliance to the water supply system.

feed main A pipe supplying risers or cross mains.

feed pump A pump which supplies feed water to a steam boiler.

feed water The water supplied to a steam boiler.

feeler gauge A series of blades of graduated thickness; used to measure the clearance in a gap.

feeler gauge

fee-plus-expense agreement Same as **cost-plus-fee agreement**.

fee simple An inheritable, possessory inter-est in land which may endure until the death of all lineal and collateral heirs of the first owner and which may be freely conveyed by its owner.

fee tail An estate of inheritance which is limited to one particular class of heirs of the person to whom it is granted.

feint A slight bend in the edge of a flashing or counterflashing to form a **capillary break**.

feldspar A group of igneous minerals, all of which are softer than quartz, having the chemical composition of calcium silicates, potassium silicates, or sodium-aluminum silicates.

felt An unwoven fabric, composed of fibers which are matted together, usually with the aid of moisture and heat, by rolling or by pressure; usually manufactured from cellulose fibers from wood, paper, or rags, or from asbestos or glass fibers.

felt-and-gravel roofing See **built-up roofing**.

felting down Rubbing a dried paint or varnish film with a wet felt pad and an abrasive, to lower surface gloss.

felt nail Same as **clout nail**.

felt paper A type of **building paper**.

female connector In general, any type of electrical **connector** having contacts which are set into recessed openings.

female coupling A **coupling** with the threads on the inside.

female thread Same as **inside thread**.

femerall See **femerell**.

femerell A ventilator, often louvered, drawing smoke through a roof when no chimney is provided. Also see **louver**.

femur The long projecting face between each channel of a **triglyph**.

fence A barrier that defines a property line, encloses, or borders on a field, a yard, or the like. For illustrations and definitions of specific types, see **barbed-wire fence, board fence, chain-link fence, picket fence, plank fence, post-and-rail fence, rail fence, split-rail fence, sunk fence, Virginia rail fence, worm fence, zigzag fence.**

fencerow Planting which forms a fence or is adjacent to a fence.

fender A protective curb or device, often of timber.

fender wall A dwarf wall built in a basement under the hearthstone of a fireplace in the story above.

fenestella **1.** A small glazed opening in a shrine to afford a view of the relics. **2.** A small niche above a **piscina** or **credence**.

fenestella, 2

fenestra bifors The ancient equivalent of a **French window**.

fenestral **1.** A small window. **2.** A framed window blind of cloth or paper used prior to the introduction of glass.

fenestra method A procedure for predicting the interior illumination provided by daylight through windows.

fenestration The arrangement and design of windows in a building.

fengite A type of translucent alabaster or marble, sometimes used for window panes in ancient times.

feng-shui A traditional Chinese technique for planning the layout of a building and for orienting rooms within it, so as to be in harmony with nature and with its surroundings.

feretory In a church, a space where major relics are kept, often treated as a chapel behind the main altar.

ferme ornée See **cottage orné**.

ferrocement, ferrocemento A composite material consisting of a number of layers of wire mesh embedded and interlayered with a cement-sand mortar; provides a relatively thin, flexible, tough membrane; has been used in experimental structures and in fabricating complicated formwork for repetitive concrete pours.

ferroconcrete See **reinforced concrete**.

ferrocyanide blue See **Prussian blue**.

ferrous metal Metal in which iron is the principal element.

ferruginous Containing iron; such rocks indicate the presence of iron by reddish-brown stains.

ferrule A metal sleeve, esp. one which is fitted with a screwed plug; serves as an opening on the side of a pipe providing access for inspection or cleaning the interior of the pipe.

fertilizer That which fertilizes, i.e., acts as a nutrient, whether organic or inorganic; may be natural or artificial.

festoon A festive decoration of pendant semi-loops with attachments and loose ends, esp. a swag of fabric, or representations of such decorations. Also see **garland**.

festoon curtain, festoon drape A front curtain on the stage of a theatre; raised by lines which pass through rings attached to the reverse side; when raised, the curtain remains partly visible, hanging in swags and framing the stage.

festoon lamp A small incandescent lamp having a tubular bulb and a base at each end.

festoon lighting Lighting by festoons of lamps connected by flexible electric wire.

festoon staining A form of **pattern staining** on exterior walls of a building; is usually caused by differences in the flow of rainwater over the surface.

festoon tab A diagonally drawn **festoon curtain**.

FG **1.** Abbr. for "flat (slash) grain." **2.** Abbr. for "fine grain."

FH **1.** Abbr. for "fire hose." **2.** Abbr. for "flat head."

FHA Abbr. for **Federal Housing Administration**.

FHC Abbr. for "fire-hose cabinet."

FHWA Abbr. for "Federal Highway Administration."

fiberboard A building material, usually composed of wood fiber or cane or other vegetable fiber, compressed with a binder into sheet form; the physical characteristics depend on the fiber, binder, density, and surface finish. Also see **hardboard, medium-density fiberboard, board insulation**.

fibered plaster Gypsum plaster containing fibers of hair, glass, nylon, or sisal.

fiberglass, fibrous glass, glass fiber Filaments of glass, formed by pulling or spinning molten glass into random lengths; either gathered in a wool-like mass or formed as continuous thread-like filaments having diameters in the range of 10 to 30 μm. The wool-like material is processed into many forms of varying densities for use as thermal and acoustical insulation. The continuous-filament type is used for textiles, glass fabrics, and electrical insulation and as reinforcement for other materials.

fiberglass cloth See **glass cloth**.

fiber house Same as **brush house**.

fiber optical system A system for conveying light through **optical fiber cable**, usually by the transmission of coherent light.

fiber-reinforced concrete See **fibrous concrete**.

fiber saturation point When drying or wetting wood, the point at which the wood fibers are saturated but there is no water in the cell cavities.

fiber stress The longitudinal compressive or tensile stress in a member, such as a beam.

fibre See **fiber**.

fibrous concrete Concrete containing asbestos, spun glass, or other fibers to reduce unit weight and improve tensile strength.

fibrous glass See **fiberglass**.

fibrous plaster, stick-and-rag work Cast plaster which has been reinforced with canvas, excelsior, etc.

fiddleback, cross figure, cross fire, ripple figure Abrupt, curly figures in wood, particularly maple and mahogany, caused by undulations in fiber alignment.

fiducial mark In surveying, an index line or point, used as a basis of reference.

field **1.** The central portion of a panel that is thicker than its edges, so that it projects above the surrounding frame or wall surfaces. **2.** That portion of the upper part of a wall between the **cornice** and **dado** or between the **frieze** and **dado.**

field bending The bending of steel **reinforcing bars** on the job rather than in a fabricating shop.

field check **1.** At a field site, a survey of existing conditions; also called a "field observation." **2.** At an existing structure, a comparison of dimensions with those shown on drawings; also called "field measure."

field concrete Concrete delivered to, or mixed, placed, and cured on the job site.

field-cured cylinders Test cylinders of concrete, cured as nearly as practicable in the same manner as the concrete in the structure, to indicate when supporting forms may be removed, additional construction loads imposed, or the structure placed in service.

field drain Same as **agricultural pipe drain**.

fielded panel See **raised panel**.

field engineer A term used by certain governmental agencies to designate their representative at the project **site**. Also see **project representative**.

field house A large, long-span structure used for athletic activities such as basketball or track events.

field impact insulation class (FIIC) A single-number rating of the insulation against impacts, provided by a floor (and associated structures) derived from field impact sound measurements in accordance with ASTM Test Method E989.

field joint A connection between adjoining members or parts, made at the time of installation.

field measure See **field check, 2**.

field-molded sealant A liquid or semisolid material molded into the desired shape in the joint where it is installed.

field observation See **field check, 1**.

field order A written order effecting a minor change in the **work, 1** not involving an adjustment in the **contract sum** or an extension of the **contract time**, issued by the architect to the contractor during the **construction phase**.

field painting The painting of structural steel or other metals after they have been erected and are in their final positions in the construction.

field representative See **project representative**.

field rivet A rivet driven into a steel structure during its erection.

fieldstone **1.** Loose stone found on the surface or in the soil. **2.** Slabby units, flat in the direction of bedding or lineation of the rock, and suitable for setting as dry-wall masonry. Glacial or alluvial boulders and cobbles, found in or on the soil, are not fieldstone in the strict sense.

field sound transmission class (FSTC) A single-number rating of the sound insulation (provided by a partition), as measured in buildings in accordance with an appropriate standard.

field supervision That portion of the architect's supervisory work which is done at the construction site.

field tile Same as **drain tile**.

field work Work done at the job site.

figure Pattern and natural markings in a wood surface formed by an unusual arrangement or color of the wood fibers and rays. These deviations produce such figures as **blister, bird's-eye, fiddleback**, etc.

figured glass Translucent sheet glass, rolled with a pattern in bas-relief on one face; light transmission is high; degree of obscurity varies, depending on pattern.

FIIC Abbr. for **field impact insulation class**.

filament An incandescent lamp filament whose form and construction are designated by a letter: S, straight wire; C, coil; CC, coiled coil.

filament lamp See **incandescent lamp**.

file A metal (usually steel) tool having a rectangular, triangular, round, or irregular section and either tapering or of uniform width and thickness, covered on one or more of its surfaces with teeth

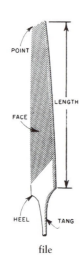

file

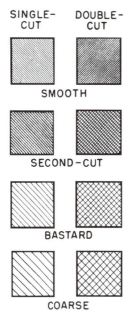

file: nomenclature

or oblique ridges; used for abrading, reducing, or smoothing metal, wood, or other materials.

fill **1.** Soil, crushed stone, or waste materials, used to raise an existing grade or as a man-made deposit. **2.** The depth or the volume of such material so added. **3.** A cementitious material such as concrete or terrazzo, which is placed over a metal substructure to provide the wearing surface of a tread or platform. **4.** Aggregate placed on a **roof decking, 2** to form the appropriate design slope.

filled-cell masonry Wall construction made with **hollow masonry units** in which all vertical cells and voids are filled by pouring **grout, 1** into them.

filler **1.** A fine mineral aggregate used as an **extender** to improve the properties of coating asphalt and plastic asphalt cement. **2.** Finely divided inert material (such as pulverized limestone, silica, or colloidal substances) sometimes added to portland cement paint or other materials to reduce shrinkage, improve workability, or act as an extender. **3.** A pigmented paste, sometimes colored, rubbed into open-grained wood surfaces to fill the pores prior to finishing. **4.** An inert material added to synthetic resin adhesives to improve their properties or reduce cost. **5.** A plate which is inserted merely to fill up space; a **filler plate**. **6.** In painting, a composition (often pigmented) used to fill pores or irregularities in a surface in preparation for the application of another coating.

filler block A concrete masonry unit used to fill in between joists or beams, providing a platform for a cast-in-place concrete slab.

filler coat A coat of paint, varnish, etc., used as a **primer**.

filler metal Metal which is added during a weld; has a melting point either approximately the same as or below that of the metals being welded.

filler plate **1.** A blank plate used to fill mortised cutouts. **2.** A steel plate used to fill an open space between structural members or parts thereof.

fillet **1.** A molding consisting of a narrow flat band, often square in section; the term is loosely applied to almost any rectangular molding; usually used in conjunction with or to separate other moldings or ornaments, as the **stria** between the flutes of columns. Also see **band**, lattice molding, fret, reglet, annulet, **supercilium**, **taenia**, **cincture**, **cimbia**, **fascia**, and **platband**; a **listel**, or **tringle**. **2.** A carved ornament representing a flowing band or ribbon. **3.** In stair construction, a thin narrow strip of wood which fits into the groove of the stair shoe or **subrail** between balusters. **4.** A **cant strip**. **5.** A concave junction where two surfaces meet.

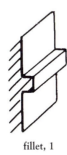

fillet, 1

fillet chisel   A mason's chisel used in the fine shaping of stone enrichments and details.

fillet gauge, radius gauge   A gauge used to determine the radius of curvature of small concave or convex surfaces.

fillet gutter   A narrow gutter on the slope of a roof against a chimney or the like, formed of sheet metal turned over a fillet of wood.

fillet weld   A weld of approximately triangular cross section joining two surfaces, approximately at right angles to each other, as in a lap joint.

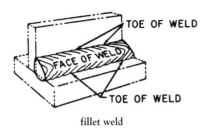

fillet weld

filling   **1.** The application of a **filler** to fill cracks, dents, and other surface imperfections. **2.** Same as **infilling**.

filling-in piece   Any timber which is shorter than similar members, as a **jack rafter**.

filling knife   A knife with a flexible blade used to apply a mastic or paste as a **filler, 3**.

filling piece   A piece of material inserted on or into another to provide a continuous surface.

fill insulation   **1.** Any thermal insulation placed in cavities of an assemblage. Also see **granular-fill insulation, loose-fill insulation, batt insulation, blanket insulation**. **2.** Any loose insulation that may be poured in place. Also see **loose-fill insulation, granular-fill insulation**.

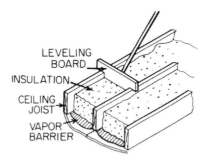

fill insulation   being placed between joists

fillister   **1.** A rabbet on the outer edge of a muntin to hold the glass and putty. **2.** A plane for grooving timber.

fill lighting   Supplementary illumination used to reduce shadows or the range of contrasts.

fill pump   A pump that supplies water to a **gravity tank** or to a pressurized storage tank; is usually of the centrifugal type because this type is readily available in a wide range of characteristics.

fill-type insulation   Same as **fill insulation**.

fill wire   Same as **shute wire**.

film   A layer of one or more coats of paint or varnish covering an object or surface.

film glue   A thin sheet of paper or scrim impregnated with a thermosetting resin; used to eliminate glue bleed-through in bonding expensive decorative veneers or in hot-pressing nonporous laminates.

filter   **1.** A device to separate solids, such as dust, from air. **2.** A device to separate solids from liquids. **3.** A **charcoal filter**. **4.** A layer or combination of layers of pervious materials designed and installed in such a manner as to provide drainage, yet prevent the movement of soil particles due to flowing water. **5.** See **heat filter**. **6.** See **light filter**.

filter bed   A bed of gravel, sand, or the like used to filter water or sewage; also see **sand filter**.

filter block   A hollow, vitrified clay masonry unit, sometimes salt-glazed, designed for trickling filter floors in sewage disposal plants.

filtration   The removal of solids and/or bacteria from water by a mechanical process in which suspended solid contaminents are removed, e.g., by passing it through a **filter bed**, sieve, or the like.

fin   **1.** An extended surface used to increase the heat transfer area, as metal sheets attached to tubes. **2.** A thin flange projecting outward from the periphery of the frame of an aluminum window to serve as a means of securing the frame in a wood or masonry opening. **3.** A narrow linear projection on a formed concrete surface, resulting from mortar flowing out between spaces in the formwork. **4.** A thin projection on a casting or forging resulting from trimming or from the metal under pressure being forced into hairline cracks in the die or around die inserts. **5.** A steel sheeting wall which projects from a main cofferdam structure.

FIN.   On drawings, abbr. for **finish**.

final acceptance   The owner's acceptance of a project from the contractor upon certification by the architect that it is complete and in accordance with the contract requirements; final acceptance is confirmed by the making of final payment unless otherwise stipulated at the time of making such payment.

final backfill   The material used in filling a trench, from bedding to the finished surface.

final completion   The completion of work and all contract requirements by the contractor.

final filter   See **afterfilter**.

final grind   See **polish grind**.

final inspection   The final review of the **project** by the **architect** prior to his issuance of the final **certificate for payment**.

final payment   Payment made by the **owner** to the **contractor**, upon issuance by the **architect** of the final **certificate for payment**, of the entire unpaid balance of the **contract sum** as adjusted by **change orders**.

final prestress   See **final stress, 1**.

final set   A degree of stiffening of a mixture of cement (or concrete or mortar) and water greater than the **initial set**; generally stated as the time required for cement paste to stiffen sufficiently to resist the penetration of a weighted test needle.

final setting time   The time required for a freshly mixed cement paste, mortar, or concrete to achieve final set.

final stress   **1.** In **prestressed concrete**, the stress which exists after substantially all losses in stress have occurred. **2.** The stress in a member after all loads have been applied.

fine aggregate   **1.** Aggregate which passes through a 9.51-mm (⅜-in.) sieve, passes almost entirely through a 4.76-mm (No. 4) sieve, and is predominantly retained on a 74-μm (No. 200) sieve. **2.** That portion of an aggregate which passes through a 4.76-mm (No. 4) sieve and is predominantly retained on a 74-μm (No. 200) sieve.

fine grading   Precise grading of ground after rough levels have been reached, to prepare for seeding, planting, or paving.

fine-grained   See **fine-textured**.

fine-grown   See **fine-textured**.

fine mineral surfacing   Inorganic material that is insoluble in water; used to surface roofing products.

fineness   **1.** A measure of **particle-size distribution**. **2.** In paints, a measure of the size of pigment particles.

fineness modulus   A measure of the fineness of an aggregate; a factor obtained by adding the total percentages of an aggregate sample retained on each of the following sieves and dividing the sum by 100: No. 100 (150 μm), No. 50 (300 μm), No. 30 (600 μm), No. 16 (1.18 mm), No. 8 (2.36 mm), No. 4 (4.75 mm), ⅜ inch (9.5 mm), ¾ inch (19.0 mm), 1½ inch (38.1 mm).

fines   **1.** In plastering, small aggregate which passes through a 74-μm (No. 200) sieve. **2.** Soil which passes through a 75-μm (No. 200) sieve. **3.** A by-product of the processing of rock; varies in particle size from powder or dust to silt or sand.

fine stuff   In plastering, lime putty used in the finish coat.

fine-textured, fine-grained, fine-grain, fine-grown   Descriptive of wood of uniform texture having small closely spaced pores or cells.

finger guard   A strip of soft material applied to the edges of a doorjamb; used to prevent possible injury to fingers inserted between door and jamb during closure.

finger joint   A **heading joint** having interlaced, finger-like projections on the ends of the joined members.

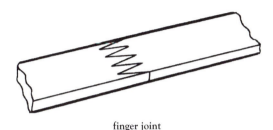

finger joint

finger plate   Same as **push plate**.

fingers   A **drag, 1**.

finial   An ornament which terminates the point of a spire, pinnacle, etc. Also see **acroterion, crop, knob, 2, pineapple, pommel**.

fining off   Applying a **finish coat**.

finish   **1.** The texture, color, and smoothness of a surface, and other properties affecting appearance. **2.** The texture and smoothness of a concrete surface after compacting and finishing operations have been performed. **3.** A **finish coat**. **4.** See **finishing**.

finish builders' hardware   See **finish hardware**.

finish carpentry   Same as **joinery**.

finish casing   The finish material around a **casing**.

finish coat, fining coat, finishing coat, setting coat, skimming coat, white coat   The final or last coat of plaster, which provides a decorative surface or a base for decoration, usually about to ³⁄₃₂ in. (1.6 to 2.4 mm) thick.

finished grade   Same as **finish grade**.

finished size   Same as **dressed size**.

finished stair string   See **face string**.

finished string   Same as **face string**.

finish floor, finished floor   The floor, usually laid over a subfloor, which provides the completed floor surface.

finish flooring   The material used for the finish floor surface, such as hardwood, terrazzo, tile, etc.

finials

finish grade   The top surface of lawns, walks, and drives, or other improved surface after completion of construction or grading operations.

finish hardware, architectural hardware, builders' finish hardware, finish builders' hardware   Hardware, such as hinges, locks, catches, etc., that has a finished appearance as well as a function, esp. that used with doors, windows, and cabinets; may be considered part of the decorative treatment of a room or building.

finishing   Leveling, smoothing, compacting, and otherwise treating surfaces of fresh (or recently placed) concrete or mortar to produce desired appearance and texture.

finishing brush   A brush used to apply water to a lime-putty finish as the finish is being water-troweled.

finishing carpentry   Same as **joinery**.

finishing coat   See **finish coat**.

finishing compound   A compound specifically designed to provide a smooth, level surface.

finishing hardware   See **finish hardware**.

finishing hydrated lime   A **hydrated lime** which is suitable for application as a **finish coat**.

finishing machine   A power-operated machine used to give the desired surface texture to a concrete slab.

finishing nail   A slender nail made from finer wire than the common nail; has a brad-type head which permits it to be set below the surface of the wood, leaving only a small hole which can be puttied easily; used in finishing work.

finishing nail

finishing off   In joinery, preparations for a finish surface.

finishings   The treatment of all surfaces in a building and the addition of those fixtures required to convert a **carcass** into a complete building; does not include **building services**.

finishing sawhorse   Same as **sawhorse**.

finishing tool   A small tool, such as a float or trowel, used in finishing a plaster surface.

finishing varnish   See **floor varnish**.

finish lime, finishing lime   See **building lime**.

finish plaster   Same as **finish coat**.

finish plate   See **armored front**.

finish size, finished size   The overall size, including trim, of any completely finished component or article.

finish string   See **face string**.

finish tile   Tile with a face that may be used as a finished wall surface.

Fink truss, Belgian truss, French truss   A symmetrical truss, esp. used in supporting large sloping roofs; in the form of three isosceles triangles—one in the center with its base along the horizontal tie, and each of the outer two having its base along the sloping sides of an upper chord.

finned tube   A metal tube having fins (i.e.,

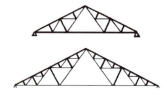

Fink truss, *above;* long-span Fink truss, *below*

metal plates, jointed to the tube, perpendicular to its length) to transfer heat from the tube to the surrounding air.

fir   A softwood of the temperate climates including Douglas fir, white fir, silver fir, balsam fir, etc.; used for framing, interior trim.

fire alarm box   A small box, usually red, having a thin sheet of glass or plastic which, if broken, activates a fire alarm system.

fire alarm system   **1.** An electrical system which is installed in a building as a protective measure against fire; sounds an alarm when actuated by a **fire-detection system**. **2.** An alarm system designed to signal the presence of a fire.

fire and extended coverage insurance   See **property insurance**.

fire area   Any area in a building, encompassed by **fire walls** and/or exterior walls, within which a fire would be confined because of the surrounding fire-resistant construction.

fire assembly   The assembly of a fire door, fire window, or fire damper, including all required hardware, anchorage, frames, and sills. Also see **self-closing fire assembly**.

fireback, chimney back   The back wall of the fireplace, constructed of heat-resistant masonry or ornamental cast or wrought metal, which not only is decorative but radiates heat into the room.

fireback   of cast iron

fire block   A **fire stop**.

fireboard, chimney board, summer piece   A board or shutter-like device to close the opening of a fireplace when not in use.

firebreak   **1.** Space between buildings, groups of buildings, or areas of a city designed to prevent the spread of fire from one building, group, or area to another. **2.** Fire-resistive floors, walls, doors, shutters, etc., designed to prevent the spread of fire within a building.

fire brick   Brick made of refractory ceramic material which will resist high temperatures; used to line furnaces, fireplaces, and chimneys; usually contains a high percentage of silica.

fire bridge   A low wall of firebrick which separates the furnace from the hearth in a reverberatory furnace.

fire canopy   A horizontal, fire-resistive construction which extends beyond the vertical line of an exterior wall; designed to prevent flames from a window from igniting the contents of floors above.

fire cement   A cementitious bonding material, such as calcium aluminate cement, esp. compounded for laying refractory brick.

fire check door   See **fire door**.

fire clay   Clay having a melting point above 1600 degrees centigrade, especially used for making **fire bricks**.

fire command station   The principal location where the status of a fire-detection system, an alarm system, and a communications-and-control system are displayed, and from which all systems can be manually controlled.

fire compartment   An area of a building enclosed within a **fire-resistive construction**; has **fire-resistive doors** that close automatically in case of fire.

fire control   Limitation of the size of a fire by (a) distributing water so as to decrease the rate of heat release, (b) pre-wetting of adjacent combustibles, and (c) controlling the gas temperature of the ceiling to avoid structural damage.

fire control damper   A device which is designed to close an air duct in the event of fire.

fire cracks   See **crazing, checking**.

fire curtain   See **asbestos curtain**.

fire cut   A diagonal cut on a joist where it enters a masonry wall; if the joist burns through somewhere along its length, injury to the wall is prevented.

fire damper   A **damper** which closes off an air duct automatically in the event of fire so as to restrict the passage of fire and smoke.

fire damper

fired brick   A brick that has been treated in a kiln at a high temperature (i.e., **burnt**), in contrast to one that has been air-dried.

fire department inlet connection   A piping connection through which the local fire department can pump water into a **standpipe system** or **sprinkler system** in a building.

fire department standpipe system   A **dry standpipe system** having no permanent water supply; the fire department supplies water to the system through a **fire department connection**.

fire detection system   A system of **sensors** and associated interconnected equipment which detects the presence of fire and provides a warning signal.

fire division wall   In fire-resistant construction, a wall which separates a building into **fire areas**, restricting the spread of fire.

fire door   **1.** A fire-resistive door assembly, including frame and hardware, which is capable of providing a specified degree of fire protection when closed. Usually provided with an automatic closing mechanism, in the event of fire. **2.** In a furnace, the doorway through which fuel is supplied.

fire-door rating A fire-endurance rating for doors, shutters, etc., established by the Underwriters' Laboratories, Inc., or other recognized and approved laboratory: *class A:* 3 hr; for doorways or other openings through a wall separating buildings or dividing a single building into fire areas; *class B:* 1 or 1½ hr; for doorways or other openings in enclosures of vertical transportation through buildings (stairs, elevators, etc.); *class C:* ¾ hr; doors in corridor and room partitions; *class D:* 1½ hr; doors and shutters in exterior walls which are subject to severe fire exposure from outside the building; *classes E and F:* ¾ hr; doors, shutters, or windows in exterior walls which are subject to moderate or light fire exposure respectively from outside the building.

fired pin A hardened steel nail which is fired into concrete by a **stud gun**, or the like.

fired strength Of a refractory concrete, the compressive or flexural strength determined after the first firing to a specified temperature for a specified period of time and subsequent cooling.

fire endurance The elapsed time during which a material, assembly, or construction provides resistance against the passage of fire (or excessive heat) through it under specified conditions of test and performance.

fire escape A continuous, unobstructed path of escape from a building for use in case of fire.

fire-escape window, emergency-exit window **1.** Any window which opens onto a fire escape. **2.** A window at ground level which is designed to open wide, as a door, for emergency exits.

fire-exit bolt See **panic exit device**.

fire exposure The subjection of a material or construction to a high heat flux from an external source, with or without flame impingement.

fire extinguisher A portable device, for immediate and temporary use in putting out a fire: *class A:* used on fires involving ordinary combustible materials (such as wood, cloth, paper, rubber, and many plastics), which require the cooling effects of water or certain dry chemical coatings to retard combustion; *class B:* used on fires involving liquids, gases, greases, etc.,

extinguished most readily by excluding air or inhibiting the release of combustible vapors; *class C:* used on fires in "live" electrical equipment; *class D:* used on fires involving certain combustible metals, such as magnesium, sodium, etc., requiring a heat-absorbing extinguishing medium not reactive with the burning metals.

fire-extinguishing system An installation of automatic sprinklers, foam nozzles, fire hoses, and/or portable fire extinguishers, designed to provide adequate fire-extinguishing capability for a room or building.

fire frame A cast-iron housing, permanently installed in a large fireplace opening to reduce its size.

fire grading The **fire-hazard classification** of a building or structure, usually specified in *hours;* see **fire-protection rating**.

fire hazard The relative danger that a fire will start and spread, that smoke or gases will be generated, or that an explosion will occur, potentially endangering the lives and safety of the occupants of the building. Also see **hazardous area**.

fire-hazard classification One of three designations: ordinary, high, or low. Based on the contents and operations conducted in the building or structure, or on the **flame-spread rating** of its interior finishes or appurtenances.

fire hydrant, fireplug A supply outlet from a water main, for use in case of fire.

fire hydrant

fire limits A boundary line establishing an area in which there exists, or is likely to exist, a fire hazard requiring special fire protection.

fire line **1.** A system of pipes and equipment used exclusively to supply water for extinguishing fires. **2.** A fire hose, particularly when in use for fire fighting.

fire load, fire loading **1.** The combustible contents or interior finish of a building per unit floor area, expressed as pounds per square foot or as Btu per square foot. **2.** The amount of fuel within a building which has the potential of burning and releasing heat to feed the growth of a fire.

firemark In colonial America, a plaque, usually cast in lead and affixed to the façade of a house, indicating that the owner of the house had contributed money to the local volunteer fire department.

firemark

fire partition In a building, a partition which has a **fire-endurance** rating of not less than 2 hr, but does not qualify as a fire wall.

fire performance characteristic A response of a product, material, or an assembly of such products and/or materials to a prescribed source of heat or flame under controlled fire conditions.

fireplace An opening at the base of a chimney, usually an open recess in a wall, in which a fire may be built.

fireplace cheeks The splayed sides of a fireplace.

fireplace crane A wrought-iron horizontal bar, once commonly attached to the rear wall of a fireplace and pivoted so that it could be swung out at any desired angle over the fire; often served as a support from which to hang pots and kettles. Also see **randle bar** and **trammel.**

fireplace damper A pivoted metal plate, set just above the throat in a chimney, that controls the **draft, 1** (i.e., the flow of air and gaseous products) through a fireplace and up the chimney;

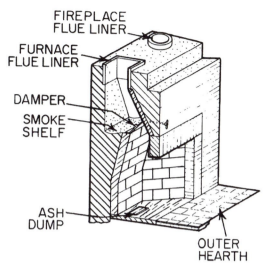

FIREPLACE FLUE LINER

FURNACE FLUE LINER

DAMPER

SMOKE SHELF

ASH DUMP

OUTER HEARTH

fireplace

may be used to close off the chimney when the fireplace is not in use.

fireplace lintel A horizontal structural member that supports the weight of the wall above a fireplace opening; same as **manteltree.** If wood, it is often plastered to increase its fire resistance; if metal, it is usually called a chimney bar.

fireplace mantel See **mantel.**

fireplace surround Around a fireplace, a framing composed of bricks, elaborate tile, marble, or decorative woodwork.

fireplace throat Same as **chimney throat.**

fireplace tile Tile used as a decorative facing around a fireplace opening; for example, **Dutch tile.**

fire plug Same as **fire hydrant.**

fire point **1.** See **flash point. 2.** The temperature at which a fuel's vapors will sustain ignition.

fireproof **1.** Descriptive of a material or construction which is unburnable, or almost so; an absolute quality which does not exist; usually refers to a material or construction which is highly fire-resistant. **2.** To apply a chemical solution to a material as a fire retardant; to **flameproof.**

fireproof curtain See **asbestos curtain.**

fireproof door **1.** A door composed entirely of fireproof materials. **2.** A **metal-clad fire door;** also called a kalamein fire door.

fireproofing Material applied to structural elements or systems which provides increased fire resistance, usually serving no structural function. Also see **sprayed fireproofing**.

fireproofing tile Tile designed for protecting structural members against fire.

fire protection Materials, measures, and practices for preventing fire or for minimizing the probable loss of life or property resulting from a fire, by proper design and construction of buildings, by the use of detection and extinguishing systems, by the establishment of adequate fire fighting services, and by the training of building occupants in fire safety and evacuation procedures.

fire-protection equipment cabinet A cabinet to house hose, fire extinguishers, or the like.

fire-protection rating The time in hours, or fractions thereof, that a material (or an assemblage of materials) can withstand fire exposure, as determined by a fire test conducted in accordance with applicable code requirements.

fire-protection sprinkler system See **sprinkler system**.

fire-protection sprinkler valve A **valve** used as an automatic means of controlling the flow of water in a fire-protection sprinkler system.

fire-protection system A system composed of appropriate electrical devices, equipment, and systems used to detect a fire, activate an alarm, and suppress a fire if detected.

fire pump A pump especially designed, tested, and **listed** for use in a fire suppression system. Since it is rarely (if ever) used, it must be tested periodically to ensure that its operating condition is satisfactory.

fire-rated door See **fire-door rating**.

fire resistance 1. The capacity of a material or construction to withstand fire or give protection from it; characterized by its ability to confine a fire and/or to continue to perform a structural function. 2. (*Brit.*) The ability of a component of building construction to satisfy certain criteria, specified by the BSI, for a stated period of time. 3. According to OSHA: so resistant to fire that, for a specified time and under conditions of a standard heat intensity, it will not fail structurally and will not permit the side away from the fire to become hotter than a specified temperature.

fire-resistance rating The time in hours that a material or construction can withstand fire exposure, as determined in conformity with generally accepted standards, or from information derived from standard tests.

fire-resistive, fire-resistant, fire-resisting Having **fire resistance**.

fire-resistive ceiling One having a **fire endurance** rating of at least 1 hr.

fire-resistive construction A building construction in which the structural members (including walls, partitions, columns, floors, and roof) are of **noncombustible** materials having fire-endurance ratings at least equal to those specified by the appropriate authorities.

fire-resistive wall A wall having a fire rating in accordance with code or underwriters' requirements governing its use; not necessarily incombustible.

fire-retardant chemical 1. A chemical or chemical preparation used to reduce flammability or to retard the spread of flame. 2. A chemical which, when added to a combustible material, delays ignition and combustion of the chemically treated material when it is exposed to fire.

fire-retardant coating 1. A material applied to the surface of a building component to increase its resistance to flaming combustion along the surface. 2. A covering which is applied (as a fluid) on a material to delay ignition and combustion of the material.

fire-retardant finish Paint which contains incombustible materials (such as chlorinated waxes and resins, silicones, antimony oxide, and other pigments) which form a protective layer over combustible surfaces to retard the rapid propagation of flame.

fire-retardant treatment The application of a **fire-retardant chemical** or a **fire-retardant coating**.

fire-retardant wood Lumber and plywood which has been impregnated, under pressure, with mineral salts; in the event of fire, the burning wood and salts emit noncombustible gases and water vapor instead of the usual flammable vapors.

fire-retarding glazing 1. Wire glass. 2. Copperlight glazing.

fire risk   **1.** The probability that a fire will occur. **2.** The potential for harm to life and damage to property resulting from the occurrence of a fire.

fire risk assessment standard   A standardized method of assessing **fire risk** of a material, product, or assembly in a specific environment or application.

fire safety plan   A description of the fire drill and evacuation procedures for a building in accordance with applicable administrative requirements.

fire screen   Any screen set in front of a fireplace to prevent flying sparks or embers from entering the room.

fire section   A sprinklered area within a building, separated from other areas by a noncombustible construction having a fire-resistance rating of at least two hours.

fire separation   A floor or wall (either without openings or with adequately protected openings) having a **fire-endurance rating** required by appropriate authorities; acts as a barrier against the spread of fire within a building.

fire separation assembly   A horizontal and/or vertical fire-resistance-rated assembly of materials having protected openings, and designed to restrict the spread of fire.

fire shutter   A metal shutter (including frame and hardware) which has a fire-endurance rating required by code. The required rating depends on the location and nature of the window or opening in which it is installed.

fireside, ingleside   The hearth or space about the fireplace.

fire sprinkler   A nozzle (sprinkler head) in a fire protection system; distributes water in a specific spray pattern.

fire sprinkler system   An integrated system of underground and/or overhead piping, with one or more automatic water supplies, to which **fire sprinklers** (i.e., sprinkler heads) are attached and placed in a systematic pattern; also called a **fire-protection sprinkler system**.

fire stair   A stair, enclosed in fireproof walls, within the body of the building which it serves, to which access may be had only through self-closing **fire doors**.

fire standpipe   See **standpipe**.

fire standpipe system   See **standpipe system**.

firestat   A thermostat in an air-conditioning system; preset at a fixed temperature, usually 125°F (52°C) in accordance with code or insurance requirements.

fire stone   Any stone, such as sandstone, that is heat-resistant and therefore especially suitable for use in fireplaces.

fire stop   In a concealed, hollow construction, a material or member which fills or seals the open construction to prevent or retard the spread of fire.

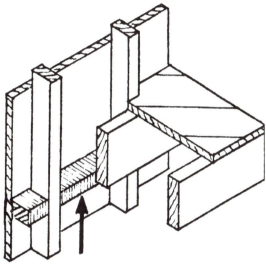

fire stop

fire-stopping   The closing of all concealed draft openings to form an effective fire barrier at floors, ceilings, and roofs by means of brick, concrete, gypsum, asbestos, mineral wool, rock wool, metal lath with cement or gypsum plaster, or other approved incombustible materials.

fire suppression   The marked reduction of the rate of heat release of a fire and the prevention of its regrowth by means of direct and sufficient application of water through the fire plume to the burning fuel surface.

fire suppression system   A system used to control or to extinguish a fire in a building. The most common types are **fire sprinkler systems** and **standpipe systems**.

fire terrace   A level space or area at a setback of an exterior wall of a building that is approximately the same elevation as that of the curb or grade level of a street that is higher than the building entrance; provides a safe termination for fire escapes from the upper stories of the building.

fire test exposure severity   A measure of the degree of fire exposure according to ASTM Test Methods E119, E152, and E163.

fire tower   In a building, a vertical enclosure (containing a stairway) having a fire-endurance rating sufficiently high to qualify as a **fire escape**.

fire-tube steel boiler   An integral steel-shell boiler in which the combustion gases pass through the tubes and the boiler water passes around them; usually shipped in one piece, ready for piping connections.

fire-tube test   A standard test for the combustible properties of treated wood; makes use of a fire-tube apparatus specified by the ASTM.

fire vent   Same as **smoke and fire vent**.

fire wall   A wall so constructed as to prevent the spread of fire from one part of a building to another.

fire window   A window and associated components, including frame, wired glass, and hardware, having a fire-endurance rating at least as high as that specified for the location in which it is to be used.

fire zone   An area of a building that has been designated by the applicable building code as being subject to a relatively high fire risk.

fir fixed   Said of unplaned timbers which are fixed only by nails.

firing   The controlled heat treatment of ceramic ware in a kiln or furnace during the process of manufacture to develop desired properties.

firing port   Same as **riflehole**.

firmer chisel   A carpenter's chisel with a blade thin in proportion to its width, esp. used for mortising.

firmer gouge   A carpenter's gouge having its bevel on the outside; similar in proportions to a **firmer chisel**; esp. used in cutting grooves.

firring   Same as **furring**.

first coat   The initial application of plaster. In two-coat work it is called the **base coat**; in three-coat work it is called the **scratch coat**.

first fixings (*usually pl.*)   Hidden blocks of wood, **grounds**, or **plugs** to which joinery is fixed.

first floor   **1.** (*U.S.A.*) The floor of a building which is at, or closest to, grade level. **2.** (*Brit.*) The floor of a building which is next above the floor at, or closest to, grade level; the latter is known as the "ground floor."

first gallery   In a theatre, a seating area in a balcony above a tier or tiers of boxes.

first mortgage   A security interest in property which takes precedence over all similar interests in the same property.

First Period Colonial architecture   A term occasionally used for architecture of the American colonies from the time of their initial settlement until the emergence of the Georgian architecture at the beginning of the 18th century; see **American Colonial architecture.**

first pipe   In a theatre stagehouse, the **pipe batten** immediately behind the proscenium; used to support lighting equipment.

First Pointed Gothic   See **Early English architecture** and **Lancet style.**

first story   In the U.S.A., the lowest story of a building which is entirely above the average grade; the **ground floor.** In many European countries, the first floor above the **ground floor.**

fish beam   **1.** A built-up timber beam composed of two beams placed end to end and secured by **fish plates** covering the joint on opposite sides. **2.** Any beam having sides which swell like the belly of a fish.

fish-bellied   Descriptive of a girder or truss having its bottom flange or chord convex downward.

fish bladder (fischblase)   An ornamental motif of the late Gothic tracery, reminiscent in form of the air-bladder of a fish.

fished joint   A **heading joint, 1** strengthened by **fishplates**.

fisheye   In plastering, a spot in the finish coat approximately ¼ in. (6.4 mm) in diameter, caused by lumpy lime.

fish glue   A glue made from fish skins and bladders; similar to animal glue.

fishing wire   Same as **snake, 1**.

fish joint   See **fished joint**.

fish mouth   In built-up roofing systems, an opening where one felt layer overlaps another; caused by a wrinkle at the overlapping edge.

fish bladder   tracery

fishplate   A wood or metal piece used to fasten together the ends of two members with nails or bolts.

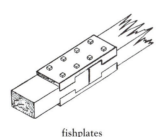

fishplates

fishscale pattern   Overlapping rows of shaped tiles or shingles that resemble overlapping fish scales; see **imbrication**.

fishtail   A wedge-shaped piece of wood used as part of the soffit form between tapered end pans in concrete joist construction.

fishtail bolt   A bolt having a split end; embedded in concrete, or the like, for use as an anchor.

fish tape   Same as **snake, 1**.

fistula   In ancient Roman construction, a water pipe of lead or earthenware.

fitch   **1.** A small thin paintbrush with a long wooden handle; used to reach recessed areas. **2.** A thin piece of wood, as a veneer. **3.** A bundle of

veneers arranged in the same order as cut from the log. **4.** A board forming part of a flitch beam.

fitment   See **fitting**.

fitting   **1.** A pipe part, usually standardized, such as a bend, coupling, cross, elbow, reducer, tee, union, etc.; used for joining two or more sections of pipe together. The term usually is used in the plural. **2.** An accessory such as a bushing, coupling, locknut, or other part of an electric wiring system which is intended to perform a mechanical rather than an electrical function. **3.** Same as **window hardware**. **4.** British for **luminaire**. **5.** A decorative or functional item or component in a building which is fixed but not built in; also called a **fitment**.

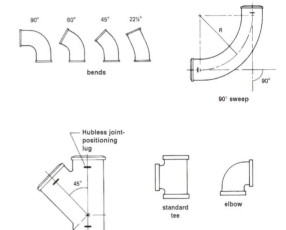

fittings, 1

fitting-up   Assembling the different members of a structure and connecting them temporarily with bolts preparatory to making the final connection.

fitting-up bolt   An ordinary bolt used to hold members together temporarily while they are being permanently connected.

five-centered arch   An arch whose intrados is struck from five centers.

five-part mansion   A pretentious colonial home connected to a **dependency** on each side of the house **hyphens**.

FIX.   On drawings, abbr. for **fixture**.

fixed-bar grille   In an air-conditioning system, a grille most commonly used for return and exhaust air openings; the position of the bars is preset and nonadjustable.

fixed beam, fixed-end beam A structural beam whose ends are fixed.

fixed-end column A column whose fixed ends prevent it from rotating.

fixed joint In a structural framework, a joint that restrains a member from turning.

fixed light, deadlight, fast sheet, stand sheet, fixed sash A window or an area of a window which does not open; glazed directly in a fixed frame that does not open.

fixed limit of construction cost The maximum allowable cost of the construction work as established in the agreement between the owner and the architect. Also see **construction budget**.

fixed retaining wall A **retaining wall** which is rigidly supported at its top and bottom; can withstand higher pressures than a **freestanding** wall.

fixed sash A **fixed light**.

fixed transom An inoperable panel or glass light over a door.

fixing **1.** Installing glass panes in a wall, partition, or ceiling. (Installing glass in windows, doors, storefronts, curtain walls, borrowed lights, etc., is termed **glazing**.) **2.** Same as **ground, 1**.

fixing block A lightweight concrete block that is nailable.

fixing brick **1.** Same as **nog**. **2.** A lightweight brick that is nailable.

fixing fillet See **ground, 1**.

fixing pad Same as **ground, 1**.

fixing slip See **ground, 1**.

fixity See **depth of fixity**.

fixture **1.** Any item which was once tangible personal property, but which by virtue of its affixation to **real property** is deemed to be permanently merged into it. **2.** An electrical device which is secured to a wall or ceiling, and used to hold lamps; a **luminaire**. **3.** See **plumbing fixture**.

fixture branch Any pipe which connects several plumbing fixtures, such as a drain serving two or more fixtures or a supply pipe between the water-distributing pipe and several fixtures.

fixture carrier A metal device designed to support an off-the-floor plumbing fixture.

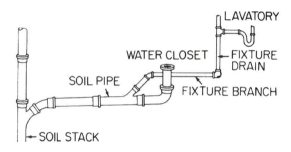

fixture branch

fixture drain The drain extending from the trap of a plumbing fixture to a junction of that drain with any other drainpipe.

fixture fitting A device used to control or guide the flow of water into a fixture or to convey water away from the fixture.

fixture joint An electric connection between two conductors, formed by crossing their bare ends, wrapping one end around the other, and then folding them over.

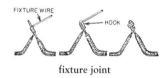

fixture joint

fixture supply The water-supply pipe connecting a plumbing fixture to a branch water-supply pipe or directly to a main water-supply pipe.

fixture trap Same as **trap, 1**.

fixture unit A measure of the probable discharge into the drainage system by various types of plumbing fixtures; expressed in units of cubic volume per minute; the value for a particular fixture depends on: its volume rate of drainage discharge; the time duration of a single drainage operation; and the average time between successive operations.

fixture-unit flow rate According to code, the total discharge flow in gallons per minute of a single fixture divided by 7.5, which provides the flow rate of that particular plumbing fixture as a unit of flow; fixtures are rated as multiples of this unit of flow.

fixture vent A **vent pipe** which leads from the drainage pipe to another vent pipe or to the atmosphere.

fL   Abbr. for **footlambert**.

FL   **1.** Abbr. for "floor line." **2.** On drawings, abbr. for **floor**. **3.** On drawings, abbr. for **flashing**.

flabelliform   Fan-shaped; said of an ornament composed of palm leaves, or the like.

flag   A **flagstone**.

flagging   **1.** **Flagstone**. **2.** A surface paved with flagstones. **3.** The process of setting flagstones.

flagpole   A pole on which a flag, banner, or emblem may be raised and displayed.

flagstone, flag, flagging   A flat stone, usually 1 to 4 in. (2.5 to 10 cm) thick, used as a stepping-stone or for terrace or outdoor paving; usually either naturally thin or split from rock that cleaves readily; sometimes produced by sawing.

flagstone: paved walk

Flamboyant style

flail   A device for breaking or crushing material by means of one or more hammers which are hinged or pivoted about a rotating axle.

flake board   Same as **particleboard**.

flaking   The loss of adhesion and cohesion of a paint film accompanied by peeling.

flambeau   A luminaire resembling a flaming torch.

flambé glaze   A flow ceramic glaze with copper, which produces a variegated effect.

flamboyant finish   A decorative coating achieved by applying transparent colored varnish or lacquer over a polished metal substrate.

Flamboyant style   The last phase of French Gothic architecture in the second half of the 15th cent., characterized by flowing and flame-like tracery.

flame   A hot (usually luminous) zone of gas and/or particulate matter in gaseous suspension that is undergoing combustion.

flame cleaning   The use of a hot flame on steel to remove paint, mill scale, moisture, and surface dirt.

flame-cut   Said of a steel plate whose longitudinal edges have been prepared by oxygen cutting.

flame cutting   A metal-cutting operation in which the separation of the metal is effected with a torch. See also **oxygen cutting** and **oxyacetylene torch**.

flame front   The leading edge of a flame propagating through a gaseous mixture or across the surface of a solid or liquid.

flame resistance   The ability to withstand flame impingement or to provide protection from it.

flame resistant   Having **flame resistance**.

flame-retardant chemical   Any chemical which, when added to a combustible material, delays ignition and reduces the spread of flame on the resulting material.

flame-retardant coating   A fluid-applied surface covering on a combustible material which delays ignition and reduces flame spread when the covering is exposed to flame.

flame-retardant treatment   The application of a **flame-retardant chemical** or a **flame-retardant coating**.

flame speed   The rate of propagation of a flame through a gaseous fuel-and-oxidizer mixture relative to a fixed reference point.

flame spread   Flaming combustion along a surface (not to be confused with the transfer of flame by air currents).

flame-spread index   A numerical designation, applied to a building material, which is a comparative measure of the ability of the material to resist flaming combustion over its surface; the rate of flame travel, as measured under the applicable ASTM test, in which a selected species of untreated lumber has a designated value of 100, and noncombustible cement-asbestos board has a value of 0.

flame-spread rating   A measurement of **flame spread** on the surface of a material (or an assemblage of materials) as determined by procedures described in the applicable code.

flame treating   A method of rendering inert thermoplastic objects receptive to inks, lacquers, paints, adhesives, etc., by bathing them in an open flame to promote oxidation of the surface.

flammability   A material's ability to burn or support combustion.

flammable   Subject to easy ignition and rapid flaming combustion.

flammable liquid   Any liquid having a flash point below 140°F (60°C) and having an absolute vapor pressure not exceeding 40 lb per sq in. (2.8 kg per sq cm) absolute at 100°F (37.8°C).

flanch, flaunch   To widen and slant the top of a chimney stack so that water is directed away from the flue.

flange   1. A projecting collar, edge, rib, rim, or ring on a pipe, shaft, or the like. 2. One of the principal longitudinal components of a beam or girder which resists tension or compression.

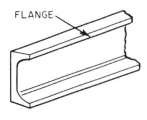

flange, 2

flange angle   One of the component parts of the top or bottom flange in a girder.

flange cut   A cut in the flange of a beam or girder to facilitate attachment or passage of another element.

flanged joint   A joint consisting of two companion flanges, bolted together and made leakproof by means of a gasket.

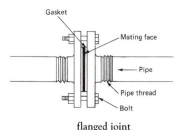

flanged joint

flange plate   1. See **cover plate, 2**. 2. In a railing system, the flat piece between the end of a railing (or railing element) and the adjoining construction or supporting member.

flange splice   A splice made in the flange of a beam or girder.

flange union   In plumbing, a pair of flanges which hold two pipes together; the flanges are screwed onto the ends of the pipes and then are held together by bolts.

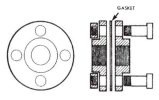

flange union

flank   A side, as of a building or arch.

flanker   A **dependency** or a service wing on a side of a building.

flanking transmission   The transmission of sound from one room to another by a path other than directly through the partition which separates the rooms.

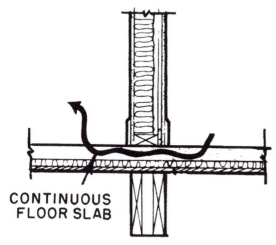

CONTINUOUS FLOOR SLAB

flanking transmission: path, indicated by arrow

flank wall   A sidewall of a building in contrast to the front or rear wall.

flank window, flanking window   Same as **sidelight**.

flanning   The internal splay of a window jamb.

flap door   A small door, hinged horizontally along the bottom, that opens downward.

flap hinge   See **backflap hinge**.

flap trap   In plumbing, a **trap** having a hinged flap which allows flow in one direction only, preventing backflow.

flap valve   In plumbing, a **check valve** in the form of a hinged disk which permits flow in one direction only.

flared eaves   That part of a roof that has a gradually diminishing slope and that projects beyond the face of an exterior wall, flaring outward near its lower end; common in rural **Dutch Colonial architecture**.

flared joint   A mechanical joint between two pieces of copper or plastic tubing; made by flaring one end of a tube in such a way as to receive a special fitting which fits in the flare; may be taken apart and reassembled without difficulty; especially useful in areas where fire hazard will

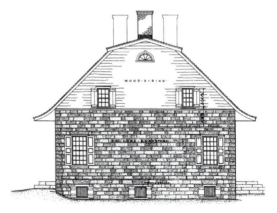

flared eaves

not permit the open flame required in soldering or brazing a joint.

flared post   A heavy post, often located at the corners of a **timber-framed house**, that has a flare at its upper end to provide a larger area for supporting the load imposed on it from above; occasionally located at the middle of a wall to provide additional support for a massive **summerbeam**.

flared post

flare fitting   A mechanical connection used with soft-metal tubing; one end of a tube is flared and provided with a mechanical seal.

flare header   In masonry, a **header** of darker color than the field of the wall.

flash   1. A color variation on the surface of a brick, produced intentionally or otherwise, due to surface fusion or vitrification of a film of different texture. 2. Abbr. for **flashing**.

flash chamber   A tank between the expansion valve and evaporator in a refrigeration system to separate and bypass any flash gas formed in the expansion valve.

flash coat   A light coat of shotcrete over a concrete surface to cover minor blemishes.

flashing   A thin impervious material placed in construction (e.g., in mortar joints and through air spaces in masonry) to prevent water penetration and/or provide water drainage, esp. between a roof and wall, and over exterior door openings and windows.

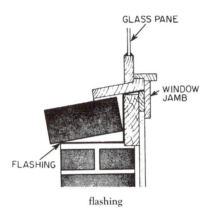

GLASS PANE

WINDOW JAMB

FLASHING

flashing

flashing block   A specially designed masonry block having a slot or channel into which the top edge of a counterflashing may be inserted and anchored. Also see **raggle, 1**.

flashing board   A board to which flashings are fixed.

flashing cement   A mixture of bitumen, a solvent, and inorganic reinforcing fibers, such as glass or asbestos fibers; applied with a trowel.

flashing compound   See **flashing cement**.

flashing ring   A collar around a pipe to secure it as it passes through a wall or floor.

flash point   The minimum temperature of a combustible material at which there is sufficient vaporization to produce a combustible mixture with air if ignited by a flame.

flash set, grab set, quick set   The rapid development of rigidity in a freshly mixed portland cement paste, mortar, or concrete, usually with the generation of considerable heat; this rigidity cannot be dispelled, nor the plasticity regained by further mixing, without the addition of water.

flash welding   A resistance welding process in which metals are joined as a result of heat,

obtained from the resistance to an electric current between the metal surfaces, and subsequent pressure.

flat   **1.** Descriptive of a roof, etc., having little or no slope. **2.** One floor of a multistory building or a dwelling unit on one floor. **3.** Descriptive of paint having very low gloss. **4.** A piece of framed stage scenery without thickness other than its framing members. **5.** A metal bar having a rectangular cross section; if fabricated of steel, must have a minimum thickness of 0.203 in. (0.516 cm) and a maximum width of 8 in. (20.3 cm).

flat arch   An arch whose soffit (i.e., lower face) is horizontal. Also called a Dutch arch, French arch, jack arch, or straight arch.

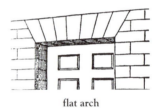

flat arch

flat arris   An arris (i.e., the external angular intersection of two surfaces), such as between two flutes of a Doric column, which has been flattened so that it is not sharply defined.

flat band   A flat, undecorated **impost**.

flat-chord truss   A truss in which the top and bottom chords are approximately flat and parallel.

flat coat   An intermediate coat of paint used as a base for a topcoat; a **filler coat**.

flat cutting   See **ripsawing**.

flat-drawn glass, flat-drawn sheet glass   See **drawn glass**.

flat enamel brush   A paintbrush, about 2 to 3 in. (5 to 7.5 cm) wide, having flagged and tapered bristles; used to apply smooth films of enamel on woodwork. Also see **flat wall brush**.

flat glass   See **window glass, plate glass, float glass, rolled glass, sheet glass**.

flat-grained   See **plain-sawn**.

flathead   **1.** A bolt or screw having a flat top surface and a conical bearing surface. **2.** A rivet head that has been flattened.

flathead dormer   Same as **shed dormer**.

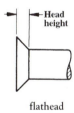

flathead

flathead rivet A rivet which has the point hammered flat instead of rounded.

flat joint Same as **flush-cut joint**.

flat-joint jointed pointing Flat-joint pointing in which the grooves are further embellished by narrow grooves along their center lines, or by grooves at top and bottom, next to the bricks.

flat keystone arch A **flat arch** with a **keystone** at its center.

flat paint A paint which dries either without gloss or with very low gloss.

flat paintbrush See **flat wall brush**.

flat piece A particle of aggregate in which the ratio of the width to thickness of its circumscribing rectangular prism is greater than a specified value. Also see **elongated piece**.

flat plate A flat concrete slab having no **column capitals** or **drop panels**.

flat pointing, flat-joint pointing The simplest form of pointing. Mortar in the joints of brickwork is finished flush with the face of the masonry with a flat trowel.

flat rolled Descriptive of a product (such as a steel plate, strip, or sheet) of a rolling mill which is equipped with smooth-faced rolls, in contrast to rolls used to manufacture special shapes.

flat roof A horizontal roof either having no slope, or a slope sufficient only to effect drainage, its pitch being usually less than 10 degrees; it may be surrounded by a parapet or it may extend beyond the exterior walls.

flat-sawn Same as **plain-sawn**.

flat seam In sheet metal work, a seam between adjacent metal sheets, formed by turning up both edges, folding them over, and then flattening; the joint, so formed, usually is soldered.

forming a **flat seam**

flat skylight A **skylight** which is essentially horizontal; has only enough slope to allow rainwater to run off.

flat slab A concrete slab which is reinforced in two or more directions, usually without beams or girders to transfer the loads to supporting members.

flat spot An imperfection on a glossy painted surface; a spot lacking gloss, usually caused by a porous spot on the undercoat.

flat spray sprinkler In a fire protection system, a **sprinkler** providing a parabolic water distribution which directs 60 to 80 percent of the total water flow initially in a downward direction toward the floor; some water is sprayed toward the ceiling.

flatting 1. Same as **flat cutting**; also see **ripsawing**. 2. Same as **flatting down**.

flatting agent A substance which lowers gloss of paints or varnishes to which it is added.

flatting down, rubbing Rubbing abrasive powder or similar material on a surface to lower the gloss and make it more uniform.

flatting oil A thin solution which is added to glossy paint or varnish so that a semigloss or matte finish may be obtained.

flat top truss Same as **Howe truss**.

flat varnish, matte varnish A varnish which dries either without gloss or with a low gloss.

flat wall brush, flat paintbrush A paintbrush usually 4 to 6 in. (10 to 15 cm) in width, with long, stiff bristles, usually made of synthetic fiber.

flaunch Same as **flanch**.

fleaking Same as **thatching**.

flèche A spire, usually comparatively small and slender, above the ridge of a roof, particularly one rising from the intersection of the nave and transept roofs of Gothic churches.

fleck A small spot, mark, or figure in wood, usually caused by wood rays, or other irregular growth characteristics, e.g., natural deposits of gummy matter.

fleet angle In hoisting gear, the maximum angle between the rope (as it comes off the drum on which it is wound) and a perpendicular to the axis of the drum.

Flemish bond

Flemish bond A brick pattern in which each course consists of **headers** and **stretchers** that are laid alternately; each header is centered with respect to the stretchers above and below it.

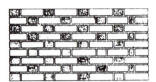

Flemish bond

Flemish cross bond Similar to **Flemish bond** but with two additional headers in place of a stretcher at intervals.

Flemish diagonal bond A bond in which a course of alternate **headers** and **stretchers** is followed by a course of stretchers, resulting in a diagonal pattern.

Flemish eaves Same as **flared eaves**.

Flemish gable A **gable** having a pediment whose outline contains two or more curves on each side of its apex.

Flemish gable

Flemish gambrel roof Same as **Dutch gambrel roof**.

Flemish garden-wall bond Similar to **Flemish bond** but with three stretchers between each header instead of a single stretcher.

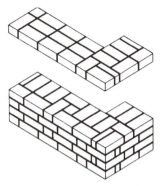

Flemish garden-wall bond

fletton An English brick made from Oxford clay; manufactured by the semi-dry-press process; represents over 40% of current British brick production.

fleur-de-lys The French royal lily, conventionalized as an ornament in Late Gothic architecture.

fleuron 1. The small flower at the center of each side of the Corinthian abacus. 2. Any small flower-like ornament in general.

fleuron, 1

flexibility The property of a material that allows it to bend without damage (and without losing its strength) and then to return to its original shape.

flexible conduit See **flexible metal conduit, flexible nonmetallic tubing, flexible metallic hose, flexible seamless tubing**.

flexible connector **1.** A nonmetallic airtight connection in ductwork, between a fan and a duct or between ducts, to prevent the transmission of vibration along the duct. **2.** In a piping system, a connector, usually fabricated of a combination of metallic mesh and a nonmetallic material; used to minimize the transmission of vibration along the piping system (as between pipes or between a pipe and a pump, etc.) or to reduce pipe misalignment. **3.** An electric connection that permits the contraction, expansion, or relative motion between connected parts of rotating machinery.

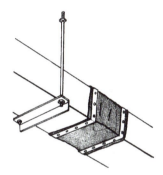

flexible connector, 1

flexible coupling A coupling, used in rotating machinery, having high transverse or torsional compliance.

flexible drop-chute A heavy elastic or rubberized canvas collapsible tube which serves as a **drop chute**.

flexible joint A joint between two conduits, ducts, or pipes that permits one of them to be deflected or moved without significantly disturbing the other.

flexible metal conduit A flexible raceway which is circular in cross section, esp. constructed for the pulling in or withdrawing of cables or wires, after the conduit and its fittings are in place.

flexible metallic hose Hose made from a continuous coil of strip metal; embodies an interlocked construction with a packing wound continuously into the grooves in the interlocked joint; suitable for use with water, oil, and gases at low pressure.

flexible metallic hose

flexible-metal roofing Roof coverings of flat sheet metal such as aluminum, copper, or galvanized iron.

flexible-metal sheeting See **sheet metal**.

flexible mounting A flexible support between rotating machinery and the foundation or slab on which it is mounted; used to reduce the transmission of vibration from machinery to the foundation or slab.

flexible nonmetallic tubing A mechanical protection for electric conductors; consists of a flexible tubing having a smooth interior and a wall of nonconducting fibrous material.

flexible pipe connection Same as **flexible connector**.

flexible seamless tubing A flexible metal tubing made from seamless, welded, or soldered tubing; commonly made from steel, bronze, stainless steel, and a variety of alloys; not susceptible to leakage; esp. used for gases under pressure and volatile gases; sometimes enclosed within a flexible braid.

flexible seamless tubing

flexural bond In **prestressed concrete**, the stress between the concrete and the tendon which results from the application of an external load.

flexural center See **shear center**.

flexural rigidity A measure of stiffness of a structural member; the product of modulus of elasticity and moment of inertia divided by the length of the member.

flexural strength That property of a solid which is an indication of its ability to withstand bending.

flexure The bending of a member, as under a load.

FLG   On drawings, abbr. for **flooring**.

flier, flyer   **1.** Any of the steps in a straight flight of stairs, each tread of which is of uniform width (as distinguished from the treads in a winding stair). **2.** A **flying shore**.

flies, fly loft   The space over a theatre stage for hanging scenery or other equipment by means of movable rigging.

flight   A continuous series of steps with no intermediate landings.

flight header   A horizontal structural member used in stair construction, at a floor or platform level, to support the end(s) of one or more **strings, 1**.

flight rise   The vertical distance between the floors or platforms connected by a flight of stairs.

flight run   Same as **run, 3**.

flint   A dense, fine-grained stone; a form of silica; naturally occurs in the form of nodules; usually gray, brown, black, or otherwise dark in color, but nodules and other chunks tend to weather white or light shades from the surface inward. Broken "flints," as the nodules are called, are used in cobble size, either whole or split (knapped) in mortared walls, esp. in England.

flint glass   **1.** A soda-lime-quartz glass having a high transparency. **2.** A glass that contains lead.

flitch   **1.** A portion sawn from a log and normally manufactured into veneer or lumber. **2.** Sheets of veneer, stacked in sequence, as cut from the log. **3.** A thick timber cut with bark on one or more edges. **4.** A board which forms part of a **flitch beam**.

flitch beam, flitch girder, sandwich beam   A beam built up of structural timbers which are bolted together with a steel plate sandwiched between them.

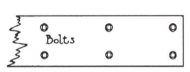

flitch beam

flitch plate   The steel plate which is sandwiched between the timbers in a **flitch beam**.

float   A flat tool with a handle on the back; used on cement or plaster surfaces for smoothing or for producing textured surfaces. Also see **angle float, bull float, carpet float, rotary float**.

float

float check   A type of **check valve**; as water flows into a atmospheric-type vacuum breaker, the float check rises and seals against the air inlet port, permitting water to flow through. When the water is turned off, the float check falls, opening the air inlet port, thereby preventing **backflow**.

float coat   A finish coat of cement applied with a float.

float-controlled valve   See **float valve**.

floated coat, topping coat   A plaster coat which has been applied with a float, usually over the **scratch coat**.

float finish   A rather rough concrete or mortar surface texture obtained by finishing with a float; rougher than a **trowel finish**.

float glass   See **plate glass**.

floating   Smoothing newly applied mortar, plaster, or concrete with a trowel or float.

floating brick   A type of very lightweight brick.

floating coat   Same as **brown coat**.

floating floor   In sound-insulating building construction, a floor slab (or floor assembly)

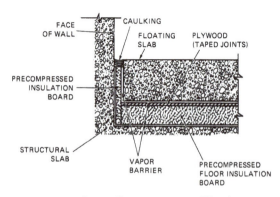

concrete floating floor construction of fiberglass insulation board

which is completely separated from (and mechanically isolated from) the structural floor by a resilient underlayment, such as fiberglass floor-isolation board, or by resilient mounting devices; used to isolate the vibration of machinery mounted on the floating floor from the building structure.

floating foundation A reinforced concrete slab used to support and distribute the concentrated load from columns in a soil having low bearing capacity; also called a raft foundation or mat foundation.

floating rule A long straightedge used as a **float**.

floating wood floor A **floating floor** consisting of wood flooring floating on a resilient layer of material which completely separates it from the building structure.

float scaffold A scaffold hung from overhead supports by ropes and consisting of a substantial platform having diagonal bracing underneath, resting upon and securely fastened to two parallel plank bearers at right angles to the span.

floatstone In bricklaying, a stone used to rub curved work smooth and remove ax marks.

float switch An electric switch which is actuated automatically when a float on the surface of a liquid reaches a preset level.

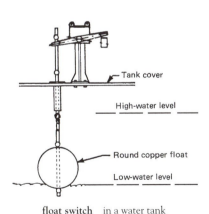

float switch   in a water tank

float trap A mechanical buoyancy-operated steam trap in which a ball float changes level as the quantity of steam condensation in the trap varies, thus controlling the discharge of steam through the trap.

float valve, float-controlled valve A **valve** which controls the flow of water; its opening or closing depends on the position of a float which rides on the surface of water in a tank, as in a water closet.

flock spraying, flocking The creation of a textured effect similar to suede or felt by blowing fibers of cotton, silk, nylon, or other material onto a tacky film of varnish.

flood coat 1. See **flow coat**. 2. In an aggregate-surfaced, built-up roof, the top layer of bitumen, which is poured on the surface.

flooding 1. The stratification of different-colored pigments in a paint film. 2. Introducing water, by gravity, into the backfill surrounding a pipe in order to compact the backfill. 3. A temporary condition of partial or complete inundation of normally dry land areas resulting from (a) the overflow of inland or tidal waters, or (b) the unusual and rapid accumulation of runoff of surface waters from any source.

flood level In a plumbing fixture, the level at which water begins to overflow the top or rim of the fixture.

flood-level rim The edge of a plumbing fixture or receptacle over which water would flow if it were full.

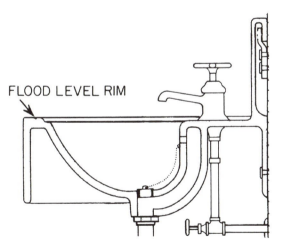

flood-level rim

floodlight 1. A **projector** type of luminaire; designed for lighting a large area or an object to a level of illumination which is considerably greater than that of its surroundings. **2.** In stage lighting, a unit of one or more lamps in a metal housing, usually nonfocusing and used to illuminate a large area diffusely.

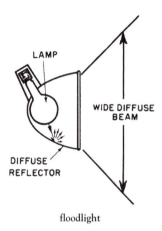

floodlight

flood plain   Any land area susceptible of being inundated by water from any source.

floor   **1.** In a room, the surface on which one walks. **2.** A division between one story and another; one story of a building. Also see **blind floor, counterfloor, earth floor, finish floor, ground floor, lowest floor, threshold floor, underfloor, upper floor.**

floor anchor   Same as **base anchor.**

floor arch   **1.** A flat concrete slab supported by beams. **2.** An arch which has a flat extrados.

floor area   See **gross floor area; net floor area.**

floor area ratio   The ratio of the total floor area of a building (excluding areas such as mechanical rooms or the areas of floors used exclusively for mechanical equipment) to the area of the lot on which the building is built.

floor batten   A batten which is fixed to a concrete subfloor and to which flooring is nailed.

floor beam   A beam supporting the floor of a building or the deck of a bridge.

floorboard   One of the boards or planks used as the finish floor, forming the walking surface of the room.

floor box   A metal **outlet box** providing for outlets from conduits concealed in the floor.

floor brick   Smooth, dense brick, highly resistant to abrasion; used for finished floor surfaces.

floor chisel   A steel chisel having a broad blade and a long shank; esp. used for ripping up floor boards.

floor clamp, floor cramp, floor dog   A clamp used to force floorboards together while nailing them to the joists.

floor clearance   The distance between the bottom of a door and the finish floor or saddle.

floor clip   Same as **sleeper clip.**

floor closer   A door-closing device which is installed in a recess in the floor below the door to regulate the opening and closing swing of the door.

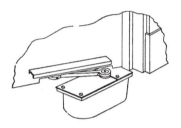

floor closer

floorcloth   A heavy canvas used as carpeting; may be decorated.

floor decking   Same as **decking, 1.**

floor dog   Same as **floor clamp.**

floor drain   A fixture providing an opening in a floor to drain water into a plumbing system; in homes, usually fitted with a deep seal trap.

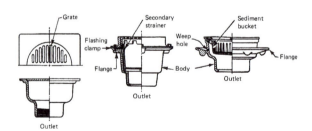

typical **floor drains**

floor fill   A **filler** between the structural floor slab and the **finish floor.**

floor flange   Same as **escutcheon, 2.**

floor framing   **Framing** consisting of common floor joists, cross bridging, solid bridging, and other members which provide support for flooring.

floor furnace   See **floor-type heater**.

floor furring   Wood furring strips fixed to a subfloor to provide clearance for piping or conduit laid directly on the subfloor.

floor guide   A groove in a floor or surface-mounted hardware on the floor, used to guide a sliding door.

floor hanger   A **stirrup, 2**.

floor hatch   A hinged panel unit which provides access through a floor.

floor hinge   Same as **floor closer**.

floor hole   According to OSHA: any opening measuring less than 12 in. (30.5 cm) but more than 1 in. (2.5 cm) in its least dimension in any floor, roof, or platform through which materials but not persons may fall, such as a belt hold, pipe opening, or slot opening.

flooring   Any material used as the finish surface of a floor, such as boards, bricks, planks, or tile.

flooring brick   A dense, hard brick that is especially resistant to heavy surface wear.

flooring cement   Same as **Keene's cement**.

flooring nail   A steel nail with a mechanically deformed shank, often helically threaded, having a countersunk or casing head and a blunt diamond point.

flooring nail

flooring saw   A handsaw which tapers to a point, with teeth on its upper edge as well as along the bottom; used for cutting holes in wood floors.

flooring strips   See **strip flooring**.

flooring underlayment   See **underlayment**.

floor joint   A joint between the sides of boards or planks which are continuous from end to end.

floor joist   Any **joist** which carries a floor.

floor light   A window in the floor which transmits light to the room below it; of heavy glass, designed to support the normal floor loads.

floor line   A line, or series of short lines, as on a wall, establishing the level of the **finish floor**.

floor lining paper   See **building paper**.

floor load   The **live load** for which a floor of a building has been designed, and which may be applied safely; usually expressed as a uniformly distributed load, except where there are concentrations of heavy machinery.

floor molding   See **base shoe**.

floor opening   According to OSHA: an opening measuring 12 in. (30.5 cm) or more in its least dimension in any floor, roof, or platform, through which persons may fall.

floor outlet   Same as **floor receptacle**.

floor panel   A prefabricated unit consisting of flooring, subflooring, and reinforcing joists; supported by columns, walls, or beams.

floor pit   A recess below a floor which provides access to parts beneath a machine, as an **elevator pit**.

floor plan   A drawing; a horizontal section taken above a floor to show, diagrammatically, the enclosing walls of a building, its doors and windows, and the arrangement of its interior spaces.

floor plate   **1.** A flat metal plate which is set in a floor; usually provided with slots into which equipment can be fastened. **2.** A steel plate having a raised pattern which provides a nonslip wearing surface.

floor plug   See **floor receptacle**.

floor pocket   A **stage pocket** set into a theatre stage floor.

floor receptacle   In an electric circuit, a receptacle which is mounted in an outlet box, set flush with the floor.

floor receptacle

floor register   A **register** which is set flush with a floor.

floor sealer   A **sealer, 1**, in liquid form when applied, which seals the pores of a floor surface such as cement or wood.

floor slab   A structural slab serving as a floor; usually of reinforced concrete. Also see **slab, 1**.

floor sleeve   A hollow metal tube which penetrates, and is set into, a floor.

floor socket outlet   Same as **floor receptacle**.

floor stilt   A device attached to a doorframe jamb to hold the bottom of the frame above the finished floor level.

floor stop   A **doorstop** which is set into the floor.

floor strutting   Same as **bridging**.

floor system   **1.** The system of structural components which separate the stories of a building. **2.** In a building, the structural floor assembly between the beams and girders.

floor tile   **1.** A resilient material such as asphalt, vinyl-asbestos, rubber, vinyl, cork, or linoleum manufactured in modular units; laid on a floor as the finish flooring. **2.** Structural tile units for floor and roof slab construction.

floor trap   In a **burglar alarm system**, a device which includes a thread or very thin electrical conductor which extends across a floor space that activates an alarm when moved or broken.

floor-type heater, floor furnace   A heater consisting of a burner, air-heating radiator, and valves which are suspended from a floor (usually in a single-story house) beneath a grille which is flush with the floor; warm air rises from the center of the grille, and return air descends around its perimeter.

floor varnish, finishing varnish   A tough, durable high-gloss, wear-resistant varnish used on wood flooring.

floor ventilation   The passage of air, between openings in a foundation wall, beneath a building.

Florentine arch   A semicircular arch having its **extrados** struck from a higher point than its intrados so that the length of the **voussoirs** is longer nearer the top of the arch.

Florentine lily   Same as **giglio**.

Florentine mosaic   A kind of mosaic made with precious and semiprecious stones, inlaid in a surface of white or black marble or similar material, generally displaying elaborate flower patterns and the like.

floriated, floreated   Decorated with floral patterns.

florid   Highly ornate; extremely rich to the point of overdecoration.

floriated   Romanesque capital

flounder house   A two- or three-story house that is one room deep and several rooms wide; its roof is in the shape of an inclined plane that runs the full length of the house, giving it the appearance of one-half of a **gable roof**.

flounder roof   Same as **shed roof**.

flow   **1.** See **cold flow**. **2.** A measure of the consistency of freshly mixed concrete, mortar, or cement paste in terms of the increase in diameter of a molded truncated-cone specimen after jigging a specified number of times. **3.** That characteristic of a paint which enables it to form a uniform, smooth surface without showing brush marks or other evidence of the method of application.

flow chart   A graphical representation of the steps taken in defining, analyzing, and solving a problem or undertaking an activity.

flow coat   A coating obtained by completely drenching an object with streams of paint and allowing the excess to drain off. Also called a **flood coat**.

flow cone   A device for measuring grout consistency; after a predetermined volume of grout is permitted to flow through an orifice of known size, the time of efflux (called the **flow factor**) is an indication of the consistency.

flow-control device   In a **controlled-flow roof drainage system**, a device that controls the rate at which rainwater is permitted to drain off a roof.

flow factor   See **flow cone**.

Flowing style An old term for the later phases of the English Decorated and the French Flamboyant styles of Gothic architecture; a term derived from the flowing quality of the tracery.

flowing tracery, curvilinear tracery, undulating tracery Tracery in which continuous curvilinear patterns (largely ogees) dominate. A characteristic feature of the Decorated and Flamboyant styles.

flowing tracery: Little St. Mary's, Cambridge (c. 1350)

flow pressure The pressure in the water-supply pipe near a faucet or water outlet while the faucet or water outlet is wide open and water is flowing.

flow promoter A substance added to a coating to enhance brushability, flow, and leveling.

flow slide The failure of a sloped bank of soil in which the soil movement does not take place along a well-defined surface of sliding.

flow test A standardized laboratory test to determine **flow, 2**.

flow trough An open channel used to convey concrete by gravity flow from a receiving hopper or truck mixer to the point of placement.

flue An incombustible, heat-resistant enclosed passage in a chimney to control and carry away products of combustion from a fireplace to the outside air. Often, several fireplaces within a home are connected to a single large flue, but it is also common to carry up one flue for each fireplace.

flue effect See **chimney effect**.

flue gathering See **gathering**.

flue grouping The inclusion of several flues in one chimney or stack to minimize the number of vertical shafts up through a building.

flue lining, chimney lining In a chimney flue, a lining consisting of special heat-resistant firebrick or other fireclay units, heat-resistant glass units, or special concrete block; used to prevent fire, smoke, and gases in the flue from spreading to surroundings.

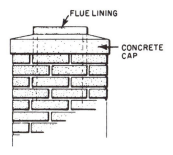

flue lining

flue pipe An airtight conduit which conveys the products of combustion from a furnace to the atmosphere or to a chimney stack.

flue surface In boiler flues, the total surface area which is exposed to high temperature or hot gases.

flueway The clear space (free open area) for the passage of flue gases within a chimney.

fluid-filled column A hollow structural-steel column which is filled with liquid; if exposed to flame, the liquid absorbs heat and rises within the closed-loop system, being replaced with cooler fluid.

fluidifier An admixture employed in grout to decrease the flow factor (time of efflux from a standard orifice) without changing its water content.

fluidity The quality of being fluid, or capable of flowing; that quality of a body which renders it incapable of resisting tangential stresses.

fluing Expanding or splaying, as the splayed jambs of a window.

flume An open channel for carrying water; usually constructed of metal, concrete, or wood.

FLUOR On drawings, abbr. for "fluorescent."

fluorescence The emission of visible light from a substance (such as a phosphor) as the result of, and during, the absorption of radiation of shorter wavelengths.

fluorescent lamp A low-pressure **electric-discharge lamp**; ultraviolet-light radiation is generated by the passage of an arc through mercury vapor; the inner surface of the lamp tube is coated with a phosphor which absorbs the ultraviolet and converts some of it into visible light.

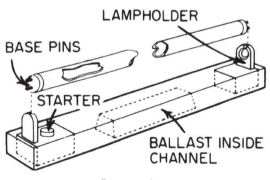

fluorescent lamp

fluorescent lighting fixture A **luminaire**, usually complete with fluorescent lamps, sockets, ballast, reflector, and a louver or diffusing medium.

fluorescent-mercury lamp See **phosphor mercury-vapor lamp**.

fluorescent paint See **luminous paint**.

fluorescent pigments Pigments of excep-

tional brilliance which absorb ultraviolet radiant energy and reemit it as visible light.

fluorescent reflector lamp A **fluorescent lamp** having reflective powder between the phosphor and the tube wall over part of the circumference; this directs a larger percentage of the light flux to one side.

fluorescent snaking The apparent swirling and twisting of the arc in a fluorescent lamp; a common phenomenon in a new lamp until it has been turned on and off a few times.

fluorescent strip A fluorescent luminaire in which the lamp(s) are mounted on a wiring **channel** containing the ballast and lamp sockets, usually without light reflectors or lenses.

fluorescent tube See **fluorescent lamp**.

fluorescent U-lamp A tubular fluorescent lamp whose bulb has a 180° bend at the center, forming a U-shaped lamp.

fluosilicate A salt, usually of magnesium or zinc, used on concrete as a surface-hardening agent.

flush Having the surface or face even or level with the adjacent surface.

flush bead See **quirk bead, 2**.

flush bolt A door bolt so designed that when applied it is flush with the face or edge of the door.

flush bolt

flush bolt backset The distance from the vertical center line of the leading edge of a door to the center line of the bolt.

flush bushing In plumbing, a bushing which has no shoulder; fits flush into the **fitting** with which it is connected.

flush chimney An **interior chimney** whose outer surface is flush with an exterior wall.

flush-cup pull   A door pull which is mortised flush into a door, having a recess to receive fingers to actuate the slide of the door.

flush-cut joint, flush joint   In brickwork, a masonry joint in which an excess of mortar is applied; then a trowel is held flat against the brick surface and moved along the surface, so as to cut away the excess mortar. The resulting joint is flush with the wall, and is usually not watertight as a result of small hairline cracks produced by the cutting action as the trowel removes the excess mortar.

flush-cut joint

flush door   A smooth-surfaced door having faces which are plane and which conceal its rails and stiles or other structure.

flush eaves   **Eaves** where there is no roof projection requiring a **plancier piece**; instead, the eaves fascia is against the wall surface and is attached directly to it.

flush glazing   Glazing in which glass is set in a recess in a frame; stops (if any are used) also are recessed; the glazing is flush with the frame jamb surface.

flush-head rivet   A rivet having a countersunk head.

flushing cistern   See **flush tank**.

flushing tank   See **flush tank**.

flushing-type floor drain   A floor drain, equipped with an integral water supply that enables the drain receptor and trap to be flushed.

flushing valve   See **flush valve**.

flush molding   Molding whose surface is in the same plane as that of the wood member or assembly to which it is applied.

flushometer, flushometer valve   A valve designed to supply a fixed quantity of water for flushing purposes; is actuated by direct water

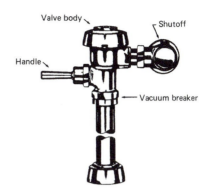

flushometer

pressure, without the use of a cistern or flush tank.

flush panel   A panel whose surface is in the same plane as the face of the surrounding frame.

flush paneled door   A **paneled door** in which, on one or both faces, the panels are finished flush with the rails and stiles.

flush pipe   A straight pipe which conveys flushing water from the source of supply to a water closet.

flush plate   A metal or plastic cover for a flush wiring device in a wiring box, providing a neat covering for an outlet or switch; supported by screws in tapped holes in the metal housing for the device; holes in the plate accommodate handles for switches or plugs for flush outlet receptacles.

flush plate

flush pointing   In brickwork, the troweling of mortar into joints by scraping a trowel against the wall surface to remove excess mortar.

flush ring   A flush door pull which is mortised into a door; has a ring pull that folds flat into the cup of the pull when not in use. (*See illustration p. 394.*)

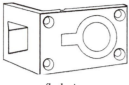

flush ring

flush siding A wood exterior covering on the walls of a colonial New England house of wood-frame construction; commonly made of pine boards that have been sawn and planed smooth. These boards, applied horizontally, are usually wider than ordinary **clapboard** and are nailed flat against the studs; the upper edge is often beveled and may be overlapped by the board above.

flush soffit The smooth underside in a flight of spandrel steps.

flush sprinkler A fire **sprinkler** (head) in which all or part of the body is mounted above the lower plane of the ceiling.

flush switch In electric wiring, a switch which is mounted in a flush wall box so that only its front face is visible.

flush tank A tank which holds a supply of water for flushing of one or more plumbing fixtures.

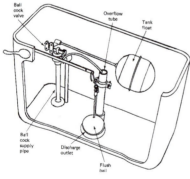

flush tank

flush valve 1. A special valve located at the bottom of the tank of a water closet, or the like; provides the discharge through which the fixture is flushed. 2. A diaphragm-type **flushometer**.

flush wall box A **wall box** which houses an electric device, embedded in a partition, ceiling, or floor so that the face is flush with the surface.

flush water See **wash water**.

flushwork (*Brit.*) Masonry which contrasts smooth ashlar with knapped flint; the split side is set flush with the wall face.

flute A groove or channel, esp. one of many such parallel grooves, usually semicircular or semielliptical in section; used decoratively, as along the shaft of a column.

fluted rolled glass Flat sheet glass, one surface of which is impressed with a pattern of narrow parallel flutes.

fluting A series of **flutes**, as on a column.

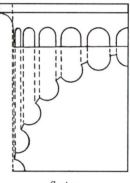

fluting

flutter echo A rapid succession of **echoes** caused by the reflection of sound back and forth between two parallel walls; initiated by a single, sharp pulse of sound.

flux 1. A fusible substance used in oxygen cutting, welding, brazing, or soldering operations; assists in the fusion of metals and the prevention of surface oxidation. 2. A bituminous material, generally liquid, used for softening other bituminous materials.

flux-cored arc welding Any one of a group of welding processes in which coalescence is produced by the heating of an arc; the arc is between the work being welded and a continuous **filler metal** electrode.

flux oil A thick, relatively nonvolatile fraction of petroleum used as **flux, 2**.

fly ash The finely divided residue resulting from the combustion of ground or powdered coal, transported from the firebox through the boiler by flue gases.

fly bridge On a theatre stage, a platform for

supporting lights or other equipment which is hung by means of rigging.

fly curtain A theatre curtain which can be raised into the **flies**.

flyer See **flier**.

fly floor, fly gallery In a theatre, a narrow balcony above the stage floor, usually on both sides of the stage, sometimes with an interconnection across the back wall.

fly gallery See **fly floor**.

flying bond Same as **monk bond**.

flying buttress A characteristic feature of Gothic construction, in which the lateral thrusts of a roof or vault are taken up by a straight bar of masonry, usually sloping, carried on an arch, and a solid pier or buttress sufficient to receive the thrust.

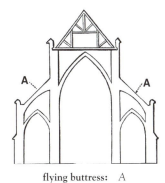

flying buttress: A

flying façade See **false front**.

flying form A large prefabricated unit of **formwork** designed for reuse.

flying scaffold Suspended staging which is hung from outrigger beams at the top of a structure by means of ropes or cables.

flying shelf A mantel or shelf above the fireplace opening which is cantilevered from the chimney construction.

flying shore A timber which provides temporary support between two walls; a horizontal supporting shore.

fly ladder A ladder, at the side or rear of a theatre stage, providing access to the **fly floor**.

fly line In a theatre stagehouse, a rope or wire line used to hang scenery or equipment from the **flies**.

fly loft See **flies**.

fly rafter A **rafter** in the projecting portion of a gabled roof.

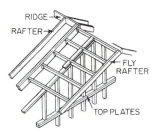

fly rafter

fly rail, pinrail, working rail In a theatre stagehouse, a railing on the stage side of the **fly floor**; used for tying off lines when scenery is hauled into the **flies**.

fly stair A stairway from the stage of a theatre to the **fly floor** and above.

FMT Abbr. for "flush metal threshold."

foam concrete See **foamed concrete**.

foam core The rigid foam material that is used in sandwich panel construction.

foamed adhesive An adhesive, the density of which has been decreased substantially by the presence of numerous gaseous cells dispersed throughout its mass.

foamed blast-furnace slag See **expanded blast-furnace slag**.

foamed concrete, foam concrete A very light, cellular concrete; made by the addition of a prepared foam or by the generation of gas within the unhardened mixture.

foamed-in-place insulation A plastic foam; prepared by mixing the ingredients with a foaming agent immediately before placement, either by pouring the material into enclosed cavities or by application with a spray gun; used for thermal insulation.

foamed plastic, plastic foam 1. A plastic expanded chemically, mechanically, or thermally, to form a lightweight closed-cell structure; used as thermal insulation. Also see **chemically foamed plastic**. 2. A resin in a sponge form, either flexible or rigid, with cells that are either closed or interconnected.

foamed polystyrene A foamed plastic weighing about 1 lb per cu ft (0.016 gm per cu cm);

grease-resistant, low in cost, high in thermal insulation value.

foamed slag   See **expanded blast-furnace slag**.

foam fire-extinguishing system   A **fire-extinguishing system** employing a special means to discharge foam, made from concentrates, over a protected area.

foam glass, cellular glass, expanded glass   A thermal insulation made by foaming softened glass to produce many sealed bubbles; has a closed-cell structure. Molded into board and blocks, usually with a density of about 9 to 10 lb per cu ft (14.4 to 16 kg per cu m).

foaming agent   A substance that is added to a material in the plastic state to generate gases within the material and cause it to assume a lightweight, foamy structure; used with concrete mixtures, gypsum, plastics, rubber, etc.

foam rubber   Same as **sponge rubber**.

FOB   Abbr. for "free on board."

fodder house   A small shedlike structure for storing coarse food for livestock.

fog curing   The curing of concrete products in a room having very high humidity (achieved by the atomization of water). Also see **moist room**.

fogón   In Spanish Colonial architecture, a cooking stove or fireplace with a chimney; usually constructed of adobe brick and finished with adobe plaster. It was commonly located across one corner of a room.

fog room   Same as **moist room**.

fog sealed   Said of a surface which has received a light surface treatment of asphalt, without a mineral cover.

FOHC   In the lumber industry, abbr. for "free of heart centers."

foil   **1.** In tracery, any of several rounded lobes that meet each other in points called **cusps**; widely used in Gothic architecture, Gothic Revival architecture, and Collegiate Gothic; see **trefoil** (three lobes), **quatrefoil** (four lobes), **cinquefoil** (five lobes), and **multifoil** (usually greater than five lobes). **2.** A metallic substance formed into very thin sheets, usually by a rolling process.

foil arch   An arch with cusps or foils on its **intrados**.

foil-backed gypsum board, insulating plaster-board   Gypsum board having an aluminum foil on one of its surfaces providing a vapor-resistant membrane and increased resistance to heat flow.

foil-backed gypsum lath   A plain **gypsum lath**, the back surface of which is covered with a continuous sheet of aluminum foil.

foil-backed gypsum wallboard   A **gypsum wallboard**, the back surface of which is covered with a continuous sheet of aluminum foil.

foiled   Decorated with foils.

foiled arch   Same as **cusped arch**.

FOK   Abbr. for "free of knots."

folded-plate construction, hipped-plate construction   Construction consisting of thin, flat elements of concrete, steel, timber, etc., which are connected rigidly at angles with each other (similar to accordion folds), forming a stiff cross section which is capable of carrying a load over a long span.

folding casement   **1.** One of a pair of **casements, 1,** with rabbeted meeting stiles which is

foils

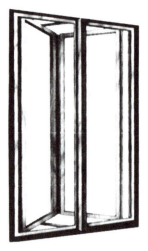

folding casement

hung in a single frame having no mullion. **2.** One of two or more **casements, 1**, which are hinged together so that they can open and fold in a confined space.

folding door **1.** One of two or more doors which are hinged together so that they can open and fold in a confined space. **2.** One of a pair of doors hung from the jambs of a single opening. Also see **accordion door, multifolding door.**

folding partition A movable door or partition comprised of a number of individual sections that are hinged and folded against each other, but can be pulled open to form a continuous vertical surface that divides a large space into two smaller ones. Compare with **falling wainscot**; also see **accordion partition, operable partition**, and **sliding door.**

folding rule A **rule** which is jointed at fixed intervals for convenience in carrying.

folding rule

folding shutter See **boxing shutter.**

folding stair A **disappearing stair.**

folding wall An **operable partition.** Also see **accordion partition.**

foliated **1.** Adorned with foils, as on tracery. **2.** Decorated with conventionalized leafage, often applied to capitals or moldings.

foliated arch An arch having **foils**; a **foil arch.**

foliated joint A joint between two boards made by overlapping two rabbeted edges, so as to form a continuous surface on each face; a form of **joggle.**

foliation **1.** The cusps or foils with which the divisions of a Gothic window are ornamented. **2.** Leaf-like decoration.

Folk architecture An imprecise term for architecture intended to provide only basic shelter suitable for the surrounding terrain and climate, with no pretense of following current styles of architecture. Such houses were built using local materials and available tools, often by the people who planned to live in them.

Folk Victorian architecture Same as **Gingerbread Folk architecture.**

foliated, 1: arches

foliated, 2: capital

follow current The current that flows through a **surge arrester** to ground, following the passage of discharge current.

follow spot A theatre spotlight used to follow a performer on the stage.

folly, eye-catcher A functionally useless structure, often a fake ruin, sometimes built in a landscaped park to highlight a view.

fonar In early Russian architecture, a type of **lantern** consisting of a cupola having many small windows.

font A basin, usually of stone, which holds the water for baptism.

food display counter A unit for the display of food, esp. prepared food; usually temperature-controlled.

food tray rail One of several rails, forming a continuous shelf, installed at the front of food dispensing units, as in a cafeteria.

foot base A molding above a plinth.

foot block A mat of concrete, steel, or timbers used to distribute the load of a post or shore on the soil that supports it.

foot bolt A bolt which is fixed at the bottom of a door and can be operated by foot; usually when the door is unbolted, the bolt head is held up by a spring.

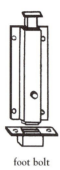

foot bolt

footbridge, pedestrian bridge　A narrow bridge designed to carry pedestrians only.

footcandle　A unit of illuminance in U.S. Customary units; equal to 1 **lumen** per square foot; equals 10.76 **lux**.

footcandle meter　Same as **illumination meter**.

foot cut　See **seat cut**.

footer　Same as **footing**.

footing　That portion of the foundation of a structure which transmits loads directly to the soil; may be the widened part of a wall or column, the spreading courses under a foundation wall, a foundation of a column, etc.; used to spread the load over a greater area to prevent or reduce settling.

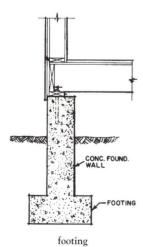

footing

footing beam　Same as **tie beam, 2**.

footing course　One of the courses of masonry at the foot of a wall, broader than the courses above.

footing piece　In **staging**, one of the horizontal transverse members which support the platform.

footing stone　A broad flat stone used as the base or bottom course of a wall.

footing stop　A board, temporarily inserted in a concrete form as a stop for concrete at the end of a day.

footlambert　**1.** A unit of **luminance** equal to $1/\pi$ candela per sq ft. **2.** The uniform luminance of a perfectly diffusing surface emitting or reflecting light at a rate of 1 lumen per sq ft.

footlight　One of a row of lights set in a trough, in a theatre stage floor, which runs across the width of the stage in front of the curtain.

footlights

footlight spot　A spotlight small enough to be mounted in the **footlights**.

foot-meter rod　A **stadia rod**, marked in feet and tenths on one side and meters and hundredths on the other side; used to determine distances and elevations in one unit of measurement and to check them by readings in the other system.

footpace　**1.** A dais. **2.** A **halfpace**.

footpath　A British term for **sidewalk**.

footpiece　In a heating, ventilating, or air-conditioning system, a piece of ductwork which provides a change in direction of air flow.

footplate　**1.** In wood-frame construction, a timber used to distribute concentrated loads, as a **plate** beneath a row of studs. **2.** A **hammer beam**.

footprint　The area on a plane directly beneath a structure (or piece of equipment), that has the same perimeter as the structure (or piece of equipment).

foot run　**1.** Same as **board measure**. **2.** A foot of length of any material.

foot scraper　Same as **boot scraper**.

foot scraper

footstall   **1.** The plinth or base of a pillar or pier, usually having a distinctive architectural treatment. **2.** A pedestal which supports a pillar, statue, etc.

footstone   A **kneeler, 1**; a **gable springer**.

footway   **1.** A pedestrian walk or footpath. **2.** A sidewalk.

force account   A term used when **work, 1** is ordered to be done without prior agreement as to lump sum or unit price cost thereof and is to be billed for at cost of labor, materials and equipment, insurance, taxes, etc., plus an agreed percentage for overhead and profit.

force cup   Same as **plumber's friend**.

forced-air furnace   A **warm-air furnace** equipped with a blower to circulate the air through the furnace and ductwork.

forced circulation   Circulation of air, water, etc., by mechanical means, such as a fan or pump.

forced-circulation register   A **register** for use with a duct system conveying air under pressure; permits the control of the discharged air in two or more directions simultaneously.

forced convection   Heat transfer resulting from the forced circulation of air, water, etc., as by a fan, jet, or pump.

forced draft   In a furnace, a draft of air which is mixed with fuel before being fed into the combustion chamber.

forced-draft boiler   A boiler having a power-operated fan which furnishes the burner and boiler with air, and also forces the products of combustion out through the chimney.

forced-draft water-cooling tower   A **water-cooling tower** having one or more fans located in the air stream entering the tower.

forced drying   A process for speeding up the drying of paint, using a moderate heat, up to 150°F (65°C).

forced fit   The joining of two parts, members, etc., without the use of fasteners, by forcing the two together.

forebay   An integral part of a structure's upper story that significantly overhangs the story below; see **forebay barn**.

forebay barn   A barn, often on a hillside, having a **forebay** (usually on its downhill side) that may be supported by a series of heavy posts or pillars.

fore choir   Same as **antechoir**.

forechurch   A consecrated extension in front of a larger church.

foreclosure   The depriving of the right to a property by legal transfer of title, esp. because of failure to maintain mortgage payments.

foreclosure sale   The optional right of the mortgagee to resort to the sale of the mortgaged property in the event of default in mortgage payments, and to apply the net proceeds realized from its disposition to the unpaid debt.

forecourt   A court forming an entrance plaza for a single building or several buildings in a group.

forend   British term for **lock front**.

fore plane   A carpenter's plane, intermediate in length and used between a jack plane and a **jointer, 4**.

forestage   **1.** That part of a theatre stage which is on the audience side of the proscenium or stage curtain. **2.** See **apron, 8**.

forging   A metal part, worked to a predetermined shape by one or more of such processes as hammering, upsetting, pressing, or rolling.

forklift truck   A power-operated vehicle having heavy steel prongs which can be moved in position under a load on **pallets, 2** and then raised; esp. used in construction for moving material around a job site.

forklift truck

form   Temporary boarding, sheeting, or pans of plywood, molded fiberglass, etc.; used to give desired shape to poured concrete, or the like. (*See illustration p. 400.*)

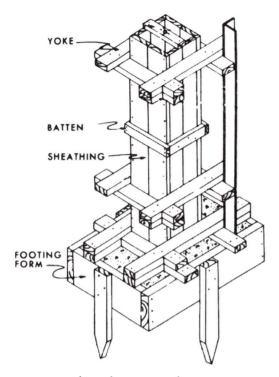

YOKE

BATTEN

SHEATHING

FOOTING
FORM

form   for a concrete column

formaldehyde, methylene oxide   A color-less, pungent, volatile liquid, readily soluble in water, widely used in the manufacture of plastics and resins and as a disinfectant.

formal garden   A garden whose plantings, walks, pools, fountains, etc., follow a definite, recognizable plan, frequently symmetrical, emphasizing geometrical forms.

form anchor   A device used to secure **form-work** to previously placed concrete of adequate strength.

format   An AIA standardized arrangement for the **project manual** including bidding information, contract forms, **conditions of the contract**, and **specifications** subdivided into sixteen divisions.

form board, form liner, form lumber   A board or a sheet of wood used in **formwork**.

form coating   A liquid coating applied to concrete **formwork** to promote ease of release of the form from the concrete.

formed plywood   Curved plywood; manufactured by being pressed between rigid forming dies.

formeret, wall rib   One of the ribs against the walls in a ceiling vaulted with ribs.

form hanger   A **hanger** used as a support for formwork which is hung from a structural framework.

forming   A process of shaping metal by mechanical action other than machining, forging, or casting.

form insulation   Thermal insulation which is applied to the outside of concrete forms between studs and over the top; used in sufficient thickness, with an airtight seal, to retain the heat of hydration so that the concrete is maintained at the required temperature for proper setting in cold weather.

form lining   A lining on the concrete-face side of **formwork** either: (a) to absorb water from the concrete, (b) to impart a patterned finish or smooth finish to the concrete surface, or (c) to apply a set-retarding chemical to the formed surface.

form nail   See **double-headed nail**.

form oil   An oil which is applied to the interior surfaces of concrete formwork so as to promote a clean break when the forms are removed.

form-pieces   A medieval term for **tracery**.

form pressure   In concrete construction, the lateral pressure which acts on the vertical or inclined surfaces of the **formwork** as a result of the fluid-like behavior of the unhardened concrete within the formwork.

form release agent   See **release agent**.

form scabbing   The removal of the surface of concrete as a result of the lack of a clean break when the forms are removed; some of the concrete adheres to the form and is pulled away.

form spreader   Same as **spreader, 2**.

form stop   In concrete **formwork**, a temporary wood piece used to limit the flow of concrete at the end of a day's work.

form stripping agent   Same as **release agent**.

form tie   Any **tie**, in tension, which is used to prevent concrete forms from spreading as a result of fluid pressure of freshly placed, unhardened concrete.

formwork   A temporary construction to contain wet concrete in the required shape while it is cast and setting.

forniciform   In the shape of a vaulted roof or ceiling.

fornix   In ancient Roman construction, a vaulted surface.

Forstner bit   A bit used for drilling blind holes in wood.

fort   A defensive work, exclusively military in nature, that is strengthened for protection against enemy attack and commonly incorporates a series of bastions (i.e., projections from the outer wall of the fort) to defend the adjacent perimeter; usually occupied by troops. See **bastion, battlement, breastwork, casemate, embrasure, loophole, rampart.**

fortress   **1.** A fortification of massive scale, generally of monumental character and sometimes including an urban core; also called **stronghold. 2.** A protected place of refuge.

45° pipe lateral   A pipe fitting similar to a **pipe tee** except that the side opening is at a 45° angle.

forum   A Roman public square surrounded by monumental buildings, usually including a basilica and a temple; the center of civic life. A forum sometimes was purely commercial in aspect.

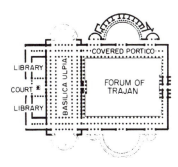

Forum   of Trajan, Rome, circa 110 A.D.

forward-curved fan   A fan having forward-curved blades; used primarily for **HVAC** applications where high-volume flow rates and low-pressure characteristics are required.

foss   A moat or ditch.

fossil resin   Naturally occurring hard resins such as copal and amber, which are mined and purified for use in varnishes.

foul drain   See **soil drain.**

foul sewer   See **soil drain.**

foul water   A combination of waste and soil water.

foundation   **1.** Any part of a structure that serves to transmit the load to the earth or rock, usually below ground level; the entire masonry substructure. **2.** The soil or rock upon which the structure rests. **3.** The structure on which the base of a machine rests or to which the feet are fastened.

foundation bolt   See **anchor bolt.**

foundation course   Same as **base course, 1.**

foundation drainage tile   Tile or piping for the collection of subsurface drainage, dispersion of septic tank effluent, and the like.

foundation engineering   That aspect of engineering concerned with the evaluation of the ability of the earth to support a load, and with the design of a substructure or transition member to transmit the load of the superstructure to the earth.

foundation failure   See **differential settlement.**

foundation investigation   A subsurface investigation.

foundation mat   See **mat foundation.**

foundation pier   A column embedded in the soil that extends from the lowest floor of a building down to the top of a **footing** or **pile cap;** where the **pier, 1** bears directly on the soil with intermediate footings or pile caps, the foundation pier is considered to be the entire length of the column below the lowest floor level.

foundation pile   A relatively long column, driven in the ground, which supports a load by bearing on firm material and/or by friction along its periphery.

foundation planting   Plants massed close to the foundation of a structure.

foundation soil   That part of the earth mass which carries the load of a structure; **foundation, 2.**

foundation stone   **1.** One of a number of stones in a foundation. **2.** Same as **cornerstone.**

foundation wall   That part of the foundation for a building which forms the permanent retaining wall of the structure below grade. (*See illustration p. 402.*)

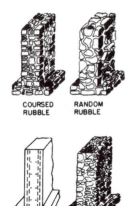

COURSED RUBBLE   RANDOM RUBBLE

CONCRETE REINFORCED   RUBBLE MASONRY

foundation walls

founding, casting Producing metal products in a foundry by pouring melted metals into molds.

fountain **1.** See **architectural fountain.** **2.** See **drinking fountain.** **3.** See **soda fountain.** **4.** See **wash fountain.**

four-centered arch An arch whose intrados is struck from four centers.

four-centered pointed arch See **Tudor arch.**

four-crib barn See **crib barn.**

four-leaved flower An ornament used in hollow moldings, resembling a flower with four petals.

four-over-four Descriptive of a **double-hung window** having four panes in the upper sash over four panes in the lower sash; see **pane.**

four-part vault A vault formed by the intersection of two **barrel vaults.**

four-piece butt match See **diamond matching.**

four-square house A one-and-a-half or two-and-a-half-story house having a square plan with one room in each corner; a central stairway; usually a steeply pitched **hipped roof** or **pyramidal roof;** often a kitchen attached to one of the rooms; also called an American four-square house.

four-square plan A **floor plan** for a house having four rooms that form a square or rectangle.

four-way reinforcement A system of **reinforcing bars** in flat-slab **reinforced concrete** construction; consists of bands of bars parallel to two adjacent edges, and other bands parallel to both diagonals of a rectangular slab.

fox bolt A bolt having a split end to receive a **foxtail wedge;** used as an anchor bolt.

foxtail Same as **foxtail wedge.**

foxtail saw Same as **dovetail saw.**

foxtail wedge, fox wedge, fox tenon A small wedge used to secure the split end of a tenon in a mortise, the split end of a bolt in a hole, or the like, by spreading the end as the wedge is driven in.

foxy timber Timber having a reddish cast indicating the onset of decay.

foyer **1.** An entranceway or transitional space from the exterior to the interior of a building. **2.** The area between the outer lobby and an auditorium. **3.** The lobby itself.

FPRF On drawings, abbr. for **fireproof.**

fps Abbr. for "feet per second."

FPT Abbr. for **fan-powered terminal.**

fractable A coping on the gable wall of a building, when carried above the roof; esp. when broken into steps or curves forming an ornamental silhouette.

fractables   on a coped gable

fracture load See **breaking load.**

fracture toughness A measure of a member's ability to absorb energy without fracture.

frake Same as **limba.**

frame The timberwork or steelwork that encloses and supports structural components of a building; see **bent frame, doorframe, space frame, window frame, framing**.

frame anchor See **doorframe anchor**.

frame building Same as **framed building**.

frame clearance The clearance between a door and the doorframe.

frame construction Any building primarily supported by wood or steel structural members, or some combination thereof; see **steel-frame construction** and **wood-frame construction**.

framed, ledged, and braced door A **framed and ledged door** with the addition of one or more diagonal braces.

framed and braced door Same as **framed, ledged, and braced door**.

framed and ledged door A door having rails and stiles framed together; filled in on one face with vertical boarding having a thickness less than the surrounding framing; the vertical boarding covers the middle and bottom rails, which are of less thickness than the top rail and stiles.

framed building A type of building construction in which the loads are carried to the ground by a framework, rather than through load-bearing walls.

framed door Any door having a rigid frame made up of a top rail, lock (center) rail, bottom rail, hanging stile, and lock stile.

framed floor See **double floor**.

framed ground One of the wood members fixed around an opening, with a tenon joint between the head and jambs, level and plumb to wall faces; used for attaching a wood **door casing**.

framed house A house of **wood-frame construction**; also see **timber-framed house**.

framed joist A joist which has been notched or otherwise cut to receive other timbers.

framed overhang The projection of an upper story of a house beyond the story immediately below it; see **overhang, false overhang, hewn overhang**.

framed overhang

framed partition, trussed partition A partition consisting of a covering applied to framing of studs, struts, and braces which form a truss.

framed square See **square-framed**.

frame gasket A resilient material, in strip form, which is attached to doorframe stops to provide tight closure of the door.

frame-high In masonry, as high as the lintel of an opening or the top of a door or window frame.

frame house A house of wood **frame construction**, usually sheathed and covered with lap or panel siding or shingles.

frame pulley A pulley, installed in a window frame, which carries a sash cord.

frame wall A wall of wood **frame construction**.

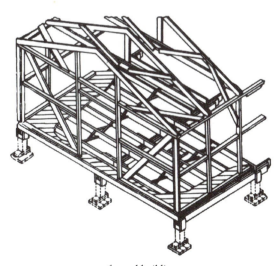

framed building

framework An assemblage of structural elements or members fitted together to form a structure, as a multistory building, a rigid-frame shed, or a truss.

framing **1.** A system of structural woodwork. **2.** The rough timber structure of a building, such as partitions, flooring, and roofing. **3.** Any framed work, as around an opening in an exterior wall. See **balloon framing, braced framing, iron framing, platform framing, post-and-beam framing, post-and-girt framing, post-and-lintel framing, skeleton framing, western framing**. Also see illustration under **timber-framed house**.

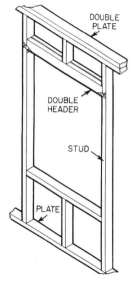

framing, 2 around an exterior wall opening

framing anchor A metal device used in light wood-frame construction for joining studs, joists, rafters, etc.

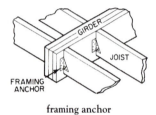

framing anchor

framing chisel See **mortise chisel**.

framing plan A plan of each floor of a building showing the makeup of beams and girders on that floor, and their connections, using a simplified system of symbols and drafting linework.

framing square See **carpenter's square**.

framing table Same as **rafter table**.

François I (Premier) style The culmination of the early phase of French Renaissance architecture named after Francis I (1515–1547), merging Gothic elements with the full use of Italian decoration. Fontainebleau is an outstanding example. (*See illustration p. 405.*)

Franco-Italianate style Same as **Second Empire style**.

frank To form a miter joint in a sash frame at the intersection of a crosspiece.

Franklin An obsolete term for a **lightning rod**.

Franklin stove A freestanding, enclosed, cast-iron stove, set on short legs with provision for air circulation around, over, and under its exterior surfaces; serves the function of a fireplace incorporating a grate; usually attributed to Benjamin Franklin. It is fuel efficient and superior to a fireplace as a means of heating a house because it is more fuel efficient and the source of heat is brought out into the room itself. The amount of heat the stove radiates can be controlled by regulating the draft through the stove by means of an adjustable opening in its front door.

frass A powdery residue in holes bored in wood by insects, usually by powder-post beetles.

frater A common eating room in a monastery.

fraternity house A building used for social and residential purposes by an association of male students called a "fraternity."

F-rating A fire performance rating of a **fire-stopping** system, measured in terms of period of time that the system will limit the passage of fire through it when tested according to the applicable code.

free area The total minimum area of the openings in an air inlet or outlet (e.g., air diffuser, grille, or register) through which air can pass; usually expressed as a percentage of the total area.

freeboard In a water tank, the vertical distance between the maximum water level and the top of the tank.

François I style: house of Agnes Sorel, Orleans

free delivery-type unit A device which takes in air and discharges it directly to the space to be treated without ductwork or other elements which impose air resistance.

free fall **1.** The descent of freshly mixed concrete into forms without dropchutes or other means of confinement. **2.** The distance through which such descent occurs. **3.** The uncontrolled fall of aggregate.

free-field room Same as **anechoic room**.

free float In **CPM** terminology, the amount of extra time available for an **activity** if every activity in the project starts as early as possible; the amount of float that can be allocated to an activity without interfering with subsequent work.

free haul The distance within which excavated material is to be moved without additional compensation.

freehold **1.** A form of tenure of property held in **fee simple, fee tail**, or for life. **2.** Property so held.

free moisture Moisture not retained or absorbed by aggregate.

freestanding Said of a structural element which is fixed by its foundation at its lower end, but not constrained throughout its vertical height.

freestone Fairly fine-grained stone that works easily; has no tendency to split in any preferential direction; esp. suitable for carving and elaborate milling; usually a sandstone or a granular limestone.

free stuff See **clear lumber**.

free water **1.** See **surface moisture**. **2.** Water that is free to move, under the influence of gravity, through a soil mass.

freeze-and-thaw tests A procedure (ASTM Test Method C666) for evaluating the resistance of concrete specimens to freeze rapidly in water and then thaw in water, and then to freeze rapidly in air and thaw in air.

freezer A mechanically refrigerated room or cabinet for the storage of frozen foods; usually maintained at a temperature of about 10°F (approx. −12°C).

freight elevator, (*Brit.*) **goods lift** An elevator used for carrying freight, on which only the operator and the persons necessary for unloading and loading the freight are permitted to ride.

French arch A **Dutch arch**.

French basement Same as **raised basement**; the main entrance to the house is one floor above.

French Canadian architecture See **Cajun cottage** and **galerie house**.

French casement window Same as **French window**.

French Colonial architecture A term descriptive of architecture developed by French colonists in New Orleans and the Louisiana Territory from about 1699 onward. Their architecture persisted until about 1830—many years after the territory was no longer French. French Colonial architecture usually characterized by a **raised basement** used for utility or commercial purposes; a symmetric façade with a centrally located front door; a porch (**galerie**); typically, a steeply pitched hipped roof, **pavilion roof**, or a shingle-covered **bonnet roof** supported by wood posts and/or brick columns; a brick chimney. In New Orleans, wrought-iron balconies, surrounding the upper stories and extending over the sidewalk; French doors, with battened or paneled shutters; transom lights or fanlights above the front doors of the more elegant homes. Also see **Cajun cottage, Creole architecture, Creole house, plantation house, raised house**. (For a description of architecture that exhibits the strong ethnic influences of the immigrant populations of the Acadians and the Creoles, see **French Vernacular architecture**.)

French Colonial architecture: Spanish Customs House, New Orleans

French door, casement door, door window

A door having a top rail, bottom rail, and stiles, which has glass panes throughout (or nearly throughout) its entire length; often used in pairs.

French door

French drain, boulder ditch, rubble drain

1. A drain consisting of a trench filled with loose stones and covered with earth. **2.** Same as **drain tile**.

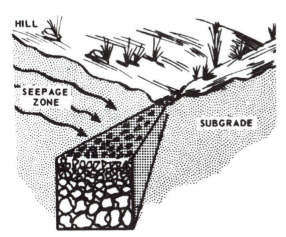

French drain

French Eclectic architecture Domestic architecture that emulates many of its French antecedents, combining elements and characteristics of a wide range of historic style of its antecedents. Typical characteristics include: a wall cladding of brick, stone, or stucco; quoins at the wall intersections; occasionally, decorative half-timbering; a cylindrical stair tow hav-

ing a steep conical roof; a small porch having a balustrade over the door; a porte cochère; a tall, steeply pitched, hipped roof with one or more gables, often tiled or shingled; flared eaves; one or more massive chimneys; arched dormers, gabled dormers, or hipped wall dormers that break the line of the cornice; French windows or double-hung windows; upper-story windows that break the roof line; an entry door having a stone or terra-cotta **door surround** or having pilasters on each side.

French embossing A method of etching glass with acid to produce lettering or ornamentation. As many as four strengths of hydrofluoric acid (or acid plus a buffering alkali) may be employed to produce an equal number of different surface textures.

French flier, French flyer A **flier** of a three-quarter-turn stair, around an open well.

Frenchman A tool used for pointing mortar joints.

French method of application A method of applying roofing shingles; at least three corners are clipped so that they form a hexagonal pattern when laid with their diagonals perpendicular to the eaves of the roof; they lap both at the top and sides.

French polish **1.** A furniture polish or finish containing shellac mixed with alcohol or oil; **French varnish**. **2.** A hand-rubbed high-gloss finish, achieved by multiple applications of such varnish.

French Revival See **French Eclectic architecture**.

French roof A term sometimes used for a **mansard roof** whose sloping sides are nearly perpendicular.

French roof

French sash See **French window**.
French Second Empire style See **Second Empire style**.

French stuc An imitation stone formed by plasterwork.

French tiles A type of interlocking roof tiles.

French truss See **Fink truss**.

French varnish See **French polish, 1**.

French Vernacular architecture In America, architecture found primarily in Louisiana and in many early settlements along the Mississippi River; it exhibits the influences of two major French-speaking immigrant populations. The first group, from Canada, the *Acadians*, whose descendants are now known as *Cajuns*, settled in the bayou districts of Louisiana during the last half of the 18th century in modest houses known as **Cajun cottages**. The second major ethnic group consisted of the *Creoles*, persons of European ancestry born in the Mississippi Valley, the Gulf Coast, or the West Indies, who usually spoke a French patois; their dwellings are known as **Creole houses**. For specific aspects of this architecture see **abat-vent, banquette cottage, barreaux, bluffland house, bonnet roof, bousillage, briquette-entre-poteaux, cabanne, columbage, faux bois, faux marbre, pièce sur pièce construction, pierro-tage, pilier, plaunch debout en terre construction, poteaux-en-terre house, poteaux-sur-solle house, raised house**.

French white See **silver white, 2**.

French window A casement window extending down to the floor; also called a **French door**.

French-window lock See **cremone bolt**.

frequency The number of oscillations per second (*a*) of the current or voltage in an alternating-current electric circuit, or (*b*) of a sound wave, or (*c*) of a vibrating solid object; expressed in hertz (*abbr.* Hz) or in cycles per second (*abbr.* cps).

fresco, buon fresco A mural painted into fresh lime plaster; in such work water-based colors unite with the base; retouching is done *a secco* (dry).

fresco secco, secco A mural, often fugitive, painted with water-based colors on dry plaster.

fresh air Air taken into a building from the outdoors.

fresh-air inlet A vent connection to a house drain, on the building side of the main drain trap.

fresh-air intake Same as **outside-air intake**.

fresh concrete Unhardened concrete capable of being consolidated.

Fresnel lens In lighting, a lens that concentrates light from a small source such as an incandescent filament; similar to but thinner and lighter than a plano-convex lens owing to steps on the convex side; used in many types of luminaires, esp. downlights and spotlights.

Fresnel lens

Fresno scraper Same as **buck scraper**.

fret **1.** An ornament, sometimes painted, incised, or raised and formed of short fillets, bands, or reglets variously combined, frequently consisting of continuous lines arranged in rectangular forms; a **meander**; a **Greek key**. **2.** Similar ornamentation in which the fillets intersect at oblique angles, as often in Oriental designs.

fret patterns

fretsaw A fine-toothed saw having a narrow blade which is held under tension, in a frame; used to cut thin wood, esp. ornamental designs.

fretwork Ornamental openwork or interlaced work in relief, esp. when elaborate and minute in its parts, and of patterns of contrasting light and dark.

friable Easily crumbled or pulverized; easily reduced to powder.

F.R.I.B.A. Abbr. for "Fellow of the Royal Institute of British Architects."

friction The resistance to relative motion, sliding or rolling, of the surfaces of bodies in contact.

friction brake A device for slowing down or stopping a moving mechanism by friction between two surfaces which rotate or slide over each other.

friction catch Any catch which, when it engages a strike, is held in the engaged position by friction.

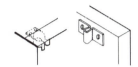

friction catch

friction-grip bolt See **high-tension bolt**.

friction head In a piping system, the **pressure drop** expended in overcoming frictional resistance to flow.

friction hinge A door or window hinge which will remain open at any selected position, because of friction in the hinge.

friction loss In concrete construction, the stress loss in a prestressing tendon resulting from friction between the tendon and other devices during stressing.

friction pile, floating pile foundation A **pile** that transfers its load to the soil through friction with the earth surrounding it; the point of the pile carries no load.

friction shoe An adjustable or preloaded friction device used to hold a sash in any open position.

friction tape A fibrous tape which is impregnated with a sticky moisture-resistant compound; used in electric wiring as a protective covering for insulation.

friction welding A method of welding thermoplastic materials whereby the heat necessary to soften the components is provided by friction.

frieze **1.** In Classical architecture and derivatives, the middle horizontal member of three main divisions of an **entablature**, above the **architrave** and below the cornice. **2.** A decorative band at or near the top of an interior wall below the cornice. **3.** In house construction, a horizontal member connecting the top row of the siding with the underside of the cornice. Also see **cushion frieze**.

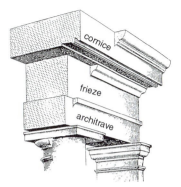

frieze, 1

from the **frieze, 2** of the Parthenon

frieze-band window One of a series of small windows that form a horizontal band directly below the cornice, usually across the main façade of a building; found especially in Greek Revival architecture.

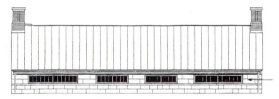

frieze-band windows

frieze panel The topmost panel in a multipaneled door.

frieze rail A door rail which is just below the frieze panel.

frigidarium The cold section of a Roman bath, sometimes including a swimming pool (piscina). Also see **bath, 3**.

frit Small friable particles produced by quenching a molten glassy material.

frithstool A seat, usually of stone, placed near the altar in some churches as a sacred refuge for those who claimed the privilege of sanctuary.

froe   A **riving knife**.

frog, panel   A depression in the bed face of a brick or building block; used to provide a better key for mortar.

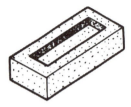

a brick having a **frog**

front   **1.** The most prominent face of a building and/or that face which contains the main entrance. **2.** The face of a lock through which the bolt or bolts move. It is usually mortised in so as to be flush with edge of door; also called a **lock front**.

frontage   The length of a lot line or a building site along a street or other public way, or along a body of water forming a boundary.

frontal   The textile or panels which form the decorative front of an altar.

frontal

front curtain   See **act curtain**.

front door   The main entrance to a building or to an apartment in a building; an **entrance** door.

front elevation   The **façade** or principal elevation of a building.

front-end loader   **1.** A bucket and lift-arm assembly designed for use on the front of a tractor; hydraulic cylinders, which raise and lower the lift arms, tip the bucket so that it may be dumped in the elevated position. **2.** The entire machine

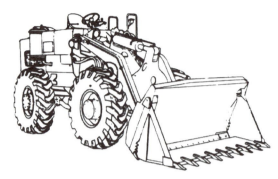

front-end loader

using the above assembly. **3.** A self-propelled machine mounted either on wheels or on crawlers and equipped with a front-mounted bucket to dig, lift, haul, and dump into stockpiles, haulers, etc.; a variety of attachments are available enabling such a machine to do other types of work, such as ripping, scraping, or ditching.

front foot   A foot measured along the front property line.

front-gabled, front-facing gable   Said of a house having a **gable** on its façade.

front girt   A structural horizontal member (**girt**) or beam in an early timber-framed house along the front face of the house; see illustration under **timber-framed house**.

front hearth, outer hearth   That part of the hearth or hearthstone which is on the room side of the fireplace opening.

frontispiece   **1.** The decorated front wall or bay of a building. **2.** An ornamental porch or chief pediment. **3.** A fancy rendering prefacing an architectural presentation, esp. a student project in architectural school.

front light   **1.** A lighting unit mounted on the auditorium side of the proscenium. **2.** A lighting fixture mounted at dead center of an **open stage**.

front lintel   A **lintel** that supports the outer leaf of a cavity wall.

front of the house   Those parts of a theatre which are on the audience side of the fire wall.

fronton   See **pediment**.

front putty   Same as **face putty**.

front stage   The forepart of the stage in a theatre, nearest the footlights.

front yard   A yard of a plot of ground facing the street; extends from the front line of the building to the front property line, and across the full width of the plot.

frost The action (or result of such action) of the freezing of water vapor on a surface (e.g., the ground) that is colder than 32°F (0°C).

frost action The freezing and thawing of moisture in materials and the resultant effects on these materials and on structures of which they are a part or with which they are in contact.

frost boil **1.** A defective spot on a concrete surface resulting from swelling and subsequent disintegration caused by the action of frost on entrapped moisture. **2.** The softening of soil during a period of thaw, owing to the liberation of water.

frost crack A lengthwise split in a growing tree caused by frost, usually confined to the base.

frosted **1.** Rusticated, with formalized stalactites or icicles. **2.** Given an even, granular surface to avoid shine; matted. **3.** Closely reticulated or matted to avoid transparency.

frosted finish See **caustic etch**.

frosted glass Glass which has been surface-treated to scatter light or to simulate frost.

frosted lamp bulb A lamp bulb that is chemically etched or sandblasted to diffuse the emitted light. Incandescent lamps usually are frosted on the inside; tungsten-halogen lamps are frosted on the outside.

frosted work A type of ornamental rusticated work, having an appearance like that of frost on plants.

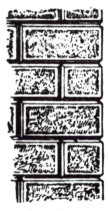

frosted work

frost heave The raising of a soil surface due to the accumulation of ice in the underlying soil.

frosting **1.** A surface haze on the surface of a paint film caused by very fine wrinkling. **2.** A lusterless finish of metal or glass.

frost line An imaginary line indicating the depth of frost penetration in the ground.

frostproof closet A **hopper, 4** which has no water in the bowl and has the trap and the control valve for its water supply installed below the frost line.

frow A **riving knife**.

frowy Descriptive of soft and brittle timber.

frt Abbr. for "freight."

FS On drawings, abbr. for "Federal Specifications."

fsp Abbr. for **fire standpipe**.

FSTC Abbr. for **field sound transmission class**.

ft On drawings, abbr. for "foot."

ft-c Abbr. for **footcandle**.

FTG **1.** On drawings, abbr. for **footing**. **2.** On drawings, abbr. for **fitting**.

FT-LB On drawings, abbr. for "foot-pound."

fuel bunker A receptacle for the storage of solid fuel.

fuel-fired boiler Automatic mechanical equipment which utilizes heat from combustion of solid, liquid, or gaseous fuels to heat water or generate steam, and having all components including burner, boiler controls, and auxiliary equipment assembled in one unit, either at the factory or on the site.

fuel load The quantity of potential fuel within a building, including its contents and fabric.

fugitive Changing in color as a result of lack of permanency in a colored pigment or medium when exposed to air, light, etc.

full Of a dimension, slightly oversize.

full bond In masonry, a bond in which all bricks are laid as **headers**.

full-bound Descriptive of a sash having stiles and rails of equal width.

full Cape house A **Cape Cod house** which has two double-hung windows on each side of the front door. (See illustration p. 412.)

full-cell process Same as **Bethell process**.

full-centered Applied to an architectural feature the outline of which follows an arc of a circle.

full coat A paint film of optimum thickness.

full Cape house

Fuller faucet A faucet, the flow through which is controlled by means of a rubber ball that is forced into the opening of the pipe.

full-façade portico A portico that extends the full width of a house and its full height.

full-façade portico

full-flush door A door of hollow-metal construction, formed from two sheets of steel. The top and bottom of the door may be either flush or closed by end channels; seams are visible on door edge only.

full frame See **braced frame**.

full glass door A door having glass (usually heat-strengthened or tempered) in the entire area between the rails and stiles; may have horizontal **muntins** dividing the glass area.

full gloss A very high gloss.

full-height porch A roofed porch, on the front of a house, that extends the full height of the house but not necessarily the full width.

full-louvered door A type of door having louvers the entire height and width of the area surrounded by rails and stiles.

full-open valve A shutoff valve whose cross section, in the open position, equals at least 85% of the cross-sectional area of the connecting pipes.

full-penetration butt weld A **butt weld** between two members in which the depth of the weld is equal to the thickness of the smaller of the two members.

full size A drawing at the same size as the object shown.

full splice A splice equal to the full strength of its members.

full-surface hinge A hinge designed for attachment on the surface of the door and jamb without mortising.

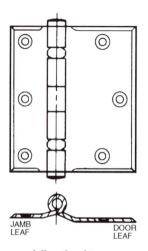

JAMB LEAF   DOOR LEAF

full-surface hinge

full torching See **torching**.

full-way valve See **gate valve**.

full-width porch A porch that extends the full width of a house, but not the full height.

fully welded seamless door A door having all joints on its faces and vertical edges continuously welded and finished flush and smooth, so as to be completely invisible.

fumed oak Oak which has been darkened by exposure to ammonia fumes.

fume hood A partial enclosure through which air is drawn to remove gases and odors within the enclosed area.

functionalism A philosophy of architectural design asserting that the form of a building should follow its function, reveal its structure, and express the nature of its materials, construction, and purpose, minimizing or eliminating all purely decorative effects. See Louis H. Sullivan's

1896 statement on this subject, ". . . form ever follows function," under **Sullivanesque**.

fundula　In ancient Rome, a blind alley; a **cul-de-sac**.

fungicide　A substance that is poisonous to fungi; retards or prevents the growth of fungi.

fur　To apply **furring**.

furnace　**1.** That part of a boiler or warm-air heating plant in which combustion takes place. **2.** A complete heating unit for transferring heat from fuel being burned to the air supplied to a heating system.

furnish　By-products from primary wood manufacturing such as planer shavings, sawdust, and slabs; used as a raw material in fabricating particleboard, fiberboard, etc.

furniture　Movable equipment or articles of convenience, such as tables and chairs, or of decoration, for exterior or interior habitable spaces.

furniture wall　A hollow metal partition containing vertical and horizontal slots through which electrical cables can be run.

furred　Provided with furring strips so as to leave an air space, as between plastering and a wall or between flooring and the subfloor.

furring　**1.** Spacers such as wood strips or metal channels which are fastened to the joists, studs, walls, or ceiling of a building so that the finish surface may be leveled. Also see **wall furring**. **2.** Grillage for the attachment of gypsum or metal lath. **3.** A method of finishing the interior face of a masonry wall to provide space for thermal insulation, to prevent moisture transmission, or to provide a level surface for finishing. **4.** Same as **scale, 8**.

furring

furring brick　A hollow brick used for furring or lining the inside face of a wall; usually the size of an ordinary brick and grooved or scored on the face to afford a key for plastering; carries no superimposed load.

furring channel　A steel channel used as **furring, 1**.

furring channel clip　Same as **channel clip**.

furring nail　A galvanized, low-carbon steel nail, usually having a flat head and a diamond point, with a washer or spacer on the shank for fastening wire lath and spacing it from the nailing member.

furring nails

furring strip　A wood strip used as **furring, 1**; also see **batten, 3**.

furring tile　Tile designed for lining the inside of exterior walls and carrying no superimposed load; has a corrugated surface to receive plaster.

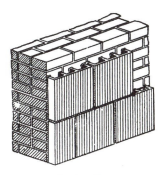

furring tile

furrowed　Said of (margin drafted) **ashlars** which have vertical grooves cut in the face.

furrowing　A technique used in bricklaying to increase the speed of work; the bricklayer creates a furrow in the mortar bed with the tip of his trowel.

fus　Abbr. for "fusible."

fusarole A molding of convex rounded section, commonly carved into beads and the like.

fuse An overcurrent protective device consisting of a metal strip, ribbon, or wire which is designed to open an electric circuit by melting if a predetermined current is exceeded.

fuse of the cartridge type

fuse block Same as **fuse board**.

fuse board A panel on which fuse holders (such as "fuse clips") are mounted.

fuse box A **cutout box** containing the fuses for an electric circuit.

fuse lighter A special device for the purpose of igniting **safety fuses**.

fusible-element sprinkler In a fire protection system, a **sprinkler** which opens under the influence of heat by the melting of a component (e.g., a fusible plug).

fusible link A metal chain link made of a low-melting-point alloy; in case of fire, the chain breaks, thereby closing a damper, door, or the like.

fusible metal An alloy having a low melting point; esp. used to release fire-protection devices in the event of fire.

fusible solder An alloy, usually containing bismuth, having a low melting point—below that of tin-lead solder, i.e., below 361°F (183°C).

fusible switch An electric switch with fuse holders.

fusible tape See **joint tape**.

fusion In welding, the melting together of **filler metal** and base metal, or of the base metal alone, which results in coalescence.

fust The shaft of a column or pilaster.

fuzzy texture A defect in a porcelain enamel surface characterized by a myriad of minute bubbles, broken bubbles, and dimples.

FW Abbr. for **flash welding**.

G

G **1.** On drawings, abbr. for "gas." **2.** On drawings, abbr. for **girder**.

ga. Abbr. for **gauge** or **gage**.

gabbro Igneous rock similar to diorite, predominantly composed of ferromagnetic minerals with crystals visible to the eye; has the same mineral composition as basalt.

gable A vertical surface on a building usually adjoining a pitched roof, commonly at an end, whose shape depends on the type of roof and parapet, although most often it is triangular; often extends from the level of the cornice up to the ridge of the roof. If the gable is on the façade, rather than the end, the building is said to be front-gabled. For definitions and illustrations of particular types, see **bell gable, broken gable, clipped gable, corbie gable, corbiestep gable, cross gable, crowfooted gable, crowstep gable, curvilinear gable, docked gable, Dutch gable, end gable, façade gable, Flemish gable, front-facing gable, hanging gable, intersecting gable, multicurved gable, parapeted gable, segmental gable, side gable, stepped gable, straight-line gable, truncated gable, tumbled-in gable, wall gable**.

gableboard See **bargeboard**.

gable coping The protective cap covering a **gable wall** that projects above the line of the roof finish.

gable dormer, gabled dormer Same as **triangular dormer**.

gabled roof See **gable roof**.

gabled tower A tower finished with a gable on two sides or on all sides, instead of terminating in a spire, or the like.

gable end A wall of a building having a gable at its end; a **gable wall**; also called a gable-end wall.

gable finish The molding or cornice around a **gable end**, usually on the eaves of a building.

gable front A façade that is **front-gabled**.

gable-front-and-wing plan The plan of a house having its long side perpendicular to the

gable end

street and having a gable on the end facing the street; a wing is added at the rear of the house.

gable-fronted Same as **front-gabled**.

gable-on-hip roof A **hipped roof** in which the hips are not carried all the way to the ridge; instead, each end roof surface turns vertically near the top so as to form a small gable that is perpendicular to the ridge.

gable-on-hip roof

gable ornamentation Any type of decorative element on the face of a gable, such as **spindlework**, near the apex of a gable.

gable post A short post located at the peak of a gable into which the **bargeboards** are fixed.

gable roof A roof having a single slope on each side of a central ridge; usually with a **gable** at one or at both ends of the roof. (*See illustration p. 416.*)

gable shoulder Projecting brickwork or masonry which supports the foot of a gable.

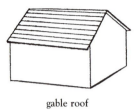

gable roof

gable springer, skew block, skew butt A **kneeler, 1** (esp. a projecting one) which is at the foot of a gable or the like.

gablet A small ornamental gable.

gable wall A wall which is crowned by a gable.

gable wall

gable window **1.** A window in a gable. **2.** A window shaped like a gable.

gaboon, okoume A wood resembling African mahogany but softer and lighter in weight.

gadroon, godroon An ornament composed chiefly of ovoid or more elongated bosses regularly repeated, side by side.

gage See **gauge.**

gaged See **gauged.**

gaged brick See **gauged brick.**

gaging See **gauging.**

gag process The process of bending structural shapes in a gag press.

gain In carpentry, a groove or notch in one piece into which another piece is fitted.

gain joint

gaine A decorative pedestal, esp. one tapered downward and square in section. Also see **estípite.**

gal On drawings, abbr. for "gallon."

galería In Spanish Colonial architecture, an open, covered porch, usually arcaded, either facing a patio or the street.

galerie A gallery or porch. In **French Vernacular architecture** of Louisiana, a roofed porch, usually open-sided, often extending across the entire front, across the front and one or more sides, or completely around the building on the upper level.

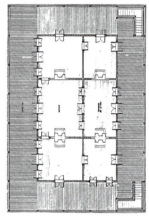

galerie surrounding a raised house

galerie house, gallery house In **French Vernacular architecture,** a farmhouse or plantation house evolved by French-speaking settlers in the Louisiana Territory; usually has a roofed **galerie** either across the façade or across the façade and one or both sides of the house; typically has gabled dormers with windows. Also see **Cajun cottage** and **Creole house.**

galilee A narthex or chapel for worship at the west end of a church.

gall Unusual growth of plant tissues; a result of the introduction of a foreign substance such as a chemical or fungus, or a result of mechanical injury.

gallery **1.** A long, covered area acting as a corridor inside or on the exterior of a building, or between buildings. **2.** An elevated area, interior or exterior, e.g., minstrel gallery, music gallery, roof gallery. **3.** An elevated section of the seating area of an auditorium, esp. the uppermost such

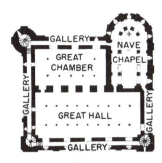

gallery, 1

space. **4.** In buildings for public worship, a similar space, sometimes set apart for special uses. **5.** A service passageway within a building, or linking a building underground to exterior supplies or exits. Some service galleries also serve sightseers, e.g., the lighting gallery in the base of the dome at St. Peter's, Rome. **6.** A long, narrow room for special activities like target practice, etc. **7.** A room, often top-lit, used for the display of art works. **8.** A building serving such art needs. **9.** See **long gallery. 10.** Any raised working platform at the side or rear of a theatre stagehouse. **11.** An **arcade, 2. 12.** (*Brit.*) A device, attached to a lampholder, for supporting a reflector, shade, etc.

gallery apartment house An apartment house having external passageways which provide entry to individual apartments on each floor.

gallery grave A prehistoric burial place consisting of a long stone-lined gallery without a tomb chamber, and covered by an artificial mound.

gallet A stone chip or **spall.**

galleting, garreting **1.** The insertion of stone chips into the joints of rough masonry to reduce the amount of mortar required, to wedge larger stones in position, or to add detail to the appearance. **2.** Pieces of tile used to provide a suitable bed for ridge tile or hip tile.

gallows bracket A triangularly shaped bracket fixed to a wall, such as one to support shelving.

GALV On drawings, abbr. for "galvanize."

galvanic corrosion An electrochemical action which takes place when dissimilar metals are in contact in the presence of an electrolyte, resulting in corrosion.

galvanize To coat steel or iron with zinc, as, for example, by immersing it in a bath of molten zinc.

galvanized iron Sheet metal of iron coated with zinc to prevent rusting; used extensively for flashings, roof gutters, gravel stops, flexible metal roofing, etc.

galvanized pipe A steel pipe or wrought-iron pipe, of standard dimensions, which has been galvanized by coating it with a thin layer of zinc.

galvanizing The process of coating steel or iron with zinc by immersing it in a bath of molten zinc.

gambrel end An end wall of a structure having a **gambrel roof.**

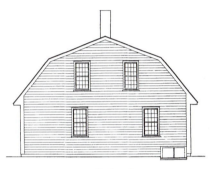

gambrel end

gambrel roof, gambrel **1.** (*U.S.A.*) A roof which has two pitches on each side; in Great Britain called a **mansard roof. 2.** (*Brit.*) A roof which has a small gable near the ridge on one end; the part of the roof below the gable is inclined. Also see **Dutch gambrel roof, English gambrel roof, Flemish gambrel roof, New England gambrel roof, Swedish gambrel roof.**

gambrel roof, 1

game room A room used primarily for recreation, often downstairs in a dwelling.

gamma protein Protein obtained from soya beans; used as a thickener in water-base paints.

gang boarding See **cat ladder.**

ganged form Prefabricated panels which are joined to make a much larger unit, for convenience in erecting, stripping, and reusing; usually braced with wales, strong-backs, or special lifting hardware.

Gang Nail A registered trademark of Gang-Nail Systems, Inc. A type of **timber connector** consisting of a metal plate having a series of spikes at right angles to it.

gang saw A powered assemblage of parallel reciprocating saw blades; used to cut a quarry block into slabs; generally utilizes a loose abrasive material with water, or diamond or tungsten carbide blade inserts, to effect the cutting.

gangway **1.** A platform or boardwalk erected over an unfinished building section to provide access for men and materials carriers. **2.** British term for **aisle**.

ganister A product made by mixing ground quartz with a bonding material such as fireclay.

gantry A framework, usually of heavy timbers, to support building equipment or to provide a working platform.

gantry crane A revolving crane, positioned atop a movable pedestal that travels along tracks; can reach a more extensive area of a construction site than a stationary crane of similar size.

gap-filling glue A glue used to join surfaces which cannot be closely fitted together.

gap-graded aggregate Aggregate having a particle-size distribution characterized by **gap grading**.

gap-graded concrete Concrete which contains **gap-graded aggregate**.

gap grading A particle-size distribution for material such as an aggregate in which particles of certain intermediate sizes are substantially absent.

gar. Abbr. for **garage**.

garage **1.** Building or part thereof where motor vehicles are kept. **2.** Place for repairing and maintaining such vehicles. Also see **attached garage, detached garage**.

garage door See **overhead door**.

garbage Animal and vegetable waste from restaurants, hotels, markets, and like installations; contains up to 70% moisture and up to 5% incombustible solids. Also see **refuse, rubbish**, and **trash**.

garbage chute See **refuse chute** and **gravity-type refuse chute**.

garbage-disposal unit Same as **waste-disposal unit**.

garçonnière A bachelor apartment. In **French Vernacular architecture**, a bachelor's residence that is separate from the main house.

garden A plot of ground used principally for growing vegetables, fruits, or flowering and/or ornamental plants.

garden apartment **1.** Ground-floor apartment with access to a garden or other adjacent outdoor space. **2.** Two- or three-story apartment buildings with communal gardens, generally located in the suburbs.

garden arch An archway in a garden, often of lattice construction, that serves as a decorative structure on which to grow vines, roses, or other climbing plants.

garden city A residential development having parking areas; esp. planned to provide considerable open space that is well planted with trees and shrubs.

garden house A structure for shelter in a garden, usually small.

garden tile Structural ceramic units made in molds and placed as stepping stones through a garden or patio.

garden wall bond See **English garden wall bond, Flemish garden wall bond, mixed garden wall bond**.

garden wall cross bond In brickwork, a bond in which a course of **headers** alternates with a course consisting of a header followed by three **stretchers**.

garderobe **1.** See **wardrobe**. **2.** A small bedroom or study. **3.** Euphemism for a latrine in medieval buildings.

garetta Same as **garretta**.

gargoyle A waterspout projecting from the roof gutter of a building, often carved grotesquely.

garland An ornament in the form of a band, a wreath, or a festoon of leaves, fruits, or flowers.

garland drain A shallow ditch or trench for draining surface or subsoil water before it reaches an excavation.

garner Same as **granary**.

gargoyle

garnet   A mineral having many varieties in color and constituents but the same general chemical formula, with an isometric crystal structure.

garnet hinge   Same as **cross-garnet hinge**.

garnet paper   An abrasive paper coated with finely powdered garnet; used in finishing and polishing surfaces.

garret   **1.** Space within a roof structure; sometimes called an **attic**. **2.** A room, usually with sloping ceilings, just beneath the roof of a house.

garreting   See **galleting**.

garrison house   **1.** An early fortified house generally constructed of stone or hewn logs, commonly with a second-story **overhang**; commonly fitted with **loopholes**; provided a family with a safe haven of refuge in times of emergency and served as a one-family dwelling in times of peace. **2.** A modern term sometimes applied to any **Colonial Revival** house having an overhanging second story.

garrison house, 1

garth   The open courtyard of a cloister, often a lawn.

gas checking   A wrinkling in a paint or varnish finish which, as it sets, is exposed to burnt coal gas.

gas concrete   Lightweight concrete produced by developing voids by means of gas generated within the unhardened mix (usually from the action of cement alkalies on aluminum powder used as an admixture). Also see **foamed concrete**.

gas distribution piping   All piping from the house side of the gas meter to the consumer service pipes used to supply fuel or illumination to a building.

gaseous discharge   The emission of light from gas atoms excited by an electric current.

gas-filled lamp   An **incandescent lamp** in which the filament operates in an inert gas atmosphere within the bulb.

gas-fired   Heated by the combustion of gaseous fuel.

gas-fired water heater   A **direct-fired water heater** using natural gas, manufactured gas, or propane gas as its source of fuel.

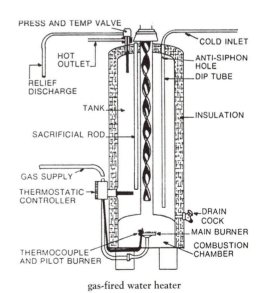

gas-fired water heater

gas flow meter   An instrument for measuring the velocity or volume of flowing gases.

gas furnace   A furnace which uses gas as a fuel.

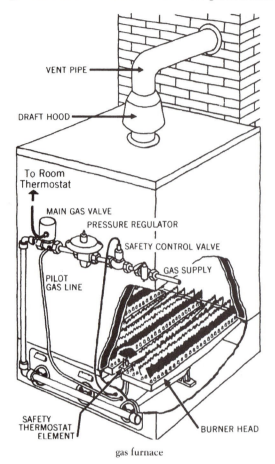

gas furnace

gasket   **1.** A continuous strip of resilient material attached to a door or doorframe to provide a tight seal between the door and frame; acts as weather stripping and as a light and sound seal. **2.** Any ring of resilient material, used at a joint to prevent leakage.

gasketed joint   A joint utilizing a gasket under compression to join cast-iron soil pipe and

gasketed joint

ductile-iron sewer and pressure pipe. The end of each pipe must be of a type suitable for the individual joint.

gas main   The line from the public utility which supplies gas to the consumer service pipes.

gas metal-arc welding   An arc-welding process in which coalescence is produced by heating with an arc between a consumable electrode (of **filler metal**) and the work.

gas meter   A mechanical instrument for measuring the amount of gas volume passing a given point.

gas meter piping   The piping from the **gas service line valve** to the outlet of the meter regulator, or to the meter if no regulator is required.

gas piping system   The collective gas service piping, gas meter piping, and gas distribution piping.

gas pliers   Sturdy pliers having concave jaws with serrated faces; esp. useful for gripping pipe or other round objects.

gas pocket, blowhole   A hole or void, as in a casting, which results from entrained air.

gas pressure regulator   A device for controlling and maintaining a uniform gas pressure; required when (a) the pressure of the gas supply is higher than the pressure at which the branch supply line or gas-utilization equipment is designed to operate, or (b) the pressure varies beyond design limits of the utilization equipment.

gas refrigeration   Refrigeration involving the use of machinery in which the refrigerant is heated by a gas flame.

gas room   A fully enclosed room, separately ventilated, in which toxic and highly toxic compressed gases and associated equipment and supplies are used or stored.

gas service-line valve   The valve located at (or below) grade on the supply side of a gas meter or service regulator.

gas service piping   The gas supply piping from the street gas main up to and including the gas service-line valve.

gas station   A building or stand where fuel for motor vehicles is sold. Facilities for motor vehicle repair are often a part of the station.

gas vent   A vent pipe leading to the outside air from a gas furnace or other gas-fired equipment for removal of gaseous products of combustion.

gas welding Any one of a group of welding processes in which coalescence is produced by heat from one or more gas flames; sometimes a **filler metal** is used; pressure may or may not be applied to the materials being welded.

gatch Plaster as used in Persia for decorative purposes.

gate A passageway through a fence, wall, or other barrier, which slides, lowers, or swings open or shut.

gate contact See **car door contact**.

gatehouse A building, enclosing or accompanying a gateway for a castle, manor house, or similar buildings of importance.

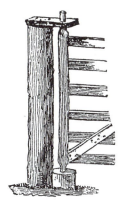
gatepost

gatehouse

gate operator An electro-mechanical device which opens or closes a gate when a switch supplies it with voltage.

gate pier A brick, concrete, or stone **gatepost**.

gatepost A post, usually one of a pair, between which a gate swings or slides; see **hanging post**.

gate tower A tower containing a gate to a fortress.

gate valve, full-way valve A flow control device consisting of a wedge-shaped gate which can be raised to allow full, unobstructed flow or can be lowered to restrict the flow passage; not intended for close fluid flow control nor for very tight shutoff. (See illustration p. 422.)

gate tower

gateway 1. A passage through a fence or wall. 2. A frame, arch, etc., in which a gate is hung. 3. A structure at an entrance or gate designed for ornament or defense. (See illustration p. 422.)

gathering A transition between two sections (as in a chimney, flue, or duct) which have different areas.

gauge, gage 1. The thickness of sheet metal or metal tubing, usually designated by a number. 2. The diameter of wire or a screw, usually designated by a number. 3. The distance between two points, such as parallel lines of connectors. 4. A strip of metal or wood used as a guide to control the thickness of a bituminous or concrete paving; called a **screed** when used in plastering. 5. A measuring instrument, esp. one for measuring liquid level, dimensions, or pressure. 6. See **mortise gauge**. 7. In roofing, the length of a shingle, slate, or tile that is exposed when laid. 8. The quantity of gauging plaster used with

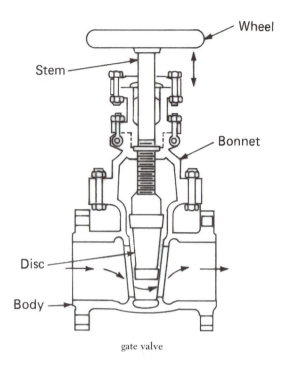

gate valve

gateway: Merton College, Oxford (1416)

common plaster (lime putty) to hasten its set-ting, etc. **9.** To mix gauging plaster with lime putty, to effect better control of the set, to pre-vent shrinkage of the lime putty, and to increase its strength. **10.** To cut, chip, or rub stone or brick to a uniform size or shape.

gauge board **1.** Same as **gauging board. 2.** A **pitch board**.

gauged Descriptive of a material which has been ground so that various pieces are of the same thickness or of a desired shape.

gauged arch An arch of wedge-shaped bricks which have been shaped so that the joints radi-ate from a common center.

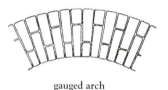

gauged arch

gauged brick **1.** A brick of special shape that has been cut with a chisel or saw and then ground (for example, on coursed sandstone) to accurate dimensions. **2.** A tapered **arch brick**.

gauged mortar Mortar consisting of a mixture of cement, lime, and sand in specified propor-tions.

gauged skim coat In plastering, a very thin final coat of gauging plaster and lime putty, troweled to a smooth, hard finish.

gauged stuff Same as **gauging plaster**.

gauged work **1.** A precise brickwork in which bricks are cut or sawn to shape and then rubbed to an exact size and smooth finish. **2.** Plastering, such as the application of moldings or orna-ments, which is done with gauged plaster.

gauge glass A device which indicates the level of a liquid in a tank, vessel, or the like.

gauge pile See **guide pile**.

gauge pressure The pressure, of a gas or liq-uid, minus the value of atmospheric pressure.

gauge rod A measuring stick for checking the accuracy of the gauge in brickwork; called a **story rod** if used to mark floor and sill levels.

gauge stick See **scantle**.

gauging board A board on which cement, mortar, or plaster is mixed.

gauging box   A **batch box**.

gauging plaster   A special gypsum plaster mixed with lime putty; used as a finish coat.

gaul   A hollow spot or area in a coat of plaster, mortar, or the like.

gauze   **1.** Any thin, open-weave, woven fabric; usually transparent. **2.** A fine wire cloth; also called **lawn**.

gazebo   A small ornamental structure, such as a pavilion, often providing a splendid view; usually built in a garden, in a park, or along a stream; same as **belvedere** or **summerhouse**.

gazebo

gazophylacium   A place where precious items were deposited, as a treasury in a palace or in a church.

GB   Abbr. for **glass block**.

GC   Abbr. for "General Contractor."

G-cramp   A large **C-clamp**, used by joiners.

geison   A projection from the face of a wall such as from a cornice or coping.

gel   A semisolid material, somewhat elastic, composed of matter in a colloidal state that does not dissolve; remains suspended in a solvent. Also see **cement gel**.

gelatin mold   A semirigid mold made from gelatin; used in making plaster casts.

gel coat   A thin, outer layer of resin, sometimes containing pigment, applied to a reinforced plastic molding to improve its appearance.

gelling   Any process whereby paint or varnish thickens to jelly-like consistency. Also see **livering**.

gemel, chymol, gimmer, gymmer, jimmer   Two corresponding elements of construction considered as a pair.

gemel window   A window built into a pair of openings; a window having two bays.

geminated   Coupled, as in **coupled columns**.

general conditions   That part of the **contract documents** (of the contract for construction) which sets forth many of the rights, responsibilities, and relationships of the parties involved. Also see **conditions of the contract**.

general contract   **1.** Under the single contract system, **the contract** between the **owner** and the **contractor** for construction of the entire **work, 1**. **2.** Under the separate contract system, that contract between the owner and a contractor for construction of architectural and structural work.

general contractor   The **prime contractor** who is responsible for most of the work at the construction site, including that performed by the **subcontractors**.

general diffuse lighting   Lighting from luminaires which distribute 40% to 60% of the emitted light upward and the balance downward.

General Grant style   A term occasionally used in the United States for the **Second Empire style** of architecture because of the number of public buildings in this style erected when he was president of the United States (1869–1877).

general hospital   An institution, consisting of a building or buildings, in which patients, irrespective of sex and age, receive diagnostic and therapeutic medical and surgical services for most forms of illness, injury, or disability.

general industrial occupancy   The use of a building of conventional design for all types of manufacturing operations, except high-hazard.

general lighting   Lighting designed to provide a substantially uniform level of illumination throughout an area.

generally accepted standard   A specification, code, rule, guide, or procedure in the field of construction, or related thereto, recognized and accepted as authoritative.

general requirements   The title of Division 1 of the AIA's **uniform system** for construction specifications, data filing, and cost accounting.

generator   A machine that converts mechanical power into electric power.

generator set   A unit consisting of an electric **generator** driven by an engine.

gentrification   The upgrading of urban property in a deteriorated area, usually resulting in the dispersal of the current residents and their replacement by a more affluent population.

geodesic dome   A structure consisting of a multiplicity of similar, light, straight-line elements (usually in tension) which form a grid in the shape of a dome.

geodetic survey   A land survey in which the curvature of the earth is considered; applicable for large areas and long lines; used for the precise location of basic points suitable for controlling other surveys.

geometrical stair   A stair constructed around a stairwell without the use of newels at the angles or turning points.

Geometric style

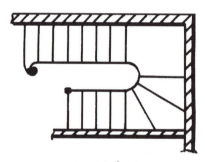

geometrical stair

Geometric style   The early development of the Decorated style of English Gothic architecture, in the first half of the 14th cent., characterized by the geometrical forms of its window tracery.

geometric tracery   Gothic openwork in the form of simple geometrical patterns, principally circles and multifoils.

Georgian style   In Great Britain, the term "Georgian" is usually applied to the prevailing architectural style during the reigns of George I through George IV, from 1714 to 1830; derived from classical, Renaissance, and Baroque forms. In America, it is applied to a similar architectural style that emerged about 1700 and flourished until about 1780. Georgian architecture is often characterized by a rectangular plan, often with symmetrical wings flanking each side; a symmetrical brick or stone façade; pedimented

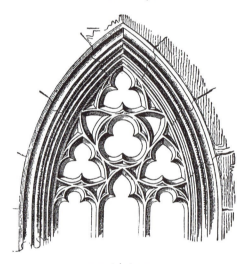

geometric tracery

gable; projecting central pavilion or a portico often with two-story columns; monumental pilasters extended the full height of the façade; a **belt course**; a slate-shingled hipped roof (often truncated and enclosed with a balustrade); a decorated classical cornice; five-**ranked** rectangular double-hung windows; lintels above rectangular windows; front windows on the ground floor, often pedimented; frequently a Palladian window; an elaborate front entrance; either a single door or a double door, with multiple panels in each leaf; often decoratively crowned; a pediment over the door; often, a projecting hood above the door; a fanlight or transom light above the door, often

Georgian architecture: typical façade

with sidelights on each side of it; decorative pilasters or engaged columns flanking the doorway. In elegant homes, the front door opened into a spacious **entrance hall**.

The introduction of the Georgian style in America varied with geographical region. In New England, two-story timber-framed houses with central chimneys predominated. In the South, brick and stone construction were widely used, with fireplace chimneys at the ends of the house; in large houses, a **raised basement** was common. Although initially relatively unpretentious, Georgian-style homes became larger, wider, and more elaborate over time. An arbitrary distinction is sometimes made by some architectural historians between *Early Georgian* and *Late Georgian*, considering the year 1750 as the approximate time of transition. However, the changes occurred gradually and at different times in different colonies.

Georgian architecture: example of a doorway

Georgian glass   Thick glass reinforced with an inner layer of steel-wire mesh.

Georgian Revival   See **Colonial Revival**.

German barn, Swiss barn   Any one of a variety of barns, often serving as a combination barn and home, built during the 18th and 19th centuries by German-speaking immigrants to the New World; especially characterized by a shingled gambrel roof or gable roof; a second floor overhanging one side of the barn, well beyond the foundation; usually an inclined driveway providing direct entry to the *threshing floor* where wheat was threshed, hay was stored, and where the family lived. The *basement* was used as a stable for horses, cattle, and sheep; often of stone construction or masonry up to the threshing floor and wood construction above. Many stone barns had long, narrow, vertical slots in the walls for supplying the barn with fresh air. Also see **bank barn, forebay barn, grundscheier, Pennsylvania barn, Sweitzer barn, slit ventilator**.

German Colonial architecture   Architecture attributed to German-speaking immigrants to America primarily in the years from about 1680 to 1780. Many of these early settlers first built a **log house** of hewn square timbers as a temporary home until they could construct more substantial housing. Common characteristics of their permanent houses included: a symmetrical façade, thick stone walls, a steeply pitched end-gabled roof usually covered with wood shingles or clay tiles; an attic story with windows at the gable ends and **shed dormers** on the roof, a porch at the gable end of the house or at the front of the house; small casement windows with battened shutters, later replaced by double-hung windows. If it was built into a hillside, it was called a *bank house*. Also see **fachwerk, grundscheier, Pennsylvania Dutch, rauchkammer, springhouse**.

German siding   **Drop siding** with a concave upper edge which fits into a corresponding groove in the siding above.

gesso   A mixture of gypsum plaster, glue, and whiting; applied as a base coat for decorative painting.

geyser   An **instantaneous-type water heater**.

GFCI   Abbr. for **ground fault circuit interrupter**.

GI   On drawings, abbr. for **galvanized iron**.

giant arbor vitae   Same as **thuya**.

giant order   See **colossal order**.

giant pilaster   Same as **colossal pilaster**.

gib   **1.** A steel strap used to clasp two members together. **2.** Same as **gib** or **jib door**.

gib-and-cotter joint   A joint in timber construction, formed with a steel strap tightly drawn in position by steel clips and wedges.

Gibbs surround   The framing of a door or window by a head composed of a (usually triple) keystone and by jambs that are bordered by protruding rectangular blocks of stone.

Gibbs surround

gib door   See **jib door**.

giglio   A Florentine emblem such as a **fleur-de-lys**.

gig stick   A **radius rod**.

gilding   **1.** Gold leaf, gold flakes, brass, etc., applied as a surface finish. **2.** The surface so produced.

gilding metal   An alloy containing nominally 95% copper and 5% zinc. Generally available as flat products, rod, and wire.

gilloche   See **guilloche**.

Gilmore needle   A device used for determining the setting time of hydraulic cement.

gilsonite, uintahite   A naturally occurring grade of asphalt used in floor tile, paints, paving, and roofing.

gimlet   A small tool with a pointed screw at one end; used to bore small holes in wood by turning it with one hand.

gimmer   See **gemel**.

gin block   A simple form of tackle block with a single wheel, over which a rope runs.

gingerbread   Highly decorative, elaborate woodwork, usually turned on a lathe and/or fashioned on a jigsaw.

Gingerbread folk architecture   A style of **folk architecture** widely applied to homes in America from about 1870 to 1910; especially characterized by the heavy use of **gingerbread**, **spindlework**, and ornate **bargeboards**. Often, these elaborate embellishments were added to an older house to update it or included in a new house to make it appear to be *au courant*. Heavily ornamented porches were common; in larger houses, many were two stories high, with decorative balustrades with spindlework balusters

Gingerbread folk architecture

and lacelike **spandrels**. Also see **Carpenter Gothic, Queen Anne style, Steamboat Gothic, Victorian architecture**.

Gingerbread style A richly decorated American building fashion of the 19th cent.

girandole A branched light holder, either standing on a base or projecting from a wall.

girder A large or principal beam of steel, reinforced concrete, or timber; used to support concentrated loads at isolated points along its length.

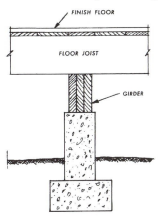

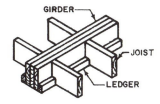

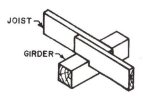

girders supporting floor joists

girder casing The material which totally encloses a girder, as one that projects below a ceiling.

girder post Any column or post which supports a girder.

girdle A band, usually horizontal; esp. one ringing the shaft of a column.

girt A horizontal structural member in the **framing, 3** of an early **timber-framed house,** typically

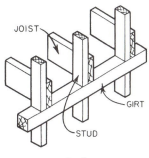

girt, 2

supporting the ends of the ceiling joists and acting as the main horizontal support for the floor above; often located about halfway between the **groundsill, 2** and the horizontal timber at the top of the wall (the **top plate**) The term *girt* often is preceded by an adjective indicating its position; for example, **front girt** denotes a heavy timber that runs horizontally along the front of the house; **rear girt** denotes a heavy timber that runs horizontally along the rear face of the house; **chimney girt** denotes a heavy timber that acts a main horizontal support between **chimney posts**. See illustration under **timber-framed house**.

girt strip Same as **ledger board**.

GL On drawings, abbr. for **glass**.

glacial till See **till**.

glacis A sloped embankment in front of a fortification, so raised as to bring an advancing enemy into the most direct line of fire.

gland joint In hot water piping, a joint that permits movement resulting from thermal expansion or contraction.

gland seal A seal used to prevent leakage between a fixed part and a movable part.

glare The sensation produced by brightnesses within the visual field that are sufficiently greater than the luminance to which the eyes are adapted to cause annoyance, discomfort, or loss in visual performance and visibility.

glass A hard, brittle inorganic substance, ordinarily transparent or translucent, produced by melting a mixture of silicates (such as sand) and a flux (such as lime and soda). Molten glass may be blown, cast, drawn, rolled, or pressed in a variety of shapes. Centuries ago, window glass was thin, generally of poor quality, often green or violet in hue, streaked with air bubbles. After about 1700, the manufacturing processes improved significantly so that the price of glass dropped significantly, the sizes of panes increased, and the use of window glass became more widespread. Also see **art glass, broad glass, crown glass, cylinder glass, figured glass, float glass, ground glass, hardened glass, heat-insulating glass, insulating glass, iridescent glass, jealous glass, laminated glass, leaded glass, opalescent glass, organic-coated glass, painted glass, plate glass, sheet glass, stained glass, tempered glass, Tiffany glass, toughened glass, wire glass.**

glass block, glass brick A hollow block of glass, usually translucent with textured faces; has relatively low thermal-insulation and low fire-resistance value; used in non-load-bearing walls.

glass bulb sprinkler In a fire protection system, a sprinkler which opens under the influence of heat by the breakage of a glass bulb; the bulb breaks as a result of the pressure exerted by the expansion of the liquid which it contains.

glass cement Any binding material used to cement glass to another piece of glass or other material.

glass cloth A closely-woven cloth fabricated of glass fibers; often used as a finishing jacket over thermal insulation for piping.

glass concrete A concrete slab or panel in which individual translucent glass lenses have been set, usually in a geometric pattern, to permit passage of light.

glass cutter A hand tool used for scoring or cutting glass; consists of a small, sharp wheel of hardened steel which is set in a handle, or a tool with a diamond point.

glass door A door of thick, heat-strengthened or tempered glass; there are no **rails** or **stiles.**

glass fiber, glass fibre See **fiberglass.**

glass house 1. British term for **greenhouse.** 2. A residence having exterior walls which are almost completely glass; an outstanding example is Philip Johnson's glass house in Connecticut.

glass paper A type of fine sandpaper, made with powdered glass as the abrasive.

glass pipe A pipe fabricated from a low-expansion borosilicate glass having a low alkali content; used primarily for the drainage of various corrosive liquids; very brittle and therefore used

only where protection is provided against mechanical damage to the pipe.

glass reinforced concrete Concrete that has been reinforced by the addition of glass fibers to the concrete mix.

glass seam A fracture in limestone that has been recemented and annealed by deposition of transparent calcite; limestone containing such a seam is structurally sound.

glass silk Same as **glass wool.**

glass size The size of a piece of glass required for glazing a given opening, allowing suitable clearance between the edge of the glass and the rebate.

glass slate Same as **glass tile.**

glass stop 1. A **glazing bead.** 2. A fitting which holds the lower end of a **patent glazing** bar; prevents the pane from sliding down.

glass tile, glass slate Tile fabricated of translucent or transparent glass; installed in a roof surface to allow light to enter the room below.

glass wool, glass silk Spun glass fibers in bulk form; resembles wool; used as thermal insulation, in air filters, and in fabricating fiberglass blankets, boards, and tile. Also see **mineral wool, fiberglass.**

glaze 1. A ceramic coating, usually thin, glossy, and glass-like, formed on the surface of pottery, earthenware, etc. 2. The material from which the ceramic coating is made. 3. To install glass in windows, doors, storefronts, curtain walls, and various other segments of building construction.

glaze coat 1. In built-up roofing having a smooth surface, the top layer of asphalt. 2. A temporary coating of bitumen used to protect the plies of built-up roofing when the application of the top pouring and surfacing is delayed. 3. A layer of thin, almost transparent, colored paint which allows an undercoat to show through.

glazed 1. Said of an opening that is filled with sheets of glass, as in a window. 2. Said of a finish that is composed of ceramic materials fused into its surface, usually making it essentially impervious to moisture.

glazed brick A brick that has been fired in a kiln hot enough to fuse the clay and sand on its surface, usually forming a dark glassy coating.

glazed door 1. Any door that has top and bottom rails and is glazed. 2. A **French door.**

glazed interior tile   A glazed ceramic tile having a body that is suitable for interior use, usually nonvitreous; not fabricated for use under conditions of excessive impact or of freezing and thawing.

glazed tile   Ceramic tile having a fused impervious glazed surface finish (clear, white, or colored) composed of ceramic materials fused into the body of the tile; the body may be nonvitreous, semivitreous, or impervious.

glazed work   Brickwork built with enameled brick or glazed brick.

glazement   A waterproof surfacing applied on a masonry surface.

glazier's chisel   A putty knife shaped like a chisel, used in setting glass.

glazier's point, sprig   A thin small three- or four-cornered piece of sheet metal, used to hold a pane of glass in a window frame while putty is applied.

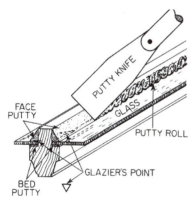

glazier's point

glazier's putty   A type of glazing compound. Also see **putty**.

glazing   **1.** Setting glass in an opening. **2.** The glass surface of a glazed opening.

glazing bar   One of the vertical or horizontal bars within a window frame which hold the panes of glass; a **muntin**.

glazing bead, glass stop   **1.** Same as **bead, 2, 3**. **2.** At a glazed opening, removable trim that holds the glass firmly in place.

glazing block   Same as **setting block**.

glazing brad   Same as **glazier's point**.

glazing clip   A metal clip used to retain a pane of glass in a metal frame while glazing compound is applied.

glazing clip

glazing color   A transparent wash, used to cover a ground coat of paint.

glazing compound   A putty-like material used to seal window glass in place; differs from **putty, 1** in that it retains its plasticity for an extended period of time.

glazing fillet   A small strip of wood used to hold glass in a rebate; a **glass stop**.

glazing gasket   A prefabricated strip of material used to seal and secure glass, or sealed glazing units, into frames and openings by a dry glazing method without using compounds or tapes.

glazing molding   **1.** A molding which serves as a glazing fillet. **2.** A **glass stop, 2**.

glazing point   Same as **glazier's point**.

glazing rabbet, glazing rebate   A **rabbet, 3** that receives the glass in a window frame or glazing bar.

glazing size   See **glass size**.

glazing spacer block   One of a number of blocks used to support glass in its frame.

glazing sprig, glazing brad   A headless nail used as a glazier's point to retain a pane of glass in a wooden opening while the putty is soft.

glazing stop   Same as **glass stop**.

glazing tape   A ribbon of resilient material for sealing a glass pane or panes in a frame, sash, or opening.

glebe house   An archaic term for **parsonage**.

gliding window   Same as **sliding sash**.

globe, light globe   **1.** A transparent or diffusing enclosure (usually of glass) to protect a light source, to diffuse and redirect the light, or to change the color of the light. **2.** An **incandescent lamp**.

globe valve   A valve in which the flow of water is controlled by a movable spindle which lowers

glory

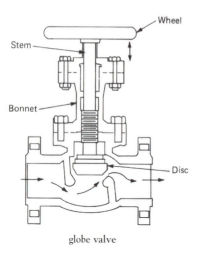

globe valve

to a fixed seat, thereby restricting the flow through the valve opening; the spindle is fitted with a washer to provide tight closure; usually enclosed in a chamber having a globular shape.

glory The luminous halo encircling the head of a sacred person and the radiance or luminous emanation encompassing the whole.

glory

gloss The degree of surface luster; ranges from a matte surface practically without sheen to an almost mirror-like glossy finish; intermediate conditions (in increasing order of glossiness) are: flat, eggshell, semigloss, and full gloss or high gloss.

glossing up The appearance of glossy areas in a matte surface when it is fingered or rubbed. Also see **burnishing**.

glow discharge An electric discharge in a gas at low pressure which produces a diffuse glow; characterized by a low cathode temperature, a low current density, and a high voltage drop.

glow lamp A **glow discharge** lamp which generates light in an ionized gas close to the electrodes; commonly used as an indicating device because of the low power consumption.

glue Any fluid adhesive substance used for joining materials, often of substantial weight; generally refers to adhesives that cure without heat: **animal glue, fish glue, emulsion glue**, etc.

glue block, angle block A block of wood, set into an interior angle formed by two boards, and glued in place to strengthen the joint.

glued-laminated timber A manufactured product consisting of four or more wood layers, none of which exceeds 2 in. (5 cm) in thickness, bonded together with adhesive; may be comprised of pieces which are end-joined to form any desired length, or which may be glued edge-to-edge to give greater width.

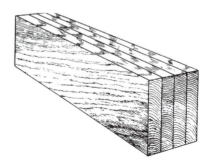

glue-laminated timber

glued-up stock Pieces of wood (including veneer or furniture) joined together by gluing.

glue line The line of adhesive between two surfaces that are glued, as between plies in plywood.

glycerol, glycerin, glycerine Colorless, odorless fluid used in mixing synthetic and natural resins for paints and varnishes; used for making distempers more pliable; used in the manufacture of some adhesives.

glyph 1. A V-shaped, vertically oriented groove used as an ornament in the **Classical Revival style** and its derivatives; usually found on a Doric frieze, as in **triglyph**. 2. A sculptured pictograph.

glyptic Pertaining to carving or engraving.

glyptotheca   A sculpture gallery.

GM   Abbr. for "grade marked."

gneiss   A coarse-grained metamorphic rock having discontinuous foliation; usually dark; composed mainly of quartz, feldspar, mica, and ferromagnesian minerals. Generally classed as **trade granite** in the building stone industry.

go-devil   A device used to clean a pipeline by placing it at the pump end of the pipeline and forcing it through the pipe by water pressure.

godown   In India and the Far East, a storehouse of any description.

godroon   See **gadroon**.

going   (*Brit.*)   **1.** The horizontal distance between two consecutive risers of a step. **2.** Of a stair or flight, the horizontal distance between the first and last risers, i.e., the run.

going rod   A rod used in laying out the **going** of a flight of steps.

gold bronze   A powdered copper alloy used in the manufacture of gold or bronze paint; usually contains copper, zinc, lead, and tin.

gold foil   See **gold leaf**.

gold leaf   Very thin sheets of beaten or rolled gold, used for gilding and inscribing on glass; usually contains a very small percentage of copper and silver. Sometimes heavy gold leaf is classified as gold foil.

gold size   A varnish used to attach gold leaf or foil to a surface; it turns sticky quickly on application, and then sets slowly.

golosniki   In early Russian architecture, acoustic resonators, made of clay, which were set into the upper portions of the walls of some churches; the mouth of the resonator faced the interior of the church and was flush with the wall surface. Similar resonators have been found in some Greek Orthodox and early Scandinavian churches.

gonge   The Anglo-Saxon term for a privy.

gont   A thin wood shingle, used for roofing in early Russian architecture.

good morning stairs   In a **full Cape house**, the front stairs leading from the front hall to the attic rooms; at the chimney block, the stairs turn both right and left, serving both sides of the house.

goods lift   British term for **freight elevator**.

goose neck   **1.** Any section of pipe, curved like the neck of a goose, or in a U-shape; sometimes flexible. **2.** In ductwork, an inverted U-shaped duct section with a screened opening; used for air intake or exhaust. **3.** A curved section of a handrail which forms its termination at the top of a newel post.

gopuram   In Hindu architecture, a tall monumental gateway.

gore   Same as **lune**.

gore lot   A small triangular lot.

gorge   **1.** In some orders of columnar architecture, a narrow band around the shaft near the top, or forming part of the capital near the bottom; a fillet or narrow member which seems to divide the capital from the shaft. **2.** A **cavetto** or hollow molding. **3.** A narrow entry into a bastion.

gorgerin   See **hypotrachelium**.

gorgoneion   In classical decoration, the mask of a Gorgon, a woman with snakes for hair, to avert evil influences.

gospel hall   House for Protestant Christian worship.

Gospel side   The north side of a church (when the main altar is at the east), from which the Gospel is read.

Gothic arch   A loose term often denoting any arch with a point at its apex, such as a **lancet arch**.

Gothic architecture   The architectural style of the High Middle Ages in Western Europe, which emerged from Romanesque and Byzantine forms in France during the later 12th cent. Its great works are cathedrals, characterized by

Gothic architecture   showing construction of a Gothic church, illustrating principles of isolated supports and buttressing

Gothic Revival

Gothic architecture: Late type Gothic base, Rouen

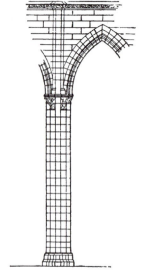

Gothic architecture: Gothic pier

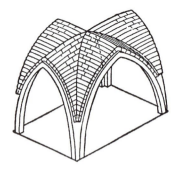

Gothic architecture: vault construction

the classical forms of the Renaissance. In France and Germany one speaks of the Early, High, and Late Gothic; the French middle phase is referred to as Rayonnant, the late phase as Flamboyant. In English architecture the usual divisions are Early English, Decorated, and Perpendicular.

Gothic Revival A movement originating in the 18th century and culminating in the 19th century, flourishing throughout Europe and the United States, aimed at reviving the spirit and forms of Gothic forms; applied to country cottages, churches, some public buildings, and castle-like structures. Gothic Revival buildings usually are characterized by ashlar masonry, **polychromed** brickwork, or wood walls, often extending into the gables without interruption; Gothic motifs such as battlements, decorative brackets, finials, foils, foliated ornaments, hood moldings, label moldings, pinnacles, pointed arches, towers, turrets; often, a porch with flattened Gothic or Tudor arches; a symmetrical façade; steeply pitched gables often decorated with ornate gingerbread bargeboards; projecting eaves; decorative slate or shingle patterns on the roof; occasionally, a flat roof with crenelated and castelled parapets; ornamental chimney stacks and chimney pots; a cast-iron decorative strip at the ridge of the roof; windows extending into the gables; often, an elaborately paneled front door set into a lancet arch; the entry door sometimes within a recessed porch or under a door hood, occasionally bordered with sidelights. The initial phase is sometimes called *Early Gothic Revival*; the latter phase is sometimes called *Late Gothic Revival* or Victorian Gothic. Also see **Collegiate Gothic, High Victorian Gothic,** and **Carpenter Gothic.**

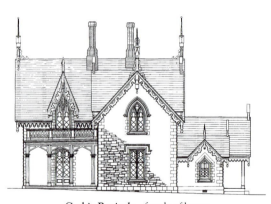

Gothic Revival: façade of house

the pointed arch, the rib vault, the development of the exterior flying buttress, and the gradual reduction of the walls to a system of richly decorated fenestration. Gothic architecture lasted until the 16th cent., when it was succeeded by

Gothic sash A term occasionally applied to a **lancet window**.

Gothic survival The survival of Gothic forms and construction techniques long after the demise of Gothic architecture (for example, as late as the 17th century); usually in a provincial context, as distinct from Gothic Revival.

gouache **1.** A method of painting, using opaque pigments pulverized in water and mixed with gum. **2.** A painting so made. **3.** An opaque color used in the process.

gouge **1.** A chisel with a longitudinal curved blade, used to cut holes, channels, or grooves in wood or stone. **2.** A form of wear in resilient floor coverings which is accompanied by removal of material and penetration considerably below the immediate floor surface.

gouge bit A bit shaped like a gouge, with the piercing end sharpened to a semicircular edge for shearing the fibers around the margin of the hole; removes the wood almost as a solid core.

gouge slip, oilstone slip, slipstone A shaped **oilstone** for sharpening gouges or shaped chisels.

gouge work An ornamental wood surface having decorative surface marks made with a chisel whose blade is curved.

government anchor A type of steel **anchor** which is inserted through a hole in the web of a steel beam; used to anchor a wall-bearing beam to masonry construction.

government house **1.** Building for the offices of the main departments of government, esp. in English colonies or Commonwealth nations. **2.** Governor's state home, esp. in a Crown colony.

GOVT On drawings, abbr. for "government."

gpd Abbr. for "gallons per day."

gpm Abbr. for "gallons per minute."

gps Abbr. for "gallons per second."

GR On drawings, abbr. for "grade."

grab bar A hand grip, usually installed in a shower, which may be used for steadying oneself.

grab bucket A **clamshell**.

grab crane A **crane** which is fitted with a **clamshell**.

grab rail Same as **grab bar**.

grab set See **flash set**.

grab bar

gradation See **particle-size distribution**.

grade **1.** The classification of materials by quality. In lumber, plywood, and building boards, the classification usually depends on the quality for one face only. **2.** The ground elevation or level, contemplated or existing, at the outside walls of a building, or elsewhere on the building site. **3.** Rate of rise or fall of a roadway, usually expressed in feet per 100 ft, in meters per kilometer, or as a percentage, ascending grades being plus, descending minus. **4.** The slope of a line of pipe with reference to the horizontal; usually expressed as the fall in a fraction of an inch per foot (or centimeters per meter) length of pipe. **5.** The **cut-off elevation** of a pile.

grade beam That part of a foundation system (usually in a building without a basement) which supports the exterior wall of the superstructure; commonly designed as a beam which bears directly on the column footings, or may be self-supporting, as a long **strap footing**.

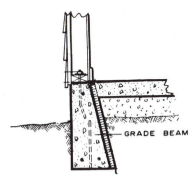

grade beam

grade correction A correction applied to a distance measured on a slope to reduce it to a horizontal distance between the vertical lines through its end points.

grade course The first course at grade level, usually waterproofed with a damp check or damp course.

graded aggregate   Aggregate having a particle-size distribution characterized by uniform grading.

graded sand   Fine aggregate (diameter under ¼ in., i.e., 6.4 mm) having a particle-size distribution characterized by uniform grading.

graded standard sand   Ottawa sand, accurately graded between the 600-μ (U.S. Standard No. 30) and 150-μ (No. 100) sieves; used in the testing of cements. Also see **Ottawa sand, standard sand**.

grade hallway   An enclosed passageway that provides a protected path of escape in the event of fire; terminates at a street or an open space or court communicating with a street.

grade line   A line usually marked with stakes or other monuments, each having an elevation referred to a common datum; by measurement or computation from such elevations and stakes, a grade is established between the terminal points.

grade passageway   Same as **grade hallway**.

grade plane   A reference plane representing the average of the ground level adjoining a building at its exterior walls.

grader, towed grader   A multipurpose machine used for leveling and crowning, mixing and spreading, ditching and bank sloping, and side casting material, or for light stripping operations; not intended for heavy excavation.

grader

grade ring   A precast concrete ring at the top of a **manhole**; used to adjust the top of the manhole so that it is set at the proper angle.

grade school   See **elementary school**.

grade slab   A reinforced concrete slab, set directly on the ground, which serves as the foundation for the structure above.

grade stake   In earthwork, a stake marking the specified level.

grade strip   A strip of wood which is nailed to the inside of a concrete form to indicate the upper line to which concrete is to be poured.

gradetto   Same as **annulet**.

gradient   **1.** The degree of inclination of a surface, road, or pipe, often expressed as a percentage. **2.** A rate of change in a variable quantity, as temperature or pressure. **3.** A curve representing such a rate of change.

gradienter   An attachment to an engineer's **transit** with which an angle of inclination is measured in terms of the tangent of the angle, rather than in degrees and minutes.

gradine   **1.** A step. **2.** A raised shelf above and at the back of an altar.

grading   **1.** The action of excavating or filling, or a combination thereof. **2.** See **particle-size distribution**.

grading curve   A graphical representation of the proportions of different particle sizes in a material; obtained by plotting the cumulative or separate percentages of the material passing through sieves in which the aperture sizes form a given series.

grading plan   A plan which shows the proposed finish of the ground surface of a given site, usually by means of contours and grade elevations.

grading rules   Specifications by which lumber, plywood, etc., are grouped according to quality.

grading timber   The sorting of timber, logs, or lumber according to the number and type of defects.

graduated course   One of a number of courses of roofing slates that diminish in gauge from the eaves to the ridge.

graecostasis   In the Roman Forum, a platform where the ambassadors from foreign states stood to hear debates and attend ceremonies.

graffito   Casual remark or depiction drawn on a wall; not synonymous with **sgraffito**.

graft   To join a scion, shoot, or bud to the stock of another similar plant.

grain   **1.** The direction, arrangement, or appearance of the fibers in wood, or the strata in stone, slate, etc. **2.** The easiest cleavage direction in a stone. **3.** Any small, hard particle, as of sand. **4.** A unit of weight measure in the English system of units; 7,000 grains equals 1 lb; used as a measure of the weight of moisture in air.

graining Simulating a grain such as wood or marble on a painted surface by applying a translucent stain, then working it into suitable patterns with tools such as graining combs, brushes, and rags. See **false woodgraining, faux bois, woodgraining**.

grain size A measure of the size of mineral particles of soil or rock; a physical characteristic of the particles of a soil which affects its mechanical properties; used in classification and identification.

grain slope The angle of grain in a piece of lumber relative to a line parallel to its length. The angle for structural timber (as for beams) is restricted to a slant of 1 part in 8.

granary A storehouse for grain, usually after it has been threshed, or for the storage of corn after it has been husked.

grandmaster key A key that operates locks in several groups, each of which has its own master key.

grandstand A structure, often with a roof, which supports standing or seated spectators at a racecourse, ball field, stadium, or similar public places.

grand tier The tier immediately above the **parterre** in an opera house, theatre, etc.

grange 1. A farm. 2. A farmhouse and its outbuildings.

granite 1. An igneous rock having crystals or grains of visible size; consists mainly of quartz, feldspar, and mica or other colored minerals. 2. In the building stone industry, a crystalline silicate rock having visible grains; this includes gneiss and igneous rocks that are not granite in the strict sense.

graniteware A one-coat porcelain-enameled article having a mottled pattern which is produced by the controlled corrosion of the metal base prior to firing.

granitic finish A finish provided by a **face mix** of **granolithic concrete**.

granolithic concrete Concrete suitable for use as a wearing surface finish to floors; made of cement mixed with specially selected aggregate (originally granite chips) of suitable hardness, surface texture, and particle shape.

granolithic finish A surface layer of granolithic concrete which may be laid on a base of either fresh or hardened concrete.

granular-fill insulation A loose-fill thermal insulation, such as vermiculite or perlite, in the form of granules, pellets, nodules, powder, or flakes; can be poured or placed by hand without mechanical means. Also see **loose-fill insulation**.

granular material Gravels, sands, or silts which exhibit no characteristics of cohesiveness or plasticity; more permeable than cohesive or plastic soils.

granulated blast-furnace slag The nonmetallic product consisting essentially of silicates and aluminosilicates of calcium which is developed simultaneously with iron in a blast furnace and is granulated by quenching the molten material in water or in water, steam, and air. Also see **blast-furnace slag**.

granulated cork Small particles of cork used as loose-fill thermal insulation, to make cork tile, etc.

grapevine ornament A **running ornament** usually consisting of a grapevine with bunches of grapes and grape leaves.

graphics The art of drawing, esp. of drawing according to mathematical rules, as in perspective, projection, etc., associated with architectural and engineering plans.

graphite, plumbago One of the forms under which carbon occurs in nature; electrically conductive; in powdered form, used as a lubricant.

graphite paint A painting compound consisting of powdered graphite and oil; used to coat metallic structures to inhibit corrosion.

grapple A **clamshell, 2** which has three or more jaws; especially suitable for handling rocks such as **rip rap**.

grappler A pointed spike that is driven into masonry to provide an eye for support of the brackets of a scaffold.

grass cloth, China grass cloth A loosely woven fabric of vegetable fibers; used for wall covering.

grass table Same as **ground table**.

grate A surface with suitable openings to support a fuel bed and permit passage of air through the burning fuel. Designed to permit removal of unburned residue, and may be horizontal or inclined, stationary or movable.

grating 1. A **grate**; also see **coke grating**. 2. A **grille**. 3. Same as **grillage**. 4. See **bar-type grating**. 5. See **plank-type grating**.

gravel A coarse granular aggregate, larger than sand; formed either naturally or by crushing rock; will pass a 76.1-mm (3-in.) sieve and be retained on a 4.76-mm (No. 4) sieve.

gravel board, gravel plank A board attached near the lower edge of a wood fenc-ing so that the fencing does not touch the ground; prevents the lower end of the fencing from rotting.

graveling-in The spreading of gravel on top of a **flood coat, 2** in **built-up roofing**.

gravel plank See **gravel board**.

gravel roofing See **built-up roofing**.

gravel stop, gravel strip, slag strip A flange, usually of a metal strip, used to prevent gravel or loose surfacing from washing off a roof; may also provide a finished edge for built-up roofing.

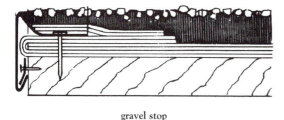

gravel stop

grave trap A rectangular **trap, 2** centrally located in a theatre stage floor, sometimes provided with a mechanism for raising and lowering.

gravitational water Same as **free water, 2**.

gravity drainage system See **building gravity drainage system**.

gravity feed Said of a chute that transports waste materials, soiled linen, etc., from one level of a building to another by the force of gravity.

gravity hinge A hinge that closes automatically as a result of the weight of a door to which it is attached.

gravity supply, gravity water system A water system in which the source of water is at a higher elevation than the place where the water is to be used.

gravity-type refuse chute A **refuse chute** in which waste material is conveyed down the chute by the force of gravity.

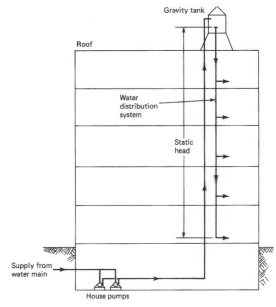

gravity supply

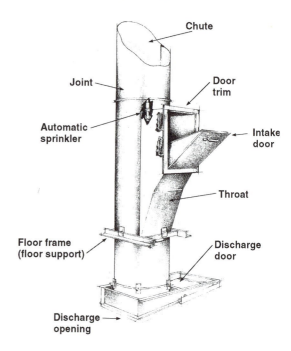

gravity-type refuse chute

gravity wall A massive concrete wall that resists overturning by virtue of its own weight.

gravity water system See **gravity supply**.

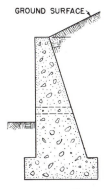

gravity wall

gravity water tank, gravity tank A water storage tank in which water is stored at atmospheric pressure and distributed by gravity flow in a **downfeed system**; the tank is usually elevated above the roof of a building and is filled by a **house pump**.

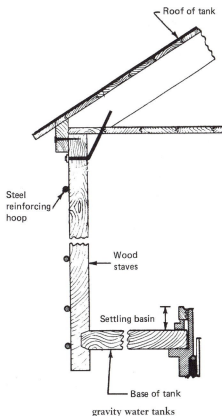

gravity water tanks

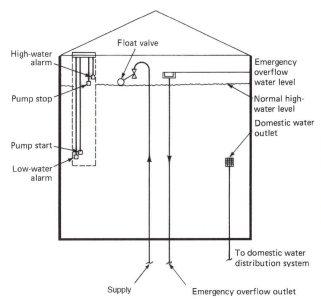

gravity water tanks

gray cast-iron pipe See **cast-iron pipe**.

gray scale A series of achromatic samples in discrete steps in lightness from white to black.

gray water **Waste water** which may be a combination of liquid and water-carried wastes, with the exception of human wastes.

gre See **grees**.

grease extractor Equipment which traps droplets of grease and greasy vapors from the exhaust air of cooking equipment.

grease interceptor See **grease trap**.

grease trap, grease interceptor A device for removing grease from waste water by allowing the retained liquid to cool and the grease to solidify; then the grease is separated by flotation; it rises to the top of the trap, where it is held.

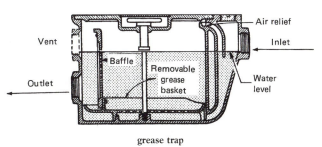

grease trap

great house The main or central residence of an estate or plantation.

great room The main room of a house of some pretension; usually the room largest in size.

grece Same as **grees**.

Greek cross A cross with four equal arms.

Greek key See **fret**.

Greek masonry See **isodomum**.

Greek Revival style An architectural style based on the reuse of ancient Greek forms in architecture. Public buildings in this style were usually symmetrical in plan and rectangular in shape. Buildings in this style are commonly characterized by: asymmetrical plan, a symmetric front-gabled façade with a classical pedimented portico extending across the building; a façade of brick, clapboard, or stone construction; a partial-height porch, sometimes with the porch roof having a raked cornice supported on round or square columns with ornamental capitals; pilasters; a frieze or a plain wide band of trim with a simple **architrave** below a heavy cornice; walls that imitate flat stonework, wood buildings often painted white; typically sparse ornamentation, including classical Greek decorative motifs; gabled or hipped roof; widely spaced double-hung windows trimmed with decorative crowns; a wide, imposing entryway, framed by pilasters or engaged columns; an entry door usually having raised panels with a horizontal line of small **lights** above the door; a vertical line of small lights on each side of the door. In America, during the height of its widespread popularity from about 1820 to the 1850s, Greek Revival was frequently called the National Style. Also see **Classical Revival style** and **Neoclassical style**.

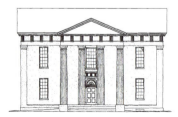

Greek Revival style

Greek theatre An open-air theatre constructed by the ancient Greeks; usually built on a hillside, with no outside facade. The **orchestra, 1,** on which the actors and chorus performed, was a full circle; behind it was the **skene**, a temporary or permanent building for the actors' use. In the classic theatre, the seating area (around and facing the orchestra) usually occupied approx. three-fifths of a circle. Also see **Roman theatre**.

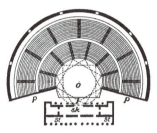

Greek theatre: *o*, orchestra; *l*, logeion; *p*, parascenium; *sk*, skene; *st*, stoa

green   1. See **green concrete. 2.** See **green lumber. 3.** See **green mortar. 4.** See **undercuring. 5.** An open space or public park in the center of a town or village. **6.** A bowling green or putting green.

greenbelt A wide area of parks, farmland, or undeveloped land surrounding a community.

green concrete Concrete which has set but not appreciably hardened.

green glass A low-grade glass which is green because of impurities in its raw materials.

greenheart A British Guiana hardwood having high density and strength; difficult to machine; used for piles, planks, etc., where strength is important.

greenhouse, glasshouse A glass-enclosed, heated structure for growing plants and out-of-season fruits and vegetables under regulated, protected conditions. Also see **conservatory, hothouse, orangery.**

green lumber Lumber which has not been dried or seasoned.

green manure Green herbaceous plants plowed under to benefit the soil.

green mortar Mortar that has set but not dried.

green room A lounge near the stage of a theatre or concert hall where actors or musicians may rest or receive visitors before or after a performance.

greensand A resin used to oxidize the soluble iron in water and then to filter it out.

greenstone A basic igneous rock having a green color due to iron-bearing silicate minerals; quarried and fabricated for structural and decorative **dimension stone**.

greensward Turf, green with grass, usually well-tended.

grees, gre, greese, gryse In medieval architecture, a step or flight of steps.

G/Rfg, G/R Abbr. for "grooved roofing."

grid **1.** See **gridiron**. **2.** See **grillage**. **3.** In surveying, closely-spaced reference lines which are perpendicular to each other; elevations usually are taken at the intersections of these lines.

grid bearing The angle in the plane of the projection between a line and a north-south grid line.

grid ceiling A ceiling with apertures through which natural or artificial light can pass.

grid foundation A **combined footing** which is formed by a number of intersecting continuous footings, loaded at their points of intersection; the area covered is less than 75% of the total area within the outer limits of the assembly.

gridiron A framework (usually of steel) over a theatre stage and immediately below the **stagehouse** roof; used as the structural support from which scenery and lighting equipment are hung. Also called a **grid**.

grid plan A **city plan** in which the streets are laid out in a rectangular pattern of lines forming rectangles of uniform size.

grid pulley, grid sheave A pulley, located on a **gridiron**, through which a cable or rope of a rigging system passes.

grid sheet system A system of **soldier beams** and **horizontal sheeting** used to brace the lateral face of a deep excavation or cut; the soldier beams receive lateral support from **wales** and braces.

grid system See **exposed suspension system**.

griffe See **spur, 1.**

griffin, griffon, gryphon A mythological beast having a lion's body with an eagle's head and wings; used decoratively.

grillage **1.** A framework of heavy timbers, steel, or reinforced concrete beams laid longitudinally

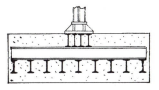

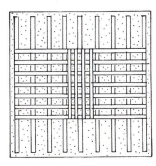

grillage, 2

and crossed by similar members laid upon them to spread a heavy load over a larger area, esp. for use where the ground is not firm. **2.** A series of steel beams, bolted together and placed over a **footing**; used to distribute a concentrated column load over the top of the footing.

grille **1.** A grating or openwork barrier, usually of metal but sometimes of wood, stone, or reinforced concrete; used to cover, conceal, decorate, or protect an opening, as in a wall, floor, or outdoor paving. **2.** A louvered or perforated covering for an air passage opening, which can be located in the wall, ceiling, or floor.

grille, 1

grillroom, *Brit.* **grille room** A room for informal dining in a restaurant, club, or hotel.

grillwork Material which functions as, or has the appearance of, a **grille**.

grinder pump A special type of solids-handling pump, designed to grind sewage solids into a fine slurry.

grindstone A rotating solid stone wheel (usually sandstone) used for grinding, shaping, sharpening, or polishing.

grinning through **1.** The visible appearance of lathing through a plaster coat. **2.** The visible appearance of an undercoat of paint through a topcoat.

grip **1.** Of a mechanical fastener: the thickness of the material or parts which the fastener is designed to secure when assembled. **2.** Of a rivet: the thickness of the plates or parts through which the rivet passes. **3.** A channel that carries away rain water from a foundation, during its construction.

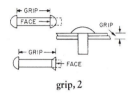

grip, 2

grip length See **bond length, development length**.

grisaille **1.** A system of painting in grey tints of various shades; used either for decoration or to represent objects, as in relief. **2.** A stained glass window executed according to this method.

gristmill A mill for grinding grain, in earlier times powered by the wind, a stream, river, or by tidal water.

grit A granular abrasive material (e.g., consisting of particles of aluminum oxide or silicon carbide) which is used to coat cloth, paper, or wheels for sanding, grinding, or polishing; also used to provide a nonslip finish to a surface.

gritblast See **sandblast**.

grizzly A stationary screen or series of equally spaced parallel bars set at an angle; used to remove oversize particles in processing aggregate or similar material.

grizzly brick Same as **salmon brick**.

grnd Abbr. for **ground**.

groin The ridge, edge, or curved line formed by the intersection of the surfaces of two intersecting vaults.

groin arch, groined arch One arched division of **cross vaulting**.

groins: A

groin centering **1.** In groining without ribs, the **centering** of timber extended during construction under the whole surface. **2.** In ribbed or groined work, the centering for the stone ribs, which need support until their arches are closed, after which the supports for the filling of the spandrils are sustained by the ribs themselves.

groined **1.** Having groins. **2.** Showing the curved lines resulting from the intersection of two semicylinders or arches.

groined rib A rib under the curve of a groin, either to mask the groin or to support it.

groined rib: A shows an enlarged section

groined vault, groin vault A compound vault in which **barrel vaults** intersect, forming arrises called **groins**.

groining Any system of vaulting implying the intersection, at any angle, of simple vaults.

groin rib See **groined rib**.

groin vault Same as **groined vault**.

grommet A metal or plastic eyelet which provides a reinforced hole for attachment.

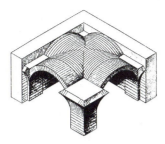

groined vault

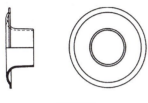

grommet

groove   A long narrow cut in the edge or face of a wood member; a groove across the grain is a **dado**; one parallel with the grain is a **plow**.

grooved joint   A joint used to connect two steel pipes or ductile-iron pipes; employs an inner elastomeric gasket and an outer split-metallic sleeve with an integral bolt for tightening the assembly.

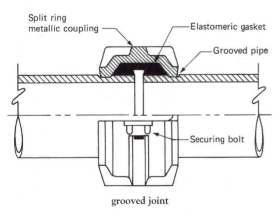

Split ring metallic coupling
Elastomeric gasket
Grooved pipe
Securing bolt

grooved joint

grooved seam   A seam in which the edges of two metal sheets are bent approximately 180°, inserted in each other, flattened, and then locked by pressure.

grooved seam

groove joint   A construction joint formed by a groove in a floor slab, wall, or pavement; used to control random cracking.

groover   A tool used to form grooves in a concrete slab before hardening; used to control crack locations or provide patterns.

groove weld   A **weld** made in a preformed groove between two members to be joined.

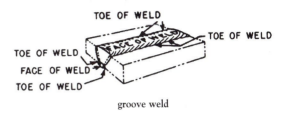

TOE OF WELD
TOE OF WELD
FACE OF WELD
TOE OF WELD
FACE OF WELD
TOE OF WELD

groove weld

grooving plane   A **plane, 1** used in carpentry, esp. to cut grooves in wood.

gross area, gross cross-sectional area   Of a concrete masonry unit, the total area of a section perpendicular to the direction of the load, including areas within the cells of the unit and within reentrant spaces, unless these spaces are occupied by portions of adjacent masonry.

gross floor area   The area within the perimeter of the outside walls of a building as measured from the inside surface of the exterior walls, with no deduction for hallways, stairs, closets, thickness of walls, columns, or other interior features; used in determining the required number of exits or in determining occupancy classification. Also see **net floor area**.

gross leasable area   The total floor area designed for tenant occupancy and tenant use.

gross load   In heating, the **net load** plus allowances for piping losses and for pickup.

gross output   The available number of Btu at a boiler outlet nozzle for satisfying the **gross load** continuously, while the boiler is operating under applicable code limitations.

gross section   Of a structural member, the total area of the cross section, making no deductions for holes within the cross section.

gross volume   **1.** In a revolving-drum concrete mixer, the total interior volume of the revolving portion of the mixer drum. **2.** In an open-top mixer, the total volume of the trough, assuming that no vertical dimension of the container exceeds twice the radius of the circular section below the axis of the central shaft.

grotesque Sculptured or painted ornament involving fanciful distortions of human and animal forms, sometimes combined with plant motifs, esp. a variety of arabesque which has no counterpart in nature.

grotto A natural or artificial cave, often decorated with shells or stones and incorporating waterfalls or fountains.

ground **1.** A nailing strip fixed in a masonry or concrete wall as a means of attaching wood trim or furring strips; also called a **common ground, rough ground, fixing, fixing fillet, fixing slip. 2.** A **plaster ground. 3.** The side of an electric circuit connected to the earth, used as a common return.

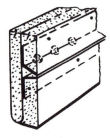

ground, 2

ground bar An electrical conductor which forms a common junction for a number of ground conductors.

ground beam **1.** A **groundsill. 2.** A horizontal heavy timber or reinforced concrete beam at or near ground level for distributing a load which it supports.

ground brush An oval or round paintbrush used for covering large areas.

ground bus A **bus** to which **grounds, 3** from individual pieces of equipment are connected; the bus, in turn, is connected to the ground at one or more points.

ground casing The **blind casing** of a window.

ground coat **1.** A first coat of paint or enamel, particularly when designed to show through a topcoat. **2.** A porcelain enamel applied directly to the base metal to function as an intermediate layer between the metal and the cover coat.

ground conductor An electrical conductor which provides an electrical connection between (a) the frame of a piece of equipment or part of a system and (b) a **ground bar** or **ground electrode**.

ground course The horizontal base course of masonry on the ground.

ground cover **1.** Low planting, often maintenance-free, used in masses. **2.** A thin plastic sheet, or the like, spread over the ground in a crawl space to minimize moisture penetration.

grounded Said of an electrical device, piece of equipment, or electrical system that is connected to the earth or to some extended electrically conducting body that serves as the earth, whether the connection is intentional or accidental.

grounded conductor An electric system or circuit conductor which is intentionally grounded.

grounded system A system of electric conductors in which at least one conductor is intentionally grounded, either solidly or through a current-limiting device.

grounded work Joinery, such as a chair rail, which is attached to a metal or wood ground.

ground electrode An electrical conductor (or group of conductors) in intimate contact with the ground; used to provide an effective electrical connection with the ground.

ground fault **1.** An electrical short-circuit involving one or more phase conductors and ground. **2.** An insulation fault between a conductor and ground or the frame of a device.

ground fault circuit interrupter (GFCI) A type of **ground fault protection** in areas where

ground fault circuit interrupter

personnel are at high risk of receiving electrical shocks (for example, in damp locations); makes use of a device designed to trip at a ground current in the milliampere range, i.e., very much below currents that are normally harmful.

ground fault protection   Protection against short-circuits produced by ground faults; may be provided by circuit breakers, relays, or ground fault circuit interrupters.

ground fill   See **fill, 1.**

ground floor   The floor of a building which is nearest the surrounding surface of the ground; usually the first floor in the U.S.A. but sometimes a floor between a basement or cellar and the first floor.

ground glass   Glass having a surface that has been roughened, usually by sandblasting or by acid, to make it nontransparent.

grounding conductor   A conductor used to connect electric equipment or the grounded circuit of an electric wiring system to a grounding electrode or electrodes.

grounding electrode   A conductor embedded in the earth, used to maintain ground potential on the conductors connected to it.

grounding electrode conductor   The electrical conductor used to connect the **grounding electrode** to the equipment grounding conductor and/or the grounded conductor of the circuit at the service equipment.

grounding outlet   An electric **outlet** which is equipped with a receptacle of the polarity type with an additional contact for the connection of an equipment grounding conductor.

grounding plug, grounding-type plug   A **plug, 5** having a blade which provides a ground connection for an electric device.

grounding plug

grounding system   A system of interconnected **grounds, 3.**

ground joint   **1.** A closely fitted joint in masonry, usually without mortar. **2.** A machined metal joint which fits tightly without packing or a gasket.

ground joist   A joist which rests on sleepers laid on the ground, stones, or dwarf walls; used in basements or ground floors.

ground-key faucet   A faucet through which flow is controlled by a slightly tapered plug with a hole in it; when the faucet is on, the fluid flows through the hole; when the plug is turned through 90°, the flow is stopped.

ground-key valve   A **valve** which controls fluid flow in a manner similar to a ground-key faucet.

ground-key valve

ground lease   A legal contract for the lease of land; contains an agreement that the lessee is obligated to pay rent each year for the use of the land for the duration of the contract; the lessee usually builds on the land but the buildings so constructed must be turned over to the land's owner at the termination of the contract.

ground light   Visible radiation from the sun and sky which is reflected by surfaces below the plane of the horizon.

ground line   The level of the surface of the ground, above (or below) which the height of a structure (or depth of excavation) is measured.

ground niche   A **niche** whose base is on a level with the floor.

ground plan, ground plot   The **plan** of a building taken at ground level.

ground plane   The horizontal plane of projection in a perspective drawing; the horizontal plane upon which the object in the drawing rests.

ground plate   A **groundsill**.

ground rent   The legally-contracted rent paid annually according to the terms of a **ground lease**.

ground ring A bare copper wire, laid underground in the shape of a loop around the exterior of a building; at the corners of the building and other appropriate locations, ground rods are installed and connected to the loop.

ground rod A metal rod or pipe which is driven into the ground to provide an electrical connection to the earth. Usually, the deeper the rod is driven beneath the earth's surface, the lower its electric resistance to ground.

groundsel Same as **groundsill**.

ground sign A sign supported by uprights or braces in or upon the surface of the ground.

groundsill, ground beam, ground plate, mudsill, sole plate In a framed structure, the **sill** which is nearest the ground or on the ground; used to distribute concentrated loads.

ground story Same as **ground floor.**

ground table, earth table, grass table A projecting course or plinth resting immediately upon the foundation; the lowest course visible above the ground.

ground wall The foundation wall of a building.

groundwater Water, near the surface of the ground, which passes through the subsoil.

groundwater

groundwater level At a particular site, the level below which the subsoil and rock masses of the earth are fully saturated with water.

groundwater recharge See **recharge.**

ground wire 1. A conductor leading to an electric connection to the earth. 2. A wire used to establish line and grade, as in shotcrete work; usually of small-gauge, high-strength steel.

groundwork Batten strips applied over roofing boards or the like; used as a base for the application of roofing materials.

grouped columns Three or more closely spaced columns forming a group, often on one pedestal.

grouped pilasters Three or more closely spaced pilasters forming a group, often on one pedestal.

group house, row house One of an unbroken line of houses having a common wall or party wall with its neighbors.

group relamping Replacing all lamps in a lighting system at one time. Also see **spot relamping**.

group vent In plumbing, a **branch vent** that serves two or more traps.

grout 1. Mortar containing a considerable amount of water so that it has the consistency of a viscous liquid, permitting it to be poured or pumped into joints, spaces, and cracks within masonry walls and floors, between pieces of ceramic clay, slate, and floor tile, and into the joints between preformed roof deck units. 2. In foundation work, mixtures of cement, cement-sand, clay, or chemicals; used to fill voids in granular soils, usually by a process of successive injection through drilled holes.

grouted-aggregate concrete Concrete that is formed by injecting grout into previously placed coarse aggregate.

grouted frame A hollow-metal doorframe which is completely filled with cement or mortar.

grouted masonry 1. Concrete masonry construction composed of hollow units where the hollow cells are filled with grout. 2. Multi-withe construction in which space between **withes** is solidly filled with grout.

grouting Filling the voids in or between aggregate, block, or tile with **grout**.

grouting sand Sand which passes through an 841µ (No. 20) sieve, and not more than 5% through a 74µ (No. 200) sieve.

grout slope   The natural slope assumed by fluid grout when injected into preplaced-aggregate concrete.

growth rate   Rate of wood growth expressed as the number of annual rings per inch measured from pith to bark; sometimes used to rate softwoods for strength.

growth ring   See **annual ring**.

grozing iron   A hot iron used by plumbers for finishing soldered joints.

grub   To clear a site by removing roots, stumps, and the like.

grub axe   A tool for digging up roots or shrubs; a **mattock**.

grub saw   A handsaw used for cutting stone, such as marble, into slabs for shelves, mantelpieces, etc.

grub screw   See **setscrew, 1**.

grummet   Same as **grommet**.

grundscheier   A barn constructed by early German-speaking immigrants to America; of varied construction, depending on available materials and the terrain; usually built on slightly sloping ground. See **German barn**.

gryphon   A **griffin**.

gryse   See **grees**.

GSA   Abbr. for "General Services Administration."

guarantee   **1.** A legally enforceable assurance of the quality or duration of a product or of **work, 1** performed. **2.** A binding commitment by one person that another will perform his contract obligations satisfactorily.

guaranteed maximum cost   An amount established in an **agreement** between **owner** and **contractor** as the maximum cost of performing specified work on the basis of cost of labor and materials plus overhead expense and profit.

guaranty bonds   **1.** See **bid bond**. **2.** See **labor and material payment bond**. **3.** See **performance bond**. **4.** See **surety bond**.

guard bar   Any bar serving as a protection or a means of security, as a **window bar, 3** or **window guard, 2**.

guard bead   **1.** A **corner bead**. **2.** A **staff bead**.

guard board   A raised timber at the edge of a scaffold that prevents workers or tools from dropping off the edge of the platform.

clip to fix a **guard board** to a scaffold

guarded   Enclosed, fenced, covered, shielded, or otherwise protected, by means of suitable barriers, rails, screens, covers or casings, mats, or platforms, to prevent dangerous contact.

guard rail   For an automatically operated door, a railing used to separate and control traffic passing in opposite directions through the door.

guardrail system   A protective railing system along the outer edges of locations of an accessible roof, balcony, landing, platform, or ramp.

guard system   A system of building components located near the open sides of elevated walking surfaces, designed to minimize the possibility of an accidental fall from the walking surface.

gudgeon   A metal pin used to hold together two blocks or slabs, as of stone.

guesthouse   **1.** A separate residence for guests, as a house on a private estate or a boarding house of high standards. **2.** A monastery building specifically for receiving visitors.

guest room   **1.** In a multiple-family dwelling, a room occupied or intended to be occupied for hire. **2.** In a single-family or two-family dwelling, a room in the main or an accessory building occupied or intended to be occupied by nonpaying guests.

guglia   An elongated finial.

guide bead   Same as **inside stop**.

guide coat   A thin coat of paint which highlights the bumps or imperfections in a sealer or filler beneath, and thus serves as a guide for rubbing them down.

guide pile   A heavy, square timber which is driven vertically downward to guide steel **sheet-piling**.

guide rail   A track that acts as a guide for a sliding window or door.

guide wire   In a theatre stagehouse: **1.** A steel cable which guides the vertical movement of a curtain. **2.** A line which guides the movement of a **counterweight arbor**.

guildhall A place of assembly for a society of craftsmen or merchants for their mutual assistance; an outgrowth of similar medieval organizations or guilds.

guilloche An ornament formed by two or more bands twisted over each other in a continuous series, leaving circular openings which are often filled with round ornaments.

guilloche

guillotine Same as **bench trimmer**.

gula **1.** A molding having a large hollow. **2.** A **cyma**. **3.** A **gorge**.

gulbishche In early Russian architecture, a terrace which surrounds a building.

gullet The concave space between saw teeth.

gulley, gully In a drainage system, a fitting at the upper end of a drain that receives the discharge from waste pipes or rain water.

gum **1.** A moderately high-density hardwood of the eastern and southern U.S.A.; whitish to gray-green in color and of uniform texture; used for low-grade veneer, plywood, and rough cabinet work. **2.** Any of a class of colloidal substances that are soluble or swell in water, exuded by or prepared from plants; sticky when moist.

gum arabic, acacia, gum acacia A white, powdery, water-soluble gum, extracted from certain acacia trees; used in the manufacture of adhesives and transparent paints.

gum bloom A defect in a painted surface, appearing as a lack of gloss or a haze, resulting from the use of incorrect reducer.

gumbo A fine-grained clay; very sticky when wet.

gum pocket See **gum vein**.

gum rosin See **rosin**.

gum seam In a piece of lumber, a **check** or **shake** filled with gum.

gum streak See **gum vein**.

gum vein, gum pocket, gum streak In hardwoods, a local accumulation or streak of resin.

gumwood Wood of the gum tree, esp. eucalyptus; used for interior trim.

gun **1.** See **spray gun**. **2.** A pressure cylinder for delivering freshly mixed concrete pneumatically. **3.** Shotcrete material delivery equipment; also see **shotcrete gun**.

gun consistency See **gun grade**.

gun finish A layer of **shotcrete** as it is applied, without subsequent hand finishing.

gun grade, gun consistency A grade of caulking or glazing compound which has the proper softness for application by a caulking gun.

gun hole, gun loop, gun port, gun slot A type of **embrasure** in a structure designed to provide protection in case of enemy attack; the opening enables a defender to fire through a wall, over a wide angle.

Gunite A proprietary name for **shotcrete**.

gunning Applying material, e.g., **shotcrete**, with the use of a gun.

gun pattern The outline of material which is discharged by a gun, as in a **shotcrete** operation.

gunshot house Same as **shotgun house**.

gun-stock post Same as **musket-stock post**.

gunstock stile A **diminished stile** in which there is a gradual change in width between the broader and narrower parts.

Gunter's chain A measuring device in land surveying, consisting of 100 metal links, equivalent to 66 ft in length.

gusset, gusset plate A plate, usually triangular in shape, used to connect two or more members, or to add strength to a framework.

gutta (*pl.* **guttae**) In Classical architecture, one of a number of pendant ornaments in a rectangular arrangement; each gutta is shaped like an inverted frustum of a cone, i.e., a cone in which the upper tip has been lopped off; usually found on the underside of the **mutules** of a Doric entablature.

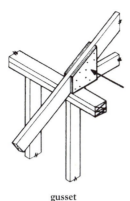

gusset

gutta: *Top,* guttae attached to mutules;
bottom, detail showing guttae

guttae band   Same as **regula** in the Greek Doric entablature.

gutter   **1.** A shallow channel of metal or wood set immediately below and along the eaves of a building to catch and carry off rainwater from the roof; also called **eaves gutter, eaves trough, roof gutter. 2.** In electrical wiring, the space provided at the sides, top, or bottom within an electric panel or switchboard to permit the installation of feeder and branch wiring conductors. Also called an eaves gutter, eaves trough, or roof gutter; see **box gutter, concealed gutter, flying gutter, standing gutter, sunk gutter, through gutter.**

gutter bearer   A member to which gutter boards are fixed.

gutter bed   A sheet of flexible metal, over the wall side of a gutter along the eaves, which prevents overflow from penetrating the wall.

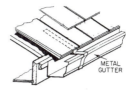

gutter, 1

gutter board, gutter plank   In a wood gutter along the eaves of a roof, a board on which the lining material of the gutter is laid.

guttered   A term sometimes used to describe a structural framing member (such as a corner post) that is either encased or cut away to disguise its appearance.

gutter hook   A light metal strap used to secure or support a metal gutter.

gutter plate   **1.** One of the sides of a **box gutter. 2.** A beam which supports a lead gutter.

gutter spout   Same as **downspout.**

gutter tool   A tool used to give the desired shape and finish to concrete gutters.

guy   A supporting rope, cable, or wire which is anchored at one end and tied to an object or structure in order to stabilize it.

guy anchor   A buried object used to secure a **guy.**

guy derrick   A **derrick** comprised of a boom and a mast supported by wire rope guys.

GV   Symbol for **gate valve.**

gymmer   See **gemel.**

gymnasium   **1.** A large room or building devoted to physical education or indoor games. In addition to the playing floor, the building form usually contains staff offices, locker and shower rooms, and spectator facilities. **2.** In continental Europe, a secondary school which prepares students for university. **3.** In Greek and Roman architecture, a large open court for exercise, surrounded by colonnades and rooms for massage, lectures, etc.; a **palaestra, ephebeion.**

gynaeceum   That part of a Greek house or a church reserved for women.

GYP   On drawings, abbr. for **gypsum.**

gypsite   Gypsum having a purity of from 60 to 90% and containing clay, loam, and sand.

gypsum   A soft mineral consisting of a hydrated calcium sulfate from which gypsum plaster is

gypsum backerboard

made (by heating); colorless when pure; used as a retarder in portland cement.

gypsum backerboard A gypsum board used as a base on which to adhere tile or gypsum wallboard; similar to, but less smooth than, wallboard; is surfaced with a gray paper.

gypsum block, gypsum tile, partition tile **1.** A hollow or solid building block, fabricated of gypsum; used in a nonbearing partition; serves as a base for plastering. **2.** A cast gypsum building block.

gypsum board A **wallboard** having a gypsum core. This noncombustible core has a paper surface.

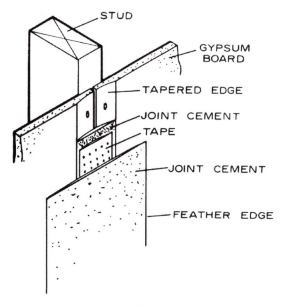

gypsum board: detail showing joint treatment

gypsum cement See **Keene's cement**.

gypsum concrete A mixture of a calcined gypsum binder and wood chips or other aggregate; when mixed with water, sets to a conglomerate mass; used for poured gypsum roof decks.

gypsum core board A **gypsum board** consisting of either a single board or factory laminated multiple boards for use as a gypsum stud or core in semisolid or solid gypsum board partitions; usually available in thicknesses from ¾ inch (19.0 mm) to 1 inch (25.4 mm).

gypsum fiber concrete Gypsum concrete in which the aggregate consists of shavings, fiber, or chips of wood.

gypsum formboard A **gypsum board** used as a permanent form for pouring gypsum roof decks.

gypsum insulation Gypsum in pellet form used as loose-fill thermal insulation.

gypsum lath, board lath, gypsum plasterboard, rock lath A base for plaster; a sheet having a gypsum core, faced with paper, which provides a good bond for plaster; usually manufactured in 16-in. by 48-in. (40.6-cm by 121.9-cm) or 24-in. by 96-in. (61.0-cm by 243.8-cm) panels, ⅜ or ½ in. (0.95 or 1.27 cm) thick with round or square edges.

gypsum-lath nail A low-carbon steel nail having a large flat head and a long diamond point; esp. used to fix gypsum lath and plasterboard.

gypsum-lath nail

gypsum molding plaster A calcined **gypsum plaster** used primarily for plaster casts or molds; occasionally used for **gauging plaster**.

gypsum mortar A plastic mixture of gypsum, water, and often sand; can be troweled in the plastic state; hardens in place when the water it contains evaporates.

gypsum neat plaster A calcined **gypsum plaster** without an aggregate, often used as a base coat.

gypsum panel A **wallboard** having a gypsum core.

gypsum perlite plaster A gypsum base-coat plaster containing perlite as an aggregate.

gypsum plank **1.** British term for **gypsum lath**. **2.** A lightweight, fire-resistant, structural precast roof deck having a gypsum core reinforced with galvanized-steel mesh.

gypsum plaster Ground gypsum that has been calcined and then mixed with various additives to control its setting and working qualities; used, with the addition of aggregate and water, for base-coat plaster.

gypsum plasterboard   See **gypsum lath**.

gypsum sheathing   A wallboard having a gypsum water-repellent core; surfaced with a water-repellent paper; usually 2 or 4 ft (61 or 122 cm) wide, 8 ft (243.8 cm) long, and ½ in. (1.27 cm) thick; used as a base for exterior wall coverings.

gypsum tile   **1.** A cast gypsum building unit. **2.** See **gypsum block**.

gypsum trowel finish   Various proprietary, factory-mixed plasters used as a finish coat, containing mainly gypsum which has been calcined.

gypsum vermiculite plaster   Gypsum base-coat plaster containing vermiculite as an aggregate.

gypsum wallboard   A **gypsum board** used primarily as an interior surfacing in a building.

H

¼H   On drawings, abbr. for "quarter-hard."

½H   On drawings, abbr. for "half-hard."

H   On drawings, abbr. for "hard."

h   Symbol for "hour."

H&M   In the lumber industry, abbr. for "hit and miss."

habit, habit of growth   The distinctive appearance and pattern of growth of a plant.

habitable room   A space used for living, sleeping, eating, or cooking, or combinations thereof, but not including bathrooms, closets, halls, storage rooms, utility and similar spaces.

habitable space   By code, a space occupied by one or more persons for living, sleeping, eating, or cooking (although a **kitchenette** is not usually deemed to be a habitable space). Compare with **nonhabitable space**.

habitacle   **1.** A dwelling or habitation. **2.** A niche for a statue.

HABS   Abbr. for **Historic American Buildings Survey**.

hachure   One of a series of parallel lines drawn on topographic maps in the direction of the slopes of hills or depressions to indicate relief features. The steeper the slopes, the heavier and more closely spaced the hachures become.

hacienda   **1.** A large estate in North and South American areas once under Spanish influence. **2.** The main house on such an estate or ranch.

hacking   **1.** Roughening a surface by striking with a tool. **2.** Laying brick so that the bottom edge is set in from the plane surface of the wall. **3.** In a stone wall, the breaking of one course of stone into courses of different height.

hacking knife, hacking-out tool   A knife used to remove old putty from a frame before reglazing.

hacksaw   A saw having a blade (typically fine-toothed) which is supported in an adjustable metal frame; used for cutting metals.

hafner ware   In northern European decorative arts of the Renaissance and derivatives, modeled, lead-glazed earthenware often used for tiled heating stoves.

haft   The handle of a tool.

hagiasterium   A sacred place; a baptismal font.

hagioscope   A **squint, 1**.

ha-ha   A barrier in the form of a trench; usually used to prevent livestock from crossing; a sunken fence.

HAIA   Abbr. for "Honorary Member, American Institute of Architects."

haikal   The central chapel of the three forming the sanctuary of a Coptic church.

hair beater   A tool formerly used by plasterers to remove hair or fiber from plaster; made of two pieces of wood lath, fastened at one end by wire.

hair checking   Same as **hairline cracking**.

hair cracking   See **hairline cracking**.

haired mortar   Mortar containing hair or fiber.

hair hook   A tool now obsolete, having several tines for mixing hair or fiber into plaster.

hair interceptor, hair trap   A device used to remove hair before it enters a drainage system.

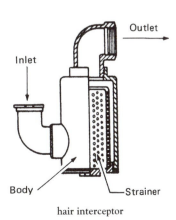

hair interceptor

hairline cracking, hair cracking, plastic shrinkage cracks Very fine cracks, in a random pattern, which usually do not completely penetrate a paint film, an exposed layer of concrete, etc.

hairline joint Between two abutting members, a joint not more than 1/64 in. (0.38 mm) wide.

hair mortar A mortar (traditionally) containing a mixture of cow's hair, lime, and sand.

hairpin **1.** The wedge used to tighten some types of form ties. **2.** A hairpin-shaped anchor set in place while concrete is plastic.

hale In Hawaii, a primitive house, especially one consisting of a wood framework covered by thatched grass.

half baluster An engaged **baluster**, projecting about half of its diameter.

half baluster

half bat, half brick, snap header A brick cut to half its length.

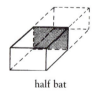

half bat

half bath A room containing a wash basin and toilet (W.C.).

half-blind dovetail Same as **lapped dovetail**.

half-brick wall A wall having a thickness equal to the thickness of a brick laid as a stretcher.

half Cape house A **Cape Cod house** that has two double-hung windows on only one side of the front door.

half column An **engaged column** projecting approx. one half its diameter, usually slightly more.

half columns

half-cut notch A simple joint between the timbers at a corner of a **log house**; formed by cutting away the lower half of the end of one timber and placing it over and at right angles to another timber in which the upper half of the end has been cut away; a spike or treenail is usually driven through the two ends to secure the joint.

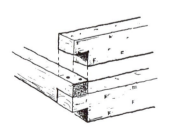

half-cut notch

half door The lower half of a **Dutch door**.

half dovetail A wood joint similar to a **dovetail** but having only one side flared; the other side is straight.

half-dovetail notch At a corner of a log house, a notch in the shape of a **half dovetail** at the end of a rectangular exterior timber; forms an interlocking joint when mated with an appropriately notched timber at right angles to it; compare with **dovetail notch**.

half-dovetail notch

half-dugout A primitive shelter, often temporary, having a significant portion of its structure dug below ground level; commonly has sod walls and a sod roof; also see **sod house**.

half figure Same as **terminal figure**.

half-gabled Descriptive of a **shed roof** having the shape of a flat inclined plane.

half-glass door A door having glass in the panel above the **lock rail**.

half hatchet A tool similar to a **lath hammer** but with a broader blade.

half header A brick, or cement block, either cut longitudinally into two equal parts or cut into four parts by cutting these halves transversely; used to close the work at the end of a course.

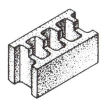

half header

half-hipped roof Same as **gambrel roof**.

half house A **Cape Cod house** or **saltbox** having two windows on one side of the front door and none on the other.

half landing Same as **halfpace**.

half-lap joint, halved joint, halving joint A joint at the intersection of two wood members of equal thickness in which half the thickness of each is removed so that they fit together to form a flush surface.

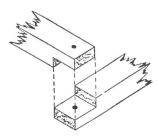

half-lap joint

half-moon A roughly crescent-shaped fortification outwork. Also see **ravelin**.

half-mortise hinge A hinge, one plate of which is mortised in the door leaf, the other being surface-mounted on the jamb leaf.

halfpace, half-space landing A stair landing at the junction of two flights which reverses the direction of horizontal progress, making a turn of 180°. Such a landing extends the width of both flights plus the well.

halfpace stair A stair making a 180° turn, usually having a **halfpace** landing.

half principal A roof member or rafter that does not reach to the ridgepole but is supported at its upper end by a purlin.

half-relief Same as **mezzo-relievo**.

half-ripsaw A handsaw similar to a ripsaw, but with teeth that are more closely spaced.

half round, half-round molding A convex strip or molding of semicircular profile.

half round

half-round file A file whose cross section is convex on one face and flat on the other face.

half slating Same as **open slating**.

half-space landing See **halfpace**.

half-space stair   Same as **halfpace stair**.

half-span roof   A **lean-to roof**.

half story   A story within a sloping roof; usually having dormer windows and occupying about half the area of the floor or floors below. Also see **garret, attic**.

half S-trap   In plumbing, same as **P-trap**.

half-surface hinge   A hinge which is applied to the surface of the door leaf and to a mortised jamb leaf.

half timber   A piece of timber measuring not less than 5 in. by 10 in. (12.7 cm by 25.4 cm) in cross section.

half-timbered   Descriptive of buildings of the 16th and 17th cent. which were built with strong timber foundations, supports, knees, and studs, and whose walls were filled in with plaster or masonry materials such as brick.

half-timbered

half-timbered construction   Building construction in which all supporting and bracing members are heavy timbers as in the medieval system of braced timber framing of a house; to provide additional rigidity and better thermal insulation, the space between the structural timbers is usually filled with brick or filled with plaster, wattle-and-daub, or a **nogging** consisting of clay (often taken from the cellar excavation) mixed with chopped straw to act as a binder. Also see **columbage, fachwerk, false half-timbering, pierotage**.

half truss   A **jack truss** whose shape is half that of a normal roof truss; partly supported by a main roof truss and at an angle to it.

half-turn   Descriptive of a stair which turns 180° or through two right angles at each landing. Also see **dogleg stair**.

halide lamp   See **metal halide lamp**.

halide torch   A test device for detecting halocarbon refrigerant leaks; usually uses alcohol and burns with a blue flame; when the sampling tube on the tester draws in refrigerant vapor, this is indicated by a change in color of the flame.

hall   **1.** The main room of a medieval or postmedieval house that served as the center of family life, usually combining the functions of a kitchen, dining room, living room, and workroom for activities such as spinning, sewing, and candle making; often called a **keeping room**; also see **hall-and-parlor plan**. **2.** An imposing **entrance hall**; also called a living hall. **3.** A large room for assembly, entertainment, and the like. **4.** A small, relatively primitive dwelling having a **one-room plan**. **5.** A **manor house**. **6.** A **corridor**.

hall-and-parlor plan   A common two-room floor plan in early colonial New England; the front door opened into a small vestibule, called a **porch**, which contained two interior doors leading to the two rooms of the house. One room, the **hall, 1**, served as the center of activity for the entire family; the other room, the parlor, contained the best furniture, as well as a bed for the parents. These rooms were separated by a wall containing a massive chimney that served them both. A loft space above was reached by a stairway in the hall. Also see **center-hall plan**.

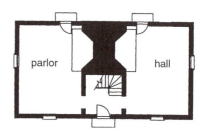

hall-and-parlor plan

hall bedroom   A bedroom having the same width as the hall, formed by sectioning off one end of the hall.

hall chamber   A bedroom directly above a **hall, 1**.

hall church   A church having aisles, no clerestory, and an interior of approximately uniform height.

hall keep A rectangular **keep** in which the great hall and bed chamber were adjacent.

hallway A corridor; a passageway.

halogen lamp See **tungsten-halogen lamp**.

halon extinguishing system A fire protection system employing halon gas as the means of extinguishing a fire used in areas of high monetary value, but now of limited application because of environmental concerns about the use of this gas.

halved-and-lapped notch Same as **half-cut notch**.

halved joint A **half-lap joint**.

halved splice Same as **half-lap joint**.

halving The cutting away of two wood members at their ends, each to half its thickness; when the two cut surfaces are placed together, a **lap joint** or **half-lap joint** is obtained.

halving joint A **half-lap joint**.

hammam An establishment for bathing in the Oriental way, with steam rooms, etc.; a Turkish bath.

hammer A hand tool having a head at right angles to the handle; used for driving nails, pounding, flattening materials, etc.

hammer beam: A

hammer-beam roof

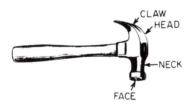

hammer: nomenclature

hammer ax A **lath hammer**.

hammer beam One of a pair of short horizontal members attached to the foot of a **principal rafter** in a roof, in place of a **tie beam**.

hammer-beam roof A roof supported by **hammer beams**.

hammer brace A bracket under a hammer beam to support it.

hammer-dressed Said of stone masonry which has been shaped and brought to a relatively smooth finish by means of a hammer only.

hammer drill A percussive-type pneumatically powered rock drill.

hammered glass Translucent glass made by embossing rolled glass on one side to resemble beaten metal.

hammer finish A paint finish which appears to have been applied over hammered metal; produced by the use of nonleafing metallic pigment plus tinting pigments which are mixed in a special binder.

hammerhead crane A heavy-duty **jib crane** with a counterbalance, giving it a T-shaped appearance.

hammerheaded Said of a chisel which is to be struck with a hammer, rather than a mallet.

hammerhead key See **double-dovetail key**.

hammer post A **pendant** which is in the shape of a pilaster; serves as an impost for a **hammer brace**.

Hamm tip A type of nozzle for a gun which delivers shotcrete; has a larger diameter at the midpoint than at either the inlet or the outlet.

hance The curve of shorter radius which adjoins the impost at each side of a three- or four-centered arch.

hance arch Same as **hanse arch**.

hand 1. The direction, left or right, of the swing of a door (when viewed from the side usually considered the outside) or associated doorframes or hardware. A **left-hand door** has hinges on the left and the door swings away; a **left-hand reverse door** swings toward the viewer. A **right-hand door** has hinges on the right and swings away. A **right-hand reverse door** swings toward the viewer. 2. Of a spiral stair, designates the direction of turn of the stair. **Right-hand** refers to a stair on which the user turns clockwise as he descends. **Left-hand** refers to a stair on which the user turns counter-clockwise as he descends.

hand brace Same as **brace, 3**.

hand clamp Same as **screw clamp**.

hand drill A hand-driven **drill, 1**.

hand file See **file**.

hand float A wooden tool used to fill in and float a plaster surface; used to produce a level base coat or a textured finish coat.

handhole Same as a **manhole**, except that it is smaller in size; often located at the termination of an underground **service entrance**.

handicap accessibility See **Americans with Disabilities Act (ADA)**.

hand level A hand-held surveying instrument used for rough checks of elevations and leveling work, usually limited in use to a radius of 200 ft (approx. 60 m) from an established elevation. Consists of a metal sighting tube (but no telescope) in which a spirit level is observed opposite the horizontal cross hair.

hand line A line used to hand-operate a counterweight, curtain, or other component in the rigging system of a theatre stage.

handling reinforcement The reinforcement of a product that is required or desirable to prevent its damage during its moving, handling, unloading, and storage, prior to its final installation.

hand plate See **push plate**.

handrail Same as **rail, 1, 2**.

handrail bolt, joint bolt, rail bolt A metal rod with threads and a nut at each end; used to bolt together two mating surfaces in a **butt joint**.

handrail height The vertical distance between the upper surface of a **top rail** and the **finish floor**.

handrailing 1. Same as **handrail**. 2. Handrail construction which includes the provision of **handrail scrolls** about landings and winders.

handrail scroll A spiral **handrail** end.

handrail wreath Same as **handrail scroll**.

handsaw Any hand-held saw for cutting wood having a handle at one end; operated manually.

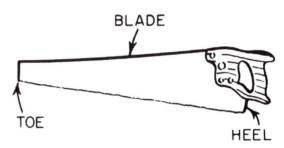

handsaw: nomenclature

hand screw Same as **screw clamp**.

hand snips Same as **tin snips**.

hangar A shed or shelter, particularly a structure for the shelter, service, and repair of aircraft.

hanger 1. A wire, strap, or rod attached to an overhead structure, used to support a pipe, conduit, the framework of a suspended ceiling, or the like. 2. A U-shaped, stirrup-like bracket used to support the end of a beam or joist at a masonry wall or girder. 3. Any device used to suspend one item or object from another item or object.

hanger, 1

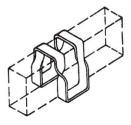

hanger, 2

hanger bolt   A bolt having a machine-bolt thread on one end and a tapered lag-screw thread on the other; used in heavy timber construction.

hanger bolt

hanging   **1.** The mounting of a door on its frame on hinges. **2.** The mounting of an operable window sash in its frame.

hanging buttress   In later Gothic architecture and derivatives, a freestanding vertical rib or buttress which is supported from a wall by a corbel rather than by its own foundation.

hanging gable   A small extension of the roof structure beyond the end wall, at the gable end of a barn or house; usually located at the ridge; encloses a heavy beam that supports the rigging used to hoist materials to upper stories.

hanging gable

hanging gutter   A metal gutter which is hung from the eaves of a roof by metal ties, sometimes with support from the fascia.

hanging pew   A **pew** raised on posts and usually set apart from the less prestigious seating, accessed by a private stair.

hanging post   The post on which a gate or door is hung.

hanging rail   The rail of a door to which a hinge is fastened.

hanging sash   A **hung sash**.

hanging scaffold   A **scaffold** that is suspended by ropes and pulleys.

hanging shingling   Shingling on vertical or near-vertical slopes.

hanging stair, hanging step   **1.** A stone step cantilevered from the wall and free at the other end. **2.** See **cantilever steps**.

hanging step   A step usually constructed without a continuous **carriage, 1** for support; instead the steps are bolted together so that each step provides support for the one above and the one below; used, for example, in architecture of the Shakers, a religious sect of English origin that settled in America in the late 18th century.

hanging stile   See **hinge stile**.

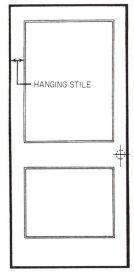

hanging stile

hanse arch, haunch arch   An arch having a crown of different curvature than the haunches, which are thus strongly marked; usually a **basket-handle** or **three-centered** or **four-centered arch**.

hard asphalt   Solid asphalt having a normal **penetration, 2** of less than 10.

hardboard   A building material manufactured of wood fiber compressed into sheets; used extensively in building, e.g., as interior panels or durable siding.

hard-burnt   Nearly vitrified; said of clay product which has been fired at a high temperature; usually has relatively low absorption and high compressive strength.

hard-burnt brick, hard-fired brick   A clay unit that has been molded to the desired shape and then treated in a kiln at a high temperature to increase its mechanical strength, moisture resistance, and weather resistance. See **brick**.

hard-burnt plaster   Same as **Keene's cement**.

hard compact soil   According to OSHA: all earth materials not classified as running or unstable.

hard-dry   Descriptive of a stage of dryness of a paint film when hard twisting pressure of the thumb will not mar the surface. It is then ready for service, rubbing, or application of a topcoat.

hardened glass   Same as **tempered glass**.

hardener   1. A chemical (including certain fluosilicates or sodium silicate) applied to concrete floors to reduce wear and dusting. 2. A material added to a paint or varnish vehicle to increase the gum or resin content, or to increase rate of oxidation, so as to cause an increase in hardness of the drying film. 3. The chemical component in a two-component coating or adhesive which causes the resin component to harden.

hard finish   A finish coat consisting of gypsum plaster and lime troweled to a smooth, hard, dense finish.

hard-finish plaster   Same as **Martin's cement**.

hard gloss paint   A high-gloss enamel, formulated with a hard-drying resin vehicle.

hard lead   See **antimonial lead**.

hard light   Light which produces well-defined shadows.

hardness   1. The resistance of wood, rubber, sealant, plastic, or metal to plastic deformation by compression or indentation; in wood, hardness is generally related to density. Common methods of measurement include the Rockwell, Brinell, Scleroscope, and Vickers tests. 2. A property of a paint or varnish film that is a measure of its ability to withstand damage from marring, abrasion, etc. 3. The degree of hardness, applied to water, based on the amount of calcium and magnesium salts in the water, expressed as grains per gallon or parts per million of calcium carbonate. 4. See **Mohs' scale**.

hard oil   A hard-drying interior oil or varnish.

hardpan   An extremely dense hard layer of soil, boulder clay, or gravel; difficult to excavate.

hard pine   Same as **yellow pine**.

hard plaster, gauging plaster, molding plaster   A quick-setting plaster to which retarder has been added to control set; used in the finish coat.

hard solder   Any solder having a melting point above solders alloyed of lead and tin, e.g., silver solder or aluminum solder; applied with a brazing torch.

hard steel   1. Steel that has undergone the process of hardening. 2. Same as **high steel**.

hard-top   A hard-surfaced road.

hardwall   A type of gypsum **neat plaster**; used as a base coat.

hardware   Metal products used in construction, such as: bolts, nails, screws (see **rough hardware**); fittings, such as catches, hinges, locks, etc. (see **finish hardware**); tools.

hardware cloth   Steel wire-woven screening; usually has a mesh ⅛ to ¾ in. (3.18 to 9.53 mm); commonly galvanized.

hard water   Water containing solutions of mineral salts (sulfates of calcium and magnesium, carbonates, and bicarbonates). Also see **water softener**.

hardwood   1. A tree belonging to the angiosperms; usually broad-leaved and deciduous, such as cherry, mahogany, maple, oak, etc. 2. Wood cut from such trees.

hardwood strip flooring   Same as **strip flooring**.

harl, harling   Same as **rock dash**.

harmonic   A component of a sound containing more than one frequency which is an integral multiple of the lowest frequency.

harped tendons Same as **deflected tendons**.

harsh mixture A concrete mixture which lacks desired workability and consistency owing to a deficiency of mortar or aggregate fines.

Hartford loop, Underwriters' loop An arrangement of the return piping connections to a steam boiler; used to balance pressures between the supply and return sides of the boiler and thus prevent boiler water from backing out of the boiler and into the return.

hasp A fastening device consisting of a loop and a slotted hinge plate, normally secured with a padlock.

hasp

hastarium In ancient Rome, a room in which sales were made by public auction, under public authority.

hatch An opening, equipped with an openable cover, in a roof or floor of a building for passage of people or goods from one level to another or for ventilation.

hatched molding Same as **notched molding**.

hatchet A combination chopping and driving tool which has a wooden handle and a steel head, with a hammer face and a blade which is notched for pulling nails.

hatchet

hatchet door Same as **Dutch door**.

hatchet iron A plumber's soldering iron having a bit which is shaped like a hatchet.

hatchway See **roof hatch**.

Hathoric, Hathor-headed Pertaining to an Egyptian column with a capital which bears masks of the Egyptian cow-head goddess Hathor.

Hathoric capital A column whose **capital** bears masks of the Egyptian cowhead goddess Hathor. Occasionally found in **Egyptian Revival**.

hathpace Same as **halfpace**.

haul, haul distance 1. The distance that an excavated material is moved from the **cut** to the **fill**. 2. The distance along the most practical route for trucks to carry excavated material from its center of mass to the center of mass of the fill.

haunch 1. The middle part between the crown and the springing of an arch. 2. The part of a beam projecting beneath a roof slab or floor. 3. That portion of a pipe barrel extending from the bottom to the springline. 4. The lower third of the circumference of a pipe. 5. The deepened section of a beam near a support.

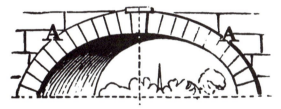

haunch: A, haunches of an arch

haunch arch See **hanse arch**.

haunch board One of the boards on both sides of a form for a concrete girder.

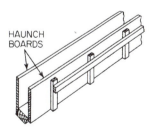

haunch boards

haunched beam A beam whose cross section thickens toward its supports.

haunched mortise-and-tenon joint A joint between two members, formed by fitting a

haunched tenon at the end of one of the members into a corresponding **mortise** in the other.

haunched tenon A tenon, part of which has a smaller width than the full width of the wood member on which it is formed.

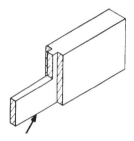

haunched tenon

haunching **1.** Placing bedding material around the haunch of a pipe. **2.** The concrete support at the sides of a drain or sewer pipe above the bedding.

haw-haw Same as **ha-ha**.

hawk A flat piece of metal or wood used by plasterers to carry plaster or mortar; held by a wooden handle on the underside.

hawkbill snips Tin snips having a curved jaw which is shaped to facilitate cutting along a curve.

hawksbeak A **beak molding, 2**.

hawksbell Same as **ballflower**.

hayband A straw rope.

hay barrack An open-sided structure for storing an overflow of hay from the main barn; usually had a four- or five-cornered roof that could move up on poles as the hay was packed beneath it.

hay barrack

haydite A lightweight aggregate, used in concrete, having an expanded cellular structure; produced by heating shale.

hay hood Same as **hanging gable**.

hayloft The upper part of a barn in which hay is stored.

hazard of contents The relative danger of fire starting and spreading, of smoke or gases being generated, of explosion or other occurrences which potentially endanger the lives and safety of the occupants of a building or structure.

hazardous area **1.** Within a building, an area which houses highly combustible, highly flammable, or explosive products or materials which are likely to burn with extreme rapidity or which may produce poisonous fumes or gases, including highly toxic or noxious alkalies, acids, or other liquids or chemicals, which involve flame, fume, explosive, poisonous, or irritant hazards. **2.** Any area in which there are fine particles or dust subject to explosion or spontaneous combustion.

hazardous substance A substance which, by reason of being explosive, flammable, poisonous, corrosive, oxidizing, or otherwise harmful, is likely to cause death or injury.

haze Dullness of a paint film resulting from formation of very fine surface imperfections.

HB **1.** Abbr. for "hollowback." **2.** Abbr. for **hose bib**.

H-bar A steel bar shaped like an H; used in structural systems; one form of main runner in a **suspended acoustical ceiling**.

H-beam A steel beam shaped like an H.

H-block A hollow concrete masonry unit having both ends open in the form of one-half of a cell.

H-brick Horizontally perforated brick.

HD On drawings, abbr. for **head**.

H/D ratio The ratio of the height **H**, to the diameter **D**.

HDW On drawings, abbr. for "hardware."

hdwd. Abbr. for **hardwood**.

head **1.** In general, the top or upper member of any structure; the top or end (esp. the more prominent end) of a piece or member. **2.** The upper horizontal cross member, between the jambs, which forms the top of a door or window frame; may provide structural support for construction above if required, as a **doorhead** or **window head**. **3.** A stone that has one end dressed to match the face because the end will be exposed at a corner or in a reveal. **4.** A roofing tile of half the usual length but of the same width; for forming the first course at the eaves. **5.** See **static head**.

headache ball   See **breaker ball**.

head casing   The horizontal casing across the top of a window or door opening.

header   **1.** A masonry unit, laid so that its ends are exposed, overlapping two or more adjacent withes of masonry and tying them together; a **bondstone**; a **bonder**. **2.** A **header joist**. **3.** A framing member which crosses and supports the ends of joists, rafters, etc., transferring the weight of the latter to parallel joists, rafters,

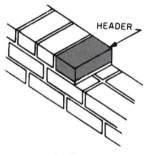

header, 1

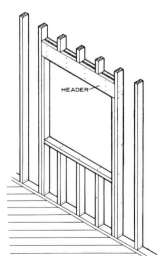

header, 3

etc. **4.** In plumbing, a pipe having many outlets which are parallel and frequently at 90° to the center line of the pipe. **5.** A chamber into which a number of pipes open. **6.** A **platform header**. **7.** A transverse **raceway** for electrical conductors which provides access to a cellular floor, thereby permitting the convenient installation of electrical conductors. **8.** The structural member immediately over a door opening.

header block   A concrete masonry unit having a portion of one **face shell** removed to facilitate bonding with adjacent masonry such as brick facings.

header bond   A pattern of brickwork consisting entirely of **headers, 1**; usually, each course of headers is displaced by half the width of one header with respect to the headers in the course above and the course below.

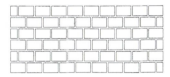

header bond

header course, heading course   In masonry, a continuous course of **headers**.

header duct   A main duct or feeder duct for bringing electrical cable from a service closet to distribution ducts.

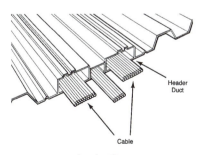

header duct

header-high   Having the height of a masonry wall to the first **header course**.

header joist, header, lintel, trimmer joist   A short structural member (as used in framing an opening) which is fastened between parallel full-length framing members at right angles to them and supports cut-off members, e.g., the common joists in framing around a rectangular opening in a wood floor. Also see **tail piece**.

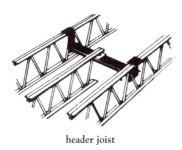

header joist

header tile   Tile containing recesses for brick headers in masonry-faced walls.

head flashing   The flashing installed in a masonry wall over a window opening or projection.

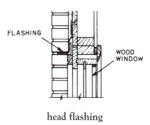

head flashing

head guard   **Cavity flashing** over a window or door frame.

heading   1. Same as **upsetting**. 2. A classification of related data used in the AIA filing system (Part Two of the **uniform system**) as the first step in subdividing each of the sixteen divisions and corresponding generally to the sections used in Parts One and Three.

heading bond   Same as **header bond**.

heading chisel   See **mortise chisel**.

heading course   In masonry, a course consisting entirely of headers; a **header course**.

heading joint   1. A joint between two pieces of timber which are joined in a straight line, end to end. 2. A masonry joint formed between two stones in the same course.

head jamb, yoke   The horizontal member forming the top of a door opening; a doorhead.

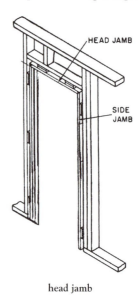

head jamb

head joint, cross joint   The vertical mortar joint between ends of masonry units.

headlap   In the lapping of roofing shingles, the shortest distance between (a) the lower edge of an overlapping shingle and (b) the upper edge of the lapped unit in the second course below.

head loss   Same as **pressure drop**.

headmold, dripstone, head molding, hoodmold, weather molding   The molding carried around or over the head of a door or window.

head nailing   The nailing of slates through holes near the heads of the slates.

head piece   1. The capping piece of a series of upright timbers. 2. The uppermost horizontal member of a wood partition.

head plate   Same as **wall plate**.

headroom, headway   1. The clear vertical space (as from floor to ceiling), esp. the height which is available for passage. 2. In the stagehouse of a theatre, the clear height over the **gridiron**.

headstock   A supporting beam for a church bell.

headstone   The principal stone in a foundation, as the cornerstone of a building or the keystone of an arch.

head up To remove the lower branches from a tree or large shrub.

headwall A masonry or concrete retaining wall at the outlet of a drain.

headway Same as **headroom**.

headwork The heads and other ornaments on the keystone of an arch.

healing The outermost layer of the roof of a building.

healing stone A roofing slate or roofing tile.

hearse **1.** A framework of metal bars or rods placed over a tomb or coffin of a noble or very important person. **2.** A canopy, usually of openwork or trellis, set over a bier, or more rarely over a permanent tomb; used especially to support candles, lighted at times of ceremony.

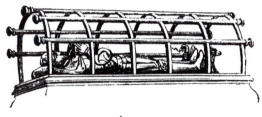

hearse

heart The center portion of a log, usually referring to **heartwood** or duramen.

heart and dart See **leaf and dart**.

heart bond In masonry, a **bond, 6** in a masonry wall, in which two **headers** meet in the middle of the wall and another header covers the joint between them.

heart-face boards Boards which are sawn so that the face side is free of sapwood.

hearth **1.** The floor of a fireplace (usually brick, tile, or stone) together with an adjacent area of fireproof material. **2.** An area permanently floored with fireproof material beneath and surrounding a stove.

hearthstone **1.** A single large stone forming the floor of a fireplace. **2.** Materials such as firebrick, fireclay products, concrete, etc., used to form a hearth.

hearth trimmer See **trimmer**.

hearting Masonry forming the interior of a wall, pier, etc., as distinguished from facework.

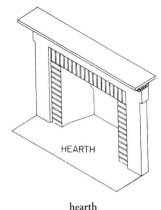

hearth

heart plank See **centerplank**.

heart shake A radial crack originating at the heart of a log; usually results from improper seasoning.

heart shake

heartwood, duramen Wood at the core of an exogenous tree; normally darker and much more durable than sapwood.

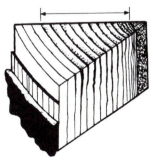

heartwood

heat The form of energy that is transferred by virtue of a temperature difference between two bodies, the transfer being from the warmer to the cooler body.

heat-absorbing glass A faintly blue-green plate or float glass, which absorbs 40% of the sun's infrared (heat) rays and approximately 25% of the visible rays that pass through it; must be exposed uniformly to sunlight (without irregular shadows) to avoid cracking due to nonuniform heating.

heat-activated adhesive A dry adhesive film that is rendered tacky or fluid by application of heat or of heat and pressure.

heat and smoke vent Same as **smoke and fire vent**.

heat balance 1. A procedure for determining the efficiency of a combustion process: all heat losses (expressed as percentages) are added together; then their total is subtracted from 100%; the remaining figure represents the efficiency. 2. The establishment of a condition of thermal equilibrium in a space, wherein the heat gains just equal the heat losses.

heat capacity, thermal capacity The amount of heat necessary to raise the temperature of a given mass by 1 degree; numerically equal to the mass multiplied by the **specific heat**.

heat conductivity See **thermal conductivity**.

heat detector An alarm-initiating device in a **fire-detection system** that detects abnormally high temperatures or rates of rise in temperature.

heated space The space within a building with a positive heat supply.

heat exchanger A device designed to transfer heat between two physically separated fluids; generally consists of a cylindrical shell with longitudinal tubes; one fluid flows on the inside, the other on the outside.

heat filter An optical filter placed in a light path to reduce heating effect of a light source; transmits the visible spectrum of the light radiated by the source, but rejects the near-infrared radiation.

heat-fusion joint A joint in which heat is used to melt the end of a plastic pipe and the socket of a plastic fitting into which the pipe is inserted. When cooled, a solid joint is formed; can be used only with plain-end plastic pipe and with fittings manufactured specifically for this purpose.

heat gain The net increase in heat within a space.

heating cable See **strip heater**.

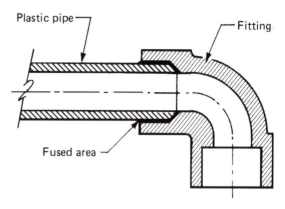

heat-fusion joint

heating capacity, recovery capacity The capacity of a water heater to raise a given number of gallons per hour (liters per hour) by a specified number of degrees, for example, from 40 to 140°F (4.4 to 60°C); usually expressed in Btu per hour (kilowatts per hour); does not include the heat losses in the system which the water heater serves.

heating degree-day See **degree-day**.

heating element See **electric heating element**.

heating load See **heat load**.

heating medium Any solid or fluid (such as water, steam, air, or flue gas) which is used to convey heat from a heat source (such as a boiler furnace), either directly or through a suitable heating device, to a substance or space being heated.

heating plant A system for heating a building or group of buildings; usually includes a boiler and a piping system with radiators, or a furnace, ducts, and air outlets.

heating rate The rate at which temperature is raised, as for example in an autoclave or kiln; usually expressed in degrees per hour.

heating system See the specific type of system, e.g., **steam heating system**.

heating unit See **electric heating element**.

heating, ventilating, and air-conditioning system (HVAC system) A mechanical system designed to satisfy the environmental conditions within an air-conditioned space, usually controlling the temperature, relative humidity, distribution and movement of air, and air cleanliness. Types of systems differ, but a basic system often includes an outside-air intake, chiller, preheater, dehumidifier, heating coil, humidifier, fans, ductwork, air outlets, and air terminals.

heat-insulating glass See **insulating glass**.

heat insulation See **thermal insulation**.

heat load, heating load The total heat per unit time that must be supplied in order to maintain a specified temperature in any space, building, or group of buildings.

heat loss **1.** The net decrease in heat within a space. **2.** See **building heat-loss factor**.

heat of hydration Heat evolved by chemical reactions with water, as during the setting and hardening of portland cement.

heat of solution The heat which is liberated by the solution of a material in a solvent.

heat pump A device that transfers heat from a cooler reservoir to a hotter reservoir by means of a **heat exchanger**, requiring the expenditure of mechanical energy in the process; used in an air

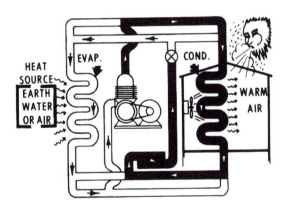

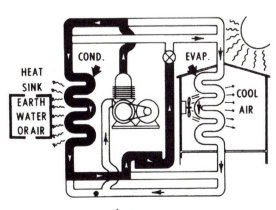

heat pump

conditioner whose cooling cycle can be reversed so that it can function as a heater.

heat recovery The extraction of heat from any heat source such as lights, engine exhaust, etc.

heat-reflective glass See **reflective glass**.

heat-resistant concrete Any concrete which does not disintegrate when exposed to constant or cyclic heating at any temperature below which a ceramic bond is formed.

heat-resistant glass Glass able to withstand higher temperatures than usual because of its low expansion coefficient.

heat-resistant paint, heat-resistant enamel A special paint (or enamel) for use in the temperature range between about 250°F and 750°F (approx. 120°C and 400°C).

heat-sealing A method of joining plastic sheets or films by the simultaneous application of heat and pressure to the areas in contact.

heat sink The medium or environment where heat is discharged after it has been removed from a heat source; usually the atmosphere or a body of water.

heat source **1.** The place or the environment from which heat is obtained. **2.** The place from which a refrigeration system removes heat.

heat-strengthened glass Annealed glass: (a) that has been cut to size, (b) heated to near its softening point, and (c) then cooled faster than normal to place the outside surfaces and edges in compression and the interior in tension; is about twice as strong as annealed glass.

heat-transfer fluid Liquid which absorbs heat energy at a heat source (for example, in a **solar collector**) and then transports this energy to a **heat exchanger** or to its point of use.

heat transmission The time rate of heat flow; usually refers to the combined effects of conduction, convection, and radiation.

heat transmission coefficient Any one of several coefficients used in the calculation of heat transmission by conduction, convection, and radiation, through various materials and structures. Also see **thermal conductance, thermal conductivity, thermal resistance, thermal resistivity, thermal transmittance**.

heat-treated glass Same as **tempered glass**.

heat treatment Heating and cooling a solid metal or alloy in order to produce changes in its physical and mechanical properties.

heave The upward movement of soil caused by expansion or displacement resulting from phenomena such as moisture absorption, the removal of overburden, the driving of piles, and the action of frost.

heave-off hinge See **loose-joint hinge**.

heavy-bodied paint A paint having a high viscosity.

heavy concrete See **high-density concrete**.

heavy-duty scaffold According to OSHA: a scaffold designed and constructed to carry a working load not to exceed 75 lb per sq ft (367.5 kg per sq m).

heavy grading The moving of large masses of earth by deep cuts and fills.

heavy joist A timber usually at least 4 in. (10 cm) thick and 8 in. (20 cm) or more in width.

heavy soil A fine-grained soil composed largely of silt or clay.

heavy-timber construction Construction in which fire resistance is obtained by using wood structural members of specified minimum size and wood floors and roofs of specified minimum thickness and composition; by using bearing walls and nonbearing exterior walls of noncombustible construction; by avoiding concealed spaces under floors and roofs; and by using approved fastenings, construction details, and adhesives for structural members.

heavyweight aggregate Aggregate of high specific gravity such as barite, magnetite, limonite, ilmenite, iron, or steel; used to produce high-density concrete.

heavyweight concrete See **high-density concrete**.

hecatompedon A building 100 ft (30.5 m) in length or width; esp. the cella of the great temple of Athena, the Parthenon, at Athens.

hecatonstylon A building having a hundred columns.

heck **1.** A door having its upper part hinged independently of its lower part, or one with an open or latticework panel. **2.** A latticed gate.

hectare A metric unit of area equal to 10,000 square meters; approximately 2½ acres.

hectastyle Same as **hexastyle**.

hedge **1.** A barrier or fence formed by bushes or small trees growing close together; **2.** A closely grown row of any kind of shrubbery.

hedgerow Trees and shrubs in a row forming a fence which encloses or separates fields.

heel **1.** The lower end of an upright timber, esp. one resting on a support. **2.** The lower end of the **hanging stile** of a door. **3.** The floor brace for timbers that brace a wall. **4.** The trailing edge of the blade of a bulldozer, or the like.

heel cut Same as **seat cut**.

heelpost **1.** A post or stanchion at the free end of the partition of a stall. **2.** A post to receive the hinges of a gate (either part of the gate or the stationary support).

heel stone A stone at the bottom of a gate pier; used to mount the bottom hinge pin for the gate.

heel strap A steel fastener used to join a rafter to its tie beam.

height **1.** The distance between two points aligned vertically. **2.** In buildings, the distance vertically from the average grade at front sides and/or rear of a building (or the average elevation of the curb or curbs of the streets faced by the building) to the average level of the roof.

height board A gauge used in the construction of stairs for setting the heights of the risers.

held water Same as **capillary water**.

helical hinge A special type hinge for a **double-acting door**.

helical reinforcement A steel **reinforcing rod** in the form of a helix.

helical stair A **spiral stair**.

helicline A spiral ramp.

heliodon A device used to orient a light source (representing the sun) with respect to an architectural model; calibrated in terms of latitude, time of day, and season of the year; used to study daylighting techniques and to illustrate the shadows cast by direct sunlight.

helioscene Same as **shade screen**.

heliport A facility where helicopters land, take off, and are maintained or repaired.

helix **1.** Any spiral, particularly a small volute or twist under the abacus of the Corinthian capital. **2.** The volute of an Ionic capital.

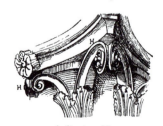

helix, 1: *H*

helix stair   Same as **spiral stair**.

Hellenic   Pertaining to the classical Greek period, roughly from 480 B.C. to the death of Alexander in 323 B.C.

Hellenistic   Characteristic of the style of Greek art after the death of Alexander in 323 B.C.

helm roof   A roof having four faces, each of which is steeply pitched so that they form a spire; the four ridges rise to the point of the spire from a base of four gables.

helm roof

helve   The handle of an ax, adz, hatchet, etc.

hem   The projecting spiral of a volute of an Ionic capital.

hemicycle   1. A semicircular arena. 2. A room or division of a room in the form of a semicircle. 3. A semicircular recess.

hemiglyph   The half channel on each of the two sides of a triglyph.

hemihydrate   A hydrate which contains one-half molecule of water to one molecule of the compound; the most common such material is partially dehydrated gypsum (plaster of paris).

hemihydrate plaster   Same as **plaster of paris**.

hemitriglyph   The portion of a triglyph which sometimes occurs in an internal angle of a returned frieze which has triglyphs in it.

hemlock   Wood of a coniferous tree of the U.S.A. Also see **eastern hemlock, western hemlock**.

hemlock spruce   See **eastern hemlock**.

hench   1. The narrow side of a chimney stack. 2. Same as **haunch**.

henhouse   See **poultry house**.

Henri II (Deux) style   The second phase of the early French Renaissance, named after Henri II (1547–1559) who succeeded Francis I. Italian classic motifs began to supplant the Gothic elements, both in architecture and in decoration.

Henri II style: west side of the Court of the Louvre

Henri IV (Quatre) style

The west side of the Court of the Louvre (1547–1559) is an outstanding example.

Henri IV (Quatre) style The early phase of the Classical period of French architecture, named after Henry IV (1589–1610), preceding the architecture of Louis XIII and Louis XIV. It is particularly strong in domestic architecture and town-planning arrangements. The Place des

Henri IV style: Place des Vosges, Paris (1605–12)

Vosges in Paris (1605–12) is the outstanding example.

HEPA filter A high efficiency particulate absolute filter capable of trapping and retaining at least 99.9% of asbestos fibers greater than 0.3 microns in length.

heptastyle A portico having seven columns, at one or at each end.

heptastyle

Heraeum A temple or sacred enclosure dedicated to the goddess Hera.

herbaceous border A permanent border of nonwoody perennials, often against an evergreen background or a stone wall.

herm A rectangular post, usually of stone and tapering downward, surmounted by a bust of Hermes or other divinity, or by a human head.

herm

hermitage **1.** A private retreat. **2.** A secluded hideaway. **3.** A house of certain monastic orders.

heroum A building or sacred enclosure dedicated to a hero, usually erected over a grave.

herringbone bond In masonry, a type of **raking bond** in which the rows of **headers** are laid at right angles to each other so as to form, in plan, a series of zigzags.

herringbone bridging A system of braces between **joists** to stiffen the joists, to hold them in place, and to distribute their load; these braces alternate in direction along the joists, giving rise to a herringbone-like pattern. Also called herringbone strutting, cross bridging, diagonal bridging.

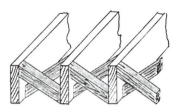

herringbone bridging

herringbone matching See **book matching**.

herringbone pattern A way of assembling, in diagonal zigzag fashion, brick or similar rectangular blocks for paving and for masonry walls; also strips of wood or other finishing materials having rectangular shapes for facing walls or ceilings.

herringbone pattern   in brickwork

herringbone strutting Same as **cross bridging**.

herringbone work In masonry, a pattern in which the masonry units are laid at an angle of 45° to the general direction of the row; reversing the inclination in alternate rows forms a zigzag effect.

herse Same as **hearse**.

Hertfordshire spike Same as **needle spire**.

hertz A unit of **frequency**, abbr. **Hz**; one cycle per second.

hesitation set See **false set**.

hessian Same as **burlap**.

hewn **1.** Roughly dressed, as stone shaped with mallet and chisel. **2.** Roughly shaped with an ax, as hewn logs.

hewn-and-pegged joint A **mortise-and-tenon joint** formed by cutting a tenon to fit a corresponding mortise, joining these two members, and then securing them with a wood pin. Such joints are used, for example, in **post-and-girt framing**.

hewn overhang In an early timber-framed house, the modest projection of an upper story beyond the story immediately below it, usually no more than a few inches. A heavy timber post extended from the foundation of the house to the upper story; this post was hewn away from just below the upper story down to the **ground-sill**, thereby creating the appearance of an upper story slightly overhanging the lower one. Compare with **framed overhang**.

HEX On drawings, abbr. for "hexagon" or "hexagonal."

hexagonal method of application See **French method of application**.

hexapartite vault Same as sexpartite vault.

hexastyle, exastyle Having six columns, as at one end or at each end of a portico.

hexastyle

hex barn A barn decorated with painted *hex* symbols called *hexenfoos*, i.e., colorful geometric patterns set within circles, particularly found on barns in **Pennsylvania Dutch** regions. The sym-

hexenfoos on a **hex barn**

bols probably were originally intended to protect the animals from harm cast by the "evil eye."

HF On drawings, abbr. for "hot finished."

HGT On drawings, abbr. for **height**.

H-hinge, parliament hinge, shutter hinge A type of **strap hinge** with leaves enlarged so that when the hinge is open, it forms the letter H.

hickey, hicky **1.** A threaded fitting for mounting a lighting fixture in an outlet box, or on a stud or pipe. **2.** A tool for bending conduit or pipe.

hickey, 2

hick joint See **rough-cut joint**.

hickory A tough, hard, strong wood of North America; has high shock resistance and high bending strength.

HID Abbr. for "high-intensity discharge."

hidden nailing Same as **blind nailing**.

hide glue See **animal glue**.

hiding power, covering power The ability of a paint film to obscure completely any pattern, marks, or color on the surface to which it is applied.

hieroglyph A figure representing (*a*) an idea, and intended to convey a meaning, (*b*) a word or root of a word, or (*c*) a sound which is part of a word; esp. applied to the engraved marks and symbols found on the monuments of ancient Egypt.

hieron The sacred enclosure of a temple or shrine.

high altar The primary altar in a church.

high-alumina cement See **calcium aluminate cement**.

high-bay lighting A lighting system with luminaires of the direct or semidirect type, mounted high above the floor; used principally in industrial installations.

high-bond bar A **deformed bar**.

high brass See **common brass**.

high-build coating A coating composed of a series of uniform tile-like films which are applied in thicknesses (minimum 5 mils) greater than those normally associated with paint films and thinner than those normally applied with a trowel.

high-calcium lime A lime which contains mostly calcium oxide or calcium hydroxide and not over 5% magnesium oxide or hydroxide.

high-carbon steel A steel having a carbon content between 0.6% and 1.5%.

high chair Same as **bar support**.

high-challenge fire hazard A fire hazard typically produced by a fire in combustible piled-high storage.

high-density concrete, heavy concrete, heavyweight concrete Concrete of exceptionally high unit weight, usually consisting of heavyweight aggregates; used esp. for radiation shielding.

high-density overlay An overlay consisting of paper that is impregnated with a thermosetting resin and then applied to plywood; provides a smooth, hard, wear-resistant surface for high-quality concrete formwork and decking.

high-density plywood Plywood made from resin-impregnated veneer and formed with heat at pressures of 500 lb per sq in. (35 kg per sq m) or more; usually density is at least twice that of normal plywood; is difficult to work with ordinary hand tools because of its extreme hardness.

high-discharge mixer See **inclined-axis mixer**.

high-early-strength cement, extra-rapid-hardening cement, type III cement Cement producing earlier strength in mortar or concrete than regular cement.

high-early-strength concrete Concrete which, through the use of high-early-strength cement or admixtures, is capable of attaining specified strength at an earlier age than normal concrete.

high explosive A material that detonates almost instantaneously.

high gloss See **gloss**.

High Gothic Same as the **Decorated style**, the second of the three phases of English Gothic architecture.

high hat **1.** A recessed **downlight**. **2.** A black circular tube which is mounted on the front of a spotlight to reduce the stray light on the sides of the main beam.

high-hazard contents Building contents that are liable to burn with extreme rapidity or from which poisonous fumes or explosions are to be feared in the event of fire.

high-hazard industrial occupancy Use of a building having **high-hazard contents**.

high-intensity discharge lamp One of the group of mercury, metal halide, or high-pressure sodium lamps.

high-joint pointing Pointing done during the progress of the work, while the mortar is still soft, first by trimming the joints flush with the face of the wall, and then scraping grooves along the edges of the brick at both sides of the joint.

high-lift grouting The technique of grouting masonry in which each **lift, 7** is raised 12 ft (3.7 m) or more in height.

highlight **1.** In a field of view, a local region that is emphasized, usually by increased local illumination. **2.** An area on a metal surface which has been most exposed to a buffing or polishing operation, and hence has the highest luster.

high-light window Same as **clerestory, 2**.

high-magnesium lime A lime produced by calcining dolomitic limestone or dolomite; contains more magnesium oxide than limes made from calcite or high-calcium limestones and marbles; ranges from 37 to 41% magnesium oxide content. Incorrectly called "dolomitic lime."

high-melting-point asphalt Roofing asphalt which melts at a high temperature; used on steep slopes and to attach insulation and/or vapor barriers to the structural deck.

high-output fluorescent lamp A **rapid-start fluorescent lamp** designed to operate on higher current than usual, resulting in a corresponding increase in flux (lumens) per unit length of the lamp.

high polymer A substance composed of a large molecule which usually but not always consists of repeat units of the low molecular weight; one having a molecular weight greater than 10,000.

high-pressure boiler A **boiler** that provides steam at pressures above 15 lb per sq in. (103.4 kPa) or hot water at temperatures exceeding 250°F (121°C).

high-pressure laminates Laminates molded and cured at pressures not lower than 1,000 lb per sq in. (70 kg per sq cm) and more commonly in the range of 1,200 to 2,000 lb per sq in. (84 to 140 kg per sq cm).

high-pressure mercury lamp A **mercury-vapor lamp** that operates at a partial pressure of mercury of about 1 atmosphere or more.

high-pressure overlay Any plastic laminate composed of phenolic or melamine-impregnated papers (often printed or patterned for decorative effects) which are pressed into hard sheets at high pressures. Such sheets have excellent wear resistance; often glued to wood substrates for tabletops and doors.

high-pressure sodium lamp A **sodium-vapor lamp** in which the partial pressure of the vapor during operation is about 0.1 atmosphere; produces a yellowish light having a wide spectrum, in contrast to the light produced at low pressures, which is characterized by sodium emission lines.

high-pressure steam heating system A **steam heating system** employing steam at pressures usually above 100 lb per sq in. (7 kg per sq cm).

high relief, alto-relievo, alto-rilievo Sculpture relief work in which the figures project more than half their thickness.

high relief

High Renaissance A term referring primarily to the culmination of the Italian Renaissance style in the 16th century (*cinquecento*). Saint Peter's in Rome is the most famous example.

high-rise A building having a large number of floors, usually constructed where land costs are high.

high-rise building A building having many stories; sufficiently tall so the use of an elevator is essential; also see **skyscraper**.

high school, secondary school In the U.S.A., a school which provides education beyond elementary school, usually from grade 9 to grade 12 but sometimes including grades 7 and 8.

high-silicon bronze See **silicon bronze**.

high-silicon iron pipe Same as **acid-resistant cast-iron pipe**.

high steel Steel containing a comparatively large amount of carbon (0.5 to 1%).

high-strength bolt A bolt made of either high-strength carbon steel or quenched and tempered alloy steel.

high-strength low-alloy steel Steel having a chemical composition specifically developed to impart higher mechanical property values and, in some cases, greater resistance to atmospheric corrosion than is obtainable from conventional carbon steels.

high-strength steel Steel which has a high yield point, e.g., 6000 pounds per square inch (4.4 MPa).

High-Tech architecture A mode of architecture in which the **building services** are not only revealed, but are emphasized. For example, ducts and pipes may be painted in bright colors to indicate their respective functions. An outstanding example is the Pompidou Centre in Paris.

High Renaissance: interior of St. Peter's, Rome

high-temperature brazed joint A gastight joint which is brazed at temperatures higher than 1500°F (816°C) but less than the melting temperatures of the joined parts.

high-temperature-water heating system A heating system in which water having supply temperatures above 350°F (177°C) is used as a medium to convey heat from a central boiler, through a piping system, to suitable heat-distributing means.

high-tensile bolt See **high-tension bolt**.

high-tensile reinforcement Steel reinforcing bars for concrete having a minimum yield strength above a specified value.

high-tension bolt A high-strength bolt which is tightened with a calibrated torsion wrench; used in place of a rivet.

high tomb Same as **altar tomb**.

high-velocity duct system A duct system in which the air velocities are 2,400 ft (approx. 730 m) per minute or higher.

High Victorian architecture See **Victorian architecture**.

High Victorian Gothic A very elaborate, highly detailed interpretation of the **Gothic Revival** in its last phase, from about 1860 to 1890; may have bands of **polychromed** masonry and multicolored brickwork or roofing tiles; is heavy in appearance, as exemplified by its massive gables and porches; sometimes called Late Gothic Revival or Ruskinian Gothic. Some architectural historians avoid this designation, regarding the adjective "Victorian" merely as descriptive of an age that encompassed a number of specific exuberant, ornate, and highly decorative architectural styles.

High Victorian Italianate A term some-times applied to the latter phase of **Italianate style**, from the 1860s to 1880; often more elabo-rate than the earlier Italianate style.

hiling The covering or roof of a building.

hinge A movable joint used to attach, support, and turn a door (or cover) about a pivot; consists of two plates joined together by a pin which sup-port the door and connect it to its frame, enabling it to swing open or closed. Also see **action hinge, butterfly hinge, butt hinge, dove-tail hinge, gravity hinge, H-hinge, HL-hinge, pintle hinge, side hinge, strap hinge**.

hinge backset The horizontal distance from the edge of a door hinge to the **stop** side of the door.

hinged latch bolt Same as **swinging latch bolt**.

hinge jamb The doorjamb to which hinges are attached.

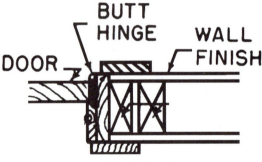

hinge jamb

hinge joint Any joint which permits action similar to a hinge and in which there is no appreciable separation of adjacent members.

hingeless frame See **rigid frame**.

hinge post See **hanging post**.

hinge reinforcement A metal plate attached to a door or doorframe to receive a hinge.

hinge stile The vertical structural member of a doorframe on which the hinges are fixed, and about which the door pivots; also called a hang-ing stile.

hinge strap A metal strap, often ornamental, which is fixed to the surface of a door to give the appearance of a strap hinge.

hip 1. The external angle at the junction of two sloping roofs or sides of a roof. 2. The rafter at the angle where two sloping roofs or sides of

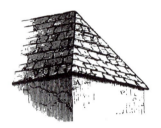

hips, 1 (flush panel type)

roofs meet. 3. The joint of a bridge truss where the top chord meets the inclined end post.

hip-and-valley roof A roof constructed so that it has both hips and valleys.

hip-and-valley roof

hip bevel 1. The angle between two slopes of a roof which are separated one from the other by a hip. 2. The bevel that must be given to the end of a rafter so that it will conform to the oblique construction at a hip.

hip capping The top strip of roofing felt or other protective covering over a hip.

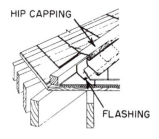

hip capping

hip hook, hip iron A metal strip, usually of wrought iron, installed at the foot of a hip rafter; used to fix the hip tiles in place.

hip iron A **hip hook**.

hip jack A **jack rafter**, one end of which termi-nates at the hip of a roof.

hip joint Same as **hip, 3**.

hip knob A finial or other similar ornament placed on the top of the hip of a roof or at the apex of a gable.

hip molding A molding on the rafter that forms the hip of a roof.

hip-on-gable roof Same as **jerkinhead roof**.

hipped dormer A **dormer** whose roof has flat surfaces that slope upward at the front of the dormer, as well as on both sides, in a manner similar to that of a **hipped roof**.

hipped end The sloping triangularly shaped end of a hipped roof.

hipped gable See **jerkinhead**.

hipped-gable roof A seldom-used term for **jerkinhead roof**.

hipped-plate construction See **folded-plate construction**.

hipped roof, hip roof A roof comprising adjacent flat surfaces that slope upward from all sides of the perimeter of the building, requiring a **hip rafter** along each intersection of the inclined surfaces; also see **pyramidal roof**.

hippodrome **1.** A circus. **2.** A modern sports arena of any shape.

hip rafter, angle rafter, angle ridge A rafter placed at the junction of the inclined planes forming a hipped roof.

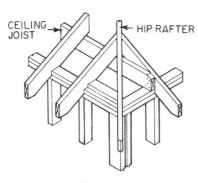

hip rafter

hip rib On domed roofs, a curved **hip rafter**.

hip roll, ridge roll A rounded strip of wood, tile, metal, or composition material which is used to cover and finish the **hip** of a roof.

hip roof, hipped roof A roof which slopes upward from all four sides of a building, requiring a hip rafter at each corner.

hip roof

hip skylight A **skylight** having sloping sides that meet to form **hips, 1**.

hip tile A saddle-shaped tile used to cover the hips of a roof.

hip vertical The upright tension member which is attached to the **hip, 3** of a truss, carries a floor beam at its lower end.

Hispanic Colonial architecture See **Spanish Colonial architecture**.

Historic American Buildings Survey (HABS) A collection of **measured drawings**, photographs, and records of American buildings, constructions, and sites that (a) are of particular historic interest, significance, or are representative of a particular architectural style; (b) represent important methods of construction; (c) were designed by a major architect; and/or (d) are typical of work by an ethnic group within the United States. Housed in the Library of Congress, HABS represents an important, useful, and significant resource. Address: National Park Service, Department of the Interior, P.O. Box 37127, Washington, DC 20013-7127.

historic marker See **marker**.

historic preservation See **building preservation**.

hit-and-miss window A window, the upper sash of which is glazed, the lower sash containing two movable panels that are slotted; one panel slides completely across the other, providing an opening for air which may be adjusted as required.

Hittite architecture The distinctive rugged architecture created in central Anatolia at the time of the Hittite Empire (14th to 13th cent. B.C.), preeminent for its fortifications, citadels, and temples.

HL-hinge   A type of **H-hinge** that has a horizontal extension added to a foot of the hinge.

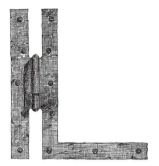

HL-hinge

HMD   Abbr. for **hollow-metal door**.

hoarding, hoard   **1.** A rough and temporary wall or fence, usually at a construction site. **2.** A covered wooden gallery projecting from the top of the wall of a medieval fortress to shelter the defenders and to increase facilities for defense.

hob   A flat projecting shelf at the side of a fireplace where pots or pans may be placed to keep warm.

hod   A wood or metal container, usually V-shaped with a long handle and having one end open; used in masonry work to carry plaster or lime putty to the mortarboard.

hoe   See **backhoe**.

hogan   The traditional single-family dwelling of the Navajo Indians of the American Southwest; typically has a framework constructed of logs, poles, branches, and sticks that is covered with a layer of bark and then a thick layer of mud or sod. A smoke hole, centered at the top of the structure, provides light and carries off fumes and smoke from an open firepit located directly below; there are no windows.

hog-backed   Cambered; applied esp. to the ridge of a roof which appears to sag in the middle.

hoggin   **1.** A graded gravel (or the like) used as a base for paths, sidewalks, roads, etc. **2.** A mixture of gravel and sand with clay.

hogging   The drooping of the extremities and consequent convex appearance of any timber supported in the middle.

hog's-back tile   A ridge tile whose section is not quite half round.

hoist   **1.** In building, a machine for lifting workers and materials to upper stories during erection of the structure. **2.** A machine that provides power drive to a cable drum used to pull or lift a load.

hoisting machine   A power-operated machine, used for lifting or lowering a load, that utilizes a drum and wire rope (excluding elevators); includes but is not limited to a cableway, crane, or derrick.

hoist tower   In building erection, a temporary (sometimes portable) structure that provides guideways for a platform that lifts materials to upper stories.

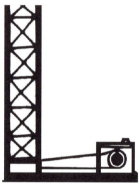

hoist tower

hoistway   A passage through which an object may be raised; for example, an elevator shaft.

hoistway door   A door between an elevator shaft or hoistway and the floor landing, normally closed except when the elevator is stopped at the floor for passengers or freight.

hoistway door interlock   A device used to prevent the operation of a **hoisting machine** unless the hoistway door is locked in the closed position; used to prevent the opening of this door from the landing side unless the car is within the landing zone and is either stopped or being stopped.

hold-down bolt   See **anchor bolt**.

hold-down clip   **1.** In a suspended acoustical ceiling, a flexible metal clip used to hold an acoustical ceiling board or lay-in panel in firm contact with the supporting members of an exposed suspension system. **2.** In roofing, a flexible metal clip used to hold adjacent lengths of capping in place.

holder bat An **escutcheon, 2** having a projecting lug on one side for attaching it to a wall.

holdfast A device for securing anything in its place, as a hook, bolt, spike, etc.

hold harmless **1.** See **contractual liability. 2.** See **indemnification.**

holding-down bolt Same as **anchor bolt.**

holding period Same as **presteaming period.**

hole saw See **crown saw.**

holiday, skip **1.** A small area on a painted surface which the brush skipped over, leaving it bare. **2.** An area on a built-up roof surface which the mop (used to coat the surface) skipped over, leaving it uncovered by bitumen.

holing The punching of holes in slates before fixing on a roof.

hollow-backed Said of a piece of wood, stone, etc., whose unexposed face has been hollowed out so that it fits against an irregular surface more tightly.

hollow bed In masonry a **bed joint** in which there is no mortar at the center of a stone (or in which the stone is not flat but hollowed) so that contact is made only along the edges.

hollow block A **hollow masonry unit.**

hollow brick **1.** (*U.S.A.*) A hollow clay masonry unit whose net cross-sectional area in every plane parallel to the bearing surface is not less than 60% of its gross cross-sectional area measured in the same plane. **2.** (*Brit.*) A brick having holes through it which total at least 25% of its volume, the holes being not less than ¾ in. (1.91 cm) wide or ¾ sq in. (4.84 sq cm) in area.

hollow chamfer A **chamfer** which is concave.

hollow clay tile Same as **structural clay tile.**

hollow concrete block A concrete **hollow masonry unit.**

hollow-core construction A construction having a lightweight inner core which is faced on both sides by a material such as plywood or hardboard.

hollow-core door A flush door of hollow-core construction.

hollow glass block See **glass block.**

hollow gorge Same as **Egyptian gorge.**

hollow masonry unit A masonry unit whose net cross-sectional area in any plane parallel to the bearing surface is less than 75% of its gross cross-sectional area measured in the same plane.

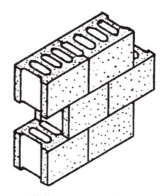

hollow masonry units

hollow-metal Said of an assembly that is fabricated of formed light-gauge metal.

hollow-metal door A metal door (commonly of the flush type), fabricated of sheet steel and reinforced by light metal channels; has a hollow core, sometimes filled with a light filler material.

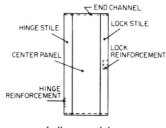

hollow-metal door

hollow-metal fire door A hollow-metal door fabricated of sheet steel, No. 20 gauge or heavier, and filled with an approved fire-proof insulating material.

hollow molding, gorge, trochilus A concave, often circular molding; a **cavetto** or **scotia**.

hollow newel, hollow newel stair **1.** The newel or central shaft of a winding stair built as a hollow cylinder. **2.** The open well in such a stair when built without the hollow enclosure.

hollow newel stair See **open-newel stair**.

hollow partition See **cavity wall**.

hollow plane A carpenter's molding plane with a convex blade for forming concave or hollow moldings.

hollow relief Same as **sunk relief**.

hollow roll A type of joint (between two sheets of metal roofing) in the direction of maximum slope of the roof; the two pieces are turned up at the joint and then bent to form a hollow cylindrical roll.

hollow square molding A common Norman molding consisting of a series of indented pyramidal shapes having a square base.

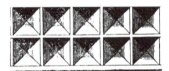

hollow square molding

hollow tile Same as **structural clay tile**.

hollow-tile floor slab A reinforced concrete floor slab, cast over rows of structural clay tile.

hollow-unit masonry Masonry constructed of **hollow masonry units** laid in mortar.

hollow wall, hollow masonry wall See **cavity wall**.

Holy door In a Greek Orthodox church, the door to the **iconostasis**.

holy-water stone A stone basin for holding holy water, placed near the entrance of a church.

home for the aged An institution which provides primarily domiciliary or custodial services and minimal nursing and medical care to aged persons.

homestall See **homestead, 2**.

holy-water stone

homestead **1.** In the United States, under the Homestead Act of 1862, a tract of unoccupied public land, 160 acres in area, that could be permanently acquired after five years of continuous occupancy and the payment of a fee. The Act was passed by the Congress to promote westward expansion and for the purposes of revenue; this quantity of acreage was deemed adequate for the support of one family. Any citizen who settled on such survey public land could purchase it from the government if he was the head of a family and over 21 years of age. **2.** The house built on such a tract. **3.** (*Brit.*) A group of buildings and the land forming the home of a family.

homogeneous material A material whose characteristics or properties are not a function of the position within the material.

hone Same as **oilstone**.

honed finish A very smooth stone surface, just short of polished; imparted by a rubbing process, either hand or mechanical.

honeycomb **1.** Any hexagonal structure or pattern, or one resembling such a structure or pattern. **2.** Voids left in concrete owing to failure

honeycomb, 1

of the mortar to fill effectively the spaces among coarse aggregate particles. **3.** A type of flaw in metal caused by corrosion or imperfect casting.

honeycomb brickwork   In a brick wall, the omission of some **headers** or **stretchers** either to provide ventilation or to serve as a decorative element.

honeycombing   Checks or splits that develop inside a piece of wood during drying; usually not visible on the surface.

honeycomb slating   Similar to **diagonal slating** except that the bottom corners are removed from the slates.

honeycomb structure   An arrangement of soil particles having a comparatively loose, stable structure resembling a honeycomb.

honeycomb vault, honeycomb work   See **muqarnas**.

honeycomb wall   A brick wall having a pattern of openings; equal in thickness to the width of one brick; either gaps are left between stretchers or bricks are omitted to provide openings; used to support floor joists and provide ventilation under floors.

honeysuckle ornament   A common name for the **anthemion**, common in Greek decorative sculpture.

honeysuckle ornament

honing gauge   A device for holding a chisel at the same angle while it is sharpened on a flat stone.

hood   **1.** A cover placed above an opening or an object to shelter it. **2.** A cover placed over a fire or chimney to create a draft and to direct the smoke, odors, or noxious vapors into a flue; may be supported or hung in space, or attached to a wall; sometimes furnished with a grease filter or extractor, a light fixture, and fire-extinguishing system.

hood, 1

hooded crown   The upper termination of a window that is covered by a **hood, 1**.

hoodmold, hood molding   The projecting molding of the arch over a door or window, whether inside or outside; also called a **dripstone**.

hook   **1.** A curved or bent metal device used for attachment. **2.** A bend in the end of a **reinforcing bar**; also see **hooked bar**.

hook-and-butt joint, hook butt scarf, hook scarf   A type of **scarf joint** for joining timbers endwise so that they lock into each other.

hook-and-eye fastener   A two-piece metal fastener consisting of a hook, bent to the required shape, and an eye through which the hook fits.

hook bolt   A bolt having one end in the form of a hook.

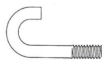

hook bolt

hooked bar   A steel **reinforcing bar**, for use in reinforced concrete, with the end bent into a hook to provide anchorage.

Hooke's law   A law stating that the deformation of an elastic body is proportional to the force applied, provided the stress does not exceed the elastic limit of the material.

hook strip   A wood board, attached to a wall of a closet, to which clothes hooks are fastened.

hoop iron Thin strips of iron used to bond masonry.

hoop-iron bond In masonry, a **chain bond** formed by metal straps or hoop iron.

hoop reinforcement In concrete columns and piles, steel rings (other than helical) which are placed around the reinforcing bars or rods of the **main reinforcement** to tie them together.

hopper **1.** A funnel-shaped bin or chute; used to store loose construction materials, such as crushed stone or sand. **2.** One of two barriers on both sides of a **hopper light** to prevent airflow through the side openings at the ends of the inward-sloping pivoted **sash (ventilator, 2)**. **3.** A water tank which releases its contents through a pipe at the bottom; esp. used with a water closet. **4.** A water-closet bowl, esp. one that is funnel-shaped. **5.** See **collection hopper**.

hopper frame A type of window frame having an upper **sash (ventilator, 2)** which is hinged along the bottom and opens inward; some frames of this type contain several such sashes.

hopper head A funnel-shaped **leader head**.

hopper light **1.** A window sash which opens inward and is hinged at the bottom; when open, air passes over the top of the sash; also called **hopper vent or hopper ventilator**. **2.** A window sash which opens inward and is hinged at each side; when open, most of the air passes over the top of the sash but there is some flow through a narrower opening along the bottom.

hopper light

hopper vent, hopper ventilator See **hopper light, 1**.

hopper window A **hospital window**.

HOR On drawings, abbr. for **horizontal**.

horizon The apparent or visible junction of the earth and sky, as seen from any specific position.

horizon cloth A **cyclorama** fabricated of canvas.

horizon light A lighting unit used to illuminate a **cyclorama** from below, e.g., from a light trough.

horizontal At right angles to the direction of gravity; on the level; parallel to the horizon; neither vertical nor inclined.

horizontal angle An angle in a horizontal plane.

horizontal-axis mixer A concrete mixer having a revolving drum which rotates about a horizontal axis.

horizontal bracing Any bracing which lies in a horizontal plane.

horizontal branch A **branch drain** with a horizontal extension from a waste, soil, or vent stack, or from a building drain, which receives the discharge from a single fixture or a group of fixtures and conducts it to the soil or waste stack or to the building drain.

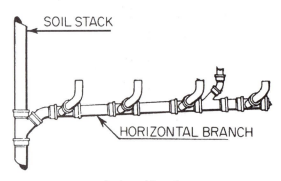

horizontal branch

horizontal bridging **1.** Any **bridging** in a horizontal plane. **2.** Bridging which is perpendicular to, and lying in the planes of, the flanges of joists or beams.

horizontal cell tile A structural masonry ceramic tile having cells whose axes are horizontal when the tile is placed in the wall.

horizontal bridging, 1

horizontal sheeting

horizontal circle A graduated circle fixed to the lower plate of a **transit**, by means of which horizontal angles can be measured.

horizontal control In surveying, a basic framework of points whose horizontal position and interrelationship have been determined accurately.

horizontal cornice The level cornice of the pediment under the two inclined cornices.

horizontal diaphragm A **diaphragm** used to distribute forces in a horizontal plane.

horizontal exit A means of passage from one building into another building occupied by the same tenant, or from one section of a building into another section of the same building occupied by the same tenant, through a separation wall having a specified fire-resistance rating.

horizontal line A line perpendicular to the vertical.

horizontal panel On a wall, a panel whose longest dimension is horizontal.

horizontal pipe Any pipe which is horizontal or makes an angle of less than 45° with the horizontal.

horizontal plane A plane perpendicular to the direction of a plumb line.

horizontal sheeting In excavation work, timber planks, sheets of steel, panels of concrete, or the like, which are placed between **soldier piles** to provide a restrain to retain the soil.

horizontal shore 1. A beam or truss that spans vertical posts and supports the formwork for pouring of concrete floor slabs. 2. A **flying shore**.

horizontal shoring 1. Adjustable span members, of either the beam or truss type; used to support concrete forms over relatively long spans, thereby reducing the number of vertical supports. 2. A number of **horizontal shores** acting collectively.

horizontal sliding door A door and frame with a track arrangement permitting the door to slide horizontally.

horizontal sliding window, horizontal slider A window having sashes (in a vertical plane) which slide in horizontal grooves or tracks; when closed, the stiles of the sashes meet and may interlock.

horizontal spring hinge A spring hinge that is mortised horizontally into the bottom rail of a door and fastened to the floor and head frame with pivots.

H or M In the lumber industry, abbr. for "hit or miss."

horn 1. Any projecting end of one of the members of a right-angle wood framing joint. 2. The

horn, 1

extension of a sash stile below the bottom rail of an upper-hung sash, either for styling or to serve as a stop. **3.** A horizontal extension of a windowsill beyond the jamb. **4.** Same as **spur, 1. 5.** A **volute, 1. 6.** An **acroterion, 2**.

hornwork   Fortress outwork with two half bastions.

hors concours   Describing an invited exhibit or exhibitor, ineligible for an award in a competition owing to acknowledged superiority.

horse   **1.** See **sawhorse**. **2.** See **carriage**. **3.** Framing used as a temporary support.

horse block   A block or platform, often set near a door, on which one steps when mounting or dismounting from a horse.

horsed joint   Same as **saddle joint, 1**.

horse mold   A **running mold**.

horsepower   A unit of power equal to 746 watts.

horsepower-hour   A unit of work or energy equal to the work done by a machine having a power output of 1 horsepower over a period of 1 hour.

horse scaffold   A scaffold for light or medium duty, composed of horses supporting a work platform.

horse shed   A rough structure having one or more open sides, once used to provide temporary shelter for horses.

horseshoe arch, Arabic arch, Moorish arch   A rounded arch whose curve is a little more than a semicircle so that the opening at the bottom is narrower than its greatest span.

horsing   Same as **outrigger shore**.

horsing up   Building up a desired plaster shape with a **running mold**.

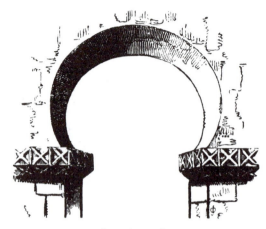

horseshoe arch

hortus   **1.** A pleasure garden or pleasure ground of the ancients, similar in style and arrangement to the garden of a modern Italian villa. **2.** Any type of garden in ancient Rome.

hose bib   Same as **sill cock**.

hose cock   Same as **sill cock**.

hose-stream test   A test in which, after a period of fire exposure, a wall partition or door is subjected to the impact, erosion, and cooling effects of a stream of water from a fire hose directed first at the middle and then at all parts of the exposed face.

hose thread   A standard screw thread used for attaching a garden hose; has 12 threads per inch on a ¾ in. pipe size.

HOSP   On drawings, abbr. for **hospital**.

hospice   A resort for travelers which includes lodging and entertainment.

hortus

hospital A building or part thereof used for the medical, obstetrical, or surgical care of four or more patients on a 24-hr basis.

hospital arm pull A handle for opening a hospital door without the use of hands, by hooking an arm over the handle.

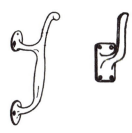

hospital arm pull

hospital door A flush door (with or without a glass **light**) large enough to permit the passage of hospital beds, stretchers, etc.; usually equipped with special hardware.

hospital frame A doorframe with **terminated stops**.

hospitalium 1. A guest chamber in a Roman house. 2. A conventional entrance for strangers in a dramatic performance.

hospital stop See **terminated stop**.

hospital window, hopper window A **hopper light, 1** having a **hopper, 2** on each side to prevent drafts.

hospitium An inn or a place for the reception of strangers.

hostry An inn.

hot-air furnace A heating unit enclosed in a casing from which warm air is circulated through the building in ducts by gravity convection or by fans.

hot-air heating A system of heating by which air, warmed above a fire chamber, is distributed through ducts.

hot-air-seasoned Same as **kiln-dried**.

hot-applied sealant A compound which is applied in a molten state and cured primarily at ambient temperature.

hotbed A small low enclosure heated by fermented manure or electric cables and usually covered with glass; used for forcing bedding plants and vegetables to grow out of season or for protecting tender exotics.

hot-cathode lamp An **electric-discharge lamp** which produces light by means of an **arc discharge**; the cathodes are heated either by the discharge or by an external source.

hot cement Cement which is at a high temperature, usually owing to inadequate or insufficient cooling after manufacture.

hot closet A **closet** adjacent to a fireplace or oven; used for drying out damp clothes.

hot-dip galvanizing A protective coating applied to ferrous metal by dipping in a bath of molten zinc.

hot-driven rivet Any **rivet** that is preheated before placement.

hotel A building in which lodging and other services, often board, are provided primarily to transients and, less often, to permanent residents.

hot food table See **steam table**.

hot glue A glue which must be heated before use. Also see **hot-setting adhesive**.

hothouse A **greenhouse** that is usually artificially heated; also see **conservatory** and **orangery**.

hot-laid mixture A mixture that is spread and compacted in a heated condition.

hotmelt A thermoplastic material used as a coating, sealer, or adhesive for wood and other materials.

hot-melt sealant Same as **hot-applied sealant**.

hot-pressing The pressure forming, between heated platens, of plywood, laminates, particleboard, fiberboard, etc.; usually requires thermosetting resins and heat for curing.

hot-rolled finish The finish on a metal surface obtained by rolling the metal while hot; results in a dark, oxidized, relatively rough surface.

hot rolling The shaping of plate metal by rolling very hot slabs of metal.

hot-setting adhesive An adhesive that requires a temperature of 212°F (100°C) or higher to set it.

hot spraying A paint-spraying technique which uses heat rather than solvent to lower the viscosity of the paint; permits use of a lower spraying pressure and lessens the loss due to overspray.

hot surface **1.** A surface which is very alkaline. **2.** A surface which is highly absorbent. **3.** A surface at a high temperature.

hot-water blending See **blending**.

hot-water heater See **domestic hot-water heater**.

hot-water heating Heating which utilizes a system in which hot water circulates through pipes, coils, and radiators.

hot-water heating system A heating system in which water having supply temperatures lower than 250°F (121°C) is used as a medium to convey heat from a central boiler, through a piping system, to suitable heat-distributing means.

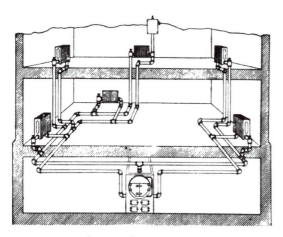

hot-water heating system

hot-water recirculation system A hot-water distribution system in which additional piping and a return pump are incorporated so as to return the unused hot water to the heater. The water is recirculated through the heater to compensate for system losses due to convection, radiation, and conduction.

hot-water storage tank A tank that meets code requirements for storing hot water. These requirements depend on its size and pressure as well as the authority having jurisdiction. The volume of the tank usually selected so that 60 to 80 percent of the volume of water in the tank may be drawn off before the temperature drop of the water in the tank is unacceptable.

hot-water supply A combination of equipment and piping capable of providing a continuous supply of hot water for domestic purposes, usually between about 120° and 140°F (approx. 50° and 60° C).

hot-wire anemometer An **anemometer** which measures the velocity of airflow by the effect of the airflow on the temperature of a wire resistor which is connected to an electrical circuit.

hot working The process of forming a metal when its temperature is higher than its recrystallization temperature.

hound's-tooth Same as **dog's-tooth course**.

house **1.** A building or dwelling for human residence. **2.** A theatre, as a **legitimate house**. **3.** (*Colloq.*) The auditorium in a theatre; the audience space.

house-and-a-half Same as **three-quarter Cape Cod house**.

house board A permanently connected electric switchboard in a theatre, often controlling only the houselights.

house connection Same as **building sewer**.

house curtain See **act curtain**.

housed Said of a piece or a member which is fitted into another.

housed joint, dado joint A joint between two wood members, usually at right angles; the full thickness of the edge or end of one member is inserted in a corresponding housing in the other.

housed joint

house drain Same as **building drain**.

housed stair Same as **box stair**.

housed string, housed stringer, housed stair string Same as **close string**.

household All persons, including family members and any unrelated persons, who occupy a dwelling unit.

houselights Lights in an auditorium which provide general illumination in the seating areas, before and after performances and during intermissions.

house pump A pump which fills a **gravity tank** serving as the water supply for a building.

house raising See **barn raising**.

house sewer Same as **building sewer**.

house slant A T- or Y-shaped connection between a sewer and a **building sewer**.

house tank **1.** A water **storage tank** for a building. **2.** A **gravity tank**.

house trap Same as **building trap**.

housing **1.** A notch or groove cut in one wood member, usually to receive another wood member, as in a **housed joint**; also called a **trench**. **2.** A shelter or dwelling place, or a collection of such places. **3.** A niche for a statue.

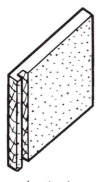

housing, 1

housing project See **project, 3**.

housing unit A house, apartment, group of rooms, or a single room occupied or intended for occupancy as separate living quarters.

hovel **1.** A shed open at the sides and covered overhead for sheltering livestock, produce, or people. **2.** A poorly constructed and ill-kept house.

hoveling **1.** Constructing a chimney by covering the top, leaving openings in the sides, or by carrying up two sides higher than the other two. **2.** A chimney so constructed.

Howe truss A **truss** having upper and lower horizontal members, between which are vertical and diagonal members; the vertical members of the web take tension, and the diagonal members are under compression.

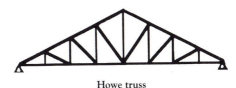

Howe truss

Hoyer effect In prestressed concrete, the frictional forces resulting from the tendency of the tendons to assume their original diameter (i.e., their diameter before prestressing).

hp, HP **1.** Abbr. for **horsepower**. **2.** Abbr. for "high pressure."

H-pile **1.** Any steel H-section used as a **bearing pile**. **2.** A steel H-beam used as a **pile**.

H-plan The basic **plan** of a building having the shape of a capital letter **H**, with two open courtyards.

HPS Abbr. for "high-pressure sodium."

HP-shape A standard structural hot-rolled steel I-shaped column section; used for piles of a specified category designated by the prefix HP, placed before the size of the member.

H PT On drawings, abbr. for "high point."

HR On drawings, abbr. for "hour."

Hrt. In the lumber industry, abbr. for "heart."

Hrt.CC In the lumber industry, abbr. for "heart cubic content."

Hrt.FA In the lumber industry, abbr. for "heart facial area."

Hrt.G In the lumber industry, abbr. for "heart girth."

H-runner In a ceiling suspension system, a light metal member shaped like the letter H on its side; one side of the H is attached to a chan-

H-runner

nel, and the other (lower) side fits into the kerfs of ceiling tiles.

HSE   On drawings, abbr. for **house**.

H-section   Same as **H-beam**.

HTR   On drawings, abbr. for "heater."

hub   **1.** The core of a building usually containing one or more stairs and elevators, from which corridors radiate. **2.** The part of a lock through which the spindle passes to actuate the mechanism. **3.** A stake marking a theodolite position in surveying. **4.** See **bell**. **5.** The thickened inner portion of a gear or wheel, i.e., the portion closest to the shaft.

HUD   Abbr. for "Department of Housing and Urban Development."

hue   The subjective perception of color, e.g., red, yellow, green, blue, purple, or some combination thereof. White, black and gray colors possess no hue.

hull   An obsolete term for the **framework** of a building.

humidifier   A device for adding moisture to air.

humidistat, hygrostat   A regulatory device, actuated by changes in humidity, used for the automatic control of relative humidity.

humidity   Water vapor within a given space or environment.

humiture   A combined measurement of temperature and humidity; computed by adding the temperature in degrees Fahrenheit to the numerical value of the relative humidity and dividing by 2; expressed to the nearest integral value.

humus   A brown or black material formed by the partial decomposition of vegetable or animal matter; the organic portion of soil.

hung ceiling   Same as **suspended ceiling**.

hungry, starved   Descriptive of a paint film which shows the minute detail of the background on which it was applied, giving the appearance of skimpiness.

hungry joint   A masonry joint lacking sufficient mortar to be weatherproof.

hung sash, hanging sash   A **sash** hung on a cord or chain at each side which is attached to a balance or counterweight; moves in the vertical direction.

hung slating   **1.** Slates covering a wall or other vertical surface, rather than a roof (sloping) or floor (horizontal). **2.** Slates supported by wire clips rather than by nails.

hung window   A window containing one or more hung sashes.

hurricane test, dynamic test   A dynamic test for windows and curtain walls simulating the forces and buffeting of a hurricane; both structural strength and water leakage are evaluated.

hut   **1.** A rough and plain habitation; often a temporary shelter for soldiers. **2.** A rustic cabin or similar slight structure.

HVAC system   Abbr. for **heating, ventilating, and air-conditioning system**.

HVY   On drawings, abbr. for "heavy."

HW   On drawings, abbr. for "hot water."

HWRC system   See **hot-water recirculation system**.

HWY   On drawings, abbr. for "highway."

hybrid   Said of a plant produced by crossing two distant varieties or species.

hybrid beam   A fabricated metal beam composed of flanges with a material of a specified minimum yield strength different from that of the web plate.

hybrid solar energy system   A solar energy system that combines the characteristics of two separate heating systems, e.g., a solar energy system and a conventional energy system.

HYD   On drawings, abbr. for "hydraulic."

hydralime   Same as **hydrated lime**.

hydrant   **1.** An apparatus for drawing water directly from a main; consists of a hollow metal cylinder provided with one or more nozzles to which a hose may be attached, or with a valve or faucet, used for supplying large quantities of water. **2.** See **fire hydrant**.

hydrate   **1.** To combine with water or elements of water. **2.** Hydrated lime.

hydrated lime   **1.** Same as **dry hydrate**. **2.** Quicklime mixed with water, on the job, to form a lime putty; **slaked lime**.

hydration   **1.** The formation of a compound by combining water with some other substance. **2.** In concrete, the chemical reaction between cement and water. **3.** The chemical reaction by which a substance (such as portland cement or plaster) combines with water, giving off heat to form a crystalline structure in its setting and hardening.

hydraulically designed (sprinkler) system A sprinkler system in which the pipe sizes are calculated on the basis of the pressure loss to provide a prescribed number of gallons of water per square foot (liters per minute per square meter) of floor area, or flow per sprinkler, with a reasonable degree of uniformity over the area.

hydraulic cement See **cement**.

hydraulic collapse The collapse of thin pile casing as a result of the hydrostatic pressure in the ground.

hydraulic elevator An elevator powered by the energy of a liquid under pressure in a cylinder which acts on a piston or plunger to move the elevator car. Also see **plunger hydraulic elevator; roped hydraulic elevator**.

hydraulic excavator A machine that uses power from hydraulic cylinders to pull a bucket at the end of a boom toward the machine through earth or rock, then to raise the bucket, permitting disposal of the spoil away from the excavation.

hydraulic fill Fill that has been moved and placed by flowing water.

hydraulic friction The friction that resists the flow of a fluid along the piping or ductwork in which it is conveyed and at obstructions.

hydraulic glue A waterproof glue.

hydraulic gradient **1.** The loss of **head** per unit distance of flow. **2.** In a drainage system, the slope of a drainage line between the trap outlet and vent connection.

hydraulic hydrated lime A dry, cementitious, hydrated product obtained by calcining a limestone containing silica and alumina to a temperature short of incipient fusion; there is sufficient calcium oxide to permit hydration, but sufficient unhydrated calcium silicates to give the dry powder its hydraulic properties.

hydraulic jack A **jack** operated by means of a liquid, usually oil, acting against a piston; a small force, applied by means of a lever attached to a small piston, produces a very large force on a large piston.

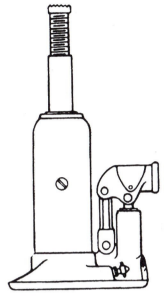

hydraulic jack

hydraulic jump A phenomenon at the transition from high to low velocity in the horizontal pipe at the base of a vertical drain (i.e., a drainage stack) where the flow of water changes from a vertical to horizontal direction; results in a discontinuity in flow at a short distance downstream from the base of the drainage stack.

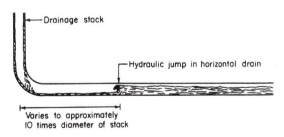

hydraulic jump

hydraulic lift Same as **hydraulic elevator**, esp. one for raising automobiles.

hydraulic lime A lime that contains more than 10% silicates; will harden under water.

hydraulic monitor A device for directing a high-pressure stream of water; used for a variety of purposes, e.g., in cleaning a surface.

hydraulic mortar A mortar that is capable of setting and hardening under water.

hydraulic pump A component unit in the hydraulic system of a construction machine; the prime mover that forces fluid to flow through the system.

hydraulic radius The ratio of the cross-sectional area of fluid flow through a pipe to the wetted perimeter of the pipe.

hydraulics The branch of engineering which treats the motion of fluids.

hydraulic splitter A device for cracking rock or concrete by means of an expanding wedge inserted in a hole or holes drilled in the material; hydraulic power provides the force needed to expand the wedge.

hydraulic spraying See **airless spraying**.

hydraulic test A test for pressure tightness in a plumbing line, using water under pressure.

hydrophobic cement An unhydrated cement which has been treated to reduce its tendency to absorb moisture.

hydropneumatic tank system A domestic water supply system in which water is pumped from the supply system into a pressure tank for storage. Air in the tank is compressed by the water entering the tank. As the pressure in the tank increases, the pressure in the water distribution system also increases, since it is fed from the tank.

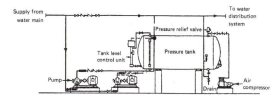

hydropneumatic tank system

hydrostatic head The pressure in a fluid at a given point expressed in terms of the vertical height of the liquid column above that point which would produce the same pressure.

hydrostatic pressure The pressure equivalent to that exerted on a surface by a column of water of a given height.

hydrostatic strength Of a pipe, the capability of withstanding internal pressure of a specified magnitude under specified conditions.

hydrostatic test On a concrete pipe, a test to determine capability of the pipe (or its joints) to withstand internal hydrostatic pressure.

hygrograph A self-recording **hygrometer**.

hygrometer An instrument for measuring humidity conditions (usually **relative humidity**) of the surrounding air.

hygrometric expansion The expansion and contraction of materials (particularly those of organic origin) as they absorb or give off moisture.

hygroscopic Readily absorbing and retaining moisture from the air.

hygrostat See **humidistat**.

hymn board A notice board in a church, on which the numbers of hymns and psalms are posted.

hypaethral, hypethral Describing a building which is open, or partly open, to the sky.

hypaethron An open court or enclosure; a place or part of a building that is roofless.

hyperthyrum A frieze and cornice arranged and decorated in various ways for the lintel of a door.

hyphen A connecting link (for example, a covered walkway) between a large, centrally located house and its dependencies or wings; the house and its hyphens may be in a straight line or form a curve. Also see **five-part mansion**.

hypobasis **1.** The lower base or the lowermost division of a base. **2.** A lower base which is below a more important one.

hypocaust A central heating system of ancient Rome; hot gases from a furnace were conducted to rooms above, through a hollow floor and through tile flues within walls.

hypogeum In ancient architecture, any underground chamber or vault, esp. an underground burial chamber.

hypophyge A depression of curved profile beneath some feature, such as the hollow molding beneath some archaic Doric capitals.

hypopodium Same as **hypobasis, 2**.

hyposcenium In the ancient Greek theatre, the low wall beneath the front part of the **logeion**.

hypostyle hall **1.** A large space with a flat roof supported by rows of columns. Prevalent in

hypostyle hall, 1: sectional view of Temple of Rameses II, Thebes

ancient Egyptian and Achaemenid architecture. **2.** A structure whose roofing was supported, within the perimeter, by groups of columns or piers of more than one height; clerestory lights sometimes were introduced.

hypotrachelium, gorgerin In some columns, that part of the capital between the termination of the shaft and the annulet of the echinus, or the space between two neck moldings.

hypsometric map See **relief map**.

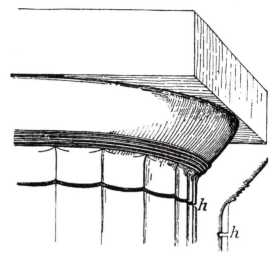

hypotrachelium: *h*

Hz Abbr. for **hertz**.

I

IALD Abbr. for "International Association of Lighting Designers."

IB Abbr. for **I-beam**.

I-bar Steel or iron bar whose cross section is similar to an I.

I-beam A rolled or extruded structural metal beam having a cross section resembling the letter I.

ICE Abbr. for the "Institution of Civil Engineers," London.

ICEA Abbr. for "Insulated Cable Engineers Association."

ice dam A buildup of snow and ice at the eaves of a sloping roof.

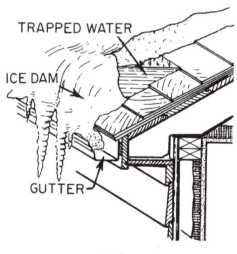

TRAPPED WATER

ICE DAM

GUTTER

ice dam

icehouse A building for storing ice that is usually cut during the winter from frozen lakes, rivers, or ponds for use later in the year; often located in a shady area; usually has overhanging eaves and thick exterior walls that are packed with thermal insulation and painted white to reduce the absorption of heat radiated from the sun.

ichnography The tracing of ground plans; the representation of a ground plot.

ICI Abbr. for "International Commission on Illumination."

iconostasis A screen in a Greek Orthodox church, on which icons are placed, separating the chancel from the space open to the laity.

ID On drawings, abbr. for "inside diameter."

IDSA Abbr. for "Industrial Designers Society of America."

IEE Abbr. for "Institution of Electrical Engineers," London.

IEEE Abbr. for "Institute of Electrical and Electronics Engineers."

IERI Abbr. for "Illuminating Engineering Research Institute."

IES **1.** Abbr. for the "Illuminating Engineering Society of North America." **2.** Abbr. for (British) "Illuminating Engineering Society."

IF Abbr. for "inside face."

igloo, iglu A hemispherical shell, built by Eskimos of blocks of ice or packed snow as a temporary dwelling for a single family; usually about 10 to 15 feet (3 to 4.5 m) in diameter at its base, with the floor often partially below the surrounding terrain. Daylight within was provided by one or more blocks of relatively transparent freshwater ice, or by an opening covered with a piece of translucent seal intestine. Entry was usually along a domed passageway.

igneous rock A class of rock formed by change of the molten material to the solid state; generally termed **granite** if coarse-grained.

ignitability The ease with which **ignition** of a material can be initiated.

ignition The initiation of combustion, as evidenced by flame, glow, or explosion.

ignition temperature Of a material, the minimum temperature required to initiate combustion.

I-house A side-gabled house, usually one-and-a-half or two stories high, one room deep, and two rooms wide; the two rooms usually have an entrance hall between them containing a central stairway.

IHVE Abbr. for "Institution of Heating and Ventilating Engineers."

IIC Abbr. for **impact isolation class**.

ILI Abbr. for "Indiana Limestone Institute."

illite A clay mineral, a hydrous silicate of potassium, aluminum, iron, and magnesium; swells considerably on wetting and shrinks proportionately on drying.

illuminance The density of luminous power, also called "illumination." One lumen of luminous flux, uniformly incident on 1 square foot of area, produces an illuminance of 1 footcandle; in SI units, one lumen of luminous flux, uniformly incident on 1 square meter of area, produces an illuminance of 1 lux.

illuminated sign A sign designed or arranged to emit or reflect light from an attached artificial source.

illumination The luminous flux density incident on a surface, i.e., the luminous flux per unit area; usually expressed in lumens per square foot or footcandles, and lumens per square meter or lux.

illumination meter, *Brit.* **illumination photometer** An instrument for measuring the **illumination** on a surface; usually consists of barrier-layer cells connected to a meter calibrated directly in a set of illumination units.

illumination photometer (*Brit.*) See **illumination meter**.

ILLUS On drawings, abbr. for "illustrate."

ilmenite A mineral which is commonly used as an aggregate in high-density concrete; also called **iron titanate**.

image Any representation of form or features, but esp. one of the entire figure of a person; a statue, effigy, bust, relief, intaglio, etc.

imaret A type of hostelry for the accommodation of Muslim pilgrims and other travelers in the Turkish empire.

imbow Same as **embow**.

imbrex **1.** A tile, semicircular in shape, which fits over the joints in a tile roof. **2.** One of the scales in ornamental **imbrication**.

image

imbricate To overlap in regular order, as shingling, tiles, etc.

imbrication Overlapping rows of shaped tiles or shingles that resemble overlapping fish scales.

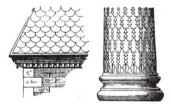

imbrication

IMC Abbr. for **intermediate metallic conduit**.

IMechE Abbr. for "Institution of Mechanical Engineers."

immersion heater A heater in which the **electric heating element**, submerged in a water tank, is controlled by a thermostat built into the tank or in contact with the water.

immersion vibrator A vibrator which is inserted in the fresh concrete during the **agitation, 1** process.

impact factor In structural design, that factor by which a static load effect must be multiplied in order to find the increment of the dynamic effect of applying the load other than statically.

impact insulation, impact isolation 1. The use of structures and materials designed to reduce the transmission of **impact noise** in a building. **2.** The degree by which transmission of **impact noise** is reduced by use of materials and structures for that purpose.

impact insulation class (IIC)   A single-number rating used to compare and evaluate the performance of floor-ceiling constructions in isolating impact noises.

impact load   The dynamic effect on a structure, either moving or at rest, of a forcible momentary contact of another moving body.

impact noise   Sound generated by impact and carried through a structure; typically, footsteps, the slamming of a door.

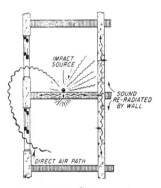

transmission of **impact noise**

impact noise rating (INR)   A rating, expressed by a single number, which is a rough measure of the effectiveness of a floor construction in providing isolation against the noise of impacts; in general, the higher the number, the greater the effectiveness.

impact resistance   The resistance of surface (or a material or product) to a shock, such as a hard blow.

impact strength, impact energy   The amount of energy required to fracture a material; a measure of the material's resistance to mechanical shock.

impact test   A method of determining the resistance of a specimen to fracture upon the application of a dynamic physical shock.

impact wrench   A wrench, driven pneumatically or electrically, which produces a series of impulsive torques.

impages   **1.** The broad transverse band on a door, which stretches from stile to stile and divides the panels horizontally from one another; a **door rail**. **2.** The border or framework of a panel of a door.

impasto   In painting, the thick laying of pigments.

impedance   In alternating-current electric circuits, a quantitative measure of the opposition to the flow of current upon the application of voltage; measured in ohms.

impeller   The rotating member in a **pump** consisting of a disk with vanes attached to it; moves liquid by accelerating the liquid radially outward.

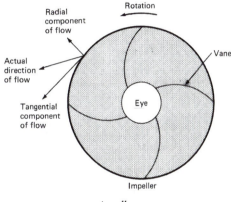

impeller

impending slough   The consistency of shotcrete which contains the maximum amount of water that can be used without flow or sag after placement.

imperfect arch   A **diminished arch**.

impermeable   Said of a soil whose particles are so closely spaced that the passage of water is either prevented or very slow.

impervious   In ceramics, that degree of vitrification evidenced visually by complete resistance to dye penetration; generally signifies zero absorption of water, except for floor and wall tile, which may absorb up to 0.5% water.

impervious soil   A fine-grained soil, such as clay, having pores too small to permit water to pass except by slow capillary creep.

impetus   The span of a building, roof, or arch.

IMPG   On drawings, abbr. for "impregnate."

implied indemnification An indemnification which is implied by law rather than arising out of a contract.

impluvium In ancient Roman dwellings, a cistern set in the **atrium** or **peristyle** to receive water from the roofs.

impluvium, A

imposed load All loads, exclusive of **dead load**, that a structure is to sustain.

impost **1.** A masonry unit or course, often distinctively profiled, which receives and distributes the thrust at each end of an arch. Also see **abutment, springer**. **2.** A vertical member in a gemel or double window taking the place of a mullion; an **integral mullion**.

impost block, dosseret, supercapital A transitional member, often tapered, placed above a column capital to receive the thrust of vaults or arches.

impregnated cloth A cloth impregnated with resin, varnish, shellac, etc.

impregnated timber Timber into which a flame retarder, insect poison, and/or fungicide has been forced under pressure.

impregnation The process of adding chemical preservatives, resin, or fire retardants to wood under pressure. Also see **Bethell process**.

improved land Land which has been provided with water, sewers, sidewalks, and other basic facilities for residential or industrial development.

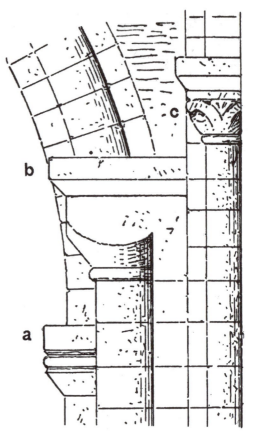

imposts, 1: *a*, impost of great arch; *b*, impost of apse vaulting; *c*, impost of wall arcades

improved wood Wood impregnated with resin and cured with heat and pressure to increase its strength, durability, and moisture resistance.

improvement A structure or public utility or any other installation or physical change made in a property to increase its value and utility or to improve its appearance.

in. Abbr. for "inch."

inactive leaf, inactive door That leaf of a pair of doors which does not contain a lock, and to which the **strike plate** is fastened to receive the latch or bolt of the **active leaf**; usually it is fixed in a closed position by bolts at the top and bottom of the door.

in-and-out bond In masonry, a **bond, 6** formed by headers and stretchers alternating vertically, esp. when formed at a corner, as by quoins.

in antis See **anta** and **distyle in antis**.

in-and-out bond: A, header; B, stretchers

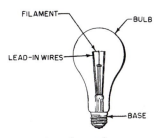

incandescent lamp

in antis

inbark   See **bark pocket**.

inbond   In masonry, bonded or forming a bond across the thickness of a wall; composed largely or entirely of **headers** or **bond-stones**.

INC   **1.** On drawings, abbr. for "incorporated." **2.** On drawings, abbr. for "incoming."

Inca architecture   The architecture of the Inca Empire in Peru from the 12th cent. until the Spanish conquest in the 16th cent., particularly fortified towns with massive stonework.

incand   Abbr. for "incandescent."

incandescence   The emission of visible light as a result of heating.

incandescent daylight lamp   An incandescent lamp having a blue-green glass bulb which makes the emitted light whiter by absorbing part of the yellow and red light; approximately 35% less efficient than the standard incandescent lamp.

incandescent direct-light lamp, bird's-eye lamp   An incandescent lamp, usually with a PS- or A-shaped bulb which is silvered from the maximum diameter to the base, leaving a clear

or frosted hemispherical region opposite the base end.

incandescent lamp, incandescent filament lamp   A lamp from which light is emitted when a tungsten filament is heated to incandescence by an electric current.

incandescent lamp base   See **lamp base**.

incandescent lamp filament   See **filament**.

incandescent lighting fixture   A **luminaire**, usually complete with incandescent lamp(s), socket(s), reflector, and often with a louver or diffusing medium.

incandescent special-service lamp   One of a class of lamps with special properties to meet particular needs, such as vibration service lamps, rough service lamps, cold service lamps, etc.

incasement   Same as **encasement**.

in cavetto   The reverse of relief, differing from intaglio in that the design is impressed into plaster or clay.

incavo   The hollowed or incised part of an intaglio.

incense cedar   A close-grained wood having a fragrant resinous odor; highly resistant to moisture.

incertum opus   See **opus incertum**.

inches of mercury   A unit used as a measure of pressure; equal to the pressure exerted by a column of mercury 1 inch (2.54 cm) high; equivalent to a pressure of 3386.4 newtons per square meter.

inch of water   A unit of pressure equal to the pressure exerted by a column of liquid water 1 in. high at a temperature of 39.2°F (4°C).

inch stuff   Building materials having a nominal 1-in. (2.5-cm) thickness, although actually measuring less.

INCIN   On drawings, abbr. for **incinerator**.

incinerator An apparatus in which solid, semi-solid, or gaseous combustible wastes are ignited and burned.

incipient decay Early stages of decay in wood in which the color has changed but the strength and hardness have not yet been affected.

incise **1.** To decorate by cutting or indenting a surface, as ceramic ware. **2.** To perforate the surface of timbers, poles, posts, etc., to increase penetration of wood preservatives.

INCL On drawings, abbr. for "include."

inclination The angle which a line or surface makes with the vertical, horizontal, or with another line or surface.

incline A sloping surface, i.e., neither horizontal nor vertical; a **slope**.

inclined-axis mixer, high-discharge mixer A truck equipped with a body for mixing concrete; consists of a revolving drum which rotates about an axis inclined to the bed of the truck chassis.

inclined end post An inclined compression member at the end of a **truss**.

inclined lift A powered passenger lift, installed on a stairway; used to raise or lower a person from one floor to another.

inclined shore A **raking shore**.

inclinometer A device for measuring the horizontal movement within a soil mass.

inclusion The presence of foreign matter in a finished material.

incombustible Same as **noncombustible**.

increaser In plumbing, a tapered coupling for joining a pipe or conduit to another of larger size.

incrustation **1.** The deposition of materials on the interior of pipes, vessels, or equipment from chemicals in the conveyed liquid. **2.** A decorative skin or coating of rich materials applied over commoner construction.

IND On drawings, abbr. for "industrial."

indemnification A contractual obligation by which one person or organization agrees to secure another against loss or damage from specified liabilities.

indent The gap left by the omission of stone, brick, or block units in a course of masonry; used for bonding future masonry.

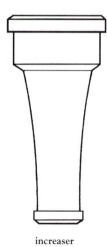

increaser

indented bar A type of **deformed bar**.

indented bolt A type of anchor bolt with surface indentations to increase its grip.

indented joint A joint used in joining timbers end to end; a notched **fishplate** is attached to one side of the joint to fit into 2 corresponding notches in the joined timbers; the entire assembly is fastened with bolts.

indented molding, indenting A molding with the edge toothed or indented in triangular tooth-like shapes.

indented molding

indented wire A type of wire having surface indentations to improve its bond when used in concrete reinforcement or for pretensioning tendons.

independent-pole scaffold Same as **double-pole scaffold**.

index of key words Part Four of the **uniform system** for construction specifications, data filing, and cost accounting.

index of plasticity See **plasticity index**.

Indian architecture The architecture of the Indian subcontinent, originally a timber and mud-brick architecture of which nothing survives. Early Buddhist monuments, chaitya halls, stupa rails, and toranas clearly imitate wood

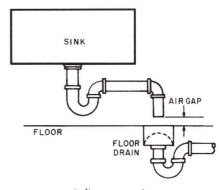

Indian architecture

construction, and timber buildings appear on relief representations. All surviving architecture is of stone, using exclusively a structural system of post and lintel, brackets, and corbels. The basically simple Indian architectural forms are generally obscured and overwhelmed by a rhythmical multiplication of pilasters, cornices, moldings, aediculae, roofs, and finials, and an exuberant and sensuous overgrowth of sculptural decoration.

Indian oak   See **teak**.

indicator bolt   A door bolt which indicates whether a **water closet** is vacant or occupied.

indicator button   A device incorporated in the lock of a door of a hotel room to indicate whether or not the room is occupied.

indicator light, indicator lamp   Same as **pilot light, 1**.

indicator valve   A **valve** whose design includes some mechanism to show that the device is open or closed.

indigenous   Said of a plant or tree which is native to the area in which it is grown.

indirect drain pipe   Same as **indirect waste pipe**.

indirect expense   Overhead expense; expense indirectly incurred and not directly chargeable to a specific project or task.

indirect footlight   A footlight unit with light sources placed so that the light rays strike the

area to be illuminated from a reflecting surface rather than directly.

indirect heating   See **central heating**.

indirect lighting   Lighting from luminaires which distribute 90% to 100% of the emitted light upward so that illumination is provided primarily by reflected light rather than by direct light.

indirect luminaire   A **luminaire** which emits 90% to 100% of its total output above a horizontal plane through it.

indirect solar water heating system   A solar water heating system employing a closed circulation loop through a **heat exchanger**; the fluid which flows through the **solar collector** is isolated from contact with other fluids in the system.

indirect system   A heating, air-conditioning, or refrigeration system in which a fluid is circulated to the space or material to be heated or cooled, or is used to heat or cool air which is so circulated; the fluid (such as air, water, or brine) is heated or cooled by products of combustion, by electric heating, or by a refrigerant.

indirect waste pipe   A **waste pipe** which does not connect directly with the building-drainage system, but discharges into it through a properly trapped fixture or receptable.

indirect waste pipe

indirect water heater   A water heater in which the temperature of the water in the system is increased by means of a remotely-located **heat exchanger**.

individual sewage-disposal system   A system of sewage treatment tanks and disposal facilities, designed for a single building, establishment, or lot, not served by a public sewer.

individual vent Of a plumbing fixture, a pipe which vents a fixture drain and which is connected to the main vent above it.

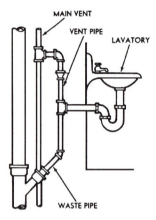

individual vent

individual water supply A supply other than an approved public water supply which serves one or more families.

induced draft The forced movement of air or gases caused by the suction created by the inlet side of a fan.

induced-draft boiler A boiler system having a power-operated fan at its discharge end; the fan draws air through the burner and boiler, conveying the products of combustion to the atmosphere through a short chimney.

induced-draft water-cooling tower A **water-cooling tower** having one or more fans located in the saturated air stream leaving the tower.

induced siphonage Siphonage of water from a fixture trap (i.e., the drawing away of water that forms a trap seal); usually due to an improperly installed vent pipe. As a result, when another fixture on the same vent pipe discharges, siphonage may be induced.

induction **1.** In air conditioning, the entrainment of air in a room by the flow of a stream of **primary air** from an air outlet. **2.** The process by which current in one conductor induces an electric current in a nearby conductor.

induction brazing A **brazing** process in which the required heat is obtained from the resistance of the work to an induced electric current.

induction heating In piping, the heat treatment of completed welds by the heat generated by the use of induction coils around the piping.

induction motor An alternating-current motor having its primary winding, on one member (which is usually the stator), connected to the source of electric power; a secondary winding on the other member (usually the rotor) carries the induced current.

induction soldering A soldering process in which the required heat is obtained from the resistance of the work to an induced electric current.

induction welding A welding process in which coalescence is produced by the heat obtained from resistance of the work to an induced electric current, with or without the application of pressure.

industrial area Any area devoted predominantly to manufacturing.

industrialized building system A building system of mechanized production design in which the subsystems and components have been integrated into an overall process, utilizing factors of planning, design, programming, production, transportation, and on-site assembly techniques. Also see **systems building**.

industrial design The art of utilizing the resources of technology to create and improve products and systems which serve human beings, taking into account factors such as safety, economy, and efficiency in production, distribution, and use. Such design may be expressed partly in external features, but predominantly in integrative structural relationships, responding to the perennial human need for meaningful form.

industrial lift A nonportable, power-operated hoisting and lowering mechanism for raising or lowering material vertically, operating entirely within one story of a building.

industrial occupancy **1.** Use of a building for the manufacture of products of any kind. **2.** Use of a building for processing, assembling, mixing, packaging, finishing or decorating, repairing, and similar operations. Also see **general industrial occupancy, high-hazard industrial occupancy, special-purpose industrial occupancy**.

industrial tubular door   A door constructed from tubular steel with locked seams; the corners are welded and all joints are ground smooth; the door panels consist of one or two sheets securely fastened to stiles and rails.

industrial waste   A waterborne waste resulting from an industrial process; differs in composition from domestic sewage wastes.

inelastic behavior   Deformation of a material that does not disappear on removal of the force that produced it.

inert base   A paint base which does not provide hiding, color, or drying properties. Its main function is to provide **solids**, usually at low cost.

inertia block   A concrete block which serves as a base for mechanical equipment such as fans or pumps; the block is mounted on a resilient support to reduce the transmission of vibration to the building structure.

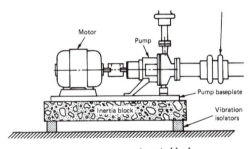

pump on an **inertia block**

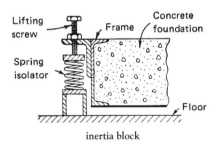

inertia block

inert pigment   **1.** A nonreactive pigment. **2.** An extender pigment, used to provide **solids** and bulk.

infant school (*Brit.*)   A form of primary school which gives instruction to 4- to 7-year-old children in preparation for grammar school.

infilling   Material used to fill the spaces, within a frame, between structural members of a building; provides additional thermal insulation, fire resistance, and stiffness. Also see **fill insulation**.

infiltration   **1.** The seepage or flow of air into a room or space through cracks around windows, under doors, etc. **2.** In a concrete sewer pipe laid in soil, the volume of groundwater that enters the pipeline system.

infirmary   A place which provides uncomplicated medical and nursing care, usually for residents or members of an institution, such as a school.

inflammable   Same as **flammable**.

inflatable gasket   A gasket whose effectiveness depends on a seal provided by inflation with compressed air.

inflatable structure   See **pneumatic structure**.

inflected arch   Same as **inverted arch**.

inflection point   Same as **point of inflection**.

inflow   The volume of any type of water entering a sewer pipe from outside sources not included under **infiltration**.

INFO   On drawings, abbr. for "information."

information outlet   In a telephone wiring system in a building, a connection device designed for a fixed location (usually on a wall) in which telephone wiring terminates; the outlet contains a female **jack** to receive a male plug that is inserted into it. Such outlets are used to connect a telephone, FAX, telephone answering machine, etc., to a telephone line.

infrared   That region of the electromagnetic spectrum at wavelengths immediately above the visible spectrum; the heat in this region of the spectrum which is generated by a light source usually is undesirable (since it represents a loss in efficiency), but such heat is used in industrial applications for drying, baking a surface, etc.

infrared drying   Drying by use of infrared lamps to decrease drying time.

infrared lamp   An incandescent lamp having a higher percentage of the radiant power in the infrared region than a standard incandescent lamp; has longer average life owing to the lower filament temperature; may have a red glass bulb to reduce the radiated visible light.

infrasound Acoustic oscillations having a frequency below the low-frequency limit (approximately 16 Hz) of audible sound.

in-glaze decoration A ceramic decoration applied on the surface of an unfired glaze and then matured with the glaze.

ingle A fireplace; a hearth.

inglenook A fireplace hearth in a corner of a room; often provided with seating; same as **chimney corner.**

ingot A mass of molten metal which has been poured into a mold to solidify; it differs from a casting in that it requires rolling or forging to become a finished or semifinished product.

ingot iron Same as **mild steel, 1.**

ingrown bark, inbark See **bark pocket.**

inhibiting pigment A pigment (such as lead and zinc chromate, zinc oxide, red lead, zinc metal, and barium metaborate) added to paint to inhibit or prevent rust and corrosion of metals or the formation of mildew.

inhibitor A substance added to paint to retard drying, skinning, mildew growth, etc. Also see **corrosion inhibitor, inhibiting pigment, drying inhibitor.**

initial backfill The material used in filling a trench from the top of the bedding to a specified height above a pipe which is laid in the trench.

initial drying shrinkage The difference between the initial length of a moist concrete specimen and the length of the specimen after it is first dried and has reached a stable length; usually expressed as a percentage of the initial moist length.

initial prestress The **prestressing** stress (or force) applied to **prestressed concrete** at the time of stressing.

initial rate of absorption See **absorption rate.**

initial set **1.** A degree of stiffening of a mixture of cement (or concrete or mortar) and water less than **final set**; generally stated as the time required for cement paste to stiffen sufficiently to resist the penetration of a weighted test-needle. **2.** Of a mastic compound, adhesive, or coating, the stage in curing or drying when the surface has become sufficiently firm to be unmarked when touched with the finger.

initial setting time The time required for a freshly mixed cement paste, mortar, or concrete to achieve **initial set.**

initial stress Stress in a **prestressed concrete** member before any loss of stress occurs.

injection burner A gas burner that employs a gas jet to thrust air for combustion into the burner and mix it with the gas.

injection molding A molding procedure whereby a heat-softened plastic material is forced from a cylinder into a relatively cool cavity which gives the article the desired shape.

inlay, intarsia, marquetry **1.** A shaped piece of one material embedded in another as part of a surface ornamentation. **2.** Such ornamentation as a whole. Also see **encaustic tile.**

inlay of black and white marble

in-line centrifugal fan A **centrifugal fan** which is specially designed to be connected to the ductwork in direct line with the discharge from the fan housing.

in-line pump A pump supported directly by the system piping (i.e., the piping carries the weight of the pump); usually mounted vertically to save floor space, with its weight centered over the piping.

inn **1.** A place which provides eating and drinking, but no lodging, for the public; a **tavern.** **2.** A **hotel.** **3.** A student hostel or residence. **4.** A **hospice.**

inner bead Same as **inside stop.**

inner casing   See **inside casing**.

inner court   **1.** An open, unoccupied space surrounded on all sides by the **exterior walls** of a building or structure. **2.** An open, unoccupied space surrounded by the exterior walls of a building and an interior lot line of the same premises.

inner hearth   That part of a hearth contained within a fireplace; the **back hearth**.

inner sanctum   A most sacred place.

inorganic material   A material which is composed of minerals, or made from minerals; not animal or vegetable in origin.

inorganic silt   See **silt**.

inosculating column   Same as **clustered column**.

inpaint   To renew damaged areas on paintings or painted surfaces by repainting.

INR   Abbr. for **impact noise rating**.

inrush current   See **lamp inrush current**.

INS   On drawings, abbr. for "insulate."

insanitary   Injurious to health or contrary to sanitary principles.

inscription   Lettering, often monumental, decorating architecture inside or out.

insect screen, window screen   A very light woven-wire used to prevent insects from flying through open windows or doors.

insect wire screening   A woven wire screening having a mesh small enough to provide protection against insects.

insert   **1.** A nonstructural repair to correct an appearance defect in laminated timber. **2.** An inlay of wood veneer, a patch, or a plug used to fill holes in plywood. **3.** See **patch, 2**.

insert card reader   A device for providing access to a locked door. The cardholder must insert a card (usually having a magnetic strip) into the device to unlock the door.

inserted column   A column which is partially inserted in a wall; an **engaged column**.

inserted grille   A grille that is fabricated separately for mounting in a prepared opening in a door.

inserted tenon   See **false tenon**.

inset dormer   A **dormer** that is partially set *below* a sloping roof, unlike the usual dormer that projects entirely *above* the sloping roof.

inset porch   Same as **integral porch**.

inside-angle tool   A **float** used in shaping inside angles in plastering and masonry.

inside caliper   A type of **caliper** which is especially designed for measuring the inside diameter of a cylinder or the distance between shapes.

inside caliper

inside casing, interior casing   The **inside trim** around the interior of a door or window frame.

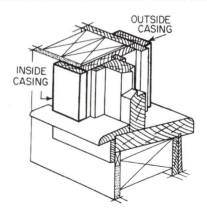

inside casing

inside chimney   Same as **interior chimney**.

inside corner molding   A molding covering the joint at the internal angle of two intersecting surfaces, as the metal coves used with plastic laminates, etc.

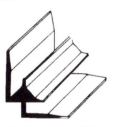

inside corner molding

inside-door lock, room-door lock A lock having a spring bolt (operated by a knob) and a dead bolt operated by a key.

inside finish See **interior trim**.

inside glazing External glazing which is installed from inside the building. Also see **internal glazing**.

inside lining See **inside casing**.

inside micrometer A micrometer especially designed for the accurate measurement of the inside diameter of a cylinder, such as a pipe.

inside stop, bead stop, inner bead, stop bead, window bead, window stop In a double-hung window, a strip of wood fixed to the casing, along the inner edge of the inner sash; restricts the motion of the sash to a vertical plane.

inside thread The thread on the inside of a pipe, fitting, or machine screw.

inside trim **1.** Any trim on the interior of a building. **2.** Trim around door or window openings; also called **inside casing**.

in situ In place, as in **cast-in-place concrete**.

in situ concrete See **cast-in-place concrete**.

insoluble residue That portion of an aggregate or cement which is not soluble in diluted hydrochloric acid.

inspection **1.** Examination of work completed or in progress to determine its compliance with contract requirements. **2.** Examination of the work by a public official, owner's representative, or others. **3.** The process of measuring or checking materials, workmanship, or methods for conformance with quality controls, specifications, and/or standards.

inspection chamber A shallow **manhole**.

inspection eye Same as **cleanout, 1**.

inspection fitting Same as **cleanout, 1**.

inspection junction Same as **cleanout**.

inspection list A list of items of work to be completed or corrected by the **contractor**.

inspector **1.** See **building inspector**. **2.** See **owner's inspector**. **3.** See **resident engineer**.

instal Abbr. for "install" or "installation."

instantaneous-type water heater A heater in which there is an exceedingly rapid increase in water temperature as the water flows through tubes surrounding an electric heating coil; best

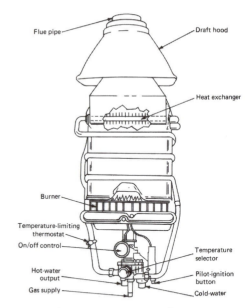

instantaneous-type water heater

suited for applications requiring a continuous flow of hot water. Must be used with care when the demand is low because accurate temperature control at low flow rates usually is poor.

instant lock A lock which is actuated automatically (by a spring) as the door is closed.

instant-start fluorescent lamp A **fluorescent lamp** designed to be started by high voltage without preheating of the electrodes; usually has single-pin base connections; a **slim-line lamp**.

InstCES Abbr. for "Institution of Civil Engineering Surveyors."

institutional occupancy The use of a building for the medical treatment or care of persons suffering from illness or infirmity; for the care of infants, convalescents, or aged persons; or for penal or corrective purposes.

instructions to bidders Instructions contained in the bidding requirements for preparing and submitting bids for a construction **project**. Also see **notice to bidders**.

insul Abbr. for "insulate" or "insulation."

insula **1.** In Roman town planning, a block of buildings surrounded by streets. **2.** A Roman apartment house occupying such a block.

insulated flange A **coupling** used in metal pipes to interrupt the electrical transmission path that would otherwise exist.

insulating board See **board insulation**.

insulating cement **1.** A combination of hydraulic-setting cement (or other bonding ingredient) and a loose-fill insulation, mixed to a workable putty-like consistency; used in insulation applications to fill voids, joints, etc. **2.** A mixture of dry granular, fibrous, flaky, or powdery materials that develops a plastic consistency when mixed with water, and when dried in place; forms a coherent covering that provides substantial resistance to heat transmission.

insulating concrete Concrete having low thermal conductivity; used as thermal insulation.

insulating fiberboard Fibrous insulating material (such as wood, cane, or other vegetable fibers) and binder, formed into a board. Manufactured units vary widely in thickness, linear dimensions, density, thermal resistance, and mechanical strength.

insulating form board Insulation board used as a permanent form for poured-in-place gypsum or lightweight-concrete roof decks.

insulating glass Two sheets of glass that are assembled and sealed around their edges as a single unit; the space between the glass sheets is dehydrated or filled with a gas. Such a unit is effective in reducing the transfer of heat through it.

insulating glass unit A panel of **double glazing** which is sealed around its periphery; provides increased resistance against the transmission of heat and sound.

insulating material See **electrical insulation, thermal insulation**.

insulating oil A type of oil used within the enclosure of a transformer, switch, or other electric device, for insulating and cooling purposes.

insulating plasterboard See **foil-backed gypsum board**.

insulating strip An **expansion strip**.

insulating varnish A varnish used as insulator on wire or electric circuits.

insulation See **electrical insulation, thermal insulation**.

insulation board See **board insulation**.

insulation lath Gypsum lath having an aluminum foil laminated to its back in order to provide a vapor barrier and reflective insulation against thermal losses.

insulation resistance The resistance to the flow of current through an insulating material resulting from an impressed direct voltage; usually expressed in ohms.

insulation test A test to determine the resistance of electrical insulation to the flow of direct current.

insulator See **electrical insulator**.

insurance See: **builder's risk insurance; completed operations insurance; comprehensive general liability insurance; contractor's liability insurance; employer's liability insurance; liability insurance; loss of use insurance; owner's liability insurance; professional liability insurance; property damage insurance; property insurance; public liability insurance; special hazards insurance; steam boiler and machinery insurance; workmen's compensation insurance**.

INT **1.** On drawings, abbr. for "intake." **2.** On drawings, abbr. for "interior." **3.** On drawings, abbr. for "internal."

intaglio **1.** Incised engraving, as opposed to carving in relief. **2.** The work producing such an object.

intaglio rilevato See **sunk relief**.

intake An opening through which water or air (or any other fluid) enters a system, chamber, plenum, pipe, or machine. Also see **outside-air intake**.

intake belt course A projecting course of masonry at a level where the wall is reduced in thickness.

intake door A door that penetrates a wall enclosing a **refuse chute** and through which waste material is deposited directly into the chute. (See illustration p. 504.)

intarsia Mosaic inlay, especially a form of wood inlay.

integral frame A type of doorframe; the trim, backbends, rabbets, and stops are all formed from one piece of metal for each jamb and for each head.

integral garage A garage that is part of the structure of a building.

integral lean-to In a colonial timber-framed house in America, a **lean-to** that was part of the original house construction, not a later addition or separate structure. This construction permitted the use of continuous rafters between the

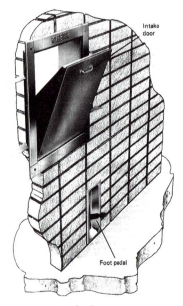

intake door

roof ridge and the eaves of the lean-to, thus providing a long, sloping roof of uniform pitch.

integral lock A type of **mortise lock** having its cylinder in the knob.

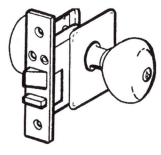

integral lock

integral mullion See **impost, 2**.

integral porch A porch whose floor is set within the main structure of a house, rather than being attached to the house, as in a **projecting porch**.

integral waterproofing The so-called "waterproofing" of concrete by the addition of an **admixture** during the mixing of the cement.

integrated ceiling A suspended ceiling system in which the acoustical, illumination, and air-handling components are combined as an integral part of a grid system.

integral porch

intercepting chamber A **manhole**.

intercepting drain A drain located between the water source and the protected area.

intercepting sewer A sewer which receives the dry-weather flow from a number of branch sewers or outlets (and sometimes a determined quantity of storm water).

interceptor A device to trap, remove, or separate deleterious, hazardous, or undesirable matter (such as oil, grease, gasoline, sand, and sediment) from normal waste conveyed through it, permitting normal sewage or liquid wastes to discharge into the disposal terminal by gravity.

intercolumniation **1.** The clear space between two adjacent columns, usually measured at the lower parts of the shafts. **2.** The system of

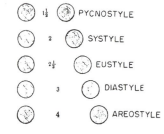

Diagram of **intercolumniation**

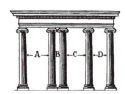

Examples of **intercolumniation:** A areostyle; B coupled columns; C diastyle; D eustyle

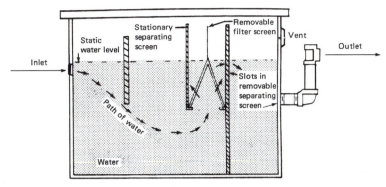

oil **interceptor**

spacing between columns which determines the style: *pycnostyle,* 1½ diameters; *systyle,* 2 diameters; *eustyle,* 2¼ diameters; *diastyle,* 3 diameters; *areostyle,* 4 diameters.

intercom   See **intercommunication system.**

INTERCOM   On drawings, abbr. for "intercommunication system."

intercommunication system   A communication system within a building or group of buildings with a microphone for speaking and a loudspeaker for listening at each of two or more locations.

interconnection   Any physical connection or arrangement of pipes between two otherwise separate building water-supply systems whereby water may flow from one system to the other, the direction of flow depending upon the pressure differential between the two systems; also called a **cross-connection.**

inter-crimp   In **wire cloth,** extra corrugations in the wires between points of crossing; usually applied to fine wire cloth having a wide mesh, to assure proper locking of the wires.

intercupola   **1.** The space between two cupolas. **2.** The space between two shells of a cupola.

interdentil   The space between two dentils.

interdome   The space between the inner and outer shells of a dome.

interduce   Same as **intertie.**

interface   The common boundary, often a plane surface, between two bodies or materials.

interfenestration   The space between windows in a façade consisting chiefly of the windows with their decorations.

interfilling   Same as **infilling.**

interglyph   The space between two grooves or cuts, as in a triglyph; usually a flat surface below which the groove itself has been sunk.

intergrown knot, live knot   A knot whose growth rings are intergrown with the surrounding wood.

interior casing   See **inside casing.**

interior chimney   A chimney that is built within the walls of a structure; often categorized according to its location, for example, an **end chimney;** compare with **exterior chimney.**

interior door   A door installed in an interior wall of a building, separating rooms or spaces within it.

interior finish   The exposed interior surfaces of a building, such as plaster or wood, or applied materials such as wallpaper, paint, or trim. Interior finishes may be classified according to an ASTM test for the surface burning characteristics of building materials, class A being the best and class E being the poorest in ability to resist fire propagation.

interior glazed   Said of glazing that has been set from within a building.

interior hung scaffold   A scaffold suspended from the ceiling or roof structure.

interior lot   A lot bounded by a street on one side only.

interior stair   A stair, within a building, that serves as an **exit** required by code.

interior trim, inside finish   Trim used on the interior of a building, esp. around door and window casings, baseboards, stairs, etc.

interior-type plywood   A plywood, bonded with glue, that has limited moisture resistance;

not durable when exposed to frequent or continuous wetting.

interior wall A wall within a building, entirely surrounded by the **exterior walls**.

interjoist The space between two joists.

interlace, entrelacs An ornament of bands or stalks elaborately intertwined, sometimes including fantastic images. Also see **knot**.

an ornament with **interlace**

interlaced arches See **interlacing arcade**.

interlaced fencing, interwoven fencing, woven board Fencing made from weaving thin, flat boards together.

interlacement band Same as **guilloche**.

interlacing arcade Arches resting on alternate supports in one row, the arches overlapping in series where they cross. Also see **intersecting arcade**.

interlacing arcade

interlocked Two or more components, members, or items of equipment which are arranged mechanically or electrically to operate or to be placed in some specific relationship with each other.

interlocked grain, twisted grain Wood in which the fibers are angled in different directions every few annual rings; produces ribbon-stripe grain when quartersawn.

interlocking joint **1.** A form of **joggle** in which a rib or other protrusion on one stone complements a routed groove or slot on another; prevents relative displacement. **2.** A joint formed between sheet-metal parts by engaging their edges which have been preformed to provide a continuous locked splice.

interlocking tile A single-lap tile made so that an edge of one tile fits under a groove along an edge in the next tile in the same course.

intermediate course Same as **binder course**.

intermediate floor beam In floor framing, any floor beam between the end floor beams.

intermediate metal conduit (IMC) See **electrical metallic conduit**.

intermediate rafter See **common rafter**.

intermediate rail A horizontal member of a door which is between the **top rail** and the **bottom rail**.

intermediate rib **1.** A rib in vaulting subordinate to the primary ribs. **2.** In a sexpartite vault, the transverse rib in the middle of the bay, above the intermediate and smaller piers.

intermediate stiffener Any one of the stiffeners on a beam or girder between the end stiffeners.

intermediate-temperature-setting adhesive An adhesive that sets in the temperature range 87° to 211°F (31° to 99°C).

intermediate truss The center truss of a three-truss span.

intermetium In an ancient Roman circus, a long barrier running down the arena between the two **metae**.

intermittent-flame-exposure test Part of an ASTM fire test of roof coverings; specified gas flames are applied to the test specimen for 3 to 15 cycles, according to the classification of roof covering.

intermittent weld A weld whose continuity is broken by recurring unwelded spaces.

intermodillion The recess between two **modillions**.

intermutule The space between two mutules, as in an architrave.

internal dormer A vertical window in a sloped roof; unlike the usual **dormer window**, it is not covered by a small pitched roof, but projects down from (and is set below) the slope of the main roof.

internal glazing Glazing installed in internal partitions. Also see **inside glazing**.

internally fired boiler A boiler whose furnace is wholly or partly surrounded by water.

internal-partition trap In plumbing, a **trap, 1** forming a seal by use of an internal partition; usually considered undesirable because of the possibility of holes developing in the partition.

internal-quality block A masonry block suitable only for concealed work.

internal-quality brick Brick suitable only for concealed work.

internal stress The stress that exists in a component (for example, at a joint) in the absence of applied external forces.

internal thread Same as **inside thread**.

internal treatment Water treatment by chemicals fed into a boiler rather than into the water before it enters the boiler.

internal vibration Energetic agitation of freshly mixed concrete by means of a vibrating device which is inserted into the concrete at selected locations.

intern architect One pursuing a program of training in practice under the guidance of practicing architects, with the objective of qualifying for registration as an **architect**.

International Revival A term occasionally used to describe a 1970s adaptation of the **International style** that emphasizes the use of pure geometric forms.

international rubber hardness degree A measure of hardness, the magnitude of which is derived from the depth of penetration of a specified indenter into a test specimen; 0° represents a material showing no measurable resistance to indentation, and 100° represents a material showing no measurable indentation.

International Standards Organization, International Organization for Standardization (ISO) A body which promotes the development of world-wide standards and which publishes such standards.

International style An architectural style that is minimalist in concept, devoid of regional characteristics, stresses **functionalism**, and rejects all nonessential decorative elements; it emphasizes the horizontal aspects of a building; developed during the 1920s and 1930s, in western Europe principally in the **Bauhaus** school, and also in America. Buildings in this style are usually characterized by simple geometric forms, often rectilinear, making use of reinforced concrete and steel construction with a nonstructural skin; occasionally, cylindrical surfaces; unadorned, smooth wall surfaces, typically of glass, steel, or stucco painted white; a complete absence of ornamentation and decoration; often, an entire blank wall; often a cantilevered upper floor or balcony; open interior spaces; a flat roof without a ledge; eaves that terminate at the plane of the wall; large areas of floor-to-ceiling glass or curtain walls of glass; metal window frames set flush with the exterior walls, often in horizontal bands; casement windows; sliding windows; glass-to-glass joints at the corners, without framing; plain doors that conspicuously lack decorative detailing. Houses are commonly asymmetric; in contrast, commercial buildings in this style are not only symmetric, but appear as a series of repetitive elements.

International System of Units (SI) A system of units based on the following fundamental quantities: metre, kilogram, second, ampere, kelvin, candela, and mole.

interpier sheeting Horizontal **sheeting** (usually wood) placed horizontally between underpinning pits; used where continuous underpinning is not required.

inter pit sheeting The **interpier sheeting** which is between concreted underpinning pits.

interrupted acoustical ceiling A discontinuous, suspended acoustical ceiling; the top of a partition extends through the upper surface of the ceiling. The partition may or may not extend upward to the overhead structure.

interrupted arch A segmental pediment whose center has been omitted, often to accommodate an ornament.

interrupted arch molding A common Norman molding consisting of a series of interrupted arches.

interrupted arch molding

intersecting arcade Arches resting on alternate supports in one row, the arches meeting on one plane at the crossings. Also see **interlacing arcade**.

intersecting arcade

intersecting gable See **cross gable**.

intersecting tracery Tracery formed by the curving upward, forking, and continuation of the mullions, springing from alternate mullions or from every third mullion and intersecting each other.

interstitial condensation Condensation of water vapor *within* an element of a building, e.g., within a wall.

interstitium The crossing in a cruciform church.

intertie In framing, a horizontal member, between the sill and head, which extends from one stud to the next in order to stiffen them.

inter-tie Same as **nogging piece, 1**.

intertriglyph The space between two triglyphs in a Doric frieze; a **metope**.

interwoven fencing See **interlaced fencing**.

intgl Abbr. for "integral."

intonaco The fine finish coat of plaster made with white marble dust to receive a fresco painting.

intrados The inner curve or face of an arch or vault forming the concave underside.

intruder alarm system See **burglar alarm system**.

intumescence The process of swelling up, as with the application of heat, such as vermiculite that is heat-treated for use in thermal insulation.

intumescent Said of a material that swells and chars when exposed to flame and that forms an insulating fire-retardant barrier between the flame and material.

inverse condemnation A legal doctrine holding that, in certain circumstances, where private property is destroyed or substantially diminished in value by government action, the conduct of the government is regarded as the *taking* of the property and the owner of the property must be compensated in fair value by the government.

inverse-square law A law which applies to a light source (or to a sound source) that is in a space far away from any reflecting surface: the intensity at a point, as measured on a surface which is perpendicular to a line drawn between the point and the source, varies inversely with the square of the distance between the point and the source. (For sound waves, this decrease in intensity is equivalent to a drop in sound-pressure level of 6 dB for each doubling of distance from the source.)

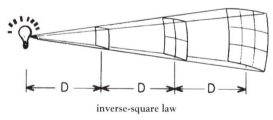

inverse-square law

invert In plumbing, the lowest point or the lowest inside surface of a channel, conduit, drain, pipe, or sewer pipe.

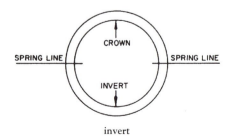

invert

inverted arch   An arch with its intrados below the springing line; esp. used to distribute concentrated loads in foundations.

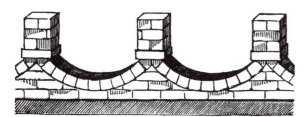

inverted arch

Ionic order: *above,* capital; *below,* base

inverted joint   A **fitting, 1** which is turned upside down, reversed in position, or turned in an opposite direction.

inverting ballast   A lamp **ballast, 1** designed to operate on direct current.

invisible hinge   A hinge so constructed that no parts are exposed when the door is closed.

invitation to bid   A solicitation of competitive bids. The term usually is employed in connection with private construction projects, but also may be used for government projects, for the purchase of supplies or other goods, or in connection with the sale of property. Also see **advertisement for bids**.

invited bidders   The bidders selected by the architect and the owner as the only ones from whom bids will be received.

involute   **1.** A curve traced by a point at the end of a string as the string is unwound from a stationary cylinder. **2.** Curved spirally.

inwrought   Closely combined or profusely embellished.

Ionic   **1.** Pertaining to, or characteristic of, Ionia, the eastern part of the Greek world. **2.** Same as **Ionic order**.

Ionic capital   The topmost member of a column of the Ionic order; the twin **volutes** in the Greek Ionic order are larger and more conspicuous than the corresponding volutes in the Roman Ionic order.

Ionic order   One of the five orders in Classical architecture, originated by the Ionian Greeks. Usually characterized by columns usually having 24 **flutes** separated by narrow fillets; an **entablature**, a frieze without triglyphs; dentils in the cornice; elegant detailing; less elaborate than the **Corinthian order** and less heavy in appearance than the **Doric order**. Pilasters in the Ionic order often have fluted shafts with a capital consisting of a band of anthemions, with egg-and-dart moldings above.

ionization-type detector   A type of fire detector that uses a radioactive source to develop a current across an air gap within the detector; when products of combustion enter the detector, they alter the flow of current and activate an alarm; particularly useful where early-warning detection is essential either because of special safety requirements or because protection is required for property of high value.

IPS   **1.** Abbr. for "iron-pipe size"; a nominal dimension, inside diameter. **2.** Abbr. for "International Pipe Standard." **3.** Abbr. for "inside pipe size."

IR   Abbr. for "inside radius."

iridescent glass   A translucent glass having an iridescence similar to that of a soap bubble; see **opalescent glass**.

Irish moss   An Atlantic Coast seaweed; used to make size for paint.

iron   A ductile metallic element from which **pig iron** and steel are made; used in its relatively crude form for making tools, castings, and so on. Also see **bar iron, cast iron, malleable iron, ornamental iron, wrought iron**.

iron back   A cast-iron **fireback**.

iron blue   See **Prussian blue**.

iron cement   A cement composed of cast-iron borings or filings, sal ammoniac, and additives; used for mending or joining cast-iron parts.

iron core Of stairs, a steel bar enclosed by a wooden handrail.

iron framing A system of structural ironwork for buildings, first developed at the end of the 18th century. The Crystal Palace, constructed in New York City in 1853, provided a dramatic example of its application in America. Also see **cast iron** and **cast-iron front**.

iron oxide A principal ingredient in a family of inorganic pigments, ranging from yellow through red and from purple to black; used extensively in paints.

iron pipe size The nominal inside dimension of a pipe.

iron titanate See **ilmenite**.

ironwork Objects or parts of objects made of **cast iron** or **wrought iron**; initially utilitarian,

later often elaborate and ornamental; also see **cast-iron lacework**.

irregular pitch A roof whose slope is not constant.

irrigation pipe Any type of pipe through which water is distributed for irrigation.

irrigation system See **lawn sprinkler system**.

I-section A cross section having an I-shape, e.g., an I-beam with a top and bottom flange connected by a vertical web.

Islamic architecture, Muslim architecture The architecture of the peoples of Islamic faith, also called Mohammedan, which from the 7th century onward expanded throughout the Mediterranean world and as far as India and China, and beyond, producing a variety of great regional works and local decorative styles. It is characterized by domes, horseshoe and round arches, tunnel vaults and richly decorated orna-

ironwork

Islamic horseshoe arch

mentation which is geometric because of the ban on human and animal representation. Also see **Muslim architecture**.

island-base kitchen cabinet   A free-standing kitchen cabinet placed below a counter or work surface; the ends of the cabinet are exposed.

ISO   Abbr. for **International Standards Organization**.

isocephalic   In bas-relief, having the heads nearly on a horizontal line; esp. said of the heads of human figures in a frieze or band.

isocephalic: from the frieze of the Parthenon

isodomum   In ancient Roman masonry and Greek, an extremely regular masonry pattern in which stones of uniform length and uniform height are set so that each vertical joint is centered over the block beneath. Horizontal joints are continuous, and the vertical joints form discontinuous straight lines; **opus isodomum**.

isodomum

isofootcandle line   See **isolux line**.

isolated   Said of a space not readily accessible to persons unless special means for access are used.

isolating switch   A switch for isolating an electrical circuit from its source of power; it is intended to be operated only after the circuit has been opened by some other means.

isolation joint   A joint, such as an expansion joint, between two adjacent structures which are not in physical contact.

isolation strip   Same as **expansion strip**.

isolation transformer   In an electrical system, a transformer that prevents one section of the system from undesirably influencing another section.

isolator   See **vibration isolator**.

isolux diagram   See **isolux line**.

isolux line   A line through all points on a surface where the illumination is the same; called an **isofootcandle line** if the illumination is expressed in footcandles. A series of such lines for various illumination values is called an "isolux diagram."

isometric drawing   A form of three-dimensional projection in which all of the principal planes are drawn parallel to corresponding established axes and at true dimensions; horizontals usually are drawn at 30° from the normal horizontal axes; verticals remain parallel to the normal vertical axis.

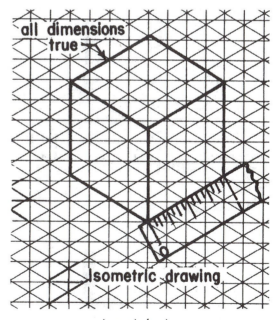

isometric drawing

isothermal   Said of a process which takes place at constant temperature.

isotropic   Said of a material which has the same physical properties in all directions.

IST Abbr. for **inside trim**.

ISWG Abbr. for "Imperial standard wire gauge."

Italianate style An eclectic style of Italian-influenced residential and commercial architecture; fashionable in England and America from the 1840s to around 1890. Italianate style residential buildings may be classified as: **Villas**: Domestic architecture intended to resemble prosperous farmhouses or country manor houses of northern Italy; usually two stories high, with an attic story; **Town houses**: Urban row houses, commonly three or four stories in height with a flat or very low-pitched roof; mullions divide both the upper and lower window sashes vertically into two panes. **Commercial Italianate style** buildings: a raised pediment above the roofline at the center of the façade, often with the name of the building and/or the date of its completion, and a cast-iron façade. **Palazzi**: See **Italian Renaissance Revival**.

Italianate style buildings are commonly characterized by a two-storied structure with exterior wall surfaces of smooth ashlar masonry, and rough-cast brick, stucco, or wood clapboard siding; classical columns, and pilasters; balustraded balconies; a **belt course** encircling the building; wide, projecting cornices with decorative brackets for support; corner quoins; a square tower; a porch; a gabled roof and/or **hipped roof**; a cupola or belvedere, chimney shafts with ornate caps; narrow double-hung window sashes commonly having arched (rather than rectangular) upper sashes; windows often topped with a segmental arch, with a hooded crown, or with a crown supported by decorative brackets; a pair of decora-

tively paneled double doors at the main entrance, the upper parts of which are glazed; often, a round-topped door or a door set in a round arch. The latter phase of Italianate style, sometimes referred to as High Victorian Italianate, is usually more highly decorated than its earlier counterpart. Also see **Tuscan Villa style**.

Italian molding A wide, heavy **bolection molding**, often used to surround a fireplace.

Italian order Same as **Composite order**.

Italian Renaissance Revival An architectural style emulating the Renaissance palazzi of Northern Italy; most popular from 1800s to about 1930. Buildings in this style are usually characterized by façades that are commonly symmetrical and essentially flat; rectangular or square in plan; usually two or three stories high; masonry or stucco walls; a different architectural treatment on different stories; an elaborate **belt course** between stories; a massive cornice that rests directly on the architrave (the frieze being omitted); pilasters, rusticated quoins, dentils, and decorative detailing; a recessed entry porch flanked with classical columns or pilasters; prominent arcading on the ground floor of public buildings and a recessed arcaded gallery on the floors above; commonly, a low- to moderate-pitched, ceramic-tiled hipped roof; widely overhanging eaves with decorative brackets below; occasionally, a flat roof with a balustrade or roofline parapet above an elaborate cornice; commonly, a different type of window on each story; on the ground floor, elaborate, tall, narrow windows placed in a regular pattern, set symmetrically on both sides of the main entrance; the second-story window heads often pedimented

Italianate style villa

Italian Renaissance Revival

and supported by **ancons** in elaborate buildings; windows on the uppermost story are usually the smallest and simplest, being square in shape; arches frequently above exterior doors; a hooded entryway; an entablature, supported by pilasters, over the entrance. Sometimes called Italian Renaissance style or Second Renaissance Revival, this style is occasionally subdivided into the *North Italian* or *Venetian mode* and the *Romano-Tuscan* or *Florentine mode*.

Italian Renaissance style Same as **Italian Renaissance Revival**.

Italian roof See **hipped roof**.

Italian tile Same as **mission tile**.

Italian tiling Same as **pan-and-roll roofing tile**.

Italian Villa style A term often used as a synonym for **Italianate style**.

itinera versurarum The side entrances from the wings to the stage of an ancient Roman theatre.

ivory black See **animal black**.

iwan A large vaulted hall having one side open to a court; prevalent in Parthian, Sassanian, and Muslim architecture.

izba A Russian **log cabin**, log house, or hut.

Izod impact test A type of **impact test** in which a single impact is delivered by a falling pendulum.

J

J Symbol for **joule**.

J&P Abbr. for "joist and planks."

jacal **1.** A rectangular structure, either partially enclosed or open on all four sides, used as a temporary storage place, such as for grain; usually a flat roof supported by two to four posts on each side of the structure (depending on its size) and often covered with a layer of adobe mud or straw. **2.** In the American Southwest, a crude house having walls built of closely spaced upright sticks, or poles driven into the ground, and small branches interwoven between them; then covered with mud or an adobe clay; usually plastered to provide additional weather protection; a flat roof is supported by horizontal logs and then covered with thatching, often with a layer of adobe atop the thatching. **3.** Same as **wigwam**.

jack **1.** A portable machine, variously constructed for exerting great force for moving a heavy body through a short distance. Also see **hydraulic jack; jackscrew**. **2.** An electrical receptacle into which a **plug, 7** is inserted to make electrical contact between communication circuits.

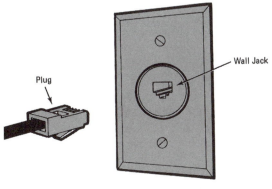

jack, 2

jack arch Same as **flat arch**.

jack boom A **boom** which supports sheaves that carry lines to a working boom.

jacked pile A **pile** (usually sections of pipe spliced together) which is forced into the ground to a bearing stratum, jacking it against a building or structure above; used primarily for underpinning.

jacket **1.** A metal or cloth covering over the heat insulation which is applied to exposed heating pipes and ducts. **2.** An outer casing around a pipe or vessel, the space between being filled with a fluid for cooling, heating, or maintaining a fixed temperature.

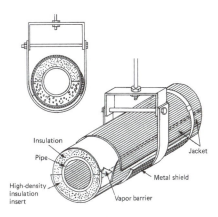

jacket, 1

jackhammer **1.** An **airhammer**. **2.** A hand-operated, pneumatic, rock drill.

jacking The imposition of a static driving force on a pile by the use of jacks; a technique widely used for installing piles in the underpinning of structures.

jacking device **1.** A device used to raise a vertical **slipform**. **2.** A device used to stress the tendons in prestressed concrete.

jacking dice In foundation work, blocks used as temporary fillers during jacking operations.

jacking force The force exerted temporarily by the device which introduces tension in **tendons** in **prestressed concrete**.

jacking plate A steel plate, atop a **pile** during jacking operations, which is used to transmit the load of the jack to the pile.

jacking stress The maximum stress occurring during the stressing of a **tendon** in **prestressed concrete**.

jack lagging The rough **lagging, 2** in **centering** an arch or vault.

jack pile Same as **jacked pile**.

jack plane A carpenter's **plane**, of medium size; used for coarse work.

jack post A post comprising two telescoping sections, so that it is adjustable in height; used to support a floor beam.

jack rafter Any rafter that is shorter than the usual length of the rafters used in the same building; esp. occurs in hip roofs.

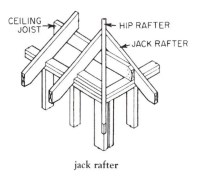

jack **rafter**

jack rib Any rib in a framed arch or dome shorter than the others.

jackscrew A jack in which a screw is used for lifting; carries a plate which bears on the load.

jack shore A telescoping, or otherwise adjustable, single-post metal shore.

jack timber A timber in a framework which, being intercepted by some other piece, is shorter than the rest.

jack truss A roof truss which is smaller in size than the others, usually because of location, as in a **hip roof**.

Jacobean architecture An imprecise term, applied to an English architectural style of the early 17th century that adapted the Elizabethan style to continental Renaissance influences; applied to buildings erected during the reign of

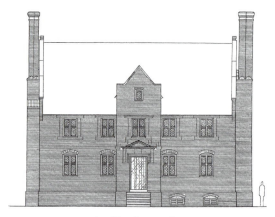

example of **Jacobean architecture**

James I (1603–1625) and thereafter. Large houses were usually two to three stories high and might have elaborate multicurved Flemish gables, Tudor arches, and decorative chimneys, and casement windows (separated by stone or cement mullions) that had small, diamond-shaped panes of glass held in place by grooved strips of lead.

Jacobethan style, Jacobethan Revival A mode of **Tudor Revival architecture**, of limited popularity from the 1800s to about 1920, that was a blend of Jacobean and Elizabethan architecture; hence, the compound term. Such buildings are often characterized by front-facing gables that rise above the roofline; elaborate brickwork or stonework; quoins at the corners of the building; occasionally, turrets or towers; stone **straight-line gables** or **multicurved gables**, tall decorative chimneys; rectangular window frames, usually containing small, leaded panes of glass set in casement sashes.

jagging Notching or indenting, as on beams.

jail **1.** A prison. **2.** A building or place for the legal detention of persons.

jal-awning window A window having a number of top-hinged out-swinging pivoted **sashes (ventilators, 2)** one above the other, which are operated by one or more controls, with individually operated locking mechanisms.

jalousie A shutter or blind with fixed or adjustable slats which exclude rain and provide ventilation, shade, and visual privacy.

jalousie window A window consisting of a series of overlapping horizontal glass louvers which pivot simultaneously in a common frame and are actuated by one or more operating devices so that the bottom edge of each louver swings toward the exterior and the top edge swings toward the interior during opening.

jamb One of the vertical members at each side of an opening such as a doorframe, window frame, or fireplace.

jamb block

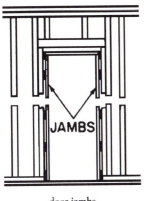

door **jambs**

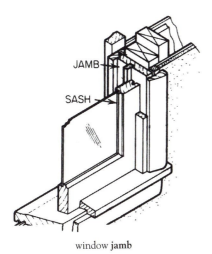

window **jamb**

jamb anchor A metal device inserted in the back of the jamb of a doorframe or window frame to anchor the frame to the wall.

jamb block, sash block A concrete masonry unit which has an end slot (rabbet) for use at an opening to receive a jamb.

jamb depth The overall depth of a door-frame, measured from one face to the other.

jamb entension The section of a metal door jamb which extends below the level of the finish floor for attachment to the rough floor.

jamb horn The part of the jamb of a window frame which extends beyond the sill or head jamb.

jamb lining 1. A strip of wood which is applied to the inside edge of a window jamb to increase its width. 2. Same as **door case**.

jamb post An upright timber at the side of an opening; a wood **jamb**.

jamb shaft A small shaft having a capital and a base, placed against or forming part of the jamb of a door or window; occurs mostly in medieval architecture. (*See illustration p. 518.*)

jambstone A stone which forms a **jamb** of a door.

jamb stove An 18th cent. cast-iron stove at the back wall of a fireplace; projects into and heats the room adjoining the back of the fireplace.

jam nut Same as **locknut**.

janua In ancient Roman architecture, a front door which opens on the street.

Janus Same as **bifrons**.

japan A short-oil varnish, usually dark in color, which produces a hard glossy surface.

Japanese architecture Architecture of timber construction exclusively, from the 5th cent. A.D. under the strong influence of China. Simple pavilion-like structures consist of a wooden framework of uprights and tie beams supported by a platform, with nonbearing plaster or wood panel walls, sliding partitions, and doors and windows of lightweight material—often paper.

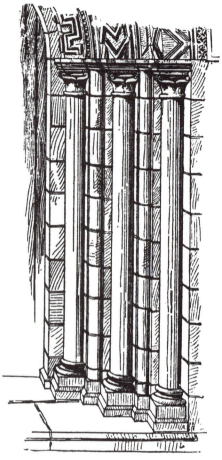

jamb shaft

The tiled, hipped roofs are widely projecting and upward-turning, on elaborate bracket systems. Stone is used only for pillar bases, platforms, and fortification walls. Great emphasis is put on the integration of buildings with their surroundings, with verandas providing the transition. Proportions of floor dimensions, height, and length of walls follow fixed standards. Modern Japanese architecture, though under strong Western influence, has developed a reinforced concrete style of its own, steeped in its tradition of timber construction.

Japanese ash, tamo   A light, yellowish wood having a grain similar to oak; esp. used for veneer.

Japanese lacquer   See **Chinese lacquer**.

Japanese tung oil   See **tung oil**.

jardin anglais   Literally, an **English garden**.

jaspé   Mottled and marbled to resemble variegated stone, and to mask signs of use; e.g., jaspé linoleum.

jawab   A false building or structure which is constructed for aesthetic reasons, to achieve a desired balance or proportions.

jaw crusher   A machine for crushing rock between two inclined jaws.

JB   Abbr. for **junction box**.

JCT   On drawings, abbr. for "junction."

jealous glass   Any nontransparent glass, for example, ground glass.

jedding ax   A stonemason's tool; a **kevel, 1**.

Jeffersonian Classicism   See **Classical Revival architecture**.

jemmy   Same as **jimmy**.

jenny   A machine which shoots out a jet of steam; used for cleaning surfaces.

jerkinhead, clipped gable, hipped gable, shreadhead   The end of a roof when it is formed into a shape intermediate between a gable and a hip; the gable rises about halfway to the ridge, resulting in a truncated shape, the roof being inclined backward from this level.

jerkinhead

jerrybuilt   Built in a flimsy manner.

Jerusalem cross   A Greek cross with a smaller Greek cross inscribed in each of the four spaces between the arms.

Jesse window   A painted window containing a decorative genealogical tree representing the genealogy of Christ.

jesting beam   A beam introduced for the sake of appearance and not for use.

jetted pile   A pile which has been sunk by **jetting**.

jetting **1.** The sinking of **piles** or **well points** by the use of a water jet, e.g., through a hole in a cast concrete pole or by inserting a pile in a hole produced by jetting; esp. used where pile driving may damage neighboring buildings. **2.** The compacting of backfill around a pipe by introducing water under pressure in the trench in which the pipe is laid.

jetty A projecting part of a building, as a bay window or the upper story of a timber house.

jib **1.** Of a crane or derrick, see **boom, 2. 2.** Same as **gib** or **jib door.**

jib boom A piece which extends the upper end of a **boom, 2.**

jib crane A **crane** having a swinging boom.

jib door, gib door A door which is flush with, and treated in the same manner as, the surrounding wall so as to be concealed; has no visible hardware on the room side.

jib window Same as **jib door.**

jig A device for guiding or holding a part or parts in correct mechanical alignment, either in the process of fabrication or in the final assembly of the parts.

jigger saw Same as **jigsaw.**

jigsaw An electrically powered saw having a narrow blade which moves with a reciprocating motion, in a vertical direction, through the surface of a table on which work is placed; esp. used for cutting curves and ornamental patterns.

jimmer See **gemel.**

jimmy, jemmy A short **crowbar.**

jinnie wheel Same as **gin block.**

jitterbug A **tamper,** usually pneumatic, for concrete.

job **1.** Same as **project. 2.** Same as **work, 1.**

job captain A member of the architect's staff normally responsible, on a given project, for the preparation of drawings and their coordination with other documents.

job site The **site, 1** of a construction project.

job superintendent See **superintendent.**

jog Any irregularity in a line or surface.

joggle **1.** A notch or projection in one piece of material which is fitted to a projection or notch in a second piece to prevent one piece from slipping on the other. **2.** A **stub tenon** on the end of a timber which prevents the timber from moving laterally; also called a **joggle joint, 2. 3.** An enlarged area on a post to support the foot of a strut.

joggle beam A built-up beam, the parts of which are fixed in place by joggles.

joggle joint **1.** A joint between two blocks of material (such as masonry) which fit one into the other by a **joggle, 1. 2.** Same as **joggle, 2.**

joggle joints

joggle piece A **joggle post, 2.**

joggle post **1.** A post made of two or more pieces of timber joggled together. **2.** A **king post** having shoulders or notches at its lower end to support the feet of struts.

joggle tenon Same as **stub tenon.**

joggle truss A roof truss with a single post placed centrally and fitted to the chord by a sub-tenon or the like, the chord being on top, and the post hanging downward and having its lower end connected with the ends of the chord by oblique braces.

joggle work In masonry, construction in which stones are keyed together by **joggles, 1.**

joiner's chisel Same as **paring chisel.**

joiner's finish See **carpenter's finish.**

joiner's gauge A **marking gauge.**

joinery The craft of woodworking by joining pieces of wood, esp. of the finish and trim workings of the interior of a structure, such as doors, paneling, sashes, etc., as distinguished from **carpentry,** which suggests framing and rough work.

joining The junction of two separate plaster applications of the same coat, usually within a single surface plane.

joint **1.** The space between adjacent surfaces (as between masonry units), or the place where two members or components are held together by nails, fasteners, cement, mortar, etc. **2.** In steel construction, the area where two or more steel surfaces are attached; often characterized by the type of weld or fastener employed. Also see **masonry joint** and **wood joint.**

joint bolt See **handrail bolt**.

joint compound In gypsum board construction, a compound used for taping and/or finishing joints.

joint efficiency In welding, the ratio of the strength of a joint to the strength of the **base metal**; expressed in percent.

jointer **1.** A metal tool used to cut a joint partly through fresh concrete. **2.** In masonry, a tool for filling the cracks between courses of bricks or stones. **3.** In masonry, a bent strip of iron inserted into a wall to strengthen a joint. **4.** In carpentry, a long plane, esp. used to square the edges of boards or veneer so that they will make a close joint with other pieces.

jointer plane Same as **jointer, 4**.

joint fastener See **corrugated fastener**.

joint filler **1.** Any putty-like material used to fill joints, as in plasterboard construction. **2.** A strip of extruded resilient material used for filling a joint.

jointing **1.** In masonry, the finishing of joints between courses of bricks or stones before the mortar has hardened. **2.** The machining of a true and flat surface on one face or edge of a wood member. **3.** The first operation in sharpening a cutting tool, whereby the tips of all teeth or knives are ground or filed to the intended cutting circle.

jointing compound Any material used to seal a plumbing joint.

jointing rule A long straightedge used by masons in drawing lines and in pointing.

jointless flooring Any type of flooring (e.g., terrazzo) that can be laid without construction joints.

joint mold, section mold A shaped template, usually of plywood or zinc; used for casting a plaster member.

joint movement The difference in width of a joint between its fully open and fully closed positions.

joint reinforcement Any type of steel reinforcement, such as reinforcing bars or steel wire, which is placed in or on mortar bed joints.

joint reinforcement tape Any strip of fabric, woven fiberglass, metal, mesh, paper, or other material, used with a cementitious material to reinforce the joint between adjacent gypsum boards.

joint residue An accumulation of foreign matter, old sealant material, and protrusions that must be removed from the walls of a joint prior to sealing.

joint rod, joint rule A piece of metal, usually 2 to 24 in. (approx. 5 to 60 cm) long and 4 in. (10 cm) wide with a 45° angle cut at one end, used to form and shape mitered plaster joints in cornice work.

joint runner In plumbing, an incombustible material (such as asbestos) used to hold molten lead that is poured in the bell of a joint, such as a bell-and-spigot joint.

joint runner

joint sealant **1.** An impervious **sealant** used to fill joints or cracks in concrete or mortar. **2.** See **preformed sealant**. **3.** See **jointing compound**.

joint shingle A wood roofing shingle that is attached by nailing edge to edge rather than overlapping.

joint tape A tape used to cover joints formed by adjacent sheets of wallboard.

joint tenancy Ownership of property by two or more persons in which, upon the death of one, his interest devolves upon the other or others until a sole owner survives.

joint venture A collaborative undertaking by two or more persons or organizations for a specific project (or projects) having many of the legal characteristics of a partnership.

joist   One of a series of parallel beams of timber, reinforced concrete, or steel used to support floor and ceiling loads, and supported in turn by larger beams, girders, or bearing walls; the widest dimension is vertically oriented. Also see **binding joist, boarding joist, bridging joist, ceiling joist, common joist, floor joist, principal joist, sleeper joist.**

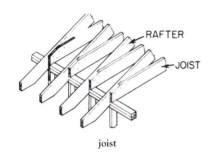

joist

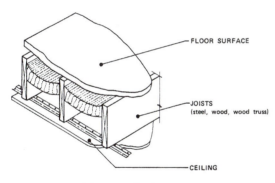

joists   in a flooring system

joist anchor   A **beam anchor.**

joist bridging   Same as **cross bridging.**

joist hanger   A metal angle or strap used to fix a **joist** to a beam or girder.

joist trimmer   Same as **trimming joist.**

joule   A unit of energy or work; equals the work done by a force of 1 newton which acts over a distance of 1 metre in the direction of the force.

JR   On drawings, abbr. for "junior."

JT   On drawings, abbr. for "joint."

jube   A screen separating the chancel from the nave or aisles, or both.

judas, judas-hole, judas window   A small trap or hole in a door for peering or watching, as in a prison door.

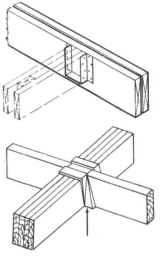

joist hangers

judgment lien   A charge against property of a judgment debtor (one against whom a judgment has been rendered by a court and who has not paid it) to secure payment of the judgment; may arise automatically in some states by operation of law, and in other states may require certain procedural steps on the part of the judgment creditor; acts as an encumbrance on the property until discharged, usually through satisfaction of the judgment.

jube

Judendstil

Jugendstil "Youth style"; the German version of Art Nouveau.

jumbo A traveling support for concrete forms.

jumbo brick A brick larger in size than standard.

jump A step in a masonry foundation.

jumper **1.** A short length of electric cable fitted with connectors at both ends, connected across a device in an electric circuit so that the current bypasses the device. **2.** A steel bar which is moved up and down manually in a borehole in the ground; used as a drilling or boring tool.

jumper tube A pipe or hose which is used to bypass the usual flow of a liquid or gas.

jump joint Same as a **butt joint** or **flush joint**.

jumpover See **return offset**.

junction box In electric wiring, a box which protects splices in conductors or joints in runs of raceways or cables; has a removable cover to provide easy access.

junior beam One of the standardized categories of hot-rolled steel, shaped I-beams.

junior channel A lightweight structural channel.

junior college A post-high school institution which offers a 2-year program of study of a ter-

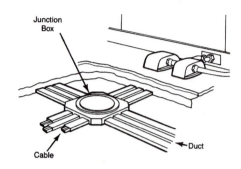

junction box

minal nature or in preparation for continued college studies.

junior mortgage One in which the lender's claim against the owner is subordinate to that of a first mortgage holder or another claim which has priority.

jute A plant fiber; forms a cheap, strong, durable yarn; used in the manufacture of canvas and hessian and for the backing of carpet to add strength and stiffness.

jutty A **jetty**.

jut window Any window that projects from the line of the building, as a **bow window** or **bay window**.

K

k **1.** Prefix for "kilo," indicating multiplication by 1000. **2.** Symbol for "co-efficient of thermal conductivity."

K **1.** Abbr. for **key**. **2.** Abbr. for **kip**. **3.** Abbr. for **kitchen**. **4.** Symbol for "Kelvin."

Kaaba A cube-shaped, flat-roofed building in the center of the Great Mosque at Mecca; the most sacred shrine of the Muslims.

Kabah Same as **Kaaba**.

kal'a, qala'a An Arabic fortress or stronghold built on a hill.

kalamein door A door of composite construction, usually having a wood core and clad with galvanized sheet metal, sometimes with panels of sheetrock or asbestos.

kalamein fire door See **metal-clad fire door**.

kalsomine Same as **calcimine**.

kaolin A mineral, usually white, composed principally of hydrous aluminum silicate, of low iron content; used in the manufacture of white cement.

kaolinite One of the clay materials consisting of a hydrous aluminum silicate.

kasr, qasr An Arabic palace, castle, or mansion.

katabasis In the Greek Orthodox church, a place under the altar for relics.

KD **1.** Abbr. for **kiln-dried**. **2.** Abbr. for **knocked down**.

KDF Abbr. for "**kalamein door** and frame."

keblah See **kiblah**.

keel An appendage of a molding, usually a fillet, on the furthest projection of a molding.

keel arch Same as **ogee arch**.

keel molding A **brace molding** in which the ogee curves meet sharply at a point or fillet more or less resembling the shape of a ship's keel.

Keene's cement, flooring cement, gypsum cement, hard-burnt plaster, tiling plaster A hard, white, high-strength, quick-setting finishing plaster; takes a high polish;

keel molding: *a*

made by burning gypsum at a high temperature, grinding to a fine powder, and then adding alum (to accelerate the set).

keep, donjon The stronghold of a medieval castle, usually in the form of a massive tower, and a place of residence, esp. in times of siege.

keep

keeper Same as **strike plate**.

keeping room A room at the back of a colonial New England house, which served as a combination kitchen, living room, and workroom.

Kelly ball test, ball test A test which uses a device consisting of a metal plunger (having a hemispherical bottom) which is guided by side stirrups; indicates the consistency of fresh concrete by the depth of penetration when the plunger drops.

kelvin (K) The International Standard unit of temperature. Absolute zero equals 0 K = −273.16°C = 459.69°F. A temperature increase of 1 K is numerically equal to an increase of 1°C.

Kentish tracery Circumscribed tracery motif, with foils separated by barbs or with forked cusps.

keratin A proteinaceous material used as a retarder for plaster.

kerb British variant of **curb**.

kerf **1.** In a suspended acoustical ceiling, a groove cut into the edges of an acoustical tile to receive **splines** or supporting members of the ceiling suspension system. **2.** A slot or cut made in a material such as wood or metal.

kerfing Making a series of parallel saw cuts partway through the thickness of a piece of wood to enable the piece to bend toward the kerfed side.

kerkis In an ancient Greek theatre, one of the wedge-shaped sections of seating of the theatre, divided by radiating staircases.

kettle crane Same as **fireplace crane**.

kevel, cavel, cavil **1.** A stone mason's axe with a flat face for knocking off projecting angular points, and a pointed peen for reducing a surface to the desired form; also called a **jedding axe**. **2.** A heavy timber, as a timber bolted between two stanchions.

kevil Same as **kevel**.

key **1.** A wedge which passes through a hole in a projecting tenon to secure its hold. **2.** A piece of metal or wood which is inserted in a joint to prevent movement between adjacent surfaces. **3.** A piece inserted in the back of a board to prevent warping. **4.** The last board in a series of floorboards, tapering in shape, and serving to hold the others in place when driven home. **5.** The property of a material that facilitates the bonding of another material to it. **6.** The roughening on the underside of veneer or similar material to assist it in holding glue. **7.** The roughened surface on the back of tile or the like to assist it in holding mortar. **8.** In plastering or similar work, that part of the plastic material that is forced between and enters the holes in (or clings to the roughened surface of) the

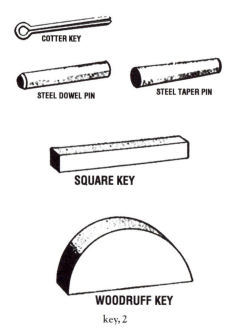

COTTER KEY

STEEL DOWEL PIN   STEEL TAPER PIN

SQUARE KEY

WOODRUFF KEY

key, 2

backing lath. **9.** A **keystone**. **10.** A groove cut in a surface into which fits a corresponding projection from a member above, as a keyed footing. **11.** A detachable metal instrument which operates a lock; it is inserted into the lock and moves a bolt, latch, or catch.

key banding, key pattern Same as **Greek key**.

key block A **keystone**.

key bolt Same as **cotter pin**.

key brick A brick which is tapered toward one end; used in brick arches.

key console A **console, 1** which acts as the **keystone** of an arch.

key course **1.** A course of keystones in an arch; used in a deep archway where a single keystone will not suffice. **2.** A course of keystones used in the crown of a barrel vault.

key drop A keyhole cover, usually attached to the escutcheon by a pivot.

keyed Said of a concrete form, or the like, which is fixed in position in a recess or notch.

keyed-alike cylinders Lock cylinders which are designed to be operated on by the same key, as opposed to master-keyed cylinders, which may be opened by the same master key but are keyed differently.

keyed beam A compound beam having mating grooves between adjacent layers to resist horizontal shearing stresses at the interfaces.

 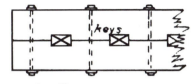

keyed beam

keyed brick A brick having a recess in one face (usually of the dovetail type); used to provide a mechanical key for plasterwork or rendering.

keyed-differently cylinders Lock cylinders requiring specific individually designed keys for their operation.

keyed-in frame A door frame erected with wall materials forced behind the frame **backband**; the wall thickness is equal to or greater than the opening between the backbands, but is not wider than the **jamb depth**.

keyed joint **1.** A joint between two timbers that is located or secured by a **key, 1** or **key, 2**. **2.** A joint left recessed or raked out as preparation for receiving a plaster or stucco coating.

keyed pointing See **key joint pointing**.

keyed tenon Same as **tusk tenon**.

key escutcheon Same as **key plate**.

keyhole saw A **compass saw** having an especially narrow blade and fine teeth.

keying in The bonding of a new brick wall to an existing one.

key interlock A mechanism that permits operation, insertion, or removal of a key to a piece of equipment only if certain conditions have been met or prescribed operations have been completed; may be required to meet specified safety conditions and to prevent improper (or unauthorized) operation of the equipment.

key joint pointing, keyed pointing Pointing in which the soft mortar is pressed and worked into shape by means of a tool having a convex edge.

keypad lock A door lock that opens when the correct set of digits has been "punched in."

key pattern See **labyrinth fret**.

key joint pointing

key pile The last **pile** driven into a bay of **sheet-piling**; usually slightly tapered.

key plan A small-scale plan of a building or building group which indicates the placement of the principal elements of the scheme.

key plate A small plate or escutcheon having only a keyhole.

keystone, key block The central, wedged-shaped masonry block of an arch; often embellished. Until this block is in place, the arch cannot support any superimposed weight.

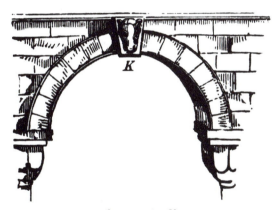

keystone, 1: *K*

keystone arch Any **arch** having a keystone at its center, but commonly a **flat arch** or a **round-topped arch**.

key switch In an electric circuit, an on-off switch which can be actuated only by the insertion of a **key, 11**.

key valve A **valve** which can be operated only by the insertion of a **key, 11**.

keyway **1.** The aperture in a lock cylinder which receives the key and closely engages with it throughout its length. **2.** A slot used to interlock slabs of masonry walls built at different times.

k factor See **thermal conductivity**.

kg Abbr. for "kilogram."

khan Same as **caravansary**.

khaya Closely resembles but is not a true **mahogany**; lighter, usually softer, and more strongly figured than mahogany; esp. used for paneling and veneer.

khory In early Russian architecture, a gallery.

kiblah, keblah, qibla In Islam, the required orientation of the prayer niche, toward Mecca.

kick In a brick, a shallow indent or **frog**.

kickboard Same as **toeboard**.

kicker **1.** Same as **starter frame**. **2.** A piece of wood which is attached to a formwork member to take the thrust of another member.

kicker plate A **plate, 2** used to anchor a stair to concrete.

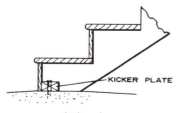

kicker plate

kicking piece A short timber which is fixed to a **wale** so as to take up the thrust of the end of a diagonal strut.

kickout In excavation work, the accidental release or failure of a shore or brace.

kickpipe A section of pipe which provides mechanical protection for an electric cable where it projects from a floor or deck.

kickplate **1.** A protective plate applied on the lower rail of a door to prevent marring. **2.** A vertical plate forming a lip or low curb at the open edge of a stair platform or floor, or at the back edge or open end of a stair tread.

kick rail A short rail mounted on a door near its lower edge, used to kick the door open, primarily on institutional doors.

kick roof A roof having **flared eaves**.

kick strip Same as **kicker, 2**.

kieselguhr See **diatomite**.

kill To seal, **6**.

killesse Same as **coulisse, 1**.

kiln A furnace, oven, or heated enclosure used: (a) for burning or firing brick and tile; (b) for drying timber.

kiln brown stain, chemical brown stain A brown-colored stain that develops during kiln-drying or air-drying of lumber as a result of changes in the wood extractives.

kiln-dried, hot-air-dried Dried or seasoned artificially in a kiln; excess moisture has been driven off by heating; usually has a **moisture content, 1** of 6 to 12%.

kiln-fired brick See **burnt brick**.

kiln-run Brick or tile, all from one kiln, which has not been sorted or graded for size or color variation.

kiln scum See **scum**.

kiln white, kiln scum A white scum that has formed on a brick surface during firing as the result of drier scum and kiln atmosphere. Also see **scum**.

kilo (k) Prefix, used in the International System of Units, denoting multiplication by 1000.

kilogram The International Standard unit for mass; equals 1000 grams.

kilonewton An International Standard unit of force equal to 1000 newtons, 0.2248 kips, or 224.8 pounds.

kilovolt A unit of electromotive force equal to 1,000 volts.

kilovolt-ampere In an electric circuit, the product of the current in amperes and the applied voltage (expressed in volts), divided by 1,000.

kilowatt A unit of power equal to 1,000 watts; equivalent to approx. 1.34 horsepower.

kilowatt-hour A unit of energy equal to 1,000 watt-hours; equal to the work expended in 1 hour at a rate of 1.34 horsepower.

kingbolt A tie rod or long bolt which takes the place of a **king post**.

king closer, beveled closer A rectangular brick, one end of which has been cut off diago-

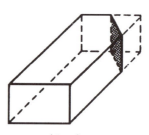

king closer

nally to half the width of the brick (a **three-quarter brick**); used as a **closer** in brickwork.

king piece   Same as **king post**.

king pile   **1.** A **pile** along the center line of a wide trench which supports timbers that run to it from both sides of an excavation. **2.** A pile which provides added support for a precast concrete or sheet steel pile wall.

king post   **1.** In a truss, as for a roof, a vertical member extending from the apex of the inclined rafters to the tie beam between the rafters at their lower ends. **2.** See **joggle post, 2.**

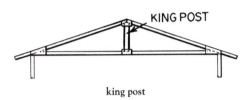

king post

king-post truss   A structural support for a roof formed by two inclined rafters joined at the apex of their intersection; a horizontal **tie beam, 2** connects the rafters near their lower ends, and a vertical central member, called the *king post*, connects the apex with the midpoint of the **tie beam.**

king rod   Same as **kingbolt.**

king-table   In medieval architecture, the **string-course**, with ballflower ornaments, usually under parapets.

kiosk   **1.** A small pavilion, usually open, built in gardens and parks. **2.** A similar structure, often enclosed, for the sale of merchandise such as newspapers or magazines.

kiot   In early Russian architecture, a niche to house one or more icons.

kip   A unit of force; equals 1000 pounds (4448 newtons).

kirk   A church, especially in Scotland.

kiss mark   A mark on a brick face produced during firing; results from the method of stacking.

kistvaen   See **cistvaen.**

kitchen   A room intended for the preparation and cooking of food, often where meals are also eaten; if prepared in a structure detached from the main house, then called an **outkitchen.** Also see **summer kitchen.**

kitchen cabinet   A case or box-like assembly consisting of doors, drawers, and shelves primarily used for storage for food, utensils, linen, etc.

kitchenette   A small room or an alcove fitted with the essential conveniences of a kitchen.

kitchen garden   A private garden especially for raising vegetables and herbs.

kite winder   On a staircase, a **winder** which is triangular in shape.

kitsch   Art or architecture that is sentimental or banal in tone; considered to have little or no aesthetic value.

klinkart   A yellowish long, hard brick; primarily used in paving.

km   Abbr. for "kilometer."

kN   Abbr. for **kilonewton**, a unit of force.

knapped flint   A flint stone that has been broken or chipped to obtain a desired shape; often set in patterns in a wall, with the split face showing.

knapping hammer   A steel hammer for breaking stone; used for splitting cobbles and for shaping paving stones or producing roughly sized material; usually has two square (or rectangular) faces, or one such face and a wedge peen.

knaur   See **knur, burl, 1.**

kneading compaction   The compaction of a plastic soil by the action of a **sheepsfoot roller.**

knee   **1.** A piece of wood having a bend, either natural or artificially set; a **crook, 2. 2.** A part of the back of a handrail having a convex upper surface. **3.** See **label stop, 2.**

knee brace   A corner brace; a diagonal member placed across the angle between two members that are joined; serves to stiffen and strengthen a framework so constructed.

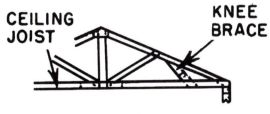

knee brace

knee iron   A **kneepiece, 2**, fabricated of iron.

kneeler, kneestone, skew   **1.** A building stone which is sloped on top and flat on the bottom, as the stone that supports inclined coping on the slope of a gable. Also see **footstone; gable springer**. **2.** The stone that breaks the horizontal-vertical unit-and-joint pattern of a normal masonry wall to begin the curve or angle of an arch or vault.

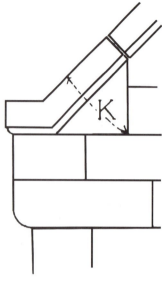

kneeler, 1: K

knee piece **1.** Same as **knee rafter**. **2.** An angular piece of timber used in a roof to strengthen a joint where two timbers meet.

knee rafter **1.** A **principal rafter** having a bend in it. **2.** A brace between a **principal rafter** and a **tie beam**.

knee roof A **curb roof**.

kneestone See **kneeler**.

knee timber A timber having a natural curve or **knee 1**.

knee wall A wall which acts as a **knee brace** by supporting roof rafters at some intermediate position along their length; shortens the span of the rafters.

knife-blade fuse A **cartridge fuse** having a metal blade at each end of a cylindrical tube for making contact with the fuse within.

knife consistency, knife grade A grade of caulking or glazing compound which has the proper firmness for application with a putty knife.

knife file A file having a blade-like cross section, with a sharp edge; used to finish narrow grooves.

knife grade See **knife consistency**.

knife switch A type of electric switch consisting of one or more movable copper blades which are hinged and which make contact with stationary forked contact jaws by being forced between them.

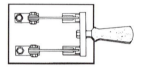

knife switch

knob **1.** A handle, more or less spherical, usually for operating a lock. **2.** A similar protuberance, useful or ornamental, such as a **boss**.

knobbing, knobbling, skiffling In stone-cutting, a preliminary process, usually the knocking off of pieces projecting beyond the required dimensions.

knob bolt A door lock with a bolt controlled by a knob on one or both sides.

knob latch A door latch with a spring bolt controlled by a knob on one or both sides.

knob lock A door lock with a spring bolt controlled by one or both knobs, and a dead bolt controlled by a key.

knob rose A round disk or plate fastened to the face of a door around the hole in the door through which the doorknob spindle passes.

knob rose

knob shank The projecting stem of a knob into which the spindle is fastened.

knob top That part of a doorknob which the hand grasps.

knocked down (KD) Prefabricated, but not assembled; said of items delivered to the jobsite for assembly there.

knocked-down frame A doorframe furnished by the manufacturer in three or more basic parts for assembly in the field.

knocker See **door knocker**.

knockings In stone masonry, the smaller pieces knocked off in dressing stone.

knocking up Preparing and mixing a batch of concrete, mortar, or plaster.

knockout A partially punched-out circular area in the surface of an electrical outlet, junction box, or panel box; can easily be removed with a hammer, pliers, or screwdriver to provide access for the attachment of a raceway cable or fitting.

knop Same as **knob, 2**.

knot **1.** In medieval architecture, a bunch of leaves, flowers, or similar ornament, as the bosses at the intersections of ribs, and bunches of foliage in capitals. **2.** An ornamental design resembling cords which are interlaced. **3.** The hard, cross-grained mass of wood formed in a trunk at the place where a branch joins the trunk. **4.** In fabric construction, the presence of an imperfection that will cause a surface irregularity.

knot brush A brush having its bristles grouped in one to three thick knots (of round or oval shape); used for distempers.

knot-cluster A compact, roughly circular group of three or more knots in wood, each surrounded by contorted grain.

knot garden A complicated garden design, usually small in area, and making use of plants set in geometric patterns, low hedges of shrubs trimmed into ornamental shapes as borders, and green foliage set off by sharp color contrast.

knothole A hole in a board or plank caused when a **knot, 3** drops out of the piece of wood.

knotted pillar, knotted shaft A form of pillar, occurring in Romanesque architecture, so carved as to appear as if knotted in the middle.

knotting, knot sealer A sealer (such as shellac, aluminum paint, or varnish) for knots in new wood; used to prevent bleed-through of resin into paints.

knotty pine Wood of the pine tree cut so that the knots form a decorative pattern; used for interior paneling and cabinets.

knotted pillar

knotwork A carved ornamental arrangement of cord-like figures knotted together as in some kinds of fringe, used to decorate voussoirs, moldings, etc.

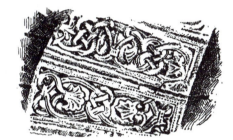

knotwork

knuckle One of the cylindrically projecting parts of a **hinge** through which the pin passes.

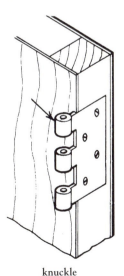

knuckle

knuckle bend A bend having a short radius.

knuckle joint **1.** See **curb joint**. **2.** A type of hinged joint between two rods.

knulling **1.** A convex rounded molding of slight projection, consisting of a series of more or less elaborate members separated by indentations. **2.** Same as **knurling**.

knur, knurl A knot or **burl, 1** in wood.

knurling **1.** A series of small ridges, usually milled on a surface, in order to provide a better surface for gripping or turning; also called **milling**. **2.** Same as **knulling**.

KO On drawings, abbr. for **knockout**.

koa A hard, light red to dark brown wood with a golden luster from the Hawaiian Islands; takes a fine polish, being marked with wavy lines; used for veneer, cabinets, and interior finish.

kondo The main, "Golden Hall" of a Buddhist monastery in Japan.

konistra In the ancient Greek theatre, the **orchestra**.

korina, limba A hardwood of central and west Africa, light to moderately heavy, having a straight grain and fine texture; one variety is light cream to pale yellow in color, while the other is light brown; used for paneling.

KP Abbr. for **kickplate**.

kPa Symbol for "kilopascal," a unit of pressure equal to 1000 pascals.

KP&D Abbr. for "kickplate and drip."

kraft paper A heavy, high-strength paper, sized with resin, usually brown in color; used as a **building paper**.

kremlin **1.** In Russia, the citadel of a town or city, serving as an administrative and religious center. **2.** (initial cap.) The citadel of Moscow, a 90 acre (36 hectares) area surrounded by 15th-century crenelated walls, entered by five steepled gate towers.

krepidoma Same as **crepidoma**.

ksi Abbr. for "kilopounds per square inch."

K-truss, K-type truss A truss in which the arrangement of the **panels, 7** has the appearance of the letter **K**.

kVA Abbr. for "kilovolt-ampere."

Kremlin

K-truss

k-value See **thermal conductance**.

kW **1.** Symbol for "kilowatt"; a unit of power. **2.** On drawings, abbr. for **kilowatt**.

kWh **1.** Symbol for "kilowatt hour"; a unit of energy equal to 3.6 megajoules. **2.** On drawings, abbr. for **kilowatt-hour**.

kyanize, kyanise To preserve wood against decay by steeping it in a mercuric chloride solution.

L

L **1.** On drawings, abbr. for "left." **2.** Abbr. for **lambert**.

labeled **1.** Carrying an identification of a recognized testing laboratory which certifies the results of appropriate fire tests conducted on essentially identical materials or construction, as a **labeled door, labeled frame**, or **labeled window**. **2.** According to the **NEC**, materials or equipment carrying an identifying label, symbol, or other identifying mark of an organization that is acceptable to the authority having jurisdiction. The label indicates compliance with appropriate standards or performance in a specified manner.

labeled door A fire-rated door carrying a certified rating by the Underwriters' Laboratories, Inc.

labeled frame A doorframe that conforms to all applicable requirements and tests of the Underwriters' Laboratories, Inc., and bears their label.

labeled window A window that conforms to all applicable requirements, in respect to fire resistance, of the Underwriters' Laboratories, Inc., and bears their label designating the fire rating.

label molding, label A square-arched **dripstone** or **hoodmold**; extends horizontally across the top of an opening and returns vertically downward for a short distance.

label molding

label stop **1.** The termination of a hoodmold or arched dripstone in which the lower ends are turned away from the opening horizontally. **2.** Any decorative boss or other termination of a dripstone, hoodmold, sill, etc.; a **knee** (*Brit. colloq.*).

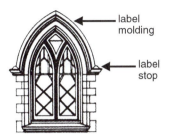

label molding and label stop

label stop, 2

labor and material payment bond A bond of the **contractor** in which a **surety** guarantees to the **owner** that the contractor will pay for labor and materials used in the performance of the contract. The claimants under the bond are those having direct contracts with the contractor or any subcontractor.

laboratory fume hood Same as **exhaust fume hood**.

labyrinth **1.** A maze of twisting passageways. **2.** In medieval cathedrals, the representation of such a maze inlaid in the floor. **3.** A garden feature of convoluted paths outlined by hedges, usually above eye level; also called a maze. (*See illustration p. 532.*)

labyrinth fret, key pattern, meander A fret with many involved turnings. (*See illustration p. 532.*)

labyrinth, 2

labyrinth fret

lac A resinous insect secretion used as a base for shellac, lacquer, and varnish.

laced beam Same as **lattice beam**; see **lattice girder**.

laced column A composite column in which the components are connected by **lacing, 1**.

laced valley, woven valley A valley of a shingle, slate, or tile roof formed by interweaving shingles, slates, or tiles from the two intersecting surfaces.

laced valley

lacewood A coarse-grained wood from Australia, pale pink to pinkish brown in color, moderately hard and heavy, with a lace-like figure; used for interior trim, paneling, and plywood.

lacework Architectural decorations resembling lace. Also see **cast-iron lacework** and **jigsaw work**.

lacing **1.** A system of members (e.g., bars or batten plates) used to connect two component elements of a composite girder, strut, or column to make them act as one member. **2.** Same as **lacing course**. **3.** Timbers placed behind or around other supports as bracing. **4.** Small boards which close up the spaces between lagging planks or sheeting to prevent dirt from entering an excavation. **5.** The interlocking of sections of sheet pile to form a wall.

lacing course A course of brick or tile inserted in a rough stone or rubble course as a **bond course**.

laconicum The sweat room in a Roman bath.

lacquer Any glossy enamel which dries quickly by evaporation of the volatile solvents and diluents. Also see **Chinese lacquer**.

lacunar, laquear A **coffer** or **coffering**.

lacunaria The ceiling of the ambulatory around the cella of a temple, or of the portico.

ladder A frame, usually of wood or metal, consisting of two side pieces (called "stiles") which are connected by crosspieces, usually round (called "rungs"); used as a means of climbing up or down.

ladder cable tray A continuous steel or aluminum support for wiring or cables.

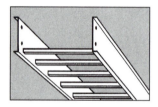

ladder cable tray

ladder core A hollow core consisting of strips of wood, wood derivative, or insulation board, with the strips running either horizontally or vertically throughout the core area and with air cells and/or spaces between the strips; used as the core in interior doors.

ladder ditcher See **ladder trencher**.

ladder jack scaffold A light-duty scaffold supported by brackets attached to ladders.

ladder trencher A **ditcher** which digs trenches; utilizes buckets mounted on a pair of chains that travel on the exterior of a boom.

ladies' room, women's room In a public building, a room containing toilet and lavatory facilities for the use of ladies.

ladkin, latterkin A pointed piece of hardwood used for clearing out the grooves of the cames, which hold panes of glass in stained-glass windows and casements.

ladrillo In Spanish Colonial architecture and derivatives, an adobe brick that has been kiln-dried rather than sun-dried, thereby providing increased durability, increased mechanical strength, and greater moisture protection.

Lady chapel A major chapel dedicated to the Virgin Mary, on the axis of a church at its east end.

LAG On drawings, abbr. for **lagging**.

lag bolt, coach screw, lag screw A bolt having a square head and a thin, coarse-pitched thread.

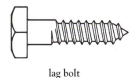

lag bolt

lagged pile A **pile** having longitudinal pieces (i.e., lags) which are fastened to it for providing mechanical protection and increased friction and bearing area.

lagging **1.** Thermal insulation for pipes, tanks, ducts, etc.; sometimes **block insulation**, pre-shaped to conform to the curved surface. **2.** The planking, consisting of narrow strips, extending from one rib of the **centering** of an arch or vault to another; provides direct support for the voussoirs until the arch or vault is closed in. **3.** Boards which are joined, side by side, lining an excavation. **4.** Horizontal members between **soldier piles**.

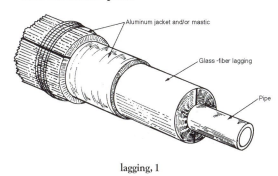

Aluminum jacket and/or mastic

Glass-fiber lagging

Pipe

lagging, 1

lag screw See **lag bolt**.

laid-dry masonry Same as **dry masonry**.

laid-on molding, planted molding A molding that is worked separately and fastened to the work by brads.

laid-on stop See **stop, 1**.

laitance A layer of weak, nondurable material containing cement and **fines** from aggregates, which is brought to the surface of overwet concrete by the bleeding of water to the top.

laja In Spanish architecture and its derivatives, same as **flagstone**.

lake Any of a number of bright pigments which are prepared from animal, vegetable, or coal-tar coloring matter, or formed synthetically; used in paints.

lake sand Sand consisting mainly of rounded particles as contrasted with **bank sand** which has sharp edges; the latter is preferred in plastering.

Lally column A proprietary name for a cylindrical column which is concrete filled; used as a structural column to support beams or girders.

LAM On drawings, abbr. for **laminate**.

Lamassu The monumental human-headed, winged bulls that guarded the entrances to Mesopotamian palaces and temples.

lambert A unit of **luminance** equal to $(1/\pi)$ candela per sq cm; equal to the uniform luminance of a perfectly diffusing surface emitting or reflecting light at the rate of 1 lumen per sq cm. Abbr. L.

Lambert's cosine law A law stating that the luminous intensity, in any direction from a plane surface, varies as the cosine of the angle between that direction and the perpendicular to the surface.

lambrequin An ornamental horizontal band, often fringed, lobed, or notched along its lower edge.

lamb's-tongue **1.** The end of a handrail which is turned out or down from the rail and curved so

lamb's-tongue, 1

as to resemble a tongue. **2.** A carpenter's molding plane having a deep and narrow blade more or less resembling a tongue and curved so as to cut a **quirk bead**. **3.** A molding cut from such a plane, usually two ovolos separated by a fillet and set off by fillets at the other ends.

lamella A reinforced concrete, metal, or wood member joined with similar members in a criss-cross pattern so as to form an arch or vault.

lamella roof A vaulted roof-framing system composed of lamellae.

laminar flow See **streamline flow**.

laminate **1.** A product made by bonding together two or more layers of material, e.g., **plywood, laminated wood**, etc. **2.** To unite layers of material with an adhesive.

laminated arch A wooden arch made of several layers or laminations of thin boards bolted or glued together.

laminated beam A beam built up by gluing together several pieces of timber; may be either straight or curved.

laminated glass, safety glass, shatterproof glass Two or more plies of plate glass, float glass, or sheet glass, bonded to a transparent plastic sheet between them to form a shatter-resisting assembly.

laminated joint A **finger joint**.

laminated plastic A plastic material consisting of superimposed layers of a synthetic resin-impregnated or resin-coated filler which have been bonded together (usually by means of heat and pressure) to form a single piece.

laminated timber See **glued-laminated timber**.

laminated wood Board or timber built up of plies which are joined together by gluing; usually the grain of all plies is parallel.

lamp A man-made light source which produces radiation in or near the visible region of the spectrum; often called a **bulb** or **tube** to distinguish it from the complete lighting unit consisting of the source and associated parts such as reflectors, etc.

lamp ballast See **ballast**.

lamp base, *Brit.* **lamp cap** That part of a lamp which connects to the lamp holder; provides electrical contacts.

lampblack, vegetable black A fine black pigment consisting of particles of carbon; collected from the soot of burning oil.

lamp bulb The glass envelope enclosing the luminous element or material of an electric lamp; usually made of glass, quartz, or similar material; its shape usually is designated by a letter (e.g., T—tubular, G—globe, etc.), followed by a number which indicates the maximum diameter of the bulb in eighths of an inch.

lamp cap (*Brit.*) See **lamp base**.

lamp depreciation The decrease in luminous output of a lamp during its operating life.

lamp holder, lamp socket A device which mechanically supports a lamp for the purposes of making electrical contact with the lamp.

lamp inrush current The initial surge of current when an incandescent filament lamp is turned on; may be as much as 50 times the rated current and may last several tenths of a second for high-wattage lamps.

lamp jacket The second, or outer, bulb used on some lamps.

lamp life See **rated lamp life**.

lamp post A standard support for a luminaire, provided with the necessary internal attachments for wiring and the external attachments for the bracket.

lamp socket See **lamp holder**.

lanai A living room or lounge area which is entirely, or in part, open to the outdoors.

lancet, lancet window **1.** A narrow window with a sharp pointed arch typical of English Gothic architecture from ca. 1150 to ca. 1250. **2.** One light shaped like a lancet window.

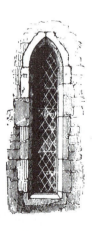

lancet

lancet arch   A sharply pointed two-centered arch whose centers of curvature are much farther apart than the width of the arch; an **acute arch**.

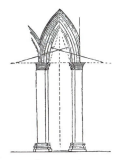

lancet arch

lanceted   Having a lancet window or arch.

Lancet style   The style of Early English architecture distinguished by its use of the **lancet arch**; sometimes called First Pointed Gothic.

lancet window   A narrow window having the shape of a **lancet arch**.

lanciform   Having a sharp point.

land   **1.** Part of the surface of the earth not permanently covered by water. **2.** Any immoveable improvements or fixtures attached thereto.

land boundary   A line of demarcation between adjoining parcels of land. The parcels of land may be of the same or different ownership, but were distinguished at one time in the history of their descent by separate legal descriptions.

land-clearing rake   A blade-like device which is attached to the front of a tractor; used to cut and collect brush which is removed in clearing a construction site.

land drain   Same as **agricultural pipe drain**.

landfill   The disposal of garbage, refuse, and trash by burying it under layers of earth in low ground or in excavated pits.

landing, pace, stair landing   The horizontal platform at the end of a stair flight or between two flights of stairs.

landing door   See **hoistway door**.

landing newel, angle newel   A **newel** which is located on a stair landing or at a point where stairs change direction.

landing tread   On a stair landing, the board directly over the uppermost riser; has an edge matching that of the nosing on the stair treads and has the same overhang.

landmark   **1.** Any building, structure, or place that has a special character, special historic interest, and/or special aesthetic interest, or value, as part of the development, heritage, or cultural characteristics of a nation, state, city, or town. **2.** A monument, fixed object, or marker on the ground that designates the location of a land boundary. **3.** A formal designation of such status for a building by a national or local authority. Also see **National Historic Landmark** and **National Register of Historic Places**.

landscape architect   **1.** A person trained and experienced in the design and development of landscapes and gardens. **2.** A designation reserved for a person professionally qualified and duly licensed to perform landscape architectural services.

landscaped roof   A roof intended to be landscaped; the weight of the landscaping materials is considered to be a **dead load**, computed on the basis of the soil's being saturated with water.

landscape improvement   Any physical betterment of **real property**, or any part thereof, as a result of natural or artificial landscaping.

landscape screen   See **office landscape screen**.

landscape window   A **double-hung window** whose upper sash is decorated with small panes of colored glass; the lower sash, of clear glass, is a single pane and is larger than the upper sash.

land survey   A survey of landed property establishing or reestablishing lengths and directions of boundary lines. Land boundaries are usually defined by ownership, commencing with the earliest owners through successive ownerships and partitions. Land surveying includes the reestablishment of original boundaries and the establishment of such new boundaries as may be required in the partition of the land.

land tie   A **tie rod** or chain used to secure a retaining wall or the like.

land tile   Porous clay tile pipe laid with butt joints.

land-use analysis   The study of an existing pattern of use, within an area, to determine the nature and magnitude of deficiencies which might exist and to assess the potential of the pattern relative to development goals.

land-use plan The projection of a future pattern of use within an area, as determined by development goals.

land-use survey A study and recording of the way in which land is being used in an area; usually classified as commercial, industrial, public, residential, etc.

lane **1.** A narrow passageway bordered by trees, fences, or other lateral barrier. **2.** That part of a roadway which accommodates a single line of vehicles.

languet An ornamental band, often enriched, consisting of a series of upright, tongue-shaped elements.

lantern A windowed superstructure crowning a roof or dome; a **lantern light**.

lantern

lantern cross A cross atop a **lanterne des morts**.

lanterne des morts A graveyard lantern; a slender tower-like structure, usually in the form of a hollow column, terminated by a pierced turret containing a light which shone through the openings; many such towers were in France in medieval times.

lantern light A relatively small structure, having openings in its sides, above the roof of a building to provide light on its interior.

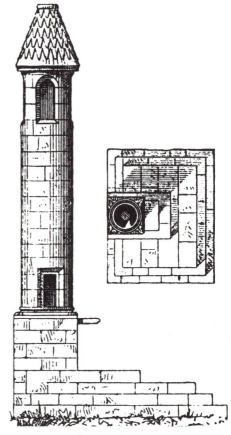

lanterne des morts

lantern skylight A small **skylight** atop a building to provide light and ventilation in the space below.

lap **1.** To overlap or partly cover one surface with another, as in shingling. **2.** The length of the overlap, as the distance one tile extends over another.

lap adhesive An adhesive used to seal the laps and sides of a jacket that surrounds thermal insulation around a pipe.

lap cement A type of asphalt used as an adhesive between the laps of roll roofing.

lap dovetail Same as **lapped dovetail**.

lapies A bedrock surface, beneath the soil, roughened as a result of action by a solution of limestone, gypsum, or other soluble rock; usually deeply trenched along joints. Such a bedrock presents hazards and results in excessive costs for footings and foundations.

lapis   Same as **milliarium**.

lapis lazuli   A rich blue semiprecious stone; either used decoratively or ground and powdered for use as an ultramarine pigment.

lap joint   **1.** A joint in which one board, plank, metal plate, etc., overlaps the edge of another piece; the overlapping part of each member is cut away to half thickness, resulting in flush surfaces. **2.** A joint formed by placing one piece partly over another and uniting the overlapped portions.

lap joint, 2

lap notch   Same as **half-cut notch**.

lapped dovetail, drawer dovetail   A dovetail at an angle in which the pegs of one member do not pass through the full thickness of the other; esp. used at the front of a drawer.

lapped dovetail

lapped tenons   Two tenons which enter a common mortise from opposite sides and overlap one another.

lapping   In reinforced concrete, the overlapping of steel reinforcing bars, or other reinforcement, so there is continuity of tensile stress in the reinforcement when the concrete member is subjected to a flexural or tensile load.

lap-riveted   Said of two plates overlapped and then joined by riveting.

lap scarf   A flush joint formed by fitting one end of a length of wood gutter into the opposite end of another.

lap seam   A joint formed by overlapping the edges of metal sheets or plates and joining them by riveting, welding, soldering, or brazing.

lap siding   See **clapboard**.

lap splice   **1.** A connection of reinforcing steel made by lapping the ends of bars. **2.** A splice made by placing one piece on top of another and fastening together with pins, nails, screws, bolts, rivets, or similar contrivances.

lap weld   A weld in which the ends of the pieces are overlapped and then joined by welding.

lap weld

laquear   Same as **lacunar**.

lararium   In Roman houses, a small shrine to the household gods (lares).

larch, tamarack   A fine-textured, strong, hard, straight-grained wood of a coniferous tree; heavier than most softwoods.

larder   A room where food is stored.

large knot   A knot in wood which is greater than $1\frac{1}{2}$ in. (3.8 cm) in diameter.

larmier, lorymer   **1.** A **corona**. **2.** Any horizontal member or stringcourse similar in profile to a corona and projecting from a wall to throw off rain; a **roll molding, drip**, etc.

larnite   A mineral which is a major constituent of portland cement; beta dicalcium silicate.

larry   A hoe having a long handle and a blade which usually is perforated; used for mixing mortar or plaster.

laser   A device that emits a powerful beam of coherent light in an intense beam; used, for example, on building projects to provide a means of ensuring that construction is along a straight line, or to ensure that the construction is carried out to precisely the same height.

LAT   **1.** On drawings, abbr. for "latitude." **2.** On drawings, abbr. for "lateral."

lat   In Indian architecture, an isolated shaft or pillar serving various purposes, as for bearing inscriptions or religious emblems or for a statue or image.

latch   A simple fastening device having a latch bolt, but not a **dead bolt**; contains no provisions for locking with a key; usually openable from both sides.

simple **latch**

latch bolt   A spring bolt, one edge of which is beveled; when the door or window to which it is attached is closed, the bolt is forced inward; when in the fully closed position, the bolt springs back into a fixed notch or cavity.

latchet   Same as **tingle, 2**.

latchkey   A key used to raise and throw back the latch of a door.

latch plate   An **escutcheon** that protects the area of a door around a **latch**.

latchstring   A string for raising the latch of a door from the outside; it is fastened to the latch and passed through a hole above it in the door.

Late Gothic Revival   The last phase of the **Gothic Revival** in the early part of the 20th century, in which an attempt was made to emulate its Gothic architecture prototype with some degree of accuracy; for example, see **Collegiate Gothic**.

latent heat   The amount of heat which is absorbed or evolved in changing the state of a substance without changing its temperature, e.g., in freezing or vaporizing water.

later   A brick, formed in a mold and dried in the sun or baked in a kiln by the early Greeks and Romans; much larger and much thinner than modern bricks; each brick was stamped with the name of the maker and the year in which it was made.

lateral   Same as **lateral sewer**.

lateral buckling, lateral-torsional buckling   The buckling of a structural member which involves lateral deflection and twist.

lateral load   1. See **wind load**. 2. See **earthquake load**.

lateral reinforcement   That part of the steel reinforcement for a **reinforced concrete** column in the form of transverse hoops, links, or helixes around the vertical reinforcing steel rods.

lateral scroll   A fitting which curves in a horizontal plane and is used to terminate a stair handrail.

lateral sewer   A sewer which discharges into a branch or other sewer and has no other common sewer tributary to it.

lateral support   The bracing for a wall, beam, or structural member, either horizontal (by roof or floor constructions) or vertical (by pilasters, columns, or cross walls).

lateral-torsional buckling   See **lateral buckling**.

latest event occurrence time   In **CPM** terminology, the deadline by which time an **event** must be completed if the project is not to be delayed.

latest finish date   In **CPM** terminology, the latest point in time by which no further work must be done on an **activity** if the project is not to be delayed.

latest start date   In **CPM** terminology, the latest possible point in time by which an **activity** must be started if the project is not to be delayed.

Late Victorian architecture   A term occasionally applied to architecture in the **Queen Anne style**. See **Victorian architecture**.

latewood   See **summerwood**.

latex   An emulsion of finely dispersed particles of natural or synthetic rubber or plastic materials in water.

latex foam   **Sponge rubber** made from latex.

latex paint   A paint containing latex in a water suspension (i.e., natural or synthetic rubber or plastic particles suspended in water) combined with pigments and other additives acting as binders.

latex patching compound   A compound which consists of a latex (usually **styrene-butadiene rubber**), portland cement, and an aggregate; moisture-, mildew-, and alkali-resistant; used for patching or leveling a floor.

latex sealant   A compound of **latex** which cures primarily through water evaporation.

lath A building material used as a base for the application of plaster; see **expanded metal lath, gypsum lath, metal lath, split lath, wood lath**.

lath brick A long, narrow brick.

lathe A machine for shaping circular pieces of wood, metal, etc., by rotating the material about a horizontal axis while a stationary tool cuts away the excess material.

lath hammer, lathing hammer, lathing hatchet A hammer which has a small hatchet blade on the side opposite the hammer head; the blade has a small lateral nick for pulling out nails; esp. used for cutting and nailing wood lath.

lathhouse A structure made of laths or slats to shelter growing plants requiring shade and wind protection.

lathing **1.** A quantity of **laths**. **2.** The erecting or placing of laths.

lathing board See **backup strip**.

lathing hammer, lathing hatchet See **lath hammer**.

lath laid-and-set In plastering, a method of finishing the ceilings and partitions of houses with two-coat work, in which the first coat is called **laying**, and is often scratched with a broom.

lath scratcher A tool, made from pieces of wood lath, for scratching and roughening base-coat plaster to improve the bond of the next coat.

latia In Spanish Colonial architecture, one of a number of light, relatively straight saplings, usually about 3 feet (1 m) long, that has been stripped of its bark and laid across log beams (**vigas**) of a structure, either diagonally so as to create a herringbone ceiling pattern or laid at right angles to the vigas. A matting of reeds, placed over the latias, is then covered with a layer of tamped earth, dried mud, or adobe mixed with grass, to serve as a roof.

latia labrada A **latia** that has been split along its length; usually laid across **vigas** with its flat side down.

Latin cross A cross with the lower arm substantially longer than the other three.

latitude **1.** The perpendicular distance in a horizontal plane of a point from an east-west axis of reference. **2.** In surveying, the north-south component of a traverse course.

latrina An ancient Roman term for a bath or place to wash, or a water closet in a private home.

latrine **1.** A public toilet. **2.** A privy.

latrobe A stove or heater set under a mantelpiece, heating the room by direct radiation and one or more rooms above by hot air.

latterkin See **ladkin**.

lattice **1.** A network, often diagonal, of strips, rods, bars, laths, or straps of metal or wood, used as screening or for airy, ornamental constructions. **2.** A regular member triangularly braced, e.g., a lattice girder, a lattice truss.

lattice beam See **lattice girder**.

lattice boom A **boom** of lattice-type construction, usually fabricated of steel angles or tubing.

lattice girder, lattice beam An open girder in which the web consists of diagonal pieces arranged like latticework.

lattice molding A wood molding, rectangular in section and broad in relation to its projection, resembling the wood strips used in latticework.

lattice porch A porch enclosed by a **lattice,** usually of wood strips; provides limited privacy, yet permits breezes to flow through the porch.

lattice truss A **truss** consisting of upper and lower horizontal chords, connected by web members which cross each other; usually stiffened by joining at the intersections of the braces.

lattice window A window casement, fixed or hinged, with glazing bars set diagonally.

latticework Reticulated or net-like work formed by the crossing of laths or narrow, thin strips of wood or iron, usually in a diagonal pattern.

lauan See **Philippine mahogany**.

laundry chute, clothes chute A shaft for conveying soiled clothing, bed linen, etc., by gravity from an upper to a lower floor of a building.

laundry room A room equipped with one or more washing machines, washtubs, driers, ironing boards, etc., for household linen and/or personal effects.

laundry tray, laundry tub, set tub A deep wide sink or tub, usually of porcelain, slate, or soapstone; used for washing clothes, etc. (*See illustration p. 540.*)

LAV On drawings, abbr. for **lavatory**.

laundry tray

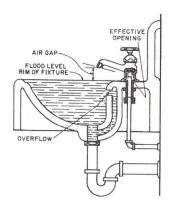

lavatory, 1

lavabo In monasteries of the Middle Ages, a large stone basin from which the water flowed through a number of small orifices around the edges, for the convenient performance of ablutions before religious exercises or meals.

lavabo: Abbey of Valmagne

lavatory **1.** A basin with water supply and drainage piping, for washing the hands and face; a washbasin. **2.** A room containing a washbasin and a water closet, but not a bathtub; a "powder room." **3.** Same as **toilet, 2** or **water closet, 2**. **4.** A small stone basin with a hole at the bottom to carry off water through a drain beneath; usually placed near the altar in an ancient church; used by the priest for washing his hands.

lavatory, 4

lawn **1.** An open space of ground of some size, covered with grass and kept smoothly mown. **2.** Same as **gauze, 2**.

lawn sprinkler system A system of devices, usually installed below ground level, to scatter or spray water droplets over a lawn, golf course, or the like.

law of reflection As applied to rays of light, sound, or radiant heat which strike a surface: the angle of reflection is equal to the angle of incidence, and the reflected and incident rays are in the same plane with a perpendicular to the surface.

lay bar A horizontal **glazing bar**.

lay board A board which is fixed on the rafters of a pitched roof to take the feet of the rafters, forming a subsidiary roof transverse to the main roof.

layer   Same as **course**.

layer board   Same as **lear board**.

laying   See **lath laid-and-set**.

laying length   The length of an installed pipeline, measured along its centerline.

laying off   The elimination of roller marks or brush marks on a wet paint surface by the application of light brush strokes.

laying out   The marking of a material, indicating where cuts are to be made, in preparation for work to be done.

laylight   A glazed opening in a ceiling to admit light (either natural or artificial) to a room below.

layout   A plan showing a scheme for an arrangement of objects and spaces.

lay panel   A wall panel whose horizontal dimension is greater than its vertical dimension.

lay-up   **1.** In reinforced plastics, the reinforcing material placed in position in the mold. **2.** The resin-impregnated reinforcement. **3.** The assembling of veneers for fabrication as plywood.

lazaret, lazarette, lazaretto, lazar house   A segregated area for infectious medical patients, esp. for their quarantine.

lazy susan   A circular, revolving shelf; sometimes used in corner kitchen cabinets.

lb   Abbr. for "pound."

L-beam   A beam whose section has the form of an inverted L; usually placed so that its top flange forms part of the edge of a floor.

Lbr   Abbr. for **lumber**.

LCL   **1.** Abbr. for **light center length**. **2.** Abbr. for "less than carload."

LCM   Abbr. for **loose cubic meter**.

L&CM   Abbr. for "lime and cement mortar."

L-column   That portion of a precast concrete frame composed of the column, haunch, and part of the girder.

LCY   Abbr. for **loose cubic yard**.

LDG   On drawings, abbr. for **landing**.

leaching   The process of separating a liquid from a solid (as in waste liquid) by percolation into the surrounding soil.

leaching basin   A drainage pit with sand and gravel sides constructed to allow water to dissipate.

leaching cesspool   A **cesspool, 1** in which the solids present are retained and the liquid seeps into the surrounding soil.

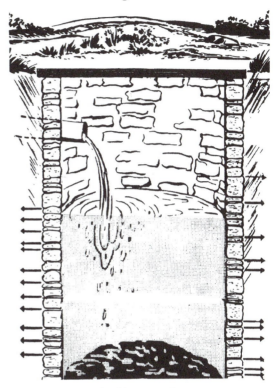

leaching cesspool

leaching field   Same as **absorption field**.

leaching pit   See **leaching well**.

leaching well, leaching pit   A pit, or a receptacle having porous walls, which permits its liquid contents to seep into the ground, but retains the solids.

lead   **1.** One of the sections of a masonry wall built up at each corner; supports a line between them which serves as a guide for constructing the remainder of the wall. **2.** (*pl.*) See **leads**. **3.** A soft, malleable, heavy metal; has low melting point and a high coefficient of thermal expansion; very easy to cut and work.

lead bat   See **lead wedge**.

lead burning   The welding of sheet lead.

lead-capped nail   Same as **lead head nail**.

lead chromate   One of a series of opaque pigments, orange to yellow in color, with high tinting strength.

lead chrome green　See **Brunswick green**.

lead-covered cable　An electric cable which is provided with a covering of lead to exclude moisture and to provide mechanical protection.

lead-covered cable

lead damp course　A **damp course** fabricated of sheet lead.

lead dot　A device for fastening sheet lead to a stone surface.

lead drier　One of many organic lead salts which are soluble in paints and varnishes; used to speed the drying and hardening of the oil vehicle.

leaded brass　An alloy of copper and zinc to which lead has been added to improve machinability.

leaded glass　See **leaded light**.

leaded light　A window having small diamond-shaped or rectangular panes of glass set in lead **cames**.

leaded zinc oxide　One of a series of mixed white pigments consisting of zinc oxide and basic lead sulfate; used principally in exterior house paints.

leader　**1.** A **downspout**. **2.** A duct for conducting hot air to an outlet in a hot-air heating system.

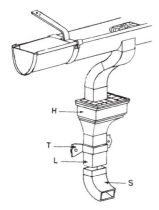

leader:　L; leader head, H; leader shoe, S; leader strap, T

leader head, conductor head, rainwater head　An enlargement or catch basin to receive rainwater from the gutter at the top of a **leader**.

leader head

lead flat　A flat roof which is covered by lead sheet laid over boarding.

lead foil tape　A tape, typically about ½ inch wide and 0.002 inch thick (12.5 mm × 0.05 mm), which is cemented to a window or panel to detect its breakage; forms part of an alarm circuit through which a small electric current flows. If the window or panel is broken, the tape is severed and the circuit is interrupted, thereby activating an alarm.

lead-free paint　A paint which contains no white lead or similar lead compounds.

lead glazing　A **leaded light**.

lead head nail　A roofing nail having a plain shank; makes a leakproof joint when driven through a metal roof.

leading edge, lock edge, strike edge　The vertical edge of a swinging door or window which is opposite the hinge edge.

lead in oil　White lead ground in linseed oil; formerly in wide use, now replaced largely by titanium dioxide pigments.

lead joint　A joint in a water pipe in which molten lead has been poured, as in a **bell-and-spigot joint**.

lead-lag ballast　A ballast for two fluorescent lamps, one of which operates on leading current and the other on lagging current; tends to reduce the stroboscopic effect.

lead-lined door, radiation-retarding door　A door which is lined internally with lead sheets to prevent the penetration of x-ray radiation.

lead-lined frame, radiation-retarding frame A doorframe internally lined with sheet lead to prevent the penetration of x-ray radiation; always used with **lead-lined doors**.

lead monoxide Same as **litharge**.

lead nail A nail for fixing a lead sheet to a roof. Such nails are often fabricated of a copper alloy.

lead naphthenate A liquid drier added to paints containing drying oils to promote rapid drying and hardening.

lead paint Any paint containing white lead.

lead pipe Pipe fabricated from 99.7 percent pig lead; various lead alloys are also available for special applications such as drainage. Lead pipes are interconnected by **wiped joints, burned joints**, or **flanged joints**.

lead pipe cinch An easy type of joint used in fabricating pipe from elongated sheets of lead. First, the lead sheets are formed in a cylindrical shape with a flat overlap perpendicular to the cylinder; then, the flat overlap is folded over and crimped, thereby forming a sealed joint.

lead plug **1.** A small cylinder of lead which is forced into a hole in a masonry wall; serves as a point of attachment for a screw or nail driven into it. **2.** A piece of lead between adjacent stones, for holding them together; formed by pouring molten lead in a groove cut in the jointing faces.

lead primer See **red lead**.

lead roof A flat roof covered with sheet lead.

leads Short lengths of electric conductors, usually insulated; usually used in the plural.

lead safe See **drip sink**.

lead-sheathed cable Same as **lead-covered cable**.

lead shield A type of **anchor**, for an expansion screw or bolt, which consists of a lead sleeve that surrounds it.

lead slate, copper slate, lead sleeve A cylindrical sleeve, formed of sheet lead or sheet copper, used around a pipe where it penetrates a roof to make the intersection watertight.

lead sleeve See **lead slate**.

lead soaker See **soaker**.

lead spitter A tapered connector between a lead gutter and a downpipe.

lead tack **1.** A lead strip used to secure the free edge of flashing; one end of the tack is fixed to

the structure and the other end is folded over the free edge of the sheet metal. **2.** A rectangular piece of lead which is attached to a lead pipe and enables it to be secured to a wall or other support.

lead-up Same as **starter frame**.

lead wedge A tapered strip of lead used to secure a flashing to a masonry wall.

lead wing In **patent glazing**, a strip of lead around a pane of glass to secure it and to prevent the entry of water.

lead wool A wool-like material of fine strands of lead; sometimes used as caulking in pipe joints.

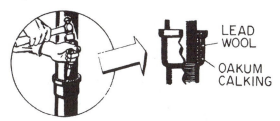

lead wool applied as caulking

leaf **1.** A hinged part; a separately movable division of a folding or sliding door. **2.** One of a pair of doors or windows. **3.** One of the two halves of a **cavity wall**.

leaf and dart, heart and dart In Greek architecture and derivatives, a pattern of alternating, conventionalized, deltoid and lanceolate leaves, usually applied to a **cyma reversa**.

leaf and dart

leaf and square A small tool used by plasterers in ornamental work; has a leaf-shaped blade at one end and a rectangular blade at the other.

lean clay A clay having low values of **liquid limit** and **plasticity index**.

lean concrete Concrete of low cement content.

leaning tower A tower, usually detached and slender for its height, which overhangs its base; the most famous example of such a tower is at

Pisa, Italy, where the 179 ft (54.6 m) tower is 16.5 ft (5 m) out of perpendicular.

lean lime An impure lime; has lower plasticity than pure lime.

lean mix, lean mixture **1.** A concrete or mortar mixture with relatively low cement content. **2.** A plaster which is not workable.

lean mortar Mortar which is deficient in cementitious components; is sticky and adheres to the trowel; is difficult to spread.

lean-to A small extension to a building with a roof (having but one slope) whose supports lean against the building.

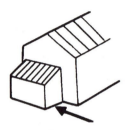

lean-to

lean-to house A seldom-used term used for a **saltbox house**.

lean-to roof, half-span roof A roof having a single pitch, carried by a wall which is higher than the roof.

lear board, layer board A board which is fixed across the rafters to provide a bearing surface for a roof gutter lining.

lease A contract transferring the right of possession of buildings, property, etc., for a fixed period of time, usually for periodical compensation called **rent**.

leasehold A tenure by lease; real estate held under a lease.

LECA Abbr. for "light-expanded clay aggregate."

Le Chatelier apparatus A device used in the testing of hydraulic cements to measure **soundness, 2**.

lecithin A liquid, obtained in refinement of soya beans or cottonseed; used in paints to promote pigment wetting and to control pigment settling and flow properties.

lectern In a church or lecture hall, a stand with a slanting top to hold a book, speech, or music at the proper height for reading.

ledge **1.** A small projecting member or molding. **2.** A wood member across a number of boards to hold them together. **3.** An unframed member which stiffens a board, or a series of boards or battens. **4.** See **bedrock**.

ledged-and-braced door A **batten door** with diagonal bracing to provide additional reinforcement.

ledged door Same as **battened door**.

ledgement table, ledgment table A band course, stringcourse, or belt course, usually molded; esp. one carried along the lower portion of a building.

ledger **1.** In formwork, a horizontal member which is supported by hangers or by upright posts and carries joists. **2.** A horizontal member which is housed in the studs of balloon framing and carries joists. **3.** In scaffolding, one of the horizontal members fastened to uprights which support the **put-logs** and which are at right angles to the wall; they carry the boards on which the workmen stand. **4.** A flat slab of stone, such as that laid horizontally over a grave.

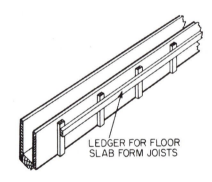

LEDGER FOR FLOOR
SLAB FORM JOISTS

ledger, 1

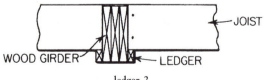

JOIST

WOOD GIRDER — LEDGER

ledger, 2

ledger board **1.** A **ribbon strip**. **2.** One of a number of horizontal boards, joined by vertical supports, as in a fence.

ledger plate **1.** Same as **ledger strip**. **2.** Same as **ledger, 1**.

ledger strip **1.** On a beam which carries joists flush with the upper edge of the beam (or girder), a strip of lumber which is nailed to the side of the beam (along its bottom edge), forming a seat for the joists and helping to support them. **2.** A **ribbon strip**.

ledgment, ledgement A horizontal, decorative **stringcourse** of brick or stone.

left-hand door See **hand**.

left-hand lock A lock for use on a **left-hand door**.

left-hand reverse door See **hand**.

left-hand stairway A stairway having the rail on the left side, in the ascending direction.

legal open space An **open space** on a premise, such as a yard or court that is permanently dedicated to public use, and that abuts the premise.

leg drop A narrow curtain, usually hung as one of a pair, on each side of a theatre stage, parallel to the footlights.

legget, leggatt A tool used by reed thatchers to align the reeds.

legitimate house A theatre in which stage plays are produced professionally.

Leipzig yellow See **chrome yellow**.

LEMA Abbr. for "Lighting Equipment Manufacturers' Association."

lemon spline A strip of wood or metal, shaped like a slice of a lemon, which is inserted in a slot formed by two members, each of which is grooved and butted against the other.

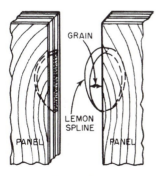

lemon spline

lengthening joint Any joint (e.g., a halved, lapped, or scarfed joint) used to increase the length of a timber.

lens **1.** A glass or plastic having smooth, regular opposite surfaces, shaped to control transmitted light by refraction; used in a lighting unit to focus, disperse, or collimate light rays. **2.** A combination of such elements.

lens panel, lens plate A transparent material in which an array of individual lens elements has been formed; covers lamps in a luminaire to control the direction of emitted light.

leopardwood Same as **letterwood**.

leper's squint See **low-side window**.

Lesbian cyma A **cyma reversa**.

Lesbian leaf Same as **water leaf, 2**.

lesche In ancient Greece, a public portico, clubhouse, or the like, frequented by the people for conversation or the hearing of news; such buildings were numerous in Greek cities, and their walls often were decorated by celebrated painters.

lesene See **pilaster strip**.

lessee The person receiving a possessory interest in buildings, property, etc., by **lease**.

lessor The person granting a possessory interest in buildings, property, etc., by **lease**.

let in In joinery, to insert, to embed, or to house; to secure a timber by inserting it in another.

let-in brace A diagonal brace that is **let in** to a stud.

letter agreement, letter of agreement A letter stating the terms of an **agreement** between addressor and addressee, usually prepared to be signed by the addressee to indicate his acceptance of those terms as legally binding.

letter box Same as **mail box**.

letter-box backplate A plate, attached to the interior side of a door, which permits the passage of mail but conceals the opening in the **letter-box plate**.

letter-box hood Same as **letter-box backplate**.

letter-box plate, letter plate A plate, attached to the exterior side of a door, having an opening through which mail may be passed; often has a **letter-box backplate**.

letter chute See **mail chute**.

letter-drop plate A **letter-box plate**, often with a **letter-box backplate**.

letter of intent A letter signifying an intention to enter into a formal **agreement**, usually setting forth the general terms of such agreement.

letter plate   See **letter-box plate**.

letter slot   See **mail slot**.

letterwood, leopardwood, snakewood   A mottled wood of Guiana; has high elasticity; used for decorative veneer.

letting of bid   See **bid opening**.

levecel   An **appentice**.

level   **1.** A surveying instrument for measuring heights with respect to an established horizontal line of sight; consists of a telescope and attached spirit level, a rotatable mounting, and a tripod. Also see **wye level** and **dumpy level**. **2.** The position of a line or plane when parallel to the surface of still water. **3.** See **spirit level**. **4.** Of an acoustical quantity, 10 times the logarithm (base 10) of the ratio of the quantity to a reference quantity of the same physical kind.

level control   A series of bench marks or other points of known elevation, established throughout a project.

leveling   **1.** In paints, see **flow, 3**. **2.** A surveying procedure of determining the difference in elevation between two points by means of a level or transit and a leveling rod. A spirit level is used on the level or transit to establish a horizontal line of sight.

leveling coat   A thin coat of plaster to provide a level surface.

leveling course   See **asphalt leveling course**.

leveling device   On an elevator car, a mechanism which automatically controls the movement of the car near a landing so that the car stops at the landing.

leveling instrument   An instrument to determine the differences in elevation between points.

leveling rod, leveling staff   A straight rod or bar, designed for use in measuring a vertical distance between a point on the ground and the line of collimation of a leveling instrument which has been adjusted to a horizontal position; usually made of wood and has a flat face which is graduated in terms of some linear unit and fractions thereof, the zero of the graduations being at one end of the rod; may have the graduations on a metal face. On some rods the graduation marks are designed to be read by the observer at the leveling instrument; another type, a "target rod," carries a target which is

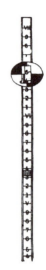

leveling rod

moved into position according to signals made by the man at the instrument; when the target is bisected by the line of collimation, it is read by the rodman.

leveling rule   A very long **level**, used by plasterers to indicate whether any part of a horizontal surface is higher than another.

leveling staff   See **leveling rod**.

level surface   A surface which at every point is perpendicular to a plumb line or the direction in which gravity acts; parallel to the surface of still water.

lever arm   In a structural member, that length of the member between the center of the tensile reinforcement and the center of action of the compression.

lever board   Same as **louver board**.

lever handle   In builders' hardware, a horizontal handle for operating the bolt(s) of a lock.

lever shears   See **alligator shears**.

lever tumbler   A flat tumbler in a lock; has a pivoted motion which is actuated by the turning of the key, thereby controlling the lock.

lever-type operator   In a casement window, a substitute for a **roto operator**.

lewis   Any of several metal devices used in hoisting stone blocks, columns, or other heavy masonry units; consists of a dovetailed tenon, made in sections, which is fitted into a dovetailed recess cut in the masonry unit.

lewis

lewis bolt **1.** A bolt with a wedge-shaped end inserted like the shank of a **lewis** in a hole drilled in a stone and fastened therein by pouring melted lead or concrete into the unfilled part of the hole. **2.** An eyebolt similarly inserted and used like a lewis for lifting heavy stones.

lewis hole A dovetailed recess which is cut in a masonry unit for the reception of a **lewis**.

lewising tool A masonry chisel used for cutting **lewis holes**.

LFT Abbr. for "linear foot."

LG On drawings, abbr. for "long" or "length."

lgr In the lumber industry, abbr. for "longer."

lgth In the lumber industry, abbr. for "length."

LH On drawings, abbr. for "left hand."

L-head The top of a shore which is formed with a braced horizontal member projecting on one side, forming an inverted L-shaped assembly.

liability insurance Insurance which protects the insured against liability on account of injury to the person or property of another.

Liberty See **Neo-Liberty** and **Stile Liberty**.

library A place for maintaining a permanent collection of books for public or private use; in a home, usually consists of a single room, but in a public or private facility, may occupy an entire building.

LIC On drawings, abbr. for "license."

license A written document authorizing a person to perform specific acts, such as the construction or alteration of a building, or the installation, alteration, use, and/or operation of service equipment therein.

licensed architect See **architect, 2**.

licensed contractor A person or organization certified by governmental authority, where required by law, to engage in construction contracting.

licensed engineer See **professional engineer**.

lich-gate See **lych-gate**.

lich-stone See **lych-stone**.

lien A right enforceable against specific property to secure payment of an obligation.

lien waiver See **waiver of lien**.

lierne rib In Gothic vaulting, any small subordinate rib which is inserted between the main ribs, more often as an ornament than for reasons of construction.

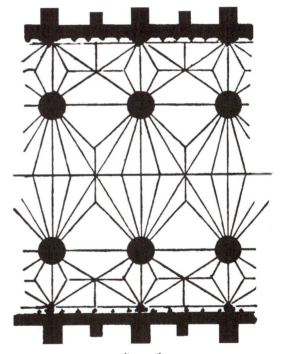

lierne ribs

lierne vault A **vault** in which **lierne ribs** are used.

life cycle cost The cost of a building or equipment (or the like) based not only on the initial expenditure, but also on its maintenance and operating costs over its entire lifetime.

life performance curve For a source of light, a curve showing the variation of some characteristic of the source throughout its lifetime (e.g., lumens vs. life).

lift   **1.** An elevator used on the stage of a theatre, in the orchestra pit, or on the apron. **2.** British term for **elevator**. **3.** A handle or projection from the lower sash in a hung window, used as a grip in raising the sash; also called a **sash lift**. **4.** One of a number of frames of scaffolding erected one above another in a vertical direction. **5.** The concrete placed between two consecutive horizontal construction joints; usually consists of several layers or courses. **6.** In reinforced concrete construction, that portion of a wall, pier, abutment, etc., placed in a single pour. **7.** The amount of grouting or mortar placed at a single time in a building structure. **8.** In a multi-level excavation, a bench or step.

lift gate   A gate that opens by moving in a vertical direction, in contrast to one that swings about hinges along one edge.

lift hole   A small hole in a pipe or pipe section which is used to insert a device for handling the pipe.

lifting, raising   In paints, the softening and swelling of a film of old dry paint when a new topcoat is applied over it.

lifting beam   Same as **strongback**.

lifting pin   A **lewis**.

lift joint   The joint formed between two successive **lifts, 5**.

lift latch, thumb latch   A type of door latch which fastens a door by means of a pivoted bar that engages a hook on the doorjamb; a lever which lifts the pivoted bar is used to unfasten the door. Also see **Norfolk latch, Suffolk latch, thumb latch**.

lift latch

lift-off butt hinge   A special type of **butt hinge** which has a pin permitting the door to be raised off the hinge.

lift-off hinge   See **loose-joint hinge**.

lift platform   Same as **elevator car platform**.

lift shaft   See **hoistway**.

lift slab   **1.** A method of concrete building construction in which floor (and roof) slabs are cast, usually at ground level, and then raised into position by jacking. **2.** A slab which is a component of such construction.

lift well   British term for elevator **hoistway**.

ligger   **1.** A horizontal timber secured to uprights and supporting floor timbers, scaffolding, or the like; a **ledger**. **2.** A long stick (often of willow) used along the ridge of a thatched roof. **3.** A mortar board. **4.** A board pathway over a ditch.

light   **1.** An aperture through which daylight is admitted to the interior of a building. **2.** A pane of glass, a window, or a compartment of a window. **3.** An artificial source of illumination. Also see **ceiling light, dead light, divided light, dome light, elliptical fanlight, fanlight, lantern light, leaded light, pavement light, quarter-round light, semicircular light, semielliptical light, sidelight, skylight, sodium light, sunburst light, transom light**.

light alloy   Any alloy of aluminum.

light bridge   A **bridge, 3**, fixed or suspended above a theatre stage, to which lighting equipment is attached and/or from which it is operated.

light bulb   **1.** Same as **incandescent lamp**. **2.** See **lamp bulb**.

light-center length   The distance between the center of the light-generating element of a lamp (e.g., the filament of an incandescent lamp) and an arbitrary point on the lamp base; for each type of lamp base, the reference point is defined by convention.

light control-console   A **console, 3**, in an auditorium, usually with a view of the stage; used to control the lighting—in the auditorium and on the stage.

light court   A recess formed by the outer walls of a building and used to provide light and air through windows to adjoining spaces within the building.

light dimmer   Same as **dimmer**.

lightfast   Descriptive of paint or pigment which is color-stable when exposed to sunlight.

light filter   A device for changing the magnitude and/or the spectral composition of the radiant light flux which is transmitted through it; designated as selective (colored) or neutral, according to whether or not the spectral distribution of the incident flux is altered.

light globe   See **globe**.

light-hazard occupancy   An occupancy in which the quantity and/or combustibility of its contents is low; if a fire should occur, a relatively low rate of heat release is expected.

lighthouse   A tall structure, such as a tower, with a powerful source of light on top; located on a seacoast or other water channel to provide guidance for mariners at sea. Lighthouses were important facilities in establishing seafaring commerce and continued to be influential until the latter part of the 20th century, when they were largely replaced by electronic guidance systems.

lighting   1. The various processes, systems, forms, and/or equipment used to provide light and illumination. 2. See **accent lighting, cove lighting**, etc.

lighting batten   A **batten, 9** for lighting equipment.

lighting booth   A booth, usually with a view of the stage, where the light-control console is located.

lighting cost, cost of light   In lamp evaluation, the cost of light rather than total system cost; commonly expressed as the cost per million lumen-hours; depends on lamp cost, operating energy cost, and lamp replacement cost.

lighting fitting   British term for **luminaire**.

lighting fixture   An electrical component used to hold a lamp, fluorescent light, or the like; often includes a shade or light reflector; may be entirely functional in appearance or decorative in design.

lighting instrument   A **luminaire**, esp. one that is portable and can be aimed, focused, or adjusted, as in theatre lighting.

lighting outlet   An **electrical outlet** intended for the direct connection of a lampholder, a lighting fixture, or a pendant cord which terminates in a lampholder.

lighting panel   1. An electric panel containing fuses or circuit breakers used to protect branch circuits serving lighting fixtures. 2. A panel for switching or controlling lights and lighting circuits.

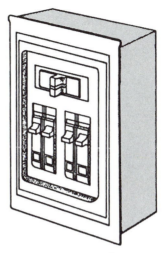

lighting panel

lighting panelboard   A **panelboard** which has 10% or more of its overcurrent devices rated at no more than 30 amperes.

lighting track   A special type of **surface raceway** with preassembled electrical conductors in an open U-track; designed so that a lighting fixture (equipped with a special connector) may be inserted into the open U-track; the fixture is then twisted 90° to make contact with the conductors on the track.

lighting unit   A **luminaire**; esp. a portable luminaire.

light loss factor   A factor used in calculating the illumination provided by a lighting system after a given period of time and under given conditions; includes the effects of temperature, voltage, ballast variations, dirt on luminaire surfaces, dirt on the room surfaces, maintenance procedures, and atmospheric conditions. There are two categories: losses which can be recovered by replacing old lamps or cleaning surfaces, and nonrecoverable losses, such as those due to component deterioration or uncontrollable voltage drops.

lightly coated electrode   See **coated electrode**.

lightness   The whiteness of a painted surface as measured by the amount of light reflected from it.

lightning arrester   A device which is connected in an electric wiring system (usually between a line voltage terminal and ground) to protect the wiring system from damage from lightning or any other abnormally high surge of voltage.

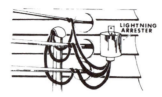

lightning arrester

lightning conductor, lightning rod A metallic cable or rod, running from the highest point on the roof of a building (and insulated from it) to the ground; protects the building, should lightning strike, by providing a direct path to ground.

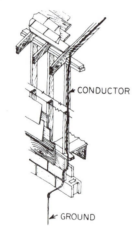

← CONDUCTOR

← GROUND

lightning conductor

lightning rod A rod-like electrical conductor attached to the highest exterior point of a building; provides a direct electrical path to the ground if lightning strikes the building, furnishing protection against lightning-induced damage; invented in 1752 by Benjamin Franklin, who established that lightning is an electrical phenomenon.

lightning shake Separation between annual rings of wood, caused by lightning damage to the tree cambium during growth.

light pipe Same as **lighting batten**.

lightproof blind A vertically operable lightproof shade which travels in guides that are fixed to the window jambs; when in the down position, the window is eliminated as a natural source of light.

light-reflective glass See **reflective glass**.

light resistance The ability of a material, such as a plastic, to resist fading after exposure to sunlight or ultraviolet light.

light source A See **standard source A**.

light source B See **standard source B**.

light source C See **standard source C**.

light tormentor A vertical pipe at either side of a theatre or auditorium proscenium, used for mounting lighting units.

lightweight aggregate Aggregate of low-bulk specific gravity, such as expanded or sintered clay, foamed slag, fly ash, exfoliated vermiculite; used as an ingredient in lightweight concrete.

lightweight concrete Concrete of substantially lower density than that made from gravel or crushed stone; usually made with lightweight aggregate.

light well A shaft within a building, open to the outer air at the top, used to admit daylight and air through windows opening onto the shaft.

lignin **1.** An organic substance in wood that, with celluloses, forms the principal constituent of wood tissue. **2.** A crystalline product recovered from paper pulp; used in the manufacture of plastics, as a binder in wood chipboard, and for anticorrosive coatings.

limba A straight-grained, fine-textured wood of the limba tree; esp. used for paneling.

lime A white or grayish-white caustic substance, calcium oxide, usually obtained by heating limestone or marble at a high temperature; used chiefly in plasters, mortars, and cements. In the past, in many areas along the seacoast where limestone was scarce, seashells were heated to obtain lime. Also see **lime mortar** and **shell lime**.

lime-and-cement mortar Hydrated lime, lime putty, or slaked lime mixed with portland cement and sand; forms a cement mortar used in masonry and in portland cement plaster (stucco).

lime burning The calcining (heating) of **lime**.

lime concrete A concrete made from a mixture of lime, sand, and gravel, widely used before the lime matrix was replaced by portland cement.

limed rosin Rosin reacted with lime; used as a binder in paints.

lime mortar A mortar made by mixing lime putty and sand; now little used because of its slow hardening.

lime paste Lime soaked with water to form a putty.

lime plaster A base-coat plaster consisting of lime and aggregate.

lime putty, plasterer's putty A hydrated lime which has been slaked with sufficient water to form a thick paste; used in plastering.

lime rock A natural, consolidated or partially consolidated form of limestone; mostly of calcium carbonate, but containing some silica.

limestone Rock of sedimentary origin composed principally of calcite or dolomite or both; used as building stone or crushed-stone aggregate or burnt to produce **lime**.

lime-tallow wash A mixture of lime and water with tallow; used on roofs, walls, and other external surfaces.

limewash A mixture of lime and water; used to coat internal and external surfaces; a **whitewash**.

limewood See **basswood**.

limit control A safety device on a boiler, refrigerator, or air-conditioning system which shuts off the system and actuates alarms when unsafe conditions are detected. Also see **limit switch**.

limit design Structural design based on any chosen limit of usefulness, such as a plastic limit, stability limit, elastic limit, fatigue limit, or deformation limit.

limited combustible material A building construction material which does not comply with the NFPA definition of **noncombustible material**. The materials in this classification must not exceed a potential heat value of 3500 Btu per pound (8141 kJ/kg); in addition, they must comply with at least at least one other applicable requirements of the applicable NFPA standard.

limiter A special-purpose fuse (usually of high current-interrupting rating) designed to protect an electrical circuit or equipment from the effects of high **available short-circuit current** by limiting the amount of current permitted to flow through it.

limit of proportionality See **proportional limit**.

limit switch An electric switch, operated by a power-driven machine or by the movement of the car which it drives, which alters or controls the electric circuit associated with the machine, e.g., a switch which slows down and stops an elevator car or dumbwaiter car automatically at or near the top or bottom terminal landing; operates independently of the device which normally controls movement of the car.

limonite A naturally occurring mineral which is used in high-density concrete because of its high density and water content, making it effective in radiation shielding.

LIN On drawings, abbr. for "linear."

linden See **basswood**.

line **1.** A system of cables and/or wires (along with poles to support them) used for the general distribution of electricity. **2.** A flexible cable, chain, rope, or the like.

linear diffuser, slot diffuser, strip diffuser An **air outlet** where the ratio of length to width of the outlet usually exceeds 10:1; the width of the outlet usually is not greater than 4 in. (10 cm).

linear light source A light source whose dimension along a line is significantly greater than its other dimensions as, for example, a line of fluorescent lamps.

linear packer An automatic **refuse compactor** similar to a **carousel packer**, but the bags, contained on a linear carriage, move along a straight line; especially suitable for use in very narrow locations. (*See illustration p. 552.*)

linear plan A house **plan** that is either one room wide and two or more rooms deep, or one room deep and two or more rooms wide.

linear prestressing Prestressing as applied to linear structural members, such as **reinforced concrete** beams or columns.

linear-type heat detector In a fire detection system, a heat sensor that can be activated anywhere along its length; employs a heat-sensitive cable whose electrical conductivity depends significantly on temperature. (*See illustration p. 552.*)

line drilling In rock excavation by blasting, drilling a series of closely spaced holes, about 4 in. (10 cm) apart, at the perimeter of the cut, so as to break the rock along a line.

line drop The decrease in voltage in the conductors of an electric circuit resulting from their resistance.

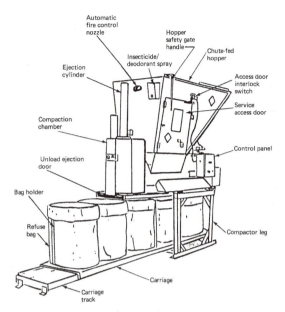

linear packer

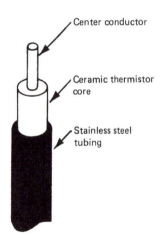

linear-type heat detector

line level A special **spirit level** used in checking the floor of an excavation, in laying pipe, and for similar work; each end of the level has a hook, permitting it to be hooked over a horizontally stretched line; is especially light and short.

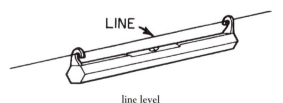

line level

linenfold, linen pattern, linen scroll A form of carved paneling representing a symmetrical fold or scroll of linen.

linenfold

line of collimation See **line of sight**.

line of levels In surveying, a continuous series of measured differences of elevation.

line of pressure A line indicating the points of pressure between the voussoirs of an arch or buttress.

line of sight, line of collimation The line extending from an instrument along which distant objects are seen, when viewed with the telescope or other sighting device. Also see **sight line**.

line of travel See **walking line**.

line pin In bricklaying, a steel pin used as a support for the line by which a bricklayer aligns his work.

line pipe A welded or seamless pipe, available with the ends plain, beveled, grooved, expanded, flanged, or threaded; principally used to convey gas, oil, or water.

liner 1. In fabrication of stone veneer (principally marble), stone bonded to the back of the thin facing sheets to add strength, rigidity, bearing surface, or depth of joint. 2. A tool used by painters. 3. A **sleeve piece** used in plumbing. 4. Same as **jamb lining**.

liner plate A prefabricated plate of stamped steel; has corrugations to provide stiffness; provided with flanges so that similar units can be bolted together to form a support system for a tunnel, shaft, or pit.

LIN FT On drawings, abbr. for "linear foot."

lining 1. Material which covers any interior surface, such as framework around a door or window, or boarding which covers the interior surfaces of a building. 2. Same as **flue lining**.

lining out Marking timber for cutting.

lining paper 1. A paper, usually waterproof, fastened to the studding of frame buildings before nailing on the weatherboarding; used under slates and shingles in roofing. 2. An undercoat paper, applied to a surface as a base for a decorative wallpaper.

lining plate In sheet-metal roofing, a metal strip which is attached to the eaves to secure the lower edge of the roofing sheets.

lining tool A slanting-edged tool used by painters in drawing lines.

link dormer A dormer which joins one part of a roof to another, or one which houses a chimney.

link dormer

linked switch Two or more electric switches which are mechanically connected by operating arms or levers, so as to operate at the same time or in a desired sequence.

link fuse An exposed **fuse** which is mounted on electrically insulated supports.

linoleum A resilient floor-covering material made by combining an oxidized linseed-oil binder and ground cork and bonding to a burlap or canvas backing; relatively low in cost; has poor stain resistance and low abrasion and dent resistance.

linseed oil A commonly used drying oil in paints and varnishes. Also see **raw linseed oil**.

lintel A horizontal structural member (such as a beam) over an opening which carries the weight of the wall above it; usually of steel, stone, or

steel **lintel**

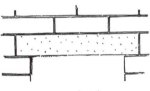

stone **lintel**

wood. Also see **door lintel, eyebrow lintel, fireplace lintel, splayed lintel, through lintel**.

lintel block, U-block A concrete masonry unit having a single core with an open end; usually placed with its open end upright; such blocks form a continuous beam when filled with grout and proper reinforcement.

lintel course In stone masonry, a course set at the level of a lintel, commonly differentiated from the wall by its greater projection, its finish, or its thickness, which often matches that of the lintel.

lintol Same as **lintel**.

lip 1. A rounded overhanging edge or member. 2. See **lip strike**.

lip block In timberwork supporting an excavation, a short timber which is fixed to the top of a strut and which projects over a **wale**.

lipping A strip of wood that covers the edge of a built-up door so that the joints between the core and veneer are not visible.

lip strike The projection from the side of a **strike plate** which the bolt of a lock strikes first, when a door is closed; projects out from the side of the strike plate to protect the frame. (*See illustration p. 554.*)

lip strike

lip union   A pipe **union** having a lip to prevent the gasket from being squeezed into the pipe.

liquefaction   **1.** The sudden, large decrease of shearing resistance of a cohesionless soil caused by a collapse of the soil structure, produced by shock or small shear strains, associated with a sudden but temporary increase of pore water pressures. **2.** The process of transforming a soil from a solid state to a liquid state, usually as a result of increased pore pressure and reduced shearing resistance. For example, an action in which a soil deposit (e.g., loose sand) loses its shear resistance temporarily and takes on the character of a liquid; such action, for example, may occur during an earthquake.

liquid-ash removal system   A system for the removal of molten ash (continuously or intermittently, as desired) from the bottom of a furnace, by a piping arrangement operated by compressed air.

liquid asphaltic material   An asphaltic product so soft that its consistency cannot be measured at normal temperature by a **penetration, 2** test.

liquidated damages   A sum specified in a contract whereby damages in the event of breach are to be determined. In a **construction contract**, liquidated damages usually are specified as a fixed sum per day for failure to complete the **work, 1** within a specified time. If set at a level consistent with a reasonable forecast of actual harm to the **owner**, liquidated damage clauses will be upheld and will preclude use of standards for computation of damages that would otherwise be imposed by law. If the amount prescribed for liquidated damages is unreasonably high, the provision will be denominated an illegal "penalty" by the courts and held invalid; in such case, damages will be determined pursuant to otherwise applicable rules of law.

liquid chiller   **1.** See **compressor-type liquid chiller**. **2.** See **absorption-type liquid chiller**.

liquid drier   See **soluble drier; drier**.

liquid-immersed transformer   A **transformer** having its core and coils submerged in an insulating liquid such as oil.

liquid indicator   A device, frequently combined with a strainer, located in the liquid line of a refrigeration system and having a sight port by which the liquid flow may be observed for presence of bubbles.

liquid limit   The water content corresponding to the limit between the liquid and plastic states of consistency of a soil.

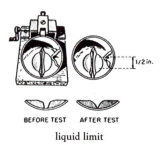

BEFORE TEST   AFTER TEST

liquid limit

liquid line   A tube or pipe carrying the refrigerant liquid from the condenser or receiver of a refrigeration system to a pressure-reducing device.

liquid-membrane curing compound   A material, laid down in the form of a liquid, which acts as a **sealant**.

liquid petroleum gas   Any material which is composed predominantly of any of the following hydrocarbons or mixtures of them: propane, propylene, butane, and butylenes.

liquid receiver   A vessel permanently connected to a system by inlet and outlet pipes for the storage of (condensed) refrigerant.

liquid roofing   A seamless roofing material, applied in liquid or semiliquid form, to produce a waterproof membrane.

liquid-volume measurement   The measurement of grout according to the total volume of its liquid and solid constituents.

liquid waste   The discharge from any fixture, appliance, area, or appurtenance which does not contain fecal matter.

liquified natural gas (LNG)   A product of natural gas essentially consisting of methanes;

stored under pressure to maintain its liquid state; used as a fuel for heating and cooking.

liquified petroleum gas (LPG)   A petroleum derivative, primarily butane and propane, stored under pressure to maintain its liquid state; used as a fuel for heating and cooking.

L-iron   Same as **angle iron**.

lisena   A Romanesque pilaster strip.

listed   Equipment, materials, or products included in a list published by an organization acceptable to the **authority having jurisdiction**; the organization is concerned with the evaluation and periodic inspection of production of listed items; a listed item must meet appropriate standards or must have been tested and found suitable for use in a specified manner.

listel, list   A **fillet, 1**.

listing   The sapwood cut from the edge of a board.

lite   Same as **light, 2**.

liter, litre   A metric unit of volume equal to 1/1000 cubic meter; equal to 61.03 cubic inches.

litharge   A yellow lead monoxide (a powder of lead oxide); used as a pigment, as a drier, and as a catalyst in paints. Also see **massicot**.

lithopone   A white pigment consisting of zinc sulfide and barium sulfate, having moderate hiding power; high-strength lithopone contains a higher percentage of zinc sulfide.

lithostrotum opus   In ancient Greece and Rome, any ornamental pavement, such as mosaic.

litmus   An organic chemical indicator of acidity or alkalinity; is red in color for **pH values** below 4.5 and blue above 8.3.

little house   An 18th-century euphemism for an outdoor toilet; a **privy**.

live   **1.** Connected to a source of voltage. **2.** Said of a room having an unusually small amount of sound absorption.

live boom   A **boom** on a power that can be raised or lowered without interrupting the digging operation.

live edge   The edge of a painted surface which can be blended with fresh paint without having the lap show.

live-front   Descriptive of a piece of electric equipment which is so constructed that there are

live parts which can be touched from the front of the assembly.

live knot   See **intergrown knot**.

live load   The moving or movable external load on a structure; includes the weight of furnishings of a building, of the people, of equipment, etc., but does not include wind load.

liveness   The acoustical quality of a **live room**.

live part   Any electric component or part which is designed to operate at a voltage different from that of the earth.

livering   The thickening of paint or varnish to an unusable rubbery consistency.

live room   A room characterized by an unusually small amount of sound absorption.

live steam   Steam that has not as yet given up any of its energy and has not yet condensed, e.g., steam emerging from a boiler.

living hall, living stair hall   A large room at the entry to a house, especially in an elegant home; frequently contains an imposing staircase, fireplace, and seating area; often, simply called the *hall*; also see **entrance hall**.

living room   A space in a dwelling for social use of the residents.

living unit   A dwelling or portion thereof, providing complete living facilities for one family, including permanent provisions for living, sleeping, eating, cooking, and sanitation.

LL   On drawings, abbr. for **live load**.

L&L   Abbr. for "latch and lock."

LL&B   Abbr. for "latch, lock, and bolt."

lm   Abbr. for **lumen**.

LM   On drawings, abbr. for **lime mortar**.

LNG   Abbr. for **liquid natural gas**.

lng, Lng   Abbr. for "lining."

LOA   On drawings, abbr. for "length overall."

load   **1.** A force, or system of forces, carried by a structure, or a part of the structure. **2.** Any device or piece of electric equipment that receives electric power. **3.** The power delivered to such a device or piece of equipment. **4.** The amount of heat per unit time imposed on a refrigeration system; the required rate of heat removal.

load-bearing partition   A partition capable of supporting a load in addition to its own weight.

load-bearing tile   Tile, used in masonry walls, which carries superimposed loads.

load-bearing wall   A wall capable of supporting an imposed load in addition to its own weight.

load-carrying band   A flat piece of metal which is welded to a side or end of a grating panel, used in a cutout to transfer the load from unsupported to supported bearing bars.

loader   A self-powered machine equipped with a front-mounted bucket and lift arms for pushing and raising a load of earth or other construction materials; usually mounted on wheels or crawler-track undercarriage.

loader

load factor   **1.** In structural design, the factor by which a working load is multiplied to determine the **design ultimate load**. **2.** In air conditioning, the ratio of the average load on a system to the maximum load capacity. **3.** In plumbing, the percentage of the total flow rate (expressed in **fixture units**) which is likely to occur at any point in the drainage system; represents the ratio of the probable load to the potential load.

load factor design   A method of structural design based on the use of a given **working load** times a multiple; also see **limit design**.

load-indicating bolt   A special type of high-strength bolt having a small projection which compresses as the bolt is tightened; the amount of projection can be measured with a feeler gauge, thereby acting as a measure of the bolt tension.

loading cycles   In structural design, the number of repetitions of load assumed to act on a structure during its lifetime; used as a criterion in determining the fatigue strength of the structure.

loading dock   See **loading platform, 1**.

loading dock leveler   An adjustable-level platform or ramp which facilitates the handling of goods or materials to or from trucks, at a loading dock or at pavement level.

loading dock seal   A resilient pad around the door of a loading dock to provide a tight seal between the door and a truck which has backed into the loading dock.

loading dock shelter   A waterproof canopy which extends out from a building to provide weather protection between loading dock doors and the opening of a truck.

loading door   A theatre stage door through which scenery, properties, and other equipment are moved.

loading hopper   A **hopper, 1** in which concrete or other free-flowing material is placed for loading by gravity into buggies, etc.

loading platform, loading dock   **1.** An elevated platform at the shipping or delivery door of a building or adjacent to the stage of a theatre; usually at the same height as the floor of a motor truck or railroad car to facilitate loading or unloading. **2.** A platform on a theatre stage for storing **counterweights, 2**.

loading ramp   A device or facility (hinged, mechanical or hydraulic) to provide for differences in the heights or to span gaps between a loading surface and a carrier.

load-transfer assembly   A unit which is designed to link or support dowel bars in the desired position during concreting operations.

loam   In building construction, a mixture composed chiefly of moistened clay, sand, and silt, or some mixture including these ingredients. Once used as a **mortar** when combined with lime, or used as a plaster with the addition of chopped straw.

lobby   A space at the entrance to a building, theatre, etc.

lobe   A segment of a circle in tracery; a **foil**.

lobed arch   A **cusped arch**.

local buckling   The buckling of a compression element which may precipitate the failure of the whole structural member.

local lighting   Lighting which illuminates a relatively small area without illuminating the general surroundings significantly.

local vent, local ventilating pipe A pipe on the fixture side of a trap through which vapor or foul air is removed from the room or fixture.

local vent stack A vertical pipe, to which connections are made from the fixture side of traps, and through which vapor and/or foul air may be removed from the fixture.

location plan Same as **site plan**.

location survey The establishment on the ground of points and lines in positions which have been determined previously by computation or by graphical methods, or by a description obtained from data supplied by documents of record, such as deeds, maps, or other sources.

lock A mechanical device that secures a door, gate, cabinet, or the like; may be operated by a key or by a **dead bolt**. The earliest door locks had a hardwood casing with working parts fabricated of metal; later, these were replaced by all-metal locks. A further significant advance in lock design was the invention of the pin-tumbler cylinder lock in 1848. Also see **box lock, case lock, door lock, rim lock, stock lock**.

lock backset The distance from the edge of a door to the center line of the lock cylinder.

lockband A course of **bondstones**.

lock bevel The direction in which a latch bolt is inclined.

lock block In a hollow-core flush door, a block of wood (the thickness of the door stile) to which the lock is fitted.

lock clip A flexible metal part which is attached to the inside of a door face to position a **mortise lock**.

lock corner A corner (as of a drawer) which is secured by an interlocking construction, such as a **dovetail**.

lock edge See **leading edge**.

locker A lockable cupboard for storage of personal property for protection from theft.

locker plant A public facility containing lockable cupboards rented for cold or frozen storage of privately owned food.

lock face The exposed surface of a mortise lock which shows in the edge of a door after installation of a lock.

lock faceplate Same as **lock front**.

lock front, *Brit.* **forend** On a door lock or latch, the plate through which the latching or locking bolt (or bolts) projects.

lock front bevel The angle of a lock front when not at right angle to the lock case, allowing the front to be applied flush with the edge of a beveled door.

locking device Any device used to secure a member, unit, or assembly in position, e.g., to hold a cross brace in scaffolding to the frame or panel.

locking stile See **lock stile**.

lock jamb See **strike jamb**.

lock joint See **lock seam**.

lock keeper The box on a doorjamb into which the bolt of a lock protrudes.

lock miter A **miter joint** having interlocking edges.

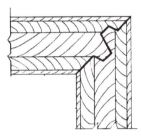

lock miter

locknut 1. A nut which is designed so that it will not come loose, locking in place when tightened. 2. A supplementary nut, screwed down on another nut to prevent it from shaking loose.

lock plate 1. Same as **strike plate**. 2. Same as **box strike plate**.

lock rail An intermediate horizontal structural member of a door, between the vertical **stiles**, at the height of the lock. (*See illustration p. 558.*)

lock reinforcement A reinforcing plate attached inside of the lock edge or lock stile of a door to receive a lock.

lock reinforcing unit A metal device used in a metal door to contain and support a lock.

locksaw A **compass saw** with a tapering flexible blade; used for cutting the seats for locks in doors.

lock seam, lock joint A joint or seam in sheet-metal roofing; the two edges are bent over in the form of hooks which are inserted in each other; then they are dressed down to form a seam.

lock seam door

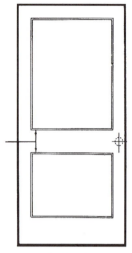

lock rail

lock seam door A door which has its face sheets secured in place by an exposed mechanical interlock seam on each of its two vertical edges.

lockset A complete lock system including the basic locking mechanism and all the accessories, such as knobs, escutcheons, plates, etc.

lockshield valve Same as **key valve**.

lockspit A small cut with a spade, or a small open trench, to mark a line of work, as fencing or the like.

lock stile, closing stile, locking stile, striking stile The vertical structural member of a

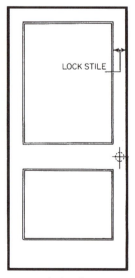

lock stile

door (or a casement sash) which closes against the jamb (or mullion) of the surrounding frame; the side away from the hinges.

lock strike Same as **strike plate**.

lock-strip gasket, structural gasket A gasket in which the sealing pressure is produced by forcing a keyed lock strip into a groove in one face of the gasket.

lockup A building or room for the temporary detention of prisoners by police.

loculus In ancient tombs, a recess for a sarcophagus or cinerary urn.

locust, black locust, red locust Wood of the locust tree; coarse-grained, strong, hard, decay-resistant, and durable; used in construction, esp. for posts.

locutorium Same as **locutory**.

locutory A place for conversation; esp. the parlor of a monastic establishment.

lodge **1.** A small house in a park, forest, or domain; a temporary habitation; a hut. **2.** The meeting place of a fraternal organization. **3.** A porter's or gatekeeper's house at the entrance to the grounds of an estate.

lodging chamber Same as **bedroom**.

lodging house A building containing rooms used or rented for sleeping purposes by two or more paying guests; the minimum and maximum numbers of rooms may be specified by the applicable local code.

loess A uniform wind-deposited accumulation of silty material having an open structure and relatively high cohesion due to cementation of clay or calcium-like material at grain contacts.

loft **1.** Unceiled space beneath a roof, often used for storage. Also see **attic, garret**. **2.** Upper space in a barn, e.g., cockloft, hayloft. **3.** Upper space in a church or concert hall, e.g., choir loft, organ loft. Also see **rood loft**. **4.** Unpartitioned space in a **loft building**. **5.** In a theatre stagehouse, the space between the top of the proscenium and the grid.

loft building A building, containing open, unpartitioned floor space, used for commercial or industrial purposes.

loft ladder A **disappearing stair**.

log cabin A general term often applied to two different types of dwellings, both of which are constructed of logs. A *log cabin* is constructed of straight, relatively smooth, round logs stripped of their bark and laid horizontally, one above the other, to form a structure. In contrast, a **log house** is constructed of logs that are *hewn* to form square timbers before they are assembled as a structure. The construction of these two types of dwellings differs with regard to the tools, skill, and time required for their construction. In both, the logs are notched or otherwise fastened together to prevent their spreading at the corners and to provide rigidity and strength, but in a log cabin the logs protrude beyond the joints; in the log house, the square-hewn timbers do not protrude beyond the joints. Log cabin construction requires only an ax, a minimum of skill, and a minimum of construction time. The walls are usually waterproofed by an infilling between the cracks, such as clay. Typically, both types have a **pitched roof**. The earliest log cabins in America usually consisted of a single room; they usually had a **battened door**, and where brick or stone was scarce, a **clay-and-sticks chimney**. Compare with **log house**; also see **dogtrot cabin, double-pen cabin, notch, planking, saddlebag cabin, vertical log cabin**.

log cabin

log-cabin siding An exterior wood siding, used on a small structure, which gives it the appearance of having been constructed of logs.

loge **1.** A box in a theatre. **2.** The front section of a mezzanine or lowest balcony in a theatre; usually separated by an aisle and/or railing from the section behind it.

logeion, logeum The raised platform for the actors in the Hellenistic theatre, corresponding to the modern stage.

loggia An arcaded or colonnaded porch or gallery attached to or contained within a larger structure; usually located in a prominent part of the building; open on at least one side to provide a protected outdoor sitting area, sometimes contains an upper story.

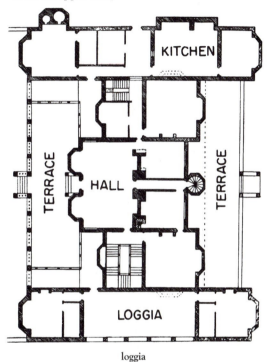

loggia

log house A house constructed of squared timbers that have been hewn from round logs, thus requiring an adze and/or other tools to shape them; the timbers are laid horizontally and notched or otherwise fastened to prevent their spreading at the corners and to provide rigidity and strength, and do not protrude at the corners as they do in a **log cabin**. The house usually has a shingled, pitched roof; often a chimney on a gable-end wall. Compare with **log cabin**, which is much easier to build.

log notch See **notch**.

Lombard architecture North Italian pre-Romanesque architecture in the 7th and 8th cent., during the rule of the Lombards, based on Early Christian and Roman forms. (*See illustration p. 560.*)

Lombard style **1.** A synonym occasionally used for the **Italianate style**. **2.** A term once

London stock brick

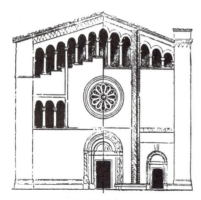
Lombard architecture

applied to **Romanesque Revival**, now usually called Richardsonian Romanesque style.

London stock brick Originally, handmade bricks produced in the vicinity of London, made on a "stock," i.e., a block of wood that locates the mold on the mold table; now machine-made brick of a coarse-textured yellow.

long-and-short work In rubble masonry, quoins which are placed alternately horizontally and vertically.

long-and-short work

long column A concrete column whose load capacity must be reduced, according to code requirements, because of its slenderness.

long float A **float** so long that two men are required to handle it.

long gallery A **gallery** in the upper stories of an Elizabethan or Jacobean manor house; often used as a promenade or family room.

long grip The **grip** of a bolt or rivet which is longer than five times its diameter.

long header A **header** which runs the full depth of a thick wall.

longhouse **1.** A multifamily dwelling usually having a rectangular plan divided by a central aisle along the length. **2.** A 20th-century term for a building that once provided both the domestic quarters for a family and housing for animals.

longitudinal axis An axis along the lengthwise direction of the figure or body, usually passing through its center of gravity.

longitudinal bar A steel **reinforcing bar** used in longitudinal reinforcement.

longitudinal bond A masonry bond in which occasional courses are laid with all **stretchers**; sometimes used in thick walls.

longitudinal bracing Bracing extending lengthwise of the structure, or parallel to its center line.

longitudinal joint Any joint which fastens two pieces along their length.

longitudinal reinforcement Steel **reinforcement, 1** for concrete which is essentially parallel to the horizontal concrete surface, or to the long axis of a concrete member.

longitudinal section In graphic representation, a **section, 1** taken along the longest axis.

longitudinal shear A **shear, 1** which is parallel to the longest axis of a member.

long-life lamp Any lamp type having a design life longer than the conventionally set value for its general class; an incandescent lamp of this type provides lower luminous output than a standard lamp of the same wattage.

long nipple A nipple having a considerable unthreaded length.

long nipple

long-oil alkyd An alkyd resin in which over 60% of the solids consist of an oxidizing oil; used for brushing enamels.

long-oil varnish See **long varnish**.

long-radius elbow An **elbow, 1** having a radius larger than standard to reduce friction losses and improve flow characteristics.

long room Primarily in the 17th and 18th centuries, a room for social gatherings, usually attached to a tavern.

long screw A pipe **nipple** usually 6 in. (15 cm) in length, with one thread much longer than usual.

long ton The equivalent of 2,240 lb (1,016 kg).

long varnish, long-oil varnish An oleoresinous varnish containing 20 to 100 gal oil per 100 lb (2 to 10 liter oil per kg) gum or resin; more durable, more flexible, less glossy, and softer than **short-oil varnish**.

lookout **1.** A rafter or joist at the ridge of a roof that projects beyond an end wall of a building; may support the overhanging portion of the roof or cornice; also called a rafter lookout. **2.** An elevated place or structure that provides a wide view for observation of the countryside, particularly against marauders.

lookout tower A **belvedere**.

lookum A small roof or penthouse used to shelter a wall crane, hoisting wheel, or the like.

loom See **flexible nonmetallic tubing**.

loom house Same as **spinning house**.

loop **1.** A loophole. **2.** A circuit vent.

loophole **1.** See **arrow loop**. **2.** In a fortification, one of a number of long, narrow slits in the walls, usually widening inward to permit small arms to be fired over a wide angle at an enemy. **3.** Same as **slit ventilator**.

looping in A method of avoiding splices in residential electric wiring by carrying the conductor or cable to and from the outlet to be supplied.

loop vent **1.** A vent arrangement for a group of plumbing fixtures; consists of a vent pipe which is connected to the waste or soil branch immediately before the first fixture of the group and immediately before the last fixture of the group; the two connections are then "looped" together and connected to the **vent stack**. **2.** The same as a **circuit vent** except that it loops back and con-

nects with a **stack vent** extension of the soil stack instead of a separate **vent stack**.

loop window A long, narrow, vertical opening, usually widening inward, cut in a medieval wall, parapet, or fortification for use by archers; an **arrowloop**.

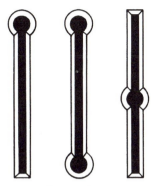

loop windows

loose-box See **box stall**.

loose core See **strip core**.

loose cubic yard (or meter) A unit to express the volume of **loose material**.

loose-fill insulation Thermal insulation in the form of granules, nodules, fibers, powder, flakes, or shreds; may be hand-packed, pneumatically placed, or poured into cavities or over supporting membranes. Also see **granular-fill insulation**.

loose grid In a theatre **stagehouse**, a counterweight system using rope ties at the pinrail, instead of fixed counterweights.

loose insulation Same as **loose-fill insulation**.

loose-joint hinge, heave-off hinge, lift-off hinge, loose-joint butt A door hinge having two knuckles, one of which has a vertical pin

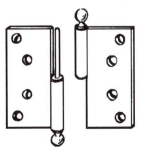

loose-joint hinge

loose knot

(at its center) that fits in a corresponding hole in the other; by lifting the door up, off the vertical pin, the door may be removed without unscrewing the hinges.

loose knot   A knot in wood which is not firmly in place and may fall out.

loose-laid membrane   A ballasted roofing membrane that is only attached to the substrate along the edges and at penetrations through the roof.

loose lintel   A **lintel** that is not attached to another structural member but is merely placed across an opening in a wall during construction to support the weight of the wall above.

loose material   Soil or rock in a blasted, broken, or loose state.

loose molding   A removable wood glazing bead.

loose-pin hinge   A hinge having a removable pin which permits its two parts to be separated.

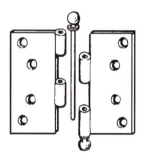

loose-pin hinge

loose side, slack side   The side of knife-cut wood veneer, next to the knife, which has numerous small checks as a result of the cutting operation.

loose stop   A nailed-on or planted stop bead; a **planted stop**.

loose tongue   **1.** Same as **cross tongue**. **2.** A spline in a **spline joint**.

loose-tongue miter   A mitered joint having matching grooves into which a common key or tongue is fitted to align or strengthen the joint.

loricula   Same as **squint, 1**.

lorymer   A **larmier**.

loss of gloss   A paint defect in which a dried film of paint loses gloss, usually over a period of several weeks.

loss of prestress   In **prestressed concrete**, the reduction of the prestressing force which results from the combined effects of creep in the steel and creep and shrinkage of the concrete; normally does not include friction losses but may include the effect of elastic deformation of the concrete.

loss of use insurance   Insurance protecting against financial loss during the time required to repair or replace property damaged or destroyed by an insured peril.

lost ground   Soil which runs from outside to within an excavation, as around or through sheeting, or as a **boil** on the bottom.

lost-head nail   A thin nail having a head only slightly larger than the diameter of the nail itself; usually nailed below the surface of the wood.

lot   A parcel of land that is described on a recorded plat or by a survey.

lot depth   The distance from the front of a lot to the extreme rear line of the lot.

lot front   The boundary line of a lot that abuts a street, or, if it abuts more than one street, then the street designated by the owner.

lotiform   Having the shape of a lotus bud or flower, as used in some Egyptian column capitals.

lotiform capital

lot line   The legally defined boundary or limit of a parcel of land.

lot-line wall   A wall adjoining and parallel to the lot line, used only by the party upon whose lot the wall is located.

lotus capital   In ancient Egyptian architecture, a capital having the shape of a lotus bud.

loudness   The intensive attribute of an auditory sensation, in terms of which sounds may be rank-ordered on a scale extending from soft to loud; depends primarily on sound pressure,

ELEVATION

PLAN

lotus capital

but also on the frequency and wave form of the sound stimulus; expressed in units called **sones**; 2 sones is just twice as loud as 1 sone.

loudness level   Of a sound, the sound-pressure level of an equally loud 1,000-Hz pure tone, expressed in units called **phons**.

loudspeaker   An electroacoustic device, used to radiate acoustic power in air, the acoustic waveform of the reproduced sound being essentially equivalent to that of the electrical input.

Louis XIV, Louis Quatorze style   The style of the high Classical period in France under the rule of Louis XIV (1643–1715) in architecture, decoration, and furniture, culminating in the building of Versailles.

Louis XV, Louis Quinze style   The Classical and Rococo style in France under the rule of Louis XV (1715–1774) in architecture, decoration, and furniture. *(See illustration p. 564.)*

Louis XVI, Louis Seize style   The later Rococo and classicist phase of the 18th century in

Louis XIV style: central compartment, northern façade, Louvre

Louis XIV style: overdoor panel

Louis XIV style: Pavilion, Hotel Soubise, Paris (c. 1730)

Louis XVI, Louis Seize style

Louis XV style

Louis XV style: doorway of Hotel de Clermont-Tonnerre, Paris

Louis XVI style

Louis XVI style

Louis XVI style

France under the rule of Louis XVI (1774–1792), terminated by the French Revolution.

Louisiana Vernacular architecture See **French Vernacular architecture, Cajun cottage, Creole house**.

lounge An informal sitting room, esp. in a hotel, theatre, or institutional building.

louver **1.** An assembly of sloping, overlapping blades or slats; may be fixed or adjustable; designed to admit air and/or light in varying degrees and to exclude rain and snow; esp. used in doors, windows, and the intake and discharge of mechanical ventilation systems. **2.** A dome or turret rising from the roof of the hall of a medieval English residence, originally open at the sides to allow the escape of smoke from the open hearth below; also called a **lantern**.

louver board One of the narrow boards, placed at an angle, in a **louver** or **louver window**; also called a **luffer board**.

louver door A door containing a louver, usually with horizontal blades, providing for the passage of air while the door is closed.

louver, 2

louver door

louvered ceiling A ceiling system consisting of multicellular louvers which shield the light sources mounted above it.

louvered shutter See **shutter**.

louver shielding angle The angle between the horizontal plane of a louver grid and the plane beyond which the louver conceals all objects above it.

louver window **1.** A window having louvers which fill all or part of the opening instead of glass. **2.** An open window in the tower of a church.

louver window

louvre Same as **louver**.

low-alkali cement A portland cement containing a relatively small amount of sodium or potassium or both.

low-alloy steel Steel having an alloy content of less than 8%.

low bid A bid stating the lowest bid price, including selected alternates, and complying with all bidding requirements.

lowboy A type of trailer for hauling construction equipment, with reduced ground clearance that facilitates loading of machinery without an auxiliary ramp.

low-carbon steel Steel having a carbon content less than 0.20%.

low-density concrete Concrete whose oven-dry unit weight of less than 50 pounds per cubic foot (800 kg/m³).

low-emissivity glass Same as **reflective glass**.

lower lateral bracing Same as **bottom lateral bracing**.

lowest responsible bidder, lowest qualified bidder The bidder who submits the lowest bona fide bid and is considered to be fully responsible and qualified to perform the **work, 1** for which the bid is submitted. In the case of private construction contracts, the decision as to the bidder's responsibility and qualification usually is made by the owner and the architect. In public contracts, a decision disqualifying a low bidder may have to be made on a reasonable basis rather than an arbitrary one.

lowest responsive bid The lowest bid which is responsive to and complies with the bidding requirements.

low-hazard contents Building contents having such low combustibility that no self-propagating fire therein can occur.

low-heat cement, type IV cement A cement in which there is only limited generation of heat during setting, achieved by modifying the chemical composition of normal portland cement.

low-lift grouting In masonry wall construction employing hollow concrete blocks, a technique in which wall sections are built as high as 5 feet (1.7 m); then, the cells of the masonry blocks are filled with grout.

low-noise lamp An incandescent lamp having a special internal construction to minimize the generation of audible noise, esp. when operated on certain types of **dimmers**.

low-pressure boiler According to the ASME Boiler Code, a boiler whose maximum safe working *gauge* pressure for steam service is 15 pounds per square inch.

low-pressure laminate A laminate molded and cured in the range of pressures from 400 lb per sq in. (28 kg per sq m) down to and including the pressure obtained by the mere contact of the plies.

low-pressure mercury lamp A mercury-vapor lamp whose partial pressure during operation does not exceed 0.001 atmosphere; fluorescent and germicidal lamps are included in this category.

low-pressure overlay A thermosetting resin-impregnated, wear-resistant paper, often with a decorative wood-grain print which has been applied, under pressure, at a high temperature to plywood, fiberboard, particleboard, etc., usually at a pressure of 150 to 250 lb per sq in. (7.5 to 10.5 kg per sq m).

low-pressure sodium lamp A **sodium-vapor lamp** having a relatively low partial pressure; produces a deep yellow light that is essentially monochromatic; widely used where the color of the lighting is not important (as, for example, in lighted parking lots) because of its high **efficacy**.

low-pressure steam curing   Same as **atmospheric steam curing**.

low relief   Same as **bas relief**.

low-side window, leper's squint, offertory window, squint   A small low window, usually on the right side of the chancel, through which the altar may be seen.

low-silicon bronze   See **silicon bronze**.

low steel   A soft steel containing a small amount of carbon (less than 0.25%).

low-studded   Having short studs.

low-temperature recovery   The ability of a sealant to recover its original form at low temperature when the deforming load is removed.

low-temperature-water heating system   Same as **hot-water heating system**.

low voltage   According to ANSI/IEEE standards, a nominal system voltage of 1000 volts or less.

low-voltage lighting control   A system of switches, control transformers, relays, and auxiliary devices to control a number of lighting circuits remotely, from one or more locations.

low-water alarm   In a system in which water is supplied to a building from a **gravity tank**, an alarm indicating that the pump supplying the tank has not activated at the low-water condition and that water in the tank is dangerously low.

low-water cutoff   A device required by the ASME Boiler Code on any steam boiler that is automatically fired; prevents the continued firing of a boiler that contains insufficient water.

lozenge   **1.** A rhomb or, more rarely, a rhomboid; usually one of a series. **2.** In a double lancet window, a small light which pierces the space between the heads of the two lancets.

lozenge fret, lozenge molding   A type of **diamond fret**.

LP   On drawings, abbr. for "low pressure."

L&P   Abbr. for "lath and plaster."

LPG   **1.** Abbr. for **liquid petroleum gas**. **2.** Abbr. for **liquified petroleum gas**.

LP gas   Same as **liquid petroleum gas**.

L-plan   A **plan** having the shape of a capital letter L.

LPS   Abbr. for "low-pressure sodium."

lozenge, 2

lozenge fret

LR   Abbr. for **living room**.

LS   **1.** Abbr. for "left side." **2.** Abbr. for **loudspeaker**.

L-shore   A **shore** having an L-head.

LT   On drawings, abbr. for **light**.

lucarne   A small dormer window in a roof or spire.

lucome window   A term once used for a window in the gable end of a house, usually providing light for a room in a loft or attic.

lucullite   A variety of black marble used in ancient Roman construction; first brought to Rome from Assan on the Nile River.

luffer   An obsolete term for **louver**.

luffer board   Same as **louver board**.

lug   **1.** In electric wiring, a device for terminating a wire or cable; the lug is bolted to an electric

lugs, 1

terminal. **2.** A small projection attached to any member or component for use in handling, assembling, or installing.

lug angle   See **clip angle**.

lug bolt   A round bolt to which is welded a flat iron bar.

lug sill   A sill with its ends extending beyond the window or door and built into the masonry at the jambs.

lukovitsa   In early Russian architecture, an onion dome.

lumber   Timber sawn or split in the form of beams, boards, joists, planks, etc., esp. that which is smaller than heavy timber.

lumber core, stave core   Wood core consisting of narrow strips of lumber edge-glued together; usually held in place by veneer which is glued to both faces with the grain of the veneer at 90° to that in the core.

lumen (lm)   The SI unit of luminous flux equal to the luminous flux received on a unit surface, all points of which are equidistant from a point source having a uniform intensity of 1 candela.

lumen maintenance curve   See **life performance curve**.

lumen method, flux method   A procedure in lighting design used to determine the number and types of lamps or luminaires required to provide a desired average level of illumination on a **work plane**; takes into account both direct and reflected light flux.

lumiline lamp   A tubular incandescent lamp having a **lamp base** at each end.

luminaire   **1.** A complete lighting unit consisting of one or more **lamps**, together with components which are designed to distribute the light, to position and protect the lamps, and to connect the lamps to the electric power supply; also called a **lighting fixture**. **2.** The above lighting unit without lamps in it.

luminaire classification   **1.** For indoor luminaires, a classification system based on the percentage of flux which is emitted by the luminaire, above (or below) a horizontal plane through the center of the luminaire. **2.** Floodlights: a measure of the beam spread in terms of beam angle ranges: type I, beam angle 10° to 18°; II, 18° to 29°; III, 29° to 46°; IV, 46° to 70°; V, 70° to 100°; and VI, above 100°.

luminaire dirt-depreciation factor   A factor (used in illumination calculations) which relates the initial illumination provided by a clean, new luminaire to the reduced illumination that it will provide as a result of the accumulation of dirt on the luminaire at the time when it is next scheduled for cleaning.

luminaire efficiency   The ratio of luminous flux emitted by a luminaire to total flux emitted by the lamp or lamps in the luminaire.

luminance   The luminous intensity of any surface in a given direction per unit of projected area of the surface, as viewed from that direction; a directional property of luminous radiation.

luminance contrast   The relationship between the luminance of an object and the luminance of the immediate background.

luminance factor   The ratio of the luminance of a surface or medium under specified conditions of incidence, observation, and light source to the luminance of a lossless, perfectly diffusing surface or medium under the same conditions.

luminance meter, brightness meter   A visual instrument or a photoelectric instrument used to measure luminance.

luminescence   The emission of light not ascribable directly to incandescence.

luminosity   The ratio of luminous flux to the corresponding radiant flux at a particular wavelength; expressed in lumens per watt.

luminous ceiling   A ceiling area-lighting system comprising a continuous surface of transmitting material (of a diffusing or light-controlling character) with light sources mounted above it.

luminous efficacy   A measure of the effectiveness with which a light source converts electric power into luminous flux; the ratio of the total luminous flux emitted to the electric power input, expressed in lumens per watt.

luminous energy   The time integral of luminous flux; given by the product of the luminous flux and the time that the flux is maintained, if the luminous flux is of constant value; usually expressed in lumen-hours.

luminous flux   The rate of flow of light energy through a surface.

luminous intensity   The luminous flux per unit solid angle in a specific direction from a point source of light; in practice, an interior source may be considered a point source if the distance exceeds 5 to 10 times the maximum source dimension of the **luminaire**; in U.S. Customary units, expressed in **candlepower**; in SI units, expressed in **candelas**.

luminous-intensity distribution curve A polar plot representing the light intensity as a function of angle about a light source.

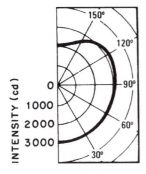

luminous-intensity distribution curve

luminous paint 1. Phosphorescent paint, which, after activation, continues to emit light (even in darkness) for several hours. 2. Fluorescent paint, which has a high light reflectivity because it reflects absorbed ultraviolet energy as visible light.

luminous transmittance Of a lens, light diffuser, or the like: the ratio of the total transmitted light to the total incident light.

lump lime A high-quality quicklime.

lump sum agreement Same as **stipulated sum agreement**.

lunding beam See **tie beam**.

lune A tapering wedge-shaped unit forming the covering of a hemisphere.

lunette 1. A crescent-shaped or semicircular area on a wall or vaulted ceiling, framed by an arch or vault. 2. An opening or window in such an area. 3. A painting or sculpture on such an area.

luster 1. An iridescent decorative surface appearance. 2. A surface or coating which imparts a gloss, sheen, glitter, or sparkle.

lute 1. A scraper having a straight cutting edge; used to level plastic concrete. 2. A bricklayer's

straightedge used for striking off clay from a brick mold. 3. See **sulfur cement**.

Lutheran window Same as **dormer window**.

luthern Same as **dormer window**.

lux The SI unit of **illuminance** equal to the illumination on a surface, all points of which are at a distance of 1 meter from a uniform point source of 1 candela; 1 lux is equal to 1 lumen per square meter (1 lm/m^2).

LWC Abbr. for **lightweight concrete**.

lx Abbr. for **lux**.

lyceum A building for general education by means of public discussions, lectures, concerts, etc.

lych-gate, lich-gate A roofed gateway at the entrance to a church or cemetery where a coffin may be placed temporarily before proceeding to the grave.

lych-gate

lychnoscope Same as **low-side window**.

lych-stone A stone at the entrance to a churchyard, intended to receive a bier.

lying panel 1. A panel so placed that the fibers of the wood lie in a horizontal position. 2. A panel whose longer dimension is in a horizontal position. 3. Same as **lay panel**.

lysis A plinth or step above the cornice of the podium of some Roman temples; when present in a columnar edifice, it constitutes the stylobate proper.

M

m Abbr. for "meter."

M **1.** Abbr. for "thousand." **2.** On drawings, abbr. for **bending moment**.

macadam, tarmac, tarmacadam **1.** A paving for roads or other surfaces, formed by grading and compacting layers of crushed stone or gravel; then the top layer(s) are usually bound by asphaltic material, acting to stabilize the stone, provide a smoother surface, and seal against water penetration. **2.** The crushed stone used in a macadamized surface.

macadam aggregate A product manufactured by crushing stone, slag, or gravel and then screening it to a uniformly coarse size; when compacted, void spaces are relatively large.

Macassar ebony A hard, very heavy wood of the East Indies; black with red or brown streaks; used for decorative paneling and applications requiring high-impact or wear resistance.

macellum A Roman meat or produce market in a covered hall.

maceria In ancient Roman construction, a rough wall having no facing; constructed in a wide variety of materials.

maceria

machicolation An overhanging defensive structure at the top of a medieval fortification, with floor openings through which boiling oil, missiles, etc., could be dropped on attackers.

machicolation

machine bolt A threaded bolt having a straight shank and a conventional head such as a square, hexagonal, button, or countersunk type.

machine bolt

machine burn A darkening or charring of a surface due to overheating of the cutting knives or abrasive belts during machining of the material.

machine finish See **smooth machine finish**.

machine gouge A groove which results when a machine cuts below the desired line of cut.

machinery room See **mechanical equipment room**.

macroscopic Visible to the unaided eye.

made ground, made-up ground **1.** Solid ground formed by filling in an artificial or natural pit with hard rubble such as broken brick, concrete, etc., or with rubbish. **2.** See **fill, 1**.

made-up ground Same as **made ground**.

madrasah A theological school, generally arranged around a courtyard, from the 11th cent. A.D. on, in Anatolia, Persia, and Egypt.

maeander   See **labyrinth fret**.

maenianum   **1.** In ancient Rome, a balcony or gallery for spectators at a public show. **2.** Originally, the balcony in the Forum at Rome, for spectators of the gladiatorial combats.

magazine   A storage place for ammunition and explosives; also see **powder house**.

magazine boiler   A coal- or coke-fired boiler (in a hot-water or central heating system) which has a bunker fitted to it, large enough to contain 24 hours of fuel.

magnesia   A fine white powder of magnesium oxide.

magnesia cement   Magnesium oxide mixed with water, often with the addition of asbestos fibers; used to cover steam pipes, furnaces, etc.

magnesia insulation   Magnesium carbonate hydroxide, with or without admixture of fiber reinforcement or other materials; a good thermal insulator because of the great number of closed air cells it contains; molded into rigid boards, blocks, or shapes conforming to piping.

magnesite   A natural magnesium carbonate.

magnesite flooring   A flooring material composed of calcined magnesite, magnesium chloride, sawdust, ground quartz or silica, and fine powdered wood waste; used as a finishing surface on concrete floor slabs.

magnesium   A gray-white, light metal (64% the weight of aluminum); easily drawn and machined; immune to alkalies.

magnesium alloy   Any of a number of alloys of magnesium; the usual additives are aluminum, manganese, silicon, silver, thorium, and zirconium, used singly or in combination.

magnesium carbonate   See **magnesia insulation**.

magnesium hydroxide   A white powder which is slightly soluble in water; in dolomitic-type limes used in plaster, its presence helps the lime to spread more easily.

magnesium lime   Lime manufactured from limestone; contains some magnesium; used as finish lime in plastering or as mason's lime in mortar.

magnetic bearing   The **bearing, 4** of a line where the reference meridian is the local magnetic meridian.

magnetic catch   A door catch that uses a magnet to hold the door in a closed position.

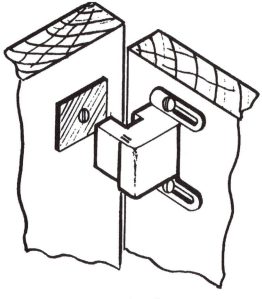

magnetic catch

magnetic core   See **core, 11**.

magnetic declination   At a particular location, the horizontal angle between true meridian (true north-south line) and magnetic meridian (direction of compass needle).

magnetic switch   An electric switch whose switch contacts are controlled by means of an electromagnet; esp. used in the control circuits for motors.

magnetite   A natural black oxide of iron, containing from about 65 to 72% iron and sometimes a small amount of nickel and titanium; used as an aggregate in high-density concrete.

mahlstick, maulstick   A stick used by painters as a rest for the hand while painting.

mahogany   **1.** A straight-grained wood of intermediate density, pinkish to red-brown in color; found principally in the West Indies, and Central and South America. Used primarily for interior cabinetwork and decorative paneling. **2.** Wood from a number of tropical species which resemble mahogany, generally classified as to origin, i.e., African mahogany, Philippine mahogany, etc.

mail box A multiple arrangement of boxes for receipt and/or distribution of mail at a central point in a building; mainly used in apartment or office buildings.

mail chute, letter chute A small shaft for conducting letters from an upper floor to a post-box on the first floor.

mail slot, letter slot A small opening, often with a hinged closer, which is set in an exterior door, sidelight, etc., and through which mail is delivered.

main **1.** In an air-conditioning system, a major duct or pipe for distributing to or collecting from various branches. **2.** In any system of continuous piping, the principal artery of the system to which branches may be connected.

main bar A steel reinforcing bar in **main reinforcement**.

main beam A **principal beam** used to carry a load, which transmits the load directly to the columns.

main cable An electric cable which distributes power to a group of buildings.

main contractor Same as **general contractor**.

main couple The principal truss in a roof.

main diagonal A diagonal member of a web, joining the top and bottom chords of a **truss**.

main member, primary member In a structural system, a member or component part which is essential to the overall stability of the structure.

main rafter A **common rafter**.

main reinforcement In **reinforced concrete**, steel reinforcement which resists stresses resulting from applied loads and moments, as opposed to reinforcement intended to resist secondary stresses.

main runner A large supporting runner for a suspended ceiling; a primary member of the suspension system; usually 1½-in. (3.8-cm) metal channels, held by hangers or rods from the building structure; used to support furring channels or rods to which lath is attached.

main sewer **1.** A **public sewer**. **2.** A sewer to which one or more **branch sewers** are connected and which serves a large area; also called a **trunk sewer**.

main stack In plumbing, a soil stack which runs in a line from the **building drain** up through the roof, where the upper end is open to the air.

maintainer Same as **motor grader**.

maintenance bond A bond that provides a guarantee to an owner that the contractor will rectify defects in workmanship or materials reported to the contractor within a specified time period following final acceptance of the work under contract.

maintenance curve For a light source, same as **life performance curve**.

maintenance factor The ratio of illumination on a given area after a period of time to the initial illumination on the same area; used in lighting calculations to account for the depreciation of lamps or reflective surfaces (or the like). Also see **light loss factor**.

maintenance finish A heavy-duty paint, varnish, or lacquer used to protect and decorate industrial, institutional, and commercial buildings and structures.

main tie In a roof truss, a member which connects the feet of the rafters.

main trap See **building trap**.

main vent The principal artery of the venting system to which vent branches may be connected; also called **vent stack**.

maison de maître See **Creole house**.

maison de poteaux-en-terre See **poteaux-en-terre house**.

maisonette Same as **duplex apartment**.

majolica A type of pottery decorated with an opaque white glaze and a colored overglaze; a type of **faïence tile**.

makeup water Water which is supplied (as to a steam boiler or cooling tower) to compensate for losses by evaporation and leakage.

makore, African cherry, cherry mahogany A moderately hard, heavy wood of West Africa, pinkish to red-brown in color; resembles mahogany and American cherry; used for cabinets, flooring, and plywood.

maksoorah In a mosque, an area which is enclosed by a screen or partition and which is reserved for prayer or surrounds a tomb.

malachite A carbonate of copper; green in color; harder than marble; usually employed as a highly polished veneer.

male connector   Any type of electrical **connector** having contacts which project into the recessed opening of a female connector.

male plug   An electric **plug, 5** inserted into a **receptacle** to form an electric connection.

male thread   **1.** A thread on the outside of a pipe. **2.** Same as **external thread**.

mall   **1.** A public plaza, walk, or system of walks, often set with trees and designed for pedestrian use. **2.** See **shopping mall**. **3.** A heavy wood mallet; a maul.

malleability   The property of a metal that permits mechanical deformation by extrusion, forging, rolling, etc., without fracturing.

malleable brass   Same as **Muntz metal**.

malleable iron   **1.** A white **cast iron** that has been annealed; malleable cast iron. **2. Wrought iron**. A low-carbon **cast iron** that has been annealed and allowed to cool slowly; capable of being beaten into shape to form decorative **ironwork**.

mallet   A short-handled wooden hammer, used by carpenters, stonecutters, etc., chiefly for driving another tool, as a chisel; the head may be of a soft material such as plastic.

mallet-headed chisel   A steel mason's chisel having a rounded head.

malm   **1.** Earth containing a considerable quantity of chalk in fine particles; a calcareous loam. **2.** A **malm brick**.

malm brick   A brick made of true or artificial **malm**, the latter consisting of comminuted chalk mixed with sand and **pan breeze**.

malm rubber   A relatively soft **malm brick** which can be rubbed to a desired shape.

Maltese cross   A cross formed by four equal triangles or arrowheads joined at their points.

maltha   **1.** In ancient Roman construction, a type of bitumen, various cements, stuccos, and the like, used for repairing cisterns, roofs, etc. **2.** A bituminous substance midway in consistency between asphalt and petroleum.

malus   In ancient Roman theatres and amphitheatres, one of the poles over which the **velarium** was stretched.

MAN.   On drawings, abbr. for "manual."

mandapa   A large, open porch or hall of a Hindu temple.

mandatory and customary benefits   See **benefits**.

mandatory standard   A standard with which it is obligatory to comply; established by an authority endowed with the necessary legal power.

mandoral   Same as **mandorla**.

mandorla, vesica piscis   An aureole, almond-shaped, depicted around the full form of a sacred person.

mandrel, mandril   **1.** A temporary internal support for a light-gauge metal shell during a pile-driving operation; takes the impact of the pile hammer during driving and is then withdrawn before concrete is placed in the shell; also called a **pile core**. **2.** A cylindrical bar or spindle, used chiefly as a support during machining or forming operations.

manganese   A metallic element used as an alloying element in steel as a hardener and deoxidizer; also used as an alloying element in other metals such as copper to introduce high mechanical damping.

manganese drier   Manganese acetate used in paints to speed its rate of drying.

manganese greensand   See **greensand**.

manganese steel   A very hard, brittle steel containing from 11 to 14% manganese and 1.5% carbon; must be treated by cooling in water to remove extreme brittleness; used where high resistance to abrasion is necessary.

manger   A trough in a stable for feeding cattle.

manhole   A covered opening in a street which provides access for cleaning and repairing of a sewer beneath, or for repairing a conduit for electric underground piping or electric cables.

man-hour   A unit of work equal to the output of one man working for 1 hour.

manifold   A section of duct, a fitting, or a pipe with a number of branches which are close together.

Mannerism   Transitional style in architecture and the arts in the late 16th cent., particularly in Italy, characterized in architecture by unconventional use of classical elements.

manometer   An instrument for the measurement of pressure; a U-shaped glass tube partially filled with water or mercury, one side of which is connected to the source of pressure. The amount

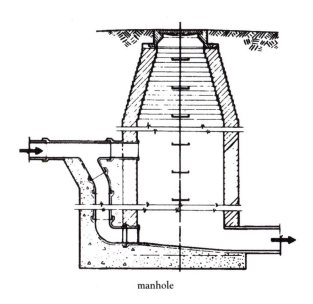

manhole

of displacement of the liquid is a measure of the magnitude of the pressure.

manor house **1.** Usually, an imposing house in a countryside, often the residence of a land-owner with considerable acreage. **2.** A relatively simple one-room house of early colonists in America, having a gable roof, clapboard walls, a battened door, a window at the front of the house with solid shutters, and a chimney at one or at each end.

mansard roof **1.** (*U.S.A.* and *Brit.*) A roof having a double slope on all four sides, the lower slope being much steeper. **2.** (*U.S.A.*) Same as

mansard roof

gambrel roof. **3.** A **hipped roof** usually having a double slope or compound curve on all four sides of the roof, the lower slope usually being much steeper than the upper slope; alternatively, the sides may have a concave-, convex-, or S-shape. **4.** A sloping roof that projects from the wall of a building and has a double slope, the lower slope being steeper than the upper.

Mansard style **1.** A term sometimes used as a synonym for **Second Empire style** in the United States. **2.** An architectural style that makes use of, or suggests, a **mansard roof**.

manse The dwelling of a clergyman.

mansion **1.** A very large, imposing, stately residence. **2.** In colonial times, the residence of a landholder. **3.** A **manor house**; also called a mansion house.

mantel **1.** A projection or facing around a fireplace opening, often decorative. **2.** Same as **mantelshelf**.

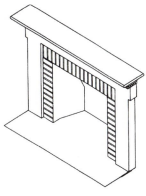

mantel, 2

mantel board A wood **mantelshelf**.

mantelpiece **1.** The fittings and decorative elements of a mantel above a fireplace. **2.** A shelf above a mantel; often called a **mantelshelf**. **3.** The construction that serves as a support for the masonry above a fireplace. **4.** A **mantelshelf**.

mantel register, cast-iron register A relatively inexpensive prefabricated cast-iron mantelpiece which screws onto the fireplace and forms the fireplace surround.

mantelshelf That part of a mantelpiece which constitutes a shelf.

manteltree A wood, stone, or iron structural member that spans the opening over a fireplace.

Often, a large horizontal oak timber that serves to support the wall construction above, typically placed high enough above the hearth to prevent its igniting; sometimes plastered to improve its fire resistance.

mantle 1. Same as **mantel**. 2. The outer covering of a wall which differs from the material of the inner surface.

mantrap A short narrow section of corridor purposely constructed to permit passage by only one person; has interlocking doors at both ends; used in some high-level security installations.

manual batcher A **batcher** equipped with gates or valves which are operated manually.

manual call point A British term for **fire alarm box**.

manual fire alarm system A **fire alarm system** that is manually operated, so arranged that the operation of any one station will ring all signals throughout the building as well as at one or more selected locations.

manual fire pump A pump supplying water to a sprinkler or standpipe system which is not activated automatically and must be started by hand.

manually-propelled mobile scaffold See **mobile scaffold**.

manual operation Said of functioning of equipment or devices that are capable of being operated directly by hand without any other source of power.

Manueline architecture The last phase of Gothic architecture in Portugal, so named after King Manuel I (1495–1521).

manufactured building A structure which is substantially or wholly made in a manufacturing plant for installation or assembly at a building site.

manufactured home A **manufactured building** intended as a dwelling.

manufactured house Same as **prefabricated house**.

manufactured sand A fine aggregate produced by crushing rock, gravel, or slag.

map A graphic, planar depiction of the earth's surface, or a portion thereof, drawn to scale.

map cracks, map cracking See **checking**.

maple A hard, tough, moderately high-density wood of North America and Europe, light to dark brown in color; has a uniform texture; used for flooring, wood turning, etc. Also see **bird's-eye maple**.

maqsura An enclosure in a mosque which includes the praying niche, made usually of an openwork screen; originally meant for the sultan during public prayers.

marb Abbr. for **marble** or "marbleized."

marble A metamorphic rock composed largely of calcite or dolomite; often highly polished to enhance its appearance; available in different colors that result from differences in mineral content.

marbled, marbleized Having the appearance of marble, or made to look like marble by a special application of paint, as in marbleized woodwork, or by integral treatment, as in marbleized plastic tile.

marbling, marbleizing The use of antiquing techniques to achieve the appearance of marble in a paint film.

marezzo, marezzo marble A cast imitation marble produced with Keene's cement. Also see **artificial stone**.

margin 1. The exposed flat surface of the stiles and rails which form the framing around a panel. 2. The projecting surface above the stair nosings in a **close string**. 3. The mitered border around a hearth. 4. The exposed surface of a slate or tile which is not covered by the one above.

marginal bar A glazing bar which divides a glazed opening so that a central glazed opening is surrounded by narrow panes at the edges.

margin draft In masonry, the plain-dressed border on the face of a hewn block; the middle part of the face may be dressed or left rough; also see **draft, 2**.

margin light See **side light**.

margin of safety Same as **factor of safety**.

margin strip In flooring, a wood member which forms a border.

margin trowel A plasterer's trowel which has a box-like shape or sides which turn up so that it is especially useful for working corner angles.

margin trowel

marigold window A round window whose mullions of tracery radiate; a **rose window**.

marine glue Any glue which is insoluble in water; usually contains a solution of rubber and/or resins.

marine paint A paint formulated to withstand exposure to sunlight and to fresh and salt water.

marked face The front or face side of a piece of lumber.

marker A sign, plaque, or monument that designates a building, site of historic importance, or boundary.

market cross Same as **cross, 2** or a cross located at the principal market place of a town.

market house, market hall Often, a one- or two-story rectangular building where butchers, fishmongers, grocers, and peddlers sell their goods on the ground floor often open to the outdoors; sometimes arches or heavy posts support a second story that may house municipal offices.

marketplace A building or open place in which produce, usually of local origin, is sold.

marking gauge, butt gauge A carpenter's tool for scribing a line parallel to an edge; consists of an adjustable faceplate (which is run along the edge) mounted on a rod containing a marking point.

mark out In carpentry, to lay out the lines where cuts are to be made.

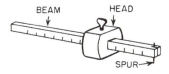

marking gauge

marl An earthy deposit; a mixture of clay and carbonate of lime.

marl brick, marl stock A superior brick made from **marl**.

marmoratum In ancient Roman construction, a cement formed of pounded marble and lime mortar which were well mixed; used in building walls, terraces, etc.

marmoset, marmouset An antic figure, usually grotesque, introduced into architectural decoration in the 13th cent.

marouflage A technique for fastening canvas (or the like) to a wall by means of an adhesive.

marquee, marquise A permanent roof-like shelter over an entrance to a building.

marquee

marquetry Inlaid pieces of a material, such as wood or ivory, fitted together and glued to a common background. Also see **inlay** and **intarsia**. (*See illustration page 578.*)

martello tower A defensive form, of 16th cent. Italian origin.

martin hole See **owlhole**.

Martin's cement, hard-finish plaster Similar to Keene's cement but contains potassium carbonate as an additive in place of alum.

martyrium A place where the relics of a martyr are deposited.

mascaron, mask The representation of a face, a human or partly human head, more or less caricatured, used as an architectural ornament. (*See illustration page 578.*)

mash hammer, mash In stoneworking, a short-handled heavy hammer with two round or octagonal faces.

marquetry

mascaron

mashrebeeyeh   See **meshrebeeyeh.**

mask   See **mascaron.**

masking   **1.** Preparing surfaces adjacent to paintwork with a temporary covering of masking tape, or tape plus paper, to keep them free of paint. **2.** Screening off part of a theatre stage from view of the audience. **3.** The action of rendering one sound inaudible or unintelligible as the result of the presence of another (usually louder) one.

masking tape   An adhesive-backed paper tape used in **masking, 1.**

masonry   **1.** The art of shaping, arranging, and uniting stone, brick, building blocks, etc., to form walls and other parts of a building. **2.** Construction using **masonry units** of such materials as clay, shale, glass, gypsum, or stone, set in mortar; this term includes **concrete masonry units** but excludes reinforced concrete.

masonry anchor   The metal piece inside the throat of a hollow-metal doorframe which secures the frame to a masonry wall.

masonry block   Same as **masonry unit.**

masonry bond   See **bond.**

masonry-bonded hollow wall   A wall built of masonry units so arranged as to provide an air space within the wall, and in which the facing and backing of the wall are bonded together with masonry units.

masonry cement   **Hydraulic cement** for use in mortars for masonry construction where greater plasticity and water retention are desired than are obtainable by the use of portland cement alone; such a cement always contains one or more of the following materials: portland cement, portland-pozzolan cement, natural cement, slag cement, and hydraulic lime, and usually contains one or more of the following: hydrated lime, pulverized limestone, chalk, talc, pozzolan, clay, and gypsum; many masonry cements also include entrained air and a water-repellent.

masonry course   A layer of masonry units running (essentially) horizontally in a wall.

masonry drill   Same as **star drill.**

masonry filler unit   A **masonry unit** which is used to fill the space between joists or beams, providing a platform for a cast-in-place concrete slab.

masonry guard   A **plaster guard.**

masonry joint   Any joint between masonry units bonded with mortar. See **colonial joint, concave joint, excess joint, extruded joint, flat joint, flush-cut joint, hick joint, hungry joint, keyed joint, raked joint, rodded joint, rough-cut joint, ruled joint, scored joint, scribed joint, skintled joint, spalled joint, struck joint, tooled joint, troweled joint, V-joint, weather joint, weatherstruck joint.** Also see **pointing.**

masonry mortar   See **masonry cement** and **mortar**.

masonry nail   A hardened-steel nail with a knurled or fluted shank; esp. used for fastening to masonry.

masonry nail

masonry panel   See **prefabricated masonry panel**.

masonry reinforcement   See **reinforcement**.

masonry tie   **1.** See **wall tie**. **2.** See **tie, 1**.

masonry unit   A natural or manufactured building unit of stone, burnt clay, glass, gypsum, etc.

masonry veneer   A masonry facing laid against a wall and not structurally bonded to the wall.

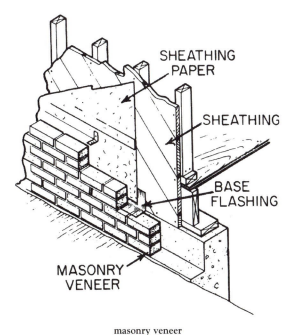
masonry veneer

mason's adjustable multiple-point suspension scaffold   A scaffold having a continuous platform supported by bearers suspended by wire rope from overhead supports, so arranged and operated as to permit the raising or lowering of the platform to desired working positions.

mason's ax   See **axhammer**.

mason's hammer   A hammer with a heavy steel head, one face of which is shaped like a chisel for trimming brick or stone.

mason's hammer

mason's joint   Same as **mason's V-joint pointing**.

mason's lead   See **lead, 1**.

mason's level   A level similar to a **carpenter's level** but longer.

mason's lime   See **building lime**.

mason's mark   See **banker-mark**.

mason's measure   A measure of the quantity of masonry units required for a job; corners are counted twice, and no allowance is made for small openings.

mason's miter, mason's mitre   A masonry joint having the appearance of a miter joint but actually shaped from a single solid stone.

mason's putty   A lime putty to which portland cement and stone dust have been added; esp. used in ashlar work.

mason's scaffold   A totally self-supporting scaffold, having two rows of standards, capable of carrying unusually heavy loads.

mason's stop   Same as **mason's miter**.

mason's V-joint pointing   Pointing in which the mortar is given a profile similar to a flattened V; may also have a flat fillet at top and bottom.

masonwork   Same as **masonry**.

mass bell   Same as **sanctus bell**.

mass burning rate   The loss of mass per unit by materials burning under specified conditions.

mass color   When viewed by reflected light, the color of a pigment-vehicle mixture which is thick enough to completely obscure the background.

mass concrete   Any volume of cast-in-place concrete intended to resist applied loads by virtue of its mass; generally cast as a monolithic structure; usually incorporates a high proportion of large coarse aggregate and a low cement content.

mass curing   The **adiabatic curing** of concrete in sealed containers.

mass diagram   A calculation employing a graph portraying the cumulative quantities of **cut and fill** along the center line (*cut* is shown as a positive quantity and *fill* is shown as a negative quantity); used to determine the **haul**.

mass foundation   Any support for a structure which is enlarged beyond the size required for adequate strength; used to provide additional inertia to dissipate or alleviate the undesirable effects of vibration or impact.

massicot   A yellow amorphous powder, the crystalline form of which is **litharge**; used as a pigment.

mass retaining wall   A **gravity wall**.

masstone   The undiluted color of a pigment or pigmented paint film.

mast   **1.** A tower which carries one or more load lines. **2.** The load-bearing component of a derrick, or the like.

mastaba   A freestanding tomb used in ancient Egypt, consisting of a rectangular superstructure with inclined sides, from which a shaft leads to underground burial and offering chambers.

mastaba

mast arm   A bracket attachment to a lamppost or pole from which a **luminaire** is suspended.

master key   A key that will operate a number of different locks, each of which is different.

master plan   A plan, usually graphic and drawn on a small scale but often supplemented by written material, which depicts all the elements of a project or scheme.

master plumber   An individual licensed and authorized to install and to assume responsibility for contractual agreements pertaining to plumbing, and to secure any permits required for plumbing installations.

MASTERSPEC   A proprietary master specification for the construction industry developed by the American Institute of Architects.

master switch   A single electric switch in a wiring system which controls the supply of power to a building, or the action of relays or any other remotely operated devices.

mastic   **1.** Any heavy-bodied, dough-like adhesive compound. **2.** A sealant with putty-like properties. **3.** A protective coating applied by trowel or spray on the surface of thermal insulation to prevent its deterioration and to weatherproof it.

mastic asphalt   See **asphaltic mastic**.

mat   **1.** See **matte**. **2.** See **mattress**. **3.** A very heavy, flexible blanket of steel mesh, woven wire rope, or chain; used to confine fragments of rock during blasting.

match   In comparing two materials or constructions: an exact or approximate replication.

matchboards   Boards which have a tongue along one edge and a groove along the other; when installed, the tongue of one board fits into the corresponding groove of the adjacent board and holds it securely. Also see **dressed and matched boards**.

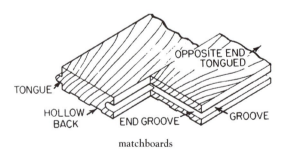

matchboards

matched joint, match joint   The joint along the edge between two matchboards.

matched lumber   Lumber having dressed edges and prepared for tongue-and-groove joints.

matched roof boards Matchboards used as roof sheathing.

matched siding Same as **drop siding**.

matching A system of **matchboards**, or of sheets of wood veneer, arranged to emphasize grain pattern, as in **book matching** or **herringbone matching**.

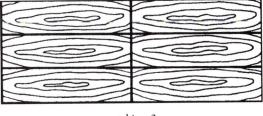

matching, 2

match plane One of a pair of planes used to prepare **matchboards**; one cuts the tongue along the edge, and the other cuts the groove.

material hose Same as **delivery hose**.

material platform hoist A suspended platform, manually or power operated, for conveying building materials and supplies; usually controlled from a point outside the conveyance.

materials cage An open platform on a vertical hoist, used for lifting materials to upper floors during construction of a building.

materials tower Same as **hoist tower**.

material supplier Same as **supplier**.

mat foundation A large, thick concrete slab that sustains the load imposed by a number of columns and/or walls; also called a raft foundation or floating foundation.

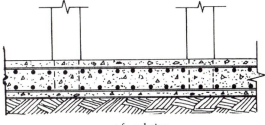

mat foundation

Matheson joint In wrought-iron pipe, a **bell-and-spigot joint**.

MATL On drawings, abbr. for "material."

matrix 1. In mortar, the cement paste in which the fine aggregate particles are embedded. 2. In concrete, the mortar in which the coarse aggregate particles are embedded.

mat sink Same as **mat well**.

matsu A common Japanese pine; used in house construction.

matte, mat, matt A surface finish which is dull, with little or no gloss or sheen, and with low light reflectivity.

matte dip A liquid dip composed of two parts by volume of sulfuric acid to one part by volume of nitric acid and saturated with zinc oxide or sulfate; used to obtain a matte finish on metals.

matte-surfaced glass Glass, one or both sides of which have been etched, ground, sandblasted, etc., to provide diffusion of light.

matte varnish See **flat varnish**.

mattock A tool for loosening soil in digging; shaped like a pickax, but having one of its ends broad instead of pointed.

mattress A layer or slab of concrete, laid directly on the ground, which acts as a footing or the like.

mature tree A tree having a trunk diameter greater than that specified in the applicable code.

maturing The aging and/or proper hardening of a material, e.g., mortar, plaster, concrete, etc.

maturing bin See **boiling tub**.

mat well At the entrance of an exterior door, a depression in the floor to hold a fiber doormat.

maul, mall 1. A heavy, wooden **mallet**. 2. See **beetle**.

maul

maulstick A **mahlstick**.

mausoleum 1. A commemorative edifice for the reception of a monument; a **cenotaph**. 2. A sepulchral chapel to contain tombs.

MAX On drawings, abbr. for "maximum."

maximum acceptable pressure In a water distribution system, the highest water pressure that will not result in the premature or accelerated damage of any component in the system.

maximum demand **1.** The greatest **load, 3** delivered to an electric system over a definitely prescribed time interval. **2.** The greatest flow of water (or waste discharge) for all the fixtures in a plumbing system in a building during a definitely prescribed time interval.

maximum overall length **1.** For a lamp bulb having a single base, the dimension from the base to the point on the bulb farthest away. **2.** For a lamp bulb with a base at each end, the maximum dimension from base to base.

maximum rated load As applied to scaffolds, the total of all loads including the working load, the weight of the scaffold, and such other loads as may be reasonably anticipated.

maximum size of aggregate The largest size of aggregate particles present in sufficient quantity to affect the physical properties of concrete; generally designated by the sieve size on which the maximum amount permitted to be retained is 5 or 10% by weight.

maximum temperature period In **autoclave curing,** the time interval over which the maximum temperature is held constant.

maximum working pressure The maximum pressure at which piping materials of the "standard" or "normally used" type are safe to use.

Maya architecture The architecture of the Mayan people in Central America and Mexico from the 4th to the 15th cent., principally of pyramid temples with steep stairways.

Mayan arch A corbeled arch of triangular shape common in the buildings of the Maya Indians of Yucatán.

maze Same as **labyrinth, 3.**

M.b.m., MBM In the lumber industry, abbr. for "thousand (feet) board measure."

MC **1.** Abbr. for "moisture content." **2.** Abbr. for "metal-clad." **3.** Abbr. for "mail chute."

MC asphalt Same as **medium-curing asphalt.**

MCM Abbr. for "thousand circular mills." See **wire size.**

meager lime Low-purity lime containing at least 15% impurities.

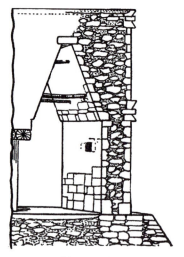

Mayan arch

meal house A structure once used for storing grain that had been ground.

meander Same as **Greek key.**

mean gradient Average slope (for example, of a water pipe or drain pipe).

means of egress A continuous path of travel from any point in a building or structure to the outside at ground level.

means of escape See **fire escape.**

measured drawing An architectural drawing of an existing building, object, site, structure, or detail thereof; accurately drawn to scale on the basis of field measurements.

measurement standard A prescribed procedure for conducting a measurement in such a way as to obtain reliable, reproducible results with a specified level of accuracy.

measuring chain **1.** See **chain.** **2.** See **Gunter's chain.**

measuring frame Same as **batch box.**

meat house Same as **smoke house.**

MECH On drawings, abbr. for "mechanical."

mechanical analysis The process of determining particle-size distribution in an aggregate or in a soil, sediment, or rock. Also see **sieve analysis** and **particle-size distribution.**

mechanical application The application of plaster or mortar by pumping and spraying, rather than by hand with a trowel.

mechanical bond **1.** The keying of a plaster coat: (*a*) with another coat or a plaster base below or (*b*) as a result of plaster which is partially troweled through metal lath. **2.** In reinforced concrete construction, a bond between concrete and specially shaped steel reinforcing bars or rods.

mechanical connection The joining of two or more elements by mechanical fasteners such as bolts, rivets, or screws (but not by nonmechanical means, such as by adhesives).

mechanical core Prefabricated piping for plumbing and/or heating, prefabricated ductwork, and/or prefabricated electric wiring, ready for field installation with a minimum amount of labor at the site.

mechanical-draft chimney A chimney in which the draft is produced, wholly or partly, by an auxiliary blower that either forces air into the furnace or draws the gases and smoke from the furnace and discharges them into the chimney.

mechanical-draft water-cooling tower A **water-cooling tower** in which air is moved through the tower by one or more fans built into the tower.

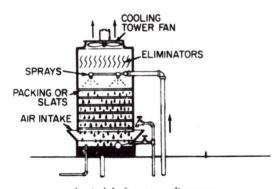

mechanical-draft water-cooling tower

mechanical drawing A precise drawing, produced with the aid of instruments, as compasses, triangles, T-squares, etc.

mechanical equipment room, machinery room A room containing a permanently installed refrigeration or air-conditioning system, or major parts thereof.

mechanical equivalent of heat The number of units of mechanical energy equal to one unit of heat, e.g., 778.2 ft-lb (107.6 kg-m) equals 1 Btu; 4.187 joules equals 1 calorie.

mechanical joint **1.** A gastight and watertight joint formed by joining metal parts through a positive-holding mechanical assembly (such as flanged joint, screwed joint, flared joint). **2.** In piping, a joint which typically consists of: (a) a flange which is integrally cast with the bell of the pipe, (b) a rubber gasket which fits into the recess in the socket, (c) a follower ring which compresses the gasket, and (d) nuts and bolts used to tighten the joint.

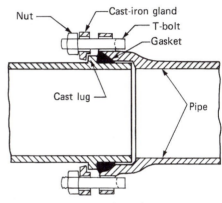

typical **mechanical joint**

mechanically foamed plastic A cellular plastic whose structure is produced by physically incorporated gases.

mechanically galvanized nail, peen-coated nail A nail which is zinc-coated by tumbling in a container with powdered zinc and small glass beads.

mechanical operator A mechanism for opening and closing side-by-side windows in factories, gymnasiums, etc., either by manual operation with a hand crank, handwheel, or hand chain, or by an electric motor drive.

mechanical property A property of a material that is associated with elastic and inelastic reaction when force is applied, or that involves the relationship between stress and strain.

mechanical room See **mechanical equipment room**.

mechanical saw See **band saw, circular saw, jigsaw**.

mechanical stoker A device which automatically feeds a solid fuel (such as coal) into a combustion chamber of a boiler or furnace, and provides air for proper combustion; may include a means for automatically removing solid products of combustion.

mechanical trowel A trowel consisting of power-driven metal or rubber blades for smoothing.

mechanical ventilation The process of supplying outdoor air to a building or removing air from it by mechanical means, e.g., with fans; the air which is supplied may or may not be heated, cooled, or air-conditioned.

mechanic's lien A lien on privately owned real property created by state statute in favor of persons supplying labor or materials for a building or structure or improvements thereof, generally for the value of the labor or materials supplied by them. In some states, a mechanic's lien also exists for the value of professional services. Laws differ greatly among states as to the circumstances in which such a lien may arise, the sum for which it may be imposed, and the procedures whereby the sum due may be collected or the lien discharged. In most circumstances, clear title to the property cannot be obtained until the claim on which the lien is based has been settled.

mechanized parking equipment Devices in mechanical parking garages that are used exclusively for conveying automobiles, by means of a power-driven transfer device, directly into parking spaces or cubicles.

MED On drawings, abbr. for **medium**.

medallion 1. An ornamental plaque (often round, oval, or square, but may be of any other form) representing an object or design in relief, such as a figure, flower, or head. 2. A ceiling ornament, often cast in plaster, at the center of which is often hung a chandelier or luminaire; also called a rose or rosette.

medallion molding A molding consisting of a series of medallions, found in the later and richer examples of Norman architecture.

medicine cabinet A storage cabinet for medical supplies, toilet articles, and the like.

Medieval architecture Architecture of the European Middle Ages, from about the 5th to

medallion molding

the 15th centuries. Found, in particular, in the pre-Romanesque, Romanesque, and Gothic styles.

Mediterranean Revival An imprecise term (*not* a Revival architecture, as the name implies) for a mixture of Mission Revival, Italian Villa style, and Spanish Colonial Revival, particularly in the latter part of the 20th century; usually applied to a one- or two-story house with a red tile roof and stuccoed walls, usually having rounded or arched windows; occasionally referred to as **Mediterranean style**.

medium The liquid or semiliquid ingredient of a paint which controls ease of application, appearance, gloss, adhesion, durability, and chemical inertness.

medium-carbon steel Steel having a carbon content between 0.3 and 0.6%.

medium-curing asphalt Liquid asphalt composed of **asphalt cement** and a kerosene-type diluent of medium volatility.

medium-curing cutback See **medium-curing asphalt**.

medium-density fiberboard, medium-density hardboard Fiberboard having a density of from 30 to 50 lb per cu ft (480 to 800 kg per cu m); used for structural building applications, coreboards, etc.

medium-density overlay An overlay of paper impregnated with a thermosetting resin; applied by a hot-press to plywood, fiberboard, particleboard, etc., usually to improve its appearance and durability.

medium-duty scaffold A scaffold designed and constructed to carry a working load not to exceed 50 lb per sq ft (245 kg per sq m).

medium oil varnish A varnish containing between 5 and 15 gal oil per 100 lb (0.5 and 1.5 liter oil per kg) gum; used for interior paints and varnishes.

medium relief   Same as **mezzo-relievo**.

medium steel   Steel neither very hard nor very soft, usually contains from 0.25 to 0.5% carbon.

medium-temperature water-heating system   A heating system in which water having supply temperatures between 250°F (121°C) and 350°F (177°C) is used as a medium to convey heat from a central boiler, through a piping system, to suitable heat-distributing devices.

medium voltage   According to ANSI/IEEE standards, a nominal system voltage of between 1000 and 72,500 volts.

medullary ray, pith ray   In a cross section of a tree or log, one of the ribbons of tissue extending radially from the pith; may vary from microscopic to 4 in. (10 cm) or more in oak; used to store and transport food horizontally within the tree.

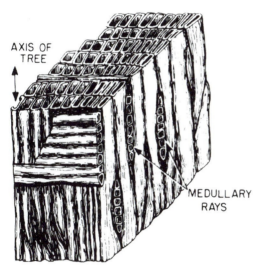

medullary rays

meeting house   A house of worship for some Protestant faiths; also may serve as a center of community activity; usually a notably plain structure, often having a square **floor plan**.

meeting post, miter post   The outer stile of a lock gate which meets, at the middle of a gateway, the corresponding stile of the companion gate.

meeting rail   In a double-hung window, the horizontal member at the top of the lower sash or the horizontal member at the bottom of the upper sash.

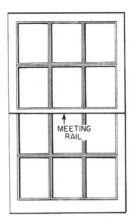

meeting rail

meeting stile   One of the abutting stiles in a pair of doors or sashes.

megalithic   Built of unusually large stones.

megalithic monument

megalopolis, megapolis   A thickly populated urban region usually consisting of one or more large cities and surrounding suburbs.

megapolis   Same as **megalopolis**.

megaron   **1.** In many Greek temples, a space divided off and sometimes subterranean, where only the priest was allowed to enter. **2.** The great central hall of a palace.

megascopic   Visible to the unaided eye.

megilp   In painting, a vehicle made of oil of turpentine and pale drying oil in equal proportions.

mehrab   Same as **mihrab**.

MEK   See **methyl ethyl ketone**.

melamine formaldehyde   A colorless alkyd-type synthetic resin which is resistant to alkalies and most acids; used for surfacing plywood, chipboard, etc.

melon dome A melon-like ribbed dome (either an exterior or interior dome), especially found in Islamic architecture.

MEMB On drawings, abbr. for "membrane."

member In structural engineering, a component part of a structure, complete in itself.

membrane In built-up roofing, a weather-resistant (flexible or semiflexible) covering consisting of alternate layers of felt and bitumen; fabricated in a continuous covering and surfaced with aggregate or asphaltic material.

membrane curing A process in which either a liquid sealing compound (e.g., bituminous and paraffinic emulsions, coal-tar cutbacks) or a nonliquid protective coating (e.g., sheet plastics) functions as a film to restrict evaporation of mixing water from a fresh concrete surface.

membrane fireproofing A lath and plaster membrane that provides resistance to fire and extreme heat.

membrane roofing See **membrane**.

membrane theory In the design of thin shells, a theory assuming that a shell cannot resist bending because it deflects, and that the only stresses in any section are shear stress and direct compression or tension.

membrane waterproofing A **membrane** applied to a surface to make it impervious to water.

MEMO On drawings, abbr. for "memorandum."

memorial An architectural or sculptural object or plaque commemorating a person or an event.

memorial arch An arch commemorating a person or event, popular during the Roman Empire, and again at the time of Napoleon and later.

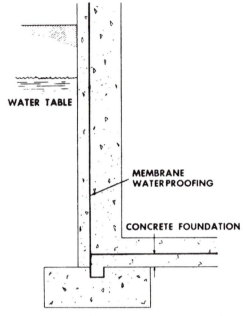

membrane waterproofing

memorial arch: at the Forum, Rome

memorial park A cemetery, usually having grave markers flush with the ground in large open meadows bordered by groves of trees.

memorial stone, memorial tablet A stone or tablet set up, or placed on or in a wall, to commemorate some person or event.

memory The quality of a material that enables it to return to its original shape after it has been compressed or stretched.

mending plate A steel strip, usually predrilled with staggered screw holes; used to strengthen joints in wood construction.

menhir A prehistoric monument consisting of a single large standing stone, sometimes rudely sculptured.

mensa **1.** The stone slab or other piece forming the top of an altar. **2.** The upper surface of an altar.

mensao Same as **menhir**.

mensole Same as **keystone** of an arch.

men's room In a public building, a room containing toilet and lavatory facilities for the use of men.

mensuration **1.** The process or art of measuring. **2.** The branch of mathematics dealing with the determination of length, area, or volume.

MER Abbr. for **mechanical equipment room**.

mer The smallest repetitive unit in the structure of a high polymer.

mercantile occupancy The use of rooms, stores, markets, buildings, or structures for the display and sale of merchandise.

merchant bar iron Obsolete name for wrought iron bars and rods.

merchant pipe A pipe which is not of standard full weight; usually 5 to 8% lighter.

mercury-contact switch A wall-mounted switch used in interior electric wiring; contains a sealed glass tube of mercury which provides a silent contact when the switch is turned on.

mercury lamp A high-intensity electric-discharge lamp consisting of an electric arc in mercury vapor in a sealed tube, which in turn may be enclosed in an outer glass envelope; the light produced appears blue-white, but contains only violet, blue, green, and yellow components; usually operates slightly above atmospheric pressure.

mercury switch Same as **mercury-contact switch**.

mercury-vapor lamp An **electric-discharge lamp** consisting of an electric arc in mercury vapor in a sealed tube, which in turn may be enclosed in an outer glass envelope; the light produced appears to be blue-white, but contains only violet, blue, green, and yellow components. The lamp is said to be "low pressure" if the partial pressure of the vapor is below 0.001 atmosphere, and "high pressure" if about an atmosphere.

meridian stone A stone placed along a meridian (i.e., an accurately determined line running north and south) to delineate the eastern or western boundary of a town or village.

merlon In an embattled parapet, one of the solid alternates between the embrasures. Also see **battlement**.

meros The frontal area between two grooves of a triglyph.

mesaulos In an ancient Greek house: **1.** A passageway connecting the **andron** with the **gynaeceum**. **2.** The door in this passageway.

mesh **1.** The number of openings per inch in **wire cloth**; a 100-mesh screen has 100 openings per inch in each direction. **2.** A network of metal wires or the like. **3.** Expanded metal, light-woven steel, or welded steel used as reinforcement in concrete.

mesh-core door, cellular-core door A hollow-core door of wood construction; the core consists of a cellulose mesh grid or honeycomb which is encased by wood rails and stiles; face panels are fixed to the core with a waterproof adhesive.

mesh partition A partition constructed of a framework which is closed by heavy wire mesh; acts as a barrier against unauthorized entry, but provides for the passage of air, heat, and light; does not obstruct operation of a sprinkler system; used to protect and secure an area, such as a stockroom.

meshrebeeyeh, mashrebeeyeh, moucharaby, mushrabiya **1.** An elaborately turned wood screen enclosing a balcony window in an Arabic structure. **2.** Such a screen otherwise used. **3.** A balcony with a parapet and machicolations projected over a gate to defend the entrance; the parapet may be either embattled or plain. (*See illustration on page 588.*)

merlon

meshrebeeyeh, 1

mesh reinforcement

meshrebeeyeh, 3

mesh reinforcement   In reinforced concrete, an arrangement of steel bars or wire normally in two directions at right angles, tied or welded at the intersections or interwoven.

Mesoamerican architecture   Architecture of the area of Mexico and Central America in which the presence of certain pre-Hispanic cultural traits permits the classification of cultures of the region as one civilization; includes central and southern Mexico, the Yucatán peninsula, Guatemala, El Salvador, and parts of Honduras, Nicaragua, and northern Costa Rica.

Mesopotamian architecture   Architecture developed by the Euphrates and Tigris Valley civilizations, from the 3rd millennium to the 6th cent. B.C. Primarily a massive architecture of mud bricks set in clay mortar or bitumen. The heavy walls were articulated by pilasters and recesses; important public buildings were faced with baked or glazed brick. Rooms were narrow and long and generally covered by timber and mud roofs, but in certain cases also by tunnel vaults; columns were seldom used; openings usually were small.

messmate   A variety of eucalyptus wood; used as timber for rough work.

messuage   A dwelling with all attached and adjoining buildings and curtilage together with adjacent lands used by the household.

MET.   On drawings, abbr. for "metal."

meta   In a racetrack, a column or monument to mark a turn.

metal-arc welding   See **arc welding**.

metal ceiling   See **pressed-metal ceiling**.

metal-clad cable   See **armored cable**.

metal-clad fire door, Kalamein fire door   A flush door consisting of a wood core, or stiles and rails and heat-insulated panels, covered with sheet steel.

metal curtain wall   An exterior building wall which carries no roof or floor loads and consists entirely or principally of metal, or a combination of metal, glass, and other surfacing materials supported by a metal framework.

metal extrusion   Same as **extrusion, 1**.

metal floor decking   Formed sheet metal **decking, 2** for structural load-carrying purposes in floor construction.

metal grating   An open metal flooring for pedestrian and/or vehicular traffic, covering floor depressions or openings.

metal halide lamp, metallic-additive lamp   An **electric-discharge lamp** in which the light is produced by the radiation from a mixture of a metallic vapor (e.g., mercury) and the products of the dissociation of halides (e.g., halides of thallium, indium, sodium, etc.).

metal lath, metal lathing, steel lathing   A base for plaster fabricated: (*a*) by slitting metal and then stretching it to form a diamond-shaped mesh or (*b*) by punching and forming sheet metal. Usually classified as **rib lath, diamond-mesh lath, sheet lath,** or **wire lath**.

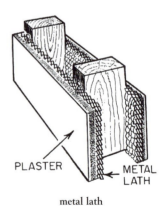

metal lath

metal leaf   A very thin sheet of metal, such as gold or silver, used in decoration or in lettering; after application, the surface may be protected against oxidation by a thin coating of shellac or lacquer.

metallic-additive lamp   See **metal halide lamp**.

metallic area   Of a wire rope, the sum of the cross-sectional areas of all of the strands of which it is composed.

metallic paint   A paint or lacquer containing metal flakes which reflect light.

metallic-sheathed cable   See **armored cable; BX**.

metallic tubing   See **electrical metallic tubing**.

metallize   To apply a coating of metal on a base material, usually by spraying the coating metal in a molten state.

metallized lamp bulb   A lamp bulb having a metallic-film coating on a portion of either the inner or the outer surface to change the direction of the emitted light.

metal-molding   See **surface metal raceway**.

metal pan   See **perforated metal pan**.

metal primer   The first coat of paint on metal; a **primer, 1** coat.

metal roof covering   Sheet metal or shingles, corrugated or otherwise shaped, for application on a roof framework or on a solid roof surface; also see **sheet-metal roofing**.

metal sheeting   Same as **sheet metal**.

metal siding   An exterior wall **siding** fabricated of metal, usually aluminum.

metal structural cladding   A nonload-bearing **cladding** for exterior walls and sloping roofs; fabricated of metal.

metal tie   See **tie, 1; see wall tie**.

metal valley   A **velley gutter** lined with metal.

metal window   A metal frame, with or without a sash, which accommodates glazing.

metamer   A light of the same color as another light, but of different spectral power distribution.

metamorphic rock   Rock which has been altered in appearance, density, and crystalline structure (and in some cases mineral composition) by high temperature and/or high pressure; e.g., slate is a metamorphic rock derived from shale.

metatome   The space between two dentils.

meter, metre (m)   The International Standard unit of length; equal to 39.37 **inches**.

meter-candle, metre-candle   See **lux**.

meter rod   Same as **precise leveling rod**.

meter stop   An off-on valve in a water service pipe for stopping the flow of water to a building.

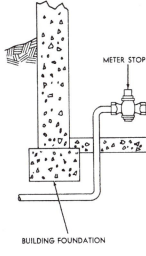

meter stop

metes and bounds   The boundaries, property lines, or limits of a parcel of land, defined by distances and **bearings, 4**.

methylated spirit   A mixture of ethyl alcohol and a small amount of methyl alcohol; used industrially as a solvent for paints, lacquers, and varnishes.

methyl cellulose   A granular, white flaky material which acts as a water-soluble thickener and stabilizer; used in water-based paints.

methyl chloride   A gas which liquefies under compression; used as a refrigerant.

methyl ethyl ketone, MEK   A strong, aromatic, flammable solvent used in paints, varnishes, and lacquers.

methyl methacrylate   A tough, rigid, transparent acrylic plastic having good resistance to common solvents and acids; subject to crazing.

metoche   Same as **metatome**.

metope   The panel between the triglyphs in the Doric frieze, often carved. Also see **triglyph**. (*See illustration on page 590.*)

metre   See **meter**.

metric modular unit   A brick whose dimensions are multiples of 10 cm.

metric sabin   A unit of sound absorption equivalent to 1 sq m of perfectly absorptive surface.

metric ton   Same as **tonne**.

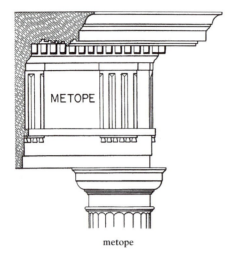

metope

meurtrière   Same as **gun hole.**

mews   **1.** The royal stables in London, so called because they were built where the king's hawks were kept; hence, a place where carriage horses are kept in cities or large towns. **2.** An alley or court in which stables are or once were located.

MEZZ   On drawings, abbr. for **mezzanine.**

mezzanine, entresol   **1.** A low-ceilinged story or extensive balcony, usually constructed next above the ground floor. **2.** In a theatre, the lowest balcony or the forward part of the first balcony. **3.** A space under the stage used for the manipulation of scenery in connection with a plateau lift system.

mezzo-relievo   Midway between **high-relief** and **bas-relief.**

MF   Abbr. for "mill finish."

MFG   On drawings, abbr. for "manufacturing."

MG   On drawings, abbr. for "motor generator."

MH   On drawings, abbr. for **manhole.**

MI   On drawings, abbr. for **malleable iron.**

MIA   Abbr. for "Marble Institute of America."

mica   A naturally occurring silicate; used in paints to improve suspension and brushing properties and to improve resistance to moisture penetration; also used as a filler in plastics and in electrical and thermal insulators.

mica pellets   Pellets of **exfoliated vermiculite.**

mica powder   Very small flakes of mica (or ground mica) used in the manufacture of asphalt shingles and roofing and as a filler in paints.

microbar   Same as a dyne per square centimeter.

micron   A unit of length equal to a thousandth part of a millimeter or a millionth of a meter.

microorganisms   In paint technology, bacteria and fungi which are harmful to liquid paint and dry paint films. Bactericides and fungicides are added to paints to inhibit the growth of these organisms.

microphone   A device which converts sound waves into essentially equivalent electric waves; the sound waves move an element in the device which generates an electric voltage.

microsand   An aggregate, essentially free of clay and shale, that is sufficiently fine to pass through a No. 100 (150 μm) sieve.

microscopic   Observable only with the aid of a microscope.

microstrainer   A fine sieve used in the initial stage of water filtration.

microwave motion detector   A device that generates a train of microwaves having a fixed frequency in a space that is to be protected. If an intruder enters and moves in the protected area, waves reflected off the intruder's body will be of a slightly different frequency. This change in frequency is detected, thereby activating an alarm.

Middle Pointed style   Same as **Decorated style** of Gothic architecture.

middle post   **1.** A **king post. 2.** A **lock rail.**

middle rail   An intermediate horizontal structural member of a door between the stiles; if it contains a lock, it is called a **lock rail.**

middle strip   In flat concrete slab framing, the slab portion which occupies the middle half of the span between columns.

midfeather   **1.** See **parting slip. 2.** A longitudinal division or partition, as a **withe** in a chimney or as in a cased frame.

midrail   A rail approximately midway between the guardrail and **platform**, secured to the uprights erected along the exposed sides and ends of platforms.

mid-wall column   A column which carries a part of a wall much thicker than its own diameter.

mid-wall column

Miesian A term descriptive of the style of Ludwig Mies van der Rohe (1886–1969), a German-American architect who was a principal exponent of the **International style**. An outstanding example of his work is the Seagram Building in New York City (1958), designed by Mies with Philip Johnson (1906–).

migration The spreading or creeping of a sealant onto adjacent surfaces, usually to the detriment of bond.

mihrab A niche in the mosque or any religious Muslim building indicating direction of prayer toward Mecca. Focal point of decoration with dome in front.

mil, MIL **1.** A unit of measure equal to a thousandth of an inch (0.0254 mm). **2.** On drawings, abbr. for "military."

mildew A fungus that grows and feeds on paint, cotton and linen fabric, etc., which are exposed to moisture; causes discoloration and decomposition of the surface.

mildewstat A chemical agent which inhibits the growth of mildew.

mild steel **1.** Nearly pure iron having a very low carbon content, usually between 0.15 and 0.25%; a ductile, rust-resistant material used in boilers, tanks, enamelware, etc. **2.** Same as **low steel**.

milestone, milepost A marker showing the distance in miles from a designated location; before the 19th century, such markers were especially helpful to those traveling between outlying communities.

mihrab   with the **minbar** on the right

mile-yard A unit equivalent to hauling one cubic yard a distance of 1 mile; used (in the U.S.A.) in determining the cost of movement of excavations.

milk house Before the 19th century, a small subsidiary structure in which milk and other dairy products were stored at a lowered temperature with cooling usually provided by slowly running cold spring water or the runoff from an **icehouse**; typically had overhanging eaves to shade it, and double walls and ceiling filled with a thermal insulator, such as sawdust; commonly had a concrete floor to promote cleanliness and louvers for ventilation; was separated from the barn for reasons of sanitation. This term replaced by the word *dairy* in the 1800s; health regulations have now made such structures obsolete.

milkiness A white, semiopaque discoloration in a clear varnish film.

milk of lime A slaked lime and water solution.

mill **1.** To remove metal by a circular tool having teeth, as by use of a **milling machine**. **2.** A machine for rolling plates, shapes, rails, etc. See **bark mill, bolting mill, gristmill, sawmill, textile mill, tide mill, water mill, windmill**.

mill construction See **heavy timber construction**.

milled lead Same as **sheet lead**

milled surface The surface obtained when metal is removed by a **milling machine**.

mill file A single-cut file having a rectangular cross section.

mill finish The finish on a metal sheet, bar, etc., which is produced by cold rolling or extrusion.

milliarium A column placed at intervals of one Roman mile (equivalent to 0.92 mile or 1.48 km) along a Roman road to indicate distance.

milliarium aureum A golden column erected by Augustus in 29 B.C. at the point where the principal roads of the Roman empire terminated.

millilambert A unit of **luminance** equal to $1/(1,000\,\pi)$ candela per sq cm.

milling **1.** In stonework, the processing of quarry blocks, through sawing, planing, turning, and cutting techniques, to finished stone. **2.** In metalwork, the process of dressing a surface with various shapes of rotary cutters to produce a flat or grooved surface. **3.** See **knurling**.

milling machine A machine consisting of a rotating mandrel carrying a milling cutter, and a movable table, operated by a feed screw, to which is bolted the object to be milled.

milliphot A unit of illumination equal to $1/1,000$ lumen per sq cm.

mill length, random length Run-of-the-mill length of pipe, usually 16 ft to 20 ft (approx. 4.9 m to 6 m).

mill-mixed, ready-mixed Descriptive of a product that is formulated and dry-mixed by the manufacturer; only the addition of water is required at the job site.

mill practice Standardized fabrication or rolling procedures of a specific mill or of an industry, usually applicable to structural steel.

mill run Products from a mill which have not been graded or inspected.

mill scale A loose coating of oxide which forms on iron or iron products when heated.

millwork Ready-made products which are manufactured at a wood-planing mill or woodworking plant: moldings, doors, door frames, window sashes, stair work, cabinets, etc.; normally does not include flooring, ceilings, and siding.

milori blue High-quality pigment of the ferric-ferrocyanide family mixed with gypsum or barium sulfate; used in lacquers.

mimbar Same as **minbar**.

min, MIN **1.** Abbr. for "minute." **2.** On drawings, abbr. for "minimum."

minah See **minar**.

minar, minah A tower, usually a memorial monument, found esp. in India.

minaret A tall tower in, or contiguous to, a mosque with stairs leading up to one or more balconies from which the faithful are called to prayer.

Persian portal with dome, flanked by **minarets**

minbar The pulpit in a mosque.

minchery A nunnery.

minch house A roadside inn.

mineral aggregate See **aggregate**.

mineral black, slate black Black pigment obtained from crushing and grinding black earth deposits, such as slate, coal, coke, or shale.

mineral dust A very finely divided mineral product, the greatest bulk of which will pass through a 74-micron (No. 200) sieve; the most common such material is pulverized limestone.

mineral fiber A fiber manufactured from glass, rock, or slag (with or without a binder) generally for use in fabricating heat insulation.

mineral fiber pad In a perforated-metal-pan acoustical ceiling assembly, the porous sound-absorptive element laid into the pan; may be enclosed in a thin, sound-transparent envelope of paper or plastic.

mineral fiber tile An acoustical tile formed of mineral or glass fiber and a binder.

mineral-filled asphalt Asphalt containing an appreciable percentage of very finely divided mineral matter which passes through a 74-micron (No. 200) sieve.

mineral filler Any finely ground mineral substance, usually inert, used as a **filler**.

mineral flax Fibrous asbestos; used in the manufacture of asbestos cement products.

mineral granules A natural or synthetic aggregate used to surface roofing material.

mineral-insulated cable An electric cable consisting of one or more conductors embedded in an insulating material of a highly compressed refractory mineral; has an outer sheath of continuous seamless tubular copper.

mineral pigment See **earth pigment**.

mineral spirit, petroleum spirit A flammable thinner having a low-aromatic hydrocarbon content obtained in petroleum distillation; widely used in paints and varnishes. Also see **odorless mineral spirit**.

mineral streak A dark green or brown stain in hardwoods; usually results from an injury during growth.

mineral-surfaced felt A heavy, saturated roofing felt which is coated on both sides with asphalt; the top surface is covered with particles of slate or stone; used on both sloped and flat roofs.

mineral wool A wool-like material of fine inorganic fibers such as asbestos or those made from molten rock, slag, or glass; used as loose fill or formed into blanket, batt, block, board, or slab shapes for thermal and acoustical insulation; also used as reinforcement for other materials such as insulating cements and gypsum wallboard.

minimalist architecture Architecture that follows the doctrine that the use of all decorative elements, including ornamentation and color, should be held to an absolute minimum. This tenet considers all such architectural features to be nonessential and of negative aesthetic value, thus promoting the concept attributed to Mies van der Rohe that "less is more."

minimum acceptable pressure In a water distribution system, the lowest water pressure permitting safe, efficient, and satisfactory operation at the most hydraulically remote fixture or component in the system.

minium Naturally occurring **red lead** oxide; used as a pigment.

Minoan architecture The architecture of Bronze Age Crete, which reached its apogee between the 19th and 14th cent. B.C. Most important were its palaces, in which a great number of rectangular rooms of various sizes, serving different functions and connected by long labyrinthine passages, were clustered around a large central courtyard. Gate buildings with columnar porches provided access to the otherwise unfortified compounds, which were generally constructed on sloping sites, utilizing terracing and split and multilevel organization of buildings with a great number of open and enclosed stairs; light wells, air shafts, elaborate drainage and sewage systems, and flushing toilets were the engineering features. Foundation walls, piers, lintels, and thresholds were built in ashlar stone; upper walls and stories in timber framework with rubblestone masonry faced by stucco and decorated by wall paintings. Ceilings were of wood, as were the frequently used columns with their typical downward-tapering shape.

minor change A change of minor nature in the work not involving an adjustment in the **contract sum** or **contract time**, which may be effected by **field order** or other written order issued by the architect.

minster A monastic church; since many English cathedrals were originally associated with monasteries, the term applies to them by extension.

minstrel gallery A small balcony on the inside of a church or manor house hall, usually over the entrance.

minute One division of a **module, 3**.

mirador In Spanish architecture and derivatives, a lookout, whether an independent structure, a bay window, or a roof pavilion.

mirror **1.** A nearly perfect reflecting surface. **2.** A small oval ornament surrounded by a molding.

MISC On drawings, abbr. for "miscellaneous."

miscellaneous storage According to NFPA standards concerning the storage of goods in a building, storage that does not exceed 12 feet (3.7 m) in height and which is incidental to another occupancy use group.

miserere, subsellium A ledge on the bottom of a hinged seat in a church; when the seat is raised, the ledge provides some support for a worshiper or choir singer who, in standing, leans against it.

miserere

misericord **1.** In monastic architecture, a room or separate building where monastic rule was relaxed. **2.** Same as **miserere**.

mismatched **1.** Said of adjacent boards or veneers in which there is an absence of symmetry. **2.** Said of a poorly fitting joint.

mismatch lumber Lumber or boards which are dressed and match but have edge details that do not fit properly.

mission In Spanish Colonial architecture, a church and complex of buildings usually dependent for support on a monastic order or a larger church.

Mission architecture Church and monastic architecture of Spanish religious orders, especially in the Americas in the 18th century, displaying considerable regional variation as a result of influences of skills of local laborers and the availability of construction materials; relatively unadorned in some regions but considerably more elaborate in others, often with

mission architecture

ornamentation imitative of the elaborate and lavish **Baroque** or the **Churrigueresque style**. Mission architecture usually exhibits many of the following characteristics: thick, massive walls of adobe brick, laid with lime mortar where available, commonly with wall buttresses to provide additional stability; adobe wall surfaces usually coated with lime-and-sand stucco to reduce the effects of erosion; tamped earth floors, commonly decorated with square tile, arcaded walkways with arches usually built around the patios; commonly, multicurved gables, a belfry, bell tower, or twin bell towers; a flat roof or a low-pitched roof with shaped parapets, usually supported by round logs; thatched or tile roofs; grilles covering windows facing the street; a massive wood door at the main entrance, sometimes heavily carved or paneled, often set in an elaborately sculptured portal. Compare with **Mission Revival**; also see **Spanish Colonial architecture**.

mission parapet In Spanish Colonial architecture, a low, **freestanding** wall at the edge of a roof (i.e., a **parapet**) whose upper edge has two or more curves on each side of the uppermost point.

Mission Revival, Mission style An architectural style popular in the southwestern United States and in Florida from about 1890 to 1930 and beyond; suggestive or imitative of the earlier **Mission architecture**, although usually much simpler because of the absence of sculptured ornamentation; compare with **Spanish Colonial Revival**. Buildings in this style are usually characterized by: stucco-finished exterior walls, occasionally with terra-cotta ornamentation; balconies or balconets; semicircular arches; a roof supported by massive piers with broad arches between them, forming arcaded walkways; multicurved gables; a low-pitched red **mission-tile** roof; often a hipped roof; open eaves having exposed rafters and a significant overhang; roof ridges topped with a red-tiled protective cap; commonly, dormers; tile-faced bell towers; roof drainage provided by waterspouts that pierce the parapets; typically, double-hung rectangular windows; a main entry door often located within a recessed porch.

mission tile **1.** A red-clay roofing tile, approximately semicylindrical in shape; laid in courses, with adjacent tiles having their convex side alternately up and down; also called **Spanish tile**. **2.** Same as **pantile, 2.**

mission tile

mist coat A sprayed coat of very dilute paint.

miter, mitre The oblique surface forming the beveled end or edge of a piece where a **miter joint** is made.

miter arch, mitre arch Two straight blocks of stone set diagonally over an opening, the upper ends resting against each other.

miter arch

miter block In joinery, a wood block arranged for sawing pieces at an angle of 45°.

miter board, miter shoot A board on which material to be planed is laid; guides or stops hold the material at the prescribed angle so that the ends of the miters can be planed at the correct angle.

miter box A device for guiding a handsaw at the proper angle in making a miter joint; often a narrow wooden box having a bottom and two sides in which kerfs are cut (usually at an angle of 45°) for guiding the saw.

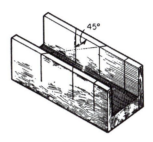

miter box

miter brad Same as **corrugated fastener**.

miter cap, mitre cap A shaped wood block, supported by the newel post, which receives the mitered handrail.

miter clamp, miter cramp A clamp used to hold together a miter joint during gluing.

miter cramp See **miter clamp**.

miter cut Any oblique cut across two pieces of board or molding, so that when joined they form an angle.

miter dovetail See **secret dovetail**.

mitered-and-cut string Same as **cut-and-mitered string**.

mitered closer A brick **closer** cut at an oblique angle.

mitered fitting A fitting especially manufactured for use with **beveled pipe**.

mitered hip A **close-cut** hip.

mitered valley A valley which is **close-cut**.

miter ending The end of a member having an angular, dovetailed, or square member which is designed to fit into an adjacent matching member so as to provide a continuous profile at the joint.

miter gauge   A gauge for determining the angle of a miter.

mitering machine   A machine for sawing or cutting the ends of pieces to be joined to a true angle of 45°, in order that they may be united by a **miter joint**, or for cutting the pieces to any desired angle to make a bevel joint.

miter joint   A joint between two members at an angle to each other; each member is cut at an angle equal to half the angle of the junction; usually the members are at right angles to each other.

miter joint

miter joint   with spline

miter knee   The miter joint between the horizontal handrail at a stair landing and the adjacent angled handrail of the descending stairs.

miter plane   A carpenter's plane generally used for preparing miter joints or butt joints.

miter post   A **meeting post**.

miter rod   A flat steel plate having one end cut at a 45° angle; used by plasterers in finishing reentrant corners.

miter saw   See **tenon saw**.

miter shoot   See **miter board**.

miter square   **1.** In carpentry, a square with a handle having one edge with a bevel at an angle

of 45°; used for laying out miter joints. **2.** A **bevel square** with a blade having a fixed angle of 45° for marking miters prior to cutting.

miter valve   A valve having a disk that fits in a seat at a 45° angle to the axis of the valve.

mitre   British variant of **miter**.

mix   A type of concrete mixture (e.g., **lean mix**).

MIX.   On drawings, abbr. for "mixture."

mix design   Same as **proportioning**.

mixed arch   A three- or four-centered arch; a **composite arch**.

mixed garden wall bond   In brickwork, a bond similar to **English garden wall bond**, except that the course of **headers** is replaced by one consisting of alternate headers and **stretchers**.

mixed garden wall bond

mixed glue   A ready-mixed synthetic resin glue.

mixed-grained lumber   Edge-grained and flat-grained lumber in any combination.

mixed-in-place pile   A soil-cement pile, formed in place by forcing a grout mixture through a hollow shaft into the ground where it is mixed with in-place soil.

mixed occupancy   In a building, two or more classes of occupancy so intermingled that separate safeguards for each class are impractical; the building construction, fire protection, exit facilities, and other safeguards meet the requirements for the most hazardous occupancy unless otherwise specified.

mixed use   **1.** Descriptive of a district that has been zoned to permit more than a single use, for example, commercial and residential. **2.** Descriptive of a building that has more than one use.

mixer   A machine employed for blending the constituents of concrete, grout, mortar, or paint.

mixer efficiency   The adequacy of a mixer in rendering a homogeneous product within a stated period; determinable by testing samples, which are extracted from various portions of a freshly mixed batch, for differences in physical properties.

mixer truck   See **truck mixer**.

mixing box   **1.** A device used to reduce the air velocity in the duct of a medium- or high-pressure, high-velocity **HVAC** system; incorporates a valve which controls the volume of flow for distribution of air within a room and for mixing hot and cold air. **2.** See **dual-duct system**.

mixing cycle   In mixing concrete in a batch mixer, the time taken for a complete cycle, i.e., the elapsed time between successive discharges of the mixer.

mixing plant   See **batch plant**.

mixing speed   In mixing a batch of concrete, the rate of rotation of a mixer drum or of the paddles in an open-top, pan, or trough mixer, expressed in rpm or in feet per minute (or meters per minute) of a point on the circumference of the drum at its maximum diameter.

mixing time   The period of time during which the constituents of a batch of concrete are mixed in a fixer.

mixing valve   A valve which mixes liquids, by either automatic or manual regulation.

mixing varnish   A varnish which is added to a pigmented paint to increase its gloss or improve its sealing properties.

mixing water   The water in freshly mixed sand-cement grout, mortar, or concrete, exclusive of any previously absorbed by the aggregate.

mix proportion   In a given concrete mixture, the ratio of cement to sand to gravel, in terms of either dry, loose volume or dry weight.

Mixtec architecture   A type of Mesoamerican architecture, circa 1000 A.D., in the state of Oaxaca, Mexico; usually characterized by great mass, use of interior stone columns, and emphasis on horizontal lines; minutely detailed fretwork on paneled friezes; use of **scapulary tablets** on building façades.

mixture   **1.** The assembled, blended, commingled ingredients of mortar, concrete, or the like. **2.** The proportions for their assembly.

MK   On drawings, abbr. for "mark."

ML   On drawings, abbr. for "material list."

mldg, Mldg   Abbr. for "molding."

MLMA   Abbr. for "Metal Lath Manufacturers Association."

mm   Abbr. for "millimeter."

MN   On drawings, abbr. for "main."

MO   On drawings, abbr. for "month."

moat   A broad, deep trench surrounding the ramparts of a town or fortress; usually filled with water.

mobile form   Same as **slipform**.

mobile scaffold   A portable rolling scaffold supported by casters.

mock-up   A model of an object in the course of design, as a section of a window or its parts; built to scale or at full size, for purposes of studying construction details, judging appearance, and/or testing performance.

MOD   On drawings, abbr. for "model."

mode   See **architectural mode**.

model   **1.** A representation or reproduction, usually at small scale, for purposes of study or to illustrate construction. **2.** A pattern of an item to be reproduced, often in quantity.

model code   (U.S.A.) A proposed building code that is written and published by building-official associations (e.g., BOCA, ICBO, and SBCC); available for adoption by states, counties, and municipalities.

modeling, *Brit.* **modelling**   Forming or shaping a clay or plaster surface.

Modern architecture   A loose term applied since the late 19th century to buildings in a variety of styles, in which emphasis is placed on functionalism, rationalism, and current methods of construction, in contrast with architectural styles based on historical precedents and traditional methods of building. This category often includes **Art Deco, Art Moderne, Bauhaus, Contemporary style, International style, Organic architecture, Streamline Moderne**.

Moderne   An imprecise term occasionally applied to Art Moderne, PWA Moderne, Streamline Moderne, and Art Deco.

Moderne Style   Same as **Style Moderne**; also see **Art Deco**.

Modernismo The Spanish, particularly Catalan, version of Art Nouveau.

Modernistic style See **Art Deco** and **Art Moderne**.

Modern style An imprecise term that often includes **Contemporary style** and **Shed style**.

modification **1.** A written amendment to the **contract document** signed by both parties. **2.** A **change order**. **3.** A written or graphic interpretation issued by the architect. **4.** A written order for a minor change in the **work, 1** issued by the architect.

modified asphalt An asphalt that has been modified by the addition of a synthetic resin or rosin ester.

modified portland cement, type II portland cement A cement used in general construction where moderate heat of hydration is required.

modillion A horizontal bracket or console, usually in the form of a scroll with acanthus, supporting the corona under a cornice. If in the form of a plain block, it is a **block modillion** or **uncut modillion**. Found in Corinthian, Composite, and, less frequently, Roman Ionic orders.

modillion

modillion cornice A cornice supported by a series of **modillions**, often found in Composite and Corinthian orders.

modular construction **1.** Construction in which a selected unit or module, such as a box or other subcomponent, is used repeatedly in the aggregate construction. **2.** A system of construction employing large, prefabricated, mass-produced, partially preassembled sections or modules which are subsequently put together in the field.

modular dwelling A **manufactured home** consisting completely or in part of **module, 4**.

modular masonry unit A brick or block whose nominal dimensions are based on a 4-in. (10.16 cm) module.

modular ratio The ratio of the modulus of elasticity of steel to that of concrete.

modular system, modular design A method of designing or constructing buildings and equipment in which modules are widely used.

module **1.** A distinct component forming part of an ordered system. **2.** A repetitive dimensional or functional unit used in planning, recording, or constructing buildings or other structures. **3.** A standard, usually of length, by which the proportions of a building are determined. **4.** A unit of a building structure which is based on a standard pattern of standard dimensions.

modulus of elasticity In an elastic material which has been subject to strain below its elastic limit, the ratio of the unit stress to the corresponding unit strain.

modulus of resilience The amount of elastic energy absorbed by a unit volume of a material when it is loaded to its elastic limit in tension.

modulus of rigidity, modulus of shear In an elastic material which has been subjected to stress, the ratio of the shearing stress to the shearing strain.

modulus of rupture A measure of the ultimate load-carrying capacity of a beam; equal to the ratio of the bending moment at rupture to the section modulus of the beam.

modulus of subgrade reaction Same as **coefficient of subgrade reaction**.

modulus of toughness The amount of energy per unit volume which is absorbed by a structural material when subject to shock or impact, up to the point of fracture.

moellon Stone rubble used as filling between the facing walls of a structure.

Mogen David See **Star of David**.

Mogul architecture The later phase of Indian **Islamic architecture**, named after the Mogul dynasty (1526–1707), typified by monumental palaces and mosques and detailed decorative work. The Taj Mahal is the most famous example.

mogul base A large, screw-in type of base for an incandescent lamp of 300 watts or higher.

Mohammedan architecture See **Muslim architecture, Islamic architecture**.

Mohs' scale A scale which rates the scratch hardness of a mineral on a scale of 1 (talc) to 10 (diamond).

moist room A room in which the atmosphere is maintained at a selected temperature, usually 73.4°F (23°C), with a relative humidity of at least 98%, for the purpose of curing and storing cementitious test specimens.

moisture barrier **1.** A **vapor barrier**. **2.** A **damp course**.

moisture content **1.** The weight of water, usually expressed as a percentage of the total dry weight of a material. **2.** The weight of water in a given soil mass.

moisture expansion **1.** See **bulking**. **2.** An increase in dimension or bulk volume of a material or manufactured article caused by the absorption of water or water vapor.

moisture gradient The difference in moisture content between the inside and outside of a piece of wood.

moisture migration Same as **moisture movement**.

moisture movement **1.** The process by which moisture moves through a porous medium, such as a wall construction, as a result of differences in vapor pressure. **2.** The effects of such movement on the dimensions of a material such as concrete, mortar, cement paste, or rock.

moistureproofing The application of a **moisture barrier**.

MOL Abbr. for **maximum overall length**.

mold, mould **1.** A concave and/or convex form from which castings or pressings are replicated. **2.** A **template** or **pattern**. **3.** Same as **molding**.

molded brick **1.** A specially shaped brick, usually for decorative work. **2.** Ordinary brick which is neither cut with a wire nor pressed.

molded-case circuit breaker A relatively light, fast-acting electrical **circuit breaker** assembled as an integral unit in a supporting and enclosing housing of molded insulating material.

molded insulation A thermal insulation material that is premolded to fit the surface contours of pipes, pipe fittings, valves, etc.

molded plastic skylight A **skylight** molded of transparent or translucent plastic, which allows the passage of light to the space below.

molded plywood Plywood formed and cured into a curved shape.

molding A member of construction or decoration so treated as to introduce varieties of outline or contour in edges or surfaces, whether on projections or cavities, as on cornices, capitals, bases, door and window jambs and heads, etc.; may be of any building material, but almost all derive at least in part from wood prototypes (as those in classical architecture) or stone prototypes (as those in Gothic architecture). Moldings are generally divided into three categories; rectilinear, curved, and composite-curved. Also called a **mold**. For special definitions and illustrations, see **applied molding, beadmolding, bead-and-reel**

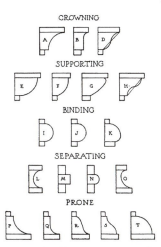

sections of classical **moldings:** A, cavetto; B, congé; D, cyma recta; E, quarter round; F, ovolo; G, echinus; H, cyma reversa; I, half round; J, torus; K, thumb; L, half hollow; M, fillet; N, bead; O, scotia; P, cavetto; Q, scape; R, cyma recta; S, cyma reversa; T, ovolo

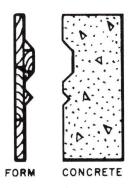

mold for finishing concrete

molding, bolection molding, cyma, dripmolding, egg-and-dart molding, half-round molding, head molding, hip molding, hood molding, Italian molding, label molding, laid-on molding, ogee, ovolo molding, planted molding, quarter-round molding, rope molding, scotia, stop molding, struck molding, sunk molding, tongue-and-dart molding, treacle molding, weather molding.

molding machine   A high-speed machine for planing, shaping, and cutting moldings.

molding pattern   See **WP-series molding pattern**.

molding plastic   A partially polymerized resin, usually in powdered form, which is molded under heat and pressure; often filler materials and pigments are added.

molding powder   See **molding plastic**.

mold stone   The **jambstone** of a door or window.

molecular sieve   An adsorbent composed of porous aluminosilicates with pores of uniform molecular dimensions which will selectively absorb molecules of the substance to be gathered.

mole drain   A subsurface channel for draining water.

moler brick   **1.** An insulation brick made from moler earth, a type of diatomaceous material. **2.** A brick made from any diatomaceous earth, i.e., any diatomite.

molybdate orange   Bright orange pigment consisting of mixed crystals of lead chromate, lead molybdate, and lead sulfate; used in paint because of its high opacity.

moment   The property by which a force tends to cause a body, to which it is applied, to rotate about a point or line; equal in magnitude to the product of the force and the perpendicular distance of the point from the line of action of the force.

moment of inertia   Of a body around an axis, the sum of the products obtained by multiplying each element of mass by the square of its distance from the axis.

momentum   Of a moving body, the product of the mass of the body and its velocity.

monastery   A building complex of a monastic order.

monial   Same as **mullion**.

monitor, monitor roof   A raised section of a roof, usually straddling a ridge; has openings, louvers, or windows along the sides to admit light or air.

monitor skylight   A **skylight** placed in a raised section of a roof, often straddling a ridge.

monk bond   Similar to **Flemish bond** but with two stretchers instead of one between each header.

monkeytail   The vertical scroll at the bottom of a handrail of a stairway.

monkeytail bolt   An **extension flush bolt**.

monkey wrench   A wrench having one jaw fixed and the other jaw (which is adjusted by a screw) movable.

monkey wrench

monolith   An architectural member (as an obelisk, the shaft of a column, etc.) consisting of a single stone.

monolithic   **1.** Shaped from a single block of stone, as a monolithic column. **2.** Composed of monoliths. **3.** Characterized by massiveness and complete uniformity. **4.** Said of concrete which is cast in a single piece. **5.** Said of a concrete pavement or floor whose surface layer is formed integrally with the slab below.

monolithic concrete   Reinforced concrete cast with no joints other than construction joints.

monolithic screed   **Screed, 4** laid in a single layer without joints.

monolithic surface treatment, dry shake   The treatment of the surface of unformed concrete by sprinkling a mixture of dry cement and sand on it after the water has mostly disappeared from the surface, following the **strike-off**; it is then worked in by **floating**.

monolithic terrazzo   A terrazzo topping which has been applied directly on a specially prepared concrete substrate; no underbed is used.

mono lock   See **preassembled lock**.

monomer   An organic liquid having a relatively low molecular weight which reacts with itself (or other compounds of low molecular weight) to create a solid polymer.

monopteron　In Greek architecture, a circular peripteral building, as a temple, having only a single row of columns.

monopteron

monostyle　**1.** Having but a single shaft; applied to medieval pillars. **2.** Having the same style of architecture throughout.

monotriglyphic　In the Doric order, having one **triglyph** over the space between two columns.

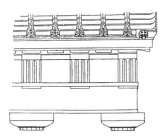

monotriglyphic

monstrance　See **ostensory**.

montant　That part of a framed stile which is in contact with the rail.

Monterey style, Monterey Revival　An architectural style that came into existence in Monterey, California, between about 1835 and 1840; typically, a two-story house with a full-façade balcony supported by plain wood posts and enclosed by wood railings. A modified version of this style was revived from about 1920 to 1960, combining Spanish Colonial architecture with some elements of early New England colonial architecture; in this 20th-century version, the balcony is typically cantilevered rather than

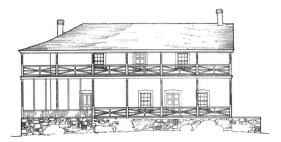

Monterey style

supported by wood columns from ground level, as in the earlier Monterey style. Nineteenth-century houses in this style usually were characterized by: thick whitewashed adobe walls; a low-pitched gable roof or hipped roof with its ridge parallel to the façade, usually covered with hand-split wood shingles, but sometimes with tiles; occasionally a decorative chimney cap or chimney hood; double-hung wood-frame windows with mullions; often, window shutters; occasionally, full-length windows opening onto the balcony; a relatively simple paneled entry door. Doors in 20th-century houses in this style are often imitative of those found in Colonial Revival architecture, including paneling, a fanlight over the door and sidelights flanking the door; occasionally, some elements of Greek Revival are included in the wood trim around doors and windows.

montmorillonite　One of the common clay minerals which typically swells upon wetting and becomes soft and greasy.

monument　**1.** A permanent natural or artificial object marking the corners and boundaries of real property or establishing the location of a triangulation or other important survey station. **2.** A stone, pillar, megalith, structure, building, or the like, erected in memory of the dead, an event, or an action.

monumental stone　A **dimension stone** of adequate size and quality for use in carving a monument or a memorial.

Moorish arch　Same as **horseshoe arch**.

Moorish architecture　The **Islamic architecture** of North Africa and the regions of Spain once under Islamic domination.

Moorish Revival　A rarely used mode of **Exotic Revival** architecture from about 1845 to 1890.

moot hall

Usually characterized by the use of **horseshoe arches, multifoil arches**, and window tracery.

moot hall   A place of public assembly; a hall for meeting, debate, or judgment; a town hall.

mop-and-flop   A roofing procedure in which roofing elements (such as felt plies or cap sheets) are initially placed upside down adjacent to their ultimate locations on the substrate; then they are coated with adhesive, turned over, and adhered to the substrate.

mopboard   A **baseboard**.

mopping   Applying hot bitumen with a mop or mechanical applicator on the felt of a built-up roof membrane, on a roof-deck, or the like.

mop plate   A narrow plate fixed to the bottom of a door for protection against soiling from a mop; similar to a **kickplate**.

mop sink   A type of **sink** having a deep basin, usually used by janitors.

mopstick handrail   A handrail having a circular cross section except for a small flat on the underside.

Moresque architecture   Same as **Moorish architecture**.

morgue, mortuary   A room or building for the holding and/or identification of dead bodies prior to burial or cremation.

Mormon thatched-roof shed   Same as **jacal, 1**.

morning room   A family, or private, sitting room, usually sunlit early in the day.

mortar, mortar mix   A plastic mixture of cementitious materials (such as plaster, cement, or lime) with water and a fine aggregate (such as sand); can be troweled in the plastic state; hardens in place. When used in masonry construction, the mixture may contain masonry cement or ordinary hydraulic cement with lime (and often other admixtures) to increase its plasticity and durability. Also see **clay-and-hair mortar, gypsum mortar, lime mortar**.

mortar aggregate   An **aggregate** consisting of natural or manufactured sand.

mortar bed   **1.** A **mortar box**. **2.** A thick layer of mortar used to seat a structural member.

mortarboard, fat board, spot board   A board, usually set on legs to form a table, used to mix lime putty and gauging plaster.

mortar box, mortar bed   A shallow, trough-like box in which mortar or plaster is mixed.

mortar brick   A type of brick used primarily in the 18th and 19th centuries; usually consisted of a mixture of sand and lime, to which water was added; then molded into bricks and allowed to harden in the open air; primarily used in regions where clay for making a better grade of bricks was unavailable.

mortar cube test   A test of the compressive strength of a material; a sample is formed into a cube, dried according to a standard procedure, and then crushed.

mortar fillet   Same as **cement fillet**.

mortar joint   See **masonry joint**.

mortar mill   A mixing and stirring machine for combining lime, sand, and other materials to make mortar.

mortar mix   See **mortar**.

mortar tray   A template designed to facilitate the laying of two ribs of mortar in conjunction with V-brick.

mortgage   A loan in which property is used as security for the debt.

mortgagee   The lender from whom a mortgage is obtained.

mortgage lien   A charge against property as security for the payment of a loan.

mortgagor   The borrower who obtains a mortgage.

mortice   British variant of **mortise**.

mortise   A hole, cavity, notch, slot, or recess cut into a timber or piece of other material; usually receives a **tenon**, but also has other purposes, as to receive a lock.

mortise-and-tenon joint, mortise joint   A joint between two wood members that is formed by fitting a **tenon** at the end of the one member into a **mortise** in the other member; the mortise and the tenon are usually cut or shaped with a mallet and chisel. After fitting the tenon into the mortise, a hole is drilled through them with an auger; then a wooden peg (**treenail**) is driven into the hole to secure the joint. Also called a mortise-and-pegged joint.

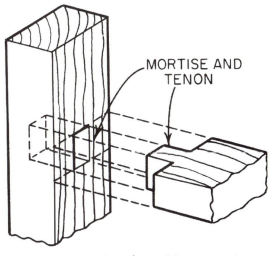

mortise-and-tenon joint

mortise bolt A door bolt designed to be mortised into a door rather than applied to its surface.

mortise chisel, framing chisel, heading chisel, socket chisel A steel chisel for woodworking; has a heavy body with a socket shank; esp. used for cutting mortises.

mortise chisel

mortised astragal On a door having two leaves, a two-piece **astragal** having one part recessed in the edge of each door.

mortised astragal

mortise gauge A tool (similar to a **marking gauge**) having two scribes for marking parallel lines; can be adjusted to the required distances from a working edge in preparing mortises or tenons.

mortise joint See **mortise-and-tenon joint**.

mortise latch A **mortise lock**.

mortise lock A lock designed to be installed in a mortise rather than applied to a door's surface.

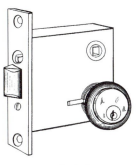

mortise lock

mortise machine A machine which cuts square or rectangular holes, usually with a chisel, or circular holes with a circular cutting bit.

mortise pin A pin which locks a mortise-and-tenon joint by being driven either through the extended tenon or through both the mortise and the tenon.

mortise preparation On a door or doorframe, the drilling, tapping, and reinforcing for hardware which is to be mortised into it.

mortuary See **morgue**.

mortuary temple A temple for offerings and worship of a deceased person, usually a deified king, as distinguished from a **cult temple**.

mosaic **1.** A pattern formed by inlaying small pieces of stone, tile, glass, or enamel into a cement, mortar, or plaster matrix. **2.** A form of surface decoration, similar to marquetry, but usu-

mosaic, 1

ally employing small pieces or bits of wood to create an inlaid design.

Moslem architecture See **Muslim architecture**.

mosque A Muslim house of worship.

mosque

MOT On drawings, abbr. for "motor."

motel A roadside building or group of buildings which contains hotel and parking accommodations primarily for transient motorists, often with individual exterior entrances to each room.

motif A principal repeated element in an ornamental design.

motion detector A device to detect intrusion within an area to be protected. The device radiates waves (electromagnetic or ultrasonic, at a fixed frequency) that are reflected back to the device. If an intruder moves within the protected space, a change in frequency results which is detected and which activates an alarm.

motor A machine which converts electric power into mechanical power by means of a rotating shaft.

motor branch circuit A **branch circuit** which supplies electric power to one or more motors and their associated controllers.

motor-circuit switch A switch intended for use in an electric-motor branch circuit; rated in horsepower and capable of interrupting the maximum operating overload current of a motor of the same rating at the rated voltage.

motor controller A **controller** which governs the power delivered to a motor (or group of motors).

motor-generator set A machine that consists of a motor which is mechanically coupled to an electric generator.

motor grader A dirt-moving machine for leveling and planing the surface to fine tolerances by means of a blade (or moldboard) than can be set and held at precise slope and elevation. Controls at the operator's station raise and lower, turn, and tilt the moldboard.

motor starter A **motor controller** used only for connecting and disconnecting a motor.

motte A steep mound of earth surrounded by a ditch and surmounted by a timber stockade and tower; the main feature of a Norman castle.

mottle 1. The pattern or arrangement of spots and cloudings forming a mottled surface, esp. in marble, or in wood veneer as a result of unusual variation in fiber growth or fiber arrangement. Also see **fiddleback, quilted figure, blister figure**. 2. See **mottling**.

mottler In painting, a brush having a flat thick shape; used for graining and marbling.

mottling Spotty round marks which appear as a defect in a sprayed film of paint.

moucharaby See **meshrebeeyeh**.

mouchette In 14th cent. Gothic tracery and derivatives, a typical small motif, pointed, elongated, and bounded by elliptical and ogee curves; a dagger motif with a curved axis.

mould, moulding British variants of **mold, molding**.

mouse, duck A lead weight on a string; used to pull a sash cord over a sash pulley, to clear a blocked pipe, etc.

mouse-tooth pattern, mouse-tooth finish See **tumbling course** and **straight-line gable**.

movable form In the placement of concrete, a formwork which has been so sized in its manufacture or construction as to be suitable for repetitive use in a series of pours.

movable partition A **demountable partition**.

movement In wood, same as **working**.

movement joint Same as **expansion joint**.

moving ramp A continuously moving system on which passengers stand, to be carried along a horizontal plane or up an inclined plane.

moving staircase, moving stairway See **escalator**.

moving walk A continuously moving passenger-carrying device on which passengers stand or walk; the passenger-carrying surface remains parallel to its direction of motion and is uninterrupted.

mow The loft in a barn for storage of hay.

Mozarabic architecture Northern Spanish architecture built after the 9th cent. by Christian refugees from Moorish domination, characterized by the horseshoe arch and other Moorish features.

mpl Abbr. for **maple**.

MR Abbr. for **mill run**.

M-roof A roof formed by joining two parallel gable roofs, creating a valley between them, resembling the capital letter M in section.

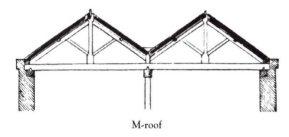

M-roof

MRT Abbr. for "mean radiant temperature."

MRTR On drawings, abbr. for **mortar**.

mucilage **1.** An adhesive prepared from a gum and water. **2.** A liquid adhesive which has low bonding strength.

muck **1.** An organic soil of very soft consistency; also called muck soil. **2.** Material to be excavated; clay, dirt, loam, stone, etc. **3.** The material so excavated.

muck soil Same as **muck, 1**.

mud A mixture of soil with sufficient water to make it soft.

mud-and-sticks chimney Same as **clay-and-sticks chimney**.

mud brick A term occasionally used for **adobe** that has been shaped in a brick form and then sun-dried.

mud-capping The blasting of a boulder by placing a quantity of explosives against it without confining the explosives in a drill hole.

Mudejar architecture A Spanish style created by Moors under Christian domination in the 13th and 14th cent., but retaining Islamic elements such as the horseshoe arch.

mudflow Movement of soft weak soil having the consistency of mud.

mud house Any primitive dwelling having walls of unbaked earth; often constructed of molded sun-dried blocks of mud usually mixed with straw, manure, or other material to provide increased mechanical strength.

mud-jacking A process of raising a concrete slab on ground where it has settled or been depressed; a hole is drilled through the slab, then a mixture of mud and cement is pumped beneath the slab under pressure, thereby raising it.

mud plaster A plaster that is usually a mixture of heavy clay and water, often containing chopped straw or manure to improve its mechanical strength when dry.

mud room In regions of heavy precipitation, a small room adjacent to an exterior door, used for temporary storage of dirty or wet boots or outer garments.

mud sill The lowest horizontal timber at the base of a **timber-framed building**, usually laid directly on the ground; used to distribute concentrated loads.

mud slab A layer of concrete, 2 in. (5 cm) to 6 in. (15 cm) thick, below a structural concrete floor or footing over soft, wet soil.

mud wall A wall usually constructed of a mixture of clay and a binder such as chopped straw; often, gravel is added.

muffle **1.** A material used to build up the core of a large plaster molding. **2.** To deaden sound.

muffler See **sound attenuator**.

Mughal architecture See **Mogul architecture**.

mulch Material such as leaves, hay, straw, or the like, spread over the surface of the ground to protect the roots of newly planted shrubs or trees, of tender plants, etc., from the sun or from the cold.

mullion A vertical member separating (and often supporting) windows, doors, or panels set in series. Also see **door mullion**. (*See illustration on page 606.*)

mullion cover A loose piece of metal trim which screws or snaps in place on the interior side of the mullion of a window.

MULT

mullions: *a*

MULT   On drawings, abbr. for "multiple."

multibag packer   See **carousel packer** and **linear packer**.

multicentered arch   An arch having a shape composed of a series of circular arcs with different radii, giving an approximation to an ellipse. These arcs are symmetrically disposed about a vertical axis and occur in odd numbers.

multicolor finish   A speckled paint finish containing small individual colored particles.

multiconductor cable   An assemblage of several electrical conductors having a common outer jacket.

multicurved gable   A gable having an outline containing two or more curves on each side of a central ridge; for example, see **Flemish gable**.

multicurved parapet   At the edge of a roof, a **freestanding** wall whose outline contains several curves on its upper surface, as in a **mission parapet**.

multicurved parapet

multi-element prestressing   Prestressing of **reinforced concrete** which is accomplished by stressing an assembly of several individual structural elements to produce one integrated structural member.

multifoil   Having more than five foils, lobes, or arcuate divisions.

multifoil: arch

multifoil: window

multifolding door   A door composed of large panels hung on a ceiling track; when the door is open, the panels stack against each other and are housed in a relatively small space.

multimedia filter   In a water supply system, a **bed-type filter** containing several different filtration media (e.g., coal, sand, and garnet).

multi-outlet assembly   A metallic or nonmetallic assembly used in electric wiring; a type of surface-mounted or flush raceway designed to hold conductors and attachment plug receptacles; assembled in the field or at the factory.

multiple dwelling   A building for residential use which houses several separate family units, usually three or more.

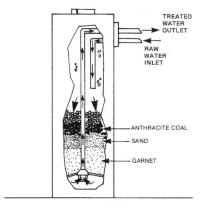

multimedia filter

multiple-family Said of a building in which more than two families or households live independently of each other and do cooking within their own living quarters.

multiple-folding rule A folding rule up to 8 ft long used where precision accuracy is not required.

multiple frame A framework of beams and columns extending over more than one bay in a horizontal direction.

multiple glazing Glazing comprised of more two or more sheets of glass with space between them, e.g., see **double glazing**.

multiple hoistway A **hoistway** for more than a single elevator or dumbwaiter.

multiple-layer adhesive A film-type adhesive inserted between dissimilar materials in order to bond them together; often a different type of adhesive is used on each side of the film.

multiple-layer weld A weld in which more than one pass or deposit of filler metal is required to obtain the required dimensions of the weld.

multiple of direct personnel expense A method of compensation for professional services based on the direct expense of professional and technical personnel, including cost of salaries and mandatory and customary benefits, multiplied by an agreed factor.

multiple-window operator See **mechanical operator**.

multiplier The factor by which an architect's **direct personnel expense** is multiplied to deter-

mine compensation for his professional services or designated portions thereof.

multi-ply construction Laminated construction having more than three plies. Also see **balanced construction**.

multistage stressing The prestressing of **reinforced concrete** performed in stages as the construction progresses.

multistory Having several stories, usually more than five.

multistory frame, skeleton construction A building framework of more than one story in which loads are carried to the ground by a system of beams and columns.

multi-unit wall A masonry wall composed of two or more withes.

multiway deflection The deflection of air, from an **air outlet**, in several directions, usually at 90° to each other.

multizone system An air-conditioning system which is capable of handling several individually controlled **zones** simultaneously.

municipality A town, city, or district possessing corporate jurisdiction.

municipal planning See **city planning** and **community planning**.

muniment house, *Brit.* **muniment room** A secure structure or area for storing and displaying important documents, official seals, etc.

munnion **1.** A mullion. **2.** A muntin.

muntin **1.** A secondary framing member to hold panes within a window, window wall, or glazed door; also called a **glazing bar, sash bar, window bar,** or **division bar**. **2.** An intermediate vertical member that divides the panels of a door. (*See illustration below and on p. 608.*) Also see **curved muntin**.

muntin, 1

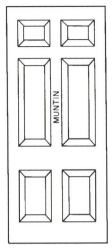

muntin, 2

Muntz metal, malleable brass, *Brit.* **yellow metal**   A copper-zinc metal alloy having 60% copper and 40% zinc; used in castings and in extruded, rolled, and stamped products.

muqarnas, honeycomb work, stalactite work   An original Islamic design involving various combinations of three-dimensional shapes, corbeling, etc.

mural   **1.** Pertaining to a wall. **2.** A mural painting, decorative or figurative.

mural arch   An arch in a wall which was constructed in the plane of the meridian; used for attachment of astronomical instruments in the Middle Ages.

murus   A wall of stone or brick, built as a defense and fortification around an ancient Roman town. Also see **paries.**

museum   An institution for the assembly and public display of any kind of collection, esp. one of rare and/or educational value.

mushrabiya   See **meshrebeeyeh.**

mushrebeeyeh   Same as **meshrebeeyeh.**

mushroom column   In reinforced concrete construction, a structural column, suggestive of a mushroom shape, that flares at the top to counteract sheering stresses.

mushroom construction   A type of **flat slab** construction which utilizes column capitals and drop panels.

mushy concrete   A concrete of relatively fluid consistency; used where mobility after initial placement is important, as between narrowly spaced forms or where reinforcement is closely spaced.

musivum   Same as **opus musivum.**

musket-stock post   A principal vertical structural support, in an early **timber-framed house,** having the shape of an inverted musket stock; the additional thickness at the top provides an added bearing surface to support the imposed load.

muqarnas

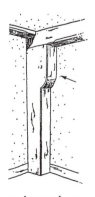

musket-stock post

Muslim architecture, Muhammadan architecture, Saracenic architecture Architecture developed from the 7th to the 16th cent. A.D., in the wake of the Muhammadan conquests of Syria and Egypt, Mesopotamia and Iran, North Africa and Spain, Central Asia and India, countries from which it absorbed in turn elements of art and architecture. A new building type was developed from the Christian basilica—the multiaisled, arcaded, columnar, or pillared mosque; a new type of domed mosque, tomb, or madrasah from the vaulted, centrally organized Byzantine and Sassanian structures. Uses many variations of basic architectural elements; pointed, horseshoe, "Persian," multifoil, and interlacing arches; bulbous, ribbed, conical, and melon domes; tunnel, cross-rib, and stalactite vaults; a wide variety of crenelations. Surfaces are covered by abundant geometric, floral, and calligraphic decorations executed in stone, brick, stucco, wood, and glazed tile.

mute A mortised **rubber silencer** for a door.

mutule A sloping flat block on the soffit of the Doric cornice, usually decorated with rows of six **guttae** each; occurs over each triglyph and each metope of the frieze.

Mycenaean architecture Architecture of the heroic age in southern Greece from the 17th to 13th century B.C. Exemplified in the earliest

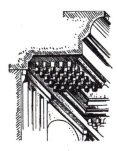

mutule

phase by shaft graves cut into the sloping rock, with sidewalls of stone masonry and a timber roof; in the middle period by monumental beehive tombs constructed of superimposed layers of enormous stone blocks progressively projecting to create a parabolic corbeled vault, with a stone-faced, inclined access passage leading to the entrance composed of upward-slanting jambs and a heavy stone lintel supporting a characteristic Mycenaean relief triangle; in the late period by fortified palaces having Cyclopean walls, underground passages with corbeled vaults, postern gates, and cisterns, laid out on an irregular ground plan, with distinctive **propylaea**, one or more unconnected columnar halls with porches facing individual courts, and long corridors linking auxiliary and storage rooms.

mynchery Old Anglo-Saxon term for **nunnery**.

N

N **1.** On drawings, abbr. for "north." **2.** On drawings, abbr. for **nail**. **3.** Symbol for **newton**.

N1E In the lumber industry, abbr. for "nosed one edge."

N2E In the lumber industry, abbr. for "nosed two edges."

NAAMM Abbr. for "National Association of Architectural Metal Manufacturers."

nab The **strike plate** of a door lock.

nail A straight, small, rigid, slender shaft of metal, one end of which is usually pointed; the other end has a head that may be driven with a hammer; used as a fastener to join separate pieces of wood, to attach tiles to a wood sheathing on a roof, and so on. Nails were hand-wrought until the invention of machines for their manufacture in the early 19th century. See **cut nail, dog nail, hand-wrought nail, wire nail, wrought nail.**

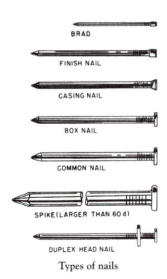

BRAD

FINISH NAIL

CASING NAIL

BOX NAIL

COMMON NAIL

SPIKE (LARGER THAN 60 d)

DUPLEX HEAD NAIL

Types of nails

nailable concrete Concrete into which nails can be driven; usually made with a suitable lightweight aggregate, with or without the addition of sawdust.

nail claw A straight steel bar having a curved end which is slotted; used to lift and pull nails from material into which they have been driven.

nailer Same as **nailing strip**.

nailer joist Same as **nailing joist**.

nail float See **devil float**.

nailhead **1.** An ornament, often highly decorated, resembling the head of a nail. **2.** The enlarged top of a nail.

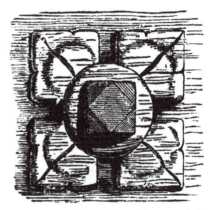

decorative **nailhead** on a wooden quatrefoil

nailhead molding A molding decorated with a series of quadrangular pyramidal projections resembling the heads of nails.

nailhead molding

nailing In roofing, the process of fixing roofing materials to the substrate. In **exposed nailing**, the nails are left exposed to the weather. In **con-**

cealed **nailing**, the nails are protected by the next sheet of roofing material.

nailing anchor   See **wood stud anchor**.

nailing block   A **wood brick**.

nailing ground   A **ground** to which trim can be nailed.

nailing joist   A steel joist which has a **nailing strip** permanently attached to it.

nailing marker   A small mark cut into one member to position a nail for correct entry into a second wood member.

nailing strip   A wood strip, attached to a surface; used as a base for nailing or fastening another material.

nail plate   A metal plate which is placed over the two ends of pieces of wood that are to be joined (in the same plane); it is secured to each end by screws or nails driven into the wood through holes in the plate.

nail punch   Same as **nail set**.

nail set   A short steel rod, usually tapered; used to drive a nail or brad below, or flush with, a wood surface.

nail set

naked flooring   The timber or framework on which floor boarding is laid.

naked wall   A wall with lath in place, ready for plastering.

nanometer   A unit of length used to express wavelengths of light in and near the visible spectrum; 1 nanometer equals 10^{-9} meter or 10 angstroms. *Abbr.* nm.

naos   See **cella**.

naphtha   A distillate of petroleum or coal; generally has low solvency and high volatility; used as a solvent in paints and varnishes.

naphthenate   A drier used in paints; made with naphthenic acid and lead, cobalt, calcium, or manganese salt.

napkin pattern   Same as **linenfold**.

Naples yellow, antimony yellow   A light yellow pigment; the true pigment is a basic antimonate of lead, but is imitated by mixtures.

narrow-light door   A door having a narrow rectangular **fixed light**, usually placed in a vertical position near the **lock stile**.

narrow-ringed, close-grained, close-grown, fine-grained, slow-grown   Descriptive of wood having narrow annual rings.

narrow side   Of a door, the face of a door which contacts the doorframe stops.

narthex   An enclosed porch or vestibule at the entrance to some early Christian churches.

NAT   On drawings, abbr. for "natural."

natatorium   **1.** A swimming pool. **2.** A building containing a swimming pool.

National Building Code   See **BOCA National Building Code** and **Uniform Building Code**.

National Electrical Code   A nationally accepted guide to the safe installation of wiring and equipment; not intended as a design specification but rather for the practical safeguarding of persons and of buildings and their contents from hazards arising from the use of electricity for heat, light, power, and other purposes. Provides rules, recommended by the National Fire Protection Association, governing the installation of interior electric wiring. These rules, subject to revision every three years, a standard of the National Board of Fire Underwriters, have been incorporated in many municipal ordinances; city or state regulations take precedence where they differ from the rules of the Code.

National Electrical Manufacturers Association   A trade association of electrical manufacturers setting standards of construction quality and dimensional uniformity.

National Electrical Safety Code (NESC)   Rules, prepared by the NESC and approved by **ANSI**, which govern: (a) methods of grounding; (b) installation and maintenance of electric-supply stations and equipment, of overhead supply and communication lines, and of underground and electric-supply and communications lines; and (c) operation of electric-supply and communication lines and equipment.

National Fire Protection Association An organization devoted to all aspects of fire safety.

National Historic Landmark See **landmark**.

National Register of Historic Places A U.S. government organization that maintains lists and files of documentation of buildings, structures, objects, districts, and sites of national, state, or local significance. Buildings on the Register may be marked with plaques that provide historical information about them. Also called the National Register. Address: National Park Service, U.S. Department of the Interior, P.O. Box 37127, Washington, DC 20013-7127.

National style A term sometimes used as a synonym for **Greek Revival style** during the height of its popularity, from about 1830 to 1850.

National Trust for Historic Preservation A national, nonprofit private organization chartered by the U.S. Congress to encourage public participation in the preservation of buildings, objects, and sites that have been significant in American history. Address: 1785 Massachusetts Avenue, NW, Washington, DC 20036.

native asphalt Same as **natural asphalt**.

natte A basket weave, as a pattern carved or painted to imitate interlaced **withes, 2** of matting.

natte

natural asphalt Asphalt occurring in nature, produced from petroleum by natural evaporation or distillation; usually not suitable for paving purposes until refined and softened to proper consistency by combining with flux oil.

natural bed Of a stone, a plane parallel to its natural strata.

natural cement A product obtained by finely pulverizing calcined argillaceous limestone which has been burnt at a temperature no higher than necessary to drive off carbon dioxide.

natural circulation The circulation of air or water due to differences in density rather than to the actions of a pump or blower.

natural clay tile A ceramic tile made from clays that produce a dense body, having a distinctive, slightly textured appearance.

natural-cleft Describing stone that has been split (cleaved) parallel to its stratification, yielding an irregular but nearly flat surface.

natural convection The circulation of air or water due to differences in density resulting from variations in temperature in the space or medium where the circulation takes place.

natural draft The flow of gases in a chimney due to the difference in temperature and density between the gases within the chimney and the outside air.

natural-draft boiler A boiler system in which a chimney is required to draw the products of combustion through the boiler or furnace.

natural-draft chimney A chimney that draws the gases and smoke of combustion from a furnace because of the natural draft it develops; operates without auxiliary mechanical-draft equipment.

natural environment The aggregate of the natural external surroundings and conditions, in contrast to the built environment (i.e., those surroundings and conditions resulting from construction by human beings).

natural finish Any finish resulting from the application of a transparent substance (such as a varnish, water-repellent preservative, sealer, or oil) which does not affect significantly the original color or grain.

natural finish tile Ceramic facing tile having unglazed or uncoated surfaces which have been fired to the natural color of the material used in forming the body of the tile.

natural foundation A foundation which requires no special preparation of the soil below to support the structure.

natural frequency One of a number of frequencies at which a system or object tends to vibrate if subject to a mechanical displacement or impact and then allowed to vibrate freely.

natural gas A combustible hydrocarbon gas having a calorific value of about 1000 Btu per cubic foot (8,900 kilocalories per cubic meter) of gas; the most commonly available gas from utility companies.

natural grade The elevation of the original or undisturbed natural surface of the ground.

natural pigment See **earth pigment**.

natural pozzolan A raw or calcined natural material (such as volcanic ash) which has **pozzolanic** properties.

natural resin A solid, thermoplastic organic substance which occurs in nature; is flammable and a nonconductor of electricity.

natural sand Sand which is the result of natural disintegration and abrasion of rock.

natural-seasoned lumber See **air-dried lumber**.

natural stone True stone, as distinguished from imitations. The term is a redundancy, as stone is, by definition, natural in its occurrence.

natural ventilation Ventilation by air movement caused by natural forces, rather than by fans.

naval stores 1. Oils, resins, tars, and pitches obtained from the oleoresin of pine trees. 2. Obsolete name for resin and turpentine.

nave 1. The middle aisle of a church. 2. By extension, both middle and side aisles of a church from the entrance to the crossing or chancel. 3. That part of the church intended primarily for the laity.

nave arcade The open arcade between the central and side aisles.

NBC Abbr. for "National Building Code."

NBFU Abbr. for "National Board of Fire Underwriters."

NBS 1. Abbr. for "National Bureau of Standards." 2. Abbr. for "natural black slate." 3. Abbr. for "New British Standard."

NC Abbr. for "noise criterion."

NAVE

NAVE ARCADE

nave, 1; nave arcade

NC curves A series of curves of octave-band sound spectra, used to provide a single-number rating of the noisiness of an indoor space. A measured octave-band spectrum is compared with this set of curves to determine the NC level of the space in which the measurements were made.

NCM On drawings, abbr. for "noncorrosive metal."

NCSBCS Abbr. for the "National Conference of States on Building Codes and Standards."

neat Descriptive of plaster or cement mixed without the addition of any material except water. See **neat cement**.

neat cement 1. Hydraulic cement in the unhydrated state. 2. Cement mortar made without the addition of sand.

neat cement grout **1.** A fluid mixture of hydraulic cement and water, with or without admixture. **2.** The hardened equivalent of such mixture.

neat cement paste A mixture of hydraulic cement and water, both before and after setting and hardening.

neat gypsum plaster See **gypsum neat plaster**.

neat line, net line **1.** A line which defines the limits of work, such as an excavation, cut stone, etc. **2.** The true face line of a building regardless of the projections of the stones; a line back of, or inside of, incidental projections.

neat plaster Plaster made without aggregate.

neat size The exact size after preparation.

neat work Brickwork set at the base of a wall above the footings.

nebulé molding, nebuly molding A characteristic Norman molding with an undulating lower edge.

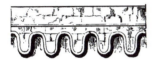

nebulé molding

NEC Abbr. for **National Electrical Code**.

neck **1.** In the classical orders, the space between the bottom of the capital and the top of the shaft, which is marked by a sinkage or a ring of moldings. **2.** A section of the branch duct that connects an **air diffuser** with the main supply duct.

necking **1.** Same as **neck**. **2.** A molding or group of moldings between a column and capital. **3.** Any ornamental band at the lower part of a capital; a **hypotrachelium**. **4.** An irrecoverable reduction in cross section of a sealant under stress.

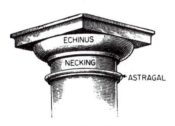

necking, 2

neck molding A **necking** which takes the form of a molding of any type; same as **necking, 2**.

necessarium The privy of an ancient castle or of a monastery.

necropolis **1.** A city of the dead; a large cemetery in ancient Egypt, Greece, Phoenicia, Carthage, etc. **2.** An ancient or historic burial place.

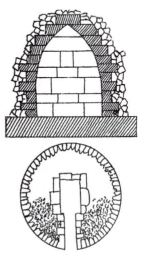

necropolis of Tantalus, Sipylus; section (*above*) and plan (*below*)

needle **1.** A piece of timber laid horizontally and supported on props or shores under a wall or building, etc.; provides temporary support while the foundation or part beneath is altered, repaired, or underpinned. **2.** A short timber, or the like, which passes through a hole in a wall; used to support a shore, a scaffold, etc.

needle bath A **shower bath** containing pipes with a large number of tiny holes through which a spray of water strikes the bather in tiny jets.

needle beam A crossbeam supporting a load; used in **underpinning** foundation walls; attached to columns at its ends, clear of the existing footing.

needle beam scaffold Same as **needle scaffold**.

needle pile A very slender steel **pile** used in underpinning operations.

needle scaffold A scaffold which is hung from **needles**.

needle spire A slender **spire** surmounting the center of a tower roof.

needle valve A type of **globe valve** in which the throttling is performed by a tapered pin moving in and out of a conical seat to adjust the fluid flow.

needlework A form of construction combining a framework of timber and a plaster or masonry filling; common in medieval houses.

needling Needle beams which provide temporary support.

NEG On drawings, abbr. for "negative."

negative easement An **easement, 1** which limits the possible use that the owner of land may otherwise be entitled to.

negative friction In foundation engineering, the additional load on a pile resulting from the settling of fill, which tends to drag the pile downward into the soil.

negative-slump concrete Concrete whose consistency has a **zero slump** before and after the addition of water.

negligence Failure to exercise that degree of care which a reasonable and prudent person would exercise under the same circumstances.

negotiation phase See **bidding or negotiation phase**.

NEMA Abbr. for **National Electrical Manufacturers Association**.

Neo-Adamesque style See **Neo-Federal style**.

Neo-Baroque Said of a mode of architecture (in the late 19th century and early 20th century) more or less patterned after **Baroque** architecture developed in the 17th century.

Neo-Byzantine Same as **Byzantine Revival**.

Neoclassical Revival A mode of architecture primarily since about 1965; a rather free interpretation of the **Neoclassical style** with little attempt to emulate the original style accurately; usually has a pedimented **portico** with full-height columns.

Neoclassical style An architectural style based primarily on the use of forms of Classical antiquity used in both public buildings and opulent homes; aspects of this style are imitative of the earlier **Classical Revival style** (often called "Early Classical Revival") that was most popular from about 1770 to 1830; others are imitative of the **Greek Revival style** that was popular from about 1830 to 1850. Buildings in this style are generally characterized by: a smooth ashlar façade, an attic story, an enriched entablature, and a parapet; a symmetrical façade, commonly having a visually important full-width portico with full-height wood or stone classical columns or with square columns (sometimes paired) and full-height pilasters, or a one-story-high portico; an unadorned roof line; often a side-gabled roof, hipped roof, or gambrel roof; a moderate overhang at the eaves or boxed eaves; balustrades frequently located just above the eaves; commonly ornamented with statuary; a wide frieze below the cornice; double-hung, symmetrically arranged, with lintels above the windows; in homes, usually six-over-six or nine-over-nine double-hung windows; a doorway at the center of the façade, capped with a decorative lintel or with a broken pediment; ornamental elements usually surround the door. The terms **Classical Revival, Neoclassical Revival,** and **Neoclassicism** are sometimes used as synonyms for the Neoclassical style.

Neoclassicism A reinterpretation of the principles of Classical architecture in the late 18th and the early 19th century, and beyond. This term often includes the Federal style, Classical Revival style, and Greek Revival style and is generally characterized by: monumentality,

Neoclassicism of the 19th cent.

colossal porticos, and columns; strict use of the Greek and Roman orders; sparing application of ornamentation, an unadorned roof line, and an avoidance of moldings. The term **Neoclassical style** is occasionally used as a synonym.

Neo-Colonial architecture In American architecture of the last half of the 20th century, a term applied to buildings more or less patterned after 19th-century **Colonial Revival** architecture but usually a poorer version of the original; occasionally called Neo-Colonial Revival.

Neo-Eclectic architecture One of any number of domestic modes of architecture during the second half of the 20th century that freely borrows from, but does not copy, an earlier traditional style and detailing, making little effort to be precise in imitating its prototype; some features of **Post-Modern architecture** can be called Neo-Eclectic. For examples, see **Neo-Classical Revival, Neo-Colonial architecture, Neo-French, Neo-Mansard, Mediterranean Revival, Neo-Tudor architecture, Neo-Victorian.**

Neo-Federal style An inexact term applied to architecture loosely based on the American **Federal style** of architecture; moderately popular in the 1920s and beyond.

Neo-French architecture A free interpretation of **French Eclectic architecture** in the latter part of the 20th century (especially in America, but also elsewhere), often vaguely recalling farmhouses in Normandy. Usually characterized by: steeply pitched, hipped roofs, sometimes with flared eaves; a cylindrical tower with a conical roof; occasionally, false half-timbering; often, rounded or segmental arches over the windows that extend above the line of the eaves.

Neo-Georgian A loose term, descriptive of an architecture that emulates features and details of **Georgian architecture**, including a symmetrical façade, but commonly historically inaccurate; found primarily in the 19th and 20th centuries, but continue to be built today.

Neo-Gothic A term descriptive of the reuse of Gothic forms during the second half of the 19th century and the early part of the 20th century; see **Gothic Revival**; also see **Collegiate Gothic** and **Steamboat Gothic.**

Neo-Grec A term descriptive of architecture, primarily in the 1870s, that sought to follow the trabeated, rectangular construction of the early Greeks (see **Greek Revival**); especially usually characterized by the use of brickwork and ironwork.

Neo-Greek Revival A term for architecture loosely based on the **Greek Revival style**, usually historically inaccurate.

Neo-Liberty A mid-1900 emulation of **Art Nouveau**.

Neo-Mansard A loose term applied to architecture since about 1960 that makes use of some form of **mansard roof**, but usually has little else in common with the **Mansard style**.

Neo-Mediterranean See **Mediterranean Revival**.

neon An inert gas which produces a reddish orange glow when used in an electric discharge lamp.

neon lamp 1. A **cold-cathode lamp** whose principal light radiation is due to passage of an electric current through neon gas. 2. Any cold-cathode glass-tubing lamp, such as that used for electric signs, regardless of the type of gas that fills the lamp or the presence of phosphors or filters to control color.

neoprene A synthetic rubber which has high resistance to sunlight and oil; used in sheet form as roof membranes and flashings, as gasketing, in vibration control, etc.

Neo-Romanesque A term sometimes used as a synonym for **Richardsonian Romanesque style**, particularly in its early phases, or for **Romanesque Revival**. Also see **Rundbogenstil**.

Neo-Tudor Descriptive of a **Neo-Eclectic architecture**, vaguely imitative of its earlier **Tudor architecture** and **Tudor Revival** prototypes. Houses are usually one or two stories with front-facing gables, and generally usually characterized by: **false half-timbering** and **strapwork** employed as decorative elements; masonry or stucco walls on the ground floor, sometimes with a different treatment on the walls of the floor above; occasionally, an overhanging upper story; a shingle-covered, steeply pitched roof; prominent chimney stacks; groups of tall, narrow windows separated by mullions, often set with small panes of leaded glass that are either diamond-shaped or square-shaped, set diagonally.

Neo-Victorian A term descriptive of a **Neo-Eclectic architecture** somewhat imitative of features and details of the traditional 19th-century **Queen Anne style, 2**; especially usually characterized by porches of wood construction having wood brackets and abundant **spindlework**.

NEPA Abbr. for "National Environmental Policy Act."

nerve Same as **nervure**.

nervure Any one of the ribs of a groined vault, but esp. a rib which forms one of the sides of a compartment of the groining.

NESC Abbr. for "National Electrical Safety Code."

net cross-sectional area In masonry units, the gross cross-sectional area of a section minus the average area of ungrouted **cores** or cellular spaces.

net cut In an excavation on a hillside (in a particular area), the required **cut** minus the required **fill**.

net fill In an excavation on a hillside (in a particular area), the required **fill** minus the required **cut**.

net floor area The actual occupied area of a building, not including accessory unoccupied areas or thickness of walls; used in determining the required number of exits.

net line See **neat line**.

net load In a heating system, the **gross load** minus all losses between the source of heat and the terminal heating units (such as radiators).

net mixing water See **mixing water**.

net positive suction head The absolute pressure available at the inlet to a pump; the most important factor in determining the performance of a pump.

net room area The wall-to-wall floor area of a room.

net section The net or available area of a cross section of a beam after deducting for holes for rivets, bolts, etc.

net site area The total area which is within the property lines of a project, but not including any streets which may be included within.

net tensile strain The **tensile strain** at nominal strength, exclusive of strains due to effective prestress, creep, shrinkage, and/or temperature.

net tracery Tracery with repetitive motifs or openings.

net tracery

network **1.** An aggregate of interconnected electric conductors consisting of high-voltage feeders, step-down transformers, protective devices, mains, and services. **2.** In CPM terminology, the same as **arrow diagram**.

neutral axis An imaginary line in a beam, shaft, or other member, subjected to bending, where there is no tension or compression and where no deformation takes place.

neutral conductor **1.** In an electric circuit consisting of three or more conductors, the electric conductor that usually is so energized that the voltages between it and the other conductors are equal in magnitude. **2.** In a three-phase three-wire electrical circuit: a conductor whose potential differences between it and each of the other conductors are equal in magnitude and equally spaced in phase.

neutralizing The treatment of concrete, cement, or plaster with solutions of weak acid salts to neutralize the lime before painting.

neutral plane See **neutral surface**.

neutral soil Soil which is in the range from slightly acid to slightly alkaline, usually considered to be in the range of **pH values** from 6.6 to 7.3.

neutral surface, neutral plane An imaginary surface within a beam, subjected to bending, where there is neither compression nor elongation.

New Brutalism   See **Brutalism**.

newel   **1.** The central post or column around which the steps of a circular staircase wind, and which provides support for the staircase. **2.** A **newel-post**.

newel, 1

newel cap   The terminal feature of a newel-post; often molded, turned, or carved in a decorative shape.

newel collar   A turned wood collar used to lengthen the base of a newel.

newel drop   An ornamental, terminal projection of a newel-post, often through a soffit.

newel joint   The joint between a **newel-post** and the handrail or between the newel-post and the **string** of a stair.

newel-post   A tall and more or less ornamental post at the head or foot of a stair, supporting the handrail.

newel stair   **1.** A **screw stair**. **2.** Same as **solid newel stair**.

New England connected barn   See **continuous house**.

New England gambrel roof   A **gambrel roof** in which the upper and lower slopes are of approximately equal length; the lower slope has a steeper pitch, usually about 60 degrees.

New England method   See **pick and dip**.

New Shingle style   A term occasionally used to classify a late-20th-century wood-shingled house having many of the basic characteristics of

newel-post: *N*

a **Shingle style** house built between about 1880 and 1900.

newton (N)   The unit of force in the International System of Units; the force necessary to produce an acceleration of 1 metre per second-square in a body having a mass of 1 kilogram.

new town   A new, essentially self-sufficient city, built in a previously undeveloped area, which provides residential, commercial, industrial, educational, recreational, and public facilities.

new wood   Virgin wood, never having been worked by a tool.

New York leveling rod   A two-piece **leveling rod** with a movable target.

NFC   Abbr. for "National Fire Code."

NFPA   Abbr. for the **National Fire Protection Association**.

NFSA   Abbr. for "National Fire Sprinkler Association."

NGR stain, non-grain-raising stain   One of many liquid wood stains, based on alcohol or other solvent; almost totally free of water.

nib   Any projecting piece, part, or particle.

nibbed tile   A roofing tile having a small projection at its head for convenience in hanging the tile on a batten.

nib guide   A straight piece of wood, nailed on the base-coat plaster of the ceiling, which acts as a guide on which a cornice mold is run.

NIC   Abbr. for "not in the contract."

niche   A recess in a wall, usually to contain sculpture or an urn; often semicircular in plan, surmounted by a half dome.

niche

nicked-bit finish   A stone surface having parallel, raised projections of various sizes and spacing formed by an irregularly notched planer blade.

nickel   A silver-white metal; widely used as an additive to steel and cast-iron alloys; also used in electroplating metals which require resistance to corrosion.

nickel steel   Steel containing 3 to 5% nickel and 0.2 to 0.5% carbon; the nickel increases the strength and the elastic limit of the alloy; has better properties (such as greater strength, more ductility, and higher corrosion resistance) than carbon steel.

nidge, nig   In masonry, to dress the face of a stone with a sharply pointed hammer instead of a chisel and a mallet.

nidged ashlar, nigged ashlar   Stone dressed on the surface with a pick or sharp-pointed hammer.

nig   Same as **nidge**.

nigged ashlar   See **nidged ashlar**.

night latch, night bolt, night lock   An auxiliary lock having a spring latch bolt which functions independently of the regular lock of the door; may be opened by a knob or handle from the inside but only by a key from the outside.

night vent   See **ventlight**.

nimbus   A halo or disk of light surrounding the head in representations of divine and sacred personages.

nine-over-nine   A term descriptive of a **double-hung window** having nine **panes** in the upper sash and nine panes in the lower sash.

NIOSH   Abbr. for "National Institute of Occupational Safety and Health."

nippers   A form of hand pincers with cutting jaws that meet parallel to each other rather than at an angle; used for cutting wire, thin metal rods, or the like.

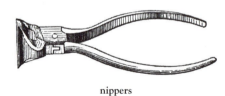

nippers

nipple   A short length of pipe with threads at each end; used to join couplings or fittings.

nipple

Nissen hut   A semicylindrically shaped prefabricated building of corrugated steel, usually thermally insulated.

nit   A unit of **luminance** equal to 1 candela per square meter. *Abbr.* nt.

nitrile rubber A synthetic rubber which has good resistance to oils and solvents; produced by copolymerizing butadiene and acrylonitrile.

nitrocellulose See **cellulose nitrate**.

NLMA Abbr. for "National Lumber Manufacturers Association."

nm Abbr. for **nanometer**.

NO. On drawings, abbr. for "number."

nobble To shape stone roughly, usually at the quarry.

node **1.** In electric wiring, a junction point at which several distribution or wiring conductors come together. **2.** A **panel point**.

nodus In ancient Roman construction, a **keystone**, or a **boss** in vaulting.

noel An old English term for **newel**.

no-fines concrete A concrete which contains little or no **fine aggregate**.

nog A brick-shaped piece of wood inserted in an internal masonry wall; often, one of a number of such pieces; also called a wood brick.

nogging The **infilling**, such as between the logs in a log cabin or between the framing members of a **timber-framed house**; used to increase the rigidity of the framing system, provide increased thermal insulation, and improve fire resistance.

nogging piece A horizontal timber fitted between the quarters of brick nogging and nailed to them in order to strengthen the brickwork.

noise Any sound which is unwanted because it is annoying, interferes with speech and hearing, or is intense enough to damage hearing.

noise absorption See **sound absorption**.

noise control The technology of obtaining an acceptable noise environment, consistent with economic and operational considerations.

noise criterion curves See **NC curves**.

noise insulation See **sound insulation**.

noise isolation class (NIC) A single-number rating derived from measured values of noise reduction between two enclosed spaces that are connected by one or more paths.

noise level The **sound level** of a source of noise; expressed in decibels, *abbr.* dB; measured with a **sound-level meter**.

noise reduction, NR The difference in decibels between the average sound pressure levels produced in two rooms by a sound source in one of them.

noise reduction coefficient, NRC The average of the sound absorption coefficients of an acoustical material at frequencies of 250, 500, 1,000, and 2,000 Hz, expressed to the nearest integral multiple of 0.05.

NOM On drawings, abbr. for "nominal."

nominal diameter A designation used to specify the size of a pipe, bolt, rivet, reinforcing steel bar, or rod, not necessarily equal to the exact diameter.

nominal dimension **1.** In masonry, a dimension greater (by the thickness of a mortar joint) than the dimensions of the actual masonry unit; in the United States, not exceeding ½ inch (13 mm). **2.** In lumber, a dimension that may vary from the actual dimensions as provided for in the local building code.

nominal mix The proportions of the constituents of a proposed concrete mixture.

nominal size The dimensions of sawn lumber before it is dried or surfaced. Also see **dressed size**.

nominal strength The strength of a structural member calculated in accordance with provisions and assumptions of the strength design method of the applicable code, before the application of any strength-reduction factors.

nonagitating unit A container for carrying concrete from a central location, where it is mixed, to the job site; the unit does not agitate the concrete enroute to the work.

non-air-entrained concrete Concrete in which neither an air-entraining admixture nor an air-entraining cement has been used.

nonautomatic sprinkler system A **sprinkler system** in which all pipes and sprinkler heads are maintained dry and which is supplied with water through a fire department **siamese connection**.

nonautomatic standpipe system A **standpipe system** in which all piping is maintained dry and which is supplied with water through a fire department **siamese connection**.

nonbearing partition See **non-load-bearing partition**.

nonbearing wall A wall supporting no load other than its own weight; a **non-load-bearing wall**.

noncohesive soil A soil such as gravel or sand in which the particles do not stick together, as opposed to a sticky clay or claylike silt.

noncollusion affidavit A notarized statement by a bidder that he has prepared his bid without collusion of any kind.

noncombustibility That property of a material which enables it to withstand high temperature without ignition.

noncombustible 1. In building construction a material of which no part will ignite and burn when subjected to fire. 2. A building material having a structural base of noncombustible material, as defined above, with surfacing not over ⅛ in. (0.32 cm) which has a **flame-spread rating** not higher than 50. 3. A material, other than those falling into the above two categories, which has a flame-spread rating not higher than 25 and which shows no evidence of continued progressive combustion.

noncombustible construction Construction in which the walls, partitions, and structural members are of **noncombustible** materials and assemblies, but which does not qualify as **fire-resistive construction**.

noncombustible material A material that will not ignite, burn, support combustion, or release flammable vapors when subject to fire or heat, in the form in which it is used and under conditions anticipated; any material that passes ASTM Test Method E136 is considered noncombustible.

nonconcordant tendons **Tendons**, in a statistically indeterminate structure, which are not coincident with the pressure line caused by the tendons.

nonconcurrent forces Forces that do not have a common point of intersection.

nonconcurrent loads Two or more elements of live or dead **loads** that, for design purposes, are considered not to act simultaneously.

nonconforming Said of any building or structure which does not comply with the requirements set forth in applicable code, rules, or regulations.

nonconforming work Work that does not fulfill the requirements of the **contract documents**.

noncoplanar forces Forces that do not lie in a single plane.

nondestructive test A test of a material, component, or assembly which does not damage the item being tested; usually carried out with ultrasonics or x-rays.

non-displacement pile A **pile** which is formed by boring or other excavation method.

nondrying Said of an oil, compound, etc., which does not oxidize in air and therefore does not form a surface skin after application.

nondrying oil An oil which does not oxidize readily; esp. useful as a plasticizer.

nonelectric-delay blasting cap A blasting cap with an integral delay element in conjunction with and capable of being detonated by a detonation impulse or signal from a miniaturized detonating cord.

nonevaporable water The water that is chemically combined during cement hydration; not removable by specified drying.

nonferrous Containing no, or very little, iron.

nonflammable Not combustible; also see **flammable**.

nonfreeze sprinkler system A **fire-protection sprinkler system** designed for installation in areas subject to freezing temperatures; usually a **dry-pipe sprinkler system**.

non-grain-raising stain See **NGR stain**.

nonhabitable space By code: a space used for a bath, boiler room, closet, dressing room, heater, kitchenette, laundry, locker, pantry, storage, toilet, utility; or for service and maintenance of a building; or used for access and vertical travel between stories; compare with **habitable space**.

nonhydraulic lime A calcium- or dolomite-type lime; used as a finish or mason's lime.

non-load-bearing partition An interior partition which divides spaces within a building but does not support floor joists or carry overhead partitions.

non-load-bearing tile Ceramic tile designed for use in masonry walls carrying no superimposed loads.

non-load-bearing wall A wall capable only of supporting its own weight and (if it is an exterior wall) capable of resisting the force of the wind blowing against it; it cannot support an imposed load. Compare with **load-bearing wall**; also called a nonbearing wall.

non-lustrous glaze Said of an inseparable ceramic glaze that has fire-bonded and non-lustrous finish.

nonmetallic sheathed cable Two or more insulated electric conductors having an outer sheath of nonmetallic, flame-retardant, moisture-resistant material.

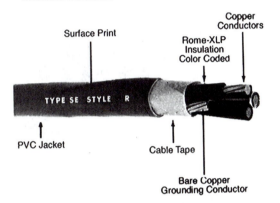

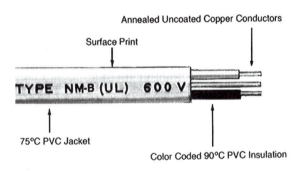

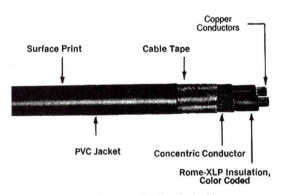

types of **nonmetallic sheathed cable**

nonmetallic tubing See **electrical nonmetallic tubing**.

nominal load The magnitude of the load specified by the applicable code.

nonplanar frame A structural frame which is composed of individual members in which at least one of the members is noncoplanar with the others.

non-pressure pipe Pipe designed for use in conveying a liquid only by gravity; does not have a pressure rating.

nonprestressed reinforcement In prestressed concrete construction, reinforcing steel which is not subjected to prestressing or posttensioning.

nonpublic fixture A plumbing fixture intended for the use of a family or an individual (for example, a W.C. in a residence or apartment or a private toilet in a hotel or motel room).

nonrenewable fuse A fuse in an electric circuit which must be replaced after it has interrupted the circuit by melting.

nonreturn valve A combination **check valve** and **globe valve** used at the discharge of a high-pressure boiler.

non-sag sealant A compound that exhibits little or no flow when applied in vertical or inverted joints.

nonsimultaneous prestressing In **prestressed concrete** construction, the posttensioning of tendons individually, rather than simultaneously.

nonsiphon trap In plumbing, a **trap, 1** whose seal (usually between 3 and 4 in.; approx. 7.5 and 10 cm) is not easily broken; the diameter is not greater than 4 in. (10 cm), and the water held in the trap is not less than 1 qt (0.95 liter).

nonslip concrete Concrete having a roughened surface, e.g., as a result of the sprinkling of grains of an oxide to the surface before it hardens or as the result of the roughening of the surface with a coarse-bristled stiff brush before the concrete sets; especially used for steps.

nonslip nosing On a stair, a **nosing strip** having a rough surface.

nonstaining cement **Masonry cement** containing not more than a specified amount of water-soluble alkali as measured by a specified test method.

nonstaining mortar   A mortar having a low free-alkali content to avoid efflorescence or staining of adjacent stone by the migration of soluble materials.

nonstop switch   A manual switch in an elevator car, which prevents the elevator from making registered landing stops.

nonvitreous tile   Ceramic tile having a degree of vitrification evidenced by a water absorption greater than 3%; an exception is nonvitreous floor and wall tile, which has a water absorption above 7% but less than 18%.

nonvolatile   In a paint film, that portion which remains after the water, solvents, and diluents have evaporated.

nook   An alcove opening off a room to provide additional or more intimate space, sometimes at a fireplace or adjoining a kitchen for dining.

nook shaft   A column or colonnette set in a square break, as at the angle of a building, or where the jamb of a doorway meets the external face of a wall.

NOP   Abbr. for "not otherwise provided for."

noraghe   Same as **nuraghe**.

Norfolk latch   A type of **thumb latch** for a door that has a long metal plate behind the latch to protect the door finish; compare with **Suffolk latch**.

normal cement   Same as **ordinary portland cement**.

normal consistency   **1.** The degree of wetness exhibited by a freshly mixed concrete, mortar, or neat cement grout whose workability is considered acceptable for the purpose at hand. **2.** The physical condition of neat cement paste 30 sec after completion of mixing, as determined with the **Vicat apparatus** in accordance with a specified method.

normal consolidation   The condition that exists if a soil deposit never has been subjected to an effective pressure greater than the existing pressure, and if the deposit is completely consolidated under the existing overburden.

normal haul   A **haul** whose cost has been included in the cost of the excavation; no additional charges are due for haulage.

normal stress   The component of **stress** which is perpendicular to the plane on which the force is applied.

normal-weight aggregate   An aggregate having characteristics between those of a **lightweight aggregate** and a **heavyweight aggregate**.

normal-weight concrete   Concrete having a unit weight of approximately 150 lb per cu ft (2,400 kg per cu m), made with aggregates of normal weight.

Norman architecture   The Romanesque architecture of England from the Norman Conquest (1066) until the rise of the Gothic around 1180.

Norman architecture

Norman brick   A brick whose nominal dimensions are 2⅔ in. by 4 in. by 12 in. (8.5 cm by 10.2 cm by 30.5 cm).

Normandy cottage   See **French Eclectic architecture** and **Neo-French architecture**.

Normandy joint   In plumbing, a joint between two unthreaded pipes which are connected by a sleeve; the ends of the sleeve are made tight by packing rings which are compressed between bolting rings and the sleeve.

Norman style   Same as **Romanesque style**.

north aisle   The aisle of a church on the left side of a church as one faces the altar; so called

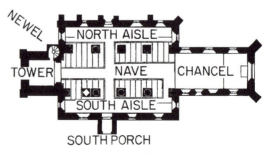

north aisle

because medieval churches almost invariably had their sanctuaries at the east end and the main doors at the west end.

north-light roof In the northern hemisphere, a **sawtooth roof** in which the glazing faces north.

north porch A porch which shelters the entrance to a church; located on the left side of the church as one faces the altar.

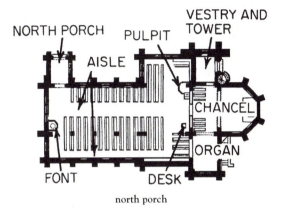

north porch

Norway spruce See **spruce**.

nose See **nosing**.

nose key Same as **foxtail wedge**.

nosing, nose The prominent, usually rounded, horizontal edge which extends beyond an upright face below; as the projection of a tread beyond a riser.

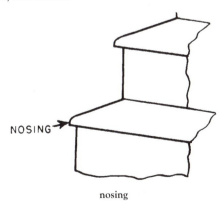

nosing

nosing line, nose line The slope of a stair determined by a line connecting the lead edge or nosing of the stair treads.

nosing strip In stair construction, a molding which has the same profile as the nosing on the stair treads.

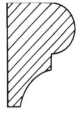

nosing strip

no-slump concrete Freshly-mixed concrete with a **slump** of less than ¼ inch (6 mm).

notch A cutout in a log or timber, usually at or near one of its ends, that is used to form a rigid joint when mated with another appropriately cutout log or timber at right angles to it; for example, at the corners of a **log cabin** or **log house**. See **corner notch, diamond notch, double-saddle notch, dovetail notch, half-cut notch, half-dovetail notch, halved-and-lapped notch, lap notch, log notch, round notch, saddle notch, single notch, single-saddle notch, square notch, V-notch.**

notchboard A stringer in a flight of stairs.

notched bar test A type of **impact test** in which the specimen is in the form of a notched metal bar. Also see **Izod impact test**.

notched molding, notch ornament An ornament produced by notching the edges of a band or fillet.

notched rafter A **rafter** having a notch on the underside near its lower end; this enables it to be fitted over, and fastened to, a horizontal timber supporting the rafter.

notching Joining of timbers, usually meeting or crossing at right angles, by cutting a notch in one or both pieces.

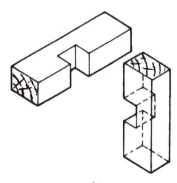

notching

notch joist A joist having one end notched to fit over a wood girder which supports it; the lower edge of the joist is supported by a **ledger, 2**.

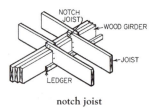

notch joist

notch ornament See **notched molding**.

notice to bidders A notice contained in the bidding requirements informing prospective bidders of the opportunity to submit bids on a **project** and setting forth the procedures for doing so.

notice to proceed Written communication issued by the **owner** to the **contractor** authorizing him to proceed with the **work, 1** and establishing the date of commencement of the work.

novelty flooring Flooring which is laid in an unusual pattern.

novelty siding See **drop siding**.

nozzle **1.** The projecting part of a faucet, or the end of a pipe or hose. **2.** A **welding nozzle**. **3.** In a fire **sprinkler system**, a sprinkler which provides a special water discharge pattern, directional spray pattern, or other unusual characteristic.

NPL On drawings, abbr. for **nipple**.

NPS On drawings, abbr. for "nominal pipe size."

NR See **noise reduction**.

NRC Abbr. for **noise reduction coefficient**.

nt Abbr. for **nit**.

N-truss A **Pratt truss**.

NTS Abbr. for "not to scale."

nt wt Abbr. for "net weight."

nucleus In ancient construction, the internal part of the flooring, consisting of a strong cement, over which the pavement was laid, bound with mortar.

nugget In seam welding, spot welding, or projection welding, the **weld metal** which joins the parts.

nugget size The width or diameter of a **nugget**, measured in the plane of the interface between the pieces which are joined.

nuisance **1.** A public nuisance is said to exist in a building, structure, or premise: (a) if it is insufficiently cleaned, drained, lighted, or ventilated for the intended usage, (b) if it poses conditions detrimental to public health or dangerous to human life, and/or (c) if its air or water supplies are unwholesome. **2.** A continuing legal wrong, usually committed by an owner or occupant of property on neighboring persons or property.

nulling A quadrant-shaped detail on decorative moldings, esp. in Jacobean architecture.

nunnery A convent for females.

nuraghe

nuraghe, noraghe Prehistoric round towers and agglomerations of stone huts peculiar to Sardinia.

nursery **1.** A room or place set apart for small children. **2.** A place where plants, shrubs, and small trees are grown, usually for transplanting elsewhere.

nursery school A school for children of about 3 to 5 years of age.

nurse's call system In a hospital, an electrically operated system by which patients or personnel can summon a nurse from a bedside station or from a duty station.

nursing home A building or part thereof used for the lodging, boarding, and nursing care, on a 24-hr basis, of four or more persons who, because of mental or physical incapacity, may be unable to provide for their own needs and safety without the assistance of another person; provides facilities and services primarily for in-patients who require nursing care and related medical services less intense than those given in a general hospital or an extended-care facility.

nut A short metal block having a central hole which is threaded to receive a bolt, screw, or other threaded part.

SQUARE   HEXAGONAL   JAM   CASTELLATED

WING   CAP   THUMB   STOP

common types of **nuts**

nutmeg ornament A common ornamental feature of Early English work in the north of England, resembling a half a nutmeg.

nymphaeum A room decorated with plants, sculpture, and fountains (often decorated with nymphs), and intended for relaxation.

O

OA On drawings, abbr. for "overall."

O/A Abbr. for "on approval."

OAI Abbr. for **outside air intake**.

oak A tough, hard, high-density wood of the temperate climates; rather coarse-textured, ranging in color from light tan to pink or brown; used for both structural and decorative applications, such as framing timbers, flooring, and plywood.

oakum A caulking material made from old hemp rope fibers that have been treated with tar.

oak varnish A long-oil varnish for indoor use; contains pigment which gives it a light yellow-tan color.

OB On drawings, abbr. for "obscure."

obelisk **1.** A monumental, four-sided stone shaft, usually monolithic and tapering to a pyramidal tip. **2.** In Egyptian art, such a shaft mostly covered with hieroglyphs; originally erected as cult symbol to the sun god.

obelisk

oblique arch Same as **skew arch**.

oblique butt joint, oblique joint A butt joint which does not form a 90° angle to the axis of the piece.

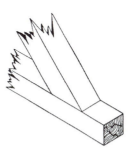

oblique butt joint

oblique grain Same as **diagonal grain**.

oblique section In a **mechanical drawing**, a section taken through an object at an angle (other than 90°) to its longest axis.

OBS **1.** On drawings, abbr. for "obsolete." **2.** Abbr. for "open back strike."

obscure glass, visionproof glass Translucent sheet glass, usually having one face roughened.

obscuring window A window glazed with frosted or stippled glass or the like; used to provide privacy.

observation of the work A function of the architect in the **construction phase**, during his periodic visits to the site, to familiarize himself generally with the progress and quality of the **work, 1** and to determine in general if the work is proceeding in accordance with the contract documents.

observatory **1.** A structure, generally with a rotatable dome, in which astronomical observations are carried out. **2.** A place, such as an upper room, which affords a wide view; a lookout.

obsidian A natural volcanic glass, usually black, with a bright luster; has relatively low water content.

obtuse angle arch   A type of **pointed arch**, formed by arcs of circles which intersect at the apex; the centers of the circles are nearer together than the width of the arch.

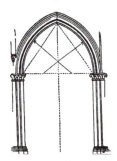

obtuse angle arch

o.c., oc, OC   Abbr. for **on center**.

occupancy   The use, or intended use, of a building.

occupancy permit   Same as **certificate of occupancy**.

occupancy rate   The total number of persons per room, housing unit, etc.

occupant load   The total number of persons that may occupy a building (or portion thereof), an elevator, etc., at any one time.

Occupational Safety and Health Administration (OSHA)   An organization within the U.S. Department of Labor, whose responsibilities include safety in the workplace; publishes standards in the U.S. Code of Federal Regulations that govern safety in buildings during construction and during occupancy. These regulations may be obtained directly from OSHA: Occupational Safety and Health Administration, U.S. Department of Labor, 200 Constitution Avenue, NW, Washington, DC 20210.

occupiable room   A space for short-term human occupancy as distinct from a space for human habitation.

occurrence   In insurance terminology, an accident or a continuous exposure to conditions which result in injury or damage, provided the injury or damage is neither expected nor intended.

ocher, ochre   A naturally occurring yellow-brown hydrated iron oxide; used as a pigment in paint and a filler in linoleum.

OCT   On drawings, abbr. for "octagon."

octagon barn   A barn having an eight-sided plan; relatively few of such structures were built prior to 1880, stimulated by interest in **octagon houses**.

octagon house   An eight-sided house, usually two to four stories high, built primarily in the last half of the 19th century, although the octagon plan was employed in some classical buildings. Often characterized by: a large porch; exterior walls usually of wood or concrete; a low-pitched roof, often topped with an eight-sided cupola; occasionally a raised basement.

octagon house

octastyle   A temple façade or portico having eight columns in the front or end row.

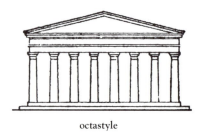

octastyle

octave   The interval between two frequencies having the ratio of 2:1.

octave band   The frequency range between two frequencies whose ratio is exactly 2:1.

octave-band analyzer   An electronic instrument for measuring **octave-band sound-pressure level**; consists of a microphone, amplifier, electric filters, an indicator, and appropriate controls.

octave-band sound-pressure level   The **sound-pressure level** of the sound within a specified octave band.

octopartite vault One of the vaults covering a square space, enclosed by walls, with eight oblique cells.

oculus 1. See **roundel**. 2. See **bull's-eye, 2. 3.** An opening at the crown of a dome.

OD On drawings, abbr. for "outside diameter."

odeion Same as **odeum**.

odeum, odeon A small ancient Greek or Roman theatre, usually roofed, for musical performances.

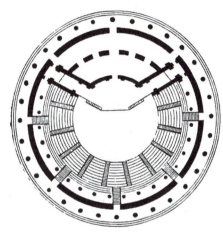

odeum, Athens

odorless mineral spirit A thinner composed of branch-chained aliphatic hydrocarbons; used in paints because of its exceptionally low odor level.

odorless paint A paint such as a water-base latex paint or an oil- or alkyd-base paint which contains an odorless mineral spirit as a thinner; produces a minimum amount of odor during application.

odor test Same as **scent test**.

oecus In a house in the ancient Roman empire, an apartment, hall, or large room.

oeil-de-boeuf, oxeye See **bull's-eye, 2**.

OFF. On drawings, abbr. for "office."

off-center 1. Having an axis not along the geometric center line. 2. Not at the center point.

off-count mesh In a wire cloth, a **count** which is not the same in both directions.

offertory window See **lowside window**.

office building A building used for professional or clerical purposes, no part of which is used for living purposes, except by the janitor's family.

office divider Same as **partial-height partition**.

office landscape screen A fixed or movable, free-standing, rearrangeable interior space divider; may incorporate acoustical properties.

office occupancy The use of a building for the transaction of business or for similar purposes.

official map One legally established by a municipality, which depicts existing parks, streets, and drainage systems; land reservations and rights-of-way for the future expansion of these systems usually are depicted.

offlet Same as **grip**.

offsaw Descriptive of the actual size of a timber after it has been sawn.

offset 1. A horizontal ledge on a wall (or other member or construction), marking a decrease in its thickness above; also called a **watertable**. 2. A bend in a pipe. 3. A change in the direction of a pipeline (other than 90°), e.g., by a combina-

offset, 2

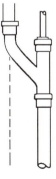

offset, 3

tion of elbows or bends, which brings one section of the pipe out of line with but into a line parallel to another section. **4.** A short line perpendicular to a surveyed line, measured to a line or point for which data are desired, thus locating the second line or point with reference to the first or surveyed line.

offset bend   In a **reinforcing bar**, any bend that displaces the center line of a section of the bar to a position parallel to the original bar (the displacement usually is relatively small); commonly used in reinforced concrete columns.

offset block   A concrete masonry unit which is not rectangular; usually used as a corner block to maintain the masonry pattern on the exposed face of a single-withe wall whose thickness is less than half the length of the unit.

offset chimney   Same as **stepped-back chimney**.

offset digging   Digging with a **ladder ditcher** whose boom is displaced from the line of travel of the ditcher.

offset elbow   A pipe fitting whose shape has the outline of the letter S, used for connecting lengths of straight pipe that are parallel to, but displaced from, each other.

offset line   A secondary survey line roughly parallel and close to a primary survey line to which it is referenced in measured offsets.

offset pipe   See **offset, 3**.

offset pivot   A pin-and-socket hardware device with a single bearing contact, by means of which a door is suspended in its frame, allowing it to swing about an axis which normally is located about ¾ in. (1.9 cm) out from the door face.

offset screwdriver   A screwdriver whose head is set 90° to the shaft.

offset screwdriver

off-white   White containing a slight amount of gray, yellow, or other light color.

o.g., O.G.   Abbr. for "ogee."

OG   **1.** Abbr. for "ogee." **2.** Abbr. for "on grade."

ogee, OG   **1.** A double curve, formed by the union of a convex and concave line, resembling

ogee, 2   *left*, Early English period; *center*, Decorated period; *right*, Perpendicular period

an S-shape. **2.** A molding having such a shape, an **ogee molding**.

ogee arch   A pointed arch composed of reversed curves, the lower concave and the upper convex.

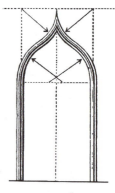

ogee arch

ogee molding   See **ogee, 2**.

ogee plane   A carpenter's plane with a reverse curved blade for shaping ogee moldings.

ogee roof   A roof whose section is an **ogee, 1**.

ogee roof

ogival arch   Same as **ogee arch**.

ogive   **1.** In general, a pointed arch. **2.** Strictly, the diagonal rib in Gothic vaults.

O/H   Abbr. for "overhead."

ohm   The unit of electrical resistance of a conductor such that a constant current of 1 ampere in it produces a decrease in voltage across it of 1 volt.

Ohm's law   A law stating that the current in an electric circuit is directly proportional to the electromotive force (voltage) in the circuit and inversely proportional to the resistance in the circuit.

OHS   On drawings, abbr. for "oval-headed screw."

oil   A lightly viscous neutral liquid belonging to one of three classes: (*a*) animal oil, (*b*) mineral oil, or (*c*) vegetable oil.

oil-base paint   See **oil paint**.

oil-bound distemper   A distemper which contains a drying oil.

oil buffer   A **buffer** consisting of a cylinder and a piston or plunger where the oil in the cylinder acts as a medium to absorb and dissipate the kinetic energy of an impact, such as that of a descending elevator car or counterweight acting on the piston or plunger.

oil burner   In a furnace or boiler, a burner in which fuel oil is vaporized or atomized and then mixed with air and ignited; the resulting flame is directed upon the surface to be heated.

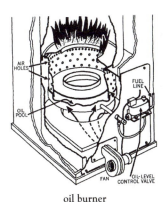

oil burner

oil-canning, tin-canning   A slight buckling in sheet metal, causing a wavy or uneven appearance.

oil color   An oil-base paint containing a high concentration of colored pigment; commonly used for tinting paint.

oilet   See **oillet**.

oil-filled transformer   A **liquid-immersed transformer** in which the liquid is a hydrocarbon or mineral oil.

oil furnace   A **furnace** that is fired by oil.

oil-immersed fuse   A fuse that is either totally or partially immersed in an insulating dielectric liquid of a transformer or switchgear.

oil-immersed switch   A switch which is immersed in a special insulating fluid, usually oil.

oil-immersed transformer   See **oil-filled transformer**.

oil interceptor   Same as **interceptor**.

oil length   In a varnish, the number of gallons of oil per 100 lb of gum or resin.

oillet, oillette   A small opening, or circular loophole, in a fortification of the Middle Ages.

oil of turpentine   See **turpentine**.

oil paint   A paint in which a drying oil is the vehicle for the pigment.

oil preservative   An oil-soluble chemical used to treat wood for protection against decay and insects. Also see **creosote, pentachlorophenol**.

oil separator   In a refrigeration system, a device for separating oil and oil vapor from the refrigerant, usually installed in the compressor discharge line.

oil stain   A stain containing dye or pigment mixed with oil or oil varnish which penetrates the surface to be finished.

oilstone   A fine-grained stone used to impart a sharp edge on tools; oil is used to lubricate the rubbing surface.

oilstone slip   See **gouge slip**.

oil switch   Same as **oil-immersed switch**.

oil varnish   A high-gloss varnish for interior use; made by heating or blending a drying oil with a gum or resin.

oil white   A house-paint pigment consisting of lithopone and white lead or zinc white.

okoume   See **gaboon**.

okwen   See **zebrawood**.

Old English style   Same as **Domestic Revival style**.

old wood   Wood which has been worked previously and is reused.

oleoresin   A natural **resin** containing essential oils; used in adhesives, varnishes, and various compounds.

oleoresinous varnish   A varnish consisting of a drying oil compounded with a hardening resin.

olive butt   Same as **olive knuckle hinge**.

olive hinge   Same as **olive knuckle hinge**.

olive knuckle hinge   A **paumelle** hinge with knuckles forming an oval shape.

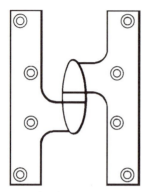

olive knuckle hinge

Olmec architecture   Architecture of the most ancient civilization of Mesoamerica (1500–400 B.C.) usually characterized by: a north-south orientation of the ceremonial center, stepped pyramids, sloping walls, ceremonial courtyards, and platforms on which to construct temples.

omnidirectional microphone   A microphone which is equally sensitive in all directions.

on-center   Same as **center-to-center**.

on-condition maintenance   Maintenance of machinery when **condition monitoring** equipment indicates that a mechanical failure is about to occur.

one-and-a-half-story   See **story-and-a-half**.

one-and-one-half-bay cottage   Same as **three-quarter Cape Cod house**.

one-and-one-half-story house   A one-story house having a loft space between the ceiling of the first floor and the roof directly above; windows in the gable-end walls and/or dormers provide light and ventilation in this loft space, providing the additional half-story.

one-bay cottage   Same as **half Cape house, 1**.

one-brick wall   See **whole-brick wall**.

one-centered arch   Any arch struck from a single center, such as a round, segmental, or horseshoe arch.

one-line diagram   A representation of an electrical system by means of single lines and graphic symbols showing the major components of the system.

one-over-one   **1.** A two-story cottage having two rooms, one directly over the other; usually the result of the expansion of a cottage having a **one-room plan** by the addition of a floor above it. **2.** A term descriptive of a **double-hung window** having one pane in the upper sash and one pane in the lower; see **pane**.

one-part adhesive   An adhesive that sets without the addition of a catalyst or hardener.

one-pipe system   A plumbing system in which a single pipe carries both soil and waste.

one-room cottage   A cottage having a **one-room plan**, usually with a loft space above.

one-room plan   The earliest and simplest **floor plan** for a dwelling, especially used in 17th century and beyond; consisted of a single room, usually called a **hall** or **keeping room**, that served as a combination living room, dining room, kitchen, and workroom; cooking was done in a large fireplace set into a massive chimney. In some regions, the front door of the house opened into a small vestibule called a *porch*, but in other regions, the door opened directly into the hall; access to a loft above was provided either by a staircase in the vestibule or by a ladder in the hall. Many such houses were enlarged by the addition of a second room at ground level, called the *parlor*, giving rise to the **hall-and-parlor plan**; the parlor served as a combination living room and sleeping room for the parents. Also see **one-over-one, 1**.

one-room cottage

one-room schoolhouse   A school in which all elementary-grade students were once taught in a single room. Such schools were common in sparsely populated areas before the 20th century;

many had a bell at the ridge of the roof for summoning students at the start of the school day.

one-sided connection A connection of one structural member to a second which is not symmetrical about the component part of the member being connected.

one-time fuse Same as **nonrenewable fuse**.

one-way joist construction A type of framing system for floors or roofs in a concrete building; consists of a series of parallel joists which are supported by girders (perpendicular to the joists) between columns.

one-way slab A rectangular reinforced concrete slab which spans a distance very much greater in one direction than the other; under these conditions, most of the load is carried on the shorter span.

one-way system In reinforced concrete, a system of steel reinforcement within a slab that is assumed to bend in one direction only.

on-grade **1.** Directly on the ground. **2.** At ground level.

onion dome In Russian Orthodox church architecture, a bulbous dome which terminates in a point and serves as a roof structure over a cupola or tower.

on-off sprinkler In a fire protection system, a **sprinkler** similar in performance characteristics to a conventional sprinkler but having the additional feature of closing when the temperature drops to a preselected value.

onyx A banded, varicolored form of quartz, closely related to agate; cut into slabs, polished, and used for decorative building stone.

oolite A granular limestone, each grain of which is more or less spherical and made up of concentric coats of carbonate of lime formed around a nucleus.

oolitic limestone A type of limestone characterized by minute spherical calcareous particles.

opa In a classical temple, a cavity which receives a roof beam.

opacity The quality of being opaque, as the capacity of a paint to cover or obliterate a background over which it is applied.

opaion **1.** In ancient Rome and Greece, an opening (as in a roof) for smoke to escape. **2.** In Greek architecture, a lacunar.

church surmounted by an **onion dome**

opal A hydrous form of silica containing 2 to 10% combined water; reacts with cement alkalies and may be highly detrimental as an aggregate in concrete.

opalescent glass A multicolored iridescent glass first used by the painters Louis Comfort Tiffany (1848–1933) and John La Farge (1835–1910) in the late 19th century; now often referred to as *Tiffany glass*.

opalescent glaze A glaze having a milky appearance.

opal glass A diffusing glass of milk-white appearance formed by incorporating material of high refractive index in the glass to scatter light.

opaline chert **Chert** that is principally or entirely of opal.

opal lamp bulb A bulb in which part or all of the glass envelope has a white, highly diffuse finish.

opaque Impervious to the transmission of visible light.

opaque ceramic-glazed tile A facing tile whose surface faces are covered by an inseparable fire-bonded, opaque, colored ceramic glaze of bright satin or glass finish.

open assembly time The time between the application of glue to joints (or wood veneer) and the assembly.

open bidding The submitting or receiving of bids or tenders from all interested contractors.

open boarding Roofing boards which are laid with a gap between adjacent boards.

open building system A building system which is designed so that its subsystems are interchangeable with like subsystems, its subassemblies are interchangeable with like subassemblies, and its components or building elements are interchangeable with like building components or elements of other systems.

open cell In foam rubber, cellular plastics, etc., a cell which interconnects with other cells.

open-cell foam A cellular plastic in which there is a predominance of interconnected cells.

open-circuit grouting A system for pumping grout in which there is no provision for recirculating the grout to the pump.

open construction Said of a **building component, building assembly**, or **building** which is manufactured in such a way that all portions can be readily inspected at the installation site without disassembly or destruction.

open cornice, open eaves Overhanging eaves where the rafters are exposed at the eaves and can be seen from below.

open cornice

open crenelation A wood **crenelated molding** of perforated, open design; often used in Gothic Revival buildings in Colonial America.

open cut An excavation, open to the sky, which has been cut from the ground surface downward, in contrast to tunnel excavation.

open defect An unfilled hole or gap in lumber, plywood, or wood veneer.

open eaves See **open cornice**.

open-end block 1. An A-block or an H-block concrete masonry unit. 2. A standard block having recessed end webs.

open-end mortgage A mortgage which permits the mortgager to borrow additional funds for improvements after the original loan has been made and permits him to repay them over an extended amortization period.

open exterior space Space without roof and/or side closure, capable of serving for egress to a street or other public space.

open floor A floor whose joists are visible from the floor below.

open-frame girder Same as **Vierendeel truss**.

open-graded aggregate An aggregate containing little or no mineral filler, or in which the void spaces in the compacted aggregate are relatively large.

open-grain, open-grained Having a coarse texture. Also see **coarse-textured, wide-ringed**.

open heart molding A common Norman molding consisting of a series of overlapping shapes resembling the outlines of a heart.

open impeller In a pump, an **impeller** that does not have shrouds (i.e., disks that enclose the impeller vanes); usually used where the water being pumped contains suspended solids.

open impeller

open industrial structure A structural platform used for required access to industrial operations conducted in the open air, such as oil refining and chemical processing; often, a roof or canopy is provided for shelter, but there are no walls.

opening door See **active leaf**.

opening leaf See **active leaf**.

opening light In a window, the light (as a sash) that opens and closes, in contrast to a **fixed light**.

opening of bids Same as **bid opening**.

opening protective A device for protecting an opening from the passage of flame, smoke, or hot gases.

opening size See **door opening**.

open mortise See **slot mortise**.

open-newel stair A spiral stair constructed around an open cylindrical space without a central post, in contrast to a **solid-newel stair** built around a post.

open parking structure A structure, normally open to the outdoors on two or more sides, for the temporary storage of motor vehicles.

open pediment Same as **broken pediment, 1**.

open plan A building plan with a minimum of internal subdivision between spaces designed for different usage.

open-plan educational building An educational building, or portion thereof, having corridors that do not comply with code requirements for exterior exit corridors.

open-plan office A large space, divided by free-standing, partial-height partitions; usually designed to accommodate a large number of office workers.

open plumbing Plumbing which is exposed; the traps and drainage pipes, beneath the fixtures, are accessible, ventilated, and open to inspection.

open riser The space between two adjacent treads in a stair when such space is not filled by a solid riser.

open-riser stair A stair not having risers.

open roof, open-timbered roof A roof construction in which the rafters and roof sheathing are visible from below; there is no ceiling.

open shaft A vertical duct or small enclosed passage within a building, open to the outer air at the top, and used to ventilate interior spaces connected to it. Also see **light well**.

open sheathing See **open sheeting**.

open sheeting, open sheathing, open timbering Horizontal or vertical planks or boards placed at intervals along the face of an excavation; used where the soil is sufficiently firm to make close sheeting unnecessary and where groundwater is not a problem.

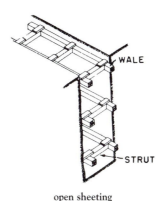

open sheeting

open shelving Shelving which is exposed, not concealed by a door or cabinet.

open slating, spaced slating In roofing, a slating pattern in which spaces are left between adjacent slates in a course.

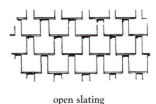

open slating

open solar energy system A solar energy system whose storage tank is open to atmospheric pressure.

open space In urban planning, the designation given parks, recreational and natural areas, or other land not occupied by buildings.

open sprinkler A **fire sprinkler** (i.e., sprinkler **head**) with a normally open nozzle.

open stage In a theatre, a stage platform not bounded by a proscenium arch.

open stair, open-string stair A stair whose treads are visible on one or both sides. (*See illustration p. 638*)

open stairway A stairway, one or both sides

open string

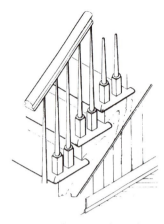

open stair, open-string stair

of which are open to a room in which it is located.

open string An inclined board in a vertical plane, parallel to the slope of a stair (i.e., a **string**), whose upper edge is cut to fit the profile of the treads and risers of the steps; the treads of the stairs project beyond the face of the string and are visible; compare with **closed string**.

open-string stair See **open stair**.

open system A fluid piping system in which the circulating fluid is connected to an open-vented elevated tank, to a cooling tower, or the like; the tank serves as a reservoir to accommodate the expansion and contraction of the fluid, and as a convenient location for inspecting the condition of the fluid.

open tendering See **open bidding**.

open-timbered Having timberwork exposed; having the wooden framework not concealed by sheathing, plaster, or other covering.

open-timbered roof Same as **open roof**.

open-timber floor A floor in which the floor joists and construction are exposed on the underside.

open timbering See **open sheeting**.

open time The time interval between the spreading of an adhesive and the completion of the bond.

open-top agitating truck A special truck which serves as an **open-top mixer**, maintaining previously mixed concrete in a uniform condition by means of agitator rotor blades; has a specially shaped watertight metal body with smooth, streamlined surfaces and a discharge gate at the rear.

open-top mixer A mixer filled through an opening at its top; for concrete, usually a pan or drum within which mixing blades revolve about the vertical axis; for mortar, usually a trough within which mixing paddles revolve about the horizontal axis.

open valley A type of **valley** on a roof. The valley formed at the intersection of two roof surfaces is lined with metal or mineral-surfaced roofing, and the shingles or slates are not laid to this intersection, leaving the metal lining exposed.

open valley

open web A **web, 1** composed of a group of members (in a crisscross or zigzag array) instead of solid plates.

open-web steel joist A steel truss having an **open web** whose component parts are either hot-rolled structural shapes or cold-formed light-gauge steel shapes.

open well A floor opening, a series of such openings, or an **atrium** of two or more stories that does not meet code requirements (with respect to enclosure) for a **covered shaft**.

open-wire circuit An electric circuit consisting of conductors which are separately supported on insulators.

open wiring Electric wiring which uses cleats, flexible tubing, knobs, and tubes to protect and support insulated conductors run on or in a building; not concealed by the building structure.

openwork 1. Any work, esp. ornamental, characterized by perforations. 2. In fortifications, any work not protected at a **gorge, 3** by a parapet or otherwise.

operable partition A partition composed of a number of large panels which are hung from a ceiling track, permitting the panels to be moved easily from their closed position (in which the panels form a partition) to an open position (in which the panels are stacked against each other); the panels also may be supported by a floor track.

operable transom A panel or glass light, above a door, which may be opened for ventilation.

operable wall Same as **operable partition**.

operable window A window which may be opened for ventilation, as opposed to a **fixed light**.

opera house A theatre intended primarily for the public performance of operas.

operating pressure The pressure indicated by a gauge in part of a system, when the system is in normal operation.

opisthodomos, epinaos, opisthodomus, posticum The inner portico at the rear of the cella of a classical temple, corresponding to the pronaos in front.

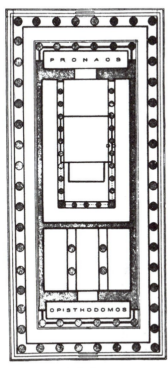

opisthodomos

OPNG On drawings, abbr. for "opening."
OPP On drawings, abbr. for "opposite."

opposed-blade damper A **damper, 1** through which the airflow is adjusted by means of two sections of damper blades on a common linkage, arranged so that adjacent blades rotate in opposite directions.

opposed-blade damper

optical detector See **photoelectric smoke detector**.

optical fiber cable An optical signal transmission medium consisting of (a) a glass fiber or plastic fiber (or filament) surrounded by protective cladding, (b) strengthening material, and (c) an outer jacket. Signals may be transmitted, along the cable, as light pulses introduced into the fiber by a laser or light-emitting diode. Its advantages over the transmission of electrical signals along (metal) wire cable include low attenuation along the cable, freedom from electromagnetic interference and electrical grounding problems, small physical size, light weight, and large transmission bandwidth.

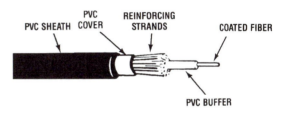

optical fiber cable

optical plummet A device on some transits and theodolites; used to center the instrument over a point, in place of a plumb bob, which moves in a strong wind.

optical refinements. In Greek architecture and derivatives, a set of adjustments of normal shaping and spacing made supposedly to counteract the somatic peculiarities of human vision. Also see **entasis**.

optical smoke detector See **photoelectric smoke detector**.

optimum moisture content That content of water in soil at which the maximum dry unit weight can be attained as a result of a given compaction effort.

optimum reverberation time In a room or auditorium designed for speech, the **reverberation time** that provides the highest speech intelligibility consistent with other requirements. In a room or auditorium designed for music, the **reverberation time** that provides optimum conditions for playing and listening to music. These optimum values depend on the use of the room, its volume, and may depend on frequency.

option An agreement between an owner and prospective user of a property which, for a specified sum, grants the latter the right to buy or rent the property within a specified period of time.

opus Alexandrinum A mosaic of relatively large pieces of marble or stone, cut to shape and arranged in geometric patterns, usually a mosaic pavement consisting of geometrical figures in black and red tesserae on white ground.

opus antiquum Same as **opus incertum**.

opus incertum In ancient Rome, masonry formed of small rough stones set irregularly in mortar, sometimes traversed by beds of bricks or tiles.

opus incertum

opus interrasile Decoration produced either by cutting away the ground and leaving the pattern or by cutting out the pattern so that the openings form the design.

opus isodomum Same as **isodomum**.

opus latericium, opus lateritium Roman masonry of brick or tiles, or of a brick or tile facing on a concrete core.

opus lithostrotum Same as **lithostrotum opus**.

opus musivum A Roman mosaic decoration employing small cubes of colored glass or enameled work.

opus pseudoisodomum In ancient Roman masonry, coursed ashlar having courses of unequal height.

opus quadratum Masonry of squared stones in regular ashlar courses.

opus quadratum

opus reticulatum A decorative Roman wall facing, backed by a concrete core, formed of small pyramidal stones with their points embedded in the wall, their exposed square bases, set diagonally, forming a net-like pattern.

opus reticulatum

opus sectile See **sectile opus**.

opus signinum A kind of tough stucco or cement used by ancient Romans to coat the interior of aqueducts, etc.

opus spicatum Same as **spicatum opus**.

opus tectorium A type of stucco used in ancient Rome; used to cover walls in three or four coats, the finishing coat being practically an artificial marble, usually polished to serve as a surface for paintings.

opus tesselatum A pavement with designs executed in pieces of different-colored **tesserae**, of larger size and more regular form than the pieces used in mosaic.

opus testaceum   In ancient Roman masonry, a facing composed of fragments of broken tile.

opus vermiculatum   See **vermiculated mosaic**.

OR   Abbr. for "outside radius."

orange peel, orange peeling   **1.** In a paint film, a surface defect characterized by a rough texture resembling orange peel; results from the poor flow of paint or a poor application technique. **2.** In ceramics, an irregular waviness of porcelain enamel surface; resembling an orange skin in texture; sometimes considered a surface defect.

orangery   A building, or a part of a building, once found in especially stately homes, for cultivating orange trees and other ornamental trees in a cool climate where they would not otherwise grow; usually had large, tall windows along its southern exposure; now often used for social and exhibition purposes. Also see **conservatory, greenhouse, hothouse**.

orange shellac   A refined lac (a secretion of insects), which is soluble in alcohol; contains some wax and resin; used as a coating on floors and other wood surfaces.

oratory   A small private chapel furnished with an altar and a crucifix.

An ancient **oratory** in Ireland

orb   **1.** A plain circular boss, as a decorative accent where two or more ribs (of a vault) cross. **2.** The medieval name for the tracery of blank windows or stone panels.

orbital sander   An electric-powered hand tool used in rapid sanding, usually for coarse work; the base of the machine, to which sanding paper or abrasive cloth is clipped, moves in an elliptical pattern.

orchestra   **1.** In the early Greek theatre, the place occupied by the dancers and chorus about the altar of Dionysos; later, the circular space reserved for the dancers and chorus, between the proscenium and auditorium. **2.** In the early Roman theatre, a semicircular level space between the stage and the first semicircular rows of seats, reserved for senators and other distinguished spectators. **3.** In an auditorium, the seating area on the main floor, or a forward section of seats on the main floor.

orchestra circle   See **parquet circle**.

orchestra pit   A pit immediately in front of, or wholly or partly under, the forestage of an auditorium.

orchestra shell   A massive, sound-reflective structure which closes off the flies and wings of a theatrical stage to form a performing area for music, or is used in an open-air theatre to direct sound to the audience.

ord   Abbr. for "order."

order   **1.** In **Classical architecture**, an arrangement of a particular style of column together with the entablature (which it supports) and standardized details, including its **base** and **capital**. The Greeks developed the Corinthian order, Doric order, and Ionic order; the Romans added the Composite order and Tuscan order. For each

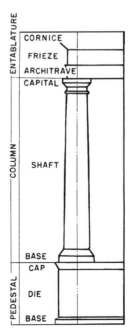

Doric **order, 2**

An arch of two **orders, 3,** each having its carved hood molding

order, the height and spacing of the columns is established in terms of a specified number of diameters of the lower part of the columns; the design of the base and capital is also prescribed. The height of the **entablatures** is determined by the height of the columns. **2.** In masonry, one ring of several around an arch.

ordinance A law or rule adopted by a local governmental authority.

ordinary A village tavern in an early American community.

ordinary construction Construction in which the exterior bearing walls (or the bearing portions of exterior walls) are of noncombustible materials having a minimum fire endurance of 2 hr and stability under fire conditions; the non-bearing exterior walls are of noncombustible construction; the roof, floors, and interior framing are wholly or partly of wood (or other combustible material) of smaller dimensions than required for **heavy-timber construction.**

ordinary-hazard contents Building contents which are liable to burn with moderate rapidity and give off a considerable volume of smoke, but in so doing will not release poisonous fumes or gases that could result in an explosion.

ordinary-hazard occupancy An occupancy in which it is expected that there will be a relatively moderate rate of heat release if a fire should occur *and* (Group 1) the quantity of combustibles

is moderate, and the heights of the stockpiles of combustibles do not exceed 8 feet (2.4 m), *or* (Group 2) the quantity of combustibles is moderate to high, and the heights of the stockpiles of combustibles do not exceed 12 feet (3.7 m).

ordinary portland cement, Type I portland cement A portland cement used for general construction which is produced without any of the special distinguishing qualities imparted to other types.

Oregon pine Common **Douglas fir.**

or equal See **approved equal.**

organic Said of a material or compound derived from vegetable or animal life.

Organic architecture Architecture whose design is established in accordance with processes of nature rather than based on an imposed design; a design philosophy of Frank Lloyd Wright (1867–1959) based largely on his early-20th-century assertion that a building (and its appearance) should follow forms that are in harmony with its natural environment. The materials used on the exterior should be sympathetic to the building's locale, thereby relating the building to its setting, as if it were the result of natural growth. Thus, use should be made of low-pitched overhanging roofs to provide protection from the sun in the summer and to provide some weather protection in the winter, and maximum use should be made of natural daylighting.

organic clay A clay with a high organic content.

organic-coated glass Glass that is coated and bonded on one or both sides with an applied polymeric coating.

organic coating A coating (such as paint, lacquer, enamel, or film) in which the principal ingredients are derived from animal or vegetable matter or from some compound of carbon.

organic silt A silt with a high organic content.

organic soil Soil with a high organic content; in general, organic soils are very compressible and have poor load-sustaining properties.

organ loft In a church, the gallery or loft where the organ is located, usually high above the floor.

organ screen **1.** An ornamental screen of stone or timber which closes off the organ chamber in a church. **2.** A **rood screen** which supports an organ.

oriel **1.** In medieval English architecture, chiefly residential, and derivatives: *(a)* a bay window corbeled out from the wall of an upper story; *(b)* a bay projecting, inside or out, extending a room; *(c)* a windowed bay or porch at the top of exterior stairs. **2.** *(rare)* In medieval Continental structures and derivatives, a subsidiary bay, or a corbeled, enclosed feature, exterior or interior.

oriel

Oriental Revival A term descriptive of a mode of **Exotic Revival** architecture that is suggestive of the architecture of the Middle East and/or Far East.

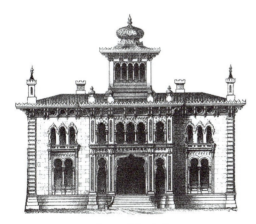

Oriental Revival

orientation **1.** The placement of a structure on a site with regard to local conditions of sunlight, wind, and drainage. **2.** The siting of a Christian church so that the main altar is housed toward the east end of the building, a common ritual disposition.

ORIG On drawings, abbr. for "original."

original construction That part of a building that was constructed at a time when the building was first erected, as opposed to additions, alterations, and reconstructions at a later date.

orillon Same as **crossette**.

O-ring A resilient ring used as a gasket in sealing a joint.

orle, orlet A narrow band, or series of small members, taking the form of a border.

orlo **1.** A plinth which supports the base of a column. **2.** The smooth surface between parallel flutes or grooves. **3.** An **orle**.

ormolu **1.** Gold crushed with mercury to form a paste. **2.** An article or ornamental appliqué of bronze, first coated with such paste, then heated to evaporate the mercury, leaving pure gold evenly and securely deposited. **3.** Any metal or substitute finished to resemble mercury-gilded bronze.

ormolu varnish A varnish having the appearance of gold or gilded bronze.

ornament In architecture, every detail of shape, texture, and color that is deliberately exploited or added to attract an observer.

ornamental cast iron See **cast-iron lacework**.

ornamental ironwork Ironwork that is merely decorative (such as **cast-iron lacework**), as opposed to ironwork having a structural function.

ornamental plaster A **plaster** element, decorative in nature, such as a ceiling medallion; usually cast using **plaster of paris**.

ornate Highly ornamented.

orpiment An arsenic sulfur compound; used in paints as a yellow pigment.

orthographic projection Projection in which exact views of an object are constructed by extending perpendiculars from points on the object to the plane of projection.

orthography In drafting, a geometrical representation of an elevation or section of a building.

orthostat One of many large stone slabs, set as a revetment at the lower part of the cella in a classical temple, or at the base of a wall in the ancient architecture of Anatolia, northern Syria, and Assyria.

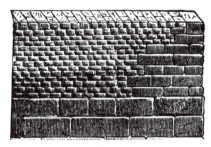

orthostat

orthostate **1.** A stone taller than wide. **2.** A stone in the lower course of a wall, higher than the regular blocks of the courses above, sometimes serving as a high base for a wall of sun-dried brick.

orthostyle Said of a colonnade in a straight line.

orthotropic Having dissimilar elastic properties in two mutually perpendicular directions; i.e., orthogonal-anisotropic.

OSHA **1.** Abbr. for "Occupational Safety and Health Administration," Department of Labor. **2.** Abbr. for "Occupational Safety and Health Act."

osier See **withe, 2**.

Osiride, Osirian column In ancient Egypt, a type of column in which a standing figure of Osiris is placed before a square pier; it differs from the classical caryatid in that the pier, and not the figure, supports the entablature.

ossature The framework or skeleton of a building or part of a building, as the ribs of a groined vault or the frame of a roof.

ossuary, bone house, ossarium A storage place for the bones of the dead; either a structure or a vault lined with such bones ornamentally arranged.

ostensory, monstrance A device in which the Eucharistic wafer may be displayed.

ostiole A small entrance.

ostiolum A small opening; a small door.

Ottawa sand Naturally rounded grains of nearly pure quartz, produced by processing silica sand obtained from deposits near Ottawa, Ill.;

used in mortar test specimens in testing hydraulic cement. Also see **standard sand, graded standard sand**.

Ottoman architecture The later phase of Turkish **Muslim architecture**, from the 14th century onward, much influenced by Byzantine forms.

Ottonian architecture The pre-Romanesque round-arched architecture of Germany during the rule of the Ottonian emperors in the second half of the 10th cent.

oubliette A secret dungeon in the deepest parts of a medieval stronghold, having as its only entry a trapdoor through which prisoners were dropped.

oundy molding See **wave molding**.

outage A failure in the electric power supplied by a utility company.

out and out Same as **overall**.

outband In masonry, a jambstone which is laid as a **stretcher** and cut to take a frame.

outbond Bonded, or forming a bond, along the face of a wall; composed largely or entirely of **stretchers**.

outbuilding A building subsidiary to, but separate from, a main house or building.

outcrop That portion of a rock formation or stratum that breaks the surface of the ground.

outdoor-air intake Same as **outside-air intake**.

outer court A space partially bounded by building walls or property lines but open to the sky and, on one side, to the street or other public space.

outer hearth See **front hearth**.

outer lining Same as **outside casing**.

outer string The **string** at the outer and exposed edge of a stair, away from the wall.

outfall The place of ultimate deposit of drainage or sewage waters.

outfall sewer A sewer that receives the sewage from a sewage collection system and carries it to the point of final discharge or treatment. It is usually the largest sewer in the system.

outhouse **1.** A detached outdoor structure housing a primitive toilet; usually constructed of wood, rather than the proverbial brick. **2.** A small accessory building generally located at the rear of a house and used for domestic animals, storage, and so on.

outkitchen A kitchen once a subsidiary to, and separate from, a large main house. This separation avoided overheating the house during hot summer weather, minimized the possibility of accidentally setting the house on fire, and minimized cooking odors in the house.

outlet **1.** In an electric wiring system, a point at which current is taken to supply appliances, portable equipment, etc. **2.** In a gas pipe system, a threaded connection or bolted flange to which a gas-burning appliance may be attached; according to code, the outlet must be located in the room or space where the appliance is, or may be, installed.

outlet box In an electric wiring system, a metal box at an outlet which encloses one or more **receptacles**.

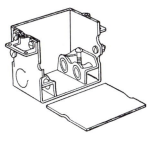

outlet box

outlet ventilator A louvered opening in an attic space to provide an outlet to the outdoors.

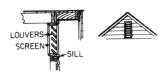

outlet ventilator

outline lighting An arrangement of incandescent lamps or gaseous tubes which outlines and emphasizes certain features such as the shape of a building or the decoration of a window.

outlooker **1.** Same as **outrigger**. **2.** A covering over a doorway or opening in the face of a building to provide a small degree of shelter; also see **hanging gable**.

out-of-center Same as **off-center**.

out-of-plumb Not truly vertical, according to a **plumb line**.

out-of-sequence service A service performed in other than the normal or natural order of succession.

out-of-true Not in exact alignment (as a part which is slightly twisted).

out of winding Said of a member that is free from twist.

outrigger A beam at the ridge of a roof that extends beyond the end wall of the building to serve as a support for hoisting tackle or the like; also called an outlooker or lookout.

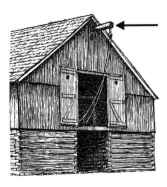

outrigger, 1

outrigger scaffold A **scaffold** supported by brackets fastened to the wall of a building.

outrigger shore, horsing A temporary bracket to support a projecting feature.

outshot An addition to a building that it adjoins, but is structurally independent of; it often results in an **L-plan**.

outside-air intake An opening or inlet through which outside air is brought into an air-conditioning system or into a boiler room. Also called a fresh-air intake.

outside architrave See **outside casing**.

outside caliper A type of **caliper** which is especially designed for measuring the outside diameters of round or cylindrical objects.

outside casing, outside architrave, outside facing, outside lining, outside trim In a cased window frame, the members of the jamb or head which face outside of the building and appear as trim. (*See illustration p. 646.*)

outside chimney Same as **exterior chimney**.

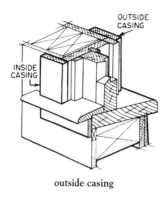

outside casing

outside corner molding A molding covering the salient angle of two intersecting surfaces either to protect the corner or to cover the exposed edge of the surface material as in wood veneer, plastic laminates, etc. Also see **corner bead**.

outside corner molding

outside facing See **outside casing**.

outside finish, exterior finish The surface treatment or decorative trim on the exterior of a building.

outside foundation line A line indicating the location of the outer side of a foundation wall.

outside glazing External glazing installed from outside of the building.

outside gouge A **gouge** which has a bevel ground on the convex side of its cutting edge.

outside lining See **outside casing**.

outside string Same as **outer string**.

outside studding plate In wood-frame construction, a **soleplate** or a double top plate, usually the same size as the studding.

outside thread A **thread** on the external surface of a pipe or cylinder.

outstanding leg One of the legs of a structural angle member; usually not connected to another structural member.

out-to-out measurement A measure of the outside-to-outside distance across a piece.

outwindow A projecting **loggia** or the like.

oval A marble chip which has been tumbled until a smooth oval shape has resulted; used for terrazzo concrete.

oval window A window having the shape of an ellipse or a shape between an ellipse and a circle.

ovendry wood, bone-dry wood Wood from which no moisture can be removed when exposed to a temperature of 212°F (100°C).

overall, overall dimension A total outer dimension of a building material, including any projection, such as a tongue.

overbreak Any excavation beyond the limits set by the **neat line**.

overburden **1.** The entire thickness of soil over rock or over a specific bearing stratum. **2.** An undesirable top layer covering rock, gravel, or other useful material wanted for construction.

overcloak In sheet-metal roofing, the part of a sheet that laps over an adjacent sheet beneath it.

overconsolidated soil deposit A soil deposit that has been subjected to an effective pressure greater than the pressure of the present overburden.

overcurrent An electrical current which is abnormally high, usually as a result of a short circuit.

overcurrent protection A form of protection in an electric circuit which prevents damage resulting from excessive current; interrupts the flow of current at a predetermined value.

overcurrent relay A relay used to provide **overcurrent protection**.

overdesign As applied to structural design, a design based on requirements higher than service demands, usually as a means of compensating for unknown and/or anticipated deficiencies.

overdoor, sopraporta A wall area, more or less ornamented, directly above a doorway.

overfire air Secondary air which is introduced in a furnace above the grate to complete combustion and to produce turbulence, thereby increasing the efficiency of the combustion process.

overdoor panel

overfloor duct A duct (usually fabricated of metal) that is designed to house and protect communications wiring across floor surfaces.

overflow, overflow pipe 1. A pipe used to remove excess water and/or to prevent flooding in certain sanitary fixtures, storage tanks, and plumbing fittings. 2. An outlet for a storage tank; used to prevent flooding or to set the water level in the tank.

overflow channel An overflow passageway (forming an integral part of a fixture) which provides a means for removing excess water and preventing overflow.

overflow drain A component in a roof drainage system, used to protect the roof against damage resulting from the water load imposed by blocked or partially-blocked roof drains.

overglaze decoration A ceramic or metallic decoration applied and fired on the previously glazed surface of ceramic ware.

overgrain Regraining a grained, painted surface to cause a deepening or exaggeration of the grained effect.

overgrainer A special type of flat bristle brush, with thin, long bristles, used in imitating the natural grain of woods.

overhand work The laying of bricks in an outer wall by bricklayers within the building, standing either on a floor or on a scaffold.

overhang 1. The projection of an upper story or roof beyond a story immediately below. 2. See **jetty**. 3. In a truss, the extension of the top chord of a truss beyond the heel, measured horizontally. 4. Same as **overshoot**.

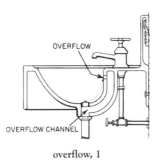

overflow, 1

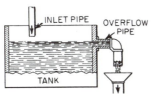

overflow, 2

overhang, 1

overhaul The movement of excavated material beyond a distance for which there are no haulage charges.

overhead balance A type of balance for a sash; installed in the head jamb of a window frame; usually consists of a coiled steel tape under spring tension.

overhead concealed closer A door closer concealed in the head of a doorframe; has an arm which connects with the door at the top rail.

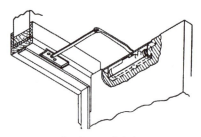

overhead concealed closer

overhead door A door, of either the swing-up or the roll-up type, which, when open, assumes a horizontal position above the door opening; may be a single leaf or constructed of several leaves; often used as a door on a garage.

overhead entrance conductor A **service entrance conductor** between (a) the terminals of service equipment and (b) a point usually outside (and clear of) the building, where it is spliced to an overhead service conductor between the last pole and the premises served.

overhead expense An **indirect expense**.

overhead shovel A **tractor** having a shovel which digs at the front end and dumps its load at the rear end; often used in confined areas.

overhead-type garage door See **overhead door**.

overhung door A door that opens outward and is hinged along the top.

overhung impeller pump A **centrifugal pump** whose **impeller** is mounted on the end of a shaft that overhangs its bearings.

overjacket See **jacket**.

overlapping astragal, wraparound astragal A vertical molding attached to the meeting edge of one leaf of a pair of doors as protection against

overlapping astragal

weather and to minimize the transmission of smoke, light, etc., between the doors.

overlay flooring Same as **strip flooring**.

overlay glass See **cased glass**.

overload **1.** A load on a structure in excess of that for which it was designed. **2.** Electric current, power, or voltage in excess of that for which a device or circuit was designed.

overload capacity The **overload, 2** which, if exceeded, will result in permanent damage to the equipment considered.

overload relay A **relay** in the circuit of a motor which causes the motor to be disconnected from its source of power if the current to the motor exceeds a predetermined value.

overmantel An ornamental panel or structure above a mantelpiece. When Victorian architecture was popular, a mirror was often set in the overmantel to reflect light into the room from a candelabra placed on the mantelpiece.

oversail To project beyond the general face of a construction.

oversailing A term descriptive of a surface that projects beyond the general face of the wall immediately below. For example, an *oversailing course* of brickwork projects beyond the general face of a wall; an *oversailing gable end* is a gable end that overhangs the floor immediately below it.

oversailing course A masonry course which projects beyond the general face of a wall.

oversanded Descriptive of mortar or concrete containing more sand than necessary to produce adequate workability and a satisfactory condition for finishing.

overshoot The projection of an upper story beyond the wall of the story below, commonly on the front of the house but sometimes on the sides as well; frequently called a *jetty*. Also see **framed overhang** and **hewn overhang**.

overshot Same as **jetty**.

oversite concrete An underlayer of concrete below a slab or other flooring; so placed to prevent disturbance of the ground below, to provide a relatively even and firm surface for the placement of the next layer, and to keep out ground air and moisture.

oversize brick A brick that is 2½ in. by 3½ in. by 7½ in.

overstory **1.** An upper floor. **2.** Same as **clerestory**.

overstretching The stressing of steel **tendons** to a value higher than designed for the initial stress; this is done (a) to overcome frictional losses, (b) to overstress temporarily the steel to reduce creep in the steel which occurs after anchorage, and (c) to counteract the loss of prestressing force that is caused by the subsequent prestressing of other tendons.

overthrow A panel of ornamental metalwork placed like a lintel above metal gates.

over-tone In painting, same as **mass color**.

overturning Failure of a retaining wall as a result of pressure of the earth, which overcomes the stability of the wall; the resistance to overturning is directly proportional to the weight of the wall and the width of the base.

overvibration Excessive use of vibrators during placement of freshly mixed concrete, causing segregation and excessive bleeding.

OVHD On drawings, abbr. for "overhead."

ovolo A convex molding, less than a semicircle in profile; usually a quarter of a circle or approximately a quarter-ellipse in profile.

ovum In classical architecture and derivatives, an egg-shaped ornamental motif.

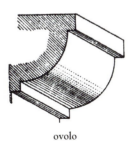

ovolo

owlhole An opening in an exterior wall of a barn that permits mice-eating birds such as owls or martins to enter; often cut in a distinctive or decorative pattern near the top of a **gable end**.

owner **1.** The architect's client and party to the **owner-architect agreement**. **2.** One who has the legal right or title to a piece of property.

owner-architect agreement A contract between the architect and client for professional services.

owner-contractor agreement A contract between the owner and contractor for a construction project.

owner's inspector A person employed by the **owner** to inspect construction in the owner's behalf.

owner's liability insurance Insurance which protects the **owner** against claims arising from his ownership of property and which may be extended to cover claims which may arise from operations of others under the construction contract.

oxeye A **bull's-eye, 2**.

oxeye molding A concave molding less hollow than a **scotia** but deeper than a **cavetto**.

oxeye window, oxeye Same as **bull's-eye window**.

oxidation Reaction of a chemical compound with oxygen, as in a paint film in which oil reacts with oxygen to form a hard dry film.

oxidized asphalt Same as **blown asphalt**.

oxidized sludge Sewage in which the organic matter has been combined with oxygen and has become stable.

oxter piece An upright timber used in **ashlaring**.

oxyacetylene torch A torch utilizing the flame produced by the combustion of **acetylene** with oxygen.

oxyacetylene welding A welding process utilizing heat from a gas flame produced by the combustion of **acetylene** and oxygen.

oxychloride cement, sorel cement A strong, hard cement composed of magnesium chloride and calcined magnesia; sometimes fillers are added.

oxygen cutting A metal cutting operation in which the separation of the metal is effected by

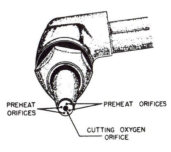

oxygen cutting tip

chemical reaction, between oxygen and the metal, at a high temperature.

oxygen starvation Localized corrosion of metals in the presence of an electrolyte, due to a smothering or poultice action or resulting from a crevice between metal parts or between the metal and another material.

oyelet, oylet Same as **eyelet**.

oz Abbr. for "ounce."

ozone An unstable form of oxygen that is a powerful oxidizing agent; produced by electric discharges and by ultraviolet energy; used as a deodorant and to control mildew, fungus, and bacteria; excessive amounts are harmful to human tissue.

ozone lamp An **electric-discharge lamp** which emits minute quantities of radiant power at a wavelength of 184.9 nanometers, producing ozone.

P

P **1.** On drawings, abbr. for "page." **2.** Abbr. for "pole."

Pa Symbol for **pascal**; a unit of pressure.

P&G Abbr. for "post and girder."

P&T Abbr. for "post and timbers."

P1E Abbr. for "planed one edge."

P1S Abbr. for "planed one side."

P1S2E Abbr. for "planed one side and two edges."

P4S Abbr. for "planed four sides."

PA On drawings, abbr. for **public address system**.

pace A seldom-used term for **stair landing**.

Pacific red cedar See **thuya**.

packaged air conditioner See **room air conditioner**.

packaged attenuator Same as **sound attenuator**.

packaged boiler A boiler unit having all components including boiler, burner, controls, and auxiliary equipment assembled as a unit.

packaged building See **manufactured building** and **precut building**.

packaged concrete A concrete mixture of dry ingredients in a package; requires only the addition of water to produce concrete.

package dealer A person or organization assuming responsibility under a single contract for the design and construction of a project to meet the specific requirements of another.

packaged fan equipment See **air-handling unit**.

package stability The ability of a liquid, such as paint or varnish, to retain its original quality after prolonged storage.

package trim Factory-made door and window **trim**, ready for installation; delivered to the jobsite in packages.

packed chord A composite **chord, 1** which consists of several longitudinal structural members that are bolted together.

packer **1.** A device, usually expandable, which is inserted into a hole to be grouted; prevents return of the grout around the injection pipe. **2.** Same as **compactor, 2**.

packing **1.** The stuffing or a thin ring of elastic material around a shaft or valve stem, or around a joint, to prevent fluid leakage. **2.** Small stones embedded in mortar; used to fill the cracks between the larger stones.

packing piece, stool A block which is used to raise one or more members above others.

pack set The condition induced in stored cement (whether in stationary containers or during bulk shipment) of reduced ability to flow freely; usually caused by interlocking of particles, by mechanical compaction, or by electrostatic attraction between particles.

pad See **padstone**.

padauk A hard, heavy wood, red with black stripes, from India; used in cabinetmaking and veneer.

paddle A flat plastering tool used to clean out or to finish an angle or corner.

paddle mixer A mixer for concrete or mortar having power-operated mixing blades which revolve about an axis.

paddock A small field near a house or barn in which animals, usually horses, are enclosed.

pad foundation An isolated, concrete slab **on-grade, 1** that serves as a foundation.

pad-mounted transformer A transformer designed to be mounted directly on a **pad foundation** with high- and low-tension cables coming directly into the terminal compartments which are part of the transformer housing.

pad saw A small **compass saw**.

padstone, pad A strong block bedded on a wall to distribute a concentrated load; a **template, 2**.

pad support In an acoustical ceiling assembly with a perforated metal pan, a device (such as a

page

wire grid) for holding the sound-absorptive element out of contact with the perforated pan.

page A short thin wedge.

pagoda A multistoried shrine-like tower, originally a Buddhist monument crowned by a **stupa**. Stories may be open pavilions of wood with balconies and pent roofs (prevalent in Japan) or built-in masonry, of diminishing size with corbeled cornices.

paillasse Same as **palliase**.

paillette In decorative work, a bit of metal or colored foil used to obtain a jeweled effect.

paillon Bright metal foil, used to show through a thickness of enamel or paint to alter its color and give it brilliance.

pai-lou, pai-loo A monumental Chinese arch or gateway with one, three, or five openings; erected at the entrance to a palace, tomb, or processional way. Usually built of stone in imitation of wood construction.

pai-lou at Amoy

paint A liquid solution of pigment in a suitable vehicle of oil, organic solvent, or water; liquid when applied but dries to form an adherent, protective, and decorative coating. Often categorized according to the solvent used for thinning, for example, water-thinned paint or solvent-thinned paint. Also see **acrylic paint, cement-water paint, epoxy paint, latex paint, synthetic rubber-base paint, vinyl paint, water-based paint.**

paint base The vehicle into which pigment is mixed to form a paint; commonly alkyd, latex, acrylic.

paint bridge A platform or gallery, of fixed or adjustable height, beside or above the stage of a theatre or in a paint loft; esp. used to paint scenery.

paint brush A tool for applying paint, consisting of a flexible brush composed of long filamentary material bound to a handle.

paint drier See **drier**.

painted glass A decorative glass that is colored by the application of an enamel paint onto a glass surface that is then heated in a kiln at a high temperature; see **stained glass**.

painter's putty See **putty**.

paint frame A movable frame, which can be raised or lowered, used to hold stretched canvas (and/or "flats") on which stage scenery is being painted.

paint kettle, paint pot An open can with a bail (wire handle) for carrying or hanging on ladders while painting.

paint loft In a theatre, a narrow vertical loft containing paint frames and/or paint bridges.

paint oil See **drying oil**.

paint pad A tool for applying paint, consisting of short filament material or an open-cell resilient material which is connected to a handle; designed to apply paint by a wiping action.

paint remover A liquid which is applied to a dry paint or varnish to cause it to soften or lose adhesion so that it may be removed easily.

paint roller A cylindrical tube which is coated on the outside with nonwoven fibers such as nylon, mohair, and lamb's wool and mounted on a roller with a handle; used for application of paint or varnish.

paint spray booth See **spray booth**.

paint sprayer See **spray gun**.

paint system The surface coating on a painted object; built up from some combination of the following coats: sealer or primer, stain, filler, undercoat, topcoat, varnish coat.

paint thinner See **thinner**.

paired brackets Two closely spaced brackets that form a pair; also called coupled brackets.

paired gables A façade having two gables that form a pair; for example, sometimes found in the façades of Gothic Revival structures of wood construction.

palaestra A Greek or Roman building for athletic training, smaller than a gymnasium, consisting of a large square court with colonnades, rooms for massage, baths, etc.

palazzo In Italian cities, a large, separate dwelling, often lavish; one of the major categories into which the **Italianate style** is often divided.

Palazzo style See **Italian Renaissance Revival** in which palazzi were widely imitated.

paldao See **dao**.

pale **1.** A flat strip (slat) or round stake, usually of wood; set in series to form a fence. **2.** An area enclosed by such stakes.

pale-bodied oil See **boiled oil**.

pale brick Same as **salmon brick**.

palestra Same as **palaestra**.

paling See **pale**.

palisade A series of stout poles, pointed on top and driven into the earth, used as a fence or fortification. Also see **stockade**.

palisado house A primitive house or building, usually built in frontier areas; walls were once constructed by setting two parallel rows of logs upright into the ground, and then filling the space between the rows with mud and twigs, or clay mixed with stones.

palisander See **Brazilian rosewood**.

palladiana See **berliner**.

Palladian dormer A **dormer** having a window, divided in three parts, that is suggestive of a small **Palladian window**.

Palladian door A door topped with a rounded arch; flanked by vertical rectangular areas of fixed glass on each side that are narrower and usually not as high as the door; suggestive of the appearance of a **Palladian window**.

Palladianism A term descriptive of a style of building that follows the strict use of Roman forms, as set forth in the publications of the Italian Renaissance architect Andrea Palladio (1508–1580), particularly under the influence of Lord Burlington in the 18th century.

Palladian motif, Serlian motif, Venetian motif A door or window opening in three parts, divided by posts, with a lintel flat over each side but arched over the center.

Palladian window A large window divided in three parts: a central sash that is arched at the top and two sashes on each side of it that are smaller than the central sash; the smaller sashes are rectangular, topped with flat lintels. Compare with **three-part window**.

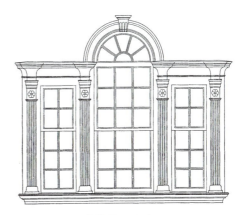

Palladian window

pallet **1.** A flat piece of wood laid in joints of brickwork to allow fastening of woodwork to wall. **2.** A portable platform used to facilitate handling by a forklift.

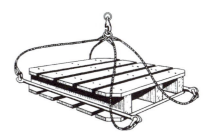

pallet, 2

pallet brick, pallet slip A brick esp. made with a groove along one edge to receive a **pallet, 1**.

palliase In masonry, a supporting bed.

palmate **1.** A column capital resembling the leaves of a palm tree. **2.** A **palmette**.

palm capital A type of Egyptian capital resembling the spreading crown of a palm tree. (See illustration p. 654.)

palmette An ornament derived from a palm leaf. (See illustration p. 654.)

palmiform Having the form of a palm leaf or the crown of a palm tree.

pampre An ornament consisting of vine leaves and grapes used to fill cavettos and other continuous hollows in a group of moldings.

pan **1.** A **wall plate**. **2.** A part of an exterior wall; esp. in half-timbered construction, the wall

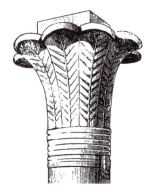

palm capital

palmette

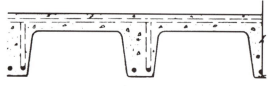

pan construction   section view

spaces between the timbers. **3.** A major vertical division in a wall. **4.** A structural panel. **5.** A form, frequently of molded fiberglass, used in pouring concrete floors or roofs. **6.** The re-cessed bed for the leaf of a hinge.

panache   The curved surface of a **pendentive**.

pan-and-roll roofing tile   Single-lap roofing tile of two types used in combination: a flat, tapered undertile having flanges, and a half-rounded tapered overtile.

pan breeze, breeze   Small bits of coke and furnace clinker from the pan beneath a coke oven; suitable for use as aggregate in lightweight concrete block.

pancarpi   Garlands or festoons of flowers, fruits, etc.

pan construction   A concrete floor or roof construction in which a prefabricated form (**pan, 5**) is used repeatedly, giving the underside of the construction a waffle-like appearance.

pane   **1.** A flat sheet of glass, cut to fit a window or door or part of a window or door; often of

small size, the larger ones usually being called *sheets*. After installation in a window sash, a pane is often referred to as a *light*. A window sash may be divided into a number of small lights, often for decorative or stylistic purposes. The configuration of a **double-hung window** having divided lights is often specified by the number of panes in the upper sash followed by the word *over* and then the number of panes in the lower sash; for example, a "six-over-three pattern" indicates that the upper sash is divided into six panes and the lower sash is divided into three panes. **2.** A panel of a door, wainscot, or the like. **3.** A rectangular division or plane surface of a building. **4.** A British term for **peen**.

panel   **1.** A large, relatively thin board or sheet of lumber, plywood, or other material used as a wall covering. **2.** A thin board, plywood sheet, or similar material with all its edges inserted in a groove of a surrounding frame of thick material. **3.** A portion of a flat surface recessed or sunk below the surrounding area, distinctly set off by molding or some other decorative device. **4.** A section of floor, wall, ceiling, or roof, usually prefabricated and of large size, handled as a single unit in the operations of assembly and erection. **5.** A length of formed metal sheet, or an assembly of such sheets, usually with insulation between, as used for wall enclosure on industrial-type buildings. **6.** A **frog**. **7.** That portion of a truss between adjacent **panel points** lying in the same chord. **8.** Same as **panelboard**.

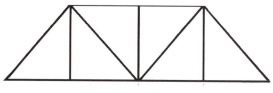

panel, 7; panel point

panel board   **1.** In an electrical installation, a single panel or group of panel units designed for assembly in the form of a single panel; includes buses, and may include switches as well as automatic overcurrent protective devices for the control of electric circuits; designed to be placed in a cabinet or cutout box placed against a wall or partition so that it is accessible from the front only. **2.** See **control board**.

panel box   A small **panel board** providing many of the same functions as a larger panel board.

panel construction, panellized construction   A method of building construction which uses panels as major elements or components.

panel divider   A molding which separates two wood panels along their common edge.

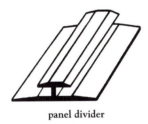

panel divider

panel door   A door having **stiles, rails,** and sometimes **mutins** which form one or more frames around (thinner) recessed panels.

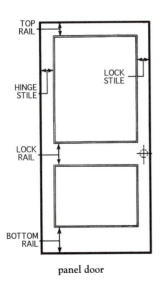

panel door

paneled door   Same as **panel door**.

panelescent lamp   See **electroluminescent lamp**.

panel heating   A system for heating a room or space by panels (in the walls, floor, ceiling, or along the baseboard) in which there are electric heating elements, hot-air pipes, or hot-water pipes.

panel house   A brothel in which the rooms are lined with sliding panels which facilitate robberies of house patrons.

paneling   A wall or ceiling treatment made up of **panels, 4.**

paneling

panel insert   A metal panel usually used to convert a half-glass recessed panel-type door to an all-metal unit.

panel lamp   A small lamp or a luminaire used to provide local lighting on instrument panels and the like.

panel length   In a truss, the distance between two adjacent joints along either the upper or the lower chord.

panel lining   **1.** Door **lining** having panels similar to those on the door. **2.** Lining around a window frame which matches the sash paneling.

panel load   The load at a **panel point** of a truss.

panel mold   See **pan mold**.

panel molding   A molding surrounding a panel. See also **bolection molding, drop molding**.

panel pin   A very slender wire nail with a small head; usually used in finished work.

panel point, node   A point where members of a **truss** intersect.

panel radiator   A **radiator** which is set into a wall panel or baseboard.

panel saw A small saw having closely set teeth; used in cutting thin panels and the like.

panel strip A narrow piece of metal or wood used to conceal a joint between two sheathing boards forming a panel.

panel tracery Same as **perpendicular tracery**.

panel wall A non-load-bearing wall between columns or piers in skeleton construction; such walls are supported at each story by the building frame.

panelwork Same as **paneling**.

panework **1.** In **Tudor Revival**, the decorative panels formed by half-timbering. **2.** Same as **pane, 3**.

pan fraction In the **sieve analysis** of aggregate, soil, etc., that fraction of the total sample retained on any sieve compared with the initial sample tested.

panhead rivet A rivet having a head whose shape is that of a truncated cone.

panic bolt See **panic exit device**.

panic exit device, fire-exit bolt, panic bolt, panic hardware A door locking device used on exit doors; the door latch releases when a bar, across the inside of the door, is pushed.

panic exit device

panic hardware See **panic exit device**.

panier See **corbeil**.

pan mixer See **open-top mixer**.

pan mold, panel mold A mold used to cast plaster panels.

pannier Any basketlike architectural member, once especially applied to **capitals** resembling baskets.

panopticon A building (often a jail) planned with corridors which radiate from a single, central point. A person located at the central point can observe each of the converging halls.

panorama A building containing an exhibit of an extended pictorial representation of landscape or some event of note; usually depicted of a large, wide area.

pantheon **1.** A temple dedicated to all the Gods. **2.** (*Cap.*) The Rotunda in Rome, formerly a temple to all the gods, now a church. **3.** The Pantheon in Paris, the former church of Sainte-Geneviève, now a shrine to national heroes.

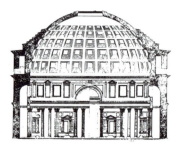

Pantheon, 2

pantile A roofing tile which has the shape of an S laid on its side.

pantile

pantograph A drafting instrument for copying drawings, plans, etc., either on the same scale or on an enlarged or a reduced scale.

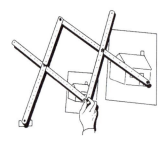

pantograph

pantry **1.** A serving room between kitchen and dining space. **2.** A room for storage of food supplies; a larder. **3.** A room for preparing refreshments, not complete meals.

pan-type humidifier A shallow pan having a relatively large area, filled with water which evaporates as air passes over the pan; a heating element in the pan may be used to increase evaporation.

pan-type tread A section formed from sheet metal to receive a fill and to provide, when filled, either a tread or a combination tread and riser.

pap A downward outlet from an eaves gutter.

paper-backed lath Any lath having a paper backing.

paper felt A type of **building paper**.

paper form A **form** for concrete made of a heavy paper material.

papier-mâché A material composed principally of paper; usually prepared by pulping a mass of paper (sometimes glue is added) to a dough-like consistency and molding to a desired form.

papyriform A capital of an Egyptian column having the form of a cluster of papyrus flowers.

papyriform

papyrus column A column having a **papyriform** capital.

p.a.r. Abbr. for "planed all round."

PAR See **PAR lamp**.

PAR. On drawings, abbr. for **paragraph**.

parabema Same as **diaconicon**.

parabolic arch An arch similar to a three-centered arch but whose intrados is parabolic, with a vertical axis.

parabolic reflector A light reflector whose surface is a paraboloid, i.e., a surface generated by rotating a parabolic section about its axis; if a small light source is placed at the focal point of the reflector, the reflected light will be concentrated in a nearly collimated beam parallel to the axis of the reflector.

paracyl reflector A cylindrical light reflector whose cross section is that of a semicircle joined to part of a parabola; they are joined so that the focus of the parabola is the center of the semicircle, at which point a **linear light source** is placed; esp. used for **wall-washing**.

paradise **1.** The court of the atrium in front of a church. **2.** The **garth** of a cloister. **3.** A Persian pleasure garden, usually elaborately planted.

paradisus Same as **paradise**.

parados **1.** An entrance to the orchestra of a Greek theatre. **2.** Earthworks behind a fortified place.

paragraph In the AIA documents, the first subdivision of an **article**, identified by two numerals, e.g., 3.3; may be further subdivided into subparagraphs and clauses.

parallel-blade damper A **damper, 1** through which the airflow is adjusted by means of damper blades on a common linkage, arranged so that adjacent blades rotate parallel to each other, providing little control of airflow; used primarily as an on-off control.

parallel-blade damper

parallel-chord truss See **flat-chord truss**.

parallel coping A coping which is flat, not sloped to shed water.

parallel gutter   See **box gutter**.

parallel stair   A stair consisting of flights which parallel each other and are separated only by one or more intermediate platforms.

parallel-wire unit   In posttensioning, a tendon which is composed of a number of strands (or wires) that are approximately parallel.

parapet   **1.** A low guarding wall at any point of sudden drop, as at the edge of a terrace, roof, battlement, balcony, etc. **2.** A defense wall. **3.** In an exterior wall, fire wall, or party wall, the part entirely above the roof.

parapeted gable   A **gable** having a face that rises above the cornice line and carries a parapet; for examples, see **corbie gable, Flemish gable, mission gable, multicurved gable, straight-line gable**.

parapet gutter   A gutter which is constructed behind a parapet wall.

parapet skirting   Roofing felt which is turned up against a parapet wall.

parapet wall   That part of a wall which is entirely above the roof.

para red   A class of organic red and maroon dyes and pigments; used in paints.

parascenium   A wing-like projection extending forward, at the ends of the **skene**, in ancient Greek theatres.

paraskenion   Same as **parascenium**.

parastas   **1.** The end of a wall, terminating in an **anta**, such as that enclosing the pronaos of a temple. **2.** A pedestal-like wall, as the abutment of the end of a monumental stairway.

paratorium   The place at the east end of a basilican church, usually on the north side, for the offerings; in some Greek churches, located on the south side.

paratory   In a church, a place where any preparation is made; a vestry or sacristy.

parcel   Of land, a contiguous land area which is considered as a unit, which is subject to a single ownership, and which is legally recorded as a single piece.

parclose, perclose   **1.** In medieval churches and derivatives, a screen dividing a special space from general space. **2.** The parapet round a gallery.

parent material   The material from which a soil has been formed.

paretta   Rough-cast masonry having a surface of protruding pebbles.

parge   To apply a parge coat; also see **parget, 3**.

parge board   Same as **bargeboard**.

parge coat, pargeting, pargework   **1.** Elaborate plasterwork; especially an ornamental facing for plaster walls decorated with figures in low relief. **2.** The interior lining of a chimney flue used to improve its fire protection and to provide a smooth surface. **3.** A coat of cement mortar on the face of rough masonry construction.

parget, pargeting, pargetting, pargework, parging   **1.** Elaborate plasterwork; esp. an ornamental facing for plaster walls, sometimes decorated with figures in low relief or indented; often used on the exterior of houses in the Tudor period. **2.** An interior lining of a flue to provide a smooth surface and to aid in fire protection. **3.** In masonry construction, a coat of cement mortar (generally containing damp-proofing ingredients) on the face of rough

parget, 1

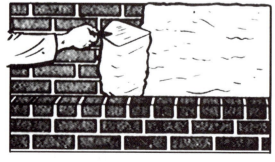

applying a **parget, 3**

masonry, the earth side of foundation and basement walls, or the like; a **parge coat**.

Parian cement, Parian plaster Similar to **Keene's cement**, but contains borax as an additive in place of alum.

paries In ancient Roman construction, a wall of a house or other edifice. Also see **murus**.

paring Trimming or reducing in size or thickness, by cutting or shaving of small portions from the surface or extremity.

paring chisel A long-handled chisel used for cutting away wood by hand alone, not by striking with a mallet.

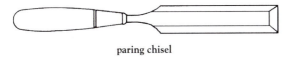

paring chisel

paring gouge A long, thin, concave gouge for woodworking which is beveled on its inner edge.

Paris blue See **Prussian blue**.

parish house A building for the secular activities of a parish.

Paris white Same as **whiting**.

park An area, usually of public land set aside for recreation and leisure, usually owned and managed by a municipality, a state, a nation, or held by royal grant, or in some cases by private organizations.

parkerized Descriptive of iron or steel which has received a rustproofing treatment by being dipped in a boiling solution of manganese dihydrogen phosphate; this protective coating also improves the bonding of paints and lacquers.

Parker's cement Same as **Roman cement**.

Parker truss A type of **truss** whose upper **chord, 1** is polygonal in form.

parking garage A garage for passenger vehicles only, exclusively for the purpose of parking or storing of automobiles and not for automobile repairs or service work.

parking lot, parking area, *Brit.* **car park** An open space for short-term storage of motor vehicles.

parking space A marked-off portion of a parking area for short-time storage of a single motor vehicle.

parking structure **1.** A building for short-term storage of motor vehicles, having two or more tiers or levels and at least two open sides, and with the top tier either roofed or not. **2.** A machine for automatic short-term storage of motor vehicles.

parking tier One of several levels or stories devoted to the temporary storage of motor vehicles.

PAR lamp A **reflector lamp**, usually incandescent, with a thick glass envelope, the back interior side of which has a parabolic shape with a reflective coating; used with a lensed front of the envelope to provide desired spread of the light beam.

PAR lamp

parlatory A room in a monastic establishment where visitors may be received.

parliament hinge See **H-hinge**.

parlor **1.** In a house, a room primarily for entertaining and conversing with guests. **2.** In a hotel, a room for receptions.

parlor chamber A bedroom above the parlor in a two-story house having a **hall-and-parlor plan**.

parodos One of the two side entrances to an ancient theatre between the seats and the stage; used principally by the chorus, but also by the public.

parpend A little used synonym for **perpend**.

parpend stone See **perpend**.

parquet **1.** Inlaid wood flooring, usually set in simple geometric patterns. **2.** Same as **parquetry**. **3.** The lower floor of a theatre, or the section of seats in an opera house, music hall, or theatre extending from the musicians' area to the **parquet circle**.

parquet circle, orchestra circle, parterre In a theatre or opera house, the part of the main floor at the rear of the **parquet, 3**, usually under the galleries or balconies.

parquetry A flat inlay pattern of closely fitted pieces, usually geometrical, often employing two or more colors or materials; used for ornamental parquet flooring or wainscoting, in stone or wood.

parquet strip flooring Same as **strip flooring**.

parrel, chimney breast A chimneypiece or the ornaments of a chimneypiece collectively.

parsonage The residence of a parson, provided by the church.

part Abbr. for **partition**.

parterre 1. See **parquet circle**. 2. An ornamental arrangement of flower or gravel beds of various sizes and shapes.

Parthenon 1. Originally, the room behind the cella in the great temple of Athena Parthenos on the Athenian Acropolis. 2. More commonly, the name of the entire temple.

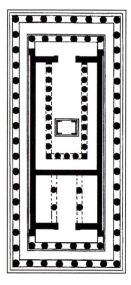

Parthenon, 2

Parthian architecture An architectural style developed under Parthian domination (3rd cent. B.C. to 3rd cent. A.D.) in western Iran and Mesopotamia, combining classical with autochthonous features. Its major achievement is the monumental *iwan* covered by a barrel vault in stone or brick.

parti A scheme or concept for the design of a building.

partial cover plate A **cover plate, 1** attached to

the flange of a girder which does not extend the full distance between the supports of the girder.

partial-height partition In an open-plan office, a free-standing partition which provides visual privacy and some (but usually little) sound attenuation between adjacent offices.

partial occupancy Occupancy by the **owner** of a portion of a project prior to final completion.

partial payment A **progress payment**.

partial prestressing The **prestressing** of concrete to a level of stress such that tensile stresses exist in the precompressed tensile zone of the prestressed member, for **design loads, 1**.

partial release In a prestressed concrete member, a release of part of the total prestress initially held entirely in the prestressed reinforcement.

particleboard A large class of **building boards** made from wood particles and a binder; usually has a density of 25 to 50 lb per cu ft (400 to 800 kg per cu m); often faced with veneer. Also see **chipboard; coreboard**.

particle shape The shape of a particle of aggregate. Also see **angular aggregate, cubical aggregate, elongated piece, flat piece**.

particle size 1. In evaluating the efficiency of a filter for removing particles from an air stream, the minimum particle diameter in microns that will be removed by the filter. 2. In paints, the diameter of a pigment or latex particle; usually expressed in mils or microns.

particle-size distribution A tabulation of the percentages of the various sizes of particles in a sample of soil or aggregate for concrete as determined by **sieve analysis**.

particulate grout A grouting material which is characterized by undissolved particles in the mix.

parting agent A material applied to one or both surfaces of a sheet to prevent adhesion to other sheets; a **release agent**.

parting bead A long narrow strip between the upper and lower sashes in a double-hung window frame, enabling them to slide past each other; also called **parting stop, parting strip**.

parting lath A **parting strip** made of wood lath.

parting slip, midfeather, wagtail A long thin strip of wood in the box jamb of a **cased**

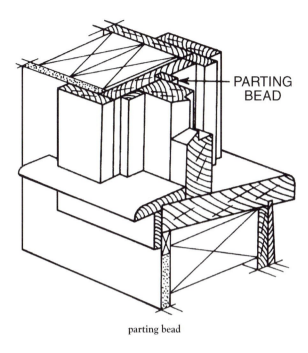

PARTING
BEAD

parting bead

frame which separates the sash weights from each other; also called a **parting strip, parting bead**.

parting stop   See **parting bead**.

parting strip   **1.** A narrow strip used to keep two parts separated, such as a **parting slip**. **2.** A **parting bead**.

parting tool, V-tool   A narrow-bladed hand tool having a V-shaped gouge; used in woodworking for cutting grooves, in wood turning, or for cutting pieces in two.

parting wall   Same as **party wall**.

partition   **1.** A dividing wall within a building; may be bearing or non-load-bearing. **2.** In sound-transmission considerations, any building component (or a combination of components), such as a wall, door, window, roof, or floor-ceiling assembly, that separates one space from another.

partition block   A concrete masonry unit for use in non-load-bearing walls; usually has solid, rectangular end faces and a nominal thickness of 4 in. (10 cm) or 6 in. (15 cm).

partition cap, partition head, partition plate   The uppermost horizontal member of a partition; the top **plate** of a partition on which the joists rest.

partition head   See **partition cap**.

partition infilling   **1.** Same as **fill insulation**. **2.** See **infilling**.

partition plate   See **partition cap**.

partition stud   See **stud**.

partition tile   Tile for use in building interior partitions, subdividing areas into rooms, or similar construction, carrying no superimposed loads.

partly cloudy sky   In daylighting, a sky having between 30% and 70% cloud cover.

partn   Abbr. for **partition**.

parts per million   The parts of a substance per million parts (by weight) of a solution; equal to 0.0001%. *Abbr.* ppm.

party arch   An arch on the line separating the property of two owners.

party fence   A fence that separates two properties.

party wall   A wall used jointly by two parties under easement agreement, erected upon a line dividing two parcels of land, each of which is a separate real estate entity; a common wall.

party-wall house   Same as **row house**.

parvis   **1.** The open square in front of a large church. **2.** An enclosed court or room in front of a church.

pascal (Pa)   The Standard International unit of pressure; 1 pascal is equal to 1 newton per square meter.

pas-de-souris   In a castle, the steps leading from the moat to the entrance.

pass   A single progression of a welding operation along a joint, resulting in a **weld bead**.

PASS.   On drawings, abbr. for "passenger."

passage grave, chamber tomb   In prehistoric Europe, a chamber approached by a long passage, of megalithic construction, covered and protected by an artificial mound.

passageway, passage   A space connecting one area or room of a building with another.

pass door   A door through the proscenium wall, from stage to the auditorium.

passenger elevator   An elevator exclusively for the use of passengers. Also see **freight elevator**.

passenger elevator car   See **elevator car**.

passenger lift   See **elevator car**.

passings   The amount of overlap between sheets of flashing etc.; same as **lap, 2.**

passion cross   Same as **Calvary cross.**

passivation   Treatment of a metal surface which leaves a protective coating, rendering the surface less reactive chemically.

passive solar energy system   A building subsystem in which solar energy is collected and transferred predominantly by natural means; uses natural convection, conduction, or radiation to distribute thermal energy through a structure, within the limits of the indoor design temperature conditions. Compare with **active solar energy system.**

pass-through   An opening in a partition for passing things from one adjoining space to another, usually between a kitchen and a dining space in a dwelling, but also between any two spaces in a building.

paste filler   In painting, a **filler, 3** in paste form; usually thinned with solvent prior to application.

paste paint   A mixture of oil, pigment, and some solvent in paste form; requires mixing with additional solvent and/or oil to produce a usable paint.

pastiche   A mixture of materials, forms, motifs, and/or styles; often incongruous.

pastophorium, pastophorion   In the early church, one of the two apartments at the sides of the bema or sanctuary; this arrangement has been retained in the modern Greek Orthodox church.

pastoral column   A tree trunk used as a column, for example, as used in **cottage orné.**

Pat.   In the lumber industry, abbr. for "pattern."

pat   As applied to a specimen of neat cement paste, a sample about 3 in. (7.6 cm) in diameter and ½ in. (1.3 cm) in thickness at the center and tapering to a thin edge; applied on a flat glass plate to determine the setting time.

patand   See **patten.**

patch   **1.** In stone masonry, a compound used to fill natural voids or to replace chips and broken corners or edges in fabricated pieces of cut stone; applied in plastic form; mixed or selected to match the color and texture of the stone. **2.** In carpentry and joinery, a piece of wood or veneer glued into a recess to replace defective portions or voids; an **insert** or **plug.**

patch board, patch panel   A board or panel where electric circuits are terminated with jacks and plugs, and where they may be interconnected temporarily by means of a cord called a "patch cord."

patch panel   See **patch board.**

patent board   A **building board** manufactured under a patented process.

patent glazing   A system of glazing which employs any of a variety of commercially available devices for securing the glass sheets without the use of putty.

patent hammer   A two-faced hammer, each of whose faces is composed of a number of parallel thin chisels; used for dressing stone.

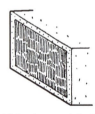

patent hammer

masonry surface which has been tooled with a **patent hammer**

patent knotting   In painting, a knot sealer; a solution of shellac and benzine or similar solvent. Also see **knotting.**

patent light   Same as **pavement light.**

patent plaster   **1.** A gypsum plaster that is mixed with sand; used as a base-coat plaster. **2.** A plaster manufactured under a patent process whose exact constituents are secret; a chemical plaster. **3.** Same as **cement plaster.**

patent plate   Same as **plate glass.**

patent stone   See **artificial stone.**

patera   A **roundel**, often decorated with leaves, petals, or the like; sometimes used as a decorative element, such as on a **corner block**. Also see **rosette**.

architectural **paterae**

paternoster   A small round molding cut in the form of beads like a rosary; a **bead molding**.

path   A **footway**; a footpath.

patience   Same as **miserere**.

patin   See **patten**.

patina, patination   **1.** A greenish brown crust which forms on bronze. **2.** Any thin oxide film which forms on a metal; often multicolored. **3.** A film, similar in color, which forms on a material other than metal. **4.** Such effects artificially induced, or imitated. **5.** A green coating on the surface of copper or copper alloys that have been exposed to the atmosphere for a long time.

patio   **1.** An outdoor area or courtyard, open to the sky but enclosed, or partially enclosed, by the walls of a building. Although the term originally described such an area in a Spanish house, it is now widely used for any outdoor recreational space that is adjacent to a house; also see **placita**. **2.** A large quadrangle of an early Spanish-American mission, usually surrounded on all four sides by a series of abutting structures for protection.

patland   In carpentry of the Early English period, the sill or lower frame member.

patten, patand, patin   **1.** The base of a column or pillar. **2.** A base or a **groundsill** which supports a column, post, or pillar.

pattern   **1.** A model made in some easily worked material (such as plaster or wood) which serves as a guide, with respect to form and dimensions, in laying out any piece of work, esp. to preserve and secure uniformity and accuracy. **2.** A design, considered as a unit, of which an idea can be given by a fragment, as a diaper pattern. **3.** In molding, a form used to provide the interior shape of the mold.

pattern book   In the 18th and 19th centuries, a book on architectural practice that once served as a builders' manual, builders' guide, or handbook containing plans and/or patterns of houses and building details such as columns, cornices, doors, porches, and windows.

pattern cracking   Fine openings on concrete surfaces in the form of a pattern; results from a decrease in volume of the material near the surface and/or an increase in volume of the material below the surface.

patterned brickwork   Masonry of bricks of more than one color, direction, texture, or **bond, 6**, so as to form a decorative design.

patterned glass   Glass that has a textured pattern on one side (the other side being smooth).

pattern staining   In plastering, dark areas, particularly on the interior side of exterior walls or ceilings; results from different thermal conductances of the backings.

paumelle   A type of door hinge having a single joint of the pivot type, usually of modern design.

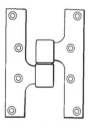

paumelle hinge

pavement   The durable surfacing of a road, sidewalk, or other outdoor area.

pavement base   In a pavement, the layer between the surfacing material and the subbase or subgrade.

pavement light   Heavy glass disks or prisms set into a pavement to convey light to a space beneath.

pavement saw   A self-propelled machine, equipped with a rotating blade, that cuts a narrow kerf in a new concrete slab to provide a localized joint for the control of cracking due to expansion.

pavement sealer   See **asphalt pavement sealer**.

pavement structure   All courses of selected material placed on a foundation or subgrade soil, other than layers or courses constructed in grading operations.

paver **1.** A **paving stone, paving brick,** or **paver tile. 2.** A self-propelled machine that places concrete.

paver tile Unglazed porcelain or natural clay tile, formed by the dust-pressed method; similar to ceramic mosaic tile in composition and physical properties but thicker.

pavestone A **paving stone.**

pavilion **1.** A detached or semidetached structure used for entertainment or (as at a hospital) for specialized activities. **2.** On a façade, a prominent portion usually central or terminal, identified by projection, height, and special roof forms. **3.** In a garden or fairground, a temporary structure or tent, usually ornamented.

pavilion roof **1.** A roof hipped equally on all sides, so as to have a pyramidal form; a pyramidal hipped roof. **2.** A similar roof having more than four sides; a polygonal roof. **3.** A steeply pitched **hipped roof** whose upper termination is usually a ridge somewhat shorter than the length of the building.

pavimentum In ancient Roman construction, a pavement formed by pieces of crushed stone, flint, tile, and other materials set in a bed of ashes or cement and consolidated by beating down with a rammer.

paving aggregate Materials such as crushed stone, gravel, sand, slag, seashells, and mineral dust, used in pavements.

paving asphalt A dark brown to black sticky residue, predominantly derived from the refining of crude oil; used as the binder in **asphaltic concrete.**

paving breaker, chipper A hand-held compressed-air-powered tool for cutting pavement or rock; delivers repetitive blows by means of a pointed or chisel-shaped bit.

paving brick A vitrified brick, esp. suitable for use in pavements where resistance to abrasion is important; a **pavior.**

paving stone, pavestone A block or chunk of stone, shaped or selected by shape for a paved surface.

paving train An assemblage of equipment designed to place and finish a concrete pavement.

paving unit Any prefabricated unit used for surfacing the ground.

pavior, paviour **1.** A brick used for paving. **2.** A **clamp brick** of second quality which is hard, well-shaped, and of good appearance and color.

pavonaceum An ancient method of laying tiles that are rounded at one end, so that in overlapping each other they present a scalloped appearance.

pavonazzo, pavonazzeto **1.** Various red and purplish marbles and brescias. **2.** A marble, used by the ancient Romans, characterized by very irregular veins of dark red with bluish and yellowish tints.

pawn A covered passageway or **gallery.**

PAX On drawings, abbr. for "private automatic (telephone) exchange."

payment request See **application for payment.**

PBX See **private branch exchange.**

pc Abbr. for "piece."

PC **1.** Abbr. for **portland cement. 2.** Abbr. for "power circuit." **3.** On drawings, abbr. for "piece." **4.** On drawings, abbr. for "pull chain." **5.** Abbr. for "Producers Council."

PCA Abbr. for "Portland Cement Association."

pcf Abbr. for "pounds per cubic foot."

PCSA Abbr. for "Power Crane and Shovel Association."

p.e. Abbr. for "plain edged."

PE **1.** In the lumber industry, abbr. for "plain end." **2.** Abbr. for **polyethylene.**

P.E. Abbr. for **professional engineer.**

peacock's-eye Same as **bird's-eye.**

pea gravel Small-diameter (¼ to ⅜ in. or 6.4 to 9.5 mm) natural gravel, screened to specification.

pea gravel grout A **grout** to which pea gravel has been added.

peak arch A **pointed arch.**

peaked roof A roof of two or more slopes that rises to a ridge or peak.

peak-head window **1.** A window that has a triangular head, such as a **lancet window;** often found in **Gothic Revival** church architecture. **2.** Same as **lancet window.**

peak joint At the ridge of a roof, the joint between members of a roof truss.

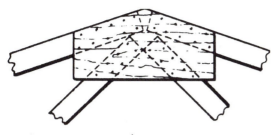

peak joint

peak load The maximum load carried by a device, system, or structure over a designated time period.

peak-load controller An automatic electrical monitor and controller which can be used to limit the maximum power demands of a building.

peak sound pressure The maximum instantaneous sound pressure (a) for a transient or impulsive sound of short time duration, or (b) for a sound of long duration, over a specified time interval.

pean See **peen**.

peanut gallery The topmost balcony in an auditorium.

pear drop 1. A pear-shaped pendant, often used as a handle or support. 2. In 18th cent. architecture, a support for a small arch.

pearl essence A translucent, lustrous pigment obtained from fish scales or compounded synthetically; used as a pigment in lacquers to obtain a pearl-like finish.

pearlite Same as **perlite**.

pearl lamp British term for a **frosted lamp bulb** which is etched on its inner surface.

pearl molding A molding decorated with a continuous series of pearl-like shapes.

pearl molding

peat A fibrous mass of organic matter in various stages of decomposition, generally dark brown to black in color and of spongy consistency.

peat moss 1. Moss entering into the composition of, or producing, peat; used as mulch. 2. The debris of mashes and bogs, somewhat compressed and partially decomposed; used as mulch.

pebble dash Same as **rock dash**.

pebble wall 1. A wall built of pebbles in mortar. 2. A wall faced with pebbles embedded, at random or in pattern, in a mortar coating on the exposed surface.

peck In timber, decay resulting from fungus in isolated spots.

pecked finished Same as **picked finish**.

pecky timber, peggy timber Fungus-spotted wood, such as pecky cypress or pecky cedar; the decay stops when the wood is dried.

pectinated Having teeth like a comb.

pedestal 1. A support for a column, statue, urn, etc., consisting in classical architecture of a base, dado, or die and a cornice, surbase, or cap; in modern design often a plain unornamented block. 2. An upright compression member the height of which does not exceed three times its least lateral dimension.

cornice

dado

base

pedestal

pedestal pile A **cast-in-place pile** which is constructed so that some concrete is forced out at the bottom of the casing, forming a pedestal shape at the foot of the pile.

pedestal urinal A **urinal** which is not connected to the wall for support but is mounted on a single pedestal.

pedestal washbasin A washbasin which is supported from the floor by a column-like base.

pedestrian bridge See **footbridge**.

pedestrian control device Any device, esp. a **turnstile**, but including a gate, railing, or post, used to control or monitor the flow of pedestrian traffic, to control access to a given area, etc.

pede window In a church, a window oriented with respect to a larger one so as to symbolize one of the feet of Christ.

pediment 1. In Classical architecture, a triangular gable usually having a horizontal cornice, with raked cornices on each side, surmounting or crowning a portico or another major division of a façade, end wall, or colonnade. 2. A gable above or over a door, window, or hood; usually has a horizontal cornice, crowned with curved sides, or may also be crowned with another configuration (such as broken sides) or its base may be broken in the middle. For definitions and illustrations of specific types, see **angular pediment, broken pediment, broken-scroll pediment, center-gabled pediment, curved pediment, open pediment, pointed pediment, round pediment, scroll pediment, segmental pediment, split pediment, swan's-neck pediment, triangular pediment**.

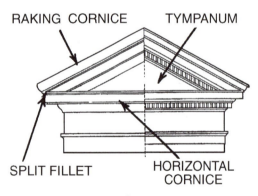

RAKING CORNICE   TYMPANUM

SPLIT FILLET   HORIZONTAL CORNICE

pediment

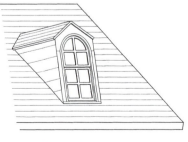

pedimented dormer

pediment arch A **miter arch**.

peel, pele In northern England and Scotland in the Middle Ages, a small, emergency defense structure, generally a low, fortified tower, usable as a dwelling place.

peel

peeling 1. A process in which thin flakes of mortar are broken away from a concrete surface, as by deterioration or by adherence of surface mortar to forms as they are removed. 2. A defect in a paint film or plaster finish which causes the film or finish to lose its adhesion to the substrate, so that it can be removed in strips.

peel tower Same as **peel**.

peen, pean The end of a hammer opposite the flat hammering face; may terminate in a cone-shaped, rounded, or sharply pointed face.

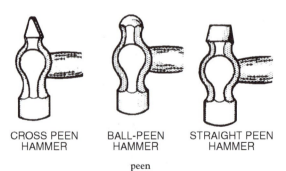

CROSS PEEN HAMMER   BALL-PEEN HAMMER   STRAIGHT PEEN HAMMER

peen

peen-coated nail See **mechanically galvanized nail**.

peening The working of a metal by means of hammer blows.

peg 1. A pointed **pin** of wood, metal, or any other material; usually used as a fastener. 2. A cylindrical piece of wood used as a **dowel pin** to fasten wood members.

pegboard, perforated hardboard A hard composition fiberboard material in sheet form, usually about ¼ in. (0.6 cm) thick, having regular rows of holes in it, through which hooks or pegs may be fastened.

peggies Slates of random length and width.

peggy timber Same as **pecky timber.**

peg mold A **running mold.**

peg stay A type of casement stay used to hold a **casement, 1** open.

pein Same as **peen.**

pellet **1.** Any small, round, decorative projection; usually one of many. **2.** A circular wood plug which covers a countersunk screw.

pellet molding A molding decorated with a series of small, flat disks or hemispherical projections.

pellet molding

pelmet A valance or cornice, sometimes decorative, built into the head of a window to conceal the drapery track or blind brackets or fittings.

pelmet board A board, at the head of the interior side of a window, which acts as a pelmet.

pelmet lighting See **valance lighting.**

pen **1.** A synonym for *room* in a four-sided enclosure constructed of logs. Thus, a one-room log cabin is often called a *single-pen cabin,* and a dogtrot cabin (consisting of two single-room cabins) is often called a *double-pen cabin.* **2.** An enclosure for animals; for example, a pigpen.

penal sum The amount named in a contract or bond as the damages or penalty to be paid by a signatory thereto in the event he fails to perform his contractual obligations or does not do so within the time prescribed by the contract.

penalty-and-bonus clause See **bonus-and-penalty clause.**

penalty clause A contract provision setting forth the damages a party must pay in the event

of his breach. If such a clause is regarded by the court as too harsh to be regarded as a fair estimate of probable damages, it will normally be held invalid. See **liquidated damages.**

penciled Descriptive of a mortar joint in a brick wall used in the early 19th century when extremely thin mortar joints were fashionable. They were prepared as follows: First, the wall, with mortar joints flush with the brick surface, was painted the color of the brick; then a narrow white line painted along the center of the mortar joints.

pencil rod Any rod having a diameter approximating that of a lead pencil.

pendant, pendent, pendent drop **1.** A suspended feature or hanging ornament used in the

pendant, 1: A

pendant, 2   on an Early New England house

vaults and timber roofs of Gothic architecture or Gothic Revival; also called a pendent. **2.** A carved or turned wood ornament that terminates the bottom end of second-floor posts in **framed overhang** construction, also called a drop or corner drop; or such an ornament on each side of the front door. **3.** An electrical device or piece of equipment that is suspended from overhead by means of a flexible cord carrying the current.

pendant luminaire   A suspended **luminaire**.

pendant post   In a **hammer-beam roof**, the lower post at the foot of the truss.

pendant sprinkler   A **sprinkler** in a fire-protection system designed in which the water stream is directed downward against a deflector disk, developing a spray pattern.

pendant switch   An electric wiring switch which is suspended from overhead at the end of a two-conductor cord; used to control lamps or other devices that are mounted overhead, beyond the reach of a person standing on the floor.

pendant switch

pendent   Same as **pendant**.

pendentive   **1.** One of a set of curved wall surfaces which form a transition between a dome (or its drum) and the supporting masonry. **2.** In medieval architecture and derivatives, one of a set of surfaces vaulted outward from a pier, corbel, or the like.

pendentive bracketing   Corbeling in the general form of a pendentive; common in Moorish and Muslim architecture.

pendentive cradling   The curved ribs in arched and vaulted ceilings, used to carry or support the plasterwork.

pendent post, pendant post   **1.** In a medieval principal roof truss, a short post placed against the wall, its lower end supported on a

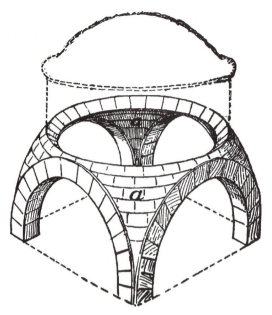

pendentives, 1:   *a*

pendentive, 2

corbel or capital, and its upper end carrying the tie beam or hammer beam. **2.** The support of an arch across the angles of a square.

pendent sprinkler   A **fire sprinkler** (i.e., sprinkler head) designed to be installed below the piping in a sprinkler system; the water stream discharged by the head is directed downward against a deflector (a flat-toothed disk) that develops the sprinkler spray pattern.

pendice   See **penthouse**.

pendiculated   Supported by a **pendicule**.

pendicule   A small pillar which serves as a support.

pendill   Same as **pendant, 2**.

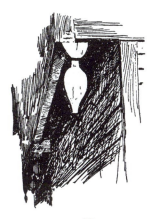

pendill

pendulum saw   See **swing saw**.

penetralia   **1.** The interior part of a building, as a sanctuary. **2.** An inner apartment.

penetrating finish   A low-viscosity oil or varnish which penetrates wood, leaving a very thin film at the surface.

penetration   **1.** The intersection of two vaulting surfaces. **2.** The consistency of a bituminous material expressed as the distance (in hundredths of a centimeter) that a standard needle vertically penetrates a sample of the material under known conditions of loading, time, and temperature. Unless otherwise specified, the load, time, and temperature are understood to be 100 g, 5 sec, and 25°C (77°F), respectively.

penetration resistance   **1.** The resistance by a subsoil to penetration by pile, casing, or sampling device; measured by the number of blows of a hammer of specified weight, falling through a specified distance to drive it a specified distance. **2.** See **standard penetration resistance**.

penetration test   A test which measures the relative density of silt or sand at the bottom of a borehole. Also see **dynamic penetration test** and **static penetration test**.

peninsula-base kitchen cabinet   A kitchen cabinet which extends outward at right angles from a row of cabinets and has one exposed end.

Penn plan   Similar to the **Quaker plan**, but having an **interior chimney** rather than an **exterior chimney**.

Pennsylvania Dutch   The German-speaking immigrants and their descendants who settled in Pennsylvania primarily during the 18th century. For examples of their architecture, see **bank barn, forebay barn, German Barn, hex barn, Pennsylvania Dutch barn, pfeiler, rauchkammer, springhouse**.

Pennsylvania Dutch barn, Pennsylvania barn   A two-story barn, built into the slope of a hill, whose upper structure overhangs the story below on the downhill side.

penny, penny-size   **1.** A unit denoting the length of a nail; for the **common nail**, and others which have been standardized, it also is an indication of the shank and head diameter. **2.** (*Abbr.* d) A suffix indicating the size of a nail; the size specifies the length of the nail and the number of nails per pound, e.g., a 2d nail is 1 in. long and there are 875 per pound.

pent   **1.** Same as **chimney pent**. **2.** Same as **pent roof**. **3.** A small room, lean-to, or shed, often with one or more open sides.

pentachlorophenol   A toxic, oil-soluble chemical; widely used as a wood preservative for protection against decay and insects.

pentacle   In Gothic tracery a five-pointed star motif with a pentagon in the center.

pentastyle   A term descriptive of a portico having five columns in front.

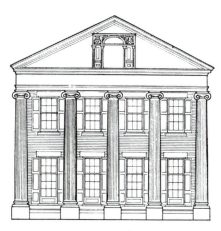

pentastyle

penthouse, pendice, pentice A structure occupying usually less than half the roof area of a flat-roofed building, and used: **1.** to house equipment for elevator, ventilation or air conditioning, or other mechanical or electrical systems serving the building, or **2.** to house one or more apartments, access to which is gained by a stair or stairs, or a separate elevator but usually not by the building's main elevators. **3.** An **appentice**.

pentice **1.** A small **pent roof, 1** on a side of a building, often restricted to the area over a door. **2.** See **penthouse**.

pent roof **1.** A small eaves-like projection from the façade of a house between the first and second floors; has a single straight slope; may provide very limited shelter for a window or door directly below, but is usually merely decorative. Frequently called a **visor roof**; also see **skirt-roof**. **2.** Same as **shed roof**.

pepperbox A small cylindrical tower or turret resembling the shape of a pepperbox used to sprinkle ground pepper; often has a conical roof.

pepperbox turret A turret circular in plan and with some form of conical or domical roof.

peppermint test A **scent test**, in a plumbing system, using oil of peppermint as the source of odor.

percentage agreement An agreement for professional services in which the compensation is based upon a percentage of the **construction cost**.

percentage fee Compensation based upon a percentage of **construction cost**. Also see **fee**.

percentage humidity The ratio of the weight of water vapor in a pound of dry air to the weight of water vapor that would be present if the same weight of air were saturated; the ratio is expressed as a percentage.

percentage reinforcement The ratio of cross-sectional area of reinforcing steel to the effective cross-sectional area of a member, expressed as a percentage.

percentage void The percentage of superficial area which is lost by holes, perforations, or cores.

percent fines **1.** The percentage of material in aggregate finer than a given sieve, usually the 74-μm (No. 200) sieve. **2.** The amount of fine aggregate in a concrete mixture expressed as a percentage, by absolute volume, of the total amount of aggregate.

percent saturation The ratio of the volume of water in a given soil mass to the total volume of intergranular space, expressed as a percentage.

percent voids See **percentage void**.

perch A unit of cubic measure used by stone masons; usually 16½ ft by 1½ ft by 1 ft (5.03 m by 0.46 m by 0.30 m).

perched water table A **water table** (usually of limited area) maintained above the normal free water elevation by the presence of an intervening relatively impervious confining strata.

perclose See **parclose**.

percolation The **seepage** of water through a porous material, such as soil.

percolation test A test to determine the rate at which a particular soil absorbs **effluent**; a hole is dug in the soil and filled with water, then the rate at which the water level drops is measured.

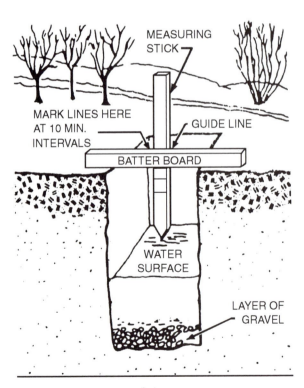

percolation test

percussion drill A **drill, 3**, usually driven by compressed air, in which the drilling action is the result of a series of impacts transmitted by a drill rod to a drill bit.

perennial A plant or shrub whose life cycle is greater than 2 years.

PERF On drawings, abbr. for "perforate."

perfect diffusion 1. *(in lighting)* The condition in which light flux is uniformly scattered in all directions so that the luminance (radiance) is equal in all directions. 2. *(in room acoustics)* The condition in which sound waves travel in all directions with equal probability so that the sound level of the reflected sound is equal throughout the room.

perfection A long red cedar shingle having a butt thickness of ⁹⁄₁₆ in. (1.4 cm).

perforated brick *(Brit.)* A brick or block in which holes passing through it exceed 25% of its volume, and in which the holes are not small (as defined under **solid masonry unit, 2**); up to three holes, not exceeding 5 sq in. (32.5 sq cm) each, may be incorporated as an aid to handling.

perforated facing In an acoustical assembly, any flexible or rigid perforated sheet or board designed as a protective surface allowing free access of sound to an underlying layer of sound-absorptive material.

perforated gypsum lath A **gypsum lath** which has perforations to provide mechanical keying of the base-coat plaster.

perforated hardboard See **pegboard**.

perforated metal Sheet metal usually having a regular pattern of perforations; available in many designs.

perforated metal pan, metal pan The exposed finish portion of an acoustical ceiling

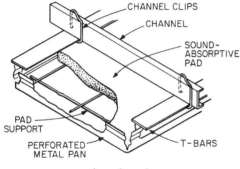

perforated metal pan

assembly, in which the metal pan contains and protects a separate pad or layer of sound-absorptive material.

perforated tape A type of tape used in finishing joints between gypsum boards.

perforated tape   covering a joint

perforated tracery Same as **net tracery**.

perforated wall See **pierced wall**.

performance bond A bond of the contractor in which a surety guarantees to the owner that the work will be performed in accordance with the **contract documents**; frequently combined with the **labor and material payment bond**; except where prohibited by statute.

performance curve A graphic representation of an operating characteristic of a piece of equipment, such as a fan; shows how such a characteristic varies as a function of a single parameter (for example, volume flow rate *vs.* fan speed).

performance requirement A requirement that a material, device, piece of equipment, or a system must possess a stated characteristic.

performance specification A **specification** based on the performance required of a given assembly, component, device, equipment, or material. Often such a specification refers to relevant standards.

performance standard In building construction, a **standard** which defines the required performance of the building (taken as a whole) or of specified building components.

perget Same as **parget**.

pergola 1. A garden structure with an open wooden-framed roof, often latticed, supported by regularly spaced posts or columns. The structure, often covered by climbing plants such as vines or roses, shades a walk or passageway. 2. A colonnade which has such a structure.

pergula   Same as **pergola**.

periaktos   In an ancient Greek theatre, one of the two pieces of machinery placed on both sides of the stage for shifting scenes.

peribolos, peribolus   A wall enclosing a sacred area such as a temple or church grounds.

periclase   A crystalline mineral which is sometimes found in portland cement, portland cement clinker, and certain slags.

peridrome   In an ancient peripteral temple, the open space or passage between the walls of the cella and the surrounding columns.

peridromos   The narrow passage around the exterior of a peripteral building behind the surrounding columns.

periform   Pear-shaped; said of a roof in the form of a pear (as some baptisteries and Eastern churches) or said of a molding having a pear shape.

perimeter beam   A wood beam attached to the edges or exposed ends of floor joists.

perimeter bracing   A vertical bracing element that is located at the perimeter of a building; also called peripheral bracing.

perimeter drain   A **drain** at the base of a foundation wall that carries water away from it.

perimeter grouting   Grouting, at relatively low pressure, around the perimeter of an area which is subsequently grouted at a higher pressure.

perimeter heating system   A warm-air heating system in which the ducts are embedded in the concrete slab of a basementless house, around the perimeter of the rooms; heated air from the furnace is carried through the ducts to registers placed in or near the floor; air is returned to the furnace from registers near the ceiling.

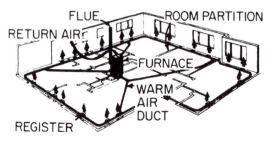

perimeter heating system

perimeter raceway   Same as **baseboard raceway**.

Period Revival   Not a specific architectural style, but rather a term that usually denotes a historic revival of some **architectural mode**; for examples, see **Colonial Revival, Georgian Revival, Mission Revival, Pueblo Revival, Spanish Colonial Revival, Tudor Revival**.

peripheral bracing   Same as **perimeter bracing**.

periphery wall   An **exterior wall**.

peripteral   A term descriptive of a classical building that is surrounded by a single row of columns.

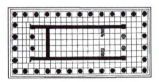

peripteral

peripteros, periptery   A building having a peristyle of a single row of columns.

peristalith   A circle of upright stones surrounding a burial mound.

peristasis   The ring of columns which encircles a peripteral building.

peristele   One of the upright stones in a **peristalith**.

peristerium   The inner or second ciborium.

peristyle   1. A colonnade surrounding either the exterior of a building or an open space, e.g., a courtyard. 2. The space so enclosed.

perithyride   Same as **ancon**.

perling   Same as **purlin**.

perlite   A siliceous volcanic rock; under heat it expands to 15 to 20 times its original volume, forming an excellent lightweight aggregate; used in plaster or gypsum wallboard, as loose-fill thermal insulation, and as an aggregate in concrete.

perlite plaster   Gypsum plaster which contains perlite as an aggregate instead of sand.

perlitic   Said of a material having a structure similar to that of **perlite**.

perm   A unit of water vapor **permeance**; in U.S. Customary units, 1 perm equals one grain of water vapor transmitted per one square foot per hour per inch of mercury pressure difference.

PERM On drawings, abbr. for "permanent."

permafrost Permanently frozen soil, subsoil, or other deposits in arctic or subarctic regions.

permanence Of an adhesive bond, the bond's resistance against deteriorating influences.

permanent bracing Bracing so designed and installed as to form an integral part of the final structure; may also serve as erection bracing.

permanent construction A term that usually encompasses construction at a job site other than the following: land preparation (such as clearing, grading, and filling); excavation for a basement, cellar, footings, foundations, or piers; erection of temporary forms; the installation on the property of accessory buildings such as garages or sheds not occupied as dwellings and not part of the main building.

permanent form Any concrete **form** that remains in place after the concrete has developed its design strength.

permanent formwork, permanent shuttering A type of **formwork** that remains in place after the concrete work has set.

permanent load The load which is permanently supported by a structure, such as the dead load or any fixed loads.

permanent set The change in length (expressed as a percentage of the original length) by which an elastic material fails to return to original length after being stressed for a standard period of time. Also see **set**.

permanent shore A **dead shore**.

permeability **1.** The property of a porous material which permits the passage of water vapor through it. Also see **permeance**. **2.** The property of soil, rock, or mantle which permits water to flow through it.

permeability test A test to determine movement through concrete of water under pressure.

permeameter An apparatus which measures the **permeability, 2** of soils and other similar materials.

permeance A measure of a material's resistance to water-vapor transmission, expressed in **perms**. Equal to the ratio of (a) the rate of water vapor transmission through a material or assembly between its two parallel surfaces to (b) the vapor pressure differential between the surfaces.

permit A document issued by a governmental authority having jurisdiction to authorize specific work by the applicant.

PERP On drawings, abbr. for "perpendicular."

perpend, perpend stone A rectangular stone set with its longest dimensions perpendicular to the face of a masonry wall; extends through the entire thickness of the wall so that it is exposed on both faces of the wall.

Perpendicular style, Rectilinear style The last and longest phase of Gothic architecture in England, ca. 1350–1550, following upon the Decorated style and eventually succeeded by Elizabethan architecture. Characterized by vertical emphasis in structure and frequently elaborate fan vaults. Its final development (1485–1547) is often referred to as Tudor architecture.

perpendicular tracery, rectilinear tracery Tracery of the Perpendicular style with repeated perpendicular mullions often rising to the curve of the arch, the mullions crossed at intervals by horizontal transoms producing repeated vertical rectangles.

perpendicular tracery

perpendiculum A plumb line, employed by ancient masons, bricklayers, etc.

perpend wall, perpeyn wall A wall built of perpends or of ashlar stones, all of which reach from one side to the other.

perpend wall

perpeyn Same as **perpend**.

perron **1.** A formal terrace or platform, esp. one centered on a gate or doorway. **2.** An outdoor flight of steps, usually symmetrical, leading to a terrace, platform, or doorway of a large building.

perron, 2

Persian A **telamon**, esp. one portrayed in Persian dress.

persienne An exterior **louver window** having adjustable slats.

person According to most **codes**: an individual, partnership, corporation, or other legal entity.

persona A mask of terra-cotta, marble, etc., designed to imitate the human face or the head of an animal, usually in grotesque form, em-

Persian

persona

ployed as an antefix in buildings, as an ornament for discharging water, or as a gargoyle.)

674

personal injury In insurance terminology, injury or damage to the character or reputation of a person, as well as bodily injury. Personal injury insurance usually covers such situations as false arrest, malicious prosecution, willful detention or imprisonment, libel, slander, defamation of character, wrongful eviction, invasion of privacy, and wrongful entry. Also see **bodily injury**.

personal property Movables and other property not classified as **real property**.

perspective **1.** The technique of representing solid objects upon a flat surface. **2.** A picture or drawing employing this technique.

perspective center The point of origin or termination of bundles of perspective rays.

perspective drawing A graphic representation of a **project** or part thereof as it would appear three-dimensionally.

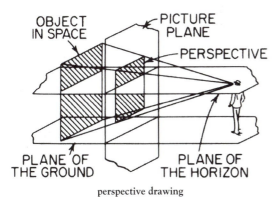

perspective drawing

perspective plane Any plane containing the perspective center.

perspective projection The projection of points by straight lines drawn through them from some given point to an intersection with the plane of projection.

PERT **1.** Acronym for "project evaluation and review technique." **2.** See **program estimation revaluation technique**.

pertica In medieval churches, a beam behind the altar from which relics were suspended on festival days.

PERT schedule A PERT chart of the activities and events anticipated in a work process. Also see **critical path method**.

pervious cesspool See **cesspool, 1**.

pervious soil A soil which allows relatively free movement of water.

pessulus A bolt for fastening a leaf of an ancient Roman door. Their doors, usually having two leafs, had two (sometimes four) bolts fixed to them—one at the top and one at the bottom of each leaf.

petal One of the overlapping shingles or tiles in **imbrication**.

pet cock, draw cock A small valve installed in a piping system or on a piece of equipment to drain it or to release air pockets.

Petersburg standard See **Petrograd standard**.

Petit truss A modified form of the **Pratt truss**, having subdiagonals.

petrifying liquid **1.** A low-viscosity penetrating solution of a waterproofing material for use on masonry surfaces. **2.** An additive for distempers.

Petrograd standard A British unit of timber measure: 165 cu ft (4.67 cu m).

petrographic analysis A laboratory determination of the mineralogical and chemical character of rocks; by extension, an analysis of the constituents of concrete, yielding the approximate cement content.

petroleum asphalt Asphalt which is refined directly from petroleum; of two types, *asphalt base* and *paraffin base*.

petroleum hydrocarbon Any of a number of solvents obtained from crude petroleum; used to lower the viscosity of oils and resins contained in paints.

petroleum spirit See **mineral spirit**.

pew In a house of worship, one of a number of fixed benches with backs; also see **box pew**.

pew

pew chair A hinged seat, attached to the end of a church pew.

pfa Abbr. for British term **pulverised-fuel ash**.

PFD On drawings, abbr. for "preferred."

pfeiler A pillar or pier that supports the **forebay** in a Pennsylvania Dutch barn.

ph Abbr. for **phot**.

pH A measure of the acidity or alkalinity of a solution; numerically equal to 7.0 for a neutral solution; the pH value increases with increasing alkalinity and decreases with increasing acidity. Also see **pH value**.

PH **1.** On drawings, abbr. for "phase." **2.** Abbr. for **Phillips head**.

1PH Abbr. for "single phase."

3PH Abbr. for "three phase."

phantom line A broken line indicating an alternative position of delineated parts of an object, repeated detail, or the relative position of an absent part; usually a fine line of alternating long and short dashes.

phased application The application of built-up roofing plies in two or more operations, usually at least one day apart.

phenol A class of acid organic compounds used in the manufacture of epoxy resins, phenol-formaldehyde resins, plasticizers, plastics, and wood preservatives.

phenol-formaldehyde resin, phenolic resin A thermosetting, waterproof, low-cost, mold-resistant, high-strength synthetic resin made from phenol and formaldehyde; has good resistance to aging; used extensively in the manufacture of adhesives, exterior and marine plywood, laminated products, and molded articles.

phenolic resin See **phenol-formaldehyde resin**.

Philadelphia leveling rod A two-piece leveling rod, with graduation marks so styled that it may be used as a **self-reading leveling rod**.

Philippine ebony See **ebony**.

Philippine mahogany, red lauan, white lauan The wood of trees of several genera found in the Philippines; not a true mahogany, but resembles true mahogany in grain; density ranges from very light to quite heavy; whitish-yellow to pink, brown, or dark red in color; the heavier, darker woods are generally durable and quite strong and are used like true mahogany; the lighter-weight, colored woods are used for interior carpentry, plywood, and general construction.

Phillips head A screw having a special head with crossed slots which are perpendicular to each other.

phon A unit of loudness level.

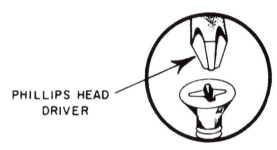

Phillips head shown with a Phillips head driver

phosphated metal A metal surface which has been pretreated with hot phosphoric acid, to prepare it for receiving a finished coating.

phosphor A substance capable of luminescence, such as a fluorescent powder which absorbs ultraviolet power and reemits it as visible light; used to coat the inside of various electric-discharge lamps.

phosphorescence The emission of light as the result of the absorption of electromagnetic radiation; continues for a noticeable length of time after excitation.

phosphorescent paint See **luminous paint**.

phosphor mercury-vapor lamp A high-pressure **mercury-vapor lamp** consisting of an arc tube enclosed by a phosphor-coated glass envelope; the phosphor generates colors not produced by the arc.

phot A unit of illumination equal to 1 lumen per square centimeter. *Abbr.* ph.

photoelectric cell A device incorporated in an electric circuit; in response to light that falls on the cell, the electrical output or the resistance varies; used in measuring devices and in control devices that depend on illumination level or the interruption of a light beam.

photoelectric control A control function which is actuated by a change in incident light.

photoelectric smoke detector A sensor used to initiate a fire alarm when smoke reduces the light received by a photoelectric cell in a device containing a light source; most effective in the early detection of fires in the smoldering stage.

photogrammetry The technology of obtaining reliable distance measurements by photograph.

photographing Same as **telegraphing**.

photometer Any instrument that measures photometric quantities such as luminance, luminous intensity, luminous flux, and illumination.

photometry The measurement of quantities associated with light.

Phrygian marble Same as **pavonazzo, 2**.

phthalocyanine pigments Exceptionally durable, permanent green and blue pigments used in paints, enamels, and plastics.

pH value A number denoting the degree of acidity or of basicity (alkalinity); 7 is a neutral value; acidity increases with decreasing values below 7; basicity increases with increasing values above 7.

physical disability, physical handicap Legally, any of the following handicaps: an impairment requiring the use of a wheelchair; an impairment causing difficulty or insecurity in walking or climbing stairs or requiring the use of braces, crutches, or other artificial supports; impairment (partial or total) of hearing or sight, causing likelihood of exposure to danger in public places; or impairment due to conditions of aging or incoordination. Also see **Americans with Disabilities Act**.

physical stability The ability of a product to maintain its physical dimensions and properties when exposed to conditions normally encountered in its service environment.

piache A covered arched walk, or portico.

piano hinge See **continuous hinge**.

piano nobile In Renaissance architecture and derivatives, a floor with formal reception and dining rooms; the principal story in a house, usually one flight above the ground.

piazza **1.** A public open space or square surrounded by buildings. **2.** A term occasionally used for a raised porch or veranda in French Vernacular architecture or in American Colonial architecture and derivatives (especially in the South); often supported by columns or posts.

piazza house A term occasionally used for a **Charleston house**.

pick A hand tool used for loosening and breaking up closely compacted soil and rock; consists of a steel head which usually is curved, with a point on one or both ends, mounted on a wooden handle.

pick and dip, Eastern method, New England method A method of laying brick whereby the bricklayer simultaneously picks up a brick with one hand and, with the other hand, enough mortar on a trowel to lay the brick.

pickax A **pick** or **mattock**.

pick dressing The first rough dressing of hard quarried stone by use of a heavy pick or wedge-shaped hammer.

picked finish In stone masonry, a surface finish covered with small pits produced by a pick or chisel point striking the face perpendicularly.

picket Same as **pale, 1**.

picket fence A fence formed of a series of vertical pales, posts, stakes, rods, etc. (sometimes sharpened at the upper end) which are joined together by horizontal rails.

picking, stugging, wasting Same as **dabbing**.

picking up The blending of a coat of freshly applied paint with another over which it is applied. Also see **pulling up**.

pickled Said of a metal surface which has been treated with a strong oxidizing agent, such as nitric acid, to clean, to provide a strong inert oxide film, and to increase corrosion resistance.

pickup The unwanted adherence of solids in contact with the open surface of a sealant.

pickup load The abnormal rate of heat consumption that takes place when a heating system is first turned on; represents the heat dissipated in bringing the piping and radiators to their normal operating temperature.

picnostyle, pycnostyle See **intercolumniation**.

picowatt (pW) A unit of power equal to a millionth of one-millionth of a watt (i.e., 10^{-12} W).

picture molding, picture rail Any of numerous types of moldings or other such devices formed so as to support picture hooks at or near the ceiling.

picture plane In perspective drawing, a plane upon which can be projected a system of lines or rays from an object to form an image or picture.

Picturesque Gothic A term sometimes applied to **High Victorian Gothic architecture**.

Picturesque Movement A movement established by a group of architects from about 1840 to 1900, particularly in Europe, wedded to the concept that architectural ideals should look away from formal Classical architecture and instead should embrace the romanticized past. The term "Picturesque" is not indicative of a particular architectural style, but is suggestive of a number of styles or modes of architecture that were related to the romanticized past, including: **Exotic Revival, Gothic Revival, Italianate style, Queen Anne style, Richardsonian Romanesque style, Second Empire style, Stick style, Swiss Cottage architecture**.

picture window In a home or apartment, a large, fixed window, often between two narrower operable windows; usually located so as to present the most attractive view of the exterior.

pieced timber **1.** A timber made from two or more pieces of wood fitted together. **2.** A damaged timber repaired with a fitted piece of wood.

piece mark A mark placed on an individual piece of an assembly, designating its location in the assembly as indicated in shop drawings.

pièce sur pièce construction In French Vernacular architecture, a method of construction brought to Louisiana from Canada by the Acadians (now known as *Cajuns*); used in building small houses of well-finished, heavy, rectangular hewn timbers (*pièces*). Each timber, laid horizontally, had a dovetail notch at each end, forming a strong, interlocking rigid joint with another appropriately notched timber at right angles to it.

pien, piend **1.** The ridge of a roof. **2.** An **arris**; a salient angle.

pien check, piend check In a stair constructed with hanging steps of stone, a rabbet cut along the lower front edge of a step which fits into the back of the step next below it.

piend rafter Same as **hip rafter**.

pien joint In a stone stair, the joint between two steps which are secured by a **pein check**.

pier **1.** A column designed to support concentrated load. **2.** A member, usually in the form of

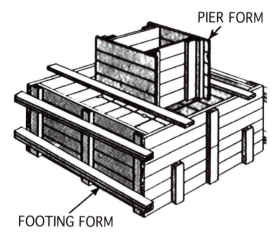

typical concrete form for a **pier, 1** and its footing

a thickened section, which forms an integral part of a wall; usually placed at intervals along the wall to provide lateral support or to take concentrated vertical loads.

pier-and-spandrel Descriptive of a wall construction having the vertical metal columns which project beyond the plane of the windows and the **spandrels**.

pier arch An arch resting on piers, esp. one along a **nave arcade**.

pier block See **double corner block**.

pier bonding A method of bonding piers to walls by bond bricks or stones.

pier buttress A **pier, 1** which receives the thrust of a flying buttress.

pierced louver, punched louver A louver that is formed in the face sheets or panels of a door.

pierced wall, perforated wall, screen wall A nonbearing masonry wall in which an ornamental pierced effect is achieved by alternating rectangular or shaped blocks with open spaces.

pierced work Ornamentation characterized by patterns formed by perforations; also see **gingerbread** and **openwork**.

pier glass A tall, narrow mirror, often running from floor to ceiling, which covers the whole or a large part of the wall between two windows.

pierrotage In French Vernacular architecture of the southern United States, lime mortar or clay mixed with small stones; used as infilling between half-timbering with diagonal braces (columbage); also see **bousillage**.

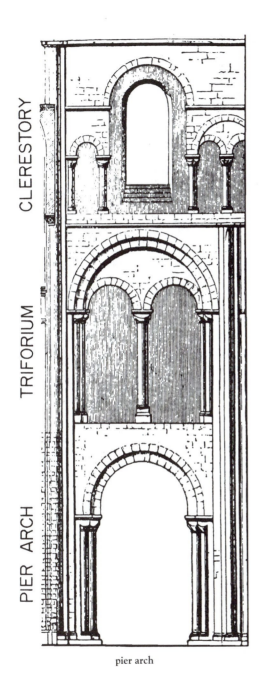

CLERESTORY

TRIFORIUM

PIER ARCH

pier arch

piezometer A device for measuring liquid pressure; used to measure the **pore water pressure** in soil.

pigeonhole 1. One of a series of small compartments. 2. A seat in the top row of a gallery or in the uppermost gallery in a theatre.

pigeonhole corner An acute angle formed in a brick wall, using square-ended bricks that have not been shaped.

pigeonholed wall Same as **honeycomb wall**.

pigeonnier, pigeon house Same as **dovecote**.

pigeon roof A roof having four steeply sloping sides that meet in a point, occasionally with a decorative element atop it; also called a pyramid roof.

pig iron Crude high-carbon iron ore that has been smelted and cast into ingots; may be remelted and used as a source of material for architectural cast-iron products, or may be further refined for use in producing steel.

pigment 1. A finely ground inorganic or organic powder which is dispersed in a liquid vehicle to make paint; may provide, in addition to color, many of the essential properties of a paint—opacity, hardness, durability, and corrosion resistance. 2. Coloring matter, usually in the form of an insoluble fine powder, used to color concrete, etc.

pigment figure A pattern in wood consisting of variations in color rather than variations in grain; found in such woods as rosewood and zebrawood.

pigment-to-binder ratio The ratio of the weight of pigment to the weight of binder in a paint, e.g., the number of pounds of pigment per 100 lb of binder.

pigment volume concentration See **PVC, 1**.

pigtail A flexible conductor which is attached to an electric component, providing a means of connecting the component to a circuit.

pigtail splice A type of connection made between two electric conductors; formed by placing the ends of the conductors side by side and then twisting the ends of the two conductors around one another.

pig tin A metal which is at least 99.80% pure tin.

pila 1. In churches in Italy, a holy-water font, consisting of a bowl mounted on a shaft, as distinguished from a font hanging from or secured to a wall or pier. 2. A square block or epistyle, just over the columns, to support a rooftimber. 3. A mortar which is valuable or curious on account of its antiquity or design.

pilaster

pilaster   **1.** An engaged pier or pillar, often with capital and base. **2.** Decorative features that imitate engaged piers but are not supporting structures, as a rectangular or semicircular member used as a simulated pillar in entrances and other door openings and fireplace mantels; often contains a base, shaft, and capital; may be constructed as a projection of the wall itself.

pilasters

pilaster base   Same as **base block**.

pilaster block   See **double corner block**.

pilastered chimney   A chimney shaft having **pilasters** on its faces to provide a decorative effect and/or to enhance its structural strength.

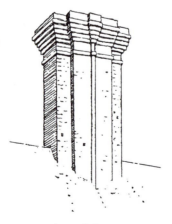

pilastered chimney

pilaster face   The form for the front surface of a pilaster, parallel to the wall.

pilaster mass   An engaged pier built up with the wall, usually without the capital and base of a pilaster.

pilaster side   The form for the side surface of a pilaster, perpendicular to the wall.

pilaster strip, lesene   Same as **pilaster mass** but usually applied to slender piers of slight projection; in medieval architecture and derivatives, often joining an arched corbel table.

pilastrade   A row of **pilasters**.

pile   **1.** A concrete, steel, or wood column, usually less than 2 ft (0.6 m) in diameter, which is driven or otherwise introduced into the soil, usually to carry a vertical load or to provide lateral support. **2.** See **carpet pile**. **3.** A term used to indicate the number of rooms in a house from front to rear; for example, a double-pile house has two rooms between the façade and the rear wall of the house.

pile bearing capacity   The load on a pile, or the load per pile, on a group of piles, required to produce a condition of failure.

pile bent   Piles which are driven in a row which is transverse to the long dimensions of a structure and which are fastened together by a **pile cap** and sometimes bracing.

pile butt   The head of a pile.

pile cap   **1.** A slab or connecting beam which covers the heads of a group of piles, tying them together so that the structural load is distributed and they act as a single unit. **2.** A metal cap which is placed, as temporary protection, over the head of a precast pile while it is being driven into the ground.

pile core   Same as **mandrel, 1**.

pile cushion   A device placed between the **drive cap** and the top end of a concrete pile as protection against crushing and spalling.

pile driver   A machine for delivering repeated blows to the top of a pile for driving it into the ground; consists of a frame which supports and guides a hammer weight, together with a mechanism for raising and dropping the hammer or for driving the hammer by air or steam.

pile driving cap   See **drive cap**.

pile eccentricity   The deviation of a pile from its plan location, or the out-of-plumbness of a pile; reduces the vertical load capacity.

pile encasement A protective covering on a **pile**.

pile extractor A machine for pulling piles from the ground, e.g., by means of a double-acting pile hammer attached to a pile, each blow of which produces an upward force on the pile.

pile foot The lower end of a pile.

pile foundation A system of piles, pile caps, and straps (if required) that transfers the structural load to the bearing stratum into which the piles are driven.

pile friction The sum of friction forces acting on an embedded pile; is limited by (a) the adhesion between the pile and the soil and/or (b) the shear strength of the soil adjacent to the pile.

pile hammer Equipment employing a weight (hammer) which strikes a pile or beam, forcing it into the ground; the weight may fall freely, under the action of gravity, or be powered by steam, compressed air, or a diesel engine.

pile head The upper end of a pile.

pile height See **carpet pile height**.

pile helmet Same as **pile cap, 2**.

pile hoop Same as **drive band**.

pile load test A test in which a load (usually 150% or 200% of the design load) is applied on a pile to verify or aid in the selection of a design load.

pile penetration The depth which is reached by the tip of a **pile**.

pile rig Same as **pile driver**.

pile ring Same as **drive band**.

pile shoe A pointed or rounded metal device on a **pile foot** to aid in pile driving.

pile tolerance 1. The permitted deviation of a pile from the vertical. 2. The permitted deviation in the horizontal plane.

pile tower Same as **peel**.

pilier In **French Vernacular architecture** of Louisiana, a stack of rectangular blocks of (rot-resistant) cypress wood used to support a Creole house, transferring the structural load from the **groundsill** to the earth below.

pilier cantonné High Gothic form of the **compound pier**, with a massive central core to which are attached at 90° intervals four colonettes sup-

porting the arcade, the aisle vaultings, and the responds of the nave vaults.

piling The property of a paint which causes it to gain viscosity rapidly during application, making it difficult to apply a smooth uniform film.

piling pipe A seamless pipe or welded pipe, having beveled ends for welding or plain ends, where the cylinder section acts as a shell to form cast-in-place concrete piles or as a permanent load-carrying member.

pillar A column, pier, pilaster, or post that is capable of providing major vertical support.

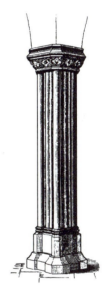

pillar: Perpendicular style

pillar bolt A stud bolt which projects; used for supporting a part near its outer end.

pillar-stone 1. Same as **cornerstone**. 2. A stone memorial, usually pillar-shaped.

pillow capital See **cushion capital**.

pillowed See **pulvinated**.

pillowwork The decorative treatment of any surface with pillow-like projections.

pilot boring In foundation construction, a preliminary boring or series of borings used to determine boring requirements.

pilot hole A hole which serves as a guide for a nail or screw, or for drilling a larger-size hole.

piloti (pl. **pilotis**) One of a number of isolated columns, posts, or piles that support a building, raising it above ground level; the ground floor is open to the exterior.

pilot lamp   Same as **pilot light, 1**.

pilot light   **1.** A light which is associated with and indicative of the operation of a circuit, control, or device. **2.** A small flame (which burns constantly) used to ignite the burner in a gas appliance.

pilot nail   A temporary nail which is used to hold boards or timbers together until the permanent nails are driven in.

pilot punch   A machine punch in which the cutting tool is provided with a small central plug which fits into a hole in the material and acts as a guide for punching a larger hole.

pilot valve   An automatic valve that regulates the air pressure in a compressor.

pin   **1.** A peg or bolt of wood, metal, or any other material, which is used to fasten or hold something in place, fasten things together, or serve as a point of attachment or support. **2.** A round bar of steel used to connect members of a truss.

pinacotheca   A picture gallery.

pinaculum   In ancient Greek or Roman architecture, a roof terminating in a ridge (the ordinary covering for a temple; in contrast, private houses had flat roofs).

pinax   A decorative panel which fills the intercolumniations of the **proskenion** or the thyromata (pl. of **thyroma**) at the back of the stage of an ancient Greek or Roman theatre.

pincers   A tool having two hinged jaws which can be closed tightly; used for gripping objects.

pinch bar, claw bar, ripping bar, wrecking bar   A steel bar with a U-shaped claw at one end and a chisel point at the other; often used as a lever for lifting heavy objects.

pin-connected truss   Any truss having its main members joined by pins.

pin drill   A drill for boring **pin holes, 5** in truss members.

pine   The wood of a number of species of coniferous evergreen distributed throughout the world; may be divided into two classes: soft (white) pine and hard (pitch) pine. An important source of construction lumber and plywood.

pineapple   **1.** An ovoid, imbricated finial. **2.** A decorative molding.

pineapple, 2

pineapple ornament   A decoration, usually carved in wood or cast in plaster, that resembles the cone of a pine tree; often found as a **pendent** or **finial.**

pine oil   A strong, high-boiling-point solvent obtained from the resin of pine trees; used in paint to provide good flow properties in application.

pine shingles   Shingles of pine wood; much used in Europe and, at one time, in the U.S.A.

pine tar   A viscous black substance, used in roofing, which is manufactured by distilling pine wood.

pin hinge   A hinge having a pin on which the hinge pivots; also see **loose-pin hinge.**

pinhole   **1.** In wood, a round hole usually less than ¼ in. (0.6 cm) in diameter, caused by the boring of a beetle or worm in standing timber. **2.** In a plaster coat, a surface defect resulting from trapped air bubbles. **3.** In a paint film, one of many small holes caused by: (*a*) impurities (in the paint, on the paintbrushes or rollers, or on the surface being painted); (*b*) solvent bubbling; or (*c*) moisture. **4.** In the surface of a ceramic body, glaze, or porcelain enamel, an imperfection characterized by a depression resembling a pinprick. **5.** A hole in a structural member through which a **pin, 2** passes and connects with another member.

pin joint   A joint in which one member is fastened to another by a pin so that rotational movement at the point of joining is not restricted.

pin knot   **1.** (*U.S.A.*) A knot in wood that is no larger than ½ in. (1.27 cm) in diameter. **2.** (*Brit.*) A knot in wood less than ½ in. (0.64 cm) in diameter.

pinnacle   **1.** An apex. **2.** In Gothic architecture and derivatives, a small, largely ornamental body or shaft terminated by a pyramid or spire.

3. A turret, or part of a building elevated above the main building.

pinnacle, 2: St. Mary's, Oxford

pinned joint   A joint that is secured by the use of wood dowels rather than by wedges.

pinner   In masonry construction, a small stone which supports a larger one.

pinning   **1.** Fastening or securing with a **pin**. **2.** A **foundation** or **underpinning**.

pinning in   The operation of filling in the joints of masonry with spalls or chips of stone.

pinning up   The operation of driving in wedges in order to bring an upper work fully to bear on **shoring** or underpinning beneath.

pinrail   See **fly rail**.

pin spot   A spotlight focused to a narrow beam.

pintle   A pin on which something is hung and about which it revolves; esp. one that projects upward.

pintle hinge   A **hinge** that pivots about an upright pin or bolt.

pin tumbler   A lock mechanism having a series of small cylindrical pins which form obstacles to rotation of the locking mechanism unless actuated by the proper key.

pipe   A continuous tubular conduit, generally leakproof, for the transport of liquids and gases.

pipe batten   A **batten, 9** used to hang scenery from stage rigging in a theatre.

pipe bend   A pipe **fitting, 1** used to achieve a change in direction.

pipe bracket   Any of a variety of shaped metal assemblies used to support a pipe from a wall or floor.

pipe chase   See **chase**.

pipe column   A column made of steel pipe; may be filled with concrete.

pipe coupling   A **coupling**.

pipe covering   A wrapping around a pipe which acts as thermal insulation and/or a vapor barrier.

pipe cross   A pipe **fitting, 1** having four openings in the same place, at right angles to each other.

pipe cross

pipe cutter   A hand tool for cutting pipe or tubing; one end of the tool, which partially encircles the pipe, carries one or more sharp wheels; the cutting edge of the wheels is forced against

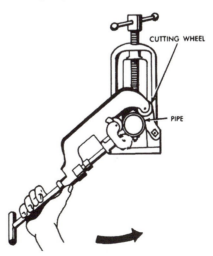

pipe cutter   cutting pipe

the pipe by a screw on the other end of the tool; cutting is effected by rotating the tool around the pipe.

pipe die Any of several types of adjustable tools for cutting threads on pipes used in plumbing.

pipe duct A duct in which only pipes are run.

pipe elbow See **elbow, 1**.

pipe exfiltration See **exfiltration, 2**.

pipe expansion joint A device, other than a fabricated U-bend, which expands or contracts to compensate for pipe contraction or expansion.

pipe fitting See **fitting, 1**.

pipe gasket A **gasket, 2** in a piping system.

pipe hanger A device to support a pipe or group of pipes from a slab, beam, ceiling, or other structural element.

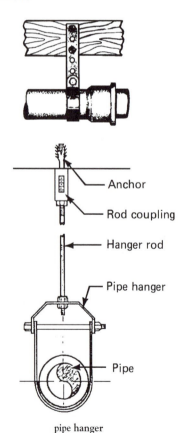

pipe hanger

pipe heating cable See **strip heater**.

pipe hook A device for supporting a pipe from a wall.

pipe infiltration See **infiltration**.

pipe insulation Thermal insulation (such as fiberglass or foamed plastic) usually manufactured in hemicylindrical shapes for pipes of various diameters.

45° pipe lateral A pipe fitting similar to a pipe tee except that the side opening is at a 45° angle.

pipelayer An attachment for a tractor or other prime mover that consists of a winch and a side boom for lowering sections of pipe into a trench.

pipeline heater A heater for a pipeline, usually wrapped around the piping and heated by an electric current; used to prevent the liquid in the piping from freezing or, changing its viscosity.

pipeline refrigeration Refrigeration provided by piping a refrigerant to a group of buildings from a central refrigerating plant.

pipe pile **1.** A pipe section heavy enough to be driven without a **mandrel, 1** having its lower end either open or closed; after the pipe is driven to its final position, it is filled with concrete. **2.** A pipe (either close-ended or open-ended) which serves as a pile.

pipe plug A threaded pipe fitting with male threads; used to close the end of a **ferrule** or a pipe having female threads.

pipe plug

pipe reducer For a pipe, see **reducer**.

pipe ring Any of a variety of circularly shaped metal assemblies used to support a pipe loosely from a suspended rod.

pipe run The path taken by piping.

pipe saddle A vertical support on which a pipe rests.

pipe schedule (sprinkler) system A fire sprinkler system in which the sizing of the pipes supplying the sprinklers is determined from a schedule based on occupancy classification; a specified number of sprinkler (heads) may be supplied for a specific size of pipe.

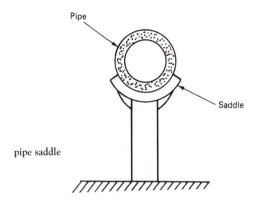

pipe saddle

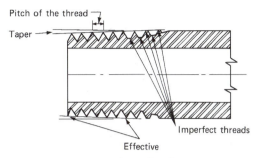

tapered pipe thread

pipe sleeve **1.** A cylindrical insert, placed in a form for a concrete wall, in a location where a pipe is to pierce the wall; the insert prevents concrete from flowing into the cylindrical opening. **2.** A pipe **coupling**.

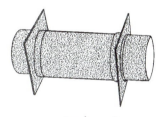

pipe sleeve, 1

pipe stock A device to hold a pipe die.

pipe stop A spigot in a pipe.

pipe strap A thin metal strip used to hang pipe.

pipe support A mount for supporting a large pipe; often on a **saddle, 3**. A support of this type may include a roller to permit movement of the pipe caused by its expansion and contraction.

pipe tee A T-shaped pipe fitting with two outlets, one at 90° to the connection to the main line.

pipe thread A V-cut screw thread, cut on the inside or the outside of a pipe (or on a pipe fitting, coupling, or connector); the diameter of the thread is not constant, but tapers.

pipe tongs A tool used by plumbers or pipe fitters to screw or unscrew lengths of pipe or pipe fittings.

pipe trim The exposed metal appurtenances of plumbing fixtures, such as faucets, spigots, and exposed traps.

pipe vise A vise for holding pipe or tubing during cutting or threading operations; the pipe is held either in V-shaped serrated jaws or (for larger pipe) by chains.

pipe wrench A hand tool having one jaw movable and the other relatively fixed, the two being shaped so as to tighten when placed on a pipe and rotated in one direction.

pipe wrench

piping **1.** The movement of soil particles by water which percolates through the soil, leading to the development of erosion channels. **2.** A run of pipe.

piping loss The loss of heat from piping between the source of heat and radiators.

pirca A type of crude wall construction using dry-laid unshaped stones, found in the Andes.

pisay Same as **pisé**.

piscina A shallow basin or sink, supplied with a drain pipe, generally recessed in a niche. (*See illustration p. 686.*)

pisé **1.** Same as rammed earth. **2.** A mixture of clay and chopped straw, sometimes with the addition of gravel; particularly used in wall construction. **3. Cob** used as a wall material.

pishtaq In Muslim or Persian architecture, a monumental gateway marking the entrance to a mosque, caravanserai, madrasah, or mausoleum.

pit **1.** An **orchestra pit. 2.** A small circular hole in a paint film; also see **pockmarking**. **3.** An excavation; a hole in the ground.

piscina

pit boards Horizontal boards used as **sheeting** to retain earth around a pit.

pitch **1.** The slope of a roof, usually expressed as a ratio of vertical rise to horizontal run, or in inches (centimeters) of rise per foot (meter) of run. **2.** See **grade. 3.** The slope of a stair flight, i.e., the ratio of the rise to the run of the flight. **4.** The distance between centers of bolts, rivets, and other fasteners in the same line. **5.** See **carpet pitch. 6.** In acoustics, that attribute of auditory sensation in which sounds may be ordered on a scale from low to high; depends primarily on the frequency of the sound stimulus. **7.** Any of various **resins. 8.** A dark, viscous, distillate of tar; used in caulking and paving; also called **pitch mastic.** Also see **coal tar pitch. 9.** In masonry, to square a stone with a chisel.

pitch board, gauge board A template, usually a right triangle in shape; used as a pattern to lay out the outline of stairs or the like; in stair construction, the base of the triangle is the exact width of the treads of the steps, and the perpendicular is the height of the riser.

pitch dimension Of stairs, the distance between the bases of the top and bottom risers in a flight, measured parallel to the slope.

pitched roof **1.** A steep gable roof having the same pitch on each side of a central ridge. **2.** Occasionally, a synonym for a **gable roof.**

pitched-roof dormer A dormer having a triangularly shaped gable.

pitched skylight A **skylight** whose members are inclined or pitched.

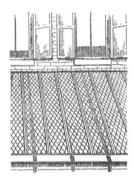

pitched skylight

pitched stone A rough-faced stone having each edge of the exposed face pitched at a slight bevel, nearly in the plane of the face.

pitcher house A wine cellar.

pitch-faced In masonry, having all arrises cut true and in the same plane, but with the face beyond the arris edges left comparatively rough, being simply dressed with a pitching chisel.

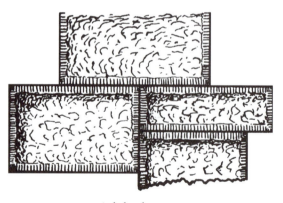

pitch-faced masonry

pitch fiber pipe Same as **bituminized fiber pipe.**

pitchhole A recess or depression occurring in the surface of a stone which has otherwise been more or less dressed to a true face for setting.

pitching chisel, pitching tool A mason's chisel having a wide, thick edge; used in rough **dressing.**

pitching piece   See **apron piece**.

pitching tool   See **pitching chisel**.

pitch knot   A knot associated with a local area of pitch or resin; usually found in softwoods.

pitch mastic   See **pitch, 8**.

pitch pine   Same as **yellow pine**.

pitch pocket   **1.** A defect in softwoods; consists of an opening in the grain that contains pitch or resin. Also called a **resin pocket**. **2.** A metal flange around the base of any roof-penetrating member (or component) which is filled with pitch or flashing cement to provide a seal.

pitch streak, resin streak   A local accumulation or streak of highly resinous wood in softwoods.

pith   The soft central core of a log.

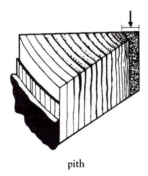

pith

pith fleck   A short dark streak in wood resembling pith, but caused by insect attack during growth.

pith knot   A knot with a small pith hole in the center.

pith ray   See **medullary ray**.

pitot tube   A device, used in conjunction with a suitable manometer or other pressure-reading

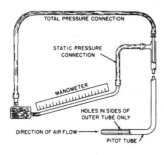

pitot tube

instrument, for measuring the velocity of air in a duct or water in a pipe.

pit-run gravel, bank-run gravel   Ungraded gravel as it is taken directly from a gravel pit.

pit sawing   An old method of handsawing timber lengthwise; the log is supported over a pit to provide easy access by men using a double-ended saw.

pitting   **1.** The development of small cavities in a surface, owing to phenomena such as corrosion, cavitation, or (as in concrete) localized disintegration. **2.** In plastering, see **popping**. **3.** The development of localized surface defects on a metal surface, e.g., small depressions, usually caused by electrochemical corrosion. **4.** The localized corrosion in the form of cavities which takes place on the surface of a metal.

pivot   **1.** A hinge. **2.** The axle or pin about which a window or door rotates.

pivoted door   A door hung on pivots (either center pivots or offset), as distinguished from one hung on hinges or on a sliding mechanism.

pivoted window   A window having a sash (ventilator) which rotates about fixed vertical or horizontal pivots, located at or toward the center, in contrast to one hung on hinges along an edge. Also see **vertically pivoted window**.

pivot window   A window that turns about hinges usually aligned along a vertical axis.

pixis, pix   A shrine to contain the host or consecrated wafer.

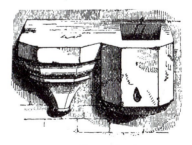

pixis and image bracket

PL   **1.** On drawings, abbr. for **pile**. **2.** On drawings, abbr. for **plate**. **3.** On drawings, abbr. for **plug**. **4.** On drawings, abbr. for "power line." **5.** Abbr. for "pipe line."

placage An ornamental thin masonry facing (revetment) of a building.

placard Same as **pargeting**.

placeability See **workability, 1**.

place brick Same as **salmon brick**.

placement The **placing** and **consolidation, 1** of concrete.

place of assembly **1.** A building (excluding dwelling units), or portion thereof, in which a specified number (the actual number depends on the local code) of persons may gather for recreational, educational, political, social, or other purposes, such as to await transportation, or to eat or drink. **2.** An outdoor space where a number of persons in excess of a specified minimum may gather for any of the above purposes.

placing **1.** The deposition and compaction of freshly mixed mortar or concrete in the place where it is to harden. **2.** The process of applying plastic terrazzo mix to the prepared surface.

placita A central enclosed courtyard in Spanish Colonial ranches in the Americas, surrounded by a high adobe wall; usually entered through a massive gate.

plafond A **ceiling**, esp. one of decorative character; flat or arched.

plain ashlar Stone facing that has been smoothed with a tool.

plain bar A **reinforcing bar** without surface deformations, or one having deformations that do not conform to the applicable requirements.

plain concrete, unreinforced concrete **1.** Concrete without reinforcement or reinforced only for shrinkage or temperature changes. **2.** Concrete without some other specific admixture or element, in contrast with concrete containing such an admixture or element, e.g., non-air-entrained concrete.

plain-cut joint In masonry, same as **rough-cut joint**.

plain lap Same as **lap joint, 2**.

plain masonry Masonry without reinforcement, or reinforced only for shrinkage or temperature change.

plain rail In a double-hung window, a **meeting rail** having the same thickness as other members of the frame of the sash.

plain reinforcement In reinforced concrete, any **reinforcement, 1** other than deformed reinforcement.

plain-sawn, bastard-sawn, flat-grained, flat-sawn, slash-sawn Descriptive of wood sawn so that the annual rings intersect the wide face at an angle of less than 45°.

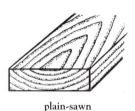

plain-sawn

Plains cottage, Plains house Typically, a relatively simple single-family, single-story house, constructed primarily of sod, having two to five rooms; primarily built in the 19th century in those parts of the Great Plains where sod was usually the only construction material conveniently obtainable; also see **sod house** and **straw bale house**.

plain tile A flat rectangular roofing tile of concrete or burnt clay; each tile has two projecting nibs for hanging the tile from battens.

plaisance Same as **pleasance**.

plan **1.** A two-dimensional graphic representation of the design, horizontal dimensions of a building, and location, as seen in a horizontal plane viewed from above, in contrast to a graphical representation representing a vertical plane (such as a **section, 2** or an **elevation, 1**). See **center-hall plan, city plan, cruciform plan, community plan, floor plan, four-square plan, gable-front-and-wing plan, gable-front plan, Georgian plan, ground plan, hall-and-parlor plan, hall-house plan, H-plan, linear plan, L-plan, one-room plan, open plan, Penn plan, Quaker plan, reflected ceiling plan, side-hall plan, single-room plan, three-room plan, T-plan, two-room plan, U-plan. 2.** When used in the plural, a set of drawings, including elevations and sections, that collectively define a building. **3.** See **city plan** and **town plan**.

planar frame A structural frame composed of individual members all of which are in the same plane.

planch (*Brit.*) **1.** A floorboard. **2.** A plank floor.

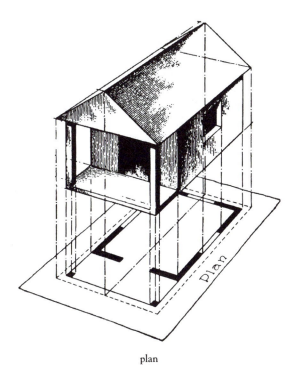

plan

planching Same as **flooring**.

plancier, planceer, plancer, plancher **1.** The soffit or underside of any projecting member, as a cornice. **2.** A **planch**.

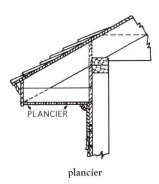

plancier

plancier piece A board which forms a **plancier**.

plan deposit See **deposit for bidding documents**.

plane **1.** A tool for smoothing wood surfaces; consists of a smooth soleplate, from the underside of which projects slightly the cutting edge of an inclined blade; there is an aperture in front of the

blade for the shavings to escape. **2.** A surface, any section through which by a like surface is a straight line. **3.** Of a column, the surface of a longitudinal section through the axis of the column.

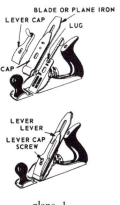

plane, 1

plane ashlar A stone block having tool marks on its surfaces.

planed lumber Same as **dressed lumber**.

planed matchboards See **dressed and matched boards**.

plane of weakness Of a structure under stress, that plane along which fracture is most likely to take place, as a result of design or accident or the properties of the structure and its loading.

plane surveying A branch of the art of surveying in which the surface of the earth is considered a plane surface; curvature of the earth is neglected, and computations are made using the formulas of plane geometry and plane trigonometry.

plane table In surveying, a device for plotting the lines of a survey directly from the observations; consists essentially of a drawing board on a tripod, with a ruler, the ruler being pointed at the observed object by the use of a telescope or other sighting device.

plane tile See **ridge tile**.

planimeter A mechanical integrator for measuring the area of a plane surface usually within a given perimeter on a map.

planing A process for smoothing the surface of a material by shaving off small fragments.

planing machine **1.** A stationary machine for planing wood. **2.** A portable machine for planing the surface of a wood floor.

planing skip See **skip**.

planish finish A bright smooth finish on a metal; usually obtained by beating the metal with a special hammer or by passing it through rollers.

plank A long, wide, square-sawn thick piece of timber; the specifications vary, but often the minimum width is 8 in. (20 cm), and the minimum thickness is 2 to 4 in. (5 to 10 cm) for softwood and 1 in. (2.5 cm) for hardwood.

plank fence Same as **board fence**.

plank frame **1.** Any framework consisting only of nailed planks. **2.** A frame construction consisting of girts, plates, posts, and sills as bearing members and heavy planks as nonbearing partitions and walls.

plank-frame house A type of 17th-century colonial house constructed of heavy wood planks, usually erected vertically by setting them into grooves in a **sill plate, 1** for support; they were then drilled and pegged at their lower ends, or otherwise held firmly in place.

plank house A large house, generally rectangular, constructed of planks; used and built by Indians and, less frequently, by Eskimos.

planking **1.** A flooring surface or covering made of planks. **2.** The laying of planks. **3.** See **decking**. **4.** In log cabin construction, a term occasionally applied to logs that have been hewn only on two opposite sides.

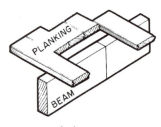

planking, 1

planking and strutting Temporary timbers at the side of an excavation.

plank-in-the-ground construction See **plaunch debout en terre construction**.

plank-on-edge floor, solid-wood floor A floor formed by joists in contact with one another (rather than spaced apart), their upper edges forming a continuous surface upon which finish flooring is applied.

plank truss A **roof truss** constructed of planks.

plank-type grating An aluminum extrusion used primarily as a structural flooring member and consisting of a **tread plate** reinforced by integral I-beam ribs, with perforations in the tread plate between the ribs.

planning **1.** The process of studying the layout of spaces within buildings and of buildings and other facilities or installations in open spaces in order to develop the general scheme of a building or group of buildings. **2.** See **community planning**.

planning grid An arrangement of one or more sets of regularly spaced parallel lines, with the sets at right angles or other selected angles to each other, and used like graph paper by architects and engineers to assist with modular planning.

plano-convex A shape of sun-dried brick, flat on one side, convex on the other, typical of early Mesopotamian construction.

plantation house The principal house of a plantation in the **antebellum** American South, typically having many of the following characteristics: two stories; a projecting two-story portico with Classic columns and a recessed central bay; thick brick walls at ground level (often stuccoed); in areas having a high water table, a **raised basement**, which often served as the location for service facilities, pantries, a wine cellar,

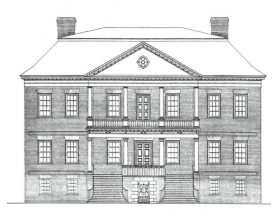

plantation house: Drayton Hall, South Carolina

servants' rooms, and sometimes for a dining room; a spacious veranda extending along the façade at the second-story level where the air circulation was much better than at ground level, and often along the sides and the back as well; many tall French windows for cross-ventilation.

planted   In joinery and plastering, fabricated or made on a separate piece of **stuff**; afterward fixed in place, as a **planted molding**.

planted molding, applied molding   A molding which is nailed, laid on, or otherwise fastened to the work rather than cut into the solid material.

planted stop, loose stop   A fillet or molding which is nailed to a doorframe, window frame, or lining, against which a door or casement is stopped; a **stop, 1**.

planter   A permanent, ornamental container to receive planted pots or boxes, often nonmovable and integral with the finish of a building.

planting   In masonry, laying the first courses of a foundation on a level bed.

planting box   A box, usually wooden, designed to hold growing plants and to fit inside a permanent receptacle.

plant mix   **1.** Any mixture produced at a mixing plant. **2.** A mixture, produced in an asphalt mixing plant, consisting of a mineral aggregate uniformly coated with asphalt cement or liquid asphalt.

plaque   A tablet that is affixed to the surface of a wall or set into a wall; often inscribed to commemorate a special event or to serve as a memorial.

plaque rail   See **plate rail**.

plaster   Usually a mixture of gypsum or lime with sand and water, producing a paste-like material that is applied in the plastic state, usually over **lath** fastened to a surface such as a wall or ceiling, or sometimes directly onto brick; it forms a hard surface when the water it contains evaporates. In some remote early settlements, when lime or gypsum was not available, a so-called plaster of fine white clay mixed with chopped straw was sometimes troweled onto a surface to produce a smooth finish on a wall or ceiling. Cow hair, cow dung, and/or chopped straw often was added to the plaster mixture to increase its mechanical strength when it dried.

Gypsum later supplanted lime as the plaster of choice because of its superior properties. Also see **mud plaster, ornamental plaster, plaster of paris**, and **stucco**.

plaster aggregate   Graded mineral particles and/or wood fibers for mixing with gypsum and cement-base plasters and with finish plaster to produce plaster mixes.

plaster arch   An untrimmed plaster opening.

plaster base   Any suitable surface for the application of plaster, such as gypsum lath, metal lath, wood lath, masonry block, or brick.

plaster-base finish tile   Ceramic tile whose surfaces are intended for the direct application of plaster; may be smooth, scored, combed, or roughened.

plaster-base nail   Same as **gypsum-lath nail**.

plaster bead, plaster head, plaster staff   A metal angle bead that is a built-in edging, reinforcing a plaster angle; a **corner bead**.

plasterboard   Same as **gypsum lath**.

plasterboard nail   A **gypsum-lath nail**; has a flat head, mechanically deformed shank, and diamond point.

plasterboard nail

plaster bond   The adhesion of plaster to a surface by a **mechanical bond, 1** or a **chemical bond**.

plaster ceiling panel   A raised or sunken section of a ceiling, forming a panel.

plaster cornice   A plaster molding where the wall and ceiling meet, crowning the top of the wall.

plaster cove   A plastered concave surface at the wall-ceiling junction.

plasterer's putty   See **lime putty**.

plaster ground   (*usually pl.*)   A wood strip, metal bead, or screed attached around a door, window, etc., as a guide for plastering to a given thickness; also serves as a fastener for trim; a **ground, 2**. (*See illustration on p. 692.*)

plaster guard   On a hollow metal doorframe, a shield attached behind the hinge and strike reinforcement to prevent mortar or plaster from

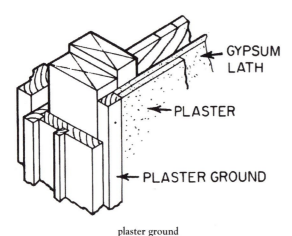

plaster ground

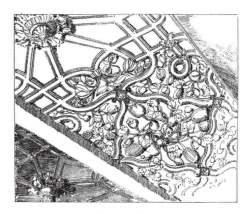

plasterwork, 1

entering the mounting holes when the frame is grouted.

plaster head   A **plaster bead**.

plaster lath   See **metal lath, gypsum lath**, etc.

plaster of paris, hemihydrate plaster   **1.** Calcined gypsum, containing no additives to control the set; a rapid-setting plaster used mainly for ornamental casting. **2. Gauging plaster**.

plaster ring   A cylindrical metal ring, set in a plaster ceiling, which serves as a guide for plastering to a given thickness; also serves as a fastener for trim.

plaster ring

plaster set   See **false set**.

plaster staff   See **plaster bead**.

plaster wainscot cap   A horizontal wood strip which covers the joint between wainscoting and the float finish surface above.

plasterwork   **1.** Cast **ornamental plaster**, commonly cast with **plaster of paris**, typically on a ceiling. **2.** Any surface finished with **plaster**.

plastic   **1.** A natural or artificially prepared organic polymer of low extensibility, as compared with rubber; can be molded, extruded, cut,

or worked into a great variety of objects, rigid or nonrigid, relatively light, which are formed by condensation polymerization and by vinyl polymerization; **plastics**. **2.** Characteristic of concrete, mortar, or plaster which is easily spread with a trowel.

plastic cement   A **flashing cement**.

plastic conduit   Plastic conduit or tubing used to enclose electric wiring.

plastic consistency   The condition of freshly mixed cement paste, mortar, or concrete such that deformation will be sustained continuously in any direction without rupture.

plastic cracking   Cracking that occurs in the surface of fresh concrete soon after it is placed and while it is still plastic.

plastic deformation   See **plastic flow**.

plastic design   Same as **ultimate-strength** design.

plastic emulsion   A **latex** emulsion.

plastic filler   Same as **plastic wood**.

plastic floor covering   See **vinyl-asbestos tile**.

plastic flooring   See **vinyl tile**.

plastic flow, plastic deformation   The deformation of a plastic material beyond the point of recovery, accompanied by continuing deformation with no further increase in stress; results in a permanent change in shape.

plastic foam   See **foamed plastic**.

plastic glue   A synthetic resin glue; also see **epoxy**.

plasticity   **1.** That property of freshly mixed cement paste, concrete, mortar, or soil which determines its resistance to deformation or its ease of molding. **2.** The ability of a plaster or lime putty to hold or retain water, so that it can be troweled easily.

plasticity index Numerical difference between the **liquid limit** and the **plastic limit**.

plasticizer **1.** An additive that increases plasticity of a cement paste, mortar, or concrete mixture. **2.** An additive in a paint formulation to soften the film, thus giving it better flexibility, chip resistance, and formability. **3.** A chemical agent added to a plastic composition to improve its flow and processability and to reduce brittleness.

plastic laminate Multiple layers of resin-impregnated paper, fused together under heat and pressure to form a hard, durable (often decorative) finished surfacing material.

plastic limit The lowest water content at which a soil becomes plastic.

plastic loss Same as **creep**.

plastic mortar A mortar of plastic consistency.

plastic paint, texture-finished paint, textured paint A heavy-bodied, thixotropic paint which can be worked after application, by stippling or by paint rollers having a textured pattern, to produce various textured or pattern surfaces.

plastic pipe Pipe formed from a material that contains one or more organic polymeric substances. Advantages may include: low initial cost, light weight, high flexibility, good corrosion resistance, and availability in long lengths. Disadvantages generally include: poor fire resistance, production of toxic gas upon combustion of some types of plastics, poor resistance to solvents, low pressure ratings at high temperatures, and (in some plastics) the susceptibility to change as a result of prolonged exposure to sunlight.

plastics See **plastic, 1**.

plastic shrinkage cracks See **hairline cracking**.

plastic skylight See **molded plastic skylight**.

plastic soil A soil exhibiting **plasticity**.

plastic structural cladding Plastic panels which are fastened directly to and supported by roof or wall framing, forming a finished roof or wall surface.

plastic wood A putty-like, rapid-drying filler; composed primarily of nitrocellulose and wood flour dispersed in volatile solvents; used for repairing holes and cracks in wood.

plastic yield Same as **plastic flow**.

plastigel A **plastisol** to which a gelling agent has been added to increase its viscosity.

plastisol A plastic resin, such as a vinyl resin, which has been dissolved in a plasticizer; a pourable liquid, used for casting; solidifies when baked.

plat A map, plan, or chart of a city, town, section, or subdivision, indicating the location and boundaries of individual properties.

platband **1.** Any flat, rectangular, horizontal molding, the projection of which is much less than its height; a **fascia**. **2.** A decorative lintel or false flat arch over a doorway, etc. **3.** The fillets between the flutes of a column; **stria**.

plate **1.** A thin, flat sheet of material. **2.** In wood frame construction, a horizontal board or timber connecting and terminating posts, joists, rafters, etc. **3.** A timber laid horizontally (and on its widest side) in a wall or on top of a wall or on the ground to receive other timbers or joists. Also see **ground plate, wall plate, partition plate, pole plate, sill plate**. **4.** Plated metalware. **5.** A flat, rolled-metal product having the following dimensions: hot-rolled steel, minimum thickness 0.18 in. (0.46 cm) and a width exceeding 6 in. (15.2 cm); stainless steel, minimum thickness $\frac{3}{16}$ in. (0.48 cm) and a width exceeding 10 in. (25.4 cm); aluminum, minimum thickness 0.25 in. (0.64 cm), no minimum width specified; copper alloys, thickness exceeding $\frac{3}{16}$ in. (0.48 cm)

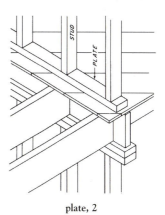

plate, 2

and a width greater than 12 in. (30.5 cm). Also see **crown plate, curtail plate, false plate, gallery plate, head plate, pole plate, rafter plate, raising plate, roof plate, sill, sill plate, soleplate, top plate, wall plate.**

platea   In ancient Rome, a wide passageway or a wide street.

plate anchor   See **sill anchor.**

plate beam   See **plate girder.**

plate bolt   A bolt in a building foundation which secures the **plate** or **sill.**

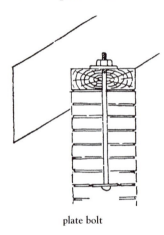

plate bolt

plate cut   See **seat cut.**

plated parquet   Parquetry having inlaid hardwood pieces applied to a framed backing.

plated truss   A wood **truss** assembly in which the truss joints are held together and reinforced with steel plates.

plate girder, plate beam   A steel girder built up of plates and angles (or other structural shapes), welded or riveted together.

plate glass   A high-quality **glass** sheet having both its flat sides plane and parallel so that it is free of distortions and flaws; has much greater mechanical strength than ordinary window glass; usually formed by a *rolling process,* then ground and polished, but can also be formed by the *float-glass process,* in which molten glass floats on a layer of molten metal to smooth out surface irregularities, producing a flat sheet of glass when the temperature of the molten metal is gradually reduced.

plate rail, plaque rail   A narrow shelf or rail along the upper part of the walls of a room, grooved to hold chinaware plates or decorations.

Plateresque architecture   A richly decorative style of Spanish architecture of the 16th century; said to resemble the intricate work of Spanish silversmiths in delicacy, hence its name (*plata* is the Spanish word for silver). Particularly applied to many Spanish Colonial buildings in the Americas from the 16th into the 18th centuries.

plate tracery   Tracery whose openings are or seem to be pierced through thin slabs of stone.

plate tracery

plate-type tread   A tread, or a combination of tread and riser, fabricated from metal plate, floor plate, tread plate, or some combination of such plates.

plate vibrator   A mechanically driven **tamper** having a flat base.

platform   **1.** A raised floor or terrace, open or roofed. **2.** A stair landing; also see **stair platform. 3.** A **grillage.**

platform framing   A system of **framing** for a building of wood construction several stories high, in which the studs are only one story high; the floor joists for each story rest on the **top plates** of the story below or on the **soleplate** of the first story; the bearing walls and partitions rest on the subfloor of each story, i.e., rest on the rough floor that serves as the base for the **finish floor.** Also called western framing. Compare with **balloon framing.**

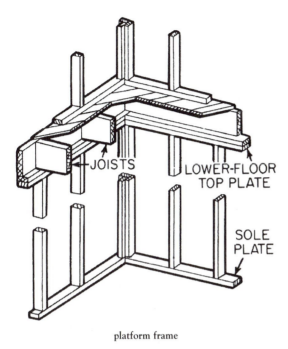

platform frame

platform framing, western framing A method of timber building construction making use of a **platform frame**.

platform header A horizontal structural member which supports a stair platform construction but carries no stringers.

platform ladder A ladder which is self-supporting and has a platform at the working level.

platform roof A roof which terminates in a horizontal plane; any roof which is truncated.

platform stair Same as **dogleg stair**.

platted molding Same as **reticulated molding**.

plaunch debout en terre construction In **French Vernacular architecture** a system of construction, once widely used in Southern Louisiana, in which closely spaced planks were driven several feet into the ground; the space between the planks was filled with **bousillage**, then the wall was covered with horizontal clapboards.

play The separation between moving parts to reduce friction.

playfield An area designed for field games.

playhouse 1. A place of assembly for dramatic presentations. 2. A small building serving children as a make-believe home.

play lot A playing area for children.

plaza A public square that is usually centrally located, in Spain and in communities of Spanish heritage.

pleached Said of the branches of trees, shrubs, vines, etc., which are united by weaving, braiding, or plaiting.

pleasance A pleasure garden intended for enjoyment; often secluded.

pleasance chamber In a royal palace, a room of state.

plenishing nail A large nail for fastening the planks of floors to the joists.

plenum 1. In suspended ceiling construction, the space between the suspended ceiling and the main structure above. 2. A **plenum chamber**.

plenum barrier In suspended ceiling construction, a material or structural barrier erected in a **plenum** over a partition; used to reduce sound transmission between adjoining rooms by way of this path over the partition.

plenum cable A jacket having low flame- and smoke-producing properties; specifically designed for use in the **plenum, 1** formed by the space between a suspended ceiling and the structural floor above; such space often is used for return air in a heating and/or cooling system in a building.

plenum chamber In an air-conditioning system, an enclosed volume which (in a supply system) is at a slightly higher pressure than the atmosphere and is connected to a number of branch supply ducts, or which (in a return system) is at a slightly lower pressure than the atmosphere and is connected to a number of return grilles; a **plenum, 1**.

plenum fan A backward-curved airfoil impeller that is housed in a rectangular plenum; has

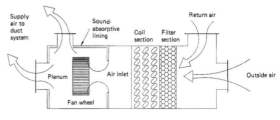

plenum fan

ducted inlet and outlet connections; it is *not* enclosed in a typical volute scroll.

plexiform   Having the appearance of network, weaving, or plaiting, as in Celtic and Romanesque ornamentation.

plf   Abbr. for "pounds per linear foot."

PLG   On drawings, abbr. for **piling**.

pliers   A hand tool, pincer-like, with scissors action, usually with serrated jaws; used for gripping, holding, bending, and cutting.

plinth   **1.** A square or rectangular base for column, pilaster, or door framing. **2.** A solid monumental base, often ornamented with moldings, bas reliefs, or inscriptions, to support a statue or memorial. **3.** A recognizable base of an external wall, or the base courses of a building collectively, if so treated as to give the appearance of a platform.

PLINTH

plinth, 1

plinth block   See **skirting block**.

plinth brick   A brick having a **chamfer, 4** on its face or on one of its ends; usually used as one of the bricks in a **plinth course**.

plinth course   **1.** A masonry course which forms a continuous **plinth**. **2.** The top course in a brick plinth.

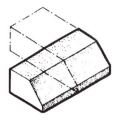

plinth **course**   of brick

PLMB   On drawings, abbr. for **plumbing**.

plot   **1.** A parcel of land consisting of one or more lots or portions thereof, which is described by reference to a recorded plat or by survey. **2.** A small area of ground.

plough   See **plow**.

plow, plough   **1.** A carpenter's **plane** which cuts grooves. **2.** A **router**. **3.** See **groove**.

plow and tongue joint   Same as **tongue-and-groove joint**.

plowed bead   Same as **quirk bead, 2**.

plow groove   A groove on the edge of a board, esp. for a **tongue-and-groove joint**.

plowshare twist, plowshare vault   A vault in which the surface between the stilted wall rib and the diagonal rib is warped like a plowshare.

plow strip   A strip of wood having a groove running along the edge, esp. used to fix the edge of a drawer bottom.

plucked finish   A stone surface which is rough in texture; produced by setting a planer blade so deep that it removes stone by spalling rather than by shaving.

plug   **1.** A small cylinder or dowel of wood (or other material) driven into a wall, to which a fastener is fixed. **2.** A small piece of wood, plywood, veneer, etc., fitted into a recess to patch a defect; an insert or patch. **3.** A fibrous or resinous material used to fill a void and otherwise patch a surface. **4.** In plumbing, a drain-opening stopper; a fitting for closing the end of a pipe. **5.** A **receptacle plug**. **6.** An **attachment plug**. **7.** A device for connecting wires to a **jack**.

plug, 4

plug center bit   A **center bit** ending in a small cylindrical plug instead of a point; used to enlarge a hole previously made or to form a counterbore around it.

plug cock   Same as **ground-key faucet**.

plug cutter   A small bit, operated by a power drill, for cutting out plugs used to cover recessed screwheads in a hardwood floor.

plug-driving gun   A **stud gun**.

plug fan   Same as **plenum fan**.

plug fuse　**1.** A **fuse** mounted in an insulated porcelain container fitted with a threaded, metal screw base; has a small window on the face of the fuse for observing the condition of the fuse element. **2.** An **Edison-base fuse** or a **type-S fuse**.

plug fuse

plugging　Filling a hole, drilled in masonry, with a fiber, plastic, or wood plug into which a screw can be driven.

plugging chisel, plugging drill　Same as **star drill**.

plug tap　Same as **ground-key faucet**.

plug tenon　Same as **stub tenon**.

plug valve　Same as **ground-key valve**.

plug weld　A weld made through a circular hole in one member of a **lap joint, 2** or **tee joint**, joining one member to the other.

plum, plum stone　A large random-shaped stone which is dropped into freshly placed mass concrete to economize on the amount of concrete mortar required.

plumb　Exactly vertical.

plumbago　Same as **graphite**.

plumb bob, plummet　A shaped metal weight which is suspended from the lower end of a line to determine the vertical.

plumb bond　In masonry, any bond in which the vertical joints are precisely in line.

plumb bond pole　In masonry construction, a pole used to ensure that the vertical joints are plumb.

plumb cut, ridge cut　A cut in a vertical plane, as the cut on a rafter where it butts vertically against a **ridgeboard**.

plumber's friend, force cup, plumber's helper, plunger　A tool consisting of a rubber suction cup attached to a handle; set over a plumbing trap (or the like) and worked with a pumping action to clear the trap of minor obstructions.

plumb bob

plumber's furnace　A portable gasoline-fired heater; used by plumbers to melt solder or lead, or to heat soldering irons, etc.

plumber's rasp　A coarse rasp, esp. used by plumbers to file lead.

plumber's round iron　A **soldering iron** used by plumbers to solder seams in tanks.

plumber's soil　A mixture of lampblack, glue, and water; painted on the surface of a pipe, outside a joint, to prevent solder from adhering; used to ensure a clean edge in wiped joints.

plumber's solder　A soft solder containing approximately two parts of lead to one part of tin; used in making **wiped joints** and seams.

plumbing　**1.** See **plumbing system**. **2.** The work or business of installing in buildings the pipes, fixtures, and other apparatus for bringing in the water supply and removing liquid and waterborne wastes.

plumbing appliance　A class of plumbing fixtures intended to perform a special function; their operation may depend on the setting of controls or on the characteristics of heating elements, motors, or pressure- or temperature-sensing elements.

plumbing appurtenance　A manufactured device or assembly of prefabricated components which act as an adjunct to the basic piping system and plumbing fixtures; usually performs a

plumbing fitting

useful function such as operating, maintaining, or servicing the plumbing system; does not add either to the water demand or to the discharge load of fixtures or of the drainage system.

plumbing fitting   Same as **fitting, 1**.

plumbing fixture   A receptacle which receives and discharges water, liquid, or waterborne wastes into a drainage system with which it is connected.

plumbing official   The officer or other designated authority charged with the administration and enforcement of the applicable plumbing code.

plumbing system   The combination of supply and distribution pipes for hot water, cold water, and gas, and for removing liquid wastes in a building; includes: the water-supply distributing pipes; the fixtures and fixture traps; the soil, waste, and vent pipes; the building drain and building sewer; and the storm-drainage pipes; with their devices, appurtenances, and connections all within or adjacent to the building.

plumbing trap   See **trap, 1**.

plumbing trim   See **trim, 3**.

plumb joint   In sheet-metal work, a joint made by lapping the edges and soldering them together flat.

plumb level, pendulum level   A level consisting of a bar and a plumb line; the bar is set in true horizontal position by placing it at a right angle to the plumb line.

plumb line   A cord or line, having a metal bob or weight attached to one end, which indicates the true vertical direction.

plumb pile   A **pile** which is vertical.

plumb rise   The overall vertical measurement at the end of a **truss** where the top and bottom chords meet.

plumb rule   A narrow board with parallel edges having a straight line drawn through the middle and a string attached at the upper end of the line; used by carpenters, masons, etc., for determining a vertical.

plume   Wood veneer having a large featherlike figure, usually cut from a crotch.

plummet   A **plumb bob**.

plum stone   A **plum**.

plunger   See **plumber's friend**.

plumb rule

plunger hydraulic elevator   A **hydraulic elevator** in which the piston (called a "plunger") is attached directly to the car frame or platform; the driving mechanism includes the cylinder, piston, pump, and associated valves.

plus sight   Same as **backsight**.

pluteus   In ancient Roman architecture, a dwarf wall or parapet; esp. one closing the lower portion of the space between the columns of a colonnade.

ply   One of a number of thin sheets in a layered construction, as in plywood, laminated panels, roofing felt, etc.

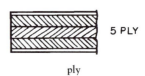

ply

plymetal   Plywood clad on one or both sides with sheet metal.

ply plastic   Same as **molded plywood**.

PLYWD   On drawings, abbr. for **plywood**.

plywood   Structural wood made of three or more layers of veneer (usually an odd number), joined with glue; usually laid with the grain of adjoining plies at right angles.

plywood squares, plywood parquet   Plywood esp. fabricated for use as flooring; has an exposed face veneer of birch, oak, or other serviceable hardwood.

PNEU   On drawings, abbr. for "pneumatic."

pneumatically applied concrete See **shot-crete**.

pneumatically applied mortar See **shotcrete**.

pneumatic caisson Same as **caisson, 1**.

pneumatic control system A system in which control is effected by air, under pressure; e.g., an air-conditioning system controlled by pneumatically operated thermostats or humidistats.

pneumatic dispatch system See **pneumatic tube system**.

pneumatic drill A drill powered by compressed air from an auxiliary external source.

pneumatic ejector A special type of device designed to receive and dispose of liquids and sewage from subbuilding drainage systems.

pneumatic feeding The delivering of shotcrete with equipment which moves the material by means of a pressurized air stream.

pneumatic hammer See **air hammer**.

pneumatic placement Of concrete, slurry, or plaster, etc.: delivery by piping or hose to the final location on a jobsite; the material may be pumped in its normal wet consistency, either for deposit in place or for spraying, or its constituents may be pumped in the dry state with water added at the nozzle from which it is sprayed.

pneumatic riveter A tool, driven by compressed air, which is used to drive **rivets**.

pneumatic structure A very lightweight enclosed structure, usually fabricated of a membrane of an impervious material and supported by the difference in air pressure between the exterior and the interior of the structure rather than by a structural framework. Fans must maintain the interior pressure slightly in excess of normal atmospheric pressure to prevent the structure from slowly deflating and collapsing. Used primarily as a temporary enclosure or to house sports facilities such as tennis courts and swimming pools. Also called an air-supported structure.

pneumatic test See **air test**.

pneumatic tube system A system for sending small items or papers from one location to another in a building. The item to be sent is placed in a small cylinder that fits snugly in a tube that connects the two locations. Then, the cylinder moves rapidly through the tube to its destination as a result of a force provided by air pressure or a vacuum.

pneumatic water supply A building water-supply system in which water is distributed from an enclosed storage tank containing water and compressed air; system pressure is maintained by the compressed air.

PNL On drawings, abbr. for **panel**.

Pnyx A public place of assembly in ancient Athens near the Acropolis; an open, paved, semicircular area surrounded by a wall; speakers addressed the people from a platform.

PO Abbr. for "purchase order."

poché In an architectural drawing, the blackened portions representing solids.

pocket **1.** A recess in masonry to receive the end of a beam. **2.** The slot in the pulley stile of a double-hung window frame, through which the sash weight is passed into the sash weight channel; a sash pocket. **3.** A recess at the head or jamb of a wall opening to receive a curtain. **4.** A recess in the interior jamb of a window to receive a folding shutter when open. **5.** A recess in a wall to receive a folding door in the open position. **6.** See **stage pocket**. **7.** A well-defined opening between the annual rings which develops during the growth of a tree.

pocket butt A type of **butt hinge** mounted on the third leaf of three-ply inside shutters; permits the leaf to enter its **pocket, 4** without jamming.

pocket chisel Same as **sash chisel**.

pocket door A door that slides into a hollow wall at the side of a doorway; often advantageous

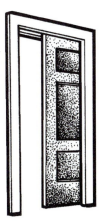

pocket door

because such a door requires no room for swinging; may be single or biparting.

pocket-head window A window in which a part of the sash slides upward through an opening in the head of the window frame.

pocket piece In a double-hung window frame, a small wood piece in the pulley stile which may be removed to insert sash weights or to replace the sash cord.

pocket rot A type of decay in trees consisting of holes (pockets) surrounded by sound wood.

pockmarking An undesirable depression in a paint film. Also see **cratering, pitting, pinhole, 3**.

podium **1.** In general, an elevated platform, such as one for a speaker's stand. **2.** The platform in a concert hall for the conductor. **3.** The high platform on which Roman temples were generally placed.

poecile A stoa or porch on the agora of ancient Athens having walls adorned with paintings of historical and religious subjects.

poikile Same as **poecile**.

point **1.** See **glazier's point**. **2.** A mason's tool; see **wasting**. **3.** See **pointing**.

point-bearing pile Same as **end-bearing pile**.

pointed arch Any arch with a point at its apex, characteristic of, but not confined to, Gothic architecture.

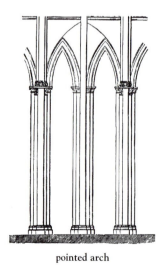

pointed arch

pointed architecture Characterized by Gothic arches.

pointed ashlar Stonework having face markings produced with a pointed tool.

pointed dormer Any **dormer** having a point at its apex.

pointed pediment A **pediment** having a triangular shape; also called a triangular pediment.

Pointed style A seldom-used term for **Gothic Revival**.

pointed work In masonry, the rough finish that is produced on a stone by repeated impacts of a pointed tool striking its face.

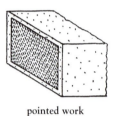

pointed work

pointel, pointelle **1.** A pattern in a pavement, formed by small squares or lozenges laid diagonally. **2.** Any similar pattern.

pointing **1.** In masonry, the final treatment of joints by the troweling of mortar or a putty-like filler into the joints; also see **flush pointing, recessed pointing, tuck pointing**. **2.** The material with which the joints are filled. **3.** The removal of mortar from between the joints of masonry units and the replacing of it with new mortar; **repointing**. **4.** In stone carving, creating points from a model and establishing their position on the stone that is to be carved.

pointing trowel A mason's trowel used in **pointing** or removing old mortar from masonry joints.

pointing trowel

point of contraflexure Same as **point of inflection**.

point of delivery Same as **point of service, 3**.

point of inflection The point on the length of a structural member subjected to flexure at which the direction of curvature changes and at which the bending moment is zero.

point of service **1.** The location at which **service cables** installed by an electrical utility company joins the customer's **service entrance conductors** in one or more terminating enclosures. **2.** The location at which a customer's service entrance conductors joins the electrical utility company's facilities in a transformer, vault, or enclosure. **3.** The initial junction of the customer's gas piping with either the gas company's piping extending from the gas main and/or the regulator which reduces the pressure of an undiluted liquefied petroleum gas to the pressure normally delivered to appliances.

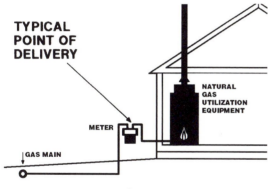

point of service, 3

point of support The point on a member where its load is transmitted to a support.

point-of-use heater An **instantaneous-type water heater** in a remote location far from other fixtures using hot water.

point source A light source whose dimensions are insignificant compared with the distance at which it is used; e.g., a fluorescent lamp is a point source when viewed from a large distance but a line source when viewed close to the source.

Poisson's ratio In a material under tension or compression, the absolute value of the ratio of transverse strain to the corresponding longitudinal strain.

POL On drawings, abbr. for "polish."

polarized receptacle An electric **receptacle** having contacts arranged so that a mating plug can be inserted in it in only one orientation.

polarized receptacle

pole A long, slender, tapering piece of wood; a pale, prop, stake, or stay.

pole foundation A foundation system using wooden poles, partly buried in excavated holes, for both lateral and vertical support.

pole-frame construction Same as **bent-frame construction**.

pole piece A **ridgeboard**.

pole plate A horizontal timber resting on the ends of the tie beams of a roof; supports the lower ends of the common rafters, directly above the wall; raises the rafters above the top plate of the wall.

pole-platform construction A pole-foundation structure in which the tops of the poles extend above the surface of the ground and support a platform; this platform acts as the base for a building superstructure.

pole-type transformer A **transformer** suitable for mounting on a pole or similar structure. (*See illustration p. 702.*)

poling board (*Brit.*) One of a number of vertical boards in **open sheeting**.

polish In plastering, to give a sheen or gloss to the finish coat.

polished finish In stonework, a finish so smooth that it forms a reflecting surface; usually obtained by chemical treatment and prolonged mechanical buffing of a stone surface on which there are no voids.

polished plate glass Same as **plate glass**.

polished work Stonework that has been polished to a mirror-like finish with an abrasive.

polish grind, final grind In concrete work, the final operation, in which fine abrasives are

polishing varnish

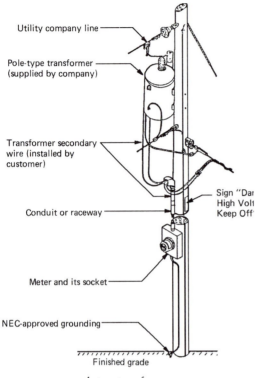

Utility company line

Pole-type transformer
(supplied by company)

Transformer secondary
wire (installed by
customer)

Conduit or raceway

Sign "Dai
High Volt
Keep Off'

Meter and its socket

NEC-approved grounding

Finished grade

pole-type transformer

used to hone a surface to its desired smoothness and appearance, as for terrazzo concrete.

polishing varnish, rubbing varnish A hard varnish which can be polished by rubbing with an abrasive and mineral oil.

poll The broad end or striking face of a hammer.

polychromatic finish 1. A multicolored paint finish. **2.** A paint containing reflecting metallic flake and fine transparent pigments which appear as a variety of colors when viewed from different angles.

polychromed 1. Said of a building façade exhibiting a distinctive masonry pattern of contrasting colors, usually in the form of horizontal bands across the façade and/or bands around arches, doorways, or windows; a feature of the latter phase of **High Victorian Gothic. 2.** Said of surfaces (such as pipes or ducts) that are painted different colors, often to indicate their respective functions.

polychromy The practice of decorating architectural elements, sculpture, etc., in a variety of colors.

polyester resin One of a group of synthetic resins which undergo polymerization during curing; advantageous because high pressure is not required for curing; has excellent adhesive properties, high strength, good chemical resistance; esp. used in laminating and impregnating materials.

polyethylene A low-cost plastic; used as piping in cold-water domestic supply lines and in cold-water lines of air-conditioning systems; in sheet form, it is especially used for membrane waterproofing.

polyfoil Same as **multifoil**.

polygonal masonry Masonry which is constructed of stones having smooth polygonal faces.

polygonal masonry

polygonal roof See **pavilion roof, 2.**

polymer One of a group of high-molecular-weight resin-like, organic compounds whose structures usually can be represented by repeated small units. Some polymers are elastomers, some are plastics, and some are fibers.

polymer-cement concrete Concrete produced by a mixture of hydraulic cement, aggregate, water, and a polymer or a **monomer.**

polymer concrete Concrete in which an organic polymer is used as the binder.

polymeric poured floor A floor covering which is composed of a polymeric material poured on a substrate; converts to a thick built-up floor covering; may incorporate mineral or plastic chips, desiccants, fillers, or pigments.

polymerization A chemical reaction in which the molecular weight of the molecules formed is a multiple of that of the original substances.

polymethyl methacrylate A polymer of **methyl methacrylate.**

polypropylene A plastic polymer of propylene; a tough material having good resistance to heat and chemical action.

polystyle Composed of many columns.

polystyrene foam See **foamed polystyrene**.

polystyrene resin A synthetic resin which is formed by the polymerization of styrene upon heating; uses include paint for concrete.

polythene Same as **polyethylene**.

polyurethane finish An exceptionally hard and wear-resistant paint or varnish made by the reaction of polyols with a multifunctional isocyanate.

polyvinyl acetal A vinyl plastic produced from the condensation of polyvinyl alcohol with an aldehyde. There are three main groups: polyvinyl acetal, polyvinyl butyral, and polyvinyl formal; used in lacquers and adhesives. Polyvinyl acetal resins are thermoplastics which can be processed by casting, extruding, molding, and coating.

polyvinyl acetate, PVA A colorless, thermoplastic, water-insoluble resin; used as a latex binder in certain paints.

polyvinyl chloride, PVC A water-insoluble resin thermoplastic resin that is highly resistant to chemicals and corrosion; widely used for pipe fittings, piping in cold-water systems, and piping in sewage and waste lines.

pommel, pomel A rounded finial.

ponded roof A roof designed to retain water on the roof's surface to provide for evaporative cooling.

ponding **1.** The accumulation of water in a depression on an otherwise level surface. **2.** The process of flooding the surface of a newly placed concrete slab with a thin layer of water to ensure continued hydration; usually requires the use of temporary dams of earth or other material around the perimeter.

pontifical altar An isolated altar, such as under the dome of St. Peter's at Rome, covered by a **baldachin**; usually placed in the great Roman basilicas.

pony wall Same as **dwarf wall, 2**.

pool See **swimming pool**.

poorhouse A building, often supported by a community or by a religious organization, that provide housing and minimal services for the indigent; also see **almshouse** and **bettering house**.

poor lime Lime containing a significant proportion of material that is insoluble in acids; not a pure lime.

popcorn concrete A **no-fines concrete** which contains insufficient cement paste to fill voids between the coarse aggregate; the particles are bound only at points of contact.

poplar See **yellow poplar**.

popout The breaking away of small portions of a concrete surface, owing to internal pressure, leaving a shallow, typically conical depression.

popping, blowing, pitting, pops Shallow conical depressions, ranging in size from pinheads to diameters of ¼ in. (64 mm), just below the surface of a lime-putty finish coat; caused by the expansion of coarse particles of unhydrated lime or of foreign substances.

poppyhead, poppy An ornament generally used for the finials of pew ends and similar pieces of church furniture.

poppyhead

population composition The distribution within a group of people of specified individual attributes such as sex, age, marital status, education, occupation, and relationship to the head of household.

pop valve A safety valve designed to open abruptly when the pressure exerted by the fluid on the valve overbalances the force exerted by a spring which normally keeps the valve closed.

PORC On drawings, abbr. for "porcelain."

porcelain A glazed or unglazed vitreous

ceramic whiteware used for electrical, chemical, mechanical, structural, or thermal components.

porcelain enamel, vitreous enamel A substantially vitreous (glassy) inorganic metal oxide coating, bonded to metal by fusion at a temperature above 800°F (427°C); not a true porcelain.

porcelain enamel ware See **double-faced ware.**

porcelain tile A dense, fine-grained, smooth ceramic mosaic tile or paver; has sharply formed face, usually impervious; usually made by the dust-pressed method. Colors of the porcelain type usually are clear and luminous or a granular blend thereof.

porcelain tube A ceramic tube having a slight shoulder on one end; in exposed electric wiring, used to carry an insulated conductor where it passes through a wood joist, stud, etc.

porch **1.** An exterior structure that shelters a building entrance. **2.** An exterior structure that extends along the outside of a building; usually roofed and generally open-sided, but may also be partially enclosed, screened, or glass-enclosed; it is often an addition to the main structure; also called a **veranda, galerie,** or **piazza;** if set within the building structure, it is said to be an *integral porch.* **3.** A small vestibule inside the front door of a 17th-century colonial American house, usually containing a steep stair leading to the loft space above. Also see **carriage porch, double-decker porch, double-tiered porch, engaged porch, full-façade porch, full-width porch, gabled porch, inset porch, integral porch, lattice porch, portale, projecting porch, raised porch,** shed-roof porch, sleeping porch, storm porch, two-tiered porch, wrap-around porch.

porch chamber A bedroom above an unheated entrance porch or veranda of a house.

porch lattice Along the side of a porch or veranda below floor level, an open lattice where the foundation is not continuous.

porch rail A molded wood member extending between columns or posts of a porch, veranda, etc., and joining either the tops or bottoms of the balusters.

porcupine boiler A vertical, cylindrical **boiler** having many short dead-end tubes projecting from the cylindrical surface to provide additional heating surface.

pore water The free water that is present in soil.

pore water pressure The pressure of water which is present in saturated soil.

porosity A ratio, usually expressed as a percentage, of the volume of voids in a material to the total volume of the material, including the voids. The voids permit gases or liquids to pass through the material.

porous fill Same as **drainage fill.**

porous wood Any hardwood having a structure which includes hollow tube-like cells called "pores" or "vessels."

porphyry Igneous rock characterized by large conspicuous crystals which are set in a matrix of finer crystals; used as decorative stone and in building construction.

porta The gate of an ancient Roman city.

portal **1.** An impressive or monumental entrance, gate, or door to a building or courtyard, often decorated. **2.** A structural framework consisting of a beam supported by two columns to which it is connected with sufficient rigidity to hold virtually unchanged the original angles between the intersecting members.

portal crane A **gantry crane.**

portale In Spanish architecture and derivatives, a covered porch, usually long and narrow, along the front or side of a house, whose roof is supported by wood posts capped with **bolsters, 1;** provides direct access to individual room entrances.

portal frame Same as **portal, 2.**

PORT CEM On drawings, abbr. for **portland cement.**

porch

portal

portcullis A defensive grating, of massive iron or timber, movable vertically in retaining grooves cut in the jambs of a fortified gateway.

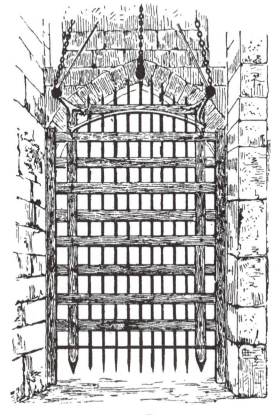

portcullis

porte cochère **1.** A carriage porch. **2.** A covered carriage or automobile entryway leading to a courtyard.

porte cochère, 1

porte cochère, 2

porthole Same as **access door**.

portico **1.** A covered entrance whose roof is supported by a series of columns or piers, commonly placed at the front entrance to a building. **2.** A stoa.

portico

portico-in-antis A portico that is recessed within a structure instead of projecting from the façade; also see **anta**.

porticus Same as **portico**.

portland blast-furnace slag cement, blast-furnace slag cement 1. An interground mixture of portland cement clinker and granulated blast-furnace slag; *type IS* cement. 2. A uniform blend of portland cement and fine granulated blast-furnace slag.

portland cement A cementitious binder used in most modern structural concrete; manufactured by grinding and "burning" a mixture of limestone with clay or shale with a small amount of gypsum. It is mixed with water and an aggregate (such as sand and/or gravel) to form a thick, heavy liquid that dries as a monolithic product. Although **cement** was developed by the ancient Romans, *portland cement* was first developed in England in 1824; since then, its tensile strength has greatly increased.

portland cement clinker A partly fused **clinker** primarily consisting of hydrated calcium silicates.

portland cement concrete See **concrete**.

portland cement paint See **cement paint**.

portland cement plaster A plaster which is a portland cement (or a combination of such cements) mixed with masonry cement or portland cement and lime; then mixed with an aggregate.

portlandite A common product resulting from the hydration of portland cement; calcium hydroxite.

portland-pozzolan cement 1. An interground mixture of portland cement clinker and pozzolan; type IP cement. 2. A uniform blend of portland cement and fine pozzolan.

Portland stone, Portland limestone An oölitic limestone which is quarried on the Isle of Portland, off the coast of England; widely used as a building stone in London.

POS On drawings, abbr. for "positive."

posada In Spanish architecture and derivatives, an **inn**.

positioned weld A **weld** made in a joint which has been so placed as to facilitate the making of the weld.

position indicator In an elevator system, a device designed to indicate the position of a car in its hoistway.

positive cutoff A **cutoff, 2** which extends downward to an impervious lower boundary, completely blocking the path of subsurface seepage.

positive-displacement Descriptive of equipment in which wet-mix **shotcrete is** delivered by being pushed through the material hose in a solid mass by a piston or auger.

positive heat supply Heat that is supplied to a space with direct design intent, such as by installed heating devices, or heat that is supplied to a space indirectly, such as by means of uninsulated surfaces of a furnace or boiler.

possum-trot cabin Same as **dogtrot cabin**.

possum-trot plan, dogtrot plan Log-cabin plan of a house with two parts separated by a **breezeway**, all under a common roof.

post A strong, stiff, vertical structural member or column, usually of wood, stone, or metal, capable of supporting a framing member of the structure above it and/or providing a firm point of lateral attachment. Posts may divide the structural framework of a building into **bays**. The term *post* may be preceded by an adjective indicating its location (such as a corner post) or by an adjective indicating its shape (such as a musket-stock post). For definitions and illustrations of specific types of posts, see **angle post, chimney post, corner post, crown post, doorpost, flared post, gabled post, gate post, gun-stock post, hanging post, jack post, jamb post, king post, musket-stock post, prick post, principal post, shouldered post, splayed post, sure post, teagle post, wall post**.

post-and-beam construction See **post-and-lintel construction**.

post-and-beam framing Same as **post-and-lintel construction**.

post-and-girt framing Since medieval times, a system of structural wood-frame construction characterized by the use of **heavy corner posts**, horizontal **girts** to support the superimposed loads, and **summerbeams** to support the floor joists; largely replaced by **balloon framing** in the early 19th century. Structural members were interconnected by **mortise-and-tenon joints** that were held fast by wood **pins** or dowels.

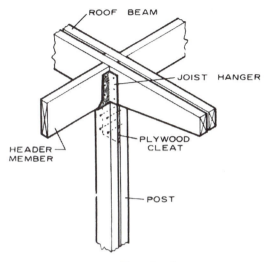

post-and-beam framing

post-and-lintel construction
A type of construction characterized by the use of vertical columns (posts) and a horizontal beam (lintel) to carry a load over an opening—in contrast to systems employing arches or vaults.

post and pane, post and petrail
A system of construction consisting of timber framings filled in with brickwork or lath and plaster; half-timbered construction.

post-and-rail fence
A fence having a series of posts set into the ground, usually interconnected by several horizontal rails between consecutive posts.

postbuckling strength
The load which can be carried by a structural member or by a plate after it has been subjected to buckling.

Post-Colonial period
A term sometimes applied to the years in America from about 1780 to 1830 during which time many buildings were built in the **Classical Revival style** or **Federal style**.

post-completion services
Additional services rendered after issuance of the final **certificate for payment**, such as consultation regarding maintenance, processes, systems, etc.

posted occupancy and use
A sign for display, usually required by the applicable building code, that indicates the legally acceptable number of occupants of a building; the code may also require an indication of code-accepted usage, floor load, and fire grade.

postern
1. A minor, often inconspicuous, entry. **2.** A small door near a larger one. **3.** Any small door or gate, esp. one far from the main gate in a fortified place.

postern, 2

post hole
A hole which is dug in the ground to hold a fence post.

post house
A house or inn along a post road (i.e., a road over which mail was once carried) with facilities for keeping horses and carriages used by mail couriers and travelers.

postiche
Superadded; done after the work is finished, esp. when superfluous, inappropriate, or in poor taste.

posticum
See **opisthodomus**.

postigo
In Spanish architecture and its derivatives, a **wicket** or peep window or small door set into a door of much larger size.

post-in-the-ground house
Same as **poteaux-en-terre house**.

postique
Same as **postiche**.

postis
In ancient Roman construction, the jamb of a door, supporting the lintel.

Post-Medieval architecture
A term often applied to architecture in the 17th century and early 18th century describing dwellings that exhibited many of the characteristics of timber-framed medieval houses, with steeply pitched roofs, very large fireplaces, large chimney stacks, and small casement windows.

Post-Modern architecture
From the late 1960s on, a term describing architecture that connotes a break with the canons of **International Style** modernism. Functionalism and emphasis on the expression of structure are rejected in favor of a greater freedom of design,

Post-Modernism

including Classical historic imagery. This leads to a new interplay of contemporary forms and materials with frequent historic allusions, often ironic, as, for example, in the use of nonsupporting Classical columns and medieval arches. Post-Modern architecture also accepts the manifestations of commercial mass culture, such as bright colors, neon lights, and advertising signs. Also see **Neo-Eclectic**.

Post-Modernism   In architecture, the term Post-Modernism connotes the break with the canons of International Style modernism. Functionalism and emphasis on the expression of structure are rejected in favor of a greater freedom of design. There is a new interplay of contemporary forms and materials, with frequent historic allusions, often ironic, as for example in the use of non-supporting classic columns, medieval arches and even port-holes. Post-Modernism also accepts the manifestations of commercial mass culture: bright colors, neon lights, and advertising signs of the Las Vegas type. Most influential for the formulation of a post-modernist program were the writings of Robert Venturi. The A.T.&T. building in New York by Philip Johnson and John Burgee can be considered one of the earliest major examples of Post-Modernist architecture.

post office   An office or building where letters and parcels are received and sorted, and from where they are distributed and dispatched to various destinations.

post pole   A single vertical member which supports loads.

postscenium,   postscaenium   1. In   the ancient theatre, the rooms behind the stage where the actors dressed and where machines were stored. **2.** The back part of the stage of a theatre, behind the scenes.

post shore   Same as **post pole**.

posttensioning   A method of prestressing reinforced concrete in which tendons are tensioned after the concrete has hardened.

potable water   Water which is fit to drink and satisfies the standards of the appropriate health authorities.

potato barn   A special-purpose barn for the long-term storage of potatoes; sunk below ground level to provide a cool temperature the year round.

poteaux-en-terre house   In French Vernacular architecture, a Cajun dwelling of the earliest settlers, primarily in the Louisiana Territory. To serve as vertical supports, closely spaced posts were driven into the ground and the space between them was filled with a mixture of clay and Spanish moss or clay and small stones. Compare with **poteaux-sur-solle house**.

poteaux-sur-solle house   In early French Vernacular architecture, a Cajun dwelling similar to a **poteaux-en-terre house** but supported by a hewn-log structural framework that usually rested on **sills, 1** (i.e., heavy horizontal timbers supported by cypress blocks placed under the sills). The space between the hewn logs was filled with **pierrotage** or **briquette-entre-poteaux**; then plastered and whitewashed in a manner similar to that of medieval half-timbering. The houses commonly had a shingle-covered bonnet or hipped roof. Individual rooms were provided access from a porch that ran across the face of the house.

potential transformer   Same as **voltage transformer**.

pot floor   A floor of **structural clay tile**.

pothead   A device used to provide a weathertight seal at the end of an electrical cable, serving as an insulated egress for the conductor(s).

pot life   **1.** The period of time during which a thermosetting plastic or rubber composition remains suitable for its intended use after mixing with a reaction-initiating agent; **working life**. **2.** The length of time a paint material is useful after its original package is opened, or after catalyst or other ingredients are added; also called **usable life, spreadable life**.

pot metal   **1.** Cast iron of a quality once used for making cooking pots. **2.** An alloy of copper and lead, once used for plumbing fixtures.

pottery   **1.** Any fired clayware which is produced by a clay worker. **2.** The low-fired, porous, colored body ware, in contrast to white or buff-colored earthenware.

poultry house   A place for housing fowl; once considered essential on most rural houses, farms, or estates before refrigerators because this provided a source of fresh eggs and freshly killed meat; also see **dovecote**.

pounced   Decorated with indentations or perforations.

pound-calorie The amount of heat required to raise one pound of water one degree centigrade.

pour coat, top mop **1.** On a built-up roof, the top coating of bitumen. **2.** The final pouring of hot bitumen in which the gravel or slag surfacing is embedded.

poured concrete See **concrete**.

poured floor See **polymeric poured floor**.

poured joint An electrical joint that is insulated by means of an insulating medium which is poured around it and which subsequently solidifies.

pouring rope See **asbestos joint runner**.

powdered asphalt Hard asphalt which is crushed or ground to a fine state; softened by combining it with flux oil.

powder house An isolated storage place for gunpowder; once found in areas subject to enemy attack; also called a powder magazine.

powdering Decoration by means of numerous small figures, usually the same figure often repeated.

powder molding A technique for producing objects of varying sizes and shapes by melting polyethylene powder, usually against the inside of a mold.

powder post A condition of wood which has decayed to powder, or has been eaten by worms which leave holes full of powder.

powder room **1.** The anteroom of a women's toilet, in which makeup and clothing are adjusted; by extension applied to a women's toilet itself. **2.** The small first-floor toilet room in a house.

power The rate at which work is performed, energy is transformed or transferred, or energy is consumed; usually expressed in watts or horsepower.

power buggy A materials-handling machine, about the size of a wheelbarrow, driven by a gasoline-powered engine or electric motor.

power cable An assembly of one or more electric conductors with one or more of the following protective coverings: insulation, inner jacket, protective armor, and outer jacket.

power cart Same as **power buggy**.

power circuit protector A low-voltage, fused, nonautomatic circuit breaker; has a circuit-breaker-type operating mechanism but is pro-

power buggy

tected by fuses rather than by a direct-acting or relay-operated tripping device.

power conditioner A packaged unit on an electric power line which provides **clean power**; may contain surge arresters, harmonic filters, isolation transformers, and voltage regulators.

power consumption The power used multiplied by time; measured in **kilowatt-hours, horsepower-hours**, etc.

power drill A **drill, 1** driven by an electric motor which transfers power to the chuck when a trigger-type switch is closed.

power elevator An **elevator** whose motion is driven by the application of a mechanical force other than that supplied by hand or gravity.

power factor In an alternating current, the ratio of the average power (expressed in watts) to the apparent power (expressed in volt-amperes).

power float See **rotary float**.

powerhouse A building in which electricity or other form of power is generated.

power level See **sound power level**.

power of attorney An instrument authorizing another to act as one's agent. Also see **attorney-in-fact**.

power-operated scaffold Any form of **scaffold** that is propelled vertically by the use of power machinery.

power outage See **outage**.

power panelboard A **panelboard** which serves branch circuits supplying motors and other heavy power-consuming loads.

power sander A portable, electric hand tool having a moving abrasive surface; used for smoothing and polishing; also see **sanding machine**.

power shovel **1.** A power-operated machine used to excavate and load dirt, rock, or debris by means of an open-ended bucket at the end of an arm which is suspended from a boom; cables or hydraulic rams force the arm (and therefore the bucket) forward and upward, into the material; then the bucket is raised and its load is dumped. **2.** A machine having a scoop or bucket for digging up or removing loose material.

power shovel

power take-off On construction equipment, any device for driving an auxiliary attachment or tool using the torque or power of the prime mover's motor or engine.

power transformer In an alternating current electrical system, a device for transforming the source of electrical supply from one voltage to another.

power trowel A **mechanical trowel.**

power wrench See **impact wrench.**

poyntel Same as **pointel.**

pozzolan, pozzolona, pozzuolana A siliceous or siliceous and aluminous material, which in itself possesses little or no cementitious value but will, in finely divided form and in the presence of moisture, chemically react with calcium hydroxide at ordinary temperatures to form compounds possessing cementitious properties.

pozzolan cement Pozzolan interground with lime; a natural cement used in ancient times.

pozzolanic Of or pertaining to **pozzolan.**

pozzuolana See **pozzolan.**

PP-AC Abbr. for "air-conditioning power panel."

PPGL On drawings, abbr. for "polished plate glass."

ppm Abbr. for **parts per million.**

PR On drawings, abbr. for "pair."

praecinctio In the ancient Roman theatre, a walkway between the lower and upper tiers of seats, running parallel to the rows of seats.

praetorium Same as **pretorium.**

prairie box A **Prairie style** house having a square floor plan, usually having a symmetrical façade and a room in each of the four corners of the house, a **hipped roof**, and occasionally **hipped dormers**; somewhat popular in the early 1900s; also called an American four-square house.

prairie cottage A cottage constructed of air-dried adobe bricks; built by settlers on the prairies of the western United States where stone was scarce, but clay suitable for brick making was usually available close to the surface of the ground. Sand, ashes, and linseed oil were often added to the clay. After the bricks air-dried for 10 to 12 days, they were laid with mortar in a construction that required minimal technical skill. **Battened doors** were common. The roof, usually shingled or thatched, had a large overhang to protect the adobe walls against erosion by rain. Contrast with a **Prairie style** house.

Prairie School A highly original group of influential architects in Chicago, closely associated with the early work of Frank Lloyd Wright (1867–1959) and, to a lesser extent, with Louis H. Sullivan (1856–1924) and their followers. The Prairie School was also influenced by the Arts and Crafts Movement in England. Many of the early works created by this school are in the **Prairie style.**

Prairie style A style of American domestic architecture that originated with the **Prairie School**, popular primarily in the Midwest from about 1900 to 1920. A house in this style often is characterized by: a two-story height with wings and/or porches of one story, integrated with its site to provide a low, horizontal appearance; the central portion of the house usually higher than the adjacent flanking wings; traditional building materials; exterior walls commonly of light-colored stucco, light-colored brick, or concrete block; contrasting wood trim between stories; a **porte cochère** and/or a porch having a roof typically supported by heavy columns that are either square in cross-section or have slanted sides; a terrace and/or balcony;

often, **Sullivanesque** friezes and/or door surrounds; a broad, low-pitched roof; eaves with a considerable overhang; hipped or gabled dormers; a prominent, large, relatively low rectangular chimney; often, a series of windows below the roof overhang; commonly, diamond-shaped window panes set in lead **cames**; commonly, **one-over-one** double-hung sashes or tall casement windows, often grouped in sets of two or three; doors having windows, often glazed with highly decorative geometric patterns.

Prairie style

prang   In Thai architecture of the 13th to 18th cent. A.D., a sanctuary consisting of a tower-like main temple with a porch structure.

Pratt truss   A **truss** having parallel chords, vertical members in compression, and diagonal members (which slant toward the center) in tension.

PRCST   On drawings, abbr. for "precast."

preaction sprinkler system   A **dry-pipe sprinkler system** which is activated by a smoke- or heat-sensing device, thereby opening a control valve and admitting water.

preaching cross   A cross erected in the immediate vicinity of a small chapel (on a highway or in an open place) to mark a place where monks or others could assemble for religious purposes. Also see **weeping cross**.

preaction sprinkler system   A fire **sprinkler system** using automatic **sprinklers** (heads) attached to a piping system; is controlled by a supplemental fire detection system, that is installed in the same area as the sprinklers; actuation of the detection system opens a valve which permits water to flow into the piping and to be discharged from the sprinklers; differs from a **deluge sprinkler system** in that *automatic* sprinklers are used rather than *open* sprinklers. There is no water in the piping under ordinary circumstances.

preassembled lock, mono lock, rigid lock, unit lock   A lock all of whose parts are

preaching cross   at Inverary, Argyllshire, Scotland

assembled as a unit at the factory; requires little or no disassembly when installed in a rectangular notch cut into the door edge.

preboring   Drilling a **pilot hole**.

precast   Said of a concrete member that is cast and cured in other than its final position.

precast concrete pile   See **precast pile**.

precast concrete wall panel   A **precast concrete** exterior panel or area separator; may be load-bearing or non-load-bearing.

CHANNEL

DOUBLE-TEE

precast concrete   (double-tee plank)

precast pile   Any reinforced concrete pile which is not cast in its final position.

precast stone   Same as **artificial stone**.

precinctio   Same as **praecinctio**.

precipitation   At a given location, the total measurable supply of water received directly as rain, snow, hail, or sleet; usually expressed in inches (millimeters) per day, month, or year.

precipitator   See **electrostatic precipitator**.

precise level   An instrument designed specifically for obtaining precise results by direct leveling techniques; essentially the same as an engineer's level with micrometers and also a prism arrangement permitting the simultaneous observation of the rod reading and the level bubble.

precise leveling rod   A precision leveling rod; the graduations are on a ribbon of special alloy whose precision is little affected by temperature; the ribbon is maintained under constant tension.

precoating   See **tinning**.

Pre-Columbian architecture   Architecture of the indigenous peoples of the Americas prior to their contact with European civilization.

precompressed zone   In **prestressed concrete**, that portion of a flexural structural member which is compressed by prestressing tendons.

preconsolidation   The condition of a highly compressed soil, usually resulting from other than natural causes, e.g., resulting from vibration of the soil or the loading of the soil by a large heap of excavated material.

preconsolidation pressure   The greatest effective pressure to which a soil has been subjected.

precure   To cure a glued joint prior to pressing or clamping.

precut building   A **manufactured building** composed largely of elements cut to size in a factory and moved to the erection site for assembly.

predella   **1.** The bottom tier of an altar-piece, between the principal panel or bas-relief and the altar itself. **2.** The broad platform on which the altar rests. **3.** An altar ledge.

preemption   The right to purchase property before, or in preference to, others.

prefab   A factory-built house of standard dimensions; does not include a mobile home or trailer having less-than-standard dimensions.

PREFAB   On drawings, abbr. for "prefabricated."

prefabricate   To fabricate components or units prior to their installation at the site, usually at a mill or plant away from the site.

prefabricated building   See **manufactured building**.

prefabricated construction   A construction method relying primarily on the use of standardized manufactured components; consists largely of assembling these parts rather than fabricating them at the site.

prefabricated flue   A metal vent for fuel-fired equipment, consisting entirely of factory-made parts.

prefabricated house   A house assembled from components cut to size at a factory, or assembled from building modules shipped to the construction site.

prefabricated joint filler   A compressible material used to fill control joints, expansion joints, contraction joints, and the like; either used exposed or as a backing for a joint sealant.

prefabricated masonry panel   A wall panel fabricated of masonry units which are bonded together at a manufacturing plant and then transported to the job site as a construction unit, ready for erection.

prefabricated pipe conduit system   Prefabricated mechanical service conduits laid underground or above grade, carrying insulated piping for one or more utilities.

prefabricated tie   A **wall tie** used in hollow-wall construction; consists of two heavy parallel wires which are tied together, at regular intervals, by short wires which are welded to them at right angles; each of the long parallel wires is bonded in one of the wall sections.

prefabricated unit   A built-up section, forming an individual structural element of a building (for example, a built-up beam, column, girder, plank, strut, or truss), which is prefabricated prior to its incorporation into the structure; usually includes any required means for erection and connection at the building site to complete the structural frame.

prefabricated wall   Same as **demountable partition**.

preferred angle   **1.** Any angle of pitch of stairs between 30° and 35°. **2.** Any angle of pitch of a ramp less than 15°.

prefilter In air-conditioning systems, a **filter, 1** before the main filter to remove the larger particles; usually has a lower efficiency than the main filter and has a low pressure drop characteristic.

prefinished door, prefitted door A door prefitted to an opening; both faces are factory-finished to specification and accommodations are provided for locks and hinges.

preformed asphalt joint filler A premolded strip of asphalt cement, mixed with a fine substance such as sawdust or cork; used as a **joint filler**.

preformed foam Foam produced in a foam generator prior to introduction of the foam into a mixer with other ingredients to produce cellular foam.

preformed joint sealant Same as **preformed sealant**.

preformed sealant A sealant preshaped by the manufacturer so that only a minimum of field fabrication is required prior to installation.

preheat coil In an air-conditioning system, a coil used to preheat air which is below freezing to a temperature somewhat above freezing, in advance of other processing.

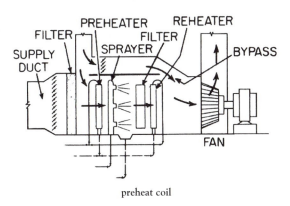

preheat coil

preheater See **preheat coil**.

preheat fluorescent lamp, switch-start fluorescent lamp A **fluorescent lamp** in which the electrodes must be preheated in order to start the arc; the preheating is initiated by either a manual switch or an automatic-starting switch.

preheating The partial heating of water in a domestic water system by circulating it through a first-stage **heat exchanger** before circulating it through the final heater.

prehung door An assembly consisting of a door on its frame, together with all necessary hardware and trim, ready for installation.

preliminary drawings Drawings prepared during the early stages of the design of a project.

preliminary estimate See **statement of probable construction costs**.

premature stiffening See **false set**.

premises Land and/or its appurtenances.

premises wiring The interior and exterior electrical wiring of a building that extends from (a) the load end of the **service drop** or **service lateral** conductor to (b) the outlets; includes power, lighting, control, and signal circuit wiring in addition to all associated hardware, fittings, and wiring devices.

premium-grade lumber The highest grade of lumber available both in material and workmanship; intended for the finest work; compare with **custom-grade lumber** and **economy-grade lumber**.

premixed plaster A **mill-mixed** plaster.

premolded asphalt panel A panel, usually made under pressure, with a core of asphalt, minerals, and fibers, covered on each side by a layer of asphalt-impregnated felt or fabric, coated on the outside with hot applied asphalt.

prepacked concrete See **preplaced-aggregate concrete**.

prepared roofing See **asphalt prepared roofing**.

prepayment meter A coin-operated water or gas meter; dispenses a fixed quantity of fluid after the money is inserted.

preplaced-aggregate concrete, prepacked concrete Concrete produced by placing coarse aggregate in a form and later injecting a portland cement-sand grout, usually with admixtures, to fill the voids.

pre-posttensioning A method of fabricating **prestressed concrete** in which some of the tendons are pretensioned and others are posttensioned.

prepreg In a reinforced plastic, the reinforcing material containing or combined with the full complement of resin before molding.

prequalification of prospective bidders
The process of investigating the qualifications of prospective bidders on the basis of their competence, integrity, and responsibility relative to the contemplated project.

pre-Romanesque architecture The several regional and transitional styles between the fall of the Roman Empire and the emergence of Romanesque architecture in the 11th cent., including Lombard, Carolingian, and Ottonian.

presbytery, presbyterium The actual sanctuary of a church beyond the choir and occupied only by the officiating clergy.

prescription specification The specification by name of products, equipment, or systems to be used.

presence chamber, presence room The room in which a great personage receives his guests or those entitled to come before him; a hall of state.

preservation See **building preservation**.

preservative **1.** A product, such as **creosote**, used to make wood waterproof or immune against attack by insects, etc. **2.** A protective coating on a metal surface.

pre-shimmed sealant A **sealant** (e.g., strip of resilient plastic or rubber) which has encapsulated solids or discrete particles which limit its deformation within a joint under compression.

pre-shimmed tape sealant A **pre-shimmed sealant** in tape form.

preshrunk **1.** Descriptive of concrete which has been mixed for a short period in a stationary mixer before being transferred to a transit mixer. **2.** Descriptive of grout, mortar, or concrete that has been mixed 1 to 3 hr before placing to reduce shrinkage during hardening.

presidio In Spanish architecture and its derivatives, a frontier outpost or fort.

pressed brick Brick that has been subjected to pressure so as to provide sharp edges and smooth surfaces before being treated in a kiln.

pressed edge That edge of a footing along which the greatest soil pressure occurs under conditions of **overturning**.

pressed glass Any unit of glass pressed into shape, such as **glass block, pavement light**, etc.

pressed-metal ceiling A sheet-metal ceiling embossed in a decorative pattern; usually coated with a layer of tin and lead or a coat of paint primer as a protection against oxidation; much used on the ceilings of stores after about 1875, especially during the early part of the 20th century.

pressed reflector lamp Same as **PAR lamp**.

pressed steel Steel which has been pressed into shape between dies to form a building component.

pressure The force per unit area exerted by a homogeneous liquid or gas on the walls of its container.

pressure bulb The zone in a loaded soil mass bounded by an arbitrarily selected isobar of stress.

pressure cell A device for measuring the pressure within a soil mass or the pressure of soil against a rigid wall.

pressure connector, solderless connector A device which establishes a connection between two or more electric conductors, or between one or more conductors and a terminal, by means of mechanical pressure and without the use of solder.

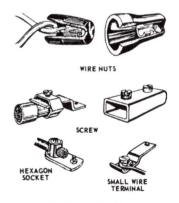

WIRE NUTS

SCREW

HEXAGON SOCKET

SMALL WIRE TERMINAL

pressure connectors

pressure creosoting The forcing of creosote, under pressure, into timber as a preservative.

pressure drainage A condition in which a static pressure may be imposed safely on the entrances of sloping building drains through soil and waste stacks connected thereto.

pressure drop The decrease in fluid pressure between two ends of a duct or pipeline, between two points in a system, across valves and fittings, etc., due to frictional losses; in a water-piping system a drop in fluid pressure also occurs between two points as a result of the difference in elevation between the two points.

pressure forming In plastics, a thermoforming process in which pressure is used to push the sheet to be formed against the mold surface in contrast to the use of a vacuum to pull the sheet flat against the mold.

pressure gauge An instrument for measuring fluid pressure.

pressure gun Same as **caulking gun**.

pressure head See **static head**.

pressure-locked grating A grating in which the cross bars are locked mechanically to the **bearing bars** at their intersections by deforming or by swaging the metal.

pressure pipe Pipe which is designed to resist a continuous pressure exerted on it by the medium which it conveys.

pressure-reducing valve, reducing valve **1.** A **pressure regulating valve**. **2.** A valve that maintains a predetermined pressure by means of an automatic valve controller.

pressure regulating valve (PRV) A device used to reduce and maintain the water pressure automatically with predetermined design parameters, for both dynamic flow and static conditions.

pressure regulating valve station, PRV station An installation of multiple **pressure regulating valves** in a single zone of a water supply system in a building.

pressure regulator **1.** In a fire sprinkler system, a device that limits water pressure, under both flow and no-flow conditions, in those portions of the system where it is probable that the pressure may exceed 175 pounds per square inch (11,400 kPa). **2.** A **pressure-reducing valve**.

pressure-relief damper A **relief damper** installed in a system which relieves pressure in excess of a preset limit.

pressure-relief device A disk which is designed to open or a device which is designed to rupture automatically in order to relieve pressure within a system.

pressure relief hatch See **smoke and fire vent**.

pressure relief valve In a **pressure tank** for

pressure-relief damper

water storage, a pressure-actuated safety valve that is designed to open and relieve pressure automatically if the pressure within the tank exceeds the value for which it was designed to operate safely.

pressure-relieving joint In panel-wall masonry, an open joint left at specified horizontal intervals to allow for expansion and contraction; commonly below horizontal supporting hangers at each floor to allow for expansion and contraction and to prevent the weight of higher courses from being transmitted to the masonry below. Such joints are stopped with flexible caulking compound to exclude moisture.

pressure-sensitive Capable of adhering to a surface when pressed against it.

pressure-sensitive adhesive A viscoelastic material which remains permanently tacky in a solvent-free form; will adhere instantaneously to most solid surfaces with the application of very slight pressure.

pressure tank A closed cylindrical steel container designed to store water under pressure.

pressure-treated lumber Lumber that has been impregnated under pressure with a chemical preservative or fire retardant.

pressure-type vacuum breaker A **vacuum breaker** containing an independently operating, internally-loaded check valve and an independently operating air inlet valve on the discharge side of the check valve.

pressure weather stripping Weather stripping which is designed to provide a seal of constant pressure by means of spring tension.

pressure wire connector   A device that establishes an electrical connection between conductors (or between a conductor and a device) solely by mechanical pressure.

pressure zone   An area of a building (it may be an entire floor, several floors, or the entire building) supplied with water having a common pressure origin or a common water supply.

pressurized stairway enclosure   A stairway enclosure whose interior is maintained at a slightly elevated pressure to minimize smoke contamination during a fire.

presteaming period   The period of time between the molding of a concrete product and the start of the temperature rise in the curing process.

prestressed concrete   Concrete in which internal stresses are introduced of such magnitude and distribution that the tensile stresses resulting from the service loads are counteracted to a desired degree; in reinforced concrete the prestress commonly is introduced by tensioning the tendons.

prestressed concrete wire   Steel wire having a very high tensile strength, used in prestressed concrete by embedding it under tension in the concrete.

prestressed pile   A concrete **pile** which is prestressed or posttensioned in order to eliminate or reduce cracking during its transportation to the construction site, during driving, and while in service.

prestressing   Applying a load to a structure, deforming it so that it will withstand a working load more effectively or so that it will deflect less.

prestressing cable   See **tendon**.

prestressing steel   High-strength steel (in the form of bars, rods, wires, etc.) which is used to prestress concrete.

presumptive bearing pressure   The vertical bearing pressure which is permitted in the absence of extensive investigation and testing.

pretensioned concrete   Concrete which has been subjected to **pretensioning**.

pretensioning   A method of prestressing **reinforced concrete** in which the tendons are tensioned before the concrete has hardened.

pretil   In Spanish architecture and its derivatives, a **parapet,** a breast-high wall, or a brick **coping** atop a wall.

pretorium   In the ancient Roman Empire, the official residence of a provincial governor; a hall of justice; a palace.

preventive maintenance   The maintenance of machinery in which mechanical components are replaced periodically at fixed time intervals regardless of the machinery's mechanical condition. Contrast with **on-condition maintenance**.

pricking coat, pricked-up coat   Same as **scratch coat** (i.e., first coat of plaster).

pricking up   Scoring a first coat of plaster on lath.

prick post   In a wood-framed structure, a secondary post or side post.

prick punch   A pointed steel **punch** which is struck with a hammer; used to mark metal or sheet metal.

prick punch

prie-dieu   A small desk before which a person may kneel when praying.

priest's door   The door by which the priest enters the chancel from the side.

primacord   A detonating fuse having a core contained within a waterproof covering; used to detonate explosives.

primary air   **1.** In a water heater, the air which is fed to the burner to be mixed with gas. **2.** The air which is delivered to any type of air outlet or **grille** by a supply duct.

primary battery   Two or more **primary cells**.

primary blasting   The blasting operation by which the original rock formation is dislodged from its natural location.

primary branch   **1.** A drain which slopes from the base of a soil stack or waste stack to its junction with a building drain. **2.** In a building, the largest single branch of a water-supply line or an air-supply duct.

primary cell   A cell that generates electric current by electrochemical means; the discharge of

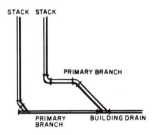

primary branches, 1

electric current causes one of the electrodes in the cell to be consumed; usually a cell cannot be recharged from an external source of electric power, although some can be recharged to a limited extent.

primary consolidation, primary compression, primary time effect The reduction in volume of a soil mass caused by the application of a sustained load on the mass; principally due to the squeezing out of water from the voids in the mass, accompanied by a transfer of the load from the soil water to the soil solids.

primary distribution feeder A **feeder** which operates at the primary voltage supplying a distribution circuit.

primary entrance The principal entrance to a building expressly utilized for day-to-day pedestrian ingress and egress.

primary excavation The excavation of soil which has not previously been moved.

primary fluid, primary refrigerant The **refrigerant** in a refrigeration system which takes up heat, by evaporation.

primary light source 1. A source in which light is produced directly from a transformation of energy. 2. The principal, or most obvious, source of light when several sources of light are present.

primary member See **main member**.

primary time effect See **primary consolidation**.

primavera A relatively lightweight, yellowish white to brown wood of Central and South America, frequently with ribbon-stripe figures; used for cabinets, plywood and interior finish.

prime coat, priming coat A first coat with a **primer, 1**.

prime contract A contract between the **owner** and **contractor** for construction of a **project** or portion thereof.

prime contractor Any contractor on a **project** having a contract directly with the **owner**.

prime mover 1. Any machine that converts fuel (e.g., diesel oil, gasoline, or natural gas) or steam into mechanical energy. 2. A powerful truck, tractor, or the like.

prime professional Any person or firm having a contract directly with the **owner** for professional services.

primer 1. A paint, applied as a first coat, which serves the function of sealing and filling on wood, plaster, and masonry; inhibits rust and improves the adhesion of subsequent coats of paint on metal surfaces. 2. A thin liquid bitumen solvent; applied to a roof surface to absorb dust and to improve the adhesion of subsequent applications of bitumen. 3. A cartridge or container of explosives into which a detonator or detonating cord is inserted or attached.

prime standby power source See **standby power generator**.

prime window The window to which a storm window is attached.

priming The application of a **primer**.

princess post In a truss, a vertical post between the **queen post** and the wall to supplement the support of the queen post.

principal 1. One on whose behalf or in whose name binding transactions may be entered into by another, usually called the **agent**. 2. One for whose debt or default another (called a "surety") promises to make good. 3. In professional practice, any person legally responsible for the activities of such practice. 4. In a framed structure, a most important member, such as a truss which supports the roof.

principal beam The largest or main beam in a framework.

principal brace 1. Same as **sway brace**. 2. A brace supporting a principal rafter.

principal elevation The façade or front **elevation** of a building.

principal façade The architectural front of a building, often distinguished from the other faces by the use of better materials and greater elaboration of architectural or ornamental details; usually faces a street, but occasionally faces a mews or court.

principal joist In a timber-framed house, a large **joist** that carries much of the floor load.

principal post A **corner post** in a timber-framed house.

principal purlin In timber-framed construction, a **purlin** that is somewhat heavier than a **common purlin**; usually runs parallel to the ridge of the roof about halfway between the ridge and the **top plate**. The only purlin on each side of the roof ridge, it is framed into and joins the principal rafters, thus providing lateral stability for the entire roof framing system and support for a number of **common rafters**.

principal rafter In a timber-framed house, one of several such rafters that extend from the ridge of the roof down to the **wall plate**; somewhat heavier than a **common rafter**; often located at a corner post, story post, or chimney post and framed into a **tie beam**. Principal rafters, together with the principal purlins, form a roof framing system having considerable stability. Also called a **blade**.

principal roof, principal rafter roof A roof supported by **principal rafters**.

print 1. A plaster cast of a flat ornament. 2. See **printing**.

printing Forming a permanent impression in a semihardened paint film as a result of pressure from an object placed on it.

print room In English 18th cent. interiors and derivatives, a room decorated by affixing prints to the walls.

priory A religious house governed by a prior or prioress.

prismatic billet molding A common Norman molding consisting of a series of prisms, with alternate rows staggered.

prismatic billet molding

prismatic glass Rolled glass ⅛ to ¼ in. (3.2 to 6.4 mm) thick, one face of which consists of parallel prisms that refract the transmitted light, thereby changing the direction of the light rays.

prismatic rustication In Elizabethan architecture, rusticated masonry with diamond-shaped projections worked on the face of every stone.

prism glass Same as **prismatic glass**.

privacy landscape screen See **office landscape screen**.

private area The area, whether within or outside a building, which is reserved for the exclusive use of a single family.

private branch exchange (PBX) A private telephone switching system located on the customer's premises, usually serving an organization (such as a business or government agency). It switches telephone calls within a building and also to an outside telephone network.

private residence A separate dwelling (or separate apartment) occupied only by the members of a single family unit.

private sewage disposal system A system composed of a septic tank with its effluent discharging into: (a) a subsurface **absorption field**, (b) one or more **seepage pits**, or (c) some combination of (a) and (b) or any other facility permitted by code.

private sewer A sewer privately owned; controlled by public authority only to the extent provided by law.

private stairway A stairway serving one tenant only and not for general public use.

privy An outhouse which serves as a toilet.

privy chamber Same as **presence chamber**.

prize house In tobacco-growing states of the southern United States, a structure that once housed a press (called a *prize*) for compacting cured tobacco leaves.

proaulion In the early Church, and in the modern Greek Church, the porch or vestibule of the church; an outer porch before the narthex.

procathedral A church used as the cathedral church of a diocese while the proper church remains unfinished or under repair.

processed shake A sawn cedar shingle; textured on one surface to resemble a **shake**.

processional path A continuation of the choir **aisles** behind the high altar in an apsidal (and sometimes in a **square-ended**) church.

processional way A monumental roadway for ritual processions in an ancient city, e.g., Babylon.

ancient Egyptian **processional way**

procoeton In ancient Greece and Roman dwellings, an antechamber or room preceding other rooms or chambers.

Proctor compaction test A test to determine the optimum moisture content of a soil; the soil is compacted according to a specified procedure, and then compacted samples of the soil are weighed.

Proctor penetration needle A needle, 0.05 to 1 sq in. (0.32 to 6.45 sq cm) in area, used with a spring balance, to measure the resistance of fine-grained soil to penetration.

Proctor penetration resistance See **standard penetration resistance**.

prodomos **1.** A lobby or vestibule. **2.** A **pronaos**.

producer A manufacturer, processor, or assembler of building materials or equipment.

production drawings See **working drawings**.

production greenhouse A **greenhouse** for growing large numbers of plants and flowers on a production basis or for research, without public access.

professional adviser An architect engaged by the **owner** to direct an authorized design competition for the selection of an architect.

professional engineer A designation reserved, usually by law, for a person or organization professionally qualified and duly licensed to perform such engineering services as structural, mechanical, electrical, sanitary, civil, etc.

professional liability insurance Insurance designed to insure an architect or engineer against claims for damages resulting from alleged professional negligence.

professional practice The practice of one of the environmental design professions in which services are rendered within the framework of recognized professional ethics and standards and applicable legal requirements.

profile **1.** A guide used to set out brick work or block work accurately. **2.** A **soil profile**. **3.** A vertical section of the surface of the ground, or of underlying strata, or both, along any fixed line. On a highway, the profile is usually taken along the center line. **4.** In architectural drawing, the outline of a vertical section. **5.** British term for **batter board**.

program A statement prepared by or for an owner, with or without an architect's assistance, setting forth the conditions and objectives for a building project including its general purpose and detailed requirements, such as a complete listing of the rooms required, their sizes, special facilities, etc.

program evaluation and review technique (PERT) A management control technique applied to building construction; determines what must be done to complete construction by a given date. Current construction progress is monitored on a computer and compared with the planned schedule so as to provide a management tool for further planning and decision making.

progress chart A chart prepared by a contractor, brought up to date monthly; the principal trades of the project are tabulated vertically and the scheduled construction time shown horizontally, from left to right; there are two sets of bars for each trade, one showing the scheduled starting and completion dates, and the other showing the actual status of the work at the date of issuance.

progressive kiln, continuous kiln, step-kiln A dry kiln arranged so that green lumber enters one end and is dried in progressive steps as it moves to the opposite end, where it is removed.

progressive scaling The disintegration, as of concrete, which at first appears as surface scaling, but gradually progresses deeper.

progress payment A partial payment made during progress of the **work, 1** on account of work completed and/or materials suitably stored.

progress schedule A diagram, graph, or other pictorial or written schedule showing proposed and actual times of starting and completion of the various elements of the work.

PROJ On drawings, abbr. for "project."

project **1.** A construction undertaking, composed of one or more buildings and the site improvements, planned and executed in a fixed time period. **2.** In an office, a job or a commission. **3.** A planned, large apartment building or housing complex, usually built at minimum cost with government funds for low-income families; also called a **housing project. 4.** The total construction designed by the architect, of which the work performed under the **contract documents** may be the whole or a part.

project budget The sum established by the owner as available for the entire project, including the construction budget, land costs, equipment costs, financing costs, compensation for professional services, contingency allowance, and other similar established or estimated costs.

project cost The total cost of a **project** including professional compensation, land costs, furnishings and equipment, financing and other charges, as well as the **construction cost.**

projected window A window having one or more rotatable **sashes (ventilators, 2)** which swing either inward or outward.

projecting belt course A course of masonry, often elaborate, which projects beyond the face of the wall.

projecting brick One of a number of bricks which project beyond the face of a wall, usually forming a pattern.

projecting bricks

projecting porch A porch that extends beyond the face of a house, in contrast to an **integral porch** set within the main structure of the house.

projecting porch

projecting scaffold A work platform cantilevered from the face of a building by means of brackets secured to the building face.

projecting sign A sign attached to, and extending outward from, a building's face.

projection **1.** In masonry, stones which are set forward of the general wall surface to provide a rugged or rustic appearance. **2.** Any component, member, or part which juts out from a building.

projection booth A booth, usually at the rear of an auditorium, for the operation of motion-picture projectors, slide projectors, or follow spots.

project manual The manual prepared by the architect for a project, including the bidding requirements, **conditions of the contract**, and the technical **specifications**.

projector   **1.** A lighting unit which concentrates the light within a limited solid angle by means of mirrors and lenses; provides a high value of luminous intensity in one direction. **2.** A line dropped perpendicularly from a point to a plane surface.

project representative   The architect's representative at the project site who assists in the administration of the construction contract; when authorized by the owner, a full-time project representative may be employed.

project site   See **site**.

projet   A scheme for a project presented by drawings and/or models as an exercise in the study of design by architectural students.

promenade   A suitable place for walking for pleasure, as a mall.

promenade tile   Same as **quarry tile**.

promoter   Same as **catalyst, 1**.

prompt box   Same as **prompter's box**.

prompter's box   A small box for the prompter at the center of the footlights, esp. in an opera house; projects slightly above the floor of the stage and has an opening facing the performers.

pronaos   The inner portico in front of the naos, or cella, of a classical temple.

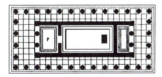

pronaos: *P*

proof stress   A stress, either compression or tension, which is applied to a material to determine the magnitude required to produce a specified permanent deformation usually specified as a percentage of the original length.

prop   A **post** or **shore**.

propeller fan   An axial-flow fan that operates against little or no static pressure; used chiefly for exhaust and circulation purposes.

property   **1.** Any asset, real or personal. **2.** An ownership interest.

property damage insurance   Part of general

propeller fan

liability insurance covering injury to or destruction of tangible property, including loss of use resulting therefrom, but usually not including property which is in the **care, custody, and control** of the insured.

property insurance   Insurance on the work at the site against loss or damage caused by perils of fire, lightning, extended coverage (wind, hail, explosion, except steam boiler explosion, riot, civil commotion, aircraft, land vehicles, and smoke), vandalism and malicious mischief, and additional perils (as otherwise provided or requested). Also see **special hazards insurance**.

property line   A recorded boundary of a plot.

property-line wall   A wall erected on or along a **property line**.

property room   A storage room for any object used on a stage except costumes, lights, and scenery.

property survey   See **boundary survey**.

proportional dividers   A drafting instrument used in reducing or enlarging drawings; consists of two legs whose ends are pointed and cross each other (like the letter X) at a pivot point whose position can be adjusted; the distance between the two pointed ends on one side of the pivot is proportional to the distance between the pointed ends on the opposite side.

proportional dividers

proportional limit   The greatest stress which a material is capable of sustaining without any deviation from Hooke's law.

proportioning   The selection of proportions of ingredients for mortar or concrete to make the most economical use of available materials to produce mortar or concrete of the required properties.

proposal   See **bid**.

proposal form   See **bid form**.

propylaeum   **1.** The monumental gateway to a sacred enclosure. **2.** (*pl., cap.* Propylaea) Particularly, the elaborate gateway to the Acropolis in Athens.

Propylaea, 2

propylon   In ancient Egyptian architecture, a monumental gateway, usually between two towers in outline like truncated pyramids, of which one or a series stood before the actual entrance or pylon of most temples or other important buildings.

propylon

proscenium   **1.** In the ancient theatre, the stage before the scene or back wall. **2.** The frame or arch that separates the stage from the seating areas of an auditorium. **3.** The **proscenium arch**.

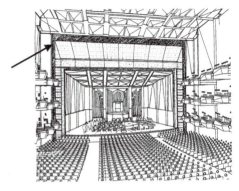

proscenium, 2   Benaroya Hall (1998), Seattle

proscenium arch   An arch or any equivalent opening in the **proscenium wall** through which the stage is seen by the audience.

proscenium box   A box adjacent to the proscenium wall; a **stage box**.

proscenium door   A door in a proscenium wall through which actors can move on and off the forestage.

proscenium stage   A theatre stage which is framed by a proscenium arch.

proscenium theatre   A theatre in which the stage is framed by a proscenium arch.

proscenium wall   A fire-resistive wall which separates a stage or enclosed platform from the public or spectators' area of an auditorium or theatre.

proscription   The acquisition of title to **real property** by one who openly and continuously is in adverse possession of it for a period sufficiently long that the statute of limitations bars the previous owner from reclaiming it (usually 20 years).

proskenion   In the ancient Greek theatre, a building before the **skene**; the earliest high Hellenistic stage; later, the front of the stage.

prospect   A scenic view, usually from an elevated position.

prospect tower   Same as **lookout tower**.

prostas   **1.** In ancient Greek architecture, a vestibule or antechamber. **2.** Same as **prostasis, 1**.

prostasis **1.** The portion of the front of a classical temple in antis which lies between the **antae**. **2.** A pronaos before a cella.

prostoon Same as **portico**.

prostyle Having a portico of columns at the front of a building only.

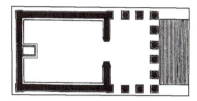

prostyle temple shown in plan

protected construction In fire-protection systems, all structural members that are constructed, chemically treated, covered, or protected so that the individual components, or combinations of such units, meet the specified values of fire-resistance ratings for the application.

protected corner The corner of a concrete slab provided with a means of transferring at least 20% of the load from that corner to the corner of an adjacent slab, either by mechanical means or by **aggregate interlock**.

protected equipment Electrical equipment (e.g., a motor or transformer) on the load side of a circuit breaker.

protected metal sheeting Sheet metal which is coated with a layer of bitumen or other material to protect it from corrosion.

protected noncombustible construction Noncombustible construction in which bearing walls (or bearing portions of walls), exterior or interior, have minimum fire-endurance ratings of 2 hr and are stable under fire conditions; roofs and floors, and their supports, have 1-hr fire-endurance ratings; stairways and other openings through floors are enclosed with partitions having 1-hr fire-endurance ratings.

protected opening In a wall or partition, an opening which is fitted with a door, window, or shutter having a fire-endurance rating appropriate to the use of the wall.

protected ordinary construction Construction in which roof and floors and their supports have 1-hr fire endurance, and stairways and other openings through floors are enclosed with partitions having 1-hr fire endurance, and which meets all the requirements of ordinary construction.

protected shaft Any type of shaft or stairwell that is enclosed within fire-rated walls, doors, or other openings.

protected waste pipe A **waste pipe** from a plumbing fixture which is not directly connected to a drain, soil pipe, vent pipe, or waste pipe.

protected wood-frame construction Construction meeting all the requirements of wood frame construction, and in which roof and floors and their supports have 1-hr fire endurance, and stairways and other openings through floors are enclosed with partitions having 1-hr fire endurance.

protection See **building protection**.

protection screen Similar to a **detention screen** except that the screen mesh is not put in tension and the construction may be somewhat lighter; usually used with psychiatric windows.

protective covenant **1.** An agreement, in writing, which restricts the use of real property. **2.** A restriction, which affects the use of real property, that appears in a legal document conveying title to the property.

protective ground An electrical connection or connections to an **approved ground** for establishing and maintaining a common potential on conductors connected to it.

protective lighting Lighting which is intended to facilitate the nighttime policing of industrial properties (or the like).

protective membrane A surface material that meets code requirements for an outer layer of a fire-resistive assembly containing concealed spaces.

protectory An institution for care and education of children who are delinquent or homeless.

prothesis In a Greek church, a chapel beside the sanctuary, usually on the north side of the bema.

prothyron In ancient Greece, a porch or vestibule in front of the door of a house.

proto-Doric Of a style apparently introductory to the Doric style. (*See illustration p. 724.*)

proto-Ionic Of a style apparently introductory to the Ionic style. (*See illustration p. 724.*)

protome

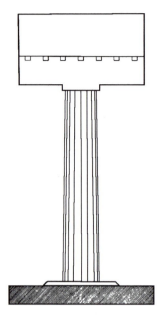

proto-Doric column

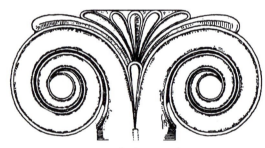

proto-Ionic capital

protome In classical architecture and derivatives, a projecting half figure, animal or human, used in a decorative scheme.

protomic capital A **capital** decorated with projecting half figures, animal or human or some combination thereof.

protractor An instrument graduated in angular degrees for measuring or laying out angles.

proximity switch A **sensor** and associated equipment which is actuated by the presence of nearby objects.

Prussian blue **1.** A class of deep blue pigments of ferric-ferrocyanides; tends to fade in light tints; reactive with alkalies; **ferrocyanide blue**. **2.** Any color produced with Prussian blue, e.g., **Chinese blue**.

PRV See **pressure regulating valve**.

pry bar A heavy steel bar, pointed at one end and shaped like a chisel at the other end; used for prying.

prytaneum A public hall in ancient Greek states and cities where public officials received and entertained distinguished guests, honored citizens of high public merit, etc.

p.s.e. Abbr. for "planed and square-edged."

pseudisodomum In Greek or Roman masonry, ashlar of regular cut stone in which the heights of the courses are not uniform.

pseudisodomum

pseudodipteral In classical architecture, having an arrangement of columns similar to the dipteral, but with the essential difference of the omission of the inner row, thus leaving a wide passage around the cella.

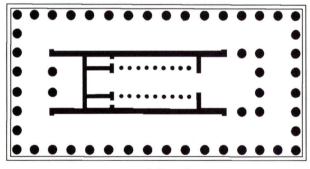

pseudodipteral

pseudoheader Same as **clipped header**.

pseudoperipteral Describing a classical temple or other building having columns all the way around, those on the flanks and rear being engaged, not freestanding.

pseudoprostyle In Classical architecture, same as **prostyle** but without a **pronaos**, the

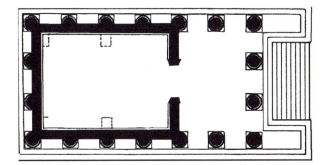

pseudoperipteral

columns of the portico being set less than the width of an intercolumniation from the front wall, or being actually engaged in it.

pseudothyrum A secret door, providing ingress and egress to a premise without being observed.

psf Abbr. for "pounds per square foot."

psi Abbr. for "pounds per square inch."

psia Abbr. for "pounds per square inch absolute."

psig Abbr. for "pounds per square inch gauge (pressure)."

p.s.j. Abbr. for "planed and square-jointed."

psychiatric window A corrosion-resistant window of a heavy-duty awning type with interior protection screens, designed for use in mental or psychiatric institutions; it is free of parts that can be removed by the patient and has a sill which can be cleaned easily.

psychrograph A self-recording **psychrometer**, providing simultaneous readings of dry-bulb and wet-bulb thermometers.

psychrometer An instrument used to measure humidity in the atmosphere from two thermometers which are similar except that the bulb of one is kept wet, the bulb of the other being dry.

psychrometric chart A chart showing the relationship between dewpoint temperature, drybulb temperature, wet bulb temperature, humidity ratio, and relative humidity.

psychrometry The study of moist air.

PT **1.** On drawings, abbr. for "part." **2.** On drawings, abbr. for "point."

pteroma In Classical architecture, the enclosed space of a portico, peristyle, or stoa, generally behind a screen of columns.

pteron **1.** In a Classical temple, the passageway between the walls of the **cella** and the columns of the **peristyle**. **2.** The side of a Classical temple or the row of columns along one side of the temple.

p.t.g. Abbr. for "planed, tongued, and grooved."

PTN On drawings, abbr. for **partition**.

P-trap A P-shaped trap forming a water seal in a waste or soil pipe; esp. used for sinks and lavatories.

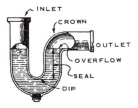

P-trap

public-address system Same as **sound-amplification system**.

public area Any area which is free and open to the general public at all times.

public corridor A corridor or enclosed passageway connecting a room or suite with a stairway, fire tower, or other designated exit, but intended to serve only the occupants of the floor on which it is located.

public garage Garage for temporary parking or storage of motor vehicles. Usually excludes repair and maintenance of such vehicles.

public hall A hall, corridor, or passageway within a building but outside all apartments or suites of private rooms.

public house Same as **tavern**.

public housing Low-cost housing, owned, sponsored, or administered by a municipal or other governmental agency.

public liability insurance Insurance covering liability of the insured for negligent acts resulting in bodily injury, disease, or death of others than employees of the insured, and/or property damage.

public nuisance See **nuisance**.

public sewer A common **sewer** directly controlled by the public authority.

public space **1.** An area within a building to which there is free access by the public, such as a foyer or lobby. **2.** In some codes, an area or piece of land legally designated for public use.

public system A water or sewerage system which is owned and operated by a local governmental authority or by a local utility company controlled by a governmental authority.

public-use area Rooms or spaces that are available to the general public.

public utility A public service such as water, gas, electricity, telephone, sewers, etc.

public water main A water-supply pipe for public use, controlled by public authority.

public way Any parcel of land unobstructed from the ground to the sky, appropriated for the free passage of the general public; a minimum width usually is specified by code.

pudding stone A composite rock containing rounded pebbles or gravel embedded in a siliceous matrix; see **cyclopean concrete**.

puddle To compact loose soil by first soaking it and then permitting it to dry.

puddle, clay puddle, puddling Clay to which a little water has been added and which then has been tempered, to make it homogeneous and to increase its plasticity; used to prevent the passage of water.

puddled adobe construction A primitive wall construction once used in what is now the American Southwest; built up of successive layers of an **adobe** mixture containing enough water so that it could be poured. The first layer was poured directly on the ground and allowed to dry before the next layer was poured on top of it; successive layers were built up until the wall reached its full height. Such walls eroded easily.

puddle weld A type of **plug weld** for joining two sheets of light-gauge material; a hole, burned in the upper sheet, is filled with a puddle of weld metal to fuse the upper sheet to the lower.

puddling **1.** Inducing compaction in mortar or concrete by the use of a tamping rod. **2.** See **puddle**.

pueblo Communal dwelling, usually of stone or adobe, built by the Pueblo Indians of southwestern U.S.A.; built in excavated hollows in the faces of cliffs or on the plains, valleys, or mesas. Usually entered by means of ladders.

pueblo architecture Communal housing, as much as five stories high, containing a large number of individual family units, built by unrelated tribes of New Mexico and Arizona known as "Pueblo Indians." Buildings are constructed of adobe or a combination of adobe and stone and have massive exterior walls coated with an adobe plaster; windows of small size; stepped-back roof lines; flat roofs supported by roof beams; interior walls finished with adobe plaster. Entry to the rooms through a hatchway in the roof, reached by a ladder.

Pueblo Revival, Pueblo style In the southwestern United States, primarily from about 1910 to 1940, an architectural mode intended to suggest pueblo architecture; usually includes a mixture of **Spanish Colonial Revival** and **Mission Revival**. Such buildings are usually characterized by: earth-colored stucco walls that provide a low-profile, adobe-like appearance; rounded corners at wall intersections; occasionally, battered walls; brick flooring on the porches and terraces; stepped-back roof lines in imitation of pueblo architecture; parapeted flat roofs drained by waterspouts; rows of wood beams protruding through the exterior walls, providing structural support for the roof; casement windows, usually recessed, with roughly hewn lintels; and **battened doors**.

puff pipe A short vent pipe on the outlet side of a trap, to prevent siphonage.

pugging Heavy loose material, such as ashes or sand, placed as a filler between the **joists** in floor-ceiling assemblies; formerly used to improve the sound insulation between the rooms above and below the floor.

pug mill A machine for mixing and tempering clay.

pug-mill brick Same as **adobe quemado**.

pull A handle for opening a door, window, drawer, etc.

pull box In electric wiring, a box (with a removable cover) that is inserted in one or more runs of raceway to facilitate the pulling of conductors through the raceway.

pull-chain operator A chain used to control the amount of opening of a device such as a **damper, 1**.

pulldown handle A **pull** on the upper sash of a double-hung window; fixed to the bottom rail.

pulley **1.** A wheel having a grooved rim for car-

pull-chain operator

rying a rope or other line and turning in a frame; a **pulley sheave. 2.** A **pulley block** containing one or more pulley sheaves.

pulley block   A frame or case containing one or more **pulley sheaves**; a **block, 6**.

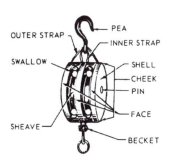

pulley block

pulley mortise   See **chase mortise**.

pulley sheave   The grooved roller over which a cord or rope runs in a pulley block.

pulley stile, hanging stile, sash run, window stile   The upright of a window frame in which the sash pulleys are installed and along which the sash slides.

pull hardware   A fixed handle or grip used to pull a door open.

pulling   In painting, the resistance to movement while brushing, resulting from high viscosity of the paint.

pulling over   In wood finishing, the smoothing of a nitrocellulose lacquer by rubbing with a solvent-soaked cloth.

pulling tension   The amount of pull placed on a cable during its installation.

pulling up   The softening of a previous coat of paint as the next coat is applied.

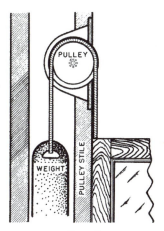

pulley stile

pull scraper   A hand scraper consisting of a steel blade at right angles to the handle; esp. used for smoothing wood or for removing thick finishes.

pull shovel   Same as **backhoe**.

pull switch   Same as **chain-pull switch**.

pulpboard   A solid board usually composed of wood pulp. Also see **fiberboard**.

pulpit   An elevated enclosed stand in a church in which the preacher stands.

pulpit

pulpitum **1.** In a Roman theatre, the part of the stage adjacent to the orchestra; corresponds to the **logeion** of a Greek theatre. **2.** The **tribune, 1** of an orator.

pulsation In a furnace, the panting of the flames; an indication of rapid, cyclical changes of pressure in the furnace.

pulverised-fuel ash British term for **fly ash**.

pulvinarium A room in an ancient Roman temple in which was set out the couch (*pulivar*) for the gods at a special religious feast.

pulvinated, pillowed Cushion-shaped, bulging out, as in the convex profile of the frieze in some Ionic orders.

pulvinus **1.** The baluster at the side of an Ionic capital. **2.** An **impost block**, a **dosseret**.

pulvinus, 1

pumice Lava having a highly porous, loose, spongy, or cellular structure; of relatively high silica content; used in powdered form as an abrasive in polishing, etc.

pumice concrete A lightweight concrete that has pumice as the coarse aggregate and provides relatively good thermal insulation.

pumice stone A solid block of **pumice**; used to polish or rub painted or varnished surfaces.

pumicite Naturally occurring, finely divided pumice.

pump A device or machine that compresses and/or transports fluids, usually by pressure or suction, or both; may be used to remove water from a construction site or to convey water from one elevation to another. See **water pump**.

pumped concrete Any concrete which is transported through a hose or pipe by means of a pump.

pumping The displacement and ejection of water and suspended fine particles at joints, cracks, and edges.

pumpkin dome Same as **melon dome**.

punch **1.** A small sharply pointed metal tool which is struck with a hammer and used for centering, marking, or starting holes. **2.** A steel driving tool with a sharpened edge, used to cut holes in sheet metal.

punched louver See **pierced louver**.

punched work Same as **broached work**. Also see **broach, 2**.

puncheon **1.** A short, upright piece of timber in framing; a short post; an intermediate stud. **2.** A split log or heavy slab with the face smoothed. **3.** A short post used as a spacing support in temporary timbering around an excavation.

punching shear **1.** The shear stress calculated by dividing the load on a column by the product of its perimeter and the thickness of the base or cap, or by the product of the perimeter taken at one-half the slab thickness away from the column and the thickness of the base or cap. **2.** The failure of a base when a heavily loaded column punches a hole through it. **3.** The punching of a hole through a base by a heavily loaded column as a result of failure of the base.

punch list **1.** The architect's list of work to be corrected or performed by the contractor. **2.** See **inspection list**.

punkah A type of fan (used in Asia, esp. in India) in the form of a swinging screen; consists of cloth stretched on a rectangular frame, hung from the ceiling and kept in motion by a cord pulled by a servant.

punning A form of light ramming.

pura In Bali, a terraced sanctuary consisting of three courts enclosed by walls, connected by richly decorated gates.

Purbeck marble A gray marble obtained from the upper Purbeck strata in southern England.

purchase money mortgage A mortgage that secures a loan the proceeds of which are used to finance the purchase of property. Colloquially, the term generally is employed only to denote a mortgage taken by the seller of property to secure later payment to him of the unpaid portion of the purchase price.

purchaser One who buys or contracts to buy real property. Also see **vendor**.

pure tone Sound waves in which only a single frequency is present; the wave form is that of a **sine wave**.

purfle   To edge ornamentally, as if with elaborate needlework or lacework.

purge   To evacuate air or gas from a duct line, pipeline, container, space, or furnace; e.g., to blow out gas from a refrigerant-containing vessel.

purge valve   See **air purge valve**.

purging   **1.** The process of voiding a pipe of fuel gas and replacing it with air. **2.** The process of replacing the air in a gas pipeline with fuel gas.

purlin, purline   A piece of timber laid horizontally on the **principal rafters** of a roof to support the common rafters on which the roof covering is laid. Compare with **subpurlin**; also see **common purlin** and **principal purlin**.

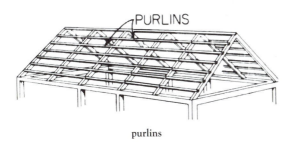

purlins

purlin cleat   A fastener used to secure a purlin to its support.

purlin plate   In a **curb roof**, a purlin which is located at the curb and which supports the ends of the upper rafters.

purlin post   One of the struts which support a purlin to prevent it from sagging.

purlin roof   A roof construction in which **purlins** are laid between the principal rafters; they support the boards that run between the ridge and eaves of the roof.

purpleheart, purple wood   The heartwood of any of several leguminous South American trees; hard, durable, fine-grained wood which is brown in color but turns purple on exposure; esp. used for inlays and veneer.

purpose-made brick   A specially shaped brick.

push bar   A heavy bar fixed across a glazed door or horizontally pivoted window sash; used to open or close the door, while providing protection for the glass.

push button   A device in an electric circuit consisting of a button that must be pressed to activate or disconnect the circuit.

push drill   A small, slender hand drill which is operated by pushing it; a spiral ratchet rotates the bit.

push hardware   A fixed bar or plate used to push a door open.

push joint   Same as **shoved joint**.

push-on joint   A joint having an elastomeric **gasket, 2** that is compressed in the annular space between a bell end (or a socket) and a spigot-end of a pipe.

push plate, finger plate, hand plate   A plate applied to the lock stile of a door to protect it against soiling and wear.

push-pull rule   A flexible steel rule which coils into a case when not in use.

puteus   In ancient Roman construction, an opening or manhole in an aqueduct.

puteus

putlog   In bricklaying, one of a number of short pieces of timber on which the planks forming

putlogs shown in **putlog holes:**   *b*

the floor of a scaffold are laid, one end resting on the ledger of the scaffold and the other in a **putlog hole**.

putlog hole A hole left in a masonry or concrete wall to provide support for a horizontal framing member of scaffolding, and filled to match the wall after the scaffolding has been removed.

putti Plural of **putto**.

putto In Renaissance architecture and derivatives, a decorative sculpture or painting representing a chubby, usually naked infant.

putto

putty **1.** A heavy paste composed of pigment, such as whiting, mixed with linseed oil; used to fill holes and cracks in wood prior to painting to secure and seal panes of glass in window frames; also called **painter's putty**. **2.** In plastering, a fine cement consisting of lump lime slaked with water; **lime putty**. Now, other compounds, premixed or in powdered form to be combined with water, are widely used.

putty coat In plastering, the smooth trowel finish coat, composed of **lime putty** and **gauging plaster**.

putty knife A knife with a broad flexible blade used for laying on putty.

putty knife

puzzolano Same as **pozzolan**.
PVA See **polyvinyl acetate**.

PVC **1.** Pigment volume concentration; the percentage of pigment by volume in the total volume of a paint film. **2.** Abbr. for **polyvinyl chloride**.

PWA Moderne An architectural style that combined elements of **Art Deco, Streamline Moderne**, and the **Beaux-Arts style**; applied in the design of many large public buildings, civic centers, theaters, and other buildings constructed between 1933 and 1944 by the Public Works Administration (PWA), an agency of the U.S. Government created during the Great Depression.

pycnostyle See **intercolumniation**.

pylon **1.** Monumental gateway to an Egyptian temple, consisting of a pair of tower structures with slanting walls flanking the entrance portal. **2.** In modern usage, a tower-like structure, as the steel supports for electrical high-tension lines. **3.** In a theatre, a movable tower (usually part of a set) for carrying lights.

pylon, 1

pyramid A massive funerary structure of stone or brick with a square base and four sloping triangular sides meeting at the apex; used mainly in ancient Egypt. In Central America stepped pyramids formed the bases of temples; in India some temples had the shape of truncated pyramids.

pyramidal hipped roof Same as **pavilion roof, 1**.

pyramidal house A one- or two-story house having a **pyramidal roof**.

pyramidal light A skylight having the shape of a polygon, and in which the glazing slopes to a point.

pyramidal roof A **hipped roof** that usually has four or six sloping surfaces, terminating in a peak.

pyramidion A small pyramid, such as the cap of an obelisk.

pyramid roof A roof which has four slopes terminating at a peak.

pyramid roof

pyriform Same as **periform**.

pyriform profile

pyrometer An instrument for measuring high temperatures.

Q

qala'a See **kal'a.**

qasr See **kasr.**

qibla See **kiblah.**

QR On drawings, abbr. for **quarter round.**

qt Abbr. for "quart."

QTR **1.** Abbr. for "quarry-tile roof." **2.** On drawings, abbr. for **quarter.**

QUAD. On drawings, abbr. for **quadrangle.**

quadra **1.** A square frame or border enclosing a bas-relief. **2.** The **plinth** of a podium. **3.** Any small molding of plain or square section, as one of the fillets above or below the scotia of an Ionic base.

quadrangle, quad **1.** A rectangular courtyard or grassy area enclosed by buildings or a building. Most often used in connection with academic or civic building groupings. **2.** Buildings forming a quadrangle.

quadrant **1.** An angle-measuring instrument used for measuring elevations. **2.** A **quarter-round** molding. **3.** A device for fastening together the upper and lower leaves of a Dutch door. **4.** A **quadrant stay.**

quadratura In Baroque interiors and derivatives, painted architecture, often continuing the three-dimensional trim, executed by specialists in calculated perspective.

quadrel A square brick, tile, or stone; a **quarrel.**

quadrifores ianuae Ancient Roman doors with hinged leaves like shutters, with two leaves on each side.

quadriga In classical ornamentation and derivatives, the representation of a chariot drawn by four horses, i.e., a royal or divine accouterment. Also see **triga, biga.**

quadripartite Divided by the system of construction employed, into four compartments, as a vault.

quadripartite vault A groined vault over a rectangular area, the area defined by ribs on each side and divided into four parts by intersecting diagonals.

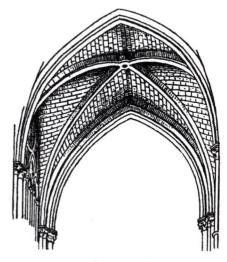

quadripartite vault

quadriporticus An **atrium** which is nearly square and surrounded by colonnaded porticoes.

quadrivalve One of a set of four folds or leaves forming a door.

quaggy timber Defective wood with numerous shakes. Also see **ring shake, starshake, heart shake.**

Quaker plan In the late 17th and early 18th centuries, the **plan** of a three-room stone or brick house found primarily in Pennsylvania; typically had one large room with a fireplace in one corner and an **exterior chimney,** and two small rooms along side it, one serving as a vestibule and the other as a bedroom. Also see **Penn plan.**

quaking concrete A concrete of medium consistency suitable for massive construction, such as heavy walls and abutments; shakes likes jelly when rammed in the plastic state.

QUAL On drawings, abbr. for "quality."

qualification test The evaluation of a product (new, existing, or modified) to determine its acceptability for a given job or function or to

733

determine if it conforms to requirements of an applicable specification.

quality assurance The inspection, testing, and other relevant actions taken (often by an owner or his representative) to ensure that the desired level of quality is in accordance with the applicable standards or specifications for the product or work.

quality control The inspection, analysis, and other relevant actions taken to provide control over what is being done, manufactured, or fabricated, so that a desirable level of quality is achieved and maintained.

quality of steam The dryness of saturated steam expressed as a percentage of perfect dryness.

quantity distance tables Same as **American table of distances**.

quantity survey A detailed analysis and listing of all items of material and equipment necessary to construct a project.

quantity surveyor British term for an individual who has received special training in the various aspects of building construction costs and contract procedures, including advising the client on the selection of a contractor. There is no direct counterpart for this position in the U.S.A. Also see **building surveyor**.

quarrel A small pane of glass, usually diamond-shaped or square-shaped and set diagonally; framed and held in place by slender, grooved strips of lead (**cames**).

quarrels

quarry 1. An open excavation at the earth's surface from which building stone is extracted. 2. Same as **quarry glass**.

quarry-faced Descriptive of the freshly split face of ashlar, as it comes from the quarry,

squared off only for the joints; usually used in massive masonry work.

quarry-faced   masonry

quarry glass A small, square piece of glass; usually set diagonally.

quarry run Building stone as it is supplied from the quarry, unselected for color and texture.

quarry sap The natural moisture in stone as it comes from the quarry ledge; varies in amount with the porosity.

quarrystone bond In masonry, an arrangement of stones in an uncoursed **rubble wall**.

quarry tile, promenade tile Unglazed ceramic tile, machine-made by the extrusion process from natural clay or shales; sometimes used for factory floors.

quarter 1. A small timber used as an upright stud in partitions to which the laths are nailed. 2. A square panel.

quarter bend A 90° change in direction, as in piping.

quarter-cleft Same as **quarter-sawn**.

quarter closer, quarter closure A brick which has been cut to one-quarter of its normal length but is of normal thickness and width; used to complete a course or to space normal-sized bricks.

quarter-cut, radial-cut Said of veneer which has growth rings at right angles (or nearly at right angles) to the face of the veneer.

quartered Same as **quartersawn**.

quartered partition A partition formed with **quarters, 2**.

quarter-girth rule A method sometimes used to compute the volume of wood in a log.

quarter grain The grain of **quarter-sawn** wood.

quarter-hollow molding A concave molding; same as **cavetto**.

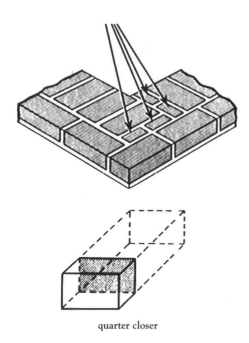

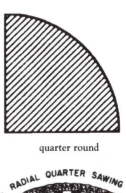

quarter round

quarter closer

quartering   **1.** A method of obtaining a representative sample by dividing a circular pile of a larger quantity into four equal parts and discarding opposite quarters, continuing the process until the desired size of sample is obtained. **2.** Studs in a building wall. **3.** A small **scantling**.

quartering house   A subsidiary building that provided housing for servants in the 17th century; usually near or adjoining a principal structure in the mid-Atlantic area of America.

quarterpace, quarterpace landing, quarter-space landing   A stair landing, often square in plan, between two flights which make a right-angle (90°) turn.

quarterpace stair   A stair having a **quarter-turn**. Compare with **halfpace stair**.

quarter panel   A **quarter, 2**.

quarter round   A convex molding the profile of which is exactly or nearly a quarter of a circle. An edge or corner when rounded, as in tile or plaster work, is called a **bullnose**.

quarter-round light   A window, often one of a pair, that has the shape of one-quarter of a complete circle.

quartersawn, rift-sawn   Descriptive of lumber sawn so that the growth rings intersect the

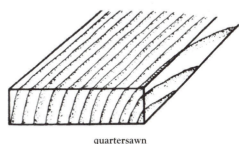

quartersawn

wide face at an angle of 45° or greater. Also see **edge-grained**.

quarter section   A square tract of land that is one-half mile on each side.

quarter-space landing   See **quarterpace**.

quarter-turn   Descriptive of a stair which, in its progress from top to bottom, turns 90°.

quarter-turn stair   Same as **quarterpace stair**.

quartz   The most abundant form of mineral silica; very hard, will scratch glass.

quartz glass, silica glass Glass consisting entirely of pure, or nearly pure, amorphous silica; has the highest heat resistance and ultraviolet transmittance of all glasses.

quartz-halogen lamp A lamp having a tungsten filament in a quartz envelope; quartz is used instead of glass to permit higher temperatures, higher currents, and therefore greater light output.

quartz-iodine lamp Obsolete term for a **tungsten-halogen lamp**.

quartzite A variety of sandstone composed largely of granular quartz which is cemented by silica forming a homogeneous mass of very high tensile and crushing strengths; esp. used as a building stone, as gravel in road construction, and as an aggregate in concrete.

quartzitic sandstone A type of sandstone in which most of the grains are quartz and the cementing material is silica; intermediate between normal sandstone and quartzite.

quatrefoil A four-lobed pattern divided by **cusps**; also see **foil**.

quatrefoil

Quattrocento architecture Renaissance architecture of the 15th cent. in Italy.

Queen Anne arch An arch over the triple opening of the so-called Venetian or Palladian window, flat over the narrow side lights, round over the larger central opening.

Queen Anne arch

Queen Anne style 1. English architecture during the reign of Queen Anne, from 1702 to 1714; primarily country houses and many houses in the suburbs of London, often of red brick.

Characterized by a dignified simplicity and moderateness in scale; avoidance of the appearance of massiveness; hipped roofs hidden behind parapets; sash windows. 2. An eclectic style of domestic architecture primarily of the 1870s and 1880s in England and the United States; misnamed after Queen Anne; actually based on country-house and cottage Elizabethan architecture. A blending of Tudor Gothic, English Renaissance, Flemish, (and in the United States on Colonial elements), houses in this style usually are characterized by an asymmetrical façade with emphasis on verticality; often, a front-facing gable; commonly, timber-framed and irregular in plan and elevation; decorative trusses, bracketed posts, **gingerbread** in the form of spindlework, finials, and cast-iron cresting; textured shingles, masonry with variations in wall surface treatment and color; carved ornamentation, and patterned horizontal siding; contrasting wall materials used in combination with the various stories decorated differently; one or more conspicuous porches often set within the main structure of the house; typically, an irregularly shaped, steeply pitched roof, ornamented gables and

home in **Queen Anne style**, 2

ridges, overhanging eaves, bargeboards, second-story projections, various-shaped ornamental dormers, cresting, finials, pendants, and/or pinnacles; shingles laid in decorative patterns; tall ornamented chimneys; frequently, a tower; a paneled main entry door typically located off the central axis of the façade. Occasionally called *Victorian Queen Anne style* to avoid confusion with the 18th-century **Queen Anne style, 1** from which it differs markedly.

queen bolt Same as **queen rod**.

queen closer A brick which has been cut in half along its length; it is of normal thickness but half normal width; used to complete a course or to space normal-sized bricks.

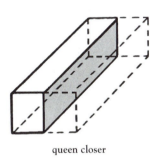

queen closer

queen closure Same as **queen closer**.

queen post One of the two vertical supports in a **queen-post truss**.

queen-post roof A roof supported by two queen posts.

queen-post roof

queen-post truss, queen truss A roof truss having two vertical posts between the rafters and the tie beam; the upper ends of the vertical posts are connected by a **straining piece, 1** (such as a tie rod or cable).

queen rod, queen bolt A metal rod which serves as a **queen post**.

queen truss See **queen-post truss**.

quenched Said of a metal which was first heated and then cooled by contact with a liquid, gas, or solid, for the purpose of hardening or tempering.

quetta bond A bond in brickwork having vertical voids in which reinforcement is placed (usually connecting to foundations, floors, and roof); the voids then are filled with mortar.

quick-break Descriptive of a device having a high-opening speed regardless of how it is operated.

quick-change room In a theatre, a dressing room on or near the stage, where actors may make quick changes of costume or makeup.

quick-closing valve A valve or faucet whose automatic closure is fast-acting.

quick condition A soil condition in which water flows upward with sufficient velocity to reduce significantly the bearing capacity of the soil through a decrease in intergranular pressure.

quick-disconnect device **1.** A hand-operated device that provides a means for connecting and disconnecting a gas appliance. **2.** A connector (to a gas supply) that is equipped with an automatic means for shutting off the supply when the device is disconnected.

quick-hardening lime A **hydraulic lime**.

quicklime See **lime**.

quick-response early-suppression sprinkler A **fast-response sprinkler** that is listed as providing fire suppression of specific hazards.

quick-response extended coverage sprinkler A fire sprinkler that is listed as providing the characteristics of both a **quick-response sprinkler** and an **extended coverage sprinkler**.

quick-response sprinkler A fire sprinkler that combines the characteristics of a **fast-response sprinkler** and a **spray sprinkler**.

quicksand Fine sand, sometimes with an admixture of clay, which is saturated with water so that it has no bearing capacity at its surface; fine sand in a **quick condition**.

quick set See **flash set, false set**.

quick sweep Descriptive of any carpentry or joinery work having a small radius of curvature.

quilted figure See **blister figure**.

quilt insulation A blanket-type thermal insulation having, on one or both principal faces, a flexible facing that is stitched or quilted.

quincunx An arrangement of elements so that four are symmetrically placed around a central one.

quinquefoil, quintefoil See **cinquefoil**.

quirk **1.** An indentation separating one element from another, as between moldings, or between the abacus and echinus of a Doric capital. **2.** A V-groove in the finish-coat plaster where it abuts the **return** on a door or window; reduces the possibility of cracking by freeing the two surfaces.

quirk bead, bead and quirk, quirked bead **1.** A bead with a quirk on one side only, as on the edge of a board. **2.** A **recessed** or **double-quirked bead**, where the bead is flush with the adjoining surface and separated from it by a quirk on each side. Also called **flush bead**. **3.** A **return bead**, in which the bead is at a corner with quirks at either side at right angles to each other. **4.** A bead with a quirk on its face.

quirk beads

quirk molding, quirked molding A molding characterized by a sudden and sharp return from its extreme projection or set-off and made prominent by a quirk running parallel to it.

quitclaim deed A written instrument whereby the seller conveys only whatever interest he has in property, but makes no warranties or representations as to the nature of that interest or as to the absence of any limitations or restrictions thereon, or even that he has any right to the property at all.

quoin, coign, coin In masonry, a hard stone or brick used, with similar ones, to reinforce an external corner or edge of a wall or the like; often distinguished decoratively from adjacent masonry; may be imitated in non-load-bearing materials. Occasionally imitated, for decorative purposes, by wood that has been finished to look like masonry.

stone **quoins** set in brickwork

quoin bonding In masonry, bonding at a corner with alternating stretchers and headers.

quoin header A quoin which is a header in the face of a wall and a stretcher in the face of the return wall.

quoining Any architectural members which form a **quoin**.

quoin post Same as **heelpost, 2**.

quoin stone A **quoin**.

Quonset hut A prefabricated structure, developed during World War II, that has a semicylindrical shape; commonly constructed of corrugated steel fastened to arched steel ribs that are rigidly fastened to a concrete slab floor.

quotation A price quoted by a contractor, subcontractor, material supplier, or vendor to furnish materials, labor, or both.

R

R **1.** Abbr. for "radius." **2.** Abbr. for "right." **3.** Symbol for the capacity of a **pile** (for example, 3R indicates three times design capacity). **4.** Symbol for the thermal resistance of a material or component of construction. **5.** Symbol for electrical resistance.

R.A. Abbr. for "registered architect."

rab A rod or stick used by masons in mixing hair with mortar.

RAB On drawings, abbr. for **rabbet.**

rab and dab Same as **wattle and daub.**

rabbet, rebate **1.** A longitudinal channel, groove, or recess cut out of the edge or face of a member; esp. one to receive another member, or one to receive a frame inserted in a door or window opening, or the recess into which glass is installed in a window sash. **2.** A **rabbet joint. 3.** A shallow recess in one body to receive another, as at the edges of a pair of doors or windows so shaped as to provide a tight fit; one half of the edge projects beyond, and serves as a stop for, the other edge of each leaf. **4.** A **rabbet plane.**

rabbet, 1

rabbet bead A bead in the reentrant angle of a rabbet.

rabbet depth In glazing, the depth of the glazing rabbet; equal to the sum of the **bite** and the **edge clearance.**

rabbeted doorjamb, rabbeted frame A doorjamb with a **rabbet, 3,** to receive a door.

rabbeted lock, rebated lock A lock or latch in which the face is flush with the rabbet on a rabbeted doorjamb.

rabbeted lock

rabbeted siding Same as **drop siding.**

rabbeted stop A **stop, 1** which is integral with a door or window frame.

rabbet joint An edge joint formed by fitting together rabbeted boards or timbers.

rabbet joint

rabbet plane A **plane, 1** for cutting a groove along the edge of a board; open on one side and having the plane iron (which does the cutting) extend to the open side.

rabbet size In glazing, the actual size of the rabbeted glass opening; equal to the glass size plus two edge clearances.

raceway Any channel designed to enclose and loosely hold electric conductors; may be of metal or of an insulating material; various types include rigid conduit, flexible metallic conduit, nonmetallic conduit, metallic tubing, underfloor raceways, cellular floor raceways, surface metal raceways, structural raceways, wireways and busways, and auxiliary gutters or moldings.

raceway cable distribution system A system for distributing cable in an open or closed metal tray that is suspended within a false ceiling from the structural floor above; generally used in large buildings where complex cable distribution systems require special support.

rack-and-pinion elevator An elevator having electrically driven rotating gear pinions mounted on the car; rotation of the gear pinions moves the car up or down on a stationary gear rack which is mounted vertically in the hoistway.

racked Descriptive of **timbering** which is braced, providing additional support to prevent deformation.

racking The distortion or movement of a frame.

racking load A load applied in the plane of an assembly in such manner as to lengthen one diagonal and shorten the other.

rack saw A saw having wide teeth.

rad Abbr. for **radiator**.

rad and dab Same as **wattle and daub**.

radial arch roof A roof supported by a system of arches radiating from a central point.

radial-arm saw, radial saw A circular saw which is suspended from, and moves along, a cantilevered arm, mounted above the saw table; the blade can be set at any angle (or tilted) with respect to the work.

radial bar Same as **radius rod, 2**.

radial-blade fan A heavy-duty industrial fan used for severe service, e.g., where foreign material (such as wood chips) passes directly through the fan.

radial brick, radius brick An **arch brick, 1**.

radial-cut See **quarter-cut**.

radial grating Nonrectangular grating, in which the **bearing bars** extend radially from a common center and the **cross bars** have a pattern of concentric circles.

radially-cut grating Rectangular grating that is cut into panels shaped as annular segments, for use in circular or annular areas.

radial road One of a group of roads which radiate outward from the center of a city, as spokes on a wheel.

radial saw See **radial-arm saw**.

radial shrinkage The shrinkage of wood across the growth rings during drying; the loss in dimension along the radius of a log.

radial step Same as **winder**.

radiance The rate of radiant emission per unit solid angle and per unit projected area of a source in a stated angular direction from the surface.

radiant glass Glass containing radiant heating elements.

radiant heating Heating which results from heat transmitted by **radiation**, as contrasted with heat transmitted by conduction or convection.

radiant heating system A system for heating a room or space by means of heated surfaces (such as panels heated by the flow of hot water or electric current) which provide heat primarily by **radiation**.

radiant panel test An ASTM standard method of test for the surface flammability of a material, using a radiant heat source.

radiating brick An **arch brick, 1**.

radiating chapels Chapels projecting radially from the curve of an ambulatory or rarely of an apse.

radiation The transmission of heat through space by means of electromagnetic waves; the heat energy passes through the air between the source and the heated body without heating the intervening air appreciably.

radiation-retarding door See **lead-lined door**.

radiation-retarding frame See **lead-lined frame**.

radiation-shielding concrete High-density concrete suitable for enclosing nuclear installations; its aggregate has a high specific gravity; contains a high proportion of atoms having a high atomic weight or consisting of minerals and synthetic glasses of substantial boron content.

Also see **heavyweight aggregate, boron-loaded concrete**.

radiation-shielding door   See **lead-lined door**.

radiator   A heating unit usually exposed to view within the room or space to be heated; transfers heat by radiation to objects within visible range, and by conduction to the surrounding air, which in turn is circulated by natural convection; usually fed by steam or hot water.

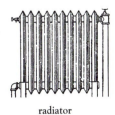

radiator

radius brick   See **arch brick, 1**.

radius diffusion   The horizontal axial distance an airstream travels after leaving an **air outlet** before the maximum stream velocity is reduced to a specified terminal value.

radius gauge   See **fillet gauge**.

radius of gyration   In mechanics, the distance from the axis to a point such that, if the whole mass of a body were concentrated at it, the **moment of inertia** would remain unchanged.

radius rod   **1.** A plastering tool; a wooden arm fixed at one end to a mold and attached at the other end to a center about which it swivels; a gig stick. **2.** A long wooden arm with a marker at one end for tracing large curves.

radius shoe   A zinc plate attached to one side of a plasterer's **radius rod** at midpoint.

radius tool   A **radius rod**.

radon   A gaseous emanation produced by the radioactive decay of radium, given off by some soils and rocks; it may collect and constitute a health hazard in buildings with poor ventilation.

rafter   One of a series of inclined structural members from the ridge of the roof down to the eaves, providing support for the covering of a roof. For special types of rafters, see **beveled rafter, binding rafter, common rafter, compass rafter, compound rafter, fly rafter, hip rafter, jack rafter, knee rafter, notched rafter, principal rafter, valley rafter**.

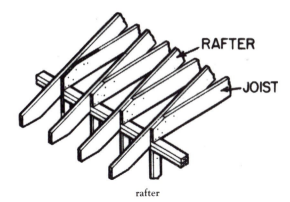

rafter

rafter fill   Same as **beam fill**.

rafter house   In the Chesapeake Bay area of colonial America, a house of a relatively temporary nature, in which the lower ends of the roof rafters rested directly on the ground; a forerunner of the modern **A-frame house**.

rafter lookout   See **lookout, 1**.

rafter plate   A **plate, 2** which supports the lower end of rafters and to which they are fixed.

rafter table   A table of values, usually on a steel square, used by carpenters to determine the lengths and angles of cut for rafters for a roof.

rafter table

rafter tail   The part of a rafter which overhangs the wall.

raft foundation   Same as **floating foundation**.

rag bolt   Same as **lewis bolt**.

rag felt   An **asphaltic felt** fabricated from the fibers of rags; used for roofing paper and shingles.

raggle, reglet, raglin   **1.** A manufactured unit, often of terra-cotta, having a groove to receive flashing; also called a **raggle block** or **flashing block**. **2.** A groove cut in stone or brickwork to receive flashing. (*See illustration p. 742.*)

raggle block   See **raggle, 1**.

raglet   A **raggle**.

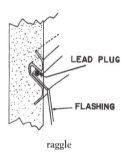

raggle

raglin A **raggle**.

rag-rolled finish A decorative effect on a painted surface; made by rolling a piece of twisted rag over a coat of wet paint so as to remove portions of it and show the color of the base coat. A similar effect can be achieved with a special paint roller.

rag rubble Rubblework of thin small stones.

ragstone **1.** A rough, shelly, sandy limestone with layers of marl and sandstone. **2.** In masonry, stone quarried in thin blocks or slabs.

ragwork **1.** Crude masonry, laid in a random pattern of thin-bedded, undressed stone (like flagging); most commonly set horizontally. **2.** Polygonal rubble which is set on edge as exterior facing.

ragwork, 1

rail **1.** A bar of wood or other material passing from one post or other support to another; a hand support along a stairway. **2.** A structure consisting of rails and their sustaining posts, balusters, or pillars, and constituting an enclosure or a line of division, as a **balcony rail**. **3.** A horizontal piece in a frame or paneling as a **door rail**, or in the framework of a window sash.

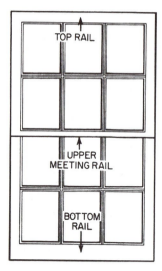

rail, 3

rail bead A **cock bead** when on a uniform continuous surface, and not at an angle, reveal, or the like.

rail bolt A **handrail bolt**.

rail fence A fence in which the rails are set into the posts; adjoining rails either butt against each other or overlap. Also called a **zigzag fence**.

railing **1.** Rails, collectively, or a combination of rails. **2.** Any openwork construction or rail used as a barrier or the like.

rail pile A **pile** fabricated from railroad rails which are welded together and driven as a unit.

railroad flat A narrow apartment whose rooms are in a straight line; one must pass through each room to get to the next one because there is no internal corridor. Only the front and rear rooms have windows; air shafts along one or both sides of the apartment provide ventilation and a little light in the interior rooms. Primarily constructed on the east coast of America in the 1880s; also called a **dumbbell tenement**.

rail steel reinforcement Steel **reinforcing bars** that have been hot-rolled from standard T-section rails.

rainbow roof **1.** Same as **compass roof**. **2.** Same as **ship's bottom roof**.

rain cap A device which is installed at the upper termination of a chute or vent, above the roof of a building, to prevent rain from entering the interior of the chute; often includes a screen to prevent the entry of birds.

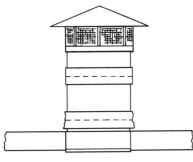

rain cap   with a birdscreen

raindrop figure   A mottled figure in wood veneer; resembles a raindrop pattern.

rain leader   See **downspout**.

rainproof   Constructed, protected, and/or treated to prevent rain from interfering with the successful operation of apparatus.

raintight   Constructed, protected, and/or treated so that exposure to intense rainfall will not result in the entrance of water.

rainwater conductor   Same as **downspout**.

rainwater conductor head, rainwater hopper head   Same as **leader head**.

rainwater head   See **leader head**.

rainwater hopper   A hopper-shaped **leader head**.

rainwater pipe   A **downspout**.

rainwater shoe   At the foot of a **downspout**, a short fitting with a bend to discharge the rainwater clear of the building.

raised barn   Occasionally, a synonym for a **bank barn**.

raised basement   A **basement** whose floor level is much higher than usual, so that its ceiling is well above (usually one story above) ground level.

raised cottage   **1.** Cottage on stilts or built-up piers to protect it from groundwater. **2.** Same as **raised house**.

raised floor   A floor fabricated entirely of square plates that rest on interlocked pedestals attached to the structural floor of a building. The plates usually are fabricated of aluminum and are covered with cork, carpet, or vinyl tiles. The plates can be removed to provide conve-

nient access to the cables beneath; used extensively in computer rooms.

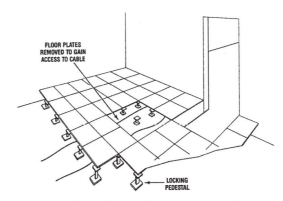

raised floor   showing floor plates on pedestals

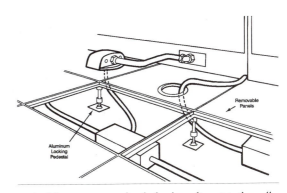

raised floor: cutaway detail of a plate adjacent to the wall

raised flooring system   A system of flooring consisting of completely removable and interchangeable floor panels which are supported on adjustable pedestals and/or stringers to allow free access to the area beneath.

raised girt, flush girt, raised girth   A **girt** which is parallel to the floor joists and level with them.

raised grain   **1.** In dressed softwood lumber, surfaces in which the hard summerwood is raised above the soft springwood. **2.** In hardwoods, fibers protruding above the normal surface; usually caused by wetting.

raised house   In the American South, a house or cottage having a **raised basement**; this cellar, whose floor is at ground level, often functions as a service area, shop, office, or stable. The main floor (one story above) contains the family living quarters. The exterior walls typically are whitewashed brick, stone, plaster, or stucco. A porch (**galerie**), extends across the entire façade and sometimes along both sides as well; French doors opening onto the porch promote the flow of air during very hot weather. Also see **plantation house**.

raised house   (1801)

raised joint   Same as **excess joint**.

raised molding   Same as **bolection molding**.

raised panel, fielded panel   A panel with the center portion thicker than the edges or projecting above the surrounding frame or wall surface. When exposed on both sides (as on both sides of a door), it is called a **double raised panel**.

raised table   A flat horizontal raised surface which is large in area compared to its elevation above its surroundings.

raising   See **lifting**.

raising bee   See **barn raising**.

raising hammer   A hammer with a long head and a rounded face, used in lifting sheet metal.

raising piece   A piece of timber laid on a brick wall, or on the top of posts or puncheons of a timber-framed house, to carry a beam or beams; a template.

raising plate   A horizontal timber resting on a wall, or upon vertical timbers of a frame, and supporting the heels of rafters or other framework; also called a **wall plate**.

rajones   The term for **shingles** in Spanish Colonial architecture in the American Southwest.

rake   1. A slope; an inclination; e.g., the inclination (from the horizontal) of an auditorium floor. 2. A board or molding along the sloping edge of a **gable**; covers the edges of the siding. 3. On the roof of an early colonial house, a flat board covering the lower ends of the rafters.

raked   Said of any surface that is inclined with respect to the horizontal, such as a *raked molding*, or the inclined surface of a *raked cornice* in a **triangular pediment**.

rake dimension   Same as **pitch dimension**.

raked joint   A joint made by removing the surface of mortar, while it is still soft, with a square-edged tool; is difficult to make watertight; produces marked shadows and tends to darken the overall appearance of a wall.

raked joint

raked molding   Same as **raking molding**.

rake-out, raking out   In masonry, preparing mortar joints for **pointing**.

raker   1. A tool for raking out decayed mortar from the joints of brickwork, preparatory to repointing them. 2. Any inclined member, as a brace, or **pile**. 3. A **raking shore**.

raker pile   Same as **batter pile**.

raking   Inclining; having a rake or inclination.

raking arch   Same as **rampant arch**.

raking back   Same as **racking**.

raking bond   A method of bricklaying in which the bricks are laid at an angle in the face of the wall; either **diagonal bond** or **herringbone bond**.

raking coping   A coping set on an inclined surface, as at a gable end.

raking cornice   A cornice following the slope of a gable, pediment, or roof.

raking cornice

raking course   A course of bricks laid diagonally between face courses of a thick wall to strengthen it.

raking flashing   A flashing, parallel to the roof slope, which is used to cover the intersection of a chimney and a sloping roof.

raking molding, raked molding   **1.** Any molding adjusted at a slant, rake, or ramp. **2.** Any overhanging molding which has a rake or slope downward and outward.

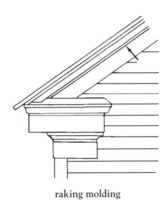

raking molding

raking-out   In brickwork, preparing mortar joints for pointing.

raking pile   A **pile** that is not driven vertically; a **batter pile**.

raking riser   On stairs, a riser which is not perpendicular to the tread, but inclined inward to permit more footroom on the tread below.

raking shore, inclined shore   An inclined member which supports a wall; a **raker, 3**.

raking stretcher bond   Similar to **stretcher bond**, except that each stretcher is displaced with respect to the one below, so that it overlaps it by a quarter of a brick rather than a half brick.

raking stretcher bond

ramada   **1.** In Spanish architecture and derivatives, a rustic arbor or similar structure. **2.** An open porch.

rambler   A one-story dwelling; a ranch house.

rammed earth   A material usually consisting of clay, sand, or other aggregate (such as sea shells) and water, which has been compressed and dried; used in building construction.

rammer   A power-driven tool used to compact soil or other granular material.

ramp   **1.** A sloped surface connecting two or more planes at different levels. **2.** A concave sweep in a vertical plane. **3.** The paved area of an airport between the terminal building and the taxiways, used to park airplanes during loading and unloading.

ramp and twist   Any surface that rises and twists simultaneously.

rampant arch, raking arch   An arch in which the impost on one side is higher than that on the other.

rampant arch

rampant vault   A continuous wagon vault, or a cradle vault, whose two abutments are located on an inclined plane, such as a vault supporting or forming the ceiling of a stairway. (*See illustration p. 746.*)

rampart   An elevated earthen wall for purposes of defense, located on the inner side of a ditch surrounding a bastioned **fort**.

ramped step   A step with a sloping tread.

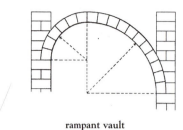

rampant vault

ramped steps   See **stepped ramp**.

ram's-horn figure   A curly, wavy figure in wood veneer, like **fiddleback**.

rance   A **shore**.

ranch house   A rambling one-story house, especially popular in the mid-20th century; usually designed to emphasize the horizontal aspects of the house. Typically characterized by: an asymmetrical plan; exterior wall cladding of stucco, brick, wood, or some combination thereof; a low-pitched roof with eaves having a moderate-to-wide overhang, a hipped, cross-gabled, or side-gabled roof; exposed rafters; **ribbon windows**, windows decorated with shutters; frequently, glass sliding doors that open onto a porch or patio at the side or rear of the house; an attached garage.

ranch-type shingle   A rectangular (usually asbestos-cement) shingle which is lapped at the top and on the side.

rand (*Brit.*)   A border, or a fillet cut from a border in the process of straightening it.

randle bar   A horizontal iron bar, built into a **jamb** of a fireplace, that projected over the fire so that pots could be suspended from it for cooking; also see **chimney hook, fireplace crane, trammel**.

random ashlar   Masonry in which rectangular stones are set without continuous joints and appear to be laid without a fixed pattern; also called random bond or random work.

random bond   See **random ashlar**.

random course   One of a number of horizontal stone masonry courses which are of unequal height.

random length   In piping, see **mill length**.

random line   In surveying, a trial line toward a fixed terminal point which is invisible from the initial point.

random noise   A type of **noise** comprised of transient disturbances which occur at random times; its instantaneous magnitudes are specified only by probability distribution functions which give the fraction of the total time that the magnitude lies within a specified range.

random range ashlar   Same as **random work**.

random rubble   Same as **rubblework**.

random shingle   One of many shingles of uniform length, but of any width.

random slate   One of many slate shingles installed in irregular pattern, using varying sizes.

random tooled ashlar   See **random work**.

random widths   Boards, lumber, shingles, etc., of nonuniform widths.

random work, broken ashlar, random range ashlar, random range work   1. Random stonework. 2. Masonry of rectangular stone not laid in regular courses, but broken up by the use of stones of different heights and widths, fitted closely.

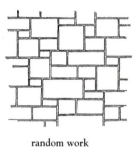

random work

range   1. In masonry, a row or course, as of stone. 2. A line of objects in direct succession, as a range of columns.

range closet   A latrine having a number of seats.

ranged rubble   Same as **rubblework**.

range hood   An open metal enclosure over cooking surfaces through which air is drawn in from the surrounding spaces, entraining grease, heated air, and odors.

range-in, wiggling-in   A trial-and-error procedure for placing a surveyor's instrument on a previously established line.

range masonry, rangework   See **coursed ashlar**.

range pile   A **pile** which serves as a guide for locating other piles.

range pole   Same as **range rod**.

ranger   Same as **wale**.

range rod, range pole A wood, fiberglass, aluminum, or steel lining pole used by surveyors as a sighting rod for locating points or directions of lines in marking alignment; approx. 1 in. (2.5 cm) thick and 6 to 10 ft (approx. 2 to 3 m) long; usually painted with alternate red and white bands.

rangework Masonry in which the stones are of equal height within each course, but all courses need not be of the same height.

ranging bond In masonry, a **chain bond** formed by small strips of wood at the face of the wall, commonly laid in the joints, and projecting slightly to provide a nailing surface for battens, furring, etc.

ranging pole Same as **range rod**.

ranked A term preceded by a digit (usually from two to nine) that indicates the number of windows across an upper floor of the façade of a house. For example, a six-ranked house has six windows across the upper floors; on the ground floor, the entry door is tallied as one of the windows, so it has five windows plus the door.

rapid-curing asphalt Liquid asphalt composed of asphalt cement and a naphtha or gasoline-type diluent of high volatility.

rapid-curing cutback Same as **rapid-curing asphalt**.

rapid-hardening cement A **high-early-strength cement**.

rapid-start fluorescent lamp A **fluorescent lamp** designed for operation with a ballast having a low-voltage winding for preheating the electrodes and for initiating an arc; may be operated on preheat fluorescent circuits; does not require a starter or the use of high voltage.

rasp A coarse file having its surface dotted with protruding pointed teeth.

ratchet brace A **brace, 3** with a ratchet-driven chuck, permitting its use in confined spaces where complete circular sweeps of an ordinary brace would be impossible.

ratchet brace

ratchet drill A hand-driven **drill, 1** which has a ratchet-driven chuck; used in confined spaces.

ratchet drill

ratchet screwdriver See **spiral ratchet screwdriver**.

rated current The current that an electrical device can carry, under specified conditions, without resulting in overheating or mechanical overstress.

rated horsepower Of an engine or prime mover, the maximum horsepower that can be provided under normal, continuous operation.

rated lamp life 1. The average life of a lamp of a given type, as determined from a large sample operated under laboratory conditions; the average life of a group of lamps which are operated under variable conditions may not equal the rated lamp life. 2. For lamp types whose luminous output drops to a very low value before the lamps cease to operate: the time when the output of a large sample of lamps under controlled laboratory conditions reaches a specified fraction of the initial output.

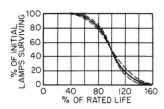

% **rated lamp life** vs. % of initial lamps which survive
A life expectancy curve for incandescent lamps

rated load In vertical transportation, the load in pounds or kilograms which an elevator, lift, dumbwaiter, or escalator is designed to lift at its **rated speed**.

rated speed The speed in feet (or meters) per minute at which a device, apparatus, conveyance, elevator, etc., is designed to operate in the upward direction with the rated load.

rate of decay Same as **decay rate**.

rate of growth Same as **growth rate**.

rath A primitive fort in Ireland, many of which still exist today; the defensive structure includes ramparts of stone or earth as well as some rudimentary form of housing.

rating correction factor The fraction by which the rated electrical load or current must be multiplied to obtain the appropriate figure to estimate the total load for design purposes.

ratio of reduction See **reduction ratio**.

rat stop In masonry wall construction, a barrier to prevent rats from burrowing down along the exterior of a foundation wall.

rat-trap bond A modification of **Flemish bond** with the stretchers laid on edge.

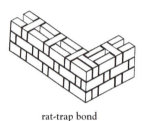

rat-trap bond

rauchkammer A room in a garret in a Pennsylvania Dutch colonial house that was set aside for the curing of meat. An opening in the chimney stack that passed through this space allowed smoke to enter the garret, and the meats to be cured were hung from hooks attached to the underside of the roof framing.

ravelin, demilune In fortifications, a projecting outwork forming a salient angle.

raveling In asphalt pavement, the progressive disintegration by the dislodgement of aggregate particles, from the surface downward or from the edges inward.

raw linseed oil Linseed oil which has been refined but has not undergone further treatment, such as boiling, blowing, or bodying.

raw sewage Untreated sewage.

raw water 1. In ice making, any water used for ice making except distilled water. 2. Water, from any source, that requires treatment before it can be used, e.g., as in steam generation.

ray See **medullary ray**.

rayon Continuous-filament yarn composed of regenerated cellulose; similar in chemical structure to natural cellulose fiber but contains shorter polymer units; usually made by the viscose process.

Rayonnant style The middle phase of French Gothic architecture in the 13th and 14th cent., characterized by radiating lines of tracery.

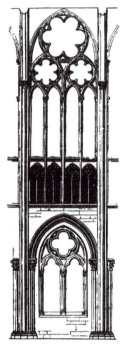

Rayonnant style

RBM Abbr. for **reinforced brick masonry**.

RC, R/C Abbr. for **reinforced concrete**.

RC asphalt Same as **rapid-curing asphalt**.

RC curves (room criterion curves) A series of curves of octave-band sound spectra; used to provide a single-number rating of the noisiness of an indoor space. A measured octave-band spectrum is compared with this set of curves to determine the RC level of the space in which the measurements were made.

RCD Abbr. for "residual current device."

RCP Abbr. for "reinforced concrete pipe."

¼ RD On drawings, abbr. for **quarter-round**.

½ RD On drawings, abbr. for **half-round**.

RD 1. Abbr. for **roof drain**. 2. On drawings, abbr. for "round."

reach The section of a sewer between structures.

reach-in refrigerator A prefabricated reach-in compartment for cooling food and/or beverages.

reaction pile   Same as **anchor pile**.

reaction wood   Wood which results from abnormal growth.

reactive aggregate   Aggregate containing substances capable of reacting chemically with the products of solution or hydration of the portland cement in concrete or mortar under ordinary conditions of exposure; in some cases causes harmful expansion, cracking, or staining.

reactive concrete aggregate   See **reactive aggregate**.

reactive silica material   Any material, such as fly ash, natural pozzolan, or pulverized silica, which reacts at high temperatures with portland cement or lime during autoclaving.

readily accessible   Providing direct access (e.g., to piping, wiring, air-conditioning controls, etc.) without requiring the removal or movement of a panel or similar obstruction.

ready condition   Said of a **wet alarm valve** in a fire sprinkler system in which the piping is filled with water from a water supply of stable pressure; in this condition, there is no water flow from any outlet of the system downstream from the alarm valve **sealing assembly**.

ready-cut house   Same as **prefabricated house**.

ready-mixed   See **mill-mixed**.

ready-mixed concrete   Concrete for delivery to a site in an unhardened state for immediate use.

ready-mixed glue   See **mixed glue**.

real estate   Property in the form of land and all its appurtenances, such as buildings erected on it.

real property   Land, everything growing on it, and all improvements made to it. It usually includes rights to everything beneath the surface, and at least some rights to the airspace above it.

reamer   A tapered bit having sharp, spiral, fluted cutting edges along the shaft; used to enlarge an opening, to cut the burrs from the inside of pipe, etc.

reaming iron   A **reamer** for use in enlarging rivet holes.

rear arch   **1.** An inner arch of an opening which is smaller in size than the external arch of the opening and may be different in shape. **2.** See **arrière-voussure**.

rear girt   A **girt** that runs horizontally along the rear wall of a house; see illustration under **timber-framed house**.

rear vault   **1.** A small vault over the space between the tracery or glass of a window and the inner face of the wall. **2.** An **arrière-voussure**.

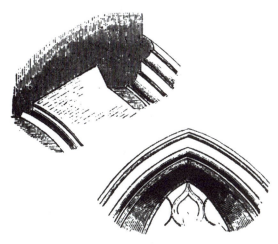

rear vault, 1

rear yard   The yard across the full width of a plot, extending from the rear line of a building to the rear property line.

reasonable care and skill   See **due care**.

reason piece   Same as **raising piece**.

rebar   A steel bar having ribs or slightly projecting patterns on its surface to provide a greater bond with concrete when used in **reinforced concrete**.

rebate   See **rabbet**.

rebound   Wet **shotcrete** which bounces off a surface against which it is projected.

receptacle   A device which is installed in an **outlet box** to receive a plug for the supply of electric current to an appliance or portable equipment.

reamer

receptacle outlet An outlet where one or more **receptacles** are installed.

receptacle plug A device, usually connected to an electric cord, which is inserted in a **receptacle** to establish an electric connection with the electrical supply.

reception wall Same as **retention wall**.

receptor **1.** A channel-shaped, telescoping member which adapts the frame of a window to the size of the window opening; an adapter. **2.** The shallow base pan for a shower.

receptorium A kind of parlor which usually adjoined an ancient Roman basilica.

recess **1.** Any shallow depression in a surface. **2.** A shallow depression in a floor; a **sinkage**.

recess bed See **wall bed**.

recessed arch An arch with a shorter radius set within another of the same shape.

recessed bead See **quirk bead, 2**.

recessed dormer A **dormer**, part or all of which is set below the main roof surface; also called an inset dormer.

recessed fitting Same as **drainage fitting**.

recessed fixture A **lighting fixture** which is recessed into a ceiling so the lower edge of the fixture is flush with the ceiling.

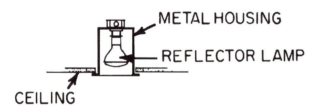

recessed fixture

recessed head For a mechanical fastener, a head having a specially formed indentation which is centered in its top surface.

recessed joint Same as **recessed pointing**.

recessed pointing In masonry, a **joint** in which the mortar is pressed back, about ¼ in. (6 mm) from the wall face, to protect the mortar from peeling.

recessed sprinkler In a fire-protection system, one of many **pendant sprinklers** located within cups recessed into the ceiling.

recessed pointing

recharge, groundwater recharge The replenishment of water in the ground, e.g., through injection or infiltration from trenches outside the construction area.

reciprocating drill Same as **push drill**.

reciprocating saw Similar to a **saber saw** but with a heavier blade and a motor with greater power.

recirculated air Air which is withdrawn from an air-conditioned space and passed through the air conditioner before being supplied once again to the conditioned space.

reconditioned wood Hardwood lumber that has been steam-dried to correct defects, such as collapse, warp, etc., that occurred during the original drying process.

reconstituted stone Same as **artificial stone**.

reconstructed stone Same as **artificial stone**.

record drawings Construction drawings revised to show significant changes made during the construction process, usually based on marked-up prints, drawings, and other data furnished by the contractor to the architect.

record sheet On a construction job, a sheet or printed form for keeping a record, usually of materials delivered, number of men working at the various trades, hours worked, etc.

recovery capacity See **heating capacity**.

RECP On drawings, abbr. for **receptacle**.

rec. room Abbr. for "recreation room."

rectangular tie A **wall tie** of heavy wire that has been bent into the shape of a closed rectangle, about 2 in. by 6 in. (5 cm by 15 cm).

Rectilinear style See **Perpendicular style**.

rectilinear tracery See **perpendicular tracery**.

rectory The residence of a rector.

recycled concrete Hardened concrete which has been crushed for re-use as an aggregate.

redan A diminutive **ravelin**.

red brass, rich low brass A metal alloy con-

rectangular tie

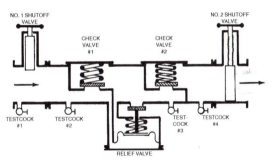

reduced-pressure-principle backflow preventer

taining 85% copper and 15% zinc; has high corrosion resistance; can take a high polish; generally available in flat sheets, rod, wire, and tube.

red cedar See **eastern red cedar.**

red fir Same as **Douglas fir.**

red gum Same as **gum, 1.**

red heart Decayed heartwood; in some woods it is red in color although it is commonly called **brown rot.**

red lauan See **Philippine mahogany.**

red lead A lead compound, lead tetroxide; bright red to orange-red in color; used in corrosion-resistant paints as a rust inhibitor on iron and steel.

red locust See **locust.**

red oak An oak of eastern North America; the wood is a light brown or red color; relatively heavy, hard, strong, coarse-grained; used esp. for clapboards, also for interior finish.

red ocher A mixture of hematites; any of a number of natural earths used as red pigments.

redoubt A small fortification detached from the principal site.

red oxide A natural or synthetic inorganic red pigment; used in paints to provide a lightfast color at a low cost; grades vary in purity, particle size, and brightness.

red rosin paper A type of **building paper.**

red-shortness Brittleness of iron or steel at a red hot temperature.

reduced level The level at a construction site after excavation, usually with respect to a given **datum.**

reduced-pressure-principle backflow preventer A **backflow preventer** that consists of two independently-operating check valves that are spring-loaded in a *closed* position and are separated by a chamber in which there is an automatic relief vent to the atmosphere that is spring-loaded in the *open* position.

reduced size vent A **dry vent** that is smaller than one specified by code.

reducer **1.** A thinner or solvent; used to lower the viscosity of a paint, varnish, or lacquer. **2.** A **reducing pipe. 3.** A **reducing valve.**

reducer, 2

reducing coupling Same as **reducer, 2.**

reducing joint A joint between two lengths of electric conductors of unequal size.

reducing pipe A pipe coupling, with inside threads, having one end with a smaller diameter than the other; both openings have the same center line; for connecting pipes of different size.

reducing pipe fitting Any **fitting, 1** which is used to connect pipes of different size.

reducing valve See **pressure-reducing valve.**

reduct A small piece cut from a larger piece, member, etc., to make it more uniform or for symmetry.

reduction of area The difference between the original cross-sectional area of a test specimen before being subjected to tension and the area of its smallest cross section after rupture; expressed as a percentage of the original cross-sectional area of the specimen.

reduction ratio In stone crushing, the ratio of the maximum dimension of stone before crushing to the maximum dimension after crushing.

redwood A very durable, straight-grained, high-strength, moderately low-density softwood from the Pacific Coast of the U.S.A.; esp. resistant to decay and insect attack; light red to deep reddish brown in color; used primarily for construction, plywood, and millwork, where durability is required.

redwood bark Shredded bark of the redwood tree; sometimes used as loose-fill thermal insulation.

reed **1.** A small convex molding, usually one of several set close together to decorate a surface. **2.** (*pl.*) Same as **reeding**. **3.** A straw-like material prepared for thatching a roof.

reed house Same as **brush house**.

reeding An ornament of adjacent, parallel, protruding, half-round moldings (reeds); the reverse of **fluting**. Also see **cabling**.

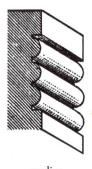

reeding

reel and bead See **bead and reel**.

reentrant angle An internal angle usually less than 90°.

reentrant corner An internal or inside corner; usually used to describe angles less than 90°.

REF On drawings, abbr. for "refer" or "reference."

refectory A hall in a convent, monastery, or public secular institution where meals are eaten.

reference line Any line which can serve as a reference or base for the measurement of other quantities.

reference mark A supplementary mark of permanent character close to a survey **station**, to which it is related by an accurately measured distance and azimuth (or bearing); the connection between a survey station and its reference mark or marks must be of sufficient precision and

refectory

accuracy to permit the reestablishment of the station on the ground from its marks.

refined tar **1.** Tar from which water has been evaporated or distilled until a desired consistency is reached. **2.** A bituminous product produced by fluxing tar residuum with tar distillate.

reflectance The ratio of the reflected flux to the flux incident on a surface.

reflectance coefficient, reflectance factor Same as **reflectance**.

reflected glare Glare resulting from specular reflection of high brightness in polished or glossy surfaces in the field of view. Also see **specular surface**.

reflected plan A plan, viewed from above, laid out as if it were projected downward on an upper surface (such as a ceiling); thus a member seen on the left from below appears to the right on the plan.

reflection The change of direction which a ray of light, sound, or radiant heat undergoes when it strikes a surface; also see **law of reflection**.

reflective glass Window glass which has been coated on the outside with a transparent metallic coating to reflect a significant fraction of the light and radiant heat which strikes it.

reflective insulation **1.** Thermal insulation in sheet form which has one or both surfaces faced with a reflective foil of comparatively low heat emissivity; used in building construction with a reflective surface facing an air space, to reduce the transfer of heat (by radiation) across the air space. **2.** Thermal insulation whose performance depends on the reduction of transfer of radiant heat across air spaces by the use of one or more surfaces having high thermal reflectance and low emittance.

reflectometer A photometer for measuring the reflectance of a material.

reflector 1. A device that redirects light or sound by reflection. 2. The device on a luminaire which controls the distribution of light from the lamp by reflection.

reflector lamp An incandescent lamp in which part of the bulb serves as a reflector, e.g., a **PAR lamp**.

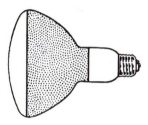

reflector lamp

reflux valve See **check valve**.

REFR 1. On drawings, abbr. for **refractory**. 2. On drawings, abbr. for "refrigerate."

refraction The change in direction of a light ray or a sound ray in passing from one medium to another.

refractory A material, usually nonmetallic, used to withstand high temperatures.

refractory aggregate A material having refractory properties; when bound together into a conglomerate mass by a matrix, forms a refractory body.

refractory brick A brick capable of withstanding high temperatures.

refractory cement Cement esp. manufactured for use in furnace and oven linings; often a mixture of fireclay with crushed brick, silica sand, or sodium silicate.

refractory concrete Concrete having refractory properties; suitable for use at high temperature; usually made with calcium aluminate cement and refractory aggregate.

refractory insulating concrete Refractory concrete having low thermal conductivity.

refractory insulation Thermal insulation which may be used at temperatures above 1500°F (816°C).

refractory materials Materials (such as bricks or blocks) that do not deform significantly or change chemically when subject to high temperatures.

refrigerant The medium of heat transfer in a refrigeration system which absorbs heat by evaporation at low temperature and pressure and gives up heat on condensing at higher temperatures and pressures.

refrigerant compressor unit A packaged unit comprising a pump suitable for compressing refrigerant gas, associated controls and accessories, and a prime mover which may be an integral part of the compressor or mounted with the compressor on a common base.

refrigerant condenser See **condenser**.

refrigerant condensing unit See **condensing unit**.

refrigerating medium Any substance whose temperature is such that it is used to lower the temperature of other bodies or substances below the ambient temperature.

refrigeration The process by which heat is absorbed from a body or substance by expansion or vaporization of a **refrigerant**, lowering its body temperature and maintaining the temperature below its surroundings.

refrigeration cycle A repetitive sequence of thermodynamic processes in which a **refrigerant** absorbs heat from a controlled space at relatively low temperature; then the heat is rejected elsewhere at a higher temperature, and the process is repeated.

refrigeration system A closed-flow system in which a **refrigerant** is compressed, condensed, and expanded to produce cooling at a lower temperature level and rejection of heat at a higher temperature level for the purpose of extracting heat from a controlled space.

refrigerator A container and a means of cooling it, such as a commercial refrigerator, service refrigerator, etc.

refusal The depth below which a pile cannot be driven.

refuse An approximately even mixture of **garbage** and **rubbish** by weight; contains up to 50% moisture and 7% incombustible solids. Also see **trash**.

refuse chute A means of transporting waste materials by chute, from the point of disposal in high-rise residential (or office building) to a

refuse compactor

refuse collection room at the base of the chute. See also **gravity-type refuse chute**.

refuse compactor A motor-driven machine having a ram that reduces the volume of waste material by subjecting it to pressure and forcing it into a removable container or package.

Reg Abbr. for "regular."

REG 1. On drawings, abbr. for **register**. 2. On drawings, abbr. for "regulator."

Regency Revival A mode of Revival architecture, found to a limited extent in America in the 1930s, that borrowed features of its Georgian and **Regency** style prototypes; usually two stories high with a hipped roof; had brick walls with **quoins** at the corners and sometimes at the main entrance, often painted white; double-hung windows with shutters; an entrance porch; and, typically, a small octagonal window above the door.

Régence style The decorative and elegant Rococo style flourishing under the regency of Philip of Orleans (1715–1723) during the minority of Louis XV.

Regency style The colorful neoclassic style, often combined with oriental motifs, prevalent in England between 1811 and 1830, during the Regency and reign of George IV. Later, very occasionally emulated in America as **Regency Revival**; often combined with oriental motifs.

regenerative heating Heating by the use of heat which is rejected in one part of the cycle and utilized in another part of the cycle, by heat transfer.

regia On the ancient Roman theatre stage, the central door, leading to the palace of the main hero; the royal door.

register 1. A grille having a **damper, 1** for regulating the quantity of air passing through it. 2. A list of buildings, constructions, objects, or sites that are of historic local, state, provincial, or national interest. Such lists are maintained by designated governmental agencies.

registered architect Same as **architect, 2**.

regle A groove or channel by which the movement of anything, as that of a sliding or lifting door or sash, is guided.

reglet 1. A fillet or small flat-faced projection, as used in a fret molding or to cover a joint between two boards. 2. A **raggle**.

regrating The cleaning of masonry by removing a thin surface layer, exposing fresh stone.

regressed luminaire A **luminaire** which is mounted above the ceiling with its opening above the ceiling line.

regula In the Doric entablature, one of a series of short fillets beneath the taenia, each corresponding to a triglyph above.

regular coursed rubble Same as **coursed ashlar**.

regulated-set cement A hydraulic portland cement which contains an additive to control its set and early strength.

regulation Any rule prescribing permitted or forbidden conduct, whether established by legislation or the action of an administrative agency; also see **building code**.

regulator In a gas supply system, a device for controlling and maintaining a uniform gas supply pressure.

regulus metal See **antimonial lead**.

rehabilitation See **building rehabilitation**.

reheat coil 1. In an air-conditioning system, a coil which heats air in the supply duct to control its temperature. 2. A coil which is heated to control the temperature of air being furnished to individual **zones, 1**.

reheating In an air-conditioning system, the heating of air which has already been conditioned, e.g., the heating of air supplied to one zone of the system in order to maintain temperature control in that zone.

reimbursable expenses Amounts expended for or on account of the project which, in accordance with the terms of the appropriate agreement, are to be reimbursed by the **owner**.

REINF On drawings, abbr. for "reinforce" or "reinforcing."

reinforced bitumen felt A light roofing felt

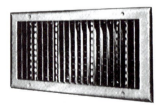

supply **register**

saturated with bitumen and reinforced with a jute cloth.

reinforced blockwork In masonry, **blockwork** in which steel reinforcement is added to resist tensile, compressive, or shear stresses.

reinforced brick masonry See **reinforced-grouted brick masonry**.

reinforced cames Lead bars reinforced with a steel core; used in **leaded lights**.

reinforced column A concrete column containing reinforcement such as steel rods or wire mesh.

reinforced concrete, beton armé, ferroconcrete, steel concrete Concrete containing reinforcement designed on the assumption that the concrete and reinforcement act together in resisting forces.

reinforced concrete masonry Concrete masonry construction in which steel reinforcement (in excess of a specified minimum percentage) is so embedded that the materials act together in resisting forces. Where hollow concrete masonry units are used, certain cores (including those containing the embedded reinforcement) are filled solidly with grout. In multiwithe construction in which the reinforcement is embedded between the withes, the space between the withes is filled solidly with grout.

reinforced-grouted brick masonry, reinforced brick masonry Grouted brick masonry in which reinforcement is provided in the horizontal joints and in grouted vertical joints between withes.

reinforced masonry Masonry units in which reinforcement, usually steel mesh or rods, is embedded in such a manner that the two materials act together in resisting forces.

reinforced membrane A roofing or waterproofing membrane which is reinforced with felts, mats, fabrics, fibers, or the like.

reinforced plastic A plastic having imbedded high-strength fillers to provide mechanical properties which are superior to those of the base material.

reinforced T-beam A concrete T-beam that has been reinforced with steel rod before the concrete is poured.

reinforcement 1. In **reinforced concrete**, metal bars, rods, wires, or other slender members which are embedded in concrete in such a manner that the metal and the concrete act together in resisting forces. 2. Material added to provide additional strength.

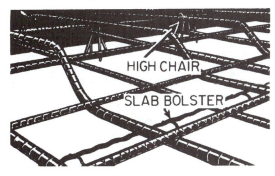

reinforcement, 1

reinforcement displacement The movement of steel reinforcement in the forms from its specified position.

reinforcement ratio At any section of a reinforced concrete structural member, the ratio of the effective area of the reinforcement to the effective area of the concrete.

reinforcement weld Along a **groove weld**, weld metal in excess of the specified weld size.

reinforcing bar A steel bar used in concrete construction (e.g., in a beam or wall) to provide additional strength; also see **deformed bar, reinforcing rod**.

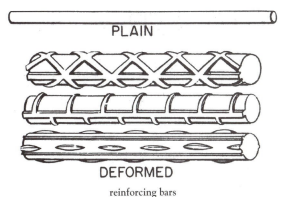

reinforcing bars

reinforcing plate An extra plate used to reinforce or strengthen a member.

reinforcing rod Any of a variety of steel rods used in **reinforced concrete**.

reinforcing rods in place for a footing

reinforcing tape A high-strength tape which resists stretching, wrinkling, and tearing; lies flat and may be lightly sanded; may be used to add strength and crack resistance along flat joints and inside corners.

reinforcing unit In a metal door, a box-shaped reinforcement in which a bored lock is installed; provides support for the latch, both vertically and horizontally.

reja In Spanish architecture and its derivatives, a grille or grating over windows facing the street, often projecting from the face of a house into the street.

rejointing Same as **repointing, 3**.

relamping See **spot relamping** and **group relamping**.

related trades In building construction, trades whose work is required to complete a system within a building (such as a **HVAC** system), part of a building, or the entire project; or trades using similar tools.

relative compaction The dry density of soil in the field expressed as a percentage of the density of the soil after it has been subjected to a standard amount of compaction.

relative consistency Of a soil, the ratio of the **liquid limit** minus the natural water content to the **plasticity index**.

relative density For a given **void ratio** of soil, the ratio between: (*a*) the difference between the void ratio of the soil in its loosest state and the given ratio and (*b*) the void ratio in the loosest state minus the void ratio in the densest state.

relative humidity The ratio of the weight of water vapor actually in humid air to the maximum possible weight of the water vapor that the air could contain at the same temperature; usually expressed as a percentage.

relative settlement See **differential settlement**.

relaxation of steel **1.** The decrease in stress in steel as a result of creep within the steel under prolonged strain. **2.** The decrease in stress in steel as a result of decreased strain of the steel, such as results from shrinkage and creep of the concrete in a prestressed concrete unit.

relay An electromechanical device in which changes in the current flow in one circuit (that flows through the device) are used to open or close electric contacts in a second circuit.

release agent In formwork, any material that is used to prevent the bonding of concrete to a surface.

release of lien Instrument executed by one supplying labor, materials, or professional services on a project which releases his mechanic's lien against the project property. Also see **mechanic's lien**.

release paper A protective sheet having an adhesive film on one side; may be easily removed from the surface to which it is applied.

relief Sculptured work, carving, casting, or embossing that is raised above the plane of its background. Also called relievo; see **bas-relief, demi-relief, high relief, mezzo-relievo, sunk relief**.

relief

relief cut A preliminary cut with a jig saw or band saw to prevent the saw from binding, when cutting a curve in a piece of wood.

relief damper, relief opening A damper in an air-conditioning system which opens automatically, relieving the buildup of air pressure within the building or air-conditioned space.

relief map, hypsometric map A map depicting the configuration of the earth's surface, called the "relief," by means of contours, form lines, hachures, shading, tinting, or relief models.

relief opening See **relief damper**.

relief valve A valve installed in a system to relieve pressure in excess of a preset limit by discharging a portion of the contents of the system.

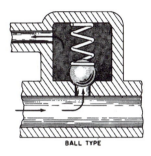

BALL TYPE

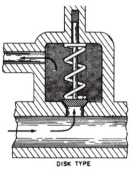

DISK TYPE

relief valves

relief vent A branch from the vent stack, connected to a horizontal branch between the first fixture branch and the soil or waste stack, whose primary function is to provide for circulation of air between the vent stack and the soil or waste stack.

relieve To lighten a color in order to reduce its intensity.

relieved work Ornamentation done in relief.

relieving arch Same as **discharging arch**.

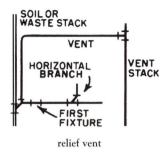

relief vent

relievo Same as **relief, 1**.

relish In carpentry and joinery, the projection or shoulder at the side of, or around, a tenon.

relocatable partition See **demountable partition**.

REM On drawings, abbr. for "removable."

remainder An interest in property that confers a right to possession in someone other than the grantor or his heirs upon the termination of a prior interest, such as following the death of a life tenant.

remodeling See **alterations**.

remoldability The ease with which freshly mixed concrete responds to an effort to remold it, as by jigging or by vibration, causing it to reshape its mass around reinforcement and to conform to the shape of the formwork.

remolded soil Soil that has had its natural structure modified by manipulation.

remolding test A test to determine the **remoldability** of concrete.

remote-control circuit An electric circuit that controls another circuit which is at a distance.

removable mullion A **door mullion** which can be removed temporarily from a doorframe to permit large objects to be moved through the frame.

removable stop 1. A **stop** which is removable to permit the installation of a glass pane, fixed panel, or door. 2. A **glazing bead, 2**.

Renaissance architecture, Renaissance Classical architecture The architectural style developed in early 15th cent. Italy during the rebirth (*rinascimento*) of classical art and learning. It succeeded the Gothic as the style dominant in all of Europe after the mid-16th cent., and evolved through the Mannerist phase into Baroque and in the early 17th cent. into classicism. Initially characterized by the use of the classical orders, round arches, and symmetrical composition.

Renaissance Revival A term occasionally used as a synonym for **Italian Renaissance Revival**.

render 1. To give a mechanical drawing, as in elevation, a more or less complete indication of shades and shadows; in ink, color, or other media. 2. To apply plaster directly to brickwork, stonework, tile, etc.; esp. to apply the first coat.

render, float, and set Three-coat plastering executed directly on stone or brick.

render and set To apply two-coat plastering directly on stone or brick walls.

rendered Said of any piece of wood that is split rather than sawn.

rendered brickwork Brickwork which has been coated with a facing of waterproof material.

rendering 1. Applying a coat of plaster directly on an interior wall or stucco on an exterior wall. 2. A perspective or elevation drawing of a project or portion thereof with artistic delineation of materials, shades, and shadows.

rendering coat The first coat of plaster on brickwork or stonework.

rendu An architectural rendering of a design problem.

rent See **lease**.

rent lath Lath which has been split instead of sawn.

rent pale A narrow wood strip, esp. of oak which has been split instead of sawn.

REP. On drawings, abbr. for "repair."

repair Replacement or renewal (excluding additions) of any part of a building, structure, device, or equipment with like or similar materials or parts, for the purpose of maintenance of such building, structure, device, or equipment.

repeating theodolite A **theodolite** so designed that successive measures of an angle may be accumulated on the graduated circle, and a final reading of the circle made which represents the sum of the repetitions.

REPL On drawings, abbr. for "replace."

replum In door construction of the ancients, an upright rail (from sill to lintel) which divides a doorframe in two parts; used with a door having two leaves, which close against it.

repointing Same as **pointing, 3**.

repoussé Raised in relief by embossing or by beating on the underside with a hammer.

reprise In masonry, the return of a molding in an internal angle.

REPRO On drawings, abbr. for "reproduce."

reproducible Said of a drawing, copy, or the like, which is capable of being used as a master-to-be in a reproduction process.

REQD On drawings, abbr. for "required."

rere-arch Same as **rear arch**.

reredorter A privy behind a monastery or convent.

reredos An ornamental screen or wall at the back of an altar.

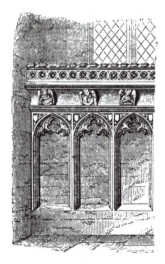

reredos

reredosse In an ancient hall, the open hearth upon which a fire was lit, immediately under the **louver, 2**.

res In the lumber industry, abbr. for "resawn."

resealing trap On a plumbing-fixture drain pipe, a **trap, 1** which is designed so that the rate of flow at the end of a discharge from the fixture seals the trap but does not cause self-siphonage.

reservoir A receptacle or enclosed space for the collection or retention of water, which is supplied to it by natural springs, drainage, or artificial means.

reshoring A temporary vertical support for forms or a completed structure, placed after the original shoring support has been removed.

residence casement **1.** Any casement used in residential construction. **2.** A lightweight, relatively low-cost, steel or aluminum casement window.

resident engineer A person representing the owner's interests at the project site during the **construction phase**; a term frequently used on projects in which a governmental agency is involved. Also see **owner's inspector**.

residential-custodial care facility A building, or part thereof, used for the lodging or boarding of four or more persons who are incapable of self-care because of age or physical or mental limitation.

residential occupancy Occupancy of a building in which sleeping accommodations are provided for normal residential purposes; includes all buildings designed to provide sleeping accommodations except those classified under institutional occupancy.

resident inspector **1.** See **owner's inspector**. **2.** See **resident engineer**.

residual deflection A deflection resulting from an applied load which remains after the removal of the load.

residual deformation The nonreversible deformation that remains in hardened concrete after a sustained load has been removed.

residual soil Soil formed in place by weathering of the underlying mineral materials.

residual sound The composite sound from many sources and many directions (near and far) remaining when all uniquely identifiable discrete sound sources are eliminated.

residual stress A stress that remains in an unloaded member after it has been formed into a finished product, such as that induced in steel shapes by cold bending, cooling after rolling, or welding.

residual tack See **aftertack**.

resilience The capacity of a material to recover its original size and shape after deformation.

resilient channel In sound-insulating construction, a fabricated metal strip having two faces with flexible interconnection; used for attaching gypsum board to studs or joists without a solid connection so as to reduce the transmission of noise and vibration.

resilient clip In sound-insulating construction, a flexible metal device for attaching gypsum board or metal lath to studs or joists to reduce transmission of noise and vibration.

resilient connector In a piping system, a flexible connector which joins pipe to another pipe that is subject to vibration or joins a pipe to a pump; can be deformed and deflected without leakage or rupture.

resilient floor A wood floor, laid on battens, having the quality of springiness (e.g., a floor supported by spring clips); especially used as a dance floor, gymnasium floor, etc.

resilient flooring A manufactured interior floor covering, in either tile or sheet form, which is resilient.

resilient hanger **1.** See **resilient clip** and **resilient channel**. **2.** A hanger, **1** which incorporates a metal or elastomer spring, providing a resilient method of attachment.

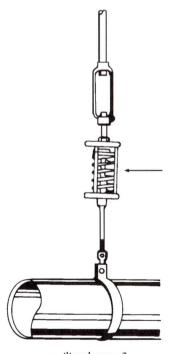

resilient hanger, 2

resin A nonvolatile solid or semisolid organic material, usually of high molecular weight; obtained as gum from certain trees or manufactured synthetically; tends to flow when subjected to heat or stress; soluble in most organic solvents but not in water; the film-forming component of a paint or varnish; used in making plastics and adhesives.

resin-bonded Descriptive of timber which has been glued with a synthetic resin.

resin chipboard A **particleboard** in which the binder for the wood chips is a resin.

resin concrete Concrete in which an organic polymer is used as the binder.

resin-emulsion paint A water paint consisting of a water emulsion of an oil-modified alkyd or other resin; when dry, leaves a tough film of resin.

resin-impregnated wood, resin-treated wood Wood whose fibers are impregnated with synthetic resin to provide improved hardness, moisture resistance, durability, etc.

resin pocket See **pitch pocket**.

resin streak See **pitch streak**.

resin-treated wood See **resin-impregnated wood, compregnated wood**.

resistance See **electrical resistance, thermal resistance**, etc.

resistance brazing A brazing process in which the heat required is obtained from the resistance to electric current in a circuit of which the work is a part.

resistance welding A group of welding processes in which coalescence is produced by the heat obtained from resistance of the work to the flow of electric current in a circuit of which the work is a part, and by the application of pressure.

resistivity See **electrical resistivity**.

resistor A device used in an electric circuit to control the flow of current.

resonance The state existing in a system which is set into oscillation (e.g., a panel which is set into vibration by sound waves) by a steady oscillatory force, when a change in frequency of excitation, however small, causes a decrease in the response of the system.

resonance frequency A frequency at which **resonance** occurs.

resorcinol adhesive An adhesive which is water-soluble for a period of 2 to 4 hr, and then insoluble and chemically resistant.

respond A support, usually a corbel or pilaster, affixed to a wall to receive one end of an arch, a groin, or a vault rib.

respond

responsible bidder See **lowest responsible bidder**.

ressant, ressaut 1. Medieval name for **ogee, 2. 2.** A projection of any member or part from another, such as a projecting portion of a molding. **3.** A **roll molding**.

ressault See **ressant**.

restaurant A building (or part of a building) or any place used as a place where meals or sandwiches are prepared and/or served to its clientele.

rest bend A right-angle **fitting, 1** for a pipe with an integral seat which may be mounted on a support.

restoration See **building restoration**.

restricted list of bidders See **invited bidders**.

restriction On land, an encumbrance limiting its use; usually imposed for community or mutual protection.

restrictive covenant An agreement between

two or more individuals, incorporated within a deed which stipulates how land may be used. The constraints may include: the specific use to which a property can be put, the location and dimensions of fences, the setback of buildings from the street, the size of yards, the type of architecture, the cost of the house, etc. Racial and religious restrictions on inhabitants are legally unenforceable.

resurfacing The placing of a supplemental surface on an existing surface to improve its conformation or to increase its strength.

RET. On drawings, abbr. for "return."

retable A decorative screen set up above and behind an altar, generally forming an architectural frame to a picture, bas-relief, or mosaic.

retainage A sum withheld from progress payments to the contractor in accordance with the terms of the **owner-contractor agreement**.

retaining wall A wall, either freestanding or laterally braced, that bears against an earth or other fill surface and resists lateral and other forces from the material in contact with the side of the wall, thereby preventing the mass from sliding to a lower elevation. Also see **cantilever wall, counterfort wall, gravity wall**.

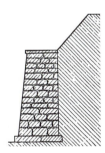

retaining wall

retardation Reduction in the rate of hardening or setting; an increase in the time required to reach initial and final set or to develop early strength of fresh concrete, mortar, plaster, or grout.

retard chamber A device in a fire **sprinkler system** used to minimize false alarms caused by surges or fluctuations in its water supply system.

retarded hemihydrate A calcined gypsum plaster having a retarder added to control the setting action.

retarder **1.** In paint, varnish, or lacquer, a high-boiling solvent used to lower evaporation rate of the volatile ingredients. **2.** An admixture which delays the setting of cement paste or the setting of mixtures such as mortar or concrete containing cement. **3.** An additive, mixed with plaster to control the rate of hardening.

retarding admixture Same as **retarder, 3**.

retempering **1.** The addition of water and remixing of concrete or mortar which has started to stiffen. **2.** The addition of a small amount of water to plaster or mortar as it begins to set; improves spread and workability, but weakens the plaster.

retention **1.** The withholding of a portion (usually 10%) of a periodic payment to a contractor, by prior agreement, for work completed. The retention is held in escrow for a stipulated time period after the acceptance of the completed work by the architect and owner/payee. **2.** The amount of preservative, fire-retardant salt, resin, etc., retained by treated or impregnated wood.

retention money Same as **retention, 1**.

retention wall A thin wall or barrier which forms a gap between it and the external wall of a building (the space between being filled with a waterproofing material).

reticulated Covered with netted lines; netted; having distinct lines crossing in a network.

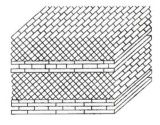

reticulated masonry

reticulated molding A molding decorated with fillets interlaced to form a network or mesh-like appearance.

reticulated molding

reticulated tracery Tracery whose openings are repetitive like the meshes of a net.

reticulated work Same as **opus reticulatum**.

reticulatum opus Same as **opus reticulatum**.

reticuline bar Of a grating, a sinuously bent connecting bar extending between two adjacent **bearing bars**.

retrochoir A chapel behind the high altar of a church but in front of the Lady chapel if there is one.

retrofit The addition of new building materials, building elements, and components, not provided in the original construction. See **building retrofit**.

return The continuation of a molding, projection, member, or cornice, or the like, in a different direction, usually at a right angle. For example, see **cornice return** and **label return**.

return air Air returned from an air-conditioned or refrigerated space to the central plant for processing and recirculation.

return air fan A fan which withdraws air from an air-conditioned space and returns it (or part of it) to the central air-conditioning system.

return-air intake An opening through which **return air** reenters an air-conditioning system; usually provided with a damper to regulate the flow of return air.

return bead The continuation of a bead in a different direction, usually at a right angle. Also see **corner bead, quirk bead**.

return bend A pipe **fitting, 1** or a preformed piece of tubing which provides a 180° change in direction.

return bend

return-circulation system See **hot-water recirculation system**.

return duct A duct carrying **return air**.

returned end The end of a molding having a shape which is the same as the profile of the molding.

returned molding A molding continued in a different direction from its main direction.

returned molding

return fan A fan that removes air from an air-conditioned space.

return grille A **grille, 2** through which return air is extracted; usually not provided with an adjustment for volume of airflow.

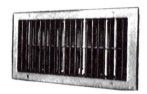

return grille

return mains Pipes or conduits which return a heating or cooling medium from the heat transfer unit to the source of heat or refrigeration.

return offset, jumpover In plumbing, a double **offset, 3** installed in a pipeline to pass around an obstruction.

return offset

return period See **average frequency of occurrence**.

return pipe In a heating system, a pipe through which water that is produced by the condensation of steam is returned to the boiler.

return system **1.** An assembly of connected ducts, or passages or plenums, and fittings through which air from an air-conditioned space is delivered to the return fan. **2.** In a piping system, the pipes through which water is returned to a pump.

return wall A short wall usually perpendicular to, and at the end of, a freestanding wall to increase its structural stability.

REV On drawings, abbr. for "revise."

revalé A stone molding, carved in place.

reveal **1.** The side of an opening for a door or window, doorway, or the like, between the doorframe or window frame and the outer surface of the wall; where the opening is not filled with the door or window, the whole thickness of the wall. **2.** The distance from the face of a door to the face of the frame on the pivot side.

reveal lining Moldings or any other finish applied over a reveal.

reveal pin, reveal tie An adjustable clamp, placed horizontally across an opening in a wall; used to hold scaffolding against the wall.

revent pipe That part of a vent pipeline which connects directly with an individual waste pipe or group of waste pipes underneath or back of the fixture, and extends to either the main or branch vent pipe; also called an **individual vent**.

reverberation The persistence of sound in an enclosed space (such as a room or auditorium) after a source of sound has stopped.

reverberation chamber A room, having a long reverberation time, which is especially designed for the measurement of the **sound absorption coefficients** of an acoustical material or the **sound power** of a sound source.

reverberation time A measure of reverberation in an enclosed space; the time required for **sound-pressure level** to decrease 60 dB after the source has stopped.

reverse A template that has the reverse profile of a molding it is intended to match.

reverse-acting diaphragm valve A valve which opens when pressure is applied on a diaphragm and closes when pressure is released.

reverse-acting thermostat An instrument which activates a control circuit upon sensing a predetermined high temperature.

reverse bevel A bevel on the latch bolt or lock of a door, opening outward from a building, etc., which is the reverse of an ordinary lock bevel.

reversed door See **reverse-swing door**.

reversed loader A **front-end loader** on a wheel tractor which has the driving wheels in front and the steering wheels at the rear.

reversed zigzag molding A compound ornamental **zigzag molding** commonly used in Norman architecture.

reversed zigzag molding

reverse-flight stair See **dogleg stair**.

reverse-swing door, reversed door A door which opens in a direction opposite the usual direction; a door to a room which swings outward.

reversible grating A grating which is constructed so that it may be installed with either side exposed, with no difference in appearance or carrying capacity.

reversible lock A lock which, by reversing the latch bolt, may be used either way; on certain types of locks, other parts also must be changed.

reversible window A window in which the **sash** may be turned so that the glass surface that normally faces the exterior is turned toward the interior for purposes of cleaning.

reversion Chemical reaction leading to the deterioration of a sealant, backup, or filler; due to moisture trapped behind the sealant.

revertible flue A flue or breeching designed so that at some point in the travel of the flue gases they are forced to flow downward instead of in the normal upward direction.

revestry Old form of **vestry**.

revet To face a sloping wall or foundation, an embankment, or the like, with stone, concrete, or a similar material.

revetment **1.** Any facing of stone, metal, or wood over a less attractive or less durable substance or construction. **2.** A retaining wall or breast wall; a facing on an embankment to prevent erosion.

revibration One or more applications of vibration to concrete after completion of placing and initial compaction but preceding initial setting.

Revival architecture Architecture that makes use of elements of an earlier style that it seeks to emulate, borrowing many of the features of its prototype, as described under the term **architectural mode**. For example, see **Adam Revival, American Colonial Revival, American Renaissance Revival, Byzantine Revival, California Mission Revival, Carpenter Gothic Revival, Chateauesque Revival, Classical Revival style, Classic Revival, Colonial Revival, Dutch Colonial Revival, Early Classical Revival, Early Gothic Revival, Early Romanesque Revival, Egyptian Revival, Exotic Revival, Federal Revival, French Revival, Georgian Revival, Gothic Revival, Greek Revival style, International Revival, Italian Renaissance Revival, Jacobethan Revival, Late Gothic Revival, Mediterranean Revival, Mission Revival, Monterey Revival, Moorish Revival, Neoclassical Revival, Neoclassical style, Neoclassicism, Neo-Colonial, Neo-Eclectic, Neo-French, Neo-Georgian, Neo-Gothic, Neo-Grec, Neo-Greek Revival, Neo-Romanesque, Neo-Tudor, Neo-Victorian, Oriental Revival, Period Revival, Pueblo Revival, Regency Revival, Renaissance Revival, Romanesque Revival, Second Renaissance Revival, Spanish Colonial Revival, Spanish Pueblo Revival, Territorial Revival, Tudor Revival, Tuscan Revival.**

revolving-blade mixer Same as **open-top mixer.**

revolving door An exterior door consisting of four leaves (at 90° to each other) which pivot about a common vertical axis within a cylindrically shaped vestibule; prevents the direct passage of air through the vestibule, thereby eliminating drafts from outside.

revolving-drum truck mixer A truck which mixes concrete during its transport to a construction site. Previously proportioned materials from a batch plant are transferred to the truck drum where all mixing takes place.

revolving door: plan

revolving shelf See **lazy susan.**

revolving shovel A **shovel** in which the digging machinery can rotate independently from the supporting structure.

rez-de-chaussée The ground floor of a building.

RF On drawings, abbr. for **roof.**

Rfg Abbr. for "roofing."

RFP Abbr. for "request for proposal."

rgh, Rgh In the lumber industry, abbr. for "rough."

Rh Abbr. for **Rockwell hardness.**

RH **1.** Abbr. for **relative humidity. 2.** Abbr. for "right hand." **3.** Abbr. for "round head."

Rhenish brick A type of lightweight brick.

rheology The science dealing with flow of materials, including studies of deformation of hardened concrete, the handling and placing of freshly mixed concrete, and the behavior of slurries, pastes, and the like.

rheostat An electric device having a resistance which can be adjusted; used to control the flow of electric current, as, for example, in one type of **dimmer.**

RHN Abbr. for **Rockwell hardness number.**

rib **1.** A curved structural member supporting any curved shape or panel. **2.** In vaulted roofs, the moldings which project from the surface and

rib, 1 of an arch

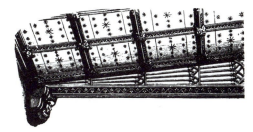

ribs, 2   dividing a ceiling into squares

separate the various roof or ceiling panels. **3.** A raised ridge or fold which is formed in sheet metal (or a formed section attached thereto) to provide stiffness.

RIBA   Abbr. for **Royal Institute of British Architects**.

riband, ribband   Same as **ribbon strip**.

ribbed arch   An arch composed of individual curved members or ribs.

ribbed fluting   **1.** (*Brit.*) Flutes alternating with fillets. **2.** See **cabled fluting**.

ribbed panel   A reinforced concrete panel composed of a thin slab reinforced by a system of ribs.

ribbed slab   Same as **ribbed panel**.

ribbed vault   A vault in which the ribs support, or seem to support, the web of the vault.

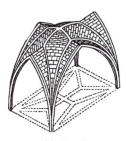

ribbed vault

ribbing   An assemblage or arrangement of ribs, as timberwork sustaining a vaulted ceiling.

ribbing up   Laminating circular joinery by gluing up layers of veneer with parallel grain direction.

ribbon   **1.** A **ribbon strip**. **2.** A long thin strip of wood, or a series of such strips uniting several parts. **3.** In stained glass work or the like, a strip or bar of lead to hold the edge of the glass. Also called a **came**.

ribbon board   **1.** A **ribbon strip**. **2.** A horizontal member in formwork used to prevent the spreading of a **wall box**.

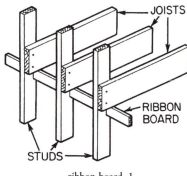

ribbon board, 1

ribbon course   A course in roofing, in which the exposed depth of tile, slate, etc., from one course to the next is alternately large and small.

ribbon development   An urban extension primarily in the form of a single depth of buildings along roads radiating from a city, along a highway between two cities, or along the bank of a river.

ribbon loading   In batching concrete, the loading of all the solid ingredients (and sometimes water) into the mixer at the same time.

ribbon rail   A metal rail which joins the tops of metal balusters.

ribbon saw   Same as **band saw**.

ribbon strip, girt strip, ledger board, riband, ribband   A wood strip or board let into the studs to add support for the ends of the joists; also called a girt strip or ledger board.

ribbon-stripe veneer, ribbon-grained veneer, stripe veneer   Wood veneer having alternate light and dark stripes running parallel to the grain. Also see **interlocked grain**.

ribbon window, ribbon lights   On the façade of a building, a horizontal band of at least three windows, separated only by **mullions**; occasionally called a window band.

rib lath, stiffened expanded metal   Expanded-metal lath having V-shaped ribs to provide greater stiffness and to permit wider spacing of framing members.

rib vault   Same as **ribbed vault**.

Richardsonian Romanesque style

Richardsonian Romanesque style, Romanesque Revival The massive architectural style, from 1880 to 1900 and beyond, as practiced by Henry Hobson Richardson (1838–1886) and his followers; an outgrowth of earlier architecture making use of architectural elements of the **Romanesque style**, chiefly in public buildings, churches, railroad terminals, and universities designed from 1840 to 1880. Buildings in this style usually exhibit many of the following characteristics: a façade of rough-cut rock-faced masonry, and different colors and textures of stone, occasionally in combination with decorative brickwork; massive semicircular arches, sometimes in combination with flat arches; clustered arches or piers; a decorative **tympanum**; parapeted gable ends; short, thick columns, occasionally with **cushion capitals**; bands of engaged colonettes; decorative plaques; a roof covering of slate or tile; one or more cross gables; decorative cresting or decorative tile at the ridge of the roof; a tower with a steep roof and/or topped with a finial; a steeply pitched, hipped roof with little roof overhang at the eaves; a decorative chimney; double-hung windows, often arched or rectangular; deeply recessed window opening; window openings framed by round arches having hooded moldings, often with label stops; often, a circular or semicircular window in a wall gable; doors usually deeply set within massive semicircular or segmental masonry arches ornamented with Romanesque decorations. Also called Neo-Romanesque or Romanesque Revival. See **Victorian Romanesque**.

Richardsonian Romanesque

rich concrete Concrete having a high cement content.

rich lime A **fat lime**.

rich low brass See **red brass**.

rich mix A **fat mix**.

rich mixture Same as **fat mix**.

rich mortar A **fat mortar**.

RICS Abbr. for "Royal Institution of Chartered Surveyors."

riddle A sieve, esp. a coarse one for sand.

rider cap Same as **pile cap**.

rider shore A heavy timber whose lower end abuts another timber laid against the back of the outer **raking shore** rather than against the ground.

ridge **1.** The horizontal line at the junction of the upper edges of two sloping roof surfaces. **2.** The internal angle or nook of a vault.

ridge batten Same as **ridge roll**.

ridge beam A beam at the upper ends of the rafters, below the ridge of a roof; a **crown plate, 2**.

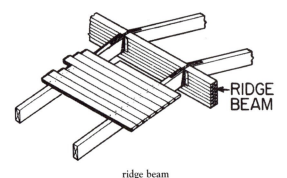

←RIDGE BEAM

ridge beam

ridgeboard, ridgepole A longitudinal member at the apex of a roof which supports the upper ends of the rafters. Also called a ridge beam, ridgepiece, ridgeplate, or ridgetree.

ridgecap, ridge capping, ridge covering Any covering (such as metal, wood, shingle, etc.) used to cover the ridge of a roof.

ridge course The last or top course of roofing tiles, roll roofing, or shingles.

ridge covering See **ridgecap**.

ridge crest The ornamentation of the ridge of a roof.

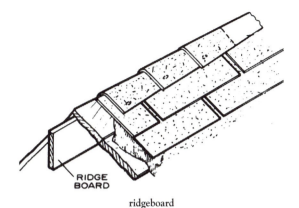

ridgeboard

ridge roll

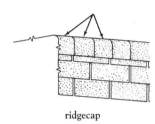

ridgecap

ridge cresting   See **cresting**.

ridge cut   See **plumb cut**.

ridge fillet   A fillet between two depressions, as between two flutes of a column.

ridge molding   A molding of sheet metal, copper, zinc, or lead which covers the ridge of a roof.

ridgepole   See **ridgeboard**.

ridge rib   **1.** A horizontal rib marking the crown of a compartment of vaulting, characteristic of English Gothic architecture from the early 13th cent. on, but occasionally found on the Continent. **2.** A **rib** which follows the ridge of a vault.

ridge roll   **1.** A wood strip, rounded on top, which is used to finish the ridge of a roof; often covered with lead sheeting. **2.** A metal, tile, or asbestos-cement covering which caps the ridge of a roof; also called a hip roll or ridgecap.

ridge roof   A pitched roof; the rafters meet at the apex of a ridge; the end view is that of a **gable roof**.

ridge stop   In roofing, a metal **flashing** used at the intersection of a ridge and a wall rising above it.

ridge terrace   On a slope, the area behind a contour line of a slope which forms a ridge that retains the rainwater that falls on the slope above it.

ridge tile, crown tile   A tile which is curved in section, often decorative, used to cover the ridge of a roof.

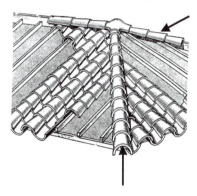

ridge tile

ridgetree   An archaic form of **ridgepole**.

ridge ventilator   A **roof ventilator** that straddles a ridge of the roof of a barn; usually square in plan and constructed of wood and/or metal.

ridging   **1.** In built-up roofing, a failure characterized by long narrow blisters in the roof surface. **2.** The covering of the ridge of a roof.

riding house   A structure especially designed for teaching the skill of horse riding. (*See illustration p. 768.*)

riding shore   Same as **rider shore**.

riding trail   See **bridle path**.

riebeckite asbestos   A type of mineral derived from a monoclinic amphibole.

riffler   A file which is curved and grooved for working in depressions.

rifle hole

riding house

rifle hole A slot in an exterior wall of structures such as blockhouses, forts, and garrison houses, used for defensive purposes. The sides of the slot are splayed so the opening is wider at the inner face of the wall than at the exterior face, permitting a rifleman on the interior to fire over a wide angle.

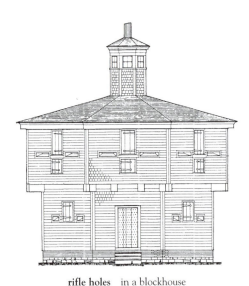

rifle holes in a blockhouse

rift The direction in which stone splits most readily; characteristic of granite or other stone not having visible stratification or foliation.

rift-grained See **edge-grained**.

rift sawn See **quartersawn**.

rigger A long-haired, slender brush used in precision painting.

rigging See **stage rigging**.

rigging line A rope or wire used in **stage rigging**.

rigging loft A space above the stage of a legitimate theater; designed and used for the flying and storage of scenery and scenic elements.

riggot An open rainwater drain, such as a gutter.

right angle An angle of 90°.

right-hand door See **hand**.

right-hand lock A lock for use on a **right-hand door**.

right-hand reverse door See **hand**.

right-hand stairway A stairway having the rail on the right side, in the ascending direction.

right line A straight line between two points.

right-of-way Any strip or area of land, including surface and overhead or underground space, which is granted by deed or easement for the construction and maintenance of specified linear elements such as power and telephone lines; roadways; gas, oil, water, and other pipelines; sewers.

rigid arch An arch which has no joints, being continuous and rigidly fixed at the abutments.

rigid concrete pavement Reinforced portland concrete pavement on a gravel base and subbase; usually has transverse joints for controlling expansion and contraction.

rigid connection A connection between two structural members which prevents one from rotating with respect to the other.

rigid foam **1.** See **cellular plastic**. **2.** See **foamed plastic, 1**.

rigid frame A structural framework in which all columns and beams are rigidly connected; there are no hinged joints and the angular relationship between beam and column members are maintained under load.

rigid insulation Thermal insulation whose density is high enough so that a sheet of this insulation will stand upright if supported only along one edge of the sheet.

rigidity That property of a material which resists a change in its physical shape.

rigidized Said of light-gauge sheet metal which is embossed or textured by a rolling process to provide additional stiffness.

rigid lock See **preassembled lock**.

rigid metal conduit A **raceway** for electric wires or cables, made of metal pipe of standard thickness and weight permitting the cutting of standard threads.

rigid pavement A pavement which provides high bending resistance and which distributes loads to the foundation over a relatively large area.

riglet Same as **reglet**.

rim **1.** The border or outer edge of anything which is circular or continuously curved. **2.** Descriptive of any **finish hardware** which is designed for application to the face of a door or window, rather than for mortising.

rim latch A surface-mounted latch.

rim lock A face-mounted door lock. Compare with **box lock**.

rinceau In classical architecture and derivatives, an ornamental band of undulant and recurving plant motifs.

rinceau

rind gall A defect in timber caused by a bruise in the bark which produces a callus on the wood over which later layers grow without consolidating.

ring course In an arch, an outer course of stone or brick.

ringed column See **banded column**.

Ringelmann chart A chart used as the basis for evaluating the density of smoke discharged from chimneys.

ring gasket Same as **gasket, 2**.

ring-groove nail Same as **ring-shank nail**.

ringhiera In Italian Medieval architecture, a balcony (on the front of the town hall) from which speeches and decrees were read.

ringlock nail Same as **ring-shank nail**.

ring louver, *Brit.*, **spill ring** In lighting, a louver system in the form of concentric annular rings; used in luminaires having circular apertures.

ring-porous wood Hardwood having springwood pores which are larger and more distinct than those produced later in the growing season.

ring scratch awl A **scratch awl** esp. used in sheet-metal fabrication.

ring shake, cup shake, shell shake, wind shake A separation in wood between or along the annual rings.

ring-shank nail A nail having a number of ring-like grooves around the shank to increase its holding power.

ring stone One of the stones of an arch which show on the face of the wall, or the end of the arch; one of the voussoirs of the face forming the archivolt.

ring-type hanger A type of hanger primarily used to support pipes; either fabricated in one piece or split in two halves which are fastened.

rink **1.** A bounded space of ice, usually enclosed, for skating, curling, or ice hockey matches. **2.** A bounded space, usually enclosed, with a smooth floor, of wood or asphalt, for roller skating.

rip To cut wood lengthwise, parallel to the grain.

riparian right The right of a landowner to use water from a river or other body of water on which his land abuts.

ripper **1.** An attachment with long angled teeth that fits on the rear of a tractor or is towed by it; penetrates and loosens subsurface layers of earth to a depth of up to 3 ft (approx. 1 m). **2.** A tool used for removing damaged slates on a roof; consists of a long steel blade with a notched hook at one end for withdrawing nails. **3.** A towed machine, provided with teeth to loosen hard soil and soft rock. (*See illustration p. 770.*)

ripping See **ripsawing**.

ripping bar Same as **pinch bar**.

ripping chisel

ripper, 1

ripping chisel In woodworking, a bent chisel used in clearing out mortises or seams.

ripping size The size of lumber, as it comes from the operation of **ripsawing**, that is required to obtain a specified finish size.

ripple figure Same as **fiddleback** or **curl**.

ripple finish A crackled or wrinkled paint finish, usually obtained by baking. Also see **wrinkling**.

riprap **1.** Irregularly broken and random-sized large pieces of quarry rock; individual stones ranging from very large (2 to 3 cu yd, approx. 1.5 to 2.3 cu m) to small (½ cu ft, approx. 0.014 cu m); used for foundations and revetments. **2.** A foundation or parapet of stones thrown together without any attempt at regular structural arrangement.

ripsaw A saw, the teeth of which have a chisel-like ripping action; used for cutting wood in the direction of the grain.

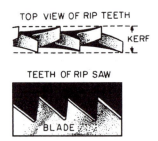

TOP VIEW OF RIP TEETH

KERF

TEETH OF RIP SAW

BLADE

ripsaw

ripsawing, flat cutting, ripping Sawing lumber parallel to the grain direction.

rise **1.** The height of a flight of stairs from landing to landing. **2.** The height between successive treads of a stair. **3.** The vertical distance such as that used to express the height of a roof slope compared to horizontal distance or run, or the vertical measurement from the face of one stair tread to the next. **4.** In an arch, the vertical distance from the springing line to the highest point of the intrados. **5.** Of elevators, same as **travel**.

rise-and-fall table A circular-saw assembly in which the table, rather than the saw, is movable.

rise and run **1.** The pitch of an inclined surface or member, usually expressed as the ratio of the vertical rise to the horizontal run. **2.** The slope of a building element expressed as the vertical increase in height for a selected distance in the horizontal direction.

risen molding Same as **bolection molding**.

riser **1.** The vertical face of a stair step. **2.** Any upright face, as of a seat, platform, etc. **3.** A platform on the stage of a theatre or concert hall on which a performer is placed. **4.** A water-supply, drainage, gas, steam, or vent pipe which extends vertically, one full story or more, to service several branches or a group of fixtures. **5.** An electrical cable which extends vertically, one full story or more, to distribute electrical power to electric panels on the different floors of a building. **6.** A duct, which extends vertically, one full story or more, to distribute air to branch ducts on the different floors of a building. **7.** A vertical supply pipe for a fire **sprinkler system**.

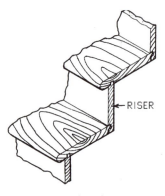

RISER

riser, 1

riser board In formwork, the board that forms the vertical face of a step.

riser diagram A diagram (two-dimensional, in a vertical plane) which shows the major items of electrical equipment in a building; displays, floor by floor, the feeders and major items of equipment.

riser height The vertical distance between the top surfaces of two successive treads.

riser pipe A **riser, 4**.

rising arch An arch having a **springing line** which is not horizontal.

rising damp The upward movement of moisture in a wall or other structure standing in wet soil or water.

rising hinge, rising butt hinge A door hinge having a spiral groove winding about its knuckle, or having the joints of the knuckle oblique, so that when opened, the door is lifted and clears the carpet.

rising main Same as **riser, 4** or **riser, 5**.

rive To split wood along the grain, as in making shingles.

rived board, riven board A board that has been shaped by splitting it along the grain instead of sawing it.

riveling See **wrinkling**.

riven laths Wood laths made by splitting instead of sawing.

rivet A short pin, of a malleable metal such as iron, steel, or copper, with a head at one end; used to unite two metal plates by passing it through a hole in both plates and then hammering down the point to form a second head.

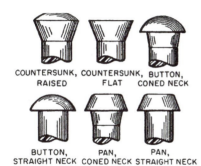

COUNTERSUNK, RAISED   COUNTERSUNK, FLAT   BUTTON, CONED NECK

BUTTON, STRAIGHT NECK   PAN, CONED NECK   PAN, STRAIGHT NECK

rivet heads

rivet centers The distance between the centers of rivets along a straight line, as along a bearing bar in a **riveted grating**.

riveted grating A grating composed of straight **bearing bars** and bent connecting bars, which are joined at their contact points by riveting.

riveted joint A connection between two members which are riveted together.

riveted truss Any truss having its main members riveted together.

rivet hole A hole through which a **rivet** is driven.

riveting The fastening of plates or parts by means of rivets.

riveting hammer A hammer having a long head, a flat face, and a narrow peen; used for swaging down rivets or beating sheet metal.

rivet set, rivet snap, setting punch, snap A tool for shaping the head of a **rivet**.

rivet snap See **rivet set**.

rivet set

riving knife, froe, frow A tool for splitting shingles and the like.

R/L Abbr. for "random lengths."

R lamp A **reflector lamp** (usually incandescent) having a thin glass envelope, the back interior side of which is aluminum-coated to serve as a light reflector; this reflecting surface is shaped so as to provide a desired beam spread.

RM On drawings, abbr. for **room**.

rms Abbr. for "root mean square."

road oil A heavy petroleum oil, usually one of the grades of **slow-curing asphalt**.

rocaille An ornament, usually asymmetrical, consisting of rock, plant, and shell forms in combination with artificial forms; widely used during the 18th century when **Rococo** was popular.

rock **1.** Solid natural mineral material, occurring in fragments or large masses and requiring mechanical or explosive techniques for removal. **2.** Stone in a mass. **3.** A stone of any size.

rock asphalt Porous rock such as sandstone or limestone that has become impregnated with natural asphalt through a geological process.

rock-cut Said of a temple or tomb excavated in native rock without the aid of masonry, or with but little masonry; usually presents an architectural front with dark interior chambers, of which sections are supported by masses of stone left in the form of solid pillars.

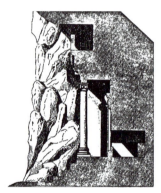

rock-cut tomb at Telmissus

rock dash An exterior **stucco** finish containing crushed rock, large pebbles, or shells that are imbedded in a stucco base; also called pebble dash or slap dash.

rock drill A machine or device for drilling a hole in rock so that it may be blasted; usually driven by compressed air, but also may be driven by electricity or by steam.

rocket tester Same as **smoke rocket**.

rock-faced A term descriptive of the rough face of stone as it is split at the quarry or dressed to resemble such a natural face; squared off only along the edges.

rock fill A **fill, 1** comprised of large, loosely placed rocks.

rock flour A very finely powdered rock material; also see **silt**.

rocking frame A flat mechanically powered, oscillating bed; used to compact concrete, which is in the plastic state, in precast units temporarily set on the bed.

rock lath See **gypsum lath**.

rock pocket A porous, mortar-deficient portion of hardened concrete; consists primarily of coarse aggregate and open voids; results from the leakage of mortar from the concrete form, separation (segregation) during placement, or insufficient consolidation.

rock rash A patchwork appliqué of oddly shaped stone slabs; used on edge as a veneer; often further embellished with cobbles or geodes.

Rockwell hardness A measure of the resistance of a material to indentation; determined by use of a machine which presses a steel ball or a spheroconical ball indentor into the material under arbitrarily fixed test conditions; expressed by the **Rockwell hardness number**—the higher the number, the harder the material.

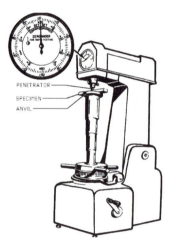

PENETRATOR
SPECIMEN
ANVIL

Rockwell hardness tester

Rockwell hardness number A measure of Rockwell hardness; determined by use of a machine having an indentor which can be loaded; the number is derived from the net increase in depth of impression that the indentor makes in the material as the load on the indentor is increased from a fixed load to a higher load, and then returned to the minimum load.

rock wool A type of **mineral wool** made by forming fibers from molten rock; used in thermal insulation.

rockwork **1.** **Quarry-faced** masonry. **2.** Stonework in which the surface is left irregular and rough.

Rococo A style of architecture and decoration, primarily French in origin, which represents the final phase of the Baroque around the middle of the 18th cent.; characterized by profuse, often semiabstract ornamentation and lightness of color and weight.

Rococo

rod 1. In plastering, a **straightedge**, usually of wood, for leveling the face of a wall. 2. A solid (metal, wood, or plastic) product that is long in relation to its cross section. 3. A **leveling rod**.

rod bender A powered device, with movable rollers and clamps, used to bend steel **reinforcing rods** to shapes required in reinforced concrete.

rod cutter A bench-type device, with a guillotine-like wedge, used to cut steel **reinforcing rods**.

roddability The susceptibility of fresh concrete or mortar to compaction by means of a **tamping rod**.

rodded joint A masonry term occasionally used for a **concave joint**.

rodding 1. The strengthening of stone slabs or panels (usually marble) by cementing reinforcing rods into routings in the back. 2. The consolidation of mortar or concrete by the repeated insertions and withdrawals of a rod. 3. The clearing of an obstruction in a drain.

rodding eye Same as **cleanout**.

rode A medieval English form of **rood**.

rod level An accessory for use with a leveling rod or a stadia rod to assure a vertical position of the rod prior to instrument reading.

rod target A target carried on a **leveling rod** or a **range rod** and upon which sights are made in surveying.

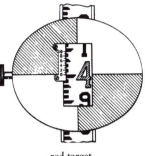

rod target

roe figure A type of grain in wood; esp. found in tropical woods with a spiral grain which have been **quarter-sawn**.

roll 1. A rounded strip fastened to, and running along, the ridge of a roof. 2. In a roof covered with sheet metal, one of a number of rounded strips placed under the metal sheeting at intervals, to prevent movement of the sheets resulting from expansion and contraction. 3. Any type of rounded molding. 4. A quantity of any material wound in cylindrical form.

roll-and-fillet molding A molding of nearly circular cross section with a narrow band or fillet on its face.

roll-and-fillet molding

roll billet molding A common Norman molding consisting of a series of **billets, 1** which are cylindrical in cross section, usually staggered in alternate rows.

roll billet molding

roll capped Said of **ridge tiles** having a roll along the apex.

rolled Said of metal which has been shaped, either hot or cold, by being passed between rollers.

rolled beam, rolled steel beam A metal beam fabricated of steel made in a rolling mill.

rolled glass A flat glass sheet produced by passing a stream of molten glass between two steel rollers; usually in widths up to 12 ft (3.66 m) and thicknesses from ⅛ to 1 in. (3.2 to 31.8 mm). Embossed rollers are used to produce patterned surfaces.

rolled steel beam See **rolled beam**.

rolled strip roofing See **asphalt prepared roofing**.

roller 1. See **paint roller**. 2. A self-propelled or towed device to compact soil.

roller coating 1. Applying a coat of paint with a **paint roller**. 2. A method of paint application whereby an object is coated between two rollers wet with paint.

roller-coating enamel An enamel made esp. for application on strip steel, aluminum, or other metal surfaces, using a roller-coating machine.

roller latch A type of door latch; has a roller under spring tension instead of a beveled spring bolt; the roller engages a **strike plate** having a recess formed to receive it.

roller latch

roller strike A **strike plate** which has a cylindrical roller at the point where the latch bolt of a lock makes contact with the strike plate; used to minimize friction.

rolling The use of heavy metal or stone rollers on terrazzo topping to extract excess matrix.

rolling curtain A theatre stage curtain that rolls up on a horizontal drum or roll.

rolling cyclorama A **cyclorama** which can be rolled around a vertical drum usually by means of an electric motor.

rolling grille door A vertically moving rolling door made up of a grille which is guided in a track; has a horizontally mounted overhead rolling mechanism.

rolling shutter door Same as **roll-up door**.

rolling shutters See **roll-up door**.

roll insulation A flexible blanket-type thermal insulation in roll form; esp. used between studs or joists in frame construction.

roll joint In sheet-metal work, a joint formed by rolling the edges of adjoining sheets together and then flattening the roll.

roll molding Any convex, rounded molding, which has (wholly or in part) a cylindrical form.

rollock Same as **rowlock**.

roll roofing See **asphalt prepared roofing**.

roll-up door, rolling shutters A door made up of small horizontal interlocking metal slats which are guided in a track; the configuration coils about an overhead drum which is housed at the head of the opening; either manual or motor-driven.

rolock See **rowlock**.

rolock arch Same as **rowlock arch**.

rolok See **rowlock**.

Roman arch A semicircular arch. If built of

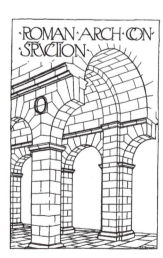

Roman arch construction

stone, all units are wedge-shaped; the usual arch in Roman architecture.

Roman brick Brick whose nominal dimensions are 2 in. by 4 in. by 12 in. (5 cm by 10 cm by 30 cm).

Roman bronze A copper-zinc alloy to which a small quantity of tin has been added to give it greater corrosion resistance and hardness.

Roman cement A quick-setting **natural cement** that can harden under water and is relatively impervious to water; made of a finely pulverized calcined argillaceous limestone that has been treated in a kiln at a temperature no higher than that necessary to drive off carbon dioxide.

Roman Classicism See **Classical Revival style**.

Romanesque Revival **1.** Same as **Richardsonian Romanesque style**. **2.** A term sometimes applied to the early works of James Renwick (1818–1895) and Richard Upjohn (1802–1878) using elements of the **Romanesque style**.

Romanesque style An architectural style emerging in Western Europe primarily in the 11th century and lasting until the advent of Gothic architecture in the 12th century; based on Roman and Byzantine elements; found especially in churches and castles; usually characterized by round arches and by massive articulated walls, barrel vaults, groined vaults, ribbed vaults; semicircular arches; served as the basis for the **Richardson Romanesque style** and occasionally used as a synonym for it.

Romanesque style

Roman mosaic A pavement that is **tessellated**.

Roman order **1.** A seldom-used term for the **composite order**. **2.** Same as **arch order, 1**.

Roman Revival See **Classic Revival**.

Roman theatre An open-air theatre constructed by the ancient Romans; sometimes built on a hillside, but more often on level ground—usually with a richly decorated outer façade, with a colonnade gallery and vaulted entrances for the public. The **orchestra, 2** usually was a half-circle; behind it was a stage having a richly decorated proscenium and stage background. Also see **Greek theatre**.

Romantic style A loose term embracing a variety of modes of architecture, often including **Exotic Revival, Gothic Revival, Greek Revival style, Italianate style**.

Roman tile A channel-shaped, tapered, single lap, roofing tile.

rondel See **roundel**.

rood A large crucifix, esp. one set above the chancel entrance.

rood altar An altar standing against the nave side of a rood screen.

rood arch The central arch in a rood screen; rarely, the arch between nave and chancel over the rood.

rood beam A horizontal beam extending across the entrance to the chancel of a church to support the rood.

rood loft A gallery or elevated platform established upon the rood screen.

rood screen An ornamental altar screen that separates the **nave** of a church from the **chancel**; intended to carry a large crucifix (*rood*).

rood spire A spire over the crossing of the nave and transepts.

rood stairs Stairs by which the rood loft is approached.

rood tower A tower built over the crossing and hence approximately above the rood.

roof The top covering of a building, including all materials and constructions necessary to support it on the walls of the building or on uprights; provides protection against rain, snow, sunlight, extremes of temperature, and wind. For definitions and illustrations of the different types, see **barrel roof, bellcast roof, bonnet roof, bowed roof, broken-pitch roof, bunker fill roof, butterfly roof, candle-snuffer roof, canopy roof, collar-beam roof, compass roof, conical roof,**

curb roof, deck roof, double-gable roof, double-hipped roof, double-pitched roof, dropped roof, dual-pitched roof, Dutch gambrel roof, Dutch hipped roof, Dutch roof, Dutch slice-hip roof, earth roof, English gambrel roof, flat roof, Flemish roof, flounder roof, French roof, gable-on-hip roof, gable roof, gambrel roof, Gothic roof, helm roof, hip-on-gable roof, hipped-gable roof, hipped roof, hip-on-gable roof, hyperbolic paraboloid roof, Italian roof, jack roof, jerkinhead roof, kick roof, knee roof, landscaped roof, lean-to roof, mansard roof, monitor roof, M-roof, New England gambrel roof, ogee roof, open roof, pavilion roof, pent roof, pigeon roof, pitched roof, ponded roof, principal roof, purlin roof, pyramidal roof, queen-post roof, rainbow roof, ridge roof, round roof, saddle-back roof, saltbox roof, segmental roof, shed roof, ship's bottom roof, single-pitched roof, skirt-roof, slice-hip roof, sod roof, span roof, square roof, Swedish gambrel roof, terrace roof, thatched roof, truncated roof, umbrella roof, visor roof, wagon roof, whaleback roof.

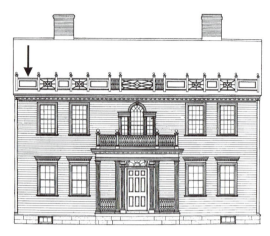

roof balustrade

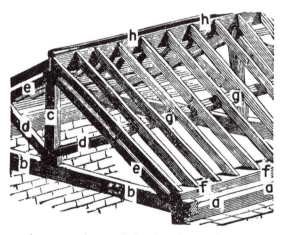

timbers in a **roof:** *a*, wall plate; *b*, tie beam; *c*, king post; *d*, strut; *e*, principal rafter; *f*, pole plate; *g*, purlin; *h*, ridgeboard

roofage   Same as **roofing**.

roof balustrade   A railing with supporting balusters on a roof, often near the eaves or surrounding a **widow's walk**.

roof board   One of a number of boards that cover the upper surface of rafters so as to serve as a base for the application of a roof covering, such as shingles.

roof cladding   See **roofing, 1**.

roof comb, roof crest   A wall along the ridge of a roof; used to give an appearance of additional height.

roof covering   **1.** All the materials laid on the roof frame; includes sheathing, the outer cladding materials, asphalt paper, etc. **2.** A **roof covering, 1** which is not readily flammable and does not slip from position. The following classes have these and additional properties: *Class A* is effective against severe fire exposure, does not carry or communicate fire, and affords a fairly high degree of fire protection to the roof-deck. *Class B* is effective against moderate fire exposure, does not readily carry or communicate fire, and affords a moderate degree of fire protection to the roof-deck. *Class C* is effective against light fire exposure, does not readily carry or communicate fire, and affords a slight degree of fire protection to the roof-deck.

roof crest   See **roof comb**.

roof cresting   See **cresting**.

roof-deck   **1.** The flat portion of a roof, used as a terrace, for sunbathing, etc.; compare with **deck roof**. **2.** The structural material between the roof supports used as a base for the roof covering system; may be metal, concrete, wood, gypsum, or a combination of these or similar materials.

roof decking   Prefabricated units, usually in the form of long structural panels, which span the roof framing system and form a **roof-deck, 2**.

roof dormer   See **dormer**.

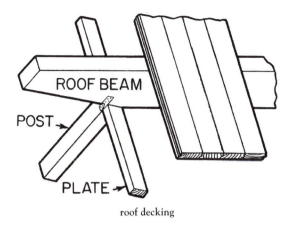

roof decking

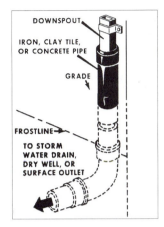

lower portion of a **roof drainage system**

roof drain   A drain designed to receive water collecting on the surface of a roof and to discharge it into a leader or a downspout.

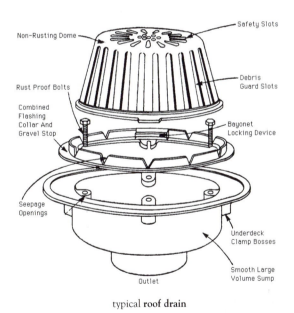

typical **roof drain**

roof drainage system   On the roof (or at the roof line) of a building, a system composed of storm-water collection devices, and piping connected to these collection devices; transports the rainwater off the roof and out of the building.

roofed ingle   A **chimney corner**.

roofer   A term once used for a **roof board**.

roof flange   A flange which fits around a pipe that penetrates a roof; used on the upper side to provide a raintight installation.

roof framing   The assemblage of roof members which provide support for the roof covering.

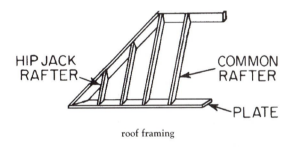

roof framing

roof gallery   See **widow's walk**.

roof garden   A garden or restaurant, or the like, on a roof.

roof guard   Same as **snow guard**.

roof gutter   See **gutter, 1**.

roof hatch   A hinged panel unit, providing a weathertight means of access to a roof.

roofing   Any material (or any combination of materials) used as a roof covering, such as corrugated metal, sheet metal, shingles, slate, thatch, or tile; usually provides waterproofing, windproofing, and thermal insulation.

roofing assembly   The combination of all of the elements used in constructing a roof: the roof deck, substrate or thermal barrier, insulation, vapor retarder, underlayment, interlayment, base plies, and roof covering.

roofing bond A guarantee by a surety company that a roofing manufacturer will repair a roof membrane or covering under the conditions listed in the bonding contract.

roofing bracket A bracket, used on a sloping roof, which is fastened to the roof or is supported by ropes fastened over the ridge and secured to a suitable object.

roofing felt See **asphalt prepared roofing**.

roofing nail A short nail having a barbed or ring shank and a comparatively large flat head; may be galvanized or bright; often provided with a neoprene, lead, or plastic washer; used to secure roofing felt or shingles to a roof-deck or roof boards.

LARGE HEAD, PLAIN SHANK

NEOPRENE WASHER ATTACHED, PLAIN SHANK

NEOPRENE WASHER ATTACHED, SCREW SHANK

BARBED SHANK WITH LEAD WASHER

roofing nails

roofing paper See **asphalt prepared roofing, asphalt paper, building paper**.

roofing putty A heavy asphaltic material used to caulk metal roofs.

roofing sand A fine, white silica sand.

roofing slate See **slate**.

roofing square An area of 100 sq ft (9.3 m²) of roofing surface.

roofing system An assembly of components which provide **roofing**.

roofing tile A tile for roofing, often fabricated of clay or slate that has been treated in a kiln at an elevated temperature; also available in many types of materials and a variety of configurations; see **clay tile, mission tile, pantile, ridge tile, Spanish tile**.

roof insulation 1. A board-type product, usually of low or medium density, made of mineral fibers, cellular glass, foamed plastic, lightweight concrete, wood fiberboard, or other materials, one or both sides of which may be faced with

another material; provides thermal insulation in a roofing system. **2.** Lightweight concrete which is used primarily for thermal insulation over a structural roof system.

roof ladder A **cat ladder**.

roof light Same as **skylight**.

roof-light sheet A sheet of transparent material used to glaze an opening in a roof.

roof line The contour or shape of a roof.

roof live load The load exerted on a roof other than the roofing system and its supporting members; the **live load** on the roof.

roof pitch The slope of a roof, usually expressed as the angle of pitch in degrees or as a ratio of vertical rise to the horizontal run.

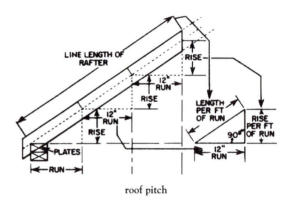

roof pitch

roof plate A horizontal structural member that receives and supports the lower ends of the rafters of a roof; same as **top plate, 1** or **wall plate**.

roof principal A **roof truss**.

roof purlin Same as **purlin**.

roof saddle A **saddle, 3**.

roof scuttle A **roof hatch**.

roof sheathing The boards or sheet material, especially plywood, fastened to the roof rafters, onto which the shingle or other roof covering is laid.

roof sign A board, poster, lighting display, or the like, erected and maintained on or above the roof of a building, usually to advertise or impart information.

roof slating See **slating**.

roof space Space (generally unused) between the roof and the ceiling of the highest room.

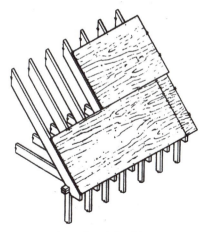

plywood **roof sheathing**

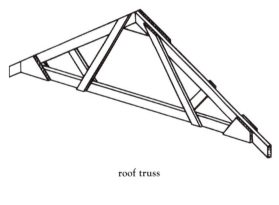

roof truss

roof ventilators

roof structure A structure on a roof or above any part of a building, such as a cooling tower or sign support.

roof tank A water-storage tank on a roof.

roof terminal The termination of a vent pipe at the roof.

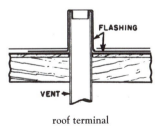

roof terminal

roof tie 1. A **collar beam**. 2. A **tie beam**.

roof tile See **roofing tile**.

rooftop The roof of a house or other building.

rooftree The **ridgeboard** of a roof.

roof truss A structural support for a roof.

roof valley See **valley**.

roof vent 1. A ventilation device for an attic or roof cavity. 2. Above a legitimate theater, one of two or more vents above the **stagehouse**, constructed to open automatically in case of fire, with an aggregate clear opening area of not less than 5 percent of the area of the stage.

roof ventilator A **ventilator, 1** on the roof of a building, usually designed to exclude rain and snow. Also see **ridge ventilator**.

rookery 1. A tenement or dilapidated group of dwellings. 2. A building with many diverse occupants and rooms, such as a boardinghouse.

room In a building, a particular portion, an enclosure or division separated from other divisions by partitions.

room air conditioner, packaged air conditioner, unit air conditioner, unit cooler A factory-made encased unit which is designed to deliver conditioned air to an enclosed space without the use of ducts; usually mounted in a window or in an opening in a wall, or as a console.

room criterion curves See **RC curves**.

room-door lock An **inside-door lock**.

room velocity The velocity of air in the occupied zone of an air-conditioned space, expressed in feet per second (m/s).

root That portion of a tenon in the plane of the shoulders.

root cellar A structure, either partially or wholly below ground level, that is used to store root crops, such as potatoes and beets, at a cool temperature; also see **potato barn**.

rooter   A heavy-duty **ripper** intended to remove roots of trees.

rope   A strong thick line, comprised of a number of twisted or braided strands of fiber (such as hemp) or of wire (see **wire rope**).

rope caulk   A preformed bead of tacky caulking compound; often contains twine reinforcement to facilitate handling.

rope drum   The drum of a **hoist, 2** on which the hoisting cable or rope is wrapped.

roped hydraulic elevator   A **hydraulic elevator** in which the piston is connected by wire ropes (cables) to the elevator car for hoisting it; the driving mechanism includes a hydraulic cylinder, piston, sheaves (and their guides), tanks, hydraulic pump, and associated valves.

rope molding   A bead or torus molding carved in imitation of a rope; also see **cabling**.

rope suspension equalizer   A device installed on an elevator car or counterweight to equalize automatically the tensions in the hoisting wire ropes.

ropiness   Hills and valleys in a paint film created by bristles in a brush when the paint is applied; usually caused by the poor flow of the paint or by brushing into a semidried film.

rosace   See **rosette, 1**.

rose   A metal plate attached to the face of a door, around the shaft for the doorknob; sometimes acts as a bearing surface for the knob.

rose bit   A bit used to countersink holes in wood.

rose molding   An ornament used esp. in Norman architecture, chiefly during its later and richer period.

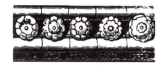

rose molding

rose nail   A nail with a conical head which is hand-hammered into triangular facets.

rosette   **1.** A round pattern with a carved or painted conventionalized floral motif; a **rosace**. **2.** A circular or oval decorative wood plaque used in joinery, such as one applied to a wall to receive the end of a stair rail. **3.** An ornamental nailhead or screwhead.

rosette, 1

rose window, Catherine-wheel window, marigold window, wheel window   A large, circular medieval window, containing tracery disposed in a radial manner.

rose window

rosewood   See **bubinga, Brazilian rosewood, East Indian rosewood**.

rosin, colophony   A resin obtained as a residue in the distillation of crude turpentine from the sap of pine trees (**gum rosin**) or from an extract of the stumps and other parts of them (**wood rosin**).

rostral column   A column, in honor of a naval triumph, ornamented with the rostra or prows of ships.

rostrum   A platform, elevated area, pulpit, or the like for addressing an audience.

rot   Decomposition in wood by fungi and other microorganisms; reduces its strength, density, and hardness. Also see **brown rot, white rot**.

rotary cutting, rotary slicing   A method of cutting wood veneer in which a log is fixed in a lathe and rotated against a knife so that the veneer is peeled from the log in a continuous sheet; used to produce softwood veneer and low-grade hardwood veneer.

rotary drill   A machine for opening holes in rock or earth by means of a cutting bit at the end of a metal shank; usually turned by a hydraulically or pneumatically driven motor.

rotary float, power float A motor-driven revolving disk that smooths, flattens, and compacts the surface of concrete floors or floor toppings.

rotary float

rotary trowel Same as **rotary float**.

rotary veneer Wood veneer obtained by **rotary cutting**.

roto operator A gear-driven device, turned with a small crank handle or knob; used to open and close jalousies, awning windows, casement windows, and fanlights.

roto operator

rotten knot See **unsound knot**.

rottenstone A soft, friable limestone; in pulverized form, used for polishing soft metal surfaces and wood.

rotunda 1. A circular building, especially one with a dome. 2. A circular hall in a large building, esp. one covered by a cupola.

rough arch Same as **discharging arch**; built with rectangular bricks and wedge-shaped mortar joints.

rough ashlar A block of stone, as brought from the quarry.

rough-axed brick An **axed brick**.

roughback 1. A side cut of stone (a slab) having one side sawn and the other rough; cut from a block fed through a gang saw. 2. In masonry, a concealed end of a stone laid as a bondstone.

rough bracket A bracket under stair steps, fastened to the supporting carriage.

rough brick arch A brick arch made up of rectangular bricks that are neither cut nor tapered to **voussoir** shape; the required curvature is achieved by additional mortar in the joints.

rough buck See **subframe, 1**.

rough carriage A **carriage, 1** which is unplaned, usually concealed from view.

roughcast Same as **rock dash**.

roughcast glass See **rough plate glass**.

rough coat A **scratch coat** of plaster.

rough-cut joint, flat joint, flush joint, hick joint The simplest joint in masonry; made by holding the edge of the trowel flat against the brick and cutting in any direction, so that the mortar in the joints is made smooth with the wall surface. Because this cutting action produces a small hairline crack, the joint is not always watertight.

rough-cut joint

roughened finish tile Tile whose plane die surfaces are entirely broken by mechanical means, such as wire cutting or wire brushing, to provide for a more effective bond for mortar, plaster, or stucco.

rough floor A layer of boards or plywood, nailed to the floor joists, which serves as a base or subfloor for the **finish floor**.

rough flooring Material used for the rough floor, either sheets of plywood or rough boards (often unplaned).

rough grading Cutting and filling of earth preliminary to the final work.

rough grind The initial smoothing operation in which coarse abrasives are used to cut the projecting chips in hardened terrazzo down to a level surface.

rough ground **1.** A piece of linear blocking used to fix the approximate position of a desired planar surface. **2.** See **ground, 1**.

rough hardware In building construction, hardware meant to be concealed, such as bolts, nails, screws, spikes, and other metal fittings.

roughing-in **1.** The first coat of plaster in three-coat plasterwork. **2.** The rough work in any phase of construction. **3.** Installing the concealed portion of a plumbing system to the point of connection for the fixtures.

roughing-out In carpentry, a preliminary shaping operation.

rough lumber Sawn lumber that has not been planed; also called undressed lumber.

rough opening An opening in a wall, or the framework of a building, into which a doorframe or window frame, subframe, or **rough buck** is fitted.

rough plate glass, roughcast glass Translucent, rolled sheet glass, one face of which has a slightly rimpled texture.

rough rendering The application of a coat of a plaster without smoothing the surface, which is left rough.

rough rubble A well-bonded **rubble wall**.

rough service lamp An incandescent lamp designed to resist failure due to impact; uses extra filament supports which result in lowered efficiency.

rough sill **1.** In frame construction, the **sill, 1** on which the building frame is erected. **2.** The wood piece laid across the bottom of a rough opening to act as a base for a window construction.

rough string, rough stringer **1.** A notched, generally unplaned, inclined board which supports the steps of a wooden stairway, usually concealed from view. **2.** A **carriage, 1**.

rough work The rough framework of a building, including framing, boxing, and sheeting.

round **1.** A wood plane for cutting grooves. **2.** See **round molding**. **3.** A cylindrical metal rod.

round arch A **semicircular arch**.

Round Arch style An architectural style used infrequently in the mid-19th century; characterized by arcaded round arches, primarily in masonry buildings; also see **Rundbogenstil**.

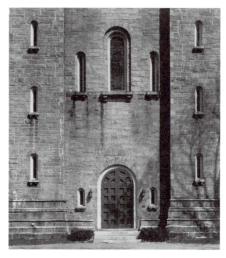

Round Arch style

round barn A barn having a circular plan; see **circular barn**.

round billet molding Same as **roll billet molding**.

round church One whose plan is a circle; by extension, a church designed around a central vertical axis such as those of polygonal or Greek-cross form, though these are more accurately described as churches of the central type.

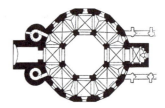

round church, plan

round dormer A **dormer** having a circular window in its face.

rounded forend See **rounded front**.

rounded front, *Brit.* **rounded forend**   A **lock front** which is shaped to conform to the rounded edge of a **double-acting door** (swinging door).

rounded step   See **round step**.

rounded tile   **1.** Same as **Mission tile**. **2.** One of the **tiles** in a course of tiles whose lower edges are semicircular; has the appearance of a series of **scallops**; see **imbrication**.

roundel   **1.** A small circular panel or window; an **oculus**. **2.** In glazing, a bull's-eye or circular light like the bottom of a bottle. **3.** A small **bead molding** or **astragal**. **4.** In stage lighting, a glass or gelatin color filter used in a **borderlight**.

round-headed   Same as **round-topped**.

roundhouse   A house that is round in plan, with no exterior corners.

round knot   A knot sawn across so that it is approximately circular.

round molding, round   A fairly large molding, the section of which is circular (or nearly circular) and convex.

round notch   A synonym for **saddle notch**.

round pediment   A rounded **pediment, 2** used ornamentally over a door or window.

round pediment

round ridge   The ridge of a roof, finished with a rounded surface.

round roof   Same as **rainbow roof**.

round step, rounded step, round-end step   A step having a bullnose.

round timber   Felled trees which have not been converted to lumber.

round-topped   A term **descriptive** of a window, door, or arch having a semicircle at its head.

round-topped roll   In sheet-metal roofing, a joint which is formed over a **roll, 1, 2**.

round tower   In early Christian architecture, esp. in Ireland, a conically capped circular tower of stone construction; used for defense.

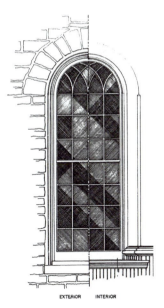

EXTERIOR   INTERIOR

round-topped window   with curved muntins

rout   To groove, furrow, hollow out, or otherwise machine a wood member with a **router**.

router   **1.** A **router plane**. **2.** A machine tool having a rapidly revolving vertical spindle and cutter; used for routing, cutting mortises, etc. **3.** A chisel having a curved point; used for cleaning out grooves, mortises, etc.

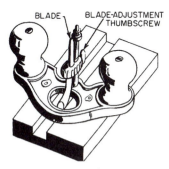

BLADE   BLADE-ADJUSTMENT THUMBSCREW

router plane

router gauge   A tool similar to a **marking gauge**, but having a narrow chisel as a cutter instead of a marking point; esp. used in inlaid work, cutting out the narrow channels in which metal or colored woods are laid.

router patch   A piece of plywood or veneer

having parallel sides and rounded ends; used to repair a defect in a surface.

router plane, plough, plow   A plane used for cutting and smoothing grooves which have their bottoms parallel to the surface; has a handle at each end and a centrally located cutting tool.

rover   Any member, as a molding, that follows the line of a curve.

row house, row dwelling   **1.** One of an unbroken line of houses sharing one or more sidewalls with its neighbors. A **group house**. **2.** One of a number of similarly constructed houses in a row; usually in a housing development.

rowlock, rolok, rollock   **1.** A brick laid on its edge so that its end is visible. **2.** One ring of a **rowlock arch**.

rowlock

rowlock arch   An arch wherein the bricks or small voussoirs are arranged in separate concentric rings.

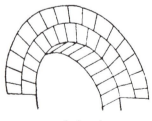

rowlock arch

rowlock bond   Same as **rat-trap bond**.

rowlock cavity wall, all-rowlock wall, rolock wall, rolok wall, rowlock-back

wall, rowlock wall   A brick **cavity wall** built with all bricks laid on edge.

rowlock cavity wall

row spacing   In timber construction, the distance between rows of bolts or similar fastenings measured from center to center of the rows.

royal   A cedar shingle, about 24 in. (61 cm) long and ½ in. (1.25 cm) thick at the butt.

Royal Institute of British Architects (RIBA)   Founded in 1835, the RIBA has been the authoritative organization for the profession of architecture in Britain; it qualifies candidates for admission to the Institute, recognizes a number of schools of architecture, and awards prizes for outstanding work. Address: 66 Portland Place, London, W1N 4AD

rpm   Abbr. for "revolutions per minute."

RSJ   Abbr. for "rolled steel joist."

RT   Abbr. for "raintight."

rubbed brick   A brick having a **rubbed finish, 2**.

rubbed finish   **1.** A stone finish between **smooth machine finish** and **honed finish**, obtained by mechanical rubbing. **2.** A finish obtained by using an abrasive to remove surface irregularities from concrete or brick. **3.** On a varnished or shellacked wood surface, a dull finish, usually produced by rubbing with a pad which is saturated with pumice and water or oil.

rubbed joint   An edge joint formed by coating the contacting surfaces with glue and rubbing them together until glue no longer is expelled; subsequent clamping need not be applied.

rubbed work   Work in brick, concrete, wood, or stone having a **rubbed finish**.

rubber   **1.** A highly resilient material, capable of recovering from large deformations quickly;

manufactured from the juice of rubber trees as well as of other trees and plants. **2.** Any of various synthetically produced materials having similar properties; an **elastomer**. **3.** A **cutter**.

rubber-emulsion paint See **latex paint**.

rubber set See **false set**.

rubber silencer, bumper A resilient part, such as a rubber button, attached to the stop on a doorframe to reduce noise caused by slamming of the door.

rubber tape A tape of rubber or a rubber-like compound; used to provide electrical insulation at joints.

rubber tile A hard-wearing flooring material; composed principally of natural or synthetic rubber with a filler of clay and fibrous talc or asbestos; usually set in mastic over a wood or concrete subfloor.

rubber-tired roller A self-propelled or towed vehicle which rolls on a parallel series of pneumatic tires set on one or two axles; used to compact soil.

rubbing See **flatting down**.

rubbing block In marble polishing, a block of sandstone with which the preliminary operation of smoothing is done by hand.

rubbing brick Same as **rub brick**.

rubbing down An intermediate step in finishing a painted surface; rubbing with a mild abrasive before applying the topcoat.

rubbing stone A stone for polishing or erasing the toolmarks on a stone, or on bricks for gauged work after they have been rough-shaped.

rubbing varnish See **polishing varnish**.

rubbish A mixture of combustible waste such as paper, cardboard cartons, wood scrap, and combustible floor sweepings; contains up to 20% by weight of restaurant or cafeteria waste but contains little or no treated papers, plastic, or rubber wastes. Also see **garbage, refuse**, and **trash**.

rubble Rough stones of irregular shapes and sizes; used in rough, uncoursed work in the construction of walls, foundations, and paving.

rubble arch See **rustic arch**.

rubble ashlar wall A **rubble wall** which has an ashlar facing.

rubble concrete **1.** Concrete similar to **cyclopean concrete** except that small stones (such as

rubblework

one man can handle) are used. **2.** Concrete made with rubble from demolished structures.

rubble drain See **French drain**.

rubble masonry Same as **rubblework**.

rubble stone masonry Stone masonry composed of irregularly shaped units bonded by mortar.

rubble wall A wall, either coursed or uncoursed, of rubble.

rubblework Stone masonry built of **rubble**.

rub brick A silicon carbide brick used to smooth and remove irregularities from hardened concrete surfaces.

rudenture Same as **cabling, 2**.

ruderation The process of paving with pebbles or small stones and mortar.

rule An instrument having straight edges, usually marked off in inches or centimeters and fractions thereof; used for measuring distance and for drawing straight lines.

common types of **rules**

ruled joint   Same as **scribed joint, 2.**

rule joint   A pivoted joint in which two flat strips can be turned edgewise toward or from each other, but in no other direction.

ruling pen   A pen used to draw lines of even thickness; commonly consists of two blades which hold ink between them, the distance between the points being adjusted by a screw.

Rumford fireplace   An efficient fireplace invented by Benjamin Thompson (1753–1814), originally of Massachusetts, who later achieved distinction as Count Rumford. His innovative fireplace design increased the efficiency of radiated heat and lessened the emitted smoke, benefits that were achieved by significantly reducing the size of the massive colonial fireplace opening and by introducing a constriction in the chimney directly above the hearth so as to increase the draft through the chimney.

run   **1.** In roofing, the horizontal distance from the face of a wall to the ridge of the roof. **2.** In stairways, the width of a single stair tread. **3.** The horizontal distance covered by a flight of steps. **4.** The runway or track for a sash. **5.** A small stream of paint flowing vertically on a painted object; usually occurs with enamels if an excessively thick coat is applied; also called **tear. 6.** That section of pipe or fitting continuing in a straight line in the direction of flow in the pipe to which it is connected.

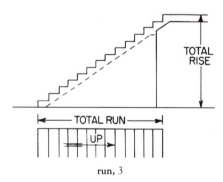

run, 3

Rundbogenstil   A German architectural style of the mid-19th century; especially characterized by round arches, often with Romanesque or Italianate features; the prototype of the **Round Arch style.**

rung   A bar, usually round in cross section, forming the step of a ladder.

runic cross   See **Celtic cross.**

Runic knot   An interlaced or twisted ornament common in Anglo-Saxon architecture.

run line   A thin line of paint, applied by a lining tool run along a straightedge.

run molding   A molding of plaster, and occasionally of cement or other such material, formed by passing a metal or wood template over the material while wet.

runner   **1.** A metal supporting member which is attached to structural steel members or concrete; used to support partitions, acoustical ceiling tile, etc. Also see **main runner. 2.** Same as **ledger, 1.**

running   **1.** Linked in a smooth progression, inclining to the right or the left, within a band; applied to various ornamental motifs. **2.** Forming a cornice in place with a **running mold.**

running bond   Same as **stretcher bond.**

running dog   See **Vitruvian scroll.**

running ground   Earth in a plastic or semi-plastic state, sand, etc., which will not stand without sheeting.

running mold, horse mold   A template shaped to the configuration of a cornice and mounted on a wooden frame; used by plasterers to run a molding; travels sideways along the ceiling line to build up a desired shape as plaster is applied.

running off   Applying the final coat of plaster to a molding.

running ornament, running mold   Any molding ornament in which the design is continuous, in intertwined or flowing lines as in foliage, meanders, etc.

running ornament

running screed   A narrow strip of plaster used in place of a running rule to guide the running of a cornice or molding.

running shoe   A piece of metal on a **running mold** to prevent wear and allow it to slide freely on the running rule and nib guide.

running trap   A depressed U-shaped section of pipe in a drain; allows the free passage of fluid, but always remains full, whatever the state of the pipe, so that it forms a seal against the passage of gases.

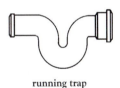

running trap

run-of-bank gravel   See **bank-run gravel**.

run of rafter   Same as **run, 1**.

run-to-breakdown maintenance   The replacement of machinery parts only after a machinery breakdown has occurred. Contrast with **on-condition maintenance**.

runway   1. In the theatre, a narrow projection of the stage, over the orchestra pit and sometimes into the aisles of an auditorium, permitting the actors to perform in close proximity to the audience. 2. A path taken by buggies of concrete on decking over an area of concrete placement.

rupture disk   A safety device, used in a system under pressure, consisting of a frangible disk which ruptures when a predetermined pressure is exceeded.

rupture member   Any safety device which will rupture automatically at a predetermined pressure.

rupture modulus   See **modulus of rupture**.

rupture strength   See **modulus of rupture**.

Ruskinian Gothic   See **High Victorian Gothic**.

Russo-Byzantine architecture   The first phase of Russian architecture (11th to 16th century) derived from the Byzantine architecture of Greece; mainly stone churches characterized by cruciform plans and multiple bulbous domes.

rust   A substance, usually in powder form, of light brownish red color, accumulating on the face of steel or iron as a result of oxidation; ultimately weakens or destroys the steel or iron on which it is allowed to form.

rustic   1. Descriptive of rough, hand-dressed building stone, intentionally laid with high relief; used in modest structures of rural character. 2. A grade of building limestone, characterized by coarse texture.

rustic arch, rubble arch   An arch laid up with rough or irregular stones, the spaces between them being filled with mortar.

rusticated   Said of cut stone having strongly emphasized recessed joints and smooth or roughly textured block faces; used to create an appearance of impregnability in banks, palaces, courthouses, etc. The border of each block may be rebated, chamfered, or beveled on all four sides, at top and bottom only, or on two adjacent sides; the face of the brick may be flat, pitched, or diamond-point, and if smooth may be hand- or machine-tooled.

rusticated column   See **banded column**.

rusticating   Applying a coarse texture on the face of clay bricks or stone.

rustication   Same as **rustic work**.

rustication strip   A strip of wood, or the like, which is fixed to the surface of a concrete form to produce a groove or rustication in the concrete.

rustic brick   Brick that has been covered with sand on the surfaces to be exposed before being fired; so treated to provide a decorative effect.

rustic finish, washed finish   A type of terrazzo topping in which the matrix is recessed by washing prior to setting, so as to expose the chips without destroying the bond between chip and matrix; a retarder sometimes is applied to the surface to facilitate this operation.

rustic joint   In stone masonry, a deeply sunk mortar joint that has been emphasized by having the edges of the adjacent stones chamfered or recessed below the surface of the stone facing.

Rustic order   Same as **Tuscan order**.

rustic quoin   A quoin treated with sunken joints, the face of the quoins being generally roughened and raised above the general surface of the masonry.

rustic siding   See **drop siding**.

rustic slate   One of a number of slate shingles of varying thickness, yielding an irregular surface when installed.

rustic stone   Any rough, broken stone suitable for rustic masonry, most commonly limestone or sandstone; usually set with the elongate dimension exposed horizontally.

Rustic style   A vague term denoting an **architectural mode** rather than an **architectural style**, often applied to hunting lodges or log cabins in forested areas of the northeastern United States.

rustic woodwork

Characteristics include: wall construction of logs (often peeled), saddle-notch corner joints, and rough-cut lumber; a fieldstone chimney; a moderately to steeply pitched roof covered by hand-split wood shingles, a roof overhang with exposed rafters; one or more balconies or porches with flat balusters having decorative cutouts or stickwork. Occasionally called Adirondack Rustic style or Teddy Roosevelt Rustic style.

rustic woodwork Decorative or structural work constructed of unpeeled logs or poles.

rustic work **1.** Decorative or structural work constructed of logs from which the bark has not been peeled. **2.** Roughly faced stonework; the separate blocks are marked by deep **chamfers**.

rust-inhibiting paint An **anticorrosive paint**.

rust joint A watertight connection between two sections of iron pipe made by filling the hub with any compound, such as iron cement, that induces rusting; the compound also may be used to cure a leaky joint.

rust pocket A **cleanout** at the base of a pipe which permits removal of accumulated rust debris.

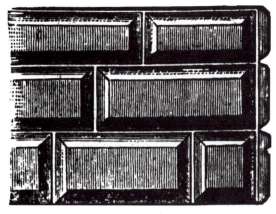

rustic work

rutile A common mineral, red-to-brown or black in color; contains 60% titanium; used in paints, as a coating on welding rods to stabilize the arc, and as an opacifier in ceramic glaze and in glass.

R-value A measure of the thermal resistance of a material or component.

R/W **1.** On drawings, abbr. for **right-of-way**. **2.** Abbr. for "random widths."

R/W&L Abbr. for "random widths and lengths."

S

s Symbol for "second."

S **1.** On drawings, abbr. for "side." **2.** On drawings, abbr. for "south." **3.** Abbr. for "seamless."

S&E In the lumber industry, abbr. for "surfaced one side and edge."

S&G Abbr. for "studs and girts."

S&M Abbr. for "surfaced and matched."

S1E In the lumber industry, abbr. for "surfaced one edge."

S1S Abbr. for "surfaced one side."

S1S1E Abbr. for "surfaced one side and one edge."

S1S2E Abbr. for "surfaced one side and two edges."

S2E Abbr. for "surfaced two edges."

S2S Abbr. for "surfaced two sides."

S2S&CM Abbr. for "surfaced two sides and center matched."

S2S&SL Abbr. for "surfaced two sides and shiplapped."

S2S1E Abbr. for "surfaced two sides and one edge."

S4S Abbr. for "surfaced four sides."

S4S&CS Abbr. for "surfaced four sides and caulking seam."

S/A Abbr. for "shipped assembled."

Sabbath house, Sabbath-day house In colonial New England, a small house having but a single room with a fireplace at one end, usually located near a house of worship; used on Sundays by a family as a place in which to warm and feed themselves during breaks in the all-day religious services, because such services typically were conducted in unheated **meeting houses**. Occasionally several families shared a two-room house with a centrally located fireplace; others had a small two-story house for this purpose, with the ground floor used as a stable. Also see **Sunday house**.

saber saw A power-driven saw with an oscillating blade which extends through the base of the saw; has an action similar to that of a jigsaw.

sabin A unit of sound absorption equivalent to 1 sq ft of perfectly absorptive surface. Also see **metric sabin**.

sable, sable pencil A fine paintbrush made of hair of the tail of the sable.

sable writer A long **sable**, esp. one used in lettering signs.

sacellum A small Roman sanctuary, usually an unroofed enclosure with a small altar. Sometimes, a roofed funerary chapel.

sack See **bag**.

sack finish See **sack rub**.

sack rub, sack finish A finish for formed concrete surfaces; designed to produce even texture and fill all pits and air holes; after the surface is dampened, mortar is rubbed over it; then, before it dries, a mixture of dry cement and sand is rubbed over it with a wad of burlap or a sponge-rubber float to remove surplus mortar and fill voids.

sacrarium Any consecrated place, in Roman or medieval architecture; a shrine, a chapel, or a sacristy for keeping liturgical objects.

sacrarium: Pompeii

sacrificial anode A metal plate used in **cathodic protection** (i.e., the protection from corrosion) of piping or other equipment to which it is electrically connected. This metal

sacrificial protection

plate must be more corrodible than the piping to which it is attached.

sacrificial protection The use of a metallic coating, such as a zinc-rich paint, to protect steel. In the presence of an electrolyte, such as salt water, a galvanic cell is set up and the metallic coating corrodes instead of the steel.

sacrificial timber A timber which is purposely oversized to enhance its fire resistance.

sacristy A room in a church, near the chancel, where the robes and altar vessels are stored, where the clergy vest themselves for services, and where some business of the church may be done; usually a single room, but sometimes a very large one.

sacristy

saddle **1.** Same as **threshold**. **2.** A **cricket**. **3.** Any hollow-backed structure suggesting a sad-

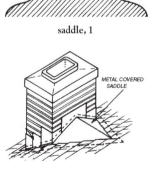

saddle, 1

saddle, 2

dle, as a ridge connected to two higher elevations or a **saddle roof**. **4.** A floor mount for a heavy pipe.

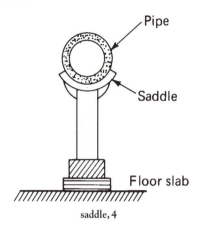

saddle, 4

saddleback **1.** A **saddle joint**. **2.** A coping stone having its top surface sloped with its high point along the center ridge, so that rainwater spills on either side; also called **saddle-backed coping**.

saddleback, 2

saddleback board Same as **threshold**.

saddle-backed coping See **saddleback, 2**.

saddleback joint Same as **saddle joint, 1**.

saddleback roof Same as **saddle roof**.

saddlebag cabin Two one-room log cabins that are connected and share a shingled roof having a single pitch on each side of a central ridge. The two cabins have separate entrances and usually there is no interior door between them; there is often a full-width porch across the entire façade. In the Northern United States, a central chimney is common, so the cabins are usually joined back-to-back, sharing the same chimney stack; in contrast, in the South, there is a chimney at the end of each cabin. Compare with **center-hall cabin**.

saddle bar One of the horizontal iron bars across a window opening which secure the **leaded lights**.

saddle bead A type of glazing bead used to secure two panes of glass.

saddle bend A saddle-shaped bend in a conduit, where it crosses another conduit, in order to clear it.

saddle board A board at the ridge of a pitched roof which covers the joint at the ridge. Also see **comb board, ridgeboard**.

saddle coping A **saddle-backed coping**; see **saddleback, 2**.

saddle fitting A fitting for making a connection to a pipe which is already installed; clamped to the outside of the pipe and sealed with a gasket.

saddle flange A curved flange, usually welded or riveted to a tank, boiler, or the like; shaped to fit the curved surface and receive a threaded pipe.

saddle flashing Flashing over a **cricket**.

saddle joint 1. A stepped joint in a projecting masonry course or in a coping; used to prevent the penetration of water. 2. A vertical joint in sheet-metal roofing; formed by bending up the end of one sheet and folding it downward over the turned-up edge of the adjacent sheet.

saddle joint

saddle notch At a corner in **log cabin** construction, a rounded notch cut near one end in the lower surface of a horizontal log; forms an interlocking joint when mated with a similarly notched log set at a right angle to it. Occasionally, this term is also used for a **double-saddle notch**, which is cut in *both* sides of a round log; in such instances, the logs at right angles are unnotched.

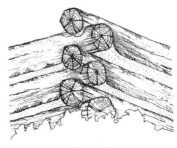

saddle notches

saddle piece In sheet-metal roofing, a metal **cricket**.

saddle roof A roof having a concave-shaped ridge with gables at each end of the roof, this configuration being suggestive of a saddle.

saddle scaffold A scaffold erected over the ridge of a roof; esp. used for repairing chimneys.

saddle stone 1. An **apex stone**. 2. Obsolete term for a stone containing saddle-shaped depressions.

saddle tenon See **bridlejoint, 2**.

saddle tie 1. For wire hangers, the attachment of wire hangers to main runners. 2. For furring, the attachment of furring members to framing members of wall or ceiling assemblies by the use of a single or double strand of wire.

sadl Abbr. for **saddle**.

SAE Abbr. for "Society of Automotive Engineers."

SAF On drawings, abbr. for "safety."

safe 1. A tray with a waste pipe; placed below a fixture to catch overflow, below a pipe to catch leakage, etc. 2. A built-in or portable steel-enclosed repository, designed to protect stored materials against fire and/or burglary.

safe area An exterior or interior space that serves as a means of egress from a building by providing a transitional area from, or a normal means of entry to, an assembly space.

safe leg load That load which can be imposed safely on the frame leg of a scaffold.

safe load A load on a structure which does not produce stresses in excess of allowable stresses.

safety See **elevator car safety**.

safety arch A **discharging arch**.

safety belt A device, usually worn around the waist, which is attached to a structure or lifeline to prevent a worker from falling.

safety cage A lightweight rig, usually used with a power-operated winch, sometimes used in place of a scaffold for relatively minor jobs.

safety chain A chain attached to a piece of equipment to prevent its falling should the equipment fastener fail.

safety curtain See **asbestos curtain**.

safety factor See **factor of safety**.

safety fuse A flexible cord containing an internal burning medium by which fire is conveyed at

safety glass

a continuous and uniform rate for the purpose of firing blasting caps.

safety glass **1. Wire glass**. **2. Tempered glass**. **3. Laminated glass**.

safety lighting See **emergency lighting**.

safety lintel An auxiliary lintel, usually of wood, placed behind a stone lintel in the aperture of a door or window.

safety nosing For a stair, **nosing** having an abrasive nonslip surface flush with the tread surface.

safety shutoff device In a gas burner, a device that will stop the gas supply if the gas flame is extinguished.

safety switch A switch used in interior electric wiring which is mounted inside a metal box and operated from outside the housing by means of a handle connected to the switch mechanism.

safety switch

safety tread A tread on a stair, esp. to prevent the foot from slipping; usually has a roughened surface or strips which are roughened.

safety valve See **pressure-relief valve**.

safe waste The waste pipe from a **safe**.

safe working pressure The maximum working pressure for a given vessel, boiler, flask, or cylinder, allowable under the American Society of Mechanical Engineers Boiler Code; usually stamped on the unit.

safflower oil A drying oil obtained from safflower seeds; used in paints; has properties similar to linseed oil.

safing A barrier which is placed in an air duct around a component (such as a filter) to ensure

that air flows through the component rather than around it.

sagging **1.** A defect characterized by a wavy line or lines appearing on those surfaces of porcelain enamel that have been fired in a vertical position. **2.** A defect characterized by irreversible downward bending in a ceramic article insufficiently supported during the firing cycle. **3.** The excessive flow of a wet paint film on vertical surfaces resulting in drips, runs, or curtains in the film when it dries. **4.** The flowing of a sealant within a joint, so that it loses its original shape. **5.** See **curtaining, 3**.

sagitta The **keystone** of an arch.

sahn Central court of a mosque.

sailing course An **oversailing course**.

sailor A brick that is laid on end (i.e., positioned vertically), with its wider face showing on the wall surface; compare with **soldier**.

sail-over Any projection or jutting beyond the general wall surface.

Saint Andrew's cross bond See **English cross bond**.

Saint Augustine house In Saint Augustine, Florida, after it was settled by the Spanish in 1565, a two-story house with very thick walls constructed of blocks of **tabby** or **coquina,** usually roofed with hand-split cypress shingles; one room on the ground floor facing the street, with windows protected by gratings (**rejas**) and solid-wood interior shutters; two rooms on the upper floor, accessible by way of an exterior stairway; usually one or two balconies. Also see **palma house** and **tabla**.

sala In Spanish architecture and its derivatives, a reception room, main hall, or living room in a house; usually has windows facing the street that are protected by grilles or wood gratings (**rejas**), and also by heavy interior shutters.

salamander A portable stove used in cold weather to heat the air around freshly placed concrete in order to sustain proper curing conditions.

sal ammoniac, ammonium chloride A material used in a soldering flux and as an ingredient in iron cement.

sales square In the U.S.A., the quantity of prepared roofing required to cover 100 square feet (9.3 m²) of deck.

saliens An artificial fountain in which water shoots up through a constricted tube, under its own pressure.

salient Describing any projecting part or member, as a salient corner.

salient corner A corner which projects outward; the opposite of a reentrant corner.

sally A projection, as the end of a rafter beyond the notch which has been cut to fit over a horizontal beam.

sally port An underground passage or concealed gate which serves to link the central and outer works of a fortress.

salmon brick A poor quality brick that lacks weather resistance; so named because of its pink color; commonly used to fill spaces between interior structural timbers in a **timber-framed house** in order to provide increased structural rigidity and improved thermal insulation.

salomónica A twisted or spiral column.

salon **1.** A room used primarily for exhibition of art objects. **2.** A drawing room. **3.** A small, stylish place of business.

saloon **1.** A place where intoxicating liquors are sold and consumed; often the social center in many early towns of the Western United States. **2.** A variant form of **salon**.

saltbox house In colonial New England, a timber-framed house, commonly two and one-half stories high, having a **hall-and-parlor plan**; gables at each end wall; a sloping roof with slope on the rear side of the ridge much longer and less steep than the slope on the front side. This roof contour gave the house a shape resembling a box for holding salt used at that time in the British colonies.

saltbox house

saltbox roof Any roof having a configuration similar to that of a **saltbox house**. In the South, often called a *catslide*.

saltbox roof

salt-glazed brick, brown-glazed brick Brick having a glossy finish, obtained by thermochemical reaction between silicates of clay and vapors of salt or other chemicals, produced in a kiln.

salt-glazed tile Facing tile whose surface faces have a lustrous glazed finish, obtained from the reaction of the silicates of the clay body with vapors of salt or other chemicals produced in a kiln.

salutatorium In medieval churches, a porch or a portion of the sacristy where the clergy and the people could meet and confer.

samel brick Same as **salmon brick**.

sample A small specimen of material, or a single unit of many such items to be furnished, which is in conformity with the requirements for the specifications; furnished for review and approval; establishes standards by which work will be judged.

SAN On drawings, abbr. for "sanitary."

sanctuary **1.** In a church, the immediate area around the principal altar; the chancel. **2.** The sacred shrine of a divinity.

sanctum sanctorum **1.** The innermost or holiest place of a tabernacle or temple, the "holy of holies." **2.** Any especially private place or retreat which may not be entered except by special permission.

sanctus bell A bell hung in an exterior turret or a bell cot over or near the chancel arch, which was rung to fix the attention of those not in the church to the service of the mass.

sanctus bell

sand **1.** Granular material which passes through a 9.51-μm (⅜-in.) sieve, almost entirely passes through a 4.76-mm (No. 4) sieve, and is predominantly retained on a 74-μm (No. 200) sieve; results from natural disintegration and abrasion of rock or processing of completely friable sandstone. **2.** That portion of an aggregate passing through a 4.76-mm (No. 4) sieve and predominantly retained on a 74-μm (No. 200) sieve. Also see **sieve number**.

sandal brick Same as **salmon brick**.

sand asphalt **1.** A hot-laid mixture of local sand and asphalt cement, prepared without special control of aggregate grading. **2.** A mixture of local sand, with or without a mineral filler, and a liquid asphaltic material.

sandbag In the backstage of a theatre, a canvas bag filled with sand which is used to counterbalance hanging scenery or other equipment.

sandblast To use sand, propelled by an air blast, on metal, masonry, concrete, etc., to remove dirt, rust, or paint, or to decorate the surface with a rough texture.

sand boil The ejection of sand and water resulting from **piping**.

sand box See **sand jack**.

sand clay A mixture of sand and clay in which the two materials have been blended so their opposite qualities tend to maintain a condition of stability with various moisture contents.

sand-coarse aggregate ratio The ratio of fine to coarse aggregate in a batch of concrete, by either weight or volume.

sand-dry Descriptive of a stage in drying of a paint film at which sand will not adhere to the surface.

sanded bitumen felt See **asphalt prepared roofing**.

sanded fluxed-pitch felt A felt that is saturated with a fluxed coal tar, coated with the same material, and then sanded on both sides to prevent sticking in the roll.

sanded grout Grout which incorporates fine aggregate or sand into the mixture.

sanded plaster Gypsum plaster with sand aggregate.

sand equivalent A measure of the amount of clay contamination in fine aggregate.

sander **1.** A **power sander**. **2.** A **sanding machine**.

sand-faced brick A **brick** whose faces have been sprinkled with sand before placing it in a kiln at an elevated temperature.

sand filter A bed of fine sand which is laid over graded gravel; used to remove impurities from a water supply.

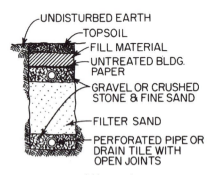

sand filter: plan

sand filter trenches A system of trenches, consisting of perforated pipe or drain tile surrounded by clean, coarse aggregate containing an intermediate layer of sand as filtering material and provided with an underdrain for carrying off the filtered sewage.

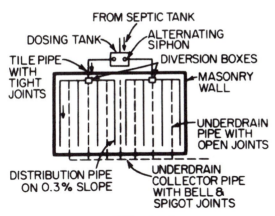

sand filter trench

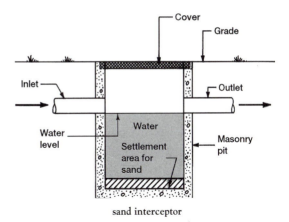

sand interceptor

sand finish **1.** A textured-finish plaster surface; the plaster contains sand, lime putty, and gauging or Keene's cement. **2.** A finish obtained by rubbing the coat to a smooth finish.

sand-float finish In plastering, a rough sand finish obtained by using a wooden **float**.

sand grout, sanded grout Any portland cement grout into which a fine aggregate is incorporated.

sanding, flatting down, rubbing Smoothing a surface with abrasive paper or cloth, either by hand or by machine.

sanding block A device which holds a piece of sandpaper for sanding by hand.

sanding machine A stationary, electrically powered machine having a moving abrasive surface (usually sandpaper); used for smoothing surfaces; the abrasive surface usually is a belt, disk, or spindle. Also see **power sander**.

sanding sealer A priming coat which seals or fills, without hiding, the grain of wood; a hard film, usually sanded before the application of subsequent coats.

sanding skip See **skip**.

sand interceptor, sand trap A small catch basin designed and constructed to prevent the passage of sand (and other solids) into a drainage system; requires periodic cleaning.

sand jack A box having tight joints which is filled with dry, clean sand on which rests a tight-fitting plunger; the plunger supports the bottom of posts used in **centering**; when it is desired to lower the centering, a plug in the bottom of the box is removed, allowing the sand to run out.

sand-lime brick Brick made with sand and slaked lime rather than with clay; usually a light gray or off-white color.

sandpaper A tough paper which is coated with an abrasive material such as silica, garnet, silicon carbide, or aluminum oxide; used for smoothing and polishing; graded by a grit numbering system according to which the highest grit numbers (360 to 600) are used for fine polishing, and the lowest grit numbers (16 to 40) are used for coarse smoothing. Alternatively, sandpaper may be designated by the "0 grade" system, according to which "very fine" includes grades from 10/0 to 6/0, "fine" from 5/0 to 3/0, "medium" 2/0, 1/0, ½; "coarse" 1, 1½, and 2; "very coarse" 2½, 3, 3½, and 4.

sandpile A filling of compacted sand which has been rammed into a hole left by a pile that has been driven into the ground and then withdrawn.

sand plate A flat steel plate which is welded to the bottom of legs of bar-supports.

sand pocket A small region in mortar or concrete which contains fine aggregate, but little or no cement.

sand-rubbed finish In stonework, a type of surface formerly obtained by rubbing with a sand-and-water mixture under a block; now such a finish is obtained with a rotary or belt sander.

sand-sawn finish In stonecutting, a fairly smooth surface resulting from using sand as the abrasive agent carried by the gang saw blades.

sandstone Sedimentary rock composed of sand-sized grains, naturally cemented by mineral materials. In most sandstone used for building,

795

quartz grains predominate; often used for decorative elements in buildings because it is easy to carve.

sand streak A streak in the surface of formed concrete; caused by **bleeding, 4**.

sand-struck brick See **soft-mud brick**.

sand trap See **sand interceptor**.

sandwich beam See **flitch beam**.

sandwich construction A composite construction consisting of relatively thin layers of a material (having high-strength properties) bonded to a thicker, weaker, light core material; results in high ratios of strength to weight and stiffness to weight.

sandwiched girder Same as **flitch beam**.

sandwich panel A panel of **sandwich construction**; made by bonding facing sheets, of high strength and density, to a relatively light core.

sanitary base, sanitary shoe A congé, usually associated with ceramic tile work.

sanitary bend A **pipe bend** having a radius of curvature large enough to provide good hydraulic-flow characteristics and prevent solids from accumulating at the bend.

sanitary building drain A building drain which conveys the discharge of plumbing fixtures.

sanitary building house sewer A **building sewer** that carries sewage only.

sanitary cove On a stair, a metal piece serving as a transition between the tread surface and the riser face; used to facilitate cleaning.

sanitary cross A type of **pipe cross** used as a fitting for a soil pipe; designed with a slight curve in each of the 90° transitions so as to channel flow from branch lines toward the direction of the main flow.

sanitary cross

sanitary drainage Water and waste material originating at plumbing fixtures, floor drains, etc.

sanitary drainage fixture unit See **fixture unit**.

sanitary engineering The application of engineering to the control of environmental conditions related to public health, such as water supply, sewage, and industrial waste.

sanitary landfill Garbage that is buried to a depth which is sufficient to control vermin, odors, etc.

sanitary sewage, domestic sewage The **sewage** containing human excrement or household wastes which originates in a **water closet**.

sanitary sewer A sewer which carries sewage (liquid or waterborne waste from plumbing fixtures) and to which storm and surface water, street runoff, and groundwater are not admitted intentionally.

sanitary shoe Same as **sanitary base**.

sanitary stop See **terminated stop**.

sanitary tee A **tee, 2** used as a fitting for a soil pipe; designed with a slight curve in the 90° transition so as to channel flow from a branch line toward the direction of the main flow.

sanitary tee

sanitary ware Porcelain enamel ware, such as bathtubs, sewer pipes, toilet bowls, washbasins, etc.

Santa Fe style An **architectural mode** that is a combination of Pueblo Revival and Spanish Colonial Revival architecture.

santorin A lightweight, gray, volcanic tuff; used as **pozzolan**.

sap **1.** The fluid which circulates in trees, plants, etc. **2.** Same as **sapwood**. **3.** See **quarry sap**.

sapele, sapele mahogany A light-to-dark red-brown wood of central and western Africa; hard, relatively dense, frequently with ribbon-stripe grain; often decoratively figured.

sap gum Wood of **gum, 1** from either young trees or the outer portion of logs.

sapling-frame construction Same as **bent-frame construction**.

saponification The conversion into soap which occurs when an alkali, such as the lime in cement, reacts with oils in paint; destroys the adhesion and strength of oil-based paint films.

sap stain **1.** Same as **blue stain, 1. 2.** A stain used in wood finishing to make sapwood the color of heartwood.

sapwood, alburnum The wood of a tree between the bark and heartwood; normally lighter in color than the heartwood; equal in strength to heartwood but usually not as decay-resistant.

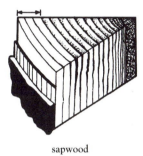

sapwood

Saracenic architecture Same as **Muslim architecture**.

sarasin A **portcullis**.

sarcophagus An elaborate coffin for an important personage, of terra-cotta, wood, stone, metal, or other material, decorated with painting, carving, etc., and large enough to contain only the body. If larger, it becomes a **tomb**.

sarcophagus of Roman Imperial time

sarking, sarking board A thin board for sheathing, as under tiles or slates in roofing.

sarking felt Same as **underlayment, 2**.

sarrasine A **portcullis**.

sash, window sash Any framework of a window; may be movable or fixed; may slide in a ver-

tical plane (as in a double-hung window) or may be pivoted (as in a casement window); a pivoted sash also is called a **ventilator, 2**. See **window sash**.

sash adjuster Same as **casement adjuster**.

sash and frame A **cased frame** and a **double-hung window**.

sash balance A spring-loaded device, usually a **spring balance** or **tape balance**; used to counterbalance a sash in a **double-hung window**; eliminates the need for sash weights, sash cords, and pulleys.

sash bar A secondary framing member to hold panes within a window, a window wall, or a glazed door; same as **muntin**.

sash block See **jamb block**.

sash casing Same as **sash pocket**.

sash center A support for a horizontally pivoted sash or transom; composed of two parts, a socket which is attached to the frame or jamb, and a pin on which the sash pivots.

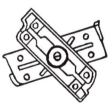

sash center

sash chain A metal chain used to connect a vertically hung sash with its counterweight; used in place of a sash cord.

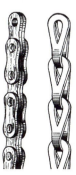

sash chains

sash chisel A chisel having a wide blade, sharpened on both sides; used for cutting the **mortises** in **pulley stiles**.

sash cord, sash line In a double-hung window, a rope connecting a sash with its counterweight, passing over the sash pulley.

sash-cord iron A small metal holder inserted in the edge of the sash of a double-hung window to which sash cord or sash chain is attached.

sash counterweight See **sash weight**.

sash door See **half-glass door**.

sash fast, sash fastener, sash holder A fastener, screw, or latch for holding two window sashes together to prevent their being opened; often attached to the meeting rails of a **double-hung window**.

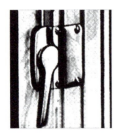

sash fast

sash fillister **1.** A rabbet cut in a **glazing bar** to receive the glass and glazing compound or putty. **2.** A special plane for cutting such rabbets.

sash hardware All window accessories, including sash chains or cords, sash fasteners, sash lifts, sash weights, etc.

sash holder See **sash fast**.

sash lift See **lift, 3; window lift**.

sash lifts

sash lift and hook, sash lift and lock A sash lift having a locking lever which holds the window fixed by means of a **strike** in the window frame; raising the sash releases the strike.

sash line A rope by which a sash is suspended in its frame; also called a **sash cord**.

sash lock **1.** A sash fast. **2.** A **sash fast** controlled by a key. **3.** An upright mortised lock.

sash plane A carpenter's plane for trimming the inside of a window frame or doorframe; has a special notched cutter.

sash plate In a horizontally pivoted sash or transom, one of a pair of plates providing the pivot mechanism.

sash pocket See **pocket, 2**.

sash-pole socket, sash socket A metal plate attached to a sash (or a transom) which is beyond hand reach; the sash can be raised or lowered by means of a pole having a hook at the far end, which is inserted in the socket.

sash pull A small metal plate sunk in a sash rail, or a handle attached to the rail, for raising or lowering the sash.

sash pulley, axle pulley In a double-hung window, a pulley mortised into the side of the frame near the top; the sash cord or sash chain passes over this pulley to the counterweight.

sash pulley

sash ribbon A metal tape used in place of a **sash cord**.

sash run See **pulley stile**.

sash saw A small saw, similar to but smaller than a **tenon saw**, used for cutting the tenons of sashes.

sash sill See **sill, 3**.

sash socket Same as **sash-pole socket**.

sash spring bolt See **window spring bolt**.

sash stop A small strip nailed or screwed around a cased frame to hold a sash (of a double-hung window) in place; also called a **window stop**.

sash stuff Wood which has been cut to stock sizes and shapes and prepared for making window frames.

sash tool A round brush used for painting frames, glazing bars, and other details of sash windows.

sash weight, sash counterweight A weight (usually of cast iron) used to balance a vertically sliding sash.

sash window Any window having a sliding (vertically or horizontally) or hung sash, but usually a **double-hung window**.

Sassanian architecture Architecture prevalent in Persia under the Sassanian dynasty (3rd to 7th cent. A.D.); excelled in large palace complexes with open *iwans* and the extensive use of barrel vaults and parabolic domes on squinches of brick or rubblestone, set in plaster mortar and constructed without centering. The massive walls were covered with stucco decor or articulated by pilasters and cornices.

Sassanian architecture gallery in palace at Serbistan

säteri roof In Swedish architecture of the 17th and 18th centuries, a type of hipped roof with vertical breaks which were often provided with windows.

satin finish See **scratch-brushed finish**.

satin sheen The subdued gloss of a paint film.

satinwood A hard, fine-grained, pale to golden yellow wood of the gum arabic (acacia gum) tree; esp. used in cabinetwork and decorative paneling.

satisfaction Cancellation of an encumbrance on real property, usually by payment of the debt secured by it.

satisfaction piece A document, prepared and executed in such manner as to be appropriate for recording in real estate records, evidencing the fact that an encumbrance has been discharged.

saturant In roofing, a bituminous material, having a low softening point, used for impregnating the felt in **asphalt prepared roofing**.

saturated air Air containing the maximum amount of water vapor possible at a given temperature; the partial pressure of the water vapor is equal to the vapor pressure of water at the same temperature.

saturated color See **saturation, 2**.

saturated felt, saturated roofing felt See **asphalt prepared roofing**.

saturated surface dry The condition of an aggregate particle or other porous solid when the permeable voids are filled with water but the exposed surfaces are dry.

saturated vapor pressure The pressure above a liquid at constant temperature which is confined so that the vapor from the liquid accumulates above it; the value depends on the temperature and the properties of the liquid.

saturation **1.** The condition under which air at a given temperature and pressure holds the maximum amount of water vapor without causing precipitation. **2.** The degree of purity of a color. A color is said to be saturated when it contains no white.

saturation coefficient See **C/B ratio**.

saturation line A line indicating the **groundwater level**.

saturation temperature The air temperature at which, for any given water vapor content, the air is saturated; any further temperature reduction results in condensation.

saucer dome A dome that is very shallow; its radius of curvature of the dome is very large compared with its rise.

sauna A steam bath, of Finnish origin, in which steam is produced by spraying water on very hot stones; in some modern units, heated surfaces other than stone are used.

sausage compactor Same as **extruded compactor**.

savino **1.** One of many saplings used in roof construction in **pueblo architecture**; such saplings are laid across the roof beams (**vigas**) to provide support for fiber matting, then covered by a thick layer of earth or dried mud that acts as a roof. **2.** Red cedar posts once used in Spanish Colonial homes.

savinos

saw   A cutting tool having a thin, flat metal blade, band, or stiff plate with cutting teeth along the edge; worked either by a reciprocating motion (as in a handsaw) or by a continuous motion (as in a band saw).

saw bench   A bench on which a **circular saw** is mounted.

sawbuck   See **sawhorse**.

sawdust concrete   A concrete made of a mixture of sawdust and concrete.

sawed finish, sawn face   The surface of any stone which has been sawn, e.g., sand-sawn, shot-sawn, etc.

sawed joint   In hardened concrete, a joint cut by means of special silicon-carbide or diamond blades; generally not to the full depth of the member.

sawhorse, sawbuck   A four-legged support, usually used in pairs, to hold wood while being sawed.

saw kerf   A **kerf, 2**, or slot, which is cut into wood by a saw.

sawmill   A facility where timber is sawn by mechanical equipment into boards and planks. Many early sawmills were operated by power generated by rivers, streams, or tidal changes. The development of the *gang saw*, which contained several parallel saw blades in a single frame greatly enhanced their efficiency; this innovation was followed by the invention of the circular saw. Virtually all saws are now operated by electric power.

sawn face   See **sawed finish**.

sawn-log house   Same as **board house**.

sawn veneer   A strong, high-quality veneer cut with a thin saw, rather than sliced or rotary-cut.

sawpit   A pit dug in the ground and usually lined with boards, over which a log to be sawn was laid during a hand-sawing operation; often located on the side of a hill, for accessibility.

saw set   An instrument used to set or angle the teeth of a saw blade so as to make a **kerf** wider than the thickness of the blade in order to reduce friction.

saw table   The table or platform of a powered saw, on which the material to be sawn is held or clamped during the sawing.

sawtooth molding   Same as **notched molding**.

sawtooth pattern   On a roof, a pattern of tiles or shingles resembling the teeth of a saw.

sawtooth roof   A roof system having a number of parallel roof surfaces of triangular section with a profile similar to the teeth in a saw; usually the steeper side is glazed and often faces north.

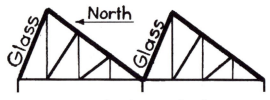

section through a **sawtooth roof**

sawtooth skylight   A **skylight** in the steeply inclined surface of a **sawtooth roof**.

sax, slate ax   A slate cutter's hammer; has a point at the back of the head for making nail holes in the slate.

Saxon architecture   See **Anglo-Saxon architecture**.

Saxon shake   A long shingle made of red cedar, usually of random width and butt thickness.

sb   Abbr. for **stilb**.

SBCC   Abbr. for "Southern Building Code Congress International," which publishes the Standard Building Code.

SB rubber   See **styrene-butadiene rubber**.

scab   A short flat piece of lumber which is bolted, nailed, or screwed to two butting pieces in order to splice them together.

scabbing hammer   See **scabbling hammer**.

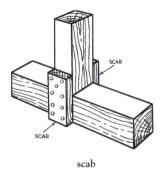

scab

scabble To dress stone with a pick, scabbling hammer, or broad chisel, leaving prominent toolmarks so that a rough planar surface results; usually preparatory to finer dressing.

scabbled rubble In masonry, **rubble** which has had only the roughest irregularities removed.

scabbling A chip or fragment of stone.

scabbling hammer, scabbing hammer A hammer with one end pointed for picking a stone; used for rough dressing.

scabellum In Roman architecture and derivates, a high, freestanding pedestal.

scaena A temporary building or booth for players behind the acting area in the ancient theatre; later the permanent back building of the theatre.

scaena ductilis In the ancient theatre, a movable screen which served as a background.

scaena frons The richly decorated front of the scaena, facing the audience.

scaffold 1. A temporary platform to support workers and materials on the face of a structure and to provide access to work areas above the ground. 2. Any elevated platform.

scaffold board One of the boards that form the work floor of a scaffold.

scaffold height The distance between successive stages of scaffolding used in masonry construction; usually about the height within which a bricklayer can work effectively.

scaffold-high Descriptive of masonry construction work sufficiently high to require a scaffold.

scaffold nail See **double-headed nail**.

scagliola Plaster work imitating stone, in which mixtures of marble dust, sizing, and various pig-

ments are laid in decorative figures; designs may be routed into a surface.

scale 1. The product resulting from the corrosion of metals. 2. A heavy oxide coating on copper and copper alloys resulting from exposure to high temperatures in an oxidizing atmosphere. 3. In drawing, a measuring instrument with graduated spaces. 4. A system of proportion by which definite magnitudes represent defined larger magnitudes, as on a map or drawing. 5. See **scaling**. 6. The outer covering of a **casing**. 7. See **architect's scale, engineer's scale**. 8. The crust on the inner surfaces of boilers, hot water heaters, and pipes formed by deposits of silica and other contaminants in water.

scaleboard Thin sheet of wood used for veneer.

scale drawing A drawing, usually considerably reduced in size from the actual or designed object, site, construction, or building, but which is drawn to **scale, 4**.

scale ornament Same as **imbrication**.

scaling Local flaking or **peeling** away of the surface portion of concrete or mortar.

scallop One of a continuous series of curves resembling segments of a circle, used as a decorative element on the outer edge of a strip of wood, molding etc.

scallops: a scalloped molding

scalloped capital The term applied to a medieval block (cushion) capital when each lunette is developed into several truncated cones. (*See illustration p. 802.*)

scalper A screen for removing oversize particles.

scalping The removal of particles larger than a specified size by screening.

scalp rock Rock which has passed over a grading screen and has been rejected; waste rock.

scamillus 1. In Classical and Neoclassical architecture, a plain block placed under the **plinth** of a column, thus forming a double plinth.

scalloped capital

2. A slight bevel at the outer edge of a block of stone, as occurs between the necking of a Doric capital and the upper drum of the shaft.

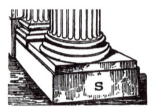

scamillus, 1

Scamozzi order   An order similar to the Ionic but having volutes of the capital which radiate at 45°.

scant   Said of lumber, panels, etc., somewhat short of a specified dimension; bare.

scantle, gauge stick, size stick   In roofing, a gauge by which slates are cut to proper length.

scantling   **1.** A piece of square-sawn timber 1⅞ in. (47.6 mm) to under 4 in. (101.6 mm) thick, and 2 in. (50.8 mm) to under 4½ in. (114.3 mm) wide. **2.** Hardwood timber cut to specified dimensions. **3.** Any square-edged piece of hardwood of nonstandard dimensions.

scape   Same as **apophyge**.

scapple   Same as **scabble**.

scapulary tablet   In **Zapotec architecture** of Mesoamerica, a rectangular framed panel cantilevered over an outward-sloping apron.

scapus   The shaft of a column.

scarcement   In building, a setback in the face of a wall, or in an earthen embankment; a footing or ledge formed by the setting back of a wall.

scarf   **1.** The end on one of the pieces of timber forming a **scarf joint**. **2.** A **scarf joint**.

scarf connection   Same as **scarf joint**.

scarf joint   **1.** A joint by which the ends of two pieces of timber are united to form a continuous piece; the mating surfaces may be beveled, chamfered, notched, etc., before bolting, gluing, welding, etc. **2.** A joint formed by bonding the beveled ends of two pieces of lumber. **3.** In welding, a butt joint between two pieces whose ends are beveled. **4.** A joint in electrical cable in which the ends are beveled before soldering.

scarf joint, 1

scarifier   A machine or an attachment for a tractor or grader having a long tooth or series of teeth that can be lowered to tear up surface soil or pavement.

scarifier

scarify   To roughen a surface by sanding or some other technique, in order to improve adhesion of paint.

scarp   A steep slope constructed as a defensive measure in a fortification.

SC asphalt   Same as **slow-curing asphalt**.

scena   Same as **scaena**.

scene dock   A place usually adjacent to, or below, the stage of a theatre where the scenery is stored.

scenery   Any or all devices ordinarily used on a theater stage, such as backdrops, borders, scrims, set pieces, side tabs, tabs, but not including props or costumes.

scenery wagon (*Brit.* **boat dock**)   A low platform on casters or rollers, used to support scenery on the stage of a theatre; permits rapid changes of scenery.

scene shop   A place where scenery is fabricated for use in a theatre or opera house.

scent test, smell test A test for leaks in a drainpipe; a material having a strong odor is introduced into the pipe and leaks are detected by tracing the scent to its source.

sceuophylacium Same as **diaconicon, 1**.

SCH On drawings, abbr. for "schedule."

schedule **1.** A detailed tabulation of components, items, or parts to be furnished, as a **door schedule**. **2.** See **steel pipe**.

schedule of values A statement furnished by the contractor to the architect reflecting the portions of the **contract sum** allotted for the various parts of the work and used as the basis for reviewing the contractor's applications for progress payments.

schematic design phase The first phase of the architect's **basic services**. In this phase, the architect consults with the owner to ascertain the requirements of the project and prepares schematic design studies consisting of drawings and other documents illustrating the scale and relationship of the project components for approval by the owner. The architect also submits to the owner a **statement of probable construction cost**.

schematic drawing See **schematic design phase**.

scheme **1.** The basic arrangement of an architectural composition. **2.** Preliminary sketch for a design.

scheme arch An arch which forms part of a circle which is less than a semicircle.

schist A rock, the constituent minerals of which have assumed a position in more or less closely parallel layers or folia; due to metamorphic action; used principally for **flagging**.

schola **1.** The apse or alcove containing a tub in Roman baths. **2.** An exedra or alcove in a palaestra for relaxation or conversation.

school An educational institution offering studies at differentiated levels to groups of pupils of various ages; instruction may be given by one or more teachers. It may be contained in a single structure or a group of separate buildings; may be under private or public auspices.

schoolhouse A building in which classes are conducted at different educational levels for students up to college age. Also see **one-room schoolhouse**.

sciagraph The geometrical representation of a building, showing its interior structure or arrangement.

scialbo Same as **intonaco**.

scintled brickwork Same as **skintled brickwork**.

scion A cutting from a woody plant that is joined onto rootstock of another plant in grafting and budding.

scissors truss A type of truss used to support a pitched roof; the **ties** cross each other and are connected to the opposite rafters at an intermediate point along their length.

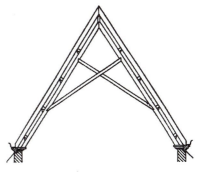

scissors truss

sclerometer An instrument for determining the degree of hardness of a material by the amount of pressure required to scratch it with a diamond point.

scoinson arch Same as **sconcheon arch**.

scollop Same as **scallop**.

scollop capital In Romanesque architecture, a **capital** similar to a **cushion capital** but having its underside scalloped.

sconce An electric lamp, resembling a candlestick or a group of candlesticks, which is designed and fabricated for mounting on a wall.

sconcheon, esconson, scuncheon **1.** The **reveal** of an aperture (such as a door or window) from the frame to the inner face of the wall. **2.** See **squinch, 2**.

sconcheon arch, scoinson arch An arch which includes the sconcheons of a door or window. (*See illustration p. 804.*)

scone Same as **split, 3**.

scoop loader Same as **front-end loader**.

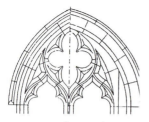

sconcheon arch

scotia

score **1.** To cut a channel or groove in a material with a hand tool or a circular saw so as to interrupt the visual effect of a surface or otherwise decorate it. **2.** To roughen the surface of a material with gouges to provide a better bond for mortar, plaster, or stucco; to **scratch**. **3.** To groove a freshly placed concrete surface with a tool to control shrinkage cracking. **4.** To roughen the top surface of one concrete pour in order to provide a better mechanical bond for the next pour.

scored finish A characteristic of a building unit having faces which have been grooved during the manufacturing process.

scored joint Same as **scribed joint, 2**.

scoria **1.** A dark, cellular volcanic rock. **2.** Blast-furnace slag or scum.

scotch See **scutch**.

Scotch bond Same as **common bond**.

Scotch bracketing Lath, attached at an angle between a wall and ceiling, which form a base for a hollow cornice.

Scotch glue An **animal glue**.

scotching Same as **scutching**.

Scotch method of application See **Dutch method of application**.

scotia A deep concave molding, esp. one at the base of a column in Classical architecture. Also called a **gorge, trochilus**.

scour The erosion of a concrete surface, exposing the aggregate.

scouring Using a wood float, in a circular motion, to smooth freshly applied mortar or plaster.

scouring action In a drain pipe, the lifting or scrubbing of loose particles (including sand, grit, and small pebbles) from the interior surface of the pipe and carrying them downstream. To achieve this action, sufficient flow velocity is required.

SCPI Abbr. for "Structural Clay Products Institute."

SCR Abbr. for "silicon-controlled rectifier."

scrabbled rubble Same as **rubblework**.

scraped finish A European style of plaster finish which is obtained by scraping the stucco finish coat with a steel tool (sometimes serrated) as the stucco is setting.

scraped joint A joint brought to an accurately plane surface by scraping.

scraper **1.** A self-propelled machine capable of digging, loading, hauling, dumping, and spreading materials; used to move earth by stripping or collecting a layer with a cutting blade while moving forward, pushing the earth into a bowl, and then unloading it. **2.** A towed machine which is used to level the surface of ground by stripping away earth, or by collecting earth and filling hollow areas. **3.** A **cabinet scraper**.

pull-type **scraper, 1**

scraper plane Same as **cabinet scraper**.

scratch To **score** or groove a plaster surface to provide a better bond for the succeeding coat.

scratch awl An **awl** used for scribing wood, plastic, or the like.

scratch awl

scratch-brushed finish, satin finish A finish obtained by mechanically brushing a surface with wire bristle brushes or by rotary buffing with an abrasive compound.

scratch coat In three-coat plastering, the first coat of plaster, which is then scratched to provide a bond for the second (brown) coat.

scratched Said of a surface in which minute groove-like breaks are made in the surface.

scratcher See **scratch tool**.

scratch tool, scratcher Any hand tool for scratching plaster to provide a mechanical bond for the following coat of plaster, such as a **drag** or **devil float**.

scratchwork Same as **sgraffito**.

SCR brick Brick whose nominal dimensions are 2⅔ in. by 6 in. by 12 in.

screed **1.** Firmly established grade strips or side forms for unformed concrete which will guide the **strikeoff** in producing the desired plane or shape; also called **screed rail**. **2.** A tool to strike off the concrete surface. **3.** A long, narrow strip of plaster, applied at intervals on a surface to be plastered; carefully leveled and trued to act as a guide for plastering to the specified thickness. **4.** A layer of mortar laid on concrete, usually to provide a uniform, level surface.

screed coat In plastering, a coat made even or flush with the screeds.

screeding Forming a concrete surface by use of screeds and a **strikeoff**.

screed rail See **screed, 1**.

screed strip A **screed, 3**.

screed wire Same as **ground wire, 2**.

screen **1.** Any construction whose essential function is merely to separate, protect, seclude, or conceal, but not to support. **2.** A covered framework, either movable or fixed, which serves to protect from the sun, fire, wind, rain, or cold. **3.** A metallic plate or sheet, a woven wire cloth, or other similar device, with regularly spaced apertures of uniform size, mounted in a suitable frame or holder for use in separating material according to size; also called a **sieve**.

screen analysis See **sieve analysis**.

screen door A lightweight exterior door consisting of solid wood or aluminum stiles and rails that serve as a framework for small-mesh wire screening; permits ventilation but excludes insects.

screen-door latch A small locking or latching device used on screen doors and operated by a knob or a lever handle; sometimes equipped with a dead bolt.

screen-door latch

screen façade A nonstructural facing assembly used to disguise the form or dimensions of a building.

screenings In passing sand or aggregate through a **sieve**, that portion which is retained on the sieve.

screen molding Any type of simple molding used to cover the exposed edge of a sheet of wire screening.

screen side Of a fiberboard or the like, that side which receives the impression of the mesh during manufacture.

screens passage In a medieval hall, the space between the screen and the doors to the service rooms (buttery, kitchen, pantry).

screen wall A screen of some solidity as differing from one which is pierced, esp. in the intercolumniations of a colonnade. Also see **pierced wall**.

screen wire cloth A light **wire cloth** used as screening in a door or window.

screw An externally threaded fastener. (*See illustration p. 806.*)

screw anchor An **anchor** (similar to an expansion bolt) having a metal shell with a screw along its central axis; when the shell is placed in a hole and the screw is driven in, the shell expands, tightly securing the anchor in the hole.

screw auger Same as **auger, 1**.

screw blank See **bolt blank**.

screw clamp Any clamp set by means of a screw, but esp. one used in woodworking which

screw dowel

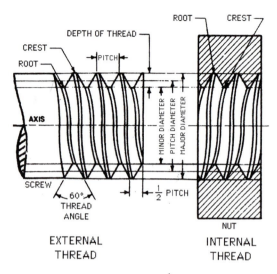

screw: nomenclature

has two large parallel jaws for holding the work to be pressed together.

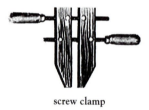

screw clamp

screw dowel A metal dowel pin provided with a straight or tapered thread.

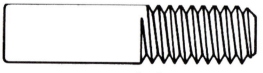

screw dowel

screwdriver A tool having a handle and a long shank, with a tapered wedge-shaped tip which fits into the recess in the head of a screw; used for driving a screw in place or removing it, by turning the head of the screw.

screwed joint A joint that uses threads on the ends of two pipes (or on a pipe and a fitting) to draw the two pieces together and form a leakproof seal.

screwed work In wood turning, work in which the cutting is done in a spiral direction, so as to leave a spiral fillet or other ornamental spiral pattern.

screw eye A screw having a loop or eye for its head.

screw jack Same as **jackscrew**.

screwless knob A doorknob attached to a spindle by means of a special wrench instead of the more commonly used side screw.

screwless rose A **rose** with concealed method of attachment.

screwnail See **drivescrew**.

screw pile **1.** A **pile** which has a broad-bladed screw attached to its foot to provide a larger bearing area. **2.** A **pile** which has a spiral blade fixed to its lower end; it is twisted into the ground rather than driven by a series of impacts.

screw stair, winding stair A circular stair whose steps wind around a central post. Also called a **newel stair** or **vice stair**.

screw thread See **thread** and **taper thread**.

scribbled ornament A decorative effect produced by lines, scrolls, or the like, irregularly distributed over a surface.

scribed joint **1.** See **coped joint**. **2.** A masonry joint in which a thin line has been cut in the face of the mortar between bricks after it has been smoothed with a metal tool.

scriber A pointed instrument used to mark lines on wood, metal, bricks, etc., to serve as a guide in sawing, cutting, etc.

scrim **1.** A coarse mesh-like material such as heavy cloth, fiberglass, or wire mesh, used to bridge and reinforce a joint or as a base for plastering or painting. **2.** A light open-weave fabric, sometimes painted or dyed, used as a **drop curtain** or part of a drop curtain; transparent, but less so than theatrical gauze.

scriptorium A writing room; specifically, the room assigned in a monastery for the copying of manuscripts.

scroll An ornament consisting of a spirally wound band, either as a running ornament or as a terminal, like the volutes of the Ionic capital or the scrolls on consoles and modillions.

scroll molding A form of **roll molding**; a large projecting molding, resembling a scroll with the free end hanging down, found in string-courses

scroll

and similar locations requiring a drip. Also see **torsade, 1**.

scroll molding

scroll pediment A little-used synonym for **swan's-neck pediment**.

scroll saw A handsaw or band saw for cutting thin boards, veneers, or plates into ornamental scrollwork; esp. used for cutting curves.

scroll step See **curtail step**.

scrollwork **1.** Ornamental woodwork that has been cut by a **scrollsaw** in decorative curved patterns often suggestive of a series of waves. **2.** Wrought-iron ornamental work in which scroll-like characters are an important element.

scrubboard A **baseboard**.

scrub plane A plane having a blade with a rounded cutting edge; used in rough carpentry work.

scrub sink A plumbing fixture usually located in the operating suite in a hospital to enable personnel to scrub their hands prior to a surgical procedure; the hot and cold water supply is activated by a knee-action mixing valve or by wrist or pedal control.

scullery A room, generally annexed to a kitchen, used to prepare food for cooking, and/or as a pantry.

scum, scumming **1.** A surface deposit sometimes formed on clay bricks; caused either by soluble salts in the clay which migrate to the surface as moisture escapes during drying (**drier scum**) or by the formation of deposits during kiln firing (**kiln scum**). **2.** A mass of organic matter which floats on the surface of sewage.

scumbling In painting, the operation of lightly rubbing a brush containing a small quantity of opaque or semiopaque color over a surface to soften and blend tints that are too bright, or to produce a special effect; the coat may be so thin as to be semitransparent.

scuncheon Same as **sconcheon**.

scupper **1.** An opening in a wall or parapet that allows water to drain from a roof. **2.** A device placed in such an opening to prevent clogging of the drain.

scupper, 2

scupper drain Same as **scupper**.

scutch, scotch A bricklayer's tool, with a cutting edge on each side, for cutting, trimming, and dressing brick or stone.

scutcheon Same as **escutcheon**.

scutching A method of finely dressing stone with a hammer, the head of which is composed of a bundle of steel points.

scuttle A hatchway or opening through a roof-deck or ceiling for access purposes, with a lid for covering it.

scuttle door A door covering a **scuttle** in a roof; usually made of sheet metal with a metal frame; often hinged and counterbalanced.

scutula A segment of marble or other material, cut in the shape of a diamond or rhombus and used for inlaying floors or pavements.

SDFU (sanitary drainage fixture unit) See **fixture unit**.

Sdg Abbr. for **siding**.

SDR See **standard dimension ratio**.

S/E Abbr. for "square-edged."

SE&S In the lumber industry, abbr. for "square edge and sound."

seal **1.** A device usually consisting of an impression upon wax or paper, or a wafer, or the inscription of the letters "L.S." (locus sigilli), sometimes used in the execution of a formal legal document such as a deed or contract. In some states, the statute of limitations applicable to a contract under seal is longer than that for a contract not under seal; in most states, the seal has been deprived by statute of some or all of its legal effect. **2.** An embossing device or stamp used by a design professional on his **drawings** and **specifications** as evidence of his registration in the state where the **work, 1** is to be performed. **3.** In a trap for a plumbing fixture, the water between the dip and the **crown weir**; a water seal. **4.** The vertical distance between the dip and the crown weir of a trap. **5.** To coat the surface fibers of wood so as to prevent penetration of moisture or successive coatings during finishing. **6.** To apply a shellac or other resin-resistant coating on knots in wood, to prevent resin staining; to **kill**. **7.** A **sealant**; a **sealer**.

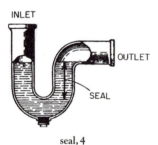

seal, 4

sealable equipment Electrical equipment enclosed in a case or cabinet that is provided with a means of locking or sealing so that *live* parts are not accessible unless the enclosure is opened.

sealant Any material or device used to prevent the passage of liquid or gas across a joint or opening; a **sealer**.

sealant backing A compressible material inserted in a joint prior to applying a sealant; limits the depth of the sealant.

seal coat, sealing coat Same as **sealer**.

sealed glass unit Same as **insulating glass unit**.

sealed refrigeration compressor A mechanical compressor consisting of a compressor and a motor, both enclosed in the same sealed housing, with no external shaft or shaft seals, the motor operating in the refrigerant atmosphere.

sealer **1.** A liquid coat which seals wood, plaster, etc., and prevents the surface from absorbing paint or varnish; may be transparent; may act as a primer for a following coat or as a finish for the surface. **2.** A coat, applied in liquid form, which is laid over a tar-like substance to prevent its bleeding through an applied paint film. **3.** A finishing coat of a bituminous substance, asphalt, concrete, etc., to seal it against moisture.

sealing compound A mastic-like material used as a **seal** or **sealer**.

sealing sleeve Same as **compression coupling**.

seal weld A weld used primarily to provide a specific degree of tightness against leakage.

seam **1.** A joint between two sheets of materials, such as metal. **2.** See **welt**.

seamer A hand tool used in making sheet-metal joints or seams.

seam face On a building stone, a face formed by a natural seam in the rock.

seaming The joining of the edges of a metal sheet or sheets by bending over or doubling and pinching them together.

seamless door **1.** A hollow-metal door formed from two sheets of steel, without seams on the door faces or on the vertical edges. **2.** A steel door of composite construction; the sheet-steel facings are bonded to a solid, structural mineral core without edge seams.

seamless floor See **polymeric poured floor**.

seamless flooring Fluid or trowel-applied flooring without aggregates.

seamless pipe Pipe without a longitudinal joint or seam.

seamless tubing Tubing having a continuous periphery, with no longitudinal seam.

seam roll Same as **hollow roll**.

seam weld A continuous weld made along a line between two overlapping members.

season crack **1.** A crack that develops in metals that have been rolled or otherwise subjected to a process developing internal stress. **2.** Same as **seasoning check**.

seasoning **1.** The drying of wood, either in air or in a kiln. **2.** The curing or hardening of concrete.

seasoning check A longitudinal crack that develops in wood during the drying process as a result of uneven or rapid seasoning.

seat **1.** In carpentry, same as **seat cut**. **2.** In plumbing, same as **valve seat**.

seat angle A short **angle iron** connected to a column to support a beam temporarily during erection.

seat cut A horizontal cut at the lower end of a **rafter** so that it may rest securely on the edge of a horizontal timber such as a wall plate; also see illustration for **bird's mouth**.

CEILING JOISTS

RAFTERS

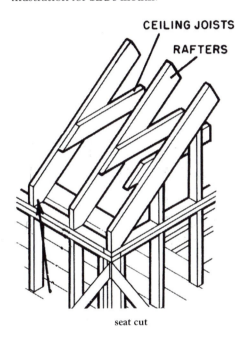

seat cut

seating **1.** Devices such as theatre seats, benches, pews, etc., used for the accommodation of groups of people. **2.** The arrangement of seats in a place of assembly. **3.** The capacity of a room or space in terms of the number of seats available; the **seating capacity**.

seating capacity The total number of seats in an auditorium.

seating section A group of seats bounded on all sides by aisles, ramps, walls, or partitions.

sec Abbr. for "second."

secco See **fresco secco**.

second A unit of secondary quality or one not meeting specified dimensions; a **cull**.

secondary air **1.** Air which is introduced into a furnace (in addition to the primary air which enters either as a mixture with fuel or as blast underneath a stoker) above or around the flames to promote combustion. **2.** Air already in an air-conditioned space, in contrast to **primary air** which is introduced into the space.

secondary air motion The motion of air in a room caused by the discharge of air from an **air diffuser** or any type of air outlet.

secondary arch See **rear arch**.

secondary beam A beam which is carried by the main beams and transmits its load to them.

secondary blasting The reduction of oversize material by the use of explosives to the dimension required for handling, including **mudcapping** and **blockholing**.

secondary branch In plumbing, any branch of a building drain or water-supply main other than a **primary branch**.

secondary combustion The unintentional combustion of fuel beyond the outlet of a furnace.

secondary consolidation The reduction in volume of a soil mass caused by the application of a sustained load to the mass, due principally to the adjustment of the internal structure of the soil mass after most of the load has been transferred from the soil water to the soil solids.

secondary distribution feeder In electric wiring systems, a **feeder** which operates at the secondary voltage supplying a distribution circuit.

secondary façade A façade not facing a public street or otherwise visible to the public, and that does not possess significant architectural features.

secondary feeders Electrical conductors between the main distribution center at the building **service entrance** and the distribution centers downstream (i.e., closer to the load).

secondary light source **1.** A light source which is not self-luminous but receives light and redirects it as by reflection or transmission. **2.** The second most important, or most obvious, source of light when several sources are present.

secondary reinforcement In **reinforced concrete**, any steel reinforcement other than **main reinforcement**.

secondary school   See **high school**.

secondary substation   Same as **distribution center**.

secondary truss member   A subsidiary member of a **truss**, used to support a main member or to transfer load from a point within a panel to one or more **panel points**.

secondary voltage   Low voltage, distributed to the different circuits within a building.

Second Classical Revival style   A term sometimes used as a synonym for **Italian Renaissance Revival**.

second coat   In plastering, the **brown coat**; in two-coat work, the **finish coat**.

Second Empire architecture   A stylistic designation for the eclectic architecture named after the French Second Empire of Napoleon III (1852–1870) or their derivatives.

Second Empire style in the United States   A grand, eclectic architectural style from about 1855 to 1890 and beyond, primarily in public buildings but also in domestic architecture; named after the French Second Empire of Napoleon III (1852–1870); frequently called *Mansard style* because it features a **mansard roof** usually having the profile of a compound curve. Buildings in this style usually are characterized by the following attributes: a central one-story pavilion projecting outward from a façade; classical pediments with elaborate heavy detailing and trim; often, a heavy cornice, typically supported by decorative brackets; commonly, a square tower located at the center of the façade;

Second Empire style

pedimented dormers; **terneplate** or multicolored slates forming decorative patterns covering the roof; a curb or railing around the roof, commonly enclosed with decorative metalwork cresting; windows having an upper sash divided in two parts by a vertical secondary framing member, over a similar lower sash; pedimented, bracketed, or hooded windows usually having square or arched heads; tall, almost floor-to-ceiling windows on the first floor; a pair of paneled entry doors having glass in the upper panels; frequently, arched doorways; usually, steps leading from the street up to the level of the doorway. Also called **General Grant style** or Second Empire Baroque.

second fixings   All carpentry and joinery installed after the plastering; may include electrical wiring and plumbing.

second-growth timber   Wood which has grown after a virgin forest has been cut down.

Second Pointed style   Same as **Decorated style**, the second of three phases of English Gothic architecture.

Second Renaissance   Same as **Italian Renaissance Revival**.

secos   Same as **sekos**.

secret dovetail, miter dovetail   A joint appearing to be a simple miter joint when assembled, but having dovetailing concealed within it.

secret dovetail

secret fixing   See **secret screwing**.

secret gate latch   A spring latch which is surface-mounted on an office gate (or the like); operated by a concealed button or actuated electrically.

secret gutter   A **concealed gutter**.

secret joggle   An interlocking joint in an ashlar **voussoir** that is not visible on the face.

secret nailing See **blind nailing**.

secret screwing, secret fixing, secret screw joint A method of joining carpentry work by screws which are hidden.

secret tenon Same as **stub tenon**.

secret valley See **secret gutter**.

SECT On drawings, abbr. for "section."

sectile opus A kind of pavement formed of slabs or tiles of glass or other material, the pieces having a uniform size (far larger than the tesserae of ordinary mosaic) and being either plain-colored or mottled and veined.

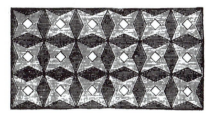

sectile opus   (two types)

section **1.** A representation of an object as it would appear if cut by an imaginary plane, show-

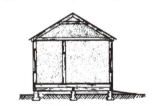

SECTION A-A

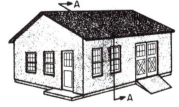

PERSPECTIVE VIEW

section, 2

ing the internal structure. **2.** A representation of a building, or portion thereof, drawn as if it were cut vertically to show the interior. **3.** Such a representation of a molding or assembly of pieces, to show the profile or makeup. **4.** In structures, a section made by a plane perpendicular to the axis of a member, structure, or any construction. **5.** A subdivision of a division of the specifications which covers the work of no more than one trade.

sectional insulation Thermal insulation fabricated in sections which fit together, such as molded pipe insulation made of two or more annular segments.

sectional ladder A portable ladder that is not self-supporting and not adjustable in length; consists of two or more sections of ladder that may be combined for use as a single ladder.

section modulus The moment of inertia of the area of the cross section of a structural member divided by the distance from the center of gravity to the farthest point of the section; a measure of the flexural strength of the beam.

section mold See **joint mold**.

sectroid A twisted surface which is between the groins of a vault.

security alarm system See **burglar alarm system**.

security cabinet door-contacts Electrical contacts mounted on the doors of vaults, security file cabinets, etc. When the door is opened, the contacts separate, thereby activating an alarm.

security glass **1.** See **bullet-resisting glass**. **2.** See **laminated glass**.

security screen Heavy screen used as a barrier against escapes or break-ins; see **detention screen, protection screen**.

security window **1.** A steel industrial-type window, generally used in stores and warehouses to provide protection against burglary. **2.** A **detention window**.

sedge A plant which grows in dense tufts in marshy places; used to form a ridge on a thatched roof.

sedile A seat (usually one of three) for the clergy to the right of an altar, often set in a canopied niche in the chancel wall. (*See illustration p. 812.*)

sediment The matter which settles to the bottom of water or any other liquid.

sedile

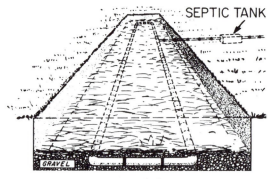

seepage bed

sedimentary rock   Rock, such as limestone or sandstone, which is formed from materials deposited as sediments, in the sea or fresh water, or on the land. Also see **stratified rock**.

sediment trap   **1.** A removable device inside the body of a drain; used to trap and retain small solids that pass through the grate. The unwanted solids that have accumulated are disposed of. **2.** In a gas supply system, a trap useful in collecting dirt or other foreign material that may be entrained in the gas flow, thus protecting the equipment operating controls.

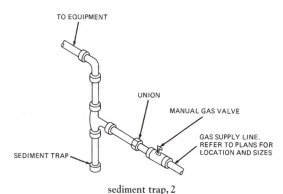

sediment trap, 2

seedy   Descriptive of a paint finish that is not smooth owing to undispersed pigment particles or insoluble gel particles in the paint.

seel   Old English for **canopy**.

seepage   **1.** The slow movement of water through a soil. **2.** The quantity of water which has slowly moved through a porous material, such as soil.

seepage bed   A trench usually exceeding 36 in. (approx. 1 m) in width containing clean, coarse aggregate and a system of distribution piping

through which treated sewage may seep into the surrounding soil.

seepage force   That force which is transmitted to the soil grains by **seepage**.

seepage pit   A covered pit with open-jointed lining through which septic-tank effluent may seep or leach into the surrounding soil.

seggio   A council chamber.

segmental arch   A circular arch in which the intrados is less than a semicircle.

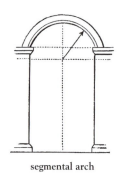

segmental arch

segmental billet   A **billet, 1** molding formed by a series of segments of cylinders.

segmental billet

segmental dormer   A **dormer** having a roof whose cross section is an arc of a circle having a large radius of curvature.

segmental dormer

segmental member A structural member made up of individual elements prestressed together so as to act as a monolithic unit under service loads.

segmental pediment A **pediment** whose upper bounding surface has the shape of an arc of a circle having a large radius of curvature.

segmental pediment

segmental vault A **vault, 1** having the cross section of a **segmental arch**.

segment head The **head** of a door in the shape of the arc of a circle.

segment saw A large-diameter, specially designed circular saw, used for cutting veneer because it makes a very narrow kerf.

segregation The differential concentration of the components of mixed concrete.

seismic load The force produced on a structural mass owing to its acceleration, induced by an earthquake.

seismic protection The application of engineering design methods and the installation of devices that make possible the continuance of essential services (such as the distribution of water, gas, electricity, telephone) in buildings during and immediately after an earthquake.

seizing The damaging of one metal surface as a result of rubbing with another metal surface.

sekos In ancient Greece: **1.** A shrine or sanctuary. **2.** The cella of a temple. **3.** A building which only the specially privileged might enter.

Sel In the lumber industry, abbr. for "select."

selected bidder The bidder selected by the **owner** for discussions relative to the possible award of the **construction contract**.

selected list of bidders Same as **invited bidders**.

selenite A variety of gypsum in transparent, foliated, crystalline form; used as decorative building stone.

selenitic cement, selenitic lime Lime cement to which 5 to 10% plaster of paris has been added to increase its hardening properties.

self-ballasted lamp A lamp of the arc-discharge type (such as a high-pressure mercury lamp) which incorporates a current-limiting device.

self-centering lath Expanded-metal rib lath used on bar joists as formwork for concrete floors, or for lathing in 2-in. (5-cm) solid plaster partitions.

self-cleansing velocity In a drain pipe, a flow velocity that is high enough to initiate **scrubbing action**.

self-clinching Said of a nail whose shank or point clinches automatically when fully driven.

self-closing device See **closing device**.

self-closing fire assembly A **fire assembly** which is kept in a normally closed position and is equipped with an approved device to ensure closing and latching after opening for use.

self-closing fire door A fire door which is equipped with a **closing device**.

self-extinguishing Said of a material that does not continue to burn after the external source of ignition is removed.

self-faced stone A stone having its natural face or surface, as a **flagstone**.

self-finished roofing felt See **asphalt prepared roofing felt**.

self-furring Said of metal lath or welded wire fabric having some means of spacing it from a wall; when plaster, stucco, or concrete is applied to the fabric, the space makes it possible to **key, 8** the applied material to the metal lath or welded wire fabric.

self-furring nail Same as **furring nail**.

self-ignition temperature The minimum initial temperature at which the self-heating properties of a material lead to its ignition; dependent on specimen size, heat-loss conditions, and possibly other variables such as moisture content.

self-leveling sealant A **sealant** which exhibits sufficient flow to level itself by gravity.

self-noise In a **sound attenuator** in an HVAC system, the noise which is generated as a result of the flow of air through the attenuator.

self-reading leveling rod A **leveling rod** with graduation marks designed to be read by the observer at the leveling instrument.

self-sealing fastener A fastener which provides a seal that is so tight that a sealant material or mechanical seal is not required.

self-sealing paint A paint which, when applied over a surface of varying porosity, seals the surface and yet dries with a uniform color and sheen.

self-service elevator See **automatic elevator**.

self-service refrigerator Any type of refrigerator found in food stores and other stores where the customer helps himself; may be of the open type or may be equipped with sliding or hinged doors.

self-siphonage The removing of water from a **trap, 1** (thereby breaking the seal) as a result of siphonage set up by the momentum of discharge from the fixture to which the trap is connected.

self-spacing tile Ceramic tile having lugs, spacers, or protuberances on the sides which automatically space the tile for grout joints.

self-spreading Said of a nail having a split shank so that its two or more legs penetrate material in different directions.

self-stressing Descriptive of expansive-cement concrete, mortar, or grout in which expansion, if restrained, induces persistent compressive stresses in the material.

self-supporting wall, self-sustaining wall A **non-load-bearing wall**.

self-tapping screw Same as **sheet-metal screw**.

self-vulcanizing Said of an adhesive that undergoes vulcanization without the application of heat.

seliana window Same as **Palladian window**.

sellary, sellaria A large sitting-room, drawing room, or reception room that is furnished with chairs or benches.

selvage, selvedge 1. The finished edge of carpeting, a fabric, etc., which prevents raveling. 2. The unsurfaced strip along a sheet of prepared roll roofing that forms the underportion of the lap. The plate through which the bolt of a lock projects.

selvage joint In roofing, a lap joint between mineral-faced **cap sheets**; mineral surfacing is omitted along the selvage to provide a better bond at the joint.

semiarch An arch having only one half of its sweep developed, as in a flying buttress.

semiautomatic arc welding Arc welding with equipment which controls only the **filler metal** feed; the advance of the welding is manually controlled.

semiautomatic batcher A **batcher** equipped with gates or valves which are opened manually to allow the material to be weighed separately, but which are closed automatically when the designated weight of each material has been reached.

semibasement A basement which is only partly below ground level.

semibungalow A bungalow or cottage having an added room or two in the attic area.

semicircular arch A round arch whose intrados is a full semicircle.

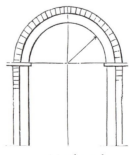

semicircular arch

semicircular dome   A dome in the shape of a half sphere.

semicircular fanlight   A **fanlight** having a semicircular shape, often located directly above the main entry of a house.

semicircular vault   A barrel or tunnel vault.

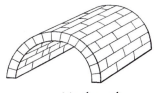

semicircular vault

semicircular window   **1.** A window having a semicircle at its head. **2.** A window having the shape of a semicircle, often placed above a door or in a **tympanum**; also called a D-window.

semi-column   Same as **half column**.

semidetached dwelling   A dwelling, one side wall of which is a party or lot-line wall.

semidetached house   One of a pair of houses joined by a party wall.

semidirect lighting   Lighting from luminaires which distribute 60% to 90% of the emitted light downward.

semidome   A dome equivalent to one-quarter of a hollow sphere, covering a semicircular area, such as an apse.

semidome: apse of Suleimanie Mosque, Istanbul 1550 A.D.

semi-drying oil   An oil having the characteristics of a **drying oil**, but to a lesser degree.

semielliptical arch   Strictly, an arch whose intrados is half an ellipse; in practice the term usually denotes a three- or five-centered arch; also called a basket-handle arch.

semielliptical fanlight   A window, over the opening of a door, which has the shape of half an ellipse; often simply called an elliptical fanlight.

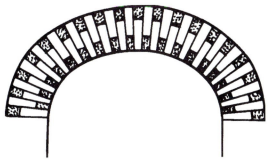

semielliptical arch

semielliptical fanlight

semiengineering brick   A brick whose strength is intermediate between a **building brick** and an **engineering brick**.

semiflexible joint   A joint in reinforced concrete in which the reinforcement is arranged so as to permit some rotation of the joint.

semigloss   A level of gloss of paint films; higher than an eggshell gloss, but lower than a full-gloss enamel. Also see **gloss**.

semihydraulic lime   A lime intermediate between a hydraulic lime and a high-calcium lime.

semi-indirect lighting   Lighting from luminaires which distribute 60% to 90% of the emitted light upward.

semi-instantaneous-type water heater   An **instantaneous-type water heater** having a sophisticated temperature control system and a tank of small storage capacity.

seminary   A place of education; a school, academy, college, or university; especially a school for the education for the priesthood.

semirigid frame   A structural framework in which the columns and beams are connected in such a way that there is some flexibility at the joints.

semirubbed finish　The surface of a split stone which has been sand-rubbed to the degree that prominences have been smoothed flat, but recessed areas still remain.

semisteel　A grade of **cast iron** of low carbon content; made by the addition of steel scrap to pig iron while molten.

semi-vitreous　Descriptive of that degree of vitrification evidenced by a moderate or intermediate water absorption, i.e., a water absorption of 0.3 to 3.0% except for floor tile and wall tile, which are considered semi-vitreous when water absorption is between 3.0 and 7.0%.

sems　(*sing. and pl.*)　A machine screw permanently combined with a lock washer which was inserted before the thread was cut.

sensible heat　Heat that changes the temperature of a material without a change in state, such as that which would lead to increased moisture content.

sensible heat factor　The ratio of the **sensible heat** to the total heat load of an air-conditioned space.

sensing device　See **sensor**.

sensor, detector, sensing device　A device which senses or detects an abnormal ambient condition, such as smoke or unusually high temperature; used to initiate an alarm signal, open a smoke hatch, etc.

SEP　On drawings, abbr. for "separate."

separate application　The application of components of a catalyzed glue or adhesive separately to opposite faces of members to be joined; curing occurs when the faces are joined.

separate-application adhesive　An adhesive consisting of two components, one part being applied to one adherend and the other part to the other adherend; the two are brought together to form a joint.

separate contract　One of several prime contracts on a construction project.

separated aggregate　**1.** A coarse aggregate which has been divided into components of two or more sizes. **2.** Fine and coarse aggregate considered separately, as differentiated from a **combined aggregate**.

separately-coupled pump　A pump which is mechanically coupled to an electric motor driven by means of a flexible coupling; both pump and motor are mounted on a structural baseplate to provide support and to maintain shaft alignment.

separate sanitary sewer　Same as **sanitary sewer**.

separate sewer　Same as **sanitary sewer**.

separate system　Same as **sanitary sewer**.

separation　The development of layers of paint of different composition in a can during storage when the materials are not completely soluble, miscible, or stable.

separator　See **interceptor**.

septic tank　A watertight, covered receptacle designed and constructed to receive the discharge of sewage from a building sewer, separate solids from the liquid, digest organic matter and store digested solids through a period of detention, and allow the clarified liquids to discharge for final disposal.

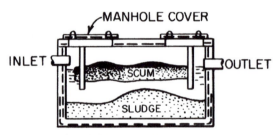

household **septic tank,** cross section

septizonium　A special type of edifice of great magnificence, consisting of seven stories of columns, one above the other, supporting seven distinct entablatures or zones.

septum　**1.** A low wall or balustrade which divided the nave of the ancient basilican church into a middle section (for the clergy) and two side sections (for the laity). **2.** A low wall around a tomb. **3.** The enclosure of the Holy Table made by the altar rails in a church.

sepulcher　**1.** A tomb. **2.** A receptacle for relics, esp. in a Christian altar. **3.** A shallow arched niche in the chancel to hold the elements of the Eucharist between their consecration on Maundy Thursday and the Easter High Mass.

sepulchral　Of, or pertaining to, a tomb.

sequence-stressing loss　In **posttensioning**, the elastic loss in a stressed tendon resulting from the shortening of the member when additional tendons are stressed.

sepulchral effigy

seraglio **1.** An enclosed or protected place. **2.** A palace.

serai Same as **caravanseray**.

serdab **1.** In ancient Egyptian architecture, a closed statue chamber. **2.** In Mesopotamian town houses, a cellar under the courtyard, ventilated and lighted by skylights, serving as a living room during the summer months.

serial distribution A group of absorption trenches (or seepage pits or seepage beds) so arranged that the total effective absorption area of one is utilized before liquid flows into the next.

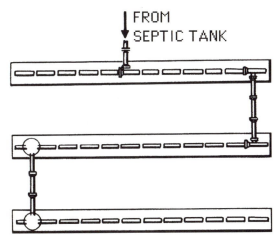

serial distribution

series circuit A circuit which supplies electric power to a number of devices connected so that the same current passes through each device in completing its path to the source of supply.

Serlian motif See **Palladian motif**.

serpent column A type of column used in Toltec architecture; features a feathered serpent whose open-fanged head serves as the base and whose tail rattlers are the roof support. Outstanding examples at Chichén Itzá and Tula, in Mexico.

serpentine A group of minerals consisting of hydrous magnesium silicate, or rock largely composed of these minerals; commonly occurs in greenish shades; used for decorative stone; the prominent constituent in some commercial marbles.

serpentine wall A wall that is not straight in plan but follows a sinuous course. Also called a crinkle-crankle.

serpentine wall

serrated Notched on the edges, like a saw.

serrated grating A grating which has the top surfaces of the bearing bars or cross bars (or both) notched by punching.

SERV On drawings, abbr. for "service."

servants' room In a large home of the past (or in a dependency of such a home), a common room in which the servants gathered, ate, and waited to be summoned. Also called a servants' hall.

service The conductors and equipment for delivering electric power from the electricity supply system to the wiring system of the premises served.

serviceability The capability of a component, material, assembly, construction, or building to perform the function(s) for which it is designed and used.

service bar A counter on which bartenders place liquor and other beverages for waiters to take to their customers.

service box 1. In the electric wiring system for a building, the box (within the building) at the point of entry of the **service conductors**. 2. A box, usually flush with the pavement, which provides access to a corporation cock.

service cables 1. The **service conductors**, in the form of a cable. 2. Those cables and neutral conductors which are furnished, owned, installed, and maintained by the utility company, from the distribution system or overhead lines to the **point of service delivery**.

service chute See **building service chute**.

service clamp Same as **saddle fitting**.

service conductors In an electric wiring system, the supply conductors between the street mains (or transformer) and the service equipment of the building supplied.

service conduit See **service pipe**.

service connection An electrical connector that attaches the utility company's conductors to the customer's wiring.

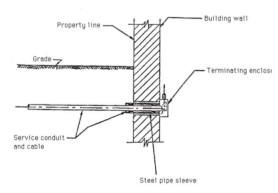

service connection

service core A multistoried space in a tall building, usually centrally located, that houses essential building services such as elevators, and/or is the wiring distribution site for services such as electricity, telephone, security, fire protection, communications systems, and plumbing lines.

service corridor A fully enclosed passageway other than a passageway required by code for exiting.

service dead load The calculated **dead load**; the calculated dead weight supported by a member.

service door, service entrance An exterior door in a building, for the delivery of equipment, supplies, etc., for the removal of waste, or for the use of servants.

service drop In the electric wiring system for a building, the portion of the **service conductors** between the last pole of the utility supply and the junction with the **service entrance conductors** of the building supplied.

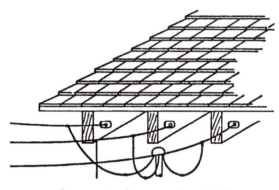

attaching a **service drop** to a residential building

service duct A conduit or tube to enclose the service cables installed by an electrical utility company.

service elbow Same as **service ell**.

service elevator A combination passenger and freight elevator.

service ell, street ell A malleable-iron fitting for threaded pipe, having a 45° or 90° bend, with an inside thread on one end and an outside thread on the other.

service ell

service entrance, service entry 1. That part of the customer's installation from the point of attachment (or termination) of the **service lateral** to and including the service equipment on the customer's premises. **2.** In a communications system, the point at which the network communications lines (e.g., the telephone company lines) enter a building.

service entrance conductors The **service conductors** which extend from the point of utility company supply through the wall of a building to the service switch for the electric wiring of the building.

service entrance conductors

service entrance switch See **service equipment, 2.**

service equipment **1.** Equipment and machinery for the provision of heat, light, sanitation, ventilation, fire fighting, transportation, refuse disposal, etc., which is a permanent part of a building and subject, therefore, to the code requirements governing the installation and use thereof. **2.** The necessary electric equipment, located near the place of entry of the supply conductors in a building, which constitutes the main control and means of cutoff for the electrical supply to the building; usually consists of a switch and fuses or a circuit breaker and required accessories.

service fitting A **service ell** or **service tee** having a male thread at one end.

service ground A ground connection to a **service conductor** or **service equipment** or both.

service head For **service entrance conductor**, a type of terminating fitting that prevents water from entering the interior of the fitting.

weatherproof **service head**

service integrated ceiling See **integrated ceiling**.

service lateral **1.** The underground service conductors between the street main, including any risers at a pole or other structure or from transformers, and the first point of connection to the **service entrance conductors** in a terminal box or meter or other enclosure, inside or outside the building wall. **2.** The duct from a pull box, manhole, or vault of a utility company's underground distribution system to the curb or property line of a parcel of property.

service live load **1.** The **live load** which is specified by the applicable building code. **2.** The nonpermanent load applied under service conditions.

service load **1.** The load which a structure is expected to support under normal usage; the **nominal load** is often taken for this value. **2.** See **working load**.

service opening Same as **intake door**.

service period In illuminating engineering, the number of hours per day for which the daylight provides a specified level of illumination.

service pipe **1.** The section of pipe which connects the public water or gas main to a termination point within a building, such as a meter or trap. **2.** In an electric wiring system, the conduit or pipe that contains underground **service conductors** and extends from the junction with the outside supply wires into the premises of the building served.

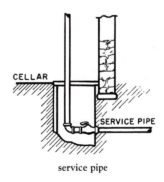

service pipe

service point Same as **point of service**.

service protector Same as **power circuit protector**.

service raceway The **raceway** (such as a rigid metal conduit or metal tubing) that encloses the **service entrance conductors**.

service refrigerator Any commercial refrigerator of the reach-in type or refrigerated display case from which an attendant serves a customer (as differentiated from a **self-service refrigerator**).

service rise See **riser, 4; riser, 5;** and **riser, 6**.

services See **building services**.

service stair **1.** A stairway primarily for servants, deliverymen, etc. **2.** A **basement stair**.

service switch The electric switch that controls all the energy registered by the meter in the system (and only that energy).

service tee A malleable-iron fitting for threaded pipe in the form of a **tee** having an outside thread on one end and an inside thread on the other and on the branch.

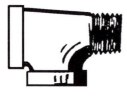

service tee

service termination The point where a utility company's conductors and/or equipment terminate and the customer's wiring begins.

service valve Any valve which isolates an apparatus from the rest of a piping system.

service wiring raceway See **service raceway**.

servient estate See **dominant estate**.

serving hatch Same as **pass-through**.

SE Sdg, S.E. Sdg. Abbr. for "square-edge siding."

set **1.** The condition reached by a cement paste, mortar, or concrete when it has lost plasticity to an arbitrary degree; usually measured in terms of resistance to penetration or deformation; **initial set** refers to first stiffening, **final set** to attainment of significant rigidity. **2.** The hydration and hardening of a gypsum plaster. **3.** To convert a liquid resin or an adhesive to a hardened state by chemical or physical action such as condensation, polymerization, oxidation, vulcanization, gelation, hydration, or the evaporation of volatile constituents. **4.** See

saw set. **5.** In plastering, to apply a finishing coat. **6.** To drive a nail below the surface of the wood (with the use of a **nail set**). **7.** The strain remaining after complete release of the load producing a deformation. **8.** Collectively, the pieces of scenery that make up a theatrical scene. **9.** In pile driving, the vertical distance a pile penetrates with a single blow of the driving hammer.

setback The minimum distance between a reference line (usually a property line) and a building, or portion thereof, as required by ordinance or code.

setback buttress A buttress near but not at the corner of a building.

set-in Same as **offset, 1**.

setoff Same as **offset, 1**.

setscrew **1.** A screw used to fix a collar, knob, or other detachable part to a shaft or part of a machine; also called a **grub screw**. **2.** A screw in a **cramp** that brings the two sides in close contact.

setscrews, 1

setting bed The mortar subsurface to which a terrazzo topping is applied.

setting block A small block of neoprene, lead, wood, or other suitable material, placed under the lower edge of a sheet of glass to support it within a frame.

setting coat See **finish coat**.

setting-in stick In plumbing, a tool for bending sheet lead.

setting out The marking of dimensions and joints on dressed lumber.

setting punch See **rivet set**.

setting shrinkage A reduction in volume of concrete prior to the final set of cement; caused by the settling of the solids and by a decrease in volume due to the chemical combination of water with cement.

setting space The distance between the finished face of a masonry panel (or veneer) and the backup wall.

setting stuff Obsolete term for **finish coat**.

setting temperature The temperature to which a liquid resin or adhesive (or an assembly involving either) must be heated in order for it to set.

setting time **1.** The length of time required for gypsum plaster to harden after the addition of water. **2.** The length of time during which a molded or extruded product must be subjected to heat and/or pressure to set the resin or adhesive. **3.** See **initial setting time, final setting time**.

setting-up **1.** The thickening which occurs when paint stands in an open can. **2.** The increasing viscosity of a paint film as it dries.

settlement **1.** The downward movement of a building structure due to consolidation of soil beneath the foundation. **2.** The sinking of solid particles of aggregate in fresh concrete or mortar after its placement and before its initial set.

Settlement phase The time period immediately following the landing of the English settlers on the American continent; during this time the colonists provided themselves with basic shelter and planted crops for the future; see **American Colonial architecture**.

settlement shrinkage The volume reduction in concrete prior to its final set, caused by the settling of the solids.

settling The sinking of pigments or other solid matter in paint with a consequent accumulation on the bottom of the can.

settling basin A basin, in a water conduit, which allows suspended debris, sand, etc., to settle.

set tub See **laundry tray**.

Seven Wonders of the World The seven most remarkable structures of ancient times: pyramids at El Gizeh, the Mausoleum at Halicarnassus, the Temple of Artemis at Ephesus, Hanging Gardens of Babylon, Colossus at Rhodes, statue of Zeus at Olympia, and the lighthouse at Alexandria; of these, only the pyramids at El Gizeh remain.

severy, civery **1.** A **baldachin**. **2.** One bay or compartment in a vaulted ceiling or structure.

SEW. On drawings, abbr. for **sewer**.

sewage Any liquid-borne waste, containing animal or vegetable matter in suspension or solution; may include liquids containing chemicals in solution; ground, surface, or storm water may become mixed with it as it is admitted into or passes through the sewers.

sewage disposal system A system for disposing of sewage, whether by means of a cesspool, septic tank, or by mechanical treatment, all of which is designed to serve a single building or group of buildings, independently of the public sewer.

sewage ejector A device for raising **sewage** by entraining it in a high-velocity jet of water, air, or steam.

sewage gas See **sewer gas**.

sewage pump **1.** A centrifugal pump of special design, having impellers that can pump large pieces of solid matter without clogging. **2.** A **sump pump**.

sewage treatment Any artificial process to which **sewage** is subjected in order to remove or alter its objectionable constituents and to render it less dangerous from the standpoint of public health.

sewage treatment plant Structures and appurtenances which receive the discharge of a sanitary drainage system and which are designed to bring about a reduction in the organic and bacterial content of the waste so as to render it less offensive or dangerous, e.g., a septic tank or cesspool.

sewer A pipe or conduit for carrying sewage and other liquid waste.

sewerage The works required to collect, treat, and dispose of sewage, including the sewer system, pumping stations, and treating works.

sewer appurtenances Constructions, devices, and appliances other than the pipe or conduit, which are appurtenant to a sewer, such as manholes, sewer inlets, etc.

sewer brick A low-absorption, abrasive-resistant brick; used in drainage structures; a **blue brick**.

sewer gas A mixture of gases, odors, and vapors found in a sewer; not of definite chemical composition; may include poisonous and combustible gases.

sewer pipe **1.** Same as **sewer**. **2.** The piping used in a sewer, e.g., **vitrified clay pipe**.

sewer tile   Impervious tile of circular cross section; designed to carry off water or sewage.

sewer trap   Same as **building trap**.

sexfoil   A **foil, 1** having six points.

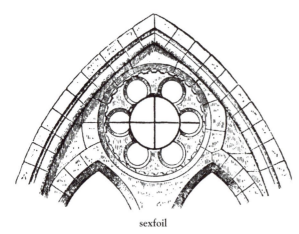

sexfoil

sexpartite vault   A ribbed vault whose lateral triangles are bisected by an intermediate transverse rib producing six triangles within a bay.

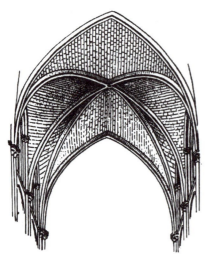

sexpartite vault

sextry   The **sacristy** of a church.

Sezession   The Austrian variant of Art Nouveau, so named because its adherents seceded from the official Academy of Art in Vienna.

SF₆   Sulfur hexafluoride; a gas used in enclosed electrical circuit breakers because of its arc-extinguishing properties.

Sftwd.   Abbr. for **softwood**.

sfu   Abbr. for **supply fixture unit**.

SGD   Abbr. for "sliding glass door."

sgraffito   A type of decoration executed by covering a surface, as of plaster or enamel, of one color, with a thin coat of a similar material of another color, and then scratching or scoring through the outer coat to show the color beneath.

SH   **1.** On drawings, abbr. for "sheet." **2.** On drawings, abbr. for "shower." **3.** Abbr. for "single-hung."

shack   Same as **shanty**.

shackle   A **clevis**.

shade   **1.** A material hung from, and coiled on, a ratcheted spring-activated roller; used to provide privacy, to darken a room, or to reduce the amount of sunlight striking a window. **2.** The result of the addition of a black dispersion to a mixture of white and color. **3.** See **shading and blending**. **4.** See **shade screen**.

shade screen, sun screen   A louvered awning used over windows; the metal blades are angled to permit good vision downward and horizontally while preventing the sun, at higher elevations, from striking the window.

shading and blending   Altering the color of a paint slightly by the addition of black tinting color to create a decorative effect of graduated colors when applied to adjacent areas. The lap areas often are brushed and rolled to achieve a subtle blending.

shading coefficient   The total amount of solar energy that passes through a glass relative to a ⅛ inch (3 mm) thick clear glass under the same design conditions; includes both solar energy transmitted directly plus any absorbed solar energy subsequently re-radiated or convected into a room; lower values indicate better performance in reducing summer heat gain and therefore air-conditioning loads.

shaft   **1.** The portion of a column, colonette, or pilaster between the base and the capital. **2.** An enclosed space extending through one or more stories of a building, connecting vertical openings in successive floors, or floors and the roof.

shafted impost   In medieval architecture, an **impost** with horizontal moldings, the section of the moldings of the arch above the impost being different from that of the shaft below it.

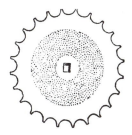

shaft   in Ionic column, section

shafted impost   A

shafting   In medieval architecture, an arrangement of shafts, wrought in the mass of a pier or jamb, so that corresponding groupings of archivolt moldings may start from their caps at the impost line.

shaft ring   See **annulet**.

shaft wall   The fire-rated wall that isolates an elevator and/or stairwell core in high-rise construction.

shake   A thick wood shingle, usually formed either by hand-splitting a short log into tapered radial sections or by sawing; usually attached in overlapping rows on wood **sheathing, 1** as a covering for a roof or wall.

Shaker architecture   Architecture of the "Shakers," a religious sect of English origin that founded its first community in America in 1776. Their structures were built of wood, stone, or bricks, which they made themselves. Their distinctive architecture is a combination of unadorned simplicity and functionality. Men and women lived in the same building in separate but equal facilities; symmetric in plan, with men on one side and women on the other. In some communities, even the hallways and stairways were separate. The large meeting rooms for religious services, usually in a separate building, had no internal partitions or posts so as to leave an unimpeded space for the fervent dancing that formed part of the religious ritual and from which the sect derived the name "Shaking Quakers" or "Shakers."

shale   Argillaceous sedimentary rock derived from clays or silts; typically thinly laminated and weak along planes; may be undesirable as a concrete aggregate.

shall   When used in a specification, the word *shall* is used with reference to the work required to be done by a contractor or supplier. It denotes the things the suppliers shall do, documents they shall supply, features they shall build into the equipment, or performance levels the equipment shall meet.

shallow-bearing foundation   A foundation that is placed directly beneath the lowest part of a building.

sham door   Same as **blind door**.

shank   **1.** One of the plain spaces between the channels of a triglyph in a Doric frieze. **2.** That part of a tool which connects the acting part with the handle. **3.** The body of a fastener, such as a nail or bolt, i.e., the portion between the head and the point.

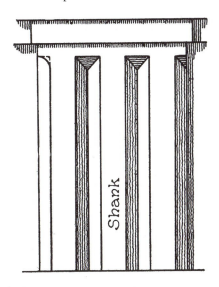

shank, 1

shanty   **1.** A hut, usually of wood; a small structure of rough character. **2.** A temporary building on a construction site used for storage or as a contractor's office.

shape   **1.** Any of a number of metal bars or beams of uniform section, as an I-beam. **2.** To cut a profile or detail, as a beaded or rounded edge on a board. **3.** To work a material to a required pattern, as on a shaper.

shaped brick   Any **brick** having a nonstandard size and/or shape.

shaped gable   A **gable, 2**, each side of which is multicurved.

shaped parapet   Any parapet whose edge does not follow a straight line; for example, one that is multicurved, as in a **mission parapet**.

shaped work   Curved carpentry or joinery.

shaper   **1.** In woodworking, a machine with a vertically revolving cutter; used for cutting irregular outlines, moldings, etc., in wood which is placed horizontally below the cutter. **2.** In metalwork, a type of machine tool; a planer in which the cutting tool moves back and forth across the work.

shaping machine   See **shaper**.

shark fin   In a roofing system, an upward-curled felt sidelap or endlap.

sharp coat   In painting, a coating of white lead in oil.

sharpening stone   Same as **whetstone**.

sharp flute   In a column, one of a series of **flutes** that are so close together that they form sharp arrises.

sharp paint   A rapidly drying paint for use as a seal coat.

sharp sand   Coarse sand whose particles are of angular shape.

shatterproof glass   See **laminated glass, bullet-resisting glass**.

shave hook   A scraping tool used to clean, shave, or cut lead pipe, prior to soldering.

shay house   Same as **coach house**.

shear   **1.** A deformation (e.g., in a beam or flexural member) in which parallel planes slide relative to each other so as to remain parallel. **2.** To cut a metal with a pair of moving blades or with one moving blade and one fixed edge. **3.** See **shears**.

shear center, center of twist, flexural center   Of any cross section of a beam, that point in the plane of the cross section through which a transverse load must be applied in order that there will be only bending of the section and no twisting.

shear connector   **1.** A connector (such as a welded stud, spiral bar, or short length of channel) which resists horizontal shear between elements of a **composite beam**. **2.** A **timber connector**, such as a **split-ring connector**.

sheared edge   An edge of a plate which has been cut in a **shearing machine**.

sheared plate   **1.** A plate which has been sheared from another larger plate. **2.** Any plate the edges of which are sheared.

shear failure, failure by rupture   Failure in which movement caused by shearing stresses in a soil mass is of sufficient magnitude to destroy or seriously endanger a structure.

shearhead   In the top of the columns of flat-plate or flat-slab construction, a unit which transmits loads from the slab to the column.

sheariness   In painted surfaces, the variations in gloss of **semigloss** or **eggshell gloss** finishes resulting from differences in film thickness.

shearing machine   A machine for cutting metal; usually consists of a movable blade which operates against a fixed cutting edge.

shearing strain   See **shear strain**.

shearing stress   See **shear stress**.

shear legs   A hoisting apparatus consisting of two or more poles, fastened together near the top, fitted with a pulley; used to lift heavy weights.

shear lug   A steel **embedment** (such as a bolt, plate, or welded stud) which is located transverse to the direction of the shear force and that transmits shear loads introduced into the concrete.

shear modulus   See **modulus of rigidity**.

shear plate   **1.** One of the reinforcement plates added to the web of a steel beam to increase the web capacity to resist shearing loads. **2.** A special round plate inserted in the face of a timber; used to develop shear resistance in a wood-to-metal or wood-to-wood joint; designed to provide greater load-carrying capacity in shear than can be achieved by a bolt alone.

shear plates, 2

shear-plate connector A **timber connec-tor** used in wood-to-wood or wood-to-steel assemblies.

shear reinforcement Reinforcement designed to resist shear stresses or diagonal tension stresses.

shears A cutting tool consisting of two pivoted blades with beveled edges facing each other.

shear splice A **splice** between two members designed to transmit shear between the two members across the splice.

shear strain, shearing strain A deformation in a structural member (measured in radians) resulting from the application of a force in a plane (or line) of a cross section of the member, perpendicular to the length of the beam.

shear strength The maximum **shear stress** which a material or soil is capable of sustaining.

shear stress, shearing stress The force per unit area of cross section which tends to pro-duce **shear**.

shear wall A wall which in its own plane car-ries **shear, 1** resulting from forces such as wind, blast, or earthquake.

sheath In reinforced concrete, an enclosure which encases posttensioned tendons to pre-vent their being bonded during the placement of concrete.

sheathed cable See **nonmetallic sheathed cable**.

sheathing, sheeting 1. The covering (usually wood boards, plywood, or wallboards) placed over exterior studding or rafters of a building; provides a base for the application of wall or roof cladding. Also see **sheeting**. 2. In colonial Amer-ica, boards on the interior of a house that served as an interior surface finish.

sheathing felt A saturated roofing felt.

sheathing paper See **building paper**.

sheave 1. Same as **pulley sheave**. 2. A grooved wheel or pulley used to assist in pulling cable; especially used in underground installations between manholes.

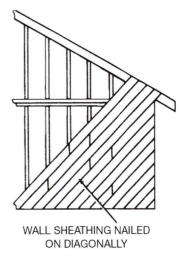
WALL SHEATHING NAILED
ON DIAGONALLY
diagonal wooden **sheathing**

sheave block An assembly consisting of a pul-ley wheel, side plates, shaft, and bearings over which a cable or rope is passed; a **pulley block**.

she bolt A type of tie and spreader bolt used with concrete forms; the end fastenings are threaded into the end of the bolt, thereby eliminating cones (which are otherwise used) and reducing the size of the holes left in the concrete surface.

shed A rough structure for shelter, storage, or a workshop. It may be a separate building or a lean-to against another structure; often with one or more open sides.

shed dormer A **dormer** window whose eave line is parallel to the eave line of the main roof instead of being gabled; provides more attic space than a gabled dormer.

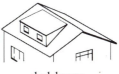
shed dormer

shed roof, pent roof A roof shape having only one sloping plane. (*See illustration p. 826.*)

Shed style In American domestic architecture of the latter half of the 20th century, an archi-tectural style characterized by its roof: usually two or more **shed roofs**, steeply sloped in differ-ent directions with no significant overhang; wall cladding that is vertical, horizontal, or sloped at

825

sheepsfoot roller

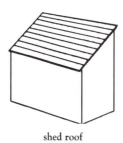

shed roof

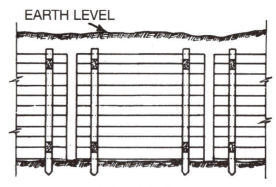

horizontal **sheeting**

an angle parallel to one of the major roof surfaces; a main doorway intentionally lacking in prominence.

sheepsfoot roller, tamping roller A self-propelled or towed drum-like roller with projecting studs that penetrate the surface of the ground; used to obtain deep compaction of fill material; esp. effective for compaction of clay soils.

sheepsfoot roller

sheer legs Same as **shear legs**.

sheet **1.** See **sheet metal**. **2.** A flat section of a thermoplastic resin, 10 mils or greater in thickness, having its length considerably greater than its width.

sheet asphalt Plant-mixed asphalt cement with graded sand which passes through a 2.00-mm (No. 10) sieve and mineral filler; its use ordinarily is confined to surface course construction and most frequently is laid on a binder course.

sheet glass Ordinary **window glass**.

sheeting, sheathing **1.** Members of wood, concrete, or steel (horizontal or vertical) used to hold up the face of an excavation. Also see **closed sheeting, open sheeting**. **2.** See **sheathing**. **3.** Boards which form the surface of concrete formwork. **4.** Same as **sheetpiling**. **5.** Any material in the form of sheets. **6.** A rock structure in which there are numerous small closely spaced fractures.

sheeting clip A metal clip esp. made for fastening various thicknesses of plasterboard, asbestos-cement board, plywood paneling, etc.

sheeting driver A type of pile driver with a hammer head designed to fit atop the shaped steel sections used as **sheet piling** or timber trench sheeting.

sheet lath A type of metal lath; fabricated by punching holes in sheet metal; heavier in gauge than expanded-metal lath.

sheet lead A cold-rolled sheet of lead, designated by the weight of 1 sq ft; e.g., a 2-lb sheet (which is $\frac{1}{32}$ in. thick) weighs 2 lb for an area of 1 sq ft.

sheet metal A flat, rolled metal product, rectangular in cross section and form, of thickness between 0.006 and 0.249 in. (0.015 and 6.32 cm), with sheared, slit, or sawn edges.

sheet-metal door See **hollow-metal door**.

sheet-metal lath See **metal lath**.

sheet-metal roofing A thin, rolled metal product used as roofing; usually flat or corrugated; also see **corrugated metal** and **zinc**.

sheet-metal screw, tapping screw A coarse-threaded, tapered screw with a slotted head for driving with a screwdriver; used for fastening sheet metal and other materials, without a tapped hole and without a nut.

sheet-metal screws

sheet-metal work Any work with sheet metal, such as the ducts in an air-conditioning system.

sheet pavement Road surfacing that is free of joints.

sheet pile One of a number of piles, interlocked or meshed with similar units, to form a barrier to retain soil or to keep water out of a foundation.

sheetpiling A barrier or diaphragm formed of **sheet piles**; used to prevent the movement of soil, to stabilize foundations, to construct cofferdams, to prevent the percolation of water, etc.

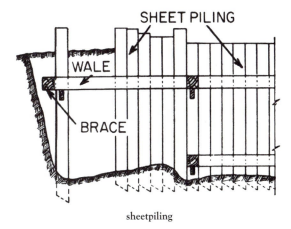

sheetpiling

Sheetrock A proprietary name for **gypsum board**.

sheet-roofing nail Same as **roofing nail**.

shelf 1. A flat surface mounted horizontally, used to support or store objects. 2. Any projecting, flat, near-horizontal surface, such as a ledge of rock.

shelf-angle An angle iron which is fixed to a girder to carry the ends of joists.

shelf bracket A structural member fastened to a wall or upright and projecting therefrom to support a shelf.

shelf cleat, shelf strip A strip of wood used to support a shelf along one edge.

shelf life The time period during which an adhesive, coating, sealant, or the like, can be stored (under specified conditions) and remain suitable for use.

shelf nog A piece of wood, built into a wall, which acts as a shelf support.

shelf pin See **shelf rest**.

shelf rest, shelf pin, shelf support A small angle bracket held in place by a pin (on the vertical side) which is inserted in one of a number of holes in a wall or cabinet so that its position can be adjusted; used in supporting a shelf.

shelf strip See **shelf cleat**.

shelf support See **shelf bracket, shelf rest**.

shell 1. A hollow structure in the form of a thin, curved slab or plate whose thickness is small compared with its other dimensions and with its radii of curvature. 2. Any framework or exterior structure which is regarded as not completed or filled in. 3. An ornament similar in design to a seashell.

shellac A resin extracted and purified from matter secreted by insects; dissolved in alcohol or a similar solvent in the manufacture of shellac varnish.

shell aggregate An aggregate composed of the crushed shells of oysters, clams, and the like; generally blended with other fine sands.

shell bit A type of **bit, 1** for boring holes in wood, shaped like a gouge.

shell construction Construction which uses thin curved concrete slabs.

shell-headed Said of a decoration, generally concave in shape, that is often similar in appearance to the shell of a sea scallop; often found at the **head** of a building component in Spanish architecture and its derivatives.

shell-headed cupboard A built-in cupboard, usually in one corner of a room, topped with a rounded arch containing a decorative element in the shape of a large seashell; common in the early 1700s.

shelling See **checking**.

shell lime Lime obtained by burning the shells of oysters, clams, or mussels; once used in making **lime mortar**, particularly where limestone was not available for this purpose.

shell shake See **ring shake**.

shelving 1. A series of shelves, as used in clothes closets, linen closets, kitchen cabinets, and other locations; often adjustable. 2. Boards used for making shelves.

sherardize To coat steel with a thin corrosion-resistant cladding of zinc.

SHGC Abbr. for **solar heat gain coefficient**.

shield A metallic layer that surrounds insulated conductors in a shielded cable; may be the metallic sheath of the cable or a metallic layer inside a nonmetallic sheath; especially effective in providing protection against electrostatic interference.

shielded conductor An electric conductor which is enclosed within a metallic sheath.

shielded joint A joint between electrical cables which has its insulation so enclosed by a conducting shield that every point on the surface of the insulation is, essentially, at ground potential.

shielded metal-arc welding Welding which utilizes the heat produced by an arc between a covered metal electrode and the work.

shift joint A vertical joint which is above a solid member of the course below.

shim A thin piece of wood, metal, or stone, usually tapered, which is inserted under one member so as to adjust its height; used in adjusting the height of one surface so that it is flush with another.

shim spacer A spacer which positions the face surface of a pane of glass between the stops and prevents glass contact with the stops.

shingle A roofing unit of wood, asphaltic material, slate, tile, concrete, asbestos cement, or other material cut to stock lengths, widths, and thickness; used as an exterior covering on sloping roofs and side walls; applied in an overlapping fashion; usually in one of the following designs: **chisel pattern, coursed pattern, diamond pattern, fishscale pattern, sawtooth pattern**. Also see **wood shingle** and **pine shingle**.

shingle backer In roofing, an underlayment applied over the roof sheathing before the shingles are laid.

shingle lap A type of **lap joint** in which the two surfaces are tapered; the thinner surface is lapped over the thicker.

shingle nail A nail for attaching shingles to a roof; usually galvanized.

shingle nail

shingle ridge finish See **Boston hip**.

shingle stain A low-viscosity, pigmented, penetrating paint for use on wood shingles to provide color and protection against moisture penetration.

Shingle style An American eclectic style of domestic architecture especially used from about 1880 to 1900; the Old English style, in using tiles rather than wood shingles, can be considered a prototype. Houses in this style are usually rambling and often asymmetrical in plan, with the exterior walls covered with unpainted wood shingles that emphasize the shingled surface and the horizontal aspects of the house; large porches set within the main structure or forming part of it; multilevel eaves with little overhang; occasionally, a tower having a conical or bell-shaped roof, usually topped with a finial; occasionally an **eyebrow dormer**; prominent arches at entryways. This style used in the latter part of the 20th century is sometimes referred to as the "New Shingle style."

Shingle style

shingle tile A flat clay tile used for roofing; applied in an overlapping pattern.

shinglewood Same as **thuya**.

shingling hatchet, claw hatchet A carpenter's tool used in shingling a roof, etc.; a small hatchet combined with a hammer and nail claw.

ship-and-galley tile A special quarry tile having an indented pattern on its face to produce an antislip effect.

shiplap, shiplap boards, shiplap siding Wood sheathing whose edges are rabbeted to make an overlapping joint.

shipper A hard-burnt brick that is sound but of inferior shape.

ship's bottom roof A pitched **gable roof** whose slope on each side of a peaked ridge is slightly bowed, rather than constant.

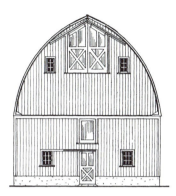

ship's bottom roof

ship scaffold Same as **float scaffold**.

ship spike Same as **barge spike**.

shivering The splintering that occurs in a fired glass or ceramic coating owing to critical compressive stresses.

shock hazard According to OSHA: considered to exist at an accessible part in a circuit between the part and ground, or other accessible parts if the potential is more than 42.4 volts peak and the current through a 1,500-ohm load is more than 5 milliamperes.

shock load During the placement of concrete, the load imposed by the impact of material such as aggregate or concrete as it is dumped or released.

shock mount Same as **vibration isolator**.

shoe **1.** A piece of timber, stone, or metal, shaped to receive the lower end of any member; also called a **soleplate**. **2.** A metal base plate for an arch or truss which resists lateral thrust. **3.** A **base shoe molding**. **4.** A subrail. **5.** A metal protective device for the point or foot of a pile.

shoe molding See **base shoe, carpet strip**.

shoe rail The molding on top of a stair stringer on which the balusters rest.

shōji A very lightweight sliding partition used in Japanese architecture; consists of a wooden lattice covered on one side with translucent white rice paper. The lattice is most often composed of small rectangles; the lower section is occasionally filled by a thin wooden panel.

shōji

shoot To straighten the edge of a board with a plane.

shooting The placement of **shotcrete**.

shooting board A device for holding a board while it is being planed or its edge is being squared.

shooting plane In carpentry, a light side plane for squaring or beveling the edge of a board; used with a **shooting board**.

shop coat A coat of paint applied to a building component in the shop before it is sent to a job site; the finish coat is applied in the field.

shop drawings Drawings, diagrams, illustrations, schedules, performance charts, brochures, and other data prepared by the contractor or any subcontractor, manufacturer, supplier, or distributor, which illustrate how specific portions of the **work, 1** shall be fabricated and/or installed.

shop front See **storefront**.

shop lumber, factory lumber Lumber which is graded according to the number of pieces, of specified size and quality, into which it may be cut.

shop painting The painting of structural steel or other metals in a shop before final installation in the construction.

shopping center A concentration of stores, markets, and service establishments, along with parking facilities; often in a suburban location.

shopping mall A **shopping center** enclosed within a large structure; often two or three stories high, often designed around a central atrium; may have numerous stores, as well as entertainment facilities such as movie theaters, fast-food outlets, restaurants, and public areas.

shop rivet   A rivet driven in the shop.

shopwork   Work done in a factory or shop in contrast to work done on the construction site.

shore   A piece of timber to support a wall, usually set in a diagonal or oblique position, to hold the wall in place temporarily.

Shore hardness number   A numerical scale for rating the hardness of a material by means of a device consisting of a small conical hammer fitted with a diamond point; the hammer strikes the material under test, and then the height of rebound (which is a measure of the hardness) is noted on a graduated scale; the higher the number, the harder the material.

shore up   To hold or support by means of **shores**.

shoring   A number of **shores** acting collectively.

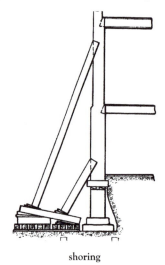

shoring

shoring layout   A pre-erection drawing which shows the arrangement of equipment for **shoring**.

short   **1.** Said of a piece of building material not up to specified length. **2.** A **short circuit**.

short brace   A **brace, 3** having a small handle for working in confined places.

short circuit   In an electric circuit, an abnormal connection, having relatively low resistance, between two points of different potential; causes an abnormally high current flow through the connection.

short column   A column whose load capacity need not be reduced because of its slenderness.

short-grained   See **brashy**.

short-length   **1.** A length of stock lumber usually less than 8 ft (244 cm) long. **2.** (*Brit.*) A length of sawn hardwood, usually less than 6 ft (183 cm) long.

short nipple   A pipe **nipple** which is slightly longer than a close nipple, having a small unthreaded portion between the pipe threads.

short-oil alkyd   An alkyd resin containing less than 40% oil in the solids.

short-oil varnish   A varnish containing little oil in comparison with the amount of resin present, less than 15 gal oil per 100 lb (1.5 liters oil per kg) resin.

short varnish   Same as **short-oil varnish**.

short working plaster   Old plaster (in the plastic state) that will not carry the proper ratio of aggregate; behaves like a lean, oversanded plaster.

shotblasting   A process similar to sandblasting except that hardened, cast-metal shot is used instead of sand.

shotcrete   Concrete or mortar which is pumped through a hose and projected at high velocity onto a surface.

shotcrete gun   **1.** A pneumatic device to deliver shotcrete under pressure. **2.** A pneumatic device to propel freshly mixed concrete.

shotgun house   Built primarily in the rural southern regions of the United States from the late 1800s to the early 1900s, a one- or one-and-a-half-story house (commonly supported on short piers), one room wide and several rooms deep, with all rooms and their doors in a straight line perpendicular to the street; a narrow gable front with a porch, and often with a similar porch at the rear.

shot hole   A **wormhole** in wood, usually more than ¹⁄₁₆ in. (1.6 mm) but not more than ⅛ in. (3.2 mm) in diameter.

shot-sawn finish   In stonecutting, the randomly scored surface resulting from chilled steel shot carried by the gang saw blades. Also see **chat-sawn finish**.

shot tower   A very high structure, usually cylindrical and constructed of brick, once used in making lead shot for muskets. At the top of the tower, a molten alloy of lead was poured through a coarse metal screen, forming small lead globules that solidified; these pellets became spherical as they dropped, finally falling into a container of water at the base of the tower.

shoulder **1.** A projection or break made on a piece of shaped wood, metal, or stone, where its width or thickness is suddenly changed. Also called **ear, elbow. 2.** The surface bordering a road, esp. where a vehicle can be parked in emergency. **3.** The angle of a bastion included between the face and the flank of a fortification. Also called **shoulder angle.**

shoulder angle See **shoulder, 3.**

shouldered arch A square-headed **trefoil arch.**

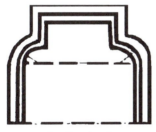

shouldered arch

shouldered housed joint A type of **housed joint**; the full thickness of the edge (or the end) of one member is inserted in the housing of another.

shouldered post Same as **musket-stock post.**

shouldering The raising of the edge of a slate with mortar so that at the lower edge it may make a closer joint with the slate which it overlaps and provide a watertight joint.

shoulder nipple **1.** A nipple, longer than a **close nipple**, with a small unthreaded space between the threads at the end. **2.** A **nipple** threaded only at its two ends, not over the entire length.

shoulder nipple

shoulder piece Same as **crossette, 2**; a bracket.

shoved joint In brickwork, a vertical joint which is filled with mortar by laying a brick in a bed of mortar and shoving it toward the last brick laid.

shovel See **power shovel.**

shovel dozer Same as **dozer shovel.**

shower bath, shower An apparatus for spraying water on the body, usually from above.

shower-bath drain The floor drain in a shower-bath compartment, stall, or enclosure.

shower head In a shower bath, a device (usually a nozzle having many fine openings) through which water is sprayed.

shower heads

shower mixer A plumbing valve for mixing hot and cold water in a shower bath to obtain the desired temperature.

shower pan In a shower compartment or stall, a metal pan with sides above the finish floor level, in which the floor drain is located.

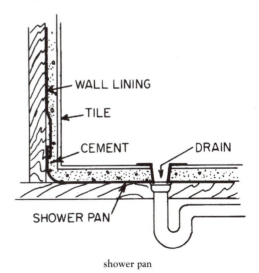

shower pan

shower partition A prefabricated panel, door, or screen, used in a shower to provide visual privacy.

shower stall door A glazed door, with or without a transom, for an individual site-built shower.

show rafter A rafter exposed below a cornice; often ornamental.

showroom A room used for displaying merchandise, goods, and the like.

show-through See **telegraphing**.

show window Any window used, or designed for use, for the display of goods or advertising material, whether it is fully or partly enclosed or entirely open at the rear; it may have a platform raised above street level.

shreadhead Same as **jerkinhead**.

shredding A short, light piece of timber, fixed as a bearer below the roof, forming a straight line with the upper side of the rafters.

shrine A receptacle to contain sacred relics; by extension, a building for that purpose.

shrine chapel A small enclosed structure containing the tomb of a sainted person.

shrinkage **1.** The reduction in dimensions of a piece of wood during drying; reduction is very slight along the grain, but a reduction of 5 to 6% in width is common for dry flat-sawn boards. **2.** The volume decrease of concrete caused by drying and chemical changes. **3.** The proportionate decrease in dimensions or volume of a material, usually as a result of a change in temperature.

shrinkage-compensating A characteristic of grout, mortar, or concrete made with an **expansive cement** in which volume increase, if restrained, induces compressive stresses which are intended to approximately offset the tendency of drying shrinkage to induce tensile stresses.

shrinkage crack A crack due to restraint of shrinkage.

shrinkage cracking Cracking of a concrete structure or member owing to failure in tension caused by external or internal restraints as reduction in moisture content develops, or as carbonation in the concrete occurs, or both.

shrinkage joint A **contraction joint**.

shrinkage limit Of a soil, that water content at which a reduction in water content will not cause a decrease in the volume of the soil mass, but an increase in water content will cause an increase in the volume of soil mass.

shrinkage loss The loss of prestress in concrete as a result of the shrinkage of the concrete.

shrinkage reinforcement In reinforced concrete, steel reinforcement which is designed to resist shrinkage stresses.

shrink-mixed concrete A concrete which is partially mixed in a stationary mixer and then given its final mix in a truck mixer.

shriving pew Same as **confessional**.

shroud A place under ground, as a crypt of a church.

shrub A woody plant with stems branching from or near the ground and, in general, smaller than a tree; a bush.

shrunk joint A joint made between the ends of two pipes (which are cool) by shrinking a heated piece over the two ends.

shuff Same as **chuff**.

shute wire In **wire cloth**, a wire running directly across the width of the cloth.

shuting Same as **eaves gutter**.

shutter A movable panel, often one of a pair used to cover an opening, especially a window opening; provides privacy and some thermal insulation when closed; also see **battened shutter, boxing shutter, folding shutter**.

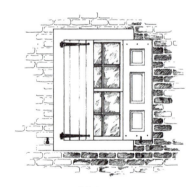

solid **shutters**

shutter bar A hinged bar that can be fastened across the interior side of a pair of shutters. When the shutters are in the closed position, completely covering the window, the shutter bar prevents their being opened, adding a measure of security.

shutter blind An outside adjustable louver used as a window blind.

shutter bar

shutter box A pocket or recess located along the interior side of a window to receive **shutters** when folded.

shutter butt A small (usually narrow) hinge, esp. used on shutters and light doors.

shutter dog Same as **shutter fastener**.

shutter fastener A pivoted device used to hold a shutter in the open position on the exterior side of a window; also called a shutter catch, shutter dog, or shutter holdback.

shutter fastener

shutter hinge See **H-hinge**.

shuttering Same as **formwork**.

shutter lift A handle fixed to a shutter for convenience in opening or closing it.

shutter operator, shutter worker A device incorporating a crank for opening or closing a shutter from inside without opening the window.

shutter worker A **shutter operator**.

shutting post The post at the side of a gate against which it shuts.

shutting shoe A device of iron or stone with a shoulder, sunk in the middle of a gateway, against which the gate is shut and secured.

shutting stile Same as **lock stile**.

siamese connection A wye connection, installed close to the ground on the exterior side of the wall of a building, providing two inlet

connections for fire hoses to the standpipes and fire-protection sprinkler system of the building.

siamese connection

SIC Abbr. for "Standard Industrial Classification."

sick house A **hospital** or **infirmary**.

SIDD See **standard inside diameter dimension ratio**.

side bearer A structural member that runs horizontally along a side wall of a house and supports a load.

side board, side cut Lumber which has been sawn from a log in such a way as to exclude the **heartwood**.

side chapel A chapel to the side of the choir.

side-construction tile Tile designed to receive its principal stress at right angles to the axes of the cells; set in place with the axes of the cells running horizontally.

side cut 1. Same as **cheek cut**. 2. See **side board**.

side-dump loader A type of **loader** having a bucket mounted on its front, with a pivot so that it can be tilted (usually by a hydraulic system); the bucket can be dumped either to the side or forward.

side flights See **double return stair**.

side gable A gable whose face is on one side (or part of one side) of a house, perpendicular to the façade.

side girt A **girt** between corner posts on the long side of a timber-framed house. See illustration under **timber-framed house**.

side grain A surface which is approximately parallel to the grain.

side gutter A small gutter on a sloped roof, located at its intersection with a dormer or chimney or other vertical surface.

side-hall plan, side passage plan A **floor plan** of a house having a corridor that runs from the front to the back of the house along one exterior wall; all rooms are located on the same side of the corridor.

side-hill barn   A term occasionally used for a **bank barn**.

side hinge   Same as **H-hinge**.

side hook   Same as **bench hook**.

side-hung window   Same as **casement window**.

side jamb   The vertical member forming the side of a door opening.

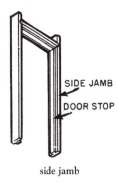

side jamb

side knob screw   A **setscrew** used to fasten a doorknob to a spindle.

side lap   The amount by which one material (or tile, shingle, etc.) overlaps the adjacent one along its side or edge.

sidelight   A framed area of glass that does not open, typically composed of a number of small fixed panes; commonly one of a pair of such lights, set vertically on each side of a door.

sidelights   with fanlight above door

side line   The boundaries of a strip of land, such as a street or right-of-way; does not apply to the ends of the strip.

side outlet   In plumbing, a pipe **fitting, 1**, either an ell or a tee, having an outlet at right angles to the plane of the run.

side post   One of a pair of truss posts, each set at the same distance from the middle of the truss, as a support to the principal rafters and to suspend the tie beams below.

side set   The difference in thickness between the two edges of metal sheet or plate.

sidesway   The lateral movement of a structure under the action of lateral loads or unsymmetrical vertical loads.

side timber   A roof **purlin** that supports common rafters.

side vent   A **vent** connecting to the drain pipe through a fitting at an angle not greater than 45° to the vertical.

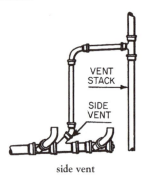

side vent

sidewalk   A paved footwalk at the side of a street or roadway.

sidewalk door   A cellar door which opens directly on a sidewalk; when closed, it is flush with the sidewalk.

sidewalk elevator   A **freight elevator** having a movable platform that operates between a sidewalk outside a building and a different level on a floor within the building.

sidewalk shed   A construction over a public sidewalk used to protect pedestrians from falling objects during the erection or repair of a building.

sidewalk vault   A space below a sidewalk directly adjacent to a building, often covered with a **hatch** that can be lifted to allow access to the basement of the building via steps down; often used for storage.

sidewall sprinkler   In a fire protection system, a **sprinkler** providing a one-sided (parabolic) water distribution outward from a wall.

side yard The yard between the side line of a building and the adjacent property line, extending from the front property line to the rear property line.

siding A finish covering on the exterior walls of a building in the form of a series of horizontal strips or boards; made of such **cladding** materials as wood or aluminum. The strips are usually applied horizontally with an overlap to provide resistance against the penetration of water. Also see **bevel siding, bungalow siding, clapboard, colonial siding, drop siding, flush siding, German siding, lap siding, matched siding, novelty siding, rabbeted siding, rustic siding, shingles, shiplap siding, vertical siding, weather slating**.

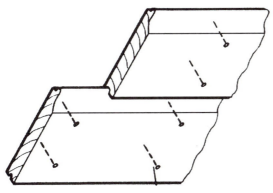

drop **siding**

siding gauge See **clapboard gauge**.

siding shingle A shingle of any of a number of materials such as wood, cement-asbestos, etc., used as a protective exterior wall covering over sheathing.

siege Same as **banker**.

siel Old English for **canopy**.

sienna A naturally occurring pigment, chiefly oxides of iron; yellow-brown when mined. When calcined, a dark, rich color; then called **burnt sienna**.

sieve See **screen, 3**.

sieve analysis, screen analysis A determination of the proportions of particles lying within certain size ranges in a granular material by separation on sieves of different-size openings.

sieve number A number used to designate the size of a sieve, usually the approximate number of sieve cross wires per linear inch.

sight glass A glass tube used to indicate the liquid level in a pipe, tank, or the like.

sighting rod Same as **sight rod**.

sight line **1.** In an auditorium, an imaginary, uninterrupted straight line drawn between the eye of a spectator and the stage area; if such a line is impeded by a column, the overhang of a balcony, etc., vision is restricted. **2.** The line of intersection of a transparent material with an opaque material.

sight rail One of a series of horizontal rails, usually boards supported at both ends, which are used to check the gradient of a pipe in a trench; the rails are adjusted by sighting a line having the desired gradient; the rails then establish a line from which the bottom of the trench can be measured.

sight rod **1.** See **leveling rod**. **2.** See **range rod**.

sight size, sight width See **daylight width**.

sigma A semicircular **portico**.

sign, signboard **1.** A display board or surface used for directions, identification, instructions, or advertising; usually consists of lettering, pictures, diagrams, decoration, etc., often in combination, on a contrasting background surface. **2.** According to OSHA: a warning of hazard, temporarily or permanently affixed or placed, at a location where a hazard exists.

signage Symbols or words whose function it is to provide directions, identification, information, orientation, warnings, regulations, or restrictions.

signal light, signal lamp Same as **pilot light, 1**.

signal sash fastener A fastening device for a sash; used to lock a double-hung window which is beyond reach of the floor; the fastener (which is operated by a long pole) has a ring on a lever which is in the "up" position when the window is unlocked.

signature stone A stone, found on many 18th- and 19th-century dwellings, carved with date of completion and the name or initials of

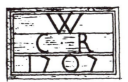

signature stone

the owner; often embedded in the wall over the entry door or in a gable.

significant architectural feature Any distinctive aspect of a building's exterior that defines its architectural character, for example, the color and texture of the building material or the style and size of its doors and windows.

significant landscape improvement In a historic district, any landscape improvement that is character defining and contributes to the special aesthetic and historic character of the designated district.

signinum opus See **opus signinum**.

sikhara, sikra Pyramidal or curvilinear tower-like upper structure of a Hindu temple.

silencer See **rubber silencer**.

silex 1. Flint or flintstone. 2. By extension, any kind of hard stone cut into polygonal blocks.

silica, silicon dioxide A white or colorless substance, nearly insoluble in water and in all acids except hydrofluoric; extremely hard; fuses to a colorless amorphous glass.

silica brick A refractory brick made from quartzite containing about 96% silica, 2% alumina, and 2% lime.

silica gel, synthetic silica A form of silica which adsorbs moisture readily; used as a drying agent.

silicate An insoluble metal salt; occurs in concrete, cement, brick, glass, clay, and many other materials.

silicate paint A paint in which sodium silicate is the binding agent.

silicious aggregate concrete A concrete produced with aggregates of normal weight that are primarily composed of silicates of silica.

silicon A metallic element, used in pure form in rectifier units; combined with oxygen, it forms **silicon dioxide**.

silicon bronze A copper alloy having silicon as the main alloying element; zinc, manganese, aluminum, iron, or nickel may be added; **high-silicon bronze** contains 96% copper and 3% silicon; **low-silicon bronze** contains 97.7% copper and 1.5% silicon.

silicon dioxide See **silica**.

silicone One of the family of polymeric materials in which the recurring chemical group contains silicon and oxygen atoms as links in the main chain; derived from silica and methyl chloride; characterized by resistance to heat and a low coefficient of thermal expansion.

silicone-carbide paper A very tough, waterproof sandpaper, shiny black in color; esp. used in wet sanding and for fine work.

silicone oil A liquid form of silicone; esp. used for lubrication at high temperatures where petroleum oil is not effective, also as a water repellent.

silicone paint Paint that is resistant to very high temperatures and therefore useful on smokestacks, heaters, stoves, and electrical insulation; requires heat to cure or set; has a high resistance to chemical attack.

silicone resin One of a class of silicones containing polymers; has excellent heat resistance, high water repellency, and chemical resistance; usually cured by heat.

silicone rubber A synthetic, remarkably stable, rubber; useful over a very wide temperature range: −65 to +350°F (−54 to 177°C).

silicon rectifier A solid-state rectifier (i.e., a device for converting alternating current into direct current) utilizing silicon wafers; especially used to control the current supplying motors, lighting circuits, etc.

silking Fine parallel lines in a paint film which follow the direction of flow or drainage of paint from the work.

sill 1. A horizontal timber, at the bottom of the frame of a wood structure, which rests on the foundation. 2. A **doorsill**. 3. The horizontal

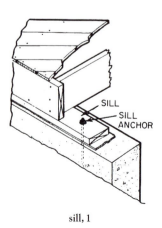

sill, 1

bottom member of a window frame or other frame.

sill anchor, plate anchor An **anchor bolt** used to fasten a **sill** to its foundation.

sill bead **1.** A **draft bead**. **2.** A **glazing bead** at a windowsill.

sill block A solid concrete masonry unit used for sills of openings.

sill cock An exterior water faucet, usually threaded to provide a connection for a hose; often located on the side of a building at the height of a sill.

sill cock

sill course In stone masonry, a **stringcourse** set at windowsill level; commonly differentiated from the wall by its greater projection, its finish, or its thickness.

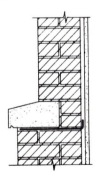

sill course

sill drip molding See **subsill, 1**.

sill high **1.** At the height of a sill above the floor. **2.** At the height of a sill above ground level.

sill plate **1.** A heavy horizontal timber at the bottom of the frame of a wood structure; the timber rests directly on a foundation; same as **sill, 1**. **2.** Same as **groundsill**.

silo **1.** A tall, enclosed structure used primarily to store grain, fodder, or chopped green plants (*silage*), or the like; commonly constructed of wood, masonry, or concrete; usually cylindrical in shape because this shape provides the tightest packing of silage and, therefore, results in the least spoilage. **2.** A sunken military structure used to shelter missiles.

silt, inorganic silt, rock flour A granular material that is nonplastic or very slightly plastic and exhibits little or no strength when air-dried; usually has a grain size between 0.002 mm and 0.05 mm in diameter.

silt grade Said of fine-grained sediment having particle sizes in the range of that for silt.

silvered-bowl lamp An incandescent filament lamp that has a hemispherical silvered reflecting coating opposite the lamp base.

silver grain The grain of quartersawn wood showing conspicuous shiny flecks or figures; particularly noticeable in oak, beech, bird's-eye maple, and sycamore.

silver-lock bond **1.** A brickwork pattern similar to English bond except that each stretcher is a **bull stretcher**. **2.** Same as **rat-trap bond**.

silver solder Any high-melting-point **solder** containing silver, usually used for soldered joints where high strength is required.

silver white **1.** Any white pigment used in paints. **2.** A very pure variety of white lead; **French white, China white**.

SIM On drawings, abbr. for "similar."

sima Same as **cyma**.

simple beam A structural beam having its ends free and resting only on supports at each end.

simple cornice A cornice consisting of only a frieze and molding.

simple vault A vault which has a smooth, continuous intrados; has no cross arches or ribs.

simplex casement A simple out-swinging **casement** window; has no mechanical device for opening and closing.

simulated masonry See **artificial stone**.

sine wave A wave form containing only one frequency; the amplitude of the periodic oscillation is a sinusoidal function of time. Also see **pure tone**.

singing gallery A gallery for singing, usually in churches of the Italian Renaissance, richly decorated with carving; a rood loft.

single-acting door, single-swing door A door provided with hinges or pivots which permit it to swing 90° in one direction only.

single-acting pump A reciprocal pump in which the reciprocating motion of a piston does work in one direction only.

single-bag compactor, single-bag packer A semiautomatic **refuse compactor** in which the refuse is crushed against a front-opening door into a specified volume.

single bridging **Bridging** between adjacent floor joists; diagonal braces are placed at the midpoint of the joists.

single-cleat ladder A ladder which consists of a pair of side rails, usually parallel, connected together with cleats that are joined to the side rails at regular intervals; also see **double-cleat ladder**.

single contract A contract for construction of a project under which a single **prime contractor** is responsible for all of the **work, 1**.

single-crib barn See **crib barn**.

single-cut file A file having serrations in one direction only.

single-duct system An air-conditioning system in which one duct conveys air, at a given condition, for a number of different spaces.

single Flemish bond In brickwork, a bond utilizing **Flemish bond** for the facework and **English bond** for the body.

single floor A floor consisting only of joists and flooring; the joists span the distance between the walls without intermediate support.

single-framed roof A roof framing system having rafters which are tied together by horizontal boards or the upper floor frame.

single house A house having a long plan that is only one room wide, with the narrow end of the house facing the street; the entrance from the street is up a short flight of stairs to the long open porch (sometimes called a *piazza*) that extends along one side of the house and provides entry into the individual rooms; for example, see **Charleston house**.

single-hub pipe A pipe having a **bell, 1** at one end and a spigot at the other.

single-hub pipe

single-hung window A window having two sashes, only one of which (usually the lower one) is movable.

single ladder A portable ladder, consisting of but one section, which is not self-supporting and not adjustable in length.

single-lap tile A curved roofing tile which overlaps only the tile in the course immediately below it.

single-line diagram Same as **one-line diagram**.

single measure Said of an object, such as a door, which is molded on one side only.

single notch Same as **half-cut notch**.

single-package refrigeration system A complete factory-made and factory-tested refrigeration system in a suitable frame or enclosure which is fabricated and shipped in one or more sections and in which no refrigerant-containing parts are connected in the field.

single-pen cabin A relatively crude one-story cabin, cottage, hut, or house having only one room.

single-pile house A house that is only one room deep; see **pile**.

single-pitched roof A roof having only a single slope on each side of a central ridge; for example, a gable roof. Compare with **shed roof**, which has a single slope but no central ridge.

single-point adjustable suspension scaffold A manually or power-operated platform designed for light-duty usage, hung by a single wire rope from an overhead support so arranged and operated as to permit the raising or lowering of the platform to the desired working position by the use of hoisting machines.

single-pole scaffold A scaffold consisting of a platform resting on putlogs or cross beams, the outside ends of which are supported on ledgers secured to a single row of posts or uprights, and the inner ends of which are supported on or in a wall.

single-pole switch In an electric circuit, a **switch** which has one movable contact and one fixed contact.

single-rabbet frame A frame having only one recess to receive a door.

single riveting A single row of **rivets**.

single-rabbet frame,   section

single-roller catch   A type of **catch** for a door; a roller, which is mounted on the door, engages a strike plate on the jamb, thereby holding the door in a closed position.

single roof   A roof supported only by **common rafters**; principals, purlins, and roof trusses are not used.

single-room plan   Same as **one-room plan**.

single-saddle notch   A synonym for **saddle notch**.

single-sized aggregate   An aggregate in which the largest portion of the particles or fragments are of sizes lying between narrow limits.

single spread   The application of adhesive to a single surface of a joint.

single-stage curing   An autoclave curing process in which the precast concrete products remain on metal pallets until stacked for delivery or yard storage.

single-suction pump   A pump having a spiral-shaped case in which water enters the impeller from only one side.

single swing frame   A frame prepared to receive one swing door.

single-throw switch   A **switch**, in an electric circuit, which can be opened or closed by the operation of a single set of contacts.

single-web girder   A built-up flanged girder whose flanges are connected by a single vertical web.

sink   A plumbing fixture usually consisting of a basin with a water supply, connected with a drain.

sinkage   See **recess**.

sink bib   A **bibcock** which supplies a sink with water.

sinker nail   A slender nail having a flat head (smaller in diameter than that of a common nail) which has a slight depression in it.

sinking   **1.** A groove or **recess**. **2.** In wood construction, the removal of some material to permit flush installation of hinges or the like.

sinking curtain   A theatre curtain which can be rolled up below the stage floor or lowered through an opening in the stage floor.

sinking in   In painting, the penetration of the paint binder into a porous substrate, causing a low gloss in the finish coat.

sink trap   Same as **trap, 1**.

sinter   To form a material from fusible powder by holding the pressed powder at a temperature just below its melting point for a period of time; the particles are fused (sintered) together, but the mass, as a whole, does not melt.

sintered fuel ash, pulverized fuel ash   Coal ash particles which have been processed so that they adhere to each other, forming pellets suitable for lightweight aggregate.

siphonage   The withdrawal of liquid, as from a **trap, 1**, resulting from suction caused by liquid flow.

siphon breaker   A **backflow preventer**.

siphon trap   In plumbing, a **trap, 1** shaped like the letter S on its side, in a vertical plane; the lower bend contains the water seal.

S-iron   An exposed retaining plate at each end of a turnbuckled tie rod between two masonry walls, to prevent them from spreading.

sisal   An organic fiber from the leaves of the sisal plant; used in making rope and cordage; sometimes mixed with plaster.

sissing   See **cissing**.

site   **1.** An area or plot of ground with defined limits on which a building, project, park, etc., is located or proposed to be located. **2.** The specific location of a building or buildings.

site drainage   **1.** A piping network installed below grade which conveys rainwater (or other wastes) to a point of disposal, such as a public sewer. **2.** The water that is drained off.

site-foamed insulation   Thermal insulation which is foamed in place at the building site.

site furnishings   Furnishings such as benches, chairs, tables, kiosks, shelters, playground equipment, and planters for outdoor use.

site investigation   An examination, investigation, and testing of the subsoil and surface of a site to obtain complete information necessary for the design of foundations and the structures on them.

site marker   See **marker**.

site plan   A **plan** of a construction site showing the position and dimensions of the building to be erected and the dimensions and contours of the lot.

sitework Exterior work on a building under construction, such as earthwork, landscaping, paving, and utility services.

Sitka spruce A soft, light, strong, close-grained wood of the West Coast of the U.S.A.; unusually free of knots; esp. used in millwork.

sitting room Same as **parlor, 1**.

sitzbath A bathtub in which one bathes in a sitting position; used esp. in hospitals or in therapeutic treatment.

SI units See **International System of Units**.

six-over-six A term descriptive of a double-hung window having six panes in the upper sash and six panes in the lower sash; see **pane**.

six-over-six window

size **1.** Same as **sizing**. **2.** To work a material to specified dimensions.

sized slate One of many shingle slates of uniform or modular size.

size of pipe (or tubing) Unless otherwise stated, the nominal size by which the pipe (or tubing) is commercially designated; actual dimensions are given in applicable specifications.

size stick See **scantle**.

sizing, size A liquid which is applied over wood, plaster, or other porous surface to fill the pores; reduces the absorption of a subsequently applied adhesive or coating; used to prepare the surface for finishing or to serve as a base for subsequent coatings.

SJI Abbr. for "Steel Joist Institute."

SK On drawings, abbr. for "sketch."

skaters' cracks In a roofing membrane, curvilinear cracks neither related to the direction of application of the membrane components nor to the substrate components.

skeen arch A **diminished arch**.

skeleton construction A type of construction, usually for high buildings, in which the loads and stresses are transmitted to the foundations by a steel framework of beams and columns; the walls are supported by the framework.

skeleton core The framework within a hollow-core door, hidden by the surface panels.

skeleton flashing Same as **stepped flashing**.

skeleton frame Any framework without its covering or panels.

skeleton-frame construction A type of steel construction, usually for buildings of considerable height, in which the loads and stresses are transmitted to the building foundation by a framework of steel columns and beams that support the walls; see **steel-frame construction** and **skyscraper**.

skeleton sheeting, skeleton timbering Same as **open sheeting**.

skeleton steps In a stair, steps which have no risers; the treads are supported on the sides.

skene The Greek term for **scaena** (Latin).

skene arch A **diminished arch**.

skenotheke In the **skene** of an ancient Greek theatre, a storeroom for the properties.

skew A **kneeler, 1**.

skew arch An arch whose vertical sides are not at an angle of 90 degrees to its face.

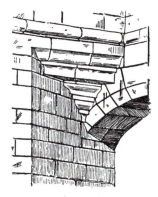

skew arch

skewback **1.** The sloping surface of an abutment which receives the thrust of an arch. **2.** The stone, or course of stones, or steel plate, providing such a sloping surface.

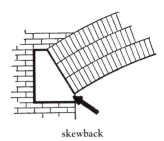

skewback

skew block See **gable springer**.

skew butt See **gable springer**.

skew chisel **1.** A woodworking chisel having the edge oblique and a bezel on each side. **2.** A chisel used in wood carving which has a bent shank to allow the edge to reach a sunken surface.

skew corbel A stone built into the bottom of a gable to form an abutment for a coping, eaves gutter, or cornice atop a masonry wall.

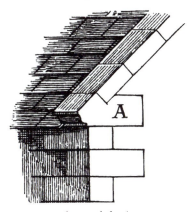

skew corbel   A

skewed Having an oblique position, or twisted to one side.

skewed connection A connection between two members which are not perpendicular to each other.

skew fillet A fillet nailed on a roof along the gable coping to raise the slates there and divert the water from the joining.

skew flashing Flashing located between a gable coping and the roof below it.

skew hinge Same as **rising hinge**.

skew nailing See **toe nailing**.

skew plane In woodworking a plane in which the mouth and edge of the iron are obliquely across the face.

skew putt Same as **skew corbel**.

skew table A variety of **kneeler**, cut integrally with the lowest section of a gable coping; serves as a lower stop for sloping sections of coping above.

skid row, skid road In the United States, an area in a community characterized by cheap barrooms, saloons, and run-down hotels; usually a gathering place for derelicts, vagrants, and down-and-out alcoholics.

skiffling Same as **knobbing**.

skim coat, skimming coat A thin coat of plaster; either the **finish coat** or a **leveling coat**.

skin A non-load-bearing exterior wall; often composed of prefabricated panels; also see **curtain wall**.

skin drying, surface drying The rapid drying of the surface of a paint film while the paint between it and the substrate remains wet.

skin friction The frictional resistance developed between soil and a structure or between soil and a pile being driven in it.

skinned bolt A bolt from which the threads have been stripped.

skinning The growth of a dry film on the surface of paint in a container; caused by oxidation of the drying oils in the paint binder.

skintled brickwork Brickwork which has been laid so as to form a wall with an irregular face.

skintled joint Same as **excess joint**.

skip **1.** An area in planed or sanded lumber or panels which was missed by the machine during the surfacing operation; also called **planing skip, sanding skip**. **2.** An uncoated area in a finished painted surface; also called a **holiday**.

skirt, skirting **1.** Same as **baseboard**. **2.** An apron, 6.

skirting block, base block, plinth block **1.** A corner block where a base strip and vertical enframement meet. **2.** A concealed block to which a baseboard is anchored.

skirting board See **baseboard**.

skirt-roof A small eavelike projection from the façade of a house between the first and second stories, usually encircling the house; provides some shelter for the windows and doors directly below it, but is primarily decorative in function. If it extends only along the front façade, usually called a visor roof.

skirt-roof

skull In welding, an unmelted residue from a liquefied **filler metal**.

skull cracker See **wrecking ball**.

sky-dome In a theatre, a half dome which curves around and over the stage and which is painted to represent the sky.

sky factor The ratio of the illumination on a horizontal plane at a given point inside a building due to the light received directly from the sky, to the illumination due to an unobstructed hemisphere of sky of uniform luminance equal to that of the visible sky.

sky light The light received from the sky exclusive of direct light from the sun.

skylight In a roof, an opening which is glazed with a transparent or translucent material; used to admit diffused light to the space below. Compare with **dome light**. Also see **hip skylight, lantern skylight, monitor skylight, pitched skylight, sawtooth skylight**.

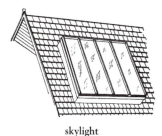

skylight

skyscraper A very tall, multistoried building, usually having **curtain walls, 1** so that the exterior walls are non-load-bearing, being supported independently at each floor by its **skeleton-frame construction**; also see **steel-frame construction** and **tripartite scheme**.

skyway An enclosed walkway, elevated above street level, that provides a passageway from one building to another.

S/L, S/LAP Abbr. for "shiplap."

SL&C Abbr. for "shipper's load and count."

slab **1.** The upper part of a reinforced concrete floor, which is carried on beams below. **2.** A concrete mat poured on subgrade, serving as a floor rather than as a structural member. **3.** A flat thick slice or plate of material such as stone, wood, concrete, etc.

slab board A board cut from the side of a log so that it has bark and sapwood on one side.

slab floor A floor of **reinforced concrete**.

slab form A **form** for pouring a concrete slab.

slab house A house built of rough-hewn planks.

slab insulation Thermal insulation which is fabricated in rigid or semirigid form; differs from block or board-type insulation only in physical dimensions. The slab designation usually is applied if the face dimension is much larger than a block but smaller than a board and if the thickness is greater than that of a board.

slab jacking See **mud-jacking**.

slab spacer In a concrete slab, a support and spacer for the steel reinforcement.

slab strip Same as **middle strip**.

slack **1.** Coal of relatively fine size, usually not exceeding 2½ in. (6.35 cm) in diameter; often screenings. **2.** Fitting loosely.

slack-rope switch A safety device which automatically cuts off the electric power from an elevator motor if the wire ropes (cables) which hoist the car should become slack.

slack side The side of wood veneer which originally faced inward in the log.

slag A grayish aggregate left as a residue of blast furnaces; used as surfacing on built-up roofing and in manufactured products such as **slag cement** and **slag wool**. Also see **blast-furnace slag**.

slag block A masonry unit made of slag concrete.

slag brick A brick made of crushed blast-furnace slag mixed with lime.

slag cement A finely divided cementitious material consisting essentially of an intimate and uniform blend of granulated blast-furnace slag and hydrated lime.

slag concrete Concrete made with blast-furnace slag as the coarse aggregate; relatively lightweight.

slag inclusion A nonmetallic solid material which is trapped within a weld.

slag plaster A plaster having crushed blast-furnace slag as the aggregate.

slag sand Slag which has been crushed to a very fine aggregate and graded; used in mortar, concrete, etc.

slag strip See **gravel stop**.

slag wool A type of **mineral wool** made by forcing steam through molten **slag**; used as thermal insulation.

slake **1.** To add water to quicklime, thereby hydrating it and forming **lime putty**. **2.** To crumble or disintegrate on exposure to air or water.

slaked lime A mixture of lime and water, used as mortar; also see **lime mortar**.

slaking box A wooden box used to **slake** quicklime.

slamming stile Same as **lock stile**.

slamming strip A strip or inlay along the edge of the **lock stile** of a flush door.

slant A sewer pipe which connects a house sewer to a common sewer.

slant range The line-of-sight distance between two points not at the same elevation.

slap dash See **rock dash**.

slasher saw A circular saw attached to a movable arm; used to cut lumber to length.

slash-grained Same as **edge-grained**.

slash-sawn See **plain-sawn**.

slat A thin, narrow strip of wood or metal, as in a window blind.

slate A hard, brittle metamorphic rock consisting mainly of clay minerals, characterized by good cleavage along parallel planes; used extensively as **dimension stone** in thin sheets for flooring, roofing, panels (both decorative and electrical), and chalkboard, and in granular form as surfacing on composition roofing.

slate-and-a-half slate Slate having the same length, but 1½ times the width, of the slate used elsewhere on a roof.

slate ax A **sax**.

slate batten, slate lath, tile batten A **batten** on which slates or tiles are hung; nailed horizontally across **common rafters** or **counter battens**.

slate black A **mineral black** obtained by grinding black slate.

slate boarding Close boarding on which roofing slates or tiles are set.

slate cramp A dovetail-shaped heavy slate, wedged at a joint between two stones to bind them together.

slate hanging Slate, usually in the form of shingles, that is hung vertically, or nearly so, on the face of an exterior wall to prevent the penetration of rainfall.

slate knife Same as **sax**.

slate lath See **slate batten**.

slate nail See **slating nail**.

slate powder A very fine powder obtained by pulverizing slate; used in paint as a dark-extender pigment.

slate ridge See **slate roll**.

slate roll, slate ridge A cylindrical rod of slate; cut with a V-shaped notch on the bottom side to fit a ridge on a slate roof.

slaters' cement A type of caulking compound used where a putty-like water-resistant material is required as a sealant; especially in roofing applications.

slaters' felt An **asphaltic paper** used as an underlayment for slate roofing.

slating **1.** The installation of slate shingles on a roof or wall. **2.** Shingles of slate, taken collectively. **3.** A roofing of slate.

slating nail, slate nail A nail having a large flat head and a medium diamond-shaped point, esp. used for fixing slates.

slating nail

slat window See **louver**.

sledgehammer, sledge A large hammer having two faces; weighs up to 100 lb (45 kg); grasped with both hands.

sleeper 1. One of a number of horizontal timbers that are laid on a concrete slab (or on the ground) and to which the flooring is nailed. 2. Any long horizontal beam, at or near the ground, which distributes the load from posts or framing.

sleeper clip A metal fastener which is attached to a concrete subfloor to fix floor battens in place.

sleeper joist Any **joist** resting directly on sleepers.

sleeper plate A **sleeper, 2**.

sleeper wall A dwarf wall which carries a joist supporting a floor; if of brick, it usually is perforated to permit the passage of air for ventilation.

sleepiness A film defect of lowered gloss in a high-gloss enamel or varnish; develops during drying.

sleeping porch A **porch**, or a room lined with windows, used for sleeping; often located in an extension to a house, above another porch, or above a **porte cochère**.

sleeve See **pipe sleeve**.

sleeve fence A short, decorative fence, usually made of light lumber and extending out from a dwelling.

sleeve piece 1. A **pipe sleeve, 1**. 2. A **thimble**.

slenderness ratio Of a column, the ratio of its effective length to its least **radius of gyration**.

sliced veneer Veneer which is machine-sliced, from the flat surface of flitch or squared log, in long, thin, straight slices.

slice-hip roof See **Dutch slice-hip roof**.

slicing cut A downward cut with a sliding movement.

slicker A **darby**.

slick line In delivering concrete by pipeline, the end section of pipeline which is immersed in the placed concrete and moved as the work progresses.

slide pile A **pile** which is driven into the earth on a hillside to consolidate the soil to prevent its sliding down the slope.

slidescape A straight or spiral chute, erected on the interior or exterior of a building, designed as a means of emergency egress directly to the street.

sliding bearing A type of support for a structure constructed so that one part slides on another.

sliding bevel See **bevel square**.

sliding door A door, mounted on track, which slides in a horizontal direction, usually parallel to one wall. Also see **accordion door, folding door**.

sliding-door lock A lock having a hook-shaped bolt which, when locked, engages a slot in a **strike plate**; esp. used on sliding doors.

sliding fire door A door hung on a sloping overhead track and held open by a fusible link or by a magnetic device; closes automatically if the fusible link is melted by heat buildup or if the magnetic device is tripped by a smoke-sensing device.

sliding form See **slip form**.

sliding sash A window or door which moves horizontally in grooves or between runners.

sliding window See **sliding sash**.

slimline lamp An instant-starting fluorescent lamp having a rugged, single-pin base.

sling See **elevator car-frame sling**.

sling psychrometer A **psychrometer** to which a handle is attached; the apparatus is whirled in the air until the reading of the wet-bulb thermometer reaches a constant value.

slip 1. A strip of wood or other material, esp. one inserted in a dovetailed groove. 2. A **parting slip**. 3. A **ground, 1**. 4. A long seat or narrow pew in a church. 5. A narrow passage between two buildings. 6. A thin layer of plaster or grout. 7. The movement which occurs between concrete and steel reinforcement in stressed reinforced concrete; an indication of anchorage breakdown.

slip-critical joint A bolt joint requiring a connection having slip resistance.

slip feather See **spline**.

slip form, sliding form In concrete construction, a form designed to move upward slowly (usually by means of hydraulic jacks or screw jacks), supported by the hardened concrete of the wall section which was poured previously.

sliphead window A window in which the upper part of the **sash** slides upward through the head of the window frame.

slip joint 1. A vertical joint between an old masonry wall and a new one; a slot is cut in the old wall into which brick from the new one is fitted. **2.** In plumbing, a connecting joint in which one pipe slips within another, a seal being effected by caulking, a gasket, or packing.

slip-joint conduit Metal conduit for electric wiring, the ends of which are joined to other pieces of conduit by means of couplings that slip over the ends; the couplings are not threaded.

slip-joint pliers **Pliers** having a joint which can be set in either of two positions, providing a jaw opening that is either wide or narrow.

slip-joint pliers

slip mortise See **slot mortise**.

slip newel A **newel** which is hollowed out at the bottom to fit over a short vertical post, or cut away at one side to fit over the end of a partition.

slip-on flange A solid, circular pipe flange which is slipped over the end of a pipe and welded in place.

slippage In built-up roofing, the lateral movement between adjacent plies; esp. occurs on sloping roofs.

slipper **1.** On a **running mold**, a metal shoe that slides on the running rule. **2.** Same as **plinth**.

slip piece A strip of wood attached to a sliding member to serve as a wearing surface.

slip-resistant tile Ceramic tile having greater nonslip characteristics than ordinary tile because of an abrasive admixture, abrasive particles in the surface, or grooves or patterns in the surface.

slip sheet A **dry sheet** of light roofing paper.

slip sill A sill no longer than the distance between the jambs of the opening, so that it can be set into the aperture after the walls are built.

slipstage A **wagon stage** on tracks.

slip stone See **gouge slip**.

slip tongue See **spline**.

slip-tongue joint A **spline joint**.

slit ventilator One of a number of long vertical slots in the masonry walls of a **German barn** to supply fresh air to the barn; occasionally called a slit window or a loophole.

slogging chisel A heavy chisel used to cut off bolt heads.

slop Same as **sludge**.

slope **1.** See **grade**. **2.** See **pitch, 3**. **3.** See **incline**. **4.** See **grain slope**.

slope correction Same as **grade correction**.

sloped footing A **footing** which has sloping top or side faces.

sloped offset chimney Same as **stepped-back chimney**.

slope map A map indicating the topography of an area along with an analysis of topographic features as they have influenced and may continue to influence land development.

slope ratio Relation of horizontal distance to vertical rise or fall; e.g., 2 ft horizontal to 1 ft vertical is designated 2 to 1 or 2:1.

slope stake A stake, driven in the ground, indicating the line where a **cut** or **fill** meets the original grade.

sloping grain **1.** Same as **diagonal grain**. **2.** Also see **grain slope**.

slop-molding, soft-mud process A method of manufacturing stock brick and multicolored brick; makes use of clay having a high water content.

slop sink A deep sink, usually set low, esp. used by janitors for emptying pails of dirty water.

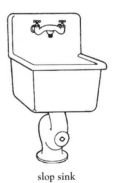

slop sink

slot diffuser See **linear diffuser**.

slot mortise, open mortise, slip mortise A **mortise** which is open on three sides of the member in which it is formed. (*See illustration p. 846.*)

slot outlet A long, narrow **air outlet**, with longitudinal vanes for directing the supply of air,

slot mortise

having an aspect ratio greater than 10:1; may be located in the ceiling, sidewalls, floor, or sill.

slot weld A weld between two members, one containing an elongated hole through which the other member is exposed; the hole is completely or partially filled with weld metal, thereby joining the two members; one end of the hole may be open.

sloughing When freshly gunned **shotcrete** is applied to a vertical surface, the slipping down of the material from the place where it was applied, usually because of the excessive use of mixing water.

slow burning A misleading term implying a general property of a material or product when it is exposed to a fire of any size or severity; meaningful only when identified with a particular test, usually applying only to very small flames for a short time period.

slow-burning construction Descriptive of buildings of timber construction designed to be fire-retardant; see **textile mill**.

slow-burning insulation Insulation which burns or chars without a flame.

slow-curing asphalt Liquid asphalt composed of **asphalt cement** and oils of low volatility.

slow-evaporating solvent A solvent which evaporates slowly because of its high boiling point; used in paint to maintain the paint film in a fluid state for a longer time than usual, thereby improving the flow properties of the paint.

slow-grown See **narrow-ringed**.

sloyd knife A woodworker's knife having a fixed, single blade; used in wood carving, slicing, and trimming.

sludge **1.** Refuse from various operations, as the waste material produced in the wet grinding of **terrazzo**. **2.** In a paint **spray booth** whose walls are washed continuously with water, the paint which accumulates in the water reservoir, sometimes reworked to make another paint. **3.** The accumulated, settled solids which are deposited

from sewage and contain more or less water to form a semiliquid mass.

sludge clear space The distance between the top of the **sludge, 3** and the bottom of an outlet device in a tank containing sewage.

sluing arch A **splayed arch**.

slum An area within a city characterized by deteriorated buildings, unsanitary conditions, and high population densities.

slump A measure of consistency of freshly mixed concrete, mortar, or stucco; equal to the decrease in height, measured to the nearest ¼ in. (6 mm) of the molded mass immediately after its removal from a **slump cone**.

slump block A concrete masonry unit which settles during curing so that the base is slightly enlarged; used in masonry wall construction.

slump cone A mold in the form of a truncated cone with a base diameter of 8 in. (20 cm), top diameter 4 in. (10 cm), and height 12 in. (30 cm); used to fabricate a specimen of freshly mixed concrete for the **slump test**; a cone 6 in. (15 cm) high is used for tests of freshly mixed mortar and stucco.

slump test A procedure using a **slump cone** for measuring the slump of concrete.

slump test

slurry **1.** A mixture of water and any finely divided insoluble material such as clay or portland cement and water. **2.** See **mud**.

slurry explosive Same as **water-gel explosive**.

slushed joint A vertical joint filled after a masonry unit is laid by slushing mortar into the joint with the edge of a trowel.

slush grouting The distribution of portland cement slurry, with or without fine aggregate, over a rock or concrete surface that is to be covered subsequently with concrete, usually by brooming it in place to fill surface voids and fissures.

slype A narrow passage as between two buildings; a **slip, 5**.

SM **1.** Abbr. for "standard matched." **2.** Abbr. for "surface measure."

smalt A deep blue pigment or coloring material; a vitreous substance made of cobalt, potash, and calcined quartz, fused and reduced to a powder.

smalto Colored glass or other pieces of vitreous material, esp. in minute regular squares, used in mosaic work.

smalto

smashing point The time beyond which it is not economical to burn old lamps because of their increasing inefficiency; based on an evaluation of the cost of operating the lighting system.

smell test See **scent test**.

smoke **1.** An air suspension of particles, usually but not necessarily solid. **2.** Carbon or soot particles less than 0.1 micron in size which result from the incomplete combustion of carbonaceous materials such as coal and oil.

smoke and fire vent A vent cover, installed on a roof, which opens automatically when the heat exceeds 160°F (71.4°C), thereby releasing the door and venting the fire.

smoke barrier Any type of continuous barrier of noncombustible construction, designed and constructed to restrict the spread of smoke in a building.

smoke chamber See **rauchkammer**.

smoke control zone A space within a building enclosed by **smoke barriers**.

smoke curtain A barrier that restricts the spread of smoke.

smoke damper A **damper, 1** arranged to seal off air flow automatically through part of an air duct system, so as to restrict passage of smoke.

smoke density The ratio of (a) the smoke emitted by a burning material to (b) the smoke emitted by a standard material.

smoke detector A device for sensing the presence of smoke in a building—usually by means of a photoelectric detector, ionization detector, ultraviolet flame detector, or a heat detector.

smoke-developed rating A relative numerical classification of a building material as determined by an ASTM test of its surface burning characteristics.

smoke door In the roof of a theatre, above the gridiron, a door which opens automatically in case of fire or when a release line is cut; confines the smoke to the backstage area.

smoke-dried lumber Lumber which has been seasoned by a process in which boards are exposed to the smoke and heat of a fire maintained beneath the stacks.

smoke exhaust system A mechanical or gravity system intended to convey smoke from one portion of a building to the outdoors; usually includes a purging-and-venting system, as well as exhaust fans.

smoke hatch Same as **smoke door**.

smoke hole In many types of primitive dwellings, a hole in the roof that permits smoke and fumes to escape from an open firepit below, also provides a source of light and ventilation in the dwelling.

smoke hood A **hood, 2**.

smokehouse An enclosed outbuilding in which meat or fish is cured with smoke to preserve it; usually has a vent, a single door, and no windows, walls typically constructed of boards, brick, logs, or stone, often with a gabled or pyramidal roof.

smoke load That fraction of the **fuel load** which has the potential of producing smoke.

smoke pipe, smoke vent **1.** A pipe or duct which carries smoke outside a building or to a flue. **2.** Same as **breeching, 1.**

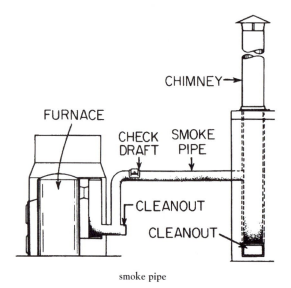

smoke pipe

smoke pocket A vertical metal slot, on both sides of the proscenium arch, in which the edges of the **asbestos curtain** move.

smokeproof tower A stairwell which provides with direct access to outdoor air at each floor level and which meets the requirements of the applicable code.

smoke rocket A device which gives off dense smoke; used in a **smoke test** of sections of piping.

smoke shelf A concave shelf on the back wall of a smoke chamber, just above the throat, to redirect downdrafts into updrafts on the front wall of a smoke chamber.

smokestack A **chimney.**

smokestop A partition to retard the passage of smoke; any opening in such partition is protected by a door equipped with a self-closing device.

smoke stop door A door or pair of doors placed in a corridor to restrict the spread of smoke and to retard the spread of fire by reducing the draft.

smoke test A test in which nontoxic, visible smoke is introduced in an air-distribution system, ductwork, piping, etc., to indicate the routes taken by air currents and/or to detect leaks.

smoke tower window In a high-rise building, an interior window, used between a stairwell and a smoke tower or smoke vent, which provides an automatic means for venting heat and smoke in the event of fire; an automatic mechanism causes the window to open quickly if sensors detect the presence of smoke or a high temperature rise.

smoke vent **1.** See **smoke pipe. 2.** See **smoke and fire vent.**

smoldering The combustion of solid materials without the accompaniment of flame.

smooth ashlar A rectangular stone block having smooth faces, ready for laying.

smooth finish See **smooth machine finish.**

smooth-finish tile Ceramic tile whose surfaces are not altered or marked in manufacture but are left flat or level as formed by the die.

smoothing plane A small fine plane used for finishing.

smooth machine finish, machine finish, smooth finish, smooth planer finish A finish on a stone surface, produced by a planer with a smooth-edged cutting tool that shaves without plucking; tool marks, if evident, are removed by a carborundum wheel, by hand scraping, etc.

smooth planer finish See **smooth machine finish.**

smooth-surfaced roofing A built-up roofing membrane which is surfaced with (a) hot asphalt applied with a mop; or (b) cold asphalt emulsion or a cutback roof coating; or (c) an inorganic top felt. It does not have a mineral surface aggregate.

SMS Abbr. for **sheet-metal screw.**

smudge **1.** A mark or smear on a surface, as from a hand or object rubbing dirt on a paint film. **2.** The scrapings and cleanings of paint pots, mixed together and used as a primer. **3.** In plumbing, a mixture of glue sizing and lampblack; painted on a lead surface to prevent solder from adhering.

snack bar An eating facility where quick, light meals, refreshments, or snacks are served, usually at a counter.

snake **1.** A long tempered-steel, resilient wire, usually having a rectangular cross section, used by electricians in pulling wires through conduit or through an inaccessible space; the snake is threaded through first, followed by the wire. **2.** A tool used by plumbers to unblock a pipe or sanitary fitting; usually a highly flexible metal wire, given a rotary motion by a crank at one end.

snake fence Same as **zigzag fence**. Also see **serpentine wall**.

snakestone A kind of hone slate or whetstone; used for polishing **scagliola** or the like.

snakewood Same as **letterwood**.

snap See **rivet set**.

snap head Same as **buttonhead**.

snap header A **half bat**.

snapped work Masonry laid with considerable use of snap headers rather than full headers.

snapping line A cord used to mark a straight line in laying out masonry, carpentry work, etc. Chalk is applied to the cord along its entire length, and the cord is held taut between two points on the surface to be marked; when the cord is raised and snapped, it leaves a chalk line on the surface.

snapping line

snap switch A manually operated **switch** used in interior electric wiring; usually used for the control of lighting or small motors.

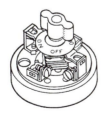

snap switch   with cover removed

snatch block A **pulley block** that can be opened on the side to receive the bight of a rope.

S-N curve Same as **stress-number curve**.

sneck In **snecked rubble**, one of the smaller stones used to fill interstices and to even out courses in a rubble wall.

snecked rubble, snecked masonry Masonry laid up with rough irregular stones, fitted so as to produce a strong bond.

snecking Same as **rubblework**.

snipe's-bill A carpenter's plane with a sharp arris used to form the **quirks, 1** in moldings.

snips Same as **tin snips**.

snow board, snow cradling A continuous narrow board or strip, secured at the foot of a roof slope, which serves as a **snow guard**.

snow fence A fence of laths wired together, set perpendicular to the direction of prevailing winds to catch drifting snow.

snow guard Any device intended to prevent snow from sliding off a sloping roof.

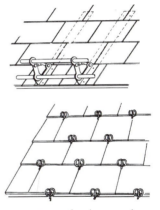

snow guards   (two types)

snow hook A device in the form of a loop of wire or a metal hook which is fastened to a sloping roof and serves as a **snow guard**.

snow house See **igloo**.

snow load The live load due to the weight of snow on a roof; included in design calculations.

snubber **1.** A component of a vibration isolator that limits the displacement of the isolator in either the vertical or horizontal direction. **2.** On a very large expulsion-type fuse, a silencer that reduces the loud noise produced in clearing heavy electrical faults. (*See illustration p. 850.*)

soakaway, soakpit A pit excavated in the earth's surface which receives excess surface water, allowing it to drain away slowly.

soaker On a slate or tile roof, a piece of metal sheeting used to make a weathertight joint at

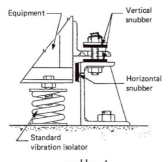

Equipment — Vertical snubber

Horizontal snubber

Standard vibration isolator

snubber, 1

the intersection between the roof and a vertical wall penetrating the roof or at a hip or valley.

soaking period In steam curing of concrete products, the time after which the steam supply to the kiln or autoclave is shut off and the products are left to soak in the residual heat and moisture of the curing kiln.

soap A brick or tile of normal face dimensions, having a nominal 2-in. (5-cm) thickness.

soapstone Massive soft rock that contains a high proportion of talc; used as dimension stone for laboratory sinks, bench tops, carved ornaments, and electrical panels. Also see **steatite**.

Society of Architectural Historians A society dedicated to the encouragement of scholarly research in the field of architectural history; founded in 1940 as the American Society of Architectural Historians, and called the Society of Architectural Historians since 1947. Address: 1365 North Astor Street, Chicago, IL 60610.

socket **1.** Same as **coupling**. **2.** British term for **bell, 2. 3.** A **receptacle outlet**.

socket chisel See **mortise chisel**.

socket fuse Same as **plug fuse**.

socketing In timber construction, the connection of one member with another by fitting it into a mating cavity in the second one.

socket outlet **1.** British term for **receptacle outlet. 2.** See **outlet**.

socket pipe A cast-iron pipe which is provided with a socket at one end and a spigot at the other end.

socket plug A pipe fitting with an outside thread and a head having a recess into which a wrench is inserted for turning it.

socket tile A **sewerpipe** of vitrified clay having **bell-and-spigot joints** between sections of pipe.

socket wrench A box wrench having a recessed socket at the end of its shank which fits over a nut.

socle A low, plain base course for a pedestal, column, or wall; a plain **plinth**.

sod The upper layer of soil covered by grass and containing the grass roots.

soda-acid fire extinguisher One that discharges water under the pressure of carbon dioxide gas produced by mixing acid and soda when the extinguisher is activated; the water may contain unreacted acid or soda.

soda fountain A system for dispensing soda water, usually equipped with a self-contained or remote refrigeration system with compartments for ice cream; may include a built-in sink and carbonator; esp. used at counters in drugstores and in restaurants.

soda-lime glass Glass manufactured by fusing sand with sodium carbonate or sodium sulfate and lime; used for window glass.

sod house, soddie A dwelling having thick walls of blocks cut from an upper layer of grassland (i.e., **sod**). Houses of this type were constructed quickly by early settlers in the Great Plains of the United States in areas where timber and stone were scarce, suitable clay was not available for making bricks in quantity, but good-quality sod was readily obtainable. Often, constructed partially underground, or built into the side of a hill to provide improved thermal insulation. The walls were usually plastered with clay to promote cleanliness and dryness within the structure, and to reduce or prevent insect infestation. Also see **Plains cottage**.

sodium light Monochromatic yellow-orange light from a low-pressure **sodium-vapor lamp**. Also see **high-pressure sodium lamp**.

sodium-vapor lamp An **electric-discharge lamp** in which light is produced by electric current flowing between electrodes in an envelope containing sodium vapor.

sod roof A roof composed of a thick layer of grassland containing roots; frequently pitched or barrel-shaped and supported by logs; usually prone to problem of water leakage. In sod houses of better quality, the sod roofs were covered with shingles (which were then covered with additional sod to prevent the shingles from being blown away). In upscale modern sod houses, an impermeable plastic sheet is set beneath the sod roof to reduce or eliminate water leakage.

soffit   The exposed undersurface of any overhead component of a building, such as an arch, balcony, beam, cornice, lintel, or vault.

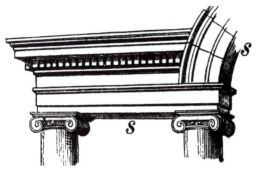

soffit   of an arch and of a lintel, S

soffit block   A concrete masonry unit used in concrete floor or roof construction where the soffit of a concrete beam is concealed by a face shell of the unit.

soffit block

soffit board   A **plancier piece**.

soffit bracket   A bracket for mounting an exposed overhead **door closer** to the underside of a doorframe head or transom bar; used for outswinging doors only.

soft brick   Same as **salmon brick**.

soft-burnt   Descriptive of a clay product which has been fired at a low temperature, resulting in relatively high absorption and low compressive strength.

softener   A flat brush of hog bristle; used to blend or soften markings in a paint coating.

softening point   An index of a bitumen's fluidity; the temperature at which a bitumen (used in roofing or road construction) softens or melts.

soft glass   A glass, usually of soda-lime composition, having a low softening point and a high coefficient of thermal expansion which renders it susceptible to thermal shock, e.g., window glass.

soft light   Light which produces soft, poorly defined shadows.

soft-mud brick   Brick produced by molding relatively wet clay (20 to 30% moisture), often by hand; if the inside of the mold is sanded to prevent sticking of clay, the product is **sand-struck brick**; if the mold is wetted to prevent sticking, the product is **water-struck brick**.

soft-mud process   See **slop-molding**.

soft particle   In an aggregate, a particle which possesses less than a specified degree of hardness or strength.

soft solder   A low-melting-point **solder**.

soft water   Water, free of magnesium or calcium salts, in which soap readily dissolves, forming a lather without being precipitated.

softwood   Wood from the evergreens; usually relatively soft and easy to cut and work, although some woods so classified in the U.S.A. are harder than others classified as hardwood.

soil   **1.** Sediments or other unconsolidated accumulations of solid particles produced by the physical and chemical disintegration of rocks; may or may not contain organic matter. **2.** Same as **sewage**.

soil absorption field   Same as **absorption field**.

soil absorption system   Any system that utilizes the soil for subsequent absorption of the treated sewage; such as an absorption trench, seepage bed, or seepage pit.

soil analysis   See **mechanical analysis**.

soil auger   See **auger, 2**.

soil binder   Soil which just passes through a 420-μ (No. 40 U.S. Standard) sieve.

soil boring   Drilling into the soil to explore the subsurface and to obtain earth samples.

soil branch   A branch line of a **soil pipe**.

soil-cement   A mixture of mineral soil, cement, and water used to make a hard surface for sidewalks, pool linings, and reservoirs, or as a base course for roads.

soil class   A numerical classification of **soil, 1** by texture, which is used by the U.S. Department of Agriculture: (1) gravel, (2) sand, (3) clay,

(4) loam, (5) loam with some sand, (6) silt-loam, and (7) clay-loam.

soil classification test A test in which soils are classified in broad groups having similar mechanical properties and strength characteristics.

soil compaction See **compaction, 2**.

soil cover Same as **ground cover, 2**.

soil creep The very slow movement of soil down a slope, under the influence of gravity.

soil drain A horizontal **soil pipe**.

soil engineering The application of the principles of **soil mechanics** in the investigation, evaluation, and design of civil works involving the use of earth materials and the inspection or testing of the construction thereof.

soil fill Same as **fill** or **backfill**.

soil horizon A layer of soil, approximately horizontal, which differs in structure and composition from the adjacent layers.

soil mechanics The application of the laws and principles of mechanics and hydraulics to engineering problems dealing with soil as an engineering material.

soil pipe, soil line A pipe which conveys the discharge of water closets or fixtures having similar functions, with or without the discharges from other fixtures. Also see **cast-iron soil pipe**.

soil pipe bend Same as **sanitary bend**.

soil plug The "plug" that is formed when an open-ended pipe pile is driven into the ground.

soil pressure Same as **contact pressure**.

soil profile The vertical section of a **soil, 1**, showing the nature and sequence of the various layers, as developed by deposition or weathering, or both.

soil sample A small specimen of soil usually taken from a **boring**.

soil stabilization The application of a chemical or mechanical treatment of a mass of soil to increase or maintain its stability or improve its engineering properties.

soil stabilizer 1. A machine, used in site preparation, that mixes in place earth and added stabilizing materials (such as cement or lime) to obtain higher soil-bearing capacity; rapidly rotating tines pick up and blend the soil with the stabilizing agent. 2. A chemical used to improve the physical properties of **soil, 1**

or to maintain or increase the stability of a mass of soil.

soil stack A vertical soil pipe carrying the discharge from toilet fixtures.

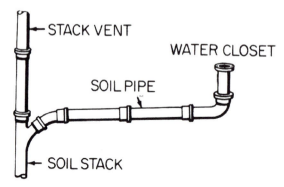

soil stack

soil structure The arrangement and state of aggregation of soil particles in a soil mass.

soil survey At a construction site, a detailed investigation of the soil, accompanied by a written report, usually including information concerning the type of soil, its thickness and strength, and the location of bedrock.

soil suspension A highly diffused mixture of soil and water.

soil vent Same as **stack vent, 1**.

solar 1. Said of radiant flux that has the sun as its source. 2. A room or apartment on an upper floor, as in an early English dwelling house.

solar collector A device designed to absorb radiation from the sun and transfer this energy to a fluid which passes through the collector.

solar constant The average rate at which radiant energy is received by the earth from the sun; equal to 430 Btu per hr per sq ft (1.94 cal per min per sq cm); a constant employed in calculating air-cooling loads due to the effects of solar radiation on buildings.

solar control glass See **coated glass** and **tinted glass**.

solar cooling system A system which converts solar energy into other forms of energy, then uses it for cooling.

solar degradation The deterioration in the properties of a material or component caused by exposure to solar energy.

solar energy system A building subsystem used to convert solar energy into thermal energy for heating and/or cooling a building or heating water for use within the building; may be of the hybrid-, open-, passive-, or thermosiphon- types.

solar fraction The ratio of the amount of input energy contributed by a solar energy system to the total input energy required for a specific application.

solar heat Heat supplied by radiation from the sun.

solar heat gain coefficient The fraction of normally incident solar energy that is transmitted through glazing under standard summer conditions.

solar heating and cooling system An assembly of (subsystems and components) which converts solar energy into thermal energy for use in combination with an auxiliary source of energy, where required, for heating and cooling a building.

solar house A dwelling designed to utilize the sun's rays to maximum advantage for heating the house and providing hot water; an auxiliary heat source is usually provided; see **active solar-energy system** and **passive solar-energy system**.

solarium A sunny room with more glass than usual, esp. one used for therapy.

solar orientation The placing of a building in relation to the sun; depending on the geographical area, the building may be oriented to maximize the amount of heat gained from solar radiation during the coldest months, or it may be oriented to minimize the amount of heat gained in the warmest months.

solar resistance That property of a material which resists decomposition resulting from (a) the exposure to the sun's ultraviolet rays and/or (b) the heat absorbed by exposure to the sun's rays.

solarscope Same as **heliodon**.

solar screen **1.** A nonstructural openwork or louvered panel of a building arranged so as to act as a sun-shading device. **2.** A perforated wall used as a sunshade.

solar screen tile Tile manufactured for masonry screen (perforated wall) construction.

solar thermal collector See **solar collector**.

solar water heater A system in which the sun's heat is gathered by a **solar collector** and used to increase the temperature of a heat-transfer fluid (such as water or a nonfreezing liquid) which flows through the pipes in the collector; the heat contained in this fluid then is conveyed and transferred to the water to be heated. Also see **direct solar water heating system** and **indirect solar water heating system**.

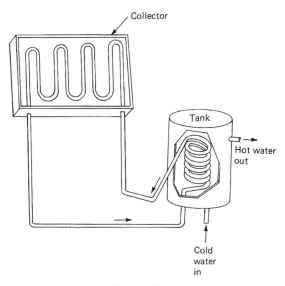

solar water heater

solder An alloy, usually having a lead or tin base, which is used to join metals by fusion; has a melting point which does not exceed 800°F (427°C).

soldered joint A gastight metal-pipe joint, made by soldering materials.

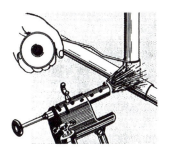

soldered joint formed with a blowtorch

soldering flux Same as **flux, 1**.

soldering gun   An electrically heated soldering iron with a pistol grip which reaches its operating temperature rapidly; has a relatively small bit.

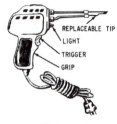

soldering gun

soldering iron   A tool for joining metals with **solder**; has a wedge-shaped metal bit, usually of copper, which is heated.

soldering nipple   A pipe **nipple** which is threaded on one end and unthreaded on the other; the plain end is soldered to the end of a pipe.

solderless connector   See **pressure connector**.

solder nipple   Same as **soldering nipple**.

soldier   **1.** A brick that is laid on end, i.e., positioned vertically with its narrower face showing on the wall surface; compare with **sailor**. **3.** Same as **soldier pile**.

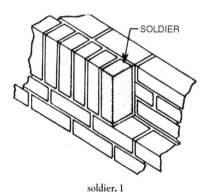

soldier, 1

soldier arch   A flat arch in brick, having the stretchers (long sides) of the uncut bricks set vertically.

soldier beam   A steel section which is driven into the ground vertically; supports a horizontally sheeted earth bank.

soldier course   A **course** of upright bricks with their narrow faces showing on the wall surface.

soldier pile, soldier   **1.** In excavation work, a vertical member which takes the side thrust from **horizontal sheeting** or from walings and which is supported by struts across the excavation. **2.** A vertical member used to prevent the movement of **formwork**; is held in place by struts, bolts, or wires.

sole   **1.** Same as **solepiece**. **2.** Same as **soleplate**.

solea   A raised walkway between the **ambo** and **bema** in an Early Christian or Byzantine church.

solenoid valve   A valve which is opened by a plunger whose movement is controlled by an electrically energized coil; the valve may be closed by the action of a spring, by gravity, or by an electrically energized coil.

solepiece   **1.** A horizontal member used to distribute the thrust of one or more uprights, posts, or struts. **2.** A member on which the foot of a raking shore rests.

soleplate   **1.** Same as **solepiece**. **2.** A horizontal timber which serves as a base for the studs in a stud partition. **3.** A plate riveted to the bottom flange of a plate girder to bear on the masonry plate.

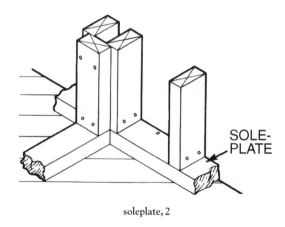

soleplate, 2

soler   Middle English term for **solar**.

solid bearing   The continuous support for a beam, along its entire length.

solid block   A masonry block which meets the specifications for a **solid masonry unit**.

solid-borne sound   See **structure-borne sound**.

solid brick   A brick which meets the specifications for a **solid masonry unit**.

solid bridging   See **block bridging**.

solid concrete block   A concrete **solid masonry unit**.

solid-core door   A door having a core of solid wood or mineral composition, as opposed to one of **hollow-core construction**.

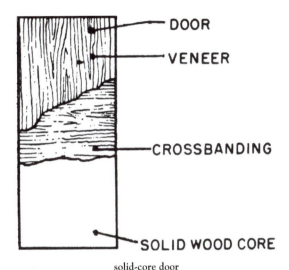

solid-core door

solid door   Same as **solid-core door**.

solid floor   See **solid-wood floor**.

solid frame   A door or window frame made from a single piece of timber as distinguished from one that is built up in sections.

solid glass door   A door in which the glass provides all or part of the structural strength.

solid masonry unit   **1.** (*U.S.A.*) A masonry unit whose net cross-sectional area in every plane parallel to the bearing surface is 75% or more of its gross cross-sectional area measured in the same plane. **2.** (*Brit.*) A solid masonry unit having small holes, less than ¼ in. (2 cm) wide or less than ¾ sq in. (5 sq cm) in area, passing through it but not exceeding 25% of its volume, or having **frogs** that do not exceed 20% of its volume. Up to three larger holes, not exceeding 5 sq. in. (32.5 sq cm) each, may be incorporated as aids to handling, within the total of 25%.

solid masonry wall   A wall built of solid masonry units, laid contiguously, with joints between completely filled with mortar.

solid molding   See **struck molding**.

solid mopping   In roofing, the application of hot bitumen over an entire roof surface, leaving no areas uncovered.

solid newel   A **newel** into which the ends of a winding stair are built, as distinguished from a **hollow newel**.

solid-newel stair   A type of spiral stair whose wedge-shaped treads (**fliers**) wind around, and are supported by, a central post (i.e., a **newel**); also called a newel stair.

solid panel   A panel which is flush with the faces of the **stiles** of a door; also see **flush panel**.

solid partition   A partition which contains no voids.

solid plasterwork   Plaster that is formed in place and has a solid core.

solid punch   A steel rod used to drive bolts out of holes.

solid rib   In the **centering** of a large arch, a profile of solid timber **framing**.

solid roll   A joint in sheet-metal roofing made over a wood **roll, 2**.

solids   Residual matter in a paint film consisting of pigments, resins, oils, driers, etc., after the volatile water or solvent has evaporated.

solids content   **1.** The percentage of solids in a liquid mix, as in an adhesive. **2.** In adhesives, coatings, or sealants, the percentage of nonvolatile material.

solid-state welding   Any welding process in which coalescence is produced without the addition of a brazing **filler metal** at temperatures below the melting point of the base metals being joined; sometimes pressure is used.

solid stop   A **doorstop, 1** which is integral with the doorframe; formed by a rabbet in the frame.

solid strutting   See **block bridging**.

solidum   The **dado** of a pedestal.

solidus   The highest temperature at which a metal is completely solid.

solid wall   **1.** See **solid masonry wall**. **2.** A wall of solid concrete.

solid waste   A collective term for *garbage, refuse, rubbish,* and *trash,* each term representing a definite category of solid-waste materials according to the classification established by the National Solid Waste Management Association.

solid web A **web** composed of one or more solid plates.

solid-web steel joist A steel truss having a **solid web**, formed by a rolled section or plate.

solid-wood floor 1. See **plank-on-edge-floor**. 2. A floor of **wood block**.

sollar, soller Same as **solar**.

Solomonic order See **spiral column**.

soluble drier, liquid drier A liquid that is soluble in oil or in solvent-based paints and acts as a **drier**.

solute, dissolved solids Solid particles of material (i.e., dissolved salts and dissolved organic materials) having a mean diameter of less than 0.000001 mm that are dissolved in water.

solvency, solvent power The degree to which a solvent holds a resin or other paint binder in solution, or reduces its viscosity.

solvent A liquid used to dissolve a solid (such as a paint resin) so that it is brushable; usually volatile; evaporates from the paint film after application; a **thinner**.

solvent-activated adhesive A dry adhesive film that is rendered tacky, just prior to use, by application of a solvent.

solvent adhesive An adhesive having a volatile organic liquid as a vehicle.

solvent molding The process of forming thermoplastic articles by dipping a mold into a solution of the resin and then drawing off the solvent, leaving a layer of plastic film adhering to the mold.

solvent power See **solvency**.

solvent-release sealant A **sealant** that cures primarily through the evaporation of the solvent it contains.

solvent-weld joint A pipe joint made by spreading a cement on two plastic surfaces to be joined. The cement reacts chemically with these surfaces, thereby dissolving the material. Then these two surfaces are placed in contact; a solid joint is formed when hardening takes place.

solvent wiping Removing oil, grease, or dirt from a surface with a cloth that has been soaked in solvent.

sommer Same as **summer**.

sone A unit of **loudness**.

sonic modulus Same as **dynamic modulus of elasticity**.

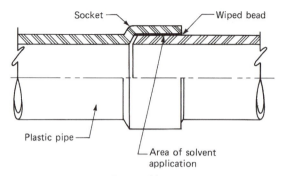

solvent-weld joint

sonic pile driver A device for driving piles into soil by means of a hammer whose head is vibrated (usually at a frequency less than 6,000 times per minute); this vibration is transmitted to the tip of the pile, resulting in a penetration that is relatively rapid and quiet.

soot door An access door to a flue for cleaning and repairing the area traversed by flue gases. Also see **ashpit door**.

soot pocket At the foot of a chimney, the place where soot collects below the smoke inlet, usually fitted with a door so that the soot can be removed conveniently.

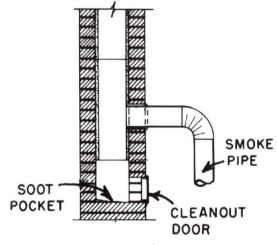

soot pocket

sopraporta See **overdoor**.

sorel cement See **oxychloride cement**.

sough A small drain at the foot of an embankment; carries the surface water from it to a side drain.

sound An oscillation in pressure of the atmosphere which is capable of being detected by the human ear.

sound absorption **1.** The process of dissipating sound energy by converting it to heat. **2.** A property possessed by materials or objects of absorbing sound energy. **3.** A measure of the magnitude of the absorptive property of a material or object; expressed in sabins or metric sabins.

sound absorption coefficient, α The fraction of the sound energy (incident at random angles on a surface) which is absorbed or otherwise not reflected by the surface.

sound-amplification system A combination of one or more microphones, amplifiers, loudspeakers, and associated electronic controls; used to increase the level of a sound source so that it may be heard clearly in all parts of an auditorium, large room, open-air theatre, etc.

sound analyzer An instrument used to measure the distribution of sound over the audible frequency range, i.e., used to obtain a **sound spectrum**.

sound attenuating door Same as **sound-rated door**.

sound attenuation The reduction in the intensity or in the sound pressure level of sound which is transmitted from one point to another. Also see **sound insulation**.

sound attenuator In ductwork, a device (usually prefabricated) especially designed to provide much greater sound attenuation than would be provided by an equal length of ductwork; the pressure drop through the device is greater than for an equal length of ductwork.

sound barrier Any solid obstacle which is relatively opaque to sound that blocks the line of sight between a sound source and the point of reception of the sound.

sound-control booth A room, usually in or adjacent to an auditorium, containing the sound-control console and associated equipment.

sound-control console A **console, 3** used to control the sound-amplification system in an auditorium.

sound-control glass See **sound-insulating glass**.

sound deadening See **sound insulation**.

sound deadening board Any material, in board form, used as a component in sound-insulating construction.

sound door See **sound-rated door**.

sound focus A relatively small area in a room or auditorium where the sound level is significantly higher than elsewhere.

sounding board A solid flat surface above a pulpit of an early church, intended to act as a sound reflector, directing a small fraction of sound of the speaker's voice toward the listeners.

sound-insulating glass **1.** Glass consisting of two or more lights which are fixed in resilient mountings, separated by spacers, and sealed so as to leave an air space between them; the air space contains a dessicant to assure dehydration of the trapped air. **2.** A single glazing unit consisting of a thick sheet of plate glass that has been laminated with a plastic.

sound insulation, sound isolation **1.** The use of structures and materials designed to reduce the transmission of sound from one room or area of a building to another or from the exterior to the interior of a building. **2.** The degree by which sound transmission is reduced by means of sound-insulating structures and materials.

sound intensity The average rate of sound energy transmitted in a specified direction through a unit area normal to this direction at the point considered.

sound isolation See **sound insulation**.

sound knot, tight knot An undecayed, solid, dead knot at least as hard as the surrounding wood, and firmly held in place.

sound level The reading of a **sound-level meter**, using one of the three weighting networks; expressed in decibels (*abbr.* dB); the weighting network used must be specified; the most widely used network for noise measurements is the A-network.

sound-level meter An instrument for the measurement of **noise levels** and **sound levels**, whose characteristics are specified by the American National Standards Institute; the instrument includes a microphone, amplifier, an output meter, and three electrical networks (called weighting A, B, and C) which weight different frequency components differently.

sound lock A vestibule or entranceway which has highly absorptive walls, ceiling, and a carpeted floor; used to reduce the transmission of noise into an auditorium, studio, or rehearsal room from the area outside.

soundness **1.** The freedom of a solid from cracks, flaws, fissures, or variations from an accepted standard. **2.** In cement, freedom from excessive volume change after setting. **3.** In an aggregate, the ability to withstand the aggressive action to which concrete containing it might be exposed, particularly that due to weather.

sound power Of a source of sound, the total amount of acoustical energy radiated per unit time.

sound-power level The **level, 4** of **sound power**, averaged over a period of time, the reference level being 10^{-12} watt.

sound pressure The minute fluctuations in atmospheric pressure which accompany the passage of a sound wave and give rise to the sensation of hearing; usually expressed in dynes per square centimeter or newtons per square meter.

sound-pressure level The **level, 4** of **sound pressure**; equal to 10 times the logarithm of the **sound pressure** squared and averaged over a period of time, the reference pressure being 0.0002 dyne per sq cm (2×10^{-5} newton per sq m); expressed in decibels (*abbr.* dB).

soundproofing The elements of construction and the design features of a building which make it relatively impervious to sound transmission from one room to another or from outside the building to the inside.

sound-rated door A door especially constructed to provide greater sound attenuation than that provided by a conventional door; usually carries a rating in terms of its **sound transmission class.**

sound ray An imaginary line emanating from a sound source which indicates the direction of propagation of the sound waves.

sound reduction index, R British term for **sound transmission loss.**

sound-reinforcement system Same as **sound-amplification system.**

sound-resistive glass See **sound-insulating glass.**

sound-retardant door See **acoustical door** and **sound-rated door.**

sound spectrum A representation of the magnitude of the components of a complex sound as a function of frequency.

sound transmission The passage of sound from one point to another, e.g., from one room in a building to another, or from the street into a room in the building.

sound transmission class, STC A single-number rating of the sound insulation value of a partition, door, or window; it is derived from a curve of its insulation value as a function of frequency; the higher the number, the more effective the sound insulation.

sound transmission loss, transmission loss, TL A measure of the sound-insulation value of a partition; the amount, in decibels, by which the intensity of sound is reduced in transmission through the partition.

sound trap Same as **sound attenuator.**

sound waves In air, succession of outwardly traveling layers of compression and rarefaction, capable of being detected by the ear.

sound wood Wood free from decay.

souse, souste Same as **corbel.**

south aisle The aisle of a church on the right side as one faces the altar; so called because medieval churches almost invariably had their sanctuaries at the east end and the main doors at the west end.

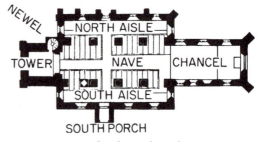

south aisle; south porch

south door A small door into the chancel (for the priest), usually on the south side of the church leading to his residence.

Southern Colonial house **1.** Any prerevolutionary house in the tradition of **American Colo-**

nial architecture of the early South. **2.** Descriptive of a full-colonnaded **Greek Revival style** mansion, usually constructed *after* the colonial period. Also see **plantation house.**

southern pine   Same as **yellow pine.**

south-light roof   In the southern hemisphere, a **sawtooth roof** in which the glazing faces south.

south porch   A porch which shelters the entrance to a church; located on the right side of the church as one faces the altar.

SOV   Abbr. for "shutoff valve."

Sovent system   A single-stack plumbing system used for both drainage and venting.

soya glue, soybean glue   A vegetable protein glue made from extracted soya bean meal; has greater adhesive power than most other vegetable glues and is more water-resistant than vegetable pastes; marketed dry; used for interior plywood.

soybean oil, soya-bean oil   A pale yellow **drying oil** obtained from soya beans; used in paints and varnishes; sometimes mixed with linseed oil.

SP   **1.** Abbr. for **soil pipe. 2.** Abbr. for **standpipe.**

SPA   Abbr. for "Southern Pine Association."

space diagram   A drawing of a structure that indicates its form as well as means of its support and loading conditions.

spaced slating   See **open slating.**

spaced steel column   A **battened column** in which the battens are attached to the longitudinal column elements by hinged connections.

space frame   Any three-dimensional structural framework (e.g., the rigid frame for a multistory building) as contrasted with a plane frame all of whose elements lie in a single plane.

space heater   A relatively small self-contained heater, usually with a powerful fan, used to heat the room or space in which it is placed; electricity or a liquid fuel supplies the heat energy.

space lattice   A **space frame** constructed of lattice girders.

spacer   **1.** In glazing, one of the small blocks of wood or other material placed on both sides of the edges of glass, during its installation, to center it, to maintain uniform width of sealant beads, and to prevent excessive sealant distor-

tion under lateral loading. **2.** A device which holds steel reinforcement in its proper position, or which holds wall forms at a given distance apart before and during concreting. **3.** See **edge spacer. 4.** See **shim spacer.**

spachtling   See **spackle.**

spackle, spachtling, spackling, sparkling   A paste, compound, or powder which can be mixed into a paste; used to fill holes, cracks, and defects in wood, plaster, wallboard, etc., to obtain a smooth surface.

spade   A tool for digging and cutting the ground, having a rather thick blade, usually nearly flat, so formed that its terminal edge may be pressed into the ground with one foot while the handle is grasped.

spading   Consolidation of mortar or concrete as the result of repeated insertions and withdrawals of a flat, spade-like tool.

spall   A small fragment or chip removed from the face of a stone or masonry unit by a blow or by action of the elements.

spalled joint   A masonry joint using mortar containing cementitious material, water, and an **aggregate** consisting largely of **spalls.**

spalling   The flaking of brickwork due to frost, chemical action, or movement of the building structure.

spalling hammer   A heavy ax-like hammer with a chisel edge; used for the rough dressing of stone by chipping off small flakes.

span   **1.** The interval between two terminals of a construction. **2.** The distance apart of any two consecutive supports, esp. as applied to the opening of an arch. **3.** A structural member (or part of a member) between two supports.

spandrel, spandril   **1.** An area, roughly triangular in shape, included between the extradoses of two adjoining arches and a line approximately connecting their crowns (or a space approximately equal to half this in the case of a single arch); in medieval architecture, often ornamented with tracery, etc. **2.** In a multistory building, a wall panel filling the space between the top of the window in one story and the sill of the window in the story above. **3.** A surface, roughly triangular in shape, as below a stair string. (*See illustration p. 860.*)

spandrel beam

spandrel, 1

spandrel beam In concrete or steel construction, an exterior beam extending from column to column usually carrying an exterior wall load.

spandrel frame Framing which is triangular in shape.

spandrel glass An opaque glass used in windows and curtain walls to conceal spandrel beams, columns, or other internal construction.

spandrel panel A panel covering a **spandrel** area.

spandrel step A solid step, triangular in section, whose hypotenuse forms part of the sloping soffit of the stair flight.

spandrel wall **1.** A wall built on the extrados of an arch, filling in the spandrels. **2.** That portion of a **skeleton wall** above the head of a window or door.

Spanish Colonial architecture Architecture, particularly in those areas of the American continents that have been subject to Spanish influence; greatly affected by local culture, customs, traditions, and availability of materials. Spanish Colonial architecture in the American southwest usually is typified by thick, solid adobe walls, often covered with a protective layer of stucco or plaster; a one-story building around an enclosed courtyard; a long, narrow, covered porch either facing the street or facing a patio; often, a balcony, commonly supported by columns at ground-floor level, each column usually topped with a **bolster**; commonly, flat roofs supported by round logs drained by waterspouts that penetrated the parapet surrounding the roof; low-pitched or medium-pitched roofs covered with red clay tiles, often with a substantial overhang, were also common; windows facing the street usually protected by ornamental grillwork; doors to the various rooms opened directly onto a covered porch or onto a patio. Also see **azotea, board house, canale, Churrigueresque style, common house, conch house, coquina, galeria, Monterey style, palma hut, plank house, Plateresque architecture, Saint Augustine house, tabby, tabla house, viga, zaguán, zambullo door.**

Spanish Colonial Revival An eclectic style loosely based on one or more phases of Spanish Colonial architecture; most common from about 1915 to the present. Buildings in this style usually characterized a façade with unadorned stucco or plastered walls; glazed and/or unglazed wall tiles; a covered porch or arcade; commonly, a patio; wrought-iron balconies or balconets; often, a low- to moderate-pitched, mission-tiled, hipped and/or gable roof multicurved **mission parapets** with decorative tilework along the outer face of the parapet; round arches over the most prominent windows; often, rectangular windows with **lintels**, sometimes crowned with an enriched cornice; window grilles; ornate, low-relief **window surrounds**; heavy wood doors, often elaborately paneled or carved; frequently,

Spanish Colonial Revival

rounded arches over the exterior doors; French doors providing easy access to a patio, balcony, or outdoor terrace.

Spanish Eclectic architecture   Same as, or an early phase of, **Spanish Colonial Revival**.

Spanish Mission Revival, Spanish Mission style   See **Mission Revival**.

Spanish Pueblo Revival   Same as **Pueblo Revival**; also see **Spanish Colonial Revival**.

Spanish Territorial style   See **Territorial style**.

Spanish tile   **1.** A red roofing tile whose horizontal cross section has the shape of the letter **S** laid on its side. **2.** Same as **mission tile**.

spanner, span piece   A horizontal cross brace or **collar beam**.

span piece   **1.** In a **collar-beam roof**, the horizontal beam which connects the rafters. **2.** A **collar-beam**.

span roof   A **pitched roof**, both sides of which have the same slope.

spar   **1.** A **common rafter**. **2.** A bar for fastening a gate or door. **3.** A heavy round timber. **4.** See **brotch**.

spar dash   Same as **rock dash**.

sparge pipe   A perforated water pipe used to flush a urinal.

spark arrester   A device (located at the top of a chimney) to prevent sparks, embers, or other ignited material above a given size from being expelled to the atmosphere. Also called a **bonnet**.

sparkling   See **spackle**.

spar piece   Same as **span piece**.

sparpiece   See **collar beam**.

sparrow peck   A textured finish, produced on a plastered surface by dabbing the surface with a stiff brush.

spar varnish   A varnish made with durable oils and resins; used on exterior wood surfaces because of its superior weather-resistant qualities.

spat   A protective covering (usually stainless steel) at the bottom of a doorframe to prevent or minimize damage in this area.

spatter dash   **1.** A wet mixture of cement and sand, thrown on a smooth surface; when hard it provides a key for a plaster coat. **2.** A finish produced by throwing a wet mixture of cement and sand on fresh mortar.

spawl   Same as **spall**.

speaking rod   Same as **self-reading leveling rod**.

speaking tube   A tube, usually of metal, used to transmit the voice from one part of a building to another, before the days of electronics.

SPEC   On drawings, abbr. for **specification**.

special assessment   A compulsory charge imposed by a government upon the owners of a restricted group of properties to defray the cost of a specific improvement or service, presumably of general benefit to the public and of special benefit to the owners of such properties.

special conditions   A section of the **conditions of the contract**, other than **general conditions** and **supplementary conditions**, which may be prepared for a particular project. Also see **conditions of the contract**.

special hazards insurance   Additional perils insurance to be included in property insurance (as provided in **contract documents** or requested by contractor or at option of owner) such as sprinkler leakage, collapse, water damage, all physical loss, or insurance on materials and supplies at other locations and/or in transit to the site.

special matrix terrazzo   Flooring consisting of colored aggregate and organic matrix.

special provisions   See **special conditions**.

special-purpose industrial occupancy   Industrial occupancy for particular types of operations, characterized by a relatively low density of employee population, with much of the area occupied by machinery or equipment; highly hazardous usage is excluded.

special-quality brick   Brick that is durable even when used under extreme conditions of exposure, as in the case of a structure that becomes water-saturated and/or frozen.

special waste   Any waste that requires special treatment before being fed into a normal drainage system.

specification   A written document describing in detail the scope of work, materials to be used, method of installation, and quality of workmanship for a parcel of work to be placed under contract; usually utilized in conjunction with working (contract) drawings in building construction.

specifications   A part of the **contract documents** contained in the **project manual** consisting of written descriptions of a technical nature of materials, equipment construction systems, standards, and workmanship. Under the **uniform system**, the **specifications** comprise sixteen **divisions**.

specific gravity **1.** The ratio of the density of a substance to the density of a reference material (usually water for liquids and air for gases). **2.** As applied to a gas piping system, the ratio of the weight of gas of a given volume to the weight of the same volume of air, both measured under the same conditions.

specific heat The ratio of the quantity of heat required to raise the temperature of a given mass of any substance 1 degree to the quantity required to raise the temperature of an equal mass of water 1 degree.

specific resistance See **electrical resistivity**.

specific retention The percentage of water which will be retained by rock or soil (against the pull of gravity) after being saturated; computed in terms of the ratio of volume of water retained to its own value.

specific surface In a unit weight of a material, the surface area of the contained particles.

specific yield The percentage of water which will be yielded by a rock or soil (by gravity) after being saturated; computed in terms of the ratio of the volume of water retained to its own volume.

SPECSystem A (proprietary) interactive expert system for writing specifications in the CSI's 16-division format.

SPECTEXT A (proprietary) guide specification published by the Construction Specification Institute (CSI); published in the CSI's 16-division format.

spectral power distribution In illumination engineering, the distribution of radiant power

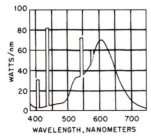

spectral power distribution: deluxe warm white fluorescent lamp

(commonly expressed in watts per nanometer) with respect to wavelength.

spectrophotometer An instrument for measuring the reflectance and transmittance of surfaces and media as a function of wavelength.

specular angle The angle between the perpendicular to the surface and the reflected ray that is numerically equal to the angle of incidence and lies in the same plane as the incident ray and the perpendicular, but on the opposite side of the perpendicular to the surface.

specular angle: angle of incidence, I, equals the angle of reflection, R

specular surface A mirror-like surface which reflects light at an angle equal to that of the incident light.

speculative builder One who develops and constructs building projects for subsequent sale or lease.

specus In early Roman architecture, the covered channel of an aqueduct in which water flows.

speer See **spere**.

spelter Same as **zinc**.

speos In ancient Egypt, a temple or part of a temple, or a tomb of some architectural importance, excavated in solid rock; a grotto temple or tomb.

spere, speer, spier, spur In medieval English residences and derivatives, a fixed screen projecting from the side of a great hall, near a door, to mitigate drafts.

spere-truss In a medieval hall of timber construction, a roof-supporting wooden arch, rising from trusses attached to the sidewalls, marking the division between the principal area of the hall and the **screens passage**.

sperone A **buttress**.

spewing The formation of a film, or the collection of particles, on a paint surface; results from the migration, to the surface, of the insoluble portion of the paint binder.

SP GR On drawings, abbr. for **specific gravity**.

sphaeristerium In ancient Rome, an enclosed place or structure for ball playing, usually attached to a gymnasium or a set of baths.

spherical vault A dome shaped like a half globe.

sphinx In Egyptian antiquity, a figure having the body of a lion and a male human head, or an animal head; commonly placed in avenues leading to temples or tombs; the most celebrated example is the Great Sphinx near the pyramids of Giza, near Cairo.

spicae testaceae Oblong bricks for pavements, used in **spicatum opus**.

spicatum opus Ancient Roman **herringbone work**.

spicatum opus

spier See **spere**.

spigot **1.** A faucet. **2.** The end of a pipe that fits into a **bell, 2**.

spigot, 2

spigot-and-socket joint See **bell-and-spigot joint**.

spigot joint See **bell-and-spigot joint**.

spike A very heavy nail, 3 in. (7.6 cm) to 12 in. (30.5 cm) in length, usually having a rectangular cross section.

spike-and-ferrule installation A type of gutter installation in which the gutter is fastened by means of long nails and metal sleeves.

spiked-and-linked chain A heavy chain, usually wrought iron, with spikes alternating with links; attached to posts to enclose a garden.

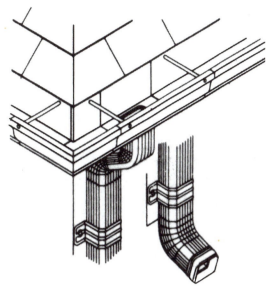

spike-and-ferrule installation

spike grid A type of **timber connector**.

spike knot, splay knot An elongated knot; the result of cutting wood approximately parallel to the length of the knot.

spile **1.** A peg or plug used to fill a nail hole. **2.** Same as **pile**.

spiling Same as **piling**.

spill, spill light Light rays, from spotlights and other focused light sources, that are not useful, e.g., producing lighting where it is not wanted on a stage.

spill ring See **ring louver**.

spill shield A type of **louver, 1** to prevent the **spill** of light.

spina A barrier dividing an ancient Roman circus lengthwise, about which the racers turned.

spindle **1.** A slender rod or pin on which anything turns, as the shaft to which a doorknob is attached. **2.** On a lock mechanism, the bar connected with the knob or lever handle that passes through the hub of the lock or otherwise engages the mechanism to transmit the knob action to the bolt(s). **3.** In woodworking, a short turned part as in a baluster.

spindle sander A **sanding machine** in which the sandpaper is carried on a small-diameter vertical drum located on the work table of the machine.

spindlework Wood details having circular cross sections, such as balusters turned on a lathe; occasionally called spoolwork.

spindlework   on porch

spine wall A **load-bearing wall** running parallel to the long axis of a building.

spinning house A subsidiary building once devoted exclusively to spinning or weaving; also called a loom house or a weaving house.

S-pipe Same as **offset elbow**.

spira The moldings at the base of a column; a **torus**.

spiral A continuously wound reinforcement in the form of a cylindrical helix.

spiral balance A **sash balance** using a spirally wound helical spring to compensate for the weight of the sash.

spiral column See **barley-sugar column, calomónica, torso**.

spiral grain Grain following a spiral course, in one direction, around the axis of a tree; produces highly figured veneer.

spirally reinforced column A column whose vertical **reinforcing bars** are enveloped by spiral reinforcement.

spiral ratchet screwdriver A screwdriver having a blade that rotates with respect to the handle, as the handle is pushed inward toward the blade; permits a screw to be driven easily and with speed.

spiral reinforcement Coiled steel wire or bar, bent to a definite pitch or spacing; used as reinforcement in **reinforced concrete**.

spiral stair, caracole, circular stair, cockle stair, corkscrew stair, spiral staircase A flight of stairs, circular in plan, whose treads

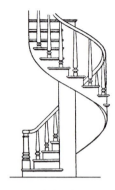

spiral stair

wind around a central newel. Also called a **helical stair, solid newel stair**.

spire Any slender pointed construction surmounting a building; generally a narrow octagonal pyramid set above a square tower.

spirelet A small spire as of a pinnacle or turret.

spire-steeple A **spire** atop a steeple.

spiriting off In finishing with **French polish**, rubbing the surface lightly with a rag soaked in methylated spirit.

spirit level A closed glass tube of circular cross section, usually set in a device or instrument; nearly filled with liquid, so that a bubble is formed, the centering of which is used to determine true horizontal or vertical directions; a level.

spirits of turpentine See **turpentine**.

spirit stain A penetrating, alcohol-soluble dye used to stain wood, producing deep color and little fiber swelling.

spirit varnish A varnish which uses a highly volatile liquid as the solvent for the resin or oil.

spitter See **lead spitter**.

SPKR On drawings, abbr. for **loudspeaker**.

SPL On drawings, abbr. for "special."

splashback Same as **splashboard**.

splash block A small masonry block laid on the ground below a downspout to carry roof drainage away from a building and to prevent soil erosion.

splashboard A board which provides protection against water splashes, as behind a sink.

splash brush In plastering, a brush for applying water on a finish coat while it is being smoothed with a trowel.

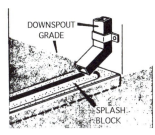

splash block

splash lap   In sheet-metal roofing, that part of a seam in a drip or roll that extends onto the flat surface of the next sheet.

splat   A strip which covers the joints between adjacent sheets of **building board**.

splay   A sloped surface, or a surface which makes an oblique angle with another, esp. at the sides of a door, window, proscenium, etc., so the opening is larger on one side than the other; a large chamfer; a reveal at an oblique angle to the exterior face of the wall.

splay brick, cant brick   A brick, one side of which is splayed (beveled).

splayed arch   An arch opening which has a larger radius in front than at the back.

splayed baseboard   A **baseboard** having its upper edge beveled.

splayed coping   See **featheredged coping**.

splayed ground   A **plaster ground** having undercut edges which provide a key for holding the plaster more securely.

splayed heading joint   An overlapping joint between boards; their ends are cut at an angle of 45° rather than 90° as in a **butt joint**.

splayed jamb   Any **jamb** whose face is not at right angles to the wall in which it is set.

splayed joint   A joint between the ends of two adjacent members, each of which is splayed so that the cross-sectional area of the members is unchanged at the joint.

splayed lintel   A **lintel** (i.e., horizontal structural member above a window) each end of which slants downward toward a centerline through the window; often has a keystone at its center.

splayed mullion   A mullion joining two glazed units which are at an angle to each other, as the mullion of a **bay window**.

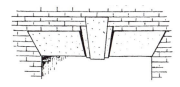

splayed lintel   with a keystone at its center

splayed skirting   A **baseboard** having its upper edge beveled.

splayed window   A window whose frame is set at an angle with respect to the face of the wall.

splay end   The smaller end of a splayed masonry unit.

splay knot   See **spike knot**.

splice   To connect, unite, or join two similar members, columns, pieces, wires, etc., usually in a straight line, by fastening lapped ends by means of mechanical end connectors, by welding, etc.

splice box   1. Same as **manhole**. 2. Similar to a **manhole**, but much smaller.

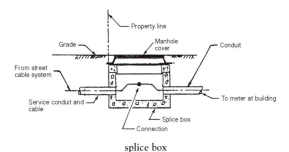

splice box

spliced pile   A **pile** composed of two or more segments that have been joined end-to-end to form a single pile.

splice plate   A metal plate used for fastening two or more members together.

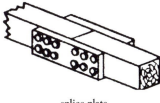

splice plate

spline, false tongue, feather, slip feather, slip tongue   1. A long thin strip of wood or metal which is inserted in a slot formed by two members, each of which is grooved and butted against the other. **2.** In a **suspended acoustical ceiling,** a strip of metal or hard fiber inserted in the slot between adjacent acoustical tiles which butt against each other, forming a concealed mechanical joint.

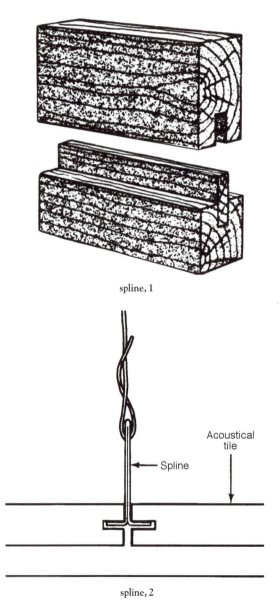

spline, 1

spline, 2

spline joint   A joint formed by inserting a **spline** in a slot cut into the two butting members.

split   **1.** A rupture in a built-up roof membrane, resulting from tensile stresses. **2.** A crack that extends completely through a piece of wood or wood veneer. **3.** A brick cut lengthwise, in two pieces, parallel to the wide face of the brick, so that it is half as thick; also called **scone.**

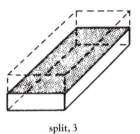

split, 3

split astragal   A vertical molding, attached to the meeting edges of each of the leaves of a pair of doors, for protection against weather; the split feature permits both leaves to be active.

split-batch charging   A method of filling a concrete mixer in which the cement, and sometimes different sizes of aggregate, may enter the mixer separately.

split block, split-face block   A solid or hollow concrete masonry unit, split lengthwise after curing; laid with the fractured surface exposed, so as to provide a rough texture.

split-conductor cable   A cable in which each conductor consists of two or more insulated conductors which are normally connected in parallel.

split course   A course of **splits, 3,** i.e., bricks cut so they are of less than normal thickness.

split dead bolt   A **dead bolt** composed of two pieces (each with its own control knob), one on each side of a door.

split-face block   See **split block.**

split-face finish   A building stone having a rough face; usually slabs of stratified stone are sawn parallel to the bedding so that the split face exposes the bedding in its natural orientation, but some stone is sawn perpendicular to bedding and then split with the exposed bedding running vertically.

split-face machine   A device for splitting slabs of stone into usable thicknesses for job-fabricated masonry patterns.

split fitting   In interior electric wiring, a conduit fitting which is split longitudinally so that it can be placed in position after the wires have been drawn into the conduit; the two parts of the fitting are held together with screws.

split frame, split jamb A doorframe with the jamb split in two or more pieces; may be used to enable a pocket-type sliding door or vertical sliding sash to enter the partition.

split lath A **wood lath** made by splitting long strips of wood; less uniform than wood lath cut with a saw.

split-level house A house having its living room area on the main floor, with stairs leading upward to the bedrooms approximately a half-story higher; and other stairs leading downward, a half-story lower, to the kitchen and/or dining areas and to a laundry or utility room; often has no attic, cellar, or porch for reasons of economy.

split pediment Same as **broken pediment**.

split pin A pin or spike which spreads when inserted, or which may be spread after insertion.

split-rail fence See **zigzag fence**.

split-ring connector A ring-shaped metal insert placed in precut circular grooves and held by bolts; used as a **timber connector**.

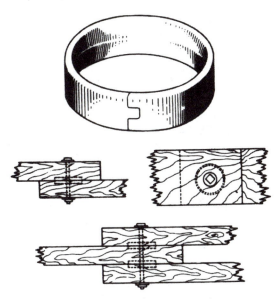

split-ring connector showing a typical joint

split rivet A small rivet having a split end for securing by spreading the ends; commonly furnished with an oval or countersunk head.

split roof A roof constructed of strips split from straight-grained timber.

split shake Same as **shake, 1**.

split stuff A timber cut to length and then split.

splitting A defect in a painted surface; results from the penetration of solvents, contained in a fresh coat of paint, into an older layer of paint over which it has been applied; likely to occur when the old layer has been sanded too much.

splitting tensile strength The tensile strength of concrete determined by a **splitting tensile test**.

splitting tensile test A test for **tensile strength** in which a cylindrical specimen is loaded to failure in diametral compression.

splocket Same as **sprocket**.

spoil Material from excavating or dredging.

spoil area A site where excavated material is deposited.

spokeshave A carpenter's tool; a kind of drawing knife or planing tool having a blade set between two handles; esp. used for shaping curved edges.

BLADE

spokeshave

sponge rubber, foam rubber Expanded rubber having a cellular structure; usually has interconnecting cells; used as resilient padding and as thermal insulation.

spontaneous ignition The initiation of combustion caused by internal, chemical reaction in which heat is liberated.

spontaneous liquefaction See **liquefaction**.

spoolwork Same as **spindlework**.

spoon In plastering, a small steel tool, used in finishing moldings by hand.

spoon bit See **dowel bit**.

spot See **spotting**.

spot board A **mortarboard**.

spot cementing The discontinuous application of a cold-liquid cementing compound.

spot elevation A point on a map or chart whose height above a specified reference datum is noted, usually by a marker and elevation value.

spot finishing See **spotting in**.

spot ground A piece of wood which is attached to a plaster base to serve as a means of gauging plaster thickness.

spot level Same as **spot elevation**.

spotlight A **floodlight** equipped with a lens and one or more reflectors to provide a narrow beam to illuminate a specifically defined area.

spotlight booth A booth in an auditorium where spotlights are mounted and controlled.

spot mopping **Mopping** of a roofing surface with hot bitumen in roughly circular areas about 1½ ft (46 cm) in diameter, leaving a gridwork of unmopped bands.

spot relamping The replacement of each lamp in a lighting system, individually, at the time it fails. Also see **group relamping**.

spotting A paint-film defect characterized by small circular or irregular areas having color or gloss different from that of the surrounding background.

spotting in, spot finishing Repairing a small area on a dry painted surface by blending a fresh coat of paint with the dry coating.

spot-weld A **weld** between two overlapping members at an isolated spot by means of heat and pressure.

spout A short channel or tube used to spill storm water from gutters, balconies, exterior galleries, etc., so that the water will fall clear of the building. Also see **gargoyle**.

spraddle Same as **bonnet roof**.

spray booth An enclosed or semienclosed area used for the spray painting of fabricated items; may be equipped with a source of filtered air to keep the atmosphere dust-free, a waterfall backdrop to trap overspray, and an exhaust system to vent the fumes of the evaporating solvents.

sprayed acoustical plaster An acoustical plaster which has been applied with a special spray gun to form a continuous surface, usually of rough texture.

sprayed asbestos Asbestos fibers intermixed with bonding and adhesive ingredients; applied to surfaces such as structural beams with a spray gun; serves primarily as fire protection. The use of this material is no longer permitted in the United States because of its carcinogenic effects.

sprayed concrete See **shotcrete**.

sprayed fireproofing A material which is sprayed directly onto structural elements (or on specially provided base, such as lath) to provide increased fire endurance. Also see **sprayed asbestos**.

sprayed insulation See **spray-on insulation**.

sprayed mortar See **shotcrete**.

spray gun A tool, operated with compressed air or fluid pressure, which expels paint, mortar, etc., through a small orifice, onto the surface being coated. Also see **concrete gun**.

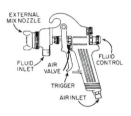

spray gun

spray lime A very fine hydrated lime; at least 95% of the particles pass through a No. 325 (45-μm) sieve.

spray-on insulation A mixture of mineral fiber with other ingredients; applied by air pressure with a **spray gun**; used to provide fire protection and/or thermal insulation.

spray painting Applying paint by means of a spray gun; provides a very uniform film, can cover evenly an object of irregular shape; esp. useful for painting large areas or mass-produced items.

spray pond An arrangement for lowering the temperature of water by evaporative cooling; the water to be cooled is sprayed by nozzles into a pond of water, cooling in the air as it falls.

spray-pond roof A roof designed to retain water in a **spray pond**, incorporating a system of spray jets; used to cool the roof.

spray sprinkler **1.** In a fire sprinkler system, a type of sprinkler that is **listed** for its capability to provide fire control over a wide range of fire hazards. **2.** A sprinkler providing a parabolic water distribution downward for a definite protection area; directs from 80 to 100 percent of the total water flow initially in a downward direction.

spread Of air supplied by a **air diffuser** in an air-conditioned space, the divergence of the airstream after it leaves the outlet.

spreadable life See **pot life, 2**.

spreader **1.** A machine for metering granular material, such as gravel or crushed stone, from a feed hopper and distributing it over a given area. **2.** A brace between two **wales**. **3.** A stiffening member temporarily attached to the base of a doorframe, extending between the jambs, to keep the frame in proper alignment during shipping and handling.

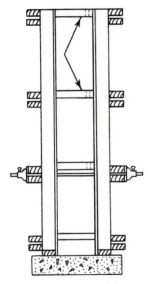

spreaders, 2 in a wall form

spreader bar A stiffening member placed at the base of a doorframe to keep it in alignment during shipment and prior to installation.

spread footing A **footing** which is especially wide, usually of reinforced concrete.

spreading rate **1.** The rate at which bitumen, roof surfacing, or other material is applied to a roof. **2.** The area covered by a gallon of paint.

spread lens A lens at the front of a directional luminaire or floodlight used to spread a relatively narrow beam; may be part of the luminaire or an auxiliary element.

spread-of-flame test A fire test of roof coverings in which a specified large flame plays on a

test roof deck continuously while exposed to a specified wind.

sprig A brad or nail without a head; also see **glazing sprig**.

sprig bit Same as **brad awl**.

spring **1.** An elastic body or device (such as a spirally wound metal coil) which stores mechanical energy when it is compressed and imparts this energy when it recovers its shape. **2.** See **springing. 3.** See **crook, 1**.

spring balance A **sash balance** in which the weight of the sash is counterbalanced by the force supplied by a spring.

spring bolt, cabinet lock A bolt having a beveled face; retracts when subject to pressure and springs back when the pressure is released; is self-acting when the door or drawer is closed.

spring bow Same as **bow compass**.

spring buffer A **buffer** consisting of a spring which stores and dissipates the kinetic energy of an impact (such as that resulting from a descending elevator car or counterweight that strikes the spring).

spring clamp A clamp esp. used to hold materials during gluing; similar to lightweight pliers in which clamping pressure is exerted by a spring.

spring clamp

spring clip Same as **resilient clip**.

spring constant Of an elastic spring, the ratio of the force applied on the spring to the resulting displacement.

springer, skewback, summer **1.** The impost or place where the vertical support for an arch terminates and the curve of the arch begins. **2.** The lower voussoir, or bottom stone of an arch, which lies immediately on an impost. **3.** The bottom stone of the coping of a gable. **4.** The rib of a groined roof or vault; also see **cross-springer**. (*See illustration p. 870.*)

spring floor Same as **resilient floor**.

spring hinge A hinge containing one or more springs; when a door is opened, the hinge returns

springhouse

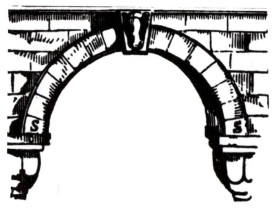

springer, 1: *S*

it to the open position automatically; may act in one direction only, or in both directions (as on a swinging door).

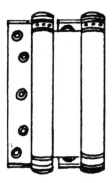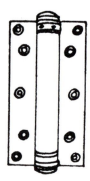

spring hinges

springhouse A small structure, typically of masonry construction, usually built into the slope of a hillside and enclosing a natural spring; the water flows into a small pool within the springhouse, keeping it cool at all times, and providing an excellent storage place for dairy products and other perishable foods.

springing, spring **1.** The point where an arch rises from its supports. **2.** The angle of rise of an arch.

springing course In masonry, the stones upon which the first stones of an arch rest.

springing line The imaginary horizontal line at which an arch or vault begins to curve; the line in which the springers rest on the imposts.

springing wall Same as a **buttress**.

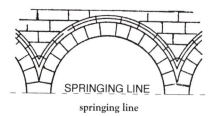

springing line

spring latch A door latch that springs into place when the door is closed.

spring line **1.** Same as **springing line**. **2.** In a transverse cross section of pipe, the line of maximum horizontal dimension.

spring lock A lock which fastens automatically by a spring when the door or lid to which it is attached is shut.

spring snib A spring-controlled sash fastener.

springwood Wood formed during the spring and early summer; characterized by cells which are larger and thinner than the cells formed later in the year.

sprinkle The distribution of additional chips on a terrazzo topping prior to rolling.

sprinkle mopping **Mopping** a roof surface with hot bitumen in a pattern applied in parallel bands.

sprinkler **1.** In a fire protection system, a device designed to release a stream of water and distribute it in a specified pattern and quantity over a designated area; usually one of many such outlet nozzles. **2.** A **fire-protection sprinkler system**.

sprinkler alarm An alarm on a **fire-protection sprinkler system** which sounds when there is flow of water in the system.

sprinklered Said of an area of a building that is equipped with a properly maintained **automatic sprinkler system**.

sprinkler head One of the many outlet nozzles in a fire-protection sprinkler system; in an automatic system, each nozzle is closed by a fusible plug that melts at a predetermined temperature; in an open-head system the individual nozzles are open, and a small group of nozzles is controlled by an automatic valve.

sprinkler system A system (usually automatic) for protection against fire which, when activated, sprays water over a large area in a systematic pattern; an integrated system of overhead and underground piping, designed in accordance with fire protection engineering standards, which includes: (a) one or more automatic water supplies, (b) a network of specially sized or hydraulically designed piping which is installed (generally overhead) throughout the building or area, (c) sprinklers (i.e., sprinkler heads) distributed in a systematic pattern which are attached to the piping, (d) a valve which controls each system riser or its supply piping, and (e) a device for actuating an alarm when the system is in operation.

sprinkler valve See **fire-protection sprinkler valve**.

sprocked eaves The eaves of a roof which have been raised by **sprockets**.

sprocket, cocking piece, sprocket piece In roofing, a strip of wood, fixed to the upper side of rafters at the eaves; raises the edge of the eaves and forms a break in the roof line.

spruce, Norway spruce, spruce fir, white deal, white fir A white to light brown or red-brown, straight- and even-grained wood; moderately low density and strength. Relatively inexpensive; used for general-utility lumber.

spruce pine See **eastern hemlock**.

sprung Said of timber or other structural members which have been bent by overloading.

sprung floor Same as **resilient floor**.

sprung molding A curved molding.

SPT Abbr. for "standard penetration test."

spud **1.** A sharp narrow bar or spade used for removing gravel and roofing from a roof. **2.** A dowel which is in the foot of a doorpost. **3.** A short pipe which serves as a connection in a piping system.

spudding drill Same as **churn drill**.

spud vibrator A type of concrete **vibrator** used to consolidate freshly placed concrete by inserting it into the mass of concrete.

spun concrete Concrete compacted by centrifugal action, e.g., in the manufacture of pipes.

spur **1.** An appendage to a supporting structure, as a shore, prop, or buttress; a decorative appendage of the base of a round column resting on a square or polygonal plinth, set at the corners, and taking the form of a grotesque, a tongue, or leafwork. Also called a **griffe**. **2.** A **spere**.

spur beam A horizontal timber, across the thickness of a wall, which is fixed to a wall plate, rafter, and ashlaring.

spur, 1

spur pile See **batter pile**.

spur shore A slanted timber holding a cofferdam around an excavation.

spur stone A stone post or block, set at the corners of archways, or the like, to protect the corners from damage by vehicles.

spur tenon Same as **stub tenon**.

sq. Abbr. for "square."

sq.E&S Abbr. for "square edge and sound."

square **1.** A measure of roofing materials; equals 100 sq ft (9.29 sq m). **2.** Any piece of material sawn or cut to be rectangular with equal dimensions on all four sides. **3.** A **steel square** for checking angles.

square and flat A frame, without molding, containing a flat panel; also see **square-framed**.

square and rabbet Same as **annulet**.

square billet A Norman molding consisting of a series of projecting cubes, with spaces between the cubes.

square bolt A door bolt which moves in a casing; similar to a **barrel bolt** but has a square rather than a circular cross section.

squared log A **balk**.

square dome Same as **coved vault**.

squared rubble Wall construction in which squared stones of various sizes are combined in patterns that make up courses as high as or higher than the tallest stones.

squared splice See **square splice**.

square-edged lumber Lumber having the edges sawn or planed, removing the **wane** to form a 90° angle; also see **square-sawn lumber**.

square-edge door A door having vertical edges that are perpendicular to the plane of its faces.

square-framed In joinery, framing having all the angles of its stiles, rails, and mountings square, without being molded.

square-headed Cut off at right angles above, as an opening with upright parallel sides and a straight horizontal lintel, as distinguished from an opening that is arched.

square-headed window A window having a straight horizontal lintel above it.

square joint See **straight joint, 2**.

square mil A unit of area equal to a square having sides equal to 0.001 in.; sometimes used to express the cross-sectional area of an electric conductor.

square miter An ordinary miter joint, where the abutting edges meet at an angle of 45°.

square notch At the corner of a log house, a joint formed by cutting away part of the upper half of one end of a timber and placing this timber at right angles to the end of another timber whose lower half has also been partially removed. A spike (or other fastener) through the overlapping timbers is required to secure the joint.

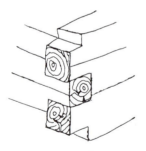

square notches

square-rigger house A colonial New England **hip roof** house with chimneys at both gable ends, or on both sides of a central hall, or centered between the front and back rooms. Many such houses had a **widow's walk** and/or cupola on the roof.

square roof A roof in which the rafters on opposites sides of the roof ridge meet at an angle of 90 degrees; each side of the ridge has a pitch of 45 degrees with respect to the vertical.

square-sawn lumber Sawn lumber having a rectangular cross section, with or without **wane**.

square shoot A wood **downspout**.

square splice, squared splice A type of half-lapped **scarf joint, 1**; may be reinforced with a fishplate; esp. used to resist tension.

square splice

square staff In plastering, a narrow wooden strip fixed as an angle bead at a salient corner of a room.

square-turned Said of ornamental balusters or the like which are molded or decorated on all four sides; not turned on a lathe.

square-turned baluster A baluster with moldings cut on four sides without the use of a lathe.

square up To plane a timber, piece of wood, etc., so that its cross section is rectangular.

squaring Adjusting or constructing so that all corners are rectangular.

squatter's right The right of one who occupies land without legal authority to acquire ownership of it through long-continued occupation. Also see **adverse possession** and **proscription**.

squatting closet Same as **Asiatic water closet**.

squeezed joint A joint formed at the surface of two pieces which have been coated with glue or cement and squeezed together.

squib See **electric squib**.

squinch **1.** Corbeling, often arcuate, built at the upper corners of a structural bay to support its tangent, smaller dome or drum. **2.** A small arch across the corner of a square room which supports a superimposed mass; also called a **sconce**.

squinch arch See **squinch, 2**.

squint **1.** A small opening, often obliquely cut, in the wall of a church, generally so placed as to afford a view of the high altar from the transept or aisles. **2.** A **squint brick**.

squint brick, squint quoin A building stone or brick of special shape; used at an oblique corner.

squint quoin See **squint brick**.

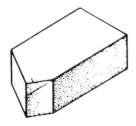

squint, 2

squint window See **squint, 1**.

SR Abbr. for "styrene rubber."

S/S Abbr. for **stainless steel**.

S-shape A standard, structural, hot-rolled steel shape of a specified category, designated by the prefix S placed before the size of the member.

SST On drawings, abbr. for **stainless steel**.

st Symbol for **strainer**.

ST **1.** On drawings, abbr. for "steam." **2.** On drawings, abbr. for **street**.

stab To roughen a surface of a brick wall with light blows of a pointed tool to provide a hold for plasterwork.

stability The resistance of a structure or element thereof to withstand sliding, overturning, buckling, or collapsing.

stabilization The action of improving the stability of the sloped surface of a soil mass.

stabilizer A substance used to increase the stability of a solution or suspension, usually by preventing precipitation.

stable A building, or portion thereof, for the housing and feeding of horses, cattle, and other domestic animals.

stable door Same as **Dutch door**.

stack **1.** Any vertical pipe, such as a soil pipe, waste pipe, vent, or leader stack. **2.** Such pipes, collectively. **3.** Any structure or part thereof which contains a flue or flues for the discharge of gases. **4.** A chimney stack. **5.** In warm-air heating systems, a vertical supply duct. **6.** A tier of book shelves.

stack bond, stacked bond **1.** In brickwork, a pattern bond; the facing brick is laid with all vertical joints continuously aligned. The brick is bonded to the backing by metal ties. **2.** In stone veneer masonry, a pattern in which units of a single size are set with continuous vertical and horizontal joints.

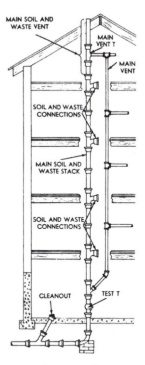

stack, 1: installation

stack bond, 2

stack cap Same as **vent cap**.

stack effect See **chimney effect**.

stack partition Any partition which carries a stack internally.

stack vent **1.** The extension (to the open air) of a soil or waste stack above the highest horizontal branch drain or fixture branch connected to the stack. Also called a **soil vent** or **waste vent**. **2.** In built-up roofing systems, a vertical outlet permitting water vapor, which is entrapped within the insulation, to escape. (*See illustration p. 874.*)

stack venting A method of venting a fixture or fixtures through the soil stack or waste stack;

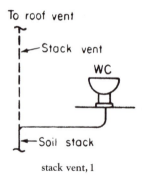

stack vent, 1

the fixtures must be grouped within a predetermined distance from the stack so that individual venting is not required.

staddle   **1.** A rack or supporting framework placed beneath a stack, such as a haystack. **2.** Any similar supporting framework.

staddle stone   One of the stones which supports a **staddle, 1**; usually mushroom-shaped.

stadia rod, stadia   A graduated rod used in the determination of distance by observing the intercept on the rod subtending a small known angle at the point of observation; the angle usually is defined by two fixed lines in the reticle of a telescope (transit or telescopic alidade).

stadium   A sports arena, usually oval or horseshoe-shaped.

staff   **1.** Ornamental plastering, made in molds and reinforced with fiber; usually nailed or wired into place. **2.** An exterior wall covering resembling stucco, used on temporary buildings. **3.** A **staff bead**. **4.** A piece used to close the joint between a wooden frame, as a window or door frame, and the masonry in which it is set.

staff angle   See **angle staff**.

staff bead   **1.** Same as **angle bead, corner bead**. **2.** A **backband**. **3.** A **brick molding**.

Staffordshire blue   A **blue brick**.

stage   **1.** A floor area or platform for dramatic, musical, or other types of performances. **2.** Same as **staging**.

stage box   A **proscenium box**.

stage door   An exterior door leading to the backstage of a theatre, used primarily by theatre personnel.

stage equipment   Equipment which is specifically fabricated for a theatre stage to facilitate the setting and striking of stage scenery.

stage grouting   Grouting in a series of steps rather than in one operation.

stagehouse   In a theatre, the part of the building on the stage side of the proscenium, including the stage, wings, and storage area.

stage left   The side of the stage to the left of an actor as he faces the audience.

stage level   The elevation of a stage.

stage lift   A section of the stage floor of a legitimate theater that can move upward or downward; designed to carry scenery between the stage storage areas, and/or for temporary use at elevations above or below the stage level, for special scenic effects.

stage peg, stage screw   A coarse-threaded hand screw, inserted into the stage floor of a theatre, to secure a brace for scenery.

stage pocket   In the backstage of a theatre, one of several metal boxes, with hinged lids, which are set into the wall or floor outside the acting area; contains jacks into which electric cables for stage lighting can be plugged.

stage rigging   Collectively, the ropes, wires, blocks, pulleys, pins, counterweights, winches, and other pieces of stage equipment required for the movement of scenery from overhead.

stage right   The side of the stage to the right of an actor as he faces the audience.

stage wagon   Same as **scenery wagon**.

stage wall pocket   A **stage pocket** set into a wall.

staggered   Descriptive of fasteners (such as nails, rivets, or screws), joints, studs, etc., arranged in two or more rows so that the beginning of each row is offset from the adjacent one(s).

staggered course   One of the courses of shingles, tiles, etc., on roofing where the butts do not form a horizontal line.

staggered partition   Same as **staggered-stud partition**.

staggered riveting   Rivets set in a zigzag pattern, so spaced that the rivets in one row are opposite the centers of the spaces of the adjoining rows.

staggered-stud partition   A partition using wood studs which are not in a straight line, but in two rows which are **staggered**; one row of studs supports the lath on one side of the wall,

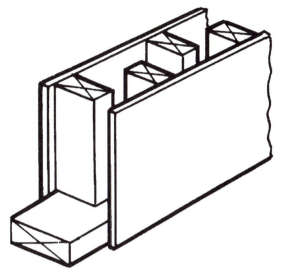

staggered-stud partition

and the second row supports the lath on the other; a fiberglass blanket may be woven between the staggered studs to improve the sound insulation value of the wall.

staging **1.** A temporary platform for workers and the materials they use in building erection; a **scaffold**. **2.** A temporary platform for workers which is supported on temporary timbering of a trench.

stain **1.** A discoloration in the surface of wood, plastic, sealant, etc. **2.** A colorant for enhancing wood grain during finishing. **3.** A **stainer**.

stained glass A decorative glass that is given a desired color, not by staining the glass, as the name implies, but by any one of several techniques. One method involves the application of an enamel paint onto a plain or tinted glass surface and firing it in a kiln. Another method fuses various metal oxides with glass while it is in its molten state; the resulting color, which has a jewel-like quality, depends on the metal oxide used. William Morris and his handycraftsmen in a studio near London may be said to have revived the modern art of making stained glass. Louis Comfort Tiffany (1848–1933) and John La Farge (1835–1910), developed yet another technique for making stained glass called *opalescent glass, Favrile glass,* or *American glass,* now often referred to as *Tiffany glass.* It is characterized by unusual combinations of colors and special effects in transparency and opaqueness, creating exaggerated color variations within the glass itself; was much used in the late 1800s and early 1900s for decorative objects, and to highlight architectural details.

stained-glass window A window whose glass is colored.

stainer, coloring pigment, tinter A pigment or dye which is used to impart color to paints.

staining The application of a liquid dye solution to a porous surface to impart color.

staining power See **tinting strength**.

stainless steel A high-strength, tough steel alloy; usually contains 4 to 25% chromium with nickel as an additional alloying element; highly resistant to corrosion and rust.

stair A series of steps (or flights of steps), connected by landings, that permit passage between two or more levels or floors. For specific types, see **box stair, bracketed stair, circular stair, cockle stair, cylindrical stair, dogleg stair, double-entry stair, double-L stair, double-return stair, double stair, fire stair, geometrical stair, good-morning stair, halfpace stair, hanging stair, helical stair, hollow-newel stair, interior stair, newel stair, open-newel stair, open stair, quarterpace stair, quarter-turn stair, reverse-flight stair, solid-newel stair, spiral stair, straight-flight stair, straight-run stair, well stair**.

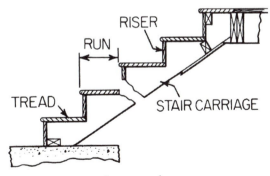

stair: nomenclature

stair bolt Same as **handrail bolt**.

stair bracket A bracket, often decorative, which is fixed to the face of an **open string**, immediately under the return nosing of each stair tread, to stiffen the tread. (*See illustration p. 876.*)

stair bracket

stairbuilder's truss   Crossed beams which support a **landing** of a stair.

stair carriage   Same as **carriage, 1**.

staircase   **1.** A flight of stairs, or a series of such flights, including supports, handrails, and framework. **2.** The structure containing a flight of stairs.

stair clip   A metal clip, or equivalent, used to hold a stair carpet in place.

stair dormer   A **dormer** of sufficient width to accommodate the upper part of a staircase leading to an upper half-floor or attic.

stair flight   See **flight**.

stair hall   A room in a home, usually of some pretentiousness, that is especially designed to contain and display a stair.

stairhead   The initial stair at the top of a flight of stairs or staircase.

stair headroom   The clear vertical height measured from the nosing of a stair tread to any overhead obstruction.

stair horse   A **carriage, 1**.

stair landing   See **landing**.

stair nosing   See **nosing**.

stair platform   An extended step or landing which breaks a continuous run of stairs.

stair rail   See **rail, 1**.

stair rise   Same as **rise, 1**.

stair riser   See **riser, 1**.

stair rod   A metal rod used to hold a stair carpet in place.

stair run   Same as **run, 2, 3**.

stair shaft   Same as **stairwell**.

stair shoe   See **shoe rail**.

stair string, stair stringer   See **string**.

stair tower   **1.** A **staircase**. **2.** A **stair turret**.

stair tread   See **tread**.

stair trimmer   See **trimmer**.

stair turret   **1.** A building containing a winding stair which usually fills it entirely. **2.** A stair enclosure which projects beyond the building roof.

stair turret

stair wall string   See **wall string**.

stairway   A **staircase**.

stairwell   The vertical shaft which contains a staircase.

stair windows   Same as **stepped windows**.

stair wire   A light **stair rod**.

stake   **1.** A small anvil used for the working of thin sheet metal, so called because it is supported by a sharp vertical prop which is inserted in a hole in the workbench; the sheet-metal worker may select one of a number of different stakes, the particular shape depending on the task. **2.** A stick of wood sharpened at one end and set into the ground to act as a boundary marker or to support or hold something.

stake-and-rider fence A **rail fence** assembled without the use of post holes, as follows: two *stakes* are crossed, forming a crotch near their upper ends; a horizontal rail (called the *rider*) is supported by the crotch, then this assembly is bound together at the crotch; a series of such assemblies is required to form the fence, often with additional horizontal rails below the rider.

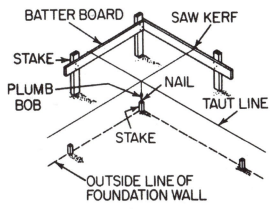

stake-and-rider fence

staking out The driving of **stakes, 2** for **batter boards**, thereby locating the corners of an excavation.

staking out

stalactite work See **muqarnas**.

stale sewage Sewage that contains little or no oxygen and is free from putrefaction.

stalk See **cauliculus**.

stall **1.** A fixed seat enclosed wholly or partially at the back and sides. **2.** (*Brit.*) In the theatre, a seat in the front division of the parquet (orchestra stalls).

stalactite work

stallboard A strong sill (and lumber framing) at the base of a storefront window which supports it.

stallboard light A **pavement light** adjacent to a **stallboard**.

stallboard riser On a storefront, the vertical surface between pavement level and the stallboard.

stamba, stambha In Hindu architecture and derivatives, a freestanding column surmounted by a large symbol.

stamped-metal ceiling See **pressed-metal ceiling**.

stamping A process used to shape a piece of sheet metal by means of a die and a punch in a drop hammer.

stanchion **1.** A prop, upright bar, or piece of timber giving support to a roof, a window, or the like. **2.** An upright bar, beam, or post, as of a window, screen, railing, etc.

standard **1.** A document prepared by a recognized standard-setting organization that prescribes methods and materials for the safe use and consistent performance of specific technologies; usually a procedure that has been developed by consensus of the interested parties. **2.** As used by governmental agencies, a document which sets certain legally permissible limits. **3.** See **measurement**. **4.** A document containing mandatory requirements indicated by the word ***shall***.

standard absorption trench An **absorption trench** which is 12 to 36 in. (approx. 30 to 90 cm) in width, containing 12 in. (30 cm) of clean coarse aggregate and a distribution pipe which is covered with a minimum of 12 in. (30 cm) of earth cover.

standard air Air having a density of 0.075 lb per cu ft (0.0012 gm per cu cm) which approximates air at 68°F (20.0°C) dry bulb and 50% relative humidity at a barometric pressure of 29.9 in. (76.0 cm) of mercury, or approximating dry air at 70°F (21.1°C) at the same pressure.

standard atmosphere A pressure equivalent to 14.7 lb per sq in. $(1.01 \times 10^6$ dynes per sq cm).

standard atmospheric pressure The pressure exerted by a standard atmosphere; also see **atmospheric pressure**.

standard cubic foot of gas The amount of gas that would occupy one cubic foot at a temperature of 60°F, saturated with vapor, and under a pressure equivalent to that of 30.0 inches of mercury column.

standard curing Subjecting test specimens of concrete to specified conditions of temperature and moisture.

standard dimensions ratio (SDR) The ratio of the average specified outside diameter to the minimum specified wall thickness of a pipe.

standard hook At the end of a steel **reinforcing bar**, a hook made in accordance with a standard.

standard inside diameter dimension ratio (SIDR) The ratio of the average specified inside diameter to the minimum specified wall thickness of a pipe.

Standard International units, SI units See **International System of Units**.

standard knot In wood, any knot 1½ in. (3.81 cm) or less in diameter.

standard penetration resistance, Proctor penetration resistance **1.** The unit load required to maintain a constant rate of penetration of a probe into a soil. **2.** The unit load required to produce a specified penetration into a soil, at a specified rate of penetration; for a Proctor needle, the specified penetration is 2.5 in. (6.35 cm) and the penetration rate is 0.5 in. (1.27 cm) per second.

standard penetration test See **penetration test**.

standard pile Same as **guide pile**.

standard pipe size See **iron pipe size**.

standard pressure Same as **standard atmospheric pressure**.

standard railing According to OSHA: a vertical barrier at floor level erected along exposed edges of a floor opening, wall opening, platform, runway, or ramp to prevent falls of persons.

standard sand **Ottawa sand**, accurately graded to pass a 850-μm (U.S. Standard No. 20) sieve and to be retained on a 600-μm (U.S. Standard No. 30) sieve; used in testing cements.

standards of professional practice Statements of ethical principles promulgated by professional societies to guide their members in the conduct of professional practice.

standard source In illumination engineering, a light source having a specified spectral distribution, used as a standard for colorimetry.

standard source A, light source A A tungsten filament lamp operating at a color temperature of 2856°K (2583°C).

standard source B, light source B A light source that approximates noon sunlight having a correlated color temperature of approx. 4874°K (4601°C).

standard source C, light source C Light which approximates a combination of direct sunlight and a clear sky having a correlated color temperature of 6774°K (6501°C).

standard special A special-shaped brick that is in general use and may be available from stock.

standard temperature and pressure A temperature of 32°F (0°C) and a barometric pressure of 29.9 in. (76.0 cm) of mercury.

standard tolerance An established **tolerance** for a particular class of product.

standard wire gauge A wire gauge formerly used in Great Britain and Canada; superseded by metric wire diameters.

standby lighting Lighting designed to supply illumination in the event of failure of the normal lighting system, so that normal activities in the area may continue.

standby power generator A packaged unit including a prime mover, electric generator, and associated controls and equipment to provide power if the normal source fails.

standing bevel   A bevel which forms an obtuse angle.

standing finish   That part of the interior fittings of a building which is permanent and fixed in place, as distinguished from doors, movable sashes, etc.

standing gutter   A **V**-shaped gutter near the lower end of a sloped roof; one side of the **V** is formed by a long board, running parallel to the eaves, whose broad side is approximately perpendicular to the sloping surface of the roof; the roof itself acts as the other side of the **V**.

standing leaf   An **inactive leaf** of a door, bolted in a closed position.

standing panel   A panel whose longer dimension is vertical.

standing room   A space set aside for spectators to stand, usually at the back of the orchestra section of a theatre.

standing seam   In metal roofing, a type of seam between adjacent sheets of material, made by turning up the edges of two adjacent sheets and then folding them over.

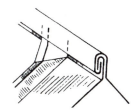

standing seam   along the ridge of a roof

standing waste   A type of device for the control of the outlet and overflow of a plumbing fixture; an overflow pipe is inserted in the outlet at the bottom of a fixture or tank, permitting water to be retained at a desired level.

stand oil   A polymerized vegetable oil, such as linseed or tung oil, which has been heated (without blowing) at a high temperature in order to thicken it to the consistency of honey; used as a medium in paints.

standpipe   A pipe or tank used for the storage of water, esp. for emergency use.

standpipe system   A system of **standpipes**, pumps, siamese connections, and piping, provided with an adequate supply of water and equipment with hose outlets for fire fighting.

standpipe   connection

stand sheet   See **fixed light**.

stanza   A room or chamber within a building, as the stanze of Raphael in the Vatican.

staple   A U-shaped piece of metal or heavy wire, with pointed ends, driven into a surface to secure a sheet of material, hold a hasp, etc.

staple gun   A tool for driving wire staples; esp. used in construction for fastening materials such as building paper, asphalt prepared roofing, and the like.

staple hammer, stapling hammer   A tool, resembling and swung like a hammer, that drives a staple when the face strikes a surface.

stapler   1. A **staple gun**. 2. A **staple hammer**.

stapling hammer   See **staple hammer**.

starch gum   See **dextrin**.

star drill   A long steel tool having a star-shaped point, used for drilling holes in concrete, masonry, and stone; it is handheld, the head being struck repeatedly with a hammer to provide the drilling action.

star drill

star expansion bolt   A type of **expansion bolt** which has a shield of two semicircular parts that are forced apart as the bolt is driven.

star molding   A common Norman molding whose surface is a succession of projecting star-like shapes.

Star of David, Mogen David A six-pointed star composed of two equilateral triangles, one superimposed upside down on the other; a symbol of Judaism.

star-ribbed vault Same as **star vault**.

starshake A number of **heartshakes** which radiate from the center of a log in a star-like pattern.

starshake

starter **1.** A device used with a **ballast** to start an **electric-discharge lamp**. **2.** An electric controller for starting an electric motor, for bringing it up to normal speed, and for stopping it. **3.** One of a series of roofing shingles applied beneath the first course of shingles, with a slight overhang at the eaves.

starter frame Shallow **formwork** which projects above floor level, for the location and subsequent construction of a column or wall.

starter strip, starting strip The first course of composition roofing material, applied along a line adjacent to the eaves.

starter tile See **eaves tile**.

starting board In the construction of **formwork**, the board at the foundation which is first nailed in place.

starting course The first course of shingles applied to roof sheathing, along a line adjacent to the eaves.

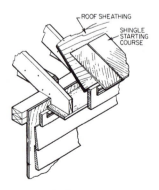

ROOF SHEATHING

SHINGLE STARTING COURSE

starting course

starting newel The newel-post at the foot of a stair.

starting step The lowest step in a flight of stairs.

starting strip See **starter strip**.

start of construction See **actual start of construction**.

star trap A type of trap in a theatre stage through which an actor, standing on a counterweighted platform, can make a sudden appearance or disappearance.

star vault, stellar vault A vault whose rib pattern suggests a star.

starved See **hungry**.

starved joint A poorly bonded glue joint resulting from an insufficient quantity of glue in the joint.

statement of probable construction cost Cost forecasts prepared by the architect during the **schematic design, design development**, and **construction documents phases** of **basic services** for the guidance of the owner.

static deflection Same as **residual deflection**.

static head, pressure head The static pressure of fluid expressed in terms of the height of a column of the fluid which the pressure could support.

static load Any load, as on a structure, which does not change in magnitude or position with time.

static penetration test A **penetration test** in which penetration into the soil results from the application of a steady force on a testing device. Also see **dynamic penetration test**.

static pressure **1.** In an air distribution system, the pressure which the fan must supply to overcome the resistance to airflow through the system ductwork and system components. **2.** The pressure which a fluid exerts on a surface at rest with respect to it. **3.** At a point, the atmospheric pressure in the absence of sound waves; usually expressed in pascals.

statics That branch of the science of mechanics concerned with forces acting on bodies in equilibrium.

static test On windows and curtain walls: **1.** A structural test, subjecting a test unit to a pressure differential equivalent to the maximum expected wind pressure. **2.** A water test simulating the flow of water down over the test unit during a hurricane.

static Young's modulus The value of Young's modulus derived from static measurements of stress-strain relationships, rather than from dynamic measurements.

station **1.** A definite point on the earth whose location has been determined by surveying methods. **2.** A point on a **survey traverse** over which an instrument is placed. **3.** On a survey traverse, a length of 100 ft measured on a given line—broken, straight, or curved.

stationary hopper A container used to receive and store temporarily freshly mixed concrete.

stationary window A window or area of a window that does not open; glazed directly in a fixed frame.

station roof **1.** A roof which is shaped like an umbrella, supported by a single post in the center; also called an **umbrella roof**. **2.** A long roof supported by a single row of posts and from cantilevers to one or both sides, as on a railway station platform.

statute of frauds A rule that certain kinds of contracts are unenforceable unless signed and in writing or unless there is a written memorandum of their terms signed by the party to be charged. In most states contracts for the sale of real property or for leases of over a specified duration must be in writing to be enforceable.

statute of limitations A statute specifying the period of time within which legal action must be brought for alleged damage or injury. The lengths of the periods vary from state to state and depend upon the type of legal action. The period commences to run under some statutes of limitations upon the accrual of a legal claim, but in others only upon the time of discovery of the act resulting in the alleged damage or injury.

statutory bond A bond, the form or content of which is prescribed by statute.

St. Augustine house See **Saint Augustine house**.

staunchion Same as **stanchion**.

stave **1.** One of a number of narrow boards used to build up a curved surface. **2.** A **rung** of a ladder. **3.** In formwork for an excavation, one of many vertical members which form a curved surface (in plan).

stave church A Scandinavian wooden church with vertical planks forming the walls.

stave church

stave core See **continuous block core**.

stay **1.** Anything that stiffens or helps to maintain a frame or other structure, as a strut or brace. **2.** See **casement stay, peg stay**.

stay bar Same as **casement stay**.

stay bolt A long metal rod having a threaded end.

stay bolt

stay plate See **batten plate**.

stay rod A **tie rod** which prevents spreading of the parts to which it is connected.

stay rope A **rope** that serves as a **guy**.

STC Abbr. for **sound transmission class**.

STD On drawings, abbr. for "standard."

Std. M Abbr. for "standard matched."

steam blow A **blister, 1**.

Steamboat Gothic A richly ornamental mode of **Carpenter Gothic architecture**, making elaborate and imaginative use of **gingerbread**; primarily found in the middle to the latter half of the 19th century, suggestive of the ornate and flamboyant decorations on steamboats on the Ohio and Mississippi Rivers.

steam boiler and machinery insurance Special insurance covering steam boilers, other pressure vessels, and related equipment and machinery; covers damage or injury to property resulting from explosion of steam boilers which is not covered by extended coverage perils.

steam box, curing kiln An enclosure for the **steam curing** of concrete products.

steam cleaner A machine that generates a high-pressure jet of steam which can be directed through a nozzle to scour dirt or grease from a surface; may use detergents or other chemicals.

steam curing The **curing** of concrete or mortar in water vapor at an elevated temperature, at either atmospheric or high pressure.

steam-curing cycle **1.** The time interval between the start of the temperature-rise period and the end of the soaking period or the cooling-off period. **2.** A schedule of the time and temperature of the periods which make up the cycle.

steam-curing room, steam kiln A chamber for steam **curing** concrete products at atmospheric pressure.

steam curtain An apparatus consisting of perforated pipes, located at the proscenium of a theatre, from which steam escapes; used to block or partially obscure a view of the stage.

steam grid humidifier, steam jet humidifier A **humidifier** in an air duct in which steam is introduced into the airstream through a series of perforated pipes.

steam heating system A system in which heat is transferred from a boiler or other source of heat to the radiators by means of steam at, above, or below atmospheric pressure.

steam humidifier A humidifier in which steam is injected directly into an airstream.

steam jet humidifier See **steam grid humidifier**.

steam kiln See **steam-curing room**.

steam pipe Any pipe in which steam is conveyed.

steam shovel A **power-shovel** operated by steam which is generated in its own boiler.

steam table A table, or a section of a counter in a cafeteria, having openings set in the top in which are fitted containers for cooked food; the containers are kept warm by steam, hot air, or hot water which circulates beneath them.

steam trap A device for allowing the passage of **condensate**, or air and condensate, and preventing the passage of steam.

steatite An industrial grade of talc of high purity; block steatite which meets a specified degree of purity is designated as **soapstone**.

steel A malleable alloy of iron and carbon produced by melting and refining pig iron and/or scrap steel; graded according to the carbon content (in a range from 0.02 to 1.7%); other elements, such as manganese and silicon, may be included to provide special properties. Also see **high steel** and **tempered steel**.

steel-cage construction Same as **skeleton construction**.

steel casement A **casement**; usually made from hot-rolled steel sections; often classified as a residence, intermediate, or heavy-intermediate steel casement.

steel concrete See **reinforced concrete**.

steel decking See **decking, 2** and **metal floor decking**.

steel-frame construction Construction in which the structural supporting elements consist of combinations of steel beams, steel girders, and steel columns, joined together at their intersections.

steel H-pile See **H-pile**.

steel joist In a building, any steel structural member that is composed of hot-rolled or cold-formed solid or open-web sections of steel or welded bars, strip- or sheet-steel members, or slotted, expanded, or otherwise deformed rolled sections of steel.

steel lathing   See **metal lath**.

steel measuring tape   A **tape measure**.

steel pipe   A pipe manufactured in any of a large number of steel alloys, either extruded (seamless) or welded (with in a seam). Its wall thickness ranges from Schedule 10 (lightest) to Schedule 160 (heaviest).

steel sheet   In steel construction work, a cold-formed sheet of metal which is shaped as a structural member to carry loads (live or dead) in lightweight concrete roof construction.

steel square   A steel **carpenter's square**.

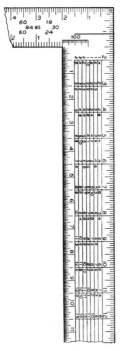

one type of **steel square**

steel stud   An upright post or support (i.e., a **stud**) fabricated of sheet steel; usually one of many in constructing a **stud partition**.

steel stud anchor   A metal piece or clip attached to the inside of a doorframe to secure the frame to a steel stud.

steel tape   See **tape measure**.

steel troweling   The use of a trowel or a troweling machine in the final stages of concrete finishing operations to impart a relatively smooth surface to a concrete floor or other unformed concrete surface.

steel wool   A matted mass of long, fine, steel fibers; esp. used for cleaning and polishing surfaces.

steening   The brick or stone lining, often laid dry, of a cesspool, cistern, or well.

steep asphalt   Roofing asphalt having a high **softening point**; esp. applied on roofs that are steep.

steeple   A tall ornamental structure; a tower, composed of a series of stories diminishing in size, and topped by a small pyramid, spire, or cupola.

steeple house   A term used by some religious faiths for a church.

steining   Same as **steening**.

stele, stela   **1.** In classical architecture and derivatives, an upright stone, usually a slab, marking a grave. **2.** A wall area set aside as a memorial.

finial to a Greek **stele**

stellar vault   See **star vault**.

stemming   A suitable inert incombustible material or device used to confine or separate explosives in a drill hole, or to cover explosives in **mudcapping**.

stench trap   **1.** A **trap, 1**. **2.** A **flap trap** in a cellar drain, preventing sewer air from entering the building.

step

step A stair unit which consists of one tread and one riser.

step bracket Same as **stair bracket**.

step brazing A method of **brazing** in which successive joints on a part are joined with **filler metals** of successively lower brazing temperatures, so that the joints previously brazed are not disturbed.

step-down ceiling diffuser A **ceiling diffuser** which projects below the plane of the finished ceiling.

step flashing Same as **stepped flashing**.

step gable See **corbie gable**.

step iron A U-shaped heavy metal loop which is set into masonry work; usually one in a series to provide convenient steps for climbing up or down a wall, chimney, etc.

step joint **1.** A notched joint for two structural timbers making an angle with each other, as a **tie beam** and **rafter**. **2.** A joint between the ends of two rails of different height and/or section.

step-kiln See **progressive kiln**.

stepladder A ladder having flat steps, or treads, in place of rungs; usually provided with a supporting frame to steady it.

step log Same as **notch-log ladder**.

stepped arch An arch in which the **voussoirs** are cut horizontally and/or vertically so they fit in with the masonry courses above and below, forming a series of steps.

stepped arch

stepped-back chimney An exterior brick chimney, rectangular in cross section, sufficiently wide at the level of the hearth to enclose a large fireplace on the interior, and then of decreasing width, in number of steps, with increasing chimney height.

stepped-back chimney

stepped column A column whose cross section changes abruptly at several points along its length.

stepped flashing A metal flashing used at the intersection of a wall and a sloping roof; the upper edge of the vertical part of the flashing steps down, following the general inclination of the roof; the horizontal edges are fastened to **raggle** cut in the brickwork of masonry walls.

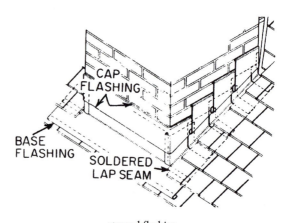

stepped flashing

stepped floor A floor on the stage of an auditorium which rises in steps, as contrasted to a raked or ramped floor.

stepped footing A **footing** consisting of a series of concrete prisms of progressively smaller lateral dimensions, one above the other, to distribute the load of a wall or column to the subgrade.

stepped foundation   A foundation cut in a series of steps in a sloping bearing stratum, to prevent sliding when subject to the bearing load.

stepped gable   Same as **corbie gable**.

stepped ramp, ramped steps   A series of ramps which are interconnected by steps.

stepped string   Same as **open string**.

stepped voussoir   A **voussoir** which is squared along its upper surfaces so that it fits horizontal courses of masonry units.

stepped windows   A series of windows set in an exterior wall adjacent to a staircase, arranged in a stepped pattern that generally follows the ascent of the steps.

stepping   **1.** Softwood lumber suitable for steps; usually pine or fir. **2.** A **step-plank**. **3.** In concrete step construction, **benching, 1, 2. 4.** In surveying, **chaining** in a series of steps, over a sloping surface, where the chains are always horizontal.

stepping off   Laying off, exactly, the required length of a rafter by the use of a framing square.

steppingstone   A flat stone set in level with the earth, or set in a pond or stream, to provide a footpath.

step-plank   Hardwood lumber, usually about 1¼ to 2 in. (3.2 to 5.1 cm) thick, esp. used as **stepping**.

step pyramid   An early type of **pyramid** having a stepped superstructure.

step pyramid

step soldering   A method of soldering in which successive joints on a part are joined with solders of successively lower soldering temperatures, so that joints previously soldered are not disturbed.

step turner   A tool, made of hardwood, used to shape a **stepped flashing**.

stereobate   The substructure, foundation, or solid platform upon which a building is erected.

In a columnar building, it includes the **stylobate** (the uppermost step or platform of the foundation upon which the columns stand).

stereochromy   A method of painting in which water glass serves as the connecting medium between the color and its substratum.

stereotomy   The art of cutting solids, e.g. stone, into certain figures or shapes.

steyre   Old English term for **grees**.

STG   On drawings, abbr. for "storage."

stiacciato   In very low relief, as if a **bas-relief** had been pressed flatter.

stick   **1.** Any long slender piece of wood. **2.** A shaped piece of wood, as a stake.

stick-and-rag work   See **fibrous plaster**.

sticker   **1.** A narrow rectangular strip of wood used to separate pieces of lumber in piles. **2.** A piece from which molding is cut. **3.** A **sticker machine**.

sticker machine, sticker molder   A machine for shaping moldings.

sticking   **1.** The shaping of molding. **2.** The cementing together of pieces of broken or separated stone, or the like.

sticking board   A frame used to position a piece of wood while a molding is being cut in it.

sticks-and-clay chimney, sticks-and-mud chimney, stick chimney   Same as **clay-and-sticks chimney**.

Stick style   An eclectic style of domestic architecture in the United States primarily from about 1860 to 1890, mainly of **wood-frame construction**; usually asymmetric in both plan and section; has applied ornamentation in the form of wood boards on the exterior surfaces that is intended to express the inner structure of the building. Buildings in this style usually include some of the following characteristics: a façade of clapboard or board-and-batten siding with structural framing materials used as exterior ornamentation or wood boards prominently applied in patterns on wall surfaces; prominent structural corner posts; spacious porches, decorated in wood with simple diagonal braces or brackets; a steeply pitched gable roof, often with intersecting gables and/or cross gables; eaves with a significant overhang, often supported by large diagonal brackets; exposed roof trusses and rafters; corbeled chimneys. (*See illustration p. 886.*)

Stick style

stickwork Wood boards applied in patterns in the horizontal, vertical, and diagonal directions, usually over the exterior wood **cladding** of a house.

sticky cement Cement having reduced ability to flow freely as a result of **pack set**, or **warehouse set**.

stiffback Same as **strongback**.

stiffened compression element A structural element, subject to compressive forces, that has been reinforced or stiffened, along a line perpendicular to its weak axis of bending, in order to provide additional strength against buckling.

stiffened expanded metal Same as **self-centering lath** or **rib lath**.

stiffened seated-beam connection A seated-beam connection that has a vertical element directly below the horizontal component of the seat in order to help support the load above.

stiffener **1.** A secondary member, usually an **angle iron** or **channel, 1**, attached to a plate or sheet to increase its stiffness and to prevent buckling. **2.** In a hollow-metal door, the internal reinforcement for door panels; usually channel iron.

stiffening angle An **angle iron** connected to the web of a girder to stiffen it against buckling.

stiff frame See **rigid frame**.

stiff leaf (*Brit.*) In medieval ornament and derivatives, a formalized leaf shape.

stiff-leg derrick A **derrick** comprised of a mast and boom, with two (relatively short) sloping fixed legs supporting the mast.

stiff-mud brick Brick produced by extruding a stiff, but plastic, clay (12 to 15% moisture) through a die.

stiffness The ratio of the force applied to a structure (or a structural element) to the corresponding displacement.

stiffness factor Of a member, the ratio of the moment of inertia of the cross section to its length.

stilb A unit of luminance equal to 1 candela per sq cm. *Abbr.* sb. The use of this term is deprecated.

S-tile A roof tile S-shaped in profile.

stile **1.** One of the upright structural members of a frame, as at the outer edge of a door or a window sash. **2.** A set of steps, or a framework of bars and steps, for crossing over a fence or wall.

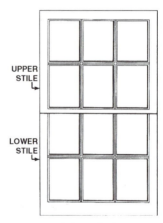

window **stile, 1**

Stile Liberty The Italian version of Art Nouveau, so named after the firm of Liberty and Co. in London.

stile plate Same as **push plate**.

stillroom A room connected with the kitchen, where coffee, tea, and the like are stored and prepared for use.

stilt **1.** A structural area or element lifting another such above its regular position. **2.** A post which raises a structure above ground or

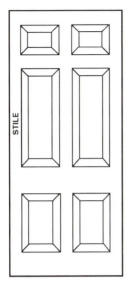

door **stile,** 1

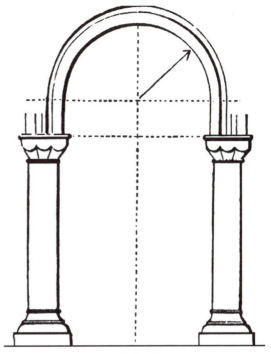

stilted arch

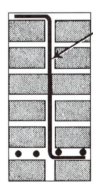

stirrup, 2

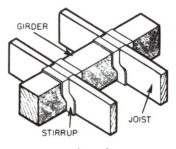

stirrup, 4

water level. **3.** A member placed above or below another vertical member for additional height. **4.** See **stilted arch. 5.** Of a door frame: see **base anchor. 6.** A brace in **bridging.**

stilted arch An arch whose curve begins above the impost line.

stilted vault A **vault** whose curve begins above the line of the **imposts.**

stipple **1.** To make dots, points, etc., on a surface (as a painted or freshly plastered surface), to achieve a decorative effect. **2.** A **stippler.**

stippled finish A dotted or a pebbly-textured finish on a surface coat of paint, plaster, porcelain enamel, etc.; produced by striking the unhardened coat with the bristles of a stippling brush.

stippler **1.** A broad flat-based brush having stiff bristles for producing a texture on a surface such as soft plaster or paint. **2.** Any tool (as a rubber sponge or a textured or tufted roller) used to create a stippled surface.

stippling Dotted or pebbly-textured finish of any kind.

stipulated sum agreement A contract in which a specific amount is set forth as the total payment for performance of the contract.

stirrup **1.** Same as **hanger. 2.** A bent rod, usually U-shaped or W-shaped; used in reinforced brick or concrete construction. **3.** A reinforcing device to resist shear and diagonal tension stresses in a beam. **4.** A metal seat, attached to a wall beam or post or hung from a girder, to receive and support a beam or joist.

stirrup strap Same as **stirrup, 4.**

stitch nailing A method of nailing two pieces of wood together by driving nails through each of the two exposed sides so they cross each other at right angles.

stitch rivet One of a number of rivets placed at intervals between two component parts to hold them together and to provide lateral stiffness.

stitch welding The joining of two or more parts by the use of intermittent welds.

STK On drawings, abbr. for "stock."

STL On drawings, abbr. for **steel**.

stoa A portico, usually detached, often of considerable extent, providing a sheltered promenade or meeting place.

stob A small post, as one of the uprights in fencing.

stock **1.** Lumber, panels, doors, windows, etc., commonly used and readily available from suppliers. **2.** The principal supporting or holding part; the part in which other parts are inserted, as the body of a tool. **3.** A tool, used in cutting threads for pipes or bolts, which holds the dies.

stockade A defensive barrier; logs or timbers driven into the ground to form an enclosure.

stock brick In any geographical area, the type of brick that is most commonly available.

stock brush In plastering, a brush for applying water to dampen a base coat which is too dry (before applying the finish coat) or to a finish coat during troweling.

stockhouse set Same as **warehouse set**.

stock lock Same as **box lock**.

stock lumber Lumber which has been cut to standard sizes and is readily available from a supplier.

stock millwork Millwork manufactured in standard sizes, patterns, and layouts, and readily available from a supplier.

stock size A size which is normally available from warehouse supplies.

stoker A mechanical device for feeding solid fuel into a furnace.

stone Any type of rock that has been selected or processed by cutting, shaping, or sizing for use in building construction or for decorative purposes; see **brownstone, cobblestone, dimension stone, fieldstone, flagstone, freestone, granite, limestone, marble, pudding stone, rib vault, rusticated stone, sandstone, soapstone**.

stone bolt In masonry construction, a bolt which is fixed in mortar for supporting a member.

stone cabin A small house built of stone, typified by homes built by German-speaking colonists in Pennsylvania; usually characterized by a roof having a very steep pitch, thick stone walls, and wooden casement windows with solid shutters.

stone chip A small, angular fragment of stone containing no dust.

stone drain Same as **French drain**.

stone dust Pulverized stone used for walks, either mixed with earth and compacted or mixed with gravel to fill the spaces between irregular stones and produce a stable surface.

stone-ender, stone-ender house A late 17th-century house having **post-and-girt framing**; basically, a one-room medieval-style cottage of the type described under **American Colonial architecture**; found primarily in Rhode Island; its most significant feature was a massive end wall built of stone that incorporated a very large fireplace chimney; an impressive chimney cap; small casement windows containing panes of glass set diagonally in lead cames; a battened door at the entry, which opened into a small room called the *porch*.

stone-filled sheet asphalt Asphalt concrete in which most of the mineral aggregate passes through a 2.00-mm (No. 10) sieve and conforms to the requirements for **sheet asphalt**; ordinarily confined to surface course construction.

Stonehenge A megalithic, prehistoric monument near Salisbury, England, in Wiltshire; the most imposing megalithic monument in existence.

stone lantern An outdoor lantern, usually Japanese, used as a permanent garden ornament.

stone masonry **Masonry** composed of field, quarried, or cast stone units bonded by mortar.

stone medallion A term occasionally used for **date stone**.

stone sand Sand manufactured from stone.

stone-setter's adjustable multiple-point suspension scaffold A swinging-type scaffold having a platform supported by hangers suspended at four points so as to permit the raising or lowering of the platform to the desired working position by the use of hoisting machines.

stone slate Thin-bedded stone slabbing or flagging, irregular in size and shape, usually limestone or sandstone; used as rough shingling on a roof; separates along its bedding, unlike true **slate**, which is a metamorphic rock that splits along its cleavage.

stoneware, earthenware A hard, vitrified, ceramic ware, usually salt-glazed; used for sanitary fixtures, pipes, and channels.

stonework 1. Masonry construction in stone. 2. Preparation or setting of stone for building or paving.

stool 1. The flat piece upon which a window shuts down, corresponding to the sill of a door. 2. A narrow shelf fitted across the lower part of the inside of a window opening; butts against the sill. 3. A **window stool**. 4. Same as **packing piece**. 5. A framed support.

stoop A platform or small porch, usually up several steps, at the entrance to a house.

stoop

stoothing (*colloq.*) Studding, lath and plaster, common grounds, etc.

stop 1. The molding or trim on the inside face of a door or window frame against which the door or window closes; a **bead, 2**. 2. The projecting boss or other ornament against which the termination of a molding abuts. 3. A button, or the

like, which serves to lock a latch bolt in the position in which it is set.

stop-and-check valve Same as **nonreturn valve**.

stop-and-waste cock A **stopcock** having a drain in the valve, used in a water piping system; when the stopcock is turned so that the water supply is shut off, the drain in the valve opens, thereby draining off the water downstream from the stopcock to a waste.

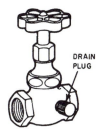

DRAIN PLUG

stop-and-waste cock

stop bead See **bead, 2**.

stop chain In a theatre stagehouse, a chain between the **gridiron** and the top of the fire curtain; used as a limiting device to restrain the curtain when it reaches the stage floor.

stop chamfer, stopped chamfer A chamfer which curves or angles, becoming narrower until it meets the arris.

stopcock A valve to shut off flow of water or gas in a branch of the building distribution network.

stope An excavation in the earth in a series of benches or tables.

stop end, stopped end 1. The closed end of gutter or ridge capping. 2. The squared-off, finished end of a wall.

stop molding A solid or struck molding which is terminated short of the end of the member into which it is cut.

stopoff A material used to limit the spread of solder or brazing **filler metal** on the surfaces adjacent to the joint.

stopped chamfer See **stop chamfer**.

stopped dado A **dado, 3** which does not cut across the full width of the piece of wood in which it is set. (*See illustration p. 890.*)

stopped end See **stop end**.

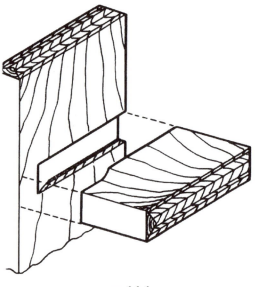

stopped dado

stopped flute In classical architecture and derivatives, a flute terminated, usually about two-thirds of the way down a column or pilaster. Below this, the shaft may be smooth or faceted, or the fluting may be incised partway, leaving a flat surface sunk between fillets. A cabled flute is sometimes called "stopped."

stopped mortise See **blind mortise**.

stopper, stopping A compound, such as **putty**, used to fill holes in wood, metal, etc.

stopping Same as **stopper**.

stopping knife A **putty knife**.

stop screw A wood screw used to fasten a **bead, 2** to a window frame.

stop stone In a pair of gates, a stone (in the ground) against which the meeting stiles close.

stop valve A valve in a piping distribution network which is used to shut off a line.

stopwork A mechanism on a lock which fixes the spring bolt in the shot-out position so that it cannot be operated by a key (or the handle) from the outside, providing additional security; can be set by a sliding button or push button.

storage capacity factor In a water heater, the ratio of the volume of the storage tank to the maximum volume of hot water probably used in a one hour period.

storage cistern A **cistern** for storing water.

storage hopper See **stationary hopper**.

storage life, shelf life The time period for which a material (such as a packaged adhesive or sealant) can be stored, under specified temperature conditions, and remain suitable for use.

storage tank A container or vessel which receives water from a source of supply and holds it while awaiting distribution to the points of consumption; a storage cistern.

storage-type water heater A water heater composed of a horizontal or vertical storage tank, a source of heat (such as an electric heating coil or heat exchanger), and various accessories for the control, safe operation, and maintenance of the heater.

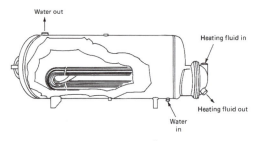

storage-type water heater

store 1. A place where goods are kept for sale; a shop. 2. A place where goods or materials are accumulated and kept for future use.

store door handle Part of a door lock, a heavy door pull, usually fixed to a surface-mounted plate; provided with a thumbpiece which operates the latch trip.

store door latch A door latch which is operated by a thumb lever that moves the spring bolt.

storefront, shop front The front of a store or shop at street level, usually having one or more windows for the display of goods or wares.

storefront sash An assembly of light metal members which form a continuous frame for a fixed-glass storefront.

storey See **story**.

storey rod See **story rod**.

storm anchor In roofing, a corrosion-resistant metal fastener having a flat base; the shank fastens the concealed lower corner of each shingle to the exposed edge of the adjacent shingle.

storm cellar A cellar used for shelter against violent storms such as cyclones, tornadoes, or hurricanes.

storm clip In **glazing**, a clip on the exterior of a glazing bar; prevents the pane from moving outward.

storm door, weather door An auxiliary door installed exterior to, and in the same doorframe as, an entrance door to a house, to provide added protection against cold and air infiltration; frequently includes glass paneling.

storm drain A drain used for conveying rainwater, subsurface water, condensate, cooling water, or other similar discharges, but not sewage or industrial waste, to a point of disposal.

storm porch An enclosed porch, or portion thereof, protecting the entrance to a house from the weather. Often erected only during the winter months.

stormproof window A window designed to resist wind, hail, snow, and rain in a storm or hurricane.

storm sash See **storm window**.

storm sewage The **sewage** flowing in combined sewers or storm sewers, resulting from rainfall.

storm sewer A **sewer** used for conveying rainwater or other similar discharges, but not sewage or industrial waste, to a point of disposal.

storm-sewer system A sewer system consisting only of sewers carrying rainwater, street wash, cooling water, and similar discharges, but excluding sewage and industrial waste.

storm sheet A sheet of roofing material having one edge curved downward at the eaves to provide protection against rain.

storm water Water flowing on the surface of the ground, resulting from heavy rainfall.

storm-water conductor In a roof drainage system, a pipe (located within a building) that carries off the drainage; if the pipe is attached to the outside of the building, it is called a **downspout** or **rainwater leader**.

storm window, storm sash An extra window, usually placed on the outside of an existing window as additional protection against severe weather.

story (*Brit.* **storey**) **1.** The space in a building between floor levels, or between a floor and a roof above. In some codes and ordinances a basement is considered as a story; generally a cellar is not. **2.** A major architectural division even where no floor exists, as a tier or a row of windows.

story-and-a-half The designation for a house (or building) in which the ceilings of the second-story rooms at the eaves are comparatively low.

story drift The difference in horizontal deflection between the top and bottom story of a building.

story height The vertical distance from the **finish floor** on one level to the finish floor on the level above.

story post One of several upright posts that support a beam on which a floor rests.

story rod, height board, story pole A wood rod equal in length to the distance between two floors; may be divided into equal parts, each equal to the height of a step for use in stair construction. Also see **gauge rod**.

stoup A basin for holy water, sometimes freestanding but more often affixed to or carved out of a wall or pillar near the entrance of a church.

stovepipe A metal pipe for conducting smoke, gases, etc., from a stove to a chimney flue.

stove room A term once applied to any room heated by a stove.

stoving See **baking**.

St. Petersburg standard See **Petrograd standard**.

Stpg Abbr. for "stepping."

Str. Abbr. for "structural."

STR. Abbr. for **strike**.

straddle pole In a **saddle scaffold**, the sloping pole laid on the roof's surface.

straddle scaffold Same as **saddle scaffold**.

straight arch A brick arch whose soffit (i.e., lower face) is horizontal; the brick joints on each side of its midpoint slant downward toward the centerline; also called a Dutch arch, flat arch, French arch, or jack arch.

straightedge, rod **1.** A rigid, straight piece of wood or metal used to **strike off** a concrete, mortared, or plastered surface; a **screed, 2. 2.** A long piece of seasoned, planed wood having straight, parallel edges; used in construction to lay out straight lines and to align framing.

straight-edge gable   Same as **straight-line gable**.

straight flight, straight stair   A stair extending in one direction only, with no turns or winders.

straight-grained   **1.** Descriptive of wood in which the grain is more or less parallel to the sawn edges. **2.** Descriptive of quarter-sawn lumber in which the grain appears as straight lines.

straight jacket   A stiff timber which is fixed to a wall so as to increase its rigidity and to reinforce it.

straight joint   **1.** In a wood floor, a continuous joint formed by the ends of parallel boards; the joint is perpendicular to the length of the boards. **2.** In carpentry, a joint between two timbers which are laid edge to edge without a tongue and groove, dowels, or overlap to bind them; also called a **square joint**. **3.** A continuous vertical straight-line joint formed by the ends of masonry units.

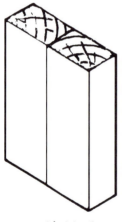

straight joint, 2

straight-joint tile   A tile designed to be laid in single-lap fashion so that the edges in successive courses run in a straight line from the eave to the ridge.

straight-line edger, straight-line ripsaw   A mechanically fed saw used to straighten the edges of veneer and lumber.

straight-line gable   A term descriptive of a parapeted **end gable**, the face of which rises above the roof line; the edge of the parapet forms a straight line at a steep pitch with respect to the horizontal; especially found in Dutch Colonial architecture and Jacobethan architecture; occasionally called a straight-edge gable.

straight-line theory   In the analysis of reinforced concrete members, theory based on the assumption that stresses and strains in a member under flexure vary in proportion to the distance from the neutral axis.

straight lock   A lock which is designed to be fixed on the face of a door, requiring no preparation other than the cutting of a keyhole.

straight nailing   Same as **face nailing**.

straight-peen hammer   A hammer having a blunt chisel-shaped **peen** whose edge is parallel to the handle.

straight-run stair   Same as **straight-flight stair**.

straight stair   See **straight flight**.

straight tee   A **tee** having all openings of the same size.

straight tee

straight tongue   A **tongue** along one edge of a board.

strain   A change in the form or shape of a body or material which is subjected to an external force.

strain energy   The work which is done in deforming a body.

strainer   A device for withholding foreign matter from a flowing liquid or gas; a sieve.

strain gauge   A very fine wire or thin foil which exhibits a change in resistance proportional to the mechanical strain imposed on it; usually mounted on or bonded to some type of carrier material or wound on a jig or fixture; used in the experimental determination of stresses.

strain hardening   The hardening of a metal produced by **cold working** it.

straining arch   An arch used as a strut, as in a flying buttress.

straining beam, straining piece, strutting piece   In a truss, a horizontal strut above the tie beam or above a line joining the feet of the rafters, commonly between the joists at midspan; esp. in a queen post truss, the strut between the upper ends of the two queen posts.

straining piece **1.** Same as **straining beam**. **2.** Any member which is fixed between opposing struts to take their thrusts.

straining sill In a timber roof, a **straining beam** which is placed on the upper surface of the tie beam of a roof truss, between posts, to resist the inward thrust from struts.

strake **1.** On the siding of a house, a run of clapboard. **2.** In a tall steel chimney, a row of steel plates.

strand **1.** A number of individual steel wires twisted together. **2.** A number of individual steel wires laid together (not twisted). **3.** In prestressed concrete, a type of prestressing **tendon**.

stranded wire A group of small wires which is used as a single wire.

strand grip In prestressed concrete construction, a device used to anchor a prestressing **tendon**.

S-trap An S-shaped **trap, 1**.

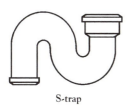

S-trap

strap **1.** A metal plate placed across the junction of two or more timbers to which it is bolted or screwed. **2.** See **tie beam, 1. 3.** See **pipe strap. 4.** A metal component designed to join a truss and wall plate to a wall.

strap anchor Same as **strap, 1.**

strap bolt **1.** Same as **lug bolt. 2.** A bolt having the middle part of its shank flattened, so that it can be bent in a U-shape.

strap footing, strip footing A **continuous foundation** in which all loads occur in a straight line.

straphanger A **hanger, 1** in the form of a strap.

strap hinge A surface-mounted hinge with long flaps of metal on each side, by which it is secured to a door and adjacent post or wall.

strap joint A **butt joint** between two pieces that are secured by a riveted strap between them.

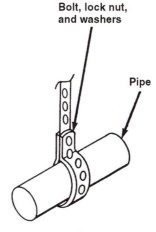

Bolt, lock nut, and washers

Pipe

straphanger

strap hinge

strapped elbow Same as **drop elbow.**

strapped wall See **battened wall.**

strapping **1.** Battens which support a lath-and-plaster construction. **2.** Same as **banding, 4.**

strapwork **1.** Any type of ornament consisting of narrow fillets or bands that are folded, crossed, or interlaced. **2.** Interlacing decorative bands found within gables; especially found in Tudor architecture and Tudor Revival, as well as in northern Europe. (*See illustration p. 894.*)

stratification **1.** The separation of overwet or overvibrated concrete into horizontal layers with increasingly lighter material toward the top; water, laitance, mortar, and coarse aggregate tend to occupy successively lower positions in that order. **2.** A layered structure in concrete resulting from the placement of successive batches that differ in appearance.

stratified rock Layered earth materials, deposited as successive beds of sediment and

strapwork on a Tudor style house

solidified by compaction, cementation, or crystallization; same as **sedimentary rock**, although not all the latter shows visible stratification.

stratum A bed of sedimentary rock or earth.

straw bale house A dwelling whose walls are constructed of bales of straw, compressed and wire-tied or string-tied into large units and built up on a concrete slab as if they were oversized bricks; they are reinforced with vertical poles that pierce the bales. When thoroughly dry, the walls are usually finished with a coat of stucco or adobe plaster to promote sanitation, fire safety, and protection against the weather; the bales provide excellent thermal insulation. Especially found in the farm regions of midwestern United States.

strawboard, compressed straw slab Straw mixed with a bonding ingredient and compressed into a board-type material.

straw-hat theatre A theatre used only in the summertime.

straw shed An extension at the rear of a barn, usually on one side, used primarily for the storage of straw; it may also be a two-story structure in which the upper story is used to store hay and the lower story is used to store farm machinery.

stray light Incidental light reaching an area from sources used to light other areas.

streamlined specification A specification containing adequate technical information for the construction of the **work, 1** but written in an abbreviated manner.

streamline flow The flow of a liquid or gas past a solid body in a manner so that the velocity of the fluid, at every point, does not change with time.

Streamline Moderne, Streamline Modern A phase of Art Deco that emphasizes the contours that offer minimum resistance to fluid flow, resulting in emphasis on the horizontal aspects of design. Usually characterized by curved end walls, rounded corners; glass block; flush windows; white or light-colored stucco walls; horizontal stainless-steel railings.

stream shingle Flat pieces of thin-bedded or foliated rock taken from the channel of a small, high-gradient stream; has a sloped overlapping pattern resembling shingling.

street A public thoroughfare, usually paved, including all area within the right-of-way, such as sidewalks; a public way.

street elbow Same as **service ell**.

street elbow

street ell See **service ell**.

street floor **1.** In a building, that floor which is nearest to street level; usually not more than a half story above or below street level; often the main floor of the building. **2.** To qualify as a street floor under certain codes in the U.S.A., the floor level may not be more than 21 in. above or more than 12 in. below grade level at the main entrance.

street furniture The benches, signs, lights, fixtures, and receptacles provided as part of the design of a street right-of-way.

street lighting luminaire A complete lighting device consisting of a light source together with its appurtenances such as a globe, reflector, refractor, housing, and such support as is integral with the housing; the pole, post, and bracket are not included.

street lighting unit The assembly of a pole or lamppost with a bracket and a **street lighting luminaire**.

street line **1.** A lot line dividing a lot or other area from a street. **2.** A side boundary of a street, defined by the instrument creating that street as having a stated width.

street main   See **gas main** and **water main**.

street pavement   The exposed or wearing surface of a roadway.

street projection   Any part of a structure that extends beyond the street building line, including but not limited to architectural features, marquees, fire escapes, flagpoles, marquees, and signs.

street wall   The wall of the building nearest a street line abutting the property.

strength   Of a material, the capability of the material to resist physical forces imposed on it.

stress   The internal forces set up at a point in an elastic material by the action of external forces; expressed in units of force per unit area, e.g., pounds per square inch or kilograms per square millimeter.

stress analysis   See **structural analysis**.

stress concentration   Localized stress (usually as a result of localized loading or changes in geometry) which is significantly higher than the average stress.

stress corrosion   Corrosion of a metal which is accelerated by stress.

stress corrosion cracking   Failure in a metal as a result of cracks caused by the simultaneous interaction of sustained tensile stress at an exposed surface with the chemical or electrochemical effects of the environment to which it is exposed.

stress-corrosion cracking   A failure of metals by cracking as a result of corrosion and stress.

stress crack   An external or internal crack in a plastic caused by internal or external tensile stresses; environmental conditions frequently accelerate the development of such cracks. Also see **crazing**.

stress cracking   The cracking of a weld or a base metal which contains residual stresses.

stress diagram   See **stress-strain diagram**.

stressed sandwich panel   Same as **stressed-skin panel**.

stressed-skin construction   Construction in which a thin material, on the exterior surface of a building, is utilized to carry loads.

stressed-skin panel   A panel composed of a core which is faced on both sides with plywood

or another suitable sheet material, providing strength for the complete assembly.

stress-graded lumber   Lumber graded for strength according to growth rate, grain slope, and defects.

stressing end   In **prestressed concrete**, the end of the tendon from which the load is applied, when tendons are stressed from one end only.

stress-number curve   In fatigue testing, a curve showing the relation between the value of stress and the number of cycles at that value of stress required to produce failure in the test specimen.

stress range   The difference between the maximum and minimum values of stress in a member which result from different loading conditions.

stress relaxation   The time-dependent decrease in **stress** in a constrained material under a constant **load, 1**.

stress-relief heat treatment, stress relieving   The uniform heating of a material or structure to a temperature high enough to relieve the major portion of the residual stresses, followed by uniform cooling.

stress relieving   See **stress-relief heat treatment**.

stress-strain diagram   A diagram in which corresponding values of stress are plotted against strain; values of stress usually are plotted as ordinates (vertically) and values of strain as abscissas (horizontally).

stretch   An area of **patent glazing**.

stretcher   A masonry unit laid horizontally with its length in the direction of the face of the wall. (*See illustration p. 896.*)

stretcher block   A concrete masonry unit which is laid as a **stretcher**.

stretcher bond, running bond, stretching bond   In masonry, a bond in which bricks or stones are laid lengthwise; all courses are laid as **stretchers** with the vertical joints of one course falling midway between those of adjacent courses. (*See illustration p. 896.*)

stretcher course, stretching course   A course consisting only of **stretchers**.

stretcher face   The long face of an exposed brick which is laid as a **stretcher**.

stretcher leveling   The flattening of metal sheets by stretching them mechanically.

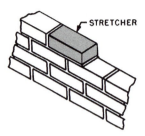

stretcher laid in a wall

STRETCHER (3 CORE)   STRETCHER   STRETCHER (2 CORE)

hollow-masonry-unit **stretchers**

stretching bond   Same as **stretcher bond**.

stretching course   A **stretcher course**.

stretching piece   A tie, strut, or brace.

stria   **1.** A **fillet**. **2.** A rib, esp. one repeated to give texture.

striated   Fluted, as a column.

striatura   The **fluting** on columns.

striga   A fluting of a column.

strigil ornament   In Roman architecture, a decoration of a flat member, as a fascia, with a repetition of slightly curved vertical flutings or reedings.

strike   **1.** In stone setting or bricklaying, to finish a mortar joint with a stroke of the trowel, simultaneously removing extruding mortar and smoothing the surface of the mortar remaining in the joint; **strike off**. **2.** A **strike plate**.

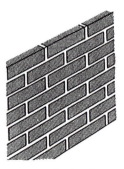

stretcher bond

strike backset   On a doorframe, the distance from the stop to the edge of the **strike plate** cutout.

strike block   A plane, shorter than a **jointer plane**, used for fitting a short joint.

strike edge   See **leading edge**.

strike jamb, lock jamb   The vertical member of a doorframe on which the strike plate is installed.

strike off   **1.** To use a straight wood or metal bar for removing material (from a newly plastered or mortared work or from a freshly laid concrete surface) which is in excess of that required to fill a form evenly or to level the surface. **2.** The wood or metal bar used for this purpose. **3.** See **strike, 1**.

strike plate, strike, striking plate   A metal plate or box which is set in a doorjamb and is either pierced or recessed to receive the bolt or latch of a lock, fixed on a door. Also see **box strike plate**.

striker   A slightly beveled metal plate, set in the jamb of a door to receive and guide a door latch to its socket in closing.

strike reinforcement   A metal tab in a hollow-metal doorframe, to which the **strike plate** is attached; strengthens the frame.

strike stile   Same as **lock stile**.

strike-through   See **bleed-through**.

striking   **1.** Cutting a molding with a plane. **2.** Removing temporary supports from a structure.

striking-off lines   In plastering, markings for cornice work, on ceilings or walls.

striking plate   See **strike plate**.

striking point   The center of curvature of a circular arc; the point from which such an arc is drawn.

striking stile   See **lock stile**.

string   **1.** In a stair, an inclined board which supports the end of the steps; also called a **stringer**. **2.** In a lattice roof truss, a horizontal tie. **3.** A **stringcourse**. Also called stringer, stringboard, or face string. For specific types, see **closed string, face string, finish string, open string, outer string, rough string, stair string**.

stringboard   Same as **face string**.

stringcourse, belt course   A horizontal band of masonry, generally narrower than other courses, extending across the façade of a struc-

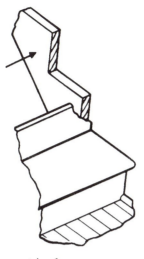

string, 1

ture and in some instances encircling such decorative features as pillars or engaged columns; may be flush or projecting, and flat-surfaced, molded, or richly carved; a **bond course**.

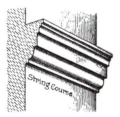

stringcourse

string development   Same as **ribbon development**.

stringer   **1.** A **string, 1. 2.** A **stringpiece. 3.** A long, heavy horizontal timber which connects the posts in a frame which supports a floor.

stringer bead   In welding, a type of bead which is made by moving the welding electrode in a direction parallel to the axis of the bead, without appreciable transverse oscillation.

stringiness   The property of an adhesive that results in the formation of filaments or threads when the adhesive transfer surfaces are separated.

stringing mortar   The process of spreading enough mortar on a bed to lay several masonry units at one time.

stringpiece   In construction or shoring, any long, heavy horizontal timber.

strip   **1.** Any material which is long and narrow, usually of uniform width. **2.** See **board, 1. 3.** To damage the threads on a nut or bolt.

strip board   See **strip core**.

strip building   Building dwellings, usually low-cost, in long parallel rows, using a minimum of land.

strip core, blockboard, loose core, strip board   A composite board; a **coreboard** whose core is made up of strips of wood, either laid separately or glued together; veneer is glued to both faces of the core strips with its grain at right angles to that in the strips.

strip diffuser   See **linear diffuser**.

stripe   See **ribbon stripe**.

stripe veneer   Same as **ribbon stripe**.

strip flooring   Hardwood **finish flooring**; narrow tongue-and-groove strips; commonly maple, mahogany, oak, etc.

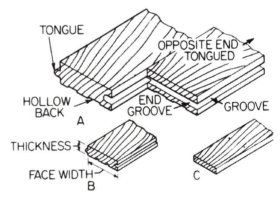

strip flooring: A, side- and end-matched; B, matched; C, square-edged

strip footing   See **strap footing**.

strip foundation   A **continuous foundation** in which the length is considerably greater than the breadth.

strip heater   An electric heater, of the self-regulating type, in the form of a strip containing an electrical heating element that is wrapped directly around a pipe; may be used to maintain the desired delivery temperature at hot-water outlets without the necessity of installing a circulating hot-water system. (*See illustration p. 898.*)

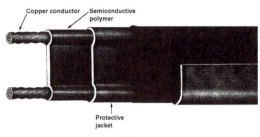

strip heater

strip lath   A narrow strip of diamond-mesh lath; applied as a reinforcement over gypsum lath joints or at a juncture of two different types of plaster bases.

striplight   1. See **fluorescent strip**. 2. A row of lamps mounted in a trough with a reflecting hood and color frames; used to flood an entire theatre stage or a selected area of the stage.

strip mopping   **Mopping** hot bitumen in strips, usually about 8 in. (20 cm) wide with 4-in. (10 cm) unmopped strips between.

stripped joint   In brickwork, a type of **raked joint**, used with bricks of rough texture.

stripped joint

stripper   A liquid designed to remove coatings by chemical and/or solvent action.

stripping   1. In grading an area in which a foundation is to be built, the preliminary operation of removing trees, shrubs, vegetation, and topsoil. 2. Removing old paint, wallpaper, distemper, etc., by the use of a blowtorch, paint remover, steam stripping appliance, stripping knife, or other scraping tools. 3. Sealing the joint between a metal sheet and a built-up roofing membrane. 4. Taping the joints between insulation boards.

stripping agent   Same as **release agent**.

stripping felt   A narrow strip of roofing used to cover a metal flange of flashing.

stripping knife   See **broad knife**.

stripping piece   In formwork, a splayed narrow member which is used to facilitate removal in a confined space.

stripping shovel   A **power shovel** which has an especially long boom, permitting it to reach farther and pile higher.

strip slates   See **asphalt shingles**.

strip soaker   In roofing, a strip of waterproof material installed under each course of shingles, slates, or tiles at a **swept valley**.

strip taping   Same as **stripping, 4**; also see **taping strip**.

strip welting   See **welting strip**.

strix   A **flute**, or concave **canal**; a fluting of a column.

stroked work   Stone which has been tooled so as to produce a finely fluted surface.

stroll garden   A garden designed to be viewed from a footpath, which usually proceeds from one of a series of vantage points to another.

strong axis   The major principle axis of a cross section.

strongback   A frame attached to the back of a concrete form to stiffen or reinforce it.

stronghold   See **fortress, 1**.

strong mortar   A **mortar** made only with portland cement, without lime; has high shrinkage.

Struc   Abbr. for "structural."

struck joint   1. A masonry joint from which excess mortar has been removed by a stroke of the

struck joint, 2

trowel, leaving an approximately flush joint. **2.** A horizontal masonry joint in which the mortar is sloped inward and downward from the lower edge of the upper brick, leaving a recess at the bottom of the joint. **3.** A **weather-struck joint**.

struck molding, solid molding, stuck molding A molding cut into rather than added to or planted on a member.

structura A general term for masonry of the ancient Greeks and Romans.

structural Said of a load-bearing member, element, etc., of a building.

structural adhesive A bonding agent used to prepare bonded joints which are able to sustain very high loads.

structural analysis, stress analysis In structural engineering, the analytical determination of the stresses in the elements of a structure resulting from an applied load.

structural bond The union of two or more masonry units so that the combination acts as a single unit and provides the same structural strength as a single unit of the same material.

structural clay facing tile Ceramic tile designed for use in interior and exterior unplastered walls, partitions, or columns.

structural clay tile A hollow masonry building unit composed of burnt clay, shale, fireclay, or mixtures thereof, having parallel cells or cores (or both) within a single tile.

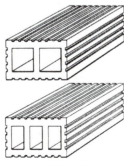

structural clay tile units

structural concrete **1.** Concrete, of a specified quality, which is used to carry a structural load or to form an integral part of a structure.

structural connection A device for uniting individual members of a structural assembly.

structural damage The loosening, twisting, warping, cracking, distortion, or breaking of any piece, or of any fastening or joint, in a structural assembly, with a resulting loss of sustaining capacity of the assembly.

structural design documents The plans, design details, and job specifications prepared by the structural designer.

structural drawings Drawings, usually prepared by a structural engineers, of the design and working drawings of a building's structure.

structural engineering That branch of engineering concerned with the design and construction of structures to withstand physical forces or displacements without danger of collapse or without loss of serviceability or function.

structural facing unit A building unit having one or more faces designed to be exposed in a finish wall; the specifications may include color, finish, and any factor affecting its appearance.

structural failure **1.** The loss of sustaining capacity or stability. **2.** Rupture of an essential component of the structure. **3.** A marked increase in strain without an increase in load. **4.** A deformation which increases much more rapidly than the increase in imposed load.

structural frame All the members of a building or structure required to transmit loads to the ground.

structural gasket See **lock-strip gasket**.

structural glass Glass, sometimes colored, which is cast in the form of cubes, rectangular (solid or hollow) blocks, tile, or large rectangular plates; used widely for wall surfacing.

structural glued-laminated timber A stress-rated assembly of especially selected and prepared wood laminations which are securely bonded together with adhesives.

Structuralism Based on the findings in anthropology, ethnology, and psychology by Claude Lévi-Strauss in his search for primordial societal constructs or patterns which serve as the basis for all later cultural developments, Structuralism in architecture connotes the referral to basic structural forms, *archeforms*, from which architectural design and construction can derive. The Dutch architect, Aldo van Eyck, is often cited as a main representative, although structural ideas have also been expressed by early Le Corbusier, by Louis Kahn, and by others.

structural lighting element A lighting element that is built into a structure or that uses the structure as a part of the **luminaire**.

structural lightweight concrete Structural concrete made with lightweight aggregate; usually weighs 90 to 115 lb per cu ft (1,440 to 1,840 kg per cu m).

structural lumber Lumber consisting of the following classifications: **1.** *Beams and stringers:* Lumber of rectangular cross section, 5 in. or more thick and 8 in. or more wide; graded with respect to its strength in bending when loaded on the narrow face. **2.** *Joists and planks:* Lumber of rectangular cross section, 2 in. to (but not including) 5 in. thick, and 4 in. or more wide; graded with respect to its strength in bending when loaded either on the narrow face as a joist or on the wide face as a plank. **3.** *Posts and timbers:* Lumber of square or approximately square cross section 5 in. by 5 in. and larger; graded primarily for use as posts or columns carrying longitudinal load but adapted for miscellaneous uses in which strength in bending is not especially important.

structural sealant A **sealant** capable of transferring either dynamic or static loads (or both) across joint members exposed to the service environments which are typical for the structure involved.

structural shape A hot-rolled steel beam of standardized cross section, temper, size, and alloy; includes angle irons, channels, tees, I-beams, and H-sections; commonly used for structural purposes.

structural steel Steel, rolled in a variety of shapes (such as beams, angles, bars, plates, sheets, strips, etc.) and fabricated for use as load-bearing structural members or elements.

structural steel fastener A fastener for connecting or attaching structural steel members to other structural steel members, to supporting elements, or to a concrete member forming a composite section.

structural tee A standard structural hot-rolled steel member shaped like the letter T and formed from cutting an I-beam in half.

structural terra cotta See **structural clay tile**.

structural timber connector See **timber connector**.

structural timbers Structural lumber of approximately square cross section that is 5 in. (12.7 cm) on a side or larger; used primarily for posts and columns.

structural wall A wall capable of supporting an imposed load.

structure **1.** A combination of units constructed and so interconnected, in an organized way, as to provide rigidity between its elements. **2.** Any edifice.

structure-borne sound Sound that reaches a point in a building, over at least part of its path, by solid-borne transmission through the building structure.

structure height **1.** The vertical distance from grade to the highest point of a structure; the overall height. **2.** For a roof structure, the mean level of the roof to the highest point of such a structure.

strut A brace or any piece of a frame which resists thrusts in the direction of its own length; may be upright, diagonal, or horizontal.

strutbeam Same as **collar beam**.

strut guide In a doorframe, a metal piece within the **throat opening** of the frame; serves as a guide for the **ceiling strut**.

strutting **1.** Diagonal braces between joists to prevent side deflection. **2.** See **cross bridging**.

strutting beam Same as **collar beam**.

strutting piece Same as **straining beam**.

Stuart architecture Architecture of the English late Renaissance (1603–1688).

stub A piece or part of something sticking out, as the **nib** on a tile.

stub mortise A mortise which does not pass through the entire thickness of the timber in which it is made; a **blind mortise**.

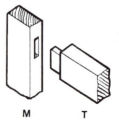

stub mortise (M); stub tenon (T)

stub mortise and tenon Same as **blind mortise and tenon joint**.

stub pile   A short, thick **pile, 1**.

stub tenon   A short tenon which does not pass completely through the material in which the mortise is cut; fits into a **stub mortise**.

stub wall   A low wall, monolithically placed with a concrete floor (or other members) so as to provide for the control and attachment of wall forms.

stuc   Plaster applied to form an imitation stone.

stucco   **1.** An exterior finish, composed of some combination of portland cement, lime, and sand, which are mixed with water, which dries to a very hard textured surface. **2.** A synthetic exterior finish such as an **exterior insulation and finishing system**, containing materials other than **stucco, 1**, for example, containing an epoxy as a binder. **3.** A fine plaster used for decorative work, moldings, or cornices. **4.** A partially or fully calcined gypsum that has not yet been processed into a finished product.

stucco mesh   A lightweight galvanized wire netting usually having a hexagonal mesh; sometimes used in stucco work.

stuck molding   See **struck molding**.

stud   **1.** An upright post or support, esp. one of a series of vertical structural members which act as the supporting elements in a wall or partition. **2.** A cylindrical rod of moderate length, threaded on one or both ends or throughout its entire length.

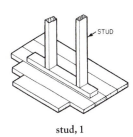

stud, 1

stud, 2

stud anchor   An **anchor** used in a wall built with steel or wood studs.

stud and mud   Same as **wattle and daub**.

stud bolt   A **stud, 2**.

studding   **1.** Same as **stud**. **2.** The material from which wood studs are cut.

stud driver   A device for driving a hardened steel nail (a stud) into concrete or other hard material; the driver, containing a stud, is held against the concrete; then a blow on the head of the driver forces the stud into the concrete.

stud gun   A **stud driver** in which the impact is provided by the firing of a blank cartridge.

studio   **1.** The working room of an artist or a place where an art form is pursued. **2.** A room equipped for the recording of music or the transmission of radio or television broadcasts.

studio apartment   **1.** An apartment consisting of a single, multifunctional room which serves as a living room, dining room, and bedroom and which contains kitchen facilities; has a separate bathroom. **2.** An apartment, with large windows and high ceilings, used as an artist's studio.

stud opening   A **rough opening** in a wood framework.

stud partition   A partition using **studs, 1** as the vertical structural members; usually faced with **wallboard**.

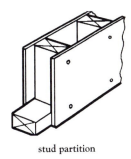

stud partition

stud shooting   **1.** Inserting studs by means of a **stud gun**. **2.** Driving a hardened steel nail or bolt into concrete by means of a **stud gun**.

stud wall   See **stud partition**.

stud welding   An arc-welding process in which coalescence is produced by heating with an arc between a metal stud and the other work part until the surfaces to be joined are properly heated; then they are brought together under pressure.

studwork   **1.** Brickwork interspaced with studs. **2.** A construction with alternating bricks and studs.

study **1.** A room or alcove of a house or apartment used primarily as a place for reading, writing, and study. It often embodies the features of a private office and private library. **2.** A preliminary sketch or drawing to facilitate the development of a design.

stuff **1.** Sawn timber; **stock lumber**. **2.** See **fine stuff**.

stuffers See **carpet stuffers**.

stuffing box A packing gland surrounding a shaft to prevent leakage; commonly used on water pumps.

stugging Same as **dabbing**.

stumper An attachment on a **bulldozer**, used in the removal of tree stumps.

stump tenon A **stub tenon** which is nonuniform in thickness, being wider at the root for additional strength.

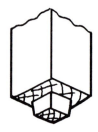

stump tenon

stump tracery Tracery, late German Gothic, whose interpenetrating bars are cut off like stumps.

stump veneer See **butt veneer**.

stumpwood See **buttwood**.

stunning The deep scoring or bruising of building stone, esp. by careless cutting.

stupa, tope A Buddhist memorial mound, erected to enshrine a relic or to commemorate a sacred site; consists of an artificial mound, raised on a platform and surrounded by an outer ambulatory with a stone railing and four gateways, crowned by a multiple sunshade.

ST W On drawings, abbr. for **storm water**.

style See **architectural style**.

Style Moderne See **Art Moderne** and **Art Deco**.

Style Rayonnant See **Rayonnant Style**.

stylobate **1.** Strictly, the single top course of the three steps of the **crepidoma** upon which the

stupa   topped by a **chattravali**

columns rest directly. **2.** Any continuous base, plinth, or pedestal, upon which a row of columns is set. Also see **stereobate**.

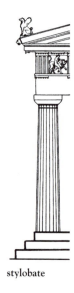

stylobate

stylolite A jointed or irregular columnar structure occasionally found in beds of limestone, uniting the adjoining surfaces of two layers of rock.

styrene-butadiene rubber A widely used synthetic rubber made by copolymerizing styrene and butadiene **monomers**.

SUB On drawings, abbr. for "substitute."

subarch One of two or more minor arches beneath and enclosed by an outer arch.

subbase The lowest projection of a base molding or baseboard with more than one horizontal subdivision.

subbase course For the support of paving materials, a layer of granular material applied to the **subgrade** in a predetermined depth; provides underpavement drainage and reduces frost damage.

subbasement The level, or levels, of a building below the basement.

subbidder One who tenders to a bidder on a **prime contract** a proposal to provide materials and/or labor.

sub-buck A **subframe, 1**.

subbuilding drainage system A **building-drainage system** which cannot drain by gravity into the sewer.

subcasing, blind casing 1. A **rough buck**. 2. A **subframe**.

subcellar The level, or levels, of a building below the cellar.

subcompartment One of the areas into which a building can be divided to provide protection against fire and smoke; the availability of such areas reduces the distance that must be travelled to a place of safety in the event of fire.

subcontract An agreement between a prime or general contractor and a subcontractor for the execution of a portion of the contractual obligation of the prime contractor to the owner.

subcontractor A person or organization who has a direct contract with a **prime contractor** to perform a portion of the work at the site.

subcontractor bond A performance bond given by a subcontractor to the general contractor which guarantees performance of a contract and the payment of bills for labor and material.

subcrust See **cushion course**.

subdiagonal In a truss, an intermediate **diagonal** of a **web, 1** joining a chord with a main diagonal.

subdivided truss Any **truss** having a secondary framework placed in one or more **panels, 7** to shorten the effective length of the panels.

subdivision A tract of land divided into residential lots.

subdivision regulations Local ordinances which specify the standards and conditions under which a tract of land can be subdivided. Originally directed at street layout and construction specifications, many regulations now stipulate the general design of street lighting and signs, sidewalks, sewage disposal, and water-supply systems; others require the dedication of land for schools, parks, and other community facilities within the subdivision.

subdrain See **building subdrain**.

subfeeder In electric wiring, a **feeder** which originates at a distribution center other than the main distribution center and supplies one or more branch-circuit distribution centers.

subfloor, blind floor, counterfloor A rough floor, laid on joists, which serves as a base for the finished floor; is used as a working platform during construction, may act as a structural diaphragm to resist lateral stresses.

subflooring The material used in constructing the subfloor; usually plywood sheets or an inferior grade of soft lumber.

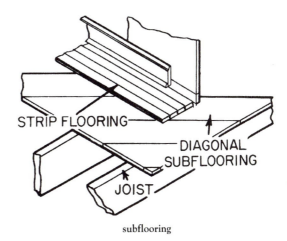

STRIP FLOORING — DIAGONAL SUBFLOORING — JOIST

subflooring

subframe, rough buck, sub-buck 1. A secondary frame, usually formed of wood members or channel-shaped metal members, which supports the finish frame of a door or window; attached to the wall in which the finished frame, **knocked-down frame**, door casing, or door lining is set; a **buck frame**. 2. A frame which supports a panel used as a wall finish.

subgrade 1. The soil prepared and compacted to support a structure or a pavement system; the base portion of any surfaced area, the elevation of which is lower than that of the finished grade. **2.** The elevation of the bottom of a trench in which a sewer or pipeline is laid.

subgrade modulus Same as **coefficient of subgrade reaction**.

subgrade reaction Same as **contact pressure**.

subheading A subdivision of a **heading** used in the **filing system** (Part Two of the **uniform system**).

subhouse drainage system Same as **subbuilding drainage system**.

subjective brightness See **brightness**.

subject to mortgage A conveyance of property will be subject to an existing mortgage if the purchaser has actual or constructive notice of it, e.g., if a mortgage of **real property** has been recorded in the land records. If there is a default in mortgage payments, the mortgagee may foreclose. The new owner usually keeps up the mortgage payments in order to preserve his interest in the property. But if he decides not to do so (if, for example, the property's value drops below that of the amount still unpaid on the mortgage), he is not personally liable to make the mortgage payments unless he has agreed to do so. See **assumption of mortgage**.

sublease A lease by a tenant to a subtenant of part or all of the premises leased by him, for part or all of the term of his lease.

sublica In ancient construction, a pile driven into the earth, or into ground covered by water, to support a structure.

sublight A small **sash** or **light** (usually fixed) at the bottom of a window.

submerged arc welding An arc-welding process resulting from heat from an arc drawn between a bare metal electrode and the work; the arc is shielded by a blanket of granular, fusible metal on the work; pressure is not used.

submersible pump A type of pump designed with an integral motor and liquid-handling section in a watertight casing that can be lowered directly into the liquid to be pumped.

suborder A secondary architectural **order**, introduced chiefly for decoration, as distinguished from a main order of a structure.

subordinate lien Any subsequent (second, third, fourth, etc.) **mortgage lien**. In the event of

foreclosure, holders of such liens may resort to the property for payment only to the extent of any surplus after prior liens have been paid off. Priority is usually determined by the chronological sequence in which the mortgages were created, but may be varied by agreement among the parties.

subparagraph In the AIA documents, the first subdivision of a **paragraph**, identified by three numerals, e.g., 3.3.3; may be subdivided into clauses.

subplatform In metal stair construction, the metal subfloor over which a fill is placed to provide a platform.

subplinth A secondary plinth sometimes placed under the usual one in column and pedestal bases.

subpost, car frame An elevator car frame all of whose members are located below the car platform.

subpurlin A light member of an intermediate system of beams which rests on and usually runs at right angles to **purlins** in a roof structure.

subrail, shoe On a staircase, a member which is fixed to the upper edge of a **close string** to receive the balusters.

subrogation The substitution of one person for another with respect to legal rights such as a right of recovery; occurs when a third person, such as an insurance company, has paid a debt of another or claim against another and succeeds to all legal rights which the debtor or person against whom the claim was asserted may have against other persons.

subsealing The placing of a waterproof material under an existing pavement, or the like, to prevent the flow of water through the pavement and to fill the voids under the pavement.

subsellium Same as **miserere**.

subsidence A sinking of an entire area, in contrast to the settlement of an individual structure.

subsill **1.** A subsidiary **sill** member fitted to a **window frame**; serves as a stop for screens; causes water to drip farther away from the wall surface; also called a **sill drip molding**. **2.** A subsidiary doorsill which is fixed to the groundsill.

subsoil The bed or stratum of earth which lies immediately below the surface soil.

subsoil drain A drain installed for collecting subsurface or seepage water and conveying it to a place of disposal.

substantial completion See **date of substantial completion**.

substantial improvement Any alteration, improvement, reconstruction, or repair of a building, the cost of which equals or exceeds a code-specified percentage of its market value: (a) either before the work is started, or (b) if the building has been damaged and is being restored, before such damage occurred.

substation The electrical equipment (e.g., circuit breakers, switches, transformers, and busses) associated with the **service entrance** or other major transformation and distribution equipment concentrated in one location in areas of building complexes or on floors of high-rise buildings.

substitution A material or process offered in lieu of, and as being equivalent to, a specified material or process.

substrate **1.** The underlying material to which a **finish** is applied, or by which it is supported. **2.** A material upon which an adhesive, film, coating, etc., is applied.

substrate failure At a joint in a concrete wall, a failure that occurs where the concrete surface is weak; caused by a sealant of high tensile strength which tears off concrete or mortar from the face of the joint.

substructure The foundation or understructure of a building; supports the superstructure.

sub-subcontractor A person or organization who has a direct or indirect contract with a **subcontractor** to perform a portion of the work at the site.

subsurface course The top course of pavement providing a surface which is resistant to traffic abrasion.

subsurface investigation The soil boring and sampling program, together with the associated laboratory tests, necessary to establish subsurface profiles and the relative strengths, compressibility, and other characteristics of the various strata encountered within the depths likely to have an influence on the design of the project.

subsurface sand filter A wide bed, consisting of a number of lines of perforated pipe or drain tile surrounded by clean coarse aggregate, containing an intermediate layer of sand as filtering material, and provided with a system of underdrains for carrying off the filtered sewage.

subsurface sewage disposal system A system for the treatment and disposal of domestic sewage by means of a septic tank and a soil absorption system.

subsurface utility Any **public utility** which is underground.

subsystem See **building subsystem**.

suburb An outlying area, in or near a city, of predominantly residential land use.

subvertical The upright member in a subdivided panel of a **truss** running from midpanel point to the chord.

subway **1.** (*U.S.A.*) An underground, intraurban passenger railway. **2.** (*Brit.*) An underground pedestrian passageway sometimes containing building maintenance and service elements.

successful bidder Same as **selected bidder**.

sucker A shoot rising from a subterranean root or stem of a plant.

suction **1.** In plastering, the absorption of water from a plaster finish coat by the base coat (or the base, such as block or gypsum lath), thus providing a better bond and causing it to adhere to the base coat. **2.** The adhesion of mortar to bricks.

suction head The energy per unit weight of fluid on the suction side of a pump.

suction lift Same as **suction head**.

suction pump A pump which raises water, or draws water in plumbing, by producing a partial vacuum within a pipe.

suction rate For bricks, same as **absorption rate**.

sudatorium In an ancient Roman bath, a hot room for inducing sweat, used by athletes.

Suffolk latch A type of **thumb latch** for doors; originally fabricated of iron wrought by hand in England. Attractive in appearance and available in many different designs; unlike the **Norfolk latch**, it has no plate behind the thumb latch to protect the door finish.

sugarhouse A building or shed, usually located in a grove of sugar maple trees, in which maple sugar is made by boiling the sap of the trees to evaporate its water content.

sugar pine   A durable, moderately even-grained wood, widely used as factory lumber, esp. for doors and frames.

suite   A connected group of rooms arranged or designed to be used as a unit.

sulfate attack   A chemical or physical reaction, or both, between sulfates (in ground water or in the soil) and concrete or mortar; primarily damaging to the **cement paste** matrix; reduced in concrete made with **sulfate-resistant cement**.

sulfate plaster   Same as **gypsum plaster**.

sulfate resistance   The ability of concrete or mortar to withstand **sulfate attack**.

sulfate-resistant cement   A portland cement which is low in tricalcium aluminate; has a reduced susceptibility to attack by dissolved sulfates in water or soils; *type* V portland cement.

sulfide staining   The formation of dark stains in a paint film, as a result of the reaction of atmospheric hydrogen sulfide with metallic compounds such as lead, mercury, or copper in the paint.

sulfoaluminate cement   See **expansive cement**.

sulfur cement   A cement of clay or other tenacious infusible substance, usually with additives such as sulfur, metallic oxides, silica, or carbon; used for sealing joints and seams and high-temperature coatings or coverings; also called **lute**.

sullage   **1.** Drainage, sewage, or waste. **2.** Sediment or silt which is carried and deposited by flowing water.

Sullivanesque   A term descriptive of the architectural style and decorative designs of Louis H. Sullivan (1856–1924), an important figure in the development of modern functional architecture. He is known for his famous statement that "Form ever follows function," and is especially noted for his **tripartite scheme** for the design of tall buildings. This term is also applied to his continuous foliated motifs, which are somewhat **Art Nouveau** in character.

Sumerian architecture   A monumental architecture developed by the Sumerians, who dominated southern Mesopotamia from the end of the 4th to the end of the 3rd millennium B.C. This architecture made use of locally available building materials: tall rushes and clay, tied bundles of reeds, and wattle and daub. To give character and structural strength to the mud-brick walls, the walls were articulated by buttresses or built with alternating pilasters and recesses.

summer   **1.** A horizontal beam supporting the ends of floor joists or resting on posts and supporting the wall above; also called a **summertree**. **2.** Any large timber or beam which serves as a bearing surface. **3.** The **lintel** of a door or window; a **breastsummer**. **4.** A stone laid on a column and serving as a support for construction above, as in the construction of an arch.

summer, 4:   *S*

summerbeam   **1.** A massive horizontal beam in the ceiling of an early **timber-framed house**; usually joined at their ends to **girts** and supporting the floor above, or acting as a binding beam running in a transverse direction, connecting one post to another. After about 1750, they were replaced by a number of heavier floor **joists**, thus making it possible to plaster the entire ceiling as a single horizontal surface. Also called a summer or summertree. See illustration under timber-framed house. **2.** Same as **breastsummer**. **3.** Same as **fireplace lintel** or **manteltree**.

summer house   **1.** A home in the country used as a summer residence. **2.** A garden house of light airy design used in the summer for protection from the sun.

summer kitchen   A supplementary kitchen located near, but detached from, a large home; especially used during hot weather to avoid overheating the house.

summer piece   A **fireboard**.

summer stone   Same as **summer, 4**.

summertree   See **summer, 1**.

summerwood   Wood which is formed during the later part of the growing season; characterized by compact, thick-walled cells; denser than **spring wood**.

sump **1.** A pit, tank, basin, or receptacle which receives sewage or liquid waste, located below the normal grade of the gravity system, and which must be emptied by mechanical means. **2.** A reservoir sometimes forming part of a roof drain. **3.** A depression in a roof deck where the roof drain is located.

sump pit A pit or tank that receives clear liquid wastes not containing organic material or compounds subject to decomposition; located below the normal grade of the **building gravity drainage system** so the discharge in the pit space must be emptied by means of a **sump pump**.

sump pump, ejector A pump used to remove the accumulated waste in a **sump**.

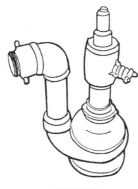

sump pump

sump vent A **vent** from a pneumatic **sewage ejector** which terminates in the open air.

sunblind Same as **shade screen**.

sunburst light A **fanlight**.

Sunday house A small house, usually consisting of a single room with a fireplace, commonly built near a house of religious worship for use one night a week. A farmer or rancher who lived some distance away would trade or sell produce on Saturday, stay overnight in the house, attend church services on Sunday, and then return home; also see **Sabbath house**.

sun deck A roof area, balcony, open porch, etc., which is exposed to the sun.

sun disk A disk with wings, emblematic of the sun, used in **Egyptian Revival** architecture.

sunk draft A margin around a building stone which is sunk below the face of the stone to give it a raised appearance.

sunken garden A garden, sometimes geometrically planned, at a level below prevailing grade, or surrounded by raised terraces.

sunken joint A type of defect in a veneer panel; a surface depression which develops above a joint in the core construction below.

sunken pit A pit which is lower (on all sides) than the surrounding area.

sunk face A building stone having a face from which material has been removed to give the stone the appearance of a sunken panel.

sunk fence A **ha-ha**.

sunk fillet A **fillet** formed by a groove in a plane surface.

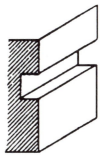

sunk fillet

sunk gutter A **concealed gutter**.

sunk molding A molding slightly recessed behind the surface on which it is located.

sunk panel A panel recessed below the surface of its surrounding framing or carved into solid masonry or timber.

sunk relief A carving or other type of relief that does not project beyond the flat surface on which it is cut; also called cavo-relievo. (*See illustration p. 908.*)

sunk shelf A narrow shelf serving as a **plate rail**.

sunk weathered Descriptive of a **weathered, 2** surface which is sunk below the original surface of the member.

sun room Same as **solarium**.

sun screen See **shade screen**.

SUP On drawings, abbr. for "supply."

superabacus An **impost block**.

sunk relief

superblock A larger than usual residential block, having no through traffic.

supercapital An **impost block**.

supercilium **1.** The fillet above the uppermost molding or cyma of a cornice. **2.** The small fillet on either side of the scotia of an Ionic base.

supercolumniation The placing of one **order** above another.

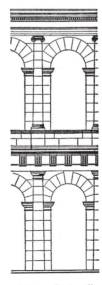

supercolumniation: Ionic pillars on Doric

superficial measure See **face measure, 1**.

super foot A square foot (0.0929 sq m).

superheated steam Steam at a temperature higher than the **saturation temperature** corresponding to the pressure.

superheater A heat exchanger for heating steam above 212°F (100°C) at atmospheric pressure.

superimposed drainage **1.** A naturally evolved drainage system having little relation to present geological structure because of erosion occurring after the system's development. **2.** A drainage system purposely designed against existing geological structure.

superimposed load The **live load** which is imposed on a structure.

superintendence The work of the contractor's representative at a construction site.

superintendent At a construction site, the contractor's representative who is responsible for continuous field supervision, coordination, and completion of the work and, unless another person is designated in writing by the contractor to the owner and the architect, for the prevention of accidents.

supermarket A large, self-service, retail market which sells food, household goods, and household merchandise.

supernatant liquid In a paint can, the liquid layer which rests upon a layer of heavier pigments and other matter in the bottom of the can.

superposition Same as **supercolumniation**.

superstructure **1.** That part of a building or structure which is above the level of the adjoining ground or the level of the foundation. **2.** Any structure built on something else, as a building on its foundation; that part of a structure which receives the live load directly.

supersulfated cement A **hydraulic cement** made by intimately intergrinding a mixture of granulated blast-furnace slag, calcium sulfate, and a small amount of lime, cement, or cement clinker; the content of sulfate exceeds that for portland blast-furnace slag cement.

supervision The observation and inspection of construction work in order to ensure conformity with the contract documents; direction of the **work, 1** by contractor's personnel. Supervision is neither a duty nor a responsibility of the architect as part of his basic professional services.

supervisory device In a fire **sprinkler system**, a device which supervises its condition of operation.

supplemental conditions Same as **supplementary conditions**.

supplemental vertical exit An enclosed stair, ramp, or escalator providing means of egress to an area of refuge at another area near the street floor.

supplementary conditions A part of the **contract documents** which supplements and may also modify provisions of the **general conditions**. Also see **conditions of the contract**.

supplementary lighting Lighting used to provide an additional quantity and quality of illumination, not obtained by the general lighting system; usually provides for specific work requirements.

supplier Any commercial firm that supplies components, fixtures, materials, or parts used on a construction project.

supply air In an air-conditioning system, the air which is delivered to the conditioned space or spaces.

supply bond A bond which guarantees that materials delivered comply with contract documents.

supply fan A fan that delivers **supply air**.

supply fixture unit A measure of the probable demand on the water supply by various types of plumbing fixtures; for a particular fixture the value of the supply fixture unit depends on its volume rate of supply, on the time duration of a single supply operation, and on the average time between successive operations.

supply grille A **grille, 2** through which air is supplied to an air-conditioned space.

supply grille

supply mains The pipes through which the heating or cooling medium of a system flows from the source of heat or refrigeration to the runouts and risers leading to the heating or cooling units.

supply opening, supply outlet Same as **air outlet**.

supply system An assembly of connected ducts, air passages or plenums, and fittings through which air, heated in a heat exchanger, is conducted from the heat exchanger to the space or spaces to be heated.

supporting clamp A clamp used to support vertical pipes, particularly where they penetrate a building slab or are in a pipe **chase**.

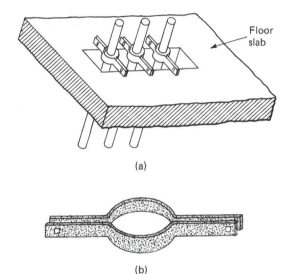

Floor slab

(a)

(b)

supporting clamp

SUPSD On drawings, abbr. for "supersede."

SUPT On drawings, abbr. for "superintendent."

SUPV On drawings, abbr. for "supervise."

SUR On drawings, abbr. for "surface."

surbase 1. The crowning moldings or cornice of a pedestal. 2. A border or molding above a base or dado. 3. The molding at the top of a baseboard. (*See illustration p. 910.*)

surbased arch An arch whose rise is less than half the span.

surcharge The vertical load applied at the ground surface or above the level of the bottom of a **footing**.

surcharged earth Earth which is above the level of the top of a retaining wall. (*See illustration p. 910.*)

surbase, 1 *a*

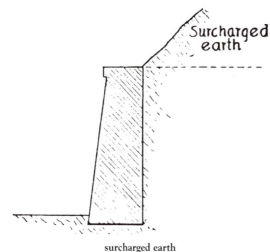

surcharged earth

surcharged wall A retaining wall carrying **surcharged earth**.

sure post A vertical timber that provides added support for a load imposed from above; for example, a vertical timber placed below a beam or sill.

surety A person or organization who, for a consideration, promises in writing to make good the debt or default of another.

surety bond A legal instrument under which one party agrees to answer to another party for the debt, default, or failure to perform of a third party.

surface-active agent **1.** In unhardened mixtures of concrete, an additive which has the ability to modify the surface tension of the mixing water, thereby facilitating the wetting and penetrating action of the water, and/or assisting the emulsifying, dispersing, solubilizing, foaming, or frothing of other additives. **2.** Same as **surfactant**.

surface arcade Same as **blind arcade**.

surface astragal A **surface-mounted astragal**.

surface bolt A rod or bolt mounted on the face of the inactive door of a pair, to lock it to the frame and/or sill; operated manually by means of a small knob.

surface bonding The bonding of dry-laid masonry by a thin layer of fiber-reinforced mortar.

surface condensation The formation of water on the exterior surface of cold pipes (or the like) when the temperature of the air falls below its dew point (i.e., the temperature at which the air is fully saturated).

surface course The exposed surface of paving designed to withstand wear by traffic.

surfaced lumber See **dressed lumber**.

surface drying See **skin drying**.

surface flame spread The propagation of flame across the surface of a material away from its source of ignition; see **flame spread index**.

surface hardware preparation The reinforcement of a metal door or frame to receive surface-mounted hardware which is applied after the door is mounted.

surface hinge A hinge, often ornamental, which is applied to the face of a door, as distinguished from one which is mounted on the edge of a door.

surface latch A **latch** which is applied to the face of a door.

surface measure See **face measure, 1**.

surface metal raceway A **raceway** which consists of a surface-mounted assembly of metal backing (providing mechanical support) and

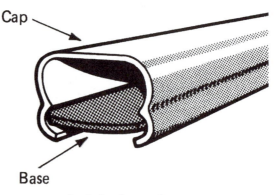

Cap

Base

detail of **surface metal raceway**

capping (providing a protective covering); used for electric wiring for branch circuits or feeder conductors.

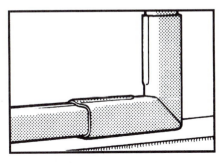

surface metal raceway: 90° bend

surface moisture, free water, surface water Water retained on surfaces of aggregate particles and considered to be part of the mixing water in concrete, as distinguished from **absorbed moisture** within the permeable voids of the aggregate particles.

surface-mounted astragal An **astragal, 3** which is mounted on the surface of a pair of doors along the joint between the meeting stiles.

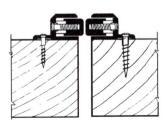

surface-mounted astragal

surface-mounted luminaire A **luminaire** that is mounted directly on the ceiling.

surface planer A machine which is used to dress or plane the surface of a material such as metal, stone, or wood.

surface retarder A **retarder** applied to the surface of newly placed concrete or to formwork; used to (a) delay setting of the cement, (b) facilitate the production of exposed aggregate finish, or (c) facilitate construction joint cleanup.

surfacer 1. A paint containing a high percentage of pigment; used as an intermediate coat to provide a smooth, uniform substrate for application of finish coats. 2. A **surface planer** for timber. 3. A machine for polishing stone surfaces; also called a **dunter machine**.

surface rib A decorative rib on the soffit of a vault.

surface sash center A **sash center** designed for surface mounting on the sash.

surface scaling See **scaling**.

surface sealer See **sealer**.

surface spread of flame See **flame spread index**.

surface texture The degree of roughness of the exterior surfaces of hardened concrete or of aggregate particles.

surface vibration As applied to concrete, see **vibration, 1**.

surface void A cavity which is visible on the surface of a solid.

surface water 1. See **surface moisture**. 2. Rainfall which runs over the surface of the ground. 3. Water carried by an aggregate except that held by absorption within the aggregate particles themselves.

surface-water drain A **storm drain**.

surface waterproofer See **waterproofing**.

surface wetting and adhesion The mutual affinity of (and bonding between) a finish and the surface to which it is applied.

surface wiring switch A switch mechanism which is designed for mounting on a surface, such as a wall, with all or almost all of the switch body extending beyond the surface on which it is mounted.

surface wiring switch

surfacing 1. The material used as a protective covering or coating as on the top side of a built-up roof, a floor, an outdoor tennis court, etc. 2. In welding, same as **cladding, 3**.

surfacing weld A weld which consists of one or more **stringer beads** or **weave beads** deposited on an unbroken surface in order to establish desired dimensions or properties.

surfactant   A chemical wetting agent; added to water to improve its penetration into a material; often useful in reducing the amount of water required in removing a material from the surface on which it has been applied.

surform tool   A cutting tool used for shaping and trimming wood; shaped either like a large, coarse, flat file or like a large, coarse, round file; has hundreds of sharp cutting teeth, pitched at an angle of about 45°, which take off wood like a plane, the chips passing through holes in the top of the tool.

surge   A sudden voltage rise and/or fall in an electrical current.

surge arrester   A protective device that limits surge currents through electrical equipment.

surge drum, surge header   An **accumulator, 1**.

surge tank   In a water-supply system, a reserve tank which supplies some of the water when there is a sudden drop in pressure, helping to maintain a more uniform flow.

Surinam mahogany   See **carapa**.

surmounted arch   A semicircular **stilted arch**.

surround   A decorative element or structure around a doorway, fireplace, or window; for example, see **arch surround, banded surround, door surround, fireplace surround, Gibbs surround, window surround**.

surround curtain   In a theatre, a curtain hung in such a manner that it envelops an area of a stage.

survey   **1.** A boundary and/or topographic mapping of a site. **2.** A compilation of the measurements of an existing building. **3.** An analysis of a building for use of space. **4.** A determination of the owner's requirements for a project. **5.** An investigation and report of required data for a project. **6.** The process of determining data relating to the physical or chemical characteristics of the earth, such as a **land survey** or **topographic survey**.

surveying   That branch of engineering concerned with a determination of the earth's surface features in relation to each other, as the relative position of points, a determination of areas, etc., and their recording on a map.

surveyor   One whose occupation is **surveying**, or who is otherwise skilled in the art.

surveyor's arrow   See **chaining pin**.

surveyor's compass   An instrument used by surveyors for measuring horizontal angles and for determining the magnetic bearing of a line of sight; consists of a pivoted magnetic needle, a graduated horizontal circle, and a sighting device.

surveyor's compass

surveyor's level   Same as **level, 1**.

surveyor's level

survey station   Same as **station, 1**.

survey traverse   In surveying, a sequence of lengths and directions of lines between points on the earth, obtained by or from field measurements and used in determining positions of the points.

suspended absorber   A sound-absorptive material, formed as a discrete structure; designed for overhead suspension within a room.

suspended acoustical ceiling   An **acoustical ceiling** which is suspended from the building structure above; usually the acoustical material itself forms a **suspended ceiling**, but it also may be secured to a backing.

suspended ceiling, dropped ceiling   A nonstructural ceiling suspended below the overhead structural slab or from the structural elements of a building and not bearing on the walls.

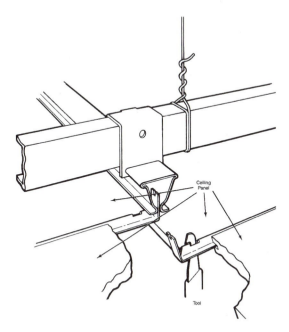

suspended ceiling

suspended floor A floor which spans the entire distance between end supports without additional support in the middle.

suspended formwork Any **formwork** which is supported on hangers.

suspended metal lath A system of metal lath suspended by wire hangers from furring channels and framing channels; the metal lath is used as a base for a plaster ceiling.

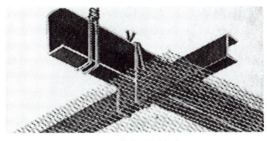

suspended metal lath

suspended scaffold A **scaffold** consisting of a number of **outriggers, 2** from which wire ropes

are wound on hand-operated winches on the scaffold platform.

suspended span A **span, 3** which is supported between two cantilevers.

suspended-type furnace A self-contained warm-air furnace designed to be suspended from the ceiling to supply heated air through ducts to spaces other than the room in which the furnace is located.

suspending agent A material, used in a paint to improve its resistance to the settling of pigments.

suspension roof A roof whose load is carried by a number of cables.

Sussex bond Same as **Flemish garden wall bond**.

sustaining wall A structural wall, such as a **bearing wall** or **retaining wall**.

SW On drawings, abbr. for **switch**.

swag A **festoon**.

swage **1.** A tool or die used to shape metal. **2.** A tool for setting the teeth on a saw by bending one tooth at a time to the proper angle. **3.** To shape metal by the use of a **swage, 1**.

swage block A heavy block of iron or steel, perforated with holes of different sizes and shapes and variously grooved on the sides; used to swage objects of larger size or to head bolts.

swage bolt, swedge bolt An **anchor bolt, 1** whose shank has been deformed by swaging to increase its resistance to being pulled out.

swage pile A **pipe pile**, having a thin wall; the bottom of the pipe is closed with a precast point.

swale **1.** A tract of low, usually wet land. **2.** A depression in a stretch of otherwise flat land.

swallow hole A term occasionally used as a synonym for **owl hole** although swallow holes are usually smaller.

swallow tail Same as **dovetail**.

swan-neck **1.** The curved portion of a handrail of stairs which joins the newel-post. The member's upper part is convex on the top; the lower part is concave on the top. **2.** A downspout connector between a gutter and the downpipe, where the eaves overhang.

swanneck chisel **1.** A long, curved **mortise chisel**. **2.** A **corner chisel**.

swan's-neck pediment A broken pediment having a sloping double **S**-shaped decorative element on each side of the pediment; said to be suggestive of the necks of a pair of swans facing each other.

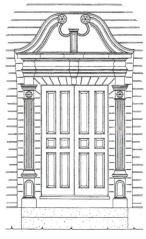

swan's-neck pediment

sward Turf, or ground covered with turf.

swatch A representative patch or sample of material, as a small piece of carpet or a sample of veneer.

sway In thatched roof construction, one of the small willow or hazelwood rods laid at right angles to the thatching to hold it down.

sway brace Same as **wind brace**.

SWBD On drawings, abbr. for **switchboard**.

sweathouse, sweat lodge **1.** A structure used for sweating of tobacco. **2.** An American Indian structure heated by steam produced by pouring water on hot stones, and used for therapeutic sweating or ritual.

sweating **1.** On a paint or varnish film, the development of gloss on a dull or matte finish; caused by rubbing the film. **2.** The joining of metal surfaces by heating and pressing them together, usually with solder between. **3.** The collecting of moisture on a surface which is below the **dewpoint** temperature, as a result of condensation of moisture from the air. **4.** See **surface condensation**.

sweat joint A gastight, metal pipe joint which is either soldered or brazed.

sweat-out A soft, damp area occurring in plasterwork; usually caused by insufficient ventilation and very slow drying; plaster thus affected does not develop good strength.

swedge Same as **swage**.

swedge bolt See **swage bolt**.

Swedish gambrel roof A roof having two flat surfaces on each side of the central ridge of the roof; similar to a **New England gambrel roof** or a **Dutch gambrel roof**, except that the upper surface is shorter and has little slope, and the lower surface is longer and has a much steeper slope than either the New England or Dutch gambrel roofs.

sweep **1.** Said of any large form or mass that curves; for example, the sweep of a curved wall. **2.** A long pole, pivoted on a vertical post, to which a bucket is attached at one end; used to raise water from a well.

sweep fitting Any **fitting** which has a large radius of curvature.

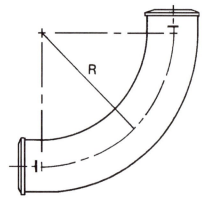

90° sweep fitting

sweep lock A **sash fast**, usually placed on the meeting rails of a window to secure the window; controlled by the action of a lever which rotates to a position where it is secured by a catch.

sweep lock

sweep strip, door sweep A flexible weather stripping used at the top and bottom edges of a revolving door.

sweep tee A **pipe tee** in which each of the two branches gradually curves away from the main run of pipe instead of turning at a right angle.

sweet gum Same as **gum, 1**.

Sweitzer barn A **Swiss barn**; see **German barn**.

swellage See **swelling**.

swell box In a pipe organ, the chamber in which the pipes of the swell organ are placed, the front being made with movable slats which can be opened or shut by means of a pedal.

swelled chamfer See **wave molding**.

swell factor Of a material such as soil, the ratio of the weight of a **loose cubic yard** (or meter) to the weight of a **bank cubic yard** (or meter).

swelling The volume increase caused by wetting, absorption of moisture, or chemical changes.

swept valley On a roof, a **valley** formed of shingles, slates, or tiles; "tile-and-a-half" units are cut with a taper, eliminating the need for a metal valley and giving the appearance of a continuous course.

S.W.G. Abbr. for Brit. **standard wire gauge**.

swift In **prestressing**, the reel or turntable on which the tendons are placed for convenience in handling and placement.

swimming pool Any basin or tank containing an artificial body of water sufficiently deep for swimming.

swimming pool paint Specially formulated water-impermeable paint having good wet adhesion; used to decorate and protect interior surfaces of swimming pools.

swing The action of a door's movement, usually on hinges or pivots, about a hanging stile.

swing check valve A type of **check valve** having a hinged gate which permits fluid to pass through the valve only in one direction; esp. used where fluid velocities are low.

swinging door See **double-acting door**.

swinging latch bolt A **latch bolt** that is hinged to a lock front and is retracted with a swinging rather than a sliding action.

swinging post See **hanging post**.

swinging scaffold, swinging stage A **scaffold** which is suspended by ropes or cables from a

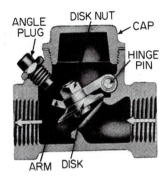

swing check valve

block and tackle attached by roof hooks; can be raised or lowered to any height.

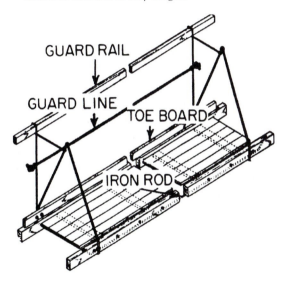

swinging scaffold

swing joint A type of joint used with threaded pipe which permits motion to occur when the pipes are heated or cooled, without bending of the pipes; esp. used in riser and radiator connections. (*See illustration p. 916.*)

swing loader A **tractor loader** which digs at it its front end, but which may dump its load on the side of the tractor.

swing leaf 1. An **active leaf** in a double door. 2. A hinged **sash** (**ventilator, 2**) in a casement window.

swing offset In surveying, the perpendicular distance from a point to a survey line found by swinging a tape about the point as a center and

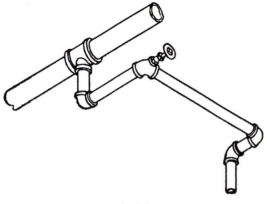

swing joint

measuring the minimum distance from the point to the line.

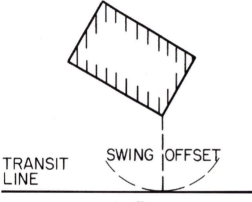

swing offset

swing saw, pendulum saw A power-operated **circular saw** suspended from above and pivoted on a long arm.

swing scaffold, swing stage Same as **swinging scaffold**.

swing-up garage door A rigid **overhead door** which opens as an entire unit.

swipe card reader A security device for providing access to a locked door. The person seeking entry is required to move a card (having a coated magnetic strip on one side) rapidly through an open-ended slot.

swirl The irregular wood grain pattern that surrounds knots or crotches, esp. found in veneer.

swirl finish A nonskid texture imparted to a concrete surface during final troweling by keeping the trowel flat and using a rotary motion.

Swiss barn See **German barn**.

Swiss Cottage architecture, Swiss Chalet architecture A domestic picturesque architecture patterned after its chalet prototype in Switzerland; usually a two-story house built of rough-cut lumber to enhance its rustic appearance; often a front-gabled, shingled roof of moderate pitch, occasionally a **jerkinhead** roof; bracketed eaves having a significant overhang; exposed rafters; often, walls of board-and-batten construction; porches typically have flat balusters with cut-outs or **stickwork**. Occasionally called Swiss Cottage style or Chalet Gothic.

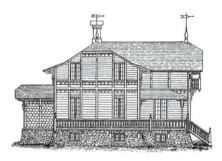

Swiss Cottage architecture

switch A device used to open or close an electric circuit or to change the connection of a circuit.

switchboard A large single electric control panel, frame, or assembly of panels on which are mounted (either on the back or on the face, or both) switches, overcurrent and other protective devices, buses, and usually instruments; not intended for installation in a cabinet but may be completely enclosed in metal; usually is accessible from both the front and rear.

switchgear Any switching and interrupting devices in combination with their associated control, regulating, metering, and protective devices.

switch mat A floor mat containing thin metal blades laminated in plastic sheets. When an intruder steps on the mat, the blades make contact and an alarm is activated.

switch plate A **flush plate** for an electric switch.

switch-start fluorescent lamp See **preheat fluorescent lamp**.

swivel joint Same as **swing joint**.

swivel spindle In door hardware, a **spindle, 1** having a joint midway along its length which permits the knob at one end to be held fixed by the stop works, while the other end is free to operate.

swp Abbr. for "steam working pressure."

sycamore A tough, yellowish wood having a close, firm texture; takes a fine polish; used for flooring and veneer.

SYM On drawings, abbr. for "symmetrical."

Symmetrical Victorian style A term once occasionally used to describe a style of **Gingerbread Folk architecture**.

SYN On drawings, abbr. for "synthetic."

Synadicum marble Same as **pavonazzo, 2**.

synagogue A place of assembly for Jewish worship.

synchronous motor A motor which rotates at a constant speed, at a number of revolutions equal to the frequency of the supply voltage divided by one-half its number of poles or windings.

synergizing agent In water conditioning, a substance which increases the effectiveness of a scale or corrosion inhibitor.

synodal hall A hall in which the clergy of a whole diocese meet.

synthetic paint A paint made with synthetically manufactured resins rather than with naturally occurring oils or gums.

synthetic resin Any of a large number of resin-like products made either by polymerization or condensation, or by modifying a natural material.

synthetic rubber An **elastomer** manufactured by a chemical process, as distinguished from natural rubber obtained from trees; rubberlike with respect to its degree of elasticity.

synthetic rubber-base paint Same as **latex paint**.

synthetic silica Same as **silica gel**.

synthetic stone Same as **artificial stone**.

Syrian arch On a classical façade, an arched entablature over the central intercolumniation.

Syrian arch

syrinx In ancient Egypt, a narrow and deep rock-cut channel or tunnel forming a characteristic feature of Egyptian tombs of the New Empire.

SYS On drawings, abbr. for "system."

system In building construction, prefabricated assemblies, components, and parts which are combined into single integrated units utilizing industrialized production techniques.

Système International d'Unités See **International System of Units**.

system riser In a fire **sprinkler system**, the aboveground supply pipe which is directly connected to the water supply.

systems building See **prefabricated construction** and **industrialized building**.

systyle See **intercolumniation**.

T

T On drawings, abbr. for **tee**.

T&G Abbr. for **tongue-and-groove**.

T&G joint See **tongue-and-groove joint**.

tab **1.** A small, narrow **drop curtain** in a theatre used to mask from view a portion of the stage. **2.** A **tableau curtain**. **3.** The lower end of a shingle.

tabby A mixture of lime and water with shells, gravel, or stones; when dry, forms a mass as hard as rock; used as a building material.

taberna In ancient Rome, a booth, shop, or stall.

tabernacle **1.** A decorative niche often topped with a canopy and housing a statue. **2.** A church for a large Protestant congregation.

tabernacle, 1

tabernacle frame The frame for a door, window, or other opening that is treated as part of a complete design with columns or pilasters and an entablature.

tabernacle work A highly decorated arcade with canopies and sculpture.

tabia A **rammed earth** mixed with lime and pebbles.

tabla house A primitive one-room house of wood-frame construction sheathed with vertical cypress rough-hewn planks (*tablas*), used by early Spanish colonists in Florida in the 16th century. Typically, had a gable roof thatched with palm leaves, a hole in the roof at the ridge to permit smoke to escape from the fireplace below, and a battened door.

tablature **1.** A tabular surface or structure. **2.** A painting or design on a part of an extended surface, as a ceiling.

table **1.** A **stringcourse** or other horizontal band of some size and weight; a horizontal molding on the exterior or interior face of a wall. **2.** A flat surface forming a distinct feature in a wall, generally rectangular and ornamented. **3.** In medieval architecture, the frontal on the face of the altar. **4.** A slab set horizontally and carried on supports.

table, 1

table, 2

tableau curtain A curtain on the stage of a theatre which pulls back as it rises, creating a single festoon on each side, giving a draped effect; may function as the **act curtain**.

tabled joint In cut stonework, a **bed joint** formed by a broad, shallow channel in the surface of one stone which fits a corresponding projection of the stone above or below.

table saw A **circular saw** which is set below the surface of a table having a slot through which the saw blade protrudes.

table stone Same as **dolmen**.

tablet **1.** A regularly shaped, separate panel, or a representation thereof, often bearing an inscription or image. **2.** A **coping stone**, set flat; also called **tabling**. **3.** A plaque, often inscribed and carved, usually affixed to a wall surface or set into the surface; sometimes used to serve as a memorial or to commemorate a special event.

tablet flower In Decorated Gothic architecture, a variation of the **ballflower**, having the form of an open flower with four petals.

tabling Same as **tablet, 2**.

tablinum In ancient Roman architecture, a large open room or apartment for family records and hereditary statues; situated at the end of the **atrium** farthest from the main entrance.

tabularium See **archivium**.

tacheometer See **tachymeter**.

tachometer See **tachymeter**.

tachymeter, tacheometer, tachometer A surveying instrument designed for use in the rapid determination of distance, direction, and difference of elevation from a single observation, using a short base which may be an integral part of the instrument.

tack **1.** A strip of metal, usually lead or copper, used as a clip to secure the edges of metal items in roof construction, such as flashings. **2.** A short, sharp-pointed nail. **3.** The property of an adhesive that enables it to form a bond of measurable strength immediately after the adhesive and adherend are brought into contact under low pressure. **4.** To glue, weld, or otherwise fasten in spots rather than in a continuous line.

tack coat See **asphalt tack coat**.

tack dry Descriptive of the stage in the drying of an adhesive at which it will adhere to itself on contact, although it seems dry to the touch.

tack-free dry Descriptive of the stage in the drying of a paint or varnish film at which it no longer feels sticky to the touch.

tack-free time The time period during which a sealant that is molded in the field remains tacky and is not yet fully serviceable.

tackle A mechanism for shifting, raising, or lowering objects or materials, such as a rope and pulley block or an assembly of ropes and pulley blocks.

tackle

tackless strip A metal strip, beneath the edge of carpeting, which is fastened to the floor, to a stair, etc.; the strip has many small hooks which point upward and slightly toward the edge; the carpeting is stretched beyond the metal strip, allowing the hooks to secure the carpet backing and hold the carpeting in place.

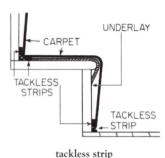

tackless strip

tack rag A rag impregnated with a slow-drying or nondrying varnish or resin; used to wipe dust, lint, and dirt from an article before it is painted.

tack range   The period of time during which an adhesive remains in the **tacky dry** condition after application to an adherend.

tack rivet   A rivet, usually temporary, to hold work during riveting; not intended as a load-carrying rivet.

tack weld   **1.** A weld used for holding metal parts in position temporarily. **2.** One of a series of welds applied where a continuous weld is unnecessary.

tacky dry, tacky   **1.** That stage in the drying of an adhesive at which the volatile constituents have evaporated or been absorbed sufficiently so as to leave the adhesive in a desired condition of tackiness. **2.** That stage in the drying of a paint at which the film appears sticky when lightly touched with the finger.

taenia, tenia   A narrow raised band or fillet, particularly the topmost member of the Doric architrave. Also see **order**.

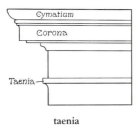

taenia

tag   **1.** In roofing, a sheet-metal strip which is folded over and used as a wedge for holding metallic sheeting in a masonry joint. **2.** A temporary sign, usually attached to a piece of equipment or part of a structure, to warn of existing or potential hazards.

tagger   A sheet of tinplate, or the like, which is of less than standard thickness.

t'ai   Chinese tower structure, rectangular in plan with several receding stories. Watchtower in the Han period; earlier, a hunting or pleasure tower.

tail   **1.** Exposed lower portion of a slate shingle. **2.** Tailing. **3.** See **rafter tail**. **4.** See **lookout**.

tail bay   **1.** In a framed floor, the space between a wall and the nearest girder of the floor. **2.** In a framed floor or roof, a **bay, 1** which is next to the end wall; one end of its joists rests on the end wall, the other on a girder.

tail beam   See **tail piece, 1**.

tail cut   **1.** A cut in the lower end of a rafter where it overhangs the wall; sometimes ornamental. **2.** The **seat cut** at the lower end of a rafter.

tailing   **1.** That portion of a projecting stone or series of stones, as in a cornice, which is built into a wall. **2.** See **tailings**.

tailing in   **1.** Securing one end or edge of a projecting masonry unit, as a cornice. **2.** To fasten one end of a timber, as a floor joist at a wall.

tailing iron   A steel member, built into a wall, to take the upward thrust of a cantilevered member, directly below it, projecting from the wall.

tailings   **1.** Stones which do not pass through the largest openings of a screen used to separate sizes (as after a crushing operation). **2.** The residue or leavings of any product.

tail joist   See **tailpiece, 1**.

tailpiece   **1.** A short beam, joist, or rafter, which is supported by a **header joist** at one end and a wall at the other; also called a **tail beam** or **tail joist**. **2.** An extension to **centering**, where there is a projection from an **impost**; can be removed easily. **3.** A **lookout**. **4.** A **pipe tee** used with a sink drain.

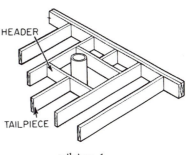

tailpiece, 1

tail trimmer   A **trimmer** placed next to a wall, into which the ends of the joists are fastened instead of supporting them on the wall.

take-up   Any device or mechanism for taking up slack.

take-up block   A guided pulley block, rigged so that its weight or spring loading prevents slack from occurring in lines passing through it.

taking   Of property, a government action that substantially disturbs or interferes with an owner's use and enjoyment of the property.

T & P valve See **temperature and pressure relief valve**.

takspan A Swedish pine shingle for roofing.

talc A soft mineral composed of hydrous magnesium silicate; a major ingredient of **soapstone**; used on roll roofing to prevent sticking in the roll.

tallboy A chimney pot of long and slender form, intended to improve the draft.

tallus See **talus**.

tallut, tallet, tallot (*Brit.*) A loft or attic.

talon molding An **ogee, 2**.

talus, tallus **1.** The slope or inclination of any work, as a **talus wall**. **2.** Coarse rock fragments, mixed with soil, at the foot of a cliff or natural slope.

talus wall A wall having an inclined face; a **battered wall**.

tamarack See **larch**.

tambour **1.** A column drum. **2.** Any generally drum-shaped member.

tamo See **Japanese ash**.

tamp To compact a material or surface, such as earth or freshly placed concrete, by repeated blows.

tamper A compaction device for consolidating a granular material such as soil, backfill, or unformed concrete; usually powered by a motor. Also see **jitterbug**.

tamper

tamping rod A straight steel rod, having a rounded tip at one end.

tamping roller See **sheepsfoot roller**.

tampion A cone-shaped hardwood tool used by plumbers; forced into the end of a lead pipe to increase its diameter.

T and G Abbr. for **tongue** and **groove**.

tang The slender projecting tongue, or prong, forming part of one object that serves to secure it to another, as the projecting tongue on a chisel that secures it to a handle.

tang

tangent Of lines, curves, and surfaces: meeting at a single point and having, at that point, the same direction.

tangential flow filtration Same as **crossflow filtration**.

tangential shrinkage The **shrinkage** across the width of **plain-sawn** lumber.

tangential stress A **shear stress**.

tangent-sawn Same as **plain-sawn**.

tanguile, tangile A hardwood which resembles true mahogany, but shrinks and swells to a greater extent when exposed to moisture; the sapwood is light red, and the heartwood is brownish red.

tanking (*Brit.*) A waterproof lining for a basement floor and walls.

tap **1.** A connection to a water supply main. **2.** A **faucet**. **3.** A tool used for cutting internal threads, as in a pipe.

tap bolt A machine bolt, threaded relatively close to the head, which is screwed into a hole in a material without the use of a nut.

tap bolt

tap borer A hand tool used by plumbers for boring tapered holes, as in a lead pipe when making a connection to it.

tape **1.** See **joint tape**. **2.** See **taping strip**. **3.** See **tape measure**. **4.** See **friction tape**. **5.** See **thermoplastic insulating tape**. **6.** See **thermoplastic protective tape**.

tape balance A **sash balance** in which the weight of the sash is counterbalanced by the force supplied by a metal tape coiled on a spring-loaded reel.

tape correction A correction applied to a distance measured with a tape to eliminate errors caused by the physical condition of the tape or by the way the tape was used.

tapeista In Spanish Colonial architecture, a crude rooflike structure supported by four posts; used as a somewhat protected open-storage area for cornstalks, hay, or the like; also see **jacal, 1**.

tape joint A flat joint, sealed with a joint compound and covered with a **reinforcing tape** which provides added strength.

tape measure, tapeline A steel ribbon used for the measurement of distances; in the U.S.A., surveyor's and engineer's tapes usually are accurately graduated in feet, tenths, and hundredths of a foot; builder's tapes are graduated in feet, inches, and fractions of an inch; also called a **steel measuring tape**.

tape measure

taper A gradual diminution of thickness in an elongated object, as in a **spire**.

tapered edge strip In built-up roofing, a tapered strip of insulation used to raise the roofing at its perimeter, where there are penetrations through the roofing.

tapered-roll pantile A roofing **pantile** having a roll that has a slight increase in width from the head to the tail of the tile.

tapered tenon A **tenon** which decreases in width from the root toward the end.

tapered valley In roofing, a **valley**, formed between shingles, slates, or tiles, which is wider at the bottom than the top.

taper pin A headless, solid pin having controlled diameter, length, and taper, with crowned ends.

taper pin

taper pipe See **diminishing pipe**.

taper thread A screw thread which is formed on a cone or the frustum of a cone; used on some types of fasteners; used in plumbing on pipes and **fittings, 1** to ensure a gastight joint.

tapestry A fabric, worked on a warp by hand, the designs employed usually being pictorial; used for wall hangings or the like.

tapestry brick Same as **rustic brick**.

tapia An adobe-like building material consisting mainly of earth or clay in which small pebbles was imbedded; this term is also occasionally applied to **puddled adobe**.

taping Measuring distance on the ground with a tape or chain.

taping arrow See **chaining pin**.

taping compound A compound that is specifically formulated and manufactured for embedding a joint reinforcing tape at a gypsum board joint.

taping pin See **chaining pin**.

taping strip **1.** A strip of roofing felt laid over the joints between adjacent precast concrete roof slabs; prevents bitumen which is applied subsequently from dripping into the space below. **2.** A strip used to cover the joint between adjacent roof insulation boards.

tapped fitting Any pipe **fitting, 1** having a tapped internal thread to receive a threaded pipe.

tapped tee In plumbing, a bell-end **tee** which has a branch that is tapped to receive a threaded pipe fitting or a threaded pipe.

tapping machine A machine designed to produce a sequence of uniform impacts on a floor surface; used to measure impact sound transmission of a floor-ceiling assembly.

tapping screw See **sheet-metal screw**.

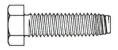

tapping screw

tar See **coal-tar pitch**.

tar-and-gravel roofing A **built-up roofing** which has a surfacing material consisting of gravel in a heavy coat of coal-tar pitch.

tar cement Heavier grades of asphalt cement which are prepared for direct use in construction and maintenance of bituminous pavements.

target In surveying, see **leveling rod**.

target leveling rod A type of **leveling rod** carrying a target, which is moved into position according to signals given by the instrument man; when the target is bisected by the line of collimation of the instrument, it is read and recorded by the rod man.

target rod See **leveling rod**.

tarmac, tarmacadam See **macadam**.

tar paper See **asphalt prepared roofing**.

tarpaulin A waterproof cloth, esp. one used in large sheets for covering anything exposed to the weather.

tarred felt Same as **asphaltic felt**.

tarsia Same as **inlay**.

tas-de-charge **1.** The lowest voussoir or voussoirs of an arch or vault with the joints horizontal instead of radial. **2.** In vaulting, that section of a group of vault ribs between the line where they spring and the line where they separate.

task lighting Lighting that is directed to a specific area to provide illumination for the performance of a visual task.

tasolera In Spanish Colonial architecture, a barn to house animals or to store agricultural produce.

tatami A thick straw mat serving as floor covering in the Japanese house. Used as standard unit of floor area, approx. 3 ft by 6 ft (1 m by 2 m).

tauriform See **bull's head**.

tavern See **inn, 1**.

tax abatement The reduction of real estate taxes on a property; usually accomplished by means of a reduction in its assessed value.

tax exemption The release of a property from the obligation to pay real estate taxes.

taxpayer A building, often temporary, which yields a minimal return on investment, usually little more than real estate taxes.

TB Abbr. for **through bolt**.

T-bar In a perforated-metal-pan acoustical ceiling assembly, a metal suspension member designed to support the metal pan by engaging its flanges.

T-beam A reinforced concrete beam or rolled metal shape having a cross section resembling the letter T.

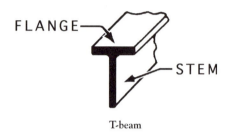

T-beam

T-bevel Same as **bevel square**.

TC On drawings, abbr. for **terra-cotta**.

tchahar taq Square open pavilion in Sassanian architecture (A.D. 224–651), composed of four columns with four arches supporting a dome, mostly over an altar.

tea garden **1.** A Japanese garden next to a teahouse, usually small and serene. **2.** An outdoor tearoom in a public garden, serving refreshments, including tea.

teagle A hoist.

teagle post In timber framing, a post supporting one end of a tie beam.

teahouse A Japanese garden house used for the tea ceremony.

teak A dark golden yellow or brown wood with a greenish or black cast, found in southeastern Asia, India, and Burma; moderately hard, coarse-grained, very durable; oil which it contains gives it a greasy feeling and makes it immune to the attack of insects; used for exterior construction, plywood, and decorative paneling; also called **Indian oak**.

tear See **run, 5**.

tearing A defect in the surface of porcelain enamel, characterized by crackle or short breaks which have been healed.

tear strength A material's resistance against being pulled apart.

tease To work out a surface defect, as on a varnished surface.

teaser A horizontal curtain or canvas-covered framework, behind and across the top of the proscenium arch of a theatre; used to conceal the **flies** and, together with the **tormentors** along the sides, to frame the opening of the stage.

tease tenon See **teaze tenon**.

teaze tenon, tease tenon A tenon, having a stepped outline, on the top of a post; esp. cut to receive two horizontal pieces of timber that cross each other (at right angles) at the post.

tebam The reader's platform in a synagogue.

tectiform Like a roof in form or use.

tectonic Of or pertaining to building or construction; architectural.

tectorial Covering, forming a roof-like structure.

tectorium opus See **opus tectorium**.

tee 1. A **finial** in the form of a conventionalized umbrella, used on stupas, topes, and pagodas. 2. Same as **pipe tee**. 3. A metal member having a constant T-shaped cross section.

tee, 1: as the finial of a pagoda

tee, 2: copper-to-copper pipe tee

tee beam See **T-beam**.

tee bevel Same as **bevel square**.

tee handle A T-shaped handle for actuating the bolt of a lock on a door; used in place of a knob.

tee head See **T-head**.

tee hinge See **T-hinge**.

tee iron 1. A flat T-shaped piece of heavy sheet metal having predrilled, countersunk holes; screwed to a joint in wood construction in order to provide reinforcement. 2. A section of steel **T-beam**.

tee joint A joint between two members which are located approximately at right angles to each other in the form of the letter T.

welded **tee joint**

teepee Same as **tipi**.

tee square See **T-square**.

tegula A tile, esp. one of unusual shape or material.

tegurium A roof over a sarcophagus, usually double-sloped and supported by narrow columns.

teja In Spanish Colonial architecture, a burnt-clay roof tile, semicircular in cross section, and usually tapered.

TEL On drawings, abbr. for "telephone."

telamon (*pl.* **telamones**) A sculptured male human figure used in place of a column to support an entablature; also called an **atlas**.

telamones at Agrigentum

telecommunications The transmission and reception of signals (such as electrical or optical) by wire, optical fiber, or electromagnetic means.

telegraphing, show-through On a decorative material covering a wall, etc., irregularities, imperfections, or patterns of an inner layer which are transmitted to the surface so that they become visible.

telephone booth An enclosure for a telephone in a public area.

telephone station A shelf unit for a telephone in a public area.

telescope house A house comprised of several units, each of descending height, giving the building the appearance of fitting together like the components of a collapsible telescope; compare with **continuous house**.

telltale Any device designed to indicate movement of formwork.

temenos A sacred enclosure surrounding a temple or other holy spot.

TEMP On drawings, abbr. for "temperature."

temper **1.** To mix lime, sand, and water in such proportions as to make mortar for masonry or plastering. **2.** To moisten and mix clay to proper consistency to form bricks, etc., prior to hardening by fire. **3.** To bring to a proper degree of hardness and elasticity for use, as steel or other metal, by heat treatment. **4.** To impregnate wood fibers or composition board with a drying oil or other oxidizing resin and subsequently to cure with heat so as to improve the strength, hardness, water resistance, and durability of the board.

tempera A rapidly drying paint consisting of egg white (or egg yolk, or a mixture of egg white and yolk), gum, pigment, and water; esp. used in painting murals.

temperature and pressure relief valve A valve that combines the functions of a **pressure relief valve** and a **temperature relief valve**.

temperature controller See **thermostat**.

temperature cracking The cracking of a concrete member due to tensile failure caused by a temperature drop (if member is subjected to external restraints) or caused by a temperature differential (if member is subjected to internal restraints).

temperature reinforcement In reinforced concrete, reinforcement designed to carry stresses resulting from temperature changes.

temperature relay A **relay** that operates at a predetermined temperature in the apparatus which it protects.

temperature relief valve A temperature-actuated safety valve designed to open automatically when the temperature of the water being heated exceeds a preset value.

temperature rise In cement, the increase in temperature resulting from the absorption of heat or from the internally generated heat, as by the hydration of cement in concrete.

temperature steel Steel reinforcement which is placed in a concrete slab, or the like, to minimize the possibility of developing cracks as a result of temperature changes.

temperature stress See **thermal stress**.

temperature stress rod In reinforced concrete, one of a number of steel rods laid perpendicular to the **reinforcing bars** or rods to prevent cracks from forming parallel to the reinforcement, as a result of stresses from drying or from thermal stresses; a type of **temperature reinforcement**.

tempered board A durable wood fiber or composition board; also see **temper, 4**.

tempered glass (*U.S.A.*), **toughened glass** (*Brit.*) Glass having two to five times the strength of ordinary glass as a result of having been prestressed by heating and then suddenly quenched; the rapid cooling produces a compressively-stressed surface layer.

tempered steel Steel that has been heated to a high temperature and then quenched, usually a number of times, a process that significantly hardens it; also called case-hardened steel.

tempered water Water in the temperature range from 85°F (29°C) to 110°F (43°C).

tempietto A small temple, especially one of ornamental character, during the Renaissance or later; many such structures were constructed in the gardens of imposing country houses.

template, templet **1.** A pattern, usually of sheet material, used as a guide for setting out work and in repeating dimensions. **2.** A piece of stone, metal, or timber placed in a wall to receive the impost of a beam, girders, etc., and to distribute its load. **3.** A beam or plate spanning a door or window space to sustain joists and transfer their load to piers. **4.** One of the wedges in a building block.

template hardware Hardware that exactly matches a master template drawing, as to spacing of all holes and dimensions.

temple **1.** An edifice dedicated to the service of a deity or deities, and connected with a system of worship. **2.** A synagogue. **3.** An edifice erected as a place of public worship, esp. a Protestant church. **4.** A pretentious edifice for some special public use. **5.** The local lodge of a fraternal organization.

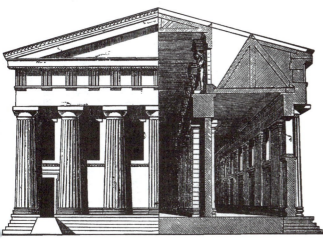

temple, 1: at Agrigentum

templet Same as **template**.

temple tower A **ziggurat**.

templon A trabeated colonnade which closes off the **bema** of a Byzantine church.

temporary (electrical) service Electrical service used for a limited time during construction, exhibits, or similar temporary purposes.

temporary shoring **Shoring** installed during construction, to support a member or a portion of the structure; removed prior to the completion of construction.

temporary stress In a precast concrete member or in a component thereof, a stress which may occur during fabrication, erection, construction, or test loading.

temse Same as **screen, 3**.

tenancy Occupation by one with less than a fee interest in property, e.g., a tenancy for life, or a tenancy for a term of years. The latter type of tenancy usually is created by lease.

tenancy in common Ownership of property by two or more persons, each of whom may freely transfer his interest; the death of one tenant does not transfer his rights to the other or others.

tenant A person or firm using a building, or part of a building, as a lessee or owner-occupant.

tenant's improvement Improvements on real property made by a tenant at his own expense. Unless otherwise agreed, they become part of the property and may not be removed by the tenant at the end of his term.

tender A proposal or bid for a contract to perform work, often on a form, completed by a contractor, giving estimated price and time to complete a contract.

tendon In **prestressed concrete**, a steel element such as a wire, cable, bar, rod, or strand used to impart prestress to the concrete when the element is placed under tension.

tendon profile In prestressed concrete, the trajectory of a prestressing **tendon**.

tenement A building having multiple housing units for rent; often, ill-maintained, overcrowded units that may barely meet minimum code requirements for safety and sanitation; usually built many years earlier and found in poorer sections of a city.

tenia See **taenia**.

tenon The projecting end of a piece of wood, or other material, which is reduced in cross section, so that it may be inserted in a corresponding

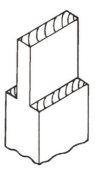

tenon

cavity (mortise) in another piece in order to form a secure joint. Also see **mortise-and-tenon joint.**

tenon-and-slot mortise A wood joint formed by a **tenon** and a **slot mortise,** usually at right angles to each other.

tenon saw A saw having a metal strip along the back to stiffen it; has many small teeth; used for fine, accurate sawing, as in forming tenons, dovetails, and miters. Also called a **miter saw.**

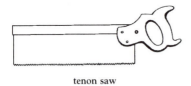

tenon saw

tensile-frame construction See **bent-frame construction.**

tensile strain The elongation of a material which is subject to tension.

tensile strength The resistance of a material to rupture when subject to tension; the maximum **tensile stress** which the material can sustain.

tensile stress The stress per square unit area of the original cross section of a material which resists its elongation.

tension The state or condition of being pulled or stretched.

tension bar A metal bar by means of which a tensile strain is applied or resisted.

tension member A structural member subjected to **tension;** a **tie.**

tension reinforcement Reinforcement designed to carry tensile stresses such as those in the bottom of a simple beam.

tension rod A rod in a truss or structure which connects opposite parts and prevents them from spreading.

tension wood Abnormal wood found on the upper side of hardwood branches and leaning trunks; characterized by abnormally high longitudinal shrinking, causing warping and splitting.

tepee Same as **tipi.**

tepidarium In ancient Roman baths, a room of moderately warm temperature.

TER On drawings, abbr. for **terrazzo.**

term Same as **terminal figure.**

terminal **1.** An electrically conductive element, attached to the end of a conductor or piece of equipment for connection to an external conductor. **2.** The ornamental finish, decorative element, or termination of an object, item of construction, or structural part.

terminal box On a piece of electric equipment (such as a motor), a box within which the leads from the piece of equipment are connected to the leads supplying the equipment with power; usually provided with a removable cover plate for access.

terminal expense An expense incurred in connection with the termination of a contract.

terminal figure, terminal statue A decorative figure in which a head, or a head and bust, or the human figure to the waist and including the arms, is incorporated with (as if it were springing out of) a pillar which serves as its pedestal.

terminal pedestal A pedestal prepared for a bust, so that the two together comprise a **terminal figure.**

terminal pedestal

terminal reheat system An air-conditioning system in which a **reheat coil** is provided for each individually controlled zone, regulating the temperature of the air being furnished.

terminal stopping device A **limit switch** for an elevator car.

terminal unit In an air-conditioning system, a unit at the end of a branch duct through which air is transferred or delivered to the conditioned space.

terminal velocity In an **air-conditioning system**, the average velocity of an airstream at the end of its throw; one of the indicators of drafty conditions and comfort level.

terminated stop, hospital stop, sanitary stop A **stop, 1** that terminates above the floor line and is closed with a 45° or 90° angle.

terminating enclosure A type of enclosure (approved by the utility company) which is installed at the **point of service** for the load-end termination of the utility company's **service cables** where they join the customer's service entrance conductors; includes concrete subway-type pull boxes, manholes, wall-mounted pull boxes, and switchboard pull sections.

terminating facility Any type of electrical terminating enclosure or transformer enclosure.

termination An ornamental element which finishes off an architectural feature such as a **dripstone**.

(a) Norman

(b) Early English style

(c) Perpendicular style

terminations of various types

terminus A bust or figure of the upper part of the human body terminated in a plain block of rectangular form; a terminal figure.

termite shield A shield of noncorroding metal or inorganic material, used as protection against the infiltration of termites in a building; so placed as to prevent their passage, usually as a projecting shield on a masonry foundation or pier (or under a wood sill or beam which it supports), or around pipes which enter the building.

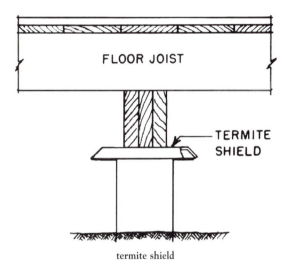

termite shield

terne metal An alloy of lead, containing up to 20% tin.

terneplate Sheet steel which is coated with **terne metal**; widely used for roofing and construction work.

terra alba A pure white uncalcined gypsum which is used as a filler in paints.

terrace **1.** An embankment with level top, often paved, planted, and adorned for leisure use. **2.** A flat roof or a raised space or platform adjoining a building, paved or planted, esp. one used for leisure enjoyment.

terrace house One of a row of houses situated on a **terrace**, or similar site.

terrace roof See **cut roof**.

terra-cotta Clay that has been molded in shape and then treated in a kiln at a high temperature; typically reddish-brown in color when unglazed;

when glazed, usually colored and used for ornamental work, such as architectural terra-cotta, and for floor tile and roof tile.

terras   Same as **trass**.

terrazzo, terrazzo concrete   Marble-aggregate concrete that is cast in place or precast and ground smooth; used as a decorative surfacing on floors and walls.

terreplein   An earth embankment, flattened at the top.

Territorial Revival   An architectural mode of limited popularity in the southwestern United States, particularly New Mexico, after about 1920; basically a modification of **Territorial style**.

Territorial style   An architectural style in New Mexico from the time it became a territory of the United States in 1848 until about 1900; typically, a one-story house usually having a flat roof with parapets, exterior walls of adobe coated with adobe plaster or stucco; an entry door commonly flanked with sidelights; brick trim around doors and windows with pedimented lintels above, sometimes with wood decorative trim suggestive of the Greek Revival style. Such houses were sometimes built around an enclosed courtyard with rooms opening onto a covered walkway around the perimeter of the courtyard.

terrone   A building material cut into rectangular units of sod from a river bottom or swamp, and then sun-baked; similar to **adobe** but stronger when dry because of the added strength provided by the sod roots; used in the form of building blocks.

tertiary beam   Any beam which transfers its load to a secondary beam, at either one end or both ends.

tessellated   Formed of small square pieces of marble, stone, glass, or the like, in the manner of an ornamental mosaic.

tessellated work   Inlay work composed of **tesserae**.

tessera   A small squarish piece of colored marble, glass, or tile, used to make mosaic patterns, either geometric or figurative.

testaceum   Same as **opus testaceum**.

test code   A measurement standard that is primarily applicable to a specific class or type of machinery or equipment.

tesserae: shown separately and combined in a mosaic

test cylinder   A cylinder of concrete 6 in. (15 cm) in diameter and 12 in. (30 cm) high; cast from a representative sample of the plastic concrete in any pour and cured under controlled conditions; used to determine its compressive strength after a specified time interval.

tester   A flat canopy, as over a bed, throne, pulpit, or tomb.

testing machine   Any device or machine used to measure accurately the properties of a material, product, assembly, etc., under controlled conditions.

test method   The technical procedures and actions that are required to determine whether or not a particular product conforms with a relevant standard.

test pile   A **pile, 1** used to determine the load that it can support without settling; this determination usually is made by placing heavy weights on a platform mounted on the top of the pile.

test pit   An excavation made to examine an existing foundation, or to determine whether an area is suitable for building construction; includes the taking of soil samples and the determining of the depth of groundwater.

test plug   In a drainage system, a plug which is installed in the system being tested for leaks. The test plug is connected to an air compressor (through a valve) that is used to inflate it and seal the drain.

test pressure   In plumbing, the water pressure or air pressure to which the pipes and **fittings, 1** are subjected when they are tested for watertightness and strength.

test tee   In plumbing, a special **pipe tee** which is inserted in a drainage system; provided with a mechanism for producing water **test pressure** to check the system for leaks.

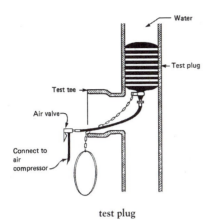

test plug

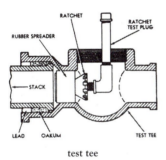

test tee

tetraprostyle: temple on the Ilissus, Athens (449 B.C.)

testudo   In Roman architecture, an arched vault or ceiling, esp. when surbased or flattened.

tetraprostyle   Said of a classical temple having a portico of four columns in front of the **cella** or **naos**.

tetrapylon   A structure characterized by having four gateways as an architectural feature.

tetrastoon   A courtyard with porticoes or open colonnades on each of its four sides.

tetrastyle   Having four columns in the front or end row; consisting of a row or rows of four columns.

textile mill   A factory in which woven fabrics are manufactured. Many early mills were located near a source of water power for operating the machinery; most were of timber construction and in constant danger of being consumed by fire. In 1832, a significant advance in fire safety occurred with the construction of a mill in Rhode Island that was especially designed to resist fire (and to burn slowly if ignited) by using thick floor planking, by minimizing the number of timber beams, and by maximizing the cross-sectional area of each beam. These design criteria, widely applied, greatly improved fire safety in the mills.

texture   The tactile and visual quality of a surface or substance other than its color.

texture brick   A **rustic brick**.

textured paint   See **plastic paint**.

texture-finished paint   See **plastic paint**.

TG&B   Abbr. for "tongued, grooved, and beaded."

thalamus, thalamium   In early Greek architecture, an inner room or chamber, esp. the women's apartment.

thatch   The covering of a roof, or the like, usually made of straw, reed, or similar materials fastened together to shed water and sometimes to provide thermal insulation; in tropical countries palm leaves are widely used.

thatched hut   See **palma hut**.

T-head   **1.** In precast framing, a segment of girder crossing the top of an interior column. **2.**

The top of a **shore** formed with a braced horizontal member which projects on two sides, forming a T-shaped assembly. **3.** In plumbing, same as **curb cock**.

theatre   A building or outdoor structure providing a stage (and associated equipment) for the presentation of dramatic performances and seating for spectators.

Shakespearian **theatre:**   Fortune Theatre, London, mid-17th cent.

theatre-in-the-round   An arena theatre; also see **arena, 2**.

theatre seating   Same as **auditorium seating**.

theatrical gauze   A stiff **gauze, 1**, usually of cotton or linen; used on the stage of a theatre for curtains or scenery.

theodolite   A precision instrument used in surveying; consists of an **alidade** which is equipped with a telescope, a leveling device, and an accurately graduated horizontal circle; also may carry an accurately graduated vertical circle.

theologeion, theologium   A small upper stage or balcony in the stage structure of the ancient theatre, on which persons representing divinities sometimes appeared and spoke.

therm   A quantity of heat equivalent to 100,000 Btu.

thermae   See **bath, 3**.

thermal barrier   See **thermal break**.

thermal break, thermal barrier   An element of low heat conductivity placed in an assembly to reduce or prevent the flow of heat between highly conductive materials; used in some metal window or curtain wall designs intended for installation in cold climates.

thermal capacity   See **heat capacity**.

thermal conductance   The time rate of flow of heat through a unit area of material from one of the faces of the material to the other, for a unit temperature difference between the two faces, under steady-state conditions.

thermal conduction   The process of heat transfer through a material medium in which kinetic energy is transmitted by particles of the material from particle to particle without gross displacement of the particles.

thermal conductivity   The rate of transfer of heat by conduction; the amount of heat per unit of time per unit area that is conducted through a slab of unit thickness of a material if the difference in temperature between opposite faces is one degree of temperature; a property of the material itself, usually represented by the letter k and called **k factor**.

thermal conductor   A material which readily transmits heat by means of **thermal conduction**.

thermal cutout   An overcurrent protective device in an electric circuit; contains a heater element and a renewable fusible member which opens when the current is so great as to produce sufficient heat to melt it; not designed to interrupt short-circuit currents.

thermal diffusivity   The thermal conductivity divided by the product of the specific heat and unit weight; an index of the ease with which a material undergoes a change in temperature.

thermal emissivity   The ratio of the rate of radiant heat energy emitted by a body at a given temperature to the rate of radiant heat energy emitted by a **blackbody, 1** at the same temperature, in the same surroundings.

thermal expansion   The change in length or volume which a material or body undergoes on being heated.

thermal insulating cement   A prepared composition, in dry form, comprising granular, flaky, fibrous, or powdery materials; when mixed with a suitable proportion of water, it develops a plastic consistency, and if applied to a surface, dries in place and forms a covering that provides thermal insulation.

thermal insulation, heat insulation A material providing high resistance to heat flow; usually made of mineral wool, cork, asbestos, foam glass, foamed plastic, diatomaceous earth, etc.; fabricated in the form of batts, blankets, blocks, boards, granular fill, and loose fill.

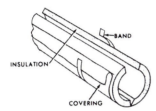

thermal insulation   for covering a pipe

thermal insulation board A preformed rigid or semirigid material in board or block form, which provides resistance to heat flow.

thermal load A load on a structure which is induced by changes in temperature.

thermal movement Changes in dimension of concrete or masonry as a result of temperature changes.

thermal protector For a motor or motor-compressor, a protective device which protects the motor against dangerous overheating, due either to failure to start or to overload.

thermal radiation The transmission of heat from a hot surface to a cooler one in the form of invisible electromagnetic waves, which, on being absorbed by the cooler surface, raise the temperature of that surface without warming the space between.

thermal resistance The reciprocal of **thermal conductance**.

thermal resistivity An index of a material's resistance to the transmission of heat; the reciprocal of **thermal conductivity**.

thermal shock The sudden stress produced in a body or in a material as a result of a sudden temperature change.

thermal stress, temperature stress Stress introduced by uniform or nonuniform temperature change in a structure or material which is constrained against expansion or contraction.

thermal transference The steady-state flow of heat from a body, through applied thermal insulation, to the external surroundings, i.e., the time rate of heat flow per unit area of the body surface per unit temperature difference between the body surface and the external surroundings.

thermal transmittance, U-value The time rate of heat flow per unit area under steady conditions from the fluid on the warm side of a barrier to the fluid on the cold side, per unit temperature difference between the two fluids.

thermal unit A unit of heat energy, such as the British thermal unit (Btu) in the English system, or the calorie in the metric system.

thermal valve A valve whose action is controlled by a thermally responsive element.

thermite welding A welding process in which the joining of the parts is produced by heating with superheated liquid metal and slag resulting from the ignition of a mixture of ferric oxide and finely-divided aluminum particles; pressure may be applied.

THERMO On drawings, abbr. for **thermostat**.

thermocouple A device consisting of two junctions of two dissimilar metals, in an electric circuit; when the two junctions are at different temperatures, a voltage is generated by the device; used for measuring temperature.

thermometer A device for measuring temperature.

thermometer well A specially designed enclosure which is connected into a piping system and into which a thermometer may be inserted to measure fluid temperature.

Thermopane™ A proprietary name for a **heat-insulating glass**.

thermoplastic A material which becomes soft and pliable when heated (without change in its other properties) and hard and rigid when cooled again.

thermoplastic insulating tape A tape composed of a thermoplastic compound; used to provide insulation at joints in an electric conductor.

thermoplastic protective tape A tape which is composed of a thermoplastic compound that provides a protective covering for electrical insulation.

thermosetting Descriptive of a material such as synthetic resin which hardens when heated or cured, and does not soften when reheated.

thermosetting resin A synthetic resin which assumes a permanent set under heat; cannot be remolded once the set has taken place.

thermosiphon solar energy system A solar energy system in which the heat transfer fluid circulates by convection as the less dense, warm fluid (air) rises and is displaced by the denser, cooler fluid (air).

thermostat An instrument which responds to changes in temperature, and directly or indirectly controls temperature.

thermostatic expansion valve A controlling device for regulating the flow of volatile refrigerant into a cooling unit, actuated by changes in cooling unit pressure and superheat of the refrigerant leaving the cooling unit.

thermostatic switch A type of switch installed inside security cabinets, vaults, etc. If the temperature within the cabinet or vault rises significantly above its normal value, the thermostatic switch closes, thereby activating an alarm.

thermostatic trap A **steam trap** utilizing a thermally actuated device to expand and close the discharge port when steam flows through it, and to contract and allow steam condensate to flow through when the temperature of the fluid drops to a predetermined value; usually used for small steam loads such as radiators.

therm window Same as **Venetian window**.

thesaurus In ancient Greece, a treasury house.

thickness gauge Same as **feeler gauge**.

thickness molding Same as **bed molding**.

thimble 1. A protective sleeve of metal which passes through the wall of a chimney to hold the end of a stovepipe or smoke pipe. 2. The socket or bearing attached to an **escutcheon** plate in which the end of the knob shank rotates.

T-hinge, tee hinge A surface-mounted door hinge in the shape of the letter T, of which one leaf, the strap, is fastened to the door, and the other (short and wide) is fixed to the doorpost.

thinner, dilutent, solvent A volatile liquid used to dilute and lower the viscosity of paints, adhesives, etc.

thinning ratio The amount of **thinner** that is recommended for a given quantity of paint.

thin-set terrazzo Same as **special matrix terrazzo**.

thin-shell concrete Thin **reinforced concrete** in the shape of a large **shell, 1** or section thereof.

thin-shell precast Precast concrete which is characterized by relatively thin slabs and web sections.

thin-wall conduit Electric conduit which has a wall thickness insufficient for providing threads; the ends are joined by couplings which slip over the ends and which are held in place by setscrews.

thixotropic That property of certain gels of becoming liquid when shaken or stirred.

THK On drawings, abbr. for "thick."

thole 1. Same as **tholos**. 2. A niche or recess in which votive offerings were made. 3. A knot or escutcheon at the apex of a timber vault.

tholobate The circular substructure of a dome.

tholos 1. In Greek architecture, any round building. 2. The corbeled, domed tombs of the Mycenaean period. 3. A domed rotunda.

tholos tomb See **beehive tomb**.

tholus Same as **tholos**.

thread The prominent spiral part of a screw; a ridge of uniform section in the form of a helix on

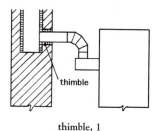

thimble, 1

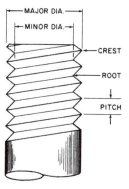

thread: terminology

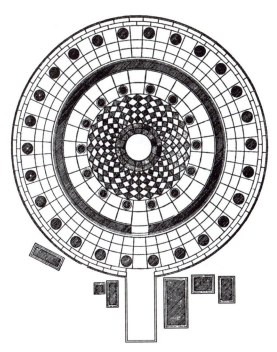

tholos, 1   at Epidaurus, plan

the external or internal surface of a cylinder. Also see **taper thread**.

threaded anchorage In posttensioning, a device used for **anchorage**; has threads to attach the jacking device more easily and to effect the anchorage.

threaded joint A mechanical joint between threaded pipes or between a threaded pipe and threaded fitting.

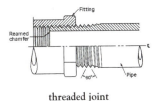

threaded joint

thread escutcheon A small metal plate placed around any small opening, as a keyhole.

three-bay threshing barn, three-bay barn Same as **Yankee barn**.

three-centered arch An arch whose inner curved surface is struck from three centers, resulting in a shape approximating one-half an ellipse. Compare with **two-centered arch**.

three-coat work In plastering, the application of three successive coats: **scratch coat**, **brown coat**, and **finish coat**.

three-decker A pulpit for a meetinghouse with the clerk's desk at the bottom, the reader's desk above it, and the pulpit on top.

three-ended barn See **straw shed**.

three-hinged arch An arch with hinges at the two supports and at the crown.

three-light window 1. A window with three panes. 2. A window which is three panes high or three panes wide.

three-part window 1. A window having three sashes of the same height and in the same plane; there is a wide rectangular **sash** at its center and a narrower sash on each side; essentially the same as a **Palladian window** with the rounded head of the center sash lopped off at the top. 2. Same as **treble sash**.

three-pinned arch Same as **three-hinged arch**.

three-ply Consisting of three layers, thicknesses, laminations, etc., as veneers in plywood; where the layers have a grain or orientation, usually the grain in adjacent layers is opposite.

three-pointed arch See **equilateral arch**.

three-point lock A device which locks the active leaf of a pair of doors at three points; sometimes required on doors having a 3-hr fire rating.

three-quarter bat Same as **three-quarter brick**.

three-quarter brick A brick which is equal to three-quarters of the length of a full-sized brick.

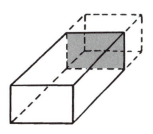

three-quarter brick

three-quarter Cape house A **Cape Cod house** that has two double-hung windows on

three-quarter Cape house

one side of the front door and only one on the other side of the door.

three-quarter closer   Same as **king closer**.

three-quarter closer

three-quarter header   A **header** whose length is equal to three-fourths of the thickness of the wall.

three-quarter house   A **Cape Cod house** or **saltbox** having two windows on one side of the front door and one window on the other side.

three-quarter-turn   Descriptive of a stair which, in its progress from top to bottom, turns 270°.

three-quarter view   A view of an object which is midway between a front and a side view.

three-room plan   A once-popular **plan** consisting of a parlor, hall, and kitchen lined up along the front of the house. The entry door, which was not centered on the façade, usually opened directly into the kitchen.

three-way strap   A steel strap which is shaped to fit and join three members of a wood truss; fastened with bolts or screws.

three-way switch   An electric **switch**, used in conjunction with a similar switch, to control lights from two different points, as from two different ends of a hallway.

three-wire system   An electric wiring system which utilizes three conductors; one of the wires (the "neutral wire") is maintained at a potential midway between the potentials of the other two.

threshing floor   The section of a barn where wheat is separated from the chaff and also where hay is stored. In some early barns, the threshing process took up an entire floor.

threshold   **1.** A strip fastened to the floor beneath a door, usually required to cover the joint where two types of floor material meet; may provide weather protection at exterior doors. Also see **doorsill. 2.** In illumination engineering, the value of physical stimulus which permits an object to be seen a specified percentage of the time with specified accuracy.

throat   **1.** A groove that is cut along the underside of a projecting member (for example, under a **belt course**) to prevent rainwater from running back across it toward the wall; also called a drip molding. **2.** Same as **chimney throat**.

throating   **1.** A **drip** or **drip mold. 2.** See **throat. 3.** A chimney throat.

throat opening   In a steel doorframe, the opening between the **backbends** of the frame.

throttling valve   In a piping system, an orifice designed to control the rate of flow through it.

through-and-through-sawn   Same as **plain-sawn**.

through arch   Any arch which is set in a thick, heavy wall.

through bolt   A bolt which passes completely through the members it connects.

through bond   In a masonry wall, the transverse bond formed by stone units or bricks extending through the wall.

through check   In a timber, a **check** which extends from one surface through to the opposite side.

through dovetail   See **common dovetail**.

through gutter   A **gutter** having parallel sides.

through lintel   A **lintel** whose thickness is that of the wall in which it is placed.

through lot   A lot, other than a corner lot, having frontage on two public streets or highways.

through penetration   An opening that passes through both sides of a fire-resistive construction.

through shake   In timber, a **shake** which extends between any two faces.

through stone   A stone that is set with its longest dimension perpendicular to the face of a

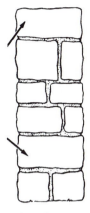

through stones
(indicated by arrows)

wall and whose length is equal to the thickness of the wall.

through tenon A **tenon** that extends completely through the piece into which its corresponding mortise is cut.

through-the-cornice wall dormer See **wall dormer**.

through-wall flashing A **flashing** which extends through a wall, from one side to the other.

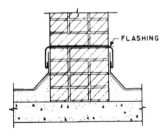

through-wall flashing

throw 1. The horizontal or vertical axial distance an airstream travels after leaving an **air outlet** to the point where the airstream velocity is reduced to a specific value; also called **blow**. 2. The effective distance between a lighting fixture and the area being lighted. 3. The maximum distance that a bolt projects when it is fully extended.

THRU On drawings, abbr. for "through."

thrust 1. The amount of push or force exerted by or on a structure. 2. In an arch, the resultant force normal to any cross section of the arch.

In medieval pointed vaulting, a section taken at the level of the head of the flying buttress; arrows indicate the directions of **thrust**

thrust bearing A support for a shaft designed to take up its end thrust.

thrust stage A stage in a theatre that does not have a proscenium; the stage is surrounded on three sides by the audience.

thuja Same as **thuya**.

thumbat In roofing, a hook for fastening sheet lead.

thumb knob Same as **turn knob**.

thumb latch A **lift latch** for securing a door in a closed position, usually by means of a flat bar that falls into a catch when pressed by the thumb; for example, see **Norfolk latch** and **Suffolk latch**.

thumb molding A narrow convex molding which is flattened in cross section.

thumb nut Same as **wing nut**.

thumb piece A small pivoted part above the grip of a door handle; pressure on this part, by the thumb, causes the latch bolt to operate.

thumb plane A very small, narrow carpenter's plane.

thumbscrew A screw having a broad head that is knurled or flattened so that it may be turned easily by the thumb and one finger.

thumb turn   Same as **turn knob**.

thurm   To work moldings, or the like, across the grain of the wood with a saw and chisel, producing an effect similar to turning on a lathe.

thuya, western red cedar, Pacific red cedar   A soft, lightweight, straight coarse-grained wood that is relatively weak; the sapwood is white, the heartwood is reddish; because of its durability it is widely used for shingles, tanks, and other exterior applications.

thymele   In the orchestra of an ancient Greek theatre, a small altar dedicated to Bacchus; usually at the center of the orchestra circle and marked by a white stone.

thyroma   1. Of an ancient house, a door which opens on the street. 2. A large doorway in the second story at the rear of the stage of the ancient Roman theatre.

thyrorion, thyroreum   Of an ancient Greek house, a passageway leading from the entrance to the peristyle.

tide mill   A mill, such as a **gristmill** or **sawmill**, operated by a waterwheel powered by tidal water confined in a reservoir after high tide. An incoming tide opens a gate, permitting tidal water to fill the reservoir; when the direction of the tide changes, the gate is closed by hand, and then the outflowing tidal water turns the mill's waterwheel.

Tidewater cottage   A one-room cottage in the Chesapeake Bay region of Virginia, after about 1630.

tie   1. Any unit of material which connects two parts, as masonry to masonry. Also see **wall tie**. 2. A framing member which sustains only a tensile load; a member in tension to prevent spreading. 3. In surveying, a connection from a point of known position to a point whose position is desired.

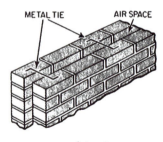

metal **ties, 1**

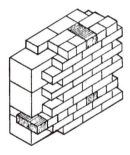

masonry **ties, 1**

tieback   A tension element used to resist the lateral force on a retaining structure.

tie bar   1. A flat bar used as a tie or a tie rod. 2. A deformed bar, embedded in a concrete construction at a joint and designed to hold abutting edges together; not designed for direct-load transfer.

tie beam   1. On individual pile caps or spread footings which are eccentrically loaded, a beam (usually of reinforced concrete) used to distribute horizontal forces to other pile caps or footings; a **strap, 2**. 2. In roof framing, a horizontal timber connecting two opposite rafters at their lower ends to prevent them from spreading; also see **collar beam**.

tied arch   An arch having a tie between the skewbacks of the arch ends in order to provide a horizontal reaction component.

tied column   A column which is reinforced laterally with ties.

tie iron   Same as **wall tie**.

tien   A basic Chinese structure used for domestic, public, and religious buildings; consists of a platform supporting a structural wooden framework of at least four columns and longitudinal and transverse tie beams, on which rest the roof trusses of the prominent, upward-curving, high-pitched, tiled roof. Enclosures and interior partitions are nonbearing screen walls.

tie piece   Same as **tie beam, 2**.

tie plate   1. Any plate used to tie together two components or parallel parts of a built-up structural-steel member. 2. Same as **batten plate**.

tie point   The point of closure of a survey, either on itself or on another survey.

tier   A row, or a group of rows placed one above the other, as rows of seats in a theatre or of beams in construction.

tier building A multistoried building, the floors of which may or may not be partitioned.

tierceron In medieval vaulting, a secondary rib springing from an intersection of two other ribs; an intermediate rib that rises between the main diagonal and transverse ribs from the impost of the pier to the ridge rib.

tie rod A rod in tension, used to bind parts of a structure together.

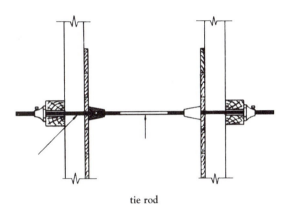

tie rod

tier structure A multistory framed building.

tie wall A wall built at right angles to a **spandrel wall** to increase its lateral stability.

Tiffany glass See **opalescent glass** and **stained glass**.

tige The shaft of a column, from the base moldings to the capital.

tigerwood A grayish to dark brown wood of western Africa; of moderate density; highly figured and with high luster; used for interior carpentry and plywood.

tight knot See **sound knot**.

tight sheathing **1.** Tongue-and-grooved boards or **dressed-and-matched boards** nailed to rafters or studs to serve as a base for an outer covering; may be fastened either at right angles or diagonal to the supports. **2.** Same as **closed sheeting** except that the vertical sheathing planks are interlocked; used in saturated soils; sometimes steel sheet piling is used instead of wood planking.

tight sheeting Same as **closed sheeting**.

tight side The side of veneer which originally faced outward in the log or **flitch** when the veneer was cut from it.

tile **1.** A glazed or unglazed ceramic unit for finishing a surface; usually thin in relation to the dimensions of its face. **2.** A surfacing unit of slate or of some other impervious composition; also see **brick-tile, chimney tile, clay tile, corner tile, crown tile, Dutch tile, encaustic tile, fireplace tile, hollow clay tile, mission tile, pantile, ridge tile, rounded tile, Spanish tile, structural clay tile**.

tile-and-a-half tile Tile having the same length, but 1½ times the width, of the tile used elsewhere on a roof.

tile batten See **slate batten**.

tileboard **1.** A wallboard used for interior finishing; usually a base sheet material overlaid with a hard, glossy decorative facing to simulate tile. **2.** Square or rectangular boards, usually made of compressed wood or vegetable fibers, often with beveled interlocking edges, used for ceiling or wall covering.

tile creasing A weather-protective barrier at the top of a brick wall; consists of two courses of tiles which project beyond both faces of the wall, so as to throw off rainwater. Also see **creasing**.

tile drain See **drain tile**.

tile field A system of **distribution tile**.

tile fillet Tiles cut to form a fillet, and set in mortar against a wall adjoining a roof surface in lieu of **flashing**.

tile hammer A brick hammer of reduced size; used to cut glazed brick and tile and, in some cases, facing brick; not used for heavy-duty work, which is performed with a **brick hammer**.

tile hanging Same as **weather slating**.

tile listing Tile used to create a splayed **fillet** at an abutment.

tile pick A sharp pointed hammer used to pick holes in tile units.

tile pin A pin passing through a roofing tile into the wood beneath to hold the tile in place.

tile shell In a **structural clay tile**, the outer shell of the hollow unit.

tile shingle See **shingle**.

tile strip Same as **slate batten**.

tile tie A heavy braided wire used to secure tile to a roof.

tile valley On a roof, the **valley** between two sloping plane surfaces formed with specially made tiles.

tiling plaster   See **Keene's cement**.

till, glacial till, boulder clay   An unstratified glacial deposit which consists of pockets of clay, gravel, sand, silt, and boulders; has not been subject to the sorting action of water; usually has good load-sustaining properties.

tilting concrete mixer   See **tilting mixer**.

tilting-drum mixer   Same as **tilting mixer**.

tilting fillet, cant strip, doubling piece, tilting piece   A thin wedge-shaped strip of wood placed under the slates or tiles of a roof to tilt the bottom course; used where needed to shed water more effectively. Also see **arris fillet**.

tilting level   A **level, 1** in which the final leveling of the instrument is obtained by small controlled amounts of rotation of the telescope about a horizontal axis.

tilting mixer   A horizontal-axis cement mixer whose drum can be tilted; the materials are fed in when the discharge opening of the drum is raised, and the mixture is discharged by tilting the drum.

tilting piece   See **tilting fillet**.

tilt-up construction   Construction of concrete wall panels which are cast horizontally, adjacent to their final positions, and then tilted up into a vertical position when hardened.

timber   **1.** Uncut trees or logs that are suitable for conversion to lumber. **2.** Wood sawn into balks, battens, boards, etc., suitable for use in carpentry, joinery, and general construction. **3.** Square-sawn lumber having: (U.S.A.) a minimum dimension of 5 in.; (Brit.) approximately equal cross dimensions greater than 4 in. by 4½ in. (101.6 mm by 114.3 mm). **4.** A heavy wooden beam used as a shoring or bracing system member.

timber bond   In masonry, a **chain bond** formed by the use of timber.

timber brick   Same as **wood brick**.

timber building   Same as **timber-framed building**.

timber connector   One of a number of metal connectors used (with bolts) to join timber in heavy construction; usually the connector has a series of sharp teeth which dig into the wood as a bolt is tightened, thereby preventing lateral movement and decreasing the number of bolts required; another type employs a sharp round ring to perform this function.

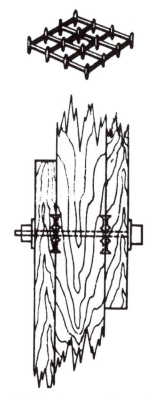

spike grid **timber connector**; joint employing two **timber connectors** is shown below

timber dog   A **dog iron** suitable for joining two timbers.

timber-framed building   A building having timbers as its structural elements (except for the foundation); for a description of the major individual components used in such a structure, see **collar beam, girt, joist, plate, purlin, rafter, summerbeam, windbrace**.

timber-framed house   A house in which the major structural components were huge timber posts and beams or girts. The space between these structural timbers was usually filled with brick, plaster, mud, **wattle-and-daub**, or the like. The exterior of the building was often coated with hard plaster and then sheathed with weatherboarding, or covered with slates or shingles as protection against the penetration of rain and to provide improved thermal insulation. (See illustration p. 941.)

timber framing   See **frame**.

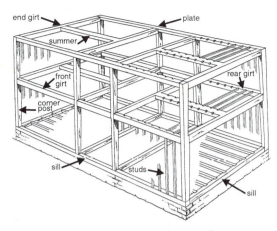

timber-framed house with terminology for many structural members

timber house A type of house, usually lofty, found in secular Gothic architecture, especially in Central Europe; characterized by a lower story of masonry which supports the timber construction above, usually with richly carved gables.

timbering Any temporary work in timber, as formwork for concrete, shoring, etc.

timber joint connector Same as **timber connector**.

timber stresses In **stress-graded lumber**, the stresses which conform to recognized values.

time Time limits or periods stated in the **contract**. A provision in a construction contract that "time is of the essence of the contract" signifies that the parties consider that punctual performance within the time limits or periods in the contract is a vital part of the performance and that failure to perform on time is a breach for which the injured party is entitled to damages in the amount of loss sustained, or is excused from any obligation of further performance, or both.

time and materials (T&M) The time and total cost of all materials required to complete a construction job; often used where the cost of the job is otherwise difficult to estimate.

time-delay fuse Any **fuse** in an electric circuit that takes more than 12 seconds to open at a 200% load.

timely completion Completion of the **work, 1** or designated portion thereof on or before the date required.

timber house: Market Place in Hildesheim, Lower Saxony, Germany

time of completion The date established in the contract, by name or by number of days, for substantial completion of the **work**. Also see **completion date** and **contract time**.

time of concentration In a storm-water drainage system, the time required for storm water to travel from the most remote portion of the tributary area to an inlet or drain.

time of haul In production of ready-mixed concrete, the period from first contact between mixing water and cement to the discharge from the mixer of the freshly mixed concrete.

time of set See **initial setting time, final setting time**.

time system A system of clocks and control devices, with or without a master timepiece, which will indicate time at various remote locations; the master timepiece may have additional facilities to program other systems, such as bells.

tin **1.** A lustrous white, soft, and malleable metal having a low melting point; relatively unaffected by exposure to air; used for making alloys and solder and in coating sheet metal. **2.** To coat with a layer of tin.

tin-canning See **oil-canning**.

tin cap A small flat metal washer used under roofing nails.

tin ceiling See **metal ceiling** and **pressed-metal ceiling**.

tin-clad fire door A door of two- or three-ply wood-core construction, which is covered with No. 30 gauge galvanized steel or terneplate or No. 24 gauge galvanized steel sheets.

tinfoil A very thin sheet of tin, now replaced by other foils such as aluminum.

t'ing A four-sided, open, wooden pavilion of Chinese origin; consists of uprights supporting an upward-curving roof by means of tie beams and brackets.

tingle **1.** A support which reduces the sag in a long line used in laying brick. **2.** A flexible metal clip used to hold a sheet of glass, metal, etc.

tinning, precoating Coating a metal with solder or tin alloy, prior to soldering or brazing it.

tinplate Thin iron or steel sheets which have been plated with tin as a protection against oxidation.

tin roofing A roof covering of flexible **tin-plate** or terneplate metal.

tin saw A saw used for cutting kerfs in bricks.

tin snips Shears with a blunt nose; used for cutting thin sheet metal.

tint A light color made by mixing a small amount of the pure color with a large amount of white.

tinted glass Glass which has been tinted, usually to filter out near-infrared solar energy, thereby reducing the solar heat gain through the glass and reducing the load on the air-conditioning system.

tinter See **stainer**.

tinting strength, staining power The ability of a pigment to modify the color of a standard white or colored paint.

tipi A relatively lightweight, transportable, conically shaped dwelling primarily of American Indians of the Great Plains; its base was generally egglike in plan, with the narrower end of the base at the entrance. The framework consisted of heavy wood poles, fixed in the ground at their lower ends and lashed together at the top. This framework was covered with decorated waterproof animal skins, sewn together with sinew and secured to the ground by pegs driven through loops at the base of the cover. Another type of tipi, used by tribes in the eastern regions of America, had a domed rather than a conical framework consisting of branches bent over, tied together, and covered by bark or animal skins sewn together with sinew to provide a waterproof covering. Also spelled tepee or teepee.

tirant **1.** A tie beam. **2.** A tie rod.

T-iron See **tee iron**.

titanium dioxide A white pigment having a very high opacity; used in paints; occurs in two crystalline forms, **anatase** and **rutile**, of which the latter has higher opacity.

titanium white A pigment consisting primarily of titanium dioxide; bright white in color; has high **hiding power** and good permanence.

title A legal right to the ownership of property. Also see **abstract of title**.

title insurance Insurance, offered by a company, that the title to property is clear or that it may be cleared by curing specified defects.

title search An inquiry into the historical ownership record of a property in order to ascertain its true ownership and the possible existence of any liens or easements on the property which might affect its sale.

tjandi A Hindu sepulchral monument, prevalent in Java from the 8th to 14th cent. A.D., consisting of a square base, a cella-like temple, and a prominent pyramidal roof structure; a small room in the base contained the urn with the ashes of the prince in whose memory the structure was erected.

T-joint   See **tee joint**.

TL   Abbr. for **transmission loss**.

TMA   Abbr. for "Tile Manufacturers Association."

tobacco barn   A barn used for curing tobacco leaves, with or without the addition of heat, by hanging them from a series of horizontal poles within the barn; occasionally called a tobacco house. Three common types of tobacco barns are designated by the curing process employed: *air-cured*, *fire-cured*, and *flue-cured*.

toe   **1.** A projection from the foot or foot piece of any object or construction to give it broader bearing and greater stability. **2.** That part of the base of a concrete retaining wall which projects in front of the face of the wall, away from the retained material. **3.** That portion of sheeting below the excavation subgrade. **4.** On a door, the lower portion of the **lock stile**. **5.** Of a weld, the junction between the base metal and the face of a weld. **6.** To drive a nail at an oblique angle.

toeboard   **1.** A board placed around a platform or on a sloping roof to prevent workmen or materials from falling. **2.** A member that forms the lowest vertical face of a kitchen cabinet, or the like, at toe level.

toe crack   A crack, at the toe of a weld, in the base metal.

toed   In carpentry, said of a board, strut, etc., having the end secured by nails driven obliquely.

toehold   A batten or board which is nailed, temporarily, to a sloping roof to act as a footing for workmen.

toe in   The small reduction in the outside diameter of a plastic pipe at its cut end.

toe joint   A joint formed between a horizontal timber and another at some vertical angle with it, as between a rafter and a wall **plate**.

toenailing, skew nailing, tusk nailing   Nailing obliquely to the surfaces being joined;

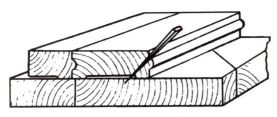

toenailing   wood-strip flooring

alternate nails may be driven at opposite angles to provide increased holding power.

toe piece   Same as **ledger, 2**.

toeplate   **1.** Same as **kickplate, 2**. **2.** A flat metal bar attached to the outer edge of a metal grating or to the rear edge of a tread, and projecting above the top surface of the grating or tread so as to form a lip or curb.

toe wall   At the bottom of an embankment, a low wall built to prevent the earth from slipping or spreading.

toggle bolt   A bolt having a nut with pivoted, flanged wings that close against a spring when it is pushed through a hole, and open after emerging from the hole; used to fasten objects to a hollow wall or to a wall which is accessible only from one side.

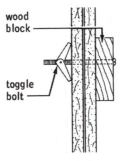

wood block

toggle bolt

toggle bolts

toggle switch   A lever-actuated **snap switch**. (*See illustration p. 944.*)

toilet   **1.** A **water closet**; **W.C. 2.** The room containing the water closet.

toilet enclosure   In a toilet room having a number of water closets, one of the compartments which provides individual privacy.

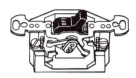

flush-mounted **toggle switch**

toilet partition One of the panels forming a **toilet enclosure**.

toilet room An enclosed space containing one or more water closets, lavatories, toilet enclosures, urinals, and other plumbing fixtures; also see **bathroom**.

tokonoma In the Japanese house, an alcove, raised above the floor, for displaying a hanging scroll and a flower arrangement.

TOL On drawings, abbr. for **tolerance**.

tolerance The permissible deviation in a specified size or dimension.

tollhouse **1.** A house near a tollgate of a highway or bridge, serving as the residence of the keeper. **2.** A tollbooth.

tom Same as **shore**.

tomb In architecture, a memorial structure over or beside a grave.

tomb chest A stone coffin-like box.

ton **1.** The equivalent of 2,000 lb (907.2 kg). Also see **metric ton**. **2.** A unit of refrigeration capacity equal to 200 Btu per minute, the equivalent cooling provided by the melting of one ton of ice in one hour.

tondino **1.** A small **tondo**. **2.** A circular molding.

tondo A circular plaque or medallion.

toner An undiluted organic pigment; contains little or no inert matter.

tongue A projecting member, either as a continuous ridge along the edge of a board or plank, or as a tenon on the end of a wood member; intended to be fitted into a corresponding groove or opening in another member to form a joint.

tongue-and-dart molding A decorative molding consisting of a tonguelike ornament alternating with a dartlike ornament.

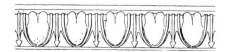

tongue-and-dart molding

tongue-and-groove boards See **dressed-and-matched boards**.

tongue-and-groove joint, T and G joint A joint formed by the insertion of the **tongue** of one member into the corresponding groove of another.

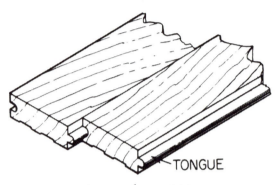

tongue-and-groove joint

tongue-and-groove material See **dressed-and-matched-boards**.

tongue-and-lip joint A type of **tongue-and-groove joint** in which the joint is concealed by a flush bead on the board with the tongue.

tongued miter A **miter joint** which incorporates a tongue.

tongue joint A split joint formed by inserting a tongue or wedge-shaped piece into a correspondingly grooved piece in another member; if metal, such a joint may be welded.

tonk strip A steel adjustable support for a shelf.

tonne A metric ton; a unit of mass equal to 1000 kilograms (approximately 2205 pounds).

ton of refrigeration A refrigerating effect equal to 12,000 Btu (3,024 cal) per hour.

ton slate Random-sized slate which is purchased by weight.

tooled ashlar Stonework having a **tooled finish**.

tooled finish, tooled surface In stonework, a fluted, flat surface that usually carries 2 to 12 concave grooves per inch (5 to 30 per centimeter); also called **tooling**.

tooled joint Any masonry joint that has been prepared with a tool before the mortar in the joint has set rigidly.

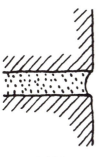

tooled joint

tooled surface   A **tooled finish**.

tooled work   See **batted work**.

tooling   **1.** Compressing and shaping the face of a mortar joint. **2.** See **tooled finish**. **3.** See **batted work**. **4.** Compacting and contouring a **sealant** in a joint.

tooling time   After the application of a sealant in a joint, the time interval during which **tooling, 3** is possible.

tool pad   A tool, consisting of handle and clamp or chuck, for holding small tool bits, such as awls, screwdriver blades, etc.

tooth   **1.** In a paint film, a fine texture imparted either by pigments or by the abrasives used in sanding; this texture provides a good base for the adhesion of a subsequent coat of paint. **2.** A **dogtooth, 2**.

toothed plate, bulldog plate   A toothed metal plate that serves as a **timber connector**.

toothed plate

toothed ring   A metal ring with toothed edges which serves as a **timber connector**.

toother   Same as **dogtooth, 2**.

toothing   Cutting out alternate courses in old work to provide a bond for new work.

toothing plane   A carpenter's plane, the cutting edge of which is formed into a series of small teeth, usually to roughen a surface.

tooth ornament, dogtooth   A decoration, generally in the hollow of a Gothic molding, consisting of four-leaved flowers, the centers of which project in a point.

tooth ornament

top-and-bottom cap   One of the horizontal metal channels, attached at the jobsite to the top and to the bottom of a **hollow-metal door** which does not have an integral flush top or bottom.

top beam   A **collar beam**.

top car clearance   The shortest vertical distance between the top of an elevator car (or crosshead, if provided on the car) and the nearest overhead obstruction when the car floor is level with the top terminal landing.

topcoat   The final coat of paint applied to a surface; usually applied over a primer and/or one or more undercoats or surfacers.

top-course tile   The uppermost course of tile, laid along the ridge of a roof; usually shorter than the others.

top cut   The vertical cut at the upper end of a rafter.

top dressing   A layer, usually thin, of manure, humus, loam, etc., to improve soil conditions in planted areas.

tope   See **stupa**.

top form   A concrete form required on the upper or outer surfaces of a sloping slab, a thin shell, etc.

top-hinged in-swinging window   A window having a **sash** (**ventilator, 2**) which is hinged at the top and swings in at the bottom.

top-hung window   A **casement window** hung by a hinge running along its upper edge.

topiary work   The clipping or trimming of plants, trees, and shrubs, usually evergreens, into ornamental and fantastic shapes.

top lap   In shingle roofing, the shortest distance between (a) the lower edge of an overlapping shingle and (b) the upper edge of the lapped unit in the course directly below.

toplighting   Lighting from above.

top mop   See **pour coat**.

topographic survey   The configuration of a surface including its relief and the locations of its natural and man-made features, usually recorded on a drawing showing surface variations by means of contour lines indicating height above or below a fixed datum.

top out   To complete the uppermost course or the highest structural member in a construction.

topping   **1.** A layer of high-quality concrete or mortar placed to form a floor surface on a concrete base. **2.** The mixture of marble chips and matrix which, when properly processed, produces a **terrazzo** surface.

topping coat   A **floated coat**.

topping compound   Same as **finishing compound**.

topping joint   In a **topping, 1**, a joint which is directly over an expansion joint in the concrete base.

topping out   The placing of a flag or banner (sometimes a tree—especially at Christmas time) at the highest point of the framework of a building when it is completed.

top plate   **1.** The top horizontal member of a frame building to which the rafters are fastened. **2.** The horizontal member at the top of the partition studs.

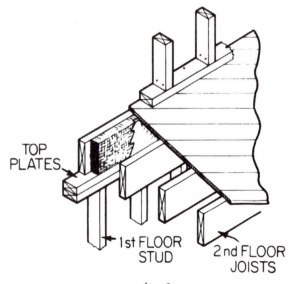

top plate, 2

top rail   **1.** The top horizontal structural member of any piece of framing, as a door or sash. **2.** A **rail** which is the top member of a railing system.

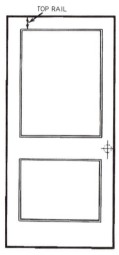

top rail   of a door

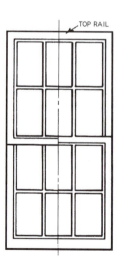

top rail   of a sash

topsoil   **1.** The surface of upper layer of soil, as distinct from the subsoil; usually contains organic matter. **2.** See **loam**.

torana, toran   A monumental and richly decorated gateway in the enclosure of a Buddhist stupa in Indian architecture.

torch brazing A brazing process in which the required heat is furnished by a gas flame.

torchère **1.** An indirect floor lamp which sends all or nearly all of its light upward. **2.** An ornamental support for a **flambeau** or other source of light.

torching The application of a lime mortar under the top edges of roof tiles or slates; in **full torching** the mortar is applied beneath the entire underside of slates between battens.

torch soldering A soldering process in which the required heat is furnished by a gas flame.

tore Same as **torus.**

torii A monumental, freestanding gateway to a Shinto shrine, consisting of two pillars with a straight crosspiece at the top and lintel above it, usually curving upward.

torii   at Nikko, Japan

tormentor In a theatre, one of a pair of curtains or a rigid framed structure running parallel to the front of the stage, just behind the proscenium; used to frame the sides of the inner proscenium opening and to conceal the offstage wings from the audience.

torn grain A fuzzy or whiskered appearance in the face of a wood **shake**, usually caused by cutting the shake with a dull saw.

torque That which tends to produce rotation; the product of a force and a lever arm which tends to twist a body, as the action of a wrench turning a nut on a bolt.

torque viscometer An apparatus for measuring the **viscosity** of slurries.

torreón A defensive tower used for protection against enemy attack; a fortification once found in some Spanish Colonial communities.

torsade, cable molding, rope molding **1.** A twisted or spiral molding. **2.** Any ornamental twist.

torsel A piece of timber, steel, or stone which supports one end of a beam or joist and distributes its load.

torsion The twisting of a structural member about its longitudinal axis by two equal and opposite **torques**, one at one end and the other at the opposite end.

torsional strength The resistance of a material to being twisted about an axis.

torsional stress The **shear stress** on a transverse cross section which results from the action of a twist.

torso A **spiral column**, in Medieval and Renaissance architecture.

torus A bold projecting molding, convex in shape, generally forming the lowest member of a base over the plinth.

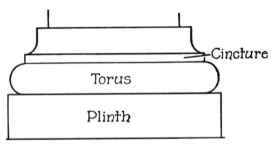

torus

torus   molding

torus roll In sheet-metal or lead roofing, a joint made at the intersection of two planes having different slopes; allows for differential movement.

toshnailing Nailing at an angle so the nailheads are not visible.

TOT. On drawings, abbr. for "total."

total float In **CPM** terminology, the difference between the amount of time available to accomplish an **activity** and the time required.

tot lot An outdoor playground for very young children.

touch catch A door **catch** which releases automatically if the closed door is pushed.

touch dry A stage during the drying of a paint film when it can be touched lightly without the paint's adhering and lifting when the finger is removed.

toughened glass British term for **tempered glass**.

toughness **1.** The ability of a structural material to resist shock or impact; its ability to absorb energy before fracture. **2.** The ability of a cladding, coating, or paint film to resist abrasion, chipping, or cracking.

tough-rubber sheath (*Brit.*) An abrasion-resistant, corrosion-resistant, waterproof, protective covering for an insulated electric cable.

tourelle A **turret**.

tourist cabin One of a number of small separate units, each providing overnight accommodations for travelers; usually consisting of a bedroom and bathroom, grouped in what was once called a *tourist court*; found along well-traveled highways during the first half of the 20th century; now replaced by motels.

towed grader See **grader**.

tower A structure or building characterized by its relatively great height as compared with its horizontal dimensions; also see **shot tower** and **torreón**.

tower bolt Same as **barrel bolt**.

tower crane A type of **crane** consisting of a fixed vertical mast which is topped by a rotating

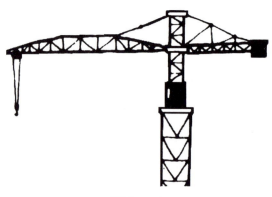

tower crane

boom, equipped with a winch for hoisting and lowering loads and placing them at any location within the diameter of the boom.

tower hoist In concrete handling in tall building construction, usually a tower, elevator bucket, and a movable receiving hopper set at the level where the concrete is placed; the bucket may be hoisted within the well of the tower frame or external to it.

town hall A public hall or building, belonging to a town, where public offices are established, the town council meets, the people assemble in town meetings, etc.

town house **1.** A comfortable-to-luxurious dwelling in an urban environment. **2.** One of a series of houses constructed in an unbroken row, separated by **party walls**, often with a relatively flat roof. **3.** An upscale **row house**.

town plan A large-scale, comprehensive map of a town or city that delineates its streets, important buildings, and other urban features in a detail compatible with the scale of the map; also see **city plan**.

town planning See **city planning** and **community planning**.

townscape **1.** A view of a town or city from a single vantage point. **2.** The planning and construction of buildings within a town or city with the objective of achieving overall aesthetically pleasing relationships.

T-plan The basic **floor plan** of a building having the shape of a capital letter **T**.

T-plate A flat metal plate in the shape of a T; used to join two timbers, one of which butts against the other, or to strengthen a joint.

trabeated **1.** Descriptive of construction using beams or lintels, following the principle of post and lintel construction, as distinguished from construction using arches and vaults. **2.** Furnished with an entablature.

trabeated system A system of building construction using beams or lintels to support the weight over an opening.

trabeation Construction using beams and posts; lintel construction.

trabes, trabs In ancient Rome, a beam, esp. a long beam supporting the joists of a ceiling.

tracery The curvilinear openwork shapes of stone or wood creating a pattern within the upper

tracery

crawler **tractor**

part of a Gothic window, or an opening of similar character, in the form of mullions which are usually so treated as to be ornamental. By extension, similar patterns applied to walls or panels. See **bar tracery, branch tracery, fan tracery**, etc.

trachelium In classical architecture, any member (usually part of the necking) which comes between the hypotrachelium and the capital.

tracing cloth A smooth linen fabric, coated with size to make it transparent and suitable for tracing.

tracing paper A transparent paper used for tracing and original drawings.

track A U-shaped member, attached to the floor and/or ceiling; used to receive metal studs for a partition, or to guide a sliding partition, door, curtain, etc.

track lighting Lighting provided by fixtures on a **lighting track**.

traction load A load on a structure exerted by a moving vehicle in the direction of its motion, caused by friction, tractive effort, or braking.

traction machine On elevators, a machine having a sheave which produces motion of the car through friction between the sheave and the wire ropes (cables) that hoist the car.

tractor A powerful engine-driven vehicle, on wheels or on tracks, used for pushing or pulling attachments or tools.

tractor loader, tractor shovel A tractor which has a bucket for digging, elevating, and dumping its load at truck height.

trade 1. A person's occupation or craft, usually involving manual skill. 2. In building construction, the classifications of work, such as masonry, carpentry, plastering, etc.

trade granite See **gneiss**.

trading post A store, usually found in sparsely settled areas, where inhabitants can exchange products they make, grow, or trap, for goods sold by the store.

traffic deck surfacing See **topping**.

traffic paint Paint specially formulated to withstand wear of vehicular traffic and to be highly visible at night; used to mark center lines on roadways, traffic lanes, crosswalks, etc.

traffic topping See **topping**.

trammel 1. In a fireplace, an adjustable hook for suspending a cooking pot from a pivoted wrought-iron horizontal bar attached to one of the fireplace walls. 2. An instrument for drawing ellipses.

trammel point One of the two metal points on a **beam compass**.

TRANS On drawings, abbr. for **transformer**.

transducer A device which converts power in one kind of system to power in another form, e.g., a loudspeaker which converts electric power to acoustic power.

transenna Latticework of marble or metal enclosing a shrine.

transenna: church at entrance of the Catacombs of St. Alexander, Rome

transept The transverse portion of a church crossing the main axis at a right angle and producing a cruciform plan.

transept aisle An aisle on the side of a transept.

transept chapel A chapel entered from a transept, usually on its east side.

transfer In **pretensioning**, the act of conveying the stress in the prestressing tendons from the jacks (or pretensioning bed) to the concrete member.

transfer bond In **pretensioning**, the **bond stress** resulting from the transfer of stress from a prestressing tendon to the concrete.

transfer column A column in a multistory framed building that is not continuous down to the foundation, but is supported at some intermediate level where the load is transferred to adjacent columns.

transfer girder A girder supporting a **transfer column**.

transfer grille In an air-conditioning system, a grille which permits air to flow from one space to another; may be one of a pair, installed on opposite sides of a wall, door, etc.

transfer length Same as **transmission length**.

transfer molding An **injection molding** using a thermosetting material.

transfer register A **transfer grille** having a mechanism for controlling the quantity of airflow.

transfer strength In **pretensioning**, the strength the concrete must attain before stress is transferred from the stressing mechanism to the concrete.

transfer switch A device arranged to switch an electrical conductor from one circuit to another without interrupting the flow of current.

transformer A device with two or more coupled windings, used to convert a supply of electric power at one voltage to another voltage.

transformer bank Two or more transformers located in the same enclosure, as in a transformer vault.

transformer box See **instrument transformer box**.

transformer room An unattended room used to house electric transformers and their auxiliary equipment.

transformer vault An unattended isolated enclosure having fire-resistant walls, ceiling, and floor, for transformers and their auxiliary equipment; often located below ground.

transillumination The illumination of a material from the rear by light which is transmitted through the material.

transit A surveying instrument used for the measurement and laying out of horizontal and vertical angles, distances, directions, and differences in elevation; a type of theodolite having an alidade with a telescope which can be reversed in direction.

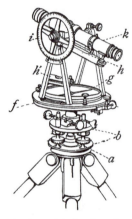

transit: *a*, tripod stand; *b*, leveling plates; *f*, vernier; *g*, compass; *h*, *h′*, levels; *i*, vertical circle; *k*, telescope

transit-and-stadia survey A survey in which horizontal and vertical directions or angles are observed with a transit and distances are measured by transit and stadia rod.

transitional style An **architectural mode** in a period between two different **architectural styles**, as for example, between late Georgian and early Federal style; such a transition may occur at different times in different parts of a country.

transit line In surveying, any line of a **survey traverse** which is projected, either with or without measurement, by the use of a **transit** or the like.

transit mix, transit-mixed concrete, truck-mixed concrete Concrete that has been mixed in a **revolving-drum truck mixer**.

transit-mix truck Same as **truck mixer**.

translation A linear displacement; in kinemat-

Transitional style: capital,
Church of St. Sebaldus, Nuremberg

ics, a motion of a body such that a set of rectangular axes, fixed in the body, remains parallel to a set of axes fixed in space.

translucent Descriptive of a material that transmits light but diffuses it sufficiently so that an image cannot be seen through the material clearly.

translucent coating A liquid formulation (such as varnish, shellac, or lacquer) which when dry forms a translucent film.

translucent concrete A combination of glass and concrete in precast or prestressed panels.

transmission coefficient See **thermal transmittance**.

transmission factor See **transmittance**.

transmission length At the end of a pretensioned tendon, the distance necessary for the bond stress to develop the maximum tendon stress.

transmission loss Of a partition, the number of decibels by which sound (incident on the partition) is reduced in transmission through it; a measure of the sound insulation value of the partition—the higher the number, the greater the insulation value.

transmissivity The capacity of a material to transmit radiant energy.

transmittance When radiant flux is incident on a medium, the ratio of the flux which emerges from the medium to the flux which is incident upon it.

transom **1.** A horizontal member, usually of wood or stone, that separates a door from a window, fanlight, or panel above it; sometimes called a transom bar. **2.** An operable window hinged to the **transom, 1** directly above a door. **3.** A crossbar in a window frame that divides a window horizontally. Also see **operable transom**.

transom bar **1.** An intermediate horizontal member of a doorframe, window frame, or similar structure. **2.** A horizontal member which separates a door from a window, panel, or louver above.

transom bracket A bracket supporting an all-glass transom over an all-glass door when the door has no metal **top rail** or **transom bar, 2**.

transom catch A fastener applied to a transom and having a ring by which the latch bolt may be retracted by means of a hook on a long pole.

transom chain A short chain used to limit the opening of a transom; usually provided with a plate for attachment at each end.

transom frame A doorframe with a **transom bar, 2** and glass, a panel, or a louver above the door opening.

transom lift A vertically operated device attached to a doorframe and an operable **transom window, 1**, by which the transom may be opened or closed.

transom lift

transom light A glazed **light** above the **transom bar, 2** of a door.

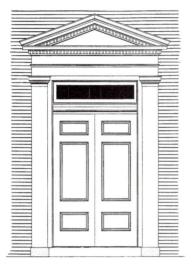

transom lights

transom window 1. A **transom light**; may be operable. **2.** Any window operated by a **transom lift**. **3.** Any window divided by a **transom bar**.

transparent coating A liquid formulation (such as varnish, shellac, or lacquer) which when dry forms a transparent film.

transtrum In ancient Roman construction, a horizontal beam.

transverse See **chambranle**.

transverse arch The arched construction built across a hall, the nave of a church, or the

transverse arch

like, either as part of the vaulting or to support or stiffen the roof.

transverse load A **load, 1** applied perpendicularly to the plane of the longitudinal axis of a structure, such as a wind load.

transverse prestress In a member, prestress that is applied perpendicular to the principal axis.

transverse reinforcement Reinforcement at right angles to the principal axis of a member.

transverse rib A rib in vaulting spanning the nave, aisle, or transept at right angles to its longitudinal axis and dividing its length into bays or compartments.

transverse rib

transverse seam See **cross welt**.

transverse section Same as **cross section**.

transverse shear A shearing action parallel to the transverse axis of a body.

transverse strength 1. The breaking load applied normal to the neutral axis of a beam. **2.** Same as **modulus of rupture**.

transyte See **tresaunce**.

trap 1. A device to maintain a water seal against sewer gases, air, and odors; also called a **stench trap**. 2. A removable section of a theatre stage floor. 3. Same as **traprock**.

trapdoor A door set into a floor, ceiling, or roof.

trapdoor monitor A section of a sloping roof which is elevated so that it is at a flatter angle than the remainder of the roof; has the appearance of a trapdoor hinged along the upper edge; does not run the full length of the roof.

trap elevator In a theatre, an elevator below the stage floor that lifts a **trap, 2**.

trapeze hanger A horizontal rigid member, suspended by rods, on which pipes are supported and/or clamped.

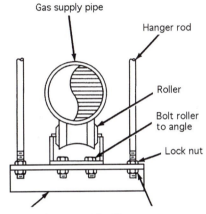

trapeze hanger   with roller support

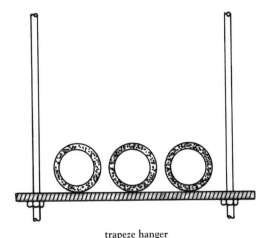

trapeze hanger

traprock A dark-colored igneous rock having a fine-grained, more or less columnar structure.

trap seal In plumbing, the vertical distance between the **crown weir** and the top of the dip of the trap.

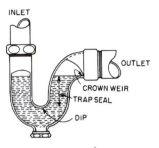

trap seal

trascoro In Spanish church architecture, a part of the choir separated from the main choir by an open passage at the crossing.

trash A mixture of highly combustible waste such as paper, cardboard cartons, wood boxes, and combustible floor sweepings; contains up to 10% by weight of plastic bags, coated paper, laminated paper, treated corrugated cardboard, oil rags, and plastic or rubber scraps; contains approx. 10% moisture, and approx. 5% incombustible solids. Also see **garbage, refuse, and rubbish**.

trash chute **1.** Any vertical smooth shaft used to conduct rubbish, trash, or garbage from the upper floors of a building to a trash storage bin or room at the bottom end of the chute. **2.** A temporary shaft erected during the construction of a multistoried building for the removal of debris. **3.** See **refuse chute**.

trass A natural **pozzolan** of volcanic origin.

trass mortar A mortar made of a mixture of lime and **trass**, with or without the addition of sand; the trass provides protection against moisture.

T-rated switch A switch whose rating satisfies the requirements of the National Electrical Code for a tungsten-filament lamp load.

travated Divided into traves.

trave **1.** A crossbeam; a beam or a timber crossing a building. **2.** One of the divisions or bays, as in a ceiling, made by crossbeams.

travel, rise Of an elevator, escalator, etc., the vertical distance between the bottom terminal landing and the top terminal landing.

travel distance At a specified point in a building, the distance between that point and a place of safety, in the event of fire.

traveler, traveler curtain On the stage of a theatre, a curtain which is drawn across the proscenium, usually from both sides.

traveling cable A cable, made up of electric conductors, which provides an electric connection between an elevator or dumbwaiter car and a fixed electrical outlet in the hoistway.

traveling crane A **tower crane** which is mounted on crawlers, rubber tires, or rails.

traveling form Same as **slipform**.

traverse **1.** A screen, railing, or other barrier across an opening to allow passage from one place to another by an official or dignitary, but to discourage unauthorized entry. **2.** Same as **survey traverse**.

travertine A variety of limestone deposited by springs; usually banded; commonly coarsely cellular; used as building stone, esp. for interior facing and flooring; some varieties are sold as **marble** in the building trade.

traviated Having a series of transverse divisions or bays, as in a ceiling.

travis See **trave, 2**.

tray ceiling Under a gabled roof, a horizontal ceiling constructed part of the way up toward the ridge.

trayle See **vinette**.

tray rail See **food tray rail**.

treacle molding A rounded molding or nosing that is deeply undercut, upward to a groove that acts as a **drip** to discharge rainwater.

tread The horizontal surface of a **step**; often has a rounded edge that extends beyond the upright face of the **riser** below it.

treading barn A circular two-story barn once specifically constructed for threshing grain. Horses or oxen were led around the second story of the barn, across layers of wheat; the grinding action of their hooves separates the wheat from the chaff; the grain fell through gaps between the floorboards into the granary in the story below.

tread length The dimension of a tread measured perpendicular to the normal line of travel on a stair.

tread plate A **floor plate** which is fabricated of metal, e.g., aluminum.

tread return In an **open stair**, the continuation of the horizontal rounded edge of the tread, beyond the stair stringer.

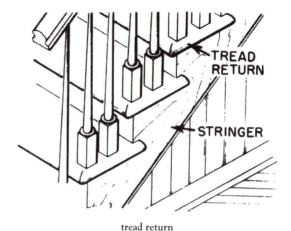

tread return

tread run The horizontal distance between two consecutive risers or, on an open-riser stair, the horizontal distance between nosings or the outer edges of successive treads, all measured perpendicular to the front edges of the nosings or treads.

tread width The dimension of a tread (measured along the normal line of travel of the stair) plus the projection of the nosing, if any.

treated wood **1.** See **fire-retardant wood**. **2.** Wood which has been subjected to a **wood preservative**.

treble sash A window having three vertically sliding sashes, one above the other, each of which closes a different part of the window; once used in large houses having very high ceilings; compare with **three-part window**.

tredyl Old English term for **grees**.

tree belt A strip between the sidewalk and curb of a road, planted with grass and sometimes with shade trees.

tree-dozer An attachment for the front of a tractor consisting of metal bars and a cutting blade; used in clearing land of small trees, bushes, and the like.

tree grate Surrounding a tree trunk set in pavement, a metal grille which is flush with the pavement.

treenail A long pin of hardwood used in **timber-framed houses** to secure a joint between two planks or timbers; also called a trenail or trunnel.

trefoil In an opening, a three-lobed pattern separated by **cusps**; see **foil**.

trefoils

trefoil arch An arch whose inner surface is struck from three centers; the configuration of the arch is determined by the position of the centers of curvature and radii of curvature of the arcs that are joined.

treillage A **trellis** support for vines or espaliers.

trellage Same as **treillage**.

trellis **1.** An open grating or latticework, of either metal or wood. **2.** An arbor or framework for the support of vines; a **treillage**.

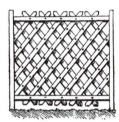

trellis

trellis molding, trellice molding An ornament, used in buildings of the Norman style, consisting of a series of overlapping zigzag lines which produce a trellis-like appearance.

trellis window A **casement window**, fixed or hinged, with glazing bars set diagonally to suggest a trellis; also called a lattice window.

tremie A pipe or tube through which concrete is deposited under water, having at its upper end a hopper for filling and a bail by means of which the assembly can be handled by a derrick.

tremie concrete Concrete placed by means of a **tremie**.

tremie seal Concrete placed under water by means of a **tremie** to seal a cofferdam or caisson so that water may be pumped out.

trenail Same as **treenail**.

trench **1.** A creep trench. **2.** A housing, **1**.

trench box, trench shield A heavily braced box of wood or steel which can be moved along a trench bottom as excavation and pipe laying

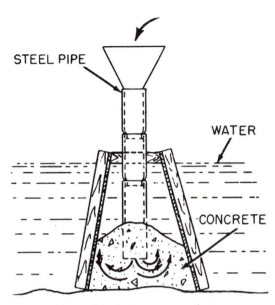

tremie   used in placing concrete under water

trench box

proceed; used where the trenches are deep and not sheathed; also used in lieu of other methods of sheathing and shoring for shallow excavations where the sides of the shield can extend from the trench bottom to the ground surface.

trench brace A device, usually adjustable in length, for supporting sheeting or other materials used to prevent collapse of the sidewalls of a ditch or trench.

trench duct A metal trough buried in a concrete floor and having removable cover plates that are level with the top of the floor; used to carry electric conductors. (*See illustration p. 956.*)

trench jack A screw jack or hydraulic jack used as cross bracing in a trench shoring system.

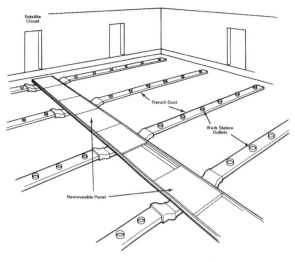

trench duct

trench shield A shoring system composed of steel plates and braces which are welded or bolted together; the shoring system supports the walls of a trench from the ground level down to the bottom of the trench; can be moved along as the work progresses.

tresaunce, transyte, trisantia In medieval architecture and derivatives, a narrow vestibule or passageway.

tresse Flat or convex **bandelets** which are intertwined; especially such interlacing ornamentation used to adorn moldings.

tresse

trestle ladder A portable ladder which is self-supporting, but not adjustable in length; consists of two sections which are hinged at the top so as to form equal angles with the base.

trevis See **trave, 2**.

trial batch Of concrete, a batch which is prepared to establish or check the proportions of the constituents.

trial pit A small-diameter hole in the ground, excavated to investigate the nature of the soil and to determine the distance to bedrock.

triangular arch **1.** An arch often formed by two large diagonal stones that mutually support each other to span an opening; also called a miter arch. **2.** A **Mayan arch**.

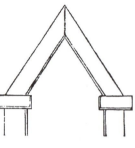

triangular arch

triangular dormer A **dormer** having a triangularly shaped gable roof.

triangular fret molding See **dovetail molding**.

triangular pediment A **pediment** having a horizontal cornice and slanting sides that meet in a point at the top so as to form a triangle; also called an angular pediment.

triangulation A method of surveying in which the stations are points on the ground which are located at the vertices of a chain or network of triangles; the angles of the triangles are measured instrumentally; then the sides are derived by computation from selected sides which are termed "base lines," the lengths of which are obtained from direct measurements on the ground.

triapsidal Having three apses, either side by side or forming a cloverleaf pattern at the sanctuary end of a church.

triaxial compression test A test subjecting a specimen to a confined hydrostatic pressure and then to an axial load until failure.

triaxial test A test subjecting a specimen to lateral and axial loads simultaneously.

tribelon In a church, a triple arcade which connects the nave with the narthex.

tribunal In an ancient Roman basilica, a raised platform for the curule chairs of the magistrates.

tribune **1.** A slightly elevated platform or dais for a speaker. **2.** The apse of a church.

tricalcium silicate A compound which is a main constituent of portland cement.

triclinium A dining room in an ancient Roman house, furnished with a low table, surrounded on three sides by couches.

triconch Having apses with semidomes on three sides of a square chamber; some churches, chapels, and tombs are built on this plan.

triforium In medieval church architecture, a shallow passage above the arches of the nave and choir and below the clerestory; characteristically opened into the nave.

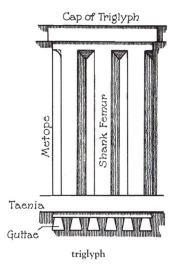

triglyph

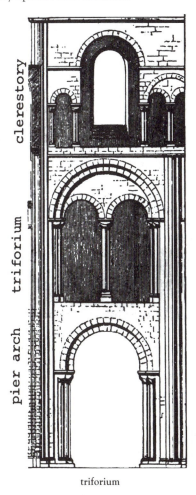

triforium

triga A chariot similar to a **quadriga** but drawn by three horses.

trigger bolt See **auxiliary dead latch**.

triglyph The characteristic ornament of the Doric frieze, consisting of slightly raised blocks of three vertical bands separated by V-shaped grooves. The triglyphs alternate with plain or sculptured panels called **metopes**. Also see **order**.

trigonum A mosaic of triangular pieces of marble, terra-cotta, glass, or other material.

trilateration A surveying method in which the lengths of all sides of a chain of triangles, polygons, or quadrilaterals (or any combination of them) are measured with an electronic instrument; the angles then may be computed from these field measurements.

trilithon Two upright monoliths spanned by a third, as at Stonehenge.

trim **1.** The visible woodwork or moldings of a room, such as the baseboards, cornices, casings, etc. **2.** Any visible element, usually of metal or wood, which covers or protects joints, edges, or ends of another material; the **finishings** around **fittings** and openings, as a door trim, window trim, etc. **3.** The exposed metal appurtenances of plumbing fixtures, such as faucets, spigots, exposed traps. **4.** The hardware applied to a door. **5.** In the theatre, to adjust the vertical position of any element of scenery or equipment hung in the rigging. **6.** Same as **trimstone**. **7.** To adjust closely. **8.** To fit up and finish.

trim band A flat piece of metal which is welded to a side or end of a grating panel and carries no load; used chiefly to improve appearance.

trim block Same as **corner block**.

trim bronze A copper-zinc alloy having a bright finish; usually a commercial bronze (90% copper) or red brass (85% copper); in strip form it is used for architectural trim.

trim hardware   Decorative finish hardware, used either to operate functional hardware or to serve as functional hardware.

trimmed joist   A joist, supported by a **trimmer**, which has the same cross section as the common joists.

trimmed opening   See **cased opening**.

trimmed rafter   A rafter, supported by a **trimmer**, which has the same cross section as the common rafters.

trimmer   **1.** A piece of timber inserted in a roof, floor, wooden partition, or the like, to support a header which in turn supports the ends of the joists, rafters, studs, etc. **2.** A small horizontal beam, as in a floor, into which the ends of one or more joists are framed; often named from the place of use as a **hearth trimmer, stair trimmer,** etc. **3.** A **trimmer arch**. **4.** Variously shaped ceramic tile used as bases, caps, corners, moldings, and angles, as necessary to complete an installation and to satisfy sanitary and architectural requirements.

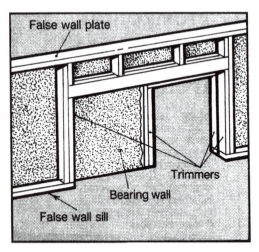

trimmer

trimmer arch   A nearly flat arch, usually a low-rise arch of brick; used for supporting a fireplace hearth; also called **trimmer**.

trimming   Trimming rafters, or trimmers and trimming joists which form an opening.

trimming joist   A joist, supporting a **trimmer**, of larger cross section but of the same length as, and parallel to, the **common joists**.

trimming machine   See **bench trimmer**.

trimming piece   Same as **camber piece**.

trimming rafter   A rafter, supporting a trimmer, of larger cross section but of the same length as, and parallel to, the **common rafters**.

trimstone, trim   In masonry, the stone used as decorative members on a structure built or faced largely with other masonry material, as brick, tile, block, or terra-cotta; includes sills, jambs, lintels, coping, cornices, and quoins.

tringle   A small square **fillet** molding or ornament.

tripartite scheme   A type of design for a multi-story commercial building, often associated with the work of Louis H. Sullivan (1856–1924). The building's façade is characterized by three principal divisions: a **base** consisting of the lowest two or three stories of the building; a **cap**, consisting of one to four stories, at the top of the building, and a **shaft**, consisting of the floors between the base and the cap. Such a building has a flat roof, projecting eaves, imposing arched or round-topped windows, vertical strips of windows separated by massive mullions, and massive arched doorways. In Sullivan's designs, the decorative elements typically consist of highly ornate friezes with interwoven foliated designs in low relief (particularly in terra-cotta) that usually appear in **spandrels, 1** and over entrances. See **Sullivanesque**.

tripartite vault   A vault, covering a triangular space, which is formed by the intersection of

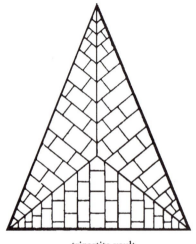

tripartite vault

three barrel vaults or three expanding vaults; esp. common in Romanesque buildings.

tripartite window, triple window **1.** Same as **three-part window**. **2.** Same as **treble sash**.

triple-hung window A window having three vertically sliding sashes, each closing a different part of the window; the weight of each sash is counterbalanced for ease of opening and closing; same as **treble sash**.

triplex cable A cable composed of three individually insulated electric conductors, twisted together and having a common outer protective covering.

triplex house A house that provides living quarters for three families, each with a separate entrance; usually has three stories, with one apartment on each floor.

tripteral Having three wings or three rows of columns.

triquetra An ornament composed of three half circles or ellipses crossed and joined together at their ends.

trisantia See **tresaunce**.

triumphal arch An arch commemorating the return of a victorious army, usually in the line of march during its triumphal procession.

trivet A low support for a surveying instrument where a tripod cannot be used.

trochilus A **cavetto** or **scotia**.

troffer A long recessed lighting unit, usually installed so that its opening is flush with the ceiling.

trolley beam An exposed steel beam, attached to the underside of the structure above; provides support for and acts as a track for a trolley crane.

trompe A piece of vaulting of conical or partly spherical shape, or resembling one corner of a cloistered vault.

trophy A sculptured composition of arms and armor as an emblem of, or a memorial to, victorious battles or triumphant military figures.

trough A channel used to carry electric conductors.

trough cable tray A continuous **cable tray** having slots for ventilation.

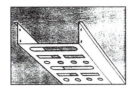

trough cable tray

trough gutter A **box gutter**.

trough mixer See **open-top mixer**.

trough roof See **M-roof**.

trowel A flat hand tool having a broad steel blade; used to apply, spread, and shape plaster or mortar or to impart a relatively smooth surface to concrete floors and other unformed concrete surfaces in the final stages of finishing operations.

trowel

trowel finish A smooth-finished surface produced by troweling.

troweling machine A motor-driven device that operates orbiting steel trowels on radial arms, which rotate on a vertical shaft; used to trowel concrete.

truck crane A materials-handling machine consisting of a crane which is mounted on a truck-type vehicle to provide mobility and maneuverability.

truck-mixed concrete Concrete that has been mixed in a **revolving-drum truck mixer**.

truck mixer A mobile unit for hauling and mixing concrete in transit; consists of a rotating drum (in which the concrete materials are placed) that is mounted on a truck chassis. (*See illustration p. 960.*)

truck zoning device On a freight elevator, a device which permits the operator to move the car within a limited distance above a landing with the car door or gate and the hoistway door open.

true bearing The **bearing, 4** of a line in relation to the local geographic meridian; used in early descriptions of land boundaries in the U.S.A.

truck mixer

true horizontal   A horizontal plane passing through a point of vision or a perspective center.

true north   The direction from an observer's position to the geographic north pole.

trullo   A dry-walled rough stone shelter, circular in plan, with a corbeled domical roof, resembling ancient structures and still used in southern Italy.

trumeau   The central support of a medieval doorway.

trumpet arch   A conically shaped **squinch, 2**.

truncated gable   Same as **jerkinhead**.

truncated roof   A **gable roof** or **hipped roof** whose top has been cut off, forming a flat horizontal surface.

trunk sewer   A sewer which receives many tributary branches and serves as an outlet for a large territory; also see **main sewer, 2**.

trunnel   See **treenail**.

truss   A structure composed of a combination of members (such as **chords, 1, diagonals**, and **web members**), usually in some triangular arrangement so as to constitute a rigid framework. See **king-post truss, plated truss, queen-post truss, Vierendeel truss**; also see **bowstring beam**.

truss beam   Same as **trussed beam**.

truss blade   Same as **principal rafter**.

truss clip   A metal component that serves as a connection between a **truss** and a **wall plate**; resists the forces of wind uplift.

trussed   Provided with some form of **truss**.

trussed beam   **1.** A beam, usually of timber, reinforced with one or more tie rods. **2.** A beam in the form of a **truss**; braced by one or more vertical posts supported by inclined rods attached to the ends of the beam.

trussed joist   A joist in the form of a truss, as a **bar joist**.

trussed partition   **1.** A **framed partition** which is self-supporting at its ends. **2.** A partition consisting of a continuously supported frame with **facing** or **infilling**.

trussed purlin   A lightweight **trussed beam** used as a purlin.

trussed-rafter roof   A pitched roof having all (or selected) opposite pairs of **common rafters** triangularly braced.

trussed ridge roof   A pitched roof having the upper ends of its rafters supported by a single truss, which runs along the ridge.

trussed-wall opening   In a framed structure, any opening in which the framing is trussed to carry the load above.

truss rod   **1.** In a truss, a metal rod used as a member under tension for stiffening. **2.** A metal rod used as a diagonal **tie**.

try square   A **square** whose legs are fixed at 90°; serves as a guide for marking lines at right angles to an edge or surface, as a scale for laying out work, and as a tool for testing the straightness and/or squareness of edges, faces, etc.

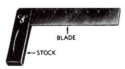

try square

T-shore   A shore having a **T-head, 1**.

T-square, tee square   A guide used in mechanical and architectural drawing; consists of two arms joined together at right angles, like

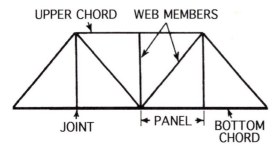

truss

the letter T; the shorter arm slides along the edge of the drawing table or drawing board, which serves as a guide; the longer arm is used to draw parallel lines or to support triangles for drawing lines at different angles.

TUB. On drawings, abbr. for **tubing.**

tube 1. A thin-walled pipe. 2. See **lamp.**

tube-and-coupler scaffold An assembly consisting of tubing which serves as posts, bearers, braces, ties, and runners, a base supporting the posts, and special couplers which connect the uprights and join the various members.

tubeaxial fan 1. A fan consisting of a propeller or disk-type wheel within a cylinder; may be either belt-driven or connected directly to a motor. 2. A type of **axial-flow fan** which is similar to a **vaneaxial fan** but without downstream guide vanes. Lower in efficiency than the vaneaxial fan, but also lower in cost.

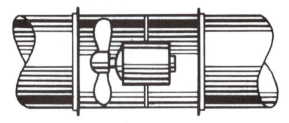

tubeaxial fan

tube pile A **pipe pile.**

tubing Any material in the form of a **tube.**

tub mixer See **open-top mixer.**

tubular discharge lamp Any **electric-discharge lamp** having a straight or curved tubular bulb.

tubular lock A type of **bored lock** in which the bolt is enclosed in a tube.

tubular saw Same as **crown saw.**

tubular scaffolding Scaffolding which is fabricated of aluminum or galvanized steel tubing, held together by clamps.

tubular-welded-frame scaffold A sectional panel or frame metal scaffold substantially built up of prefabricated welded sections which consist of posts and horizontal bearer with intermediate members.

tuck A recess in a horizontal mortar joint which is raked out to provide for **tuck pointing.**

tuck and pat pointing See **tuck pointing.**

tuck-in The part of a **counterflashing**, skirting, or roofing felt that is inserted into a chase or reglet in a wall.

tuck pointing, tuck and pat pointing, tuck joint pointing The finishing of old masonry joints: the joints are first cleaned out and then filled with fine mortar which is left projecting slightly or with a fillet of putty or lime; also called tuck-and-pat pointing or tuck-joint pointing.

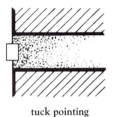

tuck pointing

Tudor arch A relatively flat, slightly **pointed arch** whose inner surface is struck from four centers; common in the architecture of Tudor England.

Tudor arch

Tudor architecture The final development of Perpendicular style architecture during the reigns of Henry VII and Henry VIII, preceding Elizabethan architecture. Characterized by **Tudor arches, diaperwork, strapwork, labels** and **label stops** over windows with mullions, ornate brick chimneys. (*See illustration p. 962.*)

Tudor chimney A term occasionally used for a **stepped-back chimney.**

Tudor flower

Tudor architecture

Tudor flower An ornament of English Perpendicular Gothic buildings; a trefoil flower developed from the upright points of the crossing or the cusps of a foliated arch.

Tudor Revival, Tudor style A term descriptive of a picturesque mode of domestic architecture prevalent from about 1880 to 1940 and beyond, emulating its Tudor architecture

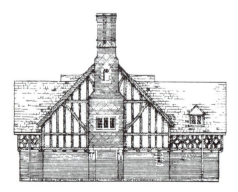

Tudor Revival

prototype. Homes in this style, usually asymmetrical in plan, often were clad in brick, or stucco in combination with wood; commonly, **false half-timbering**; surface ornamentation consisting of **strapwork**; steeply pitched gables with little overhang at the eaves; bargeboards on the gables; a shingled roof; tall, massive, elaborate chimneys often with decorative chimney pots atop the chimneys; tall, narrow, leaded windows; a decorative main entry doorway, often incorporating a **Tudor arch** or a **round-topped arch**. Compare with **Neo-Tudor architecture, Elizabethan architecture, Jacobethan architecture**.

Tudor rose A conventionalized rose pattern, usually with five petals, a superposition of white and red roses, the heraldic emblem of the Tudor dynasty.

tufa A porous limestone used in masonry construction.

tuff, volcanic tuff A low-density, high-porosity rock; composed of volcanic particles, ranging from ash size to small pebble size, which are compacted or cemented together; sometimes used as building stone or as a thermal insulation material.

tufted carpet Carpet made by punching pile yarn through a **carpet backing** material which has been previously woven; then the pile is cut.

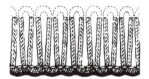

tufted carpet

tulipwood **1.** A soft, close-textured durable wood, yellowish in color; used for millwork and veneer. **2.** A rose-colored, very hard wood from Brazil; esp. used for inlay work.

tumbled Said of a metal surface that has been cleaned and polished by agitation in a rotating drum containing a polishing compound.

tumbled-in gable Same as **straight-line gable**.

tumble home, tumble in An inclination inward from the greatest breadth of a structure.

tumbler In a lock, the locking mechanism which detains the bolt until set free by a key.

tumbler switch In electric wiring, a lever-actuated **snap switch**.

tumbling See **barreling**.

tumbling course A sloping course of bricks that are set perpendicular to a **straight-line gable** in Dutch architecture or its derivatives; such an arrangement provides a better seal against the penetration of moisture through the masonry joints than one in which all courses of bricks within the gable are laid in horizontal courses up to the peak of the gable. Where a sloping course of bricks intersects a horizontal masonry course, the arrangement of brickwork so formed is called a *mouse-tooth pattern*.

tumulus A mound of earth or stone protecting a tomb chamber or simple grave; a **barrow, 2**.

tung oil A drying oil which oxidizes very rapidly, at almost twice the rate of linseed oil; forms a hard dry film when used in paints and varnishes; although "China wood oil" and "wood oil" sometimes are used as synonyms, tung oil never is extracted from wood.

tungsten-halogen lamp A tungsten-filament incandescent lamp which is filled with a gas containing halogens; the envelope, made of quartz or other material that can be subjected to high-temperature, is small compared with standard lamps of equivalent wattage; formerly known as **quartz-iodine lamp**.

tungsten steel Steel usually containing 5 to 10% (but sometimes as much as 24%) tungsten and 0.4 to 2% carbon.

tunnel test An ASTM standard test of the surface-burning characteristics of a building material.

tunnel vault A **vault** having a uniform cross section everywhere.

turbidimeter An apparatus for the measurement of particle-size distribution of a finely divided material such as portland cement, based on successive measurements of the turbidity of a suspension in a fluid.

turbidimeter fineness The fineness of a material as measured on a turbidimeter; usually expressed as the total surface area in square centimeters per gram.

turbine mixer See **open-top mixer**.

turf The upper layer of earth and vegetable mold in which the roots of grass and other small plants form a thick cover.

turf sprinkler system Same as **lawn sprinkler system**.

turnbuckle A device for connecting and tightening a line, rod, or stay; consists of a right screw and a left screw which are coupled by means of a link.

turn button, button A fastener for a window or door which rotates on a pivot and is attached to the frame.

turned bolt A machine bolt, ordinarily with a hexagonal head, whose shank is fabricated to a close tolerance.

turned drop A hanging wood ornament, formed on a lathe, but sometimes hand-carved; especially found in timber-framed early American colonial houses, often suspended from a second-floor **overhang, 1.** either at the front corners of the façade or adjacent to the front door. Sometimes simply called a drop; compare with **pendant**.

turned work In stone and wood cutting, pieces having a circular outline, such as columns, balusters, etc.; usually cut on a lathe, although some shapes are cut by hand.

turning The shaping of objects by means of cutting tools while the material, from which the objects are made, rotates rapidly on a lathe.

turning bar See **chimney bar**.

turning gouge Any one of a set of gouges having the corners of the bit rounded off; used in **turning**.

turning piece **1.** A piece of board cut to a curve to guide the mason in turning any small arch for which no centering is required. **2.** Same as **camber piece**.

turning vane One of a number of curved fins which are placed in air-conditioning ductwork

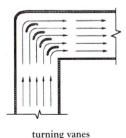

turning vanes

at a point where the duct changes direction; used to promote a more uniform airflow and to reduce pressure drop.

turn-key job   A job in which the contractor completes all work and furnishing of a building so that it is ready for immediate use.

turn knob   A small doorknob, often oval or crescent-shaped; used to control the door bolt from the inside of the door.

turn piece   A small doorknob, lever, or the like, having a spindle attached; used to operate the **dead bolt** or a bolt mortised in the door.

turnpike stair   A spiral staircase.

turnstile   A barrier which rotates on an axis and usually is so arranged as to allow the passage of a person through an opening only in one direction, one person at a time.

turn tread   A **tread** on a stair where it changes direction.

turnup   That portion of roofing material which is turned up at any vertical surface.

turpentine, oil of turpentine   A volatile liquid obtained by the distillation of the exudation from certain coniferous trees; once widely used in paint, it is now replaced by solvents obtained from petroleum or coal-tar stocks. Also see **wood turpentine**.

turret, tourelle   A diminutive tower, characteristically corbeled from a corner.

turret step   A stone step, triangular in section, which forms, with other turret steps, a spiral or solid newel stair. Turret steps are tapered and have shaped ends which, laid upon each other, constitute the central column or solid newel.

turriculated   Describing a building in which the characteristic feature is a row of turrets.

turris   A tower of a fortification, placed at intervals in the walls of an ancient city or any other fortified enclosure.

turtleback   **1.** See **blistering, 1. 2.** In plastering, a localized condition of **checking, 3**.

Tuscan order   One of the five Classical **orders**; a simplified version of the Roman Doric order to which it is similar, but has fewer and bolder moldings, unfluted columns, a plain frieze, and no triglyphs; its only decorative details are moldings.

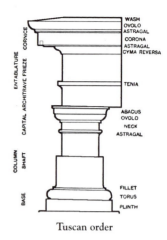

Tuscan order

Tuscan Revival   A term descriptive of late 17-century architecture that emulates and borrows features from the **Tuscan order**.

Tuscan Villa style   A style somewhat similar to that of villas in the **Italianate style**, boxlike in shape but having a symmetrical plan rather than an asymmetrical plan and a flat roof; frequently a square **belvedere** at the center of the roof; windows often round-headed.

tusk   **1.** A beveled shoulder on a tenon to provide additional strength, the mortise being cut correspondingly. **2.** A stone or brick in **toothing**.

tusk nailing   See **toenailing**.

tusk tenon   A **tenon** strengthened by having one or more steps on its lower side; the shoulder above may be beveled.

twelve-over-twelve   See **pane**.

twin archway   An opening having two archways which are side-by-side.

twin brick   Same as **double-sized brick**.

twin cable   A cable consisting of two individually insulated electric conductors, laid parallel; either bound together in a common outer pro-

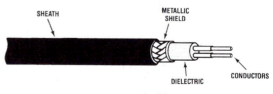

twin axial cable

tective covering or attached to each other by insulation. Also see **duplex cable**.

twin-filament lamp An incandescent lamp with two filaments that are wired independently.

twining stem molding A common Norman molding consisting of a **half round** entwined by a stylized tendril.

twin tenons (*pl.*) Same as **double tenons, 1**.

twin-twisted bar reinforcement Two **reinforcement bars** having the same nominal diameter, twisted together.

twist A warped board in which the four corners of one face are not in the same plane; a spiral distortion.

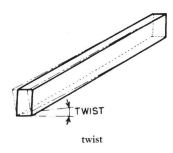

twist

twist drill A drill, with one or more helical cutting grooves; used for drilling holes in metal, wood, etc.

twisted column See **wreathed column**.

twisted grain Same as **interlocked grain**.

twisted pair Two insulated electrical conductors, twisted together without a common covering.

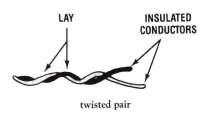

twisted pair

two-and-one-half-story house A two-story house in which the loft space between the ceiling of the second floor and the roof above is provided with natural light and ventilation either by dormers and/or by windows in the gable-end walls.

two-bay cottage A **Cape Cod house** having a façade with two windows on each side of the front door; also called a full Cape house.

two-by-four A piece of timber, nominally 2 in. (5 cm) thick by 4 in. (10 cm) wide, but actually 1⅝ in. by 3⅝ in. (4.13 cm by 9.21 cm).

two-centered arch A **pointed arch** whose inner surface is struck from two centers; the shape of the arch is determined by the position of the centers of curvature and radii of curvature of the two arcs of circles that are joined; also see **equilateral arch**.

two-coat work In plastering, the application of a first coat (the base coat) followed by a second (the finish coat).

two-family house A two-story house having two separate living quarters, with a separate entrance for each.

two-hinged arch An arch with hinges at the supports at both ends.

two-light window **1.** A window with two panes. **2.** A window which is two panes high or two panes wide. **3.** A **gemel window**.

two-over-two Descriptive of a **double-hung window** having two panes in the upper sash and two panes in the lower sash; see **pane**.

two-part adhesive An adhesive that requires the addition of an accelerator to the resin, in order to set, e.g., see **epoxy**.

two-point latch A type of door latching device; sometimes used where it is necessary to lock the inactive leaf of a pair of doors at top and bottom.

two-point suspension scaffold Same as **swinging scaffold**.

two-room plan A relatively common **floor plan** for a simple two-room dwelling in colonial architecture of New England, the mid-Atlantic area, and the South. This plan has many variations but usually consists of an all-purpose main room (the *hall*) and an adjacent room (the *parlor*) containing the best furniture and a bed for the parents. Also see **hall-and-parlor plan**.

two-stage curing A process in which concrete products are cured in low-pressure steam, stacked, and then autoclaved. See **cure; autoclave**.

two-tiered porch A two-story porch, each of which is virtually identical.

two-way joist construction Floor or roof construction in which two mutually perpendicular systems of parallel beams, in a horizontal plane, are used to support the floor or roof.

two-way-reinforced footing A **footing** in which the reinforcement runs in two directions, usually perpendicular to each other.

two-way reinforcement **Reinforcing bars** arranged in a grid pattern, so that the sets of bars are at right angles to each other.

two-way slab **1.** A concrete floor slab in which the main reinforcement runs in two directions. **2.** A rectangular, reinforced concrete slab having a span on the long side that is less than twice the span on the short side.

T-wrench A T-shaped wrench with a handle having a socket (either fixed or removable) which fits over a nut or bolt head.

tympanum **1.** The triangular or segmental space enclosed between the horizontal cornice

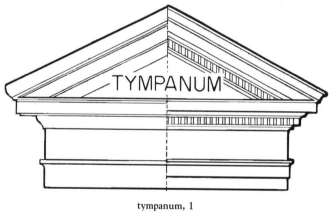

tympanum, 1

of a **pediment** and the underside of the raking or curved cornice above; sometimes decorated with decorative elements, sculpture, or a window. **2.** Any space similarly marked off or bounded, as between the lintel of a door and the arch above.

TYP On drawings, abbr. for "typical."

type-DWV tubing A copper tubing which has thinner walls than other types of copper tubing; used primarily for drainage, waste, and vent lines.

type-S fuse

type-S fuse A fuse contained in a small glass or ceramic housing, which can be screwed into a screw-shell socket; it has a window for observing whether the fuse has been "blown"; available in three, noninterchangeable sizes (15, 20, and 30 amperes).

type-X gypsum lath A **gypsum lath** which is especially manufactured to provide specific fire-resistant characteristics.

type-X gypsum wallboard A **gypsum wallboard** which is especially manufactured to provide specific fire-resistant characteristics.

Tyrolean finish A rough plaster finish obtained by flinging plaster on a wall with a hand-operated machine.

U

UBC Abbr. for **Uniform Building Code**.

U-bend A pipe **expansion bend** in the shape of the letter U.

U-block See **lintel block**.

U-bolt A rod bent in the shape of the letter U with threads for nuts on the ends.

U-bolt

U/E Abbr. for "unedged."

U-factor See **thermal transmittance**.

UFAS Abbr. For **Uniform Federal Accessibility Standards**.

U-gauge Same as **manometer**.

uintahite See **gilsonite**.

UL Abbr. for **Underwriters' Laboratories, Inc**.

UL Label An identification affixed to a building material or component, with the authorization of Underwriters' Laboratories, Inc., indicating that the labeled product: (*a*) has a rating based on the performance tests of such products; (*b*) is from a production lot found by examination to be made from materials and by processes essentially identical to those of representative products which have been subjected to appropriate fire, electrical hazard, or other tests for safety; and (*c*) is subject to the reexamination service of UL.

ultimate bearing capacity The average load per unit of area required to produce failure by rupture of a supporting soil mass.

ultimate load See **breaking load**.

ultimate set The final degree of firmness attained by a plastic compound after curing, evaporation of volatile materials, and surface polymerization.

ultimate shear strength The loading at a section resulting from the failure of a member in shear.

ultimate shear stress The stress at a section which is loaded to its maximum in shear.

ultimate strength Of a material in tension, compression, or shear: the maximum value of tension, compression, or shear, respectively, that the material can sustain without failure.

ultramarine A blue pigment used in paint; once obtained from crushed **lapis lazuli**; now manufactured synthetically by calcining aluminum silicate and sodium sulfide; has good alkali resistance, but is sensitive to acids.

ultramarine ash The residue of **lapis lazuli** after the ultramarine has been extracted; used as a pigment in paints.

ultrasonic motion detector A **motion detector** employing sound waves having a frequency above 20,000 Hz.

ultrasonic soldering A soldering process in which high-frequency sound waves are transmitted through molten solder to remove undesirable surface films from the base metal, thereby promoting wetting of the base metal with solder; usually accomplished without the use of flux.

ultrasonic testing A nondestructive method of testing metal; makes use of very-high-frequency sound waves to locate flaws in metal.

ultrasonic welding A solid-state welding process in which the metals are joined by the local application of high-frequency sound waves as the work parts are held together under pressure.

ultrasound Acoustic oscillations having a frequency above the high-frequency limit of audible sound, i.e., above 20,000 Hz.

ultraviolet radiation Electromagnetic radiation at wavelengths immediately below the visible spectrum, i.e., within the wavelength range

10 to 380 nm. May be classified as: *far ultraviolet*, 10 to 280 nm; *middle ultraviolet*, 280 to 315 nm; *near ultraviolet*, 315 to 380 nm. Also may be classified as: *ozone-producing*, 180 to 220 nm; *germicidal*, 220 to 300 nm; *erythemal*, 280 to 320 nm; *black light*, 320 to 400 nm. In either method of classification, there are no sharp demarcations between the wavelength bands.

umber A naturally occurring brown siliceous earth, containing hydrated iron oxide with small amounts of manganese oxide; used as a pigment in paint; turns red to reddish-brown when calcined, and then is called **burnt umber**.

umbral In Spanish Colonial architecture, a **lintel**.

umbrella roof In French Vernacular architecture of Louisiana, a roof having a single pitch on each side of a central ridge and covering a **galerie** on each side of the house.

unbonded member A posttensioned, **prestressed concrete** member in which tensioning force is applied against end anchorages only, the tendons being free to move within the element.

unbonded posttensioning In prestressed concrete, **posttensioning** in which the tendons are not grouted to the concrete after being stressed.

unbonded tendon In prestressed concrete, a **tendon** which is not bonded to the concrete.

unbraced frame A structural framework in which the resistance to lateral **load, 1** is provided by the bending resistance of its structural members and their connections.

unbraced length The distance between ends of a structural member (such as a column) which are prevented from moving normal to the axis of the member, by bracing, by floor slabs, etc.

unburnt brick Brick, such as adobe brick, that is sun-dried, rather than kiln-dried at an elevated temperature; compare with **burnt brick**.

uncased Said of an arch, doorway, or other opening that has no frame around it. Uncased openings are especially found in **Spanish Eclectic architecture** and its derivatives.

unclassified excavation An excavation in which there is a single unit price for removal, regardless of the proportion of **common excavation** and **rock excavation** (compare with **classified excavation**).

unconsolidated backfill The non-compacted material which is in place in a trench.

uncoursed Said of masonry which is not in layers with continuous horizontal joints, but is laid irregularly.

uncoursed masonry

unctuarium Same as **alipterion**.

uncut modillion See **modillion**.

undé, undée See **waved molding**.

underbed The base mortar, usually horizontal, on which a **terrazzo** topping is applied.

underboarding Boards that are nailed to the exterior side of the framing of a **timber-framed house** to provide a surface on which to fasten an exterior covering such as shingles or siding.

undercloak **1.** In roofing, a course of plain tiles or slate used under the first course at the eaves. **2.** Shingles installed with their thick end overhanging the edge of a gable to give a slope to the tiles laid along the edge. **3.** In sheet-metal roofing, that part of the lower sheet that makes up a seam, or the like.

undercoat **1.** A coat of paint applied on new wood, or over a primer, or over a previous coat of paint; improves the seal and serves as a base for the topcoat, for which it provides better adhesion. **2.** Any paint which acts as a base for enamel. **3.** Any **primer** which is colored.

underconsolidated soil deposit A deposit that is not fully consolidated under the existing overburden pressure.

undercourse A course of shingles or tiles which serves as an **undercloak, 1, 2**.

undercroft **1.** A vaulted basement of a church or secret passage, often wholly or partly below ground level. **2.** A **crypt**.

undercured Said of concrete, a sealant, adhesive, paint, etc., which has not had sufficient

undercourse

time and/or suitable physical environment to harden properly.

undercut **1.** In stonework, to cut away a lower part, leaving a projection above that serves the function of a **drip**. **2.** To rout a groove or channel (a drip) back from the edge of an overhanging member.

undercut door A door without louvers which is given additional clearance at the floor line to provide ventilation.

undercut tenon A **tenon** in which a shoulder is cut at an angle to the face of the tenon in order to ensure a tight fit.

underdrain A drain, installed in porous fill, for drawing off surface water or water from the soil, as under the slab of a structure.

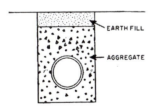

underdrain

underdrawing Same as **torching**.

underfelt A dry sheet of **asphaltic felt**. See **underlayment, 2**.

underfill A depression, on the face of a weld, which extends below the surface of the adjacent base metal.

underfloor Same as **subfloor**.

underfloor conduit system A method of distributing communications wiring within the floor of a building. Metal pipes (for housing the wiring) radiate out to the area served from a serving closet (or cabinet). Such a system is suitable for installation in buildings in which the terminal equipment locations are likely to remain fixed.

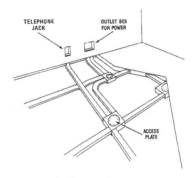

underfloor conduit system

underfloor heating Heating provided beneath a finish floor, usually by hot water pipes or electric heating cables.

underfloor raceway A **raceway**, for carrying electric conductors, which is suitable for use in a floor, as one buried within a structural concrete floor.

underglaze decoration A ceramic decoration applied directly on the (bisque) surface of ceramic ware and subsequently covered with a transparent glaze.

underground Below grade or ground level, as underground drain lines or cables.

underground distribution system An electrical supply system employing underground structures, cables, and other equipment located under designated areas along public ways or utility easements; does not include service cables in the customer's duct.

underground piping Piping in direct contact with, and covered by, earth.

underground structure Any duct, manhole, subway-type pull box, underground-type enclosure, or vault in which cables, transformers, and similar items of equipment are installed.

underlay **1.** Same as **underlayment**. **2.** Same as **carpet underlayment**. **3.** A layer, such as

underlayment

asphaltic felt, which isolates a roof covering from the substructure; underfelt.

underlayment **1.** A material such as plywood or hardboard placed on a subfloor to provide a smooth, even surface for applying the finish. **2.** The material, usually No. 15 felt, used to cover a roof deck before shingles are applied; also called **underfelt**. **3.** See **carpet underlayment**.

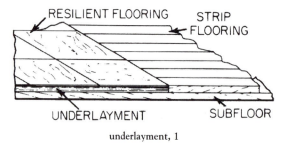

underlayment, 1

underlining felt Same as **underlayment, 2**.

underpinning The rebuilding or deepening of the foundation of an existing building to provide additional or improved support, e.g., additional support required as a result of a new excavation in adjoining property which is deeper than the existing foundation.

underpitch groin A groin formed by an **underpitch vault**.

underpitch vault, Welsh vault A construction formed by the penetration of two vaults of unequal size, springing from the same level.

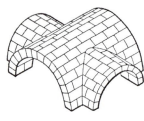

underpitch vault

under plate See **armored front**.

undersanded concrete Concrete containing an insufficient proportion of fine aggregate to produce optimum properties in the fresh mixture, esp. with respect to workability and finishing characteristics.

undersealing Same as **subsealing**.

underslating felt Same as **underlayment, 2**.

underslung car frame An elevator car frame having the fastenings or sheaves for the hoisting ropes (cables) attached at or below the car platform.

underthroating The cove of an outside cornice when treated so as to serve as a **drip**.

undertone **1.** A color modified by an underlying color, as in the effect of glazing over a thin film of paint. **2.** A secondary color of a pigment which appears when it is diluted with a large amount of white.

Underwriters' Laboratories, Inc. A non-profit nongovernment organization sponsored by the National Board of Fire Underwriters; classifies, tests, and inspects electric devices to assure their compliance with the National Electrical Code.

Underwriters' loop See **Hartford loop**.

undisturbed sample A sample of soil that has been obtained by methods in which every precaution has been taken to minimize disturbance to the sample.

undressed lumber, rough lumber, *Brit.* **unwrought timber** Sawn lumber that has not been planed.

undulating molding See **wave molding**.

undulating tracery See **flowing tracery**.

undy molding See **wave molding**.

uneven grain Wood grain in which the growth rings show an obvious difference between springwood and summerwood; found in ring-porous hardwoods (such as oak) and softwoods (such as yellow pine) that have soft, uniform springwood and hard, dense summerwood.

unframed door A door not in a frame, as a **batten door**.

ungauged lime plaster Plaster containing no gypsum; usually composed of lime, sand, and water.

unglazed tile A hard, dense ceramic tile for floors or walls; of homogeneous composition throughout, deriving its color and texture from the materials of which the body is made and from the method of manufacture.

unidirectional microphone A microphone whose response is predominantly from a single direction.

Uniform Building Code (UBC) A U.S. national **building code**, prepared and issued by the International Conference of Building Code Officials, 5360 South Workman Mill Road, Whittier, CA 90601-2294. Also see **BOCA National Building Code**.

uniform construction index An outline of building trades and products, separated into 16 divisions (illustrated under **contract documents**), that are arranged by trade and construction sequence.

Uniform Federal Accessibility Standards (UFAS) A set of standards concerning accessibility for the disabled, which are available at no charge from: U.S. Access Board, 1331 F Street NW, Suite 1000, Washington, DC 20004-1111. Also see **Americans with Disabilities Act**.

uniform grading A particle-size distribution of aggregate in which all pan fractions are present without a preponderance of any one size or group of sizes.

uniformity coefficient A coefficient related to the size distribution of a granular material, such as sand; obtained by dividing one size of grain (60% of the grains are smaller than this size, by weight) by a second size (10% of the grains are smaller than this size, by weight).

uniform load A **load, 1** uniformly distributed over all or a portion of a structure.

uniform system Coordination of specification sections, filing of technical data and product literature, and construction cost accounting, organized in 16 **divisions** based on an interrelationship of place, trade, function, or material.

uninterruptible power system An electric power system which provides continuity of power, to the apparatus or appliances being served, without discernible interruption upon failure of the normal power supply.

union A pipe **fitting, 1** used to connect the ends of two pipes, neither of which can be turned; consists of three pieces, the two end pieces (having inner threads), which are tightened around the pipe ends to be joined, and a center piece,

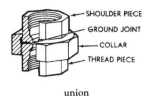

union

which draws the two end pieces together as it is rotated, effecting a seal. Also see **flange union**.

union bend See **union elbow**.

union clip A fitting for interconnecting the ends of two rainwater gutters.

union elbow A pipe **elbow, 1** having a union-type coupling on one end, so that the coupling end may be connected to the end of a pipe without turning the pipe.

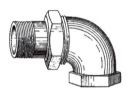

union elbow

union fitting A **union elbow** or a **union tee**.

union joint A pipe joint made with a **union**.

union tee A **pipe tee** having a union-type coupling on one end.

union vent Same as **dual vent**.

unit absorber A sound-absorptive element which is designed for application on a wall or ceiling as a single unit; usually part of a spaced array of similar units.

unit air conditioner Same as **room air conditioner**.

unitary air conditioner Equipment consisting of one or more factory-fabricated assemblies designed to perform the functions of air moving, air cleaning, cooling, and dehumidification; the assemblies usually include a fan, evaporator or cooling coil, and a compressor and condenser in combination; a heating unit also may be included.

unit construction Same as **modular construction**.

unit cooler See **room air conditioner**.

united inches The sum of the length and width (expressed in inches) of a rectangular piece of glass.

United States of America Standards Institute See **American National Standards Institute**.

unit heater A direct-heating, factory-made, encased assembly including a heating element, fan and motor, and directional outlet.

unit lock A **preassembled lock**.

unit masonry See **masonry unit**.

unit price An amount stated in a **contract** as the price per unit of measurement for materials or services as described in the **contract documents**.

unit substation One or more transformers which are mechanically or electrically connected to (and coordinated in design with) one or more switchgear or motor control assemblies, or combinations thereof.

unit-type vent An opening of relatively small area (one of a number which are distributed about a roof according to the occupancy requirements), usually having a lightweight metal frame and housing, with hinged dampers which may be operated manually or which open automatically in the event of fire.

unit vent See **dual vent**.

unit ventilator An operable air-inlet damper which furnishes outdoor air to an interior space; may be provided with a filter and heating and/or cooling coils.

unit water content 1. The quantity of water per unit volume of freshly mixed concrete. 2. The quantity of water on which the water-cement ratio is based, not including water absorbed by the aggregate.

universal Descriptive of a door lock, a door closer, or the like, which can be used on either a right-hand swing door or a left-hand swing door.

universal motor A motor capable of operating either on alternating current or on direct current.

unloader A control mechanism for an electric-motor-driven compressor; controls the pressure head of the compressor; permits the motor to be started at low starting torque by removing the load during this initial period of operation.

unprotected corner Of a slab, a corner having no adequate provisions for transfer of load, so that the corner must carry over 80% of the load.

unprotected metal construction Steel frame construction in which the framing members are not fireproofed.

unreinforced concrete See **plain concrete**.

unrestrained member A member that is permitted to rotate freely at its points of support.

unsound Descriptive of a plaster, slaked lime, cement, or other mortar which contains particles that may expand.

unsound knot, decayed knot, rotten knot A knot that is softer than the surrounding wood.

unsound plaster Hydrated lime, plaster, or mortar which contains unhydrated particles that may expand and cause popping or pitting.

unsound wood Same as decayed wood.

unstable soil Earth material that, because of its nature or the influence of related conditions, cannot be depended upon to remain in place without extra support, such as would be furnished by a system of shoring.

unstiffened member A member (or part of a member) which is subjected to compressive forces and is not reinforced in a direction perpendicular to the direction along which it will bend most easily.

unwrought timber, unwrot timber British term for **undressed lumber**.

up-and-down sash An archaic term for a rectangular window sash that moves in a vertical plane; a **double-hung window**.

up-and-over door An **overhead door** which is a single leaf.

UPC Abbr. for "Uniform Plumbing Code."

upfeed system A water distribution system in which water is supplied and fed upward through the vertical piping to the highest point of the system that may be fed, using the available pressure.

upheaval The upward push of a soil mass.

U-plan The basic **plan** of a house having a shape similar to that of the capital letter **U**.

uplift 1. The upward pressure on a structure due to the pressure of the water below. 2. The pressure acting on a material that tends to lift it off its supports or fasteners as a result of an external force (for example, wind) acting on it.

uplift capacity   A measure of the resistance of a pile to being pulled out of the ground.

upper capital   Same as **dosseret**.

upping block   Same as **horse block**.

upright   **1.** A vertical piece of timber or stone. **2.** A vertical structural member.

upset   **1.** To shorten and thicken by hammering, as a bar of heated metal struck on the end. **2.** In the region of a weld, a localized increase in volume resulting from the application of pressure. **3.** A defect in timber due to a severe blow that breaks the fibers across the grain.

upset price   See **guaranteed maximum cost**.

upsetting   The hot-forging operation by which the cross-sectional area of a metal bar or rod is increased locally.

upset welding   A resistance-welding process in which the joining of two surfaces is effected by the heat obtained from the flow of current through the resistance provided by the area of contact between the surfaces to be joined; pressure is employed in this process.

upstage   The back part of a stage, away from the audience.

up stairs   Stairs designated to be used for going up only, as in some schools and institutional buildings.

upstairs   The portion of a house or small building situated on the floors above the main or entrance floor.

upstand, upturn   The part of a roof covering that turns up against a vertical surface.

upstanding beam   In a concrete floor, a beam which projects above a concrete slab rather than below it.

UR   On drawings, abbr. for **urinal**.

urban area   An area which is within the city limits, or closely linked to it by common use of public utilities or services.

urban planning   See **city planning** and **community planning**.

urban renewal   The improvement of slum, deteriorated, and underutilized areas of a city; generally implies improvement realized through city, state, and, particularly, federal programs, including the clearance and redevelopment of slums, the rehabilitation of relatively sound structures, and conservation measures to arrest the spread of deterioration.

urea-formaldehyde   Same as **urea resin adhesive**.

urea resin adhesive   A dry powder which is mixed with water before being applied; has high early strength and good resistance to heat; not recommended for poorly fitted joints or outdoor use.

urinal   A sanitary fixture equipped with a water supply and drain for flushing away urine.

urinal (wall hung)

usable floor area   The net floor area in a building after deducting the area occupied by lobbies, corridors, rest rooms, cafeterias, etc.

usable life   See **pot life**.

USASI   Abbr. for **American National Standards Institute**.

U.S. Customary Units   The system of units ordinarily used in the U.S.A., for example, the unit of length may be the inch, foot, yard, or mile.

use district   An area, designated in the zoning ordinance of a municipality, within which specified types of land use are permitted and others forbidden.

USG   On drawings, abbr. for "**United States gauge**."

U-stirrup   In reinforced concrete construction, a **stirrup, 2** which is U-shaped.

U-tie A U-shaped heavy wire used as a **wall tie**.

utility See **public utility**.

utility pole An outdoor pole installed by a telephone or electric utility company for the support of conductors and other electric or telephone equipment.

utility sheet Mill-finished metal sheeting; available in a variety of sizes suitable for general building construction.

utility tractor A low- to medium-horsepower **tractor**; used primarily for pulling auxiliary

utility tractor

equipment, but also used in construction with attachments for trenching, dozing, breaking, etc.

utility vent A **vent, 1** which rises well above the highest water level of a fixture and then turns downward before it connects to the main vent or stack vent.

utility window A low-cost hot-rolled steel window for use in basement areaways, garages, shops, and the like; has a **hopper light** over a **fixed light**.

utilization equipment Any equipment which utilizes electric energy for mechanical, heating, lighting, or similar useful purposes.

utilization factor **1.** The maximum **demand** of a system (or part of a system) divided by its rated capacity. **2.** See **coefficient of utilization**.

U-trap A U-shaped **running trap**.

U-tube Same as **manometer**.

U-value See **thermal transmittance**.

V

V **1.** Abbr. for **volt**. **2.** On drawings, abbr. for **valve**. **3.** On drawings, abbr. for "vacuum."

V1S Abbr. for "vee one side."

VA Symbol for "volt-ampere."

vacuum breaker A **backflow preventer** which prevents a vacuum in a water-supply system from causing **backflow**.

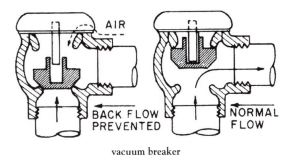

vacuum breaker

vacuum circuit breaker An electrical circuit breaker in which the contacts that perform switching and interrupting functions are enclosed in a vacuum.

vacuum concrete Concrete from which water is extracted by a vacuum process before hardening occurs.

vacuum lifting The lifting of an object, using a vacuum as the method of attachment.

vacuum pump A pump which produces a partial vacuum in an enclosed space; may be used to remove air or steam from a chamber or a system.

vacuum relief valve An automatic valve that opens and closes a vent for relieving a vacuum within a hot water supply system.

vagina The upper part of the pedestal of a **terminus**, from which the bust or figure seems to arise.

valance **1.** A frame at the top of a window to conceal the tops of decorative draperies. **2.** The draperies themselves.

valance lighting, pelmet lighting Lighting furnished by light sources that are concealed and shielded by a panel parallel to the wall at the top of a window; may provide lighting in the upward and/or downward direction.

valley The trough or gutter formed by the intersection of two inclined planes of a roof.

valley board In roofing, the board, nailed to the **valley rafter**, on which the metal gutter lies.

valley flashing The sheet metal used to line the **valley** on a roof.

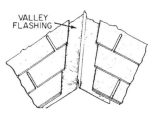

valley flashing

valley gutter The open gutter in a **valley**; has sloping sides and is exposed to view.

valley jack A rafter, shorter than the **common rafters**, one end of which is fixed to the ridge, and the other end to a **valley rafter**. (*See illustration p. 976.*)

valley rafter In a roof framing system, the rafter in the line of the **valley**; connects the ridge to the wall plate along the meeting line of two inclined sides of a roof which are perpendicular to each other. (*See illustration p. 976.*)

valley roof Any **pitched roof** that has one or more valleys.

valley shingle A shingle laid next to a **valley** and especially cut so that the grain is parallel to the valley.

valley tile A special roof tile, shaped and laid to form a **valley**.

valve A device which regulates or closes off the flow of a fluid.

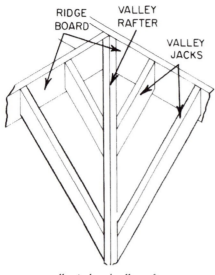

valley jack and valley rafter

vane

vaneaxial fan

valve bag   A paper bag for cement, or the like, which is completely closed except for a self-sealing paper valve through which the contents are introduced.

valve motor   In an air-conditioning system, a pneumatic or electric device which is used to control a valve from a remote location.

valve seat   The stationary portion of a valve which, when in contact with the movable portion, stops flow completely.

vamure, vaimure, vauntmure   **1.** In fortifications, a false wall; a work raised in front of the main wall. **2.** The **alure** or walkway along ramparts behind the parapet.

vanadium steel   An **alloy steel** containing a small percentage of vanadium, which raises its elastic limit and ultimate strength.

Vandyke brown, Cassel brown   **1.** A very dark deep brown pigment; usually obtained from peat or lignite. **2.** A synthetic pigment of similar color.

vane   See **weather vane.**

vaneaxial fan   **1.** A fan consisting of a disk-type wheel within a cylinder, with a set of air guide vanes located either before or after the wheel; may be either belt-driven or connected directly to a motor. **2.** An **axial-flow fan** which incorporates downstream guide vanes. It has a higher efficiency than any other type of axial-flow fans.

vaned outlet   A **register** or **grille** which is equipped with vertical and/or horizontal adjustable vanes to regulate the direction of airflow.

vane ratio   The ratio of the depth of a **vane, 2** to the minimum distance between adjacent vanes.

vanishing point   In perspective, a point toward which a series of parallel lines seem to converge.

VAP   On drawings, abbr. for "vapor."

vapor barrier   See **vapor retarder.**

vapor heating system   A steam heating system which operates at or near atmospheric pressure and returns the condensate to the boiler or receiver by gravity.

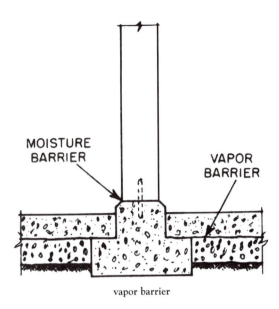

MOISTURE BARRIER

VAPOR BARRIER

vapor barrier

vapor lock   The formation of vapor in a pipe carrying liquids; prevents normal fluid flow.

vapor lock device   Any device, such as an orifice or capillary tube, which eliminates or minimizes the collection of vapor in a pipe.

vapor migration   The movement of water vapor as a result of a vapor pressure differential between a building roof or walls and the outside, resulting in vapor penetration.

vapor permeance   See **permeance**.

vapor pressure   The component of the total pressure which is caused by the presence of a vapor, as, for example, by the presence of water vapor in air.

vapor retarder   **1.** A membrane covering the outer surface of an insulated cold water pipe that is used to prevent moisture from penetrating the insulation and reaching the pipe. **2.** A layer of material or laminate used to reduce, appreciably, the flow of water vapor into a roofing system.

vapor-tight   Said of a surface that is enclosed so as to resist the passage of vapor, often including the use of a gasket around its periphery.

vapor vent, vapor relief vent   Same as **local vent**.

vapour   See **vapor**.

variable air valve (VAV)   In an **HVAC** system, a control unit consisting of a metal box containing damper-position control equipment, a controller, and a sensor. The box is usually supplied with "primary" air through a duct from the main distribution system; the output delivers air to diffusers located in the space being served.

variable-volume air system   An air-conditioning system in which the quantity of air supplied to each controlled zone is regulated automatically, from some preset minimum value to a maximum value based on the load in each zone.

variance   A written authorization, from the responsible agency, permitting construction in a manner which is not allowed by code or other regulations.

variation order   British term for **change order**.

variegated   Said of material or a surface which is irregularly marked with different colors; dappled.

varnish   A clear, unpigmented preparation consisting of resinous matter dissolved in alcohol (**spirit varnish**) or other volatile liquid, or in oil (**oil varnish**); when applied as a thin coating on a surface, it dries leaving a hard, smooth, transparent, glossy protective film.

varnish drier   See **drier**.

varnish remover   A material, usually liquid, which softens or dissolves a dry film of varnish so that it can be removed easily.

varnish stain   A varnish which is colored with a transparent material, leaving a colored coating on the surface; has less penetrating power than a true stain.

varved clay   Alternating thin layers of silt (or fine sand) and clay formed by variations in sedimentation during the various seasons of the year, often exhibiting contrasting colors when partially dried.

vase   See **bell, 1**.

vat   See **wat**.

VAT   Abbr. for **vinyl-asbestos tile**.

vault   **1.** A structure based on the principle of the arch, often constructed of masonry; typically consists of an arrangement of arches that cover the space below; also see **barrel vault, cradle vault, cylindrical vault, fan vault, groined vault, lierne vault, rampant vault, ribbed vault, segmental vault, sidewalk vault, stilted vault, tun-**

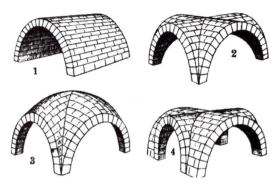

vault: 1, barrel vault; 2, intersecting vault; 3, domed vault; 4, stilted vault

nel vault, wagon vault, Welsh vault. **2.** A burial chamber, especially one under a church. **3.** An underground chamber especially designed for maintaining electrical equipment. **4.** A room for the safekeeping of valuables.

vault bay An area of vaulting limited by two transverse ribs; a **severy**.

vault door A factory-assembled door with a frame and hardware which are designed to protect a storage room against fire and/or burglars.

vaulted **1.** Constructed as a vault. **2.** Covered or closed by a vault.

vaulting **1.** Vaulted work. **2.** Vaults, collectively.

vaulting capital The capital of a pier or colonette intended to support a vault or a rib thereof.

vaulting cell One compartment of a vault which is so planned that one part can be built at a time.

vaulting course A horizontal course made up of the abutments or springers of a vaulted roof.

vaulting shaft A colonette in a membered pier that appears to support a rib in a vault.

vaulting tile A special type of hollow tile, shaped according to the specific job; used in vaulting to reduce the weight of the upper parts of large masses of masonry.

vault light Same as **pavement light**.

vault rib An arch under the soffit of a vault that seems to support it.

vault shell The **web plates** between the ribs of the vault that are, or seem to be, supported by them.

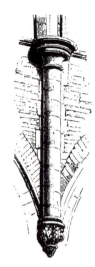

vaulting shaft

V-beam sheeting Similar to corrugated sheeting but formed of a series of angled flat surfaces instead of curved surfaces.

V-brick Vertically perforated brick.

V-cut **1.** Descriptive of lettering, inscribed in stone, in which the cuts are acutely triangular. **2.** Any saw cut or cut in wood which is V-shaped.

VDT Abbr. for "video display terminal."

VDU Abbr. for "visual display unit."

Vebe apparatus An apparatus for measuring the consistency of freshly mixed concrete; determined from a measurement of the time for a vibrated, truncated cone to be transformed into a right cylinder.

vee- See **V-**.

vee-joint See **V-joint**.

vegetable black Same as **lampblack**.

vegetable glue A water-based treated starch which spreads easily; has low strength and poor moisture resistance; esp. used for hanging wallpaper.

vegetable oil An oil extracted from vegetable matter; esp. castor, linseed, safflower, soya, and tung oil; used in paints and plastics.

vehicle In a paint, the liquid in which the pigment is dispersed.

velarium The awning sheltering the seats in an ancient Roman theatre or amphitheatre from sun and rain.

vellum glaze   A semimatte glaze having a satin-like appearance.

velocity head   Of a fluid moving with a given velocity: the equivalent height through which a body must fall to acquire the same velocity.

velodrome   A stadium or arena with a banked track designed for bicycle or motorcycle racing.

velum   Same as **velarium**.

velvet carpet   Carpet woven on a loom in a manner similar to cloth; the layers of pile yarn loops are bound to a layer of jute; then the pile is cut, forming a smooth surface.

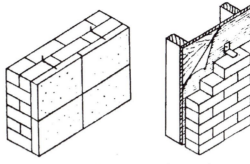

veneered construction   (two types)

velvet carpet

veneered plywood

vendor   **1.** A person or organization who furnishes materials or equipment not fabricated to a special design for the **work, 1**. Also see **supplier**. **2.** One who sells or contracts to sell real property. Also see **purchaser**.

veneer   **1.** A thin sheet of wood that has been sliced, rotary-cut, or sawn from a log; often used as the top one of several layers of plywood serving as a facing that is bonded to a less attractive wood, or as facing on a fire-rated material. **2.** An outside wall facing of brick, stone, etc.; provides a decorative, durable surface but is not load-bearing. **3.** See **brick veneer**.

veneer base   A type of gypsum lath sheeting, usually 4 ft (121.9 cm) wide, available in various thicknesses and lengths; has a gypsum core with a special paper facing which permits **veneer plaster** to be applied.

veneered construction   A reinforced concrete or steel framework (or wood construction) which is faced with a thin external layer of marble, structural glass, or some other facing material.

veneered door   A door made up of either a solid or a hollow core and veneer faces.

veneered plywood   Plywood which is faced with a decorative wood veneer.

veneered wall   A wall of **veneered construction**. For example, a wall having a facing of brick or some other weather-resistant noncombustible material that is securely attached to the backing, but not bonded to it.

veneer plaster   A one-component or two-component mill-mixed gypsum plaster; applied to a maximum overall thickness of about ³⁄₃₂ in. (0.25 cm); has good bond, high strength; is rapidly installed.

veneer tie   A **wall tie** designed to hold a veneer facing to the wall construction.

veneer wall, veneered wall   Any wall having a facing which is attached, but not bonded, to the wall. Also see **brick veneer**.

veneer wall tie   A strip of metal used to tie a facing veneer to the wall which it covers.

Venetian, Venetian mosaic   A type of **terrazzo** topping containing large chips.

Venetian arch   A **pointed arch** in which the intrados and extrados are farther apart at the peak than at the springing line.

Venetian blind   **1.** A blind made of thin horizontal slats or louvers, so connected as to overlap one another when closed, and to show a series of open spaces for the admission of light and air when open; esp. a hanging blind of which the slats are held together by strips of webbing or other flexible material. **2.** Adjustable exterior slatted shutters.

Venetian dentil A type of **dentil**; a notched ornamentation consisting of a series of cubical projections alternating with sloped surfaces.

Venetian door A door having a long narrow window at each side which is similar in form to that of a **Venetian window**.

Venetian mosaic See **Venetian**.

Venetian motif See **Palladian motif**.

Venetian red A red pigment having a high red iron oxide content.

Venetian window, Palladian window, Diocletian window A window of large size, characteristic of neoclassic styles, divided by columns or piers resembling pilasters, into three lights, the middle one of which is usually wider than the others, and is sometimes arched.

vent **1.** A pipe installed to provide a flow of air to or from a drainage system or to provide a circulation of air within such system to protect trap seals from siphonage and back pressure. **2.** A **vent connector**. **3.** A **vent system**. **4.** A **ventilator, 3**. **5.** A stack designed to allow moisture vapor or other gas from inside a building or building system to escape into the atmosphere.

VENT. On drawings, abbr. for "ventilate."

vent cap A fitting which provides protection for the open end of a vent stack, soil stack, or

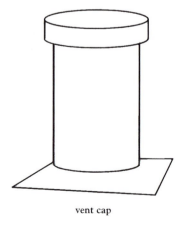

vent cap

waste stack; prevents objects from being dropped down the stack.

vent connector A metal pipe which connects the exhaust of a gas appliance to a chimney.

vented form Formwork constructed to retain the solid constituents of concrete but to permit water and air to escape.

vented wall furnace A recessed heater; a self-contained vented appliance designed for incorporation in, or permanent attachment to, the structure of a building.

vent extension A pipe from the uppermost drainage branch connection through the roof to the atmosphere.

vent flue Same as **vent, 1**.

vent header A **header, 4** (i.e., a horizontal vent pipe) that connects the tops of **vent stacks** or **stack vents** at the header; a single vent pipe extends from the header to the open air above the roof.

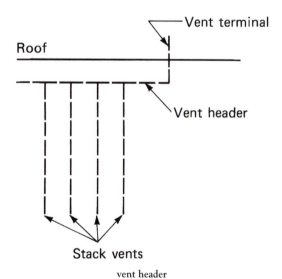

vent header

ventilated ceiling A ceiling containing a multiplicity of **air outlets** covering a significant part of the ceiling area and acting as a whole (not as individual units).

ventilating bead See **draft bead**.

ventilating brick A brick with holes in it to provide for air passage.

ventilating eyebrow Same as **eyebrow**.

ventilating jack A sheet-metal hood over the inlet to a vent pipe to increase the flow of air into the pipe.

ventilation The process of supplying or removing air, by natural or mechanical means, to or from any space; such air may or may not have been conditioned.

ventilator **1.** In a room or building, any device or contrivance used to provide fresh air or expel stale air. See **ridge ventilator, roof ventilator,** and **slit ventilator**. **2.** A framework, pivoted on hinges, in which panes of glass are set; a pivoted **sash. 3.** Same as **ventlight**.

ventilator frame An assembly consisting of two rails and two stiles, designed to support the glass of a pivoted sash (**ventilator, 2**).

venting The replacement of air that is carried out from a stack into the building drain and sewer by waste.

venting loop Same as **loop vent**.

ventlight, night vent, vent sash In a window, a small operable light (pane) with hinges along its upper edge, so that it may be swung open to provide ventilation without opening the entire sash.

vent pipe **1.** A pipe, attached to drainage pipes near one or more traps, which leads to outside air (e.g., a connection to a **vent stack**); admits air or takes air away from the drainage pipes and prevents the trap seals from being broken by air pressure within the drainage pipes. **2.** A pipe connecting a space on the interior of a building with outside air.

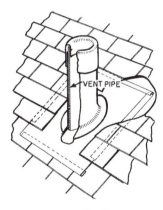

vent pipe, 2

vent sash Same as **ventlight**.

vent stack, main vent A vertical vent pipe installed primarily for the purpose of providing circulation of air to or from any part of the building-drainage system, and to prevent the water seals of the traps from being broken by siphonage.

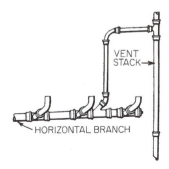

vent stack

vent system A gas vent or chimney, together with a vent connector, that forms a continuous unobstructed passageway from gas-burning equipment to the outdoor air for the purpose of removing vent gases.

veranda, verandah An open porch or balcony, usually covered, that extends along the outside of a building; sometimes called a **piazza**; also see **galerie** and **galería**.

verd antique, verde antique A dark green serpentine rock marked with white veins of calcite; takes a high polish; used for decorative purposes since ancient Rome; sometimes classed as a **marble**.

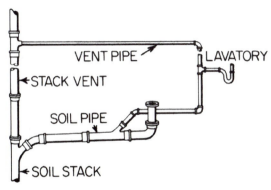

vent pipe, 1

verdigris, aerugo The greenish blue corrosion on copper that has been exposed to air for a long period of time; used as a pigment.

verge **1.** The edge projecting over the gable of a roof. **2.** The shaft of a column; a small ornamental shaft.

vergeboard Same as **bargeboard**.

verge course See **barge course**.

verge fillet A strip of wood nailed to the roof battens over a gable; covers the upper edges of the gable walls.

vermiculated Ornamented by irregular winding, wandering, and wavy lines, as if caused by the movement of worms.

vermiculated mosaic An ancient Roman mosaic of the most delicate and elaborate character; the Roman **opus vermiculatum**; the **tesserae** are arranged in curved, waving lines, as required by the shading of the design.

vermiculated work **1.** A form of masonry surface, incised with wandering, discontinuous grooves resembling worm tracks. **2.** A type of ornamental work consisting of winding frets or knots in mosaic pavements, resembling the tracks of worms.

vermiculated work

vermiculite A natural mica expanded by heat (i.e., **exfoliated**) to form lightweight thermal insulating material, used in the expanded state alone as loose-fill or as aggregate with other materials.

vermiculite concrete Concrete in which the aggregate consists of exfoliated vermiculite.

vermiculite plaster A plaster using very fine exfoliated vermiculite as the aggregate; used as a fire-retardant covering on steel beams, concrete slabs, etc.

vernacular architecture Architecture that makes use of common regional forms and materials at a particular place and time; sometimes includes strong ethnic influences of an immigrant population; usually modest, unassuming, and unpretentious, and often a mixture of traditional and more modern styles or a hybrid of several styles. Houses are often owner-built by people familiar with local materials, regional climatic conditions, and local building customs and techniques, as described under **folk architecture**.

vernier An auxiliary scale sliding against and used in reading a primary scale; the total length of a given number of divisions on a vernier is equal to the total length of one more or one less than the same number of divisions on the primary scale; makes it possible to read a principal scale much closer than one division of that scale.

versurae The side wings of the stagehouse of an ancient Roman theatre.

VERT On drawings, abbr. for "vertical."

vertical **1.** Any upright member, as in a truss. **2.** The direction of gravity, at right angles to the horizon.

vertical angle An angle in a vertical plane.

vertical bar An upright **muntin**.

vertical bond Same as **stack bond**.

vertical circle A graduated disk mounted on an instrument in such a manner that the plane of its graduated surface can be placed in a vertical plane.

vertical curve A smooth parabolic curve in the vertical plane used to connect two grades of different slope to avoid an abrupt transition in passing from one to the other.

vertical cut Same as **plumb cut**.

vertical exit Any path of travel such as a stair, ramp, escalator, or fire escape, serving as an exit from the floors above or below the street floor.

vertical-fiber brick A type of paving brick which is cut with a wire in manufacture; laid with wire-cut side facing up.

vertical firing In a furnace, burners (gas, oil, or pulverized-coal) which are arranged so that the fuel is discharged vertically—either upward from burners below or downward from burners in the top.

vertical-grained   See **edge-grained**.

vertical-log cabin   A **log cabin** whose exterior logs are oriented vertically rather than horizontally; this construction requires more time and greater skill than if the logs are oriented horizontally, as is usual. For an example of construction in which vertical logs are driven in the ground, see **poteaux-en-terre**; also see **poteaux-sur-sole**, a somewhat similar construction where the vertical logs rest on a wood foundation.

vertically pivoted window, reversible window   A window having a **sash** (**ventilator, 2**) which pivots (usually 360°) about a vertical axis at or near its center; when opened, the outside glass surface is conveniently accessible for cleaning.

vertically pivoted window

vertical meeting rail   See **meeting stile**.

vertical pipe   Any pipe or fitting which makes an angle of 45° or less with the vertical.

vertical plane   A plane at right angles to the horizontal plane and within which angles and distances are observed.

vertical-plank door   Same as **battened door**.

vertical pump   A long, slender **multistage pump** designed primarily to pump water from deep wells.

vertical riser diagram   Same as **riser diagram**.

vertical sash   Same as **vertical sliding window**.

vertical saw   A saw which operates in a vertical plane.

vertical section   A drawing depicting a view that would be seen if a vertical plane were cut through the object observed.

vertical siding   A type of exterior wall **cladding** attached to the wall in a vertical orientation; most often consists of wide, upright boards that have a tongue along one vertical edge and a groove along the opposite edge; also see **siding** and **tongue-and-groove joint**.

vertical siding

vertical sliding window   A window having one or more sashes which move only in the vertical direction; they are held in various open positions by means of friction or a ratchet device instead of being supported by sash balances or counterweights.

vertical slip form   A **form** which is jacked vertically and continuously during the placing of concrete.

vertical spring-pivot hinge   A spring hinge for a door which is mortised into the heel of the door; the door is fastened to the floor and **door head** with pivots.

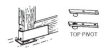

vertical spring-pivot hinge

vertical tiling   Tile which is hung vertically on the face of a wall; provides protection against moisture.

vertical tray conveyors   A vertical conveying system which is capable of carrying trays or boxes.

vertical-vision-light door   Same as **narrow-light door**.

very-high-output fluorescent lamp   A **rapid-start fluorescent lamp** designed to operate on higher current than a **high-output**

fluorescent lamp, providing a corresponding increase in light flux (lumens) per unit length of lamp.

vesica piscis A long and sometimes pointed oval form; a **mandorla**.

vesica piscis

vestiary A room for the keeping of vestments, garments, or clothes; a wardrobe.

vestibule An **anteroom** or small foyer leading into a larger space.

vest-pocket park A park which is built on a small plot of land.

vestry, revestry A chamber in a church, near the sanctuary, for the storage of the utensils used in a service and for the robes of the clergy and choir.

VG Abbr. for "vertical grain."

V-groove See **quirk, 2**.

V-gutter A **valley gutter**.

vibrated concrete Concrete compacted by vibration during and after placing.

vibrating pile driver Same as **sonic pile driver**.

vibrating roller A roller which has a motor-driven eccentric for compacting soils.

vibrating screed A machine designed to level a freshly poured concrete slab and also to act as a **vibrator**.

vibration As applied to concrete, see **concrete vibration**.

vibration isolator A resilient support for machinery, piping, ductwork, etc., which may act as a source of vibration; designed to reduce the amount of vibration transmitted to the building structure.

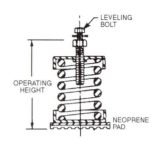

vibration isolator (coil-spring type)

vibration isolator (bonded-elastomeric type)

vibration limit The time required for fresh concrete to harden sufficiently to prevent its becoming mobile when subjected to vibration.

vibration meter An apparatus for measuring the displacement, velocity, or acceleration of a vibrating body.

vibration mount Same as **vibration isolator**.

vibration service lamp An incandescent lamp, having a tungsten filament, which is designed to withstand mechanical vibration to a greater degree than a general service lamp.

vibrator An oscillating, power-operated machine used to agitate fresh concrete so as to eliminate gross voids including entrapped air (but not entrained air) and to produce intimate contact with form surfaces and embedded materials.

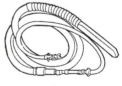

vibrator

vicarage In England, the home or residence of a vicar.

Vicat apparatus A penetration device used in the testing of hydraulic cements and similar materials to measure their consistency and their initial and final setting times.

vice See **vis**.

vice stair   A **screw stair**.

Victorian architecture   **1.** The Revival and Eclectic architecture in 19th century Great Britain, named after the reign of Queen Victoria (1837–1901); also its American counterpart. Many architectural historians avoid the term *Victorian architecture*, considering the adjective "Victorian" merely as descriptive of an age that encompassed a number of specific exuberant, ornate, and highly decorative architectural styles. **2.** A loose term that sometimes covers three picturesque phases of architecture in America: *Early Victorian* (1840–1860), *High Victorian* (1860–1880), and *Late Victorian* (1880–1890) and beyond; the adjective "Victorian" is descriptive of an age that encompassed a number of specific exuberant, ornate, and highly decorative architectural styles, such as High Victorian Italianate (1860–1885), High Victorian Gothic (1860–1890), Second Empire style (1855–1890), Stick style (1860–1885), Shingle style (1880–1890), Victorian Romanesque (1870–1900), Gingerbread Folk architecture (1870–1910), and Queen Anne style (1870–1910). The adjectives *Victorian* or *High Victorian* are sometimes applied to Gothic Revival and Italianate style to indicate their later, more detailed, and more elaborate phases.

Victorian Gothic   Same as **High Victorian Gothic**; also see **Gothic Revival**.

Victorian Queen Anne style   See **Queen Anne style**.

Victorian Romanesque   An ornate outgrowth of the Richardsonian Romanesque style from which it differs both in the use of color and in the texture of masonry, and in being less exact in adapting Romanesque style forms; popular from about 1870 to 1900; usually characterized by: rock-faced stone or decorative stonework, often polychromed; brick of different colors; panels of terra-cotta; semicircular arches or compound arches similar to those in the Romanesque style; pilastered arcades at ground level; steeply pitched wall gables; multicurved parapets; window heads framed by masonry arches; doors set within concentric rounded masonry arches or with **voussoirs** of more than one color.

Vierendeel truss, Vierendeel girder   An open-web **truss** having verticals which are rigidly connected to the top and bottom chords but without diagonals.

viga   In Spanish Colonial architecture and its derivatives, a log that has been stripped of its bark and unhewn; used as one of a number of roof beams spanning the width of a building between opposite adobe walls; usually evenly spaced along the length of the walls; often round in cross section. Typically, the vigas are overlaid with small straight saplings that are covered by a reed matting; this combination supports a roof of dried mud or adobe.

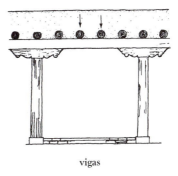

vigas

vignette   See **vinette**.

vihara   A Buddhist or Jain monastery in Indian architecture.

villa   **1.** In the Roman and Renaissance periods, a country seat with its dwelling, outbuildings, and gardens, often quite elaborate. **2.** In modern times, a detached suburban or country house of some pretension.

village green   An open space or public park, once traditionally located at the center of a village; still found in many towns today; also see **common**.

Villa style   See **Italianate style**.

vimana   **1.** A Hindu temple, mainly of the Deccan and southern India. **2.** The sanctuary in such a temple containing a cell in which a deity is enshrined.

vine   A plant whose stem is not self-supporting.

vinette, trayle, vignette   An ornament of running vine scrolls with grape clusters and leafwork.

vinyl   A thermoplastic compound made from polymerized vinyl chloride, vinylide chloride, or vinyl acetate; includes some plastics made from styrene and other chemicals.

vinette

vinyl-asbestos tile   A resilient, semiflexible floor tile; composed of asbestos fibers, ground limestone, plasticizers, pigments, and a polyvinyl chloride resin binder; has good wearing qualities, high grease resistance, and relatively good resilience.

vinyl composition tile   A resilient floor covering which is composed of a binder (one or more resins, such as vinyl chloride, compounded with suitable plasticizer and stabilizers) with fillers, and pigment.

vinyl flooring   A resilient floor covering in sheet or tile form composed of a vinyl plastic binder, mineral fillers, and pigment.

vinyl paint   A **water-based paint** containing **vinyl**.

vinyl tile   A floor tile composed principally of polyvinyl chloride but also containing mineral fillers, pigments, plasticizers, and stabilizers; does not require waxing; usually set in mastic over a wood or concrete subfloor.

Virginia house   A comparatively simple timber-framed wood house used during the 17th century, originating in the Chesapeake Bay area of the Commonwealth of Virginia; supported by posts sunk in the ground rather than by a foundation. The exterior walls were covered with a wall cladding of hand-split clapboards, which provided additional structural strength.

Virginia rail fence   Same as **zigzag fence**.

vis, vice, vise   A spiral staircase generally of stone, whose steps wind around a central shaft or newel; a **screw stair**.

viscometer   A device for determining viscosity; esp. used to measure the viscosity of slurries, including fresh concrete.

viscosimeter   Same as **viscometer**.

viscosity   The internal frictional resistance exhibited by a fluid in resisting a force which tends to cause the liquid to flow.

viscous filter   A filter for cleaning air; dirt, carried by the air, impinges on a surface covered with a viscous fluid or oil, to which the dirt particles adhere.

vise   **1.** A gripping tool, fixed or portable, used to hold an object firmly while work is performed on it; has movable jaws, similar to a clamp, which are brought together by a screw or lever. **2.** See **vis**.

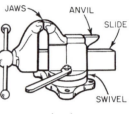

vise, 1

visibility   **1.** The quality or state of being perceivable by the eye. **2.** The distance at which an object out-of-doors can be just perceived by the eye. **3.** The size of a standard test object, observed under standardized viewing conditions, which has the same threshold as the given object.

vision cloth   A curtain on the stage of a theatre which has a gauze or scrim inset; if an actor (or scene) behind the inset is illuminated, he is visible to the audience as one appearing in a vision.

vision light   **1.** A window glazed with clear glass for viewing. **2.** A viewing window in a fire-rated door; usually **wire glass** must be used and the dimensions of the glass are limited by code.

vision-light door   A door having one small viewing window in the upper portion only, usually located on the vertical center line of the door.

visionproof glass   See **obscure glass**.

visitá   In Spanish Colonial architecture in the American Southwest, a chapel in which services were conducted by a visiting *padre* because it served too few people to have its own priest.

visor roof   A **pent roof, 1** that extends only along one face of a building, usually the façade.

vista   A usually unobstructed view into the distance; often given scale by the receding perspective of a road or a row of trees.

visual acuity   A measure of the ability to distinguish fine details; the reciprocal of the angular size of critical detail which is just large enough to be seen.

visual angle The angle which an object or detail subtends at the point of observation; usually measured in minutes of arc.

visual field The angular extent of space which can be perceived when the head and eyes are kept fixed.

visual inspection Inspection by examination without the use of testing apparatus.

visual photometer See **photometer**.

VIT On drawings, abbr. for "vitreous."

vitreous Descriptive of that degree of vitrification evidenced by low water absorption; generally signifies less than 0.3% absorption (except for floor and wall tile and low-voltage electrical porcelain, for which it signifies less than 3.0% absorption).

vitreous enamel See **porcelain enamel**.

vitreous sand Same as **smalt**.

vitrification Of a clay product, the condition resulting when kiln temperatures are sufficient to fuse grains and close the surface pores, making the mass impervious.

vitrified Same as **vitreous**.

vitrified brick Brick which has been glazed so that it is impervious to water and has a high resistance to chemical corrosion.

vitrified-clay pipe Pipe manufactured of an earthenware material which is glazed so that it is impervious to water and has a high resistance to chemical corrosion; in the U.S.A., sometimes used for house sewer pipes and underground drainage.

vitrified sewer pipe See **vitrified-clay pipe**.

Vitruvian scroll, Vitruvian wave A common motif in classical ornament: a series of scrolls connected by a wave-like band; also called a **wave scroll** or **running dog**.

Vitruvian scroll

vivarium An enclosure for raising animals and keeping them under observation.

V-joint, vee-joint A recessed masonry joint, formed in mortar by the use of a **V**-shaped metal tool.

V-notch A **notch**, in the shape of the letter **V**, cut into a log or timber near one of its ends; forms a rigid joint when mated with another appropriately notched log or timber in log-cabin or log-house construction.

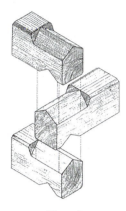

V-notch

void-cement ratio The ratio of volume of air plus water to the volume of cement.

void ratio In a soil mass, or the like, the ratio of the volume of the void space to the volume of the solid particles.

voids **1.** In cement paste, mortar, or concrete, the air spaces between and within pieces of aggregate. **2.** Volumes of air not occupied by the solid material of a soil; voids usually are partially filled with air and water.

void-solid ratio The proportion of window and door openings to wall surface area in the exterior wall of a building.

VOL On drawings, abbr. for "volume."

volatile Descriptive of a substance which passes off easily as a gas or vapor, evaporating quickly.

volatile thinner A **thinner** which evaporates especially rapidly, reducing the viscosity of a paint, adhesive, etc., without altering its other properties.

volcanic tuff See **tuff**.

volt In electric systems the unit of potential difference or electromotive force; when applied

voltage

across a resistance of 1 ohm, will result in a current flow of 1 ampere.

voltage Of an electric circuit, the greatest root-mean-square difference of potential between any two conductors of the circuit.

voltage drop The difference in electromotive force between any two points in an electric circuit.

voltage regulator An automatic electric control device whose output provides a constant voltage supply, even though the line voltage at its input may vary.

voltage-to-ground **1.** In a grounded electric circuit, the voltage between the given conductor and that point of the circuit which is grounded. **2.** In an ungrounded circuit, the greatest voltage between the given conductor and any other conductor in the circuit.

voltage transformer A transformer whose primary is connected to a medium-voltage source and whose secondary is connected to a load at lower voltage.

volt-ampere The product of 1 volt times 1 ampere; in direct-current circuits, equal to 1 watt; in alternating-current circuits, equal to one unit of "apparent power."

voltmeter An instrument for measuring the voltage drop between any two points in an electric circuit.

volume batching Measuring the constituent materials for mortar or concrete by volume, rather than by weight.

volume method A method of estimating probable total construction cost by multiplying the adjusted gross building volume by a predetermined cost per unit of volume.

volume strain See **bulk strain**.

volumeter **1.** An instrument for measuring the volume of a gas or liquid. **2.** A type of **flushometer**.

volumetric absorption The ratio of the volume of a liquid, that is absorbed by a mass to the volume of the mass.

volume yield See **yield, 1**.

voluntary standard A standard with which there is no obligation to comply, either legally or *de facto*.

volute **1.** A spiral scroll, as on Ionic, Corinthian, or Composite capitals, or on consoles, etc. **2.** A stair crook having an easement with a spiral section of stair rail.

volute, 1

vomitorium A **vomitory** in an ancient Roman theatre or amphitheatre.

vomitory An entrance or opening, usually one of a series, which pierces a bank of seats in a theatre, stadium, or the like.

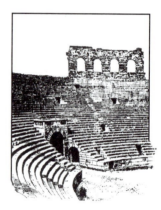

vomitories

voussoir A wedge-shaped masonry unit in an arch or vault whose converging sides are cut as radii of one of the centers of the arch or vault.

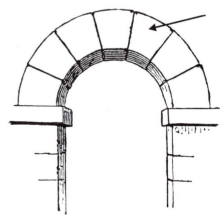

voussoirs

voussoir brick Same as **arch brick**.

VP On drawings, abbr. for **vent pipe**.

V-roof A **peaked roof, gable roof**, or the like.

VS **1.** On drawings, abbr. for "versus." **2.** Abbr. for **vent stack**. **3.** Abbr. for "vapor seal."

V-shaped joint, V-joint, V-tooled joint **1.** A horizontal V-shaped mortar joint made with a

V-shaped joint, 1

steel jointing tool; very effective in resisting the penetration of rain. **2.** A joint formed by two adjacent wood boards, in the same plane, which have faces with chamfered edges.

V-tool A **gouge** with a V-shaped cutting edge; see also **parting tool**.

V-tooled joint See **V-shaped joint**.

vug A pit-like natural cavity in stone, usually between a small fraction of an inch and a few inches in diameter; may be lined with crystals or layers of mineral materials; most common in dolomite, limestone, and marble.

vulcanization An irreversible process during which a rubber compound, through a change in its chemical structures, becomes less plastic, more resistant to swelling by organic liquids, and more elastic (or the elastic properties are extended over a greater range of temperature).

vys See **vis**.

vyse See **vis**.

W

W **1.** Abbr. for **watt**. **2.** On drawings, abbr. for "west." **3.** On drawings, abbr. for "width."

W/ On drawings, abbr. for "with."

WAF Abbr. for "wiring around frame."

wafer check valve (WCV) See **butterfly check valve**.

waffle See **dome, 2**.

waffle floor See **waffle slab**.

waffle slab A concrete slab which is reinforced by ribs in two directions, forming a waffle-like pattern.

Wagner fineness The fineness of a material, as determined by the Wagner **turbidimeter** apparatus and procedure; for a material such as portland cement, expressed as the total surface area in square centimeters per gram.

wagon ceiling A ceiling of semicylindrical shape, as a **barrel vault**.

wagon drill An assembly for positioning and handling a pneumatic drill; consists of a mast with a carrier for the drill and a wheeled carriage for moving and positioning the unit.

wagon-headed Having a continuous round arched vault or ceiling, as in barrel vaulting.

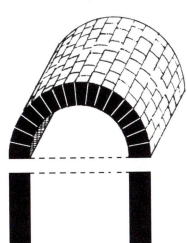

wagon-headed: vault

wagonhead vault A **barrel vault**.

wagon roof See **barrel roof, 1**.

wagon shed, wagon house A structure, separate from a main building such as a church, once used as a temporary shelter for horse-drawn wagons before the use of automobiles; usually had at least one open side so that the wagons could be driven directly into the shed without having to open doors.

wagon stage A stage mounted on wheels or rollers, usually powered; moves horizontally for the quick change of an entire theatrical setting.

wagon vault A semicylindrical vault; a **barrel vault**.

wagtail See **parting slip**.

wainscot In current usage, a decorative or protective facing, such as wood paneling, on the lower part of an interior wall or partition. In the past, this term commonly referred to the sheathing applied over an entire interior wall surface. Also see **falling wainscot**.

wainscot cap The molding which finishes the upper edge of a **wainscot**.

wainscot oak Quartersawn oak, often specially selected, used in wainscoting.

waist The narrowest thickness of the slab in concrete stairs.

waiver of lien An instrument by which a person or organization who has or may have a right of mechanic's lien against the property of another relinquishes such right. Also see **mechanic's lien** and **release of lien**.

wale, waler, whaler A horizontal timber or beam used to brace or support an upright member, as sheeting, formwork for concrete, etc. (*See illustration p. 992.*)

walk A pedestrian path or passageway.

walk-in To imbed panels of insulation in hot bitumen or adhesive by walking on them immediately after application.

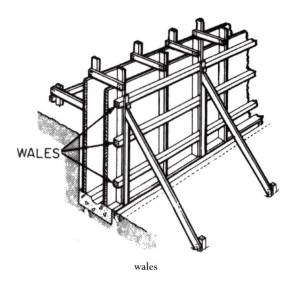

wales

walk-in box   A refrigerated cooler or freezer large enough for one or more persons to enter.

walking beam pivot   A type of retractable **center pivot**.

walking line, line of travel   The usual path taken in climbing stairs, approximately 18 in. (46 cm) from the center line of the handrail.

walk-out basement   Same as **American basement**.

walk-up   **1.** An apartment building or commercial building without an elevator. **2.** An apartment or office above the entry floor in such a building.

walkway   **1.** A passage or lane designated for pedestrian traffic, esp. one connecting various parts of an industrial plant or along roofing. **2.** A garden footpath.

wall   **1.** A structure which serves to enclose or subdivide a building, usually presenting a continuous surface except where penetrated by doors, windows, and the like. **2.** A **rampart**. **3.** A **retaining wall**. For specific types, see **battered wall, bearing wall, blank wall, blind wall, boarded wall, board wall, breakaway wall, cavity wall, common wall, composite wall, counterwall, curtain wall, dead wall, dry wall, dry-stacked surface-bonded wall, fire wall, gable-end wall, hollow wall, load-bearing wall, masonry-bonded hollow wall, mud wall, non-load-bearing wall, partition, party wall, retaining wall, serpentine wall, spandrel wall, springing wall, street wall, structural wall, sustaining wall, veneered wall**.

wall anchor   A wrought-iron clamp, often decorative, on the exterior side of a brick building wall that is connected to the opposite wall by a **tie rod** to prevent the walls from spreading apart; same as **anchor, 10**.

wall arcade   A **blind arcade** used as an ornamental dressing to a wall.

wall base   See **base, 2**.

wall beam   A metal member which acts as a **beam anchor**.

wall bearer   See **bearer**.

wall-bearing partition   A **load-bearing partition**.

wall bed, recess bed   A bed which folds and stands vertically when not in use, usually swung into a closet or recess; esp. used in apartment houses.

wallboard   A rigid sheet composed of wood-pulp, gypsum, or other materials; may be fastened to the frame of a building to provide an interior surface finish; the long edges of the board usually are tapered to provide easy treatment of the joints when board is erected. Also see **dry wall**.

wall box, beam box, wall frame   **1.** A frame or box which is set into a brick, masonry, or stone wall to receive a timber beam or joist. **2.** In electrical wiring, a metal box which is set in a wall for switches, receptacles, etc.

wall bracket   **1.** A bracket which is fixed to a wall and used to support a structural member. **2.** A bracket used to support a scaffold. **3.** A bracket used to support piping, an electrical component, or a lighting fixture.

wall chase   See **chase, 1**.

wall cladding   A nonstructural material used as the exterior covering for the walls of a building; see **cladding**.

wall clamp   A brace or tie to hold together two walls, or the two parts of a double wall.

wall cleanout   A **cleanout, 1** mounted on a wall; used where a drainage line is concealed behind a partition; a removable panel provides access to the cleanout.

wall clip   A bracket that is used to anchor a wall.

wall column   A column which is embedded, or partially embedded, in a wall.

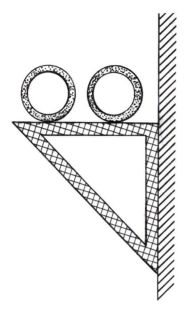

wall bracket, 3

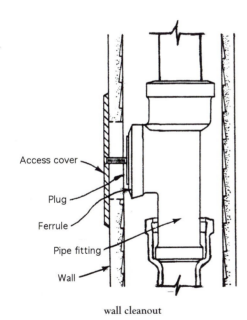

Access cover

Plug

Ferrule

Pipe fitting

Wall

wall cleanout

wall coping See **coping**.

wall covering Any material or assembly which is used as a wall facing and is not an integral part of the wall.

wall crane A **crane** having a horizontal arm (with or without a trolley); supported from a sidewall or line of columns of a building; has a maximum swing of a half circle.

wall dormer A **dormer** whose face is integral with the face of the wall below, breaking the line at the cornice of a building.

through-the-cornice **wall dormer**

wall flange Same as **wall clip**.

wall form A concrete form which is erected to provide the necessary shape, support, and finish for a concrete wall.

wall frame See **wall box, 1**.

wall furnace A self-contained, vented furnace, complete with air grilles, which is permanently attached to a wall; furnishes heated air directly to the surrounding space, either by gravity or by a mechanical blower.

wall furring Strips of wood or metal, masonry tiles, etc., applied to the rough surface of a wall so as to provide a flat plane upon which a surface material, or assembly, such as lath and plaster, wood paneling, wainscoting, etc., may be installed. Also see **furring**.

wall gable A portion of a wall that projects above the roof line in the form of a **gable**.

wall garden   A garden of plants set in the joints of a stone wall, where soil pockets have previously been arranged.

wall grille   A perforated plate, casting, molding, or framed bars or rods to cover a wall opening, radiator enclosure, etc., restricting vision but permitting the flow of air.

wall guard   A protective, resilient strip which is applied to the surface of a wall (esp. along a corridor) to prevent its being damaged by carts, wagons, and the like.

wall handrail   A **rail, 1** similar to a handrail, but attached to a wall adjacent to a stair, paralleling the pitch of the flight.

wall hanger   A stirrup or bracket built into a masonry wall to carry the end of a horizontal member.

wall height   The vertical distance to the top of a wall, measured from the foundation wall, or from a girder or other immediate support of such wall.

wall hook   **1.** A special large nail or hook used as a **beam anchor** or for holding a **wall plate** fixed in position. **2.** Same as **wall iron**.

wall-hung water closet   A **water closet** mounted on a wall, so that no part of it touches the floor.

wall-hung water closet

walling   **1.** Walls collectively. **2.** Materials for constructing walls.

wall iron   A hook or bracket fixed to a masonry wall to hold downspouts, lightning rods, etc.; a **wall hook, 2**.

wall line   A line along the exterior face of a wall.

wall opening   According to OSHA: an opening at least 30 in. (76.2 cm) high and 18 in. (45.8 cm) wide, in any wall or partition, through which persons may fall, such as a chute opening.

wall outlet   An electrical receptacle, whose face is flush with a wall, into which a plug is inserted.

wall panel   A **panel wall**.

wallpaper   Paper, or paper-like material, usually decorated in colors, which is pasted or otherwise affixed to walls or ceilings of rooms.

wall piece   See **wall plate, 2**.

wall plate   A horizontal member (such as a timber) across a timber-framed, masonry, or concrete wall to carry and distribute the load imposed by members that support the roof.

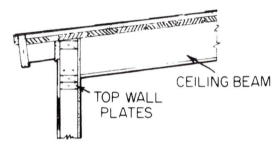

CEILING BEAM

TOP WALL PLATES

wall plate, 1

wall plug   **1.** Same as **wall outlet**. **2.** A **plug, 1**.

wall pocket   Same as **wall box**.

wall post   **1.** A post which is next to a wall, in a partition. **2.** A post, fixed to a wall, against which a fence terminates, or from which a gate may be hung. **3.** A post that supports a **wall plate**.

wall rail   Same as **wall handrail**.

wall rib   In medieval vaulting, a longitudinal rib against an exterior wall of a vaulting compartment.

wall shaft   A colonette supported on a corbel or bracket which appears to support a rib of vaulting.

wall siding   See **siding**.

wall sign   **1.** A sign mounted on, or fastened to, a wall. **2.** In some codes in the U.S.A., a sign attached to the exterior wall of a building and projecting not more than 15 in. therefrom.

wall socket   A **wall outlet**.

wall spacer   A metal tie for holding a concrete form in position until the poured concrete has set.

wall string, wall stringer   A stair string set against a wall.

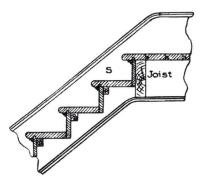

wall string *S*

wall tie In masonry, a type of anchor (usually a metal strip) used to secure facing to a backup wall or to connect the two withes of a cavity wall; mortared into joints during setting. Also see **butterfly wall tie, cavity wall tie, veneer wall tie.**

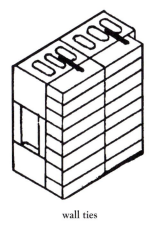

wall ties

wall tile A glazed **tile, 1** used as a facing on a wall.

wall tower A tower forming an essential part of a defensive wall, especially one having a series of towers to enhance its fortification.

wall tracery **Tracery** that is false in the sense that there is no associated **openwork**; instead, the tracery is shown in relief on a solid wall.

wall vent A ventilation device for a wall cavity, crawl space, or attic.

wall-washing Lighting a wall by luminaires located close to the plane of the wall.

wall-wash luminaire Any **luminaire** located adjacent to a vertical surface on which its light is principally directed.

wall tower

walnut A tough, dark brown-to-black wood having high strength; does not split easily; has a fine-to-coarse open grain; takes a high polish.

wane A rounded edge or bark along an edge or at a corner of a piece of lumber; usually caused by sawing too near the surface of the log.

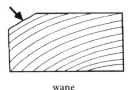

wane

ward 1. A metal obstruction in a lock; intended to prevent entrance or rotation of a key that does not fit the lock. 2. The outer defenses of a castle. Also see **bailey.** 3. A division in a hospital.

wardrobe, garderobe A room for the storage of garments.

warehouse A building designed for the storage of various goods.

warehouse set The partial hydration of cement stored for periods of time and exposed to atmospheric moisture.

warm-air furnace A self-contained unit for heating air which is circulated through it; the air either is conveyed through ducts or is discharged directly into the space being heated.

warm-air heating system A warm-air heating plant consisting of a fuel-burning furnace, enclosed in a casing, from which the heated air is distributed to various rooms of the building through ducts.

warm-setting adhesive An **intermediate-temperature-setting adhesive**.

warning pipe An **overlow pipe** whose outlet is conspicuous, so that discharge from it can be observed readily.

warp **1.** See **carpet warp**. **2.** Distortion in shape of a parallel plane surface; in lumber, usually results from a change in moisture content.

warped Said of thin-bedded rock, such as flagging, having a natural curved or a rippled finish similar to warped wood.

warping The deviation of a surface from its original or intended shape, as a concrete slab or wall surface; esp. caused by moisture and temperature differentials.

warping joint A joint permitting warping of pavement slabs when moisture and/or temperature differentials occur in the pavement.

warp wire In **wire cloth**, a wire running parallel to the length of the cloth.

warranty See **guarantee**.

warranty deed A written instrument conveying real property, in which the grantor makes legally binding representations concerning the quality of his title and its freedom from encumbrances.

Warren truss, Warren girder A form of **truss** having parallel upper and lower chords, with connecting members which are inclined, forming a series of approximately equilateral triangles.

wash **1.** The sloping upper surface of a building member, as a **coping** or sill, to carry away water; said of any other member serving such a function. See also **drip cap**. **2.** A manner of applying water color in a rendering. Also see **wall-washing**.

washable Capable of being washed repeatedly without significant erosion and without change in appearance or functional characteristics.

washable distemper A distemper which contains an emulsified oil, giving washable characteristics to a distemper coating.

washbasin Same as **lavatory, 1**.

washboard Same as **baseboard**.

wash boring The drilling of test hole in the ground to obtain soil samples that are brought up along with a mixture of water.

wash coat A very thin, semitransparent coat of paint; applied as a preliminary coating on a surface; acts as a **sealer** or **guide coat**.

washed finish See **rustic finish**.

washer A flat ring, usually thin, of metal, rubber, or other material, depending on its use; used to prevent leakage, to provide insulation; used as the bearing surface under the head of a fastener, such as a bolt, to assure tightness, relieve friction, improve stress distribution, or span large clearance holes.

FLAT WASHER   SLIT LOCK WASHER   SHAKEPROOF WASHER

washers

wash fountain A large lavatory-type vessel which supplies tempered water for group washing of hands and faces.

wash light Same as **wall-wash luminaire**.

wash primer A primer containing polyvinyl butyral, zinc chromate, alcohol, and phosphoric acid; applied in a thin film to bare steel, causes etching of the metal, thereby promoting adhesion of the subsequent coat.

washroom A room providing facilities for washing; a lavatory or toilet room.

wash water, flush water Water carried on a **truck mixer** in a special tank for flushing the interior of the concrete mixer after discharge of the concrete.

waste **1.** The discharge from any fixture, appliance, area, or appurtenance which contains no fecal matter. **2.** See **sanitary waste**. **3.** Waste material such as **garbage, refuse, rubbish,** and **trash**.

waste compactor   See **compactor, 2**.

waste-disposal unit   An electric-motor-driven device for grinding waste food and disposing of it through the plumbing drainage pipes; may be installed without a **grease trap** in a residence.

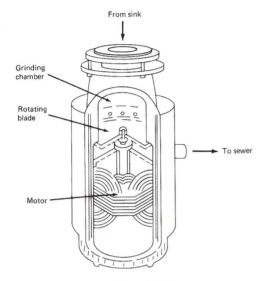

waste-disposal unit

waste-food grinder   Same as **waste-disposal unit**.

waste fuel   A fuel which is a waste by-product of some industrial process.

waste-heat recovery   The use of waste heat in a building to preheat cold water before it is fed into a hot-water heater.

waste material   See **garbage, refuse, rubbish**, and **trash**.

waste pipe   A drain pipe which receives the waterborne discharge from plumbing fixtures other than those fixtures receiving fecal matter; also see **indirect waste pipe**.

waste plug   A tapered device used to prevent the flow of water through the drain of a wash-basin or the like.

waster   A **second** or **cull**.

waste receptacle   A container for holding or facilitating the removal of refuse.

waste stack   A vertical pipe which conveys liquid wastes which are free of fecal matter.

waste vent   Same as **stack vent, 1**.

waste well   Same as **leaching cesspool**.

wasting   In stonecutting, splitting off the surplus stone with a wedge-shaped chisel (called a **point**), or with a pick, so that the faces of the stone are reduced to nearly plane surfaces; **dabbing**.

wat, vat   Buddhist monastery in Cambodia.

watching loft   **1.** Same as **excubitorium, 1. 2.** A lookout in a tower, steeple, or other high building.

watchman's system   An approved installation of equipment used to record the rounds of a watchman.

watch turret   Same as **bartizan**.

water absorption   Of a test specimen, the increase in weight after immersion in water for a specified time, expressed as a percentage of its dry weight; usually the test conditions are specified.

water analysis   A chemical analysis of the dissolved materials in water, including a determination of the amount of suspended solids and the pH value.

water back   A system of pipes or a reservoir of water at the back of a fireplace, or the like, to utilize its heat in providing a supply of hot water.

water bar, weather bar   A wood or metal strip which is fixed to the sill of an external door or a window to resist the penetration of water.

water-base paint   A paint capable of being thinned or diluted with water; for example, casein paint, latex paint, vinyl paint.

water blasting   The cutting or abrading of an exterior surface by a stream of water ejected from a nozzle at high velocity.

waterboard   An obsolete term for **watertable, 1**.

waterborne preservative   A water-soluble chemical used to treat wood for protection against decay and insects.

water cement   Same as **hydraulic cement**.

water-cement ratio   The ratio of the amount of water, exclusive only of that absorbed by the aggregates, to the amount of cement in a concrete or mortar mixture.

water channel, condensation channel   A trough-like depression in the top of the interior sill of a glazed opening to collect and drain away condensed moisture which forms on the interior face of the glass.

water check   Same as **upstand**.

water-checked casement A casement having grooves cut under the sill and meeting stile to prevent capillary movement of water.

water closet, W.C. **1.** A plumbing fixture used to receive human excrement and to discharge it through a waste pipe, using water as a conveying medium. **2.** A room containing a **water closet, 1**.

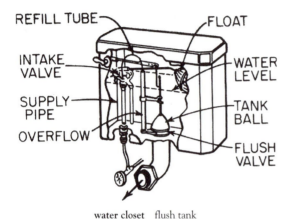

water closet   flush tank

water content Same as **moisture content**.

water cooler Same as **drinking-water cooler**.

water-cooling tower A structure, usually on the roof of a building, over which water is circulated, so as to cool it evaporatively by contact with the air.

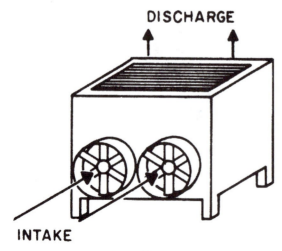

water-cooling tower

water crack In plastering, a fine crack in a coat applied before the previous coat has dried, or in a coat having excessive water in the plaster.

water curtain A **deluge sprinkler system** above a theatre proscenium.

water deactivation See **deactivation**.

water distributing pipe A pipe, in a building, which conveys water from the water service pipe to plumbing fixtures or other water outlets.

water filter A device for the removal of, or reduction of, suspended solid contaminents in water by passing the water through a porous medium.

water filtration See **filtration**.

waterflow-alarm In a fire **sprinkler system**, an alarm which is actuated when the flow through the sprinkler system is in excess of a predetermined maximum value.

water fountain **1.** See **architectural fountain**. **2.** See **drinking fountain**. **3.** See **wash fountain**.

water gain See **bleeding, 4**.

water garden A garden making use of pools in which aquatic and other water-loving plants are grown.

water gauge A **manometer** filled with water.

water-gel explosive One of a wide variety of materials used for blasting; contains substantial proportions of water and a high proportion of ammonium nitrate, some of which is in solution in the water.

water hammer **1.** In water lines, a loud thumping noise that results from a sudden stoppage of the flow. **2.** In steam lines, water of condensation that is picked up and carried through the steam main at high velocity; when direction of the flow changes, the water particles hit the pipe walls, emitting a banging noise.

water-hammer arrester A device installed in a piping system to absorb hydraulic shock waves and eliminate **water hammer, 1**.

water-hardened Said of a metal that has been quenched in water after being heated to a critical temperature.

water heater A device for heating water for domestic use, usually supplied at a temperature in the range between 120°F and 140°F (approx. 50°C and 60°C).

water joint 1. A joint in a stone pavement where the stones are intentionally placed slightly higher than elsewhere; the raised surface is intended to prevent the settling of water in the joints. 2. A **saddle joint, 1**.

water leaf 1. In early Roman and Greek ornamentation, a type of lotus leaf or an ivy motif. 2. Similar to **water leaf, 1** but divided symmetrically by a prominent rib; also called a **Lesbian leaf. 3.** Late 12th cent. capital with a large leaf at each angle, broad, smooth, curving up toward the abacus corner and then curling inward.

water leaf, 1: *left,* simple; *right,* enriched

water-leaf capital Same as **water leaf, 3**.

water level A simple device for establishing two points at the same elevation; consists of a water-filled flexible hose (from which air has been excluded) with a piece of glass tubing at each end; the water level is observed through the glass tubing.

water-level control A control used to maintain the water level in a boiler to reasonably close limits; use of the control makes it unnecessary to add large quantities of replacement water at any one time.

water lime Hydraulic lime or hydraulic cement; will set under water.

waterline Inside a cistern, the highest water level to which the ball valve should be adjusted to shut off.

water main A main supply pipe in a system for conveying water for public or community use, controlled by a public authority.

water meter A mechanical device used to measure the volume of water passing through a pipe or outlet.

water mill A mill, 3 that is powered, by running water, such as a stream; also see **tidemill**.

water motor alarm In a fire **sprinkler system**, a hydraulically actuated device that provides a local audible alarm when water flows through the **wet alarm valve**.

water outlet 1. An opening for the discharge of water that supplies a plumbing fixture, boiler, or heating system, or any device or piece of equipment which is not part of a plumbing system but requires water to operate. 2. An opening through which water is discharged into the atmosphere.

waterproof In the building trades, descriptive of any material or construction which is impervious to water.

waterproofing A material, usually a membrane or applied compound, used to make a surface impervious to water.

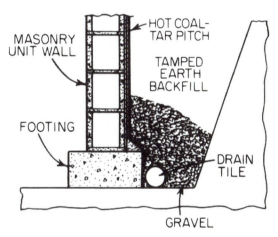

waterproofing applied to masonry wall units

waterproofing compound Any applied material which imparts the quality of **waterproofing** to a surface.

waterproof paper A water-impervious paper; usually a synthetic resin has been added to the pulp or mixed with the sizing.

waterproof portland cement A cement interground with a water-repellent material such a stearate (e.g., sodium or aluminum); reduces capillary water transmission under little or no pressure but does not completely stop water-vapor transmission.

water pump A device for raising fresh water from a lower elevation where it is available, to a higher elevation where it can be used; where electricity is not available, pumps are often powered by windmills.

water putty A type of wood filler; a powder which becomes putty-like when mixed with water; used to fill small holes and cracks in wood.

water ramp A series of pools, arranged so that water flows from one to another.

water-reducing admixture **1.** An **admixture** which either (a) increases the slump of freshly mixed concrete or mortar without increasing the water content or (b) maintains the slump with a reduced amount of water due to factors other than air entrainment. **2.** In concrete, an **admixture** which can produce a large reduction in water or flowability without an undue set retardation or entrainment of air.

water-reducing agent A material which either increases workability of freshly mixed mortar or concrete without increasing its water content or maintains workability with a reduced amount of water.

water repellent **1.** Said of a surface that is resistant to, but not impervious to, water penetration. **2.** A material used to treat a surface to increase its resistance to the penetration of water.

water-repellent cement A hydraulic cement having a water-repellent agent added during the process of manufacture.

water resistant Said of any material capable of withstanding limited exposure to water.

water retentivity That property of a mortar which prevents the rapid loss of water by absorption to masonry units; prevents bleeding or water gain when mortar is in contact with relatively impervious units.

water riser pipe See **riser, 4**.

water seal The barrier to the passage of air through a **trap, 1** in a drain, which is provided by water in the trap; a **seal, 3**.

water seasoning The seasoning of lumber by soaking it in water for a period of time prior to air drying.

water-service pipe That part of a **building main** installed by, or under the jurisdiction of, a water department or company.

watershed **1.** A dividing line between drainage areas. **2.** A **wash, 1**. **3.** A **water table, 1**.

watershed dormer Same as **shed dormer**.

water softener An apparatus which chemically removes the calcium and magnesium salts from a water supply, usually by ion exchange. Also see **zeolite**.

water spotting, white spots White marks which are left on a paint film when droplets of water evaporate, or as a result of sealing in moisture.

waterspout A duct, spout, or the like, through which rainwater is discharged from a roof or gutter; for examples, see **gargoyle** and **canale**.

water stain **1.** Discoloration in **converted timber** caused by water. **2.** A water-soluble dye used as a stain for wood that is to be finished.

water standpipe system See **standpipe system**.

water stop A diaphragm used across a joint as a sealant, usually to prevent the passage of water.

water-struck brick See **soft-mud brick**.

water supply fixture unit (WSFU) A factor so chosen that the load-producing effects of different kinds of plumbing fixtures and their conditions of service can be expressed as multiples of that factor.

water supply stub A vertical pipe less than one story in height supplying one or more fixtures.

water-supply system Of a building, the water-service pipe, the water-distributing pipes, and the necessary connecting pipes, fittings, control valves, and all appurtenances in or adjacent to the building.

water table **1.** A horizontal exterior ledge on a wall, pier, buttress, etc.; often sloped and provided with a drip molding to prevent water from running down the face of the lower portion; also called an **offset, 1**. Also see **base course, drip cap**. **2.** Same as **groundwater level**.

water tank An enclosed storage container, usually pumped to an elevated location, to increase the water pressure in a water piping system.

water tap A water outlet valve; a **faucet**.

water test **1.** A test to determine whether there are leaks in a system of piping. Also see **test plug** and **test pressure**. **2.** A test of a drainage or vent system to determine if it leaks; should not be used in locations where the temperature during the test may fall below the freezing point of water. Also see **air test**.

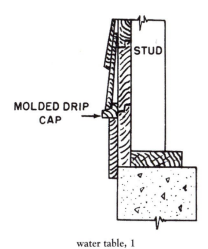

water table, 1

watertight **1.** Said of an enclosure or barrier that does not permit the passage of moisture. **2.** Said of a surface that is impermeable to water except when exposed to a hydrostatic pressure sufficient to produce structural discontinuity by rupture.

water tower A tower into which water is pumped to raise its level high enough above the level of a water distribution system so that the system will be supplied with adequate water pressure.

water valve A device in a water distribution system to start or stop, regulate, or prevent the reversal of flow of water in a system.

water vapor barrier See **vapor barrier**.

water vapor diffusion The process by which water vapor spreads or moves through permeable materials caused by differences in water vapor pressure.

water vapor permeability That property of a material which permits the passage of water vapor through it; the time rate of water vapor transmission through a unit area of flat material of unit thickness induced by a unit vapor pressure difference between two specific surfaces, under specified temperature and humidity conditions.

water vapor retarder See **vapor barrier**.

water vapor transmission (WVT) The rate of water vapor flow, under steady specified conditions, through a unit area of material between the two parallel surfaces (and normal to these surfaces).

water well See **well, 4.**

waterworks A complete system of pipelines, conduits, and so forth for distributing water from one or more reservoirs, purifying the water, and then pumping it through a distribution system for use by a community.

watt A unit of power; the power required to do work at the rate of 1 joule per second, which is equal to the power dissipated in an electric circuit in which a potential difference of 1 volt causes a current of 1 ampere to flow.

watt-hour A unit of work equal to 3,600 joules; equivalent to the power of 1 watt operating for a period of 1 hour.

watt-hour meter An electricity meter which measures and registers the active power in an electric circuit with respect to time.

wattle A framework of interwoven rods, poles, or branches.

wattle-and-daub A primitive form of wall construction consisting of upright wood poles with branches interwoven between them (*wattle*) that are then covered with plaster mixed with clay and straw (*daub*); often used to fill the space between structural timbers of **timber-framed buildings** in order to provide increased thermal insulation; also see **jacal, 2**.

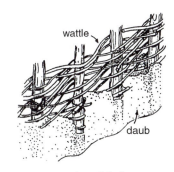

wattle-and-daub

wave front Of a sound wave, a continuous, imaginary surface which is the locus of points having the same phase at a given instant.

wavelength For light waves or sound waves, the distance between two successive points of a periodic wave in the direction of propagation, in which the oscillation has the same phase; the distance the wave travels in one period. For light waves three common units of wavelength are: micrometer, nanometer, and angstrom.

wave molding, oundy molding, swelled chamfer, undulating molding, undy molding   A molding decorated with a series of stylized representations of breaking waves.

wave scroll   Same as **Vitruvian scroll.**

wavy grain   A curly figure in wood grain, similar to **fiddleback,** but with more uniform ripples and waves.

wax   A thermoplastic solid material obtained from vegetable, mineral, and animal matter; soluble in organic solvents; used in paste or liquid form as a protective coating or polish on wood and metal surfaces and as an additive in paints.

waxing   In a finished piece of marble intended for interior use, the filling of cavities with materials patterned and colored to match.

way   A street, alley, or other thoroughfare or easement permanently established for the passage of persons or vehicles.

WB   Abbr. for "welded base."

WBT   Abbr. for **wet-bulb temperature.**

W.C.   Abbr. for **water closet.**

WCV   Symbol for "butterfly (wafer) check valve."

wd   Abbr. for **wood.**

Wdr   In the lumber industry, abbr. for "wider."

weak axis   The minor principal axis of a cross section.

weakened-plane joint   Same as **groove joint.**

wearing surface, wearing course   1. The top layer of surfacing which carries vehicular traffic. 2. Same as **topping.**

weather   That portion of a wood shingle that is exposed to the elements.

weather back   The application of weatherproofing to the back (inner side) of a wall.

weather bar   See **water bar.**

weather barrier   On the outer surface of thermal insulation, any material which protects the insulation from weather damage, including solar radiation and atmospheric contamination.

weatherboard   1. One of a number of horizontal boards commonly used as an exterior covering on **timber-framed buildings** to provide weather protection; for example, used as exterior sheathing to protect the **infilling** between the

structural timbers. The upper edges of weatherboards are commonly tapered to a thinner edge than the lower edge so they can be overlapped by the weatherboards directly above them, or they have a **rabbeted** upper edge that fits under the overlapping board above, to shed water. Also see **clapboards,** which served the same purpose but were usually not as thick as weatherboards; also see **siding.**

weatherboarding   1. A type of wood siding commonly used in the early U.S.A. as an exterior covering on a building of frame construction; consists of boards, each of which has parallel faces and a rabbeted upper edge which fits under an overlapping board above. 2. Same as **clapboard** or **siding.**

weatherboarding, 1

weather check   Same as **throat, 2.**

weathercock   A **weathervane** in the shape of a rooster.

weather door   See **storm door.**

weathered   1. Descriptive of a material or surface which has been exposed to the elements for a long period of time. 2. Having an upper surface which is splayed so as to throw off water.

weathered joint   See **weather-struck joint.**

weathered pointing   Same as **weather-struck joint.**

weather fillet   See **cement fillet.**

weathering   1. Changes in color, texture, strength, chemical composition, or other properties of a natural or artificial material due to the action of the weather. 2. See **sill offset.** 3. The cover applied to a part of a structure to enable it to shed rainwater.

weather joint See **weather-struck joint**.

weather molding A molding shaped and located to discharge rainwater; same as **dripmold**.

weatherometer A device in which specimen materials can be subjected to artificial and accelerated weathering tests, the effects of sun, rain, and temperature changes; the simulated conditions are obtained by the use of electric arcs, water spray, and heating elements.

weatherproof So constructed or protected that exposure to the weather will not interfere with successful operation or function.

weather resistance The ability of a material, paint film, or the like to withstand effects of wind, rain, sun, etc., and retain its appearance and integrity.

weatherseal channel Of a door, a top-closing channel which is set in mastic with its flanges downward.

weather slating, weather tiling Slate or tile shingles that are hung on the face of a wall to prevent the penetration of rainwater.

weather strip A strip of wood, metal, neoprene, or other material applied to an exterior door or window so as to cover or seal the joint made by it with the sill, casings, or threshold, in order to exclude rain, snow, cold air, etc.

weather-struck joint, weathered joint A horizontal masonry joint in which the mortar is sloped outward from the upper edge of the lower brick, so as to shed water readily; formed by pressing the mortar inward at the upper edge of the joint.

weather-struck joint

weathertight Sealed against the intrusion of rain, snow, cold air, etc.

weather tiling, tile hanging Tile which is hung vertically on the face of a wall; usually attached by nailing; provides protection against moisture.

weather vane A metal plate, often decorated, or in the shape of a figure or object, which rotates freely on a vertical spindle to indicate wind direction; usually located atop a spire or other elevated position on a building.

weave bead A **weld bead** which is made with oscillations along the bead which are transverse to the length of the bead.

weaving In shingled roofing, where two adjoining surfaces meet, the alternate lapping of shingles on opposite faces.

weaving house Same as **spinning house**.

web **1.** The portion of a truss or girder between the chords or flanges, whose principal function is to resist shear on the span. **2.** A core divider in a **hollow masonry unit**.

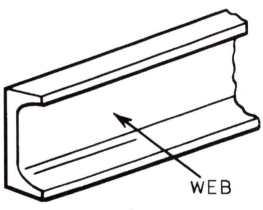

WEB

web, 1

web bar Steel reinforcement which is placed in a concrete member to resist shear and diagonal tension.

web clamp A type of clamp used to hold carpentry work during gluing; consists of a tape of nylon, or the like, with a metal fastener that is tightened with a wrench or screwdriver.

web crippling The local failure of a **web plate**, for example, as the result of a concentrated load.

web member In a **truss**, any member which joins the top and bottom chords.

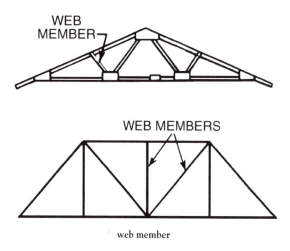

web member

web plate A steel plate which forms the **web, 1** of a beam, girder, or truss.

web reinforcement 1. Steel bars, rods, etc., placed in a **reinforced concrete** member to resist shear and diagonal tension. 2. Additional metal plates connected to the **web, 1** of a metal beam or girder to increase the strength of the **web, 1**.

web splice A splice joining two **web plates**.

web stiffener An angle iron which is connected to the **web, 1** of a beam to distribute a load or to prevent buckling.

wedge 1. A piece of wood, metal, or other hard material, thick at one end and tapering to a thin edge at the other. 2. See **lead wedge**.

wedge anchor In prestressed concrete, a device for providing the means of anchoring a **tendon** by wedging.

wedge coping Same as **featheredge coping**.

weepers Statues of mourners sometimes incorporated into tombs.

weep hole 1. A small opening in a wall or window member, through which accumulated condensation or water may drain to the building exterior, as from the base of a cavity wall, a wall flashing, or a skylight. 2. A hole near the bottom of a retaining wall, backfilled with gravel or other free-draining material, to permit water to drain to the outside of the wall, so as to prevent the buildup of pressure behind the wall.

weeping cross A type of **preaching cross** especially used for public penance.

weft See **carpet weft**.

weight batching Measuring the constituent materials for mortar or concrete by weight, rather than by volume.

weight box In a window frame, the channel in which the sash weights move up and down.

weight pocket, weight space A **weight box**.

weld To unite metals by heating them to suitable temperatures, with or without the application of pressure, and with or without the use of **filler metal**.

weld axis A line through the length of a weld that is perpendicular in its cross section.

weld bead A weld deposit resulting from a single longitudinal progression of a welding operation along a joint.

weld decay Localized corrosion at or adjacent to a weld.

welded butt splice A **reinforcing bar** splice made by welding the butted ends.

welded cover plate A **cover plate** welded to a beam or girder.

welded joint A gastight joint obtained by unit-

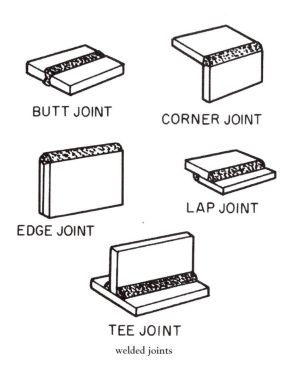

welded joints

ing metal parts, such as iron and steel that require welding, in the plastic or molten state.

welded reinforcement   Reinforcement which is joined by welding.

welded system   A piping system for conveying fluids, in which all joints are welded, usually to make the system leakproof.

welded truss   Any **truss** having its main members joined by welding.

welded tube   Tube made from a metal plate, sheet, or strip, with welded longitudinal or helical joint.

welded-wire fabric, welded wire mesh   A series of longitudinal and transverse wires arranged at right angles to each other and welded together at all points of intersection; used as reinforcement in **reinforced concrete**.

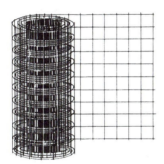

welded-wire fabric

welded-wire fabric reinforcement   The use of welded-wire fabric as **reinforcement** in concrete.

welded wire lath   Same as **wire lath**.

weld gauge   An instrument for checking the shape and size of welds.

welding cables   A pair of electric cables supplying power from a welding machine to the work being done; one lead connects the machine with the electrode holder, the other lead connects the machine to the work.

welding nozzle   A short length of pipe which is welded to a vessel at one end and is chamfered at the other end for butt welding.

welding rod   **Filler metal**, in wire or rod form, used in gas welding and brazing processes and in those arc-welding processes wherein the electrode does not furnish the filler.

welding screw   A screw provided with lugs or weld projections on the top or underside of the head to facilitate attachment to a metal part by resistance welding.

weldment   Any assembly whose component parts are joined by welding.

weld metal   The part of a weld that has been melted during welding.

weld nut   A solid nut provided with lugs, annular rings, or embossments to facilitate its attachment to a metal part by resistance welding.

well, wellhole   **1.** The clear vertical space about which a stair turns; a **stairwell**. **2.** The open vertical space between walls in which a stair or elevator is constructed. **3.** Any enclosed space of small area but of considerable height, as an **air shaft. well, 4.** See **bored well, dug well**, etc.

well, 1:   *W*

well curb   A protective structure around the top rim of a **well, 4** to prevent objects from falling into it; also provides a convenient mounting surface for a mechanism for raising a water bucket.

well curbing   Same as **pit boards**.

well-graded aggregate   Aggregate having a particle-size distribution which will produce maximum density, i.e., minimum void space.

wellhole   The open vertical space between walls in which a stair is constructed; see **well, 1**.

well house, wellhead   A shelter over a water **well, 4**.

well point A hollow rod with a perforated intake at its lower end, which is pointed; driven into the ground and connected to a pump, to remove water at an excavation site.

well points

well-point system A number of **well points** connected to a header, which is attached to a pump, to lower the water table at an excavation site.

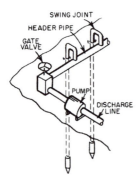

well-point system

well stair A stairwell in a **well, 1**.

Welsh arch A small flat arch consisting only of a keystone supported on each side by two projecting stretchers that are shaped to fit the keystone.

Welsh groin A groin formed by an **underpitch vault**.

Welsh vault See **underpitch vault**.

welt 1. In sheet-metal roofing, a seam which joins two sheets; formed by folding over the edges of the sheets, engaging the folded portions and then dressing them down flat. **2.** A strip of wood fastened over a flush seam or joint, or an angle, to strengthen it.

welted drip A drip formed by roofing felt at the eaves or the rake edge of a roof; a strip is folded back to return on the roof, forming the drip.

welting strip In sheet-metal roofing, a strip having one edge fixed to the roof and the other edge bent to hold the lower edge of a vertical sheet. Also see **stripping, 3**.

west end The end of a church that is opposite the sanctuary; usually where the main doors are located; so called because medieval churches almost invariably had their sanctuaries at the east end.

western frame See **platform frame**.

western framing A system of framing a building of wood construction in which all **studs** are only one story in height; the floor **joists** for each story rest on the **top plates, 2** of the story below, except for the first story, which rests on the **groundsill**. The bearing walls and partitions rest on the subfloor (i.e., on the rough floor that serves as a base for the finish floor). Same as **platform framing**; compare with **balloon framing**.

western hemlock A straight-grained, moderately low-density softwood of the western U.S.A.; white to yellowish brown in color and not as strong as Douglas fir; used for general construction and plywood.

western larch A moderately strong, heavy softwood of the western U.S.A. with coarse-textured reddish brown wood; used in general building construction, as timbers and flooring.

western red cedar A durable, straight-grained, moderately low-density wood of the western U.S.A.; used extensively for construction where durability is important, esp. for shingles and shakes. Also called **thuya**.

Western Stick style A type of one-story **timber-framed house** representing the finest of the **Craftsman style**, developed in California between about 1905 and the 1920s, exemplified in the work of Greene and Greene, Architects, who carried their architectural details to a high art; compare with **Stick style.**

West Indian mahogany   See **carapa**.

wet-alarm valve   A valve that (a) permits the flow of water into a **wet-pipe sprinkler system**, (b) prevents the reverse flow of water, and (c) incorporates provisions for actuating an alarm under specified flow conditions.

wet-bulb depression   The difference between dry-bulb and wet-bulb temperatures.

wet-bulb temperature   The temperature of a thermometer in which the bulb is enclosed in a wick that is kept moistened.

wet-bulb thermometer   In a **psychrometer,** the thermometer whose bulb is kept moistened.

wet cleaning   In the removal of asbestos, the process of eliminating asbestos contamination by using mops, cloths, and other cleaning tools which have been wetted; these items are then disposed of as asbestos-contaminated waste.

wet construction   Any construction, e.g., a wall, using materials (such as concrete, mortar, plaster, etc.) which are installed or applied in other than a dry condition.

wet glazing   A method of sealing glass in a frame by the use of a glazing compound or sealant which is applied with a knife or gun.

wet mix   Concrete containing a high proportion of water, as evidenced by its runny consistency when still in the unhardened state.

wet-mix shotcrete   A **shotcrete** in which all the ingredients (including water) are mixed before they are fed into the delivery hose.

wet-on-wet painting   A technique of spray painting a second coat before the previous coat has dried.

wet-pipe sprinkler system   A fire **sprinkler system** consisting of a network of pipes containing water under pressure. Automatic sprinklers are connected to piping so that each **sprinkler** (head) protects an assigned area of coverage; the water discharges immediately from any sprinkler opened by the heat of a fire.

wet riser   A wet **standpipe**.

wet rot   The decay of timber having a high moisture content, as a result of the attack of fungi.

wet screening, wet sieving   Screening to remove from fresh concrete, in the plastic state, all aggregate particles larger than a certain size.

wet sieving   See **wet screening**.

wet sprinkler system   Same as **wet-pipe sprinkler system**.

wet stable consistency   The consistency of cement grout or mortar at which it contains the maximum water without **sloughing**.

wet standpipe system   A **standpipe system** completely filled with water at a pressure required for immediate discharge and use.

wet storage stain   Same as **white rust**.

wet strength   The strength of an adhesive joint determined immediately after removal from a liquid in which it has been immersed.

wetting   In soldering or brazing, the spreading of a liquid **filler metal** or flux on a solid **base metal**.

wetting agent   A substance capable of lowering the surface tension of liquids, facilitating the wetting of solid surfaces, and permitting the penetration of liquids into the capillaries.

wet-use adhesive   In glue-laminated timber, adhesives which perform satisfactorily under a wide variety of conditions including exposure to the weather, dry use, marine use, and pressure treatment.

wet vent   A pipe, usually oversized, which functions both as a **fixture branch** and as a **vent**, e.g., a soil or waste pipe that also serves as a vent. (*See illustration p. 1008.*)

wet wall   See **wet construction**.

WF   Abbr. for "wide flange."

WG   Abbr. for "wire gauge."

WH   Abbr. for **water heater**.

whaleback roof   **1.** Same as **ship's bottom roof**. **2.** Same as **compass roof**.

whale house   In the early 18th century, a simple house especially favored by whalers of Massachusetts. At the rear of the house there was a kitchen with a small bedroom on each side. The kitchen fireplace was usually on the opposite side of the principal fireplace in the **hall, 1** of the dwelling.

whaler   See **wale**.

wheat-threshing barn   See **bank barn**.

wheelbarrow   A handcart usually fitted with one wheel in front and two supporting legs in back; and with two handles; used for transporting materials over short distances.

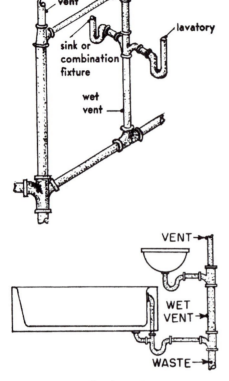

examples of **wet vents**

wheel ditcher   Same as **wheel trencher**.

wheeler   Same as **winder**.

wheeling step   Same as **winder**.

wheel step, wheeling step   A **winder**.

wheel tracery   Tracery radiating from a center, as the spokes of a wheel.

wheel window   A large circular window on

wheel window

which the radiation of tracery from the center is suggested; a variety of **rose window**; a **Catherine wheel window**.

whetstone   A piece of stone, natural or artificial, used to sharpen cutting tools.

Whipple truss   A double-intersection **Pratt truss**; has diagonal tension members and vertical compression members.

whirley crane   A large **crane** which can revolve 360°.

whispering gallery, whispering dome   A large dome or vault that reflects sounds (esp. high frequencies) along a large concave surface so that even whispers may be heard some distance away.

white cement   A pure calcite limestone cement, similar in properties to ordinary cement, but ground finer and of higher grade.

white coat   A gauged lime-putty, troweled, plaster **finish coat**.

white deal, white fir   See **spruce**.

white lauan   See **Philippine mahogany**.

white lead   Basic lead carbonate, used as a white opaque pigment in exterior house paints; also used in ceramics and putty; available either as a dry powder or as a mixture of turpentine and linseed oil in paste form.

white lead putty   A high-quality putty containing at least 10% white lead mixed with calcium carbonate and linseed oil.

white lime   1. Same as **high-calcium lime**. 2. Same as pure **lime**.

white mahogany   See **avodire**.

whitening   In the grain of finished wood, a white appearance, usually due to improper finishing techniques or spotty adhesion of the coating.

white noise   Noise having a flat spectrum over the frequency range of interest; the power per unit-frequency is substantially independent of frequency.

white oak   A hard, heavy, durable wood, gray to reddish brown in color; esp. used for flooring, paneling, and trim.

white pine   A soft, light wood; works easily; does not split when nailed; does not swell or warp appreciably; widely used in building construction.

white portland cement   A portland cement, produced from raw materials low in iron, which hydrates to a white paste; used to yield a concrete of considerable whiteness.

white rot   A type of decay in wood caused by a fungus that leaves a white residue.

white rust   White corrosion products (such as zinc oxide) on zinc-coated articles.

white spirit   Petroleum ether, distilled from crude oil; used as a solvent, esp. in varnishes.

white spots   See **water spotting**.

white walnut   See **butternut**.

whitewash   An impermanent coating applied with a brush on walls to give them a white appearance; usually a mixture of hydrated lime and water; once typically consisted of a mixture of ground-up chalk (*whiting*), lime, flour, glue, and water, sometimes with addition of tallow or soap.

whitewood   Same as **tulipwood, 1**.

whiting   Calcium carbonate pigment; used as an extender in paint, in putty, and in whitewash.

whole-brick wall   A brick wall, the thickness of which is equal to the length of one brick.

whole pitch   The pitch of a gable roof whose vertical rise is equal to the span.

whole timber   A squared timber; a **balk**.

WHSE   On drawings, abbr. for **warehouse**.

WI   **1.** On drawings, abbr. for **wrought iron. 2.** On drawings, abbr. for "water inlet."

wicket   A small door or gate, esp. one forming part of a larger one.

wicking   The action of absorption by means of capillary action.

wickiup   Same as **wikiup**.

wide-flange beam   A structural beam of rolled steel or concrete having a shape whose cross section resembles the letter H; has wider flanges than an I-beam.

wide-flange beam

wide-ringed, coarse-grained, open-grained   Descriptive of wood having wide annual rings, due to rapid growth; in softwood, usually weaker than narrow-ringed wood.

wide-throw hinge   A rectangular hinge with extra-wide leaves for clearance.

wide tolerance   A tolerance greater than **standard tolerance**.

widow's walk   A flat roof deck or raised observation platform sometimes having a view of the sea, situated on the roof of a house and enclosed by a balustrade or railing; the horizontal roof surface is usually formed by truncating the top of a hipped roof; also called a captain's walk.

wiggle nail   A **corrugated fastener**.

wiggling-in   See **range-in**.

wigwam   An Indian dwelling in the American Northeast, found in a variety of shapes; commonly, a domed structure having a framework of saplings set into the ground, bent over, and bound together. This framework was covered with a watertight surface of overlapping matting or animal skins. A hole at the top of the wigwam provided an escape for smoke from the firepit below; an opening at the side served as an entrance. Compare with **tipi**.

wikiup   A relatively small, temporary, round dwelling of the Apache Indians of the American Southwest; could be reassembled relatively easily and quickly; had a lightweight framework formed by saplings lashed together at their tops so as to form either a domed structure or a conical structure. Additional poles were placed along the sides of the framework to provide added structural strength; the framework was covered with a matting.

will   The word *will* is used in connection with acts and actions required of the owner or of the architect/engineer; it is used by the owner or purchaser as a self-imposed requirement; denotes the information the owner will supply, documents the owner will review, and approvals the owner will issue—all at the proper time.

Williot diagram   A graphical method of determining the deflections of a framed structure under load.

Wilton carpet   A velvet cut-pile carpet, woven with loops on a Jacquard loom, usually having excellent wearing qualities.

winch

winch   A machine for pulling or lifting heavy weights. It has a rotating drum around which a pulling line or rope is turned; a **hoist, 2**.

wind   British term for **twist**.

windage loss   A loss of fine droplets of water which are entrained by circulating air; this loss of water in a system (e.g., in the cooling tower of an air-conditioning system) is replaced by **makeup water**; usually expressed as a percentage of the circulation rate.

wind beam   A **collar beam**.

wind box   A plenum from which air for combustion is supplied to a stoker, gas burner, or oil burner.

wind brace   Any brace, such as a strut, which strengthens a structure or framework against the wind; usually a brace between a **principal rafter** and a **purlin** to provide the roof framing with greater rigidity.

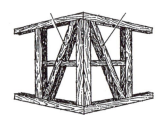

wind brace

windbreak   A dense growth of trees, fence, wall or the like, which provides protection against the wind, esp. to gardens and buildings.

wind-cut tree   A tree shaped by the force of a strong wind.

winder, wheel step   A step, more or less wedge-shaped, with its tread wider at one end than the other, as in a **spiral stair**.

wind filling   Same as **beam fill**.

wind guard   **1.** Any construction which provides protection against the wind, as a **chimney cap, 2**. **2.** Same as **draft fillet**. **3.** A **draft bead**.

winding-drum machine   On elevators, a gear-driven machine having a drum to which the wire ropes that hoist the car are fastened, and on which they wind.

winding stair   **1.** Any stair constructed chiefly or entirely of **winders**. **2.** See **screw stair**.

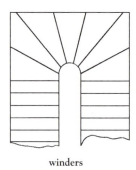

winders

winding strips, winding sticks   Two short sticks or strips of wood having parallel edges, placed on a surface to test it for flatness.

windlass   A modification of the wheel and axle used for lifting weights; usually an axle, turned by a crank, and a rope or chain wound around the axle for raising the weight.

wind load   The total force exerted by the wind on a structure or part of a structure.

windmill   A large machine in which the wind acts on a number of vanes or blades, rotating them about an axis, thereby producing mechanical power; once widely used for grinding grain, sawing timber, and pumping water. The earliest windmills in America (similar to those in the Netherlands) had four very large, slowly moving blades that were cloth-covered, and required the constant attendance of an operator. In 1854, a patent was issued for an entirely new type of windmill, having a large number of *small* blades, which was self-regulating and could operate without human intervention; this feature greatly increased its practical application, especially for pumping water. In the latter part of the 20th century, large two-bladed windmills have been assembled in large groups called "farms" for the environment-friendly generation of electrical power.

window   An opening, generally in an external wall of a building, to admit light and provide ventilation; usually glazed. The framework in which the glass is set is called a *sash*; a flat sheet of glass, cut to fit a window, or part of a window, is called a *pane*. Many early glazed openings had fixed lights (i.e., could not be opened); others were a combination of fixed lights and a casement window that opened outward. For various types of windows, see **angled bay window, art**

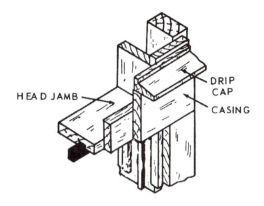

HEAD JAMB

DRIP CAP

CASING

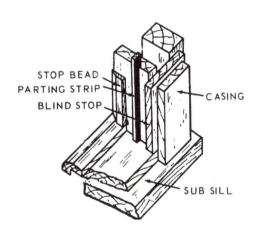

STOP BEAD
PARTING STRIP
BLIND STOP

CASING

SUB SILL

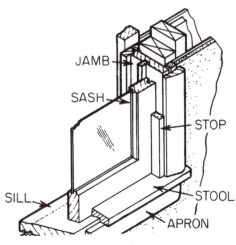

JAMB

SASH

STOP

SILL

STOOL

APRON

window: details

window, awning window, band window, bay window, blank window, bow window, bull's-eye window, camber window, cant-bay window, cantilevered window, cant window, casement window, Chicago window, circle-head window, circular window, clerestory window, compass window, cottage window, cross window, dead window, diamond window, Diocletian window, dormant window, dormer window, double-hung window, double-lancet window, drop-head window, D-window, eyebrow window, false window, fanlight, flank window, French window, frieze-band window, frieze window, gable window, hopper window, jalousie, jib window, lancet window, landscape window, lattice window, leaded window, leper's squint, louver window, low-side window, lucarne, lucome window, Lutheran window, lynchnoscope, marigold window, oculus, oeil-de-boeuf, operable window, oriel, oval window, Palladian window, peak-head window, picture window, pivot window, pocket-head window, reversible window, ribbon window, rose window, round-topped window, sash window, semicircular window, serliana window, single-hung window, skylight, sliding window, sliphead window, square-headed window, stationary window, stepped windows, storm window, three-part window, transom window, trellis window, tripartite window, triple-hung window, Venetian window, wheel window, Yorkshire light.

window apron A plain or molded wood strip which covers the edge of the plastering below a **window stool**.

window back The inside face of the portion of wall between the windowsill and the floor below.

window band Same as **ribbon window**.

window bar **1.** A muntin. **2.** A glazing bar. **3.** A bar which prevents ingress or egress through a window. **4.** A bar for securing a casement or window shutters.

window bay A **bay window**.

window bead See **inside stop, draft bead**.

window blind A shade, **blind, shade screen**, or **shutter, 1** for a window.

window board Same as **window stool**.

window bole A small, nonglazed wall opening, usually shuttered, to let in light and air.

window box Same as **weight box**.

window casing The finished frame surrounding a window; the visible frame.

window catch A fastening device, fixed to a window sash, to prevent it from being opened from the outside.

window-cill Same as **windowsill**.

window cleaner's anchor A fitting attached securely to the outside of a window frame (or to the wall just outside the frame) to which a window cleaner fastens the safety belt.

window cleaner's platform A platform operated manually or by power and suspended by cables or ropes from roof assemblies; used to support window cleaners and maintenance personnel.

window configuration The shape, number, and relationship of glass lights, mullions, mutins, tracery, and/or window frames; also see **fenestration**.

window crown The upper termination of a window, such as a pediment; often decorative.

example of a **window crown**

window divider See **mullion** and **muntin**.

window dressing The **trim, 2**, usually of wood or stone, around a window.

window frame The fixed, nonoperable frame of a window designed to receive and hold the sash or casement and all necessary hardware.

window glass, sheet glass A soda-lime-silica glass; in the U.S.A. fabricated in continuous flat sheets up to 6 ft (1.83 m) wide, in thicknesses from 0.05 to 0.22 in. (1.27 to 5.59 mm); graded AA, A, and B according to quality, but the actual quality depends on the manufacturer.

window glazing bar Same as **muntin**.

window guard 1. A **window bar, 2. 2.** A metal protective grille, often of elaborate, decorative character.

window hardware Devices, fittings, or mechanisms for opening, closing, supporting, holding open, or locking the sashes, including such items as catches, chains, cords, fasteners, hinges, lifts, locks, pivots, pulls, pulleys, sash balances, sash weights, and stays.

window head The upper horizontal cross member of a window frame.

window jack Same as **builder's jack**.

window jack scaffold A scaffold the platform of which is supported by a bracket or jack which projects through a window opening.

window lead A slender bar or rod of lead, cast with grooves to receive the glass in a window.

window ledge Same as **windowsill**.

window lift, sash lift A handle, or the like, secured to a sliding sash (usually the lower rail) to assist in raising or lowering it.

windowlight A **pane, 1** of glass which has been installed in a window; a **windowpane**.

window lining See **lining**.

window lock Same as **sash lock**.

windowpane In a window, a **pane, 1**.

window post In a framed building, one of the solid uprights between which the **window frame** is set, often two studs nailed together.

window pull Same as **sash pull**.

window sash See **sash**.

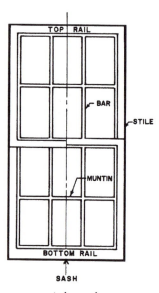

window sashes

window schedule A tabulation, usually on a blueprint or in specifications, which lists all windows required on a job, indicating the sizes, number of lights, types, locations, and special requirements.

window screen **1.** See **insect screen. 2.** An ornamental grille or lattice fitted into a window opening.

window seat **1.** A seat built into the bottom inside of a window. **2.** A seat located at a window.

window seat

window shutter See **shutter, 1**.

windowsill See **sill, 3**.

window space The total window area in a room or building.

window spring bolt A spring bolt which fixes a sash (which is not counterbalanced) in any selected position.

window stile See **pulley stile**.

window stool, window board, elbow board A horizontal board on a windowsill, fitted against the bottom rail of the lower sash and between the sash frame stiles; forms a base on which the casing rests; usually of wood, but may be of metal or other facing material.

window stop Same as **sash stop**.

window surround A decorative element or structure on the exterior wall surface around a window.

window trim The **casing** around a window; the interior decorative finishing elements.

window unit A complete window, with **sashes (ventilators, 2)** or **casements**, ready for shipment or installation in a building.

window surround

window wall A type of **curtain wall**, usually composed of vertical and horizontal metal framing members containing **fixed lights, operable windows,** or opaque panels, or a combination thereof.

window weight See **sash weight**.

window well The clear space created by a soil-retaining structure located immediately below a window whose sill height is lower than the adjacent ground level.

window yoke A **window head** which ties together the **pulley stiles**.

wind pressure The pressure on a surface produced by the wind blowing against it.

windproof Same as **windtight**.

wind shake A crack or fissure in timber caused, during growth, by wind strain.

wind shake

wind stop **1.** A **weather strip** used around a door or window. **2.** A strip, usually of wood or metal, covering the joint between a sash or casement and the adjacent stile. **3.** A wood or metal strip covering a crack of any type in a building to prevent wind from blowing in.

windtight Descriptive of construction in which all openings and cracks have been carefully sealed, using weather strips.

wind uplift A negative force (i.e., an upward pull) which acts on a roof because of wind.

wine cellar, wine vault A storage room for wine, usually underground so as to be cool and dark.

wing **1.** A subsidiary part of a building extending out from the main portion. **2.** In a theatre, the offstage space at the side of the acting area. **3.** One of the four leaves of a revolving door.

wing balcony That part of a balcony which extends along the sidewalls of an auditorium, toward the stage.

wing compass A **compass** having an arc-shaped piece (which is attached to one leg) which passes through the opposite leg and which may be clamped with a set screw to a desired opening.

wing dividers A pair of **dividers**, similar in construction to a wing compass.

wing dividers

winged bull An Assyrian symbol of force and domination, of frequent occurrence in ancient Assyrian architectural sculpture; pairs of winged human-headed bulls and lions of colossal size usually guarded the portals of palaces.

winged bull

winged disk In Egyptian Revival architecture, same as **sun disk**.

winglight See **side light, 1**.

wing nut A nut having projections so that it can be tightened with one finger and the thumb.

wing nut

wing pile A **bearing pile** (usually of concrete) which widens at the top.

wing screw A screw having a wing-shaped head, designed for manual turning without a driver or wrench.

wing wall A subordinate wall, one end of which is built against an abutment; usually acts as support for the abutment and as a retaining wall.

wiped joint A solder joint made by pouring molten solder onto the joint, and then wiping the joint with a cloth or with a small paddle so as to shape the joint as required.

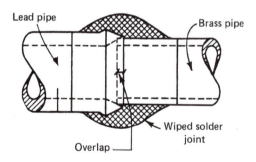

wiped joint

wire A filament or slender rod of drawn metal.

wire brad A **brad, 1**.

wire cloth A stiff fabric of fine woven wire; used in screens for excluding insects, in sieves, etc.; the number of openings per square inch is called the **mesh**.

wire comb, wire scratcher A tool for scratching a plaster base coat in order to improve the bond of the next coat.

wire-cut brick Clay that has been cut by wires

and then burnt in a kiln at an elevated temperature.

wired glass See **wire glass**.

wire gauge **1.** An instrument for measuring the thickness of wire or sheet metal; usually consists of a steel plate having a series of notches, of standard opening sizes, around the edge. **2.** One of several systems for specifying the diameter of a wire.

wire gauze **Wire cloth** of fine texture.

wire glass, wired glass, safety glass Sheet glass containing wire mesh embedded between the two faces to prevent shattering in the event of breakage.

wire holder An electrical insulator having a mounting screw or mounting bolt and a hole for securing a conductor.

wire lath Wire welded to form a netting, usually with a paper backing; used as a base for plaster.

wire mesh See **welded-wire fabric**.

wire mesh partition Same as **mesh partition**.

wire nail A nail made of wire, esp. a **finishing nail** or the like.

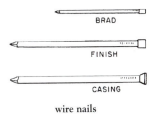

wire nails

wire nut A mechanical connector for wires which are small in size; consists of an insulating cap over a threaded or coiled metal insert; the wires to be connected are stripped of insulation at their ends and inserted in the wire nut; then the wire nut is turned by hand until the wires are securely joined.

wire nut

wire rope A rope usually fabricated of twisted **strands** of wire, usually laid over a core.

wire saw An assembly for sawing stone by a rapidly moving continuous wire that carries a slurry of sand or other abrasive material.

wire scratcher Same as **wire comb**.

wire size In the U.S.A., a size, usually stated in terms of American Wire Gauge (AWG) and/or thousand circular mills (MCM) which applies to copper conductors.

wireway Same as **raceway**.

wire wrapping A high-tensile wire which is wound, under tension, around concrete tension-resisting structural components, circular concrete walls, and the like.

wiring box In interior electric wiring, a box, usually of metal, installed at each outlet, junction point, or switch (except for exposed wiring on insulators); classified as a floor box, outlet box, sectional switch box, or utility box.

wiring device Any electrical device used to control and to provide connection points for low-voltage outlets, lighting systems, and appliances (e.g., wall switches and receptacles).

witch door A door whose lowest panels form a capital letter **X**; once thought by some to ward off evil spirits; compare with **Christian door**.

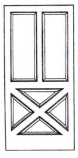

witch door

witch's hat **1.** A **conical roof** with an especially steep slope. **2.** Same as **bonnet roof**.

withdrawing room An obsolete term for **drawing room**.

withe, wythe **1.** A partition dividing two flues in the same chimney stack. **2.** A flexible, slender twig or branch; an **osier**; esp. used to tie down thatching on roofs. **3.** Each continuous

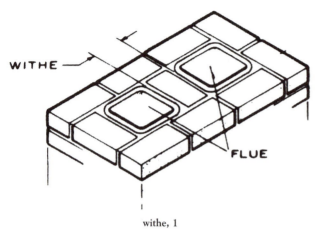

WITHE

FLUE

withe, 1

vertical section of wall, one masonry unit in thickness.

witness corner A marker set on a property line, near, but not on, a corner; used where it would be impracticable or impossible to maintain a monument at the corner itself.

WK **1.** On drawings, abbr. for "week." **2.** On drawings, abbr. for "work."

W/O On drawings, abbr. for "without."

wobble friction In prestressed concrete, the friction caused by the unintended deviation of the prestressing tendon from its specified profile.

wobble saw A **drunken saw.**

women's room See **ladies' room.**

wood The hard fibrous substance which composes the trunk and branches of a tree, lying between the pith and bark.

wood block **1.** One of many small, solid-wood blocks having plane faces, set in mastic, usually on a concrete floor slab, to form a durable floor finish. **2.** A solid piece of wood placed in a concrete formwork to prevent movement of the formwork or to fill a space.

wood brick, fixing brick, nailing block **1.** A piece of wood the size and shape of a brick; inserted in brickwork to serve as a means of attaching finishings, etc. **2.** See **nog.**

wood-cement concrete A concrete mixture using sawdust and small chips of wood as the aggregate; finished as a relatively smooth surface without visible voids.

wood chimney A chimney built of wood boards or timbers and then plastered on its interior, usually with clay, to provide a measure of fire protection. Because of its susceptibility to ignite, its use had been limited to areas where bricks and stone were not readily available. See **clay-and-sticks chimney.**

wood chipboard See **particleboard.**

wood chisel A tool having a flat cutting edge with a long stiff handle; used to cut or remove chips or strips of wood by striking the end of the handle repeatedly with a hammer, or the like.

wood dough A synthetic wood, usually made with wood fibers; used as a filler.

wood failure In plywood, the area of wood fiber remaining at the glueline following completion of a specified shear test.

wood-fibered plaster A mill-mixed gypsum plaster containing wood fiber; used **neat** or with one part of sand to one part of plaster, by weight, for greater strength.

wood-fiber insulation Thermal insulation made from wood fibers.

wood-fiber slab A slab composed of a mixture of **excelsior** and cement which is not tightly compacted; used as a base for plaster, where good thermal insulation is required.

wood filler A liquid or paste composition used to fill the pores of a wood surface before varnishing or waxing.

wood finishing The planing, sanding, and subsequent staining, varnishing, waxing, or painting of a wood surface.

wood fire-retardant treatment The impregnation of wood or wood products under pressure to reduce their flammability or combustibility.

wood flooring Flooring consisting of standard **dressed and matched boards.**

wood flour A finely ground, dried wood powder; used in the molding of plastics, in **plastic wood,** and as an extender in some glues.

wood form See **form.**

wood-frame construction Building construction in which exterior walls, load-bearing walls and partitions, floor and roof constructions, and their supports, are all built of wood.

See **balloon framing, iron framing, platform framing, post-and-beam framing, post-and-girt framing, western framing**; also see **timber-framed building, timber-framed house.** Compare with **steel-frame construction.**

wood-framed house   See **timber-framed house.**

woodgraining   Same as **false woodgraining.**

wood-grain print   A simulated wood-grain pattern, applied with patterned rolls to various wood-base substrates, such as hardboard and low-grade plywood.

wood ground   Same as **ground, 1.**

wood gutter   A **gutter, 1** along the eaves of a roof, usually made of boards but sometimes made of a solid piece of wood.

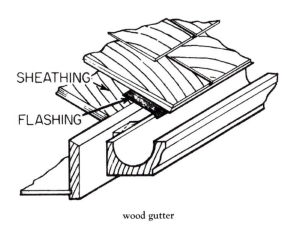

SHEATHING

FLASHING

wood gutter

wood joint   A joint formed by two boards, timbers, or sheets of wood that are held together by nails, fasteners, pegs, or the like. For specific types of wood joints, see **broken joint, butt joint, cogged joint, dado joint, dovetail joint, extruded joint, finger joint, half-dovetail, half-lap joint, hewn-and-peg joint, housed joint, mortise-and-tenon joint, rabbet joint, scarf joint, shiplap joint, spalled joint, spline joint, straight joint, tongue-and-groove joint.**

wood lath   One of many thin narrow strips of wood that serve as a base for plaster; usually nailed at regular intervals to studs or to boards in walls and ceilings. Until the early 19th century, wood lath was hand-split from larger pieces of wood; later, such strips were usually cut with circular saws, providing slats of relatively uniform width and thickness. Wood lath as a base for

plaster in new construction has now been replaced in most countries by **expanded-metal lath.**

wood molding   See **WP-series molding pattern.**

wood mosaic   **1.** See **mosaic, 2. 2.** See **parquetry.**

wood nog   See **nog.**

wood oil   **1.** See **tung oil. 2.** An oleoresin used for caulking and waterproofing.

wood preservative   A chemical used to prevent or retard the decay of wood, esp. by fungi or insects; widely used preservatives include creosote, pitch, sodium fluoride, and tar; esp. used on wood having contact with the ground.

wood rasp   Same as **rasp.**

wood roll   See **roll, 1, 2.**

wood rosin   See **rosin.**

wood screw   A helically threaded metal fastener having a pointed end; forms its own mating thread when driven into wood or other resilient materials.

wood shingle   A thin roofing unit of wood, usually cut from green wood and then kiln-dried, either split along the grain or cut to stock lengths, widths, and thicknesses; used as an exterior covering on sloping roofs and on side walls and applied in an overlapping fashion. Also see **shingle.**

wood sill   See **sill.**

wood slip   A wood **ground, 1.**

wood stud anchor, nailing anchor   A metal piece or clip which is attached to the inside of a doorframe and secures the frame to a wood stud partition.

wood treatment   **1.** See **fire-retardant wood. 2.** Treatment with a **wood preservative.**

wood turning   See **turning.**

wood turpentine, oil of turpentine   A turpentine made by the distillation of sawdust, wood chips, and waste wood; except for its characteristic odor, it differs little from true **turpentine.**

wood veneer   Same as **veneer, 1.**

wood window   A wood or wood-clad frame, with or without a ventilating sash, which accommodates glazing.

wood-wool   See **excelsior.**

woodwork Work produced by the carpenter's and joiner's art, generally applied to parts of objects or structures in wood rather than the complete structure.

woodworker's vise A vise, at the front edge of a workbench, for holding a piece of wood while it is being worked on; has jaws which are flush with the bench surface.

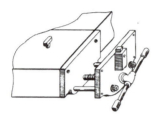

woodworker's vise

woolly grain The condition on the surface of a timber resulting from a cutting operation in which the wood fibers have been pulled to the surface instead of being cut cleanly.

work **1.** All labor necessary to produce the construction required by the **contract documents**, and all materials and equipment incorporated or to be incorporated in such construction. **2.** The produce of a force by its corresponding displacement.

workability **1.** That property of freshly mixed concrete, plaster, or mortar which determines the ease and homogeneity with which it can be mixed, applied, compacted, spread, or finished; **placeability**. **2.** The degree of ease of cutting and quality of cut that can be obtained in various woods with hand tools or machines.

work edge, face edge, working edge In carpentry, the first edge to be planed smooth; the edge from which other edges are measured or trued.

worked lumber Lumber that, in addition to being **dressed**, has been matched, shiplapped, or patterned.

work end In carpentry, the first end to be planed smooth.

worker's hoist A hoisting and lowering mechanism equipped with a platform that moves in guides in a substantially vertical direction; used primarily for raising and lowering workers to var-

ious working levels when a building is under construction.

work face, face side, working face In carpentry, the first surface to be planed smooth; the surface from which the others are measured or trued.

workhouse **1.** An institution for confining individuals sentenced to terms usually less than one year. **2.** (*Brit.*) A **poorhouse**.

working The alternate swelling and shrinking in seasoned wood, resulting from moisture content changes that occur with changes in relative humidity of the surrounding air; also called **movement**.

working drawings Drawings, intended for use by a contractor, subcontractor, or fabricator, which form part of the contract documents for a building project; contain the necessary information to manufacture or erect an object or structure.

working edge See **work edge**.

working face See **work face**.

working life The period of time during which a liquid resin or adhesive, after mixing with catalyst, solvent, or other ingredients, remains usable; **pot life**.

working load, service load The **load, 1** which a structure is expected to sustain and for which it is designed; cannot exceed the **allowable load**.

working point On a construction drawing, a point which is designated as a reference for other points.

working rail See **fly rail**.

working stage A partially enclosed portion of an assembly room or building, cut off from the audience section by a proscenium wall, and which is equipped with scenery loft, gridiron, fly gallery, and lighting equipment; the minimum depth from the proscenium curtain to the back wall may be specified by code.

working stress See **allowable stress**.

working stress design A method of design in which structures or members are proportioned for prescribed working loads at stresses which are well below their ultimate values; linear distribution of flexural stresses is assumed.

work light In the theatre, a light used to provide illumination for rehearsing, scene shifting, or other work onstage or backstage.

workmen's compensation insurance Insurance covering liability of an employer to his employees for compensation and other benefits required by workmen's compensation laws with respect to injury, sickness, disease, or death arising from their employment.

work order See **notice to proceed.**

work plane The plane at which work is usually done, at which the illumination is specified and measured; usually assumed to be a horizontal plane 30 in. (76 cm) above the floor.

works British term for **factory.**

workshop A building or room used for handicraft work.

worm fence Same as **zigzag fence.**

wormhole, bore hole A hole or tunnel of any size in wood caused by worms.

woven board See **interlaced fencing.**

woven carpet A carpet which is constructed on a loom by interlacing the **carpet warp** and filling threads, e.g., Axminster, velvet, or Wilton carpet.

woven valley See **laced valley.**

woven-wire fabric A prefabricated steel reinforcement for **reinforced concrete;** composed of cold-drawn steel wires mechanically twisted together to form hexagonally shaped openings.

woven-wire reinforcement See **welded-wire fabric.**

WP 1. On drawings, abbr. for **waterproof.** 2. On drawings, abbr. for "weatherproof."

WP-series molding pattern One of a large number of profiles of commercially available moldings listed by the Western Wood Products Association.

wrack 1. The lowest grade of softwood. 2. A cull.

wraparound astragal See **overlapping astragal.**

wraparound frame Same as **keyed-in frame.**

wraparound porch A full-width porch that continues around the sides of a house.

wreath 1. The curved portion of the string or handrail which follows a turn in a geometrical stair, usually a quarter circle, and therefore corre-

sponds to a portion of the surface of a vertical cylinder; also called a **wreath piece. 2.** A twisted band, garland, or chaplet, representing flowers, fruits, leaves, etc.; often used in decoration.

wreathed column A column entwined by a band which presents a twisted or spiral appearance.

wreathed column

wreathed stair Same as **geometrical stair.**

wreathed string See **wreath, 1.**

wreath piece A curved section of a stair **string;** a **wreath, 1.**

wrecking The act of demolishing or razing a structure.

wrecking ball, skull cracker A heavy steel ball used in structural demolition; usually swung or dropped from a crane or derrick.

wrecking bar See **pinch bar.** (*See illustration p. 1020.*)

wrecking strip A small piece or panel which is fitted into a concrete formwork assembly in such a way that it can be removed easily, ahead of the main panels or forms, thereby making it easier to strip those major form components.

wrench A hand tool consisting of a metal handle with a jaw at one end which is designed to fit the head of a bolt or nut (or to grasp a pipe or rod) so that it may be turned.

Wrightian An imprecise term suggestive of the work of Frank Lloyd Wright (1867–1959) and

wrinkling

wrecking bar

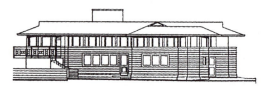

Wrightian: Glasner House, Glencoe, IL, designed by Frank Lloyd Wright

some of his followers. Wright cannot be characterized by a single architectural style; for example, some of his early buildings, closely associated with the **Prairie School,** differ markedly from his later designs. Also see **Organic architecture** and **Prairie style.**

wrinkling, crinkling, riveling **1.** The distortion in a paint film appearing as ripples; may be produced intentionally as a decorative effect or may be a defect caused by drying conditions or an excessively thick film. **2.** The crinkling of the surface skin of a sealant; affects its appearance, but usually not its sealing capability.

wrot lumber British term for **dressed lumber.**

wrought Said of an object that has been shaped by beating with a hammer.

wrought iron A commercially pure iron of fibrous nature; valued for its corrosion resistance and ductility; used for water pipes, water tank plates, rivets, stay bolts, and forged work.

wrought lumber British term for **dressed lumber.**

wrought nail A nail individually wrought by hand, often with a head forged into a decorative pattern; no longer in use.

wrt Abbr. for "wrought."

WS On drawings, abbr. for **weather strip.**

wt., Wt. Abbr. for "weight."

WT Abbr. for "watertight."

W-truss A truss whose upper and lower chords are joined by web members having the shape of the letter W.

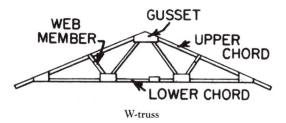

W-truss

WVT Abbr. for "water vapor transmission."

WW Abbr. for "warm white."

WWX Abbr. for "warm white deluxe."

wye **1.** A **Y-branch. 2.** A **Y-fitting.**

wye branch See **Y-branch.**

wye (Y) connection **1.** A method of connecting the ends of the windings of a poly-phase transformer; each of the three windings are joined at a common point; the other ends of the windings provide the line-to-line voltages. Compare with **delta connection. 2.** A **fire department connection** with two inlets; a **siamese connection.**

wye fitting See **Y-fitting.**

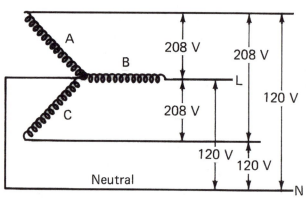

wye connection, 1

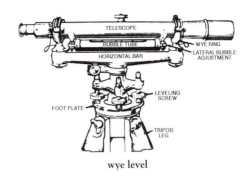

wye level

wye connection, 2

wye level A surveyor's leveling instrument having a telescope and attached spirit level, mounted in Y-shaped supports which permit it to be lifted and reversed, end for end; it is used in the direct measurement of differences in elevation.

wye tracery See **y-tracery**.

wythe See **withe**.

X

XBAR On drawings, abbr. for "crossbar."

X-brace, cross brace Any braces which cross each other to form the letter X.

X-bracing See **cross bracing, 1**.

XCU In insurance terminology, letters which refer to exclusions from coverage for property damage liability arising out of explosion or blasting (designated by X), collapse or structural damage to any building or structure (designated by C), and underground damage caused and occurring during the use of mechanical equipment (designated by U).

xenodocheum In classical architecture, a room or building devoted to the reception and accommodation of strangers or guests.

X HVY On drawings, abbr. for "extra heavy."

XL Abbr. for "extra large."

X-mark See **face mark**.

XSECT On drawings, abbr. for **cross section**.

X STR On drawings, abbr. for "extra strong."

XXH On drawings, abbr. for "double extra heavy."

xylol A colorless aromatic hydrocarbon liquid; used as a solvent for paints and varnishes.

xyst, xystum **1.** In classical architecture, a roofed colonnade for exercise in bad weather. **2.** In ancient Rome, a long, tree-shaded promenade. **3.** A tree-lined walk.

xyst, 1

Y

Yankee barn A steeply pitched, timber-framed, side-gabled wood barn of **post-and-lintel construction**, often with a gambrel roof; usually having no **forebay**; typically built against a hillside with animals housed at ground level on the lower side adjacent to the barn; similar to a bank barn.

yard That part of a building plot not occupied by the building, open to the sky.

yardage 1. The number of cubic yards excavated or filled. 2. An area or surface, expressed in square yards.

yard drain A surface drain; used to clear an open area of surface water.

yard line That section of a consumer's gas piping and fittings that extends from the **point of service, 3** (i.e., point of delivery) to the house piping.

yard lumber Lumber up to 5 in. (12.5 cm) thick intended for general building construction.

Y-branch, wye branch In a plumbing system, a **branch** in the shape of the letter Y.

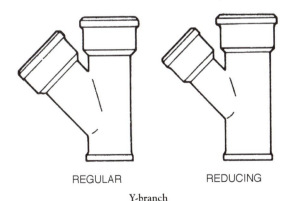

REGULAR REDUCING

Y-branch

Y-connection See **wye (Y) connection.**
yd Abbr. for "yard."
year ring Same as **annual ring.**

yellow fir See **Douglas fir.**

yellowing The development of a yellow color or cast in white or clear coatings after aging.

yellow metal Same as **Muntz metal.**

yellow ocher, yellow ochre A form of earth used as a yellow pigment; limonite.

yellow pine A hard resinous wood of the longleaf pine tree, having dark bands of summerwood alternating with lighter-colored springwood; used as flooring and in general construction.

yellow poplar, poplar A moderately low-density, even-textured hardwood of the central and southern U.S.A.; color varies from white to yellow, tan, or greenish brown; used for veneer, plywood, and lumber core for cabinetwork.

yellow poplar Same as **tulipwood, 1.**

yelm A bundle of reeds or combed straw used as thatching material for a roof.

yett A term for a massive gate, such as a portcullis, chiefly used in Scotland.

Y-fitting, wye fitting A pipe **fitting, 1**, one end of which subdivides, forming two openings at an angle, usually 45° to the run of pipe.

yield 1. The volume of freshly mixed concrete produced from a known quantity of ingredients; **volume yield. 2.** The number of product units, such as blocks, produced per bag of cement or per batch of concrete.

yield point The lowest **stress** in a material (less than the maximum attainable stress) at which the material begins to exhibit plastic properties; beyond this point an increase in strain occurs without an increase in stress.

yield strength The **stress** at which a material exhibits a specified limiting deviation from the proportionality of stress to strain.

Y-level Same as **wye level.**

yoke 1. A horizontal framework around the formwork for a column. 2. The horizontal piece forming the head of a window or door frame.

yoke relief vent

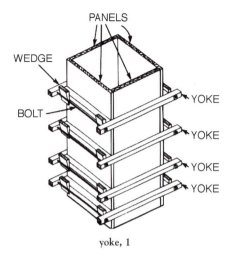

yoke, 1

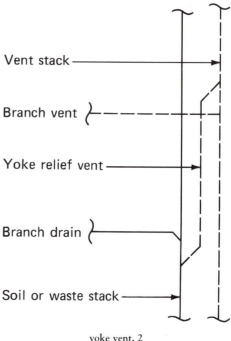

3. In plumbing, a two-way coupling for pipes, in the shape of the letter Y. **4.** A **yoke vent.**

yoke relief vent, yoke vent   See **yoke vent, 2. 1.** A pipe connecting upward from a soil stack or waste stack to a vent stack for the purpose of preventing pressure changes in the stack. **2.** A vertical or 45° relief vent of the continuous-waste-and-vent type formed by the extension of an upright wye branch or 45° wye branch inlet of the horizontal branch to the stack; becomes a dual yoke vent when two horizontal branches are thus vented by the same relief vent. **3.** A

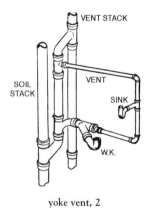

yoke vent, 2

yoke vent, 2

vent connected to a soil or waste stack that continues upward to the connection with the vent stack for the purpose of reducing pressure changes in the stack.

Yorkshire bond   Same as **monk bond.**

Yorkshire light   A window having one or more fixed sashes and a movable sash which slides horizontally.

Young's modulus   In an elastic material which has been subject to strain below its elastic limit, the ratio of the tensile stress to the corresponding tensile strain.

YP   On drawings, abbr. for **yield point.**

YR   On drawings, abbr. for "year."

YS   On drawings, abbr. for **yield strength.**

Y-tracery   A type of **tracery** in which the mullions split in the shape of the letter Y.

Z

zaguán **1.** In Spanish architecture and derivatives, an entry; often a massive wooden gate that was often sheltered and wide enough to permit large wagons or coaches to enter the courtyard (*placita*) of a **casa del rancho**. Often had a small door adjacent to, or a door set within the zaguán, for pedestrian traffic. **2.** In Spanish Colonial architecture, a **vestibule**.

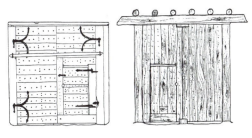

zaguán

zapata In Spanish Colonial architecture of the Americas, a horizontal piece of wood, atop a post, that provides greater bearing area to support the load imposed on the post from above; usually carved; similar to a **bolster, 1** but often more highly decorative.

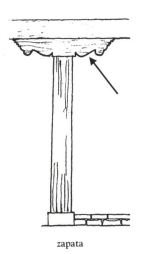

zapata

Zapotec architecture An eclectic architecture of Mesoamerica, especially in Oaxaca, Mexico. Characterized by multiterraced pyramids ascended by broad stairways, accented by wide balustrades and tablets, the use of circular supporting columns, and free-standing structures placed around a large plaza.

zax Same as **sax**.

Z-bar In a **suspended acoustical ceiling**, one form of main runner.

Z-braced battened door A **battened door** held together by two horizontal boards that are joined by a diagonal board; suggestive of the letter Z.

zebrawood, zebrano A moderately hard and heavy wood, pale yellow or pinkish brown, having pronounced dark stripes; found in central and western Africa. Used for plywood and decorative applications.

zee A metal member having a modified Z-shaped cross section; the internal angles of the Z are approximately equal to right angles.

zee

zeolite A coarse-grained chemical compound used in water-softening equipment; consists of a greenish granular material containing iron (up to 25%), a large percentage of silica, and some alumina and potash.

zeolite softening A water softening process now called **cation-exchange softening**.

zero-slump concrete Said of freshly-mixed concrete which has no measurable **slump**; compare with **no-slump concrete**.

zeta **1.** A closed or small chamber. **2.** A room over a porch of an early Christian church, where the porter or sexton lived and where documents were kept.

ziggurat A Mesopotamian temple tower; from the end of the 3rd millennium B.C. on, ziggurats rose in three to seven stages, diminishing in area and often in height square (Sumer) or rectangular (Assyria), built of mud brick and faced with baked brick laid in bitumen.

zigzag, dancette An ornamental molding of continued **chevrons**.

zigzag bond Same as or similar to **herringbone bond**.

zigzag fence A fence constructed of split rails that (in plan) alternate in direction, usually at a wide angle of about 120 degrees. At the intersection between the two stacks of rails, uprights are sometimes driven in the ground and lashed to the fence to improve its stability.

Zigzag Moderne See **Art Moderne**.

zigzag molding, dancette An ornamental molding of continued **chevrons**. Also see **reversed zigzag molding**.

types of zigzag moldings

zigzag riveting Same as **staggered riveting**.

zigzag rule A folding rule whose sections are pivoted; stiff when fully opened.

zinc A hard bluish white metal, brittle at normal temperatures, very malleable and ductile when heated; not subject to corrosion; used for galvanizing sheet steel and iron, in various metal alloys, and as an oxide for white paint pigment.

zinc chromate, buttercup yellow, zinc yellow A bright yellow stable pigment used in paints, esp. in metal primers as a rust-inhibiting pigment.

zinc coating See **galvanizing**.

zinc dust A fine gray powder of zinc metal usually of at least 97% purity; used as a pigment in paint primer for galvanized iron and other metal substrates.

zinc oxide, zinc white A white water-insoluble pigment which has low hiding power; used in paints to provide durability, color retention, and hardness, and to increase sag resistance.

zinc white See **zinc oxide**.

zinc yellow See **zinc chromate**.

zocco Same as **socle**.

zone 1. In an air-conditioning or heating system, a space (or group of spaces), served by the system, whose temperature (or humidity) is regulated by a single control. 2. A vertical or horizontal subdivision of a water supply system, sprinkler system, or standpipe system. 3. See **pressure zone**.

zoning The control by a municipality of the use of land and buildings, the height and bulk of buildings, the density of population, the relation of a lot's building coverage to open space, the size and location of yards and setbacks, and the provision of any ancillary facilities such as parking. Zoning, established through the adoption of a municipal ordinance, is a principal instrument in implementing a master plan.

zoning permit A permit issued by appropriate governmental authority authorizing land to be used for a specific purpose.

zoological garden A park, often quite large, designed for exhibiting wild animals.

zoomorph An image or symbol of some representation of an animal.

zoophoric column A column bearing a figure or figures of one or more men or animals.

zoophorus A horizontal band bearing carved figures of animals or persons, esp. the Ionic frieze when sculptured.

zotheca In Near Eastern architecture and derivatives, an alcove off a living room.

zwinger The protective fortress of a city.